LEARNING AND BEHAVIOR THERAPY

RELATED TITLES
OF INTEREST

LEARNING AND BEHAVIOR THERAPY

Edited by
William O'Donohue
University of Nevada, Reno

Allyn and Bacon
Boston   London   Toronto   Sydney   Tokyo   Singapore

Credits
Series Editor: Carla F. Daves
Series Editorial Assistant: Susan Hutchinson
Manufacturing Buyer: Suzanne Lareau

Copyright © 1998 by Allyn & Bacon
A Viacom Company
Needham Heights, MA 02194

Internet: www.abacon.com
America Online: keyword: College Online

Library of Congress Cataloging-in-Publication Data

Learning and behavior therapy / William O'Donohue, editor.
    p.   cm.
    Includes bibliographical references and index.
    ISBN 0-205-18609-2
    1. Behavior therapy.   2. Learning.   I. O'Donohue, William T.
RC489.B4L39   1997
616.89'142—dc21   97–10769
                                          CIP

Printed in the United States of America

10 9 8 7 6 5 4 3 2 1   01 00 99 98 97

DEDICATION

This book is dedicated to the first generation of behavior therapists, the founders, and teachers: H.E. Adams, W.S. Agras, T. Ayllon, N.H. Azrin, D.M. Baer, A. Bandura, W.C. Becker, S.W. Bijou, J.P. Brady, G.C. Davison, H.J. Eysenck, C.B. Ferster, C.M. Franks, J.H. Geer, I. Goldiamond, J. Greenspoon, M.C. Jones, H. Kalish, F.H. Kanfer, F.S. Keller, L. Krasner, P.J. Lang, A.A. Lazarus, D.J. Levis, O.R. Lindsley, P. London, O.I. Lovaas, I.M. Marks, J. Michael, W. Mischel, O.H. Mowrer, G.R. Patterson, G. Paul, S.J. Rachman, R. Rayner, L.J. Reyna, T.R. Risley, A. Salter, K. Salzinger, M. Sidman, B.F. Skinner, K.W. Spence, A. Staats, S.B. Stolz, L.P. Ullmann, J.B. Watson, M.M. Wolfe, J. Wolpe, A.J. Yates, among others. Their work serves as a continuing example and inspiration for subsequent generations of behavior therapists.

CONTENTS

PREFACE

In the first four decades of its existence, behavior therapy has made significant inroads into a number of clinical problems. Gordon Paul's (1966) research on systematic desensitization, for example, is widely taken to represent the first time that psychotherapy has been shown, in properly controlled conditions, to be effective. More recently, an American Psychological Association task force composed of psychologists from diverse theoretical orientations concluded that behavioral treatments for problems such as skill deficits for people with mental retardation, enuresis, panic disorder, generalized anxiety, phobias, obsessive-compulsive disorder, and oppositional defiant disorder in children can be considered "validated" (Task Force on Promotion and Dissemination of Psychological Procedures, 1995). Other therapy schools were not well represented in the task force report.

However, two problems suggest that there is reason to be concerned about the future of behavior therapy. First, for many clinical problems the magnitude of treatment effects is not large, the effects have unacceptably poor generalization, and even in the more effective treatment programs there is a sizable subset of individuals who are hot helped by the treatment. Thus, even these "effective" behavioral treatments need to be augmented and improved. These therapies can be improved by working more quickly, for more individuals, for longer periods of time. Because these problems have been well recognized for a number of years, it is unclear whether they will yield to the current set of ideas contained in behavior therapy. Second, in recent years behavior therapy has become increasingly disengaged from its roots in learning theory and research. In its beginnings behavior therapy applied what

was then current learning theory and research to clinical problems. However, as the first chapter more fully discusses, in recent years behavior therapists largely have not kept up with developments in learning theory and research. Moreover, behavior therapists have turned their attention to other information sources to find ideas upon which to base their attempts to develop more effective treatments.

This book seeks to improve behavior therapy's future prospects by providing a readable, comprehensive, and accurate description of contemporary learning research. This book is based on the presupposition that the extrapolation of learning results to clinical phenomena has been an important reason for the past success of behavior therapy, that behavior therapists have drifted away from this paradigm, and that behavior therapists can enjoy increased success in the future by returning to this paradigm.

Currently behavior therapy underutilizes contemporary learning research. As a case in point, behavior therapists by and large rely on Skinner's concept of reinforcement, despite the numerous advantages of utilizing more contemporary accounts (see Donahoe, Chapter 9 in this volume; Green & Freed, Chapter 14 in this volume; and Timberlake, 1995). Part of the reason for this state of affairs may be that keeping up with the learning literature is a fairly daunting task for the behavior therapist. This literature can be presented very technically and scattered in a number of different sources. The unique progress of behavior therapy may have been due to its reliance on extrapolating learning principles to clinical problems. Its future may depend upon returning to this core, by utilizing *contemporary* learning results.

To help to more fully understand the promise of contemporary learning research for behavior therapy, leading learning researchers have been asked to provide reviews of their areas of specialty as well as to outline some of what they see as the important clinical applications of these areas. It is the goal of this book to provide understandable, accessible, and authoritative summaries of the relevant learning literature. We hope this book benefits not only the behavior therapist but also the basic animal learning researcher. We have heard in the last several years suggestions that animal learning research is dead or dying. Although this allegation can be criticized in a number of ways, we hope that by showing the relevance and exciting possibilities of current learning research for helping with clinical problems, this book can play a role in fostering a more positive attitude toward this important research area.

I would like to express my appreciation to these researchers. The chapter authors are busy, well-respected scholars, and I am grateful that they believed that this project was sufficiently worthwhile for them to take their time to contribute chapters. Their chapters are uniformly excellent, and I greatly appreciate their exemplary scholarship.

However, the relevance to clinical problems of the learning research described in these chapters needs to be examined further. The authors of these chapters, with a few exceptions, are learning researchers, not clinicians. Thus, the relevance of the contemporary learning research they describe is certainly not exhausted by the examples contained in the chapters. Rather, it is hoped that these chapters, which faithfully summarize contemporary learning research, will be used by clinical researchers to more fully investigate the applicability of contemporary learning research to clinical problems. The first step in this process is to accurately understand contemporary learning research, and that is the purpose of this book.

I would also like to thank Mylan Jaixen, Carla Daves, and Sue Hutchinson for their expert guidance at Allyn & Bacon. My appreciation goes to Hugh Baras for his help in reviewing this manuscript. Finally, I would like to thank my family, Jane, Katie, and Anna, for their support and kindness throughout this project.

William O'Donohue
Reno, Nevada

REFERENCES

Paul, G. L. (1966). *Insight vs. desensitization in psychotherapy*. Stanford, Calif.: Stanford University Press.

Task Force on Promotion and Dissemination of Psychological Procedures (1995). Training in and dissemination of empirically-validated psychological treatments: Report and recommendations. *The Clinical Psychologist, 48,* 3–23.

Timberlake, W. (1995). Reconceptualizing reinforcement: A causal-system approach to reinforcement and behavior change. In W. O'Donohue & L. Krasner (Eds.) *Theories of behavior therapy* (59–96). Washington, D.C.: APA Books.

BIOGRAPHICAL SKETCHES

Robert W. Allan is an Associate Professor of Psychology at Lafayette College, where his research has focused on differential reinforcement and stimulus control of response topography in the pigeon.

Suzette L. Astley received a Ph.D. in psychology at Kansas State University in 1982. She is a member of the psychology faculty at Cornell College in Mt. Vernon, Iowa. She has published research on conditioned reinforcement and categorization, and has conducted research with pigeons and humans.

John J. B. Ayres received a B.A. from the College of William and Mary in 1961 and a Ph.D. from the University of Kentucky in 1965. He served in the U.S. Army Medical Service Corps at the Army Natick Laboratories, Natick, Massachusetts, from 1965 to 1967. He joined the Department of Psychology at the University of Massachusetts, Amherst, in 1967. In 1973–1974, he was a visiting professor at Western Washington State College in Bellingham, Washington, and visiting scholar at the University of Washington in Seattle. He was a visiting professor at the University of Hawaii at Oahu in 1982. He was Associate Editor of *Animal Learning & Behavior* from 1980 to 1984.

Peter Balsam became interested in psychology at the State University of New York at Stony Brook while working with Al Israel in a tutoring project. Subsequent involvement with Dan O'Leary's research on classroom management led him to choose a career in psychology. In graduate school at the University of North Carolina at Greensboro, his mentors, Aaron Brownstein, Eve Segal, Rick Shull, Kendon Smith, and Scott Lawrence, introduced him to the excitement of basic behavioral research and its applications. Since leaving graduate school he has been a Professor at Barnard College and Columbia University. He does research on conditioning and on the roles of experience in behavioral development.

Mark E. Bouton is a Professor of Psychology at the University of Vermont. His research addresses the memory processes that are represented in classical conditioning, with a recent emphasis on inhibition and behavioral phenomena that may be concerned with clinical relapse. He is a fellow of the American Psychological Association and the American Psychological Society. His research has been funded by the National Science Foundation since 1981, and he has received Fulbright and James McKeen Cattell Sabbatical awards.

Maeve Bracken (B.A., University of Ulster, 1990) is a lecturer in psychology at the University of Paisley, Scotland. She is a graduate in psychology from the University of Ulster and is currently completing a Ph.D. in psychology. Her research interests are in the fields of pure and applied behavior analysis.

Marc N. Branch is a Professor and Chairman of the Psychology Department at the University of

Florida. He is former editor of the *Journal of the Experimental Analysis of Behavior*, and former president of the Society for the Experimental Analysis of Behavior. He is president-elect of the Association for Behavior Analysis. His research interests include behavioral pharmacology as well as basic conditioning processes.

Christopher L. Cunningham is currently Professor and Interim Chairman of the Department of Behavioral Neuroscience at Oregon Health Sciences University. He earned an M.A. in psychology from the University of Iowa and a Ph.D. in psychology from the University of Oregon Medical School, and completed postdoctoral training in Pavlovian conditioning at Yale University. His current research focuses on the roles played by environment, experience, and heredity in determining the motivation effects of abused drugs. He is an Associate Editor for *Animal Learning & Behavior* and a member of the editorial board for *Alcoholism: Clinical and Experimental Research*.

Terry L. Davidson has the rank of Professor in the Department of Psychological Sciences and is a member of the Graduate Neuroscience Program at Purdue University. After obtaining his Ph.D. in psychology from Purdue University in 1981, Professor Davidson held faculty positions at St. Olaf College and at the Virginia Military Institute. In addition, he received postdoctoral training in behavioral neuroscience from the Institute of Neurological Sciences at the University of Pennsylvania. Professor Davidson's research focuses on the integration of physiological and learning mechanisms in the control of food intake and other behaviors.

James D. Deich received his B.A. in Psychology at Indiana working with William Timberlake. He took his Ph.D. with Edward Wasserman at Iowa. There he studied attention, response elicitation, response form, memory, memory for response sequences, and second-order conditioning. Post-Ph.D. work has involved the monitoring of bird's beak–mediated grasping to study skilled behavior, and its neurobehavioral control and ontogeny. This work began on a post-doc with H. P. Zeigler and has continued in collaboration with Peter Balsam. He is especially interested in the effects of task and organismal constraints on response form and organization.

James A. Dinsmoor received his M.A. in 1945 and his Ph.D. in 1949 from the Faculty of Pure Science at Columbia University. He has taught at the Newark Colleges of Rutgers University (1945–1946), Columbia University (1946–1951), and Indiana University (1951–1986), where he is now Professor Emeritus. His research has dealt with a variety of topics within the general areas of stimulus control, aversive control, and conditioned reinforcement. He has served terms as president of the Midwestern Psychological Association, the Society for the Experimental Analysis of Behavior, and most recently, Division 25 of the American Psychological Association.

John W. Donahoe is a Professor in the Biopsychology Division of the Department of Psychology and in the Neuroscience and Behavior Program of the University of Massachusetts at Amherst (e-mail: jdonahoe@psych.umass.edu). He is a behavior analyst whose major research interests are the behavioral and neural processes involved in reinforcement and stimulus control, and the use of adaptive-neural networks to explore the implications of basic biobehavioral processes for complex human behavior. His general orientation is selectionist: complex phenomena arise as the cumulative products of relatively simple processes acting over time.

John L. Falk obtained his B.A. (1950) and M.A. (1952) degrees in Psychology at McGill University in Montreal, and his Ph.D. at the University of Illinois in Champaign-Urbana in 1956. He has worked at the Yerkes Laboratories of Primate Biology and done postdoctoral work in the Department of Pharmacology at Harvard University Medical School and the Department of Nutrition at the Harvard School of Public Health.

Since 1969, he has been Professor of Psychology at Rutgers University in New Brunswick, New Jersey, and since 1990 has held a Research Scientist Award from the National Institute on Drug Abuse. He has authored approximately 175 articles and chapters in the areas of experimental analysis of behavior and behavioral pharmacology.

William A. Falls is an assistant professor of psychology in the area of neuroscience and behavior at Northern Illinois University. After receiving his B.A. from Bates College, he earned his Ph.D. at Yale University in 1993. He was a postdoctoral fellow in the Department of Psychiatry at Yale from 1993 to 1994, after which he took his current position at Northern Illinois University. Currently his research focuses on identifying the neural systems that may be involved in the reduction of fear and anxiety.

Debra Freed received her A.B. from Washington University and her M.A. from the University of California at San Diego. She then returned to Washington University, where she is a doctoral candidate in Psychology pursuing research in the areas of self-control and behavioral economics.

Leonard Green received his B.A. from the City College of New York and his Ph.D. from the State University of New York at Stony Brook. After a postdoctoral position, he ventured west of the Hudson River to Washington University in St. Louis, where he is Professor of Psychology. He is coeditor of the series *Advances in Behavioral Economics* (Ablex Publishing) and coauthor of *Economic Choice Theory: An Experimental Analysis of Animal Behavior* (Cambridge University Press). He serves on the editorial boards of the *Journal of the Experimental Analysis of Behavior* and *Behavior and Philosophy.*

Timothy D. Hackenberg is an Associate Professor in the Psychology Department at the University of Florida. He currently serves on the editorial boards of the *Journal of the Experi-*

mental Analysis of Behavior and *The Behavior Analyst.* His research interests include experimental analysis of human and nonhuman behavior.

Souhir Ben Hamida obtained her B.A. in Psychology from Cornell University with honors in all subjects in 1993. She received her M.S. in Psychology in 1996 from Northwestern University. She is currently working toward her doctorate in clinical psychology, also at Northwestern University. Her research interests include nonconscious acquisition of knowledge and its clinical implications. Currently, she is also conducting research to test evolutionary hypotheses regarding human behavior, including possible reasons for sex differences in unipolar depression.

Steven C. Hayes received his Ph.D. in clinical psychology from West Virginia University in 1977 and is currently a Nevada Foundation Professor and Chair of the Department of Psychology at the University of Nevada. An author of 15 books and more than 200 scientific articles, he is interested in basic research on language pragmatics and semantic relations, and applied research on emotional-acceptance methods in psychotherapy. In 1992 he was listed by the Institute for Scientific Information as the 30th "highest impact" psychologist in the world during 1986–1990 based on the citation impact of his writings. Hayes is Past-President of Division 25 of the APA, and past-Secretary-Treasurer of the APS. He is currently President of the American Association of Applied and Preventive Psychology.

Kenneth W. Johns is a graduate student in experimental psychology. Research interests include equivalence learning in rats. As Director of Charles's Eyes and Ears, he introduced Gentle Teaching as a therapy for the congenitally deaf and blind.

Winifred C. T. Ju is a doctoral student in Clinical Psychology at the University of Nevada, Reno. She received her B.A. degree, Cum Laude, from the University of New Mexico in 1989. Her current research interests are in the area of basic human operant learning, derived relational responding, rule-governed behavior, and verbal motivation. She is particularly interested in applying these principles to learning problems in children.

E. James Kehoe has a B.A. from Lawrence University (1971) and a Ph.D. from the University of Iowa (1976). Since 1977, he has been at the University of New South Wales, where he is currently a professor of psychology.

Alexandra Woods Logue received her Ph.D. in Experimental Psychology from Harvard University. From 1978 to 1995 she was a member of the Department of Psychology of the State University of New York at Stony Brook, ultimately as Professor and Chair. She is currently Dean of Arts and Sciences at Baruch College, City University of New York. She is a fellow of APA, APS, and AAAS, and is the author of *Self-Control: Waiting Until Tomorrow for What You Want Today* and *The Psychology of Eating and Drinking: An Introduction* (2nd ed.).

Vincent M. LoLordo studied at Brown University (B.A.) and the University of Pennsylvania (Ph.D.), where his research, including a 1966 dissertation on "Similarity of Fear of Different Aversive Events," was conducted in Richard Solomon's laboratory. After seven years on the faculty at the University of North Carolina, Chapel Hill, he moved to Dalhousie University, where he is Professor in the Department of Psychology. His extensively published research has focused primarily on simple associative learning, including Pavlovian-operant interactions, conditioned inhibition, selective associations, and associative competition. He has been the editor of *Learning and Motivation* and of *Animal Learning and Behavior* as well as an officer in national organizations.

R. E. Lubow was born in the Bronx, New York. He completed his B.A. at University Heights

College of New York University, M.S. at Washington State University, and Ph.D. at Cornell University. After several years at General Electric in Ithaca, N.Y., he received a Career Development Award from NIH and moved to North Carolina State University. Since 1971, he has been at Tel Aviv University in Israel. His research interests focus on attentional processes in animal and human learning.

Michaela Macrae has a B.Sc. in psychology from the University of New South Wales (1993). She is currently conducting doctoral work in the neuropsychology of human navigation as well as continuing research in classical conditioning.

Helena Matute is an associate professor at Deusto University, Spain. She obtained her Ph.D. in 1989 and teaches undergraduate and graduate courses on animal and human learning and related areas. Her current research interests include human causal learning, categorization, helplessness, superstitious behavior, and animal and human conditioning.

Ralph Miller is a professor and chair of Psychology at the State University of New York at Binghamton. He received his Ph.D. from Rutgers University in 1969 and has served on the faculty of the City University of New York and Cambridge University. He teaches courses on animal learning and behavior, and his research is concerned with the expression of acquired information, the role of context in modulating behavior, and causal judgment.

Susan Mineka is Professor of Psychology at Northwestern University. Her Ph.D. was in experimental psychology from the University of Pennsylvania (1974); she later completed a formal clinical retraining program. Her primary research interests are in animal models of psychopathology and in understanding the role that cognitive biases cognitive play in the etiology and maintenance of emotional disorders. She is also interested in how cognitive behavior therapy works to alleviate these disorders.

She is Past-President of the Society for the Science of Clinical Psychology, Past-Chair of APA's Board of Scientific Affairs (1994), and Past-Editor of the *Journal of Abnormal Psychology* (1990–1994).

Russell E. Morgan is a postdoctoral associate at Cornell University. His current research focuses on long-term cognitive deficits resulting from developmental exposure to lead (Pb) or cocaine. His research interests also include basic animal learning and memory processes, and the role of associative mechanisms in development of tolerance to pharmacological and environmental stressors.

Amy E. Naugle received her bachelor's degree from the University of St. Thomas in St. Paul, Minn., and is currently a graduate student in clinical psychology at the University of Nevada, Reno. Her current research focuses on empirically testing a behavior analytic model for understanding the long-term effects of childhood trauma. Ms. Naugle is also interested in Functional Analytic Psychotherapy and the emphasis on the role of the therapeutic relationship in promoting psychological change.

James B. Nelson is currently a Ph.D. candidate at the University of Vermont, where he is studying with Mark E. Bouton. His interests are in neural networking and quantitative theories of conditioning as they relate to how contexts influence learning and behavior.

John A. Nevin is Professor Emeritus of Psychology, the University of New Hampshire. After receiving his Ph.D. in experimental psychology at Columbia University in 1963, Dr. Nevin taught at Swarthmore College until 1968. He then returned to Columbia, where he was Professor and Department Chair from 1970 to 1972. From 1972 to 1995 he was Professor of Psychology at the University of New Hampshire, serving as Department Chair from 1981 to 1983, and as Editor of the *Journal of the Experimental Analysis of Behavior* from 1979 to 1983. He has published more than 80 articles and book chap-

ters on reinforcement processes, stimulus control, and signal detection. His current work focuses on the momentum of rewarded behavior and the implications of behavioral momentum for clinical, educational, and social issues.

G. Ron Norton (Ph.D., Utah State), a clinical psychologist and Professor of Psychology, has studied anxiety disorders—particularly panic disorder—for more than 20 years. He has published 2 books and approximately 100 articles and book chapters.

William O'Donohue received a doctorate in clinical psychology from the State University of New York at Stony Brook, and a masters degree in philosophy from Indiana University. He is currently an associate professor of psychology at the University of Nevada, Reno. He has coedited several books including *Theories of Behavior Therapy* and *Handbook of Psychological Skills Training* (both with Leonard Krasner).

Tatsuya Ohyama was born in Yokohama, Japan, on February 13, 1969, the year Apollo landed on the Moon. After receiving primary education in the United States, she went to high school and college in Japan, and graduated with a degree in engineering. Interested in pure science, she decided to pursue graduate study in psychology at the University of Hawaii, initially working at the Marine Mammal Laboratory and subsequently conducting research at the Bekesy Laboratory of Neurobiology on associative learning in honeybees. She is presently a second-year graduate student in psychology at Columbia University.

J. Bruce Overmier studied at Kenyon College (A.B.), Bowling Green State University (M.A.), and the University of Pennsylvania (Ph.D.). He is now Professor of Psychology at the University of Minnesota and member of the Graduate Faculties of Psychology, Cognitive Science, Neuroscience, and Psychoneuroimmunology and is Professor II at the University of Bergen (Norway). He has authored research articles and book chapters in his specialties of learning, memory, stress, psychosomatic disorders, and their biological substrates based upon research carried out with a range of animal species and human clients with specific dysfunctions. Overmier is a proponent of the interdependence of research and practice, both conceptually and functionally. He has been Editor of *Learning and Motivation* and active in national and international organizations, serving as President of MPA, two APA divisions, and the Pavlovian Society, as well as serving on the Board of Directors of APS, and as Deputy Secretary-General of the International Union of Psychological Science.

Phil Reed obtained his B.Sc. from the University of Leeds in 1984, and his D.Phil. from the University of York in 1988. He worked as a Research Fellow at the University of Oxford from 1988 to 1989 and at the University of Birmingham from 1989 to 1990. Phil Reed was a Lecturer at the University of Sussex from 1990 to 1991. He has been a Lecturer at University College London since 1991. He is currently doing research on the mechanisms of response learning and latent inhibition. He is writing two books for publication in 1996 exploring conditioning and cognition, and conditioning and clinical psychology.

David C. Riccio received his B.A. from Middlebury College, Vermont, and his Ph.D. from Princeton University. Following a three-year tour of military duty in the U.S. Navy, he began his academic career in 1965 at Kent State University, where he has remained ever since. His research has been in the areas of aversively motivated learning and memory processes. A fellow in APA and APS, he has served as President of the Midwestern Psychological Association. With N.E. Spear, he coauthored a recent text, "*Memory: Phenomena and Principles.*"

Todd R. Schachtman received his B.A. from the University of California at Berkeley after spending two years at the University of Cali-

fornia at San Diego and Berkeley. He received his M.A. and Ph.D. during the four years that he spent at the State University of New York at Binghamton. His graduate training was in animal learning and conditioning. This work focused on context effects and retrieval processes. Schachtman was a postdoctoral fellow at the University of York for 18 months doing research on attention and conditioning, context effects, and instrumental learning. As a postdoctoral fellow in Rochester for 18 months, he did work on stress, conditioning, and immunity. He has been a Professor at the University of Missouri since 1988.

Pat Stokes's interest in behavioral variability stems from and combines key elements of her prior and present professions. Trained in painting and graphics at Pratt, she supervised creative groups at several major New York advertising agencies, including Ted Bates, before being retrained as a learning psychologist at Columbia. Seeing creativity as a kind of variability (which combines novelty with usefulness) and seeing variability as a learned aspect of behavior led to a research agenda that asks two questions. First, when individuals learn to do something, do they also learn how variably to do it? Second, what in their learning history generates sustained individual differences in variability and, by extension, in creativity? This work is being conducted in collaboration with Dr. Peter Balsam at Barnard College, where Dr. Stokes is a Research Associate and an Adjunct Assistant Professor.

Kevin J. Tierney (Ph.D., Dublin University, 1986) is a lecturer in psychology at the University of Ulster in Northern Ireland. He received a doctorate in psychology from Trinity College, Dublin, and a postgraduate diploma in clinical psychology from the British Psychological Society. He was previously convenor of the Psychological Society of Ireland. He has published in the areas of molar regulatory theory, stimulus equivalence, and applied behavior analysis.

E. A. Wasserman received a Ph.D. in psychology at Indiana University in 1972, after which he was a postdoctoral fellow at the Laboratory of Experimental Psychology at the University of Sussex in England in 1972 and at the Institute of Higher Nervous Activity and Neurophysiology in the former U.S.S.R. in 1976. Since 1972, he has been on the faculty in the Department of Psychology at the University of Iowa. His general research interests have been in learning, memory, and cognition in both human and nonhuman animals. Most recently, conceptual behavior and causal perception have been his specific concerns.

Douglas A. Williams (Ph.D., Minnesota) is an Associate Professor of Psychology. Research interests lie in the continuity of learning in humans and nonhumans, in particular, negative contingency learning.

CHAPTER 1

CONDITIONING AND THIRD-GENERATION BEHAVIOR THERAPY

William O'Donohue

In its beginnings, behavior therapy was linked to learning research in an inextricable and unique manner. I will refer to this period in the history of behavior therapy as "first-generation behavior therapy." First-generation behavior therapy was a scientific paradigm that resulted in important solutions to a number of clinical problems (Task Force on Promotion and Dissemination of Psychological Procedures, 1995). For various reasons, however, many behavior therapists and researchers lost touch with developments in conditioning research and theory. Over the last three decades, behavior therapists turned their attention to topics such as therapies based on "clinical experience" (e.g., Goldfried & Davison, 1976), techniques seen independently from underlying behavioral principles (Hayes, Rincover, & Solnick, 1980), cognitive experimental psychology (e.g., Lang, 1977; Mahoney, 1974), social cognition (e.g., Abramson, Seligman, & Teasdale,

1978), cognitive accounts not based on experimental cognitive psychology (e.g., Ellis & Harper, 1975), and integrating or borrowing from other therapeutic approaches (Lazarus, 1969; but see O'Donohue & McKelvie, 1993). I will collectively refer to these developments as "second-generation behavior therapy."

Often the argument in second-generation behavior therapy for this widening of influences was that "some clinical problem has not yielded to a conditioning analysis, therefore other domains need to be explored for solutions." This is a reasonable argument, as it is imprudent to restrict behavior therapy to conditioning if there are important resources in other domains. However, there are grounds for concern because second-generation behavior therapists may have relied too heavily upon these other domains as well as relying on out-of-date conditioning research and theory. The latter is a problem to the extent that contemporary learning research extends older research, contradicts older research, or has discovered completely new relationships and principles. Clinical problems may be refractory to behavioral treatment simply because the behavior therapist is not using the more powerful regularities uncovered by recent learning research. It is possible that one of the core ideas—extrapolating results from learning research—of first-generation behavior therapy still remains a useful animating principle for contemporary behavior therapy. However, many contemporary behavior therapists still look to conditioning principles and theory developed in the 1950s and 1960s for solutions to clinical problems. In this chapter, *third-generation behavior therapy* is called for. Third-generation behavior therapists should extrapolate contemporary learning research to understand and treat clinical problems. Third-generation behavior therapy should rely on regularities found in modern accounts of classical conditioning, latent inhibition, two-factor theory, response-deprivation analysis of reinforcement, behavioral regulation, matching law, other models of choice behavior, behavioral momentum, behavioral economics, optimization, adjunctive behavior, rule-governed behavior, stimulus equivalence, and modern accounts of concept learning and causal attribution. In short, it would utilize the content of the subsequent chapters of this book.

FIRST-GENERATION BEHAVIOR THERAPY

Prior to the 1960s the founders of behavior therapy extrapolated laboratory learning results to clinical problems. For example, John Watson and Rosalie Rayner (1920) attempted to demonstrate that a child's phobia could be produced by classical conditioning. Mary Cover Jones (1924a; 1924b) showed that a child's fear of an animal could be counterconditioned by the pairing of the feared stimulus with a positive stimulus. O. Hobart Mowrer and Willie Mowrer (1938) developed a bell and pad treatment for enuresis that attempted to establish bladder distension as a conditioned stimulus for sphincter control and the inhibition of urination.

Despite the initial promise of these early extrapolations, these efforts were generally ignored in clinical practice. Psychotherapists of the period were largely interested in psychoanalysis, a paradigm with a much different focus. Behavior therapists had to compete with the many offshoots of psychoanalysis. Andrew Salter (1949) shows some of the antipathy that many behavior therapists had toward psychoanalysis:

> It is high time that psychoanalysis, like the elephant of fable, dragged itself off to some distant jungle graveyard and died. Psychoanalysis has outlived its usefulness. Its methods are vague, its treatment is long drawn out, and more often than not, its results are insipid and unimpressive. Every literate non-Freudian in our day knows these accusations to be true. But we may ask ourselves, might it not be that psychotherapy, by its very nature, must always be difficult, time-consuming, and inefficient? I do not think so. I say flatly that psychotherapy can be quite rapid and extremely efficacious. I know so because I have done so. And if the reader will bear with me, I will show him how by building our therapeutic methods on the firm scientific bed rock of Pavlov, we can keep out of the Freudian metaphysical quicksands and help ten persons in the time that the Freudians are getting ready to "help" one. (p. 1)

In the 1950s, Joseph Wolpe (1958) attempted to countercondition anxiety responses by pairing relaxation with the stimuli that usually elicited anxiety. Wolpe's work represents the real beginnings of modern behavior therapy, as his work comprised a sustained research program that affected subsequent clinical practice. The earlier work of Watson, Jones, and others was not as programmatic and for whatever reasons did not disseminate well. Wolpe's desensitization techniques and his learning account of fears generated dozens of research studies and clinical applications over the following decade. The reader is referred to Kazdin's (1978) excellent history of behavior therapy for additional examples of early learning-based therapies.

First-generation behavior therapists not only

utilized learning principles to formulate interventions, but also used learning principles to develop accounts of the origins and maintenance of problems in living. Abnormal behavior was judged to develop and be maintained by the same learning principles as normal behavior (e.g., Ullmann & Krasner, 1969). Problems in learning or problems in maintaining conditions resulted in a variety of behavior problems. Ullmann & Krasner's (1969) abnormal textbook is a useful compendium of first-generation learning-based accounts of the development and maintenance of changeworthy behavior.

Most of the initial behavioral studies were influenced by Pavlovian principles, particularly simultaneous and forward classical conditioning. This is not surprising, as some of these predated Skinner's work on operant conditioning. However, in the 1950s another stream of behavior therapy emerged: that of applied behavior analysis or behavior modification. These interventions relied on operant principles. In one of the first studies to explicitly use operant principles, Lindsley, Skinner, and Solomon (1953) initiated this stream when they operantly conditioned responses in schizophrenics, demonstrating that psychotic disorders did not obviate basic conditioning processes. Another important early operant researcher, Sidney Bijou (e.g., Bijou, 1959) investigated the behavior of both normal and developmentally delayed children through the use of functional analyses and schedules of reinforcement. Baer, Wolf, & Risley (1968) in the first issue of the *Journal of Applied Behavior Analysis* highlighted the importance of the systematic and direct application of learning principles for the future of applied behavior analysis: "The field of applied behavior analysis will probably advance best if the published descriptions of its procedures are not only precise technologically but also strive for relevance to principle. . . . This can have the effect of making a body of technology into a discipline rather than a collection of tricks. Collections of tricks historically have been difficult to expand systematically, and when they were extensive, difficult to learn and teach" (p. 96).

These cases of first-generation behavior therapy exhibit several important commonalities: (1) The clinical scientists had extensive backgrounds in basic learning research. They could reasonably be described as learning researchers seeking to understand the generalizability of laboratory research as well as examining the practical value of this research by helping to solve problems involving human suffering. (2) They were applying *what was then current learning research* to clinical problems. (3) The results of their clinical research were by and large positive, although the methodological adequacy is problematic by today's standards. (4) They saw their particular research as illustrating a much wider program of research and therapy. That is, their research did not exhaust the potential for the applicability of learning principles to clinical problems, but merely illustrated a small part of a much wider program.

During this period, behavior therapy was often defined by a direct and explicit reference to learning principles. For example, Ullmann and Krasner (1965) defined behavior modification as "includ[ing] many different techniques, all broadly related to the field of learning, *but learning with a particular intent, namely clinical treatment and change*" (p. 1; italics in the original). Wolpe (1969) stated, "Behavior therapy, or conditioning therapy, is the use of experimentally established principles of learning for the purpose of changing maladaptive behavior (p. VII). Eysenck (1964) defined behavior therapy as "the attempt to alter human behavior and emotion in a beneficial manner according to the laws of modern learning theory" (p. 1). Franks (1964) stated, "Behavior therapy may be defined as the systematic application of principles derived from behavior or learning theory and the experimental work in these areas to the rational modification of abnormal or undesirable behavior" (p. 12). Furthermore, Franks (1964) wrote that essential to behavior therapy is a "profound awareness of learning theory" (p. 12).

Although by and large these early behavior therapists agreed that learning principles should serve as the foundation of behavior therapy, the behavior therapy they advocated was not homogeneous. There was a significant heterogeneity in this early research. These researchers did not draw upon the same learning principles, nor did they subscribe to the same theory of learning. Skinner and his students emphasized operant conditioning principles; Watson, Rayner, and Jones, Pavlovian principles; and Wolpe and others Hullian and Pavlovian. Moreover, within these broad traditions different regularities were used: some used extinction procedures, others excitatory classical conditioning; some differential reinforcement of successive approximations, others counterconditioning. However, each of these is a canonical illustration of behavior therapy of this period because each shares a critical family resemblance: an extrapolation of learning principles to clinical problems.

A related but separate movement occurred during this period. This movement did not gather much momentum and has largely died out. It is best represented by the work of Dollard and Miller (1950). In their classic book, *Personality and Psychotherapy*, these authors attempted to provide an explanation of psychoanalytic therapy techniques and principles based on learning principles. Dollard and Miller attempted to explain psychoanalytic techniques by an appeal to Hullian learning principles. This movement should be regarded as separate from the first movement described above because the connection between conditioning and a therapy technique in this movement is post hoc. That is, first, therapeutic principles are described with no direct connection to learning principles, and this is followed by an attempt to understand these by learning principles. In the first movement, initially learning principles are discovered, and this is followed by the development of treatment procedures.

Today, there is little work that follows the second paradigm. Few are attempting to uncover the learning mechanisms underlying Rogerian and Gestalt techniques, object-relations therapy, etc. This is probably because today, unlike the 1950s, there is more doubt whether there is anything to explain. This movement attempted to explain how, for example, psychoanalysis worked (what

were the conditioning processes involved). However, if there is little reason to believe that these other therapies are effective, then there is little reason to explain *how* they work. Moreover, this movement failed to produce any novel treatment techniques. In its emphasis upon attempting to understand existing therapy techniques, it produced no useful innovations.

However, the model of moving from the learning laboratory to the clinic proved to be a extraordinarily rich paradigm. In the 1960s, numerous learning principles were shown to be relevant to clinical problems. Learning research quickly proved to be a productive source of ideas for developing treatments or etiological accounts of many problems in living. The development of psychotherapy had been a quasimysterious process before this point. Psychotherapies were usually developed by the unique clinical observations of the person who would become the leader of the school. Psychotherapists were no longer dependent upon the "revelations" of insightful and creative seers who founded their schools. For the first time, psychotherapists could do Kuhnian (Kuhn 1970) normal science because it is considerably more straightforward to extrapolate extant learning principles to clinical phenomena than it is to understand how, say, Freud formed and revised his assertions. "Extrapolate learning principles" is a clear and useful heuristic for the context of discovery.

Six books were critically important in extending the learning-based therapy paradigm. Wolpe's (1958) *Psychotherapy by Reciprocal Inhibition*; Eysenck's (1960) *Behavior Therapy and the Neuroses*; Franks's (1964) *Conditioning Techniques in Clinical Practice and Research*; Eysenck's *Experiments in behavior therapy* (1964); and Krasner and Ullmann's two volumes *Case Studies in Behavior Modification* (Ullmann and Krasner, 1965) and *Research in Behavior Modification* (Krasner and Ullmann, 1965). All contained an extensive set of case studies, research, and conceptual analyses that greatly extended the paradigm. Conditioned reinforcement, modeling, generalization and discrimination, satiation techniques, punishment, the effects of schedules of reinforcement, and token economies were investigated. Moreover, these principles were applied to a greater number and variety of clinical problems. Eating, compulsive behavior, elective mutism, cooperative responses, disruptive behavior, anorexia, hysterical blindness, post-traumatic anxiety, fetishism, sexual dysfunction, stuttering, tics, school phobia, tantrums, toilet training, social isolation, teaching skills to people with mental retardation, and hyperactive behavior were all addressed by learning-based treatments in these books. The matrix involving the crossing of learning principles by kinds of problematic behavior resulted in a rich research and therapy program.

Due to the initial successes in applying learning principles to clinical problems, another trend emerged. First-generation behavior therapists started working in the other direction: they began with a clinical problem and then attempted see to what extent it yielded to an analysis based on learning principles. Thus, a reciprocal relationship between the clinic and the learning lab emerged. This movement was important because behavior therapists can also be interested in uncovering basic learning processes in humans and can have a useful vantage point for generating and testing hypotheses concerning basic processes.

However, there is some danger with this approach. Unfortunately, it could be quite attractive to the behavior therapist who knew much more about clinical presentation than about learning research. This may have been the beginnings of the reliance of behavior therapists on something other than a thorough, and faithful knowledge of current learning theory and research. With the success of behavior therapy came a new kind of professional: one who was first trained to be a clinical behavior therapist rather than a learning researcher.

Care must be taken not to lose sight of another important dimension of first-generation behavior therapy: its commitment to science and research. This scientific commitment, although not unprecedented in the history of psychotherapy, was more thoroughgoing. In 1952, after more than a half-century of the dominance of psychotherapy by psychoanalysis, Eysenck correctly pointed out that there was little properly controlled research that demonstrated it was more effective than a placebo treatment. Part of Eysenck's thesis was that it may be the case that effective therapies had yet to be discovered. However, another part was that existing therapies had not been adequately evaluated with properly controlled designs. Psychotherapists were doing an inadequate job as clinical researchers by not evaluating the efficacy of their therapies. Admittedly, many of the early reports of behavior therapy were largely uncontrolled case studies that merely demonstrated its potential utility. Behavior therapists, however, quickly began to conduct unprecedentedly well-controlled research. Paul's (1966) study of the effectiveness of systematic desensitization can properly be regarded as the first research in history that was sufficiently well controlled to demonstrate that a form of psychotherapy was more effective than placebo and no treatment.

The research orientation of behavior therapists may have emanated from the school's roots in conditioning theory and research. Many then-extant forms of therapy had a much different heritage: the founder of the particular school made what were taken by some as astute clinical observations (witness Freud, Perls, Rogers; see O'Donohue & Halsey, 1997) and somehow formed this clinical experience into a more or less systematic school of therapy. It is easier to be "looser" when one is not extrapolating from a basic science. In contrast, the learning researchers/behavior therapists who composed the first wave of behavior therapy did not give up their experimental orientation when turning their attention to clinical problems. Behavior therapy from its beginnings valued science. The epistemological principles from their backgrounds in experimental psychology remained with them and became an important part of the metascience of behavior therapy. Behavior therapists were interested in process research because they had a strong prior set of expectations (i.e., learning principles) of what these process variables might look like.

First-generation behavior therapy resulted in unprecedented progress in psychotherapy. If we somewhat arbitrarily say that the modern era of psychotherapy began in roughly 1900 with Freud, then we can agree with Eysenck (1952) in that the first 50 years of psychotherapy resulted in little progress. No treatments were developed that effectively resolved the problems they attempted to address. In contrast, during the early years of behavior therapy, significant progress was made with enuresis, phobias, other anxiety problems, child-management problems, skills deficits of developmentally disabled individuals, self-injurious behavior and stereotypic behavior of autistic and schizophrenic individuals, and social and verbal problems of schizophrenia. These all were no longer completely refractory to ameliorative attempts. Moreover, as Salter (1949) described, behavioral treatment was also much quicker and less costly. In the span of a little over a decade, psychotherapy made progress that it failed to make in the preceding five decades. Surely, any reasonable observer could see that there was something special about this new movement. Today, if one looks at the Task Force on Promotion and Dissemination of Psychological Procedures (1995), this first-generation behavior therapy still accounts for a significant percentage of what are now considered "validated treatments."

The success of early behavior therapy should not have come as a complete surprise. Psychotherapists for the first time began using a strategy that had proved successful in other domains. For nearly a century, physicians had relied on experimental physiology and microbiology, and by extrapolating from the results of the basic biological sciences they had made significant clinical progress. Engineers relied upon the basic sciences of physics and chemistry and made remarkable progress solving many applied problems. The strategy used by these groups was enticing: extrapolate antecedently validated principles from basic research to applied problems.

For the first time in the 1950s and 1960s, psy-chotherapy began to use the same strategy: first nomothetics were discovered through basic research, and then these were applied to practical problems. In the learning laboratory, learning researchers derived principles applicable to human behavior. The animals used in their research were largely chosen for convenience rather than because of any strong interest in understanding the behavior of that particular species. Evolutionary theory supported some behavioral continuity across species, which further justified the study of infra-human animals. The laboratory and the animal preparation allow control that is not possible in naturalistic studies of humans. Variables can be controlled and isolated, and thus false hypotheses can more easily be refuted. Regularities emerging from the learning laboratory have relatively good epistemic credentials and a reasonable potential for revealing clinically useful regularities. The epistemic credentials of the laboratory-derived first-generation behavior therapy were far superior to the epistemic credentials of principles or regularities alleged by the clinical observers who initiated competing schools of therapy. The number of possible therapy techniques is, of course, indefinitely large, and therefore it is useful to have antecedent evidence upon which to judge which are worthy of investigation (Erwin, 1978).

An additional, somewhat more subtle, factor may also have contributed to the success of first-generation, learning-based therapies. This paradigm may have met with such unprecedented success because of felicitous correspondences between the core objects of both programs. Learning researchers attempt to uncover how experience changes behavior. In fact, a common definition of learning is that learning is experience that results in relatively enduring changes in behavior. This focus precisely addresses the general question involved in the enterprise of psychotherapy: How can therapists structure experience so that relatively enduring changes occur in the client's behavior? Thus, this paradigm might have been successful because of the confluence of the aims of these two pursuits.

Two further confluences might have accounted for the success of operant approaches. Skinner criticized research utilizing group designs. He argued that group averages are a confused and confusing scientific variable. Instead of group comparisons, Skinner argued for the intensive experimental analysis of the behavior of an individual organism. The goal was to find the controlling variables of the individual's behavior by manipulating environmental conditions to see if these were functionally related to subsequent behavior. Again, this emphasis is highly consistent with the clinician's problem situation. The clinician is rarely concerned with group averages but rather is concerned with the behavior of an individual client. Moreover, clinicians aim to find manipulable conditions to bring about desirable changes in the client's behavior.

A final confluence was that in conducting these single-subject designs, Skinnerians eschewed statistical analysis. They wanted to show that they had identified controlling variables due to the reliable, high-magnitude changes produced in the dependent variable. Although some learning researchers statistically analyzed group designs in order to find "statistically significant" differences, operant researchers wanted to demonstrate differences that would be readily apparent in any graphical display. This is fortuitous because clinicians generally want or need dependent variables to undergo large changes. The work coming out of the operant lab showed that these large changes were possible. Work coming out of group designs showed that with large enough sample sizes, small differences (that were statistically significant but often not clinically significant) were possible.

Despite the considerable advantages provided by this basic science/applied science model, it has one serious disadvantage. The limits of the basic science place limits on the applied science. Learning research was (and still is) unsettled. Pavlovians, Hullians, and Skinnerians, among others, engaged in debates concerning fundamental issues. Much of the behavior of the organism remained unaccounted for. There was a clear need for further basic research to fill the many lacunae in the learning account. At times,

behavior therapists were stymied because they relied on incorrect information, incomplete information, regularities that were weak, and regularities whose initial conditions or boundary conditions were poorly understood.

SECOND-GENERATION BEHAVIOR THERAPY

In the 1970s behavior therapy's heterogeneity increased. Systematic desensitization, implosion therapy, and two-factor accounts of anxiety disorders were examples of the continuing influence of Pavlov, Hull, and Mowrer, respectively. Those influenced by Skinner sometimes tried to distinguish themselves from those influenced by nonoperant principles and particularly from those influenced by nonconditioning factors. Operantly inclined behavior therapists sometimes called what they did *applied behavior analysis* or *behavior modification*. These terminological distinctions have not always been clear, but at times they function as code words for background allegiances regarding favored learning principles.

The increasing diversity of behavior therapy should not be surprising, as the seeds for the growth of a heterogeneous discipline were present from its beginning. For example, Ullmann & Krasner (1965) described behavior therapy as "treatment deducible from the *sociopsychological model* that aims to alter a person's behavior directly through the application of general psychological principles (p. 244, italics added). These prominent, early behavior therapists viewed behavior therapy as also relying on many social-psychological domains such as role theory, small-group research, demand characteristics, labeling, and conformity. Ullmann and Krasner attempted to set a learning-influenced behavior therapy in the larger context of a psychology of behavior influence.

Gerald Patterson (1969), another prominent early behavior therapist, agreed with the emphasis upon social-psychological principles:

> It seems to me that future trends will of necessity involve a greater reliance upon principles available from social learning. The term social

learning as used here refers to the loosely organized body of literature dealing with changes in learning, or performance, which occur as a function of contingencies which characterize social interaction. . . . Many of the mechanisms which have been described as bringing about these changes have been based upon principles from social psychology rather than learning theory: these would include such processes as persuasion, conformity, and modeling. (p. 342)

Arnold Lazarus, a student of Wolpe's, was probably one of the earliest and most significant forces for turning behavior therapists' attention to areas other than learning. Lazarus argued that learning principles were helpful but insufficient. Lazarus (1968) stated:

Why should behavior therapists limit themselves only to "experimentally established principles of learning against the background of physiology" and ignore other areas of experimental psychology such as studies on perception, emotion, cognition, and so forth? And why should behavior therapists avoid using such techniques as self-disclosure, dyadic interactions, and other methods, as long as they can be reconciled with reinforcement principles? Finally, one might inquire to what extent Wolpe's reference to a "stimulus-response model" is a vague and meaningless abstraction. If the current upsurge of interest in behavior therapy is to expand and mature, we must beware of oversimplified notions, limited procedures, and extravagant claims which would conceivably undermine our efforts. (p. 2)

Following this line of thought, Lazarus (1969) stated that the multimodal behavior therapist is "free to employ any technique, derived from any system, without subscribing to any theoretical underpinnings which do not have the benefit of empirical support" (p. 5).

Bandura's description and analysis of modeling and vicarious learning was another important influence on the development of behavior therapy during this period. Bandura (1969) stated that:

research conducted within the framework of social-learning theory demonstrates that virtually all learning phenomena resulting from di-

rect experiences can occur on a vicarious basis through observation of other persons' behavior and its consequences for them. Thus, for example, one can acquire intricate response patterns merely by observing the performances of appropriate models; emotional responses can be conditioned observationally by witnessing the affective reactions of others undergoing painful or pleasurable experiences; fearful and avoidance behavior can be extinguished vicariously through observation of modeled approach behavior toward feared objects without any adverse consequences accruing to the performer; inhibitions can be induced by witnessing the behavior of others punished; and finally, the expression of well-learned responses can be enhanced and socially regulated through the actions of influential models. Modeling procedures are therefore ideally suited for effecting diverse outcomes including elimination of behavioral deficits, reduction of excessive fears and inhibitions, transmission of self-regulating systems, and social facilitation of behavioral patterns on a groupwide scale. (p. 118)

Together, these authors argued that social psychology as well as experimental learning psychology were relevant to behavior therapy. It is also fair to say that many of those influenced by the social-learning perspective relied most heavily on learning principles. Growing from these early seeds, in the second generation, behavior therapy became more broadly defined. Instead of defining behavior therapy as the application of learning principles, behavior therapy came to be defined as the application of principles from *experimental and social psychology* (e.g., Davison & Neale, 1974; Rimm & Masters, 1974; Franks & Wilson, 1975). This, of course, included learning principles, but it also included a lot of other material.

During this period, applied behavior analysts appeared to become less attentive to the underlying learning principles. Hayes, Rincover, & Solnick (1980) found that in early volumes of the *Journal of Applied Behavior Analysis* it was nearly always the case that the articles contained references to behavioral principles. However in an analysis of later volumes, Hayes et al. found: "Overall the data show that applied behavior analysis is becoming a more purely technical effort, with less and less interest in conceptual questions. To answer these technical questions we are using relatively simple experimental designs which determine if the technique had a reliable effect, or if it is better than another technique, with little interest in the components producing the effect or the parametric boundaries of the techniques" (p. 281).

THE RISE OF COGNITIVE BEHAVIOR THERAPY

Behavior therapy is not insulated from events happening outside it. The "cognitive revolution" in psychology occurred in the 1960s, and by the 1970s many behavior therapists influenced by it began to call what they did "cognitive behavior therapy." Wilson (1982) stated:

> During the 1950s and 1960s, the behaviour therapies developed within the framework of classical and operant conditioning principles that had originally served importantly to distinguish behaviour therapy from other clinical approaches. Over the course of the 1970s, this conceptual commitment to conditioning theory peaked out—some would say even waned. In part this change reflected the shift to more technological considerations governing the increasingly broad application of behavioral techniques that had been developed and refined during the previous period of growth. Moreover, as psychology "went cognitive" during the 1970s, cognitive concepts inevitably were drawn upon to guide and explain treatment strategies. (p. 51)

Mahoney, an early leader in cognitive behavior therapy, stated a similar theme (1984): "By the late 1970s it was clear that cognitive behavior therapy was not a fad; indeed it had its own special interest group in the AABT. It had become a more frequent topic at conventions, in journals, and in research, and it had become more pervasively integrated into behavioral psychotherapies. Behavior therapy, like psychology in general, had "gone cognitive" (p. 9).

Part of this movement argued that learning research was still relevant but the research that should influence second-generation behavior therapy was *human* learning research that examined cognitive mediators of learning. The argument was that conditioning in humans is not automatic and direct, but rather is mediated by the person's verbal and cognitive abilities. Awareness, attention, expectancy, attribution, and linguistic representation were constructs thought to be necessary to account for learning. The argument was that animal conditioning models were inadequate for the study of human learning because these neglected to include the unique abilities of humans such as verbal abilities. Thus, these animal conditioning models needed to be supplemented or replaced by cognitive accounts.

Not all behavior therapists "went cognitive." Most applied behavior analysts continued to practice first-generation behavior therapy. These and others argued that the so-called cognitive revolution was in part a retreat to folk psychology rather than a progressive scientific movement. Critics were quick to point out that the new cognitive techniques generally had, at best, a rather loose connection with experimental cognitive psychology. This was serious epistemically because to the extent that this criticism was true, no longer were behavior therapists extrapolating antecedently tested principles.

It does appear that during this period behavior therapists developed treatments that had a looser relationship with conditioning: self-reinforcement, behavioral rehearsal, covert sensitization, and thought-stopping all were clinical techniques that were not derived from basic animal learning research. Conditioning principles became more of a rough heuristic during the second generation of behavior therapy. Admittedly, these techniques have a family resemblance to conditioning procedures, but their actual connection is much more ephemeral. Claims that there was a shift in regard for basic animal research have some empirical support. Poling et al. (1981) found through a citation analysis that sources that report work with nonhuman subjects have been referenced increasingly infrequently since 1965 by clinical authors.

It also may have been the case that the success and credentials of behavior therapy attracted many individuals, some who were relatively unfamiliar with learning principles. Psychotherapists and clinical researchers trained in other paradigms "converted" to behavior therapy during this period. However, such conversion rarely entailed an extensive training in learning research. Rather it more typically included training in behavior therapy techniques themselves. This trend could have hastened the view of these techniques as being more autonomous from the basic learning principles. For this group of behavior therapists, when difficulties were encountered, it was more likely that learning principles were not drawn upon. It is easier for the potential of learning principles to be seen as exhausted when one does not have an exhaustive knowledge of them.

I also conjecture that these less faithful, less accurate extrapolations from basic learning research had a higher likelihood of leading to failures. To the extent that these failures were attributed to the inadequacy or insufficiency of learning principles to gird clinical practice, a movement away from learning and toward other domains occurred. Many behavior therapists have had the experience of hearing psychotherapists say that their failed attempts at what they see as behavior therapy support their conclusions that behavior therapy is a bad form of therapy. I recall an avowed eclectic therapist telling me that behavior therapy failed her because she tried to reinforce an academically underperforming adolescent by rewarding him with a minibike at the end of the semester if he received all As and Bs. If she had even a cursory understanding of operant conditioning, she would have known: (1) that one does not reinforce organisms, but rather responses; (2) that reinforcement of successive approximations is usually a more effective strategy for producing high-magnitude changes; (3) that a large, distant reinforcer often needs to be supplemented by more proximate reinforcers; (4) that receiving a good grade is not a response; and (5) a more careful functional analysis of competing behaviors and reinforcers needed to

be done to understand controlling variables. Too often during this period, people began to practice "behavior therapy" in a superficial and rather incompetent manner.

This is not to say simply that an understanding of the growing schism between behavior therapy and basic learning research can be understood entirely by the behavior of behavior therapists. During this period, basic learning research moved on as well. It admittedly became more esoteric, more technical, and thus there were more barriers to entry to those who wanted to acquaint themselves with contemporary learning research. The difficulty of contemporary learning research helps to explain why many behavior therapists failed to keep up. If one picks up a current issue of, for example, *Journal of the Experimental Analysis of Behavior* and attempts to read one of the articles, it is likely that one will understand little. Learning research became more insular as it grew more technical, quantitative, and specialized. Learning researchers stopped writing for general psychologists and wrote increasingly for their scientific microcommunity. Learning researchers began to experience problems in knowledge utilization and dissemination—topics that are of intellectual interest in their own right.

The advent and success of behavior therapy also created certain interpersonal and professional tensions. Behavior therapists were often critical of the lack of evidence for the efficacy of other schools of therapy, of the lack of scientific commitment of these schools, of the lack of evidence that these schools' favored process variables actually were important, and of the way these schools defined abnormality. Part of the general ethos of the psychotherapy movement is to have good interpersonal relationships. But behavior therapists were increasingly critical, skeptical, and unaccepting of many of the claims of other schools, and, frankly, claimed to be practicing a superior form of therapy. These tensions were at least partly relieved when behavior therapists became more eclectic, less stridently learning-based, and accepting of techniques from other schools. If one looks at some of the external forces on the development of behavior therapy, one problem behavior therapists had to face was this sort of "foreign relations." Some sought appeasement by compromise. Eclecticism may be understandably more satisfying in certain political and interpersonal contexts.

Probably the most radical critique of first-generation behavior therapy during this period was the criticism that behavior therapy techniques were not derived from basic laboratory principles of learning. For example, Breger & McGaugh (1965) stated, "When we look at the way conditioning principles are applied in the explanation of more complex phenomena, we see that only a rather flimsy analogue bridges the gap between such laboratory defined terms as stimulus, response, and reinforcement and their reference in the case of complex behavior" (p. 344). Erwin (1978) also argued that behavior therapy techniques were not derived from learning principles. For example, the argument was that in systematic desensitization Wolpe used an imagined scene as a conditioned stimulus but that this conditioned stimulus did not have properties that laboratory conditioned stimuli have — for example, public observability, direct control by the experimenter, and invariance. Thus, the claim was that often animal laboratory research could serve as a heuristic or useful analog but that behavior therapy techniques were not derived from basic animal learning research.

This argument presents a restrictive view of the relationship between basic and applied research. It is an elementary methodological point that laboratory research trades off external validity for internal validity. Laboratory protocols simplify in order to isolate and improve control of independent variables, and to improve the accuracy of measurement of dependent variables. In doing this, the laboratory preparation often becomes idealized and removed from naturalistic phenomena. However, after regularities are discovered in the lab, the next step is to examine whether they can be extrapolated to related (but not identical) variables in the natural environ-

ment. Similar relationships can be found in laboratory preparations and naturalistic phenomena in physiology and medicine, for example. Moreover, it is not clear if it is necessary for there to be a logical entailment between laboratory preparations and behavior therapy techniques. Rather, the behavior therapy technique simply needs to be "covered" (Hempel, 1966) by regularities discovered in the lab. Most competent contingency-management procedures are subsumed under general operant principles and procedures. A particular behavior therapy technique may represent a widening of laboratory-derived regularities. This may be the case in Wolpe's systematic desensitization.

These factors contrived to create a heterogenous behavior therapy with more tenuous or even often nonexistent roots in animal learning. Kazdin (1978) stated, "By now [the mid to late 1970s] behavior modification is so variegated in its conceptualization of behavior, research methods and techniques that no unifying schema or set of assumptions about behavior can incorporate all the extant techniques. Many of the theoretical positions expressed within behavior modification represent opposing views about the nature of human motivation, the mechanisms that influence behavior and the relative influence of such factors, and the most suitable focus of treatment for a given problem (p. 374).

TOWARD THIRD-GENERATION BEHAVIOR THERAPY

It is clearly legitimate for behavior therapy to explore all areas of experimental and social psychology. However, it seems prudent that behavior therapists do this in a way that preserves the basic science/applied science relation. Extrapolating regularities found by basic researchers has epistemic advantages as described above. As previously mentioned, there is reason to be somewhat pessimistic about the usefulness of certain areas of basic psychology. Some of these areas do not share any of the three important confluences: (1) a shared search to understand how experience changes behavior; (2) a shared use of single-subject methodologies; and (3) a mutual reliance on large, "clinically significant" change.

The potential or actual usefulness of other areas of basic psychology does not reduce the relevance or importance of contemporary learning research. Nothing that occurred during the second generation of behavior therapy obviated the usefulness of conditioning research. However, learning is not a settled area. *Behavior therapists need to keep up with the evidential status of learning principles.*

An example may provide a clearer idea of what third-generation behavior therapy would look like. Third-generation behavior therapy suggests new ways of analyzing and intervening with clinically relevant behaviors. First-generation behavior therapists would examine individual contingencies to find controlling variables. However, third-generation behavior therapists would not view the behavior of the organism as controlled by a single contingency but rather as under the influence of multiple contingencies. Thus, the behavior therapist needs to understand the organism's behavior as an example of choice behavior, and as being influenced by *competing* contingencies. The matching law dictates an analysis of multiple sources of reinforcement, not just the simple, single contingency on which the first-generation behavior therapist would focus. McDowell (1982) argued:

> Hernstein's equation is considerably more descriptive of natural human environments than Skinner's earlier view of reinforcement. It is not always easy to isolate Skinnerian response-reinforcement units in the natural environment. Hernstein's equation makes efforts to do so unnecessary and moreover, obsolete. The equation can help clinicians conceptualize cases more effectively and design treatments regimens more efficiently. It also suggests new treatment strategies that may be especially useful in difficult cases. (p.778)

The matching law would predict that reducing the reinforcement of competing responses should increase responding in the other contingency. Somewhat counterintuitively (at least to first-generation behavior therapists), the frequency of a behavior can be altered not only by manipulating the contingency the behavior is involved in, but also by the contingency of a competing behavior.

As a further example, behavior therapists often wish to identify reinforcers to influence the behavior of their clients. First-generation behavior therapists used Skinner's empirical law of effect, which renders reinforcer identification a post hoc process: Reinforcers are stimuli that when presented contingently upon some response increase the frequency of that response. Third-generation behavior therapists could rely on response deprivation/free operant analysis (Timberlake, 1995) to more accurately, more fully, and antecedently identify reinforcers. Using a free operant analysis, behaviors that occur within the system can be identified as reinforcers. Further, any behavior that occurs in the situation can be deprived and function as a reinforcer. This more contemporary analysis is useful because it (1) can *antecedently* identify what will function as a reinforcer; (2) can uncover "natural" reinforcers that occur within the system; (3) precisely describes the conditions needed to produce a reinforcer (deprivation is transformed from an unclear initial condition in the empirical law of effect to having an explicit and clear role); (4) indicates that there is no special and unique class of reinforcers; (5) describes a wider range of reinforcers; and (6) indicates why something will function as a reinforcer.

Moreover, third-generation behavior therapists can rely on further behavioral principles to greatly augment the analysis of client behavior. Staddon's behavioral-regulation account of the preservation of "bliss points" can be used to make point predictions of response change under the influence of constraints such as contingencies. This analysis suggests that the organism attempts to preserve responses in fixed proportions. This can be further augmented by behavioral economics. The notion of elastic versus inelastic demand (or Staddon's defense variable and Rachlin's research on substitutability; see Green and Freed, this volume) is also relevant and potentially important. Depriving an organism of a response that is elastic or substitutable is a weaker intervention than deprivation of a nonsubstitutable or less elastic reinforcer. That is, individuals will try to preserve certain behaviors that are constrained (e.g., sleep) more than others (reading a newspaper). Under constraint, the organism will sometimes seek to make substitutions for constrained behaviors. If water is constrained and juice freely available, many subjects will not engage in a higher frequency of the instrumental response and simply drink more juice instead. Thus, in third-generation behavior therapy, concepts such as response deprivation, choice, matching law, bliss points, behavioral regulation, and substitutability, among others, will enrich and enhance the behavior therapist's analysis and treatment.

This book is an attempt to make contemporary learning research and theory accessible to behavior therapists. Additionally, it is hoped that learning researchers will be more mindful of dissemination and utilization issues and more frequently write in an accessible manner so that applied psychologists can more routinely access their important work. It is also hoped that learning researchers will conduct basic human conditioning studies to more clearly investigate the relevance to humans of their initial studies with animals. Often, basic researchers are best equipped to understand how protocols may need to be modified or augmented when applied to significant responses of humans. This would greatly aid behavior therapists' extrapolations to clinically significant behaviors.

Part of the excitement and promise of first-generation behavior therapy was that behavior therapists were not simply technicians. They knew how to faithfully execute procedures but also understood the underlying principles upon which these were based. The first-generation behavior therapists understood the basic learning principles and could creatively and opportunistically apply them. Their repertoire was complex and led to many innovative and faithful applications. It is hoped that the subsequent chapters in this book will help reinstate this deep and faith-

ful understanding of learning principles. As Kalish (1981) stated:

> The inclination to regard the methods of intervention in behavior modification as a collection of standardized techniques is especially misleading. It tends to obscure one of the most important contributions to the understanding of behavior change made by the advent of behavior modification procedures: namely, that for every so-called technique, there is a more fundamental and more general principle of behavior derived from research with animals and/or humans which can be applied to the solution of a problem in human functioning. This means, among other things, that those who intend to use behavior modification to help solve human problems should be aware of these principles and resourceful enough to propose treatment strategies which fit the case after a thorough analysis of the conditions which initiate and maintain the behavior. (p. 3)

REFERENCES

Abramson, L. Y., Seligman, M. E. P., & Teasdale, J. D. (1978). Learned helplessness in humans: Critique and reformulation. *Journal of Abnormal Psychology, 87*, 49–74.

Baer, D. M., Wolf, M., & Risley, T. R. (1968). Some current dimensions of applied behavior analysis. *Journal of Applied Behavior Analysis, 1*, 91–97.

Bandura, A. (1969). *Principles of behavior modification.* New York: Holt, Rinehart & Winston.

Bijou, S. W. (1955). A systematic approach to the experimental analysis of young children. *Child Development, 26*, 161–168.

Bijou, S. W. (1959). Learning in children. *Monographs for the Society for Research in Child Development,* 24.

Breger, L., & McGaugh, J. L. (1965). Critque and reformulation of "learning theory": Approaches to psychotherapy and neurosis. *Psychological Bulletin, 63*, 338–358.

Davison, G., & Neale, J. (1974). *Abnormal psychology: An experimental clinical approach.* New York: Wiley.

Dollard, J., & Miller, N. E. (1950). *Personality and psychotherapy.* New York: McGraw-Hill.

Ellis, A., & Harper, R. A. (1975). *A new guide to rational living.* Englewood Cliffs, N.J.: Prentice-Hall.

Erwin, E. (1978). *Behavior therapy: Scientific, philosophical, & moral foundations.* Cambridge: Cambridge University Press.

Eysenck, H. J. (1952). The effects of psychotherapy: An evaluation. *Journal of Counseling Psychology, 16*, 319–324.

Eysenck, H. J. (ed.) (1960). *Behavior therapy and the neuroses*. New York: Pergamon.

Eysenck, H. J. (ed.) (1964). *Experiments in behavior therapy*. Oxford: Pergamon.

Franks, C. M. (ed.) (1964). *Conditioning techniques in clinical practice and research*. New York: Springer.

Franks, C. M., & Wilson, G. T. (1975). *Annual review of behavior therapy theory and practice*. New York: Brunner/Mazel.

Goldfried, M. R., & Davison, G. C. (1976). *Clinical behavior therapy*. New York: Holt.

Hayes, S. C., Rincover, A., & Solnick, J. V. (1980). The technical drift of applied behavior analysis, *Journal of Applied Behavior Analysis, 13*, 275–285.

Hempel, C. G. (1966). *Philosophy of natural science*. Englewood Cliffs, N.J.: Prentice-Hall.

Jones, M. C. (1924a). The elimination of children's fears. *Journal of Experimental Psychology, 7*, 383–390.

Jones, M. C. (1924b). A laboratory study of fear: The case of Peter. *Journal of Genetic Psychology, 31*, 308–315.

Kalish, H. I. (1981). *From behavioral science to behavior modification*. New York: McGraw-Hill.

Kanfer, F. H., & Phillips, J. S. (1970). *Learning foundations of behavior therapy*. New York: Wiley.

Kazdin, A. E. (1978). *History of behavior modification*. Baltimore: University Park Press.

Kuhn, T. S. (1970). *The structure of scientific revolutions*. Chicago: University of Chicago Press.

Lang, P. J. (1977). Imagery in therapy: An information processing analysis: *Behavior Therapy, 8*, 862–886.

Lazarus, A. A. (1968). A plea for technical and theoretical breadth. *AABT Newsletter, 3*, 2.

Lazarus, A. A. (1969). Broad-spectrum behavior therapy. *AABT Newsletter, 4*, 5–6.

Lindsley, O. R., Skinner, B. F., & Solomon, H. C. (1953). Studies in behavior therapy: Status report 1. Waltham, Mass.: Metropolitan State Hospital.

Mahoney, M. J. (1974). *Cognition and behavior modification*. Cambridge, Mass.: Ballinger.

Mahoney, M. J. (1984). Behaviorism, cognitivism, and human change processes. In M. A. Reda & M. J. Mahoney (eds.), *Cognitive psychotherapies*, 3–30. Cambridge, Mass.: Ballinger.

McDowell, J. J. (1982). The importance of Herrnstein's mathematical statement of the law of effect for behavior therapy. *American Psychologist, 37*, 771–779.

Mowrer, O. H., & Mowrer, W. M. (1938). Enuresis: A method for its study and treatment. *American Journal of Orthopsychiatry, 8*, 436–459.

O'Donohue, W., & Halsey, L. (1997). The substance of the scientist-practitioner relation: Freud, Rogers, Skinner, & Ellis. *New Ideas in Psychology*.

O'Donohue, W. T., & McKelvie, M. (1993). Problems in the case for psychotherapeutic integration. *Journal of Behavior Therapy and Experimental Psychiatry, 24*, 161–170.

Patterson, G. R. (1969). Behavioral techniques based upon social learning: An additional base for developing behavior modification technologies. In C. M. Franks (ed.), *Behavior therapy: Appraisal and status*, 341–374. New York: McGraw-Hill.

Paul, G. L. (1966). *Insight vs. desensitization in psychotherapy*. Stanford, Calif: Stanford University Press.

Poling, A., Picker, M., Grossett, D., Hall-Johnson, E., & Holbrook, M. (1981). The schism between experimental and applied behavioral analysis: Is it real and who cares? *The Behavior Analyst, 4*, 93–102.

Rimm, D. C., & Masters, J. C. (1979). *Behavior Therapy: Techniques and findings* (2nd ed.). New York: Academic Press.

Salter, A. (1949). *Conditioned reflex therapy*. New York: Creative Age Press.

Watson, J. B., & Rayner, R. (1920). Conditioned emotional reactions. *Journal of Experimental Psychology, 3*, 1–14.

Task Force on Promotion and Dissemination of Psychological Procedures (1995). Training in and dissemination of empirically-validated psychological treatments: Report and recommendations. *The Clinical Psychologist, 48*, 3–23.

Ullmann, L. P., & Krasner, L. (1969). *A psychological approach to abnormal behavior*. Englewood Cliffs, N.J.: Prentice-Hall.

Ullmann, L. P., & Krasner, L. (eds) (1965). *Case studies in behavior modification*. New York: Holt, Rinehart & Winston.

Wilson, G. T. (1982). The relationship of learning theories to the behavioral therapies: Problems, prospects, and preferences. In J. Boulougouris (ed.), *Learning theory approaches to psychiatry*, 33–56. New York: Wiley.

Wolpe, J. (1958). *Psychotherapy by reciprocal inhibition*. Stanford, Calif.: Stanford University Press.

Wolpe, J. (1969). *The practice of behavior therapy*. New York: Pergamon.

CHAPTER 2

HUMANS ARE ANIMALS, TOO: CONNECTING ANIMAL RESEARCH TO HUMAN BEHAVIOR AND COGNITION

Marc N. Branch
Timothy D. Hackenberg

More than any other approach to psychotherapy, behavior therapy and cognitive behavior therapy have direct ties to research with nonhumans. The origins of many therapeutic techniques employed by behavior therapists can be traced directly to results of research with nonhumans, and general conceptualizations employed by behavior therapists often have their roots in research with nonhumans (cf. Martin & Pear, 1996). These conceptualizations are based, in the main, on the assumption that behavior is modifiable by experience, that is, that particular categories of experience can lead to particular kinds of changes in subsequent behavior.

Using nonhumans to conduct research on the effects of experience offers several advantages over trying to conduct such research directly with humans. The advantages are evident mainly in the ability to exercise experimental control. Better control is available with respect to two important dimensions. First, conditions of experiments proper can be more tightly controlled with nonhumans, and second, greater control can be exercised over the experiences of the subjects outside of the experiments. When one studies an adult human, the subject brings many years of unspecified and unknowable experience to the situation. That is an especially unsatisfying state of affairs for a science that attempts to examine the effects of experience on behavior. Allowing the main category of variables of interest to vary in an uncontrolled fashion is problematic, to say the least. By employing nonhumans, experience can be controlled to a much greater degree.

Granting that more rigorous experimental control can be brought to bear when nonhumans are the subject of experimentation that examines effects of experience, the relevance of such experiments to human behavior and therefore to behavior therapy depends on the existence of continuity of process between humans and non-humans. It is our goal in this chapter to argue that such continuity does exist. To that end, we first discuss two major lines of argument against the proposition we are supporting. Specifically, we deal with the issues of whether explicitly arranged consequences (intended as rewards) undermine "intrinsic motivation," and of whether fundamental conditioning processes can be shown to exist in verbally competent adult humans. Upon reviewing the relevant literature, we conclude that neither of these criticisms has serious merit, although both have implications for how one draws connections between nonhuman animal experimentation and human behavior. We next discuss briefly the logic and rationale underlying the extrapolation from nonhuman to human behavior, and the conditions under which such extrapolations may be warranted. The remainder of the chapter is directed at explaining how research with nonhumans informs us about human behavior, including behavior that ordinarily would be described as cognitive or under cognitive control. That is, we hope to convince even the most committed of cognitively oriented therapists that research on the behavior of nonhumans has important relevance for the effective employment and development of therapeutic techniques.

DOES EXPLICIT REWARD UNDERMINE "INTRINSIC MOTIVATION"?

Perhaps the most important central concept in the study of behavior of nonhumans is reinforcement (see Donahoe, this volume). There exists a voluminous literature that illustrates how arranging consequences for various actions can change the future probability of those actions. When the probability is increased, the process observed is referred to as reinforcement. Reinforcement is central to the study of nonhuman animal behavior, even when reinforcement itself is not the object of study. Reinforcement is employed to study discrimination, emotional responding, drug effects, and even Pavlovian

processes, among others. There exists also a substantial literature illustrating that human behavior, too, is sensitive to its consequences (e.g., Bailey, Shook, Iwata, Reid, & Repp, 1989; Sulzer-Azaroff, Drabman, Greer, Hall, Iwata, & O'Leary, 1990). Since the early 1970s, however, a challenge to the relevance of reinforcement to human behavior has emerged. Specifically, it has been argued, and some would say demonstrated, that arranging consequences for humans that are assumed to be ones that would produce reinforcement instead produces decrements in performance. The argument basically is that humans are fundamentally different from other animals when it comes to the effects of consequences. If that is true, then research with nonhuman animals that uses reinforcement is of questionable relevance to understanding human behavior.

The earliest work on "detrimental" effects of reward was reported by Deci (1971). In his original experiment, Deci had college students attempt to solve commercially available puzzles. Twenty-four subjects were divided into two groups. Each subject was exposed individually to three, one-hour sessions. In each session, a subject was asked to solve four puzzles. In the middle of each session, the experimenter left the room for eight minutes, and during this eight-minute period measurements were made of how much time a subject spent working on the puzzle. In the first session all subjects merely worked on the puzzles. In the second session, the experimental-group subjects were told they would receive $1 for each puzzle successfully solved, whereas the control-group subjects were told nothing and received nothing. The third session was like the first: the subjects were asked simply to solve the puzzles, and the key data were taken from this session. Deci hypothesized that subjects in the experimental group would spend less of the eight-minute measurement period working on the puzzles than would subjects in the control group. A one-tailed t test supported the hypothesis at the $p<.10$ level. His interpretation was that the results supported the view that, "If a person is engaged in some activity for reasons of intrinsic motivation, and if he begins to receive the external reward, money, for performing the activity, the degree to which he is intrinsically motivated to perform the activity decreases" (Deci, p. 108).

Shortly after the publication of Deci's work, Lepper, Greene, and Nisbett (1973) reported a similar effect with nursery school children, and their results have been widely cited. In their study, children were observed while engaged in drawing. Children who spent a lot of time drawing during a free-play period were selected as subjects. Three conditions were then compared. Children in an expected-reward condition were told they would receive a good-player award for drawing. Children in an unexpected-reward group received awards for drawing but were not informed in advance that they would get them, and children in a no-reward condition were given neither advance notice nor awards. In a post-manipulation free-play period, children in the expected-reward group spent less time drawing than children in the other two groups and also spent less time drawing than they had in the original free-play period. Lepper et al. concluded that their findings represented "empirical evidence of an undesirable consequence of the unnecessary use of extrinsic rewards" (p. 136). This conclusion is interesting in light of the fact that children in the unexpected-reward group showed more time spent drawing in the last free-play period than children in either of the other two groups.

These initial reports led to the generation of a substantial and complex literature on the issue of the interplay of external rewards and intrinsic motivation. A recent set of meta-analyses reported by Cameron and Pierce (1994) highlights the complexity of the resulting literature. Cameron and Pierce were able to segregate papers in the literature according to several dimensions. Studies have used a range of dependent variables including not only time spent engaged in an activity, but also verbal reports of interest or liking, as well as actual measures of accuracy of performance. There has been even wider variation in implementation of the reward phases of experiments. Here, procedures vary according to whether consequences were announced in ad-

vance, whether they were contingent on any of several aspects of performance, and whether they actually served as demonstrable reinforcers. The complexity of the research on rewards and intrinsic motivation is illustrated in the summary of the meta-analysis that was presented by Cameron and Pierce. The summary is shown in Figure 1–1.

The analysis separated studies by the four major types of dependent variable that have been employed, and these are denoted in the four boxes across the top. The row just under the boxes shows the results of the overall meta-analyses for the four dependent variables. For three of the dependent variables, the analysis reveals no overall effect, either positive or negative, of prior reward on subsequent intrinsically motivated behavior. There is a statistically significant effect for the attitude measures. These are measures of how subjects like the task with which rewards were associated, and, interestingly the overall effect is a positive, not negative, one. The effect is largest when verbal rewards were employed.

Perhaps surprisingly, the free-time measure, the measure used by Deci (1971) and Lepper et al. (1973), also revealed no overall effect. Cameron and Pierce's (1994) review included 61 experiments in which measures of time allocated to the intrinsically motivated activity served as the dependent variable. Of these, 34 reveal a negative effect of prior reward, whereas 22 show the reverse. Given the diversity of results, Cameron and Pierce performed a more detailed analysis as illustrated in Figure 1–1. Use of verbal reward (e.g., praise) yielded a positive effect of prior reward, whereas tangible rewards produced an overall negative effect. Further analyses revealed that tangible rewards produced a statistically significant deficit only when tangible rewards were announced in advance (labeled "Expected" in the figure) and were not contingent on successful performance. ("Task contingent" in the figure means that rewards merely depended upon engaging in a task, with no performance criteria.) These very narrow and specific circumstances were employed by both Deci (1971) and Lepper et al. (1973).

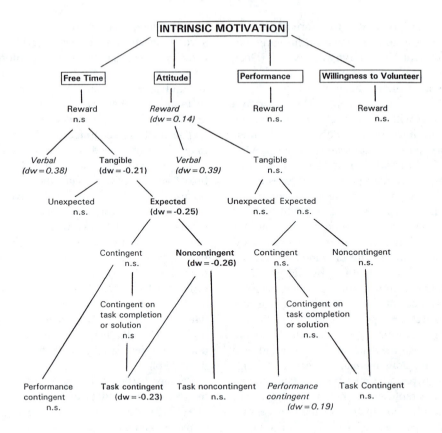

Figure 2–1. Summary of results of the overall and targeted meta-analyses of research on effects of extrinsic reward on intrinsic motivation. The four boxes across the top indicate the four major types of dependent variables employed in research. Results of overall meta-analyses for each of the four types are given in the next row. Lower rows provide findings with reward and contingency type separated. Italics indicate a statistically significant positive effect, and boldface type indicates a statistically significant negative effect. The "dw" value is a measure of the magnitude of effect. (Adapted from Cameron & Pierce, 1994)

Cameron and Pierce's (1994) review provides compelling evidence that the so-called deleterious effect of reward is a highly constrained phenomenon, at best. It is important to recall, too, that these effects, even when they do occur, have been observed in very short observation periods (cf. Dickinson, 1989). The findings of detrimental effects of rewards stand in contrast to the voluminous literature indicating large and long-lasting effects of arranging consequences contingent on specific activities (e.g, Catania, 1992).

The best conclusion at this time is that deleterious effects of reward on subsequent performance generally are rare.

It is interesting, however, that in some circumstances detrimental effects of prior reward can be observed. An understanding of the phenomenon is important because some attempts at arranging consequences can share the features that seem critical for observing deleterious effects. In many applications contingencies are announced, and in some cases consequences are provided for mere participation. These are exactly the circumstances in which detrimental effects have been observed.

Although the undermining of intrinsic motivation by extrinsic consequences is a very limited phenomenon, any thorough analysis of how consequences influence subsequent behavior must deal with the rare deleterious effects. One such account involves the interaction of self-descriptive behavior and current contingencies. In a learning-based account, people learn via reinforcement from the social community, to describe their own behavior (Skinner, 1953, 1974). Importantly, persons learn to describe both their public and private behavior (e.g., we learn to report where our arm is, what we just said, or what we just thought). The social community bases the delivery of reinforcement on correspondence between the referent and the label. The processes involved are presumed to be fundamentally the same whether the referent is public or private (Skinner, 1945). Once we have learned to listen (i.e., to react to the verbalizations of others), our own verbalizations may act as stimuli that influence what we do (see Hayes and Ju's chapter on rule-governed behavior in this volume). Just as the social community offers positive feedback for accurate self-descriptive talk, so does it approve correspondence between what we say we are doing (or going to do) and what we actually do. Self-descriptive talk, be it public or private, thus may come to exert influence over what we do, presumably through processes similar to those involved in establishing operant stimulus control of any activity. A child who plays for a long period with puzzles might, as a result of experience in developing a self-descriptive repertoire, say to herself, "I love playing with puzzles" (cf. Bem, 1972). When behavior like playing with puzzles occurs in a context in which there is no apparent external constraint, we all learn to attribute the action to internal causes, and perhaps even to call it something like "intrinsic motivation." In Western culture, the presence of external constraints (e.g., announced rewards), however, raises the specter of "control" of behavior, something we learn is bad and should be resisted. Consequently, when faced with a situation in which engaging in a normally pleasing activity results in extrinsic reward, control of behavior by private verbalizations about control may predominate over control by the rewards. That is, intrinsically motivated behavior might be suppressed by the presence of extrinsic rewards.

CAN CONDITIONING OCCUR IN VERBALLY COMPETENT HUMANS?

A second challenge to the premise that conditioning principles apply to human behavior concerns the role of awareness in conditioning. In a widely cited review paper, Brewer (1974) asked whether operant or Pavlovian conditioning had been convincingly demonstrated in adult human subjects, and concluded that these had not. Brewer defined *conditioning* as experience-based changes for which verbal involvement was shown to be completely lacking, and defined *cognitive* as everything else. According to Brewer, subjects develop "conscious hypotheses and expectations about the experiment, and . . . these produce the resulting 'conditioning' " (p. 2). Stated in a slightly different way, a subject's ongoing verbal behavior can interact with, and in some cases alter, other aspects of performance under investigation. On this point we are in complete agreement with Brewer. Humans acquire behavior not only through direct contact with contingencies, but also through verbal descriptions of those contingencies, including their own descriptions. When faced with a novel or challenging arrangement of contingencies, like those encountered in a psychology experiment, a subject is very likely to engage in overt or covert verbalizations regarding the task requirements. As mentioned previously, such self-talk can influence the degree to which other behavior is sensitive to the contingencies arranged within the experiment. Also, by virtue of long histories of describing contingencies and the correspondence between behavior and those contingencies, adult human subjects are frequently aware of—in the sense of being able to report on—

their own behavior and on some of the circumstances surrounding it. We therefore have no quarrel with Brewer's contention that adult human subjects, when asked, are often able to describe the task requirements they are responding under; this is an inevitable result of the verbal history they bring with them to the experiment. Where we part company with Brewer's position is with respect to the claims that such awareness is *necessary* for conditioning to occur; and that when awareness is present, it cannot be accounted for by straightforward behavioral processes but instead requires a cognitive account.

The second claim is addressed in a later section in which we sketch a learning-based account of verbal behavior and its relation to other behavior. The first claim is addressed here. We focus on Brewer's claims because he states explicitly what many cognitively oriented accounts only assume, namely that learning is rational and conscious. If this view is accurate, and awareness is necessary for behavior to be modified by experience, then one would expect accurate self-reports to be readily available to subjects performing laboratory tasks. If, on the other hand, awareness is not necessary for learning to occur, then one might expect to find at least occasional dissociations between task performances and self-reports of such performances. This section examines some of the empirical support for the latter case, showing some of the circumstances under which one may speak appropriately of unconscious learning—that is, of behavioral changes in the absence of corresponding verbal descriptions. Such dissociations of task performance from task-related verbalizations are important in showing that an ability to learn from experiences is a basic fact that applies to a wide range of species, whether those species can talk about the contingencies or not.

Conditioning During Altered States of Consciousness

In a series of experiments, Lindsley and colleagues established operant responding during various states of subconscious activity, including sleep (Lindsley, 1957), surgical anesthesia (Lindsley, Hobika, & Etsten, 1961), and electroconvulsive shock-induced coma (Lindsley & Conran, 1962). In the basic procedure, operation of a hand switch (by touching the thumb to the index finger of the preferred hand) reduced the intensity of a tone presented to a subject over earphones. A conjugate reinforcement procedure was used, whereby the intensity of the tone was a continuous function of response rate. Rapid responding reduced tone intensity to its minimum; sustained responding prevented its onset altogether. In the absence of responding, the tone was presented continuously at its maximum intensity. In the study examining behavior during sleep, for example, responding occurred at high, sustained rates prior to sleep (which effectively prevented the tone), and ceased altogether during periods of deep sleep (which maintained the tone at its maximum intensity). These periods of high and low responding defined end points on a continuum ranging from full wakefulness to deep sleep. Lindsley showed how these measures varied as an orderly function of sleep deprivation and drug administration. Of particular interest to Lindsley, however, were intermediate response rates, presumed to reflect various stages of subconscious activity. During the final three to four hours of the eight-hour observation time, periods of rapid responding alternated with periods of low responding. These "response bursts," which grew more frequent in the final hours of sleep, were unrelated to general body movements or to subjects' subsequent verbal reports.

An interesting example of a dissociation between the measured operant response and ongoing verbal activity on these procedures is provided by Lindsley and Conran (1962). In this study, a psychiatric patient's responding was examined before, during, and after a brief coma induced by an electroconvulsive shock procedure. As in the other studies, responses reduced the intensity of a tone in a continuous fashion. Following a near-complete suppression of responding during a 10- to 15-minute period of deep coma, responding gradually recovered to intermediate rates, which dropped tone intensity to moderate levels. Soon thereafter, the patient began to talk with the attending physician. Unlike the baseline period, however, when the patient talked to the physician and pressed the hand switch concurrently (keeping the tone off), he now talked but stopped pressing the hand switch. Because this increased the tone to its maximum intensity, the resulting conversation was strained at best: the patient tried to lip-read and talk at volumes exceeding the tone. This period of talking without pressing soon gave way to a full recovery of baseline activity, in which pressing and talking occurred together. Although lasting only a few minutes, such partial recovery of functioning (first pressing without talking, then talking without pressing) calls attention to the relationship between conditioning and its verbal accompaniments.

Because these experiments were not explicitly designed to assess the role of awareness, the verbal-report data are rather sketchy. Nevertheless, it is clear that responding was established and maintained with little or no verbal behavior appropriate to the contingencies. Summarizing the results of these studies, Lindsley et al. (1961) state: " . . . [It] was shown that differential free-operant motor responses can be produced and maintained in individuals in states in which they cannot verbally describe the responding either at the time it occurs or after it has occurred. Also, such responding occurs in states in which verbal response to questions and motor response to commands are absent" (p. 945).

In a more recent study, Boyle and Greer (1983) reported sensitivity of behavior in comatose patients to contingent music delivery. Specific target responses and potential reinforcers (musical excerpts) were selected for each of three patients who had been in varying degrees of coma for periods ranging from 10 to 38 months. The patients were generally unresponsive to stimulation and lacked verbal skills of any sort. A discrete-trial procedure was used; trials were defined by an experimenter's request to make one of a subject's three individually selected target responses and an opportunity to comply with the request. Responses within 10

seconds of the request produced 15 seconds of that patient's preferred music. Using a combination of reversal and multiple-baseline comparisons within subjects, Boyle and Greer were able to show clear effects attributable to the reinforcement contingencies in one subject and weaker but discernible effects in a second subject. Although the effects were not terribly robust, what is striking about these results is that the changes in behavior were clearly not mediated by verbal behavior: subjects were incapable of describing either the contingencies or their behavior with respect to those contingencies. Few, if any, definitions of consciousness would include this level of functioning, yet behavior was still modifiable by its consequences.

Conditioning of Covert Responses

Perhaps the most convincing demonstrations of learning without awareness were conducted by Hefferline and associates (Hefferline, Keenan, & Harford, 1959; Hefferline & Keenan, 1963; Hefferline & Perrera, 1963). In a series of experiments, these researchers successfully brought small-scale covert activity under control of its consequences. Specifically, myoelectrical activity in the thumb region of the hand (hereafter called "thumb twitching") was reinforced and extinguished, normally in the absence of corresponding verbal reports. In one experiment, for example, thumb twitching in four adult human subjects was established and extinguished through contingent delivery of points later exchangeable for money (Hefferline & Keenan, 1963). This was accomplished by reinforcing thumb twitches falling within specified target regions, determined individually for each subject. The target region for each subject was one in which very few thumb twitches occurred during a preconditioning baseline period. When point delivery was made contingent on such thumb twitches, they increased steadily relative to twitches in other (unreinforced) regions. By the end of the conditioning phase (which lasted from 60 to 90 minutes, across subjects), responding in the target region had supplanted responding in adjacent regions as the modal response class in all four subjects. To verify that the changes were indeed the result of contingent point delivery, the contingency was suspended for a brief period of time (10 to 23 minutes, across subjects), during which responding in the target region returned to approximately its baseline level. In brief post-session interviews, subjects were unable to describe the contingencies, despite responding that had clearly been under control of those contingencies.

The results of an earlier study (Hefferline et al., 1959) are even more relevant to the present issues. As in the Hefferline and Keenan experiment, thumb twitching in adult human subjects was examined before, during, and after reinforcement contingencies were applied to it. But thumb twitching in this experiment, rather than producing points, escaped from or avoided loud noise. Each thumb twitch in the target region terminated the noise (if it was on) or postponed it (if it was not) for 15 seconds. Responding was readily established by the negative-reinforcement contingency in all six subjects provided with minimal or incomplete instructions. Interestingly, behavior was less sensitive to the contingencies when subjects were provided with complete and accurate descriptions of the contingencies. Two of three subjects who were explicitly told that the effective response involved a tiny twitch of the left hand showed negligible effects of the contingencies. The instruction presumably interfered with conditioning by establishing an overt thumb twitch incompatible with the smaller reinforced variety. Thus, instructions, even when they accurately describe a set of contingencies, do not necessarily produce better conditioning with respect to those contingencies. The significance of this fact will be considered later.

In a more recent study, Laurenti-Lions, Gallego, Chambille, Vardon, and Jacquemin (1985) replicated part of the Hefferline et al. (1959) experiment with a more advanced technology, including fully automated contingencies and better instrumentation. Unlike in the earlier study, no task-relevant instructions were provided to any of the subjects. Despite the absence (or perhaps

because of the absence) of such instructions, conditioning effects were even stronger here than in the earlier experiment. Thumb twitching increased in those subjects for whom such responding terminated or postponed noise, relative to control subjects for whom no such contingency existed. Also consistent with most of the earlier results, subjects were unable to verbalize the response-reinforcement contingency.

Conditioning of Verbal Responses

One area of investigation in which the theoretical controversies over the role of awareness in human learning once raged concerns the conditioning of verbal responses. In a widely cited paper, Greenspoon (1955) reported modifying the frequency of particular classes of verbal responses in adult human subjects. Subjects were asked to say aloud as many words as possible over a 50-minute period in the presence of an experimenter. The contingencies were somewhat different for different groups of subjects. For one group, particularly relevant to the present issues, the contingencies were as follows: during the first 25 minutes of the session, the experimenter said, "mmm-hmm" whenever the subject emitted a plural noun; during the second 25 minutes of the session, the experimenter said nothing. Relative to a control group of subjects for whom no such contingency between plural nouns and experimenter feedback was arranged, the frequency of plural nouns increased during the first 25 minutes, then dropped to approximately control levels by the end of the 50-minute session. When asked at the end of the session to report on any changes in behavior or about the function of the experimenter feedback, 14 of 15 subjects in the contingent-feedback condition were unable to do so. (Data from the one subject who did report on such relations were discarded from the analysis pertaining to reinforcement effects.)

These results raised important questions about the necessity of verbal mediation in human conditioning. Although Greenspoon was interested primarily in bringing verbal behavior under operant control, his findings effectively launched an active area of research and interpretation concerned with the role of awareness in human learning. For those who held verbal mediation necessary to behavior change, experiments like Greenspoon's purporting to show learning in the absence of awareness were roundly criticized, primarily on methodological grounds. Criticisms focused on assessments of awareness and generally took one of two forms: (1) subjects may actually be aware of the contingencies, but brief postsession queries are simply not sensitive enough to detect it (Levin, 1961), or (2) subjects may verbalize partially accurate descriptions of the contingencies (so-called "correlated hypotheses") that go undetected in conventional postsession assessments of awareness (Dulany, 1961).

To respond to such criticisms, some investigators included extended postsession interviews, which provided many opportunities to reveal relations between subjects' behavioral changes and any of their correlated verbal behavior in relation to those changes (Oakes, 1967; Williams, 1977). Williams (1977), for instance, exposed subjects to a sentence-construction task, in which particular verb tenses were followed by experimenter feedback ("Correct"). Unlike in the Greenspoon (1955) study, subjects in this experiment were encouraged to develop hypotheses concerning the procedure. Specifically, they were told that the task was one involving problem solving and that they were to try to identify the basis for the experimenter's feedback. Immediately after the session, subjects were asked a series of 16 questions that probed their verbal responses to virtually every aspect of the procedure. Williams categorized as "aware" any subject who reported generating and following for even one trial any hypothesis that was even remotely related to the arranged contingencies. These subjects (which accounted for only 16 of the 64 subjects tested) were then eliminated from the analysis, despite the fact that many of them were incapable of actually describing the contingencies (and thus would have been considered "unaware" by most measures). Williams reported evidence of learning in many of the remaining subjects in the absence of any task-relevant verbalizations.

An experiment by Thaver and Oakes (1967) also used an extended postsession interview to assess awareness subsequent to a sentence-construction task. Sentences that included particular classes of verbs (either neutral or hostile) were followed by an experimenter's saying, "Good." Prior to the postsession interview, however, subjects were taken to a different room and asked to write a story in relation to each of two pictures (taken from the Thematic Apperception Test), a manipulation designed to assess transfer. The postsession interview included questions regarding the conditioning trials, the transfer test, and the relation between them. On the whole, there was clear evidence of conditioning of verbal responses, even when those considered "aware" (approximately 24% of the sample) were omitted from the analysis. Moreover, these effects appeared to transfer to the second task, as evidenced by a greater number of words thematically related to those used in the conditioning phase. Performance on this transfer task was unrelated to awareness of the contingency during the conditioning trials or of the relationship between the conditioning trials and the transfer task. In other words, behavioral changes established in one setting transferred to a new setting in the absence of verbal descriptions appropriate to either setting or to the relationship between settings.

This general pattern of results bears resemblance to a growing body of research in cognitive psychology showing transfer of experiences learned in one setting to another setting in the absence of accompanying verbal descriptions (Broadbent, FitzGerald, & Broadbent, 1986; Reber, 1989; Roediger, 1990). The distinction between learning with and without supporting verbal descriptions parallels a distinction in human memory research between explicit (declarative) and implicit (procedural) memory, "with the former referring to verbalizable knowledge and the latter to the running off of skilled behavior without the need for conscious recollection" (Roediger, 1990, p. 1048).

A particularly interesting case of such implicit/procedural learning is provided by a series of studies by Lewicki and colleagues (Lewicki, Hill, & Bizot, 1988; Lewicki, Czyzewska, & Hoffman, 1987). In the basic task, subjects are asked to locate a target stimulus that always appears in one of four quadrants on a computer screen. The location of the stimulus varies from trial to trial and follows a subtle but predictable pattern. The typical finding is that performance improves with experience on the task in ways consistent with the arranged pattern, but in the absence of any task-relevant verbal reports: when interviewed (usually extensively) after the experiment, subjects are unable to report either following a rule, or any changes in their own behavior. Thus, although their behavior could be described by a rule, there was no evidence that it was governed by one.

Evaluative Conditioning

In a series of interesting experiments, Levey and Martin have shown that neutral visual stimuli (e.g., photographs), when paired with positively valued or negatively valued stimuli, assume the valence of those stimuli, even in the absence of a supporting verbal description of the contingencies (Levey & Martin, 1975, 1983; Martin & Levey, 1978). In the basic procedure, subjects are asked to rate a series of stimuli on a scale ranging from *liked* to *disliked*. Stimuli rated neutral (those falling in the middle of the scale) are then paired with stimuli rated both highly positive (the most liked stimulus) and highly negative (the most disliked stimulus) in a Pavlovian conditioning procedure. The typical finding is that the valence of these previously neutral stimuli changes in directions appropriate to the stimuli with which they were paired. That is, the neutral stimuli paired with positive ("liked") stimuli themselves assume a more positive valence, and those paired with negative ("disliked") stimuli assume a more negative valence (as defined by postconditioning ratings). Moreover, a high proportion of the subjects are unable to identify accurately which stimuli had

been paired together during the conditioning phase, prompting the authors to conclude that awareness of the contingency is not necessary for conditioning to occur.

In a more recent follow-up study, Baeyens, Eelen, and van den Bergh (1990) replicated Levey and Martin's findings, while also addressing some methodological problems concerning their assessment of awareness. Specifically, in response to the criticism discussed earlier that postexperimental queries may not be a fully adequate test of awareness, Baeyens et al. included more extensive assessments of a subject's awareness of the contingencies. In addition to the usual postexperimental "recognition" test (in which subjects were presented with a neutral stimulus and asked which other stimulus or stimuli had followed it during conditioning phase), half of the subjects were also asked to predict which stimulus type ("liked," "disliked," or "neutral") was likely to follow a neutral stimulus on a given trial during the conditioning phase. (The subject responded during a brief interstimulus interval.) This "concurrent-awareness" procedure was designed to provide an ongoing assessment of the degree to which subjects could accurately describe contingent relations between stimuli during conditioning. By comparing the degree of awareness of subjects exposed to these conditions with those exposed to the postexperimental queries alone, it was also possible to determine the extent to which the concurrent-awareness technique not only *measures* awareness but actually *creates* it, that is, by prompting contingency descriptions that would not otherwise have been present.

The results of the conditioning phase were consistent with the prior results of Levey and Martin: preference for the neutral stimuli changed in directions appropriate to the positively valued and negatively valued stimuli they had been paired with, while those paired with neutral stimuli changed little. Also consistent with the earlier findings, these changes appeared not to depend on a subject's ability to describe the contingencies. There was evidence of greater awareness in those subjects exposed to both the concurrent-awareness and postexperimental-awareness procedures than for those exposed to the postexperimental-awareness procedure only, suggesting that repeated, ongoing prompts for verbal reports can result in more accurate contingency descriptions. Nonetheless, this greater awareness did not result in better conditioning; the changes in responding to the neutral stimuli occurred regardless of a subject's degree of awareness. In a subgroup of subjects, conditioning effects were demonstrated despite a complete lack of awareness of the contingencies (adopting the most conservative definition of awareness possible).

Although important questions about the empirical and theoretical status of evaluative conditioning remain unanswered (Shanks & Dickinson, 1990), it joins with other experimental demonstrations of behavioral changes that appear not to depend on accurate verbal descriptions of the contingencies. Of particular importance is that verbal reports, even when accurate, did not necessarily result in better conditioning. Conditioning can be just as effective with or without supporting verbal descriptions of the contingencies. We will consider the implications of this fact for a general understanding of the role of verbal functioning in conditioning in a later section.

These results are broadly consistent with other studies showing dissociations between Pavlovian conditioning and verbal indices of such conditioning (Esteves, Parra, Dimberg, & Ohman, 1994; Weiskrantz & Warrington, 1979). For example, in an experiment examining radiation-induced taste aversion in cancer patients, Smith, Blumsack, Bilek, Spector, Hollander, and Baker (1984) reported strong evidence of taste aversion conditioning in the absence of corresponding verbal measures. All 10 subjects who experienced pairings of their preferred fruit juice with radiation markedly decreased consumption of the juice on test days (9 of the 10 subjects refused to drink any of the juice after several pairings). Despite the development of such strong aversion to the juice, only 4 of the 10 subjects reported liking it any less in verbal preference ratings collected in conjunction with the consumption data.

As was the case with evaluative conditioning, results such as these indicate that behavioral changes can and do occur in the absence of corresponding verbal indices of such changes. This is not to suggest that verbal descriptions are never aligned with behavioral changes—they undoubtedly are in many circumstances. An examination of such circumstances, as in studies of rule-governed behavior and of correspondences between saying and doing, is worth pursuing in its own right. Such work will help to clarify relations between what people say and what they do and the extent to which experiences that are verbal in nature interact with currently acting contingencies. At the same time, it should be recognized that operant and Pavlovian conditioning are fundamental processes that hold true whether accompanying verbal behavior is brought to bear on them or not.

THE LOGIC OF SPECIES CONTINUITY IN BEHAVIOR

Assuming continuity in behavioral processes across a variety of species does not imply that a general process like reinforcement will look the same in all those species, or that humans are no different than other animals. Rather, it is to suggest the possibility that a capacity to learn from experiences is something basic to biological functioning—perhaps so basic that it contributes to differential survival of those that possess it. Organisms whose behavior is not modifiable by their experiences simply do not live very long or prolific lives. To be sure, the particular events that enter into reinforcement relations will differ greatly across species, each one of which displays a wonderfully diverse array of adaptations suited to particular anatomies and environments. As Wasserman (1994) writes:

Pigeons fly through the air, rats run along the ground, and monkeys swing in the trees. The skeletal, muscular, and neural systems that permit these marvelously adapted movements must surely differ in important ways among these different species. Yet, decidedly different actions systems may nevertheless accomplish similar ends. For example, the attraction of all of these different species of animals to localized signals of positive reinforcement—whether the animals fly, run, or swing to those signals—is probably so basic a behavioral predisposition that nature has organized these different actions patterns along a single common plan. (p. 222)

To speak of a broadly applicable concept such as reinforcement should do nothing but heighten our appreciation for the remarkable ways in which it may be manifest in different species and habitats. The systematic study of the adaptive fit of various species to their habitats has traditionally been one of the focal concerns of ethology and comparative psychology. These concerns have too often been viewed as orthogonal to those of the experimental psychologist interested in general laws of behavior. But this need not be the case. It is quite possible to emphasize similarities of process that extend across different species while at the same time to recognize and appreciate differences in the ways in which those processes operate for different species in specialized habitats. Whether one focuses on the similarities or the differences depends on the kind of questions one is asking. If one is interested primarily in the adaptive fit of animals to particular niches and how such adaptations are related to phylogenetic influences, then closely related species with common lines of evolutionary descent should be studied. If, on the other hand, one is interested primarily (as we are here) in general principles applicable to a wide range of species, then it may be more profitable to study distantly related species, such as pigeons and humans. Rather than illuminating phylogenetic processes, studying distantly related species may reveal behavioral processes that cut across species and the vicissitudes of particular situations. As Hodos and Campbell (1969) pointed out in their seminal paper on the uses and misuses of species comparisons,

. . . [In] comparative psychology, the study of analogous behavior in animals of divergent groups may be very useful in formulating generalizations about behavioral adaptation to spe-

cific problems of survival. Such generalizations might have broad applicability to a number of lineages of the phylogenetic tree and would greatly aid in the interpretation of data obtained through the phylogenetic approach. (p. 347)

To acknowledge that humans are biological creatures is to identify a dimension along which they are similar to other animals. It does not mean that humans are similar along all dimensions, but rather that for some purposes these other dimensions can be ignored. An analogy may be useful here. If one is studying, say, gravitational forces, by dropping objects of different mass from the top of a building, it matters little whether the objects are human bodies or rocks; what is relevant is their mass. Along this dimension, human bodies can be ordered in a more or less continuous fashion with the rest of nature. Similarly, if one is studying a general behavioral process such as reinforcement, it matters little whether the species whose behavior is under investigation is a human, a rat, or a pigeon. This does not mean that humans are the same as rats or pigeons; important differences certainly exist. It simply means that for the present purposes, the dimensions along which they differ can be ignored. For the purpose of formulating general laws of behavior, humans are no different than other biological creatures *in the same sense that* for the purpose of formulating general laws of gravity, humans are no different than other physical objects.

Assuming cross-species continuity in behavioral process is an analytic strategy that has paid off handsomely in the study of learning and conditioning. The study of learning is the study of effects of experience on later performance. As noted earlier, studying nonhumans provides the prospect of controlling relevant history, whereas, as some of the material from the previous section illustrates, that task is much more difficult with humans. Interestingly, the study of nonhuman animals can provide information on the importance of existing verbal repertoires in certain kinds of tasks with humans. Similar kinds of tasks can be arranged for humans and nonhumans, and if the performances are similar, we can begin to feel more comfortable that advanced, verbal reasoning skills are not necessary for the capabilities to be exhibited. On the other hand, if the performances are not similar, possible verbal influences (both current and past) need to be considered. In either case, it is important to study human and nonhuman behavior under circumstances as similar as possible. Otherwise, differences in performance may be mistakenly attributed to human verbal functioning or some other species-typical characteristic, when they are actually the result of more mundane differences in procedure.

We are advocating here a cautious extrapolation from nonhuman to human behavior, one based on empirically derived commonalities. Ironically, such an approach is better suited to detect genuine species differences, should they exist, than an approach that assumes species differences from the outset. That is, by assuming that humans are fundamentally similar to other animals, we are in the most favorable position to identify what is uniquely human. As Skinner (1969) pointed out, "Although it is sometimes said that research on lower animals makes it impossible to discover what is uniquely human, it is only by studying the behavior of lower animals that we can tell what *is* distinctly human" (p. 101).

THE PATH TO CONCEPTUAL CLARITY

A general contribution made by the study of nonhumans concerns conceptual precision. Because experiments with nonhumans generally involve more rigorous control of extraneous variables than do experiments with humans, they often provide clearer perspective on issues. Consider, for example, the common concept of reinforcement. This concept emerged from the study of nonhumans, specifically from situations such as the following. A hungry rat is placed in a small chamber equipped with a movable lever and a receptacle into which food can be delivered. The rat is observed in this condition, and measurement is made of the frequency with

which it presses the lever. Subsequently, electronic circuitry is arranged so that each depression of the lever results in delivery of a small piece of food to the food receptacle. The usual result is that the frequency with which the rat presses the lever increases (usually dramatically).

Even in such highly controlled environments, variability in the form of behavior is evident. A rat pressing a lever never does so in exactly the same way twice (lever presses are like snowflakes in that regard). Clearly recognizing this feature of behavior, Skinner (1935) focused on classes of behavior rather than on individual instances, and he called these classes "operants." He argued that a profitable way to classify actions is on the basis of their function. For example, in the case of the lever press, each of the varied topographies emitted has the function of depressing the lever. What counts is what the behavior accomplishes. Virtually all experimental psychologists now work from this functional perspective, and its general implications should not be lost on therapists. When targeting behavior for change, the targets are most likely to be well chosen if they represent functional classes of actions.

One of the great strengths of the concept of the operant is its broad applicability. Most important from a therapeutic perspective is that it is not limited to small pieces of behavior (although it can be applied there with success). For example, traveling to New York can be considered as a single class of actions, even though one can go by plane, rail, auto, foot, bicycle, and so on. The key to classifying behavior in this instance is that all the different forms of behavior lead to the same outcome. Once a class of behavior has been identified by its function, it is possible to perform an empirical test to see if the different forms actually "hang together" as a class of behavior. Tests are accomplished by observing whether the frequencies of occurrence of the different forms covary when manipulations are made. For example, if the frequency of all forms of going to New York is diminished after flying there and having a terrible experience, then we gain confidence that "going to New York" is a functional class of behavior for that individual.

It is often useful to distinguish between two aspects of the concept of the operant: (1) responses that are necessary to satisfy the reinforcement contingency, and (2) responses that are generated by experience with the contingency. These usages correspond to a distinction between *descriptive* and *functional* definitions of an operant class (Catania, 1973). Descriptive operants specify the requirements for reinforcement (e.g., only lever presses exceeding a minimum force requirement will produce a food pellet). Functional operants describe the actual distribution of responding that results from contact with the contingency, including those that fail to meet the requirements of the contingency (e.g., lever presses not forceful enough to produce a food pellet).

For reinforcement to occur, the class of responses specified by the reinforcement contingency and the class of responses generated by that contingency must overlap (e.g., a rat's lever press must at least occasionally produce a food pellet). In those cases in which the two classes are in close alignment, the distinction between descriptive and functional operants is unnecessary; the contingencies generate just enough behavior to meet the requirements for reinforcement. In other cases, however, contingencies may give rise to a great deal of activity, only some of which is actually necessary in satisfying the contingencies. Said another way, environmental contingencies, especially those encountered in complex environments outside the laboratory, generate not only behavior that is effective in meeting the contingencies but incidental byproducts as well. This fact is important in understanding some of the ways in which reinforcement affects human behavior. It may shed some light on seemingly irrational or wasteful activities. The "lucky" suit that must be worn to an important interview or the elaborate sequence of rituals performed before leaving the house can be understood in part as incidental byproducts of conditioning—patterns that accompany a larger reinforced unit but are not necessary in

the maintenance of that unit. As we will discuss below, the distinction between descriptive and functional operants may also help us to make sense of the varied and complex ways in which verbal behavior enters into other behavioral relations.

The behavioral process at issue here is called *reinforcement* and when abstracted can be stated as follows: If an action (e.g., lever press) results in a consequence (e.g., delivery of food) and the action becomes more frequent, then reinforcement has occurred. Here, the definition has two parts: (1) a consequence is provided; and (2) the behavior in question becomes more frequent. Catania (1992) has pointed out that the two-part definition is not restrictive enough because it does not eliminate cases of mere elicitation. An example of this that he presents is to suppose that one arranges a painful pinch to an infant each time it cries. We have an action, crying, and a consequence, pinching, and crying will become more frequent. This is not an instance of reinforcement, however, because the mere presentation of pinches will elicit crying. Consequently, a third criterion must be met for the proper application of the term *reinforcement*. This leads to a three-part definition: (1) an action must lead to a consequence; (2) the action subsequently must become more frequent; and (3) the increase in frequency must be due to arranging the consequence to follow the action, not merely to its presentation.

Let us now examine a similar case with a verbally competent adult human. Suppose we place a hungry human in an environment equipped with a lever and a food receptacle and then measure the frequency of lever pressing. Next, we deliver food occasionally independent of behavior and continue to measure lever-pressing frequency. Suppose further that lever pressing occurs very infrequently in both conditions. Next, it is arranged that each lever press results in presentation of a bit of food, and we see a dramatic increase in the frequency of lever pressing. All three of Catania's criteria have been met, thus that definition of reinforcement is satisfied, so is this not a case of reinforcement? The answer is that it might be, but it is likely that the situation is more complicated than that because we have not taken into account the person's verbal competence. It is quite likely that the experimental situation occasioned a lot of verbal activity, largely covert. Upon pressing the lever and immediately gaining access to food, the person might have said to himself, "Say, it looks like pressing this lever delivers food. I think I'll try that again." And after a few successful lever presses, the person might say something like, "I see the rule here. Press the lever, get food." Speaking humans have long histories of speaking and reacting to verbal utterances, including their own. It is therefore possible that not only is the person's behavior a result of the recently experienced contingency between lever pressing and food delivery, but also that it is influenced by his ongoing verbal behavior, which is a result of experience with contingencies well in the past. To make this more explicit, suppose there were three levers in the environment and the required action was pressing two of the three, numbers 2 and 3, in either order, for food to be delivered. Suppose the first time the person succeeded he had pressed the levers in the order 1, 2, 3, and then thought, "I see, I need to press the levers in order to get food." From then forward the person would press the levers in order, 1, 2, 3.

What role does the verbal statement play in this situation? The distinction outlined above between descriptive and functional usages of the operant may be useful here. In this context, the question boils down to this: Is lever pressing determined by the verbal statement, or are lever pressing and the verbal statement both determined by the contingencies but independent of one another? To answer this question, one would need to show how altering the verbal statement affected the lever-pressing sequence. One might, for example, require a collateral verbal task such as counting backward that is presumed to interfere with task-relevant verbalizations. If this disrupted the lever-pressing sequence, one might conclude that the verbal statement was at least partially involved. If the sequence did not change, one might conclude that the verbal state-

ment was not involved—that is, that pressing the lever and stating a rule about pressing the lever were separate responses to the situation with no necessary causal connection between them (cf. Hineline & Wanchisen, 1989).

The point of this example is to show that in the case of verbally competent humans, a change in performance produced by exposure to contingencies can be a product not only of recent exposure to that contingency, but also of a long verbal history to which researchers and therapists often have little or no access. Thus, when it comes to verbally competent humans, it may be necessary to supplement Catania's three-part definition of reinforcement in the following way: (1) behavior has a consequence; (2) behavior becomes more frequent; (3) it does so because of the contingent relation between behavior and consequence, not because of mere presentation of the consequence; and (4) *nothing else is involved*. It is the fourth criterion that is difficult to achieve with verbally competent humans. Speaking humans have long histories of both talking and listening that they bring with them to the laboratory and the clinic, and these histories can, and frequently do, play a role in determining their behavior. As suggested above, the precise ways in which verbal histories interact with other behavior depends on the contingencies. Verbal behavior sometimes controls other behavior, is sometimes controlled by other behavior, and sometimes merely accompanies other behavior without at the same time controlling it. The better understanding we have of the various ways in which verbal behavior is interrelated with other behavior, the better equipped we are in interpreting and changing human behavior, both in the laboratory and in the clinical setting.

Despite their sometimes limited accessibility, there is no reason to assume that verbal histories are fundamentally different from other behavioral histories. It is clear that reinforcement contingencies early in life play a role in learning to speak and follow rules (e.g., Baer, Detrich, & Weninger, 1988), but how these experiences interact with more recent ones is, despite its importance, a relatively little-studied issue. Here, too, research with nonhumans can be illuminating. When historical factors can be directly controlled, it is possible to systematically assess the "layering" of particular experiences and how those experiences interact with current performances (e.g., Freeman & Lattal, 1992; Wanchisen, Tatham, & Mooney, 1989; Weiner, 1964).

COMBINING CURRENT CONTINGENCIES AND PAST HISTORIES

The foregoing analyses indicate that a potentially profitable avenue of experimentation will involve the combining of particular histories with current contingencies. Just as an existing verbal repertoire can interact in important ways with current contingencies, it should be possible to establish repertoires experimentally and then see how they interact with newly arranged contingencies. Of particular relevance to behavior therapy will be experimentation that involves the establishment of stimulus-control relations (perhaps like the stimulus-control relations operative in verbal behavior) and then observe how those relations interact with new contingency arrangements.

An interesting example of this general category of research (although not one that involves establishing prior discriminative repertoires) can be found in the work of Colwill and Rescorla (1985a). These investigators trained rats to press a lever that resulted in presentation of one reinforcer (e.g., a 45-mg food pellet) and to pull a chain that resulted in presentation of a second reinforcer (e.g., 0.3 ml of 32% sucrose solution). The responses were trained in separate sessions on alternate days. Once performance of both responses had been established under intermittent reinforcement (a variable-interval 60-second schedule), flavor-aversion training was carried out over five two-day cycles. These sessions were conducted in the same environment used for response training, but the response operanda were not available. On the first day of each cycle, one of the two reinforcers (choice of rein-

forcer was balanced across subjects) was presented independently of behavior every 60 seconds, on average (i.e., according to a variable-time, or VT, 60-second schedule), for 30 minutes. The session was followed by injection of lithium chloride. On the second day of each two-day cycle, the alternate reinforcer was presented on a VT 60-second schedule for 30 minutes, but no injection occurred after the session. In this fashion, one of the two reinforcers was systematically paired with the illness-inducing injections. Over the course of this training, an aversion developed to the reinforcer paired with poisoning. Subjects either would not consume the reinforcer associated with the poison, or they would consume at most 1 of the 30 possible. Subjects reliably consumed all 30 of the reinforcers not associated with lithium chloride.

On the day after the 10-day aversion-conditioning phase, a single 20-minute test occurred. During the test, both the lever and the chain were available simultaneously for the first time. The test results were very clear: animals made many fewer of the responses that had formerly led to the reinforcer associated with the poison. Colwill and Rescorla interpreted this change to indicate that by "devaluing" the reinforcer, by pairing it with an aversive state, they diminished its effectiveness in maintaining behavior even though the "devalued" reinforcer was never experienced as a consequence of action after its devaluation. The result obtained by Colwill and Rescorla (1985a) can be reliably obtained (e.g., Colwill & Rescorla, 1985b, 1990) and serves as an illustration of how previously established behavior can interact in intriguing ways with new contingencies. It also serves to illustrate a strategy for examining these kinds of interactions, and it is these kinds of interactions that should be of relevance to behavior therapy.

IMPLICATIONS FOR BEHAVIOR THERAPY

Although it is not possible to do justice in such a short chapter to the view that an appreciation of principles derived from research with nonhumans can assist behavior therapists, a brief final summary is in order. We hope the foregoing has dispelled the perception that research with animals is irrelevant or only marginally relevant to the concerns of those trying to understand and change human behavior. Given, however, that so little is known about combining or "layering" experiences, one might wonder about how profitable it is to be concerned with developments in the literature on behavior of nonhumans. We argue that it is worthwhile not only because of occasional direct applicability of particular findings, but even more so for the general conceptual base that it provides a therapist.

What has been learned from the study of nonhumans provides a solid foundation, or conceptual base, for behavior therapy. Of special relevance is the interpretation of the roles of verbal repertoires that has been generated from a base in nonhuman research. The concepts most relevant to therapy are those outlined by Skinner (1957) and more recent work on rule-governed behavior (see Hayes, 1989, and this volume). It may be surprising to some to see Skinner's treatment of verbal behavior suggested as a base, given the widespread assumption that the view was discredited following Chomsky's (1959) scathing review. On subsequent analyses, Chomsky's (1959) criticisms, as well as those of others (e.g., Bever, Fodor, & Garrett, 1968) have been found wanting (Andresen, 1991, 1992; MacCorquodale, 1970), largely because they misrepresented Skinner's views. Verbal behavior does have functions that are operant in nature, and an operant perspective offers an avenue not only for understanding verbal behavior in therapy but also for the generation of and understanding of therapeutic strategies.

A functional view of language suggests that it is important to consider four different verbal repertoires that are present in any one-on-one therapy situation. Each participant has a speaker's repertoire and listener's repertoire, and these repertoires are functions of separate, and conceptually separable, histories. (One can find evidence of the separability of the repertoires in the fact that it is possible to "surprise" oneself while talking or thinking verbally.) Traditionally these repertoires are identified as receptive and expressive language, but by paying heed to their separate origins and to the fact that the repertoires remain to some degree independent (cf., e.g., Lamarre & Holland, 1985; Lee, 1981) provides insights that might not emerge from the traditional distinction. Such a perspective provides, for example, a good justification for "establishing rapport" with a client. Part of establishing rapport may be conceptualized as identifying aspects of a patient's listener's repertoire that allow the therapist to produce via the therapist's speaker's repertoire the desired understanding on the part of the patient. Most likely this will involve avoiding the use of technical behavioral jargon when conversing with patients. Some might claim that such avoidance makes the therapy "nonbehavioral," but from the point of view being expressed here such avoidance would represent behavioral sophistication.

Viewing verbal behavior from a functional point of view also emphasizes that the "meaning" of any particular utterance will, perforce, be somewhat different for any two people, and perhaps more important that a particular utterance may simultaneously have more than one function, or meaning. For example, the statement "I'm anxious" could mean that the person wants to avoid talking, wants to use psychological terms and impress the therapist, is desiring sympathy, is physically tired, exhibits signs of clinical anxiety, or any of several other possibilities. In fact, it is possible that all these meanings may be operative at once. The main point is that a conceptualization based on principles derived from experiments with nonhumans alerts the therapist to the multiple sources of control over behavior, including the behavior we call verbal. The astute therapist, instead of taking self-descriptive statements at face value, realizes that verbal behavior has complex functions as a result of complex histories. What clients do and what they say about what they do are often very different responses maintained by different consequences. Here we see the converse of the situations described earlier in which different forms of behavior can be construed as members of a single operant. Instead, similar forms of behavior are members of different operants that have served different functions. So again we see the utility of defining behavior by its function rather than its form.

As noted earlier, in verbally competent humans verbal behavior can play an important role in the local control of behavior. When behavior is under the control of prior verbal statements, it is said to be "rule-governed" (Skinner, 1966), and it is so if the verbal statements are generated by someone else or the person whose behavior is so controlled. Much of everyday human activity falls outside the provenance of such rules; grasping and drinking from a cup, riding a bicycle, buttoning a shirt, driving a car, playing a video game—all well-developed skills, in some cases requiring complex chains of articulated movements, that occur without the necessary support of verbal descriptions. Verbal descriptions in the form of rules can often be extracted from such experiences, but this does not imply that rules were involved in the execution of the skills to begin with. The rule may have followed the observed changes in behavior and been partly under the control of such changes. Conversely, a rule may be necessary in the establishment of a skill but may fade in its influence as the skill comes under sharper control of the contingencies. In actuality, most behavior is under the control of both rules and of naturally occurring consequences. Consider almost any skilled movement (e.g., hitting a golf ball with a golf club). When doing so, we may act in a rule-governed fashion with respect to a few aspects of the action (e.g., "keep your head down until after the hit"), but many of the actions will be a result of practice, that is, of recurrent experiences with the direct consequences of hitting the ball. The point of introducing the concept of concurrent rule-governed and other-governed behavior is to alert the cognitively oriented behavior therapist to the multiple sources of control over any activity. This point also brings to mind the idea expressed earlier in this chapter that clinically interesting (and challenging) behavior often is

the result of the melding of separately learned repertoires.

Most behavior therapy involves words and therefore can be conceptualized as involving rule-governed behavior. Therapists give advice; if the advice is followed, the behavior is rule-governed, at least to begin with. Once behavior has occurred as a result of a rule, it comes into contact with the naturally occurring consequences specified by the rule, and those experiences then also influence the future likelihood of the activity. For example, a therapist may advise a client who is attempting to control his anger to take a walk around the block when he feels himself getting angry. This enables a more adaptive response to the situation, and ultimately improved social relations. Behavior was initially established by the rule but then maintained at least in part by the consequences the new behavior made possible.

Rule-governed behavior is not always adaptive, however. Rules sometimes lock behavior into rigid patterns that are effective only in the narrowest circumstances. By precluding contact with certain experiences, rules can and often do reduce the likelihood of "learning by doing." The significance of this fact for clinical practice cannot be emphasized too strongly. The client provided with practical rules appropriate to different situations may function well in those and closely related situations, but may be at a loss should those situations change. If the goal of therapy is to develop self-sufficient skills that generalize to new settings, then rules (in the form of advice, warnings, suggestions) should be used by therapists judiciously and in full recognition of their varied and complex effects.

Words also can elicit emotional reactions, so that statements like "I feel so sad" can actually make one feel sad or exacerbate existing negative feelings. Often a therapist's goals include altering what people say to themselves, and when that is so, the therapist can rely on the literature about conditioning with nonhumans to attempt to modify either what is said (i.e., alter the patient's speaker's repertoire) or how it is reacted to (i.e., modify the patient's listener's repertoire).

CONCLUSIONS

In this chapter we have tried to convince the reader that behavioral experiments with nonhumans have relevance for understanding and changing the behavior of humans. We have done so in several ways. First, we have tried to show that two major criticisms of extrapolating from nonhumans to humans are largely, but not totally, without merit. The undermining of "intrinsic motivation" by extrinsic reinforcers is a highly constrained phenomenon, and even in those cases where it is observed it can be accounted for by an interpretation based largely on basic learning processes. The difficulty in demonstrating simple conditioning processes in adult humans is real, but it does not point to any fundamental discontinuity between humans and other animals. It merely illustrates that earlier learning, usually with regard to developing verbal repertoires (both speaker's and listener's), interacts with procedures used to study learning. It also points to the need for additional research on how developed repertoires interact with new experiences.

We also have presented a discussion of the logic of extrapolation across species. This logic applies not only to behavior but to all biological phenomena, and it asserts that extrapolation is never direct and automatic. When done with reason, caution, and empirical analyses, however, such extrapolations serve well.

Finally, we have emphasized how familiarity with basic learning processes in nonhumans can promote conceptual clarity in understanding and interpreting human behavior. We described how practices such as defining behavior functionally, treating verbal behavior as learned, and emphasizing the importance of rule-governed activity can yield coherent interpretations of current practices in behavior therapy, including cognitive behavior therapy. These practices also can assist therapists in conceptualizing virtually any presenting problem. It is our hope that behavior therapists of all ilks can realize that behavior therapy, in all its forms, can rest comfortably on the mass of data about learning processes in nonhumans. The literature on basic learning processes remains the foundation of behavior therapy.

END NOTES

Preparation of this manuscript was supported by grants DA 04074 and MH 50249 from the National Institute on Drug Abuse and the National Institute of Mental Health, respectively. Address correspondence to either author at the Department of Psychology, University of Florida, Gainesville, FL 32611.

REFERENCES

Andresen, J. (1991). Skinner and Chomsky 30 years later or: The return of the repressed. *The Behavior Analyst, 14,* 49–60.

Andresen, J. T. (1992). The behaviorist turn in recent theories of language. *Behavior and Philosophy, 20,* 1–19.

Baer, R. A., Detrich, R., & Weninger, J. M. (1988). On the functional role of the verbalization in correspondence training procedures. *Journal of Applied Behavior Analysis, 21,* 345–356.

Baeyens, F., Eelen, P., & van den Bergh, O. (1990). Contingency awareness in evaluative conditioning: A case for unaware affective-evaluative learning. *Cognition and Emotion, 4,* 3–18.

Bailey, J. S., Shook, G. L., Iwata, B. A., Reid, D. H., & Repp, A. C. (eds.) (1989). *Behavior analysis in developmental disabilities* (2nd ed.). Lawrence, Kansas: Society for the Experimental Analysis of Behavior.

Bem, D. J. (1972). Self-perception theory. In L. Berkowitz (ed.), *Advances in experimental social psychology*, Vol. 6: 1–62. New York: Academic Press.

Bever, T. G., Fodor, J. A., & Garrett, M. (1968). A formal limitation of associationism. In T. R. Dixon & D. L. Horton (eds.), *Verbal behavior and general behavior theory,* 582–585. Englewood Cliffs, N.J.: Prentice-Hall.

Boyle, M. E., & Greer, R. D. (1983). Operant procedures and the comatose patient. *Journal of Applied Behavior Analysis, 16,* 3-12.

Brewer, W. F. (1974). There is no convincing evidence for operant or classical conditioning in adult humans. In W. B. Weimer & D. S. Palermo (eds.), *Cognition and the symbolic processes,* 1–42. Hillsdale, N.J.: Erlbaum.

Broadbent, D. E., FitzGerald, P., & Broadbent, M. H. P. (1986). Implicit and explicit knowledge in the control of complex systems. *British Journal of Psychology, 77,* 33–50.

Cameron, J., & Pierce, W. D. (1994). Reinforcement, reward, and intrinsic motivation: A meta-analysis. *Review of Educational Research, 64*, 363–423.

Catania, A. C. (1973). The concept of the operant in the analysis of behavior. *Behaviorism, 1*, 103-116.

Catania, A. C. (1992). *Learning* (3rd ed.). Englewood Cliffs, N.J.: Prentice-Hall.

Chomsky, N. (1959). A review of B. F. Skinner's *Verbal Behavior. Language, 35*, 26–58.

Colwill, R. M., & Rescorla, R. A. (1985a). Postconditioning devaluation of a reinforcer affects instrumental responding. *Journal of Experimental Psychology: Animal Behavior Processes, 11*, 120–132.

Colwill, R. M., & Rescorla, R. A. (1985b). Instrumental responding remains sensitive to reinforcer devaluation after extensive training. *Journal of Experimental Psychology: Animal Behavior Processes, 11*, 520–526.

Colwill, R. M., & Rescorla, R. A. (1990). Effect of reinforcer devaluation on discriminative control of instrumental behavior. *Journal of Experimental Psychology: Animal Behavior Processes, 16*, 40–47.

Deci, I. L. (1971). Effects of externally mediated rewards on intrinsic motivation. *Journal of Personality and Social Psychology, 18*, 105–115.

Dickinson, A. M. (1989). The detrimental effects of extrinsic reinforcement on "intrinsic motivation." *The Behavior Analyst, 12*, 1–15.

Dulany, D. (1961). Hypotheses and habits in verbal "operant conditioning." *Journal of Abnormal Social Psychology, 63*, 251–263.

Esteves, F., Parra, C., Dimberg, U., & Ohman, A. (1994). Nonconscious associative learning: Pavlovian conditioning of skin conductance responses to masked fear-relevant facial stimuli. *Psychophysiology, 31*, 375–385.

Freeman, T. J., & Lattal, K. A. (1992). Stimulus control of behavioral history. *Journal of the Experimental Analysis of Behavior, 57*, 5–15.

Greenspoon, J. (1955). The reinforcing effect of two spoken sounds on the frequency of two responses. *American Journal of Psychology, 68*, 409–416.

Hayes, S. C. (ed.) (1989). *Rule-governed behavior: Cognition, contingencies, and instructional control.* New York: Plenum.

Hefferline, R. F., Keenan, B., & Harford, R. A. (1959). Escape and avoidance conditioning in human subjects without their observation of the response. *Science, 130*, 1338–1339.

Hefferline, R. F., & Keenan, B. (1963). Amplitude-induction gradient of a small-scale (covert) operant. *Journal of the Experimental Analysis of Behavior, 6*, 307–315.

Hefferline, R. F., & Perrera, T. B. (1963). Proprioceptive discrimination of a covert operant without its observation by the subject. *Science, 139*, 834–835.

Hineline, P. N., & Wanchisen, B. A. (1989). Correlated hypothesizing and the distinction between contingency-shaped and rule-governed behavior. In S. C. Hayes (ed.), *Cognition, contingencies, and instructional control,* 221–268. New York: Plenum.

Hodos, W., & Campbell, C. B. G. (1969). *Scala naturae:* Why there is no theory in comparative psychology. *Psychological Review, 76*, 337–350.

Lamarre, J., & Holland, J. G. (1985). The functional independence of mands and tacts. *Journal of the Experimental Analysis of Behavior, 43*, 5–19.

Laurenti-Lions, L., Gallego, J., Chambille, B., Vardon, G., & Jacquemin, C. (1985). Control of myoelectrical responses through reinforcement. *Journal of the Experimental Analysis of Behavior, 44*, 185–193.

Lee, V. L. (1981). Prepositional phrases spoken and heard. *Journal of the Experimental Analysis of Behavior, 35*, 227–242.

Lepper, M. R., Greene, D., & Nisbett, R. E. (1973). Undermining children's intrinsic interest with extrinsic reward: A test of the "overjustification" hypothesis. *Journal of Personality and Social Psychology, 28*, 129–137.

Levey, A. B., & Martin, I. (1975). Classical conditioning of human "evaluative" responses. *Behaviour Research and Therapy, 13*, 221–226.

Levey, A. B., & Martin, I. (1983). Cognitions, evaluations, and conditioning: Rules of sequence and rules of consequence. *Advances in Behaviour Research & Therapy, 4*, 181–195.

Levin, S. M. (1961). The effects of awareness on verbal conditioning. *Journal of Experimental Psychology, 61*, 67–75.

Lewicki, P., Czyzewska, M., & Hoffman, H. (1987). Unconscious acquisition of complex procedural knowledge. *Journal of Experimental Psychology: Learning, Memory, and Cognition, 13*, 523–530.

Lewicki, P., Hill, T., & Bizot, E. (1988). Acquisition of procedural knowledge about a pattern of stimuli that cannot be articulated. *Cognitive Psychology, 20*, 24–37.

Lindsley, O. R. (1957). Operant behavior during sleep: A measure of depth of sleep. *Science, 126*, 1290–1291.

Lindsley, O. R., Hobika, J. H., & Etsten, B. E. (1961). Operant behavior during anesthesia recovery: A continuous and objective method. *Anesthesiology, 22*, 937–946.

Lindsley, O. R., & Conran, P. (1962). Operant behavior during EST: A measure of depth of coma. *Diseases of the Nervous System, 23*, 407–409.

MacCorquodale, K. (1970). On Chomsky's review of Skinner's *Verbal Behavior. Journal of the Experimental Analysis of Behavior, 13*, 83–99.

Martin, G. & Pear, J. (1996). *Behavior modification: What it is and how to do it* (5th ed.). Upper Saddle River, N.J.: Prentice-Hall.

Martin, I., & Levey, A. B. (1978). Evaluative conditioning. *Advances in Behaviour Research & Therapy, 1*, 57–102.

Oakes, W. F. (1967). Verbal operant conditioning, intertrial activity, awareness, and the extended interview. *Journal of Personality and Social Psychology, 6,* 198–202.

Reber, A. S. (1989). Implicit learning and tacit knowledge. *Journal of Experimental Psychology: General, 118,* 219–235.

Roediger, H. L. (1990). Implicit memory: Retention without remembering. *American Psychologist, 45,* 1043–1056.

Shanks, D. R., & Dickinson, A. (1990). Contingency awareness in evaluative conditioning: A comment on Baeyens, Eelen, and van den Bergh. *Cognition and Emotion, 4,* 19–30.

Skinner, B. F. (1935). The generic nature of the concepts of stimulus and response. *Journal of General Psychology, 12,* 40–65.

Skinner, B. F. (1945). The operational analysis of psychological terms. *Psychological Review, 52,* 270–277.

Skinner, B. F. (1953). *Science and human behavior.* New York: Macmillan.

Skinner, B. F. (1957) *Verbal behavior.* New York: Appleton-Century-Crofts.

Skinner, B. F. (1966). An operant analysis of problem solving. In B. Kleinmuntz (ed.), *Problem solving: Research, method, and theory,* 225–257. New York: Wiley.

Skinner, B. F. (1969). *Contingencies of reinforcement: A theoretical analysis.* New York: Appleton-Century-Crofts.

Skinner, B. F. (1974). *About behaviorism.* New York: Knopf.

Smith, J. C., Blumsack, J. T., Bilek, F. S., Spector, A. C., Hollander, G. R., & Baker, D. L. (1984). Radiation-induced taste aversion as a factor in cancer therapy. *Cancer Treatment Reports, 68,* 1219–1227.

Sulzer-Azaroff, B., Drabman, R., Greer, D., Hall, V., Iwata, B. A., & O'Leary, S. (eds.) (1990). *Behavior analysis in education.* Lawrence, Kansas: Society for the Experimental Analysis of Behavior.

Thaver, F., & Oakes, W. F. (1967). Generalization and awareness in verbal operant conditioning. *Journal of Personality and Social Psychology, 6,* 391–399.

Wanchisen, B. A., Tatham, T. A., & Mooney, S. E. (1989). Variable-ratio conditioning history produces high- and low-rate fixed-interval performance in rats. *Journal of the Experimental Analysis of Behavior, 52,* 167–179.

Wasserman, E. A. (1994). Common versus distinctive species: On the logic of behavioral comparison. *The Behavior Analyst, 17,* 221–223.

Weiner, H. (1964) Conditioning history and human fixed-interval performance. *Journal of the Experimental Analysis of Behavior, 7,* 383–385.

Weiskrantz, L., & Warrington, E. K. (1979). Conditioning in amnesic patients. *Neuropsychologia, 17,* 187–194.

Williams, B. W. (1977). Verbal operant conditioning without subjects' awareness of reinforcement contingencies. *Canadian Journal of Psychology, 31,* 90–101.

CHAPTER 3

CLASSICAL CONDITIONING

E. James Kehoe
Michaela Macrae

Classical conditioning plays a key role in understanding both the origin and the treatment of clinical disorders. Leading textbooks and journals in behavior therapy have emphasized two fundamental principles of classical conditioning: (1) acquisition of conditioned responses (CRs) through pairings of a conditioned stimulus (CS) with an unconditioned stimulus (US) and (2) extinction of CRs through presentation of the CS alone (e.g., Davison & Neale, 1990; Rosehan & Seligman, 1984, p. 90). However, recent advances in classical conditioning have produced a rich array of research and theory to offer to clinical psychology (Bouton, 1991b; Fantino, 1992; Zinbarg, 1993). Although classical conditioning has traditionally been applied in a behavioral rather than a cognitive context, the historic division between conditioning and cognition is currently being reevaluated. In studies using humans, the impact of symbolic, propositional processes on classical conditioning has received substantial attention (Lovibond, 1993). In animal conditioning, attempts have also been made to explain classical conditioning in rule-governed terms (Dickinson, 1989).

Although the "top-down" influence of cognition on conditioning has generated much interest, a "bottom-up" approach has begun to illuminate the behavioral and neural foundations of cognition. Today, classical conditioning sits at the nexus of cognition, brain science, associative learning, and adaptive behavior. Classical conditioning figures prominently in "computational neuroscience," a joint enterprise of cognitive science and neuroscience (Gabriel & Moore, 1990). The distinctive features of computational neuroscience are its focus on learning as the key to behavioral adaptation and its reliance on the mathematical models known variously as "connectionist modeling," "neural networks," and "parallel distributed processing." Connectionist models contain networks of neuronlike units that interact on the basis of simple but dynamic connections. These models represent a dramatic departure from conventional theories of cognition that rely on manipulation of symbolic information under executive control (Estes, 1988; Gluck & Bower, 1988). The growth of connectionist modeling has reinvigorated interest in classical conditioning as a fruitful method for studying associative learning at both a behavioral and a neural level.

This chapter presents recent empirical developments in classical conditioning and discusses them from a neurocomputational perspective. It also outlines the implications of these developments for cognitive and behavioral therapies. The chapter is divided into three sections. As a point of departure, the first section concerns changes in our understanding of the fundamental character of classical conditioning. The second section describes the research and theory in transfer of training that may help to explain the elaboration of disorders and relapse after therapy. The third section concerns interactions among sequences of stimuli that have implications for understanding stimulus hierarchies that control behavior.

FUNDAMENTALS OF CLASSICAL CONDITIONING

The popular conception of the CR is that it is a highly stereotyped reaction that is "simple," "automatic," "unconscious," and "involuntary" (Gormezano & Kehoe, 1975; Lovibond, 1993). Over the past 25 years, however, there have been radical reconceptualizations of classical conditioning fueled by broad advances in behavioral, neural, and theoretical studies. Behavioral studies have shown that even the most "reflexive" of CRs are actually highly dynamic and can be adapted to suit varying environmental conditions. Neural studies have found that the pathways that subserve CRs are complex structures that are orgnized in a distributed fashion that allows a great degree of subtlety and flexibility. At a theoretical level, studies with classical condi-

tioning have yielded powerful, quantitative models of associative learning that are already being applied in areas of research outside the traditional scope of classical conditioning. Accordingly, the present section has two purposes. First, it will reintroduce readers to the basics of classical conditioning methods. Second, it will describe developments in understanding the fundamental character of classical conditioning.

Model Preparations

Neurocomputational studies of classical conditioning have relied heavily on the in-depth study of a handful of "model preparations" (Schreurs, 1989). Each of these preparations is restricted to a particular species, response, and set of stimuli. Within each preparation, progress has been made in discovering the principles governing the behavior of interest and its neural underpinnings. This model preparation approach is similar to that taken in other natural sciences, such as the use of fruit flies in the study of population genetics.

In the study of classical conditioning, the most successful mammalian preparations have used rabbits and several of their responses. In each case, the model preparations have conformed to a traditional definition of classical conditioning. This definition has four key features.

Response Origin

A target response may be either "homogeneous" or "heterogeneous" with respect to the behavior evoked by the reinforcer (Hilgard & Marquis, 1940, p. 70). In the traditional definition of classical conditioning, the target response is selected from among the URs elicited by the US (Gormezano & Kehoe, 1975). Thus, the CR and the UR are said to be homogeneous. Perhaps the most familiar example is the salivary CR based on a salivary UR elicited by a food US. In contrast, target responses may be heterogeneous; that is, they are unrelated to the URs. Heterogeneous responses are often used in instrumental conditioning. For example, pressing a lever or traversing a maze is not itself elicited by the receipt of a food reward.

Response Description

Behaviors may be anatomically defined or outcome defined (Tolman, 1932). Anatomically defined responses include both glandular secretions and muscular movements, for example, salivation and eyelid closure. In contrast, responses used in instrumental conditioning studies are usually outcome defined. That is to say, they are described in terms of how the movements of the subject operate on the surrounding environment, such as pressing a lever.

Stimulus Contingencies

The most familiar feature of classical conditioning is its "stimulus-reinforcer" contingency, that is, the dependency that the experimenter arranges between the CS and the US. In the laboratory, both the CS and the US are delivered in an entirely preprogrammed manner whether or not the CR occurs. In instrumental conditioning, however, the delivery of a reinforcer depends on a designated response by the subject (Hilgard & Marquis, 1940, p. 51; Skinner, 1938). Thus, the defining feature of instrumental conditioning is its "response-reinforcer contingency."

Nonassociative Controls

In a typical classical conditioning experiment, CR acquisition results from forward, relatively close pairings of the CS and the US. However, not all responses during the CS can be attributed to CS-US contiguity. Consequently, there has been an evolution of control methods for determining what proportion of the responses during the CS arise from CS-US contiguity (Gormezano, 1966; Gormezano & Kehoe, 1975). The most common control group receives widely spaced presentations of the CS and the US, usually in a random sequence. This "unpaired" control provides an economical means for jointly assessing contributions from different nonassociative sources. Such sources include any spontaneous occurrences of the target response, any innate tendency for the CS to evoke the target response, and pseudoconditioning, which is a sensitization-like effect arising from presentations of the US. Classical conditioning is said to occur only when the level of responding to the CS in the experimental group exceeds that of the control groups (Grether, 1938; Hilgard & Marquis, 1940, pp. 41–43).

Demonstrations of Classical Conditioning

Figure 3–1 shows the learning curves obtained in three demonstrations using rabbit preparations that meet the traditional definition of classical conditioning. The three response systems were (1) eye movements elicited by an airpuff US to the cornea (Deaux & Gormezano, 1963), (2) changes in heart rate elicited by a mild shock US to the ear (Schneiderman, Smith, Smith, & Gormezano, 1966), and (3) jaw movements elicited as part of a swallowing reflex to a water US (Sheafor, 1975). In each case, the CS was a tone, and there were four groups. First, a paired group received CS-US training, which was potentially associative in nature. Second, an unpaired control received separate but intermixed presentations of the CS and US. Third, a CS-alone control received only presentations of the CS. Fourth, a US-alone control received only presentations of the US. For the paired, unpaired, and CS-alone groups, the percentage CR measure represents the mean proportion of trials on which a CR occurred during the CS. For the US-alone groups in the left-hand and center panels, the percentage CR measure represents the mean proportion of trials on which the target response occurred before the US during a period equivalent to the CS. For the US-alone group in the right-hand panel, the single point on the figure represents responding to a test CS after US-alone presentations.

Inspection of Figure 3–1 reveals that for all three responses, CRs grew steadily in the paired groups over CS-US trials. In all three cases, the paired group showed a substantially higher level of responding than any of the control groups, thus demonstrating the associative effects of CS-US pairings. The eye-movement and heart-rate responses showed little if any evidence of response acquisition in the control groups. Accordingly, it can be safely concluded that the

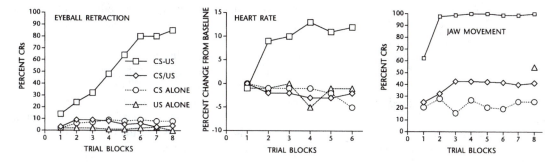

Figure 3–1. Acquisition of CRs in three response systems in the rabbit for groups receiving either paired CS-US training or a nonassociative control condition. The response systems were eyeball retraction (Deaux & Gormezano, 1963), heart rate (Schneiderman et al., 1966), and jaw movement (Sheafor, 1975).

bulk of CRs in the paired groups were associative in origin. The jaw-movement response included contributions from both pseudoconditioning and spontaneous responses during the CS. That is, in the unpaired and US-alone groups, an appreciable increase in the likelihood of a jaw movement occurred during the CS, which is indicative of pseudoconditioning. In the CS-alone group a steady level of spontaneous responding hovered around 20% CRs.

The Anticipatory CR

The CR is often assumed to be a stereotyped replica of the UR. In fact, the CR usually has its own dynamic features, especially its time course. Specifically, the CR is highly tuned to the CS-US interval. Figure 3–2 shows the time course for eyelid CRs acquired by four groups of rabbits trained with different CS-US intervals, namely 125, 250, 500, and 1,000 ms. As can be seen in

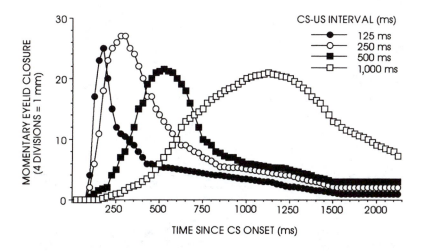

Figure 3–2. Moment-by-moment time course of CRs for groups trained with CS-US intervals of either 125, 250, 500, or 1,000 ms. The upward excursion of each line represents closure of the rabbit's third eyelid (nictitating membrane) (Smith, 1968).

Figure 3–2, closure of the eyelid was initiated shortly following the onset of the CS, but peak eyelid closure occurred around the time of US presentation at the end of the CS-US interval (Smith, 1968).

Although the eyelid CR is initiated and completed within a few hundred ms, it is highly adaptable. When the CS-US interval is altered, the CR peak disappears and then reappears at the new locus of the US (Coleman & Gormezano, 1971). Moreover, when a single CS is paired with the US at two randomly mixed intervals, the CR develops two distinct peaks, one located at each locus of US delivery (Hoehler & Leonard, 1976; Millenson, Kehoe, & Gormezano, 1977). For example, Figure 3–3 shows the time course of an eyelid CR displayed by rabbits trained with a CS that randomly signaled the US after intervals of either 400 or 900 ms. Accordingly, the rabbits acquired a CR with two peaks at the appropriate locations.

From a neurocomputational perspective, the dynamic time course of the CR solves a fundamental conundrum in timing responses for crucial events. On the one hand, early anticipation maximizes the amount of time available for plan-

ning and preparation. On the other hand, premature action can be wasteful and even deleterious to the animal. For a protective response such as eyelid closure, blinking in anticipation of a threat maximizes protection of the eye but at the same time blinds the animal. Thus, the timing of the closure must be a compromise between protection of the eye and the need for current vision, and the graded nature of the CR provides the required compromise.

Association: Contiguity and Frequency

Over the past 200 years, the Law of Contiguity has been the keystone of the major philosophical and psychological theories of knowledge, learning, and memory. The Law of Contiguity states that events that occur close together in time become strongly associated. In addition, the Law of Frequency states that the more often events are paired, the more strongly associated they will become. From a neurocomputational perspective, the laws of contiguity and frequency preclude the formation of random associations based on a one-off coincidence of events. Conversely, the

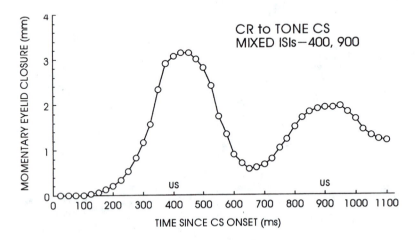

Figure 3–3. Moment-by-moment time course of CRs when one CS was followed unpredictably by the US at either 400 or 900 ms. The upward excursion of each line represents closure of the rabbit's third eyelid (nictitating membrane) (Kehoe, Graham-Clarke, & Schreurs, 1989).

laws of contiguity and frequency dictate that associations will form only between regular sequences of events in the environment.

Although associations can form on the basis of close, frequent contiguity, research in conditioning has increasingly revealed that strong associations can form between widely spaced events, sometimes on a one-off basis. The most notable example is taste aversion learning. In a typical taste aversion study, the CS is the consumption of flavored water, and the US is a nausea-inducing agent (e.g., lithium chloride, X-ray exposure). In this procedure, a taste aversion has been established on the basis of a single presentation of the CS and the US, separated by minutes or even hours (Garcia, Ervin, & Koelling, 1966; Smith & Roll, 1967; Westbrook & Homewood, 1982).

In studies using the rabbit preparations, two key findings have emerged concerning the contiguity and frequency factors. First, the eyelid preparation has been the archetype of conditioning that requires close and frequent contiguity. However, more recent results have revealed that these constraints can be loosened dramatically when only a few CS-US pairings are widely spaced. Second, the rabbit preparations differ markedly in terms of their sensitivity to these two factors. In the case of the eyelid and heart-rate responses, divergences in the rate of CR acquisition occur under common training conditions, including the same CS and the same US (Powell & Levine-Bryce, 1988; Schneiderman, 1972).

To illustrate the changes in acquisition of the eyelid CR as a result of the trial spacing, Figure 3–4 summarizes the effects of varying the number of CS-US pairings delivered in each daily session of training. The vertical axis shows the mean number of CS-US trials that were presented prior to the appearance of the first CR. Each point on the figure represents the mean for a different group of rabbits (Kehoe & Macrae, 1994).

Inspection of Figure 3–4 reveals that for one trial per session, the first CR generally appeared in fewer than a dozen trials. For those groups, the

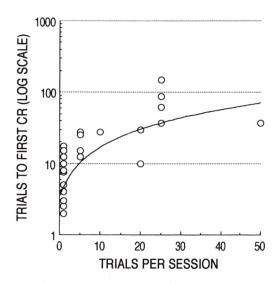

Figure 3–4. Scattergraph of the number of CS-US trials prior to the first CR as a function of the number of trials per training session. Each point represents the mean for a different group of rabbits, using the third eyelid (nictitating membrane) preparation (Kehoe & Macrae, 1994).

interval between each trial was 24 hours. As the number of trials per session increased, more trials were needed to obtain the first CR. For example, in groups trained with 25 trials per session, the first CR appeared only after 80 trials of training. For those groups, the training sessions were still separated by 24 hours, but the interval between trials within each session was around one minute. In summary, fewer CS-US pairings were needed to produce an equivalent level of CR acquisition when they were well spaced.

In addition, when the CS-US pairings are well spaced, less contiguity is needed. Figure 3–5 shows the joint effects of manipulating the CS-US interval and the number of CS-US pairings per session. As the figure illustrates, when 25 pairings are presented per session, the level of CR acquisition declines as the CS-US interval is increased, particularly when the CS-US interval is 3,200 ms. When only one or five pairings are presented in each session, the gradient is much

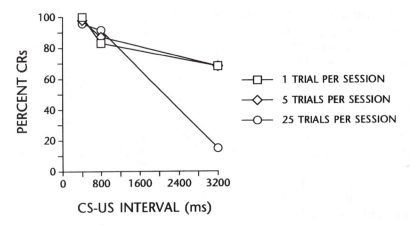

Figure 3–5. Mean CR levels as a function of CS-US interval in the rabbit's third eyelid (nictitating membrane) preparation. The rabbits were trained with either 1, 5, or 25 trials per session (Kehoe et al., 1991).

flatter, and there is considerable responding generated at the 3,200-ms CS-US interval (Kehoe, Cool, & Gormezano, 1991).

The requirements for contiguity and frequency are even looser in the heart-rate and jaw-movement preparations. In both preparations, around a dozen CS-US pairings will often produce maximum responding in a single session of training. Figure 3–6 shows the results of manipulating the CS-US interval. For the heart-rate preparation, substantial CR acquisition is obtained at intervals stretching up to 21 s. Such intervals are an order of magnitude greater than those seen in the eyeblink preparation under the same conditions (Schneiderman, 1972). In the case of the jaw-movement response, the boundary of conditioning is unknown. For intervals as long as 4 s, there is no sign of a diminishment in CR acquisition (Gormezano, 1972).

In conclusion, these findings and others like them have altered our views about the requirements for contiguity and frequency. In the late 1960s, the discovery of taste aversion learning suggested that certain types of associations, namely, taste-nausea associations, were uniquely exempt from the traditional rules. This apparent exemption led some theorists to propose that certain species were "prepared" to learn certain as-

sociations (Seligman, 1970). Although some types of associations may be easier to learn than others, the preparedness principle may be giving the wrong impression, namely, that other types of associations will usually conform to the traditional rules. However, the newer findings have revealed that for even archetypal CRs, the requirements for contiguity and frequency can vary dramatically. Most notably, for the eyeblink preparation, CR acquisition can occur either after a few, relatively widely spaced events or after many, more tightly packed events.

From a neurocomputational perspective, the newer findings will require some rethinking about the role of contiguity and frequency. As previously stated, a requirement for close and frequent pairings ensures that associations would form only between regular sequences of events. However, the picture now inclines us to recast the Law of Frequency. The traditional reading of the Law of Frequency emphasized only the number of pairings and not their rate of delivery. Instead, a trade-off clearly exists between the number of pairings and the spacing between those pairings. That is, a large number of pairings is needed when they are closely spaced, but a smaller number of pairings is needed when they are widely spaced. Thus, for relatively rare se-

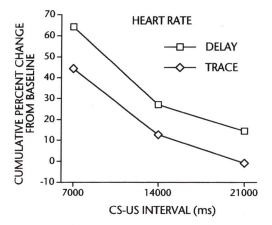

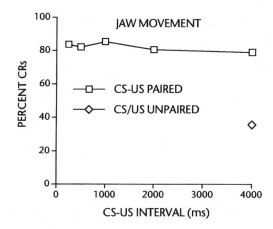

Figure 3–6. Mean CR levels as a function of CS-US interval in the rabbit's heart-rate (Schneiderman, 1972) and jaw movement preparations (Gormezano, 1972).

quences, learning can occur on the basis of a few coincidences. Moreover, the same trade-off exists between contiguity and spacing. Less contiguity is required for associations to form within rare sequences.

Neural Pathways of Conditioning

For purposes of behavioral theory, it would be convenient if all responses arising from the association of a particular CS with a particular US relied on a single central linkage. Thus, all CRs

would be indices of the same association. However, studies aimed at identifying the neural substrates of conditioning have revealed that CS-US pairings may yield multiple associative linkages, each for a different response system. In the rabbit, for example, divergent pathways subserve eyeblink and heart-rate CRs.

Figure 3–7 shows in schematic form the pathways for the eyeblink and heart-rate CRs (Kapp, Wilson, Pascoe, Supple, & Whalen, 1990; Thompson, 1986). As the figure shows, the inputs for both an auditory CS and a tactile "shock" US give rise to multiple, parallel projections into the brain. In turn, some of these projections converge at several sites. For example, a CS input projects through the cochlear nucleus and the pontine nuclei to deep cerebellar nuclei. These deep cerebellar nuclei also receive a projection from the US via the sensory trigeminal nucleus and inferior olive. This site of CS-US convergence appears to be a key site of plasticity that sends an output through the red nucleus to the accessory abducens nucleus, which is the motor nucleus for closure of the third eyelid, the nictitating membrane. While this cerebellar circuit is the key pathway for conditioning of the nictitating membrane response, a very different pathway mediates the heart-rate CR. In the heart-rate circuit, the key site of CS-US convergence is the amygdala, which sends outputs to the vagal dorsal motor nucleus that slows the heart rate.

Because the pathways that govern different CRs are complex and dispersed throughout the brain, it might seem unlikely that they would obey a common set of principles. However, across different pathways, increasing evidence exists that they share mechanisms of plasticity. This plasticity entails changes in the efficiency with which one neuron is able to activate another neuron across both neurons' synaptic cleft (e.g., Thompson, 1993, pp. 381–383; Kalat, 1995, pp. 472–484). The biochemical changes at the synaptic cleft may be common to all synapses involved in learning, even though divergent neural pathways exist that result in divergent behavior. This kind of situation is commonplace in science. Chemistry, for example, has a few basic princi-

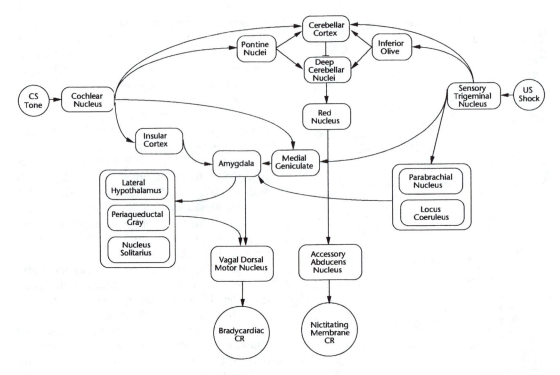

Figure 3–7. Major nuclei and their connections in pathways for conditioning of the rabbit's third eyelid (nictitating membrane) response (Thompson, 1986) and heart-rate response (Kapp et al., 1990).

ples concerning chemical bonding. However, depending on which elements are combined, the resulting molecules will have strikingly different properties. Similarly, for population genetics, the handful of basic principles concerning the recombination of genes can produce highly divergent phenotypic expressions.

Clinical Implications

A prevailing view exists that fundamental conditioning processes are simple, highly stereotyped, and automatic. However, this view of conditioning processes is outdated. Research with model preparations has shown that CRs are in fact complex, highly flexible, and adaptive. Moreover, the behavioral diversity across response systems is matched by diversity in the neural pathways that subserve them.

In the clinical context, it is commonly as-

sumed that learning occurs most quickly when the experience is intensive. For example, anxiety disorders may originate from a strong aversive association formed on the basis of a single episode in which innocuous stimuli are followed by some trauma. Our revised knowledge of conditioning principles, however, indicates that strong associations can form on the basis of much less aversive outcomes. For example, the shock US used in the rabbit preparations is reported by human volunteers as being mildly annoying and hardly traumatic. Nevertheless, with this US, a few widely spaced pairings reliably yield high levels of CR acquisition. By the same token, a few, rare encounters with events of relatively little salience may plant the seeds for a strong aversive reaction. Yet, it would not be surprising if clients were unable to recall those episodes that led to the associations that drive their behavior.

EXTINCTION, REACQUISITION, AND TRANSFER OF TRAINING

In classical conditioning, the core principle for eliminating a CR is the extinction procedure in which a CS is presented repeatedly without the US. From a neurocomputational perspective, extinction enables learners to abandon now meaningless signals. Thus, any learning system possesses the flexibility to reverse its course. From a clinical perspective, the extinction principle has provided the foundation for all exposure-based therapies, such as systematic desensitization and flooding (Marks, 1969; Stampfl & Levis, 1967; Tryon, 1976; Wolpe, 1969). To most observers, extinction of the CR would seem to suggest that the underlying association has been undone. However, closer investigations have revealed that when a CR is extinguished, the underlying association is largely preserved.

Extinction and Rapid Reacquisition

Figure 3–8 shows key findings obtained using classical conditioning of the rabbit's eyelid response (Napier, Macrae, & Kehoe, 1992). The experiment contained three groups designated as PEP, PUP, and RRP. In the initial acquisition training, groups PEP and PUP received three days of CS-US training. The top panel of the figure shows that both groups rapidly acquired CRs to levels exceeding 90% CRs. Group RRP was placed in the conditioning apparatus but received neither the CS nor US.

Following initial acquisition, group PEP received conventional CS-alone extinction presentations, while group PUP received "unpaired" presentations of the CS and US. In the unpaired procedure, the CS and US were separated by at least 30 s. Group RRP continued to sit restrained in the conditioning apparatus. The middle panel of Figure 3–8 illustrates that groups PEP and PUP showed extinction, that is, a general decline in responding across trials, from approximately 80% CRs in the first block to under 1% CRs in the last. Although extinction did occur, substantial spontaneous recovery occurred on the first three days. Even though CRs had disappeared by the end of each extinction session, they reap-

peared at the beginning of the next session. The degree of spontaneous recovery diminished over days and was eradicated by day 5 of extinction training.

Even when CRs have been thoroughly eradicated by extinction, they can rapidly reappear after just a few CS-US trials. The bottom panel of Figure 3–8 shows the course of acquisition in each group during CS-US pairings following the extinction phase. For groups PEP and PUP, these pairings represented reacquisition training, whereas for group RRP, they represented initial training. Reacquisition was clearly very rapid compared to initial acquisition. That is, groups PEP and PUP increased responding at a much faster rate than group RRP. The two experimental groups reached levels in excess of 80% CRs by the end of the first day of training, while group RRP had reached only 45% CRs.

Both spontaneous recovery and rapid reacquisition reveal that extinction leaves the underlying association at least partially intact. Indeed, even when extinction training is extended for a period three times as long as in the experiment shown in Figure 3–8, reacquisition remains just as fast (Napier et al., 1992). From a neurocomputational perspective, rapid reacquisition shows that the learning system can adapt and re-adapt its behavior without having to restart the learning process from scratch on each occasion. From a clinical perspective, the knowledge that an association can never be completely eliminated is both bad news and good news. The bad news concerns the disordered behaviors that one wants to eliminate in therapy. The principle of rapid reacquisition indicates that the potential for relapse may never be completely abolished. The good news, however, concerns the transfer of newly learned positive behaviors from the therapeutic context to everyday life. These new behaviors must be performed in everyday life without the reinforcers provided in therapy and therefore are subject to extinction. However, the principle of rapid reacquisition suggests that the new behaviors may be relearned easily when reinforcement is reintroduced, for example, in the form of brief follow-up sessions.

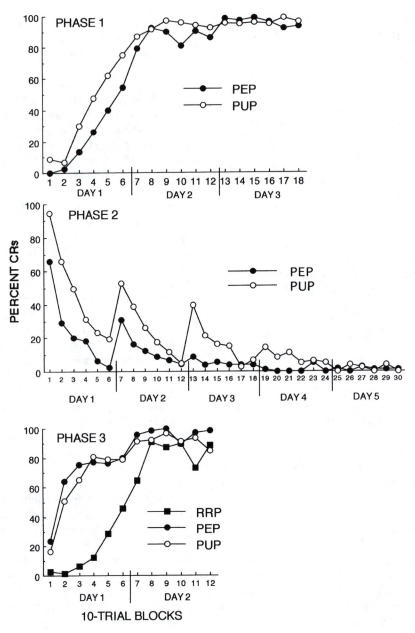

Figure 3–8. Acquisition (phase 1), extinction (phase 2), and reacquisition (phase 3) of CRs in the rabbit's third eyelid (nictitating membrane) preparation (Napier et al., 1992).

Transfer after Extinction

Rapid reacquisition is not the only evidence that extinction leaves underlying associations intact. In fact, once an association has been established, the potential for forming similar associations is increased, whether or not the original behavior has been extinguished (Kehoe & Gormezano, 1974; Kehoe & Holt, 1984; Kehoe, Morrow, & Holt, 1984; Kehoe & Napier, 1991; Schreurs & Kehoe, 1987). This effect is a type of transfer that cannot simply be attributed to stimulus generalization. Rather, it is a form of "learning to learn"—a progressive increase in the rate of learning across a series of tasks that are similar in their structure but differ dramatically in their superficial stimuli (Ellis, 1965, p. 32).

Figure 3–9 shows a demonstration of learning to learn in classical conditioning of the rabbit's eyeblink (Kehoe et al., 1984). In the initial stage of training, two groups (PPP, PUP) received CS-US pairings in which the CS was a light. A third group (UUP) served as a "no learning" control. The control rabbits received unpaired presentations of the CS and US. The left panel of the figure reveals that groups PPP and PUP showed steady CR acquisition that exceeded 90% CRs, while group UUP showed

only a few responses that never exceeded 2% (Kehoe et al., 1984).

In stage 2, group PUP underwent extinction training in which the CS and US were presented in an unpaired fashion. As depicted in the middle panel, the group showed extinction of the CR. By the end of stage 2, seven of eight rabbits had shown complete extinction of the CR. At the same time, group PPP continued to receive CS-US pairings and maintained a high level of responding. Group UUP continued to receive unpaired presentations of the stimuli and showed little responding.

In the third stage of training, all three groups received CS-US training with a new CS from a different sensory modality, namely, a tone. Learning to learn was evident in both groups PPP and PUP almost as soon as training began with the new CS. For example, both groups achieved a mean CR likelihood greater than 35% CRs within the first day of training. Thus, the prior extinction of the original CR in group PUP made little if any difference to the rate of CR acquisition to the new CS. In comparison, group UUP achieved a mean CR likelihood of only 12% CRs within the first day of training. Similar results have been obtained when extinction training in stage 2 was conducted using CS-alone pre-

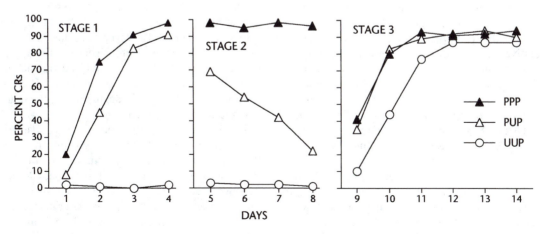

Figure 3–9. Learning to learn, transfer of training between tone and light CSs in the rabbit's third eyelid (nictitating membrane) preparation, both with and without extinction of CRs to the original CS (Kehoe et al., 1984).

sentations and when the control group received no exposure to any CS or US before the final stage of CS-US pairings. Moreover, the positive transfer between tone and light is symmetric.

Learning to learn provides a link between low-level conditioning and higher-level problem solving. Harlow contended, "[L]earning to learn transforms the organism from a creature that adapts to a changing environment by trial and error to one that adapts by seeming hypothesis and insight" (1949, p. 51). This linkage sheds new light on the long-recognized, reciprocal interaction between cognition and behavior (Bandura, 1986). At a cognitive level, the associative basis for learning to learn can be viewed as a form of rule abstraction. In turn, the rule abstraction that occurs during learning to learn translates into new, yet appropriate behavior.

Although learning to learn may provide a bridge between cognitive and behavioral processes, neither cognitive theory nor conventional associative theories have been able to explain learning to learn. Instead, a neurocomputational approach, namely, connectionist modeling, has provided principles for explaining learning to learn. Connectionist models portray the distributed nature of learning by constructing networks of neuron-like elements. Although these networks are inspired by the structure of the brain, they are not intended to model actual brain processes. Rather, they are conceptual in nature and are intended to explain behavioral laws. Figure 3–10 depicts the minimal network of associative linkages for explaining learning to learn in classical conditioning. The network contains three "sensory" units, one each for the light CS (L), the tone CS (T), and the US. The inputs for L and T converge on a shared unit (X). The output from X projects to a second unit (R) that gives rise to the CR and UR. Both of these units receive an input from the US.

In this network, initial CR acquisition to the light CS proceeds in the following fashion. At first, the L input is unable to trigger the X unit, but each L input renders the L-X connection eligible for modification during a brief period after L's onset (Sutton & Barto, 1981). If a US input

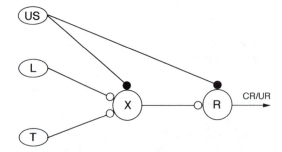

Figure 3–10. Architecture of a layered network for reacquisition and learning to learn. The L and T units represent inputs for light and tone CSs, respectively. They have adaptive connections with a hidden X unit, which in turn has an adaptive connection with a response generator unit (R). The US unit represents the input for the unconditioned stimulus, which has fixed connections to the X and R units (Kehoe, 1988).

triggers X during the eligibility period, the L-X connection will receive an increment in weight. As the L-X connection strengthens over successive L-US pairings, the L input will begin to trigger the X unit and thus render the X-R connection eligible for increments by the US input to R. CRs to L begin to appear when the L-X and X-R connections become strong enough so that L triggers X and then X triggers R.

Once the L-X and X-R connections are established, learning to learn becomes possible. In subsequent T-US training, responding does not appear immediately because the T-X connection is ineffective at first. However, once the T-X connection starts to strengthen, the earliest firings of the X unit by the T input would be translated into CRs via the previously established X-R connection. Accordingly, CR acquisition to the tone CS would be accelerated.

In summary, CR acquisition to L in a naive animal requires the successive strengthening of both the CS-specific link (L-X) and the shared link (X-R). In subsequent training with the tone, CR acquisition is accelerated because CR acquisition to tone requires only the establishment of the specific T-X link, which then capitalizes on the existing X-R link. Furthermore, this network can explain how learning to learn survives extinction of CRs to the original stimulus (L). As the L-X connection declines, it reaches a point at which it can no longer activate the X unit. Hence, the X-R link is partly protected from extinction. If there is any residual associative strength in the X-R linkage, it is available during subsequent T-US training. By the same token, this model also explains rapid reacquisition. That is, the residual associative strength in the X-R connection would be equally available if training were undertaken with the original CS (L) rather than a new CS (T) (Kehoe, 1988).

As may now be apparent, learning to learn and rapid reacquisition arise from the same associative mechanism. From a clinical perspective, this shared mechanism may mean that the high potential for relapse from therapy (i.e., the rapid reacquisition of disordered behavior) is an unavoidable side effect of learning to learn. On the other hand, learning to learn may be a substantial aid to expanding the benefits of a therapy to new contexts. For example, brief follow-up sessions could help the acquisition of new skills as well as encourage the maintenance of habits acquired in the original therapy.

More generally, the connectionist model of learning to learn suggests a new perspective on the relationship between behavioral and cognitive processes in therapy. With regard to basic classical conditioning, the model suggests that learning does not rely upon a simple CS-CR or CS-US association. Instead, CR acquisition depends on a sequence of at least two associations. From a cognitive perspective, learning to learn has usually been thought to involve the abstraction of a rule or schema about the learning task. Connectionist models, however, indicate that a sequence of associations can explain what otherwise appears to be rule-based behavior.

CONDITIONING WITH SEQUENTIAL STIMULI

Within clinical psychology, behavioral approaches to anxiety disorders have long recognized a gradient of fear. That is, successive stimuli in a sequence elicit increasing fear the closer they are to the aversive event. People tend to escape from the sequence at the earliest signs of threat. This early escape minimizes exposure to the threatening situation but also prevents people from testing the reality of their fears. Accordingly, exposure-based therapies presuppose that people must eventually confront the whole sequence of stimuli that arouse fear. Because the acquisition of fear is thought to depend on classical conditioning (Levis, 1989; McAllister & McAllister, 1986; Mowrer & Lamoreaux, 1946), studies using a sequence of CSs rather than the conventional single CS have been used to study the fear gradient and its extinction (Boyd & Levis, 1976; Levis, 1971; Levis & Stampfl, 1972).

Beyond their specific application to fear theory, studies with sequences of CSs may help illuminate the mechanism of cognitive attributions. A key feature of an attribution is the client's identification of one out of many possible sources as the cause of the client's problem (Weiner, Frieze, Kukla, Reed, Rest, & Rosenbaum, 1971). In this respect, attribution can be seen as a particular association that has been selected from among the possible associations in an aversive situation. As subsequently described, studies with sequential CSs have revealed a two-way interaction between stimuli in a sequence that may mask the underlying gradient. Such interactions give the impression that, like attributions, certain stimuli in a sequence can show conditioning on a selective basis.

Key Findings

Studies with the rabbit eyeblink preparation have commonly used a sequence of two CSs, such as a tone and a light, to signal the US (CSA-CSX-US). Although the use of two CSs may seem a small increase in complexity compared to one CS, this minimal sequence has yielded a rich and sometimes paradoxical set of findings.

Facilitation of remote associations occurs when CSA is presented several seconds in advance of CSX and the US. Ordinarily, in the rabbit eyeblink preparation, there will be little or no CR acquisition to a brief stimulus (CSA) that precedes the US by more than a couple of seconds. However, when another stimulus (CSX) is inserted just before the US, the acquisition of the CR to CSA is facilitated. That is, CR acquisition to CSA proceeds quickly and reaches a high level (Kehoe, Gibbs, Garcia, & Gormezano, 1979; Kehoe, Marshall-Goodell, & Gormezano, 1987; Kehoe & Morrow, 1984). An example of such facilitation is presented in Figure 3–11, which shows the learning curves for CR acquisition to CSA in two groups of rabbits. One group (single) had only CSA as a signal for the US (CSA———US). The other group (serial) received training with CSA-CSX-US. CSA preceded the US by 2,800 ms in both groups. In group serial, the CSX-US interval was 400 ms. There were 16 days of training, with each day containing 60 trials (Kehoe et al., 1979).

As Figure 3–11 illustrates, group single showed only weak CR acquisition to CSA. Responding to CSA never exceeded 20% CRs. However, group serial showed rapid CR acquisition to CSA that reached a maximum level of 90% CRs. Although the maximum level was not sustained, the level of responding to CSA always exceeded that of group single. This kind of facilitation has been obtained when the interval between CSA and the US has been extended to as long as 19 s.

Impairment of proximal associations often

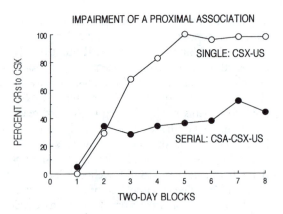

Figure 3–12. Impairment of CR acquisition to a temporally proximal stimulus (CSX) in the rabbit's third eyelid (nictitating membrane) preparation. Group serial received training with CSA-CSX-US, and group single received CSX-US training (Kehoe et al., 1979).

occurs when CSA precedes CSX by a short interval, say, less than a second. CSA has a deleterious effect on CR acquisition to CSX, even though CSX is closer to the US (Kehoe, 1979; Kehoe, 1983; Kehoe et al., 1979). For example, Figure 3–12 shows CR acquisition to CSX in two groups of rabbits. Group single had only CSX-US pairings, while group serial received training with a CSA-CSX-US sequence. In both groups, CSX preceded the US by 400 ms. In group serial, CSA preceded CSX by another 400 ms (Kehoe et al., 1979).

Group single showed unimpeded CR acquisition and attained nearly 100% CRs by the end of training. In contrast, group serial displayed an attenuated level of CR acquisition to CSX. Early in training, group serial displayed an initial rise in CRs to CSX to levels around 35% CRs. Thereafter, however, group serial showed only small additional gains and attained a level of only 45% CRs by the end of training.

Basic Principles

In addition to contiguity and frequency principles, two processes appear to underlie the findings obtained with serial compounds.

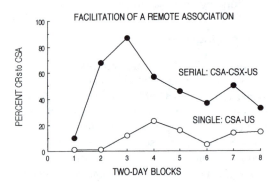

Figure 3–11. Facilitation of CR acquisition to a temporally remote stimulus (CSA) in the rabbit's third eyelid (nictitating membrane) preparation. Group serial received training with CSA-CSX-US, and group single received CSA-US training (Kehoe et al., 1979).

Second-Order Conditioning

The facilitation of responding to CSA in a serial compound appears to rely heavily on second-order conditioning (Gibbs, Cool, Land, Kehoe, & Gormezano, 1991a; Gibbs, Kehoe, & Gormezano, 1991b). Specifically, in second-order conditioning, subjects are given "second-order" CSA-CSX trials and "first-order" CSX-US trials. Figure 3–13 shows an example. As CRs are acquired on the CSX-US trials, CRs are also acquired to CSA on the CSA-CSX trials (Kehoe, Feyer, & Moses, 1981). Second-order conditioning can operate in a serial compound (CSA-CSX-US) because it contains both the CSA-CSX and CSX-US relationships.

Competitive Learning

Concurrent CSs appear to compete for a limited resource, such as associative strength or attention (e.g., Rescorla & Wagner, 1972; Sutherland & Mackintosh, 1971). That is to say, one CS loses access to the key resource because the other CS captures the resource very rapidly or has already captured all of it. Such factors as the intensity of the two CSs, their prior associative strengths, and their temporal order are commonly thought to influence their relative competitive advantage (Kehoe, 1987). In a serial compound, for example, CSA may capture the subject's attention before the onset of CSX, thus precluding CSX from gaining associative strength.

Concurrent Effects

It might seem paradoxical that CSA both relies on CSX for second-order conditioning and competes with it for associative strength. Nevertheless, second-order conditioning and competitive learning do appear to operate concurrently. In particular, Kehoe, Schreurs, and Graham (1987) conducted CSX-US training and then added CSA to form the CSA-CSX-US compound. According to competitive learning principles by themselves, the previously trained stimulus (CSX) should have a distinct competitive advantage over the added stimulus (CSA). Essentially, CSX has had the opportunity to capture nearly all of the associative strength, leaving little, if any, for CSA. Accordingly, CR acquisition to CSA should be blocked. In fact, such blocking occurs when CSA is simultaneous with CSX (Marchant & Moore, 1973). The CSA-CSX serial relationship, however, permits second-order conditioning and provides the opportunity for CSA to benefit from CSX's considerable associative strength.

Kehoe et al. (1987) observed a pattern of results that implies second-order conditioning as well as competition. That is, after prior training of CSX, there was some blocking of CR acquisition to CSA. That is, CR acquisition to CSA was slow relative to a control group that had not received initial CSX-US training. At the same time, however, responding to CSX showed a marked decline: Its response levels were cut in half. Thus, CSA's temporal primacy permitted CSA to turn around CSX's competitive advantage and effectively "steal" associative strength from CSX.

Recently, evidence has been obtained that the two processes distribute total associative strength across a sequence of CSs. Specifically, Schreurs, Kehoe, and Gormezano (1993) used

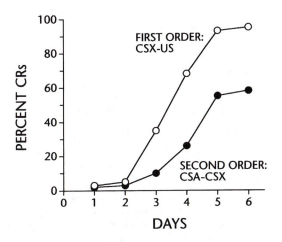

Figure 3–13. First- and second-order conditioning in the rabbit's third eyelid (nictitating membrane) preparation. The curve for the first-order trials (CSX-US) shows CR acquisition to CSX, and the curve for the second-order trials (CSA-CSX) shows CR acquisition to CSA (Kehoe et al., 1981).

either two, three, or four distinctive CSs in a sequence prior to the US. Figure 3–14 shows the level of responding (1) across all the CSs, (2) during just the last CS (X), and (3) during the first CS (A). In each case, the CSA-US interval was 2,800 ms, and the CSX-US interval was 400 ms. Regardless of the number of CSs, the total level of responding remained constant around 80% CRs. In contrast, the level of responding to both CSA and CSX declined as additional CSs were interpolated between CSA and CSX. This decline indicates that the added CSs competed successfully for a share of the total associative strength. Despite the competition, second-order conditioning was evident in that responding to CSA in all three groups exceeded that of control groups.

The Sutton-Barto Model

Despite the available evidence, it might appear impossible to reconcile second-order condi-

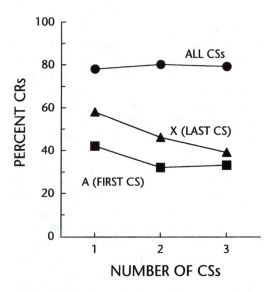

Figure 3–14. Mean CR levels in a sequence of CSs as a function of the number of stimuli in the sequence. The figure shows separate curves for responding (1) across all the CSs, (2) during the last CS (X), and (3) during the first CS (A) (Schreurs et al., 1993).

tioning with competitive learning. However, the two have been woven together in a connectionist model by Sutton and Barto (1981, 1990), who contend that learning occurs on a continuous, "real-time" basis, not just at the end of a trial when the US may or may not occur. Specifically, learning can occur whenever a discrepancy exists between associative strength at one moment and associate strength at the next. In a sequence of stimuli, such discrepancies can arise at the onset of another CS as well as at the time of the US.

Within a CSA-CSX-US trial, the associative strength of CSA (V_A) would increase at the onset of CSX in proportion to its associative strength (V_X). Later, at the point of US onset, both CSA and CSX would gain associative strength. Thus, V_A would increase at the onsets of both CSX and the US, while V_X would increase only at the onset of the US. According to a competitive learning principle, only so much associative strength can be sustained at any one time (Rescorla & Wagner, 1972). Eventually, the total of the associative strengths ($V_A + V_X$) would exceed that sustainable by the US. Consequently, at US onset, there would be decrements in both V_A and V_X. On the next trial, V_A would regain its lost value at CSX onset, while V_X would continue to suffer decrements at US onset until the sum $V_A + V_X$ stabilized at a level sustainable by the US. Thus, the Sutton-Barto model explains how CSA "steals" associative strength from CSX.

Extinction in Serial Compounds

The Sutton-Barto model might give the impression that CSA becomes independent of CSX. Most notably, Gibbs et al. (1991b) conducted training with a CSA-CSX-US serial compound (SC). As can be seen in the left panel of Figure 3–15, responding to CSA in the SC groups rose to 65% CRs, which was above the control level of 28% CRs. The control groups (UC) received separate CSA-US and CSX-US trials, thus precluding any second-order conditioning. Subsequently, half the animals in each condition received CSX-alone extinction training (E), and the other half re-

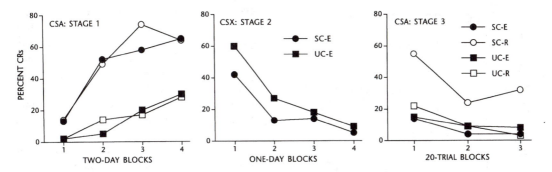

Figure 3–15. Acquisition of CRs to CSA, extinction of CRs to CSX, and extinction of CRs to CSA. Groups given CSA-CSX-US training in stage 1 are labeled as SC, and groups given uncoupled training (CSA-US/CSX-US) are labeled as UC. Groups that received extinction training with CSX in stage 2 are labeled as E, and groups that received only restraint during stage 2 are labeled as R (Gibbs et al., 1991b).

mained in their home cages (R). The results of CSX extinction in groups SC-E and UC-E are shown in the center panel of Figure 3–15.

Following extinction of CRs to CSX, all the animals were tested with CSA–alone. As can be seen in the right panel of Figure 3–15, the serial compound group that remained in their home cages (SC-R) showed a high level of responding to CSA, which remained above control levels across the CSA-alone tests. In contrast, the serial compound group that underwent CSX extinction (SC-E) showed a low level of responding to CSA, barely above the levels shown by the control groups (UC-E, UC-R). Thus, extinction of CRs to CSX abolished CRs to CSA. Thus, it might be more correct to say that CSA "borrows" associative strength from CSX rather than steals it.

Contextual Control

In addition to second-order conditioning and competitive learning, serial stimuli can exert a hierarchical influence over one another. In classical conditioning, animals can learn to modulate their responding to a stimulus on the basis of other cues, such as lights, tones, and the experimental setting (e.g., Bouton, 1991a; Holland, 1991; Kimmel & Ray, 1978; Konorski & Lawicka, 1959). Specifically, animals can learn to

respond when a stimulus is reinforced (X+) in the presence of one cue (A→X+) but to withhold responding to the same stimulus without reinforcement (X–) when it is preceded by another cue (B→X–). The target stimulus (X) is usually relatively brief, but the conditional cues can vary in their duration. In some cases, the conditional cues are short (e.g., 1 s or less), as in the serial compounds described previously (e.g., Kehoe et al., 1987). In other cases, they are longer (e.g., 60s) and continue throughout the presentation of the X stimulus (e.g., Brandon & Wagner, 1991; Macrae & Kehoe, 1995). In still other cases, a conditional cue can arise from distinctive features of a conditioning chamber present for an entire training session (Hinson, 1982).

Figure 3–16 shows a conditional discrimination using relatively long cues (78 s) provided by tone and white noise. The target stimulus (X) was a 100-ms light flash that occurred about 61 s after the onset of the conditional cues. Inspection of Figure 3–16 reveals that responding to X in A→X+ trials rose steadily over successive days to an asymptote of 69% CRs on day 9. In contrast, responding to X in B→X– trials rose only slightly to a mean level of 14% CRs by day 9. Despite the strong control that A and B exerted over responding to X, the conditional cues themselves evoked negligible responding, less than 6% CRs.

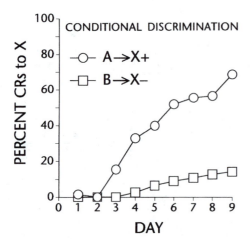

Figure 3–16. Conditional discrimination in the rabbit's third eyelid (nictitating membrane) preparation. CR acquisition during the X stimulus in A—>X+ and B—>X– trials as a function of days (Macrae & Kehoe, 1995).

Clinical Implications

Research with sequential CSs confirms, as suspected by fear theorists, that CR acquisition can be extended to the earliest signals of an aversive US. Nevertheless, CRs along the sequence remain dependent upon the associative strength of the stimulus closest to the US. Extinction of the CR to the last stimulus in the sequence causes a collapse of the gradient. Thus, the basic concept of the fear gradient and its extinction is well supported by the findings in classical conditioning.

Recent findings also demonstrate that the early stimuli in a sequence can dramatically influence the expression of the CRs to later stimuli that have been closely paired with the US. This influence has been seen both in the impairment of proximal associations and in conditional discriminations. In general, stimuli presented outside their usual reinforced sequence may elicit few CRs. The role played by prolonged "contextual" stimuli is particularly perplexing. These long stimuli themselves do not elicit CRs. They can even be conditioned to elicit responses opposite to the CR (Macrae & Kehoe, 1995).

Fears and other attributions may vary in a similar fashion. For example, a context by itself might elicit no fear until a particular trigger stimulus is introduced. At the extreme, the context may be one that is relaxing for the client until the trigger stimulus occurs. Similarly, the trigger stimulus by itself may not evoke much fear until presented in the appropriate context. Accordingly, identifying the hierarchy of stimuli that elicit fear requires the clinician to be alert to particular combinations of contexts and stimuli that might arouse fear. By the same token, fear of particular situations might be extinguished in the clinical context but remain intact in other, everyday contexts (see Chapter 4).

CONCLUSIONS

This chapter has been aimed at shifting the reader's perceptions of classical conditioning and its contribution to both behavioral and cognitive therapies. At an empirical level, manipulations using a handful of simple stimuli and their temporal relationships can yield conditioning outcomes that share key features with important cognitive phenomena. Learning-to-learn effects and the interplay between sequential stimuli certainly border on cognition. This is not to imply, however, that cognitive processes are merely some concatenation of conditioned reflexes or other simple associations. In fact, the seemingly simple matter of CR acquisition and extinction has increasingly been shown to require a more sophisticated theoretical approach than has previously been the case.

This empirical duality—the ability of classical conditioning to approximate cognitive phenomena and the sophistication of classical conditioning itself—points to a continuity between what is cognitive and what are more primitive behavioral processes. Certainly there is not an impenetrable barrier between the two. It would be premature to assert that all animals are cognitive in the same way that humans are. Nevertheless, the complexity that is evident in nonhuman animals indicates that the processes underlying cognition are biologically fundamental and start to appear at a low level of neural and behavioral organization.

Although there is hardly a comprehensive theory for classical conditioning by itself, much less a theory that includes cognition, connectionist techniques provide a set of tools that cut across associative and cognitive processes. While the models described here are small and aimed only at classical conditioning, the same class of models has become prominent in cognitive psychology. Networks containing hundreds or thousands of units have been used to explain phenomena as diverse as word recognition, categorization, visual pattern perception, and neurological disorders (e.g., Baddeley, 1990, pp. 357–378; Estes, 1988; Gluck & Bower, 1988; Rumelhart & McClelland, 1986). The results of classical conditioning have been highly useful in developing the basic learning rules and structures in connectionist models. In this fashion, classical conditioning's chief impact may be at the level of general theory. From a clinical perspective, classical conditioning may be most useful in theories that inform both cognitive and behavioral approaches rather than in quick and easy analogies to the behavior that clinicians see in their clients.

ENDNOTES

Preparation of this manuscript was supported by Australian Research Council Grant AC9231222. The authors extend their thanks to Gabrielle Weidemann for her assistance in preparing the figures. Correspondence should be sent to E. James Kehoe, School of Psychology, University of New South Wales, Sydney, NSW 2052, AUSTRALIA.

REFERENCES

Baddeley, A. D. (1990). *Human memory: Theory and practice*. Boston: Allyn & Bacon.

Bandura, A. (1986). *Social foundations of thought and action: A social cognitive theory*. Englewood Cliffs, N.J.: Prentice-Hall.

Bouton, M. E. (1991a). Context and retrieval in extinction and in other examples of interference in simple associative learning. In L. Dachowski & C. F. Flaherty (eds.), *Current topics in animal learning: Brain, emotion, and cognition*, 25–49. Hillsdale, N.J.: Erlbaum.

Bouton, M. E. (1991b). Sources of relapse after extinction in Pavlovian and instrumental learning. *Clincial Psychology Review, 11*, 123–140.

Boyd, T. L., & Levis, D. J. (1976). The effects of single-component extinction of a three-component serial CS on resistance to extinction of the conditioned avoidance response. *Learning and Motivation, 7*, 517–531.

Brandon, S. E., & Wagner, A. R. (1991). Modulation of a discrete Pavlovian conditioned reflex by a putative emotive Pavlovian conditioned stimulus. *Journal of Experimental Psychology: Animal Behavior Processes, 17*, 299–311.

Coleman, S. R., & Gormezano, I. (1971). Classical conditioning of the rabbit's (*Oryctolagus cuniculus*) nictitating membrane response under symmetrical CS-US interval shifts. *Journal of Comparative and Physiological Psychology, 77*, 447–455.

Davison, G. C., & Neale, J. M. (1990). *Abnormal Psychology* (5th ed.). New York: Wiley.

Deaux, E., & Gormezano, I. (1963). Eyeball retraction: Classical conditioning and extinction in the albino rabbit. *Science, 141*, 630–631.

Dickinson, A. (1989). Expectancy theory in animal conditioning. In S. B. Klein & R. R. Mowrer (eds.), *Contemporary learning theories: Pavlovian conditioning and the status of traditional learning theory*, 279–308. Hillsdale, N.J.: Erlbaum.

Ellis, H. (1965). *The transfer of learning*. New York: Macmillan.

Estes, W. K. (1988). Toward a framework for combining connectionist and symbol-processing models. *Journal of Memory and Language, 27*, 196–212.

Fantino, E. (1992). The concept of latent inhibition and its application to psychosomatic medicine. *Psychosomatic Medicine, 54*, 638–640.

Gabriel, M., & Moore, J. W. (eds.) (1990). *Learning and computational neuroscience: Foundations of adaptive networks*. Cambridge, Mass.: MIT Press.

Garcia, J., Ervin, F. R., & Koelling, R. A. (1966). Learning with prolonged delay of reinforcement. *Psychonomic Science, 5*, 121–122.

Gibbs, C. M., Cool, V., Land, T., Kehoe, E. J., & Gormezano, I. (1991a). Second-order conditioning of the rabbit's nictitating membrane response: Interstimulus interval and frequency of CS-CS pairings. *Integrative Physiological and Behavioral Science, 26*, 282–295.

Gibbs, C. M., Kehoe, E. J., & Gormezano, I. (1991b). Conditioning of the rabbit's nictitating membrane response to a CSA-CSB-US serial compound: Manipulations of CSB's associative character. *Journal of Experimental Psychology: Animal Behavior Processes, 17*, 423–432.

Gluck, M. A., & Bower, G. H. (1988). Evaluating an adaptive network model of human learning. *Journal of Memory and Language, 27,* 166–195.

Gormezano, I. (1966). Classical conditioning. In J. B. Sidowski (ed.), *Experimental methods and instrumentation in psychology,* 385–420. New York: McGraw-Hill.

Gormezano, I. (1972). Investigations of defense and reward conditioning in the rabbit. In A. H. Black & W. F. Prokasy (eds.), *Classical conditioning II: Current research and theory,* 151–181. New York: Appleton-Century-Crofts.

Gormezano, I., & Kehoe, E. J. (1975). Classical conditioning: Some methodological-conceptual issues. In W. K. Estes (ed.), *Handbook of learning and cognitive processes.* New York: Erlbaum.

Grether, W. F. (1938). Pseudo-conditioning without paired stimulation encountered in attempted backward conditioning. *Journal of Comparative Psychology, 25,* 91–96.

Harlow, H. F. (1949). The formation of learning sets. *Psychological Review, 56,* 51–65.

Hilgard, E. R., & Marquis, D. G. (1940). *Conditioning and learning.* New York: Appleton-Century-Crofts.

Hinson, R. E. (1982). Effects of UCS preexposure on excitatory and inhibitory rabbit eyelid conditioning: An associative effect of conditioned contextual stimuli. *Journal of Experimental Psychology: Animal Behavior Processes, 8,* 49–61.

Hoehler, F. K., & Leonard, D. W. (1976). Double responding in classical nictitating membrane conditioning with single-CS dual-ISI pairing. *Pavlovian Journal of Biological Science, 11,* 180–190.

Holland, P. C. (1991). Transfer of control in ambiguous discriminations. *Journal of Experimental Psychology: Animal Behavior Processes, 19,* 113–124.

Holland, P. C., & Rescorla, R. A. (1975). Second-order conditioning with food unconditioned stimulus. *Journal of Comparative and Physiological Psychology, 88,* 459–467.

Kalat, J. W. (1995). *Biological psychology* (5th ed.). Pacific Grove, Calif.: Brooks/Cole.

Kapp, B. S., Wilson, A., Pascoe, J. P., Supple, W., & Whalen, P. J. (1990). A neuroanatomical systems analysis of conditioned bradycardia in the rabbit. In M. Gabriel & J. Moore (eds.), *Learning and computational neuroscience: Foundations of adaptive networks,* 53–90. Cambridge, Mass.: MIT Press.

Kehoe, E. J. (1979). The role of CS-US contiguity in classical conditioning of the rabbit's nictitating membrane response to serial stimuli. *Learning and Motivation, 10,* 23–38.

Kehoe, E. J. (1983). CS-US contiguity and CS intensity in conditioning of the rabbit's nictitating membrane response to serial and simultaneous compound stimuli. *Journal of Experimental Psychology: Animal Behavior Processes, 9,* 307–319.

Kehoe, E. J. (1987). "Selective association" in compound stimulus conditioning with the rabbit. In I. Gormezano, W. F. Prokasy, & R. F. Thompson (eds.), *Classical conditioning,* 161–196. Hillsdale, N.J.: Erlbaum.

Kehoe, E. J. (1988). A layered network model of associative learning: Learning-to-learn and configuration. *Psychological Review, 95,* 411–433.

Kehoe, E. J., Cool, V., & Gormezano, I. (1991). Trace conditioning of the rabbit's nictitating membrane response as a function of CS-US interstimulus interval and trials per session. *Learning and Motivation, 22,* 269–290.

Kehoe, E. J., Feyer, A., & Moses, J. L. (1981). Second-order conditioning of the rabbit's nictitating membrane response as a function of the CS2-CS1 and CS1-US intervals. *Animal Learning & Behavior, 9,* 304–315.

Kehoe, E. J., Gibbs, C. M., Garcia, E., & Gormezano, I. (1979). Associative transfer and stimulus selection in classical conditioning of the rabbit's nictitating membrane response to serial compound CSs. *Journal of Experimental Psychology: Animal Behavior Processes, 5,* 1–18.

Kehoe, E. J., & Gormezano, I. (1974). Effects of trials per session on conditioning of the rabbit's nictitating membrane response. *Bulletin of the Psychonomic Society, 4,* 434–436.

Kehoe, E. J., Graham-Clarke, P., & Schreurs, B. G. (1989). Temporal patterns of the rabbit's nictitating membrane response to compound and component stimuli under mixed CS-US intervals. *Behavioral Neuroscience, 103,* 283–295.

Kehoe, E. J., & Holt, P. E. (1984). Transfer across CS-US intervals and sensory modalities in classical conditioning in the rabbit. *Animal Learning & Behavior, 12,* 122–128.

Kehoe, E. J., & Macrae, M. (1994). Classical conditioning of the rabbit nictitating membrane can be fast or slow: Implications for Lennartz and Weinberger's (1992) two-factor theory. *Psychobiology, 22,* 1–4.

Kehoe, E. J., Marshall-Goodell, B., & Gormezano, I. (1987). Differential conditioning of the rabbit's nictitating membrane response to serial compound stimuli. *Journal of Experimental Psychology: Animal Behavior Processes, 13,* 17–30.

Kehoe, E. J., & Morrow, L. D. (1984). Temporal dynamics of the rabbit's nictitating membrane response in serial compound conditioned stimuli. *Journal of Experimental Psychology: Animal Behavior Processes, 10,* 205–220.

Kehoe, E. J., Morrow, L. D., & Holt, P. E. (1984). General transfer across sensory modalities survives reductions in the original conditioned reflex in the rabbit. *Animal Learning & Behavior, 12,* 129–136.

Kehoe, E. J., & Napier, R. M. (1991). Temporal specificity in cross-modal transfer of the rabbit nictitating membrane response. *Journal of Experimental Psychology: Animal Behavior Processes, 17,* 26–35.

Kehoe, E. J., Schreurs, B. G., & Graham, P. (1987). Temporal primacy overrides prior training in serial compound conditioning of the rabbit's nictitating membrane response. *Animal Learning & Behavior*, *15*, 455–464.

Kimmel, H. D., & Ray, R. L. (1978). Transswitching: Conditioning with tonic and phasic stimuli. *Journal of Experimental Psychology: General*, *107*, 187–205.

Konorski, J., & Lawicka, W. (1959). Physiological mechanisms of delayed reactions: 1. The analysis and classification of delayed reactions. *Acta Biologiae Experimentalis*, *19*, 175–197.

Levis, D. J. (1971). Effects of serial CS presentation on a finger-withdrawal avoidance response to shock. *Journal of Experimental Psychology*, *87*, 71–77.

Levis, D. J. (1989). The case for a return to a two-factor theory of avoidance: The failure of non-fear interpretations. In S. B. Klein & R. R. Mowrer (eds.), *Contemporary learning theories: Pavlovian conditioning and the status of traditional learning theory*, 227–277. Hillsdale, N.J.: Erlbaum.

Levis, D. J., & Stampfl, T. G. (1972). Effects of serial CS presentation on shuttlebox avoidance responding. *Learning and Motivation*, *3*, 73-90.

Lovibond, P. F. (1993). Conditioning and cognitive-behaviour therapy. *Behaviour Change*, *10*, 119–130.

Macrae, M., & Kehoe, E. J. (1995). Transfer between conditional and discrete discriminations in conditioning of the rabbit nictitating membrane response. *Learning and Motivation*, *26*, 380–402.

Marchant, H. G., III, & Moore, J. W. (1973). Blocking of the rabbit's conditioned nictitating membrane response in Kamin's two-stage paradigm. *Journal of Experimental Psychology*, *101*, 155–158.

Marks, I. (1969). *Fears and phobias*. New York: Academic Press.

McAllister, W. R., & McAllister, D. E. (1986). Persistence of fear-reducing behavior: Relevance for the conditioned theory of neurosis. *Journal of Abnormal Psychology*, *95*, 365–372.

Millenson, J. R., Kehoe, E. J., & Gormezano, I. (1977). Classical conditioning of the rabbit's nictitating membrane response under fixed and mixed CS-US intervals. *Learning and Motivation*, *8*, 351–366.

Mowrer, O. H., & Lamoreaux, R. R. (1946). Fear as an intervening variable in avoidance conditioning. *Journal of Comparative Psychology*, *39*, 29–50.

Napier, R. M., Macrae, M., & Kehoe, E. J. (1992). Rapid reacquisition in conditioning of the rabbit's nictitating membrane response. *Journal of Experimental Psychology: Animal Behavior Processes*, *18*, 182–192.

Powell, D. A., & Levine-Bryce, D. (1988). A comparison of two model systems of associative learning: Heart rate and eyeblink conditioning in the rabbit. *Psychophysiology*, *25*, 672–682.

Rescorla, R. A., & Wagner, A. R. (1972). A theory of Pavlovian conditioning: Variations in the effectiveness of reinforcement and nonreinforcement. In A. H. Black & W. F. Prokasy (eds.), *Classical conditioning II*, 64–99. New York: Appleton-Century-Crofts.

Rosehan, D. L., & Seligman, M. E. P. (1984). Abnormal Psychology. New York: Norton.

Rumelhart, D. E., & McClelland, J. L. (eds.) (1986). *Parallel distributed processing. Vol. 1. Foundations*. Cambridge, Mass.: MIT Press.

Schneiderman, N. (1972). Response system divergencies in aversive classical conditioning. In A. H. Black & W. F. Prokasy (eds.), *Classical conditioning: Current theory and research*, 341–376. New York: Appleton-Century-Crofts.

Schneiderman, N., Smith, M. C., Smith, A. C., & Gormezano, I. (1966). Heart rate classical conditioning in rabbits. *Psychonomic Science*, *6*, 241–242.

Schreurs, B. G. (1989). Classical conditioning of model systems: A behavioral review. *Psychobiology*, *17*, 145–155.

Schreurs, B. G., & Kehoe, E. J. (1987). Cross-modal transfer as a function of initial training level in classical conditioning with the rabbit. *Animal Learning & Behavior*, *15*, 47–54.

Schreurs, B. G., Kehoe, E. J., & Gormezano, I. (1993). Concurrent associative transfer and competition in serial conditioning of the rabbit's nictitating membrane response. *Learning and Motivation*, *24*, 395–412.

Seligman, M. E. P. (1970). On the generality of the laws of learning. *Psychological Review*, *77*, 406–418.

Sheafor, P. J. (1975). "Pseudoconditioned" jaw movements of the rabbit reflect associations conditioned to contextual background cues. *Journal of Experimental Psychology: Animal Behavior Processes*, *104*, 245–260.

Skinner, B. F. (1938). *The behavior of organisms*. New York: Appleton-Century-Crofts.

Smith, J. C., & Roll, D. L. (1967). Trace conditioning with X-rays as an aversive stimulus. *Psychonomic Science*, *9*, 11–12.

Smith, M. C. (1968). CS-US interval and US intensity in classical conditioning of the rabbit's nictitating membrane response. *Journal of Comparative and Physiological Psychology*, *66*, 679–687.

Stampfl, T. G., & Levis, D. J. (1967). Essentials implosive therapy: A learning-theory-based psychodynamic behavioral therapy. *Journal of Abnormal Psychology*, *72*, 496–503.

Sutherland, N. S., & Mackintosh, N. J. (1971). *Mechanisms of animal discrimination learning*. New York: Academic Press.

Sutton, R. S., & Barto, A. G. (1981). Toward a modern theory of adaptive networks: Expectation and prediction. *Psychological Review*, *88*, 135–171.

Sutton, R. S., & Barto, A. G. (1990). Time-derivative models of Pavlovian reinforcement. In M. Gabriel & J. W. Moore (eds.), *Learning and computational neuroscience*, 497–537. Cambridge, Mass.: MIT Press.

Thompson, R. F. (1986). The neurobiology of learning and memory. *Science, 233,* 941–947.

Thompson, R. F. (1993). *The brain: A neuroscience primer* (2nd ed.). New York: W. H. Freeman.

Tolman, E. C. (1932). *Purposive behavior in animals and men.* New York: Century.

Tryon, W. W. (1976). Models of behavior disorder. *American Psychologist, 31,* 509–518.

Weiner, B., Frieze, L., Kukla, A., Reed, L., Rest, S., & Rosenbaum, R. M. (1971). *Perceiving the causes of success and failure.* New York: General Learning Press.

Westbrook, R. F., & Homewood, J. (1982). The effects of a flavour toxicosis pairing upon long-delay, flavour aversion learning. *Quarterly Journal of Experimental Psychology, 34,* 139–149.

Wolpe, J. (1969). Basic principles and practices of behavior therapy. *American Journal of Psychiatry, 125,* 362–368.

Zinbarg, R. E. (1993). Information processing and classical conditioning: Implications for exposure therapy and the integration of cognitive therapy and behavior therapy. *Journal of Behavior Therapy and Experimental Psychiatry, 24,* 129–139.

CHAPTER 4

THE ROLE OF CONTEXT IN CLASSICAL CONDITIONING: SOME IMPLICATIONS FOR COGNITIVE BEHAVIOR THERAPY

Mark E. Bouton
James B. Nelson

Pavlov's classical conditioning experiment is so well known that it is an icon of Western culture. Unfortunately, the cultural stereotype of the conditioning experiment makes it seem so simple and obvious that its enduring relevance to psychology is easy to miss. The truth is, classical conditioning is an essential phenomenon that helps humans and other animals adapt to their environments. It also involves a rich and interesting set of psychological processes that include emotion, motivation, and memory. Classical conditioning is useful as a method for studying how these processes work and how they influence behavior. The simplicity of the conditioning experiment is actually deliberate. It is deceptive too.

Let us illustrate. In a modern conditioning experiment, a rat is given pairings of a neutral cue (e.g., a tone) with an emotionally significant event, such as a brief foot shock. Typically, the rat learns to associate the tone with the shock in a few trials; the tone therefore comes to evoke a fear state that is often linked to human anxiety disorders (e.g., Mineka, 1985). In the laboratory, the tone actually evokes a whole host of behaviors and responses. For example, the rat freezes, its heart rate changes, its respiration becomes more rapid and shallow, and it becomes less sensitive to pain. As a group, these responses help prepare the rat for the upcoming aversive event (e.g., Bolles & Fanselow, 1980; Fanselow, 1994; Hollis, 1982). In modern terms, the tone evokes these behaviors because an association learned between tone and shock allows the tone to activate or retrieve a memory of shock (e.g., Davey, 1989; Rescorla, 1974). The tone has become a retrieval cue with emotional, behavioral, and adaptive impact.

In other conditioning experiments, experimenters might pair the tone with a positive, "appetitive" event, such as the presentation of food.

Here, once the subject has learned to associate the tone with food, the tone evokes a set of responses that prepares the animal for the upcoming meal (e.g., Powley, 1977; Woods & Strubbe, 1994). Appetitive conditioning appears to obey the same laws that govern fear conditioning; in our own laboratory, the parallel to date is almost perfect. Nevertheless, appetitive conditioning has direct implications for eating and food selection (e.g., Capaldi & Powley, 1990), and in the abstract, it seems more related to situations in which humans and animals associate stimuli with other positive reinforcers, such as drugs (e.g., Stewart, DeWit, & Eikelboom, 1984; Stolerman, 1992). Both appetitive and fear-conditioning experiments have many implications for clinical psychology.

This chapter introduces another layer of complexity. The fact is, no conditioning trial ever occurs in a vacuum; tone-shock or tone-food pairings always occur against a background of stimuli called a *context*. In the laboratory, the context is usually defined as the apparatus (e.g., the Skinner box) in which the animal receives the conditioned stimulus (CS, e.g., the tone) and the unconditioned stimulus (US, e.g., the shock or food). (We will expand on this definition later, and suggest that this sort of context is but one of many possible background cues.) Roughly 20 years of conditioning research suggests that what the animal knows about the context can have a powerful impact on learning about, and performing to, CSs that are presented in it (e.g., Balsam & Tomie, 1985). The effects of context have important implications for our understanding of fundamental learning and memory processes. And they may also have implications for certain clinical phenomena.

Contexts often work as CSs that control responding directly. For example, drug users may learn to associate a room "context" with drugs (e.g., Siegel, 1989). Direct associations like this between a context and a US can be extremely important. They might contribute to drug tolerance, the process by which our bodies become accustomed to drugs (see Cunningham, this volume; Siegel, 1989). Through its direct association with

the drug, the context might elicit responses that cancel the drug's usual effect, and in this manner produce tolerance. We sometimes say that drug tolerance is "context-specific"—it is lost when the drug is taken outside the usual context. Here the context plays the role of an ordinary CS, like the tone directly associated with shock or food in the previous examples.

This chapter emphasizes another kind of contextual control. Contexts can also affect learning and behavior *to CSs that are presented in them*. For example, there is ample evidence to suggest that the context has a profound effect on performance after *extinction*, the paradigm in which conditioned behavior is eliminated by presenting the tone repeatedly alone, without the US, after conditioning (e.g., Bouton, 1991a, 1991b; Bouton & Swartzentruber, 1991; see Falls, this volume). Behavior therapists have often seen extinction as an important mechanism in therapy. For example, exposure to fear-evoking stimuli alone may contribute in a major way to the effectiveness of many treatments used with anxiety disorders (e.g., Marks, 1978). Regardless of their theoretical origins, many therapies contain components designed to remove unwanted thoughts, feelings, or behaviors. Extinction is an example of such a removal procedure.

Consider the two experiments that are presented in Figure 4–1. The upper panel shows a fear-conditioning experiment in which a tone was originally paired with shock (Bouton & King, 1983, Experiment 1); the y-axis is the suppression ratio, the standard measure of fear in "conditioned emotional response" studies in which fear is indexed by the CS's ability to suppress an ongoing baseline behavior reinforced by food. (A ratio of 0 indicates maximal fear of the CS while 0.50 indicates no fear.) The lower panel shows an appetitive conditioning experiment in which a tone was originally paired with food (Bouton & Peck, 1989, Experiment 1), and the index of conditioning was the ability of the tone to evoke an excited "head jerking" response (e.g., Holland, 1977). The two experiments were very similar. In each, the conditioning phase was conducted in one context (Context A, not shown). In the second phase (shown at left), the rats received the tone repeatedly alone to extinguish performance conditioned to it. For Group Ext-A, extinction was conducted in the original conditioning context (Context A), while for Group Ext-B it was conducted in a different context (Context B). (The boxes providing the two contexts are always counterbalanced.) In either case, the procedure caused a lawful decline in responding (an increase in the suppression ratio in the fear experiment and a decrease in headjerk behavior in the appetitive experiment) over the course of extinction.

Interestingly, in both experiments, performance in the two groups was comparable in extinction regardless of the context in which extinction occurred. However, after the behavior was extinguished, the context became important. When extinction was complete, the rats were returned to the original conditioning context (Context A) and tested with the tone there. Whether the experiment involved shock or food, the results were once again the same: extinguished performance was "renewed" when the rats that had received extinction in Context B were returned to Context A. Manipulating the context had a potent impact on responding after extinction. We will have more to say about this result (the *renewal effect*) in other parts of the chapter. For now, it illustrates what we mean by contextual control, and why contextual control should be a major concern of behavior therapists. After extinction or therapy, responding depends on the context in which the conditioned stimulus is presented. Thus, *relapse* can occur after therapy when the conditioned phobic or addictive stimulus is encountered again in its original context (for reviews, see Bouton, 1988, 1991a; Bouton & Swartzentruber, 1991). We will show that contexts are important in procedures designed to eliminate unwanted cognitions or behaviors. We will also show that they are important for understanding the origin of conditioned emotions and behaviors in the first place. The purpose of this chapter is to summarize both kinds of evidence.

To frame the issue generally, there are several ways in which contexts might come to control learning and performance to a CS. Three important mechanisms are illustrated in Figure 4–2. First, the context might operate as any CS would: it might have a direct association with the US. As suggested in Panel A, the context might influence behavior controlled by the tone because it also activates the representation of shock. Panel B illustrates a second possibility.

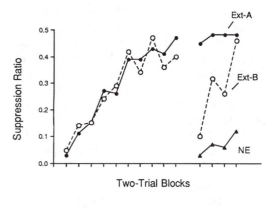

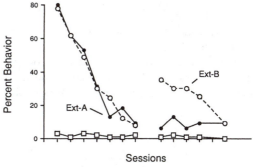

Figure 4–1. The renewal effect in fear conditioning (top) and appetitive conditioning (bottom). In both experiments, conditioning was conducted in Context A (not shown), and the extinction phase shown at left was conducted in either the conditioning context (Group Ext-A) or in a different context (Group Ext-B). Notice that the context switch between conditioning and extinction (Group Ext-B) had no effect on performance during extinction. However, when the rats were returned to Context A and tested there (right), a strong renewal of performance was observed. NE = No Extinction; open squares indicate a control group that received unpaired presentations of CS and US. Adapted from Bouton and King (1983) and Bouton and Peck (1989). Used by permission of the publishers.

Here, the context might have a direct association with the tone itself, rather than the shock. Through this sort of association, for example, the context might influence performance by affecting how the subject pays attention to the tone. Finally, as illustrated in Panel C, the context might be associated with the tone's own association with the shock. In the renewal experiments presented in Figure 4–1, Context A might signal the tone-shock association, and Context B might signal the tone–no shock association. In effect, the context might select the tone's current meaning (e.g., Bouton & Bolles, 1985). As we will see, this sort of mechanism is most responsible for the renewal effect. On the other hand, each of the mechanisms shown in Figure 4–2 can have important implications for our understanding of behavior and emotion. Let us therefore consider each of them, and their implications, separately.

DIRECT ASSOCIATIONS BETWEEN THE CONTEXT AND THE US

Perhaps the simplest way a context can affect behavior to a CS that is presented in it is through its own direct association with the US. Contexts are readily associated with shock or food when these stimuli are presented in them. If you think of the context as another CS in the background, it might influence the tone the way any extra CS should: its direct association with the US might *summate* with any association that the tone has. In Panel A of Figure 4–2, the representation of the US would be doubly activated if inputs came from both the context and the tone. We might therefore expect more behavior to the CS in the presence of strong context-US associations (see Wagner & Brandon, 1989, for a related possibility).

The renewal effect shown in Figure 4–1 could be a simple result of summation between direct context–US and CS-US associations. For example, during testing, the rats were returned to a context that could have been associated with the US during original conditioning. That association would be stronger than the one present in the extinction context, and renewal could come about if the context-US association summed with a weak tone-US association that somehow survived extinction. The fact is, the renewal effect does not seem to be controlled by this simple summation mechanism. In the conditioning literature, CS–context summation effects occasionally do occur (e.g., Durlach, 1983; Grau & Rescorla, 1984; Rescorla, 1984), but they tend to be very small or confined to special conditions in which the tone is tested almost immediately after

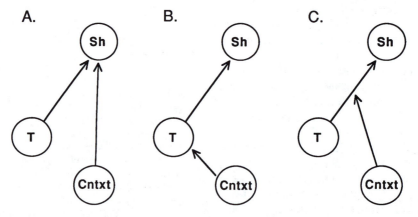

Figure 4–2. Three ways in which a context (Cntxt) can influence responding to a representative tone (T) conditioned stimulus that is associated with a shock (Sh) unconditioned stimulus. See text for explanation.

the subject is placed in the context (Miller, Grahame, & Hallam, 1990). Many researchers have failed to find CS-context summation at all under ordinary circumstances (e.g., Bouton, 1984; Bouton, Rosengard, Achenbach, Peck, & Brooks, 1993; Bouton & King, 1986; Randich & Ross, 1985). There is little question that contexts are easily associated with USs. But they do not typically summate with CSs the way ordinary CSs are expected to.

Ironically, one of the most well-documented effects of direct conditioning of the context on responding to a CS is the opposite of summation: context conditioning often actually *reduces* performance to a CS. This sort of effect is illustrated by a phenomenon known as the *US-preexposure effect*. Here, exposure to the US before conditioning slows down conditioning when a CS is later paired with the US. One of the main reasons this phenomenon occurs is that US-alone presentations condition a context-US association, and this learning interferes with responding to the CS. If the US is pre-exposed in the context in which the CS-US pairings occur, conditioning of the CS is slow. But if the US is pre-exposed in a different context, conditioning of the CS occurs at a more normal rate (e.g., Ayres, Bombace, Shurtleff, & Vigorito, 1985; Grau & Rescorla, 1984; Randich, 1981; Randich & Ross, 1985). The context controls the US-preexposure effect because the presence of contextual conditioning impairs the development of responding to the CS.

The US-preexposure effect is relevant to behavior therapists who are concerned with the origins of behavior disorders. It illustrates that pairings of a CS and an otherwise potent US can sometimes be quite ineffective at causing conditioning of the CS. The reason is that *the effectiveness of any conditioning experience is always modulated by what the subject or client knows about the context*. There are at least two ways to understand the role of context here. Many models of conditioning (e.g., Rescorla & Wagner, 1972) assume that context conditioning can interfere with *learning* about the CS (see also Pearce, 1987; Pearce & Hall, 1980; Wagner, 1978, 1981; Wagner & Brandon, 1989). When tone conditioning occurs in a context that has already been conditioned, the tone is redundant to the context as a predictor of the US. The context therefore "blocks" learning the tone-shock association (see Kamin, 1969). Alternatively, "comparator theories" propose no deficit in what the subject or client actually learns about the CS. Instead, context conditioning interferes with *performance* to the CS (Gibbon & Balsam, 1981; Miller & Schachtman, 1985). The subject always compares the strengths of the tone-US and context-US associations. If the tone has a stronger association with the US than the context does, then the animal will respond to the CS. But if the tone has a weaker association than the context, the animal will not respond to it. According to comparator theories, contextual conditioning interferes with performance because we respond to CSs only when they predict the US better than the background does. The potential for responding to the CS is held at bay by the strength of the context.

These theories have correctly identified a role of context conditioning in a number of situations in which CS-US pairings do not produce conditioning (see Durlach, 1989, for a review). In a general way, fear or conditioned responding is always a joint product of CS-US and context-US associations. However, if conditioning and testing are conducted in different contexts, it is the strength of the conditioning context, not the test context, that counts (cf. Gibbon & Balsam, 1981). For example, weak responding to a CS that is caused by pairing it with a US in a strongly conditioned context is maintained in new contexts regardless of their conditioned strengths (Ayres et al., 1985; Grau & Rescorla, 1984; Randich & Ross, 1985). And responding is not reduced when the CS is tested in a new context with stronger associations with the US (e.g., Durlach, 1983; Grau & Rescorla, 1984; Randich & Ross, 1985). These results suggest either that context conditioning present during conditioning blocks learning about the CS (e.g., Rescorla & Wagner, 1972), or that the crucial comparison that influences performance is between the CS and the current value of the *conditioning* context (Miller & Schachtman, 1985). The latter idea predicts that if the training context is extinguished *after* conditioning has occurred, then the animal should begin responding to the CS; the blocking hypothesis does not predict this, because it only considers the value of the context during conditioning. Nonetheless, the prediction has been confirmed (Matzel, Brown, & Miller, 1987; see also Miller, Barnet, & Grahame, 1992): rats that received CS-shock pairings in a highly conditioned context were relatively unafraid of the CS, but if fear of the conditioning context was eliminated by extinction, fear of the CS emerged. This result has clinical implications. Extinction of the conditioning context might cause a masked, invisible fear to emerge where one did not exist before. This phenomenon would allow anxiety disorders to appear "spontaneously," without apparent cause, in the absence of any recent conditioning experience or exposure to a traumatic US.

Despite this success of the comparator theory (Miller & Schachtman, 1985), another equally important prediction has been difficult to confirm. Just as reducing conditioning to the training context should increase performance to a CS, adding conditioning to the training context should reduce performance. (Again, because a blocking interpretation considers only the value of the context at the time of conditioning, it does not anticipate such an effect.) Despite a large number of tests, this prediction has never worked (see Miller, Hallam, & Grahame, 1990). Increasing the strength of the value of the conditioning context after CS-conditioning has no apparent impact on fear of the CS. Once responding to a CS is apparent, it is not reduced by increasing the value of the context in which conditioning occurred.

To summarize, it is clear that contexts can acquire direct associations with the US, and that such associations have an important impact on performance to the CS. Strong context-US associations seldom summate significantly to increase responding to the CS; if anything, they tend to decrease performance. The results we have discussed in this section are worth thinking about. The "classical theory" (Rachman, 1991)

of conditioning that motivated early behavior therapy suggests that pairings of CS and US are all the therapist needs to know about to understand the origin of, say, a client's anxiety disorder. But we have described situations in which a CS paired with a US showed little evidence of controlling responding; conversely, a CS might suddenly control fear in the absence of any recent pairings between CS and trauma. In both cases, the key is the context. As a general rule, if the value of the context was high during conditioning, it can reduce apparent performance to the CS, either because it blocked learning about it (Rescorla & Wagner, 1972) or because it wins a comparison/competition process that determines performance. If its value was low, more conditioning will accrue to the CS. There is even evidence that, if the value of the conditioning context is weakened after conditioning has already occurred, responding to the CS can increase—in spite of no further direct CS-US pairings. Behavior or emotion evoked by a CS depends on both CS-US and context-US associations.

DIRECT ASSOCIATIONS BETWEEN THE CONTEXT AND THE CS

Just as we learn that USs occur in particular contexts, we also learn that *CSs* occur in particular contexts. That is, in addition to everything else the animal learns during a conditioning experience, it also learns that the tone occurs, say, in Context A. This sort of context-CS learning is illustrated in Panel B of Figure 4–2. It can have important consequences on behavior. For one thing, it can provide another bridge that allows separate learning about one stimulus (e.g., the CS) to influence performance to the other stimulus (e.g., the context). For example, when a CS is first presented several times in one context (A), and then CS-food pairings occur in a second context (B), food-related behavior comes to be elicited by Context A even though it is never paired with food (Rescorla, 1984). This is an example of *sensory preconditioning*, in which a stimulus evokes responding, not because it is associated with a US directly, but because it is associated with another stimulus that is later paired with a US (e.g., Brogden, 1939; Rescorla & Cunningham, 1978b). In a related way, if CS-food pairings occur in Context A, and CS extinction occurs in a separate context, any US-related behavior that was elicited by Context A is also sympathetically reduced (Rescorla, 1984). Marlin (1982) reported similar results in fear conditioning. The presence of context-CS associations can make behavior wax and wane for subtle, nonobvious reasons.

There are still other places where context-CS associations may permit changes in behavior. Rescorla (1984) found that when a CS was first associated with food in one context and then presented repeatedly in a new context without food, the new context came to elicit food-related behavior without being paired directly with the US. The same effect has been reported in fear conditioning (Helmstetter & Fanselow, 1989). Marlin (1983) also found that when a neutral tone was presented in a context that had previously been associated with shock, the tone itself acquired the ability to elicit fear. All of these phenomena are examples of *second-order conditioning* in which initial association of a stimulus with a US makes it effective at conditioning new responding. Context-CS associations can permit anxiety, or other conditioned responses, to appear to new stimuli without their being paired directly with a US.

There are other possible consequences of learning that a context and a CS are associated. According to a major theory of conditioning developed by Wagner (e.g., 1978, 1981), once we learn that a context signals a CS, the CS is less surprising when it actually occurs. If the CS is less surprising, we are less likely to pay attention to it (or, in Wagner's terms, less likely to process it in short-term memory), and therefore less likely to learn about it. By influencing attention during conditioning, context-CS associations can interfere with learning.

This mechanism might explain an important conditioning phenomenon known as *latent inhibition* (see Lubow, 1989, and Lubow, this volume). In latent inhibition, exposure to a CS alone before conditioning makes it slow to acquire conditioned responding when it is later paired with a US. Latent inhibition is another phenomenon that cognitive-behavior therapists interested in the origins of behavior disorders need to know about. It indicates that the result of a conditioning experience depends on the novelty of the to-be-conditioned stimulus; familiar cues may be less likely to control conditioned anxiety disorders or addictive behaviors than cues that were novel when they were paired with the US. Why should novelty/familiarity be so important? According to Wagner's theory, novel stimuli are surprising, and they command attention when they are presented. In latent inhibition, the CS becomes associated with the context during pre-exposure. The context therefore makes the CS less surprising when it occurs, and reduces the learning possible with it.

This theory makes the striking prediction that if a preexposed CS is conditioned in a new context (that is, one in which it has not occurred before), then conditioning should occur at a faster (more normal) rate. Amazingly, this prediction has been confirmed in a large number of experiments (e.g., Channell & Hall, 1983; Hall & Channell, 1985; Lovibond, Preston, & Mackintosh, 1984; Swartzentruber & Bouton, 1986; see Bouton, 1993, or Hall, 1991, for reviews). Thus we can identify another major effect of context in conditioning: it controls latent inhibition. Familiar cues are difficult to condition in the same old context. But when they are presented again in a context in which they have never been presented before, they become conditionable again.

The idea that the CS can come to command less attention as a result of a learned context–CS association has implications for extinction and the renewal effect (Figure 4–1). During extinction, as in latent inhibition, the subject or client might learn to pay less and less attention to the CS (cf. Robbins, 1990). Rather than unlearn the excitatory association, the subject might come to "ignore" the CS, and performance might decline as a result. If this drop in attention was due to the context-CS mechanism proposed by Wagner, then attention to the CS might be renewed when the CS is presented outside of the extinction context, leading to renewed conditioned responding.

This is an interesting explanation of renewal, and there is evidence consistent with the idea that attention to the CS might decline in extinction (Kaye & Pearce, 1984; see also Bouton, 1986). But renewal effects also occur in situations in which attention presumably does not decline this way. For example, Peck and Bouton (1990) demonstrated renewal after *counterconditioning*. Here a tone is paired with one US (e.g., shock) in one phase and then a second US (e.g., food) in a second phase. As in extinction, fear declines in the second phase; but in this case, fear is replaced by food performance instead of nonresponding. The CS still commands enough attention to evoke vigorous *food* responding. Even here, however, renewal effects are observed. When Peck and Bouton (1990) conducted tone-shock and tone-food training in separate contexts, performance associated with the first phase was renewed after the second phase when the rat was returned to and tested in the first context. The discovery of a renewal effect in counterconditioning is important if one acknowledges a role for counterconditioning in therapy. Wolpe's pioneering work on systematic desensitization (in which a phobic stimulus is paired with relaxation during therapy) was based conceptually and empirically on counterconditioning (e.g., Wolpe, 1958). But like extinction, it leaves performance to the CS under the influence of the context, and relapse can occur. In this case, it seems unlikely that relapse is due to mere recovery of attention to the CS.

In fact, there is reason to question whether even the effect of context on latent inhibition itself is produced by the attention mechanism proposed by Wagner (e.g., Bouton, 1993; Hall, 1991). One of the main problems is that, while the theory attributes the loss of latent inhibition caused by a context switch to a recovery of the CS's surprisingness, rats do not appear to be surprised again, as judged by their orienting reactions to the CS, when the familiar CS is presented in a new context (e.g., Hall & Chan-

nell, 1985; see also Baker & Mercier, 1982). This sort of result suggests that the loss of latent inhibition that occurs with a context switch may not depend on the recovery of attention and surprise. One alternative is that the animal may learn that the CS is insignificant in the first phase, and the memory for this particular "meaning" of the CS is lost with a change of context (e.g., Bouton, 1993).

To summarize, contexts can become associated with CSs that are presented in them. This kind of learning provides a bridge that allows separate learning about the context (or the CS) to influence behavior evoked by the other stimulus. Because of a learned context–CS association, new learning about one stimulus can make performance change to the other. In an anxiety disorder, the change could once again look like the spontaneous emergence of a phobia or fear. A second possible result of a context-CS association is that the CS may command less attention in that context. This idea correctly predicts that latent inhibition will be lost after a context switch: familiar cues are ordinarily difficult to condition, but are conditionable again when they occur in a new context. However, there is reason to wonder whether that effect of context is truly due to a recovery of attention. As an alternative, latent inhibition and extinction may be due to the context signaling or retrieving the CS's current meaning, by which we mean its current relation to the US. Let us now consider this important mechanism of contextual control.

DISCRIMINATIVE CONTROL BY CONTEXTS: THE CONTEXTUAL CONTROL OF EXTINCTION

We turn now to Figure 4–2's third mechanism of contextual control (Panel C). Here the context works, not through its simple association with the tone or the shock, but through its ability to activate the overall tone-shock association. In effect, the context signals the tone's current meaning rather than the tone, or the shock, alone. The context's effect is discriminative in the sense that it can distinguish between the CS's possibly multiple meanings. This role of the context is related to *occasion setting*, a kind of behavioral control that has received some attention in the classical conditioning literature recently (e.g., Holland, 1992; Rescorla, 1985; Swartzentruber, 1995). In this type of behavioral control, a stimulus comes to control responding to a CS independently of its direct association with the US or the CS . One of the main sources of evidence for this mechanism in contextual control comes from investigations of the role of context in extinction.

As described elsewhere in this book (e.g., Falls, this volume), many theorists have assumed that extinction reduces learned behaviors and emotions because it destroys the original learning. This position is taken by several important theories of conditioning (e.g., Estes, 1955; Rescorla & Wagner, 1972), as well as by many neural network or "connectionist" theories of memory and cognition (e.g., McCloskey & Cohen, 1989). It also seems tacitly assumed by cognitive behavior therapists who hope that therapies have permanent effects. In fact, however, extinction is not unlearning. Even Pavlov knew this was true; he had discovered phenomena such as spontaneous recovery in which the extinguished response recovers naturally when time elapses after extinction. Recovery could not occur if extinction had destroyed the original learning. It is interesting to note that although spontaneous recovery is one of learning theory's best-known effects (most undergraduates learn about it at the same time they learn about extinction), no modern theory of conditioning can explain it. We will attempt to in a moment. We believe it is one of several demonstrations of the fact that performance after extinction depends inherently on the context.

Renewal

There are several phenomena besides spontaneous recovery that indicate that extinction is not unlearning. Several are listed in Table 4–1. One of the most important is the renewal effect. As we described earlier, in a typical renewal experiment, rats receive tone-shock pairings in Context A and then tone-alone trials (i.e., extinction trials) in Context B. After extinction is complete, the tone is returned to the original context and tested there again. Performance to the tone is renewed.

The renewal effect has been investigated extensively (see Bouton, 1991b, 1993 for reviews). It can occur even after a very large number of extinction trials; in one experiment, 84 trials of ex-

Table 4–1. The Contextual Control of Extinction: Phenomena Relevant to Relapse

PHENOMENON	DESCRIPTION
Renewal	Recovery of extinguished behavior that occurs when the context is changed after extinction. Most often observed when the subject is returned to the original context of conditioning. But it can also occur with mere removal from extinction context.
Reinstatement	Recovery of behavior that occurs when subject is exposed to the US alone after extinction. Strongly controlled by contextual conditioning produced when the US is presented; hence the term sometimes describes recovery that occurs when the CS is tested with stimuli that have been separately associated with the US.
Reacquisition	Recovery of responding that occurs when CS and US are paired again after extinction. Often rapid, particularly when cues in background can renew conditioned performance (as above). Can be slow when background cues continue to signal or retrieve extinction.
Spontaneous recovery	Recovery of responding that occurs when CS is tested after time has passed following the conclusion of extinction.

Note: From Bouton and Swartzentruber (1991).

tinction (following only 8 conditioning trials) did not remove the potential for renewal, even though fear performance was already gone after 20 of those trials (Bouton & Swartzentruber, 1989). This result suggests that the potential for relapse may survive well beyond the point at which an anxiety disorder has disappeared. Renewal also occurs in several variations. Most research has shown renewal when conditioning, extinction, and testing occur in Contexts A, B, and A, respectively. But it also has been observed when the three phases occur in Contexts A, B, and C (e.g., Bouton & Bolles, 1979a; Bouton & Brooks, 1993; Bouton & Swartzentruber, 1986), or in A, A, and C (Bouton & Ricker, 1994). The latter variations suggest that a return to the original context of conditioning is not necessary to create a renewal effect. Instead, a switch out of the extinction context can suffice. Extinction performance, and by implication exposure therapy, is at least partly specific to the context in which it is learned.

Renewal also happens with several kinds of contexts. For example, it occurs when the extinction context is provided by drugs. Drug states are widely known to produce internal *interoceptive* cues that can control performance (e.g., Overton, 1985; Spear, 1978). Consistent with this idea, when fear is extinguished while the rat is under the influence of either benzodiazepine tranquilizers (Librium or Valium) or alcohol, it returns when the rat is tested in the sober state (Bouton, Kenney, & Rosengard, 1990; Cunningham, 1979). The implication of this sort of phenomenon is clear. In the long run, the use of drugs in combination with exposure therapy might hurt rather than help the therapy process (e.g., Marks et al., 1993).

Renewal might also be produced by internal contexts created by moods, emotions, or stress. The results of a growing number of studies with human subjects suggest that mood states can cue information encoded while in the mood (Bower, Monteiro, & Gilligan, 1978; Eich, 1995; but see Bower, 1987). In rats, certain physiological components of stress, such as the pituitary hormone adrenocorticotrophin (ACTH), can also function

as contexts. Normally, ACTH is released during aversive learning, and perhaps through general stress. Provided that this occurs, if an avoidance response is first trained and then extinguished, the reintroduction of ACTH in the system can cause a renewal of avoidance performance (e.g., Ahlers & Richardson, 1985; Richardson, Riccio, & Devine, 1984). The implication of this line of research is once again clear. After extinction, if a client were to reexperience an emotion (or a physiological component of it) that was part of the context of the original learning, the emotion could precipitate renewal if the extinguished stimulus were encountered with it again. Relapse may occur if the wrong interoceptive stimuli are encountered after a successful therapy.

We can also say something more specific about the mechanisms that control renewal. Considerable research using physical, that is, apparatus, contexts has investigated the actual mechanisms. As we discussed earlier, one possibility is that the contexts might control because their direct associations with the US summate with those to the tone. According to many conditioning theories (e.g., Rescorla & Wagner, 1972), Context A could be associated directly with the US, while Context B acquires an inhibitory association. An inhibitory association would suppress the US representation, rather than excite it (e.g., Rescorla & Holland, 1977). In a number of experiments, we found no evidence that the two contexts acquired these properties (Bouton & King, 1983; Bouton & Swartzentruber, 1986). Furthermore, we have already noted that simple context-US and CS-US associations do not usually summate to affect performance (Bouton, 1984; Bouton & King, 1986; Bouton et al., 1993). The available data question whether the renewal effect is controlled through direct associations between the context and the US, as shown in Figure 4–2's Panel A.

We have also already discussed why it seems unlikely that renewal is controlled through Figure 4–2's Panel B—that is, through direct associations between the context and the CS . As we noted, such an association between the CS and the extinction context could theoretically make the subject pay less attention to the CS there. Removal from the extinction context could cause a recovery of attention, and hence a renewal of responding. However, this account does not explain renewal effects that occur in counterconditioning (Peck & Bouton, 1990), nor does it correspond well with the fact that orienting responses that index attention do not recover when a familiar CS is presented in a different context (e.g., Baker & Mercier, 1982; Hall & Channell, 1985). By elimination, the pattern suggests that contexts control performance through an occasion-setting mechanism related to the one sketched in Figure 4–2's Panel C. In fact, contexts interact with Pavlovian occasion setters in ways that further support this possibility (Swartzentruber, 1991). Contextual control exemplified in the renewal effect does not reduce to simple context-US or context-CS associations.

Casually speaking, in the renewal effect, Context A signals the tone-shock association, while Context B signals a tone–no-shock association. Instead of causing unlearning, extinction has given the tone a second meaning. The tone is like an ambiguous word (e.g., Bouton & Bolles, 1985; Bouton, 1994b); it has two available meanings, and the response it currently evokes depends on the current context. Your response to the word "Fire!" is very different in the movie theater and in the shooting gallery. Responding to an extinguished CS is similar; it depends fundamentally on the current context.

Reinstatement

Reinstatement (e.g., Rescorla & Heth, 1975) is another phenomenon that demonstrates both the importance of context after extinction and the fact that extinction does not destroy the original learning. In this paradigm, after extinction is complete, the subject is exposed to the US—by itself—before the tone is tested a final time. Exposure to the US after extinction can partially "reinstate" performance. This effect has been documented both in fear conditioning (e.g., Bouton, 1984; Bouton & Bolles, 1979b; Bouton & King, 1983; Rescorla & Heth, 1975; Wilson,

Brooks, & Bouton, 1995) and in appetitive conditioning (Bouton & Peck, 1989). Reinstatement suggests that the benefits of therapy can be at least partly undone if the client is exposed to the US again.

The reinstatement phenomenon is caused by conditioning of the context. When the US is presented after extinction, it conditions the background. Here, if the background conditioning is present during testing, it triggers responding to the extinguished CS. The main evidence is that reinstatement depends crucially on the test's occurring in the context in which the US was presented. If it is presented in the context in which the tone is ultimately tested, reinstatement is observed. But if it is presented in an irrelevant context, no reinstatment is observed (e.g., Bouton, 1984; Bouton & Bolles, 1979b; Bouton & King, 1983; Wilson, Brooks, & Bouton, 1995). In fact, rats exposed to the US in an irrelevant context show no evidence of reinstatement at all (Bouton & Bolles, 1979b). Once again, responding to an extinguished CS is determined by what the rat knows about the current context. For a review of other evidence supporting the role of context in reinstatement, see Bouton (1988, 1993).

One of the most important insights provided by our research on reinstatement is that responding to the extinguished CS is *particularly* sensitive to conditioning of the background. In a number of studies, we have shown that CSs that are not under the influence of extinction are not affected in the same way by contextual conditioning (Bouton, 1984; Bouton et al., 1993; Bouton & King, 1986). As discussed above, performance to a simple CS is not affected much, if at all, when it is tested in a context strongly associated with a US. Figure 4–3 shows the results of one experiment that illustrates this point (Bouton, 1984, Experiment 5). The two groups at left received conditioning with a weak shock that caused a weak conditioned fear. The groups at right received conditioning with a stronger shock and then extinction training until a similar level of fear was reached. Then, both sets of groups were exposed to foot shocks that produced fear of the context in either the original context, where testing was to occur (solid symbols), or in an irrelevant context (open symbols). Fear of the tone was then tested 24 hours later. As the figure indicates, contextual conditioning had a potent impact on fear of the extinguished tone; rats that had received extinction showed reinstated fear. But there was no effect of context conditioning in the groups that had received only conditioning: Substantial contextual conditioning in the group shocked in the same context had no impact on fear of the tone without extinction. This is exactly the sort of evidence that argues against the summation mechanism we discussed earlier. Comparable results have been produced in appetitive conditioning (Bouton et al., 1993). Responding to an extinguished tone, but not a nonextinguished one, is strongly affected by conditioning of the context (see also Bouton & King, 1986).

Why is an extinguished CS so special? Essen-

tially, reinstatement may be a renewal effect in which context conditioning provides a sort of contextual stimulus. That is, during conditioning, some conditioning of the context occurs along with conditioning of the CS. Contextual conditioning is thus part of the background in which the CS is paired with the US; it is a stimulus like Context A in the original renewal design. Extinction, on the other hand, is conducted while the background associations are relatively weak; there is no US presented in extinction to maintain contextual conditioning. Weak background conditioning is analogous to Context B in the simple renewal design. If the context is subsequently conditioned, it reintroduces a cue correlated with conditioning, and responding is renewed (see Bouton et al., 1993, for a more detailed explanation). The context arouses an expectancy of the US, which reminds the animal of the original conditioning experience.

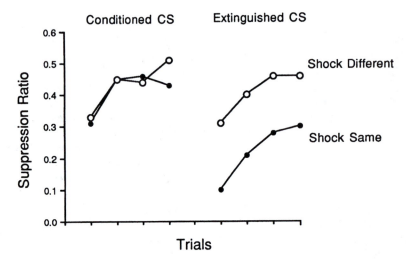

Figure 4–3. A comparison of the effects of context conditioning on fear of extinguished and nonextinguished CSs. Groups acquired similar fears of a CS through either conditioning with a weak US (left) or conditioning with a stronger US and then incomplete extinction (right). All groups then received four unsignaled shocks in either the context where the test trials shown occurred (solid symbols) or in a different context (open symbols). Contextual conditioning in the groups shocked in the same context (Shock Same) increased fear of the extinguished CS, but not the nonextinguished CS. Adapted from Bouton (1984). Used by permission of the publisher.

Reacquisition

Still other events may precipitate renewal effects. As described in Table 4–1, when CS-US pairings are resumed after extinction is complete, the extinguished response can reappear very rapidly (Napier, Macrae, & Kehoe, 1992). This finding, like the others in Table 4–1, suggests that the original learning is "saved" through extinction. However, its explanation is currently a matter of debate (e.g., Bouton, 1986; Napier et al., 1992). In the older literature, reacquisition was often begun after a time interval had elapsed following extinction, and the high responding that was observed at the start was probably no more than spontaneous recovery (e.g., Hoehler, Kirschenbaum, & Leonard, 1973; Smith & Gormezano, 1965). In other cases, presentations of the US again may themselves have cued conditioned performance. We have obtained clear evidence of this sort of effect in appetitive conditioning (Bouton et al., 1993). It is worth noting that USs involved in clinically significant conditioning episodes are likely to stimulate emotions —a type of context we identified earlier. Exposure to a US that elicits one might renew conditioned responding when they are reintroduced during the resumed CS-US pairings.

One clue about why reacquisition might occur rapidly came from the discovery that in several methods, reacquisition can be *slower* than the original learning. This is true after extensive extinction in fear conditioning (Bouton, 1986; Bouton & Swartzentruber, 1989) and after extinction in taste-aversion learning (e.g., Hart, Bourne, & Schachtman, 1995). In appetitive conditioning, reacquisition can be either rapid or slow depending in part on the number of conditioning trials (Ricker & Bouton, 1996). Slow reacquisition may tend to occur in procedures that employ relatively few initial conditioning trials. Rapid reconditioning tends to be obtained in experiments where there are many initial conditioning trials (e.g., Napier et al., 1992). One reason is that a large number of conditioning trials allows many opportunities to learn that reinforced trials predict additional reinforced trials.

Thus, when CS-US pairings are resumed after extinction, the first trial can act as a sort of contextual cue signaling other reinforced trials. Responding recovers rapidly because of a renewal effect. This sort of intertrial signaling in which certain types of trials signal other trials, has been emphasized for many years by E. J. Capaldi (e.g., Capaldi, 1994). Recent USs, their emotional aftereffects, or recent CS-US pairings can provide contextual cues with the power to produce a renewal effect.

Spontaneous Recovery

As mentioned above, spontaneous recovery is the well-known phenomenon in which responding recovers to the CS if time passes following extinction. It occurs in most of the major classical conditioning methods (e.g., Brooks & Bouton, 1993; Pavlov, 1927; Rescorla & Cunningham, 1978a; Robbins, 1990; Rosas & Bouton, 1996). The effect has also been observed in counterconditioning, where tone-food pairings follow tone-shock pairings or tone-shock pairings follow tone-food pairings. In either of these versions of counterconditioning, responding corresponding to the first phase can recover over time (Bouton & Peck, 1992). Spontaneous recovery has clear implications for relapse after therapy. Neither extinction nor counterconditioning produces effects that are necessarily permanent. Spontaneous recovery may be involved in recovery phenomena that are known to occur in humans between sessions of exposure therapy (e.g., Rachman & Lopatka, 1988).

Pavlov thought spontaneous recovery occurred because inhibition learned in extinction dissipates quickly over time. Skinner (1950) suggested that cues present during early parts of extinction sessions, such as handling cues, might undergo little direct extinction and evoke responding directly when they are introduced again at the start of the spontaneous-recovery test. Neither approach has stood up well to recent tests (e.g., Brooks & Bouton, 1993; Robbins, 1990; Thomas & Sherman, 1986). We have suggested a somewhat different approach (Bouton,

1988; Brooks & Bouton, 1993). The passage of time itself may provide a series of contexts. Therefore, just as extinguished responding may be renewed when conditioning, extinction, and testing occur in Contexts A, B, and C, renewal might occur when the three phases occur at $t1$, $t2$, and $t3$. Spontaneous recovery may be the renewal effect that happens when the extinguished CS is tested in a new temporal context. This effect, like all of the effects listed in Table 4–1, indicates that extinction is not unlearning; it is also consistent with the idea that performance after extinction depends inherently on the context in which the CS is presented.

Summary

Extinction performance is strongly influenced by the context in which the subject or client encounters the CS. Perhaps the most fundamental demonstration of this point is the renewal effect: responding to an extinguished CS may recover when it is removed from the extinction context and returned to the conditioning context. Other, equally important, effects also indicate that extinction is not unlearning. Each may boil down to renewal effects in which performance is controlled by background cues provided by an expectancy of the US, direct aftereffects of the US, emotions, recent events, or the passage of time. In addition to illustrating the fundamental importance of context in extinction, this section of the chapter has begun to expand the definition of context. It is probably safest to assume that contexts can be provided by many types of background cues. On this view, therapists need to be aware of the entire constellation of stimuli in the background when therapy or natural extinction occurs. A variety of contexts can influence performance after an extinction treatment.

This sort of analysis goes beyond an explanation of extinction (Bouton, 1993). Behavior in a variety of "interference paradigms" in which the CS acquires different meanings at different points in time may be governed by similar principles. The list of these paradigms includes latent inhibition and counterconditioning, which we have already mentioned are, like extinction, im-

portantly influenced by the context. Memories of both phases are retained and can be cued by the appropriate context; performance is also very sensitive to the passage of time. Research to date on counterconditioning provides a particularly noteworthy parallel because of its historical connection with behavior therapy. As mentioned above, we have demonstrated renewal (Peck & Bouton, 1990) and spontaneous recovery (Bouton & Peck, 1992) after counterconditioning. More recently, we have demonstrated reinstatement too (Brooks, Hale, Nelson, & Bouton, 1995). Here, tone-shock pairings caused rats to be afraid of the CS; subsequent tone-food pairings eliminated fear and replaced it with appetitive behavior. However, if the rat was exposed to shock again alone in the context in which the tone was later tested, fear performance was reinstated to the tone. The results corresponded perfectly with previous work on reinstatement after extinction. Neither extinction nor counterconditioning destroys the original learning. In these two paradigms, as well as others (Bouton, 1993), the CS acquires an ambiguous meaning, and performance is determined by contexts provided by exteroceptive cues, interoceptive cues, and cues provided by the passage of time.

CONTEXT AND MEMORY: A MEMORY MODEL OF EXTINCTION

One of the most important functions traditionally ascribed to contextual cues is the control of memory retrieval (e.g., Morgan & Riccio, this volume). The retrieval of memories in both humans and other animals depends on the degree of match between the context in which testing occurs and the context in which learning originally occurred (e.g., Estes, 1976; McGeoch, 1932; Spear, 1973, 1978; Tulving, 1974). With a match, memory retrieval occurs; with a mismatch, it is less likely to occur. Retrieval failure owing to a difference between the test and acquisition contexts is now considered one of the major sources of forgetting.

Another major source of forgetting is *interference* (e.g., McGeoch, 1932; Postman & Underwood, 1973). Interference comes in two varieties. In proactive interference, initial learning can interfere with memory for something learned at a later time. In retroactive interference, learning something later can interfere with the memory of something learned earlier. Forgetting caused by either interference or retrieval failure is available for study through experiments on classical conditioning (Bouton, 1994a). In fact, the approach to extinction sketched above invokes both processes. Extinction is one of the most fundamental of all the retroactive interference paradigms; Phase-2 learning interferes with Phase-1 performance. And relapse effects may occur when the context is changed because the subject or client fails to retrieve extinction. There are advantages to viewing conditioning and extinction from a memory perspective. And there are advantages to viewing memory from a conditioning perspective. For example, through conditioning experiments, we can begin to understand the principles that govern memory for emotionally significant material; human memory experiments usually study memory of relatively trivial verbal information (nonsense syllables, words, sentences) (e.g., Bouton, 1994; Hendersen, 1985).

Figure 4–4 shows a hypothetical memory structure that may be learned during extinction (Bouton, 1994b; Bouton & Nelson, 1994; Bouton & Ricker, 1994). It extends the kinds of conditioning models that we originally presented in Figure 4–2. During conditioning, an association between memory nodes corresponding to the tone and shock is formed. In extinction, the original association remains intact, but a new inhibitory association is learned. The new learning now inhibits activation of the memory of shock, and turns off responding to the tone. The meaning of the tone is now ambiguous; it has two available connections with the shock, and performance depends on which one is retrieved. Inhibition provided by the second association is a mechanism of retroactive interference (cf. Anderson & Bjork, 1994).

The model is specific about the context's role in extinction. Notice that the context does not work through a direct association with shock or the tone itself. Instead, it helps activate the tone's

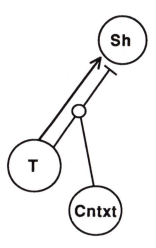

Figure 4–4. A memory model of extinction. See text for explanation. From Bouton and Nelson (1994). Reprinted by permission of the publisher.

own inhibitory association through a mechanism that is a new version of Figure 4–2's Panel C. Input from the context and the tone converge on a unit that functions as an AND gate; such a gate requires input from both the context *and* the tone to allow activation to pass to the final inhibitory association. By this means, the US node or representation is inhibited, and extinction performance is observed only when the tone is presented in the appropriate context. Outside that context, the inhibitory link cannot be activated; a recovery of responding will occur because the subject or client fails to retrieve inhibition.

The major impact of the context in extinction is thus on the CS's inhibitory meaning. This feature of the model is consistent with results we just described that suggest that not all types of knowledge or associations are context-dependent. As shown in Figure 4–4, conditioning is not readily lost with a context switch; in the model, its activation is not gated. On the other hand, extinction performance is likely to be lost with a context switch. The context's influence is mostly inhibitory. When we switch out of the extinction context, the inhibitory input is lost, and we observe a relapse or renewal effect.

This simple model provides a good description of many of our context effects. To expand it just a little, we assume that the input labeled "Cntxt" is actually provided by the possible background cues we suggested (see Bouton, 1991a, and Bouton & Swartzentruber, 1991, for reviews). We would like to emphasize that contextual cues may be provided by natural cues that change with the passage of time. As time progresses, various internal as well as external cues naturally change. If these constitute part of the background context, we can integrate the effects of retention interval with those of context. The idea, as just described, is that if we wait awhile before performing a memory test, we are testing in a new temporal context. And as the model suggests, extinction will be especially disrupted by the change.

This emphasis on temporal context provides a testable account of spontaneous recovery. We have noted that conditioning theory has all but ignored this famous phenomenon, perhaps because the effects of retention intervals have tra-

ditionally been the subject of memory theory rather than learning theory (Bouton, 1994a). A memory approach to extinction puts the problem in perspective. Renewal and spontaneous recovery may result from the same mechanism: a failure to retrieve inhibition (extinction) after moving out of the extinction context.

Douglas Brooks tested this idea with one of us (Bouton) (Brooks & Bouton, 1993, 1994). We reasoned that if spontaneous recovery and renewal result from a failure to retrieve extinction, then both effects should be abolished if we remind the animal of extinction just before the recovery test. To test the idea, we asked whether the two recovery effects could be attenuated by presenting a cue that retrieved extinction. Our first set of experiments (Brooks & Bouton, 1993) focused on spontaneous recovery. Rats received tone-food pairings, and then extinction trials with the tone alone. In the experiment shown at left in Figure 4–5 (Brooks & Bouton, 1993, Experiment 3), some of the trials of the last conditioning session were preceded by a brief cue, and some of

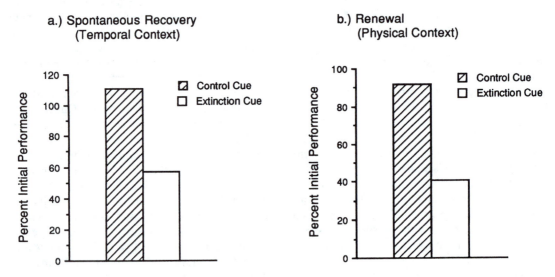

Figure 4–5. Effects of a retrieval cue for extinction on spontaneous recovery (left) and renewal (right). In either case, a cue for extinction reduced response recovery. The magnitudes of spontaneous recovery and renewal cannot be compared directly because the experiments used different methods. They are also shown for the first four-trial block and the first trial, respectively, of testing. Data from Brooks and Bouton (1993) and Brooks and Bouton (1994), respectively. Figure is from Bouton (1994b). Reprinted by permission of the publisher.

the trials of the extinction session were preceded, in an identical manner, by a different cue (counterbalanced). After a six-day retention interval that followed extinction, the tone was tested again. Our procedure produced significant spontaneous recovery; responding to the tone briefly returned to roughly 100% of the level it had reached during conditioning. However, when the cue that had been presented in extinction (the "extinction cue") was presented at the start of the recovery test, it markedly reduced recovery. In contrast, recovery was still quite strong if the cue from conditioning (the "control cue") was presented at the test instead. Spontaneous recovery was uniquely attenuated by presenting a cue that had been featured in extinction.

The right-hand part of Figure 4–5 illustrates a parallel experiment on the renewal effect (Brooks & Bouton, 1994, Experiment 3). Here the rats received tone-food pairings in Context A and then tone extinction in Context B. Control and extinction cues were introduced during conditioning and extinction sessions as before. Finally, during the test shown in the figure, the rats were returned to the original context (Context A) and tested with the tone again. Here the group given the control cue showed a substantial renewal effect—responding recovered to almost 100% of the level reached at the end of conditioning. But the effect was strongly reduced in a group that received the extinction cue at the start of the test. The results were similar to the results with spontaneous recovery. The renewal effect, like spontaneous recovery, is reduced by a cue that retrieves extinction. Spontaneous recovery and renewal seem to be produced by the same mechanism: a failure to retrieve extinction outside the extinction context.

Our retrieval cue experiments ruled out a number of alternative explanations of the attenuation effect. For example, as Figure 4–5 illustrates, to attenuate recovery, the cue must be a cue correlated specifically with extinction—equally familiar cues not correlated with extinction do not work. We also worried that presentation of any stimulus before the test might somehow disrupt responding by distracting the subject. It might

command so much attention that the rat failed to notice the tone, or it might elicit a response that competes directly with the conditioned response to the tone. The weaker effect of the control cue argues against this possibility. More impressively, even a relatively novel stimulus did not attenuate the renewal effect as much as the extinction cue (Brooks & Bouton, 1994, Experiment 2). Because novel cues command much attention—and elicit strong orienting responses—this result seems especially compelling. Furthermore, the extinction cue did not acquire excitatory or inhibitory associations with the US that we could confirm with systematic tests. Instead, we believe it may work by being coded as a part of the extinction context. Contexts are complex stimuli composed of many separate components; the extinction cue might be one of them. The results of Brooks's most recent experiments (Brooks, 1995) indeed suggest that cues featured at many points in the extinction session, either closely or remotely from the extinction trials in time, will reduce spontaneous recovery. The cue, a part of the extinction context, helps activate the inhibitory link much as the extinction context would itself.

The extinction model in Figure 4–4 handles a great deal of data on time and context effects in extinction. It provides an interesting marriage of conditioning and memory principles, and it has been extended in useful ways (e.g., Bouton & Nelson, 1994; Nelson & Bouton, 1996). Like the extinction data it summarizes, it has clinical implications. Extinction (or therapy) is not unlearning; the subject learns something new about the conditioned stimulus, and the new learning seems especially vulnerable to retrieval failure. Relapse can happen when the context changes, because the client forgets (that is, fails to retrieve) what is learned in extinction. Consistent with this idea, spontaneous recovery and renewal can both be reduced by presentation of cues that were featured in extinction. One implication is that relapse might be prevented after therapy if therapists can build reminders into long-term follow-up after therapy. Several therapies have incorporated reminders after therapy (e.g., E. B.

Foa, personal communication, August 20, 1993; George, 1989; Marlatt, 1990), with good effect, we would predict.

WHAT MAKES BEHAVIOR CONTEXT-SPECIFIC?

The extinction model recognizes that not all learning depends on context for expression in behavior. It emphasizes that extinction performance is more dependent on the context than is initial conditioning peformance. This emphasis is consistent with the results of many experiments conducted in our laboratory and others (e.g., Bouton & King, 1983; Bouton & Peck, 1989; Bouton & Ricker, 1994; Brooks & Bouton, 1994; Wilson et al., 1995; see also Grahame, Hallam, Geier, & Miller, 1990; Lovibond et al., 1984), including the two experiments depicted in Figure 4–1. Why should things work this way? What makes extinction more specific to its context than the simple excitatory CS-US association that is assumed to be learned in the first phase?

The extinction model suggests one possibility. By assuming that what is learned in extinction is inhibition (see also Konorski, 1948; Pearce & Hall, 1980; Wagner, 1981), it raises the question of whether inhibition is generally specific to its context. The idea is clinically interesting, because therapy may be viewed as a means of arranging for the inhibition of unwanted thoughts, emotions, and behaviors. Some disorders, such as Post Traumatic Stress Disorder, might involve a failure to inhibit such things (see Falls & Davis, 1995, for an illustration).

There are other ways to generate inhibition in the learning laboratory (e.g., see Williams et al., this volume). One of them is the so-called *feature-negative discrimination*. This procedure intermixes two kinds of conditioning trials. On one type of trial, a *target* stimulus, for example a tone, is presented alone and paired with the US (T+). On other trials, the target is presented together with a second stimulus, for example, a light, and on these trials it is presented without a US (LT−). The light is a conditioned inhibitor;

casually speaking, it signals "no US." It is also a feature of negative trials (ones with no US); hence the procedure is called a "feature-negative discrimination," and the light is sometimes called the *feature* stimulus.

To investigate the possibility that inhibition per se is context-specific, we have run two series of experiments exploring the effects of a context switch after feature-negative discrimination training (Bouton & Nelson, 1994; Nelson & Bouton, 1996). Remarkably, inhibition to the feature transferred extremely well across contexts. That is, inhibition to L acquired after T+/LT− training was *not* reduced when we tested it in a different context. We soon realized that the feature and the target stimulus (the tone) might *both* acquire inhibition on the nonreinforced trials. Any inhibition acquired by the target stimulus might actually be more like that acquired by an extinguished CS, because it would exist alongside excitation alternately learned on the reinforced trials. We discovered that inhibition to the target T was indeed lost after a context switch: Responding to the tone became more difficult to inhibit when we tested it outside the context in which T+/LT− training had occurred. The pattern was consistent with what we know about extinction—responding to a stimulus that is under the influence of extinction is more readily expressed after a change of context. Conditioned fears or cravings that are suppressed, that is, actively inhibited, in one context may be harder to inhibit in other contexts.

These results expanded our model of extinction, but they were not consistent with the idea that inhibition is generally specific to its context. Inhibition to the feature, like excitation in a typical experiment, was not reduced by a change of context. An alternative possibility is that inhibition may not be context-specific, but the second meaning learned about the CS may be. Inhibition is the first thing learned about the inhibitory feature, but it is the second thing learned about the CS in extinction. And it is also the second thing learned about the tone target in the T+/LT− paradigm—excitation must be learned before inhibition is possible.

Consistent with this argument, there is evidence that the second "meaning" learned about a CS is in fact often sensitive to a context switch. Swartzentruber and Bouton (1992) examined the effects of a context switch on simple fear conditioning. As usual, a CS paired with shock did not lose its ability to evoke fear when it was tested in a context that was different from the original conditioning context. However, when CS-shock pairings were preceded by presentations of the CS alone (i.e., latent inhibition training), fear conditioned to the CS in the second phase was reduced when the context was switched (see also de Brugada, Garcia-Hoz, Bonardi, & Hall, 1995). More recently, Nelson has investigated the idea that the second meaning learned about a CS, regardless of whether it is excitatory or inhibitory, is specific to the context in which it is learned. He found that responding to a CS associated with food transferred nicely to a new context. But if the CS had first been given an inhibitory meaning (by training it as a feature in a feature-negative discrimination), the excitation learned to it when it was paired with food was disrupted by a context switch. The results are summarized in Figure 4–6. Nelson is currently running experiments that ask if an excitor converted to a conditioned inhibitor (a feature in a feature-negative procedure) conversely loses its inhibition with a context switch. Regardless of whether we are speaking of inhibition or excitation, the first thing learned about a CS is not specific to the context, while the second learned about it is.

Why should a CS's second meaning be more sensitive to the context? One possibility is based on the idea that the context is important in resolving CS ambiguity; the context is not important until the CS has two meanings to disambiguate. During Phase 1, we may learn that the CS is the clearest signal that a US is about to happen. But as Phase 2 begins, and the predicted US does not happen, the subject attributes the change not to the CS but to the contextual cues present at the time. The subject or client may begin to pay attention to the context (cf. Darby & Pearce, 1995). Bouton (1994a) has discussed

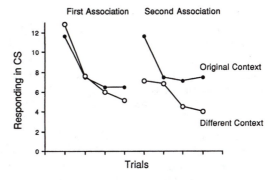

Figure 4–6. Effects of a context switch on performance when the CS-food relation is the first association (left) or the second association (right) learned about the CS. Original context = test in the context in which conditioning had occurred; Different context = test in a different but equally familiar context. In the second association condition, the CS had previously been trained as a conditioned inhibitor (a feature in a feature-negative discrimination). The four test trials shown are extinction trials. Responding was equivalent in the original context regardless of whether CS-food was the first or second association, but the context switch only disrupted performance when CS-food was the second association. The response measure is the number of times the rat inspected the cup where food was to be delivered during the CS. From an unpublished dissertation experiment by Nelson.

some reasons why learning and memory might be organized this way. He noted that a conditioning trial provides an opportunity for us to sample from, and make inferences about, the rest of the world (e.g., Staddon, 1988). If a beetle bites you, you may infer that future beetles will also bite you. As a result of associating the beetle with the bite, you will be wary of new beetles. Notice that if the world is actually composed of two types of trials (biting beetles that provide conditioning trials and nonbiting beetles that provide extinction trials), you are more likely to encounter the more common type first. An early encounter with one type of trial would, on average, reflect its dominance in the population. Subsequent samples of nonbiting beetles would likely be exceptions to the rule. In this sense, treating the second type of trial as less probable in new contexts is an adaptation to a statistical feature of sampling items from real populations. Evolution may have designed memory to treat second-learned information as an exception to the rule. It may pay to forget extinction or other second associations with changes of place or time (see Bouton, 1994a, for other reasons).

Further research is necessary, however, because first associations are still occasionally disrupted by a change of context. For example, Hall and Honey (1990) showed that a weakly learned first association (fear of a CS created by just one CS-shock pairing) may be reduced by a change of context. And there is also the case of latent inhibition; we have already mentioned that the interfering effects of preexposure to a CS can be lost with a context switch. Preexposure is a first "meaning"; why should it be lost? Our point is that the second-association hypothesis has considerable promise, but it does not explain all aspects of this complex issue.

To summarize, not all learning is disrupted by a change of context. We have shown repeatedly that while extinction is sensitive to contextual change, simple conditioning is much less so. The inhibition that may be learned in extinction is not generally context-specific; inhibition to a CS may transfer across contexts as well as excitation does (Bouton & Nelson, 1994; Nelson & Bouton, 1996). It appears that the second thing learned about a CS may be more context-dependent than the first. This feature of contextual control may be an adaptation to sampling items from real populations. There are interesting clinical implications. First, since therapy is often a kind of second learning about stimuli that the client has already learned about, context effects might generally be expected. On a more optimistic note, there is now evidence that second learning can be made to generalize to new contexts with the use of retrieval cues (Brooks & Bouton, 1993, 1994). A second implication is that we have a new reason to emphasize prevention, rather than treatment, of psychopathology. If first learning generalizes best across contexts, perhaps we should be building environments to ensure that the first things learned are healthy things. It would be better to leave the maladaptive things,

the CS-US pairings and reinforcement contingencies that create pathology, to be the context-specific, second-learned exceptions to the rule.

CONCLUSIONS

This chapter has covered a great deal of ground. The reason is that contextual stimuli turn out to be involved in a very large range of conditioning phenomena. We have described several lines of research that illustrate the context's role in effects ranging from the US-preexposure effect, latent inhibition, extinction, counterconditioning, and inhibition. This list is not exhaustive. The role of context has been one of the dominant research issues in the conditioning and learning literature during the 1970s, 1980s, and 1990s.

Although we have focused on the role of context in classical conditioning, similar principles can apply to operant conditioning, the type of learning in which behaviors (e.g., a rat's leverpress) are reinforced by their consequences. Recent research has established strong parallels between the mechanisms of classical and operant conditioning (e.g., Colwill, 1995; Colwill & Rescorla, 1986; Dickinson, 1980; Mackintosh & Dickinson, 1979; see Rescorla, 1987, for an accessible review). It has become useful, therefore, to think of Pavlovian and operant learning as examples of the same fundamental learning process: just as behavior based on Pavlovian learning reflects "knowledge" of a CS-US association, behavior based on instrumental learning may reflect knowledge of a response-reinforcer association (e.g., Mackintosh, 1983; Mackintosh & Dickinson, 1979; Rescorla, 1987). Accordingly, as a heuristic, the terms *response* and *reinforcer* could be substituted for the terms *CS* and *US*, respectively, as we have used them throughout this chapter. Consistent with this idea, the extinction of operant behavior, like classically conditioned behavior, is affected by the context (Bouton & Swartzentruber, 1991): renewal of an extinguished operant occurs when animals are returned to the original context after extinction in another context (e.g., Spear, Smith, Bryan, Gordon, Timmons, & Chizar, 1980; Thomas, McKelvie, Ranney, & Moye, 1981;

Welker & McAuley, 1978); extinguished operant responses are reinstated when the reinforcer is presented independently of the response after extinction (e.g., Reid, 1958; this effect is at least partly mediated by contextual conditioning, Baker, Steinwald, & Bouton, 1991); extinguished operants recover spontaneously over time (e.g., Ellson, 1938; Thomas & Sherman, 1986); and responding can be reacquired rapidly when the response and reinforcer are paired again after extinction (e.g., Bullock & Smith, 1953). The context is an important part of both classical and operant conditioning.

We have discussed several kinds of contexts (physical environments, US aftereffects, other recent events, drug states, emotions, and the passage of time) and several mechanisms through which contexts can control behavior and learning. Contexts may serve as conditional stimuli themselves. And they may modulate responding to CSs presented in them through their own direct associations with the US, through their direct associations with the CS, and through their ability to signal or retrieve specific CS-US relations. We have also described their role in memory retrieval, the role often emphasized in human memory research (e.g., Davies & Thomson, 1988). All of these mechanisms can play a role in generating behavior in clinical situations. It should be clear that there is a great deal involved in simple conditioning experiments. Theories about them are complex, and their application to real-world phenomena, such as issues surrounding therapy, are consequently complex, too. As this book illustrates, learning and conditioning theory continue to provide a surprisingly rich base from which to think about human behavior.

If we can identify a single take-home message from this chapter, it would be simply that all events occur in a context. The context—whether it is the physical environment, interoceptive cues, recent events, or time—is always ready to participate in learning, memory, and behavior. Responding to a CS, whether we are talking about anxiety to fear cues, cravings to drug cues, or appetite to cues that signal food, cannot be predicted from considering the CS's simple conditioning history alone. Pairings of a CS and a US do not guarantee conditioned responding, just as extended extinction training does not guarantee a lack of performance. Either kind of effect is fundamentally modulated by the context.

ENDNOTES

Preparation of this chapter was supported by Grant IBN 9209454 from the National Science Foundation. We thank Gerry Oppedisano, Juan Rosas, and Stacey Young for their comments on the manuscript.

REFERENCES

Ahlers, S. T., & Richardson, R. (1985). Administration of dexamethasone prior to training blocks ACTH-induced recovery of an extinguished avoidance response. *Behavioral Neuroscience, 99,* 760–764.

Anderson, M. C., & Bjork, R. A. (1994). Mechanisms of inhibition in long-term memory: A new taxonomy. In Dagenbach, D., & Carr, T. H. (eds.), *Inhibitory processes in attention, memory, and language,* 265–325. San Diego, Calif.: Academic Press.

Ayres, J. J. B., Bombace, J. C., Shurtleff, D., & Vigorito, M. (1985). Conditioned suppression tests of the context-blocking hypothesis: Testing in the absence of the preconditioned context. *Journal of Experimental Psychology: Animal Behavior Processes, 11,* 1–14.

Baker, A. G., & Mercier, P. (1982). Prior experience with the conditioning events: Evidence for a rich cognitive representation. In A. R. Wagner, R. Herrnstein, & M. Commons (eds.), *Quantitative analysis of behavior: Acquisition processes,* 117–144. Cambridge, Mass.: Ballinger.

Baker, A. G., Steinwald, H., & Bouton, M. E. (1990). Contextual conditioning and the reinstatement of instrumental responding. *Quarterly Journal of Experimental Psychology, 43B,* 199–218.

Balsam, P. D., & Tomie, A. (eds.) (1985). *Context and learning.* Hillsdale, N.J.: Erlbaum.

Bolles, R. C., & Fanselow, M. S. (1980). A perceptual-defensive-recuperative model of fear and pain. *Behavioral and Brain Sciences, 3,* 291–323.

Bouton, M. E. (1984). Differential control by context in the inflation and reinstatement paradigms. *Journal of Experimental Psychology: Animal Behavior Processes, 10,* 56–74.

Bouton, M. E. (1986). Slow reacquisition following the extinction of conditioned suppression. *Learning and Motivation, 17,* 1–15.

Bouton, M. E. (1988). Context and ambiguity in the extinction of emotional learning: Implications for exposure therapy. *Behaviour Research and Therapy, 26,* 137–149.

Bouton, M. E. (1991a). A contextual analysis of fear extinction. In P. R. Martin (ed.), *Handbook of behavior therapy and psychological science: An integrative approach*, 435–453. Elmsford, N.Y.: Pergamon.

Bouton, M. E. (1991b). Context and retrieval in extinction and in other examples of interference in simple associative learning. In L. Dachowski & C. F. Flaherty (eds.), *Current topics in animal learning: Brain, emotion, and cognition*, 25–53. Hillsdale, N.J.: Erlbaum.

Bouton, M. E. (1993). Context, time, and memory retrieval in the interference paradigms of Pavlovian learning. *Psychological Bulletin, 114*, 80–99.

Bouton, M. E. (1994a). Conditioning, remembering, and forgetting. *Journal of Experimental Psychology: Animal Behavior Processes, 20*, 219–231.

Bouton, M. E. (1994b). Context, ambiguity, and classical conditioning. *Current Directions in Psychological Science, 3*, 49–53.

Bouton, M. E., & Bolles, R. C. (1979a). Contextual control of the extinction of conditioned fear. *Learning and Motivation, 10*, 445–466.

Bouton, M. E., & Bolles, R. C. (1979b). Role of conditioned contextual stimuli in reinstatement of extinguished fear. *Journal of Experimental Psychology: Animal Behavior Processes, 5*, 368–378.

Bouton, M. E., & Bolles, R. C. (1985). Contexts, event-memories, and extinction. In P. D. Balsam & A. Tomie (eds.), *Context and learning*, 133–166. Hillsdale, N.J.: Erlbaum.

Bouton, M. E., & Brooks, D. C. (1993). Time and context effects on performance in a Pavlovian discrimination reversal. *Journal of Experimental Psychology: Animal Behavior Processes, 19*, 165–179.

Bouton, M. E., Kenney, F. A., & Rosengard, C. (1990). State-dependent fear extinction with two benzodiazepine tranquilizers. *Behavioral Neuroscience, 104*, 44–55.

Bouton, M. E., & King, D. A. (1983). Contextual control of the extinction of conditioned fear: Tests for the associative value of the context. *Journal of Experimental Psychology: Animal Behavior Processes, 9*, 248–265.

Bouton, M. E., & King, D. A. (1986). Effect of context on performance to conditioned stimuli with mixed histories of reinforcement and nonreinforcement. *Journal of Experimental Psychology: Animal Behavior Processes, 12*, 4–15.

Bouton, M. E., & Nelson, J. B. (1994). Context-specificity of target versus feature inhibition in a feature negative discrimination. *Journal of Experimental Psychology: Animal Behavior Processes, 20*, 51–65.

Bouton, M. E., & Peck, C. A. (1989). Context effects on conditioning, extinction, and reinstatement in an appetitive conditioning preparation. *Animal Learning & Behavior, 17*, 188–198.

Bouton, M. E., & Peck, C. A. (1992). Spontaneous recovery in cross-motivational transfer (counterconditioning). *Animal Learning & Behavior, 20*, 313–321.

Bouton, M. E., & Ricker, S. T. (1994). Renewal of extinguished responding in a second context. *Animal Learning & Behavior, 22*, 317–324.

Bouton, M. E., Rosengard, C., Achenbach, G. G., Peck, C. A., & Brooks, D. C. (1993). Effects of contextual conditioning and unconditional stimulus presentation on performance in appetitive conditioning. *The Quarterly Journal of Experimental Psychology, 46B*, 63–95.

Bouton, M. E., & Swartzentruber, D. (1986). Analysis of the associative and occasion-setting properties of contexts participating in a Pavlovian discrimination. *Journal of Experimental Psychology: Animal Behavior Processes, 12*, 333–350.

Bouton, M. E., & Swartzentruber, D. (1989). Slow reacquisition following extinction: Context, encoding, and retrieval mechanisms. *Journal of Experimental Psychology: Animal Behavior Processes, 15*, 43–53.

Bouton, M. E., & Swartzentruber, D. (1991). Sources of relapse after extinction in Pavlovian and instrumental learning. *Clinical Psychology Review, 11*, 123–140.

Bower, G. H. (1987). Commentary on mood and memory. *Behaviour Research and Therapy, 25*, 443–455.

Bower, G. H., Monteiro, K. P., & Gilligan, S. G. (1978). Emotional mood as a context for learning and recall. *Journal of Verbal Learning and Verbal Behavior, 17*, 573–585.

Brogden, W. J. (1939). Sensory pre-conditioning. *Journal of Experimental Psychology, 25*, 323–332.

Brooks, D. C. (1995). *Mechanisms by which retrieval cues for extinction reduce response-recovery*. Unpublished doctoral dissertation, University of Vermont.

Brooks, D. C., & Bouton, M. E. (1993). A retrieval cue for extinction attenuates spontaneous recovery. *Journal of Experimental Psychology: Animal Behavior Processes, 19*, 77–89.

Brooks, D. C., & Bouton, M. E. (1994). A retrieval cue for extinction attenuates response recovery (renewal) caused by a return to the conditioning context. *Journal of Experimental Psychology: Animal Behavior Processes, 20*, 366–379.

Brooks, D. C., Hale, B., Nelson, J. B., & Bouton, M. E. (1995). Reinstatement after counterconditioning. *Animal Learning & Behavior, 23*, 383–390.

Bullock, D. H., & Smith, W. C. (1953). An effect of repeated conditioning-extinction upon operant strength. *Journal of Experimental Psychology, 46*, 349–352.

Capaldi, E. D., & Powley, T. L. (eds.) (1990). *Taste, experience, and feeding*. Washington, D.C.: American Psychological Association.

Capaldi, E. J. (1994). The sequential view: From rapidly fading stimulus traces to the organization of memory and the abstract concept of number. *Psychonomic Bulletin and Review, 1*, 156–181.

Channell, S., & Hall, G. (1983). Contextual effects in latent inhibition with an appetitive conditioning procedure. *Animal Learning & Behavior, 11*, 67–74.

Colwill, R. M. (1995). In D. L. Medin (ed.), *The psychology of learning and motivation.* New York: Academic Press.

Colwill, R. M., & Rescorla, R. A. (1986). Associative structures in instrumental learning. In G. H. Bower (ed.), *The psychology of learning and motivation*, Vol. 20: 55–104. New York: Academic Press.

Cunningham, C. L. (1979). Alcohol as a cue for extinction: State dependency produced by conditioned inhibition. *Animal Learning & Behavior*, *7*, 45–52.

Darby, R. J., & Pearce, J. M. (1995). Effects of context on responding during a compound stimulus. *Journal of Experimental Psychology: Animal Behavior Processes*, *21(2)*, 143–154.

Davey, G. C. L. (1989). UCS revaluation and conditioning models of acquired fears. *Behaviour Research and Therapy*, *27*, 521–528.

Davies, G. M., & Thomson, D. M. (eds.) (1988). *Memory in context: Context in memory.* Chichester, England: Wiley.

de Brugada, I., Garcia-Hoz, V., Bonardi, C., & Hall, G. (1995). Role of stimulus ambiguity in conditional learning. *Journal of Experimental Psychology: Animal Behavior Processes*, *21*, 275–284.

Dickinson, A. (1980). *Contemporary animal learning theory.* Cambridge, Mass.: Cambridge University Press.

Durlach, P. J. (1983). The effect of signaling intertrial USs in autoshaping. *Journal of Experimental Psychology: Animal Behavior Processes*, *9*, 374–389.

Durlach, P. J. (1989). Learning and performance in Pavlovian conditioning: Are failures of contiguity failures of learning or performance? In S. B. Klein & R. R. Mowrer (eds.), *Contemporary learning theories: Pavlovian conditioning and the status of traditional learning theory*, 19–60. Hillsdale, N.J.: Erlbaum.

Dweck, C. S., & Wagner, A. R. (1970). Situational cues and correlation between CS and US as determinants of the conditioned emotional response. *Psychonomic Science*, *18*, 145–147.

Eich, E. (1995). Searching for mood dependent memory. *Psychological Science*, *6*, 67–75.

Ellson, D. G. (1938). Quantitative studies of the interaction of simple habits. I. Recovery from specific and generalized effects of extinction. *Journal of Experimental Psychology*, *23*, 339–358.

Estes, W. K. (1955). Statistical theory of spontaneous recovery and regression. *Psychological Review*, *62*, 145–154.

Estes, W. K. (1976). Structural aspects of associative models for memory. In C. N. Cofer (ed.), *The structure of human memory.* San Francisco: Freeman.

Falls, W. A., & Davis, M. (1995). Behavioral and physiological analysis of fear inhibition: Extinction and conditioned inhibition. In M. J. Friedmand & D. S. Charney (eds.) *Neurobiological and clinical consequences of stress: From normal adaptation to PTSD*, 177–201. Philadelphia: Lippincott-Raven.

Fanselow, M. S. (1994). Neural organization of the defensive behavior system responsible for fear. *Psychonomic Bulletin & Review*, *1*, 429–438.

George, W. H. (1989). Marlatt and Gordon's relapse prevention model: A cognitive-behavioral approach to understanding and preventing relapse. *Journal of Chemical Dependency Treatment*, *2*, 125–152.

Gibbon, J., & Balsam, P. (1981). Spreading association in time. In C. M. Locurto, H. S. Terrace, & J. Gibbon (eds.), *Autoshaping and conditioning theory*, 219–253. New York: Academic Press.

Grahame, N. J., Hallam, S. C., Geier, L., & Miller, R. R. (1990). Context as an occasion setter following either CS acquisition and extinction or CS acquisition alone. *Learning and Motivation*, *21*, 237–265.

Grau, J. W., & Rescorla, R. A. (1984). Role of context in autoshaping. *Journal of Experimental Psychology: Animal Behavior Processes*, *10*, 324–332.

Hall, G. (1991). *Perceptual and associative learning.* Oxford: Clarendon Press.

Hall, G., & Channell, S. (1985). Differential effects of contextual change on latent inhibition and on the habituation of an orienting response. *Journal of Experimental Psychology: Animal Behavior Processes*, *11*, 470–481.

Hall, G., & Honey, R. C. (1990). Context-specific conditioning in the conditioned-emotional-response procedure. *Journal of Experimental Psychology: Animal Behavior Processes*, *16*, 271–278.

Hart, J. A., Bourne, M. J., & Schachtman, T. R. (1995). Slow reacquisition of a conditioned taste aversion. *Animal Learning & Behavior*, *23*, 297–303.

Helmstetter, F. J., & Fanselow M. S. (1989). Differential second-order aversive conditioning using contextual stimuli. *Animal Learning & Behavior*, *17*, 205–212.

Hendersen, R. W. (1985). Fearful memories: The motivational significance of forgetting. In F. R. Brush & J. B. Overmier (eds.), *Affect, conditioning, and cognition: Essays on the determinants of behavior*, 43–54. Hillsdale, N.J.: Erlbaum.

Hoehler, F. K., Kirschenbaum, D. S., & Leonard, D. W. (1973). The effects of overtraining and successive extinctions upon nictitating membrane conditioning in the rabbit. *Learning and Motivation*, *4*, 91–101.

Holland, P. C. (1977). Conditioned stimulus as a determinant of the form of the Pavlovian conditioned response. *Journal of Experimental Psychology: Animal Behavior Processes*, *3*, 77–104.

Holland, P. C. (1992). Occasion setting in Pavlovian conditioning. In D. L. Medin (ed.), *The psychology of learning & motivation*, Vol. 28. San Diego, Calif.: Academic Press.

Hollis, K. L. (1982). Pavlovian conditioning of signal-centered action patterns and autonomic behavior: A biological analysis of function. *Advances in the Study of Behavior*, *12*, 1–64.

Kamin, L. J. (1969). Predictability, surprise, attention, and conditioning. In B. A. Campbell & R. B. Church (eds.),

Punishment and aversive behavior, 279–296. New York: Appleton-Century-Crofts.

Kaye, H., & Pearce, J. M. (1984). The strength of the orienting response during Pavlovian conditioning. *Journal of Experimental Psychology: Animal Behavior Processes*, *10*, 90–109.

Konorski, J. (1948). *Conditioned reflexes and neuron organization*. Cambridge: Cambridge University Press.

Lovibond, P. F., Preston, G. C., & Mackintosh, N. J. (1984). Context specificity of conditioning, extinction, and latent inhibition. *Journal of Experimental Psychology: Animal Behavior Processes*, *10*, 360–375.

Lubow, R. E. (1989). *Latent inhibition and conditioned attention theory*. New York: Cambridge University Press.

Mackintosh, N. J. (1983). *Conditioning and associative learning*. Oxford: Clarendon Press.

Mackintosh, N. J., & Dickinson, A. (1979). Instrumental (type II) conditioning. In A. Dickinson & R. A. Boakes (eds.), *Mechanisms of learning and motivation: A memorial volume to Jerzy Konorski*, 143–169. Hillsdale, N.J.: Erlbaum.

Marks, I. M. (1978). Behavioral psychotherapy of adult neurosis. In S. L. Garfield & A. E. Bergin (eds.), *Handbook of psychotherapy and behavior change* (2nd ed.) 493–589. New York: Wiley.

Marks, I. M., et al. (1993). Alprazolam and exposure alone and combined in panic disorder with agoraphobia: A controlled study in London and Toronto. *British Journal of Psychiatry*, *162*, 776–787.

Marlatt, G. A. (1990). Cue exposure and relapse prevention in the treatment of addictive behaviors. *Addictive Behaviors*, *15*, 395–399.

Marlin, N. A. (1982). Within-compound associations between the context and the conditioned stimulus. *Learning and Motivation*, *13*, 526–541.

Marlin, N. A. (1983). Second-order conditioning using a contextual stimulus as S_1. *Animal Learning and Behavior*, *11(3)*, 290–294.

Matzel, L. D., Brown, A. M., & Miller, R. R. (1987). Associative effects of US preexposure: Modulation of conditioned responding by an excitatory training context. *Journal of Experimental Psychology: Animal Behavior Processes*, *13(1)*, 65–72.

McCloskey, M., & Cohen, J. J. (1989). Catastrophic interference in connectionist networks: The sequential learning problem. In G. H. Bower (ed.), *The Psychology of Learning and Motivation*, Vol. 24: 109–165. San Diego, Calif.: Academic Press.

McGeoch, J. A. (1932). Forgetting and the law of disuse. *Psychological Review*, *39*, 352–370.

Miller, R. R., Barnet, R. C., & Grahame, N. J. (1992). Responding to a conditioned stimulus depends on the current associative status of other cues present during training of that specific stimulus. *Journal of Experimental Psychology: Animal Behavior Processes*, *18*, 259–264.

Miller, R. R., Grahame, R. C., & Hallam, N. J. (1990). Summation of responding to a CS and excitatory test context. *Animal Learning & Behavior*, *18*, 29–34.

Miller, R. R., Hallam, N. J., & Grahame, R. C. (1990). Inflation of comparator stimuli following CS training. *Animal Learning & Behavior*, *18*, 434–443.

Miller, R. R., & Schachtman, T. R. (1985). Conditioning context as an associative baseline: Implications for response generation and the nature of conditioned inhibition. In R. R. Miller & N. E. Spear (eds.) *Information processing in animals: Conditioned inhibition*, 51–88. Hillsdale, N.J.: Erlbaum.

Mineka, S. (1985). Animal models of anxiety-based disorders: Their usefulness and limitations. In A. H. Tuma & J. Maser (eds.), *Anxiety and the anxiety disorders*, 199–244. Hillsdale, N.J.: Erlbaum.

Napier, R. M., Macrae, M., & Kehoe, E. J. (1992). Rapid reacquisition in conditioning of the rabbit's nictitating membrane response. *Journal of Experimental Psychology: Animal Behavior Processes*, *18*, 182–192.

Nelson, J. B., & Bouton, M. E. (1996). The effects of a context switch following serial and simultaneous feature-negative discriminations. *Learning and Motivation*. In press.

Overton, D. A. (1985). Contextual stimulus effects of drugs and internal states. In P. D. Balsam & A. Tomie (eds.), *Context and learning*, 357–384. Hillsdale, N.J.: Erlbaum.

Pavlov, I. P. (1927). *Conditioned reflexes*. London: Oxford University Press.

Pearce, J. M. (1987). A model for stimulus generalization in Pavlovian conditioning. *Psychological Review*, *94*, 61–73.

Pearce, J. M., & Hall, G. (1980). A model for Pavlovian learning: Variations in the effectiveness of conditioned but not of unconditioned stimuli. *Psychological Review*, *87*, 532–552.

Peck, C. A., & Bouton, M. E. (1990). Context and performance in aversive-to-appetitive and appetitive-to-aversive transfer. *Learning and Motivation*, *21*, 1–31.

Postman, L., & Underwood, B. J. (1973). Critical issues in interference theory. *Memory and Cognition*, *1*, 19–40.

Powley, T. L. (1977). The ventromedial hypothalamic syndrome, satiety, and a cephalic phase hypothesis. *Psychological Review*, *84*, 89–126.

Rachman, S. (1991). Neo-conditioning and the classical theory of fear acquisition. *Clinical Psychology Review*, *11*, 155–173.

Rachman, S., & Lopatka, C. (1988). Return of fear: Underlearning and overlearning. *Behaviour Research and Therapy*, *26*, 99–104.

Randich, A. (1981). The US preexposure phenomenon in the conditioned suppression paradigm: A role for conditioned situational stimuli. *Learning and Motivation*, *12*, 321–341.

Randich, A., & Ross, R. T. (1985). Contextual stimuli mediate the effects of pre-and post exposure to the unconditioned stimulus in conditioned suppression. In P. D. Balsam & A. Tomie (eds.), *Context and learning*, 105–132. Hillsdale, N.J.: Erlbaum.

Reid, R. L. (1958). The role of the reinforcer as a stimulus. *British Journal of Psychology*, 49, 202–209.

Rescorla, R. A. (1972). Informational variables in Pavlovian conditioning. In G. H. Bower (ed.), *The psychology of learning and motivation*, Vol. 6: 1–46. New York: Academic Press.

Rescorla, R. A. (1974). Effect of inflation of the unconditioned stimulus value following conditioning. *Journal of Comparative and Physiological Psychology*, 86, 101–106.

Rescorla, R. A. (1984). Associations between Pavlovian CSs and context. *Journal of Experimental Psychology: Animal Behavior Processes*, 10, 195–204.

Rescorla, R. A. (1985). Conditioned inhibition and facilitation. In R. R. Miller & N. E. Spear (eds.), *Information processing in animals: Conditioned inhibition*, 299–326. Hillsdale, N.J.: Erlbaum.

Rescorla, R. A. (1987). A Pavlovian analysis of goal-directed behavior. *American Psychologist*, 42, 119–129.

Rescorla, R. A., & Cunningham, C. L. (1978a). Recovery of the US representation over time during extinction. *Learning and Motivation*, 9, 373–391.

Rescorla, R. A., & Cunningham, C. L. (1978b). Within compound flavor associations. *Journal of Experimental Psychology: Animal Behavior Processes*, 4, 267–275.

Rescorla, R. A., & Heth, C. D. (1975). Reinstatement of fear to an extinguished conditioned stimulus. *Journal of Experimental Psychology: Animal Behavior Processes*, 1, 88–96.

Rescorla, R. A., & Holland, P. C. (1977). Associations in Pavlovian conditioned inhibition. *Learning and Motivation*, 8, 429–477.

Rescorla, R. A., & Wagner, A. R. (1972). A theory of Pavlovian conditioning: Variations in the effectiveness of reinforcement and nonreinforcement. In A. H. Black & W. F. Prokasy (eds.), *Classical conditioning II: Current research and theory*. 64–99. New York: Appleton-Century-Crofts.

Richardson, R., Riccio, D. C., & Devine , L. (1984). ACTH-induced recovery of extinguished avoidance responding. *Physiological Psychology*, 12, 184–192.

Ricker, S. T., & Bouton, M. E. (1996). Reacquisition following extinction in appetitive conditioning. *Animal Learning & Behavior*. In press.

Robbins, S. J. (1990). Mechanisms underlying spontaneous recovery in autoshaping. *Journal of Experimental Psychology: Animal Behavior Processes*, 16, 235–249.

Rosas, J. M., & Bouton, M. E. (1996). Spontaneous recovery after extinction of a conditioned taste aversion. *Animal Learning & Behavior*. In press.

Siegel, S. (1989). Pharmacological conditioning and drug effects. In A. J. Goudie & M. W. Emmett-Oglesby (eds.), *Psychoactive drugs: Tolerance and sensitization*, 115–180. Clifton, N.J.: Humana Press.

Skinner, B. F. (1950). Are theories of learning necessary? *Psychological Review*, 57, 193–216.

Smith, M., & Gormezano, I. (1965). Effects of alternating classical conditioning and extinction sessions on the conditioned nictitating membrane response of the rabbit. *Psychonomic Science*, 3, 91–92.

Spear, N. E. (1973). Retrieval of memory in animals. *Psychological Review*, 80, 163–194.

Spear, N. E. (1978). *The processing of memories: Forgetting and retention*. Hillsdale, N.J.: Erlbaum.

Spear, N. E., Smith, G. J., Bryan, R., Gordon, W., Timmons, R., & Chiszar, D. (1980). Contextual influences on the interaction between conflicting memories in the rat. *Animal Learning & Behavior*, 8, 273–281.

Staddon, J. E. R. (1988). Learning as inference. In R. C. Bolles & M. D. Beecher (eds.), *Evolution and learning*, 59–78. Hillsdale, N.J.: Erlbaum.

Stewart, J., DeWit, H., & Eikelboom, R. (1984). Role of unconditioned and conditioned drug effects in the self-administration of opiates and stimulates. *Psychological Review*, 2, 251–268.

Stolerman, I. (1992). Drugs of abuse: Behavioural principles, methods and terms. *Trends in Pharmacological Sciences*, 131, 170–176.

Swartzentruber, D. (1991). Blocking between occasion setters and contextual stimuli. *Journal of Experimental Psychology: Animal Behavior Processes*, 17, 163–173.

Swartzentruber, D. (1995). Modulatory mechanisms in Pavlovian conditioning. *Animal Learning & Behavior*, 23, 123–143.

Swartzentruber, D., & Bouton, M. E. (1986). Contextual control of negative transfer produced by prior CS-US pairings. *Learning and Motivation*, 17, 366–385.

Swartzentruber, D., & Bouton, M. E. (1992). Context sensitivity of conditioned suppression following preexposure to the conditioned stimulus. *Animal Learning & Behavior*, 20, 97–103.

Thomas, D. R., McKelvie, A. R., Ranney, M., & Moye, T. B. (1981). Interference in pigeons' long-term memory viewed as a retrieval problem. *Animal Learning & Behavior*, 9, 581–586.

Thomas, D. R., & Sherman, L. (1986). An assessment of the role of handling cues in spontaneous recovery after extinction. *Journal of the Experimental Analysis of Behavior*, 46, 305–314.

Tulving, E. (1974). Cue-dependent forgetting. *American Scientist*, 62, 74–82.

Wagner, A. R. (1978). Expectancies and the priming of STM. In S. H. Hulse, H. Fowler, & W. K. Honig (eds.), *Cognitive processes in animal behavior*. Hillsdale, N.J.: Erlbaum.

Wagner, A. R. (1981). SOP: A model of automatic memory processing in animal behavior. In N. E. Spear & R. R. Miller (eds.), *Information processing in animals: Memory mechanisms*, 5–47. Hillsdale, N.J.: Erlbaum.

Wagner, A. R. & Brandon, S. E. (1989). Evolution of a structured connectionist model of Pavlovian conditioning

(AESOP). In S. B. Klein & R. R. Mowrer (eds.), *Contemporary learning theories: Pavlovian conditioning and the status of traditional learning theory*, 149–190. Hillsdale, N.J.: Erlbaum.

Wagner, A. R., & Rescorla, R. A. (1972). Inhibition in Pavlovian conditioning: Application of a theory. In R. A. Boakes & M. S. Halliday (eds.), *Inhibition and learning*, 301–336. London: Academic Press.

Welker, R. L., & McAuley, K (1978). Reductions in resistance to extinction and spontaneous recovery as a function of changes in transportational and contextual stimuli. *Animal Learning & Behavior, 6*, 451–457.

Wilson, A., Brooks, D. C., & Bouton, M. E. (1995). The role of the rat hippocampal system in several effects of context in extinction. *Behavioral Neuroscience, 109*, 828–836.

Wolpe, J. (1958). *Psychotherapy by reciprocal inhibition*. Stanford, Calif.: Stanford University Press.

Woods, S. C., & Strubbe, J. H. (1994). The psychobiology of meals. *Psychonomic Bulletin & Review, 1*, 141–155.

CHAPTER 5

CONDITIONED INHIBITION AND ITS APPLICATIONS IN PANIC AND OBSESSIVE-COMPULSIVE DISORDERS

Douglas A. Williams
Kenneth W. Johns
G. Ron Norton

Research in animal learning has been dominated by a curiosity about the origins of behavior. A good deal of informed discussion has taken place, for example, about the process by which a nonhuman organism learns to anticipate that a conditioned stimulus (CS) will be followed by a biologically salient unconditioned stimulus (US). Research has shown that conditioned responding is controlled by a process of some complexity and is not caused by reflex transfer between temporally contiguous events. Instead, the animal learns that a particular CS signals a particular US. Information about the CS-US relation produces a conditioned response (CR) that is appropriate for both the CS and the US (Holland, 1977). For example, a rat will approach and stand on its hind legs in front of a light CS that signals the delivery of an attractive sugar pellet US in the food magazine. Interest in the acquisition of new responses, such as "rearing" to a light CS, is natural. One of the most striking aspects of behavioral adaptation is the development of a new response or an increase in the frequency of occurrence of a previously learned behavior.

Much less attention has been directed at the mechanisms responsible for the suppression of a learned response. Rather than signaling an upcoming US, a CS may convey information about US absence. Pavlov (1927) studied discrimination learning of this sort in the A+, AB– paradigm, in which CS_A was followed by the US (+, US present) except when it appeared in the company of CS_B (–, US absent). He believed that CS_B acquired the ability to signal that an expected US would not be forthcoming (the animal learned that CS_B signaled "no food"), and he showed the effect could not be attributed to the AB composite stimulus simply being different from A. Pavlov's notion of learned suppression was criticized initially (Skinner, 1938), but it now receives mostly favorable reviews (Williams, Overmier, & LoLordo, 1992), although certainly not in its most detailed physiological form.

This chapter focuses on what is known about the mechanism that supports the learning of A+, AB– discriminations. This mechanism, called conditioned inhibition, is responsible for the suppression of a learned response on AB– trials. But conditioned inhibition is more than this. In an important paper, Miller and Konorski (1928) argued that conditioned inhibition is also a causal factor in the maintenance of high levels of responding in avoidance learning (see Ayres, this volume). Unfortunately, their paper was badly placed to have an immediate influence on thinking in North America. The first two sections of this chapter (Definition and Theory) review the current literature on A+, AB– discrimination learning and instrumental avoidance in animals. In keeping with the theme of this volume—the continuity between laboratory research and clinical practice—the chapter's last two sections identify some roles for conditioned inhibition in maladaptive human behavior (panic and obsessive-compulsive disorders).

DEFINITION

The many faces of conditioned inhibition are best understood by considering the selected Pavlovian and instrumental paradigms shown in Figure 5–1. In Pavlovian conditioning, the experimenter arranges the temporal relation between the CS (cue) and the US (event) and monitors the subject's response (left-hand side of Figure 5–1). Because the response is free to vary and its occurrence or nonoccurrence is irrelevant to paradigm definition in Pavlovian conditioning, no responses are shown in the left-hand side of Figure 5–1. On the other hand, in instrumental conditioning the experimenter waits for the subject to either respond or not respond and then presents an event with some specified probability. The response may be cued or uncued. Thus, no cues are depicted in the instrumental paradigms shown in the right-hand side of Figure

5–1, although the response may certainly be cued by a discriminative stimulus.

When two things (cue and event or response and event) occur at various points in the flow of time, the relation between them can be summarized by a special type of correlation coefficient that takes into account the direction of the relation (Allan, 1980). In Pavlovian conditioning the CS is a signal for the US; the US does not signal the CS. In instrumental conditioning, responding may produce a reinforcer, the reinforcer does not produce the response. The appropriate measure for an unidirectional statistical dependency is contingency, or $\Delta P = P(US|CS) - P(US|no\ CS)$, which has much the same interpretation as Pearson's r. In Pavlovian conditioning, if the CS signals every US (top right of Figure 5–1), the contingency is $\Delta P = +1.0$ and the stimulus is called a CS+. Likewise, an instrumental response may be perfectly correlated with the presentation of a particular event (top left of Figure 5–1)—the event never occurs in the absence of the response.

Of additional importance in instrumental paradigms is the valence of the positively contingent event; valence is not a basis for distinction in Pavlovian conditioning. When the event is appetitive, exposure to a positive contingency will increase responding, and this instrumental paradigm is called *positive reinforcement*. When an aversive event is made contingent on responding, whatever responding that would occur diminishes, and the paradigm is called *punishment*. Identification of the "reinforcer" as appetitive or aversive is based on empirical evidence. The reinforcing event is appetitive if the subject will work to receive it; the event is aversive if it can be used to punish an existing behavior and reduce its probability of occurrence. One unfortunate consequence of this empirical approach to classifying events is circular definition. The event is appetitive because it increases the probability of the response; the response increases because it is followed by an appetitive event. The usual way to circumvent this problem is to point to the "transsituational" properties of the event (Meehl, 1950). Although no single physical property allows for an easy distinction between aversive and appetitive events, the effect of the

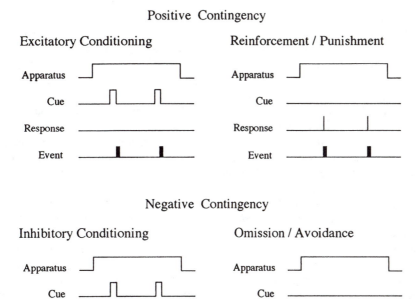

Figure 5–1. Contingency relations in Pavlovian and instrumental conditioning.

event in one situation often allows a priori prediction about its effect in another situation.

The paradigms in which conditioned inhibition plays an explanatory role are diagrammed in the lower portion of Figure 5–1. They involve either a stimulus-contingent (Pavlovian) or a response-contingent (instrumental) reduction in the probability of the target event. For example, the US may occur if and only if the CS is *not* present (lower left). In this case, there is a perfect negative contingency between the CS and the US ($\Delta P = 0.0 - 1.0 = -1.0$), and the stimulus is called a CS–. The CS– identifies each occasion on which the US is absent. On the other hand, if the instrumental response cancels the presentation of an expected appetitive event, the paradigm is called *omission* or *time-out*. *Avoidance learning* occurs when the response signals the absence of a scheduled aversive event. In the latter case, the aversive event is a reinforcer because it increases the probability of the target response by its omission.

The suggestion that conditioned inhibition has a primary role in the omission/avoidance paradigm is counterintuitive and deserves further comment. Conditioned inhibition is often equated with response suppression; however, conditioned inhibition supports the learning of a new response in the avoidance paradigm. The important point to remember is that conditioned inhibition is a label for the mechanism that is responsible for learning that two events are negatively correlated (two events occur apart from each other). Although the term *conditioned inhibition* brings to mind the early A+/AB– discrimination experiments of Pavlov (1927), the learning of the negative dependency between the response and the reinforcer in the avoidance paradigm also qualifies. What is being modeled is not suppression of responding, but the learning of a negative relation. In avoidance, the response signals a lower probability of an aversive reinforcer, and so the subject makes the response. This confusion stems in part from a historical annoyance; the Pavlovian A+/AB– paradigm is commonly referred to as the conditioned inhibition paradigm even though conditioned inhibition is a theoretical mechanism and not a specific training regimen.

One cannot stress too much the regulatory nature of the conditioned inhibition process. A conditioned inhibitory relation exists when a stimulus or response signals a reduction in the a priori probability of some event. In Pavlov's A+, AB– paradigm, CS_A signals the US, and CS_B signals the absence of the US. If the subject has no basis for expecting the to-be-omitted event, it cannot be said to have learned the negative stimulus-event or response-event relation. Thus, the apparatus cues shown in Figure 5–1 play a critical role in negative contingency learning and are not just stimuli incidental to the experiment. Placement in the apparatus must be associated with the occurrence of the US or reinforcer. It is only when the subject anticipates the US or the reinforcer that suppression of that anticipation can be said to have been caused by conditioned inhibition. This is not a particular problem in the avoidance paradigm, because the instrumental response will not occur at high levels unless the animal is sensitive to the negative relation between the response and the reinforcer. Responding increases as the subject learns that presentation of the aversive event can be prevented by responding.

On the other hand, special procedures are often necessary in Pavlovian conditioning to demonstrate the learning of negative relations. To show conditioned inhibition, the experimenter arranges the situation so that without inhibition the response will occur with high probability. For example, Rescorla (1966) trained dogs to jump back and forth over a barrier separating two compartments of a shuttle-box to avoid electric shocks. Next, in the Pavlovian conditioning stage, separate groups of dogs were exposed to either (a) positive, (b) negative, or (c) random relations between shock and an auditory CS. In this stage, the dogs were restrained in a Pavlovian harness, and shocks were delivered through electrodes attached to the dogs' legs. When the auditory CS was later presented while the dogs were shuttling to avoid shock, avoidance responding was aug-

mented in the positive group, suppressed in the negative group, and unaltered in the uncorrelated group (see Figure 5–2). As can be seen in Figure 5–2, the effects of the inhibitory CS–, like those of the excitatory CS+, lingered for some time, and responding returned to baseline levels 15 s after CS termination. In summary, the dogs of the negative correlation group learned the negative relation between the CS– and shock, and this learning undermined the motive for avoidance.

Why did Rescorla use this elaborate procedure? Without it, he would have had no method of discerning the absence of fear conditioning from conditioned inhibition. One would not have expected the dogs in either the uncorrelated group (CSo) or the negatively correlated (CS–) group to have responded fearfully to the auditory CS. Presentation of the CS– on the instrumental baseline allowed the inhibition that was learned to the CS– in the first stage to be evident in the dogs' behavior.

Not every instance of reduced responding should be unquestioningly attributed to an active process of inhibition. The failure of the organism to perform a particular response might be caused by the absence of excitatory learning as well as

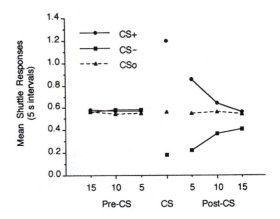

Figure 5–2. Mean number of avoidance responses prior to (pre-CS), during (CS), and after (post-CS) the presentation of a tone CS. The tone CS had previously been postively correlated (CS+), negatively correlated (CS–), or uncorrelated (CSo) with the US. (Adapted with permission from Rescorla, 1966.)

by the strengthening of other responses (response competition), forgetting, or for many other reasons. Conditioned inhibition must not be presumed; it must be shown. Rescorla (1966) used a test known as *summation*, adapted from Pavlov (1927). He declared the CS– to be inhibitory because it reduced the responding controlled by an excitatory cue when the two stimuli were presented together for the first time. In Rescorla's experiment, the apparatus cues of the shuttle-box served as the CS+ for shock (A+), and the auditory CS– (AB–) signaled the absence of the aversive reinforcer.

It is often prudent to include a *retardation* test for conditioned inhibition along with the summation test (e.g., Rescorla, 1969a). In this test, the putative CS– is paired with the US, and the number of trials it takes the CS– to evoke a CR serves as the measure of conditioned inhibition. The more slowly the CR is acquired, the stronger the inhibition. The intent of this test is to show that reduced responding in summation is due to conditioned inhibition and not to distraction. The performance of an ongoing action may be disrupted by the presentation of a distracting event. For example, the CS– in Rescorla's (1966) experiment might have been distracting, although CS+ and CSo were not. A CS that is distracting, however, should not be slow to evoke a CR upon reinforcement.

Having made these definitional points, we can proceed to the main purposes of this chapter. The next section (Theory) outlines the conditions that affect the development, transfer, and extinction of conditioned inhibition in animal learning. We begin the section by raising a general theoretical issue that has influenced research in animal learning. The last two sections examine the role of conditioned inhibition in the aetiology and maintenance of two human behavioral disorders, one based on Pavlovian learning and the other instrumentally based.

THEORY

Historically, the learning of negative relations has been modeled in one of two ways: cognitive expectancy and modulation. Cognitive expectancy theory holds that associative learning is mediated by the formation of a representation of what is likely to happen in various circumstances (Dickinson, 1980). This interpretation is best known as a theory of instrumental avoidance. For example, a well-trained rat may press a lever at regular intervals without any obvious change in its environment because it has knowledge that pressing the lever produces "no shock" (Seligman & Johnson, 1973). "No shock" became a reinforcer at the point at which the rat recognized that "shock" would occur in the absence of a lever press. Cognitive expectancy theory assumes that the animal also possesses the knowledge that it has control over the presentation of the noxious event (e.g., Seligman & Binik, 1977). With this knowledge there is no reason for the animal to be afraid. For example, most drivers stop their cars at red lights. Stopping is a habit informed by the expectation that not stopping might be dangerous. Drivers do not stop because of fear that wells up at the sight of a red light.

Exactly the same cognitive expectancy mechanism has been suggested as a model for Pavlovian A+/AB– discrimination learning, although its connection to the hypothesized avoidance mechanism is not often explicitly mentioned (see Mackintosh, 1974). For example, Konorski (1967) suggested that CS_B might evoke a mental representation of "no US" which, because of incompatibility, dampens the ability of CS_A to evoke its associate, the "US" representation.

Although methodological behaviorists would no doubt find the mentalistic nature of cognitive expectancy theory objectionable, the theory does fit with common intuition and is roughly consistent with most dictionary and textbook definitions. However, methodological behaviorists might be surprised that neobehaviorists, who are generally more accepting of the use of hypothetical entities, have also had difficulty with the concept of the omission of an event acting as a reinforcer. Building "not" into stimulus representations (e.g., "no shock") is a natural way to model conditioned inhibition, but it implies that it can be rewarding to get nothing. The objections of the neobehaviorists are summarized in the "avoidance puzzle," which Mowrer (1947) explains this way:

It is easily seen that it is rewarding to escape from such a noxious stimulus [shock]. But how can a shock which is *not experienced*, that is, which is avoided, be said to provide either a source of motivation or satisfaction (p. 108)?

The solution to the avoidance puzzle, which has the unmistakable stamp of Freud (see Mowrer, 1950, 1960), is to assume that one stimulus can change the meaning or *modulate* the effects of another stimulus. Rather than postulating that a stimulus or a response may call forth an expectation of a "nonevent," the theory of conditioned inhibition as modulation supposes that anticipations evoked by other cues can be inhibited. In instrumental avoidance learning, this modulatory mechanism appears as two-process theory (Mowrer, 1947). The first process, or component of the learning, occurs when situational cues become associated with a dangerous event (Pavlovian). The second component is instrumental reinforcement. Because the response causes the omission of scheduled USs, it is associated with reduced levels of danger. Something tangible but private occurs when the subject responds in the avoidance paradigm; the subject's fear or "tension" is reduced.

In a subsequent safety-signal revision, Schoenfeld (1950) suggested that feedback cues that accompany the response might inhibit fear because they signal a reduced likelihood of the noxious event. Solomon and Wynne (1953) noted that if the response occurred quickly enough in the presence of a signal for the aversive event, the response would have the added effect of protecting the later segments of the signal from extinction (A+, AB– where the instrumental action, B, terminates the presentation of A so that A is never fully experienced). If so, the avoidance habit will tend to become detached from the original fear reaction (McAllister & McAllister, 1991) as in the example of stopping at a red light.

Modulatory mechanisms can also be identified in theories that concern themselves with the learning of Pavlovian A+/AB– discriminations. For example, in his early writings, before postulating the existence of a "no US" representation,

Konorski (1948) suggested that a negative CS may suppress the CR by raising the threshold for activation of the US representation (see Rescorla, 1979).

Thinking about the detailed mechanism is important for two reasons. First, it implies a common mechanism in the learning of negative relations, whether one is speaking about the A+/AB– paradigm or the avoidance paradigm. Second, it provides a framework for understanding the directions that research has taken on conditioned inhibition. Evocation of a separate representation for stimulus absence (cognitive expectancy) versus qualifying or negating a positive relation (modulatory) is a subtle distinction; it does, however, have consequences for prediction. For example, cognitive expectancy theories predict that extinction of the avoidance response should occur only if the response is seen to produce the aversive event (e.g., response->shock contradicts previous learning, response->"no shock"). In the following subsections describe the conditions under which conditioned inhibition is acquired, transferred, and lost. For the most part, reference is to the Pavlovian conditioning literature. Ayres (this volume) gives broad and parallel coverage to instrumental avoidance learning.

Acquisition

A central prediction of modulatory theories is that ΔP should provide a good empirical description of the conditions that foster the development of conditioned inhibition. If a CS– acts by inhibiting (modulating) a prevailing expectation to prevent "overexpectation" of the US, the level of inhibition acquired should be just enough to bring the prevailing expectation level to its proper (i.e., lower) level. One way to test this hypothesis would be to withhold USs in the absence of the CS, that is, reduce the second term of the ΔP statistic, $P(US|no\ CS)$.

It is often helpful to visualize manipulations of this sort by illustration in a *contingency space*. This is done in Figure 5–3, which plots the probability of the US in the presence of the CS (ordinate) against the probability of the US in the

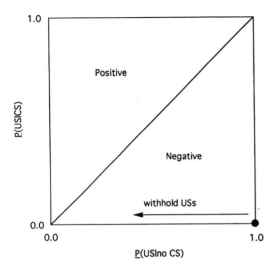

Figure 5–3. A contingency space in which the negative contingency between the CS and the US is degraded by reducing the probability of the US in the absence of the CS.

absence of the CS (abscissa). The region above the diagonal line indicates those situations in which the relation is positive; the US is more likely to occur when the CS is present than when the CS is absent, $P(US|CS) > P(US|no\ CS)$. If the relation is negative, it will fall below the diagonal line, $P(US|CS) < P(US|no\ CS)$. The vertical distance of the point from the line is a spatial representation of the magnitude of the contingency. If the starting point is a perfect negative relation, $P(US|CS) - P(US|no\ CS) = (0.0) - (1.0) = -1.0$, withholding USs in the absence of the CS would involve traveling along the horizontal axis from the most distant point in the direction of the vertical axis.

Rescorla (1969b) was the first to confirm the prediction of modulatory theories that withholding USs in the absence of the CS– attenuates conditioned inhibition. The rats that were studied in fear conditioning makes his findings all the more intriguing: The CS– was a less effective inhibitor of fear in summation and retardation tests, as *fewer* shock USs were presented to the subjects in the absence of the CS. A number of other researchers have confirmed the most ex-

treme prediction of this sort (Rescorla, 1979). If the subject has no inkling that the US might occur at this moment, the CS does not become inhibitory despite the fact that it is nominally followed by "no US" (A–, AB– is very different from A+, AB– even if the US has been experienced at some point). Baker (1977) confirmed a related prediction. He presented USs and CSs to rats on alternate days as a method for establishing conditioned inhibition. Conditioned inhibition produced by alternating CSs and USs was diminished when the USs were signaled by another CS+. That is, blocking the conditioning of apparatus cues greatly attenuated the magnitude of conditioned inhibition.

It is not at all clear from cognitive expectancy theory that conditioned inhibition and ΔP should be this closely related. In Pavlov's "method of contrasts" (A+ versus B–, or differential conditioning), however, the inhibitory CS– does not appear to cancel the expectation aroused by another cue. CS_B is presented in the middle of the intertrial interval and is temporally isolated from both the US and CS_A. Although not always effective for establishing conditioned inhibition, this method would appear to provide evidence for the learning of the "$CS_B \rightarrow$ no US" relation. This follows because there does not appear to be any US expectation to inhibit at the time of the occurrence of CS_B. As Miller, Hallam, Hong, and Dufore (1991) have shown, however, differential inhibition is mediated by a contrast with the excitatory apparatus cues in which CS_B is embedded. Following differential conditioning, they exposed subjects to the experimental context for a prolonged period in the absence of the US. This manipulation abolished differential inhibition, which suggests that anticipation of the US evoked by contextual cues at the time of the presentation of CS_B was critical to the observed inhibition.

Of greater concern for the cognitive/representational approach are reports of conditioned inhibition in situations in which the CS– signals an incomplete reduction in the probability of the US. One way to reduce the negative contingency between a CS– and a US is to withhold USs in the absence of the CS–. The other way is to directly pair the CS– with the US but with lower probability than in the absence of the CS–. In the latter case, it is hard to imagine that the CS– signals "no US"; the animal learns that one event signals a reduction in the probability of another event (modulatory). Consistent with modulation theories, Wagner, Mazur, Donegan, and Pfautz (1980) observed the development of conditioned inhibition to a CS that was continuously reinforced by a low-intensity US, provided the obtained intensity was lower than would otherwise be expected (e.g., A++, AB+ paradigm where ++ is a double intensity US). Kremer (1978) found that when two separately conditioned CSs were presented together in simultaneous compound and followed by the US, each lost some ability to evoke the CR. His animals were presumably expecting two USs to follow the compound, one for each CS; and upon receiving only one US, their expectations were lowered by the development of conditioned inhibition. (For an alternative interpretation, see Schachtman, Kasprow, Chee, & Miller, 1985.)

Other paradigms in which conditioned inhibition is generated include extinction of a CS+. As we now realize, Pavlov (1927) was correct in asserting that old learning is not erased in "extinction" (see Bouton & Nelson, 1994, this volume; Falls, this volume). Withholding the US does not reverse the process of learning and return the organism to its original state (i.e., "no US" does not replace "US"). The original learning that supported responding has not disappeared or been "extinguished," but it is temporarily suppressed by new learning. The animal learns that at this time, the CS+ will not be followed by the US. If extinction of a CS+ is cued by the presence of another CS, as in the A+, AB– procedure, CS_B acquires the lion's share of the inhibition, and the original CS_A-US association is "protected from extinction" (Soltysik, 1985). If the animal is reexposed to the CS_A in the absence of CS_B, responding is renewed.

It should be mentioned here that it is possible to force what is known about the acquisition of conditioned inhibition into the scope of cognitive/expectancy theory by interpreting "no US" as "less US." That is, the "no US" representation

could be evoked to various degrees rather than being a literal representation of US absence. Since extension of the theory in this manner is somewhat unnatural, further support for the theory would have to be found in other areas. Although this section has focused on Pavlovian conditioning, one would have little reason to suspect that cognitive expectancy theory would provide a better account of the acquisition of omission/avoidance learning. Herrnstein and Hineline (1966) found a high correlation between avoidance learning and the magnitude of shock-frequency reduction (i.e., ΔP). Thus, the avoidance response is reinforced by a decline in the probability of the aversive event; the response does not have to signal safety to be reinforced.

Transfer

Rescorla and Holland (1977) were the first to give serious consideration to the possible locus of action of conditioned inhibition. With the premise of conditioned inhibition as modulation, they identified three places in the associative system where a modulator could operate to have the effect of suppression in an A+ AB– discrimination: The inhibitory CS_B may suppress (1) the specific CR that happens to be evoked by CS_A (type A), (2) the excitatory association between the CS_A and the US (type B), and/or (3) the US representation (type C). These mechanisms are depicted in Figure 5–4. Although suppression at any of these loci would allow the organism to discriminate between the nonreinforced AB– trials and the reinforced A+ trials, Rescorla and Holland (1977) found preferential evidence for inhibition of the US representation (type C).

How did Rescorla and Holland (1977) tell where inhibition resides in the associative system? They argued that we can learn this by examining transfer of conditioned inhibition. After A+, AB– training, the usual finding is that CS_B will inhibit the CR evoked by a different CS+ that has been separately paired with the US on other trials (i.e., summation). In most cases, the same overt CR is evoked by CS_A and the second CS+. Thus, the conventional effect used to establish the existence of conditioned inhibition

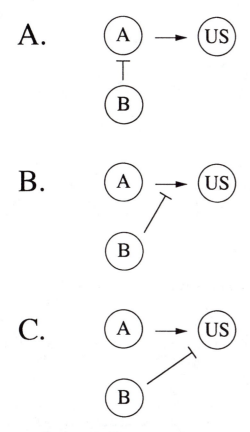

Figure 5–4. Three places in the associative system that CS_B might act upon to reduce the CR evoked by CS_A. Lines terminating with an arrow represent excitatory associations, while those terminating with a perpendicular bar present inhibitory associations.

tion. If this "neutral" CS is then paired with an important event, such as food (US), it becomes associated with that event, and it is called a CS+. Often this results in a change in the animal's orienting reaction to the CS+. For example, a rat will rear up on its hind legs when presented with a light CS+ that signals food, but the same rat will jerk its head laterally in a rapid side-to-side motion when presented with a tone CS+. One can exploit the different CR topographies supported by visual and auditory CS+s paired with food. If the presence of a CS– negates the expectancy of the food US, the CS– should suppress a different CR evoked by another food CS+.

Rescorla and Holland (1977) confirmed this prediction. A tone CS– that originally inhibited the head jerking evoked by a clicker CS+ would also inhibit rearing evoked by a light CS+ in a summation test, although the tone CS– and the light CS+ had never appeared together in the past. This summation effect with a CS+ that evoked a different anticipatory response is consistent with CS– suppression of the food expectancy, but it cannot be explained either by suppression of the CR evoked by CS_A or by suppression of the CS_A->US connection.

Using the transfer approach, Holland (1984, 1985, 1989) identified a procedural variation that affects the mode of CS_B's inhibitory action. He found that if CS_B was presented a few seconds before CS_A rather than simultaneously with it, CS_B would preferentially inhibit the associative connection between CS_A and the US. The inhibitor CS_B would not suppress the CR evoked by a second CS+ whether this new CS+ produced a CR that was similar or dissimilar to CS_A. The serial "CS_B then CS_A" procedure had apparently endowed CS_B with the ability to signal that CS_A would not be reinforced on that particular trial; it set the occasion for the nonreinforcement of CS_A (type B, called *negative occasion setting*).

This conclusion received further support in a remarkable experiment in which CS_B retained its ability to signal nonreinforcement of CS_A after being directly associated with the US. In that experiment, one group of rats received serial presentations of CS_B followed by the unreinforced CS_A (i.e., A+, B->A–). The other group received

demonstrates that CS_B has an effect beyond inhibiting the CS_A-US association (type B), but it does not distinguish between the suppression of a particular CR (type A) and the power to inhibit any CS that evokes the US expectancy (type C).

Using the behavioral observation technique developed by Holland (1977), Rescorla and Holland (1977) investigated whether transfer of inhibition across CS+s depends on the CS+s' evoking a common response. Any stimulus that is perceived by the organism will activate the perceptual system and produce a response. When the stimulus is insignificant to the animal, we call it a CS, and the response it produces is called the *orienting reac-*

the more familiar simultaneous presentations of CS_B and CS_A (A+, AB–). The inhibitory CS_B was then revalued in both groups so that it signaled the occurrence of the US. In this stage, the US occurred immediately upon termination of CS_B (i.e., B+). The surprising result was that CS_B retained its ability to signal the nonreinforcement of CS_A in the serial group. When rats of the serial group were tested with the original CS_B then CS_A discrimination trial, they responded vigorously to CS_B but did not respond to CS_A when it was preceded by CS_B. On the other hand, the B+ revaluation treatment abolished the ability of the simultaneously trained CS_B to inhibit CS_A, just as one might expect if CS_B was acting on the US representation (type C).

In summary, CS_B may inhibit responding in various ways—either by inhibiting the US representation (simultaneous) or by inhibiting the CS_A-US associative connection (serial). Although it is convenient to identify these two forms of inhibition with simultaneous and serial conditioning procedures, this empirical heuristic exaggerates the obtained difference. For example, there appears to be some retention of the original conditioned inhibition discrimination following reinforcement of CS_B with the US, even when CS_A and CS_B have been simultaneously trained (Pearce & Wilson, 1991). In addition, summation transfer is rarely complete in simultaneous conditioned inhibition. CS_B's inhibitory properties transfer from CS_A to a second CS+, but suppression is often attenuated on the transfer trial (Rescorla, 1982). Both findings suggest some specificity of action even in the simultaneous procedure.

Bouton and Nelson (1994; this volume) have suggested that rather than simply inhibit the excitatory connection, type B conditioned inhibition may toggle the CS_A-to-US inhibitory association "on" and "off" (top of Figure 5–5). They offer the following reconceptualization of Pavlovian conditioning: Excitatory conditioning is assumed to involve the formation of an association between CS_A and the US. Once this relation is learned, it is never lost. If CS_A is then nonreinforced, the excitatory association is joined by a countermanding inhibitory associa-

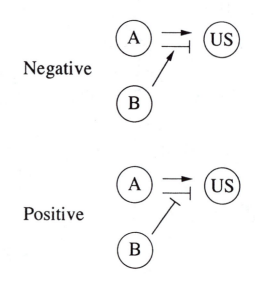

Figure 5–5. Possible associative structures for negative and positive occasion setting.

tion. This inhibitory association is acquired by CS_B if the latter CS is correlated with US omission and if it appears in simultaneous compound with CS_A (modulation of the US center, type C in Figure 5–4). If not, the countermanding inhibitory association will be acquired by CS_A itself and the opportunity will exist for the second stimulus to clarify the ambiguous role of CS_A. In the serial conditioned inhibition paradigm, for example, the presence of CS_B may enable the inhibitory link between CS_A and the US. When CS_B is absent, the inhibitory association acquired by CS_A during extinction is disabled or remains in its normally "off" state.

This increased level of complexity is an attempt to account for the finding that some CS+s are more "inhibitable" than others. In transfer, a serially trained CS_B does not usually suppress responding to a second CS+ that has been continuously reinforced. This suggests specificity of action. However, transfer does occur if the second CS+ assumed the role of CS_A in a separate discrimination with a different CS_B (Lamarre & Holland, 1987). In the latter case, the second CS+ is likely to carry an inhibitory association because it has been reinforced and nonreinforced. This appears to be the vital ingredient for transfer in serial negative discriminations and suggests an involvement of the inhibitory association in the modulation. The message in these data is that what is being modulated is as important as the training of the modulator itself.

For the sake of balanced argument, it is important to mention that Holland (1989) is not so easily persuaded that one need abandon the idea that CS_B acts in a hierarchical fashion by inhibiting a particular CS->US association. By virtue of their similarity of training, the second CS+ may be seen as interchangeable (equivalent) with CS_A. If the rats fail to distinguish the second CS+ from CS_A, CS_B would inhibit both CS+s at similar levels. Thus, the data may not imply that CS_B toggles CS_A's inhibitory association to its active state on nonreinforced trials. Instead, the CS– may prevent retrieval of the CS_A-US association (Holland, 1984; i.e., type B in Figure 5–4). At this point, it is best to suspend judgment on this issue.

It is of some interest that in addition to identifying negative modulation, a number of investigators have identified a form of positive modulation (Ross & Holland, 1981). Rather than provide information that another stimulus will be nonreinforced, a second stimulus may signal that the first stimulus (CS_A) will be reinforced (i.e., A–, AB+ rather than A+, AB–). Ross and Holland (1981) investigated the properties of CS_B in this mirror image of the conditioned inhibition paradigm using the techniques of Rescorla and Holland (1977). In this case, CS_A was an auditory stimulus, CS_B was a visual stimulus, and the US was food. When CS_A and CS_B were presented simultaneously on the reinforced AB+ trials, the rats reared to the light CS_B as if all they had learned was the light->food relation (CS_A was presumably ignored). However, when CS_B was presented a few seconds in advance of CS_A so that it no longer terminated with the US, the rats began "head jerking" and approaching the magazine in the presence of CS_A—the CR normally evoked by that auditory CS. Thus, in the serial arrangement, the light CS_B did not acquire a direct excitatory association with the US and evoke the rearing CR appropriate for a visual stimulus, but rather it modulated the head-jerking/magazine behavior supported by CS_A.

Positive modulation can be modeled by an associative structure such as that presented in the bottom of Figure 5–5 (Clark, 1992). In this case, the presence of CS_B turns off the inhibitory CS_A-US link and restores the CR. This associative structure provides an excellent fit to data suggesting that pretraining CS_A so that it carries both excitatory and inhibitory components is an essential feature of positive A+, AB– modulation (e.g., Rescorla, 1985, 1987). Swartzentruber (1995), in his thoughtful review and analysis of the literature on modulation, suggests that CS_A becomes an appropriate target for positive modulation when its excitation is currently suppressed by inhibition. That is, positive modulation is based on the removal of inhibition.

Returning to the larger question, we can ask whether the data in this section are more consistent with modulatory or cognitive expectancy mechanisms. That CS–s may have some specificity of action indicates that a CS can provide information about the conditions under which another CS will not be reinforced (i.e., modulation). Additionally, this ability to provide information about another CS's relation with the US is sometimes independent of the CS's own association with the US. In serial conditioning, the "CS–" may signal the immediate occurrence of the US but also convey information that a subsequent CS+ will not be reinforced. It is hard to see how effects like these can be mediated by the cognition that "no US" will occur. In addition, detailed analyses have cast doubt on the notion that inhibitory action on the US representation (e.g., Rescorla and Holland, 1977) is exactly the opposite to the action of an excitor as required by cognitive expectancy theory (see Rescorla, 1979; Williams et al., 1992). It is better explained by threshold modulation.

Loss and Extinction

Perhaps the most widely cited article in the area of inhibitory conditioning is that of Zimmer-Hart and Rescorla (1974; for related findings Baker, 1974). At the time of the article's publication, research in all areas of Pavlovian conditioning was heavily influenced by the

Rescorla-Wagner model (Rescorla & Wagner, 1972; Wagner & Rescorla, 1972). Many of the predictions of the Rescorla-Wagner model were counterintuitive, and early confirmation of some of these predictions intensified interest in it.

That theory viewed conditioned inhibition as the opposite of conditioned excitation. One counterintuitive prediction that received empirical support was the observation of *supernormal* levels of conditioned excitation. When a novel CS is reinforced in compound with an inhibitory CS−, the novel CS acquires more excitatory strength than it otherwise would (e.g., Rescorla, 1971; Wagner, 1971; cf. Navarro, Hallam, Matzel, & Miller, 1989; Pearce & Redhead, 1995).

Zimmer-Hart and Rescorla (1974) tested another prediction of the model. If conditioned inhibition opposes conditioned excitation, removing CS_A from the situation should undermine the basis for CS_B's inhibition. Thus, conditioned inhibition should "extinguish," or decline in strength, if CS_B is presented separately on its own (B− trials). Of the many predictions of the model, this is perhaps the most counterintuitive. It was quickly disconfirmed. Showing the organism that separate presentations of CS_B were followed by "no US" did not attenuate CS_B's ability to signal that CS_A was also followed by "no US." If anything, there was enhancement, as one might expect if the additional B− trials served as another example that CS_B would not be reinforced. Once conditioned inhibition was acquired by CS_B through involvement with CS_A, the maintenance of the power to inhibit did not require the continued presence of CS_A.

The failure of conditioned inhibition to extinguish can be viewed as highly problematic. Instead, the data seem to encourage the notion that in conditioned inhibition a cognitive expectancy of "no US" develops, and this expectation interferes with the "US" expectancy triggered by CS_A. However, the idea of conditioned inhibition as modulation was poorly developed at this time. If CS_B modulates the US representation by increasing its threshold for activation (rather than being connected to the US with an opposite or inhibitory association), the data are much less troublesome (Rescorla, 1979). A stimulus that alters the potential excitability of the US (a modulator acting on the US representation) may not undergo any detectable change in the absence of stimulation. When CS_B is presented alone, the output of the system will be zero activation of the US representation rather than negative activation, because CS_B acts by changing a threshold. Extinction is expected only if the rules of the acquisition and loss of conditioned inhibition are parallel with those used to model the strengthening and loss of conditioned excitation. A better description of the role of the CS− is to protect excitatory associations from being extinguished. Threshold modulation also allows the organism to retain a more complete representation of its past experiences so that it can benefit from the richness of the relations it has been exposed to in the environment.

A considerable degree of interest has also been shown in whether the modulatory process is retrospective in nature. For example, although nonreinforced presentations of CS_B do not cause the loss of conditioned inhibition (A+, AB−, then B−), it is possible that nonreinforced presentations of CS_A might (A+, AB−, then A−). If CS_A no longer evokes an overt CR because it is no longer followed by the US, it is possible that CS_B might lose its modulatory power because there is nothing left to modulate (inhibit). This might occur even though CS_B has not been presented since the original A+, AB− discrimination stage (this is where the term *retrospective* comes in). Miller and Schachtman (1985; see also Miller & Matzel, 1988), for example, have suggested that at the time of testing, the subject compares the expected outcome (US or no US) on A and AB trials and attributes the difference to the effect of B. If the subject does not expect the outcome on A trials because it was extinguished just prior to testing, CS_B should lose its inhibitory power.

Data on this question are mixed. Rescorla and Holland (1977) first trained rats to distinguish A+ and AB− trials. CS_A signaled the delivery of shock unless it was accompanied by CS_B. After A+, AB− training, extinction of CS_A was found to have no effect on the ability of CS_B to inhibit the shock CR evoked by a new CS+. In a second experiment, CS_B was established as an inhibitor of the food expectancy. The inhibitory power of CS_B on the second CS+ was retained even when the food reinforcer for CS_A was not only omitted but also switched from food to shock! Zimmer-Hart and Rescorla (1974) also reported that intermixing A– and AB– trials was an ineffective means of undermining the learning from previous A+ and AB– trials. On the other hand, Hallam, Matzel, Sloat, and Miller (1990) did observe a reduction in summation following extinction of CS_A. The reasons for these discrepancies are unclear.

It is worth mentioning that the findings of Rescorla and Holland (1977) are analogous to results found in the instrumental avoidance paradigm. The avoidance response may continue to occur even when the subject is no longer demonstrably afraid of the discriminative stimulus that supposedly signals the aversive event. Solomon, Kamin, and Wynne (1953) trained dogs to shuttle over a barrier to avoid shocks in the presence of a warning signal. This shuttle response was readily learned, and the dogs took very few shocks. Then, the shocker was disconnected. One might have expected the shuttle response to extinguish with some rapidity. It did not. The dogs persisted in jumping over the barrier for a minimum of 200 trials, and one dog jumped for over 600 trials until the experimenters quit. Solomon et al. (1953) also reported that their subjects showed very few signs of overt fear to the warning stimulus. Perhaps the dogs knew they could avoid the shock by jumping and so there was no reason to be fearful. In a related experiment, Kamin, Brimer, and Black (1963) trained rats to escape from a discriminative stimulus that signaled shock. This training was terminated after 1, 3, 9, or 27 consecutive trials with a successful escape response. The discriminative stimulus was then presented in a different context while the rats were pressing a lever for food. The well-trained animals that had successfully avoided shock for 27 consecutive trials showed very little fear of the discriminative stimulus, much less fear than the other groups.

The preceding findings are often cited as strong evidence against the modulatory analysis of Pavlovian conditioned inhibition and its part-

ner, two-factor theory of avoidance. For example, if the conditioned aversive stimuli, A, that initially supported avoidance learning are no longer excitatory, the avoidance response, B, might be expected to lose its capacity to inhibit fear. Maintenance of the avoidance response for prolonged periods in extinction is often seen as favoring the cognitive explanation (Seligman & Johnson, 1973). Subjects may continue to respond because their responses are associated with "no shock," not because they are presently afraid.

This interpretation has not been updated in light of new data, however, which suggests that extinction does not vanquish old learning. We now know that extinction is not unlearning. For example, the association between CS_A and the US should not be destroyed by A– extinction trials after A+, AB– training. Rather, the association should become latent (e.g., Bouton, 1994). If so, it makes perfect sense that CS_B should retain some power to negate the latent CS_A-US association even though CS_A has been operationally extinguished. The association has not really disappeared. In avoidance, the response may tend to occur for long periods in extinction because situational cues are still associated with the noxious reinforcer, although the association is currently latent. In their review of the avoidance literature, McAllister and McAllister (1991) also debunk many other myths surrounding the predictions of two-process theory. The safety signal version of two-process theory does not predict intense fear in well-trained avoidance learning (refer to Theory section).

The next two sections describe some possible roles for conditioned inhibition in the aetiology, maintenance, and treatment of panic disorder (PD) and obsessive-compulsive disorder (OCD). Our analysis of PD is based on Barlow's (Barlow, 1988; Carter & Barlow, 1995) notion of learned alarms and safety signals. In OCD, we apply a two-process avoidance model but stray from the common interpretation of OCD as merely an anxiety disorder. Our analysis is speculative in a few instances (disgust and OCD), and here it is designed to provoke thought rather than to be a recitation of fact. We hope that some of our speculations, even if they turn out to be false, will encourage the reader to look for other possible applications of conditioned inhibition (e.g., Bouton & Nelson, this volume; Mineka, 1985) and to put these speculations forward for empirical test.

LEARNED ALARMS, SAFETY, AND PANIC DISORDER

Julie, a 32-year-old married woman with two young children, experienced her first panic attack shortly after her second child was born. She felt overwhelmed by the demands of caring for two young children and trying to work part-time. She was doing the laundry early one morning when she began to feel funny. At first, she felt light-headed and slightly faint. Within minutes she began feeling very fearful, her heart raced, she became unsteady, and she thought she might vomit. She sat down, and the symptoms subsided after about 10 minutes, but vague feelings of fear continued for another hour. She phoned her husband at work and told him what had happened. Both were very concerned that she might have a serious problem. Her husband called his mother to watch the children and went home to take his wife to the hospital. The doctors ran a series of blood tests and an EKG. They found nothing wrong.

Two days later Julie had a second attack. This time she called her family doctor, who asked to see her as soon as possible. Again, the doctor could find nothing wrong but suggested that Julie might have been experiencing panic attacks and gave her a prescription for Xanax®. Julie was reluctant to take the medication because she was breast-feeding her baby. Over the next few weeks Julie had four more attacks, each of which occurred in different situations. The first attack occurred while she was driving her children to her mother's home. This attack was particularly frightening. As the attack started, Julie thought, "I might pass out and lose control of the car. My children might be killed." She made it to her mother's but refused to drive home. The last of the four attacks occurred in the early morning while she was having coffee before her children awakened. After several cups of coffee, she noticed her heart was beating faster than normal.

Her immediate thought was "Oh, no, another attack is happening." It did happen.

Approximately 3% to 5% of the adult population will develop PD at some time in their life (McNally, 1994). PD is characterized by frequent panic attacks, some of which occur "out of the blue" but more often than not during times of worry about having a future attack. Panic attacks are characterized by intense feelings of fear or terror of dying or going crazy accompanied by somatic symptoms such as difficulty breathing, racing heart, and sweating. PD, if left untreated, is usually a chronic disorder. It can, however, wax and wane over time, with some people experiencing long panic-free periods. Panic attacks occur more frequently during periods of stress.

Why some people who experience anxiety develop PD and others do not presents an interesting problem. There are several prominent theories about what causes panic attacks and why only some people with panic attacks develop PD. Klein (1993) suggests that panic attacks occur when a person's brain receives a false message that he or she is suffocating. Although there is support for this theory, it may explain only why some of the people who have experienced a panic attack develop PD. Many panickers do not experience breathing difficulties. Another prominent theory is that panic attacks occur when a person interprets normal physiological changes as a signal that a panic attack is imminent (Beck & Emery, 1985). Good evidence exists that such "catastrophic" thinking does occur in some panickers, but this does not explain why the panic attack occurred in the first place.

A theory that integrates biological and cognitive factors has been proposed by Barlow (1988), who maintains that some people have a biological predisposition to panic attacks. With minimal provocation, these people will tend to display the "emergency reaction"—the body's response to imminent danger—described by Cannon (1929). The emergency reaction is a complex set of neurophysiological responses that prepare the person for fight or flight. For example, an immediate increase in respiration allows the heart to deliver an increased flow of oxygenated blood to the large muscles. Epinephrine and norepinephrine are released into the bloodstream following sympathetic arousal of the adrenal medulla causing the release of stored energy. When a person is responding to real danger, Barlow refers to the panic response as a "true alarm." In PD, however, the fear reaction occurs in situations in which most people would not become alarmed.

About 10% to 20% of adults experience one or more panic attacks during their lifetime (Norton, Cox, & Malan, 1992). Most episodes are triggered by specific situations. If you are running with the bulls in Pamplona, it is only natural to feel panicked. Instances in which the person correctly attributes the bodily reaction to some external cause (e.g., the bull) are unlikely to cause a single panic attack to escalate into panic disorder. The person has an external cue that is predictive of the dangerous event (A+) and other cues that signal safe periods (AB−). Thus, conditioned inhibition will normally prevent nonclinical panic—a true alarm—from transforming itself into full-blown panic disorder.

Some people, however, may experience one or more panic attacks that appear to them to be uncued. (Barlow calls these uncued attacks "false alarms.") It is these people who are most at risk for PD. After the unexpected attack, they may become very apprehensive about having another attack. Because of this fear of panicking, they become acutely aware of changes in their body that might predict another attack. They may, as did Julie in our case example, misinterpret an increase in heart rate produced by drinking several cups of coffee as a sign of an impending panic attack. This triggers a cascade of events. First, the person may experience catastrophic thoughts, such as "I'm going to have an attack, and I might die." Second, they may, because of their anxiety, begin to hyperventilate. Increased respiration is a bodily symptom that is often correlated with a panic attack. Hyperventilation may lead to increasingly severe catastrophic thoughts and, ultimately, to a panic attack.

When a person has a panic attack as a result of misinterpreting changes in his or her body, Barlow refers to the attack as a "learned alarm." A learned alarm is essentially a fight-or-flight response that has become detached from external danger stimuli. The panic response is triggered by internal cues that become self-fulfilling. Somatic changes and catastrophic thinking serve as interoceptive CSs (Razran, 1961) that evoke a panic CR (A+, where A stands for interoceptive sensations or catastrophic thinking and "+" is the person's own panic response that serves as an aversive US). Because the CS and the US are highly similar (the CS is a miniature of the US), this interoceptive conditioning should be a highly prepared form of learning (Rescorla & Furrow, 1977).

Barlow's theory explains why many people with PD avoid situations such as exercise or other activities that increase anxiety. Such people have no way of discriminating A+ from AB−. They do not know whether their bodily responses will trigger a panic attack. It follows that providing panickers with a safety signal (CS_B) should reduce the probability of a panic attack. Safety signals such as a bottle of sugar pills or the presence of the therapist may provide a signal that a panic response will not occur. Indeed, some people with PD are able to engage in stressful activities if they are in the presence of someone they trust or if they have their medication, an AB− trial (Cox, Endler, Swinson, & Norton 1992). The trusted individual who could offer help is a strong safety signal (CS_B).

There is some question, however, about whether the safety effect is caused by conditioned inhibition. For example, Carter, Hollon, Carson, and Shelton (1995) examined the effect of the presence of a safe person on panic induced by CO_2 inhalation. Panickers were asked to identify a person with whom they felt safe. In the safe group, either the safe person or a psychiatrist considered safe was present during CO_2 inhalation. In the no-safe group, the safe person waited in an adjoining office. Patients in the safe group reported lower levels of affective distress and a reduced frequency of catastrophic cognitions during CO_2 inhalation. Unfortunately, Carter et al. could not determine whether the inhibition effect was learned (conditioned inhibition) or unlearned (reciprocal inhibition). The presence of the safe person may have acted as a conditioned inhibitor of the somatic CSs. Subjects in the safe group might have known that an attack was less likely to occur because such attacks have in the past been rare in the presence of the safe person (learned). On the other hand, the presence of the safe person might have suppressed physiological arousal before the CO_2 was even inhaled (e.g., Wolpe, 1995). Paniclike symptoms would be expected to be less severe when the person is feeling less stressed (unlearned).

In the animal literature, conditioned inhibition is known to dampen the expectancy of the US evoked by another cue (e.g., CS_A) . However, it has a very different effect on the processing of the US should it unexpectedly occur. When the US occurs surprisingly, after the presentation of a CS−, the unconditioned response can actually be enhanced (Desmond, Romano, & Moore, 1980). When this happens, it is usually attributed to the organism's surprise at the occurrence of the US. If the analysis of the safe person as a conditioned inhibitor is correct, the presence of the safe person during an actual attack could then aggravate the panic attack. Afterward, the realization that the conditioned inhibitor is no longer potent may potentiate the panic reaction and may serve as a new source of anxiety (supernormal conditioning). These predictions of the conditioned inhibition account have never been examined in PD.

In any case, the practitioner should be aware of the following important caveat in any effort to help patients identify safe cues. In fear conditioning in rats, conditioned inhibition is less durable over time than conditioned excitation. In fear conditioning, rats will respond with high levels of fear to both A and AB after a 35-day retention interval, although the original A+ AB− discrimination was well learned (Hendersen, 1978). Thus, if patients do not continue to employ the safety cue, they may relapse (for review of relapse, see Bouton & Swartzentruber, 1991).

DISGUST, AVOIDANCE, AND OCD

Buried within the Rat Man case history, "Notes upon a Case of Obsessional Neurosis" (Freud, 1909/1963), Freud relates an encounter with a man who was in therapy because of troubling obsessive thoughts and compulsive actions. The man, a bureaucrat, always paid with crisp, clean banknotes. Freud commented that he could tell government officials by the newness of their money. The man responded that they were not new but rather that he washed and ironed all his banknotes because they were covered in filth and that he did not want to make people ill by giving them contaminated money. Freud seized the opportunity to explore the man's sexual life, hypothesizing that obsessive concern with passing on germs is related to an underlying and displaced awareness of moral failure and unreconciled guilt. The man then recounted his premeditated sexual assaults on the daughters of close friends. When queried by Freud, he expressed no guilt concerning these attacks. Freud came to the conclusion that, like this bureaucrat, obsessive-compulsive sufferers are often troubled with the awareness of self-contamination but that there is a fundamental misattribution of its source. The man had good reason to feel self-disgust and moral pollution, but the enormity of such a self-realization made it difficult for him to acknowledge this guilt. The guilt was therefore displaced to a less reprehensible but equally contaminating cause.

Although it is commonly held by most behavior therapists that OCD is an anxiety disorder (Zetin & Kramer, 1992), we, like Freud, believe that many cases of OCD can be attributed to an overwhelming and disordered feeling of disgust/pollution (PD being a disordered alarm response). Disgust is defined as "a feeling or attitude of disdain, unpleasure, rejection, and/or incipient nausea" (English & English, 1958). It is often linked with taste and food as is indicated by its original meaning, "against taste," but this emotional response is very close to the feeling of pollution, which is a state of defilement that is not bound to taste aversion. Humans display feelings of disgust or pollution in ways that are interpretable across cultures. Disgust is one of the six characteristic human emotions that are identifiable from facial expressions along with happiness, surprise, sadness, anger, and fear (Ekman &

Friesen, 1975). Rats also make facial reactions to the taste of quinine as if they were disgusted by its bitterness (Grill & Norgren, 1978), and their orofacial responses are conditionable (Delamater, LoLordo, & Berridge, 1986). It is useful to distinguish between three possible sources for disgust or pollution: (1) physical, either directly experienced, inferred, or aroused by association with contamination (Rozin & Fallon, 1987), (2) cognitive self-judgment of moral failure, and (3) a disgust state, what Rachman (1994) has referred to as a "sense of pollution."

When the source of the disgust is physical, we perceive contamination on our person, and it is only natural for us to attempt to wash. This is an appropriate and effective means of bringing an unpleasant US to an end. The washing response acts as a conditioned inhibitor for the feeling of disgust. Following the instrumental response comes a period of relief from the unpleasant stimulus. A sense of revulsion may also be experienced when presented with an object that is known to be clean but is associated with an offensive object (Rozin & Fallon, 1987). We may also become aware of the presence of invisible contaminants, either through social taboos or by knowledge of microscopic contaminants. Awareness of nonvisible contaminants is not experienced tactually, but the individual nonetheless feels disgust and attempts to clean off the contamination. Individual differences and societal demands allow for some latitude in tolerance for contamination. For example, the preteen male is stereotypically tolerant of dirt, whereas operating room staff are justifiably zealous in their cleaning habits. That being the case, some instances of OCD may simply be an exaggerated response to actual or possible physical contamination.

The second cause of feelings of disgust—self-judgment of moral failure—is also generative of feelings of disgust. Like the disgust that arises from an awareness of the presence of harmful microorganisms, this source of disgust is not the result of exteroceptive information but rather the result of cognitive activity. It is normal that we feel guilty or disgusted with ourselves after having behaved in a way that is condemned by the moral code that we have internalized. Sometimes the real cause for our feeling of disgust is suppressed so as to maintain a self-image that is not compatible with the disgust-causing behavior. As in the case of the man who washed his money, the sense of disgust is attributed not to the real cause but to a plausible alternative. This metaphorical transformation results in a response that is appropriate to the experience of the feeling of disgust but is absolutely useless in resolving the underlying cause of the sense of disgust. The response's role as a conditioned inhibitor is not possible, because the response—washing banknotes—does not remove the real causative stimulus—guilt. Guilt is still present, and the feeling of disgust remains. The response may lessen the feelings of disgust temporarily, and in this way it may help to maintain the undesirable behavior by providing temporary relief. This type of displaced attribution is also seen in the classic literary example of Lady Macbeth, who rightly feels dirty/polluted by the blood that sprays on her hands during the assassination of the king. After washing her hands, the queen continues to attribute her feelings of pollution to her hands instead of to the guilt properly associated with regicide.

Rachman (1994) hypothesized that some cases of OCD can be explained by a continuous experience of a "sense of pollution." He describes this as a state of continual disgust. His suggestion is in line with Claude Bernard's theory of physical homeostasis (Cannon, 1932/1963). Events that impinge on the perceptual system provoke responses that are adaptive in the short term but the system then tends to return to its prestimulus state. In certain individuals, this return to homeostasis might be blocked. This is not necessarily a cause of pathology, however, as long as the cognitive-emotional system can adjust to the imbalance. If, on the other hand, this imbalance is outside the range that can be coped with cognitively, negative states will obtain and result in dysfunctional responses. If a state of disgust/pollution exists, the individual may be plagued by dysfunctional and disruptive responses that are appropriate to a feeling of disgust but provide no permanent relief. These responses could very well be species-specific defense reactions (Bolles, 1970) that would normally provide relief from physical dirt. As well, if the individual has learned from previous experiences that certain arbitrary responses soothe the feeling of "disgust," these learned behaviors could be evoked. The behavior is appropriate to the feelings of disgust/pollution but is not instrumental in altering the ongoing state. The response provides only temporary relief.

The suggestion that disgust may arise from three different sources may help explain the nature of compulsive acts in OCD, that is, the limited range of potential compulsive behaviors and why they may change over time. There are many biological hypotheses about susceptibility to OCD, such as frontal lobe dsyfunction (e.g., Abbruzzese, Bellodi, Ferri, & Scarone, 1995; Rapoport & Wise, 1988), but these hypotheses are intended to account only for the ritualistic aspects of OCD. They say nothing about the form of the compulsive action. Well over half of all OCD patients are compulsive cleaners, and most of them are hand washers. An obvious link exists between hand washing and feelings of physical disgust (first source). If OCD is a form of avoidance learning, the compulsive action should be readily provoked by suggestions of physical contamination. Hodgson and Rachman (1972) provoked obsessional thoughts in compulsive hand washers and observed increased levels of anxiety/discomfort. Anxiety and disgust are closely related. Both are highly aversive, highly arousing, and produce many of the same physiological responses (Lang, 1995).

One might expect that cognitive behavioral therapy (changing the patient's cognitions about physical dirt) might be particularly effective in such cases, so long as the feelings of dirtiness are caused by a fear of physical dirt (first source) and are not displaced cognitions (second and third sources). Good empirical support exists for the effectiveness of cognitive therapy in compulsive cleaning. Teasdale (1974) notes that compulsive, ritualistic cleaning is usually poorly controlled by physical stimuli, such as real dirt,

and the behavior is often motivated by inferred or possible contamination. If so, the compulsive action would have only a short-lived inhibitory effect because of the recueing of the action by thoughts of possible contamination. This would make compulsive cleaning an appropriate target for behavioral therapies such as response prevention and flooding. Response prevention is very effective in extinguishing the shuttle avoidance response of rats (Katzev & Berman, 1974), and it is often highly effective with compulsive cleaners (Rachman, Hodgson, & Marks, 1971).

What, then, explains the relatively high incidence of compulsive checkers, counters, and reciters, since these behaviors are not so obviously linked to feelings of disgust? Perhaps these behaviors are responses to feelings of moral reprehensibility. Self-reproach is not necessarily the result of the individual's own actions or guilt (e.g., the man who washed his money). A woman who loathes her own body may have internalized the judgment of another. She might exercise compulsively and count calories as a response to obsessive thinking about body image. Alternatively, she may feel physically unclean and wash her hands compulsively. Feelings of self-loathing are closely related to depression, and thus, it is not surprising that antidepressive drugs have some impact on some instances of OCD.

An individual who is aware of pervasive feelings of disgust that are uncued (third source) might tend to misattribute cause and effect. The cognitive system of the individual attaches an appropriate outside object (first source) or self-perception (second source) as being the cause of the sense of pollution to explain the compulsive behavior to self and to others, such as the therapist. This attachment could be to germs in the environment, body self-image, blasphemous or immoral thoughts, responsibility for harm to others, or any number of other naturally occurring causes of disgust/pollution. This misattribution may provide an explanation for the obsessional thought, a cognitive attribution of a cause for a perceived effect.

In the last two cases (second and third sources), we would expect the compulsive act to serve as an especially poor conditioned inhibitor of the feeling of disgust. The compulsive act will tend to be repeated, and because it produces no lasting relief, the person experiences anxiety over his or her inability to influence the feeling of disgust. This fits with clinical lore (Mandler & Watson, 1966) and careful observation in clinical settings that the termination of a ritualistic behavior is not always followed by anxiety reduction but sometimes is followed by an increase, especially in the case of compulsive checkers (Rachman & Hodgson, 1980). The idea that compulsive behavior is driven by three sources of disgust is also consistent with the view that OCD is multiply determined with different mediators in different clinical instances of the disorder, such as the distinction between "active" and "passive" avoidance in checking and cleaning (Rachman & Hodgson, 1980).

In summary, conditioned inhibition has an unmistakable role in both PD and OCD. Another common theme is misattribution. Julie misattributed her caffeine-induced accelerated heart rate as a cue for an impending panic attack, and the man who washed his money misattributed a feeling of disgust to contaminated banknotes. One question that merits more thought is whether the misattribution is causal or incidental. It may be that Julie experienced her panic attack after drinking coffee, not because she misattributed the increase in heart rate but because the somatic changes caused by caffeine are a CS for panic. In this case, the catastrophic ideation was present but was not necessarily causative. On the other hand, catastrophic ideation may induce a panic attack by altering somatic state. If so, causal misattribution would be a necessary link. The misattribution of the money washer is post hoc and therefore not causal. The man's feeling of guilt was aroused by his past actions, actions that he had learned were punishable.

Cognitive attribution, and more often misattribution, provides an explanation of an otherwise hard to comprehend set of behaviors. It can frequently mislead the person making the attribution and can often mislead the therapist who is called on to provide help.

REFERENCES

Abbruzzese, M., Bellodi, L., Ferri, S., & Scarone, S. (1995). Frontal lobe dysfunction in schizophrenia and obsessive-compulsive disorder: A neuropsychological study. *Brain and Cognition, 27,* 202–212.

Allan, L. J. (1980). A note on measurement of contingency between two binary variables in judgment tasks. *Bulletin of the Psychonomic Society, 15,* 147–149.

Ayres, J. J. B. (this volume). Avoidance and fear conditioning.

Baker, A. G. (1974). Conditioned inhibition is not the symmetrical opposite of conditioned excitation: A test of the Rescorla-Wagner model. *Learning and Motivation, 5,* 369–379.

Baker, A. G. (1977). Conditioned inhibition arising from a between session negative correlation. *Journal of Experimental Psychology: Animal Behavior Processes, 3,* 144–155.

Barlow, D. H. (1988). *Anxiety and its disorders: The nature and treatment of anxiety and panic.* New York: Guilford Press.

Beck, A. T., & Emery, G. (1985). *Anxiety disorders and phobias: A cognitive perspective.* New York: Basic Books.

Bolles, R. C. (1970). Species-specific defense reactions and avoidance learning. *Psychological Review, 71,* 32–48.

Bouton, M. E. (1994). Context, ambiguity, and classical conditioning. *Current Directions in Psychological Science, 2,* 49–53.

Bouton, M. E., & Nelson, J. B. (1994). Context-specificity of target versus feature inhibition in a feature-negative discrimination. *Journal of Experimental Psychology: Animal Learning Processes, 20,* 51–65.

Bouton, M. E., & Nelson, J. B. (this volume). Context and generalization in classical conditioning.

Bouton, M. E., & Swartzentruber, D. (1991). Sources of relapse after extinction in Pavlovian and instrumental learning. *Clinical Psychology Review, 11,* 123–140.

Cannon, W. B. (1929). *Bodily changes in pain, hunger, fear, and rage* (2nd ed.). New York: Appleton-Century-Crofts.

Cannon, W. B. (1932/1963). *The wisdom of the body.* New York: Norton.

Carter, M. M., & Barlow, D. H. (1995). Learned alarms: The origins of panic. In W. O'Donohue & L. Krasner (eds.), *Theories of behavior therapy: Exploring behavior change,* (209–228). Washington, D.C.: American Psychological Association.

Carter, M. M., Hollon, S. D., Carson, R., & Shelton, R. C. (1995). Effects of a safe person on induced distress following a biological challenge in panic disorder with agoraphobia. *Journal of Abnormal Psychology, 104,* 156–163.

Clark, J. M. (1992). Inhibitory mechanisms in normal and dysfunctional number processing. In J. I. D. Campbell (ed.), *The nature and origin of mathematical skills,* 411–456. Elsevier.

Cox, B. J., Endler, N. S., Swinson, R. P., & Norton, R. N. (1992). Situations and specific coping strategies associated with clinical and non-clinical panic attacks. *Behavior Research and Therapy, 30*, 67–69.

Delamater, A. R., LoLordo, V. M., & Berridge, K. C. (1986). Control of fluid palatability by exteroceptive Pavlovian signals. *Journal of Experimental Psychology: Animal Behavior Processes, 12*, 143–152.

Desmond, J. E., Romano, A. G., & Moore, J. W. (1980). Amplitude of the rabbit's unconditioned nictitating membrane response in the presence and absence of a conditioned inhibitor. *Animal Learning & Behavior, 8*, 225–230.

Dickinson, A. (1980). *Contemporary animal learning theory.* Cambridge, UK: Cambridge University Press.

Ekman, P., & Friesen, W. V. (1975). *Unmasking the face.* Englewood Cliffs, N.J.: Prentice-Hall.

English, H. B., & English, A. C. (1958). *A comprehensive dictionary of psychological and psychoanalytical terms: A guide to usage.* New York: David McKay.

Freud, S. (1909/1963). Notes upon a case of obsessional neurosis. In P. Reiff (ed.), *Three case histories.* New York: Collier Books.

Grill, H. J., & Norgren, R. (1978). The taste reactivity test: I. Mimetic responses to gustatory stimuli in neurologically normal rats. *Brain Research, 143*, 263–269.

Hallam, S. C., Matzel, L. D., Sloat, J. S., & Miller, R. R. (1990). Excitation and inhibition as a function of posttraining extinction of the excitatory cue used in Pavlovian inhibition training. *Learning and Motivation, 21*, 59–84.

Hendersen, R. W. (1978). Forgetting of conditioned fear inhibition. *Learning and Motivation, 8*, 16–30.

Herrnstein, R. J., & Hineline, P. N. (1966). Negative reinforcement as shock frequency reduction. *Journal of the Experimental Analysis of Behavior, 9*, 421–430.

Hodgson, R. J., & Rachman, S. (1972). The effects of contamination and washing in obsessional patients. *Behavior Research and Therapy, 10*, 111–117.

Holland, P. C. (1977). Conditioned stimulus as a determinant of the form of the Pavlovian conditioned response. *Journal of Experimental Psychology: Animal Behavior Processes, 3*, 77–104.

Holland, P. C. (1984). Differential effects of reinforcement of an inhibitory feature after serial and simultaneous feature negative discrimination training. *Journal of Experimental Psychology: Animal Behavior Processes, 10*, 461–475.

Holland, P. C. (1985). The nature of conditioned inhibition in serial and simultaneous feature negative discriminations. In R. R. Miller & N. E. Spear (eds.), *Information processing in animals: Conditioned inhibition,* 267–298. Hillsdale, N.J.: Erlbaum.

Holland, P. C. (1989). Transfer of negative occasion setting and conditioned inhibition across conditioned and unconditioned stimuli. *Journal of Experimental Psychology: Animal Behavior Processes, 15*, 311–328.

Kamin, L. J., Brimer, C. J., & Black, A. H. (1963). Conditioned suppression as a monitor of fear of the CS in the course of avoidance training. *Journal of Comparative and Physiological Psychology, 56*, 497–501.

Katzev, R. D., & Berman, J. S. (1974). Effects of exposure to conditioned stimulus and control of its termination in the extinction of avoidance behavior. *Journal of Comparative and Physiological Psychology, 87*, 347–353.

Klein, D. F. (1993). False suffocation alarms, spontaneous panics, and related conditions. *Archives of General Psychiatry, 50*, 306–317.

Konorski, J. (1948). *Conditioned reflexes and neuron organisation.* Cambridge, UK: Cambridge University Press.

Konorski, J. (1967). *Integrative activity of the brain.* Chicago: University of Chicago Press.

Kremer, E. F. (1978). The Rescorla-Wagner model: Losses in associative strength in compound conditioned stimuli. *Journal of Experimental Psychology: Animal Behavior Processes, 4*, 22–36.

Lamarre, J., & Holland, P. C. (1987). Transfer of inhibition after serial feature negative discrimination training. *Learning and Motivation, 18*, 319–342.

Lang, P. J. (1995). The emotion probe. *American Psychologist, 50*, 372–385.

Mackintosh, N. J. (1974). *The psychology of animal learning.* New York: Academic Press.

Mandler, G., & Watson, D. L. (1966). Anxiety and the interruption of behavior. In C. D. Spielberger (ed.), *Anxiety and behavior,* 263–288. New York: Academic Press.

McAllister, D. E., & McAllister, W. R. (1991). Fear theory and aversively motivated behavior: Some controversial issues. In M. R. Denny (ed.), *Fear, avoidance, and phobias: A fundamental analysis,* 135–163. Hillsdale, N.J.: Erlbaum.

McNally, R. J. (1994). *Panic disorder.* New York: Guilford.

Meehl, P. E. (1950). On the circularity of the law of effect. *Psychological Bulletin, 47*, 52–75.

Miller, R. R., Hallam, S. C., Hong, J. Y., & Dufore, D. S. (1991). Associative structure of differential inhibition: Implications for models of conditioned inhibition. *Journal of Experimental Psychology: Animal Behavior Processes, 17*, 141–150.

Miller, R. R., & Matzel, L. D. (1988). The comparator hypothesis: A response rule for the expression of associations. In G. B. Bower (ed.), *The psychology of learning and motivation,* Vol. 22: 51–92. New York: Academic Press.

Miller, R. R., & Schachtman, T. R. (1985). Conditioning context as an associative baseline: Implications for response generation and the nature of conditioned inhibition. In R. R. Miller & N. E. Spear (eds.), *Information processing in animals: Conditioned inhibition,* 51–88. Hillsdale, N.J.: Erlbaum.

Miller, S., & Konorski, J. (1928). Sur une forme particuliere des réflexes conditionnels. *Compe Rendu des Séances de la Société Biologique, 99*, 1155–1158.

Mineka, S. (1985). Animal models of anxiety-based disorders: Their usefulness and limitations. In A. H. Tuma & J. D. Maser (ed.), *Anxiety and the anxiety disorders*, 199–244. Hillsdale, N.J.: Erlbaum.

Mowrer, O. H. (1947). On the dual nature of learning—A reinterpretation of "conditioning" and "problem-solving." *Harvard Educational Review, 17*, 102–148.

Mowrer, O. H. (1950). Pain, punishment, guilt and anxiety. In P. H. Hoch, & J. Zubin (eds.), *Anxiety*, 27–40. New York: Grune and Stratton.

Mowrer, O. H. (1960). *Learning theory and behavior.* New York: Wiley.

Navarro, J. I., Hallam, S. C., Matzel, L. D., Miller, R. R. (1989). Superconditioning and overshadowing. *Learning and Motivation, 20*, 130–152.

Norton, R. N., Cox, B. J., & Malan, J. (1992). Nonclinical panickers: A review. *Clinical Psychology Review, 12*, 121–139.

Pavlov, I. P. (1927). *Conditioned reflexes.* Oxford: Oxford University Press.

Pearce, J. M., & Redhead, E. S. (1995). Supernormal conditioning. *Journal of Experimental Psychology: Animal Behavior Processes, 20*, 155–165.

Pearce, J. M., & Wilson, P. N. (1991). Failure of excitatory conditioning to extinguish the influence of a conditioned inhibitor. *Journal of Experimental Psychology: Animal Behavior Processes, 17*, 519–529.

Rachman, S. J. (1994). Pollution of the mind. *Behavior Research and Therapy, 32*, 311–314.

Rachman, S. J., & Hodgson, R. J. (1980). *Obsessions and compulsions.* Englewood Cliffs, N.J.: Prentice-Hall.

Rachman, S. J., Hodgson, R. J., & Marks, I. (1971). The treatment of chronic obsessional neurosis. *Behavior Research and Therapy, 9*, 231–247.

Rapoport, J. L., & Wise, S. P. (1988). Obsessive-compulsive disorder: Evidence for basal ganglia dysfunction. *Psychopharmacology Bulletin, 24*, 380–384.

Razran, G. (1961). The observable unconscious and the inferable conscious in current Soviet psychophysiology: Interoceptive conditioning, semantic conditioning, and the orienting reflex. *Psychological Review, 68*, 81–150.

Rescorla, R. A. (1966). Predictability and number of pairings in Pavlovian fear conditioning. *Psychonomic Science, 4*, 383–384.

Rescorla, R. A. (1969a). Pavlovian conditioned inhibition. *Psychological Bulletin, 72*, 77–94.

Rescorla, R. A. (1969b). Conditioned inhibition of fear resulting from negative CS-US contingencies. *Journal of Comparative and Physiological Psychology, 67*, 504–509.

Rescorla, R. A. (1971). Variation in the effectiveness of reinforcement and nonreinforcement following prior inhibitory conditioning. *Learning and Motivation, 2*, 113–123.

Rescorla, R. A. (1979). Conditioned inhibition and extinction. In A. Dickinson & R. A. Boakes (eds.), *Mechanisms of learning and motivation: A memorial volume to Jerzy Konorski*, 83–110. Hillsdale, N.J.: Erlbaum.

Rescorla, R. A. (1982). Some consequences of associations between the excitor and the inhibitor in a conditioned inhibition paradigm. *Journal of Experimental Psychology: Animal Behavior Processes, 8*, 288–298.

Rescorla, R. A. (1985). Conditioned inhibition in facilitation. In R. R. Miller & N. E. Spear (eds.), *Information processing in animals: Conditioned inhibition*, 299–326. Hillsdale, N.J.: Erlbaum.

Rescorla, R. A. (1987). Facilitation and inhibition. *Journal of Experimental Psychology: Animal Behavior Processes, 13*, 250–259.

Rescorla, R. A., & Furrow, D. R. (1977). Stimulus similarity as a determinant of Pavlovian conditioning. *Journal of Experimental Psychology: Animal Behavior Processes, 3*, 203–215.

Rescorla, R. A., & Holland, P. C. (1977). Associations in Pavlovian conditioned inhibition. *Learning and Motivation, 8*, 429–447.

Rescorla, R. A., & Wagner, A. R. (1972). A theory of Pavlovian conditioning: Variations in the effectiveness of reinforcement and non-reinforcement. In A. H. Black & W. F. Prokasy (eds.), *Classical Conditioning II: Theory and research*, 64–99. New York: Appleton-Century-Crofts.

Ross, R. T., & Holland, P. C. (1981). Conditioning of simultaneous and serial feature-positive discriminations. *Animal Learning & Behavior, 9*, 293–303.

Rozin, P., & Fallon, A. E. (1987). A perspective on disgust. *Psychological Review, 94*, 23–41.

Schachtman, T. R., Kasprow, W. J., Chee, M. A., & Miller, R. R. (1985). Blocking but not conditioned inhibition arises when an added stimulus is reinforced in compound with multiple pretrained stimuli. *American Journal of Psychology, 98*, 283–295.

Schoenfeld, W. N. (1950). An experimental approach to anxiety, escape, and avoidance behavior. In P. H. Hoch, & J. Zubin (eds.), *Anxiety*, 70–99. New York: Grune and Stratton.

Seligman, M. E. P., & Binik, Y. M. (1977). Safety signal hypothesis. In H. Davis & H. Hurwitz (eds.), *Operant-Pavlovian interactions*, 83–113. Hillsdale, N.J.: Erlbaum.

Seligman, M. E. P., & Johnson, J. C. (1973). A cognitive theory of avoidance learning. In F. J. McGuigan & D. B. Lumsden (eds.), *Contemporary approaches to conditioning and learning.* Washington, D.C.: Winston-Wiley.

Skinner, B. F. (1938). *Behavior of organisms.* New York: Appleton-Century-Crofts.

Solomon, R. L., Kamin, L. J., & Wynne, L. C. (1953). Traumatic avoidance learning: The outcomes of several extinction procedures with dogs. *Journal of Abnormal Psychology, 48*, 291–302.

Solomon, R. L., & Wynne, L. C. (1953). Traumatic avoidance learning: Acquisition in normal dogs. *Psychological Monographs, 67* (Whole No. 354).

Soltysik, S. S. (1985). Protection from extinction: New data and a hypothesis of several varieties of conditioned inhibition. In R. R. Miller & N. E. Spear (eds.), *Information processing in animals: Conditioned inhibition*, 369–394. Hillsdale, N.J.: Erlbaum.

Swartzentruber, D. (1995). Modulatory mechanisms in Pavlovian conditioning. *Animal Learning & Behavior, 23*, 123–143.

Teasdale, J. D. (1974). Learning models of obsessional-compulsive disorder. In H. R. Beech (ed.), *Obsessional states*, 197–229. London: Methuen.

Wagner, A. R. (1971). Elementary associations. In H. H. Kendler & J. T. Spence (eds.), *Essays in neobehaviorism*, 187–213. New York: Appleton-Century-Crofts.

Wagner, A. R., Mazur, J. E., Donegan, N. H., & Pfautz, P. L. (1980). Evaluation of blocking and conditioned inhibition to a CS signaling a decrease in US intensity. *Journal of Experimental Psychology: Animal Behavior Processes, 6*, 376–385.

Wagner, A. R., & Rescorla, R. A. (1972). Inhibition in Pavlovian conditioning: Application of a theory. In R. A. Boakes & M. S. Halliday (eds.), *Inhibition and learning*, 301–336. London: Academic Press.

Williams, D. A., Overmier, J. B., & LoLordo, V. M. (1992). A reevaluation of Rescorla's early dictums about Pavlovian conditioned inhibition, *Psychological Bulletin, 111*, 275–290.

Wolpe, J. (1995). Reciprocal inhibition: Major agent of behavioral change. In W. O'Donohue & L. Krasner (eds.), *Theories of behavior therapy: Exploring behavior change*, 23–57. Washington, D.C.: American Psychological Association.

Zetin, M., & Kramer, M. A. (1992). Obsessive-compulsive disorder. *Hospital and Community Psychiatry, 43*, 689–699.

Zimmer-Hart, C. L., & Rescorla, R. A. (1974). Extinction of Pavlovian conditioned inhibition. *Journal of Comparative and Physiological Psychology, 86*, 837–845.

CHAPTER 6

LATENT INHIBITION AND BEHAVIOR PATHOLOGY: PROPHYLACTIC AND OTHER POSSIBLE EFFECTS OF STIMULUS PREEXPOSURE

R. E. Lubow

To many psychiatrists and psychologists, latent inhibition (LI) probably sounds darkly Freudian or vaguely Hullian. To calm these venerable ghosts and their spirited followers, let us begin by defining and illustrating LI. The basic LI effect is demonstrated when a stimulus that is preexposed without consequences becomes less effective as a conditioned stimulus (CS) than a stimulus that has not been preexposed. Such stimulus preexposures interfere with performance on subsequent associative learning tasks.

The term *latent inhibition* dates back to a study by Lubow and Moore (1959) that was designed to provide a classical conditioning analog of *latent learning*. As such, the LI effect is "latent" in that it is not exhibited in the stimulus preexposure phase, but rather in the subsequent test phase. "Inhibition" simply refers to the fact that the effect is manifested as a *retardation* in test-phase learning rather than facilitation. Although the term *latent inhibition* is meant to be entirely

descriptive, the phenomenon itself has been subject to a number of theoretical interpretations, of which there are two major classes: reduced associability and retrieval failure.

The traditional view of LI is that stimulus preexposure results in a decreased ability to *acquire* a new association to that stimulus (e.g., Lubow, Weiner, & Schnur, 1981; Mackintosh, 1975; Pearce & Hall, 1980; Wagner, 1981). This decrement has been attributed to a variety of mechanisms that reduce attention to the preexposed stimulus (see Lubow, 1989, for a review).

Alternatively, it has been proposed that LI is a result of *retrieval failure* rather than acquisition failure (e.g., Bouton, 1993; Miller, Kasprow, & Schachtman, 1986). This hypothesis proposes that, following stimulus preexposure, the acquisition of the new association to the old stimulus proceeds normally. However, in the test stage, when the subject again encounters the target stimulus, two competing associations may be retrieved: the earlier stimulus–no-consequence association from the preexposure stage and/or the stimulus-US association of the acquisition stage. In normal LI, the nonpreexposed group performs better than the preexposed group because there is only the second association to be retrieved, whereas the preexposed group performs more poorly because the first association is the one that is retrieved.

More recently, it has been suggested that during preexposure the subject learns several associations: CS–no-consequence, CS-context, context–no-consequence association, and a higher-order conditional association whereby the context becomes an occasion setter for the expression of the CS–no-consequence association (Lubow & Gewirtz, 1995). Such an approach, for which there is not yet much supporting data, would be congruent with both acquisition and retrieval-failure interpretations of LI.

Although debate continues as to whether the disruption represents reduced associability of the CS or a retrieval deficit, there is no denying that the LI effect is extremely robust, appearing not only in many different species, including humans, but also in a variety of learning paradigms.

The large majority of LI studies are with lower animals, mainly the laboratory rat, but also aplysia, honeybees, goldfish, pigeons, and others. However, the present chapter will focus on the human literature (for a review of the animal research, see Lubow, 1989; for LI in humans, see Lubow & Gewirtz, 1995; for the neurophysiological basis of LI, see Gray et al., 1991; Weiner, 1990).

The wide distribution of LI, both in species and paradigms, suggests that it provides some adaptive value. Indeed, LI appears to serve the function of protecting the organism, animal or human, from associating random, arbitrary, inconsequential, non-predictive stimuli with other events. It helps to partition the important from the unimportant, and thus to economize on processing capacity by biasing the organism to more fully process new inputs as opposed to old, inconsequential ones. LI, which has been described in terms of the conditioning of inattention (Lubow et al., 1981; Lubow, 1989), adaptively modulates functional stimulus novelty and guards against an information-processing overload.

A recent study by Braunstein-Bercovitz (1997) illustrates the paradigmatic human LI design. As shown in Figure 6–1, there are two groups, each of which participates in the two successive phases of the procedure: preexposure and test.

In the preexposure phase, one group is presented with a stimulus that later becomes the target-stimulus. In the present example, the preexposed stimulus is a meaningless shape. Importantly, stimulus preexposure is conducted in such a manner that the subject allocates little or no attention to the to-be-target stimulus. This is accomplished by using a masking task whose function is to divert attention from the to-be-target stimulus, making it irrelevant to the demands of the preexposure task. In the Braunstein-Bercovitz (1997) study, the masking task consisted of similarity-difference judgments for the letter pairs LL, TT, TL, LT, although a variety of

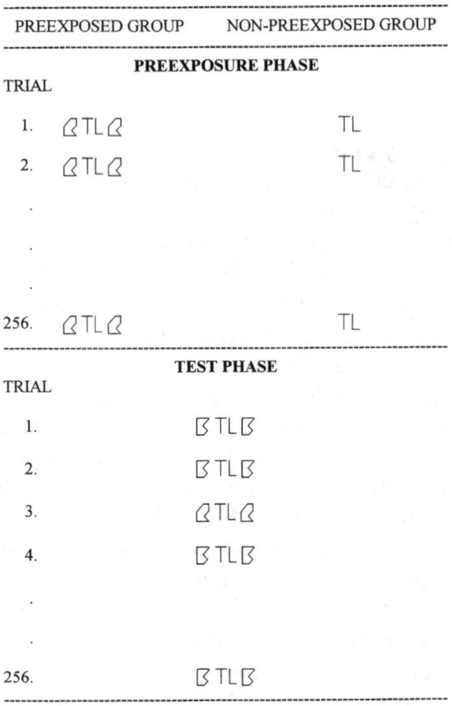

PREEXPOSED GROUP	NON-PREEXPOSED GROUP
PREEXPOSURE PHASE	
TRIAL	
1. ＱTLＱ	TL
2. ＱTLＱ	TL
.	
.	
.	
256. ＱTLＱ	TL
TEST PHASE	
TRIAL	
1. ꓭTLꓭ	
2. ꓭTLꓭ	
3. ＱTLＱ	
4. ꓭTLꓭ	
.	
.	
256. ꓭTLꓭ	

Figure 6–1. Schematic representation of a study by Braunstein-Bercovitz (1997), representing a typical human LI-experiment.

other masking tasks have been used (see Lubow & Gewirtz, 1995).

In the preexposure phase, all subjects were presented with 256 computer-generated, brief exposures to the same-different letter judgment task. In addition, subjects in the stimulus preexposed group viewed a pair of identical figures, one on each side of the letter pair (see Figure 6–1). Figure and letter presentations were initiated and terminated at the same time. Each trial, then, for the target preexposed group consisted of the simultaneous presentation of the figure and a letter-pair, while for the nonpreexposed group it consisted of the presentation of the letter-pair without the figures.

In the test phase, beginning immediately after preexposure, each subject received 256 trials. Each trial consisted of either the pair of figures (36 trials) that were preexposed, now the target, or a new pair of figures (220 trials). The subject was required to learn the relationship between the figures presented on the screen and a change in the value of a counter. For both groups, the counter was decremented when the subject pressed the bar in the presence of the target (preexposed) stimulus, and was incremented either when the subject failed to do so, or when the subject pressed the bar in the presence of the new (nonpreexposed) stimulus. The dependent variable was the number of target trials required to reach a learning criterion.

The median numbers of trials-to-criterion for the stimulus preexposed and nonpreexposed groups are shown in Figure 6–2 (Panel A). As can be seen, the preexposed group learned the association more slowly than the nonpreexposed group, thereby demonstrating the LI effect.

LI has been demonstrated many times in adult humans, both with the previously stated paradigm (Braunstein-Bercovitz, 1997), and similar ones, visual (e.g., Zalstein-Orda & Lubow, 1995) and auditory (e.g., Baruch et al., 1988; Lubow et al., 1987), as well as in eyelid conditioning (Schnur & Ksir, 1969), electrodermal conditioning (e.g., Lipp et al., 1992), and conditioned taste aversion (e.g., Arwas et al., 1989). The reliability and magnitude of the LI effect can be seen in Figure 6–2 (Panels A, B, C, D, E)

where the data from several of these studies are illustrated. LI also is evident in children, but for young ones (6–7 yrs), as for animals, a formal masking task is not required (Kaniel & Lubow, 1986; Lubow & Josman, 1993).

As noted, the role of the masking task in producing LI appears to be related to the fact that it diverts attention from the stimulus that will become the target in the test. The *formal* masking task may not be required in animal studies, because during preexposure, the novel apparatus elicits intense exploratory activity. This behavior suggests an allocation of attentional resources that would interfere with full processing of the nominally preexposed stimulus. As such, stimulus masking may be an integral part of the animal-LI studies.

LATENT INHIBITION AND BEHAVIORAL PATHOLOGY

There are at least three different ways that the data from LI research can have an impact on behavioral pathology: (1) LI may provide a useful tool for examining basic information processing in certain pathological groups, as has been done for schizophrenia (see Lubow & Gewirtz, 1995 for a review) and hyperactivity (Lubow & Josman, 1993). Once differences in the LI effect are found between the pathologic and normal groups, the theory of LI may then be of value in explicating the dysfunctional processes. (2) LI may be useful in explaining why certain therapies are not as effective as would ordinarily be expected, in particular conditioned aversion treatments of substance abuse, as used with alcoholics. In addition, the LI effect may be useful in counteracting inadvertent, undesirable side effects produced by some aversion conditioning treatments, as with the conditioned food aversions that frequently accompany radiation and chemotherapies for cancer. (3) LI research has suggested techniques that may be effective in the prophylactic treatment of certain fears and phobias. These three applications of LI research and theory to pathological behaviors will be discussed below, the first two only briefly and the last in some detail.

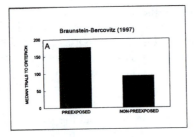

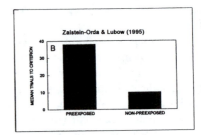

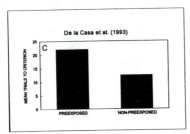

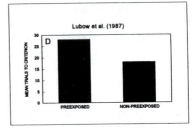

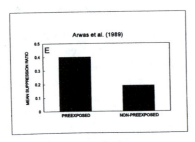

Figure 6–2. Five human-LI studies in which the target-preexposed group has a poorer learning test score than the non-preexposed group. Panels A, B, and C show the number of trials to reach a learning criterion as a function of type of target preexposure in three experiments using visual target stimuli; Panel D shows the same, but with an auditory stimulus; Panel E shows mean suppression ratios in a conditioned taste aversion study for a group receiving a familiar flavor (preexposed) and a nonfamiliar flavor (nonpreexposed). In each case, the data have been collapsed over conditions other than those of preexposure.

Latent Inhibition and Schizophrenia

In normal individuals, the exposure to irrelevant, unattended stimuli results in a decreased associability of those stimuli, namely LI. In schizophrenics this process is disrupted. Non-medicated acute schizophrenics show an attenuated LI effect (Baruch et al., 1988; Gray, N., et al., 1992). The same is true for psychosis-prone normals (De la Casa et al., 1993; Lipp & Vaitl, 1992; Lubow et al., 1992), those that score relatively high on such tests as the Schizotypal Personality Scale (STA; Claridge & Broks, 1984), which derive from DSM-III symptom lists and which putatively predict probability of a psychotic breakdown. This attenuated LI effect, a product of differences in the stimulus preexposed groups, may be related to problems in the deployment of attention (e.g., Lubow & Gewirtz, 1995), a dysfunction that is generally accepted as characteristic of schizophrenia (e.g., Braff, 1993; Neuchterlein & Dawson, 1984). More specifically, the LI deficit in schizophrenics has been attributed to a deficiency in the process that is responsible for the conditioning of *in*attention and producing LI in normals (Lubow, 1989; Lubow & Gewirtz, 1995). It has been suggested that schizophrenics, whose primary pharmacological treatment is with dopamine-receptor antagonists such as chlorpromazine and haloperidol, which produce a super-LI effect in rats, do not develop conditioned inattention to the nominally unattended stimulus. They are continuously distracted by the irrelevant incidental stimuli, maladaptively maintaining an attentional response to those stimuli.

In a further elaboration of the processes underlying the labile attentional condition that characterizes positive-symptom schizophrenics, Lubow and Gewirtz (1995) have proposed that normal LI develops as a result of conjoint stimulus-context preexposure, whereby context develops occasion-setting properties for the stimulus–no-consequence association. As an occasion setter during the test phase, context prevents the previously exposed stimulus from being primed into short-term memory (STM). This latter point, important for relating the context-LI data to schizophrenia, is speculative. Nevertheless, a number of considerations support this hypothesis (see Lubow, 1989). Normal subjects preexposed to a stimulus under masking conditions do not report awareness of that stimulus (Ginton et al., 1975). Relatedly, high-psychotic–prone subjects, who show less LI than low-psychotic–prone subjects, also have poorer recall and recognition scores for the preexposed stimuli (De la Casa et al., 1993).

Since conscious perception of a stimulus is an accompaniment of its presence in STM, these data suggest that in normals, at time of test, the preexposed stimulus does not readily gain access to STM. In other words, the high distractibility of schizophrenics is a product of the failure of stimulus–no-consequence associations to come under the control of context, thereby rendering

each presentation of the stimulus as functionally novel and, as already noted, resulting in a maintenance of attention to the stimulus and a failure to produce LI.

Indeed, adaptive behavior would seem to require that unimportant stimuli be excluded from STM, which because of its limited capacity can ill afford to be constantly disturbed by ecologically trivial events. Context, acting as an occasion setter, would serve to limit the amount of *previously insignificant* information deployed in STM. This proposal, the data on which it is based, and many of the behaviors commonly agreed to be positive symptoms of schizophrenia (agitation, delusions, hallucinations, and various thought disorders) are all congruent with the notion that in schizophrenics, STM is "preoccupied" with irrelevant stimuli.

Latent Inhibition and Conditioned Aversion Therapies Increasing Therapy Effectiveness

LI may be useful in explaining why certain types of therapies are ineffective, or in providing directions for enhancing therapeutic efficacy. For example, it has been suggested that aversion therapy for alcoholism, in which ethanol ingestion is paired with emetically induced nausea, may be a relatively weak intervention because of the patient's extensive preexposure to alcohol (e.g., Franks & Wilson, 1975). If LI is operative, such preexposure should interfere with the acquisition of the alcohol-sickness association (e.g., Elkins, 1991). However, even the strongest familiarity effects (LI) can be overcome with repeated conditioning episodes. For example, rats may acquire conditioned taste aversion to something as familiar as water, although only after many pairings with a toxicosis-producing US (Elkins, 1974; Riley, Jacobs, & Mastropaolo, 1983). In practice, then, the impeded effectiveness of aversive conditioning therapy with alcoholics due to LI can be counteracted by increasing the number of conditioning episodes. The same counsel would apply to aversive conditioning treatments for other addictive behaviors.

Decreasing Undesirable Side Effects of Some Therapies

Some types of aversive conditioning treatments inadvertently produce undesirable conditioned side effects. Such is the case with radiation and chemotherapies for cancer. Patients undergoing such therapies frequently develop severe gastrointestinal upset and nausea, and often exhibit an aversion to food, to the degree of becoming anorexic (Bernstein & Borson, 1986). The incidence of anticipatory nausea and vomiting among cancer patients receiving chemotherapy has been cited at 71% by Pratt et al. (1984), and 32% by Burish and Carey (1986). Irrespective of the large discrepancy in the estimates, the percentages are significantly high.

It has been suggested that the treatment-induced food aversion is a result of an association of the drug-elicited illness and food taste. Such conditioned taste aversion (CTA) has been repeatedly demonstrated in lower animals (Riley & Tuck, 1985). There is also an extensive literature that documents strong LI effects for CTA in animals, namely that flavor preexposure protects that flavor against the development of an aversion when it is later paired with an event that produces gastrointestinal disturbance (see Lubow, 1989, for a review). CTA and LI of CTA also have been demonstrated in experiments with healthy adult subjects (Arwas et al., 1989; Cannon et al., 1983).

Cannon et al. (1983), using healthy adults, paired a relatively novel cranberry flavor with a nausea-inducing apomorphine injection. The subjects learned an aversion to the *novel* flavor. However, the aversions were reduced markedly when subjects were given pretreatment familiarization (preexposure) to the flavor. This LI of CTA in normal adults was replicated by Arwas et al. (1989) using rotation-induced nausea as the US.

The demonstrations of CTA and LI in *healthy* humans under controlled laboratory conditions supports the contention that food aversions following chemotherapy and radiation treatments are effects of conditioning (e.g., Bernstein & Borson, 1986; Carey & Burish, 1988). Indeed,

experimental induction of CTA has recently been shown in chemotherapy-treated cancer patients (Bovbjerg et al., 1992).

Although familiar flavors acquire some immunity from conditioned aversion, in practice the repeated applications of the cancer-therapeutic procedures, as was already noted in regard to aversion therapies, may overcome such resistance.

If one accepts that chemotherapy-produced food aversions are products of conditioning, and that such conditioning is retarded for familiar flavors, then procedures for reducing those aversions become evident. During the period that patients receive chemotherapy, they should abstain from eating those foods that are part of their regular home or hospital diet and instead consume novel foods. This preemptive avoidance regimen should be adhered to even more stringently as the time interval between food consumption and therapy session is shortened. In this way, the natural protection against conditioned aversion that is offered to familiar foods is enhanced by increasing the interstimulus interval (time between flavor-CS and chemotherapy-US) and thus degrading the effectiveness of the conditioning episode.

Relatedly, Mattes (1994) offered the following rationale for a "scapegoating" procedure for reducing conditioned aversions to familiar foods: "... [B]y purposefully exposing patients to nutritionally inconsequential foods around the time of treatments, aversions will be directed to these items, thereby sparing the preferred and wholesome foods in the patient's customary diet" (p. 14). He found that patients who acquired an aversion to the novel "foil" stimulus had a 30% reduction in "dietary aversion formation" as compared with nonexposed patients or patients who did not develop an aversion to the scapegoat substance. Similar findings have been reported by others (e.g., Andresen et al., 1990; Broberg & Bernstein, 1987). Whether the results of these studies represent the operation of blocking, overshadowing, LI, or some combination of them is not entirely clear. However, irrespective of the source of the effect, the procedures do diminish some of the undesirable food-aversion side effects of the aforementioned therapies.

Preventing Fears and Phobias with Latent Inhibition Procedures

General Issues

Although there are many techniques derived from laboratory studies and theories of learning that have been used in the treatment of behavior disorders, relatively few have been proposed as a means to decrease the probability of developing a particular maladaptive behavior. Such suggestions appear only sporadically (Jaremko, 1978; Jaremko & Wenrich, 1973; Lubow, 1973; Poser, 1970; Poser & King, 1975; Siddle & Remington, 1987). However, LI does suggest a set of procedures that may be useful in reducing the incidence or severity of phobic and fear responses to a variety of common events that may produce dysfunctional avoidance behaviors, as for example school and dental-care avoidance, and such specific phobias (DSM-IV) as those associated with insects, dogs, blood, and so on.

That LI may provide an approach to the prophylactic treatment of fears and phobias follows from a basic assumption of many clinically oriented learning theorists that these deviant behaviors are the result of a conditioning process. Consequently, interfering with the association between the target stimulus and the unconditioned stimulus or response may be useful in aborting the development of such undesirable behaviors. Specific phobias, and intense though rational fears associated with surgery, hospitalization, and dental care, may be the result of early conditionings' being too rapid and too complete. Conditions that would make such learning difficult, namely LI procedures, could provide a preventive therapy, an immunization against the formation of the maladaptive behaviors.

Assuming that the rationale is correct, there are still a number of factors to be considered before implementing an immunization intervention program. Since by definition the treatment is applied *before* the onset of the behavioral problem, one has to identify in advance the target stimuli and behaviors as well as the at-risk populations. As the resources required for the intervention increase, risks, and consequences of the maladaptive behavior must be defined more carefully and restrictively.

A comparison of snake phobia and dental fear/phobia illustrates the trade-offs. Since the probability of casually encountering a snake, at least in an industrial society, is negligible, and the cost of actively avoiding them, unless one is unfortunate enough to be born into a family snake-charming business, is equally small, there appears to be no compelling reason for a parent to introduce a defanged viper into the home. On the other hand, in "modern" societies, professional dental treatment is almost inevitable, and the cost of avoiding it may be more painful and uncomfortable than the remedy itself. Indeed, in many cases the consequences of the avoidance behavior may be irreversible. Clearly, then, there is good reason to develop procedures to reduce the probability of acquiring such fears or phobias, or at least to reduce their intensity.

In theory, LI offers one approach to the prophylactic treatment of fears and phobias, at least to the extent that they have been acquired by conditioning processes (see Rachman, 1990, for an extensive discussion of this issue). Evidence for this assumption can be found in a number of retrospective studies that have surveyed the causal attributions of phobic subjects, particularly in regard to simple phobic stimuli such as dogs, spiders, blood, and injections, as well as for dental fears (for references, see Kleinknecht, 1994). If one broadens the concept of conditioning beyond physical pairings of CSs (e.g., dog) and USs/URs (e.g., bite/pain) to include symbolic and imaginal representations of CSs and USs (Marks, 1987; Rachman, 1990; Reiss, 1980), including cognitive representation of US-expectancy (Davey, 1995), then the list of specific phobias purportedly acquired by conditioning can be extended considerably (for an opposing nonassociative account see Menzies & Clarke, 1995[1]).

---

[1]Menzies and Clarke (1995) present a number of arguments against an etiology of phobias that is exclusively based on conditioning principles. However, their habituation model is also subject to such explanations (e. g., Wagner, 1981).

Whether the underlying mechanism is one based on CS-US contiguity as proposed by Wolpe and Rachman (1960) or more sophisticated contingency/expectancy models (e.g., Davey, 1995) is not of concern here. What is critical is that the conditioning episode approaches the status of a necessary condition for the acquisition of the fear/phobia. That it is not a *sufficient* condition is attested to by the fact that many, if not most, people who are exposed to the critical pairing(s) of CS and US do not develop intense fears. Although this observation has been used to discredit simple conditioning models of phobia acquisition (Rachman, 1978), the conditioning failures may be directly attributable to LI, the very reason for suggesting, in the first place, that LI can be used in the prophylactic treatment of those fears/phobias. Those people who do not develop phobias after exposure to an intense conditioning episode may well be those who have had prior neutral experiences with the CS. Conversely, the well-documented finding that phobias are not distributed equally across objects and events, that it is far more likely to suffer from a spider phobia than a spoon phobia, may simply again reflect the operation of LI (as opposed to, or in addition to, the more usual biological preparedness interpretation; e.g., Seligman, 1971). The relatively novel spider enters into new associations more easily than the familiar spoon. It is probably generally true that fear-irrelevant stimuli are experienced more frequently than fear-relevant stimuli, thereby acquiring protection against being converted into a CS (e.g., Levis & Malloy, 1982; McNally, 1987).

Empirical Support

Although there is a substantial rationale for considering stimulus preexposure as a means of preventing fears and phobias, is there any empirical support for such prophylactic treatment? In the next sections, data from such studies, pertaining to several different fears/phobias, will be examined.

Dental fears and phobias. The dental clinic is an excellent candidate for using LI procedures as a preventive measure to reduce the acquisition of fears and phobias that result from painful treatment. Not only is a large percentage of the population exposed to the fear-producing events of the dental office, but a high percentage of this group does, indeed, develop fears and phobias associated with dental treatment (Gatchel, 1989; Milgrom et al., 1995). According to Weinstein (1990), "A generation of research literature indicates that dental fear and the avoidance of dentists are major public health problems. . . ." (p. 141).

The dental clinic also lends itself to the LI-prophylactic approach because of the relatively well-defined status of the CS (appearance of syringe or drill; grinding, whirring sound and vibratory stimulation of the rotating bit; and so on) and pain-producing US, as well as UR to pain (autonomic responses such as GSR and heart rate, facial expression, increased skeletal muscle tension, withdrawal).

Some dentists have intuitively recognized the value of stimulus preexposure in reducing future fear and anxiety in the dental situation. Indeed, preexposure procedures have been reported in the dental literature since the early 1960s (Weinstein, 1990), reflecting the practice of gradually introducing the young first-time patient to the discomfort of dental treatment. Although it would seem that a thoughtful dentist would never subject the young patient, on first visit, to a painful, frightening treatment such as drilling, Weinstein (1990) found that most dentists continue to treat children such that their initial exposer to the dental-care environment is aversive.

Given the above, it is surprising that there has been such a paucity of LI-research in this area. Such investigations that do exist can be divided into two categories, direct and indirect.

Direct evidence. Only one experimental study has been conducted. Surwit (1972) obtained some evidence for the efficacy of stimulus preexposure, with 3- to 6-year-old children, for reducing initial fear in the dental situation, but not for diminished *acquired* fear, as would be needed to demonstrate LI. However, as Surwit (1972) acknowledged, there were a number of limitations in the study that may have precluded the emergence of such an effect. Of particular importance, during the stimulus preexposure session the experimenter played the role of the dentist, while during the dental treatment itself he was replaced by the real dentist (see following sections on stimulus and context-specificity of LI).

Indirect evidence. Davey (1989) divided university students into groups on the basis of their change of attitude toward dental treatment from initial to current levels, as reported retrospectively. There were two stable groups, in which reported attitude was constant from first to last treatment, one relaxed (R), the other anxious (A); and there were two variable groups, one that changed over time from R to A, and the other from A to R. Although the mean age of first dental treatment was the same for all groups, there was a significant difference in time between first treatment and first "painful or traumatic treatment." The elapsed time was longer for Group R than for Group A. Within Group R, subjects who reported a painful treatment were exposed to it at a later age than comparable subjects in Group A. "The vast majority of subjects in all groups reported regular dental treatment between their first attendance at the dentist and their first painful treatment (between 86% and 94%). . . . Group R had an extra 2–3 years of painless dental treatment before their first trauma than did subjects in Group A. . . ." (Davey, 1989, p. 55). These results, replicated by De Jongh et al. (1995), indicate that the Relaxed group received more painless treatments than the Anxious group *before* the first appearance of pain, that is, they had more stimulus preexposures. Davey (1989) concludes that "these latter facts are clearly consistent with the operation of a process of latent inhibition in Group R" (p. 55). The additional stimulus preexposures served to reduce the associability of the dental situation with pain in Group R, thereby lowering the level of fear of that situation as compared with the nonpreexposed Group A.

Although these data are, indeed, consistent with LI, alternative interpretations are possible. Adult dental fear may be a function of age of first painful experience, with early pain having more of an impact on dental fears than later pain.

Animal and related specific phobias. Among the most common phobias are those that develop to animals, from creepy crawlers such as spiders and snakes to dogs. Animal phobics are also characterized by an early age of onset. Marks and Gelder (1966) report a mean age of onset of 4.4 years (SD = 2.2) for animal phobics, substantially younger than other phobics. In a more recent study, in which 82 percent of the animal phobics reported age of onset below 9 years, Ost (1987) reached the same conclusion. These findings have obvious implications for decisions regarding age of prophylactic treatment, if indeed such treatment is warranted.

There is only one study that relates stimulus preexposure effects to an animal phobia in humans, in this case a survey of dog fears and phobias in children and adults. Doogan and Thomas (1992), as in the dental-fear studies, found that most of their dog-fearful adults reported that the fear was acquired at a relatively young age. However, only half of those adults surveyed could recall a specific event that precipitated the fear. Of these cases, the majority reported episodes that fit the conditioning paradigm, namely an aversive or traumatic encounter with a dog, a finding similar to that of Di Nardo et al. (1988) and Ost and Hugdahl (1981). However, Doogan and Thomas (1992) and Di Nardo et al. (1988) also report that these results are not too different from those obtained from low-fearful respondents, thereby calling into question the conditioning interpretation of fear/phobia acquisition. As already noted, these results can be explained by LI. Differential histories of uneventful preexposures to dogs may account for the fact that some people who experience the conditioning episode acquire the fear/phobia while others with the same conditioning experience do not. Indeed, the Doogan and Thomas (1992) survey indicates that dog-fearful adults had less exposure to dogs *prior to the conditioning episode* than the nonfearful adults, a finding consistent with an LI interpretation, and similar to that reported for dental and snake fears and phobias (Davey, 1989; De Jongh et al., 1995; Murray & Foote, 1979).

As with the dental studies, these survey data are correlational, and they permit some obvious alternative explanations. Ideally, one would want to examine the effects of stimulus preexposure from prospective studies of phobics and non-phobics. Although such data are not available from experiments with humans, there is one study with naive monkeys and phobic stimuli that does manipulate stimulus preexposure and then examines its effects on the ability of a conditioning episode to produce fear (Mineka & Cook, 1986).

Mineka and Cook (1986), who accept the relationship between specific phobias in humans and those in other primates, used rhesus monkeys as observers and models. They compared the efficacy of three manipulations to interfere with the acquisition and retention of snake phobias produced by an observational conditioning procedure. The laboratory-reared subjects were divided into three groups. One group observed a nonfearful monkey engaged in a learning task where the discriminative stimuli included a snake and snakelike objects (modeling-immunization group). A second group received the same amount of exposure to those stimuli, but directly as part of the discrimination problem (LI group). A third group was treated in the same manner as the modeling group except that neutral stimuli were substituted for the snake and snakelike stimuli (pseudoimmunization group). Following the different exposure conditions, all subjects observed a fearful monkey responding to the phobic stimuli. The acquisition and retention of fear responses to the critical stimuli were strongest in the pseudoimmunization group and weakest in the immunization group. The LI group was intermediate, although on most measures it was not *significantly* different from the immunization group. Both pre-exposure procedures showed some effectiveness in preventing the development of conditioned fear.

The Mineka and Cook (1986) procedures probably underestimate the size of the LI effect for two reasons: (1) There was a larger change of context from preexposure to acquisition in the immunization group as compared with the LI group; and, as has been demonstrated repeatedly in lower animals (for a review, see Bouton, 1990), and also in humans (Lubow et al., 1976; Zalstein-Orda & Lubow, 1995), LI is context-specific. That is, a change of context from preexposure to acquisition/test sharply reduces the magnitude of the LI effect. (2) Perhaps even more important, the immunization group was presented with the potentially phobic, to-be-conditioned stimuli under conditions of masking, a condition that enhances LI, at least in humans. During the preexposure phase, subjects in the immunization group most likely attended to the monkey model and to food reinforcement, with the result that the snake stimuli (to which there was no initial fear) were relatively unattended, the optimum conditions for producing LI. On the other hand, for the group designated "LI" by Mineka and Cook, the to-be-conditioned stimuli were the discriminative stimuli in the preexposure phase, thus assuring that the subjects attended to them, a condition that should reduce LI. If this analysis is correct, it would be appropriate to reverse the labeling of the two groups, in which case, of course, there are very strong data to support the LI-phobia-prophylaxis position.

On the basis of their data, Mineka and Cook (1986) offered the following practical advice to parents: ". . . . [P]arents who are concerned that their children might acquire their own fears through observational conditioning may be able to prevent this from occurring. Again, assuming that analogous effects are likely to occur in humans, our results suggest that giving one's children extensive exposure to a nonfearful model interacting with one's feared object should frequently accomplish this immunization" (pp. 317–318). To which, from the present analysis, one might add: Such exposures ought to be designed so that focal attention of the potentially phobic child is directed at some object or event other than the one vulnerable to fear conditioning.

MODULATING THE MAGNITUDE OF THE LATENT INHIBITION EFFECT

Many factors affect the magnitude of LI, at least in the animal literature. As such, these studies not only provide suggestions for means of increasing and decreasing LI, but they also point to potential difficulties that may be encountered in the application of LI techniques in the real world. A review of the relevant variables and supporting evidence can be found in Lubow (1989). Briefly, LI is a positive function of total amount of stimulus preexposures, as contributed to by number and duration of preexposures; intensity of the preexposed stimulus; interval between stimulus preexposures; and others, such as intervals between phases, and context, to be discussed in more detail below. Each of these, in theory, can be manipulated so as to modulate LI, and consequently to govern the magnitude of the treatment effect.

In regard to the application of LI to real-life interventions in behavioral pathology, there are at least three sets of restraints that are potentially important: stimulus- and context-specificity of LI, and the stability of LI over time.

Stimulus-Specificity of Latent Inhibition

The notion of stimulus-specificity, that the effects of preexposure are limited to that stimulus which is preexposed, is central to all theories of LI and forms the basis of *any* learning interpretation of LI effects. Such preexposures do *not* produce a generalized deficit, as might a blow on the head or US preexposure, but rather the magnitude of the learning decrement is proportional to the similarity of the preexposed stimulus to the test stimulus. Indeed, one can demonstrate an orderly stimulus generalization gradient (Siegel, 1967; for a review of the animal literature see Lubow, 1989). As would be expected from the animal literature, there is also evidence for stimulus-specificity in human LI (Lubow et al., 1982; Zalstein-Orda, 1995).

It is easy to see how such specificity might affect LI intervention programs. If one wants to immunize against snake phobia, for example, what should be the stimulus characteristics of the preexposed stimulus? Are the stimulus qualities that define the category semantically the best ones for purposes of conditioning? Will preexposure to a garter snake protect one from developing an irrational fear of a milk snake? Is it sufficient for the therapist to use an object that contains the invariant stimulus property of the category snake, namely elongated, pulsating, sinusoidal, or must the patient be exposed to a variety of exemplars from which the subject will inductively construct a model or prototype that will subsume all those instances of snake that, unless preexposed, may in the future provoke a phobic reaction?

These questions, which also are pertinent to context-specificity, relate to the problem of generalization from specific treatment events to real-world encounters, from which they inevitably differ. The absence of answers reflects the more widespread failure to address problems of generalization in behavior therapy (Rutherford & Nelson, 1988).

Context-Specificity of Latent Inhibition

Just as LI is stimulus-specific, it is also context-specific. LI is severely degraded when the environment of stimulus preexposure is different from that in which the preexposed stimulus is paired with a US. As noted earlier, there are numerous reports of context-specificity of LI in animals (for a review, see Bouton, 1990) as well as humans (Lubow, Rifkin, & Alek, 1976; Zalstein-Orda & Lubow, 1995). The implications of this specificity for the development of LI-based immunization programs are clear. Prophylactic preexposure treatments should be administered in the same environment in which the potentially phobic responses are likely to be acquired. In some cases, at least in principle, this is easily accomplished, as when one knows in advance in which dental clinic and by which dentist the child will be treated. In other cases, as with dog phobia, one cannot easily predict the context in which the potential phobia might be acquired.

Again, as with the stimulus-specificity of LI, resolution of questions in regard to countering the deleterious effects of context change on LI depends on a definition of context and the identification of its critical stimulus parameters. Unfortunately, the processing of context information, as opposed to how context affects the processing of focal information, remains a neglected area, not only in LI research but in cognitive psychology in general.

Stability of Latent Inhibition

In the same way that a useful prophylactic treatment must overcome the effects of variations in target and context from preexposure to acquisition, treatment efficacy will depend on the relative insensitivity of preexposure effects to the amount of time between preexposure and acquisition, and between acquisition and a subsequent acquisition or test session. In other words, the temporal stability of the LI effect must be considered. If, for instance, one knows that the LI effects of dental preexposure dissipate within several days, then prophylactic treatment can be scheduled accordingly. Relatedly, even if one successfully degrades first-trial CS-US association, that pairing may erode the effects of preexposure such that LI effects are no longer present on subsequent CS-US pairings. The effects of these two temporal intervals—preexposure-acquisition and time between first conditioning trial and subsequent CS presentations (with or without the US)—are described below.

Preexposure-Acquisition Interval

The animal literature provides a mixed picture of the effects of varying preexposure-acquisition interval on LI. Some studies indicate long-lasting effects of stimulus preexposure, as much as 21 days (e.g., Alvarez & Lopez, 1995), and others suggest that the effects are considerably more transient. As an example, Ackil et al. (1992) failed to obtain LI with a 10-day interval be-

tween preexposure and conditioning, although they were able to reinstate it with a reminder treatment, a single presentation of the CS prior to the conditioning episode. Unfortunately, there is only one human LI study that manipulated the time between stimulus preexposure and acquisition. Surwit and Poser (1974), using delays of 0, 1, and 24 hrs. and an electrodermal conditioning paradigm, found that, at least for some measures, LI was not affected by delay.

Post-Acquisition Intervals

Since every CS-US pairing counteracts the effects of stimulus preexposure, one needs to know how long LI is maintained after the conditioning session, at least the first one. Here, too, the data are not consistent, with some reports of no LI after a 21-day conditioning-test interval (e.g., De la Casa & Lubow, 1995) and others with a significant LI effect after as much as 10 weeks (Wickens et al., 1983).

CONCLUSIONS

The preceding review of the literature indicates that LI research and theory may play important roles in increasing our understanding of dysfunctional attentional processes in schizophrenia. Likewise, LI has offered some insights into the weaknesses of certain aversion therapies, and it has provided a tool for circumventing some of the undesirable side-effects of other therapies, as with radiation- and chemotherapy.

Finally, a convincing rationale for using LI as a preventive measure to moderate the acquisition of selected fears and phobias has been provided by laboratory studies of conditioning and LI, in both animals and humans. This proposal received some support from correlational studies that suggest that noneventful stimulus preexposure may temper the conditioning effects in selected fear-producing situations such as those encountered in the dental office or in other traumatic confrontations (Davey, 1989; De Jongh et al., 1995; Doogan & Thomas, 1992). Nevertheless, presently there is insufficient experimental evidence to sustain such a position. Such scant data that do exist fail to show unequivocally that stimulus preexposure attenuates the development of fears or phobias (Mineka & Cook, 1986; Surwit, 1972).

Considering the great potential benefit and the relatively low cost of at least some of the prophylactic programs, it can only be hoped that more experimental evidence will be made available so that one can decide if, indeed, an ounce of preexposure is worth a pound of therapy.

ENDNOTES

I thank Ruvi Dar, Michael Rosenbaum, Armonit Roter, and Avi Sadeh for helpful comments and suggestions on an earlier draft of this chapter.

REFERENCES

Ackil, J. K., Carman, H. M., Bakner, L., & Riccio, D. C. (1992). Reinstatement of latent inhibition following a reminder treatment in a conditioned taste aversion paradigm. *Behavioral and Neural Biology, 58*, 232–235.

Alvarez, R., & Lopez, M. (1995). Effects of elements or compound preexposure on conditioned taste aversion as a function of retention interval. *Animal Learning & Behavior. 23*, 391–399.

Andresen, G. V., Birch, L. L., & Johnson, P. A. (1990). The scapegoat effect on food aversions after chemotherapy. *Cancer, 66*, 1649–1653.

Arwas, S., Rolnick, A., & Lubow, R. E. (1989). Conditioned taste aversion in humans using motion-induced sickness as the US: The effects of CS familiarity. *Behavior Research and Therapy, 27*, 295–302.

Baruch, I., Hemsley, D. R., & Gray, J. A. (1988). Differential performance of acute and chronic schizophrenics in a latent inhibition task. *Journal of Nervous and Mental Disease, 176*, 598–606.

Bernstein, I. L., & Borson, S. (1986). Learned food aversion: A component of anorexia syndromes. *Psychological Review, 93*, 462–472.

Bouton, M. E. (1990). Context and retrieval in extinction and in other examples of interference in simple associative learning. In L. Dachkowski & C. F. Flaherty (eds.), *Current topics in animal learning: Brain, emotion, and cognition,* 25–53. Hillsdale, N.J.: Erlbaum.

Bouton, M. E. (1993). Context, time, and memory retrieval in the interference paradigms of Pavlovian conditioning. *Psychological Bulletin, 114*, 80–99.

Bovbjerg, D. H., Redd, W. H., Jacobsen, P. B., et al. (1992). An experimental analysis of classically conditioned nausea during cancer chemotherapy. *Psychosomatic Medicine, 54*, 623–637.

Braff, D. L., (1993). Information processing and attention dysfunctions in schizophrenia. *Schizophrenia Bulletin, 19*, 233–259.

Braunstein-Bercovitz, H. (1997). The effects of masking task load on latent inhibition in low and high schizotypals. Unpublished doctoral dissertation, Tel Aviv University.

Broberg, D. J., & Bernstein, I. L. (1987). Candy as a scapegoat in the prevention of food aversions in children after chemotherapy. *Cancer, 60*, 2344–2347.

Burish, T. G., & Carey, M. P. (1986). Conditioned aversive responses in chemotherapy patients: Theoretical and developmental analysis. *Journal of Consulting and Clinical Psychology, 54*, 593–600.

Cannon, D. S., Best, M. R., Batson, J. D., & Feldman, M. (1983). Taste familiarity and apomorphine-induced taste aversions in humans. *Behavior Research and Therapy, 21*, 669–673.

Carey, M. P., & Burish, T. G. (1988). Etiology and treatment of the psychological side effects associated with cancer chemotherapy: A critical review and discussion. *Psychological Bulletin, 104*, 307–325.

Claridge, G., & Broks, P. (1984). Schizotypy and hemisphere function I: Theoretical considerations and the measurement of schizotypy. *Personality and Individual Differences, 5*, 633–648.

Davey, G. C. L. (1989). Dental phobias and anxieties—evidence for conditioning processes in the acquisition and modification of a learned fear. *Behavior Research and Therapy, 27*, 51–58.

Davey, G. C. L. (1995). Preparedness and phobias: Specific evolved associations or a generalized expectancy bias? *Behavioral and Brain Sciences, 18*, 289–325.

De Jongh, A., Muris, P., Ter Horst, G., & Duyx, M. P. M. A. (1995). Acquisition and maintenance of dental anxiety: The role of conditioning experiences and cognitive factors. *Behavior Research and Therapy, 33*, 205–210.

De la Casa, G., & Lubow, R. E. (1995). Latent inhibition in conditioned taste aversion: The roles of stimulus frequency and duration and the amount of fluid ingested during preexposure. *Neurobiology of Learning and Memory, 64*, 125–132.

De la Casa, L. G., Ruiz, G., & Lubow, R. E. (1993). Latent inhibition and recall/recognition of irrelevant stimuli as a function of preexposure duration in high and low psychotic-prone normals. *British Journal of Psychology, 84*, 119–132.

Di Nardo, P. A., Guzy, L. T., Jenkins, J. A., Bak, R. M., Tomasi, S. F., & Copland, M. (1988). Etiology and maintenance of dog fears. *Behavior Research and Therapy, 26*, 241–244.

Doogan, S., & Thomas, G. V. (1992). Origins of fear of dogs in adults and children: The role of conditioning processes and prior familiarity with dogs. *Behavior Research and Therapy, 30*, 387–394.

Elkins, R. L. (1974). Conditioned flavor aversions to familiar tap water in rats: An adjustment with implications for aversion therapy treatment of alcoholism and obesity. *Journal of Abnormal Psychology, 83*, 411–417.

Elkins, R. L. (1991). An appraisal of chemical aversion (emetic therapy) approach to alcoholism treatment. *Behavior Research and Therapy, 29*, 387–413.

Franks, C. M., & Wilson, G. T. (1975). Behavior therapy and alcoholism. In C. M. Franks & G. T. Wilson (eds.), *Annual review of behavior therapy: Theory and practice*. New York: Brunner/Mazel.

Gatchel, R. J. (1989). The prevalence of dental fear and avoidance: Expanded adult and recent adolescent surveys. *Journal of the American Dental Association, 118*, 591–593.

Ginton, A., Urca, G., & Lubow, R. E. (1975). The effects of preexposure to a nonattended stimulus on subsequent learning: Latent inhibition in adults. *Bulletin of the Psychonomic Society, 5*, 5–8.

Gray, J. A., Feldon, J., Rawlins, J. N. P., Hemsley, D. R., & Smith, A. D. (1991). The neuropsychology of schizophrenia. *Behavioral and Brain Sciences, 14*, 1–84.

Gray, N. S., Hemsley, D. R., & Gray, J. A. (1992). Abolition of latent inhibition in acute, but not chronic, schizophrenics. *Neurology, Psychiatry and Brain Research, 1*, 83–89.

Jaremko, M., (1978). Prophylactic systematic desensitization: An analogue test. *Journal of Behavior Therapy and Experimental Psychiatry, 9*, 5–9.

Jaremko, M., & Wenrich, W. W. (1973). A prophylactic usage of systematic desensitization. *Journal of Behavior Therapy and Experimental Psychiatry, 4*, 103–105.

Kaniel, S., & Lubow, R. E. (1986). Latent inhibition: A developmental study. *British Journal of Developmental Psychology, 4*, 367–375.

Kleinknecht, R. A. (1994). Acquisition of blood, injury, and needle fears and phobias. *Behaviour Research and Therapy, 32*, 817–823.

Levis, D. J., & Malloy, P. F. (1982). Research in infrahuman and human conditioning. In G. T. Wilson & C. M. Franks (eds.), *Contemporary behavior therapy: Conceptual and empirical foundations*, 65–118. New York: Guilford.

Lipp, O. V. , Siddle, D. A. T., & Vaitl, D. (1992). Latent inhibition in humans: Single cue conditioning revisited. *Journal of Experimental Psychology: Animal Behavior Processes, 18*, 115–125.

Lipp, O. V., & Vaitl, D. (1992). Latent inhibition in human Pavlovian differential conditioning: Effect of additional stimulation after preexposure and relation to schizotypal traits. *Personality and Individual Differences, 13*, 1003–1012.

Lubow, R. E. (1973). Latent inhibition as a means of behavior prophylaxis. *Psychological Reports, 32*, 1247–1252.

Lubow, R. E. (1989). *Latent inhibition and conditioned attention theory*. New York: Cambridge University Press.

Lubow, R. E., Caspy, T., & Schnur, P. (1982). Latent inhibition and learned helplessness in children: Similarities and differences. *Journal of Experimental Child Psychology, 34*, 231–256.

Lubow, R. E., & Gewirtz, J. C. (1995). Latent inhibition in humans: Data, theory, and implications for schizophrenia. *Psychological Bulletin, 117*, 87–103.

Lubow, R. E., Ingberg-Sachs, Y., Zalstein-Orda, N., & Gewirtz, J. C. (1992). Latent inhibition in low and high "psychotic-prone" normal subjects. *Personality and Individual Differences, 13*, 563–572.

Lubow, R. E., & Josman, Z. E. (1993). Latent inhibition deficits in hyperactive children. *Journal of Child Psychiatry and Psychology, 34*, 959–973.

Lubow, R. E., & Moore, A. U. (1959). Latent inhibition: The effect of non-reinforced preexposure to the conditioned stimulus. *Journal of Comparative and Physiological Psychology, 52*, 415–419.

Lubow, R. E., Rifkin, B., & Alek, M. (1976). The context effect: The relationship between stimulus preexposure and environmental preexposure determines subsequent learning. *Journal of Experimental Psychology: Animal Behavior Processes, 2*, 38–47.

Lubow, R. E., Weiner, I., Schlossberg, A., & Baruch, I. (1987). Latent inhibition and schizophrenia. *Bulletin of the Psychonomic Society, 25*, 464–467.

Lubow, R. E., Weiner, I., & Schnur, P. (1981). Conditioned attention theory. In G. H. Bower (ed.), *Psychology of learning and motivation*, Vol. 15: 1–49. New York: Academic Press.

Mackintosh, N. J. (1975). A theory of attention: Variations in the associability of stimuli with reinforcement. *Psychological Review, 82*, 276–298.

Marks, I. M., & Gelder, M. G. (1966). Different ages of onset in varieties of phobias. *American Journal of Psychiatry, 123*, 218–221.

Marks, I. M. (1987). *Fears, phobias, and rituals*. New York: Oxford University Press.

Mattes, R. D. (1994). Prevention of food aversions in cancer patients during treatment. *Nutrition and Cancer, 21*, 13–24.

McNally, R. J. (1987). Preparedness and phobias: A review. *Psychological Bulletin, 101*, 283–303.

Menzies, R. G., & Clarke, J. C. (1995). The etiology of phobias: A nonassociative account. *Clinical Psychology Review, 15*, 23–48.

Milgrom, P., Mancl, L., King, B., & Weinstein, P. (1995). Origins of childhood dental fear. *Behavior Research and Therapy, 33*, 313–319.

Miller, R. R., Kasprow, W. J., & Schachtman, T. R. (1986). Retrieval variability: Sources and consequences. *American Journal of Psychology, 99,* 145–218. University Press.

Mineka, S., & Cook, M. (1986). Immunization against the observational conditioning of snake fear in rhesus monkeys. *Journal of Abnormal Psychology, 95,* 307–318.

Murray, E. J., & Foote, F. (1979). The origins of fears of snakes. *Behavior Research and Therapy, 17,* 489–493.

Neuchterlein, K. H., & Dawson, M. E. (1984). Information processing and attentional functioning in the developmental course of the schizophrenic disorder. *Schizophrenia Bulletin, 10,* 160–203.

Ost, L-G. (1987). Age of onset of different phobias. *Journal of Abnormal Psychology, 96,* 223–229.

Ost, L-G., & Hugdahl, K. (1981). Acquisition of phobias and anxiety response patterns in clinical patients. *Behavior Research and Therapy, 21,* 439–443.

Pearce, J. M., & Hall, G. (1980). A model of Pavlovian learning: Variations in the effectiveness of conditioned but not unconditioned stimuli. *Psychological Review, 87,* 532–552.

Poser, E. G. (1970). Toward a theory of "behavioral prophylaxis." *Journal of Behavior Therapy and Experimental Psychiatry, 1,* 39–43.

Poser, E. G., & King, M. C. (1975). Strategies for the prevention of maladaptive fear responses. *Canadian Journal of Behavioral Science, 7,* 279–293.

Pratt, A., Lazar, R. M., Penman, D., & Holland, J. C. (1984). Psychological parameters of chemotherapy induced conditioned nausea and vomiting: A review. *Cancer Nursing, 7,* 483–490.

Rachman, S. (1978). *Fear and courage.* San Francisco: W. H. Freeman.

Rachman, S. (1990). The determinants and treatment of simple phobias. *Advances in Behavioral Research and Therapy, 12,* 1–30.

Reiss, S. (1980). Pavlovian conditioning and human fear: An expectancy model. *Behavior Therapy, 11,* 380–396.

Riley, A. L., Jacobs, W. J., & Mastropaolo, J. P. (1983). The effects of extensive taste preexposure on the acquisition of conditioned taste aversion. *Bulletin of the Psychonomic Society, 21,* 221–224.

Riley, A. L., & Tuck, D. L. (1985). Conditioned food aversions: A bibliography. *Annals of the New York Academy of Science, 443,* 381–438.

Rutherford, R. B., Jr., & Nelson, C. M. (1988). Generalization and maintenance of treatment effects. In J. C. Witt, S.

W. Elliott, & F. M. Gresham (eds.), *Handbook of behavior therapy in education,* 277–324. New York: Plenum.

Schnur, P., & Ksir, C. J. (1969). Latent inhibition in human eyelid conditioning. *Journal of Experimental Psychology, 80,* 388–389.

Seligman, M. E. P. (1971). Phobias and preparedness. *Behavior Therapy, 2,* 307–320.

Siddle, D. A. T., & Remington, B. (1987). Latent inhibition and human Pavlovian conditioning: Research and relevance. In G. C. L. Davey (ed.), *Cognitive processes and Pavlovian conditioning in humans.* Chichester, England: Wiley.

Siegel, S. (1969). Generalization of latent inhibition. *Journal of Comparative and Physiological Psychological Psychology, 69,* 157–159.

Surwit, R. S. (1972). The anticipatory modification of the conditioning of a fear response in humans. Unpublished doctoral dissertation, McGill University.

Wagner, A. R. (1981). SOP: A model of automatic memory processing in animal behavior. In N. E. Spear & R. R. Miller (eds.), *Information processing in animals: Memory mechanisms,* 5–47. Hillsdale, N.J.: Erlbaum.

Weiner, I. (1990). The neural substrates of latent inhibition. *Psychological Bulletin, 108,* 442–461.

Weinstein, P. (1990). Breaking the world-wide cycle of pain, fear and avoidance: Uncovering risk factors and promoting prevention for children. *Annals of Behavioral Medicine, 12,* 141–147.

Wickens, C., Tuber, D. S., & Wickens, D. D. (1983). Memory for the conditioned response: The proactive effect of preexposure to potential conditioning stimuli and context change. *Journal of Experimental Psychology: General, 112,* 41–57.

Wolpe, J., & Rachman, S. (1960). Psychoanalytic "evidence": A critique based on Freud's case of Little Hans. *Journal of Nervous and Mental Disease, 131,* 135–147.

Zalstein-Orda, N. (1995). Effects of context on latent inhibition in human adults. Unpublished doctoral dissertation, Tel Aviv University.

Zalstein-Orda, N., & Lubow, R. E. (1995). Context control of negative transfer induced by preexposure to irrelevant stimuli: Latent inhibition in humans. *Learning and Motivation, 26,* 11–28.

CHAPTER 7

FEAR CONDITIONING AND AVOIDANCE

John J. B. Ayres

Between 1950 and 1970, psychologists were confident that the study of Pavlovian fear conditioning and avoidance learning in laboratory animals would promote the understanding and treatment of human anxiety disorders. A major source of that confidence was the publication by Dollard and Miller (1950) of their book *Personality and Psychotherapy*. In the book, Dollard and Miller showed how human neurotic symptoms could be understood as operant or instrumental avoidance behavior motivated by classically conditioned fear and reinforced by temporary reductions in fear that the symptoms produced. Their theory came to be known as two-process theory (Miller, 1948, 1951; Mowrer, 1947, 1960), a theory derived from early animal work in operant and Pavlovian conditioning and which in turn spawned decades of further research on Pavlovian fear conditioning and avoidance (Denny, 1991; Levis, 1989; Rescorla & Solomon, 1967). The

1970s, however, witnessed rising doubts about the relevance of Pavlovian conditioning models to human phobias and even about the ability of two-process theory to predict and explain animal avoidance, let alone human neurotic symptoms.

First, experimental analysts of behavior (Skinnerians) had always criticized intervening variable approaches to the study of behavior, and they readily published their objections to the construct of fear. Hineline (1973), for example, argued that the term *fear* was vague and imprecise and that it suffered from the usual problems of misunderstanding that plague any technical term taken from everyday parlance. He argued that the parsimony that patrons of the fear concept hoped to achieve was illusory. With each new fact that they tried to explain with the concept, they added some new, post hoc idea. Moreover, their measures of fear were poorly correlated, questioning whether a unitary entity was being measured.

Second, respected authorities closely aligned with clinical practice began to doubt the relevance of Pavlovian fear conditioning models even to simple phobias (for a review, see Sturgis & Scott, 1984). They argued that phobias often arose in the absence of any trauma or unconditioned stimulus (US). They cited instances, such as the London air raids, in which repeated traumas failed to induce phobias in large numbers of people. They noted that phobias attached more readily to some cues than to others, violating the equipotentiality principle that they saw as part of Pavlovian dogma. They cited forms of learning other than Pavlovian conditioning that led to phobias: vicarious learning, for example. They argued that phobias often arose from a single trauma but claimed that there was little evidence in animal research for one-trial learning.

Third, strong competitors to the two-process theory of avoidance learning emerged. Herrnstein (1969), while granting that Pavlovian conditioning occurred during avoidance learning, denied its relevance to avoidance behavior. Moreover, rather than citing the reduction of classically conditioned fear as a source of reinforcement for avoidance behavior, he stressed the fact that the behavior lowers the frequency of aversive events (Sidman, 1962). Thus, in many laboratory experiments with animals, electric shocks occur at a high rate before an avoidance response but at a low rate afterwards. The response is thereby negatively reinforced: it is strengthened by the removal of shock, an observable stimulus. On this view, fear as motivator and fear reduction as reinforcer are superfluous concepts: the behavior can be explained in terms of observables, and there is no need to appeal to nonobservables such as fear. Bolles (1970, 1971, 1972, 1975, 1978) downplayed the role of reinforcement in avoidance learning altogether and instead advanced the idea that avoidance responses in laboratory animals are examples of species-specific defense reactions (SSDRs). It does not seem unreasonable from Bolles's position to conclude that avoidance responses that are SSDRs for rats have little to do with the human condition. Is it likely that symptoms such as compulsive hand washing or heart-

rate counting or hysterical blindness or deafness could have been SSDRs for hominids during their evolution?

My goals in this chapter are to address more broadly these doubts about the relevance of Pavlovian fear conditioning to simple phobias and to human anxiety disorders. First, I want to present a definition of conditioned fear and discuss some evolutionary/adaptational ideas that give coherence to behaviors connected with it. Then I want to describe some techniques used to study fear conditioning in laboratory animals, showing how each exploits an antipredator behavior known to be adaptive in the wild. Next, I want to review the aforementioned criticisms of Pavlovian conditioning models of human phobias and, using data from the techniques described earlier, show why these criticisms are unsound. Last, I want to look at some theories of avoidance learning and related evidence to see whether fear theory really has been displaced by its competitors. Along the way, I hope that some implications for the understanding and treatment of human anxiety disorders will emerge.

FEAR CONDITIONING

Definition and Behavioral Effects of Conditioned Fear

Conditioned fear is often defined as a central state (a hypothetical construct) produced by an initially neutral stimulus (CS) after it has been consistently paired with an aversive stimulus (US). The fear state is then assumed to produce a cluster of behavioral effects or to explain those effects (cf. Davis, 1992, p. 255).

An organizing principle for anticipating the behavioral effects of fear was suggested by Ratner (1967), who proposed that in the wild, the approach of a threatening stimulus such as a natural predator would evoke a sequence of four distinct behaviors in the prey. The first to occur would be freezing (immobile crouching). Prey movement is a major cue that triggers attack in many species of predators (Fox, 1969; Herzog & Burghardt, 1974; Kaufman, 1974; Thompson, Foltin, Boylan, Sweet, Graves, & Lowitz, 1981; Van Hemel & Colucci, 1973). Therefore, freezing should and does occur in a wide range of prey species (Hofer, 1970) and is known to reduce the odds of attack (Herzog & Burghardt, 1974; Hirsch & Bolles, 1980; White & Weeden, 1966). If freezing should fail to stop the approach of the predator, the next behavior in the sequence would be flight. If flight were in vain, the prey might try to fight. Finally, if the predator caught and physically restrained the prey, the last antipredator behavior would be tonic immobility (TI). TI is a state of motor paralysis or inhibition that can last for a few seconds or for hours and "may be associated with catatonic-like waxy flexibility and fine Parkinsonian-like muscle tremors in the extremities" (Gallup, 1974, p. 837). TI has been seen in a wide variety of species, including groups as diverse as insects, crustaceans, fish, amphibians, reptiles, birds, and mammals (Ratner, 1967). Gallup and Maser (1977) have detailed at least 13 features that TI shares with the catalepsy and cataplexy seen in human catatonics (see also Ratner, Karon, VandenBos, & Denny 1981), and Suarez and Gallup (1979) have equated TI to rape-induced paralysis in human rape victims. TI reduces the chances of sustained attack by cats on Japanese quail (Thompson et al., 1981), by foxes on ducks (Sargeant & Eberhardt, 1975), and by fighting cocks on each other (Herzog, 1978). It may also reduce the odds of sustained attack by rapists on their victims (Suarez & Gallup, 1979).

Fanselow (1984b) has expanded Ratner's (1967) organizing principle, permitting a more detailed forecast of the behavioral effects of fear. According to Fanselow, fear is a "motivational system that organizes an animal's responding at many different levels (e.g., overt behavior, autonomic functioning, etc.) so that it is co-ordinated toward the function of protecting the animal from environmental threats, more particularly predation" (1984, p. 460). Fanselow proposes that fear restricts the animal's behaviors to a small number of SSDRs, behaviors with an evolutionary history of thwarting predation. Of these, the dominant behavior in laboratory rats, at least, is freezing (Fanselow & Lester, 1988).

In the laboratory, freezing tends to occur in preferred locations: next to a wall, in a corner, or in a darkened area (Aitken, 1974; Allison, Larson, & Jensen, 1967; Grossen & Kelley, 1972). Fanselow proposes that these locations may optimize the antidetection properties (crypticity) of freezing. Freezing is accompanied by heart-rate deceleration (Hofer, 1970) and shallow, rapid breathing (Hofer, 1970). Hofer described the breathing as "almost imperceptible to the eye, perhaps contributing to the likelihood of the animal being overlooked by a visually scanning predator" (1970, pp. 644–645). The heart-rate deceleration resembles that associated with increased attention and decreased reaction time (Lacey, 1967; Obrist, Sutterer, & Howard, 1972). Fanselow thus suggests that the fearful prey becomes increasingly vigilant and ready to spring into action.

While freezing, the animal also becomes analgesic. Cues that have been paired with moderate shock produce the analgesia by triggering the endogenous opioid system (Fanselow, 1984a). Cues that have been paired with more severe shock apparently produce an analgesia that is at least in part nonopioid (Fanselow, 1984a). Fanselow and Sigmundi (1982) suggested that the function of the analgesia is to reduce the likelihood of recuperative behavior (e.g., wound licking)—behavior that would disrupt the SSDRs needed for immediate survival. By disrupting freezing, for example, recuperative behavior would reduce crypsis and likely trigger further attack. Since TI is another fear response that results in immobility, we might expect similar physiological reactions during it as during freezing. Indeed, in chickens, at least, evidence exists for heart-rate deceleration and increased respiration rate during TI (Nash, Gallup, & Czech, 1976); and in rabbits, there is evidence for an analgesia that is mediated by endogenous opioids (for a review, see Porro & Carli, 1988).

One benefit of thinking of fear behaviors in terms of their adaptive value is that such thinking helps us see that some behaviors that might be offered as indices of fear probably are not. For example, Davis (1992) listed grooming in animals among the behavioral effects of fear and likened it to fidgeting in humans. He asserted that fidgeting was one of the DSM III criteria of generalized anxiety. Clearly, grooming is not a behavior that we would expect of an animal facing predation (Hirsch & Bolles, 1980), and we should be surprised to see it in laboratory animals given a CS that had been paired with a noxious US. Mast, Blanchard, and Blanchard (1982) provided relevant data using a time-sampling procedure to score the behaviors of rats during one-minute light presentations, each of which ended with a brief shock. Before the light signaled shock, grooming occurred on about 18% of the samples taken during the light. Over the last 4 days of light-shock pairings, grooming occurred on only 0.05% of those samples. This result supports our prediction based on adaptational concerns and implies that grooming is *not* an index of fear.

Popular Laboratory Measures of Conditioned Fear

In their well-known chapter on the measurement of conditioned fear, McAllister and McAllister focused on measures "in which the conditioning of fear and its measurement are generally considered to be independent" (1971, p. 107). By this they meant that the US "is assumed to have its effect on the conditioning of fear but not *directly* on the measured response." Under this constraint, they focused on four measures: (1) learning to escape fear, (2) change in performance as a result of conditioned punishment, (3) CS-evoked change in the rate of an ongoing response, and (4) CS modulation of the magnitude of an unlearned response.

In the escape-from-fear task, a CS, such as light, tone, or white noise that has previously been paired with a noxious US, such as shock, is presented in one side of a shuttle box. Leaving the box or jumping over a hurdle into an adjacent box turns off the CS. Latency to make such a response is a typical dependent measure. The latencies first decrease over trials as the escape behavior is learned, then increase as repeated CS trials with no USs cause the extinction of fear to the CS (McAllister, McAllister, Scoles, & Hampton, 1986).

In the conditioned punishment task, brief presentations of a CS that has been paired with shock are made to follow a response that is instrumental in obtaining reward. That response might be bar pressing or running down an alleyway. The CS usually results in a lowered response rate.

In the CS-evoked-change-in-rate task, a CS that has been paired with shock is presented independently of some ongoing behavior. That behavior typically is bar pressing for food or licking a dipper or the sipper tube of a water bottle. The result is that the ongoing behavior is suppressed, a result termed *conditioned suppression*. The chief difference between the conditioned punishment and conditioned suppression techniques is that in conditioned punishment, brief CSs (e.g., 1 to 2 s) are made contingent on the animal's behavior, whereas in the conditioned suppression procedure, longer CSs (e.g., 20 s to 10 min) are given independently of the animal's behavior, usually at times that the experimenter has preset.

The fourth measure the McAllisters described involved CS-evoked changes in the magnitude of an unlearned response. The example they gave was "fear potentiated startle." Here, some stimulus, usually a brief, loud tone, is presented that unconditionally evokes a startle response. The magnitude of the startle evoked by the tone alone is compared with the magnitude of the startle evoked by the tone in the presence of a CS previously paired with shock. Typically the magnitude is much greater if the tone is presented during the CS. The difference between the two magnitudes is taken as an index of fear conditioned to the CS.

A second example of the fourth measure uses tonic immobility (TI) as the unlearned response to be modulated by changes in fear. Much research has shown that the duration of TI is increased by factors thought to increase fear and is decreased by factors thought to decrease fear (for reviews that support the claims that follow about

TI, see Gallup, 1974, 1977; Gallup & Maser, 1977). A typical manipulation is to give (vs. not give) the fear-altering procedure just before manually restraining the subject for a set time, then release the subject and measure the duration of TI. Sometimes the putative fear enhancer is presented (vs. withheld) during the TI bout itself. Some of the procedures thought to be fear enhancing that increase the duration of TI are suspension over a visual cliff, exposure to (presumably predatory) experimenters, models of predators, loud noise, electric shock, and injections of adrenalin. Of most interest to students of Pavlovian fear conditioning is the fact that CSs previously paired with shock also increase the duration of TI and do so in proportion to the intensity of the shock. These procedures do not work simply by increasing arousal, because food deprivation, which should also increase arousal, has no effect on the duration of TI.

Some of the procedures thought to be fear reducing that decrease the duration of TI are ingestion of tranquilizers; presence of members of the same species; and the presence of nearby escape routes, such as bushes. But again, of most interest to students of Pavlovian fear conditioning is the fact that at least one procedure thought to establish a CS as a conditioned inhibitor of fear (Moscovitch & LoLordo, 1968) creates a CS that dramatically reduces the duration of TI. In this conditioning procedure, sometimes called *cessation conditioning*, shock USs were repeatedly presented, and the CS always began just before US cessation, then persisted into part of the inter-US interval.

Unfortunately, Pavlovian fear conditioning has been used as a tool for studying TI more than TI has been used as a tool for studying Pavlovian fear conditioning. TI awaits to be so exploited. One of its appealing features in that regard is that it requires nothing more complex than a stopwatch for its measurement.

Clearly, all four of the techniques the McAllisters discussed exploit antipredator behaviors known to be adaptive in the wild. The escape-from-fear task relies on the flight response. The conditioned suppression task relies largely on the freezing response. Animals also freeze during the CS in the fear-potentiated-startle task, and the measure accordingly exploits the animal's tendency to remain vigilant during freezing and ready to spring into action (i.e., startle). Fear-potentiated TI likewise exploits one of Ratner's (1967) four stages of antipredator behavior. As for conditioned punishment, I am not aware of a study that directly assessed freezing during the procedure, but it seems likely that freezing would occur and would correlate with the degree of response suppression.

It is worth noting that a number of high correlations have been found between some of these measures of fear. Freezing correlates highly with bar-press conditioned suppression (Ayres & Vigorito, 1984; Bouton & Bolles, 1980; Mast et al., 1982) and with the degree of potentiated startle (Leaton & Borszcz, 1985). In addition, in a study of shock intensity and dosage level of anxiolytic drugs, group mean levels of freezing and analgesia correlated highly (Fanselow & Helmstetter, 1988). And just as TI is reduced by drugs thought to be fear reducing, so are freezing and analgesia (Fanselow & Helmstetter, 1988) and fear potentiated startle (Davis, 1992). And just as TI is reduced by putative conditioned inhibitors of fear, so are conditioned suppression (LoLordo & Fairless, 1985) and fear-potentiated startle (Falls & Davis, 1995). The foregoing review thus suggests that behaviors thought to occur in response to fear are indeed coherent and may all reflect a unitary entity: fear.

Pavlovian Conditioning Models of Simple Phobia: Criticisms and Rebuttals

Earlier, I noted a number of criticisms that had been raised about animal Pavlovian conditioning models of simple phobias in humans. The following paragraphs list and discuss each criticism.

1. Phobias often arise in the absence of any trauma or US. This point has been rebutted at some length in a recent chapter by McAllister and McAllister (1995), and I shall condense their rebuttal here. The McAllisters describe two studies by Ost and Hugdahl. The first (Ost & Hugdahl, 1981) examined patients with animal or social phobias or with claustrophobia. Of these patients, only 15% could not recall some event (US) that led to the phobia. The second (Ost & Hugdahl, 1983) found that only 10% of agoraphobics could not recall such an event. These findings do not necessarily mean that there was no precipitating event in the 10% to 15% of the patients who could not recall. They may mean only that human memory is fallible. Supporting that view, Loftus (1993) found that 14% of 590 persons interviewed in a U.S. government study did not recall being injured in an accident (a US) that was known to have occurred within the past year. Likewise, she reported in another study that 25% of 1,500 persons known to have been hospitalized within the past year did not recall that hospitalization (US).

2. Repeated traumas often fail to induce phobias (e.g., London air raids). This fact should not surprise students of Pavlovian conditioning. Indeed, to use it as an argument against Pavlovian conditioning models is much like using the flight of airplanes as evidence against the law of gravity. Airplanes fly not because the law of gravity is wrong but because other principles can counteract gravity's effects. There are many ways of counteracting conditioning in situations that might otherwise favor its occurrence. For example, exposing the CS before pairing it with a US is well known to retard the acquisition of conditioned responding (Lubow, 1989; see also Lubow, this volume). In the conditioned suppression procedure with rats, the crucial parameter in producing that retardation is the total time of the so-called CS preexposure, not the number of CS preexposures per se (Albert & Ayres, 1989; Ayres, Philbin, Cassidy, Bellino, & Redlinger, 1992).

It is also difficult to establish a CS as a conditioned excitor of fear if it has first been established as a conditioned inhibitor of fear (Hammond, 1968; LoLordo & Fairless, 1985; Rescorla, 1969a). One way of viewing that situation is that it is hard to condition fear to a CS that already controls a competing emotional state. When we think about Londoners during the air raids, we need to specify the CSs that would have stood in position to become conditioned. Perhaps the CSs would have been one's home, an air raid shelter, the friends and neighbors and family with whom one hid during a raid. All of these CSs would likely have already controlled emotional responses incompatible with fear.

The sound of sirens and of planes flying overhead is another likely CS. But how many times had such sounds been experienced (and what was the total duration of that experience) before the sounds were paired with trauma? Assuming that fear had been conditioned to signs of an air raid, what would have been the role of conditioned inhibitors in preventing the expression of that fear?

It is easy to demonstrate the role of fear inhibitors in the conditioned suppression procedure with rats. Suppose every presentation of a 2-minute light ends with a brief shock except when that light appears with a 2-minute tone. The end result of such a procedure is that conditioned suppression occurs during the light alone but not during the compound of tone plus light (Rescorla, 1976; Witcher & Ayres, 1984). The tone thus inhibits the expression of fear during the light.

In the London air raids, there would clearly be many conditioned inhibitors of fear. The presence of family and neighbors, being in one's home or an air raid shelter, the existence of smoothly functioning civil defense units in the neighborhood, rescue squads, good medical facilities, temporary shelter and welfare for those made homeless—all of these things can be viewed as conditioned inhibitors of fear. All would be expected to reduce the odds that fear would result in observable symptoms. In addition, we need to consider the role of other emotional states in Londoners at the time—such states as hatred for the Germans and determination to survive and protect home and family. Wouldn't these states be likely to compete with fear conditioning and its expression?

Finally, we need to be aware that the original premise that anxiety disorders were not widespread among the Londoners who underwent bombing is a bit of an overgeneralization. Whether or not individuals acquired a phobia or strong fear depended on many factors, most of which are consistent with a Pavlovian analysis. For example, one of the most important factors was whether the individual had personally experienced a *near miss* versus a *remote miss* (Janis, 1951, p. 112). A person who experiences only remote misses receives only CS-preexposure trials, an experience known to retard fear conditioning. However, "[s]evere and prolonged fear reactions are most likely to occur among those who undergo near-miss experiences, i.e., direct exposure to the physical impact of the air attack (knocked down by blast, injured, home destroyed, etc.)" (Janis, 1951, p. 123).

3. Phobias attach more readily to some cues than to others, in violation of the equipotentiality principle. This criticism is based on the uneven distribution of phobias throughout a target population. For example, a survey of fears in a sample of 325 residents of Burlington, Vermont (Agras, Sylvester, & Oliveau, 1969) found that 39% of the sample had a fear of snakes, but only 19.8% had a fear of the dentist. This fact seems counter to what might be expected on the basis of the laws of Pavlovian conditioning. Surely more subjects in the sample suffered pain at the hands of a dentist than at the fangs of a snake. Facts like these are often taken to demand adherence to a notion of prepotency (Marks, 1969) or preparedness (Seligman, 1971; Seligman & Hager, 1972). The idea is that we are especially prepared to become phobic about things that endangered our forebears during the course of hominid evolution. It is claimed that this idea is inconsistent with the equipotentiality notion of Pavlovian conditioning models, which is that all CSs are created equal in their ability to gain control over a conditioned response. There are many things that need to be said here.

First, regarding fears of snakes, I would not be surprised if none of those Vermonters who were so afraid had ever experienced pain at the fangs of a snake. But those who would take that likely possibility as an indictment of Pavlovian conditioning models have a very narrow view of Pavlovian conditioning. Pavlovian conditioning is simply a procedure in which an experimenter (or nature) sets up a relation between two or more stimuli. In the simplest case, the relation is between only two stimuli. The usual way of describing that relation is that it is one of temporal and/or spatial contiguity. The Pavlovian conditioning result is that because of the relation that was established, the response to one of the stimuli changes. So if I see a snake (stimulus 1) and then am bitten by that snake (stimulus 2), I may respond differently the next time I see a snake. Or if I see a snake (stimulus 1) and then see my mother look at it in horror and pull away (stimulus 2), I may also react differently the next time I see one. Or if I hear the word *snake* (stimulus 1), followed by some scary account of what snakes do (stimulus 2), I may react differently to snakes in the future.

Each of the preceding examples fits the definition of Pavlovian conditioning. Very few of us have been stabbed while taking a shower, but most of us who saw Alfred Hitchcock's movie *Psycho* felt a bit of a twinge when we stepped into the shower after seeing the movie—if we were brave enough even to do so. Hitchcock was a master of Pavlovian conditioning. Even when he chose to use CSs such as showers, which, presumably, played a minor role in the history of hominid evolution, and even though he used as the US the sight of someone else being stabbed instead of ensuring that we ourselves were stabbed, he had little trouble in conditioning our fears.

Second, just as there are factors that countered phobic conditioning in the London air raids, there are factors that work against acquiring dental fears. For example, has the patient been exposed to the dentist repeatedly before the first painful experience? What sort of conditioning of competing emotional states occurred before that experience? Was the patient fussed over by the dentist or the parents, praised for being good, and given a treat at the end of those early painless visits? What was the nature of the patient's pre-conditioning history in terms of operant reinforcement for bravery, and what Pavlovian experience did the patient have with the association between bravery and respect? Did the patient have an operant/Pavlovian history in which the stimulus consequences of avoiding treatment for a little pain at time 1 were followed by much greater pain at time 2? Did the patient have a history in which a mildly painful treatment resulted in the removal of more pain or the avoidance of future pain or in the termination of CSs previously paired with pain? (More on these issues later.)

Third, another factor often overlooked in discussions about preparedness or prepotency is the role of inhibitory contexts. I discussed this role earlier in relation to the London bombings. Recall that an inhibitor of fear is a cue that denotes that an otherwise dangerous cue is not dangerous. Consider this in relation to Marks's statement: "Given equally painful experiences with automobiles, bricks, grass, animals and bicycles, humans are much more likely to become fearful of animals than of the other objects. In other words, certain stimuli seem to be like lightning conductors toward which our fears are directed" (1977, p. 179). What might be the role of fear inhibitors here? I would suggest that automobiles, bricks, grass, and bicycles usually occur in the presence of conditioned inhibitors of fear. The automobile has never hurt me when it was parked in my garage, especially with no one in it and me not fooling around with it. The stimuli of being stationary, of being empty, and of being removed from me, like the tone whose presence signals that the light will not be followed by shock, are all inhibitors of fear.

Similar claims can be made about bricks, grass, and bicycles. But these claims cannot be made about animals. When the Doberman is a block away, it could still come after me. Even the presence of its owner might not save me, even when the dog is on a leash. I've been bitten by a dog that, until the moment it bit me, seemed perfectly content with my petting it. I've seen a Rottweiler jump through its owner's plate glass door

to get at a repairman. So where are the conditioned inhibitors of fear? If automobiles, bricks, grass, and bicycles were as uninhibited as animals, I'd be afraid of them too, even if they were not a part of my ancestral experience.

Fourth, even Pavlov, who emphasized the enormous range of stimuli that could serve as CSs (Pavlov, 1927/1960, p. 38), never claimed that all CSs are equally conditionable. Indeed his demonstrations of complete overshadowing revealed the opposite: in complete overshadowing, one member of a two-element compound CS gains all the conditioned value while its mate gains none. However, that same mate, if reinforced alone, becomes highly conditioned.

Suppose that because of their evolutionary history some CSs are indeed easier to condition than others. Is that an indictment of Pavlovian conditioning models? I take it as an article of faith that every aspect of the lives of organisms is touched in some way by evolution. Why should Pavlovian conditioning be exempt?

4. Forms of learning other than Pavlovian conditioning (e.g., vicarious learning) lead to phobias. As an example of vicarious learning, Sturgis and Scott (1984) describe a case that was treated by Dr. Victor Meyer of Middlesex Hospital. The case involved two sisters who were walking in the park when one was attacked by a bird. Both sisters later developed phobias of flying birds, but the phobia was stronger in the observing sister than in the victim. Although this example was offered as showing a form of learning other than Pavlovian conditioning, it looks much like Pavlovian conditioning to me. The sight of a flying bird (stimulus 1) was followed closely by the sight of the attack and the frightened reactions of the sister (stimulus 2). After that, the reactions of the observing sister to flying birds (stimulus 1) was different. One might argue about whether the case illustrates first-order as against second-order conditioning (Rescorla, 1980), but the procedure and result clearly meet the definition of Pavlovian conditioning. But why did the observer become more fearful than the victim? Well, how badly was the victim hurt? How well did she see the whole incident in comparison to the observer? How did the past conditioning histories of the two sisters differ?

5. Phobias often arise from a single trauma, but there is little evidence in the animal experimental literature for one-trial learning. This is a very strange criticism. Reflection should reveal that evidence for learning in N trials is evidence for learning in one trial. If an animal could not learn something in one trial, then it could not learn anything in N trials. If the strength of learning were zero at the end of trial 1, then it would be zero at the start of trial 2. Since trial 2 is only one trial, and if learning can't occur in one trial, then learning would have to be zero at the end of trial 2 and at the start of trial 3, and so on. However, it is one thing to argue on logical grounds that learning *must* occur in one trial and another thing altogether to show that a single CS-US pairing can strongly affect subsequent responding to the CS.

Fortunately, the animal experimental literature contains many such demonstrations in fear conditioning. Some of these demonstrations use discrete cues presented in a conditioning chamber as CSs—cues such as a brief white noise or pure tone, whose relevance, incidentally, to the animal's ancestral history is debatable (see, e.g., Balaz, Kasprow, & Miller, 1982; Bevins & Ayres, 1992 [and references cited therein]; Burkhardt, 1980; Emmerson & DeVietti, 1982; Mackintosh, 1971; Mackintosh & Reese, 1979; Yeo, 1974). Other demonstrations have used the conditioning chamber itself as the CS (see, e.g., Bevins & Ayres, 1992; Blanchard, Fukunaga, & Blanchard, 1976; Fanselow, 1986; Kiernan & Westbrook, 1993; Maes & Vossen, 1992; Westbrook, Good, & Kiernan, 1994). In rats, such conditioning has been measured using both conditioned suppression techniques and directly observed freezing. Although shock was the US in these studies, there is no reason to believe that the generality of such one-trial fear conditioning in animals is limited to shock. Recent experiments, for example, have shown one-trial conditioning of fear to contextual cues in which a 30-second exposure to carbon dioxide served as the US (Mongeluzi, Rosellini, Caldarone, Stock, & Abrahamsen, 1996). Conditioning was assessed in terms of both freezing and analgesia measures.

AVOIDANCE LEARNING

An avoidance response (Ra) is one that prevents an otherwise scheduled event from occurring. Two-process theory makes two assumptions in explaining how such Ras are learned. First, it assumes that Ras are motivated by Pavlovian conditioned fear and/or are under the operant stimulus control of the stimulus properties of fear states. Second, it assumes that Ras are instrumental in producing temporary reductions in fear and are reinforced by those reductions. Thus, an Ra is learned not because it *avoids* some future event but rather because it *escapes* from a fear state that is currently present. Recent writers (e.g., McAllister & McAllister, 1991) advocate renaming this theory *fear theory* so as to divorce it from added assumptions made in early statements of two-process theory (e.g., Mowrer, 1947). Those added assumptions are not needed to explain avoidance and are hard to defend.

In many experiments on avoidance learning, the Ra terminates a feared discrete CS. Fear theorists assume that this CS offset can reinforce the Ra. An important elaboration of this assumption has been termed *effective reinforcement theory* (McAllister, McAllister, & Douglass, 1971). The empirical basis for this expanded assumption is the result of a shock-escape experiment by Campbell and Kraeling (1953) in which rats learned to escape more readily from a 200-V shock to a 100-V shock than they did from a 400-V shock to a 200-V shock. This result suggests that reduction in shock intensity from 200 V to 100 V is a more effective reinforcer for escape behavior than is reduction from 400 V to 200 V.

The effective reinforcement principle in fear theory applies this idea directly to the shuttle box avoidance task. For example, suppose for group 1 the CS and the context in which the CS is embedded together evoke 200 units of fear. Suppose the context alone evokes 100 units. Suppose for group 2 the CS and the context together evoke 400 units of fear and the context alone evokes 200 units. A response that terminates the CS, leaving only the context, will be more effectively reinforced in group 1 than in group 2. From this example, we see that it's not the absolute size of the drop in fear produced by CS offset that's critical. Rather, it's the size of the drop in relation to the amount of fear that continues to be evoked by the context after the CS has ended. A drop from 400 to 200 units of fear is actually less reinforcing than a drop from 200 to 100 units of fear even though the former drop of 200 units is larger (in absolute magnitude) than the latter drop of 100 units.

Although I just emphasized CS termination as a source of fear reduction in fear theory, the theory actually claims that *anything* that reduces fear following an Ra can reinforce that response. Thus, the theory holds that a conditioned inhibitor of fear, if given after a response, could reinforce the response *even if the response did not end the feared CS*. It also holds that any form of generalization decrement that reduces CS-evoked fear, context-evoked fear, or both could reinforce an Ra, provided that it follows that Ra.

An early experiment using rats (Miller, 1948) strongly supported fear theory and had enormous implications for the understanding and treatment of human anxiety disorders. The experiment was complex and has been criticized on several grounds (Bolles, 1975, p. 360; Brown & Jacobs, 1949), yet the force of those criticisms has been muted by subsequent work (e.g., Brown & Jacobs, 1949), and its conclusions have been so well supported and so influential that its recitation here seems mandatory.

Miller's apparatus was a two-chambered box. One chamber was white and had a grid floor; the other was black and had a wooden floor. Between the two chambers was a wall, the lower half of which was a guillotine door that could be dropped so that its top edge rested at floor level. Above this door was mounted a wheel, a bit like a steamboat paddle wheel. The wheel could be rigged so that turning it slightly could open the guillotine door. On a wall to the rat's left as it faced the door was mounted a small lever. The lever, too, could be rigged so that pressing it could open the door.

The study began with some initial preference testing that showed that the rat had no preference for either chamber. Next were some rather complex procedures, all of which involved shocking the rat in the white chamber. The aim was to condition fear to the white box cues. There then followed some more complex procedures, all of which involved shocking the rat in the white box and leaving that shock on until the rat ran though the open door into the black box. After 10 of these escape-from-shock trials, shock was never used again.

The results from the next three phases of the experiment, performed without shock, are of most interest. In the first of these, the rat was placed in the white box, and the door was opened. This was done for five trials. The result was that on each of the five trials the rat ran from the white box into the black box even though there was no shock in the white box. In the next phase, the rat was again placed in the white box, with the door now locked. Turning the paddle wheel above the door would open it. In this phase, 13 of 25 rats tested learned to turn the wheel enough to open the door, whereupon they ran into the black box. For the remaining 12 rats, SSDRs, mainly the SSDR of freezing in the white box, interfered with learning to wheel turn. For the 13 rats that did learn, the latency to turn the wheel decreased significantly across the 16 trials in this phase.

In the last phase, wheel turning no longer opened the door, but the lever was rigged so that pressing it did open the door. The result was that wheel turning extinguished over the course of 10 trials and was replaced by lever pressing. The latencies to lever press decreased significantly over these trials.

According to fear theory, the responses of running out of the white box in the absence of shock, wheel turning, and lever pressing were all instrumental responses that were motivated by fear, itself a Pavlovian conditioned response that was evoked by the white box. Each instrumental response was learned because it allowed the rat to exit the white box, thus ending the feared CS (escape from fear) and thereby causing fear reduction to follow the response. When one of the responses (wheel turning) lost its effectiveness, it extinguished, but fear persisted, motivating other responses (lever presses) and reinforcing them by terminating after their occurrence.

The reason the experiment was so influential was that it provided an animal model for symptom learning in human anxiety disorders. Like the wheel-turn and lever-press responses, human symptoms were held to be instrumental responses motivated by Pavlovian conditioned fear and reinforced by the temporary reductions in fear that they brought about. The implication for treatment was that human neurotic symptoms should *not* be treated directly without regard to their underlying fear motivation, because as long as the fear persisted, it would merely motivate a new symptom (lever pressing would replace wheel turning). The therapist was thus encouraged to find out what CSs evoked the Pavlovian conditioned fear and to present those CSs without USs until the fear extinguished. The symptom should then disappear.

Years later, it was shown that extinguishing only the fear while ignoring the instrumental behavior (the symptom) was also an inadequate procedure. After the instrumental behavior had disappeared, a single Pavlovian fear conditioning trial was sufficient to restore it. Indeed, the extinguished fear could spontaneously recover with the passage of time since its extinction, so that when it reappeared, the instrumental behavior would reappear, too (McAllister et al., 1986).

Sometimes the symptoms that patients develop include paralyses of one or more limbs. If it could be shown that the paralysis was not due to organic damage, fear theory also suggested a way to see whether the paralysis was being faked or was instead a true hysterical paralysis. The theory claimed that if it was a hysterical paralysis, the symptom was motivated by fear and not by a conscious verbal command. If so, then the symptom should disappear during the action of a fear-reducing drug, which would wipe out the underlying fear motivation.

In contrast, if the patient was faking the symptom, the symptom would be controlled by a conscious verbal command that the drug should leave intact. According to Dollard and Miller (1950), this drug technique was used successfully during World War II to distinguish malingerers who were trying to avoid combat by faking a paralysis from those who had true hysterical paralyses. In addition, because the hysterical paralysis was an instrumental response, it was held to be sustainable by sources of reinforcement other than the fear reduction that initially led to its learning. One such source of reinforcement might be a disability check delivered monthly as long as the symptom persisted.

Fear theory viewed symptoms as serving a function for the patient. Symptoms caused short-term reductions in fear even though they were maladaptive in the long run. Because of these short-term gains, fear theory predicted that patients should appear more content with their symptoms than an observer might have expected, based on their obviously debilitating effects. In short, the theory predicted the *belle indifference* that Dollard and Miller claimed existed in numerous cases.

Finally, as proposed by Mowrer (1947) and by Miller (1951) as well as by its current advocates (Levis, 1989; McAllister & McAllister, 1995), fear theory was not a cognitive theory or an expectancy theory. The theorists did not assume that the rat was aware that a lever press or a wheel turn would have any effect that would reduce fear. Instead, fear theorists assumed that these responses were blindly strengthened by their consequences. While that latter assumption might be unpopular in today's cognitive Zeitgeist, it, along with the mechanism of repression, which Dollard and Miller also explained in terms of fear theory, helped therapists understand how their patients could have no idea why they had their symptoms.

All of these contributions of fear theory are worth keeping in mind. If it should turn out that fear theory and its competing theories of avoidance learning are equally simple, equally testable, equally fruitful, and equally comprehensive in explaining the results of animal avoidance experiments, we should compare their contributions to the understanding and treatment of human anxiety disorders.

I should like now to review the evidence for fear theory's two major assumptions (fear motivates avoidance responses, and fear reduction reinforces avoidance responses). Then, I shall consider what is sometimes viewed as damaging evidence against fear theory. Last, I shall describe and evaluate two of fear theory's strongest competitors.

Evidence That Fear Motivates Avoidance Responses

Using dogs as subjects, Solomon and Turner (1962) mounted a panel on either side of each dog's head. The dog could push either panel with its nose. When a light was terminated, the dog had 10 seconds to push one of the panels. If it did not, shock occurred and lasted until the dog did press a panel. Shock then ended, and the light was relit. If the dog did press within the required 10 seconds, the response relit the light immediately and deleted the scheduled shock.

Once the dogs were avoiding shock regularly, they were paralyzed with the drug curare; the panels were removed, and each dog was given Pavlovian conditioning trials with two tones that differed in pitch. One tone, the CS+, was paired with shock. The other tone, the CS–, was given without shock. The purpose of paralyzing the dog and removing the panels was to prevent any panel-press behavior from occurring in the presence of either tone and thus, through any potential source of reinforcement, coming under the control of those tones. After the drug wore off, the panels were replaced, and each dog was tested to see how it would respond to the termination of the light and to each tone separately. The result was that the dogs pressed a panel when the light was terminated, just as before. Of more interest, five of the six dogs tested pressed a panel on the first presentation of the CS+ tone.

Over the course of testing, they pressed much more and with shorter latency in response to the CS+ tone than to the CS– tone.

These results were exactly what fear theory predicts. First, the dogs learned to panel press when frightened by light termination. Next, they learned to fear the (CS+) tone that was paired with shock but not the (CS–) tone that was not paired with shock. Finally, when tested with the tone that evoked fear, they did what they had been trained to do when fearful, namely press a panel. When tested with the tone that did not evoke fear, they pressed much less often, with longer latencies, or both. On the first test of CS+, the dogs had never received any reinforcement for panel pressing during that stimulus; therefore, it is unlikely that the CS+ tone itself could have gained operant stimulus control over panel pressing. It is much more likely that the stimulus consequences of fear, itself evoked by terminating the light, gained operant stimulus control over the panel press. Later, when the CS+ tone also evoked fear, that fear produced the stimulation that had previously come to control panel pressing.

Rescorla and LoLordo (1965) extended these findings in an important way. First, they used a Sidman avoidance procedure (Sidman, 1953) to train dogs to jump back and forth over a hurdle in a two-way shuttle box. (A Sidman procedure consists of programming shocks to occur at a fixed interval called the *shock-shock* [SS] *interval*. Responses postpone scheduled shocks for an interval termed the response-shock [RS] *interval*. As long as inter-response times are less than the RS interval, shocks can be postponed indefinitely.) Rescorla and LoLordo programmed shocks to occur every 10 seconds unless a jump occurred (the SS interval = 10 seconds). Each jump postponed the onset of the next shock 30 seconds (the RS interval = 30 seconds). Under this procedure, jumps occurred at a moderate rate throughout the session. This moderate rate was important because, unlike Solomon and Turner's panel press, its baseline level exceeded zero. Therefore, it might not only be increased by arousing fear but also be decreased by decreasing fear.

In the next phase of their work, Rescorla and LoLordo confined each dog to one side of the box and gave it Pavlovian conditioning trials in which a CS+ was paired with shock and a CS– was not (see next paragraph). Finally, with the dog returned to the original avoidance procedure, they tested the effects of the CS+ and the CS–. According to fear theory, the dog's jumping was motivated by fear. Therefore, CS+ trials should increase fear and make the dogs jump even faster. CS– trials, in contrast, should decrease fear and, by lessening the fear motivation, make the dogs jump slower. Both expectations were confirmed.

I should comment here on two aspects of Rescorla and LoLordo's Pavlovian conditioning procedure. First, the procedure was one that conditions fear not only to the CS+ but also to the context in which CS+ is embedded. Second, in different experiments, the researchers actually studied three different methods of making their CS– a fear inhibitor. The presumably crucial feature that all three methods shared was that they involved nonreinforcing CS– in the fear-evoking context. According to the model of Rescorla and Wagner (1972), the effects of reinforcing or nonreinforcing a CS are modulated by the conditioned values of the contexts in which the CS occurs. A feared CS loses more of its fear value if it is nonreinforced in the presence of a highly feared context (including another feared CS) than if it is nonreinforced in a neutral context (experiment by Rescorla cited in Rescorla & Wagner, 1972, pp. 72–73). Nonreinforcing the CS in a context that inhibits fear actually protects the CS from extinction (Soltysik, Wolfe, Nicholas, Wilson, & Garcia-Sanchez, 1983).

The theory and facts just cited seem to have important implications for the treatment of phobias. For example, in systematic desensitization (Wolpe, 1969), the therapist first constructs a hierarchy of the client's feared situations. The therapist also teaches the patient deep muscle relaxation techniques. On instruction from the therapist, the patient is then induced to relax. While the patient is so relaxed, the therapist, over the course of many sessions, attempts to ex-

tinquish each of the feared situations in the hierarchy, beginning with the least feared and moving toward the most feared. From the point of view of the Rescorla and Wagner model and its supporting evidence, this procedure should be less than optimal. For example, the relaxation instructions may be akin to the presentation of a conditioned inhibitor of fear. Fear inhibitors are also cues that tell the subject to relax; nothing bad will happen. Such instructions, then, might tend to protect the feared situation from extinction. Moreover, rather than extinguishing the least feared situation first and proceeding to the most feared, the model suggests that it might be best to present two or more feared situations simultaneously. A patient with a phobia of both insects and snakes might thus be asked to imagine both at once or might be presented with both at once *in vivo*.

Evidence That Fear Reduction Reinforces Avoidance Responses

If fear reduction is the reinforcer for Ras, then delaying the reduction of fear after an Ra is made should impair avoidance learning. Kamin (1957) found strong support for this prediction. He used a training procedure much like that in the first phase of Solomon and Turner's experiment except that the Ra that was required to avoid shock and to terminate the danger signal (the CS) was the response of running from one side of a two-way shuttle box to the other. If this response did not occur within 5 seconds after CS onset, shock came on and persisted with the CS until the response occurred. If the response did occur within 5 seconds, then the shock was avoided on that trial, and the CS was turned off at different times for different groups. For group 0, it was turned off immediately after the response. Thus, fear was assumed to be reduced immediately after the Ra, and optimal avoidance learning was expected. For groups 2.5, 5, and 10, however, the CS ended either 2.5, 5, or 10 seconds, respectively, after the Ra was made. The longer the delay in CS termination, the longer the time between the Ra and its presumed reinforcer (fear reduction). Avoidance learning was expected to become progressively worse, the longer this delay in reinforcement. This is exactly what Kamin found.

A conditioned inhibitor of fear, by definition, reduces fear when given to an otherwise frightened subject. If it should follow a response emitted by that subject, it should, according to fear theory, reinforce that response. Good support exists for this prediction (Rescorla, 1969b; Weisman & Litner, 1969). For example, Rescorla (1969b) first trained each of eight dogs to press a panel on either side of its head. He did so using a Sidman avoidance procedure resembling that used earlier by Rescorla and LoLordo. Rescorla took care to ensure that the two panels were pressed at the same rate. Next, while the Sidman procedure was still in effect, he gave a brief tone after each panel press. The pitch of the tone that followed a press of the left panel differed from the pitch of the tone that followed a press of the right panel. This tone preference test showed no preference for either tone. Next, with the panels removed and the Sidman procedure halted, Rescorla gave each dog a Pavlovian procedure designed to establish tone A as a conditioned inhibitor of fear while leaving tone B neutral. He did so by giving a shock after a lights-off CS except on trials in which tone A replaced the shock. That is, he nonreinforced tone A in a fear-arousing context. He did not present tone B during this phase. He ended the study with another tone preference test identical to the first.

The result in this test was that the dog learned to press whatever panel produced tone A (the presumed conditioned inhibitor of fear) in preference to the panel that produced the neutral tone. This result suggested that the conditioned inhibitor of fear was able to reinforce the response it followed. This is more evidence that fear reduction can reinforce avoidance behavior. (For an excellent paper describing the use of conditioned inhibitors of fear or "safety signals" in the treatment of maladaptive behaviors in dogs, see Tortora [1983], who also discusses possible variants of his procedure for use with human patients.)

Purported Evidence Against Fear Theory

Among the most widely cited evidence against fear theory is work that shows that fear and avoidance strengths do not vary together (Kamin, Brimer, & Black, 1963; Linden, 1969; Mineka & Gino, 1980; Starr & Mineka, 1977). The experiment of Kamin et al. will illustrate. Kamin et al. used a procedure much like that given to group 0 in the work by Kamin (1957) described earlier. There were four groups of rats. Each rat in group 1 was trained in a two-way shuttle avoidance task with a tone danger signal (CS) until it made 1 Ra. Groups 3, 9, and 27 were trained until they made 3, 9, and 27 Ras, respectively, in succession. When the avoidance criterion was met, Kamin et al. removed the rats from the two-way shuttle box and assessed their fear of the CS in a bar-press conditioned suppression task. They found that CS-evoked suppression of bar pressing increased across groups 1, 3, and 9, but decreased virtually to zero in group 27, suggesting little fear of the CS in that group.

The problem for fear theory is the weak fear of the CS in group 27. It is not hard to understand why the fear would extinguish after 27 successive Ras, because they cause the rat to receive 27 successive CSs unpaired with shock. The puzzle is that if the rat was so unafraid of the CS after these 27 Ras, what motivated the last of these responses? And if there was so little fear of the CS, how could CS termination and its consequent fear reduction have reinforced these Ras?

McAllister and McAllister (1991) have answered these questions rather easily. First, with regard to the motivation question, they note that during the run of successful Ras, the strength of the Ra increases with each reinforcement. As the instrumental behavior grows stronger, less motivation is required to energize it. Second, with regard to the reinforcement question, the McAllisters note that during the run of Ras, the CS isn't the only stimulus to undergo extinction. The context undergoes extinction as well. Thus, even though the amount of fear reduction produced by CS termination late in the avoidance run may be small, the amount of context-evoked fear that persists after CS offset is even smaller. Late in the avoidance run, the situation might be analogous to escaping from a 200-V shock to a 100-V shock, whereas early in the avoidance run the situation might be analogous to escaping from a 400-V shock to a 200-V shock. As we have seen earlier (Campbell & Kraeling, 1953), reinforcement in the former case is more effective.

Other evidence sometimes thought damaging to fear theory is that Ra learning is possible even though CS offset does not follow the Ra. If a so-called feedback signal follows the Ra while the CS persists, the Ra can be learned anyway (e.g., Bolles & Grossen, 1969). As stated earlier, fear theory is not wedded to CS termination as a reinforcer. It holds that anything that reduces fear after a response can reinforce that response. If the feedback signal has acquired fear-inhibiting powers by being the stimulus most removed from shock during avoidance training (and thus being nonreinforced in a fear-evoking context), then it should inhibit fear even if the CS persists. Even a neutral feedback signal should have some fear-reducing effect by causing generalization decrement in the fear evoked by the context (cf. McAllister & McAllister, 1992).

Another apparent puzzle for fear theory was the finding that animals could learn to avoid under Sidman avoidance schedules. That was puzzling because in Sidman procedures, such as those described earlier (Rescorla, 1969b; Rescorla & LoLordo, 1965), there is no external CS that ends after an Ra, nor is there any programmed feedback stimulus that might acquire fear-inhibiting properties and thereby reduce fear after each Ra. Anger (1963) provided a solution to this puzzle that was satisfying to fear theorists. He noted that there were temporal regularities in Sidman procedures that would make the temporal stimuli that immediately followed an Ra less aversive than those that occurred later and therefore closer to shock. This meant that an Ra would always replace a relatively aversive temporal stimulus with a less aversive one. For

fear theorists, this was a source of fear reduction that could reinforce responding.

Another way of viewing this situation is to note that whatever internal or external feedback that an Ra provides is more removed from shock than any other cue in the environment. By being nonreinforced in a fear-evoking context, that feedback, even if entirely proprioceptive, should acquire fear-inhibiting powers. Evidence that feedback signals do acquire such powers was provided by Rescorla (1968a), who first trained dogs in a two-way shuttle Sidman avoidance procedure with the RS interval = 30 seconds and the SS interval = 10 seconds. For different groups, Rescorla placed a 5-second tone CS at different points in the RS interval. Group A received the tone immediately after an Ra (mimicking response feedback and the temporal cues farthest from shock). Group S received the tone 25 seconds later (mimicking temporal cues closer to shock). A control group, group C, received the tone at random times.

After this training, Rescorla tested the effects of the tone in each group by presenting it independently of the dogs' behavior while the dogs were shuttling in extinction (i.e., without shock). He found that the tone increased the shuttle rate in group S (suggesting that it increased fear), reduced the rate in group A (suggesting that it decreased fear) and had no lasting effects in group C (suggesting that the tone was relatively neutral in that group). Likewise, Morris (1974) found that a feedback signal in a two-way shuttle avoidance task came to inhibit fear, that it did so because of Pavlovian processes, and that the inhibitory value of the feedback signal increased as a function of the intertrial interval. Morris (1975) further showed that Ra learning could be significantly enhanced by pretraining the feedback-signal-to-be as a Pavlovian fear inhibitor before using it as a feedback signal in a two-way shuttle avoidance task. More remarkably, in comparison to a feedback signal that had not been pretrained, the presentation of the pretrained feedback signal after the first Ra significantly reduced the number of trials intervening between it and the second Ra. This suggests a powerful reinforcing effect of the fear-inhibiting feedback.

Both Rescorla's and Morris's results were entirely consistent with Anger's (1963) theory in general and in particular with the idea that response feedback during Sidman avoidance can acquire the ability to reduce fear and that such fear reduction can reinforce Ras.

Shock-Frequency-Reduction Theory

Herrnstein and Hineline (1966) performed an experiment that seemed to discredit fear theory's account of Sidman avoidance. They did so by programming shocks to occur at a high rate but at random times. An Ra lowered that rate, but shocks still occurred at random times so that they might sometimes immediately follow an Ra. This would mean that even the temporal cues that immediately followed an Ra were sometimes paired with shock and were thus unsafe. It would mean that the proprioceptive cues from Ras would be paired with shock occasionally and thus would be unlikely to inhibit fear. Herrnstein and Hineline found that their rats did learn to respond under this procedure. Having eliminated reasonable sources of fear reduction for Ras, they argued that the results confirmed Sidman's (1962) suggestion that the reinforcer for the Ra was the lowering of the rate of shock that the Ra caused. Since Ras lower the rate of shocks in all shock-avoidance experiments, the researchers argued that shock-frequency reduction could explain all avoidance learning, making fear and fear reduction superfluous. Their theory was elegantly simple, and all its terms were observable. Those terms were response, consequence, and the environment (stimulus) in whose presence the response occurred. The consequence reinforced the response and brought it under the control of the environment.

The simplicity of the theory, however, left it unable to explain large portions of the aversive learning literature. For example, Miller's (1948) wheel turning and lever pressing produced no reductions in shock frequency. Since no shock was programmed when those responses were learned, the fact that the responses were learned anyway shows that shock-frequency reduction was not necessary in Miller's experiment.

Kamin's (1957) groups of rats could lower the shock frequency equally by responding, regardless of how long the CS was extended after a group's Ra. It is therefore instructive that Kamin's groups 5 and 10, which had their CS extended 5 seconds and 10 seconds, respectively, responded no more than did a control group whose responses had no effect on shock frequency. Clearly, in Kamin's experiment, shock-frequency reduction was not sufficient for Ra learning. Likewise, the shock-frequency-reduction principle cannot explain why the presentation of putative fear arousers increased the avoidance rate and why the presentation of putative fear inhibitors decreased it in the experiment of Rescorla and LoLordo (1965). It cannot explain why putative conditioned inhibitors of fear reinforced Ras in the work of Rescorla (1969b) and Weisman and Litner (1969).

To explain these data, one needs principles other than shock-frequency reduction. One likely candidate would be the principle of secondary negative reinforcement. A negative reinforcer is a stimulus whose removal after a response strengthens that response. A secondary negative reinforcer is a negative reinforcer that has acquired its ability through Pavlovian conditioning (e.g., by being paired with shock). As noted by Bolles (1975, pp. 328–329), the operations for establishing a stimulus as a secondary negative reinforcer are the same as those for establishing a CS as a fear excitor. The operation of secondary negative reinforcement (terminating the CS following the response) is the same as one of the sources of reinforcement emphasized by fear theory. To the extent that shock-frequency-reduction theorists have to rely on the same concepts as fear theorists, their view becomes less parsimonious than it might initially seem. The question then arises as to whether fear theorists must also accept shock-frequency reduction as a reinforcement principle. If so, there would be little to separate the two views.

At present, it seems unlikely that the results reported by Herrnstein and Hineline require a shock-frequency-reduction interpretation. Even though the proprioceptive consequences of Ras in their study were sometimes paired with shock, the fact remains that those stimuli on the average were further removed from shock than any other cues in the situation (cf. Dinsmoor, 1977, p. 90). Thus, most of the time those stimuli were nonreinforced in an excitatory context, which would tend to make them conditioned inhibitors of fear. The situation would be much like that in a Pavlovian conditioning experiment in which CSs and USs were distributed throughout a session such that most CSs were explicitly unpaired with USs but an occasional CS was paired. Would such a CS acquire fear-inhibiting powers? Although the evidence is sparse, one experiment of this type (Witcher & Ayres, 1980) did find evidence that such CSs can indeed become fear inhibitors.

One of the features that Hineline (1981, 1984; Hineline & Sodetz, 1987; Hineline & Wanchisen, 1989) finds attractive about shock-frequency-reduction theory is that it is a molar theory. It downplays the role of contiguous reinforcement (immediate causation) and emphasizes the long-term consequences of behavior. Ras are learned because over the long haul they reduce the frequency of shocks even though some Ras may be followed by shock. In this regard, it is worth noting that in Pavlovian conditioning, a molar theory that initially seemed promising (Rescorla, 1967, 1968b, 1969a) was ultimately unsuccessful. According to that theory, conditioning to a CS was determined by its correlation with a US as calculated over the entire course of Pavlovian training (a molar correlation). A positive correlation between a CS and shock was thought to make the CS a fear excitor. A negative correlation was thought to make it a fear inhibitor. A zero correlation was thought to leave it neutral. However, when several zero correlations were studied (Ayres, Benedict, & Witcher, 1975; Benedict & Ayres, 1972), some

of them turned the CS into fear excitors and some did not. Knowing the molar correlation was unhelpful. The molecular sequence of trial types turned out to be crucial. While the results could not be explained in terms of molar correlation, they were well explained by a molecular theory (Rescorla & Wagner, 1972) that emphasized the role of trial-by-trial events (the exact order of trial types). This experience in Pavlovian conditioning should give us pause in embracing shock-frequency-reduction theory just because it is a molar theory that frees us from the shackles of molecular constraints (immediate causation). More to the point are studies of avoidance that pit molecular considerations against molar ones. These studies speak against the importance of the molar reduction in shock frequency as the controlling variable in avoidance (e.g., Benedict, 1975; for a review, see Thomas, 1983).

SSDR Theory

Given the importance of SSDRs in the measures of fear conditioning in animals, it would be surprising if SSDRs were not also important in avoidance learning. An Ra that was an SSDR or was at least compatible with an SSDR should be easier to learn than one that was not. We have already seen in the work of Miller (1948) that almost half of his sample was unable to learn the wheel-turn response, presumably because the SSDR of freezing interfered with it. For those rats that did learn, it seems likely that the SSDR of fleeing from the white box could have led to scrabbling around the door and that such behavior would have increased the odds of wheel turning and (later) of lever pressing. These ideas are entirely consistent with the notions of early fear theorists regarding a presumed hierarchy of innate and learned responses (e.g., Miller, 1948, footnote 3).

The SSDR theory proposed by Bolles (1970, 1971, 1972, 1975, 1978), however, goes far beyond these ideas. Although the theory has changed over the years (for a summary of those changes, see Crawford & Masterson, 1982) in the most recent statement (Bolles, 1978), the issue is not simply whether the topography of an SSDR is compatible or incompatible with the instrumental Ra to be learned. Rather, the theory asserts that most Ras depend on Pavlovian, not operant or instrumental conditioning. Through Pavlovian conditioning, the animal learns which signals or places are dangerous (CS+s) and which are safe (CS–s). The SSDR that then occurs is the innate response to these signals that is best supported by the apparatus. As Bolles put it, "If we have taught a rat that it is dangerous over here and that it is safe over there, is it also necessary to teach the rat [via operant reinforcement] to run from here to there? Or can it get there all by itself?" (Bolles, 1978, p. 96). Bolles clearly thought that the flight SSDR would automatically take the rat from here to there without the aid of operant reinforcement. As support, he cited a study from his laboratory in which the latency of Ras in a shuttle avoidance task showed no change over trial blocks (Bolles, Moot, & Nelson, 1976 [for conflicting evidence, see McAllister, McAllister, Dieter, & James, 1979]). This suggested that the SSDR of flight (the Ra in that experiment) was immutable and insensitive to its consequences (i.e., was not an instrumental response).

According to Bolles, the most salient fact about Ra learning is that its speed depends so much on the apparatus. Learning is very fast in the one-way shuttle box and other apparatus where the Ra of running or jumping literally takes an animal from a dangerous to a safe place. It is slower in the two-way shuttle where shock can be delivered on either side and where the running Ra takes the animal from one dangerous place to another dangerous place. It is slowest in discrete-trial bar-press avoidance experiments in which the Ra does not move the rat from one place to another. SSDR theory was tailor-made to explain these apparatus effects. Although Bolles (1978) conceded that fear theory's effective reinforcement principle might also account for these effects, he rejected that account not for lack of plausibility but rather because he thought it was circular. "[T]he only reason the fear-re-

duction theorist thinks bar pressing produces little reduction in total fear level is that he has so much trouble reinforcing bar pressing" (Bolles, 1978, pp. 92–93).

In contrast to Bolles, I believe that fear theory's position is readily testable. In the absence of shock, one could, for example, measure the freezing that is evoked by the CS and by the context alone following CS offset. For example, if a rat that had been trained in a one-way shuttle were scored for freezing while confined at different times in the shock side and the safe side, I'd predict more freezing in the shock side than in the safe side. If a rat previously trained in a two-way shuttle were confined at different times in each side, one side with the CS and one without, I'd predict a lot of freezing in each side. If a rat that had been trained in a discrete-trials bar-press situation were observed in the Skinner box in the presence and absence of the CS but with the bar removed, I'd predict a lot of freezing in each case. I'd expect these freezing tests to suggest a continuum of effective reinforcement that was maximal in the one-way situation and minimal in the Skinner box.

When attempts have been made to directly manipulate the level of fear evoked by the CS and the context together versus the context alone, the results have supported fear theory's effective reinforcement principle (e.g., McAllister et al., 1979). One of the more elegant of these attempts was that of Callen (1986), who explored a result found repeatedly in the two-way shuttle: Avoidance performance decreases with increases in shock intensity. This is a result that makes no sense in terms of either SSDR theory or shock-frequency-reduction theory but is at least potentially understood in terms of effective reinforcement theory. That theory holds that as shock intensity increases, fear increases both to the CS and to the context without the CS. So, with a high shock, escaping from the CS-plus-context to the context alone is like escaping from a 400-V shock to a 200-V shock. With a low shock, it's more like escaping from a 200-V shock to a 100-V shock.

We've seen earlier that escape learning is better in the latter case. Callen tested this idea by contrasting between-groups versus within-subject variations in shock intensity. In the within-subject design, there were two CSs: one was the warning signal for high shock; the other warned of low shock. In this design, the fear of the context should be the same regardless of the CS. Therefore, there should be more fear reduction when the more feared CS (the one paired with high shock) terminated after the Ra, and avoidance learning should be superior when that CS served as the warning signal. This is what Callen found. In the between-groups design, there were the same two CSs, but both warned of high shock in one group and of low shock in another. Here, both context fear and fear of the CS should increase with shock intensity, and under this condition, Callen found the usual inverse relationship between shock intensity and avoidance performance.

To deny the operant nature of Ras, SSDR theory has to assert that the Ra is not modified by its consequences. This is an extremely difficult position to defend. Consider what the theory seems to predict about the following situation. Suppose fear is first well conditioned to one side of a one-way shuttle box. Next come a series of escape test trials in which a rat is allowed to flee from the conditioned side to a safe side. SSDR theory seems to predict that the flight response should be strong at the outset because fear should strongly evoke the innate SSDR of flight and because the apparatus looks like a place in which to flee. On later trials, flight should weaken as fear extinguishes. The data are, however, that the escape speed gradually increases for about 50 trials before declining (McAllister et al., 1986). The increase over the course of the 50 trials looks much like the acquisition of instrumental behavior. The behavior seems to be reinforced by its consequences.

As a second example, consider the study by Kamin (1957) that varied the delay in CS termination. In one such experiment, Kamin found that delaying CS termination after only the first Ra impaired subsequent performance. Rats for which CS termination was delayed 2.5 seconds or more after only their first Ra took significantly more trials before making their second Ra than

did rats for which the delay after the first Ra was 0 seconds. This seems to be a powerful effect of consequence on behavior (cf. Morris, 1975).

Finally, the SSDR nature of some of the Ras used in Bolles's own laboratory seems open to question. For example, in one study in which running in an activity wheel was required as the Ra, Bolles and Grossen (1969) feared that the rat would simply run continuously throughout the session. To prevent that, they adopted a procedure in which running would not function as an Ra unless the animal first came to a stop at the onset of the CS and then resumed running. One certainly has to wonder whether stopping first isn't incompatible with the flight SSDR that the running wheel would seem to support. In this sense, the behavior looks more instrumental than innate.

Although Bolles (1978) sought to downplay the instrumental nature of Ras, he did leave the door open for some instrumental Ra learning. With apparent reluctance (pp. 98–99), he conceded that *some* Ras are indeed instrumental (that they are modifiable by their consequences) and that their reinforcer was the presentation of conditioned inhibitors of fear (*safety signals* in Bolles's terminology). Believing that many trials were needed to establish a CS as a safety signal, Bolles assumed that this reinforcement mechanism would work only in situations in which the (non-SSDR) Ra was learned very slowly (as in discrete-trials bar-press avoidance tasks).

It is interesting to contrast the ways in which shock-frequency-reduction theory and SSDR theory differ from fear theory. Shock-frequency-reduction theory denies the importance of fear and fear reduction while asserting that the Ra is an operant that is reinforced by a lowered rate of shock. SSDR theory accepts the importance of fear as a motivator or evoker of SSDRs but minimizes the idea that the SSDR (the Ra) is an operant. Each theory, however, ends up having to make concessions to fear theory. By itself, shock-frequency-reduction theory cannot explain major findings in the aversive learning literature. It must also rely on the concept of secondary negative reinforcement (thus depending on Pavlovian conditioning and CS termination). Similarly, SSDR theory cannot rely entirely on Pavlovian processes and their automatic evocation of SSDRs but must concede that some Ras are instrumental and that their reinforcer is the presentation of safety signals (which fear theorists assert reduce fear).

Finally, while the implications of fear theory for the understanding and treatment of human anxiety disorders are well known, the implications of the theory's competitors are not. If we accept the premise that human symptoms are Ras, then we have to ask: Are human symptoms SSDRs? Did compulsive heart-beat counting, windowpane counting, refusing to step on cracks in the sidewalk, hand washing, etc. derive from behavior that avoided predation in hominid evolution? Are hysterical paralyses some form of freezing or tonic immobility in which only part of the body shows the phenomenon? It seems unlikely. What are the implications for treatment? Since SSDRs occur innately in response to fear, presumably we need to extinguish the fear, just as claimed by fear theory. However, since the operant nature of SSDRs is, for the most part, denied, there would seem to be little reason to attend to the operant side of the equation, which we know needs attention (McAllister et al., 1986; Tortora, 1987).

Shock-frequency-reduction theory resides within a larger theoretical framework (the experimental analysis of behavior) that has a long and distinguished history in the modification of behavior, maladaptive or otherwise. However, if we restrict our enquiry only to the shock-frequency-reduction theory of avoidance and ask what its implications are for treatment, we have to look to see how shock-frequency-reduction theorists extinguish avoidance behavior. When we do that, we find that they either eliminate shocks entirely or give them at the same rate whether the response occurs or not. The direct translation seems to be that therapists should either eliminate life's aversive events for their patients or see to it that those events occur at the same rate regardless of the patient's symptoms. Clearly, this is a plan that is both unrealistic and unpalatable.

CONCLUSIONS

1. The construct of fear has integrative value, and independent measures of it exist that are well correlated.
2. Criticisms of Pavlovian fear-conditioning models of simple phobia have been unsound.
3. Relative to its competitors, fear theory is no more complex, has been more fruitful, offers a more comprehensive explanation of the animal avoidance literature, and has contributed more to the understanding and treatment of human anxiety disorders.

ENDNOTES

This chapter is dedicated to my mother, Mrs. Joseph A. Mooney, Jr. It was prepared while I was supported by grant MH50491-01 from the National Institute of Mental Health.

REFERENCES

Agras, W. S., Sylvester, D., & Oliveau, D. (1969). The epidemiology of common fears and phobia. *Comprehensive Psychiatry, 10*, 151–156.

Aitken, P. P. (1974). Aversive stimulation and rats' preference for areas differing in novelty-value and brightness. *Animal Behaviour, 22*, 731–734.

Albert, M., & Ayres, J. J. B. (1989). With number of preexposures constant latent inhibition increases with preexposure CS duration or total CS exposure. *Learning and Motivation, 20*, 278–294.

Allison, J., Larson, D., & Jensen, D. D. (1967). Acquired fear, brightness preference, and one-way shuttlebox performance. *Psychonomic Science, 8*, 269–270.

Anger, D. (1963). The role of temporal discriminations in the reinforcement of Sidman avoidance behavior. *Journal of the Experimental Analysis of Behavior, 6*, 447–506.

Ayres, J. J. B., Benedict, J. O., & Witcher, E. S. (1975). Systematic manipulation of individual events in a truly random control in rats. *Journal of Comparative and Physiological Psychology, 88*, 97–103.

Ayres, J. J. B., Philbin, D., Cassidy, S., Bellino, L., & Redlinger, E. (1992). Some parameters of latent inhibition. *Learning and Motivation, 23*, 269–287.

Ayres, J. J. B., & Vigorito, M. (1984). Posttrial effects of presenting vs. omitting expected shock USs in the conditioned suppression procedure: Concurrent measurement of barpress suppression and freezing. *Animal Learning & Behavior, 12,* 73–78.

Balaz, M. A., Kasprow, W. J., & Miller, R. R. (1982). Blocking with a single compound trial. *Animal Learning & Behavior, 10,* 271–276.

Benedict, J. O. (1975). Response-shock delay as a reinforcer in avoidance behavior. *Journal of the Experimental Analysis of Behavior, 24,* 323–332.

Benedict, J. O., & Ayres, J. J. B. (1972). Factors affecting conditioning in the truly random control procedure in the rat. *Journal of Comparative and Physiological Psychology, 78,* 323–330.

Bevins, R. A., & Ayres, J. J. B. (1992). One-trial backward excitatory fear conditioning transfers across contexts. *Behaviour Research and Therapy, 30,* 551–554.

Blanchard, R. J., Fukunaga, K. K., & Blanchard, D. C. (1976). Environmental control of defensive reactions to footshock. *Bulletin of the Psychonomic Society, 8,* 129–130.

Bolles, R. C. (1970). Species-specific defense reactions and avoidance learning. *Psychological Review, 77,* 32–48.

Bolles, R. C. (1971). Species-specific defense reactions. In F. R. Brush (ed.), *Aversive conditioning and learning,* 183–233. New York: Academic Press.

Bolles, R. C. (1972). The avoidance learning problem. In G. H. Bower (ed.), *The psychology of learning and motivation,* Vol. 6: 97–145. New York: Academic Press.

Bolles, R. C. (1975). *Theory of motivation* (2nd ed.). New York: Harper & Row.

Bolles, R. C. (1978). The role of stimulus learning in defensive behavior. In S. H. Hulse, H. Fowler, & W. K. Honig (eds.), *Cognitive processes in animal behavior,* 89–107. Hillsdale, N.J.: Erlbaum.

Bolles, R. C., & Grossen, N. E. (1969). Effects of an informational stimulus on the acquisition of avoidance behavior in rats. *Journal of Comparative and Physiological Psychology, 68,* 90–99.

Bolles, R. C., Moot, S. A., & Nelson, K. (1976). Note on the invariance of response latency in shuttlebox avoidance learning. *Learning and Motivation, 7,* 108–116.

Bouton, M. E., & Bolles, R. C. (1980). Conditioned fear assessed by freezing and by the suppression of three different baselines. *Animal Learning & Behavior, 8,* 429–434.

Brown, J. S., & Jacobs, A. (1949). The role of fear in the motivation and acquisition of responses. *Journal of Experimental Psychology, 39,* 747–759.

Burkhardt, P. E. (1980). One-trial backward fear conditioning in rats as a function of US intensity. *Bulletin of the Psychonomic Society, 15,* 9–11.

Callen, E. J. (1986). Fear of the CS and of the context in two-way avoidance learning: Between- and within-subjects manipulations. *Animal Learning & Behavior, 14,* 80–89.

Campbell, B. A., & Kraeling, D. (1953). Response strength as a function of drive level and amount of drive reduction. *Journal of Experimental Psychology, 45,* 97–101.

Crawford, M., & Masterson, F. A. (1982). Species-specific defense reactions and avoidance learning: An evaluative review. *Pavlovian Journal of Biological Science, 17,* 204–214.

Davis, M. (1992). The role of the amygdala in conditioned fear. In J. P. Aggleton (ed.), *The amygdala: Neurobiological aspects of emotion, memory, and mental dysfunction,* 255–305. New York: Wiley-Liss.

Denny, M. R. (ed.) (1991). *Fear, avoidance, and phobias: A fundamental analysis,* Hillsdale, N.J.: Erlbaum.

Dinsmoor, J. A. (1977). Escape, avoidance, punishment: Where do we stand? *Journal of the Experimental Analysis of Behavior, 28,* 83–95.

Dollard, J., & Miller, N. E. (1950). *Personality and psychotherapy: An analysis in terms of learning, thinking, and culture.* New York: McGraw-Hill.

Emmerson, R. Y., & DeVietti, T. L. (1982). Presentation of a flashing light following one-trial fear conditioning enhances retention. *Animal Learning & Behavior, 10,* 325–329.

Falls, W. A., & Davis, M. (1995). Lesions of the central nucleus of the amygdala block conditioned excitation but not conditioned inhibition of fear as measured with the fear-potentiated startle effect. *Behavioral Neuroscience, 109,* 379–387.

Fanselow, M. S. (1984a). Shock-induced analgesia on the formalin test: Effects of shock severity, naloxone, hypophysectomy, and associative variables. *Behavioral Neuroscience, 98,* 79–95.

Fanselow, M. S. (1984b). What is conditioned fear? *Trends in Neuroscience, 17,* 460–462.

Fanselow, M. S. (1986). Associative vs topographical accounts of the immediate shock-freezing deficit in rats: Implications for the response selection rules governing species-specific defensive reactions. *Learning and Motivation, 17,* 16–39.

Fanselow, M. S., & Helmstetter, F. J. (1988). Conditional analgesia, defensive freezing, and benzodiazepines. *Behavioral Neuroscience, 102,* 233–243.

Fanselow, M. S., & Lester, L. S. (1988). A functional behavioristic approach to aversively motivated behavior: Predatory imminence as a determinant of the topography of defensive behavior. In R. C. Bolles & M. D. Beecher (eds.), *Evolution and learning,* 185–212. Hillsdale, N.J.: Erlbaum.

Fanselow, M. S., & Sigmundi, R. A. (1982). The enhancement and reduction of defensive fighting by naloxone pretreatment. *Physiological Psychology, 10,* 313–316.

Fox, M. W. (1969). Ontogeny of prey-killing behavior in Canidae. *Behaviour, 35,* 259–272.

Gallup, G. G., Jr. (1974). Animal hypnosis: Factual status of a fictional concept. *Psychological Bulletin, 81*, 836–853.

Gallup, G. G., Jr. (1977). Tonic immobility: The role of fear and predation. *Psychological Record, 27*, 41–61.

Gallup, G. G., Jr., & Maser, J. D. (1977). Tonic immobility: Evolutionary underpinnings of human catalepsy and catatonia. In J. D. Maser & M. E. P. Seligman (eds.), *Psychopathology: Experimental models*, 334–357. San Francisco: Freeman.

Grossen, N. E., & Kelley, M. J. (1972). Species-specific behavior and acquisition of avoidance behavior in rats. *Journal of Comparative and Physiological Psychology, 81*, 307–310.

Hammond, L. J. (1968). Retardation of fear acquisition by a previously inhibitory CS. *Journal of Comparative and Physiological Psychology, 66*, 756–759.

Herrnstein, R. J. (1969). Method and theory in the study of avoidance. *Psychological Review, 76*, 49–69.

Herrnstein, R. J., & Hineline, P. N. (1966). Negative reinforcement as shock-frequency reduction. *Journal of the Experimental Analysis of Behavior, 9*, 421–430.

Herzog, H. A., Jr. (1978). Immobility in intraspecific encounters: Cockfights and the evolution of "animal hypnosis." *Psychological Record, 28*, 543–548.

Herzog, H. A., Jr., & Burghardt, G. M. (1974). Prey movement and predatory behavior of juvenile western yellow-bellied racers, Coluber, constrictor mormon. *Herpetologica, 30*, 285–289.

Hineline, P. N. (1973). Varied approaches to aversion: A review of Aversive Conditioning and Learning, edited by F. Robert Brush. *Journal of the Experimental Analysis of Behavior, 19*, 531–540.

Hineline, P. N. (1981). The several roles of stimuli in negative reinforcement. In P. Harzem & M. D. Zeiler (eds.), *Advances in analysis of behavior, Vol. 2: Predictability, correlation, and contiguity*, 203–246. Chichester, England: Wiley.

Hineline, P. N. (1984). Aversive control: A separate domain? *Journal of the Experimental Analysis of Behavior, 42*, 495–509.

Hineline, P. N., & Sodetz, F. J. (1987). Appetitive and aversive schedule preferences: Schedule transitions as intervening events. In M. L. Commons, H. Rachlin, & J. Mazur (eds.), *Quantitative analyses of behavior, Vol. 5: Reinforcement value—The effects of delay and intervening events*, 141–157. Hillsdale, N.J.: Erlbaum.

Hineline, P. N., & Wanchisen, B. A. (1989). Correlated hypothesizing and the distinction between contingency-shaped and rule-governed behavior. In S. C. Hayes (ed.), *Rule-governed behavior: Cognition, contingencies, and instructional control*, 221–268. New York: Plenum.

Hirsch, S. M., & Bolles, R. C. (1980). On the ability of prey to recognize predators. *Zeitschrift fur Tierpsychologie, 54*, 71–84.

Hofer, M. A. (1970). Cardiac and respiratory function during sudden prolonged immobility in wild rodents. *Psychosomatic Medicine, 32*, 633–647.

Janis, I. L. (1951). *Air war and emotional stress: Psychological studies of bombing and civilian defense*. New York, McGraw-Hill.

Kamin, L. J. (1957). The gradient of delay of secondary reward in avoidance learning tested on avoidance trials only. *Journal of Comparative and Physiological Psychology, 50*, 450–456.

Kamin, L. J., Brimer, C. J., & Black, A. H. (1963). Conditioned suppression as a monitor of fear of the CS in the course of avoidance training. *Journal of Comparative and Physiological Psychology, 56*, 497–501.

Kaufman, D. W. (1974). Differential predation on active and inactive prey by owls. *Auk, 91*, 172–173.

Kiernan, M. J., & Westbrook, R. F. (1993). Effects of exposure to a to-be-shocked environment upon the rat's freezing response: Evidence for facilitation, latent inhibition, and perceptual learning. *Quarterly Journal of Experimental Psychology, 46B*, 271–288.

Lacey, J. I. (1967). Somatic response patterning and stress: Some revisions of activation theory. In M. H. Appley & R. Trumbull (eds.), *Psychological stress: Issues in research*, 14–42. New York: Appleton-Century-Crofts.

Leaton, R. N., & Borszcz, G. S. (1985). Potentiated startle: Its relation to freezing and shock intensity in rats. *Journal of Experimental Psychology: Animal Behavior Processes, 11*, 421–428.

Levis, D. J. (1989). The case for a return to a two-factor theory of avoidance: The failure of non-fear interpretations. In S. B. Klein & R. Mowrer (eds.), *Contemporary learning theories: Pavlovian conditioning and the status of traditional learning theory*, 227–277, Hillsdale, N.J.: Erlbaum.

Linden, D. R. (1969). Attenuation and reestablishment of the CER by discriminated avoidance conditioning in rats. *Journal of Comparative and Physiological Psychology, 69*, 573–578.

Loftus, E. F. (1993). The reality of repressed memories. *American Psychologist, 48*, 518–537.

LoLordo, V. M., & Fairless, J. L. (1985). Pavlovian conditioned inhibition: The literature since 1969. In R. R. Miller & N. E. Spear (eds.), *Information processing in animals: Conditioned inhibition*, 1–49. Hillsdale, N.J.: Erlbaum.

Lubow, R. E. (1989). *Latent inhibition and conditioned attention theory*. New York: Cambridge University Press.

Mackintosh, N. J. (1971). An analysis of overshadowing and blocking. *Quarterly Journal of Experimental Psychology, 23*, 118–125.

Mackintosh, N. J., & Reese, B. (1979). One-trial overshadowing. *Quarterly Journal of Experimental Psychology, 31*, 519–526.

Maes, J. H. R., & Vossen, J. M. H. (1992). One-trial aversive conditioning to contextual cues: Effects of time of shock presentation on freezing during conditioning and testing. *Bulletin of the Psychonomic Society, 30*, 403–406.

Marks, I. M. (1969). *Fears and phobias*. London: Academic Press.

Marks, I. (1977). Clinical phenomena in search of laboratory models. In J. D. Maser & M. E. P. Seligman (eds.), *Psychopathology: Experimental models*, 174–213. San Francisco: Freeman.

Mast, M., Blanchard, R. J., & Blanchard, D. C. (1982). The relationship of freezing and response suppression in a CER situation. *Psychological Record, 32*, 151–167.

McAllister, D. E., & McAllister, W. R. (1971). Behavioral measurement of conditioned fear. In F. R. Brush (ed.), *Aversive conditioning and learning*, 105–179. New York: Academic Press.

McAllister, D. E., & McAllister, W. R. (1991). Fear theory and aversively motivated behavior: Some controversial issues. In M. R. Denny (ed.), *Fear, avoidance, and phobias: A fundamental analysis*, 135–163. Hillsdale, N.J.: Erlbaum.

McAllister, W. R., & McAllister, D. E. (1992). Fear determines the effectiveness of a feedback stimulus in aversively motivated instrumental learning. *Learning and Motivation, 23*, 99–115.

McAllister, W. R., & McAllister, D. E. (1995). Two-factor fear theory: Implications for understanding anxiety-based clinical phenomena. In W. O'Donohue & L. Krasner (eds.), *Theories of behavior therapy: Exploring behavior change*, 145–171. Washington, D.C.: American Psychological Association.

McAllister, W. R., McAllister, D. E., Dieter, S. E., & James, J. H. (1979). Preexposure to situational cues produces a direct relationship between two-way avoidance learning and shock intensity. *Animal Learning & Behavior, 7*, 165–173.

McAllister, W. R., McAllister, D. E., & Douglass, W. K. (1971). The inverse relationship between shock intensity and shuttle-box avoidance learning in rats: A reinforcement explanation. *Journal of Comparative and Physiological Psychology, 74*, 426–433.

McAllister, W. R., McAllister, D. E., Scoles, M. T., & Hampton, S. R. (1986). Persistence of fear-reducing behavior: Relevance for the conditioning theory of neurosis. *Journal of Abnormal Psychology, 95*, 365–372.

Miller, N. E. (1948). Studies of fear as an acquirable drive: I. Fear as motivation and fear-reduction as reinforcement in the learning of new responses. *Journal of Experimental Psychology, 38*, 89–101.

Miller, N. E. (1951). Learnable drives and rewards. In S. S. Stevens (ed.), *Handbook of experimental psychology*, 435–472. New York: Wiley.

Mineka, S., & Gino, A. (1980). Dissociation between conditioned emotional response and extended avoidance performance. *Learning and Motivation, 11*, 476–502.

Mongeluzi, D. L., Rosellini, R. A., Caldarone, B. J., Stock, H. S., & Abrahamsen, G. C. (1996). Pavlovian aversive context conditioning using carbon dioxide as the unconditional stimulus. *Journal of Experimental Psychology: Animal Behavior Processes, 22*, 244–257.

Morris, R. G. M. (1974). Pavlovian conditioned inhibition of fear during shuttlebox avoidance behavior. *Learning and Motivation, 5*, 424–447.

Morris, R. G. M. (1975). Preconditioning of reinforcing properties to an exteroceptive feedback stimulus. *Learning and Motivation, 6*, 289–298.

Moscovitch, A., & LoLordo, V. M. (1968). Role of safety in the Pavlovian backward fear conditioning procedure. *Journal of Comparative and Physiological Psychology, 66*, 673–678.

Mowrer, O. H. (1947). On the dual nature of learning—A re-interpretation of "conditioning" and "problem-solving." *Harvard Educational Review, 17*, 102–148.

Mowrer, O. H. (1960). *Learning theory and behavior*. New York: Wiley.

Nash, R. F., Gallup, G. G., Jr., & Czech, D. A. (1976). Psychophysiological correlates of tonic immobility in the domestic chicken (Gallus gallus). *Physiology & Behavior, 17*, 413–418.

Obrist, P. A., Sutterer, J. R., & Howard, J. L. (1972). Preparatory cardiac changes: A psychobiological approach. In A. H. Black & W. F. Prokasy (eds.), *Classical conditioning II: Current research and theory*, 312–340. New York: Appleton-Century-Crofts.

Ost, L.-G., & Hugdahl, K. (1981). Acquisition of phobias and anxiety response patterns in clinical patients. *Behaviour Research and Therapy, 19*, 439–447.

Ost, L.-G., & Hugdahl, K. (1983). Acquisition of agoraphobia, mode of onset and anxiety response patterns. *Behaviour Research and Therapy, 21*, 623–631.

Pavlov, I. P. (1927/1960). *Conditioned reflexes*. New York: Dover.

Porro, C. A., & Carli, G. (1988). Immobilization and restraint effects on pain reactions in animals. *Pain, 32*, 289–307.

Ratner, S. C (1967). Comparative aspects of hypnosis. In J. E. Gordon (ed.), *Handbook of clinical and experimental hypnosis*, 550–587. New York: Macmillan.

Ratner, S. C., Karon, B. P., VandenBos, G. R., & Denny, M. R. (1981). The adaptive significance of the catatonic stupor in humans and animals from an evolutionary perspective. *Academic Psychology Bulletin, 3*, 273–279.

Rescorla, R. A. (1967). Pavlovian conditioning and its proper control procedures. *Psychological Review, 74*, 71–80.

Rescorla, R. A. (1968a). Pavlovian conditioned fear in Sidman avoidance learning. *Journal of Comparative and Physiological Psychology, 65*, 55–60.

Rescorla, R. A. (1968b). Probability of shock in the presence and absence of CS in fear conditioning. *Journal of Comparative and Physiological Psychology, 66,* 1–5.

Rescorla, R. A. (1969a). Conditioned inhibition of fear resulting from negative CS-US contingencies. *Journal of Comparative and Physiological Psychology, 67,* 504–509.

Rescorla, R. A. (1969b). Establishment of a positive reinforcer through contrast with shock. *Journal of Comparative and Physiological Psychology, 67,* 260–263.

Rescorla, R. A. (1976). Second-order conditioning of Pavlovian conditioned inhibition. *Learning and Motivation, 7,* 161–172.

Rescorla, R. A. (1980). *Pavlovian second-order conditioning: Studies in associative learning.* Hillsdale, N.J.: Erlbaum.

Rescorla, R. A., & LoLordo, V. M. (1965). Inhibition of avoidance behavior. *Journal of Comparative and Physiological Psychology, 59,* 406–412.

Rescorla, R. A., & Solomon, R. L. (1967). Two-process learning theory: Relationships between Pavlovian conditioning and instrumental learning. *Psychological Review, 74,* 151–182.

Rescorla, R. A., & Wagner, A. R. (1972). A theory of Pavlovian conditioning: Variations in the effectiveness of reinforcement and nonreinforcement. In A. H. Black & W. F. Prokasy (eds.), *Classical conditioning II: Current research and theory,* 64–99. New York: Appleton-Century-Crofts.

Sargeant, A. B., & Eberhardt, L. E. (1975). Death feigning by ducks in response to predation by red foxes (Vulpes fulva). *American Midland Naturalist, 94,* 108–119.

Seligman, M. E. P. (1971). Phobias and preparedness. *Behavior Therapy, 2,* 307–320.

Seligman, M. E. P., & Hager, J. (eds.) (1972). *Biological boundaries of learning.* New York: Appleton-Century-Crofts.

Sidman, M. (1953). Two temporal parameters of the maintenance of avoidance behavior by the white rat. *Journal of Comparative and Physiological Psychology, 46,* 253–261.

Sidman, M. (1962). Reduction of shock frequency as reinforcement for avoidance behavior. *Journal of the Experimental Analysis of Behavior, 5,* 247–257.

Solomon, R. L., & Turner, L. H. (1962). Discriminative classical conditioning in dogs paralyzed by curare can later control discriminative avoidance responses in the normal state. *Psychological Review, 69,* 202–219.

Soltysik, S. S., Wolfe, G. E., Nicholas, T., Wilson, W. J., & Garcia-Sanchez, J. L. (1983). Blocking of inhibitory conditioning within a serial conditioned stimulus-conditioned inhibitor compound: Maintenance of acquired behavior without an unconditioned stimulus. *Learning and Motivation, 14,* 1–29.

Starr, M. D., & Mineka, S. (1977). Determinants of fear over the course of avoidance learning. *Learning and Motivation, 8,* 332–350.

Sturgis, E, & Scott, R. (1984). Simple phobia. In S. M. Turner (ed.), *Behavioral theories and treatment of anxiety,* 91–141. New York: Plenum.

Suarez, S. D., & Gallup, G. G., Jr. (1979). Tonic immobility as a response to rape in humans: A theoretical note. *Psychological Record, 29,* 315–320.

Thomas, G. V. (1983). Contiguity and contingency in instrumental conditioning. *Learning and Motivation, 14,* 513–526.

Thompson, R. K. R., Foltin, R. W., Boylan, R. J., Sweet, A., Graves, C. A., & Lowitz, C. E. (1981). Tonic immobility in Japanese quail can reduce the probability of sustained attack by cats. *Animal Learning & Behavior, 9,* 145–149.

Tortora, D. F. (1983). Safety training: The elimination of avoidance-motivated aggression in dogs. *Journal of Experimental Psychology: General, 112,* 176–214.

Van Hemel, P. E., & Colucci, V. M. (1973). Effects of target movement on mouse-killing attack by rats. *Journal of Comparative and Physiological Psychology, 85,* 105–110.

Weisman, R. G., & Litner, J. S. (1969). The course of Pavlovian excitation and inhibition of fear in rats. *Journal of Comparative and Physiological Psychology, 69,* 667–672.

Westbrook, R. F., Good, A. J., & Kiernan, M. J. (1994). Effects of the interval between exposure to a novel environment and the occurrence of shock on the freezing responses of rats. *Quarterly Journal of Experimental Psychology, 47B,* 427–446.

White, C. M., & Weeden, R. B. (1966). Hunting methods of gyrfalcons and behavior of their prey (ptarmigan). *Condor, 68,* 517–519.

Witcher, E. S., & Ayres, J. J. B. (1980). Systematic manipulation of CS-US pairings in negative CS-US correlation procedures in rats. *Animal Learning & Behavior, 8,* 67–74.

Witcher, E. S., & Ayres, J. J. B. (1984). A test of two methods for extinguishing Pavlovian conditioned inhibition. *Animal Learning & Behavior, 12,* 149–156.

Wolpe, J. (1969). *The practice of behavior therapy.* New York: Pergamon.

Yeo, A. G. (1974). The acquisition of conditioned suppression as a function of interstimulus interval duration. *Quarterly Journal of Experimental Psychology, 26,* 405–416.

CHAPTER 8

OPERANT-RESPONDENT INTERACTIONS

Robert W. Allan

If the stimulus is already correlated with a response or the response with a stimulus, a reinforcement cannot be made contingent upon the one term without being put into a similar relation with the other. That is to say, if a reinforcing stimulus is correlated temporarily with the S in a reflex, it is also correlated with the R, or if with the R, then also with the S. It is not possible to avoid this difficulty.... (Skinner, 1937; 1972, p. 490).

Skinner's words serve as both a description and a warning—he describes the potential interrelations between stimuli and responses, and he warns future researchers that interactions between the various stimulus-response and response-stimulus relations are inevitable. Furthermore, in this 1937 paper[1] Skinner names the

procedures and response types derived therefrom as respondent and operant (Skinner, 1937; 1972, pp. 490–493). Five years earlier, Skinner (1932) made his first overt attempt to identify the two different types of responding, and their attendant conditioning procedures, although he approached the proposal with some caution (cf. Skinner, 1931, 1935a, 1935b). At the time of Skinner's proposal, Thorndike (1911) had already experimented with what was called instrumental (operant) conditioning, Pavlov (1927) had previously explored classically conditioned responses (respondents), and Miller and Konorski (1928) had already proposed the existence of at least two categories of conditioned reflexes. But it was Skinner's (1935, 1937) logical arguments that proved so successful in estab-

---

[1]This paper was written in response to Konorski and Miller (1937), who proposed two types of conditioned reflex, which they called Type I and Type II. Knowing of Skinner's interest, they sent him an advance copy of their paper, and Skinner's 1937 paper is his response. The reflex types proposed by Kornorski and Miller captured some of the same notions Skinner had been struggling with for more than five years.

lishing the bi-conditional nature of responding (cf. Williams, 1981). So successful, in fact, that subsequent generations of conditioning researchers and theorists have routinely categorized experimental procedures and responding as either operant or respondent. Although there is some disagreement concerning the criteria that are necessary and sufficient to sort responding, conditioned responses continue to be sorted into two categories largely based on the temporal and contingent relations involved in the operations engendering and maintaining responding.[2]

Ideally, researchers would like to isolate responses from each category for examination in their relatively "pure" form. Presumably, the value of such research would be the identification of the relevant factors functioning to control responses from each of the categories. Eventually, when most of the controlling factors were known, combinations of factors could then be arranged, and all behavioral output could then be adequately predicted and controlled. From its beginnings, this has been one of the goals of conditioning theory: to provide a usable set of functional descriptions relating environmental factors to the probability of behavior.

This dichotomization of behavior as either operant or respondent has a long history (Miller & Konorski, 1928; Konorski & Miller, 1937; Skinner, 1935b, 1937, 1938). At the level of experimental operations, this categorical approach to behavior has proven to be a durable distinction; both response-reinforcer (operant) and stimulus-reinforcer (respondent) contingencies have been manipulated profitably in the process of producing, experimentally manipulating, and maintaining behavior. Other theorists have proposed unified accounts of behavior. They argue that behavior is of one type and that operant and respondent conditioning operations are simply different methods of studying this single underlying behavioral disposition (e.g., Bindra, 1972; Hearst, 1975; Donahoe, Crowley, Mallard, &

Stickney, 1982; but see Mackintosh, 1974, pp. 128–139). These accounts of behavior are important, and the interested reader is encouraged to examine influential summaries of these positions (see references above). This work will take a functional approach to the question of behavioral control (Catania, 1971, pp. 196–197). The idea to be explored is that, although operant and respondent contingencies may be separately arranged, ultimately, as Skinner recognized in the quote at the beginning of the chapter, behavior is probably influenced by effects derived from the sometimes uncontrolled presence of *both* contingencies. A better understanding of the effects of these "intruding" conditions should allow for a more complete understanding of conditioned responding, regardless of its categorical type. More to the point, if we are to understand how behavior is shaped and maintained in extralaboratory conditions, an understanding of these potential intrusions is both necessary and critical to our ability to predict and control behavior.

Contingency Arrangements

Perhaps this dichotomous approach arose from the realization that there are only two ways for the environment to interact with behavior. As schematized in Figure 8–1, stimulus events can occur prior to behavior and have a direct impact

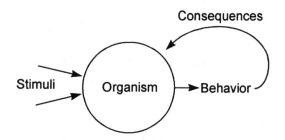

Figure 8–1. Flow chart depicting potential behavioral influences.

---

[2]A more associative view of conditioning processes is provided by Colwill and Rescorla (1986), although associative and biconditional views are not necessarily incommensurable; indeed, the associative researchers have confirmed much of what early theorists identified as being probable (e.g., Colwill & Rescorla, 1990).

on the probability of responding. In the case of an unconditioned stimulus (US), the behavior may actually be *elicited* in the sense that no prior training is needed, the response is reliably correlated with stimulus presentation, and the response rarely occurs in the absence of the stimulus. The other possibility (see Figure 8–1) is that behavior can occur and be reliably followed by environmental changes that feed back and alter the future probability of responding.[3] Generally, experimental analyses have attempted to isolate the effects of only one of these relations while holding the other constant (e.g., Jenkins, 1977), and this has proved to be a difficult task. Indeed, from a logical perspective the most likely scenario is that for any instance of responding, both antecedent and consequential events have some influence on the probability of behavior (Hearst, 1975, p. 194). Good experimental analyses, then, should assess the relative contribution of operant and respondent contingencies in the control of responding. In that process, appropriate experimental controls will be devised and used to dissociate the relative influence of these antecedent and consequential events in the support of ongoing behavior (Jenkins, 1977, pp. 51–54; Mackintosh, 1974, p. 124–128).

The difficulties encountered when developing dissociation procedures stem from the fact that differences in behavioral operations, rather than being dichotomous, may in fact be ordinally positioned on a probabilistic continuum (see Figure 8–2). At the operant extreme of this continuum the experimenter attempts to hold all stimulus-reinforcer (respondent) conditions constant so as to minimize their contribution. At the respondent end the experimenter prevents the operation of any explicit operant contingencies so as to isolate the influence of respondent factors. Of course, as already intimated, the most likely condition, either by chance or by design, is some combination of operant and respondent operations acting on *several* responses simultaneously. Indeed, there are conditions in which researchers have purposely imposed both stimulus-reinforcer (respondent) and response-reinforcer (operant) contingent relations with the purpose of examining the relative contribution of each relation to the control of responding.

As an example of unintended joint control, consider a simple multiple schedule in which a green key sets the occasion for reinforcement of key pecking on a variable-interval 30-second (VI 30 second) schedule, while a red key signals extinction (EXT). Under these schedule conditions, the probability of key pecking may be jointly influenced by the response-reinforcer (peck–food; operant) contingency and by the stimulus-reinforcer (green key–food; respondent) contingency that also attends this particular schedule (Reynolds, 1961a).[4] The problem of determining the relative contribution of each contingent relation to the control of responding is compounded when other responses are examined simultaneously. For example, in the multiple schedule described above, what if both key pecking and movement in the chamber were monitored simultaneously? Would response-reinforcer and stimulus-reinforcer contingencies have different proportional effects on each response? Do these responses compete for expression, or are they compatible in the sense that they may be performed simultaneously? What if rats' lever-pressing and salivation were both recorded (e.g., Williams, 1965)? How would these individual responses change? If the operant-respondent distinction is less dichotomous and more continuous, and if the effects of operations along this dimension are specific to the response being measured, then the problem of generating simple schedules to distinguish the relative contribution of each

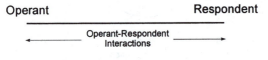

Figure 8–2. The Operant-Respondent continuum.

---

[3]As in the case of free-operant responding where consequential stimuli are highly correlated with responding.

[4]See Rescorla (1990a, 1990b) for clear demonstrations of the specificity of discriminative control.

contingency may be a difficult and thankless task (Skinner, 1938, pp. 10–12). However, the task of searching for the functional relations tying antecedent stimuli, behavior, and consequences together is an important undertaking. Research in the laboratory and in applied settings that examines these behavior relations must continue if responding is to be adequately predicted and controlled.

The remainder of this chapter represents only a précis of research on the joint operant-respondent control of behavior. If this chapter should opportune a more extended examination of the research literature, then the behavior analysis community will benefit—additional research may be prompted with a consequentially more thorough understanding of operant and respondent conditioning.

POSSIBLE INTERACTIONS

It may be useful to consider three general categories of potential operant-respondent interaction: (1) the possible intrusion of operant contingencies on explicitly arranged respondent conditioning,[5] (2) the intrusion of respondent contingencies on explicitly arranged operant conditioning (e.g., Reynolds, 1961a), and (3) an explicit arrangement of both operant and respondent contingencies (e.g., Estes & Skinner, 1941). Specific procedures have been developed to dissociate response-reinforcer (operant) and stimulus-reinforcer (respondent) effects in conditioning situations, and although each procedure has offered interesting, and sometimes successful results, there are many cases in which successful dissociation has not been made. The following sections will briefly explore each of these three categories of potential operant-respondent interaction. Attendant dissociation procedures will be considered with the hope that these approaches may find some practical use in both experimental and applied settings.

Operant Intrusion

In all respondent procedures, there is a possibility that adventitious pairings of the unconditioned response (UR), or conditioned response (CR), with the reinforcer (or US) may result in operant strengthening of that behavior. In an attempt to dissociate the potential effects of this adventitious pairing, researchers have typically applied omission training schedules specifying that reinforcers will never follow the behavior elicited by respondent contingencies. The classic study was reported by Sheffield (1965) in which he classically conditioned dogs' salivation to a tone conditioned stimulus (CS) with food as the unconditioned stimulus (US). Following establishment of a CR, an operant contingency specified that an "anticipatory" drop of salivation (a CR) during the presence of the tone CS would prevent food delivery on that conditioning trial. This arrangement assured that salivation would never be followed by the reinforcer. If, during training, food had somehow strengthened salivation via an adventitious operant contingency, then, as the logic of this arrangement suggests, salivation should have diminished rapidly and remained suppressed as long as the omission contingency was in effect. One of the dogs continued salivating for more than 800 CS-US trials with little sign of reduction in the frequency of the "anticipatory" salivation CR. In a later experiment (Miller & Carmona, 1967), when water was used as the US, dogs showed an almost immediate decline in salivation under omission conditions. These findings suggest that elicited salivation can be sensitive to response-reinforcer relations, but only under certain deprivation conditions; under food deprivation, the response seems to be insensitive to its consequences, while water deprivation conditions produce opposite results.[6]

Perhaps the most famous omission study is the Williams and Williams (1969) study of autoshaped key pecking. Brown and Jenkins (1968)

---

[5]This unplanned intrusion has been called *superstitious* or *adventitious* conditioning (e.g., Skinner, 1948; but see Staddon & Simmelhag, 1971).

[6]In the Miller and Carmona (1967) study, either salivation increases or decreases were successfully reinforced under water deprivation conditions; see also the literature on establishing operations (e.g., Michael 1982).

had previously shown that pigeons would peck a stimulus key that briefly preceded food availability. As one possible explanation of the derived key pecking, they tentatively proposed an operant, superstitious shaping interpretation of the acquired key-peck response that included gradual differential reinforcement of looking, approaching, and finally pecking at the key stimulus (cf. Hearst & Jenkins, 1974). Williams and Williams (1969) suggested that if autoshaped responses were superstitiously reinforced operants, those responses should be sensitive to a clear alteration of the response-consequence relation. Borrowing Sheffield's (1965) approach, they imposed an omission contingency on the key pecks produced under autoshaping conditions. Under one condition, if the birds pecked, the key light was immediately terminated and the potential reinforcer was canceled for that trial. Although rates of responding decreased, the probability of key pecking during any given key light presentation remained very high; sometimes over 90% of the trials were accompanied (and canceled) by key pecks. The results suggested that autoshaped key pecking was not very sensitive to its consequences, hence was probably not a superstitiously reinforced operant.

The purpose of these early omission designs was to discover whether operant contingencies were intruding on explicit respondent arrangements; in essence, to parse the contribution of respondent and operant contingencies to maintained responding. The logic is that if an adventitious (or superstitious) response-reinforcer contingency has been operating during the initial stimulus-reinforcer training phases, then the omission contingency should reverse that reinforcement trend. After all, the omission design is explicitly a negative punishment procedure, an operation that should produce effects opposite to the presumed positive-reinforcement contingency adventitiously intruding on the respondent conditions. The problem with this logic is that adventitious reinforcement could have been involved in the production and maintenance of responding, but for some unknown reason, the response could be relatively insensitive to the new, negative pun-

ishment contingency. That is, the procedures used to generate a response do not guarantee predictions of the relative sensitivity of the behavior to subsequent, altered training conditions.

Indeed, what if opposite results had been obtained in the Williams and Williams (1969) study? That is, what if all pecking had been thoroughly suppressed by the omission contingency? Would they have concluded that there was a superstitious operant contingency supporting autoshaped key pecking? Perhaps all we could say under those conditions is that whatever the source of the response (operant, respondent, or some combination), the behavior was brought under the control of this new, seemingly powerful contingency. As is the case with any new contingent relation designed to alter ongoing responding, the only logically safe conclusion is that the imposition of this new contingency either succeeds or fails to bring ongoing responding under control; the results do not indicate whether a similar category of contingency was in force when the response was originally trained (cf. Jenkins, 1977, pp. 50–51).

As it turns out, the results of Williams and Williams (1969) have not been unambiguously supported. With slight modifications of the omission design, others have discovered that autoshaped key pecking is very sensitive to its consequences (e.g., Allan & Matthews, 1991; Barrera, 1974; Hursh, Navarick, & Fantino, 1974; Schwartz & Williams, 1972; see also Peden, Browne, & Hearst, 1977). For example, in a modified autoshaping procedure (Allan & Matthews, 1991), food was presented every 30 seconds during a training phase. Filling the 30-second interval was an added clock stimulus (e.g., Ferster & Skinner, 1957, pp. 266–267) consisting of a key light whose brightness grew during each second of the inter-food interval (IFI) (see also, Dinsmoor, Dougan, Pfister, & Thiels, 1992). Food was presented briefly following the brightest key light value, and during training, key pecking was never required. After as few as 30 trials of this kind, key pecking was engendered (autoshaped) and maintained at relatively high rates with most of the pecks occurring during the brightest light values. In a second experimental phase, an explicit operant contingency was introduced in which each key peck resulted in a decrease in key brightness by one level, and an accompanying 1-second delay of food. If the pigeons continued to respond, the key-light brightness level could be driven to its starting value. When the pigeon stopped pecking, the key light began to increase again in brightness, and if the brightest key level was presented, food followed immediately. This procedure, unlike the standard omission arrangement, delivered all the reinforcers (i.e., none were canceled), and if the bird stopped responding completely, food deliveries again occurred every 30 seconds. This contingency seems, on the surface, to be much less punishing than the Williams and Williams (1969) omission contingency in which responses canceled both stimulus and reinforcer. The results, however, suggest otherwise. As depicted in Figure 8–3 (from Allan & Matthews, 1991, Figure 2), key pecking for all four birds decreased quickly with responding maintained at low levels for as long as the operant contingency was in effect. Generally, the first two or three trials of the first session in the contingent phase contained several hundred responses (thereby extending the trial from 30 seconds to, at times, more than five minutes), but the peck-stimulus-change contingency exerted thorough control thereafter. These data suggest that the autoshaped pecking generated on this schedule is extraordinarily sensitive to its consequences.

Alternatively, the argument from a purely respondent perspective could be that during the contingency phase, IFI values were altered, as was the sequence of light brightnesses predictive of food delivery. Perhaps these temporally based alterations alone were sufficient to lower the probability of continued key pecking (cf. Gibbon & Balsam, 1981). Two observations argue against this interpretation: (1) Once key pecking rates were decreased to near-zero levels, both the stimulus sequence and the IFI times returned roughly to their original values, the values that engendered key pecking earlier in training (so why would response rates remain low unless

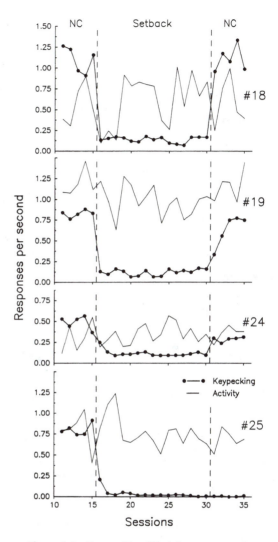

Figure 8–3. Key pecking (filled data points) and activity rates (solid line), across sessions, for individual birds. Rates from the last 5 days of noncontingent (NC) training, the 15 days of the negative punishment contingency (Setback), and 5 days after removal of the contingency are depicted. Bird numbers are indicated at the right of each plot.

the key-peck contingency was operating?); and (2) recent work has shown that if a yoked bird (whose responses have no effect) is exposed to the brightness sequences and IFI alterations produced by a bird exposed to the contingency, the

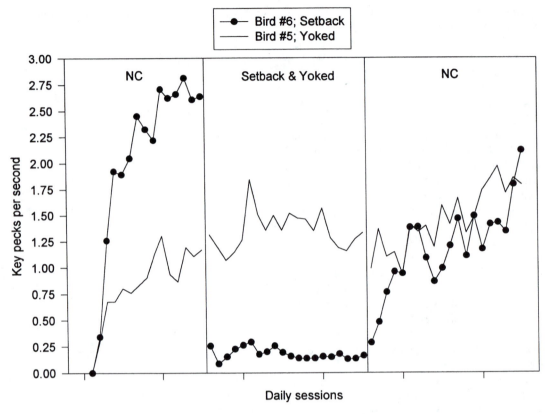

Figure 8–4. Key pecking rates across sessions, for contingent (setback; filled data points) and yoked (solid line) birds. Rates from the 15 days of noncontingent (NC) training, the 20 days of either negative punishment (Setback) or noncontingent yoked exposure, and 20 days after removal of the setback and yoked conditions are depicted. Bird numbers are indicated in the legend.

yoked bird's rates of responding remain unchanged (Allan, 1997). Figure 8–4 depicts key pecking rates for both a bird exposed to the contingency and its yoked partner. It is clear that alterations in the respondent parameters alone fail to account for the observed response-rate changes; the operant contingency is a necessary, and in this case perhaps sufficient, operation to produce response suppression.[7]

In a respondent procedure involving an aversive US, dogs were trained with a clicker as the CS

paired with brief electric shock to one leg (Wahlsten & Cole, 1972; see also Konorski & Miller, 1937). After training conditions, in which leg flexion was both the UR and the CR, the researchers introduced a negative-reinforcement contingency for leg-flexion responses during the CS. Under the contingency, leg flexion during the CS could prevent shock on that trial. Although the leg-flexion response was already being elicited by the CS on approximately 40% of the trials, when the operant contingency was installed,

---

[7]For a review of other omission studies, see Locurto (1981); for a review of several early yoked control studies, see Peden et al. (1977, p. 379).

the frequency of leg flexion increased to a much higher level (almost 80% of the trials). Control dogs not exposed to the additional operant omission contingency continued to produce lower levels of the conditioned leg-flexion response (CR). It could be argued that if "superstitious" operant contingencies were exerting control over the probability of a leg-flexion response, then adding the explicit negative reinforcement contingency should do little to rates of ongoing responding since operant contingencies were already exerting their effects. Because responding increased in frequency commensurate with the addition of the operant contingency (rates doubled), the argument could be made that "superstitious" operant contingencies were probably not contributing much to the elicitation of leg flexion during the initial respondent training phase. Once again, if there had been such a "superstitious" contingency in effect, rates of responding should have more closely approximated those observed under negative-reinforcement conditions. There is, however, the possibility that operant contingencies were in effect, but because responding was maintained on a partial, and indeed variable, schedule, rates were lower than under subsequent continuous negative reinforcement. The results, once again, suggest that elicited responding, although not originally supported by operant contingencies, may be very sensitive to its consequences. The relative sensitivity of a response is a function not only of the procedures used during training, but also of those used during the added contingent phase. Other factors, such as deprivation state and response-produced alterations of stimuli and temporal intervals, should be considered before determining that a response is insensitive to potential response-reinforcer relations (e.g., Pierce & Epling, 1991).

Additionally, there are several reports of explicit control of reflexive behavior by operant contingencies (e.g., Miller & Banuazizi, 1968; Greene & Sutor, 1971; for a review, see Miller, 1969; see also Olton & Noonberg, 1980, for a review of biofeedback). Although some of the work on operant conditioning of these reflexive responses has been called into question and some of the original experiments have not been success-fully replicated (e.g., Miller & Dworkin, 1974), if any of these studies have accurately reported the influence of operant contingencies on reflexive behavior, then consideration must be given to this potential source of control. In any case, it is possible that in explicitly respondent conditions operant contingencies may intrude and exert some level of control over ongoing responding. Even the (logically speaking) powerful omission contingency does not guarantee an accurate dissociation of operant and respondent contributions. What this means is that careful experimental work and critical examination of the data must be completed before concluding that a response is only sensitive to respondent conditioning procedures.

Respondent Intrusion

Frequently researchers will arrange conditions in which operants are brought under stimulus control (see Ferster & Skinner, 1957, Chapter 10). What this means, in its simplest form, is that responding is differentially reinforced in the presence of one stimulus (S^D) while the same behavior is extinguished in the presence of a second stimulus (S^Δ). If these two stimuli and their associated response contingencies are presented alternately, then a multiple schedule is arranged. Indeed, this is the primary arrangement used to produce a discrimination, or discriminative control of responding (this discriminative arrangement of stimulus, response, and consequence is often referred to as a three-term contingency). If the multiple schedule is successful, then responding should occur more frequently during the stimulus that is said to "set the occasion" for an active response-reinforcer contingency (Skinner, 1938, p. 178). At an operational level, the occasion-setting property of S^Ds should not be confused with eliciting properties of CSs. There is a clear operational difference between the respondent CS and the S^D, such that a respondent CS elicits behavior because of the contingent relation between CS and US (e.g., Rescorla, 1967) while the operant S^D sets the occasion for responding because of a prior history of that response's being reinforced in the presence of the

S^D. The critical difference lies in the conspicuous absence of a response contingency during the CS and the clear presence of a response contingency during the S^D. Although researchers have sometimes assumed that this qualitative, operational difference is reflected by clear, differential support of respondents by CSs and operants by S^Ds, experimental evidence has not always supported this claim (e.g., Reynolds, 1961a).

Under discriminative conditions it is certainly clear that the S^D is functioning nominally in a respondent relation that reliably pairs the S^D with the operant consequence (a putative US). Potentially, the result of these respondent pairings may be elicited behavior that may add to or compete with the discriminative control of ongoing operant responding (Rachlin, 1973; Schwartz & Gamzu, 1977; see also the phenomenon of *anticipatory* contrast, discussed below).

Potentially endemic to all three-term contingent relations is the possibility that the pairing of the S^D with a reinforcer continues to exert some control over responding even after the response-reinforcer (operant) relation is removed. The extent to which this intruding respondent relation comes to control behavior, as well as which behavior comes under control, are questions that have received considerable research attention (e.g., Williams, 1983, 1992a, 1992b).

Behavioral Contrast

In a classic series of studies, Reynolds (1961a, 1961b) described increases in rate of key pecking as a function of simply introducing an operant discrimination in a simple two-component multiple schedule (see also Smith & Hoy, 1954; Herrick, Myers, & Korotkin, 1959). During the initial phase of the experiment, both stimuli (S^D and S^Δ) set the occasion for pecking on the same-value VI schedules. After several sessions of training, responding during the S^Δ was extinguished, while responding during the S^D continued to be reinforced on the same VI schedule. Most researchers probably would have predicted that rates of responding would decrease during the S^Δ and stay

the same during the S^D, since response rate increases on the VI schedule during the S^D would not result in an increased rate of reinforcement. After all, this is the nature (and value) of VI schedules; increases and decreases in response rates do not drastically alter obtained reinforcer rates. If response rates increase or decrease during a stable VI schedule, these changes must be due to factors other than obtained reinforcer rates. Reynolds discovered that response rates did decrease during the S^Δ, but surprisingly, response rates increased during the S^D. Indeed, the observation that rates of responding in one component of a multiple schedule could be altered by changing the rates of reinforcement in a second component serves as the defining characteristic of a "contrast" effect (Reynolds, 1961a, p. 57). These results have been replicated often, and behavioral contrast effects are often immediate, large, and sustained for many sessions.

Reynolds (1961a) offered an explanation based on *relative* frequency of reinforcement obtained in each component, a view contemporaneous with the development of Herrnstein's (1961) matching law. The idea was that during the equal VI schedules, on average 50% of available reinforcers were delivered for pecking during each stimulus. After the change to multiple VI EXT, pecks were reinforced only during the unchanged VI component. Consequently, 100% of the reinforcers were obtained in the presence of that stimulus. In an impressive figure that plotted relative rates of responding to relative frequency of reinforcement, Reynolds (1961b, Figure 4) portrayed a concise predictive relation between relative frequency of reinforcement and emergent relative rates of responding (Herrnstein, 1958, 1961).[8] Reynolds (1961a) states, "The increase in relative frequency of reinforcement from 0.5 to 1.0 results in contrast, an increase in the rate of responding" (p. 70).

Subsequent researchers proposed that this kind of positive contrast (an increase in response rates during the unchanged VI component) represents the addition of elicited key pecks to the ongoing

---

[8]Herrnstein (1970) later extended this matching law analysis to account for response rate differences in single, multiple, and concurrent schedules.

emitted (VI) pecks, the former category of pecks being presumably supported by the S^D-reinforcer pairing alone (e.g., Schwartz & Gamzu, 1977). Reynolds (1961a, 1961b) relied on a very careful description of what happened during a contrast experiment; his interpretations of so-called underlying causes were kept to a minimum. But seven years later there appeared to be a logical conjoining of the contrast effect with the newly discovered autoshaping (Brown & Jenkins, 1968). Admittedly, there was a clear similarity between procedures producing behavioral contrast and those producing autoshaped pecking. In both situations, a relatively long interval with no reinforcement is followed by a stimulus that is contingently related to reinforcement. As a test of this notion, Schwartz (1973) demonstrated that key pecking could be engendered after several sessions of pigeons being exposed to a multiple variable time (VT) EXT schedule. As predicted by the contrast/autoshaping interpretation, pecks occurred only to the key light setting the occasion for the VT component. Since pecking was not required on the VT schedule, the responses supported by this multiple schedule were, in an operational sense, autoshaped. These and other findings led researchers to speculate that perhaps when behavioral contrast was observed, respondent contingencies were intruding by adding autoshaped key pecks to the operant levels of key pecking already supported by the operant contingency in force during the unchanged VI component. In this account, behavioral contrast is a function of operant rates of responding plus autoshaped rates of responding, each produced by respective respondent and operant operations. This *additivity* model interpretation has led to a considerable research endeavor examining relative rates of responding under multiple schedules (see below).

Subsequent experimental work has once again failed to support the generalizability of the additivity interpretation. For example, although behavioral contrast occurs in many species, including humans (Rovee-Collier & Capatides, 1979; Waite & Osborne, 1972), there may be differences in the way these respondent relations intrude on ongoing operant responding. For ex-

ample, behavioral contrast was not observed when treadle pressing was the required operant for pigeons (Hemmes, 1973) although more recent research suggests that this is the case only when reinforcement rates are quite low. When reinforcers are frequent during the S^D, contrast may be obtained for treadle pressing (e.g., McSweeney, 1982; McSweeney, Dougan, & Farmer-Dougan, 1986; King & McSweeney, 1987). Although there are many examples of deviation from the predictions of behavioral contrast, even Williams (1983), one of additivity theory's critics, suggests that an adequate theory of contrast effects must call on "Pavlovian contingencies," in conjunction with relative rates of reinforcement, in the explanation of behavioral contrast effects. It is clear that operationally, a high stimulus-reinforcer correlation is involved in the increased rates of responding observed in a contrast experiment.

Anticipatory Contrast

Williams (1979, 1990; see also Flaherty, 1982) has also discussed a relatively counterintuitive example of potential respondent intrusion known as *anticipatory contrast*. Essentially, in a four-component multiple schedule, pairs of components are formed. The first of each pair is the *target* component; the second is referred to as the *following* component. Reinforcer schedule values in the following component of one pair are generally manipulated during the experiment. Pigeons' response rate changes during the target component are of interest as these rates seem most affected by shifts in the reinforcing value of the *following* schedule. The counterintuitive finding is that target rates increase when the following schedule is changed to EXT in one pair of components. Even more surprising is the observation that rates do not generally increase during the target component following the EXT component. This local contrast effect is quite robust and has no clear interpretation based on "adding" autoshaped key pecks to ongoing operant responding. Of course, it is also not clear how any interpretation based on relative rates of reinforcement (e.g., Herrnstein, 1970) would handle these data (Williams, 1992a).

Subsequent studies have demonstrated that with some relatively simple manipulations of temporal, schedule, and stimulus factors, respondent intrusions may be more likely (e.g., Hassin-Herman, Hemmes, & Brown, 1992; Williams, 1992a). If components are signaled by different discriminative stimuli, if the components are all relatively long and close to being equal in duration, and if reinforcers are available in all components (except the EXT component), then anticipatory contrast is the most likely result. If, however, only the target components are signaled with different colors, if the target component durations are relatively short, and if reinforcers are only available in the following components, then autoshaped key pecking is typically produced during the target component preceding the most densely reinforced following component (Williams, 1992a). This result is exactly the opposite of anticipatory contrast, but is consistent with what a respondent-intrusion model would predict: the stimulus preceding the component with the highest rates of reinforcement should engender autoshaped key pecks (e.g., Redford & Perkins, 1974), and under selected conditions specified above, this is exactly the result. On the other hand, anticipatory contrast effects continue to elude the interpretative efforts of researchers and theorists.

Although anticipatory contrast results run counter to current respondent additivity accounts, the research on anticipatory contrast is instructive. It clearly shows that both operant and respondent conditions, often in combination, may have an impact on response rates. Furthermore, the anticipatory contrast experiments provide a warning that researchers must beware of simple interpretations and predictions. Bringing responding under discriminative control may result in increases or decreases in responding depending on the choice, arrangement, and duration of discriminative stimuli. A careful understanding of both the respondent and operant character of operations used to engender and maintain responding is extraordinarily important to successful prediction of response probability.

Feature-Positive Discrimination

On a more molecular level, Jenkins and Sainsbury (1970) reported on the effects of introducing, on a discrete-trials procedure, a small stimulus feature that was periodically superimposed on a larger stimulus background, and that set the occasion for a key peck-reinforcer contingency. The larger stimulus background without the feature signaled EXT trials. The primary result was that the key pecking of each pigeon came under control of the discrimination; that is, they pecked most frequently whenever the small feature was present. There was, however, at least one topographic feature of responding other than rate that came under the control of the small feature. While the response contingency specified that key pecks directed to any part of the key would be reinforced, the pigeons' pecks tended to be directed at the feature regardless of where it appeared on the response key. To facilitate monitoring of response location, Jenkins and Sainsbury (1970) used a key that could be revealed by opening a shutter during the trial, and that was constructed with a piece of carbon paper between the stimulus surface (where the pigeons pecked) and the substrate of the response key. They could thereby monitor response locations on each trial by simply examining the traces left by beak contacts. This combined control of response rate and location constitutes what is referred to as the *feature-positive* effect.

Once again, the control of response location was not part of the operant requirement, and yet the pigeons all tracked the feature location, providing another example of putative respondent control of this aspect of response topography. Certainly, a superstitious reinforcement account could be offered, but the results showed that all pigeons tracked the feature. Superstitious reinforcement should be strengthening different response characteristics for each pigeon as it pecks at the stimulus display. Instead, all pigeons tracked the location of the feature. Of course, this is merely a logical denial of superstitious control by the positive feature. To make the argument from a data-based perspective, Jenkins and Sainsbury (1970) exposed pigeons to several variants of the feature-positive contingency in an effort to dissociate operant and respondent controls (cf. Jenkins, 1973; Sainsbury, 1971a, 1971b). Under what are called feature-negative conditions, the unique feature was presented only during EXT trials. In this condition all birds pecked everywhere but at the feature stimulus; indeed, the discrimination was never very successfully established under feature-negative conditions. These two experimental results speak against a superstitious reinforcement explanation since there was never a contingency for pecking at a particular location.

In a replication of this tracking characteristic of the feature-positive effect, Allan (1993) used a computer touch screen to monitor peck location. In the first phase, a red 3-cm-diameter circular stimulus was presented on the computer monitor, and key pecking was maintained on a VI schedule. During the discrimination phase (multiple VI EXT), a white 3-mm diameter dot (the *feature*) was superimposed at the center of the larger circular stimulus. Reinforcers were contingent on pecking only when the feature was present. At no time during any of the experimental phases were pecks at particular locations differentially reinforced; after completion of the VI schedule, pecks anywhere on the touch screen were reinforced, but only during feature presentations. Under the initial VI-only phase, there was considerable variability in response location with less than 20% of all responses directed to the large circular stimulus (although all responses were very close to the stimulus borders). With the addition of the small feature the rates of on-stimulus pecking more than doubled. As was the case with the Jenkins and Sainsbury (1970) study, a superstitious interpretation would not necessarily predict that all birds should begin pecking at the feature, but that they would instead continue pecking at locations that had most frequently been followed by reinforcement. The results were far more orderly than a superstition interpretation would suggest. Finally, a feature-negative manipulation demonstrated that adventitious contingencies were not necessarily maintaining the location of responding.

In a second experiment, Allan (1993) used a touch screen to record pecking locations on a multiple VI EXT schedule, with four filled squares in a two-by-two configuration setting the occasion for the EXT component. When a filled triangle replaced one of the four squares, the VI component was in effect. Once again, reinforcers were never contingent on response location; pecks anywhere on the touch screen were reinforced on the VI schedule. Figure 8–5 depicts the probability of responding at each location on the touch screen as the triangular stimulus appeared in all possible positions. It is clear that the respondent pairing of a feature with reinforcement delivery is sufficient to control the loca-

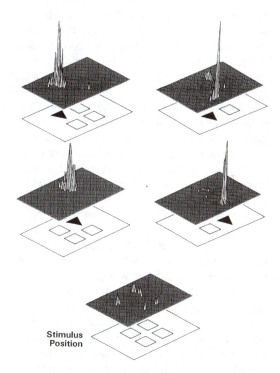

Figure 8–5. Probabilities of responding at each location in the presence of five possible stimulus displays. With a triangle present in one of the four positions, responses anywhere on the touch screen were reinforced on a VI schedule. In each case, responding tended to track the position of the triangle. When four squares were present, responding was on an EXT schedule; in this case, very few responses were emitted.

tion of pigeons' pecking. Recently, this finding has been replicated with adult humans (Mahon & Vargas, 1996; see also Sainsbury, 1971, who found a similar effect with children).

Using a more "natural" set of stimuli (e.g., Herrnstein & Loveland, 1964), pigeons were trained to peck a rather large (22-by-15-cm) touch-screen panel onto which photographic stimuli were back-projected (Allan, 1990). Stimuli consisted of a set of 40 color slides of everyday scenes, some including humans. Using a multiple VI EXT schedule, a discrimination was arranged such that the VI schedule was in effect during the slides containing one to three human figures grouped somewhere in the picture; the EXT components were signaled by slides without humans. Every 30 seconds the slides changed without respect to responding, and once again, there was no location-response contingency. Within two sessions all of the birds were responding only when slides with humans were present. Additionally, for some of the birds, pecks were directed at the human figures. Once again, these effects appear to be examples of the intrusion of respondent contingencies in the control of response location. The human figures are reliably paired with the delivery of food, thereby producing a putative autoshaping effect in which pecks are directed to the signal stimulus. When the same birds were placed in a feature-negative condition in which the presence of the humans in the slide signaled EXT, tracking responses ceased. Once again, if adventitious reinforcement was involved, these responses could have continued without punishment. Instead, feature tracking stopped almost immediately.

It seems quite clear that respondent (stimulus-reinforcer) relations (whether or not they are maintained by superstitious contingencies) can intrude on programmed operant contingencies and that they potentially may exert a powerful effect on both the frequency and location of responding. As suggested by Skinner more than 60 years ago, in any discrimination operation there are "built-in" stimulus-reinforcer correlations that may exert control over ongoing responding (Skinner, 1937, 1972, p. 490). In any setting (experimental or applied), behavior analysts must be aware of how these relationships impact the probability of behavior.

Explicit Operant-Respondent Arrangements

The Conditioned Emotional Response

Arguably, the best-studied example of an explicit combination of respondent and operant operations is the conditioned emotional response (CER). In their classic work, Estes and Skinner (1941) defined emotional responding in the rat as the reduction of ongoing operant bar pressing during the presentations of a tone that was followed by shock. Bar pressing was first maintained on a VI schedule of food reinforcement in the absence of any changing discriminative conditions. In a second phase, the respondent pairing of a 3-minute tone with a 0.5-second shock was superimposed on the VI schedule of food reinforcement. After as few as 6 to 10 tone-shock pairings, bar pressing during the tone was almost completely eliminated, even though food reinforcers would have continued to follow bar presses during the tone presentations. Estes and Skinner (1941) interpreted these findings as homologous to the disruptions of ongoing behavior that the verbal community labels "emotional."[9] It is probable, of course, that in the evolutionary history of organisms, selection was based to a large extent on the inherited ability to avoid stimuli preceding imminent danger. Presumably, in life-threatening conditions those animals possessing emotional behavior, including the attendant physiological responses (what are often called *feelings*), were more likely to survive; that is, these animals were more likely to escape the signals of imminent danger, thereby avoiding the dangerous conditions (e.g., Kamin, 1956).

---

[9]See also Holland and Skinner (1961, Set 36), for a good selection of applied examples of the conditioning of emotional responding. In addition, see Skinner (1953, pp. 160–170) for a thorough behavioral definition of the concept of *emotion*.

The literature that has grown out of this initial experiment is truly impressive. By explicitly combining operant and respondent conditioning operations, researchers have examined the contribution of various CS and US parameters (e.g., intensity, duration, probability of pairing, direction and delay of pairing, and associated random controls) to the production of the CER. In addition, other experiments have examined the contribution of various operant factors in the control of the CER; for example, the relative effects of types of reinforcers, their magnitude, and schedules of reinforcement have all been investigated. In addition, conditioning history, the age of the rats, as well as the effects of brain lesions and drugs have also been parametrically examined (see Henton, 1978). The attraction of this operant-respondent combination schedule is its presumed parallel with "real-life" conditions in which schedules often combine to generate complex performance. Also, while investigating parameters of one category of operations, the values of the other category can be maintained so that any change in responding will likely be due to the manipulated parameters. Some of this work holds a real promise of allowing researchers to dissociate the contribution of operant and respondent factors in the control of emotional behavior.

The CER findings suggest that if there are "pre-aversive" stimuli, there are also "pre-appetitive" stimuli (e.g., Herrnstein & Morse, 1957) in which, for example, a stimulus reliably predicts the response-independent delivery of food.[10] This suggests that separate pre-aversive or pre-appetitive stimulus conditions may be combined with either reinforcement or punishment operations, and the interactive results observed. For example, Sidman, Herrnstein, and Conrad (1957) reported that the pre-aversive stimuli from the CER experiments would actually function to increase rates of negatively reinforced responding. In their experiment, rats' bar pressing avoided unsignaled shock. When a stimulus that was paired with unavoidable shock was superimposed on this schedule of ongoing shock, rates of bar pressing increased during the stimulus presentation. Although the effects seem to complement those observed in CER studies, subsequent research on these explicitly combined schedules suggests that there are complex relationships between schedule of reinforcement, schedule of stimulus delivery, and shock magnitude, to mention just a few (e.g., Blackman, 1968). Clearly, the functional relations are complex, but it is the hope of researchers that with continued experimental work, common principles will emerge that may then be used to predict and control behavior. As Henton and Iversen (1978) point out, all of the combinations of pre-aversive and pre-appetitive stimuli with either positive or negative reinforcement schedules result in complex relations that generate rates of responding that are a function of several variable parameters. Generally, research programs have continued to arrange and titrate the contribution of each pair of operations to the maintenance of responding.

A Test of the "Origin Hypothesis"

In an important paper, Jenkins (1977) questioned the validity of attempting to isolate the behavioral effects of one conditioning procedure by introducing a completely new contingency after previous training with the first. The omission studies are examples of this style of research. The problem is that when new contingencies are introduced, there is a potential for new learning to occur. Instead, Jenkins proposed an exploration of the effects of varying stimulus-reinforcer (respondent), response-reinforcer (operant), and stimulus-response-reinforcer (three-term) contingencies after behavior has been maintained under explicitly combined operant and respondent conditions. In Jenkins' (1977) study, key pecking was autoshaped using an arrangement similar to the original Brown and Jenkins (1968) procedure. Although an operant contingency was later intro-

---

[10]The resemblance to autoshaping is unmistakable; the brief stimulus preceding the US delivery in an autoshaping trial may be considered pre-appetitive, in the sense that the brief stimulus supports behavior that often resembles the response to the US (e.g., Allan & Ziegler, 1994; Jenkins & Moore, 1973; Peterson, Ackil, Frommer, & Hearst, 1972).

duced such that key pecking was reinforced during the key presentation, the operational origin of the response was respondent. At the other end of the operant-respondent continuum (see Figure 8–2), head positioning was shaped by differentially reinforcing approximations to the final response, which involved breaking a pair of infrared beams 30.5 cm above the floor and at the center of the experimental chamber. The origin of this second response was clearly operant. This response was also brought under the control of a tone stimulus. At the end of 15 training sessions each response was occurring predominantly in the presence of the appropriate stimulus: key pecking in the presence of the key light and head positioning in the presence of the tone.

Based on what Jenkins (1977) called the "origin hypothesis," which suggests that responses should be sensitive only to the contingencies under which they were trained, he offered three predictions: (1) if the response-reinforcer contingency was relaxed by presenting food noncontingently after each discriminative stimulus, the autoshaped birds should continue responding (after all, their responses were originally due to a stimulus-reinforcer contingency, so why shouldn't that contingency continue to support responding?), and the head-positioning birds should stop responding; (2) if the stimulus-reinforcer correlation was degraded by reinforcing responses both in the presence and the absence of each stimulus, then the autoshaped birds should slow responding, and the head-positioning birds should continue responding during stimulus conditions and should increase response rates when the stimulus is off; and (3) when both the response-reinforcer and stimulus-reinforcer contingencies were eliminated by delivering food noncontingently during both stimulus and nonstimulus intervals, both groups should decrease response rates.

The origin hypothesis predictions were not supported. Following the removal of the response-reinforcer contingency, the autoshaped group's response rates decreased almost as much as the rates of responding in the head-positioning group. When the stimulus-reinforcer relation was degraded, response rates for both groups decreased (indeed, the head-positioning birds produced lower rates than the autoshaped birds). Finally, when both stimulus- and response-reinforcer contingencies were removed, response rates for both groups dropped to near-zero levels (as predicted). Taken together, these results suggest that regardless of response origins, behavior continues to be differentially sensitive to stimulus- and response-reinforcer manipulations (cf. Ellison & Konorski, 1964).

Several previously cited experiments are examples of the explicit arrangement of both operant and respondent operations (see the section on operant intrusions). For example, the omission contingency (Sheffield, 1965; Williams & Williams, 1969) pits a respondent operation that reliably generates key pecking against an operant contingency designed to suppress selected responses. The Wahlsten and Cole (1972) study also arranged an overlap between respondent conditioning of the leg-flexion response and operant reinforcement of that same response. These studies, however, were designed to inform the researcher as to the contribution of respondent and operant factors to the control of responding that occurred prior to the combined schedule (although see Peden et al., 1977). As Jenkins (1977) has already suggested, we will probably never know about a response's origin unless we begin with a combined schedule and then gradually alter the respective respondent and operant contingencies.

Jenkin's (1977) study also prompts another, multiple-dependent-variable research direction. Some of the experimental evidence already discussed (e.g., Allan, 1990, 1993; Ellison & Konorski, 1964; Jenkins & Sainsbury, 1970) suggests that researchers probably should be looking at several different responses simultaneously. Generally, when researchers have examined more than one response, the behavior is differentially sensitive to operant and respondent manipulations; some response frequencies increase; others decrease. Indeed, there is compelling evidence that certain responses may be naturally tied to particular stimuli (e.g., Holland,

1984), perhaps because of each species' unique interactions with the environments in which they evolved (i.e., phylogenic selection; Skinner, 1966). Multiresponse experiments, of course, require a great deal of additional observation, recording equipment and analyses, but the payoff is a more thorough understanding of the sometimes subtle effects of respondent and operant arrangements.

Henton and Iversen (1978) offer a remarkably thorough account of how respondent and operant procedures simultaneously control multiple categories of responding. They not only explore and discuss the potential interactions of respondent and operant operations, they also confront the theories that have played a role in the interpretation of those interactions. Additionally, they present the results of experiments designed to uncover potential conditioning interactions. Their approach is strikingly molecular and stands in contrast to the more molar accounts offered when average rates of responding over an entire session are offered as a demonstration of conditioning phenomena. In several experiments they present data showing the effects of reinforcers on individual responses and short sequences of responding. In many of their experiments the effects of both operant and respondent manipulations are assessed.

Conditioned Reinforcement

Of all the behavior observed and recorded in experimental and applied settings, only a small fraction is actually followed by what might be called *primary* reinforcement (e.g., biologically relevant reinforcers). For the most part, both research and applied communities have interpreted continued support of behavior in the absence of response-reinforcer contiguity as evidence for the role of *conditioned* reinforcers. This position argues that there must be something supporting continued responding and that this something must have reinforcing power. That is, a formerly "neutral" stimulus, when delivered in a response-contingent relation, may support operant responding (e.g., Skinner, 1938, p. 82, 1953, pp. 76–81; Zimmerman, Hanford, & Brown, 1967). Skinner suggested that this conditioned rein-

forcement function was derived directly from a respondent pairing of a stimulus with primary reinforcement: "If we have frequently presented a dish of food to a hungry organism, the empty dish will elicit salivation. To some extent the empty dish will also reinforce an operant" (1953, p. 76). This process implies that, for example, in discrimination schedules the S^D should come to serve as a conditioned reinforcer because of the temporal contiguity between the S^D and the delivery of the primary reinforcer. Indeed, this interpretation suggests that even in a purely respondent procedure, that is, in the absence of any response-contingency (e.g., autoshaping), the stimulus correlated with the delivery of that primary reinforcer could potentially serve as a conditioned reinforcer. Rashotte, Marshall and O'Connell (1981), for example, have demonstrated that a first-order keylight CS in an autoshaping preparation can serve to support key pecking to a second-order CS that precedes the first-order stimulus. A similar effect is observed when an operant contingency is in force. For example, a chain schedule (e.g., Catania, Yohalem, & Silverman, 1980) presents a sequence of stimuli (sometimes called *links*), with each stimulus being produced by a specified response. In the presence of the final link a response terminates the final stimulus and delivers a reinforcer at which point the chain begins again. In the presence of each stimulus (link), different schedules of reinforcement can be programmed so that many responses are emitted before the stimulus changes to the next stimulus in the chain. The relatively large number of responses can then be used to measure the relative strength or power of the potential conditioned reinforcer. If each of the stimuli in the chain can serve potentially as a conditioned reinforcer, then each stimulus should be capable of strengthening responses preceding that stimulus. If a stimulus truly serves as a conditioned reinforcer, it should support more responding than another stimulus that is not a conditioned reinforcer. Herein lies an important distinction between the aforementioned second-order autoshaping effect (Rashotte et al., 1981) and chain schedule effects (e.g., Catania et al., 1980). In second-order autoshaping the sequential stimuli change without respect to behavior; in a chain schedule each stimulus serves as both an S^D setting the occasion for a particular response and as a conditioned reinforcer for the previous response producing that stimulus.

Experimental work, however, has not always supported this notion of conditioned reinforcement. Some researchers have suggested, for example, that conditioned reinforcing effects can be interpreted as effects of discriminative stimuli setting the occasion for particular responses, and nothing else (Rachlin, 1976, pp. 416–430). Others have speculated that the behavior supposedly supported by conditioned reinforcers is simply elicited responding; that is, responding that would have been produced as a CR even in the absence of a response contingency (e.g., Staddon, 1983, p. 466). Each of these alternative explanations has its supporting experimental literature, but several experiments have demonstrated quite clearly that there are conditioned reinforcing effects in addition to the discriminative and eliciting roles that stimuli may have (for a thorough review, see Williams, 1994).

What if the sequence of stimuli, however, only functions to elicit behavior regardless of the presence of an operant contingency as Staddon (1983, p. 466) has claimed? This interpretation would predict that similar rates of responding should be produced in similarly scheduled autoshaping and chain schedules. In fact, pigeons tend to respond at very low rates to initial links in chain schedules, with rates of responding increasing as a function of the presentation of subsequent links in the chain. Of course, each link signals a decrease in time to the primary reinforcer, and the autoshaping literature indicates that such stimulus sequences do indeed support lots of pecking behavior. Catania et al. (1980) explored this explanation of maintained responding

by presenting, immediately following completion of a three-link chain schedule (chain FI FI FI), a three-component multiple schedule in which the first two component stimuli changed without a response requirement.[11] The first two components of the multiple schedule were EXT schedules; in the presence of the terminal component, an FI schedule was in effect. After completion of the multiple schedule, the chain schedule began again, and these schedules continued to alternate throughout the session. Although pecking was maintained in each of the multiple schedule components, with rates of pecking increasing as each subsequent stimulus was presented, the pigeons pecked at higher relative rates in the presence of each of the three chain stimuli, suggesting that the response-contingent stimulus transitions were serving to differentially reinforce the chain pecking behavior (but see Williams, 1994).

The intuitive appeal of the concept of conditioned reinforcement is clear. Money, for example, is a conditioned reinforcer because of its being paired with the acquisition of a variety of primary reinforcers, including food and drink.[12] Presumably, this pairing process is part respondent and part operant (in the latter case, responding is required). Consequently, people's behavior is easily maintained by money as a response outcome. Ayllon and Azrin (1968) employed this principle of conditioned reinforcement to set up what they called "token economies." In an organized effort to differentially reinforce the more productive behavior of patients in a psychiatric hospital, they used "tokens" (coins) that, once earned for any number of successfully completed jobs, could be exchanged for a host of activities, dining privileges, and objects at the institutional commissary. The success of such endeavors contributes to the strength of the arguments in favor of a principle of conditioned reinforcement.

---

[11]This is the case with most multiple schedules—discriminative stimuli change independent of the animal's behavior.

[12]Skinner referred to money as an example of a generalized reinforcer because of its ability to strengthen any number of different responses upon which was made contingent (1953, pp. 77–81). Most experiments probing the qualities of conditioned reinforcers only pair the conditioned reinforcer with a single primary reinforcer, and consequently these stimuli do not become generalized reinforcers.

Currently, one of the most popular methods of studying the effects of conditioned reinforcement is the concurrent chain schedule. Figure 8–6 depicts the order of schedule changes in a characteristic pigeon study. During the initial link of the chain, two keylights come on. Running on each illuminated key are separate but equal VI schedules. Pecks that complete the VI schedule on either key result in the change of color on the pecked key and in the simultaneous termination (blanking) of the alternative keylight. Different schedules of primary reinforcement are associated with each color in this final (terminal) link of the chain schedule. Once the terminal link schedule has been completed and the primary reinforcer has been delivered (the food hopper), the initial link is presented again, and another cycle starts. Since the VI schedules in the initial link are equal (and if all other conditions in the terminal links are equivalent) responding on the two initial link keys should be indifferent. That is, there should be no bias for one key over the other. If, however, one of the terminal link schedules is more favorable, then the terminal link stimulus, the putative conditioned reinforcer, should support a higher pro-portion of the total responses emitted during the initial links. And of course those responses should be directed toward the key on which the more favorable conditioned reinforcer is produced. For example, if pecks on one key result in access to an FI schedule, while pecks on the other key result in access to a VI value whose mean is equal to the FI value, pigeons will respond more to the key associated with the VI schedule (Killeen, 1968). Because responding in the initial link is never followed by primary reinforcement, the color changes associated with each schedule serve as conditioned reinforcers. The experimental evidence seems to support this interpretation (e.g., Mazur, 1993).

Of course, if stimuli associated with reinforcers can serve independently as conditioned reinforcers, then several other effects should logically follow. Conditioned reinforcers should also (1) support responding in extinction (e.g., Bugelski, 1938), (2) allow for the shaping of new responses (e.g., Skinner, 1938, p. 82), (3) bridge a delay between a response and the contingent primary reinforcer (e.g., Cronin, 1980), and (4) support "observing" responses (e.g., Wyckoff, 1952) that contingently present a stimulus indi-

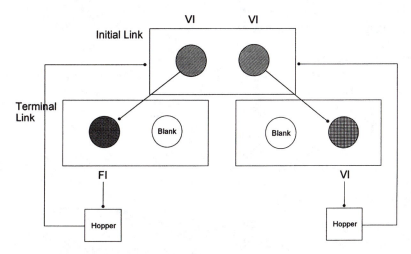

Figure 8–6. Flow chart depicting a concurrent chain schedule with equal VI schedules in the initial link and either FI or VI schedules in the separate terminal links. The chart proceeds in time from the top down, with the outermost lines indicating a re-cycling of schedule conditions.

cating which schedule of primary reinforcement is currently available. As Williams (1994) so carefully points out, there are data supporting each of these logical predictions derived from the principle of conditioned reinforcement.

It is clear that respondent conditioning is involved in the process of turning a stimulus into a conditioned reinforcer, and that these reinforcers may serve an important role in the operant support of ongoing behavior. Certainly, in the world outside the laboratory very little behavior is actually followed by primary reinforcement, so those animals whose responses are maintained by the contingent delivery of a respondently conditioned reinforcer are more likely to survive. Their behavior will be maintained even when primary reinforcers are rare.

CONCLUSIONS

The analysis of operant-respondent interactions has provided several clear messages: (1) The factors controlling any response pattern may not be commensurate with the researcher's or practitioner's design; that is, there may be operations that, if not explicitly disallowed, may intrude and exert some control over responding. (2) There are operant and respondent conditions in which it is unlikely that intrusions can be completely prevented. (3) Intrusions may enhance rates of responding; however, there are times when the intruding operation supports behavior that effectively competes with the responding of interest. (4) When designing a research program or an application, care should be taken by examining the number of responses, types of stimuli, schedules of reinforcement, schedules of stimulus presentation, and possible operant-respondent interactions.

It is very likely that almost all responses are jointly influenced by respondent and operant contingencies. Each respondent conditioning preparation has embedded in it the roots of potential reinforcement of ongoing responding. Every operant conditioning arrangement has the roots of potential pairings of accompanying stimulus events and primary (or conditioned) reinforcers, and these pairings may result in an intrusion of respondent control. Finally, there may be conditions in which some combination of both operant and respondent arrangements will assist in bringing behavior under appropriate control. If all those who work with these procedures are consistently reassessing procedures involved in behavioral control, then behavior analysis will take us more rapidly to an understanding of the relative contributions of antecedent stimulus events and response consequences to the control of behavior.

> "Such a plan cannot be carried out at a superficial level. . . . Superficial sketches of what science has to say about any subject are often entertaining, but they are never adequate for effective action. If we are to further our understanding of human behavior and to improve our practices of control, we must be prepared for the kind of rigorous thinking which science requires" (Skinner, 1953, p. 42).

REFERENCES

Allan, R. W. (1990). Concept learning and peck location in the pigeon. Paper presented at the 16th Annual Convention of the Association for Behavior Analysis, Nashville, Tenn.

Allan, R. W. (1993). Control of pecking response topography by stimulus-reinforcer and response-reinforcer contingencies. In H. P. Zeigler & H. J. Bischof (eds.), *Vision, brain, and behavior in birds*, 285–300. Cambridge, Mass.: MIT Press.

Allan, R. W. (1997). The temporal organization of responding: Selective sensitivity of schedule-induced behavior in operant suppression contingencies. Paper presented at the 68th Annual Meeting of the Eastern Psychological Association, Washington, D.C.

Allan, R. W., & Matthews, T. J. (1991). "Turning back the clock" on serial stimulus sign-tracking. *Journal of the Experimental Analysis of Behavior, 56*, 427–443.

Allan, R. W., & Zeigler, H. P. (1994). Autoshaping the pigeon's gape response: Acquisition and topography as a function of reinforcer type and magnitude. *Journal of the Experimental Analysis of Behavior, 62*, 201–223.

Ayllon, T., & Azrin, N. H. (1968). *The token economy*. New York: Appleton-Century-Crofts.

Barrera, F. J. (1974). Centrifugal selection of signal-directed pecking. *Journal of the Experimental Analysis of Behavior, 22*, 341–355.

Bindra, D. (1972). A unified account of classical conditioning and operant training. In A. H. Black & W. F. Prokasy (eds.), *Classical conditioning II: Current research and theory*, 453–481. New York: Appleton-Century-Crofts.

Blackman, D. E. (1968). Conditioned suppression or facilitation as a function of the behavioral baseline. *Journal of the Experimental Analysis of Behavior*, *11*, 53–61.

Brown, P. L., & Jenkins, H. M. (1968). Auto-shaping of the pigeon's key-peck. *Journal of the Experimental Analysis of Behavior*, *11*, 1–8.

Bugelski, R. (1938). Extinction with and without sub-goal reinforcement. *Journal of Comparative Psychology*, *26*, 121–134.

Catania, A. C. (1971). Elicitation, reinforcement, and stimulus control. In R. Glaser (ed.), *The nature of reinforcement*, 196–220. New York: Academic Press.

Catania, A. C., Yohalem, R., & Silverman, P. J. (1980). Contingency and stimulus change in chain schedules of reinforcement. *Journal of the Experimental Analysis of Behavior*, *33*, 213–219.

Colwill, R. M., & Rescorla, R. A. (1986). Associative structures in instrumental learning. In G. H. Bower (ed.), *The psychology of learning and motivation*, Vol. 20: 54–104. Orlando, Fla.: Academic Press.

Colwill, R. M., & Rescorla, R. A. (1990). Evidence for the hierarchical structure of instrumental learning. *Animal Learning & Behavior*, *18*, 71–82.

Cronin, P. B. (1980). Reinstatement of postresponse stimuli prior to reward in delayed-reward discrimination learning by pigeons. *Animal Learning & Behavior*, *8*, 352–358.

Davis, H., & Hurwitz, H. M. B. (1977). *Operant-Pavlovian interactions*. Hillsdale, N.J.: Erlbaum.

Dinsmoor, J. A., Dougan, J. D., Pfister, J., & Thiels, E. (1992). The autoshaping procedure as a residual block clock. *Journal of the Experimental Analysis of Behavior*, *58*, 265–276.

Donahoe J. W., Crowley, M. A, Mallard, W. J., & Stickney, K. A. (1982). A unified principle of reinforcement: Some implications for matching. In M. L. Commons, R. J. Herrnstein, & H. Rachlin (eds.), *Quantitative analyses of behavior: Matching and maximizing accounts*, 493–521. Cambridge, Mass.: Ballinger.

Ellison, G. D., & Konorski, J. (1964). Separation of the salivary and motor responses in instrumental conditioning. *Science*, *146*, 1071–1072.

Estes, W. K., & Skinner, B. F. (1941). Some quantitative properties of anxiety. *Journal of Experimental Psychology*, *29*, 390–400.

Ferster, C. B., & Skinner, B. F. (1957). *Schedules of reinforcement*. New York: Appleton-Century-Crofts.

Flaherty, C. F. (1982). Incentive contrast: A review of behavioral changes following shifts in reward. *Animal Learning & Behavior*, *10*, 409–440.

Gibbon, J., & Balsam, P. (1981). Spreading association in time. In C. M. Locurto, H. S. Terrace, & J. Gibbon (eds.), *Autoshaping and conditioning theory*, 219–253. New York: Academic Press.

Greene, W. A., & Sutor, L. T. (1971). Stimulus control of skin resistance response on an escape-avoidance schedule. *Journal of the Experimental Analysis of Behavior*, *16*, 269–274.

Hassin-Herman, A. D., Hemmes, N. S., & Brown, B. L. (1992). Behavioral contrast: Pavlovian effects and anticipatory contrast. *Journal of the Experimental Analysis of Behavior*, *57*, 159–175.

Hearst, E. (1975). The classical-instrumental distinction: Reflexes, voluntary behavior, and categories of associative learning. In W. K. Estes (ed.), *Handbook of learning and cognitive processes, Vol. 2: Conditioning and behavior theory*, 181–223. New York: Wiley,

Hearst, E., & Jenkins, H. M. (1974). *Sign-tracking: The stimulus-reinforcer relation and directed action*. Austin, Tex.: The Psychonomic Society.

Hemmes, N. S. (1973). Behavioral contrast in pigeons depends upon the operant. *Journal of Comparative and Physiological Psychology*, *85*, 171–178.

Henton, W. W. (1978). Concurrent classical and operant conditioning procedures. In W. W. Henton & I. H. Iversen (eds.), *Classical conditioning and operant conditioning*, 17–159. New York: Springer-Verlag.

Henton, W. W., & Iversen, I. H. (1978). *Classical conditioning and operant conditioning*. New York: Springer-Verlag.

Herrick, R. M., Myers, J. L., & Korotkin, A. L. (1959). Changes in S^D and S^Δ rates during the development of an operant discrimination. *Journal of Comparative and Physiological Psychology*, *52*, 359–363.

Herrnstein, R. J. (1958). Some factors influencing behavior in a two-response situation. *Transactions of the New York Academy of Science*, *21*, 35–45.

Herrnstein, R. J. (1961). Relative and absolute strength of response as a function of frequency of reinforcement. *Journal of the Experimental Analysis of Behavior*, *4*, 267–272.

Herrnstein, R. J. (1970). On the law of effect. *Journal of the Experimental Analysis of Behavior*, *13*, 243–266.

Herrnstein, R. J., & Loveland, D. H. (1964). Complex visual concept in the pigeon. *Science*, *146*, 549–551.

Herrnstein, R. J., & Morse, W. H. (1957). Some effects of response-independent positive reinforcement on maintained operant behavior. *Journal of Comparative and Physiological Psychology*, *50*, 461–467.

Holland, J. G., & Skinner, B. F. (1961). *The analysis of behavior*. New York: McGraw-Hill.

Holland, P. C. (1984). Origins of behavior in Pavlovian conditioning. In G. H. Bower (ed.), *The psychology of learning and motivation*, *Vol. 18*: 129–174. New York: Academic Press.

Hursh, S. R., Navarick, D. J., & Fantino, E. (1974). "Auto-maintenance": The role of reinforcement. *Journal of the Experimental Analysis of Behavior, 21*, 117–124.

Jenkins, H. M. (1973). Noticing and responding in a discrimination based on a distinguishing element. *Learning and Motivation, 4*, 115–137.

Jenkins, H. M. (1977). Sensitivity of different response systems to stimulus-reinforcer and response-reinforcer relations. In H. Davis & H. M. B. Hurwitz (eds.), *Operant-Pavlovian interactions*, 47–66. Hillsdale, N.J.: Erlbaum.

Jenkins, H. M., & Moore, B. R. (1973). The form of the auto-shaped response with food or water reinforcers. *Journal of the Experimental Analysis of Behavior, 20*, 163–181.

Jenkins, H. M., & Sainsbury, R. S. (1970). Discrimination learning with the distinctive feature on positive or negative trials. In D. I. Mostovsky (ed.), *Attention: Contemporary theory and analysis*, 239–273. New York: Appleton-Century-Crofts.

Kamin, L. J. (1956). The effects of termination of the CS and avoidance of the US on avoidance learning. *Journal of Comparative and Physiological Psychology, 49*, 420–424.

Killeen, P. R. (1968). On the measure of reinforcement frequency in the study of preference. *Journal of the Experimental Analysis of Behavior, 11*, 263–269.

King, G. R., & McSweeney, F. K. (1987). Contrast during multiple schedules with different component response requirement. *Animal Learning & Behavior, 15*, 97–104.

Konorski, J., & Miller, S. (1937). On two types of conditioned reflex. *The Journal of General Psychology, 16*, 264–272.

Locurto, C. M. (1981). Contributions of autoshaping to the partitioning of conditioned behavior. In C. M. Locurto, H. S. Terrace, & J. Gibbon (eds.), *Autoshaping and conditioning theory*, 101–135. New York: Academic Press.

Mackintosh, N. J. (1974). *The psychology of animal learning*. New York: Academic Press.

Mahon, K. L., & Vargas, J. S. (1996). Control of response topography by stimulus-reinforcer and response-reinforcer contingencies: A human analog. Poster presented at the 22nd Annual Convention of the Association for Behavior Analysis, San Francisco, Calif.

Mazur, J. E. (1993). Predicting the strength of a conditioned reinforcer: Effects of delay and uncertainty. *Current Directions in Psychological Science, 2*, 70–74.

McSweeney, F. K. (1982). Positive and negative contrast as a function of component duration for key pecking and treadle pressing. *Journal of the Experimental Analysis of Behavior, 37*, 281–293.

McSweeney, F. K., Dougan, J. D., & Farmer-Dougan, V. A. (1986). Simple and multiple schedule responding and behavioral contrast when pigeons press treadles. *Behavioural Processes, 12*, 273–285.

Michael, J. (1982). Distinguishing between discriminative and motivational functions of stimuli. *Journal of the Experimental Analysis of Behavior, 37*, 149–155.

Miller, N. E. (1969). Learning of visceral and glandular responses. *Science, 163*, 434–445.

Miller, N. E., & Banuazizi, A. (1968). Instrumental learning by curarized rats of a specific visceral response, intestinal or cardiac. *Journal of Comparative and Physiological Psychology, 65*, 1–7.

Miller, N. E., & Carmona, A. (1967). Modification of a visceral response, salivation in thirsty dogs, by instrumental training with water reward. *Journal of Comparative and Physiological Psychology, 63*, 1–6.

Miller, N. E., & Dworkin, B. R. (1974). Visceral learning: Recent difficulties with curarized rats and significant problems for human research. In P. A. Obrist, A. H. Black, J. Brener, & L. V. DiCara (eds.), *Cardiovascular psychophysiology: current issues in response mechanisms, biofeedback and methodology*, 295–331. Chicago, Ill.: Aldine.

Miller, S., & Konorski, J. (1928). Sur une forme particulière des reflexes conditionnels. *Les Comptes Rendus des Seances de la Société Polonaise de Biologie, 49*, 1155–1157. (Translated by B. F. Skinner and reprinted as: Miller, S., & Konorski, J., 1969). On a particular form of conditioned reflex. *Journal of the Experimental Analysis of Behavior, 12*, 187–189. This reprint also contains retrospective comments by Konorski.

Olton, D. S., & Noonberg, A. R. (1980). *Biofeedback: Clinical applications in behavioral medicine*. Englewood Cliffs, N.J.: Prentice-Hall.

Pavlov, I. P. (1927). *Conditioned reflexes: An investigation of the physiological activity of the cerebral cortex*. London: Oxford University Press.

Peden, B. F., Browne, M. P., & Hearst, E. (1977). Persistent approaches to a signal for food despite food omission for approaching. *Journal of Experimental Psychology, 3*, 377–399.

Peterson, G. B., Ackil, J., Frommer, G. P., & Hearst, E. (1972). Conditioned approach and contact behavior towards signals for food or brain-stimulation reinforcement. *Science, 177*, 1009–1011.

Pierce, W. D., & Epling, W. F. (1991). Activity anorexia: An animal model and theory of human self-starvation. In A. Boulton, G. Baker, & M. Martin-Iverson (eds.), *Neuromethods: Animal models in psychiatry 1*, Vol. 18: 267–311. Clifton, N.J.: Humana Press.

Rachlin, H. (1973). Contrast and matching. *Psychological Review, 80*, 217–234.

Rachlin, H. (1976). *Behavior and learning*. San Francisco: Freeman.

Rashotte, M. E., Marshall, B. S., & O'Connell, J. M. (1981). Signaling functions of the second-order CS: Partial reinforcement during second-order conditioning of the pigeon's keypeck. *Animal Learning & Behavior, 9,* 253–260.

Redford, E. M., & Perkins, C. C., Jr. (1974). The role of autopecking in behavioral contrast. *Journal of the Experimental Analysis of Behavior, 21,* 145–150.

Rescorla, R. A. (1967). Pavlovian conditioning and its proper control procedures. *Psychological Review, 74,* 71–80.

Rescorla, R. A. (1990a). Information about the response-outcome relation in discrimination learning. *Journal of Experimental Psychology: Animal Behavior Processes, 16,* 262–270.

Rescorla, R. A. (1990b). Evidence for an association between the discriminative stimulus and the response-outcome association in instrumental learning. *Journal of Experimental Psychology: Animal Behavior Processes, 16,* 326–334.

Reynolds, G. S. (1961a). Behavioral contrast. *Journal of the Experimental Analysis of Behavior, 4,* 57–71.

Reynolds, G. S. (1961b). Relativity of response rate and reinforcement frequency in a multiple schedule. *Journal of the Experimental Analysis of Behavior, 4,* 179–184.

Rovee-Collier, C. K., & Capatides, J. B. (1979). Positive behavioral contrast in 3-month-old infants on multiple conjugate reinforcement schedules. *Journal of the Experimental Analysis of Behavior, 32,* 15–27.

Sainsbury, R. S. (1971a). Effect of proximity of elements on the feature-positive effect. *Journal of the Experimental Analysis of Behavior, 16,* 315–325.

Sainsbury, R. S. (1971b). The "feature-positive effect" and simultaneous discrimination learning. *Journal of Experimental Child Psychology, 11,* 347–356.

Schwartz, B. (1973). Maintenance of key pecking by response-independent food presentation: The role of the modality of the signal for food. *Journal of the Experimental Analysis of Behavior, 20,* 17–22.

Schwartz, B., & Gamzu, E. (1977). Pavlovian control of operant behavior. In W. K. Honig & J. E. R. Staddon (eds.), *Handbook of operant behavior,* 53–97. Englewood Cliffs, N.J.: Prentice Hall.

Schwartz, B., & Williams, D. R. (1972). The role of the response-reinforcer contingency in negative automaintenance. *Journal of the Experimental Analysis of Behavior, 17,* 351–357.

Sheffield, F. D. (1965). Relation between classical conditioning and instrumental learning. In W. F. Prokasy (ed.), *Classical conditioning: A symposium,* 302–322. New York: Appleton-Century-Crofts.

Sidman, M., Herrnstein, R. J., & Conrad, D. G. (1957). Maintenance of avoidance behavior by unavoidable shocks. *Journal of Comparative and Physiological Psychology, 50,* 553–557.

Skinner, B. F. (1931). The concept of the reflex in the description of behavior. *The Journal of General Psychology, 5,* 427–458.

Skinner, B. F. (1932). On the rate of formation of a conditioned reflex. *Journal of General Psychology, 7,* 274–286.

Skinner, B. F. (1935a). The generic nature of the concepts of stimulus and response. *The Journal of General Psychology, 12,* 40–65.

Skinner, B. F. (1935b). Two types of conditioned reflex and a pseudo-type. *The Journal of General Psychology, 12,* 66–77.

Skinner, B. F. (1937). Two types of conditioned reflex: A reply to Konorski and Miller. *The Journal of General Psychology, 16,* 272–279.

Skinner, B. F. (1938). *The behavior of organisms.* New York: Appleton-Century-Crofts.

Skinner, B. F. (1948). "Superstition" in the pigeon. *The Journal of General Psychology, 38,* 168–172.

Skinner, B. F. (1953) *Science and human behavior.* New York: Free Press.

Skinner, B. F. (1966). The phylogeny and ontogeny of behavior. *Science, 153,* 1205–1213.

Skinner, B. F. (1972). *Cumulative record.* New York: Appleton-Century-Crofts.

Smith, M. H., Jr., & Hoy, W. J. (1954). Rate of response during operant discrimination. *Journal of Experimental Psychology, 48,* 259–264.

Staddon, J. E. R. (1983). *Adaptive learning and behavior.* Cambridge, Mass.: Cambridge University Press.

Staddon, J. E. R., & Simmelhag, V. L. (1971). The "superstition" experiment: A reexamination of its implications for the principles of adaptive behavior. *Psychological Review, 78,* 3–43.

Thorndike, E. L. (1911). *Animal intelligence: Experimental studies.* New York: Macmillan.

Wahlsten, D. L., & Cole, M. (1972). Classical and avoidance training of leg flexion in the dog. In A. H. Black & W. F. Prokasy (eds.), *Classical conditioning II: Current research and theory,* 379–408. New York: Appleton-Century-Crofts.

Waite, W. W., & Osborne, J. G. (1972). Sustained behavioral contrast in children. *Journal of the Experimental Analysis of Behavior, 18,* 113–117.

Williams, B. A. (1979). Contrast, component duration, and the following schedule of reinforcement. *Journal of Experimental Psychology: Animal Behavior Processes, 5,* 379–396.

Williams, B. A. (1983). Another look at contrast in multiple schedules. *Journal of the Experimental Analysis of Behavior, 39,* 345–384.

Williams, B. A. (1990). Pavlovian contingencies and anticipatory contrast. *Animal Learning & Behavior, 18,* 44–50.

Williams, B. A. (1992a). Competition between stimulus-reinforcer contingencies and anticipatory contrast. *Journal of the Experimental Analysis of Behavior, 58,* 287–302.

Williams, B. A. (1992b). Inverse relations between preference and contrast. *Journal of the Experimental Analysis of Behavior*, *58*, 303–312.

Williams, B. A. (1994). Conditioned reinforcement: Experimental and theoretical issues. *The Behavior Analyst*, *17*, 261–285.

Williams, D. R. (1965). Classical conditioning and incentive motivation. In W. F. Prokasy (ed.), *Classical conditioning: A symposium*, 340–357. New York: Appleton-Century-Crofts.

Williams, D. R., & Williams, H. (1969). Auto-maintenance in the pigeon: Sustained pecking despite contingent non-reinforcement. *Journal of the Experimental Analysis of Behavior*, *12*, 511–520.

Williams, D. R. (1981). Biconditional behavior: Conditioning without constraint. In C. M Locurto, H. S. Terrace, & J. Gibbon (eds.), *Autoshaping and conditioning theory*. New York: Academic Press.

Wyckoff, L. B., Jr. (1952). The role of observing responses in discrimination learning. *Psychological Review*, *59*, 431–442.

Zimmerman, J., Hanford, P. V., & Brown, W. (1967). Effects of conditioned reinforcement frequency in an intermittent free-feeding situation. *Journal of the Experimental Analysis of Behavior*, *10*, 331–340.

CHAPTER 9

POSITIVE REINFORCEMENT: THE SELECTION OF BEHAVIOR

John W. Donahoe

Reinforcement provides the central insight into how the environment acts upon the organism to produce, as its cumulative product, complex behavior. This chapter begins its examination of reinforcement by noting the close conceptual kinship between reinforcement as a process for changing the behavior of individuals and natural selection as a process for changing the characteristics of species. Both are seen as instances of a more general approach—*selectionism*—whereby phenomena of great complexity may arise from the repeated action of relatively simple processes acting over time. The conditions that experimental analysis has identified as necessary for reinforcement are first described followed by a principle of reinforcement based upon the fruits of those analyses. These studies are largely conducted using nonhuman animals, with which tightly controlled conditions are more nearly attainable (see Branch & Hackenberg, this volume). The chapter concludes with a presentation of a technique—*adaptive neural networks*—that may be used to explore the implications of the reinforcement principle in a more rigorous fashion than is possible using verbal interpretation alone. At various points throughout the exposition, some relations between the experimental analysis of reinforcement and applied behavior analysis are indicated: A science that has little to say about matters of general societal concern cannot long expect general societal support.

REINFORCEMENT AS SELECTION

Reinforcers are stimuli that function to strengthen the behavior they follow. Thus, reinforcers alter the behavioral repertoire of the individual in the context in which they occur. A child entering kindergarten has a large behavioral repertoire. The contingencies implemented in the classroom seek to strengthen some members of the repertoire—such as drawing pictures or copying letters while sitting quietly—by following this behavior with reinforcing stimuli—such as the approval of teachers and classmates—and seek to weaken others—such as running about and talking loudly. Over time, the behavioral repertoire changes, with members of the first set of responses increasing in frequency for most children and members of the second set decreasing. Over the much longer period during which exposure to "educational" contingencies is mandatory in our society, the cumulative effects of these contingencies produce a rich repertoire of "educated" behavior in some students and, unfortunately, an equally rich repertoire of "disaffected" behavior in others. Whichever the outcome, long-term exposure to the contingencies of reinforcement instituted by the educational system produces profound changes in the behavioral repertoire of the individual.

Complexity Through Selection Processes

Reinforcers change the frequency of responses within a population of behavior from the *same* individual. This process is conceptually related to the one whereby natural selection changes the frequency of genes within a population of characteristics of *different* individuals. In natural selection, if some characteristic affects the reproductive fitness of organisms displaying that characteristic and the characteristic is heritable (i.e., influenced by genes), the proportion of the population having that characteristic changes in subsequent generations. For example, suppose that individuals within a population differ in the quality of care they provide their offspring; that is, some individuals better nurture and protect their offspring than do others. Because their offspring are more likely to survive to the age of reproduction, such parents are said to have greater reproductive fitness. As a result, their genes (shared with their offspring) become relatively more numerous in the next generation. Over time, organisms displaying more effective parental behavior

increase in frequency in the population (as do the genes influencing such behavior). Thus, just as selection by reinforcement changes the relative frequency of members of a behavioral repertoire for a single individual, so natural selection changes the relative frequency of individuals possessing certain genes in a population of different individuals.

Figure 9–1 summarizes the sequence of events whereby selection processes potentially produce complex phenomena—whether behavioral complexity through selection by reinforcement or structural complexity through natural selection. The sequence begins with variation produced when external events act upon members of the population undergoing selection, for example, the behavioral repertoire of an individual organism. Variation is necessary because selection processes alone cannot yield diversity and complexity but merely more (or less) of the same.

The next step in the sequence occurs when a selecting factor in the environment acts upon existing variations, favoring some and disfavoring others. In the case of natural selection, the selecting factor has been identified—reproductive fitness. Identifying the selecting factor in selection by reinforcement is a primary goal of this chapter. To the degree that the selecting environment remains constant or changes gradually, selection confers direction to the process.

The third step in the sequence whereby selection produces complexity is retention. Some physical mechanism retains the selected variation so that it has an opportunity to contribute to the pool of variation acted upon by subsequent

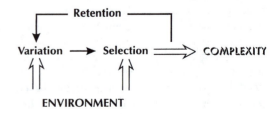

Figure 9–1. The major components of selection processes—variation, selection, and retention.

selecting environments. Thus, the effects of prior selection add to the population of variations upon which later selection operates, with diversity and complexity possible (but not inevitable) outcomes of the process. For natural selection, the enduring physical entities are genes, which mediate the characteristics that span the generations. For selection by reinforcement, the physical entities are changes in the connectivity of the nervous system (i.e., changes in synaptic efficacy), which mediate the behavioral changes that span a lifetime.

Note that selection by reinforcement and natural selection are both functional principles. Although they provide deep insights into the origins of complexity in their respective provinces, they do not specify the physical mechanisms whereby selections are retained. As a prime example, Darwin's *Origin of Species*—with all of its implications for the evolutionary process—was published before the science of genetics was known.

I would be remiss if I left this brief discussion of selection processes where it stands. As indicated thus far, the environment—through its influence on variation and selection—is the only contributor to the outcome of selection. This is an incomplete account, especially in the case of our own species. Through that human behavior known as science, we have come to understand selection processes. And as our knowledge improves of how the environment affects behavior, our ability increases to intervene effectively in the selection process. Thus, paradoxically, the more we understand about how the environment shapes behavior, the better we are able to shape our own destinies. Our behavior as scientists and as practitioners of science enhances our ability to change environmental contingencies and—by this indirect means—to change ourselves. The effect of behavior on the course of selection is known as *counterselection* (see Skinner's 1974 discussion of countercontrol). In these terms, applied behavior analysis is the systematic development and application of counterselections for the betterment of the human condition.

TOWARD A PRINCIPLE OF SELECTION BY REINFORCEMENT

Infants come into the world with a limited behavioral repertoire but one that is adequate for survival in the situations in which they usually find themselves—among nurturing families and communities. The repertoire consists of a specific set of relations between the environment and behavior, called *reflexes*. If the infant's cheek is touched, its head turns toward the touch (rooting reflex); if its lips are touched, it begins to suck (sucking reflex); and so on. These environment-behavior relations are the products of natural selection. They are what has been "taught" us by the ancestral environment.

The ancestral environment is severely limited in what it can "teach" us, however. The demands of the individual environment in which we live are highly variable, and natural selection requires relative constancy of selecting conditions if it is to have coherent cumulative effects. When nature changes, rapidly reproducing species like fruit flies change their nature; but that solution is unavailable to our species. Sensitivity to rapid changes in the environment is the province of selection by reinforcement.

Selection by reinforcement builds upon reflexive relations that are the legacy of natural selection. That is, stimuli that function as reinforcers for the infant are—in the first instance—stimuli that already elicit behavior as a part of reflexes. Both Ivan Pavlov (1927), who began the study of selection by reinforcement using a classical contingency (see Kehoe, this volume) and Edward Thorndike (1898), who began the study using an operant contingency, exploited this insight in their experimental procedures. Both Pavlov and Thorndike presented the eliciting stimulus of food, but following an environmental event—for example, the sound of a metronome—in the classical case and following behavior—for example, navigating a maze—in the operant case. The eliciting stimulus functioned as a reinforcing stimulus in both cases because it changed the environmental guidance of behavior. Pavlov's dog salivated upon hearing the metronome; Thorndike's chicks ran upon being placed in the maze. When the occurrence of a reinforcer is paired with a specified stimulus, the procedure implements what is called a Pavlovian, classical, or respondent contingency. When the reinforcer is contingent on a specified response, the procedure implements an operant or instrumental contingency (cf. Skinner, 1937, 1938).

Of course, the natural environment often implements both types of contingencies simultaneously. Environmental, behavioral, and reinforcing events are usually correlated to produce what Skinner referred to as a three-term contingency (Skinner, 1938, 1981). This chapter is largely concerned with an experimental analysis of the operant contingency, although the analysis of selection by reinforcement suggests that a single selection principle may accommodate the effects of both contingencies.

The Necessary and Sufficient Conditions for Reinforcement

What conditions has experimental analysis shown to be essential for selection to occur with an operant contingency? Two conditions have been identified: *contiguity* and *discrepancy*. Each condition is described, together with relevant experimental evidence, in the following paragraphs.

Contiguity

Events are contiguous if they occur together in time and space. Skinner's initial experiments with lever pressing in rats attest to the importance he ascribed to the presentation of food (the reinforcing stimulus) *immediately* after lever pressing (the operant). In fact, Skinner regarded the unavoidable small delay between lever pressing and the receipt of food as intolerable. To minimize the departure from contiguity, Skinner first exposed the rat to a classical contingency between the sound of the operation of the food dispenser and the delivery of food. Only after the rat avidly approached the food tray upon hearing the dispenser operate (i.e., after the sound had become a conditioned "elicitor") was the operant contingency instituted (Skinner, 1938).

The importance of contiguity between behavior and reinforcer was stressed throughout Skinner's work. In *Schedules of Reinforcement* (1957), a comprehensive study with Charles Ferster of a wide variety of operant contingencies, the specific stimulating and behavioral conditions present immediately before the reinforcer were closely examined to provide the key to understanding the global effects of operant contingencies. Skinner's unremitting emphasis upon the centrality of contiguity—what Skinner referred to as the "moment of reinforcement" (Ferster & Skinner, 1957, pp. 2–3)—is probably most apparent in the following statement: "To say that a reinforcement is contingent upon a response may mean nothing more than that it follows the response. . . . Conditioning takes place because of the temporal relation only, expressed in terms of the order and proximity of response and reinforcement" (Skinner, 1948, p. 168).

As but one example of an appeal to the conditions at the "moment of reinforcement" to account for more global effects of reinforcement contingencies, consider the following. During ratio schedules of reinforcement, reinforcers are more likely to occur after a burst of responses than after a single response. This is because ratio schedules impose a contingency between the *number* of responses and the reinforcer. Therefore, a burst of responses is more likely than is a single response to include enough responses to satisfy the contingency. Given that a burst of responses is more likely to precede a reinforcer and that the organism can discriminate having made several responses from having made only a single response, bursts should be differentially strengthened. The cumulative effect of this momentary relation between stimulus, behavior, and reinforcer was proposed as one origin of the high overall rates of responding observed with ratio schedules (cf. Morse, 1966). Subsequent experimental analysis has confirmed that animals can, indeed, discriminate the number of responses emitted (Rilling, 1967) and that bursts of responding during ratio schedules are, in fact, more likely to be followed by reinforcers than are single responses (Williams, 1968).

With operant contingencies, the experimental analysis of the effect of the time interval between the criterion response and the reinforcer presents formidable technical difficulties. Since an organism is always behaving, when the criterion response is followed by a reinforcer after a delay, other behavior has an opportunity to intervene. This intervening behavior is then in a position to be more strongly affected by the reinforcer because it occurs more closely in time to the reinforcer than the criterion response. Any behavior analyst who has shaped a pigeon to peck a disk or a retarded child to brush his teeth can testify to the problems that arise when some other response "sneaks" into the interval between the criterion response and the reinforcer. The effect of intervening behavior on the strengthening of the criterion response is nicely illustrated in an experiment by Catania (1971). Pecking one key by a pigeon in a two-key chamber was followed by a reinforcer after varying numbers of pecks on the other key. The number of intervening other-key responses was varied from 1 to 11 in different conditions. As shown in Figure 9–2, the rate of pecking the key that initiated the reinforced sequence was greatest when only one other-key response intervened before the occurrence of the reinforcer. The rate rapidly declined as the requirement was increased to 11, which consumed approximately 7 seconds.

Discrepancy

The importance of contiguity with the reinforcer was recognized early in the study of conditioning, both with the stimulus-reinforcer contingency of the classical procedure and with the response-reinforcer contingency of the operant procedure. The second requirement for selection by reinforcement was not fully appreciated until the 1970s (Rescorla & Wagner, 1972). In concert with a number of puzzling findings from several laboratories (Johnson, 1970; Thomas, 1970), Leon Kamin (1968, 1969) discovered that temporal contiguity was not sufficient for a putative reinforcer to select behavior.

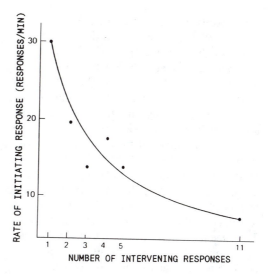

Figure 9–2. The rate of pecking on a response key that initiated a sequence of responses terminating with a reinforcer. The rate on the key is shown as a function of the number of intervening responses required on a second key before the reinforcer occurred. (Based on data in Catania, 1971.)

Using a classical procedure, Kamin first paired one stimulus (e.g., a tone) with an elicitor (electric shock) for a rat. After a sufficient number of pairings to establish conditioning to the tone, the first stimulus continued to be presented followed by the elicitor, but the tone was now accompanied by a second stimulus (e.g., a light). From other work, it was known that if a light-tone compound stimulus was paired with the elicitor from the outset of training, conditioning would occur to both stimuli. Thus, the light was clearly an adequate conditioned stimulus even when presented in the context of another stimulus, and the temporal relation between the light and the elicitor was adequate for conditioning. However, after prior tone-shock pairings, pairing the light-tone compound with shock produced little or no conditioned responding when the light was presented by itself. Kamin's finding was soon replicated with an operant procedure (vom Saal & Jenkins, 1970), and it became increasingly apparent that something in addition to contiguity was required for an elicitor to function as a reinforcer. What was it?

Although investigators describe the second condition in somewhat different terms depending on their theoretical orientations, the additional requirement may be stated in behavioral terms as follows: If an eliciting stimulus is to function as a reinforcer, it must evoke a response that is not occurring in the moment prior to its presentation (Donahoe, Crowley, Millard, & Stickney, 1982; cf. Rescorla, 1968). (As used here, the term *elicitor* designates a stimulus that, because of its history of natural selection or selection by reinforcement, reliably occasions a given response. Thus, the term is not confined to reflexive eliciting stimuli.) As applied to Kamin's experiment, because the animal was already behaving during the tone in a manner called for by its pairing with shock, the occurrence of shock-elicited responding after the light-tone compound did not provoke a change in the animal's behavior sufficient to cause the shock to select a new environment-behavior relation involving the light. This phenomenon, whereby prior conditioning to one stimulus may impair conditioning to a contemporaneous second stimulus, is known as *blocking*.

More technically, the discrepancy between the ongoing conditioned response (CR) during the tone and the unconditioned response (UR) evoked by the shock was not sufficient for the shock to foster conditioning to the light. That is, there was not a sufficient CR-UR discrepancy. Nontechnically speaking, the animal was not "surprised" when caused to engage in shock-elicited behavior because it already "expected" to behave in that manner to the tone. In the absence of "surprise," the light did not acquire control over shock-elicited responding. Subsequent work has shown that the CR-UR discrepancy must be defined quite narrowly: If the elicitor is changed slightly so that the reinforcer evoked a somewhat different UR, the stimulus could again function as a reinforcer even in the context in which it had previously appeared (Stickney & Donahoe, 1983; Brandon, Betts, & Wagner, 1994).

The necessity of discrepancy as well as contiguity for selection by reinforcement has impor-

tant implications for both experimental and applied behavior analysis: The ability of a putative reinforcing stimulus to change behavior depends on the specific history of the learner with respect to that stimulus. For example, experimental work has shown that after two stimuli (S_1 and S_2) have been individually paired with an elicitor until each stimulus separately evokes the CR, placing the two stimuli in a simultaneous compound and following them by the *same* elicitor actually weakens conditioning. The combined strength of the two CRs previously individually conditioned to S_1 and S_2 presumably exceeds the UR evoked by the elicitor, thereby rendering subsequent conditioning trials less effective (Rescorla, 1970).

As another example, suppose that a stimulus (S_1) is repeatedly presented in compound with a second stimulus (S_2) and that the compound stimulus (S_1 plus S_2) is *un*paired with an elicitor. Suppose further that S_2 *is* paired with the elicitor when presented alone. Following such training, subsequent pairings of S_1 with the elicitor produce higher levels of conditioning than would otherwise occur (Rescorla, 1971). Here, the level of ongoing CR behavior during S_1 when S_1 appeared in the unreinforced compound was presumably lower than without such training. This produced a larger CR-UR discrepancy when S_1 was finally paired with the elicitor. The larger discrepancy caused the elicitor to function as a more effective reinforcer.

In applied settings, the import of such findings is profound. A given stimulus may function as a reinforcer for some clients but not for others, depending on the client's history with respect to that stimulus. For example, a parent or teacher who lavishly and indiscriminately dispenses putative conditioned reinforcers such as praise, approval, and attention runs the risk not only of strengthening inappropriate behavior but also of undermining the effectiveness of these consequences to function as reinforcers for *any* behavior. Thus, "unconditional positive regard" produces the worst of all worlds. These unintended effects probably underlie such anomalies as the child who obeys the parent who dispenses favors stingily and ignores the "better" parent who provides would-be reinforcers at every turn.

A Unified Reinforcement Principle

Experimental analysis indicates that two conditions must be met when selection by reinforcement occurs—contiguity and discrepancy. Both conditions must be satisfied whether with an operant or with a classical (respondent) contingency. Although a common set of conditions must be present for reinforcement to occur, many differences exist between the two contingencies and their behavioral outcomes. Procedurally, operant and classical procedures implement different contingencies—stimulus-reinforcer and response-reinforcer, respectively. Their outcomes are strikingly different as well: Any member of the behavioral repertoire of the learner is potentially a candidate for selection with an operant contingency, whereas only already elicitable responses are the province of a classical contingency. The difference in their outcomes is especially important in the selection of complex behavior because the full behavioral capabilities of the learner are available only with operant contingencies.

In spite of the striking differences in procedures and outcomes, an integrated theoretical treatment of operant and classical conditioning is encouraged by Skinner's insistence upon a moment-to-moment analysis of the contingencies of reinforcement. Consider the sequence of events defining classical and operant contingencies (see Table 9–1). At the moment of reinforcement (i.e., on a single occasion when the reinforcer occurs), it is impossible for the learner to distinguish which of the contingencies is in effect. Whichever the contingency, environmental and behavioral events precede the putative reinforcing stimulus (the elicitor, or unconditioned stimulus—US), and some response is evoked by that stimulus. It is only *cumulatively* (i.e., over many occasions), as the contingencies are repeatedly encountered, that the learner can appreciate that some events reliably precede the reinforcer while others do not.

Consider a classical procedure in which Pavlov's dog might slightly move its body as it hears the sound of the metronome in the moment before

Table 9–1. Sequences of Environmental and Behavioral Events That Are Specified and Monitored in Standard Conditioning Procedures

PROCEDURE	SEQUENCE OF EVENTS	
Classical Respondent	CS (specified) Context (unspecified) Behavior (unspecified)	→ Eliciting stimulus (US) → Elicited response (UR, monitored)
Free-operant	Context (unspecified) Behavior (specified)	→ Eliciting stimulus (US) → Elicited response (UR, unmonitored)
Discriminated operant	S^D (specified) Context (unspecified) Behavior (specified)	→ Eliciting stimulus (US) → Elicited response (UR, unmonitored)

the food is presented. It is only over time that the animal can appreciate the reliability of the sound-food sequence and the unreliability of the movement-food sequence. Of course, movements can be "superstitiously" reinforced (Skinner, 1948), which only emphasizes the inability of conditions at the moment of reinforcement to distinguish a classical from an operant contingency.

Likewise, consider free-operant and discriminated-operant procedures. Although in the former case, no particular stimulus need be sensed prior to the reinforced response, *some* stimulus must have been sensed before the operant and reinforcer. It is only over time as the animal experiences repeated contiguous instances of a three-term contingency—discriminative stimulus, operant, reinforcer—that the discriminated-operant and free-operant procedure can be distinguished. Of course, the fortuitous occurrence of some stimulus prior to the reinforced response in the free-operant procedure may cause that stimulus to "superstitiously" guide the operant (Morse & Skinner, 1957), which again affirms the point that the procedures are indistinguishable at the moment of reinforcement.

Although classical, free-operant, and discriminated-operant procedures are indistinguishable at the moment of reinforcement, they are readily distinguished by the experimenter, because different events are specified and monitored in the two contingencies. In the classical procedure, the experimenter manipulates the contingency between the conditioned stimulus (CS) and the US. The experimenter monitors the UR and, after training, the CR. Whatever behavior occurs prior to the US is generally ignored. Indeed, the animal is often restrained so that its pre-CS behavior cannot be observed at all. In operant procedures, the situation for the experimenter is quite different. The experimenter manipulates the contingency between the operant and the reinforcer, and monitors the operant while leaving environmental events unmonitored in the free-operant procedure. In fact, the experimental environment is commonly designed to be homogeneous and stable so that any effects of stimuli are subtle and difficult to detect.

In both free-operant and discriminated-operant procedures, whatever responses are evoked by the reinforcer go unmonitored, although an animal salivates to food just as surely in an operant as it does in as a classical procedure (cf. Shapiro & Miller, 1965). To act as if no responses are elicited by the reinforcer in operant procedures, that no stimuli are present in free-operant procedures, and that no behavior precedes the reinforcer in classical procedures is to mistake absence of evidence for evidence of absence. Because the experimenter behaves very differently in the various procedures, we have been lured into believing that different principles are required to understand the different effects of the contingencies. Skinner's advocacy of a moment-to-moment analysis encourages us to reexamine such beliefs.

The Proposal

Given that the experimenter, not the learner, can distinguish among the various contingencies at the moment of reinforcement and that the learner's contact with the contingencies not the experimenter's description of them, is relevant, a single principle of selection by reinforcement should be sought. That principle must have very different cumulative effects when realized in the different contingencies, but the principle itself cannot change as the contingencies change. If the learner cannot discriminate among the contingencies at the moment of reinforcement, then —even if different processes were involved with classical and operant contingencies—the learner would have no basis upon which to engage one or the other process. The sequence of environmental and behavioral events does not permit the learner to distinguish among the contingencies (Donahoe et al., 1982; Donahoe, Burgos, & Palmer, 1993; Donahoe & Palmer, 1994). At every moment, stimuli are being sensed, behavior is occurring, and, perhaps, an eliciting stimulus is evoking a change in behavior.

The following is a straightforward statement of a principle that is consistent with the conditions found necessary and sufficient for selection by reinforcement: Whenever a behavioral discrepancy occurs, an environment-behavior relation is selected that—other things being equal—consists of all those stimuli and all those responses accompanying the discrepancy. This principle is called the *unified reinforcement principle* because it provides an integrated theoretical treatment of conditioning with both classical and operant contingencies (Donahoe et al., 1982). In the classical, or respondent, case, the sources of stimuli are the CS and the experimental context and the source of behavior is the elicited response, or UR. These are the events that are reliably contiguous with the discrepancy. Thus, the CS comes to control a response (the CR) that most often closely resembles the UR. In the operant procedure, the sources of stimuli are the context and, in the discriminated-operant procedure, the discriminative stimulus, and the sources of behavior are the operant and the UR. These are the events that are reliably contiguous with the discrepancy in an operant contingency. In either contingency, superstitious conditioning can occur whereby stimuli and responses contribute to the selected environment-behavior relation even though they are not reliably contiguous with the discrepancy. However, the most common cumulative effect of both contingencies is that the environment gains control over whatever behavior most reliably accompanies the discrepancy.

Interactions Between Operants and Reinforcer-Elicited Responses

If with an operant contingency both operants and elicited responses come under the control of whatever stimuli are reliably present when a discrepancy occurs, the net effect of an operant contingency depends upon any interactions between responses of these two origins. Not all reinforcers can be expected to be equally effective with all operants (see Allan, this volume). When operant and reinforcer-elicited responses are compatible, operant conditioning is facilitated; when they are incompatible, it is hindered. For example, pecking a disk is effectively reinforced with food in pigeons, where the operant and elicited response are the same form; that is, both are pecking. The influence of the form of the reinforcer-elicited response on the form of the operant is clear. When pecking is reinforced with food, pecking the disk resembles eating (nibbling movements occur as the disk is struck); when pecking is reinforced with water, pecking resembles drinking (pulsating movements of the throat occur as the disk is struck) (Jenkins & Moore, 1973). Most dramatically, when a pigeon receives food only if the disk is *not* pecked when it is illuminated just prior to food delivery, pecking is acquired even though responding reduces reinforcer frequency (Williams & Williams, 1969; see Donahoe & Palmer, 1994, pp. 51–52 for related examples).

The possibility of interactions between operants and reinforcer-elicited responses must be considered in both experimental and applied behavior analysis. As an obvious example, spanking would not effectively reduce operant crying (e.g., crying that is reinforced by parental attention) because the response elicited by spanking is also crying. Whether or not aversive stimuli ever provide a truly effective means of reducing responding is problematic. Aversive stimuli evoke escape responses that then become conditioned to the situation and thereby prevent the learner from contacting whatever reinforcers might be available in the situation (see Ayres, this volume). As an example of a facilitating interaction, a reinforcing stimulus that evoked reaching might be particularly effective with operants requiring directed arm movements.

Momentary and Molar Formulations of Reinforcement

This presentation focuses on the environmental and behavioral conditions required at the "moment of reinforcement." The cumulative effects of these momentary conditions may yield regularities between variables defined at more molar, or global, levels of analysis. For example, momentary conditions may produce orderly functional relations between variables such as the rate of responding and the rate of reinforcement, both of which are typically defined over substantial periods of time. (For work examining some of the implications of momentary analyses of reinforcement for relations between more global variables, see Hinson & Staddon, 1983; Shimp, 1969; and Silberberg, Hamilton, Ziriax, & Casey, 1978). Indeed, it is quite likely that the conditioning processes that enable organisms to be sensitive to moment-to-moment relations between events may have been naturally selected in part for the molar relations that emerged as their cumulative products. As but one possibility, processes operating at the moment of reinforcement may produce behavior that optimizes the overall rate of reinforcement under some circumstances (cf. Staddon & Hinson, 1983). This section briefly considers relations between the moment-to-moment analysis of reinforcement and some other formulations.

The Premack principle is a useful rule of thumb in applied behavior analysis (Premack, 1959, 1965). According to this view, a given response may be reinforced if a more probable (i.e., more preferred) response is made contingent on its occurrence. For instance, if a child prefers playing pinball to eating candy, eating candy may be reinforced by the opportunity to play pinball. Or, in the laboratory, if a rat prefers running in an activity wheel to licking a drinking tube, licking may be reinforced by the opportunity to run (Premack, 1963). The preference for an activity is typically measured by the number of responses (or amount of time) devoted to the activity over some extended baseline period during which the various activities are noncontingently (i.e., "freely") available. In terms of the unified reinforcement principle, which is based upon momentary relations between events, a highly preferred activity is apt to be one that is strongly evoked by whatever stimuli are present when the activity occurs. Thus, a globally defined preferred activity is likely to be the occasion for a potent elicitor and, hence, for stimuli that function as effective reinforcers.

Although the opportunity to engage in a more probable activity often strengthens a less probable activity, more recent work has shown that this probability relation is neither necessary nor sufficient for reinforcement (Timberlake, 1980;

Timberlake & Allison, 1974). If an organism is deprived of the opportunity to engage in an activity to the degree that would occur were the organism given free access to that activity, the opportunity to engage in the activity will strengthen *whatever* response permits that activity to take place. Thus, response deprivation (or, in general, the departure of responding from its preferred level of occurrence) is more predictive of the reinforcing value of the stimulus occasioning the response than is the probability of the response alone. In fact, the opportunity to engage in a lower probability response—but one of which the organism has been deprived—has been shown to strengthen a higher probability response on which the lower probability response is contingent (Timberlake & Wozny, 1979). Such findings are consistent with a unified reinforcement principle: Eliciting stimuli function as reinforcers when they produce momentary behavioral discrepancies independent of the global probability of the responses they evoke. Depriving an organism of the opportunity to make a given response is simply an effective means for ensuring that the stimuli are effective occasions for that response. The effectiveness of such stimuli as reinforcers is dependent on the degree of behavioral change they occasion, but any eliciting stimulus can potentially function as a reinforcer for any response, subject to the caveat regarding interactions between operants and reinforcer-elicited responses. (For a discussion of the implications of this reasoning for reinforcement in applied settings, see Timberlake & Farmer-Dougan, 1990.)

From the perspective of a unified reinforcement principle, functional relations between variables defined over substantial periods of time (e.g., average rates or probabilities of events) reflect the cumulative effects of processes operating on a moment-to-moment time scale. These variables do not provide direct measures of the reinforcement process. Molar variables, such as the average rate of reinforcers, are *correlated* with the fundamental variables that affect responding—that is, the moment-to-moment relation between constituents of the three-term contingency of discriminated stimulus, operant, and reinforcer—but they do not specify these variables precisely. On this view, understanding the effects of the standard schedules of reinforcement and other complex contingencies is largely the province of interpretation rather than experimental analysis (Donahoe & Palmer, 1994, pp. 125–129). Mathematical or computer-simulation techniques must supplement experimental analysis to reveal the implications of moment-to-moment processes for the interpretation of complex contingencies, and this remains an important unfinished task (cf. Williams, 1990). The necessity of interpretation for understanding complex phenomena is not confined to behavior analysis, of course. All sciences struggle to account for phenomena that are the products of a history of multiple, simultaneously acting processes—for example, many body problems in Newtonian mechanics where all the fundamental processes are known to a high degree of certainty.

TRACING THE CUMULATIVE EFFECTS OF REINFORCEMENT

Almost 100 years after Pavlov and Thorndike began the quest for a principle of reinforcement, we now appear to be approaching a genuine understanding of the essential requirements for the process and a comprehensive formulation of a principle describing that process. Moreover, applied behavior analysis increasingly demonstrates its ability to remediate dysfunctional

behavior. In spite of these advances, much of psychology does not accept the proposition that complex human behavior can emerge as the cumulative product of such a "simple" process as reinforcement. Instead, the state of psychology today parallels that of evolutionary biology in the years immediately following Darwin's proposal. Darwin had provided a functional account of a selection principle and had verbally described how that principle—acting over time—could produce the diversity and complexity of life. And yet, even members of the scientific community did not accept his insight that complex structure arose as the cumulative effect of the processes described by that principle.

The core of Darwin's proposal is now generally accepted by the scientific community. (Yet, to this day, only about half of the population at large accepts the Darwinian account.) Some 70 years elapsed between the publication of Darwin's proposal in 1859 and its acceptance by the scientific community in the 1930s. We may ask: What occurred during those 70 years to cause natural selection to be viewed as the primary engine of complex structure? By identifying the critical events and their possible modern counterparts relative to a principle of selection by reinforcement, we may hasten the recognition of the full power of reinforcement and of its potential for behavioral intervention.

As shown in Table 9–2, Darwin's functional proposal of natural selection required the occurrence of two events before it gained acceptance. First, the biological mechanisms mediating the

Table 9–2. Parallels Between Natural Selection by Reinforcement

	ORIGINS OF COMPLEX STRUCTURE	ORIGINS OF COMPLEX BEHAVIOR
Functional Principle	Natural Selection	Selection by Reinforcement
Biological Mechanism Implementing the Selection Process	Changes in Gene Frequencies (Genetics)	Changes in Synaptic Efficacies (Neurosciences)
Technique for Tracing the Selection Process	Population Genetics	Neural Networks

functional principle had to be uncovered. Mendel's work on genetics was rediscovered in the early 1900s and provided the mechanism whereby selected variations could endure and become the object of subsequent selection by later environments. Second, some more precise method for tracing the effects of natural selection over time had to be devised. Darwin had offered only a verbal account of how the evolutionary process might proceed. And although prepared minds found the parsimony of natural selection compelling, the many interacting steps required by the account left Darwin's conclusions open to unresolvable debate. The efforts of quantitative biologists such as Haldane, Fischer, and Wright addressed the problem. With the development of population genetics and, more recently, computer simulation, it became possible to trace the course of multiple, interacting processes. The conjunction of Darwin's functional principle of natural selection with the mechanisms of genetics and the techniques of population genetics led to what biologists call "the modern synthesis" (Dobzhansky, 1937). The synthesis led to the triumph of Darwinism over its creationist competitors (see Palmer & Donahoe, 1993).

If the Darwinian parallel holds, the general acceptance of reinforcement as the central insight into the origins of complex behavior awaits uncovering the biological mechanisms that mediate its effects and developing techniques that more precisely trace its implications. As shown in Table 9–2, these goals may potentially be realized through integrating behavior analysis with the neurosciences to understand the changes that occur in the nervous system when reinforcers change behavior and with quantitative techniques (adaptive neural networks) to understand how reinforcers act over time.

The remainder of this chapter provides a brief overview of these efforts, which are in their early stages of development relative to those now empowering the principle of natural selection. Contrary to common misperceptions, these developments were presaged and welcomed by Skinner as shown in the following comments:

The physiologist of the future will tell us all that can be known about what is happening inside the behaving organism. His account will be an important advance over a behavioral analysis, because the latter is necessarily "historical" —that is to say, it is confined to functional relations showing temporal gaps. . . . What he discovers cannot invalidate the laws of a science of behavior, but it will make the picture of human action more nearly complete (Skinner, 1974, pp. 236–237).

Neural Mechanisms of Selection

Figure 9–3 depicts the architecture of an adaptive neural-network with the major neural systems thought to produce selection by reinforcement and to mediate the effects of the environment on behavior. (See Donahoe, Burgos, & Palmer, 1993; Donahoe & Dorsel, in press; Donahoe & Palmer, 1994; for more detailed presentations.) The functioning of such networks is described in the following subsections. Networks of this general form are called selection networks because the effect of reinforcement is to select pathways that mediate environment-behavior relations of arbitrary form.

Selection of Environmental Relations

Environmental stimuli (S1, S2, S3) activate input units, which simulate primary sensory neurons in the brain. The input units have connections, simulating synapses, with sensory-association units. These units integrate the combinations of inputs required to activate the output units of the network. For example, a sensory-association unit might become reliably activated only when *two* stimuli occur simultaneously, thus allowing behavior to be controlled by the co-occurrence of stimuli but not by any one stimulus alone. Changes in the strength of connections to sensory-association units are governed by the simulated hippocampus, whose widely projecting outputs to sensory-association units are indicated by heavy lines with arrows. Inputs to the simulated hippocampus arise from units in the sensory-association subnetwork. The variable that determines the strength of the diffuse hippocam-

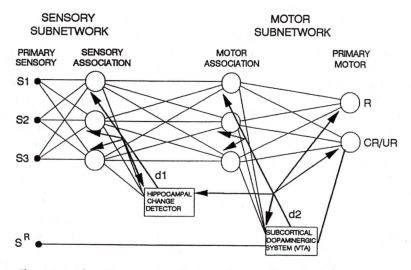

Figure 9–3. The major structures of an adaptive neural network whose architecture exemplifies a selection network. The strengths of connections to sensory-association units are modified by a diffusely projecting signal from the simulated hippocampus that is proportional to the difference (d1) in the levels of activations of hippocampal inputs from one moment to the next. The strengths of connections to motor-association and motor units are modified by a diffusely projecting signal from the simulated ventral tegmental area (VTA) that is proportional to the difference (d2) in the levels of activations of VTA inputs from one moment to the next. The reinforcing stimulus (S^R) activates its input unit, which then activates the simulated VTA.

pal output and that thereby changes the connectivity between sensory-association units is deferred for the moment.

The integration of sensory inputs is required if complex environments are to guide behavior. For example, consider the formation of equivalence classes (see Hayes & Ju, this book). A matching-to-sample procedure is used to select a number of contextual (conditional) discriminations; for example, when S1 is the sample and S2 is one of the comparison stimuli, press the display containing S2. After such training, testing reveals a number of untrained relations; for example, with S2 as the sample and S1 as one of the comparison stimuli, the display containing S1 is pressed. Murray Sidman has suggested that such emergent relations are best interpreted as indicating the formation of stimulus-stimulus relations (Sidman & Tailby, 1982). Experimental analysis at the neural

level supports Sidman's interpretation. When microelectrodes were used to record the activity of cells in the sensory-association cortex of monkeys who had received symbolic matching-to-sample training, cells were found that responded primarily to *both* of the stimuli that had served as sample and comparison stimuli on reinforced trials. Cells were not found that responded to nonreinforced pairs of sample and comparison stimuli, although they had also occurred together frequently (Sakai & Miyashita, 1991; for related work, see Tanaka, in press).

Selection of Environment-Behavior Relations

Referring again to Figure 9–3, connections from sensory-association units activate motor-association units, and these units, in turn, activate primary motor units leading to the simulated operant behavior (R) of the network. The strength of connections among motor-association and primary motor units is modified by the diffusely projecting outputs of the simulated ventral tegmental area (VTA). These nonspecific projections to the motor-association area are shown by heavy lines with arrows.

The VTA is activated by two sets of inputs. The first set comes from cells that are activated by biologically significant reinforcing stimuli (S^R_S or USs), such as the taste and smell of food. The strength of the connections from these cells to VTA is strong from the outset and is a legacy of natural selection. That is, such stimuli function as unconditioned reinforcers. The second set of inputs to VTA comes from cells in the motor-association cortex and various subcortical structures. Connections to the VTA from cells in these areas are initially weak and require strengthening by the activation of the VTA by unconditioned reinforcers. As selection proceeds, VTA neurons are increasingly driven by inputs from the second set of cells in these other areas whose connections to VTA have been strengthened by prior reinforcers. These prior reinforcers may be both unconditioned and conditioned. The pathways from these areas to VTA are thought to be the neural basis of conditioned reinforcement (Donahoe, Burgos, & Palmer, 1993). By utilizing such circuits, complex chains of behavioral relations can be automatically acquired without the need for constant and immediate environmental reinforcement. Such circuits are proposed to play an especially important role in language acquisition and in the acquisition of complex behavioral sequences generally (Donahoe, in press; Donahoe & Palmer, 1994).

Experimental analyses at the neural level are consistent with activation of the diffuse VTA reinforcement system by two sets of inputs. Using microelectrodes to monitor the activity of neurons in the VTA of monkeys, VTA neurons responded with a burst of firing when apple juice was presented. However, after several pairings in which the onset of a light preceded the apple juice, VTA neurons now fired when the light occurred and were relatively silent when apple juice was given immediately after the light

(Schultz, in press). Thus, after pairing of the light with apple juice, VTA neurons were refractory to activation by apple juice. The activation of the VTA by light was mediated by pathways from cells driven by light and demonstrates the acquired ability of light to function as a conditioned reinforcer. The inability of apple juice to function as a reinforcer when preceded by light provides a neural basis for the discrepancy requirement of selection by reinforcement. The onset of light had blocked the ability of apple juice to activate the VTA. More generally, once a stimulus acquires the ability to activate the VTA, an eliciting stimulus that would otherwise function as a reinforcer is not able to do so immediately thereafter.

Neural Mechanisms of Reinforcement

On the neural level, the process of reinforcement may be simulated in selection networks (see Figure 9–3) through the action of diffusely projecting reinforcement signals from VTA and hippocampus acting on synapses between co-active pre- and postsynaptic units (Donahoe, Burgos, & Palmer, 1993; Donahoe & Palmer, 1989, 1994). Note that that one of the outputs of VTA is to hippocampus. Signals from VTA modulate the strength of the reinforcing signal from the hippocampus to sensory-association units. Thus, reinforcers, through their direct effect on VTA and their indirect effect on hippocampal output, coordinate the modification of synaptic efficacies throughout the entire network.

Whenever a reinforcer occurs, synapses are modified between all co-active units throughout the network. At the moment of reinforcement, many of the modified synapses are irrelevant to the mediation of the reinforced behavior. However, at any moment of reinforcement, some synapses between co-active units are necessarily relevant because, were it not so, the behavior that produced the reinforcer would not have occurred. Over time, selection by reinforcement on the neural level modifies most reliably (and, hence, most strongly) those synapses that mediate the reinforced response. The emergent effect of selection is a network with a set of strengthened pathways that are sufficient to mediate the reinforced environment-behavior relation.

Experimental analyses at the cellular level are consistent with the view that the output of diffusely projecting neural systems acting at synapses between co-active neurons modifies synaptic efficacies. When activated, VTA neurons liberate a neuromodulator, dopamine. Using neuronal tissue in culture, Stein's group has found that when dopamine is microinjected into synapses within 200 milliseconds of activity in postsynaptic neurons, the firing rates of the postsynaptic neurons increase on subsequent occasions (Stein & Belluzzi, 1989). This is the cellular counterpart of the contiguity requirement at the behavioral level. The increase in firing found after activity-dependent application of dopamine is, as interpreted here, the result of an increased responsiveness of the postsynaptic neuron to neurotransmitter released by the presynaptic neuron (Donahoe & Palmer, 1994). Dopamine in conjunction with postsynaptic activity is known to initiate a series of intracellular events that produce

long-term changes in synaptic efficacy (Frey, in press; Frey, Huang, & Kandel, 1993). It is of interest that all known agents of abuse (e.g., cocaine, alcohol, and nicotine) act upon dopaminergic neural systems.

Neural-Network Simulations of Selection

The cumulative effects of the foregoing neural processes can be traced using selection networks and computer simulations (Donahoe, Burgos, & Palmer, 1993; Donahoe & Dorsel, in press). Figure 9–4 shows changes in the activations of output units for the operant (R) and elicited response (CR) when connections within the network are modified according to the unified reinforcement principle using simulated biological mechanisms of the type just described. The figure shows simulated responding during acquisition, extinction, and reacquisition.

Of particular importance is the relation between activation of the R and CR output units,

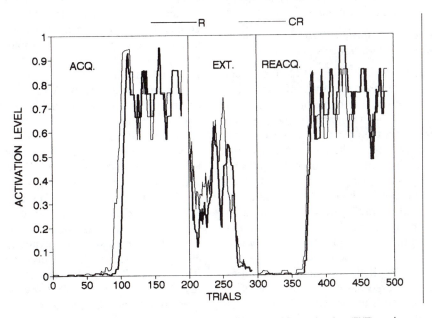

Figure 9–4. Simulated responding during acquisition (ACQ), extinction (EXT), and reacquisition (REACQ) with an operant contingency. Shown are the levels of activation of both the operant (R) and the conditioned-response (CR) output units.

simulating operant and respondent activity, respectively. Note that the CR is acquired before the R. This result occurs quite generally in the simulations for reasons described elsewhere (Donahoe & Palmer, 1994, p. 60). The presence of CR activity is highly correlated with the degree to which the simulated VTA is being activated by circuits from motor-association units and provides a measure of conditioned reinforcement mediated by these circuits. The effect of intranetwork conditioned reinforcement is most apparent during extinction when external reinforcers are not presented (Figure 9–4). Following periods of CR activation, the level of R activity increases as a result of the strengthening of connections between units that happen to be active just before the simulated VTA is activated by the conditioned-reinforcement circuits. The abrupt and transitory increases in responding produced by the conditioned-reinforcement mechanism are reminiscent of the "emotional" effects during extinction described by Skinner (1938). Note also that, as with living organisms, the simulated operant is reacquired more rapidly than it was originally acquired.

Experimental and Applied Implications of Neural-Network Simulations

Neural-network simulations of reinforcement do not, as yet, approach the power of population genetics to interpret the cumulative effects of natural selection, and it is much too soon to draw conclusions about their ultimate promise. Similarly, our knowledge of the neural mechanisms of conditioning remains incomplete. Nevertheless, many encouraging signs appear, of which a few are mentioned here. (See Donahoe & Palmer, 1994, for a preliminary but comprehensive treatment of the implications of a reinforcement principle for complex behavior when interpreted via selection networks.)

Experimentally, if the activation of respondents (CR units) precedes the activation of operants (R units) and if the activity of CR units is discriminable, then these discriminative stimuli are ideally positioned to acquire control over the operant. Such stimuli appear *immediately* before

the operant and reinforcer at a stage during acquisition when the operant has not yet been acquired (Figure 9–4, acquisition panel). If the operant is partially guided by such stimuli, variables that affect CR acquisition, such as reinforcement frequency, would be expected to affect the resistance of the operant to change (see the discussion of momentum, Nevin, this book). Similarly, extinguishing the CR would weaken the operant, because extinction eliminates some of the discriminative stimuli that would otherwise be produced by the CR. This mechanism could provide a parsimonious interpretation of what has been called the devaluation effect (Colwill & Rescorla, 1986; Rescorla, 1991), in which operant responding is altered by manipulations affecting only the stimuli that previously served as reinforcers for the operant.

The more rapid acquisition of respondents than operants also has implications for the interpretation of a number of phenomena in which the eliciting stimulus is aversive. If the eliciting stimulus is aversive (i.e., evokes unconditioned escape responses that remove the organism from the situation), the CRs are especially effective competitors with the operant. The rapid acquisition of conditioned escape responses prevents the operant from occurring; that is, the elicitor functions as a punisher. However, if the form of the operant is compatible with the conditioned escape responses, an anomalous result occurs. Under such circumstances, the aversive elicitor should function as a reinforcer! As one example, if extending the hind leg of a restrained rat is followed by shock to the tail, which is an aversive stimulus that elicits hind leg extension, then shock to the tail functions as a reinforcer for leg extension. With such an arrangement, rats receiving response-contingent shock on a fixed-interval 5-minute schedule acquired and indefinitely persisted in extending the hind leg (Donahoe & Burns, 1984, reported in Donahoe & Palmer, 1994, p. 115; for a review of the first work in this area, see Morse & Kelleher, 1977).

Implications for applied behavior analysis exist as well. As was pointed out to me during a discussion at the Shriver Center, if operants are partially guided by CR-produced stimuli, extinction of the CR is required to fully weaken control of the operant. For example, to the extent that imagining a situation in which drugs of abuse have been taken produces CRs, to that extent will stimuli be reinstated that control operant drug taking. Imagining an event is known to activate some of the very same neural systems that are activated by the events themselves (e.g., Farah, Peronnet, Gonon, & Giard, 1988). (The relation of this interpretation to previous inferred-process accounts such as Hull's r_g-s_g mechanism is appreciated; Hull, 1943. The crucial difference is that the present account appeals to structures and processes that have been previously identified through *independent* experimental analyses. The earlier accounts were largely inferences from the behavior itself; cf. Donahoe & Palmer, 1989.)

Among the many mutually beneficial relations between neural-network interpretations of reinforcement and applied behavior analysis, two merit mention here. First, self-control is generally interpreted as occurring when conditioned reinforcers are immediately available after a response that would otherwise be reinforced only after a considerable delay (see Logue, this volume). The behavior of children diagnosed with attention-deficit disorder (ADD) typically displays relatively little self-control in this sense and is sometimes alleviated with drugs that increase the levels of dopamine. Dopamine facilitates the functioning of circuits going from neurons in the motor-association area to VTA, the circuits that mediate conditioned reinforcement in selection networks. Correspondingly, behavioral interventions that implement immediate conditioned reinforcers should be effective in remediating behavior associated with ADD — and, indeed, they are (Schweitzer & Sulzer-Azaroff, 1988). Behavioral interventions should provide not only immediate conditioned reinforcers from the environment but also the covert stimuli provided by covert behavior such as imagining the ultimate consequences of the response producing the delayed reinforcer. This covert behavior then activates the circuits mediating conditioned reinforcement.

Second, beginning with work from Lovaas's group (Lovaas, Schreibman, Koegel, & Rehm, 1971), the behavior of autistic children has been attributed — in part, at least — to difficulties in sensory integration (see DeLong, 1992). (I am indebted to David Palmer for bringing this work to my attention.) In selection networks, sensory integration is accomplished through the action of the diffusely projecting outputs of the hippocampus on the connectivity of sensory-association units. A malfunction of this system for selecting connections that mediate multisensory relations would be particularly problematic for verbal behavior, for example, the visual-auditory integrations required for naming and reading.

Whether the selection of environmental relations is the core problem of autism and, if so, what specific malfunction exists in the relevant neural systems remain issues for the future. For the present, the intimate correspondence between the behavior-analytic concepts of operants and reinforcement and the neural processes simulated by selection networks bode well for the application of behavior analysis to clinical neuropsychology. The correspondence between the findings and concepts of behavior analysis and neuroscience should come as no surprise: Behavior analysis studies the guidance of behavior by the individual environment, and the ancestral environment has naturally selected neural mechanisms that mediate such relations. Accordingly, behavior analysis is uniquely positioned to lead the effort to coordinate observations at the behavioral and neural levels and, in so doing, to deepen our understanding of that most fundamental process — reinforcement.

REFERENCES

Brandon, S. E., Betts, S. L., & Wagner, A. R. (1994). Discriminated lateralized eyeblink conditioning in the rabbit: An experimental context for separating specific and general associative influences. *Journal of Experimental Psychology: Animal Behavior Processes, 20,* 292–307.

Catania, A. C. (1971). Reinforcement schedules: The role of responses preceding the one that produces the reinforcer. *Journal of the Experimental Analysis of Behavior, 15,* 271–287.

Colwill, R. M., & Rescorla, R. A. (1986). Associative structures in instrumental learning. In G. H. Bower (ed.), *The psychology of learning and motivation*, Vol. 20: 55–104. New York: Academic Press.

DeLong, R. G. (1992). Autism, amnesia, hippocampus, and learning. *Neuroscience and Biobehavioral Reviews, 16*, 63–70.

Dobzhansky, T. G. (1937). *Genetics and the origin of species*. New York: Columbia University Press.

Donahoe, J. W. (in press). Selection networks: Simulation of plasticity through reinforcement learning. In J. W. Donahue & V. P. Dorsel (eds.), *Neural-network models of cognition: Biobehavioral foundations*. Amsterdam: Elsevier.

Donahoe, J. W., Burgos, J. E., & Palmer, D. C. (1993). Selectionist approach to reinforcement. *Journal of the Experimental Analysis of Behavior, 58*, 17–40.

Donahoe, J. W., Crowley, M. A., Millard, W. J., & Stickney, K. A. (1982). A unified principle of reinforcement. In M. L. Commons, R. J. Herrnstein, & H. Rachlin (eds.), *Quantitative models of behavior*, Vol. 2: 493–521. Cambridge, Mass.: Ballinger.

Donahoe, J. W., & Dorsel, V. P. (eds.) (in press). *Neural-network models of cognition: Biobehavioral foundations*. Amsterdam: Elsevier.

Donahoe, J. W., & Palmer, D. C. (1989). The interpretation of complex human behavior: Some reactions to Parallel Distributed Processing. *Journal of the Experimental Analysis of Behavior, 51*, 399–416.

Donahoe, J. W., & Palmer. D. C. (1994). *Learning and complex behavior*. Boston: Allyn & Bacon.

Farah, M. J., Peronnet, F., Gonon, M. A., & Giard, M. H. (1988). Electrophysiological evidence for a shared representational medium for visual images and visual percepts. *Journal of Experimental Psychology: General, 117*, 248–257.

Ferster, C. B., & Skinner, B. F. (1957). *Schedules of reinforcement*. New York: Appleton-Century-Crofts.

Frey, U. (in press). Cellular mechanisms of long-term potentiation: Late maintenance. In J. E. Donahoe & V. P. Dorsel, (eds.), *Neural-network models of cognition: Biobehavioral foundations*. Amsterdam: Elsevier.

Frey, U., Huang, Y.-Y., & Kandel, E. R. (1993). Effects of cAMP simulate a late stage of LTP in hippocampus CA1 neurons. *Science, 260*, 1661–1664.

Hinson, J. M., & Staddon, J. E. R. (1983). Hill-climbing by pigeons. *Journal of the Experimental Analysis of Behavior, 39*, 25–48.

Hull, C. L. (1943). *Principles of behavior*. New York: Appleton-Century-Crofts.

Jenkins, H. M., & Moore, B. R. (1973). The form of the autoshaped response with food or water reinforcers. *Journal of the Experimental Analysis of Behavior, 20*, 163–181.

Johnson, D. F. (1970). Determiners of selective attention in the pigeon. *Journal of Comparative and Physiological Psychology, 70*, 298–307.

Kamin, L. J. (1968). Attention-like processes in classical conditioning. In M. R. Jones (ed.), *Miami symposium on the prediction of behavior*, 9–31. Miami, Fla.: University of Miami Press.

Kamin, L. J. (1969). Predictability, surprise, attention and conditioning. In B. A. Campbell & R. M. Church (eds.), *Punishment and aversive behavior*, 279–296. New York: Appleton-Century-Crofts.

Lovaas, O. I., Schreibman, L., Koegel, R. L., & Rehm, R. (1971). Selective responding by autistic children to multiple sensory input. *Journal of Abnormal Psychology, 77*, 211–222.

Morse, W. H. (1966). Intermittent reinforcement. In W. K. Honig (ed.), *Operant behavior: Areas of research and application*, 52–108. Englewood Cliffs, N.J.: Prentice-Hall.

Morse, W. H., & Kelleher, R. T. (1977). Determinants of reinforcement and punishment. In W. K. Honig & J. E. R. Staddon (eds.), *Handbook of operant behavior*, 174–200. Englewood Cliffs, N.J.: Prentice-Hall.

Morse, W. H., & Skinner, B. F. (1967). A second type of superstition in the pigeon. *American Journal of Psychology, 70*, 308–311.

Palmer, D. C., & Donahoe, J. W. (1993). Essentialism and selection in cognitive science and behaviorism. *American Psychologist, 47*, 1344–1358.

Pavlov, I. P. (1927). *Conditioned reflexes*. New York: Oxford University Press. Reprint. New York: Dover, 1960.

Premack, D. (1959). Toward empirical behavioral laws: I. Positive reinforcement, *Psychological Review, 66*, 219–233.

Premack, D. (1963). Prediction of the comparative reinforcement values of running and drinking. *Science, 139*, 1062–1063.

Premack, D. (1965). Reinforcement theory. In D. Levine (ed.), *Nebraska symposium on motivation*. Lincoln: University of Nebraska Press.

Rescorla, R. A. (1968). Conditioned inhibition of fear. In N. J. Mackintosh & W. K. Honig (eds.), *Fundamental issues in associative learning*, 65–89. Halifax, Nova Scotia: University of Dalhousie Press.

Rescorla, R. A. (1970). Reduction in the effectiveness of reinforcement after prior excitatory conditioning. *Learning and Motivation, 1*, 372–381.

Rescorla, R. A. (1971). Variation in effectiveness of reinforcement following prior inhibitory conditioning. *Learning and Motivation, 2*, 113–123.

Rescorla, R. A. (1991). Associative relations in instrumental learning: The eighteenth Bartlett memorial lecture. *Quarterly Journal of Experimental Psychology, 43B*, 1–23.

Rescorla, R. A., & Wagner, A. R. (1972). A theory of Pavlovian conditioning: Variations in the effectiveness of reinforcement and nonreinforcement. In A. H. Black & W. F. Prokasy (eds.), *Classical conditioning II*, 64–99. New York: Appleton-Century-Crofts.

Rilling, M. (1967). Number of responses as a stimulus in fixed-interval and fixed-ratio schedules. *Journal of Comparative and Physiological Psychology, 63*, 60–65.

Sakai, K., & Miyashita, M. (1991). Neural organization for the long-term memory of paired associates. *Nature, 354*, 152–155.

Schultz, W. (in press). Adaptive dopaminergic neurons report the appetitive value of environmental stimuli. In J. W. Donahoe & V. P. Dorsel (eds.), *Neural-network models of cognition: Biobehavioral foundations*. Amsterdam: Elsevier.

Schweitzer, J. B., & Sulzer-Azaroff, B. (1988). Self-control: Teaching tolerance for delay in impulsive children. *Journal of the Experimental Analysis of Behavior, 50*, 173–181.

Shapiro, M. M., & Miller, T. M. (1965). On the relationship between conditioned and discriminative stimuli and between instrumental and consummatory responses. In W. F. Prokasy (ed.), *Classical conditioning*. New York: Appleton-Century-Crofts.

Shimp, C. P. (1969). Optimal behavior in free-operant experiments. *Psychological Review, 76*, 97–112.

Silberberg, A., Hamilton, B., Ziriax, J. M., & Casey, A. C. (1978). The structure of choice. *Journal of Experimental Psychology: Animal Behavior Processes, 4*, 368–398.

Skinner, B. F. (1937). Two types of conditioned reflex: A reply to Konorski and Miller, *Journal of General Psychology, 16*, 272–279.

Skinner, B. F. (1938). *The behavior of organisms*. New York: Appleton-Century-Crofts.

Skinner, B. F. (1948). "Superstition" in the pigeon. *Journal of Experimental Psychology, 38*, 168–172.

Skinner, B. F. (1974). *About behaviorism*. New York: Harper & Row.

Skinner, B. F. (1981). Selection by consequences. *Science, 213*, 501–504.

Sidman, M., & Tailby, W. (1982). Conditional discrimination vs. matching to sample: An expansion of the testing paradigm. *Journal of the Experimental Analysis of Behavior, 37*, 5–22.

Staddon, J. E. R., & Hinson, J. M. (1983). Optimization: A result or a mechanism? *Science, 221*, 976–977.

Stein, L., & Belluzzi, J. D. (1989). Cellular investigations on behavioral reinforcement. *Neuroscience and Biobehavior Reviews, 13*, 69–80.

Stickney, K. A., & Donahoe, J. W. (1983). Attenuation of blocking by a change in US locus. *Animal Learning and Animal Behavior, 11*, 60–66.

Tanaka, K. (in press). Inferotemporal cortex and object recognition. In J. E. Donahoe & V. P. Dorsel (eds.), *Neural-network models of cognition: Biobehavioral foundations*. Amsterdam: Elsevier.

Thomas, D. R. (1970). Stimulus selection, attention, and related matters. In J. H. Reynierse (ed.), *Current issues in animal learning*, 311–356. Lincoln: University of Nebraska Press.

Thorndike, E. L. (1898). Animal intelligence: An experimental study of the associative processes in animals. *Psychological Review Monograph Supplements, 2:8*, 1–74.

Timberlake, W., (1980). A molar equilibrium theory of learned performance. In G. H. Bower (ed.), *The psychology of learning and motivation*, Vol. 14: 1–58. New York: Academic Press.

Timberlake, W., & Allison, J. (1974). Response deprivation: An empirical approach to instrumental performance. *Psychological Review, 81*, 146–164.

Timberlake, W., & Farmer-Dougan, V. A. (1990). Reinforcement in applied settings: Figuring out ahead of time what will work. *Psychological Bulletin, 110*, 379–391.

Timberlake, W., & Wozny, M. (1979). Reversibility of reinforcers between eating and running by schedule changes: A comparison of hypotheses and models. *Animal Learning and Behavior, 7*, 461–469.

vom Saal, W., & Jenkins, H. M. (1970). Blocking the development of stimulus control. *Learning and Motivation, 1*, 52–64.

Williams, B. A. (1990). Enduring problems for molecular accounts of operant behavior. *Journal of Experimental Psychology: Animal Behavior Processes, 16*, 213–216.

Williams, D. R. (1968). The structure of response rate. *Journal of the Experimental Analysis of Behavior, 11*, 251–258.

Williams, D. R., & Williams, H. (1969). Auto-maintenance in the pigeon: Sustained pecking despite contingent nonreinforcement. *Science, 12*, 511–520.

CHAPTER 10

PUNISHMENT

James A. Dinsmoor

In contemporary society, punishment is a controversial topic. The public expresses strangely contrasting views, depending upon who is administering the punishment and to whom it is being administered. If the punishment is being administered to children by their parents, then it is perfectly acceptable. A survey of 1470 adults conducted several years ago found that 84% of the respondents agreed with the statement, "It is sometimes necessary to discipline a child with a good hard spanking" (reported in Lehman, March 13, 1989). In the same vein, if we examine actual patterns of behavior, we find that almost all parents use corporal punishment of one kind or another (slapping, spanking, hitting, throwing objects, etc.) on their own children (e.g., Sears, Maccoby, & Levin, 1957); more than half of American parents continue such treatment into the adolescent years. (For a general review of current social practices, see Straus, 1994). In many cases, the parents resort to this form of discipline because they are angry and out of control (Carson, 1988, cited in Straus, 1994; Katz, 1988).

On the other hand, public campaigns have succeeded in eliminating the use of corporal punishment by members of the teaching profession, who are probably much more judicious than the average parent in determining when it is appropriate. Similarly, Lyon, Picker, and Poling (1985) have documented the decline in the use of electric shock in the conditioning laboratory since "animal rights" campaigns began. And therapists dealing with children who are hideously self-destructive and for whom no non-aversive form of treatment appears to work have found it necessary to form an organization known as the International Association for the Right to Effective Treatment to protect their therapeutic efforts from legislative interference.

DEFINITION

The lay person sometimes uses the term *punishment* rather loosely, referring to any application of electric shock or other aversive stimulus to the experimental subject, regardless of the way the stimulus is applied in relation to the subject's behavior. But in the research literature the term is usually restricted to instances in which the stimulus (a) is administered as a consequence of some recorded response and (b) reduces the future probability of that response (or affects some related measure). Sometimes, for convenience, the term is extended to a comparison procedure in which the stimulus is delivered on a response-independent basis, but it is recognized that this is a different procedure and has different consequences.

In practice, almost all of the research on punishment has been conducted with electric shock. This form of stimulation is not without its problems when used in behavioral research (for a review, see Dinsmoor, 1968). With rats, for example, the easiest way to deliver it is to place the subject on a grid floor, composed of a series of parallel rods made of brass or stainless steel, and to attach the even-numbered rods to one terminal of the shock stimulator and the odd-numbered rods to the other. But as soon as the animal chances upon a position where it is standing only on even-numbered or only on odd-numbered rods, it is out of the circuit between the two terminals, and the current no longer flows through its body. Moreover, if organic matter deposited by the subject bridges the gap between adjacent rods, some of the current will flow through an alternative path. Any variation in the contact between the subject's paws and the electrified rods as it moves across the grid also modifies the physical characteristics of the shock it receives.

Nevertheless, electric shock is the stimulus of choice for most experiments on the aversive control of operant behavior. It is quickly presented and removed and can readily be altered in intensity. It also has one overwhelming advantage over other forms of aversive stimulation: it is effective. Other stimuli, such as loud noise, bright light, immersion in water, extremes of heat or cold, noxious odors, or vibration of the test cage, are not only more difficult to implement but also have relatively little effect on the subject's behavior. By contrast, shock is capable of covering the entire range from no effect to complete suppression of the target response (Appel, 1961; Azrin, 1959). It is assumed by most writers that the behavioral principles derived from studies in which shock has been used also hold for other forms of aversive stimulation, but the discriminating reader should be aware of the danger of generalizing from so narrow a base.

BASIC PARAMETERS

Before it can be punished, behavior must occur. Furthermore, the decremental effect produced by the application of punishment can be measured only if the level of performance during the punishment can be compared with the performance at some other time, when punishment is not being applied. Therefore, the experimenter who wants to study the effects of punishment must first establish some kind of baseline performance, and the characteristics of that baseline performance will necessarily interact with the effects of the punishment to determine the final resultant.

For most comparisons, the ideal baseline is one in which the rate of responding remains relatively stable from one session to the next and from moment to moment within each session. The best arrangement for accomplishing this end is one in which the average frequency of reinforcement remains the same over an extended period of time but the occasion on which the next reinforcer becomes available is not predictable. Under a variable-interval (VI) schedule, reinforcers are "set up" by a temporal cycle of variable duration and "collected" by the next response. As the frequency with which reinforcers are delivered is determined by the average length of the temporal interval, within wide limits it is insensitive to changes in the rate of responding. On the other hand, if the subject stops responding, reinforcement of the next response becomes increasingly probable with the passage of time. The resumption of responding is selectively reinforced. With this schedule, fluctuations in the baseline performance are reduced to a minimum, so that any changes that occur in the rate of responding when punishment is applied can safely be attributed to that punishment. Because of these virtues, most of the research on punishment since Skinner (1950) first demonstrated the advantages of the VI schedule has relied on that schedule for its baseline performance.

In general, the "stronger" the baseline behavior, as measured by its rate of occurrence, the greater is its resistance to the suppressive effect of a given frequency and severity of punishment. One way of varying the rate of responding is to increase or decrease the subject's level of motivation. For example, Azrin, Holz, and Hake (1963) made their pigeons hungrier by reducing the daily allowance of food. Whenever the bird's weight dropped to a specified percentage of the weight when food was continuously available (free-feeding or satiated weight), another test session was conducted. Throughout the tests, punishment in the form of a brief electric shock was delivered following every 50th response (a schedule known as fixed ratio 50). Although these investigators did not report the rates of pecking prior to the administration of the punishment at each level of deprivation, for purposes of comparison, the absolute rates under the punishment procedure make the case. At 60% of their free-feeding weight (greatest hunger), the birds pecked the key about 3,000 times per hour, but at 85% (least hunger) they rarely pecked at all.

Effect of Punishment on Concurrent Schedules

With other variables, a more precise comparison of the effects of the same schedule and intensity of punishment on two different levels of performance can be obtained by using concurrent schedules. Under this arrangement, responses on either of two bars or either of two keys, side by side, are reinforced on two independent sched-ules, usually two VI schedules. Both levels of performance are assessed at virtually the same points in time and with the same subject, thereby eliminating possible differences in reaction between different times and different individuals.

If the shock is also delivered on a variable-interval schedule, as in experiments by Deluty (1976), de Villiers (1980), and Farley (1980), the number of shocks received can be equated for the two schedules of reinforcement. When the number of shocks is the same, the result is very simple: the absolute reduction in the number of responses and therefore in the rate of responding is the same for both performances (see also Church & Raymond, 1967). This, of course, translates into a smaller relative reduction for the high-rate (strong) performance and a larger relative reduction for the low-rate (weak) performance.

The purpose of the three studies just cited was to extend the type of mathematical model originally formulated by Herrnstein (1970) to the case where punishment is applied. In each of the three sets of data, the equations that provided the best fit all conformed to what has been called a *subtractive model*. That is, to most accurately predict the relative rates of responding, it was necessary to subtract a value representing a given frequency of punishment on each bar or each key from a value representing the frequency of reinforcement of that same response (de Villiers, 1980; Farley, 1980). *Competing response models*, in which the frequency of punishment appeared as a positive quantity in the numerator for the alternative response or was represented by an increment in reinforcement from "other sources," were rejected.

For reasons that are not clear to me, both de Villiers (1981, 1982) and Farley (1980) placed the avoidance theory of punishment within the class of models their data rejected, but that conclusion depends on where the avoidance behavior is assumed to appear within the equation. The new parameter that it was necessary to add to the original matching equation when punishment was added to the experimental procedure was a negative value, $-cp$ (the coefficient c is a scaling constant), which both authors placed just following each appearance of the positive value, r, representing the effects of reinforcement. With R representing rate of responding, the resulting equation then read as follows:

$$\frac{R_1}{R_1 + R_2} = \frac{r_1 - cp_1}{r_1 - cp_1 + r_2 - cp_2}$$

This certainly seems to be the appropriate point at which to introduce opposing avoidance behavior. When Logue and de Villiers (1981) added shock avoidance to food deliveries as a reinforcer of lever pressing on a concurrent schedule, the avoidance acted in the same direction as the food deliveries, and they added a positive quantity at this point; all that is changed in the present instance is the mathematical sign, representing the direction in which the avoidance is assumed to operate. Although there also may have been some shift in the subject's position toward key 2 as a result of avoiding key 1 (which would favor the competing response model), note that the avoidance theory of punishment was originally formulated within the context of a single-bar procedure, where there *was no* competing R_2. I see no reason why the behavior halting or reversing the subject's approach to a particular bar or key should not be subtracted directly from the rate on that same bar or key. Recently I ran across notes I had jotted down some years ago, when I was planning a similar experiment. I found that the result I had expected on the basis of an avoidance theory of punishment was an equal absolute reduction in both rates of responding, the same result these investigators actually obtained.

Although important for quantitative analysis, the equal reduction in number of responses for two performances differing in rate holds only when the number of punishments is the same for both performances, a situation that must rarely be found in nature. If the number of punishments is higher with higher frequencies of responding, as might be more typical, a different result will emerge. If all responses are punished, for example, as in an earlier experiment by Holz (1968),

the number of punishments matches the number of responses, with the result that both responses are reduced in proportion to their rate of occurrence. Another way of expressing the same result is to specify that in Holz's experiment, both responses were reduced by the same percentage, rather than by the same absolute number. Under any procedure in which the number of punishments is proportional to the number of responses, punishment should have equal *relative* effects on both responses. Note, however, that under such a procedure more punishments have been required to suppress the strong behavior to the same degree as the weak behavior.

Severity and Scheduling

Among the more obvious parameters that might be expected to influence the magnitude of the suppression produced by the application of punishment are the intensity of each shock, its duration, the type of schedule, the frequency with which the shocks are delivered (or percentage of responses shocked), and the length of the delay between the occurrence of the response and the arrival of the shock. In most cases, laboratory results have confirmed common-sense expectations. Increasing the intensity of the shock reduces the rate of the punished response in rats (Appel, 1963; Dinsmoor, 1952; Estes, 1944; Filby & Appel, 1966), in pigeons (Azrin, 1960), and in monkeys (Hake, Azrin, & Oxford, 1967). The duration of each of the individual pulses of shock has a similar effect (Church, Raymond, & Beauchamp, 1967; Deluty, 1978). Contrary to what many people might expect, however, when the number of shocks is matched, delivering them on a variable-interval schedule is more effective than delivering them on a ratio schedule (Camp, Raymond, & Church, 1966). The frequency with which shocks are delivered can be varied by changing the mean time between them on a variable-interval schedule (Farley, 1980) or by changing the ratio between responses and shocks (Azrin, Holz, & Hake, 1963; Lande, 1981). As may be seen in Figure 10–1, the rate of pecking may be reduced from approximately

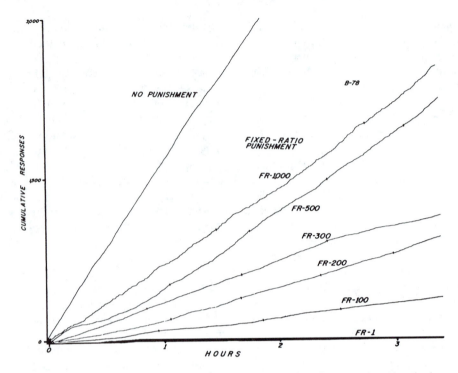

Figure 10–1. Cumulative records of one pigeon's pecking when the proportion of pecks that were punished varied between ratios of 1:1,000 (approximately 40% of unpunished rate) and 1:1 (rate near zero). Responding was maintained throughout by a 3-minute variable-interval schedule of reinforcement. The pips show when the shocks were delivered. (From Azrin, Holz, & Hake, 1963. Copyright © 1963 by the Society for the Experimental Analysis of Behavior, Inc.)

40% of the unpunished rate when only one response in a thousand is punished (fixed-ratio 1,000 schedule) to a near-zero rate when every response is punished (FR-1).

Delay of Punishment

One of the more interesting of the parameters determining the effectiveness of punishment is the length of the temporal interval (delay) between the time the response occurs and the time the punishment is delivered. As with a positive consequence, immediacy is important: even the briefest of delays greatly reduces the effectiveness of a given punishment (e.g., Camp, Raymond, & Church, 1967; Deluty, 1978). And just as in the case of a positive consequence (see

Logue in this volume), the animal's choice between a smaller, more immediate punishment and a larger, more delayed punishment depends on when the decision is made (see Figure 10–2). If the decision is made sufficiently early, it will be determined by ultimate, long-term considerations, namely the intensity and the duration of the shock that is received. The subject will "take" the smaller shock, even though it arrives sooner, in order to avoid the larger shock. But if the decision is delayed, relative time begins to play a more significant role (see Figure 10–2). For example, when viewed from a distance, a jab with a hypodermic needle may seem a small price to pay for protection against a serious disease, but as the "moment of truth" approaches, the decision becomes more and more difficult.

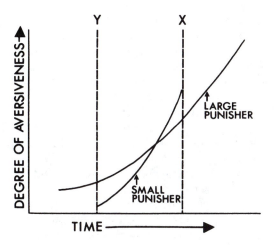

Figure 10–2. The joint effects of the intensity of the shock (large punisher vs. small punisher) and its delay following the response. When both punishers are relatively far off (*Y*), the magnitude is more important than the delay and the subject will choose the smaller punisher (self-control); but as the time for its delivery approaches (*X*), the delay becomes more important and the subject's preference switches to the larger but more remote punisher. (From Deluty, 1978. Copyright © 1978 by the American Psychological Association. Reprinted with permission.)

Laboratory data are available from Experiment 3 of a study by Deluty (1978). The small punishment was a shock of 1-second duration and the large punishment a shock of 2 seconds. Deluty varied the programmed time between the animal's decision and the first, smaller shock, if chosen, through a range from 40 seconds down to only 2 seconds; if the larger shock was chosen, it was delivered 10 seconds after the scheduled time for the small shock. At one extreme, when the alternative delays were 40 seconds for the small shock and 50 seconds for the large shock (early decision), the ratio between the two delays was fairly even, and more than 60% of all responses were made on the lever leading to the smaller shock. At the other extreme, when the alternative delays were much shorter (2 and 12 seconds) and very different (in a ratio of 1:6), about 65% of all responses were made on the lever leading to the larger but less immediate shock.

In Deluty's study, the magnitude and delay of the shock were varied, but the magnitude and delay of the reinforcer were held constant. In the world outside the laboratory, the situation may often be more complex. A problem that frequently arises in everyday living is that the short-term consequences for a given action may be reinforcing but the long-term consequences are punishing. Drinking too much alcohol at a party, for example, may produce a reinforcing state of affairs that same evening but a large punishment the following morning. Drinking some milk before the party or committing oneself to leave at a certain hour may reduce the risk. Other examples involving immediate reward but delayed punishment are eating candy or high-fat foods, running up a debt on a credit card, or engaging in unprotected sex. Impulsive actions may have disastrous consequences. Committing crimes against the person, such as assault, theft, rape, and murder, may also fit the same pattern.

Then there are the cases in which the immediate consequences are punishing but the ultimate consequences are positive. Setting the alarm clock for an early hour brings a small punishment in the morning but facilitates getting to work on time. Hitting the books may be onerous but helps a student get a good grade. Exercising regularly may entail aches and pains but benefits both health and appearance. Enduring a small, early punishment to attain a large, delayed reward is a form of self-discipline or self-control.

THEORIES OF PUNISHMENT

Historically, there have been two major ways of accounting for the effects of punishment. Early forms of Thorndike's (1911) law of effect included both a strengthening function of reward and a weakening function of punishment. Later, however, Thorndike abandoned the negative law of effect in favor of a principle that sounds very much like avoidance: "The idea of making [the] response or the impulse to make it then tends to arouse a memory of the punishment and fear, repulsion, or shame. This is relieved by making no response to the situation . . . or by making a response that is or seems opposite to the original response" (Thorndike, 1935, p. 80). It was not until 15 or 20 years after Thorndike's initial formulation, however, that the avoidance theory of punishment became widely accepted in the conditioning laboratory.

Approach and Avoidance in the Runway or Alley

One of the reasons why the treatment of punishment as a form of avoidance training has remained so popular over the ensuing years may be that the boundary between the respective procedures is often difficult to discern. Consider, for example, a human infant learning to walk. The process is punctuated by frequent falls, which must be aversive. Do these aversive stimuli influence the infant's learning by suppressing erroneous responses such as looking past obstacles, placing the feet too close together, or letting the body tilt too far to one side? Or are the necessary adjustments such as scanning the oncoming terrain, spreading the feet, and promptly correcting minor deviations in balance learned because they avoid untoward consequences?

The same problem may also arise in the laboratory. In an experimental study of what he and his mentor, Miller (1944), described as an approach-avoidance conflict, Brown (1948) trained Group I of his rats to approach the lighted end of a wooden runway or alley, where they received an allowance of wet mash as a reinforcer. The animals in Group III received exactly the same approach training as those in Group I, but before the final test "they were placed in the alley and allowed to run to food, where they received a [single, fairly severe] . . . shock" (Brown, 1948, p. 455). The rats in both groups were then strapped into small harnesses and tested at two points along the alley, one close to the beginning and the other near the food (lighted) end, to determine how hard they pulled against a calibrated spring.

Pulling toward the place where they had been fed, the rats in Group I displayed a relatively flat gradient, pulling only a little harder when they were placed near the food end than they did

when placed near the beginning of the alley; pulling in the opposite direction, however, the rats in Group III displayed a steeper gradient, pulling much harder when they were placed close to the end where they had been both fed and shocked than they did when placed near the other end of the alley.

On the basis of the differences in slope observed by Brown, Miller (1944) predicted that under suitable parametric values, unrestrained animals given both food and shock would run partway down the alley and then stop, trapped at the intersection where the opposing gradients crossed each other, equal in strength (see Figure 10–3). Moreover, the way in which greater hunger or stronger shock influenced the point where they stopped could be predicted from variations in the locus of the intersection. Miller also predicted that the animals would overshoot the stopping point and then vacillate on either side of it. All these predictions were verified in experimental work summarized (but not reported in concrete detail) in Miller's account. Although both Brown and Miller analyzed their work in terms of a conflict between the tendency to approach and the tendency to avoid the lighted end of the alley, it can also be used to illustrate the action of punishment.

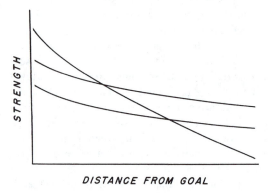

Figure 10–3. Hypothetical gradients for approach and avoidance in an alley suggested by Miller (1944). When the approach was strong, the stopping point was closer to the goal than when the approach was weak. (From Dinsmoor, 1960.)

Statement of the Avoidance Hypothesis

In order to clarify the subsequent discussion, the avoidance theory of punishment needs to be stated in greater detail. To begin with, anyone who has shaped lever pressing by the rat or key pecking by the pigeon will appreciate the fact that these recorded responses represent only one component within a longer chain of action leading to the receipt of the food. The sequence of stimuli and responses within the bar-pressing chain has been analyzed in detail, and parts of the analysis have been verified experimentally in *The Behavior of Organisms* (Skinner, 1938). The case for pecking may be less familiar, but Pear, Rector, and Legris (1982) have tracked and recorded the pigeon's repeated approaches to and withdrawals from the key under a variable-interval schedule of reinforcement. Experiments in which the subject stays closer, on average, to a stimulus that is negatively correlated and farther, on average, from one that is positively correlated with the delivery of shock indicate that these patterns of locomotion are systematically affected by these correlations (Karpicke & Dout, 1980; Leclerc & Reberg, 1980.)

In a paper published some years ago in the *Psychological Review* I analyzed in considerable detail the effect on a chain of stimuli and responses when completion of the chain is followed by shock (Dinsmoor, 1954, pp. 41–44). For present purposes, it may suffice to say that when the animal completes the chain, all the stimuli in the sequence leading up to that result are thereby paired with the shock, the stimuli arriving late in the sequence receiving the closest pairing (see LaBarbera & Church, 1974). Any response that terminates or alters the subject's contact with one of these stimuli is thereby reinforced. This is especially effective for responses that reverse the animal's progress through the chain and require additional behavior and therefore additional time before the animal can return to the same point in the sequence. In this way, the application of punishment selectively reinforces precisely those forms of behavior that most delay

the completion of the chain. (See also Dinsmoor, 1960, 1977, 1985).

Objections to the Avoidance Theory

Although Skinner (1953) endorsed essentially the same point of view, over the years a number of authors trained at Harvard University have raised objections of one kind or another to the avoidance theory of punishment. Part of their resistance may stem from the fact that without apparent exception they favor an explanatory system for the avoidance itself that is limited to a successive cataloguing of outcome measures that have been found to influence the subject's rate of responding (e.g., Herrnstein, 1969; Hineline, 1977; for a critique, see Dinsmoor, 1977). To put it another way, they consider only the correlation between the avoidance responding and changes in the shocks that are delivered, such as their frequency, their intensity, their duration, their delay, and more generally, their temporal distribution. This distal or molar treatment of avoidance studiously avoids mention of the conditioned aversive stimuli that mediate and integrate the various empirical relations between response and shock within a standard conditioning framework. Consequently, it fails to provide the necessary foundation for extending such an analysis to the effects of punishment.

Because the two-process theories of avoidance (see Ayres in this volume) and punishment rest upon principles derived from simpler, more elementary paradigms rather than from the complex arrangements found under the headings of avoidance and punishment, per se, proponents of the negative law of effect have complained that these theories are not readily subject to experimental test. This, it seems to me, is a strange complaint to be filed by advocates of an alternative theory that is completely ad hoc, namely that the decrease in the punished behavior can be explained by postulating an independent principle of learning for which there is no evidence other than the very relation it has been called up to explain. I am referring once more to the negative law of effect. To postulate a new principle each time a new empirical relation is found is to open Pandora's box: Where does the process end? How does it help us to subsume specific findings under more general principles? And what predictions that can be tested does it generate, other than the tautology that consequences that reduce responding reduce responding?

Evidence for the Avoidance Hypothesis

Just as theoretical analyses of chaining derive their underlying principles from studies of discrimination and conditioned reinforcement (e.g., Skinner, 1938), so the avoidance theory of punishment imports functional relations from experiments on escape, conditioned aversive stimulation, and avoidance. Interoceptive and exteroceptive changes in stimulation produced by the subject's own behavior have the same physical, observable status as the lights or tones presented by the experimenter. Just as we can record when a lamp was lighted, so we can record when the subject reached a specified location within the experimental chamber or when a response of specified topography occurred. The difficulty in testing theoretical formulations based on response-produced stimuli is that these stimuli are not as readily manipulated by the experimenter (but see, for example, Vandell & Ferraro, 1972). A time-honored strategem for dealing with this type of problem is to insert into the procedure manipulable stimuli that obey the same contingencies—arrive and depart under the same circumstances and therefore at the same time—as those that cannot directly be controlled by the experimenter (e.g., the response-produced stimulus used by Dinsmoor & Sears, 1973; the block counter and the chained schedule stimuli used by Ferster & Skinner, 1957; or the force feedback used by Notterman & Mintz, 1965).

It may be that the ideal experiment for the evaluation of the role of conditioned aversive stimuli in a sequence of responses leading to punishment has yet to be performed, but studies published by Dardano and Brady (1968) and by Dardano (1971) come close enough to be quite illuminating (see also Field & Boren, 1963). Two monkeys served as subjects. Both were provided with a vertical array of 20 lamps ("counter") that monitored their progress through a sequence of behavior leading to the receipt of the shock. These lamps were exteroceptive equivalents to the more natural sequence of feedback stimuli encountered en route to the shock in a conventional study of punishment.

The monkey had two levers to press. On the approach or food lever, every response (or sometimes every fifth response) moved the location where one of the lamps was lighted up one step. Deliveries of food on the same schedule maintained the animal's responding, despite the fact that whenever the top lamp was reached a brief shock was administered. (At this point in the proceedings, the location at which a lamp was lighted was reset to the bottom of the array.)

In the meantime, each response (or sometimes every fifth response) on the avoidance lever moved the location where the lamp was lighted down one step, so that by depressing this lever whenever the counter approached the top of the column, the animal could prevent itself from being shocked. According to an avoidance interpretation of punishment, this retreat from the end of the sequence was functionally equivalent to the responses by which the subject in a more conventional experiment on punishment withdraws from the lever or the key or otherwise reverses its progress toward completion of the chain and the receipt of the shock. As far as I can see, the only significant way in which this simulation departed from the standard procedure for punishment was that a subject could continue indefinitely to procure the food without ever quite completing the sequence and bringing on the shock. This feature presumably reduced the ratio of shocks to food deliveries below that found in most studies of punishment, but both subjects still performed the necessary avoidance response.

Both Dardano (1971) and Dardano and Brady

(1968) reported that when the light occupied the first position on the counter, at the beginning of the session or following a reset of the counter (delivery of a shock), the subject responded almost exclusively on the food lever until it had driven the light to a position close to the top of the column. From that point on, it responded relatively evenly on the two levers, keeping the light within a narrow range near but almost always below the 20th position (see Figure 10–4). As a consequence, neither animal received many shocks.

In subsequent sessions, during which the lamps were not operative, the behavior of the subjects was less accurate, varying within a lower range for most of the session but occasionally drifting up to the point where a shock was received. Note that under Dardano and Brady's procedure the successive responses were much less heterogeneous and the feedback stimuli much less discriminable than in a normal experiment on punishment.

An Attempted Refutation

In a status report some years ago (Dinsmoor, 1977), I answered several philosophical objections to the avoidance theory of punishment but ignored one empirical study, which the authors had admitted was not definitive. Since then, however, that study has repeatedly been cited as evidence against my point of view. Schuster and Rachlin (1968) used a concurrent chain schedule in which pecking the left key sometimes turned it red for five minutes, during which time pecking was reinforced on a VI schedule but shocks were administered at regular intervals; pecking the right key turned it orange for an equal period of time, during which pecking was punished. As might be expected, the punishment procedure, which provided an opportunity for the subject to avoid some of the shocks, was much more effective than the response-independent procedure (conditioned suppression) in reducing the rate of pecking in the presence of the stimulus. This re-

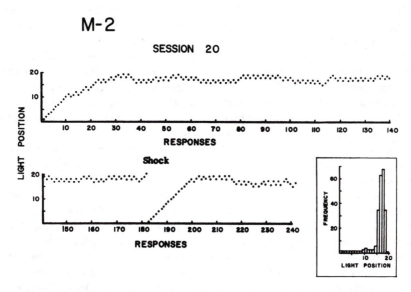

Figure 10–4. A plot of the position of the lamp that was lighted following each successive response. Pressing one lever was reinforced with food and advanced the position of the light; pressing the other lever reversed the monkey's progress toward the receipt of the shock at position 20. (From Dardano & Brady, 1968. Copyright Academic Press.)

sult certainly seems in keeping with the avoidance hypothesis.

For another comparison the authors varied the frequency with which the response-independent shocks were delivered, from a value much lower than that occurring under the punishment schedule to a value that was substantially higher. They found that the relative rate of pecking on the two keys *prior to* the production of the red or the orange (a measure of the pigeon's preference between the two stimuli) was determined by the relative frequency with which the shocks were delivered in their presence. This result, too, seems to be quite in keeping with accepted principles for the acquisition of conditioned aversive properties by a stimulus accompanied by shocks (e.g., Dinsmoor, 1962).

According to Schuster and Rachlin, however, a two-process theory of punishment implies a different result. They argued that the proprioceptive stimuli correlated under the punishment procedure with the receipt of the shock should have added to the aversiveness of the orange stimulus and led at equal frequencies of shock to a preference for the red. As there was no such preference, they concluded that in this instance —and contrary to well-established principles— the proprioceptive stimuli must not have become aversive; therefore, these stimuli could not have played the role demanded by two-process theory in mediating the suppressive effects of the punishment on the responding in the *presence* of the orange stimulus. The logic is the same as that used by Schuster (1969) to deny the existence of conditioned reinforcement. However, the authors were not aware of the complexities posed by their procedure. For example, being better predictors of the shock, the proprioceptive stimuli, in compound with the orange, might well have reduced the conditioned aversiveness of the orange alone (see Badia & Culbertson, 1972; Wagner, Logan, Haberlandt, & Price, 1968). In the absence of these proprioceptive stimuli, orange was correlated with the absence of shock. By this reasoning, the onset of the orange might well have become a much less aversive stimulus than the onset of the red. With such complex interac-

tions at work, it is difficult to know what outcome to expect.

Punishment by S–

In *Science and Human Behavior*, Skinner advanced the suggestion that, like presenting a negative reinforcer, "withdrawing a positive reinforcer" could also serve as a form of punishment (Skinner, 1953, p. 185). During the next 20 years or so, a number of investigators attempted to translate Skinner's words into experimental routines. In those early efforts, the stimulus of choice was a "time-out," during which the chamber was darkened and primary reinforcement was withheld (see Leitenberg, 1965, for citations). This stimulus often did have a suppressive effect on the behavior that produced it, but the work of these investigators was marred by two defects. First, the stimulus they used probably was not inherently neutral but may very well have possessed intrinsic properties that could account for its suppressive effect, entirely aside from its relation to the withholding of reinforcement (see Dinsmoor, Dougan, Pfister, & Thiels, 1992, for the effects of merely darkening the key). Second, as Leitenberg (1965) pointed out, production of the time-out led to a reduction in the number of reinforcers received, and that reduction could account for the corresponding reduction in the rate of responding (see also Dunn, 1990).

Both of these errors were remedied in experiments employing what is known as an *observing* procedure. Instead of using a darkening of the chamber as their physical representation of the punishing stimulus, these investigators used a stimulus like that used in other types of experiments, a color displayed on the pigeon's key. Furthermore, production of the stimulus had no effect on the schedule of primary reinforcement. Under an observing procedure, the experimental routine switches back and forth at irregular intervals between two schedules differing in their frequency of reinforcement, typically a variable-interval schedule and extinction. The pigeon has no way of altering this sequence of events, but it is furnished with a second key that produces a change in the accompanying stimulation. If the pigeon does not peck this observing key, the color displayed remains the same throughout the session, despite the alternation between the two schedules of reinforcement. On some schedule, however, usually itself a variable-interval schedule, pecking the observing key changes the display for some period of time to one that is coordinated with the ongoing schedules for the delivery of the food. During the variable-interval schedule, one color (S+) appears; during periods of extinction, another color (S–) appears. Note that pecking the observing key merely reveals which schedule is in effect; it does not alter that schedule. Observing the stimuli does not affect the frequency of primary reinforcement or the time to the next reinforcer.

To determine whether the S– had a suppressive effect on the rate of pecking the observing key, Mulvaney, Dinsmoor, Jwaideh, and Hughes (1974) and Jwaideh and Mulvaney (1976) made two such keys available on a concurrent schedule. One of these keys intermittently produced either the S+ or the S–, depending on which schedule of primary reinforcement was in effect at the time, but the other key produced only the S+, having no effect during periods of extinction (Mulvaney et al.) or periods with a lower frequency of food delivery (Jwaideh & Mulvaney). In these experiments, the rate of pecking on the key that produced both S+ and S– was lower than the rate on the key that produced only the S+. Evidently the receipt of S–, in addition to S+, had a suppressive effect on the response that produced it (see also Mueller & Dinsmoor, 1986).

Case and Fantino (1981) used a different strategy. In some sessions, pecking the observing key produced a stimulus that was not correlated with their three schedules of primary reinforcement. This procedure provided a control for the reinforcing effect of sheer change in stimulation. In other sessions, pecking the observing key was effective only when a stimulus coordinated with a particular one of the three component schedules was available. The authors found that production of the stimulus coordinated with the lowest frequency of primary reinforcement reduced the rate of pecking below the control rate recorded when pecking produced the uncorrelated stimulus. They interpreted their results in terms of a general formula for conditioned reinforcement (delay-reduction hypothesis) that for concurrent chain schedules had proved more precise than reliance on the frequency of reinforcement. If the change in stimulation was accompanied by a reduction in the delay from the onset of the stimulus to the arrival of the next reinforcer, that change was itself reinforcing, but if it was accompanied by an increase in the delay, the change was punishing.

As in the better-known case of punishment with electric shock, the effects of punishment by S– are probably mediated by avoidance of the stimulus. Pigeons face and approach a display of S+ but turn away and withdraw from a display of S– (e.g., Eldridge & Pear, 1987; Rand, 1977).

PRACTICAL IMPLICATIONS AND APPLICATIONS

A comprehensive evaluation of punishment as a means of reducing undesired behavior demands a comparison with other means of accomplishing the same end. The most obvious alternative is extinction. Of the two, Holz and Azrin (1963) and Azrin and Holz (1966) have argued that punishment is much more effective. Not only is punishment more immediate in its effects, but if the punishing stimulus is sufficiently intense, it can suppress behavior completely and permanently, even after it is no longer being administered. Extinction does not meet either of these criteria. On the other hand, I think it should be noted that the person administering the punishment (e.g., a parent punishing a child) may not be willing to resort to the degree of severity necessary to produce such a result. Milder punishment does not suppress the behavior as completely as does extinction, and in both cases a recovery occurs when the procedure is discontinued. This constitutes a major problem for practical interventions of limited duration.

Physical restraint (e.g., holding as a means of preventing a child from darting into traffic), like punishment, has an immediate effect and one that completely suppresses the undesired behavior until the restraint is lifted. Many applications of "time-out" in nursery schools and other institutions incorporate restraint as well as punishment as one of their features. The same may be said of reformatories and prisons, and that may be the main source of their effectiveness.

Another method of suppressing undesired behavior is conventionally known by the initials DRO, variously said to represent differential reinforcement of other behavior or differential reinforcement of a zero rate. Whatever the etymology, reinforcement is delivered when a specified length of time (e.g., 30 seconds) has elapsed since the last occurrence of the target response. Most comparisons of DRO have been with extinction, but for some of their animals Uhl and Sherman (1971) combined these procedures with a mild electric shock, added as punishment. They found that response elimination was more rapid when the punishment was added, but at the level of severity they used (cf. Azrin & Holz, 1966, p. 410) they concluded "that the addition of punishment to an omission or an extinction procedure actually detracts from the durability of response-elimination effects" (Uhl & Sherman, 1971, p. 64).

Stimulus Control

One way of establishing discriminative control over a given bit of behavior is to reinforce that behavior in the presence of the intended stimulus but not in its absence; another way is to punish it. In a laboratory study of this phenomenon (Dinsmoor, 1952), I found that a discrimination was quick to form when bar pressing produced food on a variable-interval schedule, but all presses in the dark (punished phase) were accompanied by the passage of an electric current through the rat's body. When the chamber was lighted (safe phase), pressing went unpunished, and higher rates were recorded.

One of the stimuli most consistently correlated with the administration of punishment as a means of controlling undesired behavior is the presence of the punishing agent. This creates a problem for the person attempting the behavioral control, as illustrated by a cat that scratches the furniture when its owner is away or teenagers who "sneak a smoke" behind their parents' backs. To deal with the problem, totalitarian regimes sometimes resort to elaborate systems of espionage directed toward their own citizens. Fortunately, perhaps, I do not know of any mechanism for the generalization and maintenance of the effects of punishment comparable to the "behavioral trap" that has been noted with positive reinforcement (e.g., Kohler & Greenwood, 1986).

Some years after my original study, Honig and Slivka (1964) obtained an entire gradient of generalization. In the presence of each of seven different wavelengths, displayed on the pigeon's key, they maintained pecking with variable-interval deliveries of grain. In the presence of the middle wavelength (550 mu), the pigeons were also shocked for 0.6 seconds each time they pecked the key. When this wavelength was present, the rate of pecking dropped to zero; with other stimuli, the rate was depressed as a function of how close each wavelength was to 550. Initially, the rates at the most extreme values tested, 490 and 610, dropped to about half of the rates before any punishment had been applied, but subsequently they recovered to a somewhat higher level, yielding a steeper gradient of generalization. Like reinforcement, then, punishment affects responding in other situations in proportion to their similarity to the one in which it is delivered.

Escape From Situation

Along with its discriminative function, a stimulus in the presence of which punishment is delivered also acquires an aversive function. During periods when an overhead light was on, Azrin, Hake, Holz, and Hutchinson (1965) reinforced pecking of the food key on a variable-interval schedule (Experiment II) and concurrently punished each peck with electric shock. By pecking an escape key, however, the pigeon could reduce the overhead illumination for a short period of time, during which time no further shocks were delivered (safe period). Six of the eight pigeons consistently pecked the escape key within a few seconds after the return of the light. Escape responses occurred even at intensities of punishment that were too low to produce significant suppression of the punished response. When pecking was extinguished on the food key, however, or the bird's hunger was reduced, responding on the escape key dwindled to a very low level.

Escape from punishment may constitute a serious problem in the practical control of behavior. Both Franks, Fried, and Ashem (1966) and Powell and Azrin (1968), for example, found that escape from the conditioning apparatus vitiated their attempts to reduce the smoking of cigarettes by the application of shock as punishment. Similarly, when seat belts first came on the market and the manufacturers of several makes of automobile installed insistent buzzers to make the occupants fasten them, many motorists disabled the buzzers instead.

Natural situations, of course, are frequently more complicated than the arrangements required for an experimental analysis of the behavior. In the experiment by Azrin, Hake, Holz, and Hutchinson (1965), described two paragraphs earlier, the schedule of reinforcement was the same in the presence of the stimulus signaling the punishment as it was in the presence of the safe stimulus, but such a consistency is not likely to hold in a complex social situation. In the laboratory, Hearst (1963) has shown that the delivery of food, for example, counteracts the effects of the shock. In a natural setting, participation on an athletic team may produce so many reinforcers of various kinds that the player will undergo considerable physical and verbal abuse without quitting the squad. If the home atmosphere is characterized by a rich schedule of positive reinforcement, it may be possible to punish the child frequently and severely without precipitating a flight to the streets, but without that counterweight severe parental discipline may have disastrous results. Educational institutions may be especially vulnerable, given the low level of reinforcement usually enjoyed by the students. Consider, for example, the possible consequences of delivering punishment while the child is learning to read. In prisons, of course, or in military service, the schedule of reinforcement may not make much difference, as escape is not ordinarily possible.

Aggression

When someone uses the word *punishment*, we envision a hierarchical situation. We think of the person administering the punishment as a parent, a teacher, an experimenter, a correctional officer, or some other figure of authority. There is an implication that the stimulus is judiciously applied for some socially approved purpose and in most cases, that the behavior of the recipient was such as to merit that treatment. The term is dispassionate. It imputes no emotion to the person who administers the punishment. But the act itself, when viewed concretely as the delivery of aversive stimulation by one individual to another, could just as readily be classified as aggression. The controlling variables (*intent, purpose*) may be different, but there is a substantial overlap between the physical characteristics of the two activities, and it is often difficult to tell them apart. It is not surprising, therefore, to find that punishment can provoke an aggressive response on the part of the individual being punished.

A program of research initiated at the Anna Behavior Research Laboratory has demonstrated that several different kinds of painful stimulation elicit behavioral topographies that look like forms of attack in a considerable variety of—although not all—species (for reviews, see Azrin, 1967; Hutchinson, 1977; Ulrich, 1966). Similarly, Azrin, Hutchinson, and Hake (1966) have shown that transitions from reinforcement to nonreinforcement may produce attacks by pigeons on other pigeons.

In social interactions outside the laboratory—provided the power of the punisher is less than absolute—an aggressive response to punishment may be intermittently reinforced by a brief or even a prolonged period of relief from the original stimulation. As Reynolds, Catania, and Skinner (1963) and Azrin and Hutchinson (1967) have shown, reinforcement of the appropriate response topography may lead to increases in what appears to be genuine attack behavior. (For a review of both human and nonhuman studies, see Ulrich, Dulaney, Arnett, & Mueller, 1973.) Another possible source of aggression is imitation. Bandura (1973) has shown that children who witness someone punching an object he called a Bo-Bo Doll become more aggressive in their subsequent behavior toward other children.

Regardless of the reasons, survey data confirm the prediction that the more parents rely on corporal punishment, the greater is the chance of the child's hitting back (Straus, Gelles, & Steinmetz, 1980). Although unpleasant for the parents, this may be one of the less significant costs of punishment: correlational data also suggest that punishment may lead to depression, child abuse, spouse abuse, and a general increase in the use of violence by the next generation (Straus, 1994).

Training Complex Behavior

It would be foolish to issue strong and sweeping statements without an empirical foundation, but logic suggests that reinforcement is likely to be more efficient than punishment in constructing complex patterns of behavior. If one form of a response is to be selected from among a broad range of competing topographies, for instance, providing a reinforcing consequence for that one desired form should take less time and less effort than providing punishing consequences for each of the possible alternatives. As the issue has not to my knowledge been tested empirically, there is some question whether behavior can be shifted along a continuum like that used in studies of response induction and shaping by the use of punishment. In studies of chaining, when a behavioral sequence leads to a reinforcer, the discriminative stimulus for each of the responses in the sequence provides a conditioned reinforcer for the preceding response, but no corresponding mechanism seems to be available in the case of punishment.

REFERENCES

Appel, J. B. (1961). Punishment in the squirrel monkey: Saimiri sciurea. *Science, 133*, 36.

Appel, J. B. (1963). Punishment and shock intensity. *Science, 141*, 528–529.

Azrin, N. H. (1959). A technique for delivering shock to pigeons. *Journal of the Experimental Analysis of Behavior, 2*, 161–163.

Azrin, N. H. (1960). Effects of punishment intensity during variable-interval reinforcement. *Journal of the Experimental Analysis of Behavior, 3*, 123–142.

Azrin, N. H. (1967). Pain and aggression. *Psychology Today, 1 (1)*, 27–33.

Azrin, N. H., Hake, D. F., Holz, W. C., & Hutchinson, R. R. (1965). Motivational aspects of escape from punishment. *Journal of the Experimental Analysis of Behavior, 8*, 31–44.

Azrin, N. H., & Holz, W. C. (1966). Punishment. In W. K. Honig (ed.), *Operant behavior: Areas of research and application*, 380–447. New York: Appleton-Century-Crofts.

Azrin, N. H., Holz, W. C., & Hake, D. (1963). Fixed-ratio punishment. *Journal of the Experimental Analysis of Behavior, 6*, 141–148.

Azrin, N. H., & Hutchinson, R. R. (1967). Conditioning of the aggressive behavior of pigeons by a fixed-interval schedule of reinforcement. *Journal of the Experimental Analysis of Behavior, 10*, 395–402.

Azrin, N. H., Hutchinson, R. R., & Hake (1966). Extinction-induced aggression. *Journal of the Experimental Analysis of Behavior, 9*, 191–204.

Badia, P., & Culbertson, S. (1972). The relative aversiveness of signalled vs unsignalled escapable and inescapable shock. *Journal of the Experimental Analysis of Behavior, 17*, 463–471.

Bandura, A. (1973). *Aggression: A social learning analysis.* Englewood Cliffs, N.J.: Prentice-Hall.

Brown, J. S. (1948). Gradients of approach and avoidance responses and their relation to level of motivation. *Journal of Comparative and Physiological Psychology, 41*, 450–465.

Camp, D. S., Raymond, G. A., & Church, R. M. (1966). Response suppression as a function of the schedule of punishment. *Psychonomic Science, 5*, 23–24.

Camp, D. S., Raymond, G. A., & Church, R. M. (1967). Temporal relationship between response and punishment. *Journal of Experimental Psychology, 74*, 114–123.

Case, D., & Fantino, E. (1981). The delay-reduction hypothesis of conditioned reinforcement and punishment: Observing behavior. *Journal of the Experimental Analysis of Behavior, 35*, 93–108.

Church, R. M., & Raymond, G. A. (1967). Influence of the schedule of positive reinforcement on punished behavior. *Journal of Comparative and Physiological Psychology, 63*, 329–332.

Church, R. M., Raymond, G. A., & Beauchamp, R. D. (1967). Response suppression as a function of intensity and duration of a punishment. *Journal of Comparative and Physiological Psychology, 63*, 39–44.

Dardano, J. F. (1971). Control of concurrent avoidance and appetitive behaviors by an indicator of shock proximity. *Journal of the Experimental Analysis of Behavior, 15*, 167–180.

Dardano, J. F., & Brady, J. V. (1968). Monitoring behavior in primates under concurrent appetitive and aversive control. *Communications in Behavioral Biology, Part A, 1*, 91–100.

Deluty, M. Z. (1976). Choice and the rate of punishment in concurrent schedules. *Journal of the Experimental Analysis of Behavior, 25*, 75–80.

Deluty, M. Z. (1978). Self-control and impulsiveness involving aversive events. *Journal of Experimental Psychology: Animal Behavior Processes, 4*, 250–266.

de Villiers, P. A. (1980). Toward a quantitative theory of punishment. *Journal of the Experimental Analysis of Behavior, 33*, 15–25.

de Villiers, P. A. (1981). Quantitative studies of punishment: The negative law of effect revisited. In C. M. Bradshaw, E. Szabadi, & C. F. Lowe (eds.), *Quantification of steady-state operant behavior*, 139–151. Amsterdam: Elsevier.

de Villiers, P. A. (1982). Toward a quantitative theory of punishment. In M. L. Commons, R. J. Herrnstein, & H. Rachlin (eds.), *Quantitative analyses of behavior, Vol. II: Matching and maximizing accounts*, 327–344. Cambridge, Mass.: Ballinger.

Dinsmoor, J. A. (1952). A discrimination based on punishment. *Quarterly Journal of Experimental Psychology, 4*, 27–45.

Dinsmoor, J. A. (1954). Punishment: I. The avoidance hypothesis. *Psychological Review, 61*, 34–46.

Dinsmoor, J. A. (1960). Studies of abnormal behavior in animals. In R. H. Waters, D. A. Rethlingshafer, & W. E. Caldwell (eds.), *Principles of comparative psychology*, 289–324. New York: McGraw-Hill.

Dinsmoor, J. A. (1962). Variable-interval escape from stimuli accompanied by shocks. *Journal of the Experimental Analysis of Behavior, 5*, 41–47.

Dinsmoor, J. A. (1968). Escape from shock as a conditioning technique. In M. R. Jones (ed.), *Miami Symposium on the Prediction of Behavior, 1967: Aversive stimulation*, 33–75. Coral Gables, Fla.: University of Miami Press.

Dinsmoor, J. A. (1977). Escape, avoidance, punishment: Where do we stand? *Journal of the Experimental Analysis of Behavior, 28*, 83–95.

Dinsmoor, J. A. (1985). The integrative power of the CS-US interval in other contexts. *Behavioral and Brain Sciences, 8*, 336–337.

Dinsmoor, J. A., Dougan, J. D., Pfister, J., & Thiels, E. (1992). The autoshaping procedure as a residual block clock. *Journal of the Experimental Analysis of Behavior, 58*, 265–276.

Dinsmoor, J. A., & Sears, G. W. (1973). Control of avoidance by a response-produced stimulus. *Learning and Motivation, 4*, 284–293.

Dunn, R. (1990). Timeout from concurrent schedules. *Journal of the Experimental Analysis of Behavior, 53*, 163–174.

Eldridge, G. D., & Pear, J. J. (1987). Topographical variations in behavior during autoshaping, automaintenance, and omission training. *Journal of the Experimental Analysis of Behavior, 47*, 319–333.

Estes, W. K. (1944). An experimental study of punishment. *Psychological Monographs, 57*, No. 263.

Farley, J. (1980). Reinforcement and punishment effects in concurrent schedules: A test of two models. *Journal of the Experimental Analysis of Behavior, 33*, 311–326.

Ferster, C. B., & Skinner, B. F. (1957). *Schedules of reinforcement*. New York: Appleton-Century-Crofts.

Field, G. W., & Boren, J. J. (1963). An adjusting avoidance procedure with multiple auditory and visual warning stimuli. *Journal of the Experimental Analysis of Behavior, 6*, 537–543.

Filby, Y., & Appel, J. B. (1966). Variable-interval punishment during variable-interval reinforcement. *Journal of the Experimental Analysis of Behavior, 9*, 521–527.

Franks, C. M., Fried, R., & Ashem, B. (1966). An improved apparatus for the aversive conditioning of cigarette smokers. *Behavior Research and Therapy, 4*, 301–308.

Hake, D. F., Azrin, N. H., & Oxford, R. (1967). The effects of punishment intensity on squirrel monkeys. *Journal of the Experimental Analysis of Behavior, 10*, 95–107.

Hearst, E. (1963). Escape from a stimulus associated with both reward and punishment. *Journal of Comparative and Physiological Psychology, 56*, 1027–1031.

Herrnstein, R. J. (1969). Method and theory in the study of avoidance. *Psychological Review, 76*, 49–69.

Herrnstein, R. J., (1970). On the law of effect. *Journal of the Experimental Analysis of Behavior, 13*, 243–266.

Hineline, P. N. (1977). Negative reinforcement and avoidance. In W. K. Honig & J. E. R. Staddon (eds.), *Handbook of operant behavior*, 364–414. Englewood Cliffs, N.J.: Prentice-Hall.

Holz, W. C. (1968). Punishment and rate of positive reinforcement. *Journal of the Experimental Analysis of Behavior, 11*, 285–292.

Holz, W. C., & Azrin, N. H. (1963). A comparison of several procedures for eliminating behavior. *Journal of the Experimental Analysis of Behavior, 6*, 399–406.

Honig, W. K., & Slivka, R. M. (1964). Stimulus generalization of the effects of punishment. *Journal of the Experimental Analysis of Behavior, 7*, 21–25.

Hutchinson, R. R. (1977). By-products of aversive control. In W. K. Honig & J. E. R. Staddon (eds.), *Handbook of op-*

erant behavior, 415–431. Englewood Cliffs, N.J.: Prentice-Hall.

Jwaideh, A. R., & Mulvaney, D. E. (1976). Punishment of observing by a stimulus associated with the lower of two reinforcement densities. *Learning & Motivation*, 7, 211–222.

Karpicke, J., & Dout, D. (1980). Withdrawal from signals for imminent inescapable shock. *Psychological Record*, 30, 511–523.

Katz, J. (1988). *Seductions of crime*. New York: Basic Books.

Kohler, F. W., & Greenwood, C. R. (1986). Toward a technology of generalization: The identification of natural contingencies of reinforcement. *Behavior Analyst*, 9, 19–26.

LaBarbera, J. D., & Church, R. M. (1974). Magnitude of fear as a function of expected time to an aversive event. *Animal Learning and Behavior*, 2, 199–202.

Lande, S. D. (1981). An interresponse time analysis of variable-ratio punishment. *Journal of the Experimental Analysis of Behavior*, 35, 55–67.

Leclerc, R., & Reberg, D. (1980). Sign-tracking in aversive conditioning. *Learning and Motivation*, 11, 302–317.

Lehman, B. (March 13, 1989). Spanking teaches the wrong lesson. *Boston Globe*, 27.

Leitenberg, H. (1965). Is time-out from positive reinforcement an aversive event? A review of the experimental evidence. *Psychological Bulletin*, 64, 428–441.

Logue, A. W., & de Villiers, P. A. (1981). Matching of behavior maintained by concurrent shock avoidance and food reinforcement. *Behaviour Analysis Letters*, 1, 247–258.

Lyon, D. O., Picker, M., & Poling, A. (1985). Use of electrical shock in nonhuman research: A survey of *JEAB* studies. *Behavior Analyst*, 8, 93–94.

Miller, N. E. (1944). Experimental studies of conflict. In J. McV. Hunt (ed.), *Personality and the behavior disorders*, *Vol. I*: 431–465. New York: Ronald.

Mueller, K. L., & Dinsmoor, J. A. (1986). The effect of negative stimulus presentations on observing-response rates. *Journal of the Experimental Analysis of Behavior*, 46, 281–291.

Mulvaney, D. E., Dinsmoor, J. A., Jwaideh, A. R., & Hughes, L. H. (1974). Punishment of observing by the negative discriminative stimulus. *Journal of the Experimental Analysis of Behavior*, 21, 37–44.

Notterman, J. M., & Mintz, D. E. (1965). *Dynamics of response*. New York: Wiley.

Pear, J. J., Rector, B. L., & Legris, J. A. (1982). Toward analyzing the continuity of behavior. In M. L. Commons, R. J. Herrnstein, & H. Rachlin (eds.), *Quantiative analyses of behavior, Vol. II: Matching and maximizing accounts*, 3–24. Cambridge, Mass.: Ballinger.

Powell, J., & Azrin, N. (1968). The effects of shock as a punisher for cigarette smoking. *Journal of Applied Behavior Analysis*, 1, 63–71.

Rand, J. F. (1977). Behaviors observed during S– in a simple discriminaton learning task. *Journal of the Experimental Analysis of Behavior*, 27, 103–117.

Reynolds, G. S., Catania, A. C., & Skinner, B. F. (1963). Conditioned and unconditioned aggression in pigeons. *Journal of the Experimental Analysis of Behavior*, 6, 73–74.

Schuster, R. H. (1969). A functional analysis of conditioned reinforcement. In D. P. Hendry (ed.), *Conditioned reinforcement*, 192–236. Homewood, Ill.: Dorsey Press.

Schuster, R., & Rachlin, H. (1968). Indifference between punishment and free shock: Evidence for the negative law of effect. *Journal of the Experimental Analysis of Behavior*, 11, 777–786.

Sears, R. R., Maccoby, E. E., & Levin, H. (1957). *Patterns of child rearing*. Evanston, Ill.: Row, Peterson.

Skinner, B. F. (1938). *The behavior of organisms: An experimental analysis*. New York: Appleton-Century-Crofts.

Skinner, B. F. (1950). Are theories of learning necessary? *Psychological Review*, 57, 193–216.

Skinner, B. F. (1953). *Science and human behavior*. New York: Macmillan.

Straus, M. A. (1994). *Beating the devil out of them: Corporal punishment in American families*. New York: Macmillan.

Straus, M. A., Gelles, R. J., & Steinmetz, S. K. (1980). *Behind closed doors: Violence in the American family*. New York: Doubleday/Anchor.

Thorndike, E. L. (1911). *Animal intelligence: Experimental studies*. New York: Macmillan.

Thorndike, E. L. (1935). *The psychology of wants, interests, and attitudes*. New York: D. Appleton-Century.

Uhl, C. N., & Sherman, W. O. (1971). Comparison of combinations of omission, punishment, and extinction method in response elimination in rats. *Journal of Comparative and Physiological Psychology*, 74, 59–65.

Ulrich, R. E. (1966). Pain as a cause of aggression. *Amerian Zoologist*, 6, 643–662.

Ulrich, R., Dulaney, S., Arnett, M., & Mueller, K. (1973). An experimental analysis of non-human and human aggression. In J. F. Knutson (ed.), *The control of aggression: Implications from basic research*, 79–111. Chicago: Aldine.

Vandell, R. R., & Ferraro, D. P. (1972). Response control of responding: Discrimination and generalization of response-produced stimuli. *Psychonomic Science*, 26, 263–266.

Wagner, A. R., Logan, F. A., Haberlandt, K., & Price T. (1968). Stimulus selection in animal discrimination learning. *Journal of Experimental Psychology*, 76, 171–180.

CHAPTER 11

EXTINCTION: A REVIEW OF THEORY AND THE EVIDENCE SUGGESTING THAT MEMORIES ARE NOT ERASED WITH NONREINFORCEMENT

William A. Falls

Pavlov (1927) observed that if a well-trained conditioned stimulus (CS) was presented several times in the absence of the unconditioned stimulus (US) with which it was originally paired, the CS would lose its ability to elicit the conditioned response (CR). He used the term *extinction* to describe the loss of the CR that occurred as a consequence of nonreinforcement. Presently, the term *extinction* (and its derivatives) is used interchangeably to describe both a procedure, "testing occurred in extinction," and the consequence of the procedure, "nonreinforcement of the CS led to extinction of the CR" (Mackintosh, 1974). Sometimes the term *extinction* is also used to describe the *mechanism* or *process* that is responsible for the loss of the CR, as in "the loss of the CR was due to extinction." This last use of the term can be misleading because it implies that the process that underlies the loss of the CR is understood when it is not.

The basic characteristics of extinction are that (1) extinction occurs only with the omission of reinforcement and does not occur if CS-US training continues and (2) extinction is an *active learning process* requiring the presentation of the CS. Therefore it differs from "forgetting," which refers to a loss of responding that results merely from the passage of time. Thus, through some learning process, presentation of the CS without the US causes a reduction in the ability of the CS to elicit a CR. What might this process be? Although there are many theories of extinction, the theories can be forced into two general classes (Mackintosh, 1974). Theories in the first class argue that the CR-producing associations (one may wish to read "memory") are *erased* as a consequence of nonreinforcement. Theories in the second class argue that the CR-producing associations are intact but are influenced (reduced or inhibited) by competing associations that are acquired as a consequence of nonreinforcement. Experiments have been unable to definitively support one or the other of these alternatives. However, what experiments have shown is that nonreinforcement may not erase all of the CR-producing associations. For example, the phenomena of spontaneous recovery, rapid reconditioning, and reinstatement all show that under certain experimental conditions the CR can return to preextinction levels. This suggests that some portion of CR-producing associations survives extinction.

This chapter begins with an overview of these extinction phenomena and the theories of extinction that have been proposed in their wake. It next discusses the paradox of avoidance behavior relevant to extinction followed by a brief overview of the salient issues in extinction of instrumental responses. It then reviews clinical implications of data related to extinction and avoidance behavior. Finally, it discusses why some traumatic memories may not be easily extinguished and how the extinction procedure may be augmented to facilitate extinction in these cases.

PHENOMENA RELATED TO THE RECOVERY OF THE CR AFTER EXTINCTION

Spontaneous Recovery

Pavlov (1927) observed that an extinguished CR would recover to a preextinction baseline with relatively minor disturbances in the experimental protocol. If left undisturbed for some period of time, an extinguished salivary CR would spontaneously recover. For example, in one experiment, three nonreinforced presentations of a well-trained CS at a 10-minute intertrial interval resulted in complete extinction of a salivation CR (from 8 drops of saliva to 0). After an interval of 20 minutes, CS was again presented, and a recovery of the CR was observed (7 drops). Spontaneous recovery is often observed in the first few CS-alone presentations that follow after

a session of nonreinforced CS presentations (Wagner, Siegel, Thomas, & Ellison, 1964).

Pavlov's Theory of Internal Inhibition

For Pavlov, spontaneous recovery indicated that extinction could not be regarded as an "irreversible destruction of the nervous associations" that first allowed the bell to elicit the salivary CR (Pavlov, 1927, p. 60). Instead, Pavlov believed that under conditions of nonreinforcement a well-trained CS became inhibited. He further assumed that the inhibition was fragile and that with the passage of time the inhibition would decay causing a restoration of the CR. Consistent with a time-dependent decay of inhibition was the observation that the restoration of the CR is more complete the greater the interval between extinction and testing.

Pavlov (1927) conceived of learning as taking place in the cortex of the animal. As a consequence of nonreinforcement, the CS produced an "inhibitory effect" in the cerebral hemispheres. Internal inhibition, as it was called, was due to a spreading wave of inhibition initiated at the cortical center that corresponded to the cerebral location of the CS. Once inhibition was initiated at the cortical center, it would irradiate over the entire cerebral cortex in a spreading wave of inhibition that would compete with the CR-eliciting properties of the CS.

In his theorizing, Pavlov (1927) attempted to describe how the nervous system functioned to produce behavior. His concept of *irradiation* of inhibition was borne out of his understanding of nervous system function. However, within a short time, Pavlov's understanding of the nervous system was no longer accurate. Konorski (1948) recognized that Pavlov's concept of irradiation of inhibition could not be reconciled with the current understanding of the nervous system. But rather than aband Pavlov's concepts, Konorski (1948) reformulated Pavlov's (1927) notions into terms that were more consistent with modern principles of neurophysiology. In doing so, Konorski provided a more detailed explanation of the mechanism of extinction.

Konorski's Theory of Extinction Via Inhibitory Association

Konorski (1948) also argued that spontaneous recovery was strong evidence that the original associations were not erased as a consequence of nonreinforcement. Like Pavlov, Konorski (1948) believed that extinction was the result of active inhibition. He conceived of *neural centers* in the brain that are activated by specific stimuli and that over the course of training developed progressively stronger associations with other neural centers. He argued that during acquisition, positive or excitatory associations were strengthened between neural centers corresponding to the CS and the US. After training, activation of the CS center alone was capable of initiating activity in the US center, thus producing a CR. If the US was subsequently omitted, negative or inhibitory associations between neural centers corresponding to the CS and US were strengthened. As nonreinforcement continued, inhibition would gradually win out over excitation, and the CR would be abolished. Importantly, despite the absence of a CR, the excitatory CS-US associations remained intact.

Konorski believed that spontaneous recovery was caused by a decay in the inhibitory associations. However, this decay process was not unique to inhibition. Konorski argued that all weak and recent associations, regardless of sign, would decay over time. Hence, newly established excitatory associations would decay in much the same way as a newly established inhibitory association. Spontaneous recovery occurred because the CR-producing associations were firmly established while inhibitory associations were more recent and more weak and therefore subject to decay. In contrast to Pavlov, Konorski did not believe that inhibition was inherently fragile. In fact, Konorski believed that with extended nonreinforcement it was possible to firmly establish inhibitory associations that would be impervious to spontaneous recovery.

Perhaps the greatest contribution of this theory came in the statement of how these associative connections were formed. Excitatory CS-US associations were strengthened when the activation of the CS center coincided with an increase in activation of the US center caused by presentation of the US. Inhibitory associations were strengthened when the activation of the CS center coincided with a *decrease* in activation of the US center. The latter occurred when the well-trained CS was presented in the absence of the US. Konorski's theory is important not only because it makes explicit the notion that extinction is the result of an accrual of competing inhibition but also because it makes specific predictions concerning the formation and detection of the competing inhibition, for example:

1. Because the strength of the CR is proportional to the number of excitatory associations, extinction of the CR will require an equal number of associations and so will also be proportional to the strength of the CR.
2. Presentation of the CS is required for extinction.
3. Extinction will not occur unless there is a fall in activation of the US center. Hence, any event that prevents the fall in activation (e.g., a US, an over-conditioned CS, or perhaps a traumatic memory) will prevent extinction.
4. If the inhibitory associations formed during extinction could be temporarily removed, the excitatory activation of the US center, and therefore the CR, would be restored.

Extinction as Unlearning

Because the acquisition of a CR is commonly thought to occur as a result of the strengthening of excitatory associations, extinction may be a symmetrical process: an unlearning or rewriting of excitatory associations. Both Skinner (1950) and Estes (1955) proposed that extinction was the result of the acquisition of a new response that was more appropriate to nonreinforcement. Importantly, the associations that were formed during nonreinforcement overwrote and therefore erased the associations that produced the original CR. Rescorla and Wagner (1972) also conceived of extinction as a *weakening* of the previously established excitatory associations (see Pearce & Hall [1980] for a review of the Rescorla-Wagner model and extinction).

If the original associations are erased, what is the cause of spontaneous recovery? Perhaps extinction does not erase all of the excitatory associations but erases enough so that they are subthreshold for performance of the CR. With the passage of time, the subthreshold associations somehow become suprathreshold, causing the CR to spontaneously recover. Estes (1955) argued that the cues present during nonreinforced CS presentations are likely to be a subset of the cues present during original training. Hence, extinction would erase only a subset of the original associations, and the CR would be abolished in the presence of this subset of cues. However, testing sometimes would later involve a different subset of the training cues whose associations have not been erased. The intact associations would produce spontaneous recovery.

Because the CR could be shown to survive extinction, Pavlov (1927) and Konorski (1948) argued that the CR-producing associations were completely intact. Extinction had to be the result of competing inhibition. However, with a few simple assumptions, an erasure hypothesis of extinction can explain why the CR returns with the passage of time. In fact, spontaneous recovery is just one example of a class of phenomena that demonstrate that the CR survives extinction. Other phenomena of this type include disinhibition, rapid reacquisition of an extinguished CR, and reinstatement of the CR by presentation of an unconditioned stimulus.

Rapid Reacquisition

In a series of experiments employing salivary conditioning in dogs, Konorski and Szwejkowska (1950) showed that while extinction of the CR generally proceeded slowly, occurring in 20 to 40 trials, reacquisition to a preextinction baseline occurred in just two to three trials (see also Konorski, 1967; Szwejkowska & Konorski, 1952). Rapid reacquisition has been demon-

strated by others as well (Frey & Butler, 1977; Smith & Gormezano, 1965) .

Recall that Konorski (1949) viewed acquisition and extinction as symmetrical processes: A complete loss of the CR is equivalent to the algebraic summation of excitatory and inhibitory associations. If the inhibitory associations are equal and opposite to the excitatory associations, reacquisition should occur at the same rate as, not more rapidly than, the original conditioning. Konorski (1948) was forced to make special assumptions about the nature of the competing inhibition to explain rapid reacquisition. Because the inhibitory associations were the most recent, they would be disrupted by reacquisition trials, resulting in net excitation and the *appearance* of rapid reacquisition. However, it may not be necessary to assume that recent associations are more fragile. Alternatively, the competing inhibitory associations may not be equal to the excitatory associations but may merely be sufficient to keep activation of the US center below threshold for performance. Because performance is near threshold, retraining would cause reacquisition that is more rapid than the original acquisition. Notice, however, that this subthreshold idea can also explain rapid reacquisition if extinction is considered to be the result of an erasure of the original CR-producing associations. Again, a phenomenon thought to support an inhibition hypothesis of extinction only indicates that some portion of the CR survives extinction.

Rapid reacquisition may not occur in all situations. Using a conditioned emotional response (CER) procedure in which conditioned fear is indexed by a suppression in operant bar pressing, Bouton (1986) compared the rates of reacquisition of three groups with different histories of acquisition and extinction. Two groups of rats received tone (CS)-foot shock (US) pairings followed by either 24 or 72 nonreinforced tone presentations (groups 24E and 72E, respectively). A control group was given equal context exposure but never received acquisition or extinction. Following these treatments, all three groups were given tone-foot shock pairings (i.e., reacquisition for groups 24E and 72E). In contrast to the data on rapid reacquisition, Bouton found that group 24E reacquired the fear to the tone CS at the *same rate* that the naive control group acquired fear to the novel tone (Bouton, 1986). Even more interesting, while both experimental groups showed equal and complete extinction of fear, group 72E showed significantly *slower reacquisition* than group 24E. More recently, Hart, Bourne, and Schatman (1995) have extended this finding showing similar slow reacquisition in conditioned taste aversion paradigm.

Slow reacquisition is consistent with the idea that extinction is caused by the accrual of competing inhibitory associations. Recall that extinction to a zero level of CR performance would occur if the inhibitory associations are equal and opposite to the excitatory associations. From this point, reacquisition would proceed at the same rate as original acquisition because neither excitatory nor inhibitory influences win out. In the Bouton (1986) experiment, group 24E and the naive control group showed comparable rates of reacquisition. Perhaps with those experimental parameters, 24 nonreinforced CS trials achieved a balance of excitatory and inhibitory associations. Carrying this one step further, perhaps if many more nonreinforced CS trials are given, extinction will be carried beyond zero (cf. Konorski, 1967; Pavlov, 1927; Rescorla & Wagner, 1972; Wagner & Rescorla, 1972). In this case, reacquisition of excitatory associations would have to first recover the net inhibition to produce a CR. Therefore, reacquisition would be much slower than acquisition to a novel stimulus. Perhaps 72 nonreinforced CS trials in the Bouton (1986) experiment succeeded in carrying extinction beyond zero. A theory of extinction based solely upon erasure of excitatory associations cannot explain slow reacquisition. In the limit, if all of the excitatory associations are erased, reacquisition should proceed at a rate similar to initial acquisition but never more slowly.

Reinstatement

A single presentation of the US can be sufficient to fully reinstate an extinguished CR. The basic finding is best exemplified by a study conducted by Rescorla and Heth (1975). In this experiment, rats were first given tone-foot shock training followed by tone-alone extinction trials. One half of the total number of rats were given a single "reminder" foot shock that was identical to the foot shock used in the original training. The remaining rats were given no treatment. Twenty-four hours later, all of the rats were tested for conditioned fear to the tone. Following nonreinforced tone presentations, the rats given no treatment after extinction showed a lack of conditioned suppression to the tone, that is, fear was extinguished. However, at testing, the group that received the reminder shock 24 hours earlier showed renewed suppression to the tone. The reminder shocks appeared to reinstate fear. A control group that was initially given unpaired tone and shock training followed by tone alone extinction trials did not show fear to the tone following a reminder shock. This suggests that the renewed fear was not the result of sensitization produced by the reminder shock. Instead, the reminder shock reinstated extinguished fear.

Reinstatement not only occurs following a single reminder shock but also occurs following systemic administration of drugs that are related to an organism's physiological response to stress. In one experiment, Richardson, Riccio, and Devine (1984) trained rats to avoid shock in a shuttle box. After they had obtained a stable avoidance baseline, the rats were given a session of avoidance trials in which shock was omitted, that is, extinction. Twenty-four hours later, the rats were tested for retention of the avoidance response. Just prior to this test, one half of the total number of rats were injected with the peptide aderenocorticotropin releasing factor (ACTH). The remaining rats were injected with water. The rats that were injected with water made few avoidance responses, indicating that the response had extinguished. In contrast, the rats injected with ACTH 24-hours earlier made significantly more avoidance responses. Like a reminder shock, systemic injection of ACTH reinstated the extinguished avoidance response.

Revaluation of the US

Reinstatement has been explained in several ways. Rescorla and Heth (1975) assume that extinction not only affects CS-US associations but also decreases how the US is represented. Nonreinforcement causes a deterioration in the representation of the US, rendering it less excitable. A reminder shock revalues the US representation of shock, therefore allowing it to be fully activated by the remaining net excitatory CS-US associations.

Rescorla and Heth's argument rests on the assumption that following extinction at least some of the associative CS-US associations remain intact. All of the evidence discussed thus far supports this assumption. Interestingly, within their model, it is possible to produce extinction nonassociatively, that is, without affecting CS-US associations at all. For example, if the US could be completely devalued, it would not allow for performance of the CR regardless of the strength of the CS-US associations (Rescorla & Heth, 1975). Therefore, according to their theory, if one could devise an extinction procedure that favors US devaluation over a reduction in the strength of CS-US associations, a reminder shock may lead to a greater magnitude of reinstatement since a reminder shock reinstates only the US representation. One such procedure involves extinction with continued US presentation.

Several reports have indicated that extinction will occur, albeit more slowly, when the US is presented in an unpaired fashion (Ayres & Decosta, 1971; Frey & Butler, 1977; Rescorla & Skucy, 1969). Rescorla and Heth (1975) argue that in comparison to a CS-alone procedure, continued reinforcement with a *gradual reduction* in US intensity should lead to extinction, but resulting more in part from a decrement in the US representation than from a change in CS-US connection. In a fourth experiment, Rescorla and Heth (1975) gave three groups of rats tone-foot shock pairings using a moderately intense US. Following acquisition, each group was subject to a different extinction procedure. Group Normal

received CS-alone presentations, group Abrupt continued to receive CS-US pairings but with a much less intense US (one that normally does not support conditioning), and group Gradual also continued to receive CS-US pairings, but the intensity of the US was gradually reduced. Extinction was continued for six sessions. All of the groups attained a criterion level of extinction within the six extinction sessions, but they extinguished at different rates. Group Normal extinguished in three days, group Abrupt in four days, and group Gradual in six days. All groups were given four reminder shocks at the original training intensity. As expected, the groups that continued to receive CS-US pairings (Gradual and Abrupt) showed a greater magnitude of reinstatement than the group that received nonreinforced CS presentations (Normal). The extinction produced with continued presentation of a less intense US resulted in an extinguished response that was more susceptible to reinstatement.

Rescorla and Heth (1975) argue that the greater susceptibility to reinstatement reflects the disproportionate contribution of US devaluation to extinction performance when the extinction procedure is carried out with continued reinforcement. However, this interpretation of extinction is derived from the assumption that reinstatement of the CR occurs by reinstating the US representation. Little direct evidence exists that extinction weakens the US representation. For example, nonreinforcement of one CS does not affect performance to another CS trained with the same US (Bouton & King, 1983). In addition, under certain conditions, presentation of the US alone may not be sufficient to produce reinstatement (Bouton & Bolles, 1979b; Callen, McAllister, & McAllister, 1984).

Facilitated Memory Retrieval

Ahlers and Richardson (1985) have offered another nonassociative account of reinstatement that is based on their findings with pretest administration of ACTH. They argue that ACTH is released during training (perhaps as a consequence of shock) and as a result becomes an element of the training memory. Subsequent pretest exogenous ACTH increases the similarity of training and testing and leads to facilitated retrieval of the training memory. To test this hypothesis, Ahlers and Richardson (1985) sought to reduce the contribution of ACTH to the training memory. They administered dexamethasone (DEX), a synthetic glucocorticoid that inhibits the endogenous release of ACTH, just prior to avoidance training. The avoidance response was then extinguished in the absence of DEX. Pretest administration of ACTH reinstated extinguished avoidance responding in rats given water during training. However, ACTH did not reinstate avoidance responding in rats given DEX during training. Thus, reinstatement by exogenous ACTH seems to depend on the participation of endogenous ACTH during training. It is possible that any postextinction event that reintroduces elements of the training memory can facilitate retrieval of the entire training memory. For example, shocks or other stressors can cause the release of ACTH, which may reinstate the CR (Ahlers & Richardson, 1985).

Reconditioning of CS-US Associations

There are, however, aspects of the effect of ACTH that cannot be easily explained by the facilitated memory retrieval hypothesis. In a subsequent experiment, Ahlers and Richardson (1989) showed that a single injection of ACTH 24 hours after extinction reinstated avoidance responding seven days later (Ahlers, Richardson, West, & Riccio, 1989). Facilitated retrieval would not persist over this long interval. Instead, effects that occur over very long intervals are oftentimes indicative of some form of learning.

Alternatively, ACTH may act to strengthen the associative CS-US associations formed during training (Bohus, Nyakas, & Endroczi, 1967; Izquierdo & Pereira, 1989). This associative effect of ACTH would be expected to persist over very long injection-to-test intervals. Consistent with this, pretraining administration of ACTH or another peptide, vasopressin, has been shown to facilitate *acquisition* of active avoidance (Bohus & Endroczi, 1965), and posttraining administration of ACTH or vasopressin has been shown to

facilitate the retention of active avoidance (Izquierdo & Pereira, 1989). Interestingly, Bohus, Nyakas, and Endroczi (1967) found that the facilitatory effect of ACTH did not occur until after a minimum amount of conditioning was demonstrated. Together these results suggest that ACTH may act to strengthen CS-US associations.

Similarly, Callen, McAllister, and McAllister (1984) argued that reinstatement was the result of reconditioning. In their experiment, fear was conditioned to apparatus cues in one side of a hurdle-jumping apparatus and then extinguished. The rats were then shocked either in the presence of these same apparatus cues or in a distinctively different apparatus. Despite the fact that both groups were shocked, reinstatement of conditioned fear occurred only in the rats that were shocked in the presence of the original apparatus cues. According to the nonassociative accounts of reinstatement (Ahlers & Richardson, 1985; Rescorla & Heth, 1975), reinstatement should occur regardless of where the shocks are given. Instead, these data show that shock must be given in the presence of the stimuli associated with original training, suggesting the possibility that reinstatement is the result of reconditioning or strengthening of residual CS-US associations (Callen et al., 1984).

Summation With an Excitatory Context

It is well established that contextual cues can acquire associative strength and can have a profound influence on acquisition and performance of CRs (Bouton, 1984; Bouton & Bolles, 1979a; Bouton & Bolles, 1979b; Dweck & Wagner, 1970; Odling-smee, 1978). One way to assess conditioning to the context is to place a weakly excitatory CS in the putative excitatory context and assess the CS's ability to elicit a CR. The weak CS does not produce a CR on its own, but when placed in compound with an excitatory context, the excitatory tendencies of both the CS and the context summate, and the CS elicits a CR. Perhaps reinstatement results from the summation of the weak extinguished CS with a context that was made excitatory by the "reminder"

US. Neither the context nor the weak CS would produce a CR on its own, but together, the combined associative strengths may result in a renewed CR. If so, reinstatement would occur only in the context where the reminder shock was given.

Rescorla and Heth (1975, Experiment 2) attempted to test this associative mechanism of reinstatement by giving the reminder shock in a context that was different from the one that was going to be used in testing. In support of their nonassociative hypothesis, they found reinstatement even though the rats were tested outside of the shocked context. However, as Bouton and Bolles (1979b) point out, the contexts used by Rescorla and Heth (1975) may not have been different enough to allow the rat to discriminate between them, as would be required to test the context dependency of reinstatement. In a direct test of context-specific reinstatement, Bouton and Bolles (1979b) gave reminder shocks to rats either in a context in which they were to be tested or in a context discriminatively different from the test context. Using the CER procedure, two groups of rats received tone-foot shock pairings followed sometime later by tone-alone extinction trials. One group (group CC) was given reminder shocks in the conditioning context, and the other group (group TC) was given the shocks in the test context. Both groups were tested for reinstatement in the test context. The results were quite clear. Reinstatement occurred only when the rats were tested in the shocked context. In addition, extinction of the shocked context prevented or erased reinstatement (Bouton & Bolles, 1979b, Experiment 2; cf. Rescorla & Cunningham, 1977). Similar results have been obtained more recently by Callen, McAllister, and McAllister (1984) using a passive avoidance procedure. It would thus appear that neither a US revaluation, facilitated retrieval, nor a strengthening of CS-US associations accounts of reinstatement are necessary. Summation of an excitatory context with residual excitation of the extinguished CS may account for the reinstatement of CRs seen following reminder shocks.

A context-US association account of rein-statement rests on the assumptions that the extinguished CS retains some level of excitation following extinction. This still leaves open the question of whether extinction is due to a build-up of competing associations or a to reduction in the number or strength of excitatory CS-US associations. Investigations of reinstatement have not provided clear evidence supporting either theory. However, similar work on the role of context in extinction suggests that little or none of the excitatory CS-US associations are erased with extinction. And more importantly, these results strongly suggest that inhibitory context-US association is formed during extinction.

Another Look at the Role of the Context

Bouton (1991) has noted that the strength of context conditioning is directly related to the amount of reinstatement observed in that context. But this context conditioning is often weak, and sensitive procedures have to be used to detect it (Bouton, 1991). So, contextual associations are weak, residual CS associations may be considered weak, yet summation of these two effects is very robust, often returning the CR to its preextinction level. Perhaps residual associations of an extinguished CS are especially sensitive to summation with weak contextual associations.

If reinstatement is due to summation of these weak associations, both an extinguished CS and a weak nonextinguished CS should produce comparable levels of conditioned responding following US exposure. To test this, Bouton (1984) arranged conditions so that an extinguished CS and a nonextinguished CS both produced comparable levels of pretest conditioned responding. This was accomplished in the following way. In one group of rats, a CS was paired with a strong shock (3.0 mA) and then followed by extinction; in the other group, the CS was paired with a weak (0.3 mA) shock and not followed by extinction. Both groups were given the intense shock alone. Despite equivalent amounts of context conditioning in both groups, only the group that had been extinguished showed enhanced fear to the CS. The context did not enhance fear to the weak CS. Hence, the contextual associations preferentially affected the extinguished CS. This result would not be expected if reinstatement was simply the result of summation of residual CS and weak contextual associations.

Bouton has argued that unlike a weak, nonextinguished CS, an extinguished CS is "ambiguous" because it has been associated with the US in some circumstances and the absence of the US in other circumstances. This ambiguity makes it susceptible to reinstatement by an excitatory context. More specifically, extinction is thought to result from a discrimination between the circumstances in which the CS is and is not followed by the US. In other words, CS-US associations are intact following extinction but are accompanied by associations that are specific to nonreinforcement. Whether or not the CR occurs in any situation will depend on which set of associations is active. Excitatory context-US associations may reinstate the CR either by retrieving the CS-US associations or by inhibiting the competing associations.

Context Specific Extinction

Context may also play a more direct role in the extinction process. In an impressive series of experiments Bouton and colleagues have shown that extinction is specific to the context in which nonreinforcement occurs (Bouton, 1991; Bouton & Bolles, 1979a; Bouton & Bolles, 1985; Bouton & King, 1983; Bouton & King, 1986). In one experiment, rats were first given tone-shock pairings in a training chamber. After conditioning, the rats were given tone-alone extinction trials in one of two different contexts. To evaluate whether extinction would be specific to the context where the tone was nonreinforced, the rats were tested either in the extinction context or in the alternate context. Rats tested in the extinction context showed extinction of conditioned fear, whereas rats tested in the alternate context showed renewed fear to the tone. The data clearly show that under circumstances in which the rat can discriminate between different contexts, extinction is specific to the context where nonreinforcement occurred.

An erasure hypothesis of extinction cannot easily explain context-specific extinction. Erasure would reduce the likelihood of the CR regardless of where it was tested. On the other hand, a competing association hypothesis can explain context specificity. Stimuli present during nonreinforcement acquire inhibitory CS-US associations that compete with existing excitatory CS-US associations. Perhaps Bouton and Bolles (1979a) succeeded in allowing the context to acquire a great deal of the inhibition. Outside that context there would be no inhibition, and the CR would be renewed. Note that this is similar to the conventional conditioned inhibition procedure in which a neutral stimulus is nonreinforced in the presence of an excitatory CS (see next subsection).

To test whether the extinction context was inhibitory, Bouton and King (1983) used a summation test in which fear to a nonextinguished light was tested in a context in which another CS had been extinguished. If the extinction context was inhibitory, fear to the nonextinguished light should be reduced because of the competing associations. Surprisingly, fear to the light was not reduced. It appears as though the extinction context was not inhibitory (Bouton & King, 1983) .

Bouton has argued that as a result of its history of reinforcement and nonreinforcement, an extinguished CS may be considered "ambiguous" (Bouton, 1984; Bouton, 1991; Bouton & King, 1986). The extinction context is not inhibitory but may act to remove the ambiguous meaning of the CS. For example, if a CS is paired with shock in one context and extinguished in another context, the former context may signal that the CS will be followed by shock, while the later context may signal that the CS will not be followed by shock. Hence, CS-US associations may be formed in both training and extinction, and the context determines which associations are selected for expression. Just how the context selects the associations is unclear. One possibility is that the extinction context plays a permissive role gating the *inhibitory CS-US associations* that are formed during nonreinforcement. (Of course, this assumes that inhibitory CS-US associations are formed during extinction. Up to this point, there has been no evidence to suggest that the CS acquires inhibitory CS-US associations.) Alternatively, the extinction context may be directly responsible for extinction, inhibiting the expression of excitatory CS-US associations. In both cases, excitatory associations are intact, and extinction is the result of the accrual of new associations. One way to begin to evaluate these alternatives is to ask whether evidence exists that an extinguished CS is inhibitory.

The Relationship of Extinction to Feature Negative Discriminations

It is well established that a neutral stimulus can acquire the ability to reduce a CR following training in which it is placed *in compound with an excitatory CS and not reinforced* (Konorski, 1948, 1967; Pavlov, 1927; Rescorla, 1969; Wagner & Rescorla, 1972). The result of this so-called feature negative discrimination procedure leaves little doubt that the neutral stimulus, referred to as a feature, has acquired the ability to somehow inhibit the production of the CR. The classic interpretation of a feature negative discrimination is that the feature inhibits the representation of the US, so when it is placed in compound with the target CS, the CR is reduced. On the face of it, the feature negative discrimination procedure does not differ substantially from the normal extinction procedure. Both involve *nonreinforcement* in the presence of an otherwise *excitatory CS,* and both result in a decrement in the CR. Therefore, one can ask whether it is necessary to assume a separate mechanism for extinction and a feature negative discrimination.

Despite all the evidence in support of the idea that extinction is caused by some form of competing association, researchers have been reluctant to entertain the notion that the CS acquires inhibitory CS-US associations. This reluctance is based on the failure to detect inhibition by an extinguished CS (Reberg, 1972; Rescorla, 1969, 1979). However, one would have no reason to suspect that an extinguished CS and a condi-

tioned inhibitor would yield the same results on a summation or retardation test. As Rescorla (1969) points out, an extinguished CS would have both excitatory and inhibitory CS-US associations (cf. Konorski, 1948; 1967). Inhibition by an extinguished CS can be detected only with the traditional procedures if the net CS-US inhibition is greater than the net CS-US excitation. A feature, on the other hand, is a neutral CS at the outset of conditioning. It only acquires inhibition and has no competing excitatory CS-US associations. Therefore, inhibition is easily detected.

The task would be to demonstrate that extinction and conditioned inhibition are functionally equivalent. One approach is to demonstrate that the inhibition and extinction procedures are interchangeable. Along these lines, Devito and Fowler (1987) conducted an experiment in which they demonstrated that conditioned inhibition can be enhanced by extinction of the conditioned inhibitor. Using a lick suppression procedure, two groups of rats given feature negative discrimination training in which a clicker was paired with shock and a tone+clicker compound was presented without shock. Group Extensive was given a total of 144 tone+clicker trials, while the other, group Moderate, was given 42 tone+clicker trials. In a third phase, both groups were given tone-alone extinction trials. A third group, group Control, was given identical training to group Moderate, but the tone-alone phase was omitted. Prior to tone-alone trials, group Extensive acquired greater inhibition to the tone than groups Moderate and Control. Following nonreinforced tone presentations, group Moderate showed the same level of inhibition as group Extensive, and they both showed reliably more inhibition than group Control. Therefore, for group Moderate, the intervening tone-alone extinction enhanced an already moderate level of inhibition. Although these data are by no means conclusive, they are consistent with the notion that feature negative discriminations and extinction operate through a similar mechanism (Devito & Fowler, 1987). This mechanism may be the accrual of inhibitory CS-US associations.

Evidence is accumulating, however, suggesting that feature negative discriminations may not always result in the feature acquiring inhibitory feature-US associations. Under some experimental conditions, the feature acquires the ability to modulate the expression of the excitatory CS-US associations (Holland, 1985, 1986, 1989, 1990; Holland & Morell, 1993). These features "set the occasion for nonreinforcement" of the CS essentially by inhibiting the ability of the training target to activate the US representation (Holland, 1985, 1990; Rescorla, 1985). Once again, the feature negative discrimination is procedurally similar to extinction, which may involve a similar occasion setting mechanism. Some stimulus present during nonreinforcement may acquire the capacity to inhibit the ability of the CS to activate the US representation. Recall that Bouton has proposed that the extinction context disambiguates the meaning of the CS. The extinction context could act like this feature and inhibit the ability of the CS to activate the US representation. In this context, the CR would be extinguished; outside this context, the modulation does not occur and the CR is renewed (Bouton, 1991). Because the CS does not inhibit the US representation and because the context does not inhibit the US representation, this hypothesis explains why there have been repeated failures to detect inhibition to the CS and the context after extinction.

Summary

Taken together, the data reviewed thus far clearly indicate that extinction does not result in a complete erasure of the original CS-US association. Despite the appearance of no further memory toward the end of an extinction session where no conditioned response whatsoever may occur, evidence of some remaining amount of CS-US association can be seen following a period of time (spontaneous recovery), presentation of a US alone (reinstatement), or testing in a different context (renewal). However, these paradigms do not directly implicate active inhibition as the mechanism of extinction. On the other hand, there is wide agreement that a closely re-lated phenomenon known as feature negative discrimination does involve some form of inhibition. In fact, it has been argued that extinction is a special case of feature negative discrimination. Whether extinction is more like traditional feature negative discrimination or like occasion setting must still be determined. Complicating this picture is the possibility that extinction can involve either process or both processes and that the contribution of one over the other is dependent on procedural differences that we do not yet understand (Falls & Davis, submitted; Holland, 1989b). Interestingly, Bouton (1991) reports that the context specificity of extinction can be reduced if extinction is also carried out in the training context. Perhaps this procedure reduces the contribution of negative occasion setting (Falls & Davis, 1993). Clearly more work is needed not only to explore the relationship between extinction and feature negative discriminations but also to determine the conditions under which feature negative discriminations result in traditional feature-US inhibition or occasion setting.

AVOIDANCE OF THE CS: IMPLICATIONS FOR EXTINCTION

Most of the experiments discussed thus far have employed Pavlovian fear-conditioning procedures to evaluate the extinction process. The advantage of these procedures is that the exact presentation and timing of stimuli can be controlled. Hence, experimenters can be reasonably assured that each stimulus is fully encountered by the animal. However, this assurance is rare outside of the laboratory and outside of these procedures. More typically, animals, if allowed, will escape from a stimulus that elicits fear. This can have a profound impact on the extinction process.

The Paradox of Active Avoidance

Consider the following experiment. A dog is placed into one side of a two-compartment box. The compartments are separated by a low barrier. After a short period of time, a tone is presented to the animal, and 5 seconds later, foot shock is presented through the floor of the box. The foot shock elicits vigorous activity, a consequence of which is that the dog jumps over the barrier and escapes the shock. A few minutes later, the same sequence is repeated. In a few trials, the dog will jump the barrier shortly after the tone is presented, thereby avoiding the shock. Over the next several trials, the time it takes for the dog to avoid the shock is reduced. Now the dog may jump the barrier immediately after the tone comes on. Depending on various parameters, the dog may make hundreds of successful avoidance responses, never getting shocked.

The explanation for this avoidance behavior seems straightforward. The tone signals that shock will occur and the dog learns to jump over the barrier to avoid getting the shock. But as Mowrer (1947, as cited by McAllister & McAllister, 1995) pointed out, how can a shock that is avoided and therefore not experienced serve to reinforce a barrier-jumping response? In addition, even if the dog is avoiding the shock when the tone comes on, why doesn't the avoidance behavior extinguish after the shock is not experienced?

Two-Factor Theory of Avoidance

To resolve this paradox, Mowrer (1947) proposed that active avoidance behavior involved a few distinct processes. Initially, the dog learns to be fearful of the CS by virtue of its being paired with shock. Fear of the CS activates the dog and eventually leads the dog to escape this aversive CS by jumping the barrier. This escape response results in a reduction of fear that reinforces the barrier-jumping response. So, when the dog is placed in the shock compartment and presented with the CS, fear elicited by the CS motivates the escape response and results in a reduction of fear, which reinforces the escape response.

Mowrer's (1947) theory resolved the avoidance paradox, although it has been criticized on two grounds. For one thing, animals well trained in active avoidance paradigms did not seem fear-

ful, but merely jumped the barrier as soon as the CS came on (Seligman & Johnston, 1973). In addition, even if fear motivated the barrier-jumping response, this response often took much longer to extinguish than fear measured in other Pavlovian conditioning paradigms.

The criticism that fear is no longer present in a well-trained dog may, however, be without empirical basis (McAllister & McAllister, 1991). Several experiments have indicated that when avoidance responding is well learned, a substantial amount of fear to the CS remains (Levis & Boyd, 1979a; Mineka & Gino, 1980; Starr & Mineka, 1977). For example, Mineka and Gino (1980) showed that rats trained to a criterion of 27 avoidance responses still showed substantial fear to the CS in a CER procedure.

To explain the very slow rates of extinction, Solomon and Wynne (1954) introduced their "conservation of anxiety hypothesis," based on a few observations. First, they noticed that over the course of training, the avoidance latencies got progressively shorter, while the signs of fear seen early in training were no longer evident. However, if the animal happened not to make a long latency response, the continued presence of the CS elicited signs of fear.

Given this behavior, the animal arranged conditions in which the CS was on for only a very short period of time. Solomon and Wynne (1954) suggested that this protected them from extinction, a conclusion consistent with later work showing that rate of extinction is directly related to the total duration of CS exposure (Malloy, 1981; Shipley, 1974). In fact, in an avoidance study in humans, subjects who failed to extinguish had shorter avoidance latencies than subjects who did extinguish (Williams & Levis, 1991).

This now, however, exposes the animal to a part of the CS that has not become extinguished and leads to a high level of fear, which then serves as a reconditioning trial, making the first part of the CS fearful once again (i.e., reinstatement). This then leads to a very short latency avoidance response and once again protects the rest of the CS from being exposed and hence protects it from extinction. In fact, Levis and Boyd (1979b) have data on rats that show a striking oscillation of avoidance latencies over trials where a long latency response tends to be followed by a short latency response, and vice versa. With extended training, the animal begins to make the avoidance response at a longer latency, thus extending the duration of CS exposure and hastening extinction.

These ideas account for a good deal of data within the literature on active avoidance, although they have not gone unchallenged. For example, Seligman and Johnston (1973) assert that although fear is necessary for the acquisition of active avoidance behavior, it does not motivate sustained asymptotic avoidance behavior. They pointed out that Solomon's dogs sometimes responded for hundreds of trials, whereas fear measured in a conditioned emotional response paradigm extinguished after only 40 trials (Annau & Kamin, 1961). Because of this, they concluded that fear would have extinguished long before avoidance behavior, and hence fear could not continue to produce the avoidance response. Instead, they proposed a more cognitive account where the avoidance response continued because the animal expected that the absence of a response will lead to a shock.

This cognitive account may not be necessary, however (Levis, 1989; McAllister & McAllister, 1991, 1995). Levis (1989) pointed out that the total duration of CS exposure in a typical Solomon avoidance study where a dog made 500 avoidance responses without receiving a shock would be about 1,000 seconds, assuming an average response latency of 2 seconds. In contrast, total CS exposure for complete extinction in the Annau and Kamin study quoted by Seligman and Johnston (Seligman & Johnston, 1973) was 2,400 seconds. Furthermore, even when animals are making short latency avoidance responses, they still appear to be fearful of the CS, provided sensitive enough tests are used. For example, Levis and Boyd (1979b) trained rats to an asymptotic level of active avoidance and showed that the

onset of the CS still caused substantial suppression of bar pressing in a conditioned emotional response paradigm. Hence, lack of exposure to the CS can account for the persistence of the avoidance response.

Eventually the avoidance response will extinguish. Although the preceding arguments describe why the escape response is slow to extinguish, they do not explain how extinction occurs. McAllister and McAllister have described how the extinction process might occur. Following Mowrer (1947), they assume that escape from the CS results in the reduction of fear and reinforcement of the escape response. Fear reduction can occur in one of two ways: either with the removal of fear-eliciting stimuli or through generalization decrement, as when a neutral stimulus or so-called feedback stimulus is presented (McAllister & McAllister, 1992). The reduction of fear results in a response of relaxation that can be conditioned to the feedback stimulus (Denny, 1991). Since relaxation is antagonistic to fear, the feedback stimuli acquire the ability to reduce fear. The instrumental avoidance response is reinforced by relaxation elicited by the feedback stimuli. Importantly, the feedback stimuli do not act as positive reinforcers of the escape response. If they did, the avoidance response would be maintained indefinitely. Instead, the avoidance response is maintained by fear reduction (i.e., relaxation). Hence, as long as fear persists, feedback stimuli will be effective as fear reducers, and the avoidance response will be maintained. Once fear is extinguished, the avoidance response is no longer reinforced and will cease to occur.

Extinction of fear occurs as a result of a competing response of relaxation. Initially, feedback stimuli and traces of the CS acquire relaxation. But as nonreinforcement continues, the CS itself can acquire the ability to elicit relaxation. Therefore, through counterconditioning of fear, fear to the CS will extinguish. As the animal exposes itself to more and more of the CS, more of the CS acquires relaxation, and the escape response stops.

EXTINCTION OF INSTRUMENTAL RESPONSES

The preceding discussion has focused on extinction of Pavlovian conditioned responses. However, biologically significant stimuli have the ability to reinforce instrumental responses, and the omission of the reinforcer after the instrumental response is acquired leads to the reduction of the response. For example, rats will learn to press a bar to receive a food reinforcer. The bar pressing will be maintained as long as food is delivered on some schedule. Once the food no longer follows a bar press, the frequency of the bar-press response will gradually decline.

Inhibitory S-R Associations

Like Pavlovian extinction, the process that underlies extinction of instrumental responses is not yet understood. Like extinction of Pavlovian CRs, extinction of instrumental responses begs the same questions: Have the associations that lead to the instrumental response been somehow masked, or have they been erased or otherwise overwritten? But answering these questions for extinction of instrumental responses may be more difficult because the nature of the associations that are formed in instrumental learning is more complex. As Rescorla (1993) points out, recent analysis of instrumental learning suggests that a variety of associations are formed as a consequence of instrumental learning procedures. For example, exists evidence to suggest that associations are formed between the instrumental response (R) and the reinforcer (more accurately referred to as the earned outcome (O), between the discriminative stimulus (S) and the reinforcer, and between the discriminative stimulus and the response. Evidence also points to higher order associations between S and the R-O association (Rescorla, 1993). It is possible that any one or a combination of these associations is affected by nonreinforcement.

Rescorla has conducted several experiments with rats that suggest that the S-O and R-O associations are intact following nonreinforcement (Rescorla, 1992, 1993). In a typical procedure, an auditory cue (S) signals that a lever press (R) will lead to a food pellet (O). After the rat has acquired this instrumental behavior, reinforcement is removed, and the lever press response extinguishes. To evaluate the integrity of S-O association, Rescorla presented the original auditory stimulus in the context of a unique response that was previously associated with the same food pellet outcome. Despite previous nonreinforcement, the original auditory cue retained its ability to augment responding. This suggests that the original S-O association was intact.

Similarly, in a test of the integrity of the R-O association, rats were presented with a unique stimulus that had previously signaled a different response that led to the same food pellet outcome. Once again, despite extinction, the bar-press response returned, suggesting that the R-O association was also intact. If both the S-O and R-O associations are intact following nonreinforcement, why does the response extinguish with nonreinforcement? Rescorla (1993) suggests that nonreinforcement results in the acquisition of an inhibitory S-R association. In a test of whether an S present at the time of nonreinforcement acquires an inhibitory association with, Rescorla (1993, Experiment 4) trained rats to press a lever for food pellets. This response was extinguished in the presence of a visual stimulus. The bar-press response was then retrained. In a subsequent test, the visual stimulus suppressed the bar-pressing response but did not affect a chain-pull response that had also been reinforced with food pellets. This suggests that nonreinforcement in the presence of the visual stimulus causes the visual stimulus to acquire the ability to inhibit the bar-press response; that is, extinction resulted in an inhibitory S-R association. Hence, like Pavlovian extinction, instrumental extinction does not appear to involve the erasure of the associations that led to the original response but rather appears to involve buildup of competing associations that mask the expression of the associations that led to the instrumental response. Moreover, the inhibition appears to be under the control of stimuli that are associated with nonreinforcement.

The Role of Competing Responses in Instrumental Extinction

In his review of the major theories of extinction, Mackintosh (1974) distinguished between the inhibition theories of extinction (Rescorla's inhibitory S-R association would come under this class) and interference theories of extinction. We have discussed the inhibition theories in some detail. The interference theories, on the other hand, believe that the omission of the reinforcer establishes a set of new responses that are incompatible with the original instrumental response. Therefore, as the strength of the new response builds, the original instrumental response is overcome. As Mackintosh (1972) points out, extinction is often accompanied by an increase in overt behaviors that appear to be incompatible with the instrumental response. However, an increase in overt behavior does not mean that these behaviors themselves are the cause of extinction. According to Mackintosh (1972), what is required is a conniving demonstration that independent manipulation of the overt behaviors systematically alters the course of extinction. For example, will prevention of these behaviors during nonreinforcement block extinction? Or will prevention of these behaviors result in reinstatement of the extinguished instrumental response? Little evidence exists that the overt behaviors themselves cause instrumental extinction.

Conditioned Frustration

These overt responses do occur, however. Perhaps they are indicative of the process that leads to instrumental extinction. That is, these overt behaviors may occur as a consequence of the process that leads to extinction. Skinner (1950) observed that when key pecking was no longer reinforced, a pigeon would begin to coo, move rapidly about the cage, defecate, or flap its wings. These behaviors gave the appearance of an emotional reaction to nonreinforcement. Several authors have suggested that the omission of reinforcement leads to the emotional response of frustration, which in turn contributes to extinction of the instrumental response (Amsel, 1958, 1962;

Skinner, 1950; Spence, 1960). Azrin, Hutchinson, and Hake (1966) provided striking evidence for frustration. In their experiment, two birds were placed in an operant box. One bird was reinforced for pecking a key, while the other bird was lightly restrained in the corner of the box. When reinforcement was discontinued, there was a high probability that the formerly reinforced pigeon would attack the restrained pigeon (Azrin, Hutchinson, & Hake, 1966). It's been argued that this aggression is due to the frustration caused by the withdrawal of reinforcement (Terrace, 1971). Although nonreinforcement may cause frustration and an overt aggressive display, little evidence exists to suggest that these behaviors cause extinction. In fact, Azrin, Hutchinson, and Hake (1966) found that both the probability of aggressive displays and the instrumental response decrease over the course of nonreinforcement. If the aggressive display were causing the decrease in instrumental performance, the aggressive displays should increase as instrumental performance decreases.

Amsel (1958, 1962) suggested that frustration could be conditioned to stimuli that preceded nonreinforcement. Importantly, because conditioned frustration was thought to be aversive and because aversive states are incompatible with instrumental performance, the presence of conditioned frustration would reduce instrumental performance. Thus, instrumental extinction can be explained through Pavlovian conditioning of frustration. To take a specific example, frustration is elicited in a rat when food reinforcement is omitted from the goal box of a maze. As a result, the goal box acquires the ability to elicit conditioned frustration, which is aversive and which the rat will avoid. The conditioned frustration grows with continued nonreinforcement, and over trials, the portions of the maze preceding the goal box also acquire the ability to elicit conditioned frustration. The tendency to avoid the cues that signal frustration competes with the tendency to approach cues that signal instrumental reinforcement, and soon the instrumental response ceases to occur.

Is frustration aversive, and can it be conditioned to stimuli associated with nonreinforcement? A variety of studies suggest that nonreinforcement is aversive (cf. Amsel, 1958, 1962). In one notable experiment, Wagner (1963) trained rats to run a U-shaped maze to a goal box where food reinforcement was provided. After this habit was established, rats were reinforced on only 50 percent of the trials. On trials in which nonreinforcement occurred, a CS of flashing lights and interrupted noise was provided. The intention was to use nonreinforcement to condition frustration to this CS. After this, the aversiveness of the CS was tested in a hurdle-jumping apparatus in which the rats could terminate the CS by jumping a hurdle. Rats exposed to the CS during nonreinforcement escaped from the CS more quickly than did control rats that had not experienced the CS. In addition, the amplitude of the acoustic startle response was facilitated during the CS in these rats as well. Facilitated startle is a reliable measure of aversive Pavlovian conditioning (Brown, Kalish, & Farber, 1951; Davis & Astrachan, 1978). Hence, these data suggest that stimuli present during nonreinforcement of an instrumental response can acquire aversive properties. To the extent that frustration is aversive and is incompatible with instrumental performance, conditioned frustration can explain extinction of instrumental responses. But as Mackintosh (1974) points out, this explanation of extinction seems to apply only to instrumental situations where food is the reinforcer. However, in situations where the instrumental response is reinforced by an aversive outcome, nonreinforcement may elicit a response of relaxation (Deny, 1991).

In summary, data suggest that nonreinforcement of an instrumental response elicits frustration, which has two primary consequences: (1) elicitation of unlearned, incompatible behavior that may interfere with the performance of the instrumental response and (2) acquisition of conditioned frustration to the stimuli preceding nonreinforcement. Conditioned frustration may result in an affective state whose consequences are incompatible with production of the instru-

mental response. As with extinction of Pavlovian CRs, direct competition between these associations leads to a reduction in responding. Also like Pavlovian extinction, the competing associations are conditioned to the stimuli that signal nonreinforcement. Therefore, any manipulation that removed these stimuli would result in a return of the instrumental response.

The Partial Reinforcement Extinction Effect

Any discussion of instrumental extinction would be incomplete without consideration of the partial reinforcement extinction effect (PREE). Simply stated, the PREE is increased resistance to extinction of an instrumental response that has been partially reinforced in training. In the most simple case, maze running that is followed by food on 75% of occasions (partial reinforcement) will extinguish less quickly than maze running that is reinforced on 100% of occasions (continuous reinforcement). Amsel (1958, 1962) argued that the PREE occurs because animals trained under partial reinforcement learn to respond under conditions of frustration. As we have seen, nonreinforcement elicits frustration that is conditioned to the stimuli preceding nonreinforcement. However, when reinforcement is partial, the rat is rewarded in the presence of cues that signal frustration. Because the rat is rewarded more than it is frustrated, the approach response prevails. When reinforcement is totally withdrawn (i.e., extinction), the rat will resist extinction and will continue to run the maze because it has learned to run in the presence of stimuli signaling frustration. On the other hand, a rat that is given continuous reinforcement does not learn to run in the presence of stimuli signaling frustration and will extinguish more quickly. As a final note, although the PREE has been demonstrated in a large number of studies and is one of the more reliable findings in instrumental conditioning, a number of studies have failed to find evidence for the PREE in Pavlovian conditioning (Berger, Yarczower, & Bitterman, 1965; Gonzalez, Milstein, & Bitterman, 1962; Longo, Milstein, & Bitterman, 1962; Thomas & Wagner, 1964; Wagner, Siegel, & Fein, 1967). Therefore, Pavlovian CRs acquired with partial reinforcement may not be more difficult to extinguish.

CLINICAL IMPLICATIONS

Therapeutic techniques such as systematic desensitization, flooding, and implosion are based on the idea that exposure to fear-eliciting stimuli will result in extinction of fear. These therapies can be successful in eliminating phobias. However, simply because the fear or phobia is no longer observable does not mean that it has been permanently removed. As we have seen, basic research has shown that extinction does not erase the original memory. The memory seems to be indelible, and extinction appears to involve a process that somehow inhibits or modulates the expression of the memory. The downside to the indelibility of the memory is that the extinction process is easily disrupted and unstable (Bouton & Swartzentruber, 1991) Therefore, under certain conditions, the extinguished memory can return. Therapists should be aware of these conditions, anticipate them, and consider them in the course of therapy.

Reinstatement

Exposure to the US itself or to some component of the original training experience can result in the return of a previously extinguished behavior. Reinstatement has four characteristics that the clinician should be concerned with. First, a single exposure to the US can result in reinstatement. Second, the effect of a single exposure to the US can persist long after US exposure. The reinstated response may remain until further extinction is carried out. Third, reinstatement can occur despite extensive nonreinforcement (Bouton & Swartzentruber, 1991). Hence, extensive behavioral therapy may not inoculate a client against the consequences of reexperiencing the

US. Fourth, and perhaps most important, reinstatement does not have to be produced by the original US. Reinstatement can occur following exposure to stimuli that are seemingly unrelated to the original US.

Recall that Bouton and colleagues have shown that reinstatement of conditioned fear will occur if a rat is placed in a context that was previously paired with shock. Hence, stimuli associated with the same US can be sufficient to reinstate extinguished memories. In addition, reinstatement may not require new learning. Reintroduction to components of the original learning may be sufficient to produce reinstatement. Ahlers and Richardson (1985) have shown that reinstatement of fear occurs if a rat is injected with the stress-related peptide ACTH. ACTH is probably an element of the original training memory. This suggests that stimuli and events seemingly unrelated to the original learning can produce reinstatement if they activate a subset of the elements of the original experience. For example, burning dinner (often mildly traumatic) could reinstate an extinguished traumatic memory if it happens to activate similar visceral responses that were activated by the traumatic experience. It is especially interesting in this regard that drugs like yohimbine, which activate the release of norepinephrine in the brain, often produce flashbacks (memory of prior trauma) in patients with post traumatic stress disorder (Southwick et al., in press). Because elevated levels of brain norepinephrine would have accompanied the traumatic event, yohimbine may reinstate a component of the traumatic memory. Presumably, any event that releases norepinephrine in sufficient quantity would also produce flashbacks.

There is evidence to suggest that extinction of stimuli capable of producing reinstatement may reduce their ability to subsequently produce reinstatement. For example, Bouton and Bolles (1979b) showed that extinction of the context in which reminder shocks occurred reduced the context's ability to produce reinstatement. Similarly, extinction carried out in the presence of exogenous ACTH reduced the ability to subsequently produce reinstatement. Although therapists cannot identify and extinguish all stimuli that could potentially produce reinstatement, they might consider identifying the stimuli that the client is likely to encounter that may be related to the original learning. Extinction of these stimuli may reduce the likelihood of reinstatement.

Context Specificity of Extinction

If extinction is carried out in a distinguishing context (e.g., the therapist's office), extinction may be evident only in that context. The response may be renewed outside of that context. The goal of the therapist should be to reduce the context specificity of extinction. Bouton (1991) reports preliminary evidence suggesting that context specificity can be reduced if extinction is carried out in the same context in which training took place. In this case, the context does not serve as a discriminative stimulus that removes the ambiguous meaning of CS. In other words, there is no salient cue to signal when or where the CS will or will not be reinforced. One way to minimize context specificity would be to conduct behavior therapy in the client's natural setting. This setting may be the context in which the stimuli to be extinguished are normally encountered. Note that this would also tend to extinguish other stimuli in the client's environment that could produce reinstatement (see reinstatement). Another way to minimize context specificity would be to vary the context in which behavior therapy is given. This would create several contexts associated with nonreinforcement and may promote generalization to yet unexperienced, novel contexts.

Another implication of context-dependent extinction is that renewed fear can occur if drugs are made part of the extinction context. If a drug is used as an adjunct to therapy, renewal could occur when the extinguished stimulus is encountered in the absence of the drug. In fact, animal experiments have shown that when benzodiazepines are given during extinction of conditioned fear, fear of the CS is renewed when testing occurs in the absence of the drug (Bouton, Kenney, & Rosengard, 1990).

Avoidance Conditioning

Mowrer (1947) believed that abnormal behaviors came about because they had for the individual the appearance of lessening or reducing anxiety. According to his theory, instrumental escape responses are motivated by fear and reinforced by the reduction of fear. When an individual performs a response to escape fear, the entire fear-eliciting stimulus is not experienced. Because extinction is a function of the amount of exposure to the CS (Shipley, 1974; Shipley, Mock, & Levis, 1971), fear will not extinguish and will continue to motivate the avoidance response (McAllister & McAllister, 1995). Flooding and implosive therapy are successful because these procedures control the exposure to the fear-eliciting stimuli, thereby ensuring extinction of fear and preventing the instrumental escape responses that would otherwise be reinforced by fear reduction (McAllister & McAllister, 1995).

Extinction of fear through flooding or implosive therapy may not extinguish the instrumental escape response but may extinguish only the fear that motivates it. If fear is reinstated or renewed, the instrumental escape response is likely to recur as well. In one experiment, McAllister, McAllister, Scoles, and Hampton (1986) gave rats CS+shock training in one side of a hurdle-jumping apparatus. Rats were then allowed to learn to escape fear by jumping the hurdle. No shock was given during escape trials. The escape response was readily learned and maintained and after 225 trials eventually ceased. Next, the rats were given a single CS+shock pairing (analogous to a reminder shock). This resulted in an immediate return of the escape response, suggesting that when fear is extinguished (as evidenced by a cessation in escape responding), the capacity to perform the escape response is maintained. Other experiments have also shown a similar dissociation of fear extinction and the extinction of the avoidance response (Miller, Mineka, & Cook, 1982; Mineka & Gino, 1979, 1980).

The implication of this is that even if fear is extinguished through flooding or implosive therapy, any event that causes fear to recur could result in a return of symptomatic escape behavior and continued maintenance of fear. Hence, therapy should not only involve the extinction of fear and consideration of the conditions in which fear might recur (see context specific extinction) but also consider the elimination of symptomatic escape behaviors, perhaps by replacing them with more appropriate behaviors (McAllister & McAllister, 1995). Therefore, if fear were to recur as a result of a change in context (i.e., renewal) and the symptomatic escape behavior not occur because it was extinguished or replaced with more appropriate behavior, the individual would experience a fuller exposure to the new context, thus providing a better opportunity for learning that this context was also safe. As Levis has stressed, central to behavior therapy is the need to repeatedly expose the patient not only to "CS patterns directly correlated with symptom onset but also to cues reactivated by the exposure procedure and those *hypothesized to be responses for symptom development*" [emphasis added] (1985, p. 67).

Conditions Under Which Extinction Might Not Occur

Levis (1985) assumes that extinction produced by behavior therapies will be directly related to the level of response that is generated during presentation of the CS pattern. This is consistent with animal work showing that the amount of extinction is a function of the initial level of conditioning. However, conditions in which an excessive response occurs to a CS may be detrimental to extinction. For example, animal research has shown that intermittent presentation of the US during nonreinforcement of the CS retards extinction (Ayres & Decosta, 1971; Frey & Butler, 1977; Rescorla & Skucy, 1969). This is understandable because US presentations can serve as additional conditioning trials or as "reminder" USs (see reinstatement). Recall that Konorski (1948) argued that extinction occurred

when the CS was presented at the time of a fall in activation of the US center. The fall in activation occurred only when the CS was presented in the *absence* of the US. Presentation of the US precludes a fall in activation of the US center and prevents extinction.

It is important to realize that there is no true distinction between a stimulus that can serve as a CS and a stimulus that can serve as a US. The distinction is based solely on the response that is elicited by the stimulus. A conditioned stimulus is initially neutral and does not elicit the CR to be measured. A US, on the other hand, elicits this or a similar response. However, once conditioned, a potent CS can function as a US to produce conditioning to a new CS (Rescorla, 1973, 1980). This is referred to as second-order conditioning and is generally weaker than primary conditioning, owing to the fact that the first-order CS is a weaker reinforcer than the original US. However, if the first-order CS is very potent (e.g., fear conditioned to a stimulus coincident with a traumatic experience), this stimulus could act like a US. This potent CS would resist extinction. In terms of Konorski's (1948) theory, if a CS has become so well trained that it activates the US center like the original US, CS-alone extinction trials *would not* accompany a fall in activation of the US center, and extinction would not occur.

This idea may be more easily understood by considering extinction in terms of relaxation (McAllister & McAllister, 1995). According to this theory, extinction of fear occurs as a result of the accrual of a competing response of relaxation. Relaxation occurs when fear is reduced, typically, when the CS is presented and nonreinforced. If the US were to occur, fear would not be reduced and relaxation would not occur. Similarly, a potent CS might also not allow for relaxation and might not extinguish. But this also tells us that any event that reduces fear at or about the time the CS is presented can produce relaxation.

Fear reduction may be aided in several ways.

Anxiolytic Drugs

Anxiolytics would certainly reduce fear and permit relaxation. However, benzodiazepines have been shown to produce state-dependent extinction (Bouton et al., 1990) in which learning in the presence of the drug does not transfer outside of the drug state (Overton, 1966). In addition, there is evidence to suggest that blockade of GABAergic mechanisms in the brain may facilitate extinction of fear (McGaugh, Castellano, & Brioni, 1990). Because benzodiazepines facilitate GABAergic systems, they may interfere with the physiological mechanisms of extinction. Therapists may want to avoid benzodiazepines as adjuncts to exposure therapy.

Safety Signals

Another way to reduce fear is by presenting a safety signal. Recall that a stimulus trained as part of a feature negative discrimination acquires the ability to inhibit fear. Presentation of a safety signal together with a potent CS should reduce fear to the CS and augment extinction. Hawk and Riccio (1977) evaluated this and found that presentation of a safety signal during nonreinforcement hastened extinction of an avoidance response. Hence, extinction to a potent CS may be aided by the presentation of a safety signal.

Neutral Stimuli

In the Hawk and Riccio (1977) study, extinction was also hastened by presentation of a novel stimulus during nonreinforcement. Pavlov (1927) observed that novel stimuli could consistently reduce the effectiveness of the CS in eliciting the CR (Pavlov referred to this phenomenon as "external inhibition"). This phenomenon has also been labeled as distraction and generalization decrement. Baum and colleagues have evaluated the effect of presenting novel stimuli during extinction of an avoidance response in rats (Baum, 1987; Baum & Gordon, 1970; Baum, Pereira, & Leclerc, 1985). In one experiment, rats were trained to escape shock by jumping from an electrified grid floor of a box to a ledge located above the floor. After attaining an escape criterion, the rats were given extinction to the apparatus by placing them onto the unelectrified grid floor with the ledge retracted. In an experimental group, a novel continuous background noise was presented during extinction and in a control group, the noise was absent. Testing occurred in the absence of the noise and involved placing the rat onto the unelectrified grid floor and recording the number of escape responses onto the ledge. Rats given extinction in the presence of the novel noise showed fewer escape responses than rats not given the noise. Hence, the novel noise hastened extinction to the apparatus cues. Similar results were also reported by Baum and Gordon (1970) and Hawk and Riccio (1977).

Despite the fact that a novel stimulus should reduce fear and allow relaxation, according to some influential theories of learning, a novel stimulus should not hasten extinction but in fact should retard extinction (Kamin, 1969; Pearce & Hall, 1980; Rescorla & Wagner, 1972; Wagner, 1980; Wagner & Rescorla, 1972). And considering the influence of context on extinction, one might expect that a neutral stimulus would become part of the extinction context. If so, extinction would not transfer outside of the presence of the neutral stimulus and might be present only in the presence of that stimulus (Brooks & Bouton, 1994). This is akin to the phenomenon of negative occasion setting discussed earlier (Bouton, 1991; Holland, 1985). Whether facilitated extinction, protection from extinction, or negative occasion setting occurs may depend on experiment parameters. More work is needed to determine the conditions under which novel stimuli may or may not hasten extinction and whether this procedure would have to be qualified by the potential for contextual effects.

Distraction

In many respects, presentation of a novel stimulus is like distracting the subject away from the fear-eliciting stimulus. Because it is difficult to define *distraction*, the term is rarely used in the animal literature. However, there have been a few studies in humans that have evaluated the effect of distraction on desensitization therapy and are therefore worth discussing in this context. (A review of this literature is beyond the scope of the present discussion, but the reader may wish to consider a recent review by Rodriguez and

Craske [1993].) Distraction from the fear-eliciting stimulus should have similar effects as presenting a novel stimulus: Fear would be reduced, allowing relaxation. Studies have shown that high levels of fear may interfere with in vivo desensitization to phobic stimuli (Borkovec & Sides, 1979; Foa & Kozak, 1986). However, the evidence is mixed as to whether distraction during exposure to the phobic stimulus can reduce fear and whether this has any effect on the long-term success of exposure therapy (i.e., extinction). As reviewed by Rodriguez and Craske (1993), the mixed results may have to do with the level of distraction and how distraction is defined. In most of these experiments, distraction involved engaging in some task while undergoing exposure, such as playing a video game or listening for target words. These tasks might produce so much distraction that the CS itself is not attended to. Herein lies the difficulty in evaluating these experiments with respect to fear reduction and relaxation. In the limit, extinction will not occur if the CS is not presented (recall Konorski, 1948). So, if the individual is fully distracted, extinction will not occur. The goal should be to partially distract the subject, reducing fear but still allowing the CS to be processed. It is interesting to speculate that the apparent therapeutic advantage of eye movement desensitization and reprocessing, EMDR (Shapiro, Vogelmann-Sine, & Sine, 1994), may be that it involves a level of distraction sufficient to produce fear reduction but without causing the subject not to attend to the CS. (See Acierno et al., 1994, and Greenwald, 1994, for reviews of EMDR.) Nevertheless, to evaluate the effect of fear reduction and distraction on desensitization, it would seem better to follow the animal experiments of Baum and colleagues (Baum, 1987; Baum & Gordon, 1970; Baum et al., 1985) and present a novel "distracting background stimulus" during exposure rather than have the subject *actively* engaging in some distracting task (cf. Singh, 1976).

In summary, an excessive amount of fear to a CS can prevent or severely retard extinction. To the extent that the potent CS behaves like a US, extinction may occur only if the exaggerated fear elicited by the potent CS is somehow reduced. The animal literature suggests that presentation of a safety signal or a neutral stimulus can hasten extinction. However, the effectiveness of these procedures as therapeutic tools has yet to be evaluated.

SUMMARY

Pavlov (1927) believed that extinction was as important to the organism as the original learning itself. Extinction provided the means to correct learned behavior to meet the organism's current circumstance, a circumstance in which the CS is no longer followed by the US. The procedural definition of extinction—presentation of the CS in the absence of the US—suggests that extinction is a simple procedure that is easily carried out. However, executing the procedure does not guarantee extinction. For example, failure to present the entire CS can retard or prevent extinction and make the memory more susceptible to reinstatement. Similarly, even though the US may be physically absent, a potent CS may act like a US and prevent extinction. And although a CS may no longer elicit a conditioned response following extinction, it is clear that many, if not most, of the original CS-US associations still exist. These associations can return with the passage of time, following presentation of a US, or when testing takes place in a context different from the one used in extinction.

The mechanistic definition of extinction remains to be written. Konorski (1948) believed that extinction was the result of the accrual of inhibition that competed with the excitatory associations for activation of the US center. However, it has been very difficult to demonstrate experimentally that the CS acquires direct inhibitory associations with the US. A more contemporary view is that extinction results from a discrimination between occasions in which the CS is and is not followed by the US center. In this scheme, some aspect of the experimental situation, such as the experiment context, serves as an occasion setter or trigger to signal whether the CS will or will not be followed by the US. The exact nature of this modulation is unclear.

REFERENCES

Acierno, R., Hersen, M., & Van-Hasselt, V. B. (1994). Review of the validation and dissemination of eye movement desensitization and reprocessing: A scientific and ethical dilemma. *Clinical Psychology Review, 14(4)*, 287–299.

Ahlers, S. T., & Richardson, R. (1985). Administration of dexamethasone prior to training blocks ACTH-induced recovery of an extinguished avoidance response. *Behavioral Neuroscience, 99(4)*, 760–764.

Ahlers, S. T., Richardson, R., West, C., & Riccio, D. C. (1989). ACTH produces long lasting recovery following partial extinction of an active avoidance response. *Behavioral and Neural Biology, 51*, 102–107.

Amsel, A. (1958). The role of frustrative nonreward in noncontinuous reward situations. *Psychological Bulletin, 55*, 102–119.

Amsel, A. (1962). Frustrative nonreward in partial reinforcement and discrimination learning: Some recent history and a theoretical extension. *Psychological Review, 69*, 306–328.

Annau, Z., & Kamin, L. J. (1961). The conditioned emotional response as a function of the intensity of the US. *Journal of Comparative and Physiological Psychology, 54(4)*, 428–432.

Ayres, J. B., & Decosta, M. J. (1971). The truly random control as an extinction procedure. *Psychonomic Science, 24(1)*, 31–33.

Azrin, N. H., Hutchinson, R. R., & Hake, D. F. (1966). Extinction-induced aggression. *Journal of the Experimental Analysis of Behavior, 9*, 191–204.

Baum, M. (1987). Distraction during flooding (exposure): Concordance between results in animal and man. *Behavior Research and Therapy, 25(3)*, 227–228.

Baum, M., & Gordon, A. (1970). Effects of a loud buzzer applied during response prevention (flooding) in rats. *Behavior Research and Therapy, 8*, 287–292.

Baum, M., Pereira, J., & Leclerc, R. (1985). Extinction of avoidance responding in rats: The noise intensity parameter in noise facilitation of flooding. *Canadian Journal of Psychology, 39(3)*, 529–535.

Berger, B. D., Yarczower, M., & Bitterman, M. E. (1965). Effect of partial reinforcement on the extinction of a classically conditioned response in the goldfish. *Journal of Comparative and Physiologica Psychology, 59*, 399–405.

Bohus, B., & Endroczi, E. (1965). The influence of pituitary-adrenocortical function on the avoiding conditioned reflex in rats. *Acta Physiological Hungary, 26*, 183–189.

Bohus, B., Nyakas, C., & Endroczi, E. (1967). Effects of adrenocorticotropic hormone on avoidance behavior of intact and adrenalectomized rats. *International Journal of Neuropharmacology, 7*, 307–314.

Borkovec, T. D., & Sides, J. K. (1979). Critical procedural variables related to the physiological effects of progressive relaxation: A review. *Behavior Research and Therapy, 17*, 119–125.

Bouton, M. E. (1984). Differential control by context in the inflation and reinstatement paradigms. *Journal of Experimental Psychology: Animal Behavior Processes, 10(1)*, 56–74.

Bouton, M. E. (1986). Slow reacquisition following extinction of conditioned suppression. *Learning and Motivation, 17*, 1–15.

Bouton, M. E. (1991). A contextual analysis of fear extinction. In P. R. Martin (ed.), *Handbook of behavior therapy and psychological science: An integrative approach*, 435–453. New York: Pergamon.

Bouton, M. E., & Bolles, R. C. (1979a). Contextual control of the extinction of conditioned fear. *Learning and Motivation, 10*, 455–466.

Bouton, M. E., & Bolles, R. C. (1979b). Role of contextual stimuli in reinstatement of extinguished fear. *Journal of Experimental Psychology: Animal Behavior Processes, 5(4)*, 368–378.

Bouton, M. E., & Bolles, R. C. (1985). Context, event-memories, and extinction. In P. D. Balsam & A. Tomie (eds.), *Context and learning*, 133–166. Hillsdale, N.J.: Erlbaum.

Bouton, M. E., Kenney, F. A., & Rosengard, C. (1990). State-dependent fear extinction with two benzodiazepine tranquilizers. *Behavioral Neuroscience, 104(1)*, 44–55.

Bouton, M. E., & King, D. A. (1983). Contextual control of conditioned fear: Tests for the associative value of the context. *Journal of Experimental Psychology: Animal Behavior Processes, 9(3)*, 248–256.

Bouton, M. E., & King, D. A. (1986). Effect of context with mixed histories of reinforcement and nonreinforcement. *Journal of Experimental Psychology: Animal Behavior Processes, 12(1)*, 4–15.

Bouton, M. E., & Swartzentruber, D. (1991). Sources of relapse after extinction in Pavlovian instrumental learning. *Clinical Psychological Review, 11*, 123–140.

Brooks, D. C., & Bouton, M. E. (1994). A retrieval cue for extinction attenuates response recovery (renewal) caused by a return to the conditioning context. *Journal of Experimental Psychology: Animal Behavior Processes, 20(4)*, 366–379.

Brown, J. S., Kalish, H. I., & Farber, I. E. (1951). Conditioned fear as revealed by magnitude of startle response to an auditory stimulus. *Journal of Experimental Psychology, 41*, 317–328.

Callen, E. J., McAllister, W. R., & McAllister, D. E. (1984). Investigations of the reinstatement of extinguished fear. *Learning and Motivation, 15*, 302–320.

Davis, M., & Astrachan, D. I. (1978). Conditioned fear and startle magnitude: effects of different footshock or back-shock intensities used in training. *Journal of Experimental Psychology: Animal Behavior Processes, 4*, 95–103.

Denny, M. R. (1991). Relaxation/relief: The effect of removing, postponing or terminating aversive stimuli. In M. R. Denny (ed.), *Fear, avoidance and phobias: A fundamental analysis*, 199–229. Hillsdale, N.J.: Erlbaum.

Devito, P. L., & Fowler, H. (1987). Enhancement of conditioned inhibition via an extinction treatment. *Animal Learning and Behavior, 15(4)*, 448–454.

Dweck, C. S., & Wagner, A. R. (1970). Situation cues and correlation between CS and US as determinants of the conditioned emotional response. *Psychonomic Science, (18)*, 145–147.

Estes, W. K. (1955). Statistical theory of spontaneous recovery and regression. *Psychological Review, 62(3)*, 145–154.

Falls, W. A., & Davis, M. (1993). Visual cortex ablations do not prevent extinction of conditioned fear to a visual conditioned stimulus. *Behavioral and Neural Biology, 60*, 259–270.

Falls, W. A., & Davis, M. (submitted). External inhibition of fear-potentiated startle: Inhibition of an associative process.

Foa, E. B., & Kozak, M. S. (1986). Emotional processing of fear: Exposure to corrective information. *Psychological Bulletin, 99*, 20–35.

Frey, P. W., & Butler, C. S. (1977). Extinction after aversive conditioning: An associative or nonassociative process? *Learning and Motivation, 8*, 1–17.

Gonzalez, R. C., Milstein, S., & Bitterman, M. E. (1962). Classical conditioning in the fish: Further studies of partial reinforcement. *American Journal of Psychology, 75*, 421–428.

Greenwald, R. (1994). Eye movement desensitization and reprocessing (EMDR): An overview. *Journal of Contemporary Psychotherapy, 24(1)*, 15–34.

Hart, J. A., Bourne, M. J., & Schachtman, T. R. (1995). Slow reacquisition of conditioned taste aversion. *Animal Learning and Behavior, 23(3)*, 297–303.

Hawk, G., & Riccio, D. C. (1977). The effect of a conditioned fear inhibitor (CS–) during response prevention upon extinction of an avoidance response. *Behavior Research and Therapy, 15*, 97–101.

Holland, P. C. (1985). The nature of conditioned inhibition in serial and simultaneous feature negative discriminations. In R. R. Miller & N. E. Spear (eds.), *Information processing in animals: Conditioned inhibition*, 267–298. Hillsdale, N.J.: Erlbaum.

Holland, P. C. (1986). Temporal determinants of occasion setting in feature-positive discriminations. *Animal Learning and Behavior, 14*, 11–120.

Holland, P. C. (1989a). Acquisition and transfer of conditional discrimination performance. *Journal of Experimental Psychology: Animal Behavior Processes, 15(2)*, 154–165.

Holland, P. C. (1989b). Transfer of negative occasion setting and conditioned inhibition across conditioned and unconditioned stimuli. *Journal of Experimental Psychology: Animal Behavior Processes, 15(4)*, 311–328.

Holland, P. C. (1990). Forms of memory in Pavlovian conditioning. In J. L. McGaugh, N. M. Weinberger, & G. Lynch (eds.), *Brain organization and memory: Cells, systems and circuits*, 78–105. New York: Oxford University Press.

Holland, P. C., & Morell, J. R. (1993). Summation and transfer of negative occasion setting. *Animal Learning and Behavior, 21(2)*, 145–153.

Izquierdo, I., & Pereira, E. M. (1989). Post-training memory facilitation blocks extinction but not retroactive interference. *Behavioral and Neural Biology, 51*, 108–113.

Kamin, L. J. (1969). Predictability, surprise, attention and conditioning. In B. A. Campbell & R. M. Church (eds.), *Punishment and aversive behavior*, 279–296. New York: Appleton-Century-Crofts.

Konorski, J. (1948). *Conditioned reflexes and neuronal organization.* London: Cambridge University Press.

Konorski, J. (1967). *Integrative activity of the brain.* Chicago: University of Chicago Press.

Konorski, J., & Szwejkowska, G. (1950). Chronic extinction and restoration of conditioned reflexes: I. Extinction against the excitatory background. *Acta Biologiae Experimentalis, 15(12)*, 155–170.

Levis, D. J. (1985). Implosive theory: A comprehensive extension of conditioning theory of fear/anxiety to psychopathology. In S. Reisster & R. Bootzin (eds.), *Theoretical issues in behavior therapy*, 49-82. New York: Academic Press.

Levis, D. J. (1989). The case for a return to a two-factor theory of avoidance: The failure of non-fear interpretations. In S. B. Klein & R. R. Mowrer (eds.), *Contemporary learning theories: Pavlovian conditioning and the status of traditional learning theory*, 227–277. Hillsdale, N.J: Erlbaum.

Levis, D. J., & Boyd, T. L. (1979). Symptom maintenance: A infrahuman analysis and extension of the conservation of anxiety principle. *Journal of Abnormal Psychology, 88*, 107–120.

Longo, N., Milstein, S., & Bitterman, M. E. (1962). Classical conditioning in the pigeon: Exploratory studies of partial reinforcement. *Journal of Comparative and Physiological Psychology, 55*, 983–986.

Mackintosh, N. J. (1974). *The psychology of animal learning.* New York: Academic Press.

Malloy, P. F. (1981) *Incubation of human fear: Effects of UCS intensity, CS exposure, and individual differences.* Ph.D. dissertation, SUNY Binghamton.

McAllister, D. E., & McAllister, R. W. (1991). Fear theory and aversively motivated behavior: Some controversial issues. In M. R. Denny (ed.), *Fear, avoidance, and phobias:*

A fundamental analysis, 135–163. Hillsdale, N.J.: Erlbaum.

McAllister, W. R., & McAllister, D. E. (1992). Fear determines the effectiveness of a feedback stimulus in aversively motivated instrumental learning. *Learning and Motivation, 23,* 99–115.

McAllister, W. R., & McAllister, D. E. (1995). Two factor theory: Implications for understanding anxiety based clinical phenomena. In W. O'Donohue & L. Krasner (eds.), *Theories of behavior therapy: Exploring behavior change,* 145–171. Washington, D.C.: American Psychological Association.

McAllister, W. R., McAllister, D. E., Scoles, M. T., & Hampton, S. R. (1986). Persistence of fear-reducing behaviors: Relevance for the conditioning theory of neurosis. *Journal of Abnormal Psychology, 95,* 365–372.

McGaugh, J. L., Castellano, C., & Brioni, J. (1990). Picrotoxin enhances latent extinction of conditioned fear. *Behavioral Neuroscience, 104(2),* 264–267.

Miller, S., Mineka, S., & Cook, M. (1982). Comparison of various flooding procedures in reducing fear and in extinguishing jump avoidance responding. *Animal Learning and Behavior, 10(3),* 390–400.

Mineka, S., & Gino, A. (1979). Dissociative effects of different types and amounts of nonreinforced CS exposure on avoidance extinction and the CER. *Learning and Motivation, 10,* 149–160.

Mineka, S., & Gino, A. (1980). Dissociation between conditioned emotional response and extended avoidance performance. *Learning and Motivation, 11,* 476–502.

Mowrer, O. H. (1947). On the dual nature of learning—A reinterpretation of "conditioning" and "problem-solving." *Harvard Educational Review, 17,* 102–148.

Odling-smee, F. J. (1978). The overshadowing of background stimuli by an informative CS in aversive Pavlovian conditioning with rats. *Animal Learning and Behavior, 6,* 43–51.

Overton, D. A. (1966). State-dependent learning effects produced by depressants and atropine-like drugs. *Psychopharmacologia, 10,* 6–31.

Pavlov, I. P. (1927). *Conditioned reflexes.* Oxford: Oxford University Press.

Pearce, J. M., & Hall, G. (1980). A model of Pavlovian conditioning: Variations in the effectiveness of conditioned but not unconditioned stimuli. *Psychological Review, 87,* 332–352.

Reberg, D. (1972). Compound tests for excitation in early acquisition and after prolonged extinction of conditioned suppression. *Learning and Motivation, 3,* 246–258.

Rescorla, R. A. (1969). Pavlovian conditioned inhibition. *Psychological Bulletin, 72(2),* 77–94.

Rescorla, R. A. (1973). Second-order conditioning: Implications for theories of learning. In F. J. McGuigan & D. B. Lumsden (eds.), *Contemporary approaches to conditioning and learning,* 127–150. Washington, D.C.: V. H. Winston.

Rescorla, R. A. (1979). Conditioned inhibition and excitation. In A. Dickinson & R. A. Boakes (eds.), *Mechanisms of learning and motivation: A memorial volume to Jerzy Konorski,* 83–110. Hillsdale, N.J.: Erlbaum.

Rescorla, R. A. (1980). *Pavlovian second-order conditioning: Studies in associative learning.* Hillsdale, N.J.: Erlbaum.

Rescorla, R. A. (1985). Conditioned inhibition and facilitation. In R. R. Miller & N. E. Spear (eds.), *Information processing in animals: Conditioned inhibition,* 299–326. Hillsdale, N.J.: Erlbaum.

Rescorla, R. A. (1992). Associations between an instrumental discriminative stimulus and multiple outcomes. *Journal of Experimental Psychology: Animal Behavior Processes, 18(1),* 95–104.

Rescorla, R. A. (1993). Inhibitory associations between S and R in extinction. *Animal Learning and Behavior, 21(4),* 327–336.

Rescorla, R. A., & Cunningham, C. L. (1977). The erasure of reinstated fear. *Animal Learning and Behavior, 5(4),* 386–394.

Rescorla, R. A., & Heth, C. D. (1975). Reinstatement of fear to an extinguished conditioned stimulus. *Journal of Experimental Psychology: Animal Behavior Processes, 1,* 88–96.

Rescorla, R. A., & Skucy, J. C. (1969). Effect of response-independent reinforcers during extinction. *Journal of Comparative and Physiological Psychology, 67(3),* 381–389.

Rescorla, R. A., & Wagner, A. R. (1972). A theory of Pavlovian conditioning: Variations in the effectiveness of reinforcement and nonreinforcement. In A. H. Black & W. F. Prokasy (eds.), *Classical conditioning II: Current research and theory,* 64–99. New York: Appleton-Century-Crofts.

Richardson, R., Riccio, D. C., & Devine, L. (1984). ACTH-induced recovery of extinguished avoidance responding. *Physiological Psychology, 12,* 184–192.

Rodriguez, B. I., & Craske, M. G. (1993). The effects of distraction during exposure to phobic stimuli. *Behavioral Research and Therapy, 31(6),* 549–558.

Seligman, M. E. P., & Johnston, J. C. (1973). A cognitive theory of avoidance learning. In F. J. McGuigan & D. B. Lumsden (eds.), *Contemporary approaches to conditioning and learning,* 69–110. Washington, D.C: V. H. Winston.

Shapiro, F., Vogelmann-Sine, S., & Sine, L. (1994). Eye movement desensitization and reprocessing: Treating trauma and substance abuse. *Journal of Psychoactive Drugs, 26(4),* 379–391.

Shipley, R. H. (1974). Extinction of conditioned fear in rats as a function of several parameters of CS exposure. *Journal of Comparative and Physiological Psychology, 87,* 699–707.

Shipley, R. H., Mock, L. A., & Levis, D. J. (1971). Effects of several response prevention procedures on activity, avoidance responding and conditioned fear in rats. *Journal of Comparative and Physiological Psychology, 77*, 256–270.

Singh, R. (1976). Desensitization procedure employing external inhibition. *Journal of Behavior Therapy and Experimental Psychiatry, 7*, 379–380.

Skinner, B. F. (1950). Are theories of learning necessary? *Psychological Review, 57(4)*, 193–216.

Smith, M., & Gormezano, I. (1965). Effects of alternating classical conditioning and extinction sessions on the conditioned nictitating membrane response in the rabbit. *Psychonomic Science, 3*, 91–92.

Solomon, R. L., & Wynne, L. D. (1954). Traumatic avoidance learning: The principle of anxiety conservation and partial irreversibility. *Psychological Review, 61*, 353–385.

Southwick, S. M. et al. (in press). Abnormal noradrenergic function in posttraumatic stress disorder. *Archives of General Psychiatry.*

Spence, K. W. (1960). *Behavior theory and learning.* Englewood Cliffs, N.J.: Prentice-Hall.

Starr, M. D., & Mineka, S. (1977). Determinants of fear over the course of avoidance learning. *Learning and Motivation, 8*, 332–350.

Szwejkowska, G., & Konorski, J. (1952). Chronic extinction and restoration of conditioned reflexes: IV. The dependence of the course of extinction and restoration of conditioned reflexes on the "history" of the conditioned stimulus. *Acta Biologiae Experimentalis, 16*, 95–113.

Terrace, H. S. (1971). Escape from S–. *Learning and Motivation, 2*, 148–163.

Thomas, E., & Wagner, A. R. (1964). Partial reinforcement of classically conditioned eyelid responses in the rabbit. *Journal of Comparative and Physiological Psychology, 58*, 157–158.

Wagner, A. R. (1963). Conditioned frustration as a learned drive. *Journal of Experimental Psychology, 66*, 142–148.

Wagner, A. R. (1969). Stimulus selection and a "modified continuity theory." In G. H. Bower & J. T. Spence (eds.), The *psychology of learning and motivation*, 1–41. New York: Academic Press.

Wagner, A. R. (1980). S.O.P: A model of automatic memory processing in animal behavior. In N. E. Spear & R. R. Miller (eds.), *Information processing in animals: Memory mechanisms*, 5–47. Hillsdale, N.J.: Erlbaum.

Wagner, A. R., & Rescorla, R. A. (1972). Inhibition in Pavlovian conditioning. In R. A. Boakes & M. S. Halliday (eds.), *Inhibition and learning*, 301–336. London: Academic Press.

Wagner, A. R., Siegel, S., & Fein, G. G. (1967). Extinction of conditioned fear as a function of percentage of reinforcement. *Journal of Comparative and Physiological Psychology, 63(1)*, 160–164.

Wagner, A. R., Siegel, S., Thomas, E., & Ellison, G. D. (1964). Reinforcement history and the extinction of a conditioned salivary response. *Journal of Comparative and Physiological Psychology, 58(3)*, 354–358.

Williams, R. W., & Levis, D. J. (1991). A demonstration of persistent human avoidance in extinction. *Bulletin of the Psychonomic Society, 29(2)*, 125–127.

CHAPTER 12

CHOICE AND MOMENTUM

John A. Nevin

What proportion of a person's behavior is likely to be devoted to a response of social or clinical significance, whether it be desirable or undesirable? And how persistent is that response likely to be in different circumstances? This chapter will review basic research on the allocation of behavior between alternatives under constant conditions, including cases where only one alternative is well defined. It will also review research on the persistence of responding when behavior is disrupted by a change of conditions. Finally, it will discuss some applications of these findings in clinical situations.

The allocation of responding between two or more well-defined alternatives—hereafter termed *choice,* without implying that organisms actively select and initiate their own behavior—and the rate of responding when only one alternative is defined, are both encompassed by a single formulation of behavior in relation to relative rates of reinforcement known as *the matching law* (Herrn-

stein, 1970). The matching law describes behavior under constant, stable conditions, but the real world is anything but constant. The next question is how reinforcement schedules affect resistance to change—characterized, metaphorically, as behavioral momentum—when conditions are altered. Research suggests that steady-state choice and response rates depend primarily on response-reinforcer relations, whereas resistance to change depends primarily on stimulus-reinforcer relations (Nevin, 1992b). The clinical implications of this distinction are especially important.

CHOICE AND MATCHING

Paradigms

The classic study of free-operant choice behavior was conducted by Herrnstein (1961), who trained food-deprived pigeons to peck at either of two lighted keys for food reinforcers. Food was scheduled intermittently according to two variable-interval (VI) schedules that operated concurrently and independently. One arranged reinforcers for the first peck on one key after an unpredictable time averaging t_1 seconds, and the other arranged reinforcers for pecks on the other key after times averaging t_2 seconds. Each VI value can be translated into a reinforcer rate: for example, a VI schedule with an average of 40 seconds between reinforcers arranges 90 reinforcers per hour. Throughout this chapter, VI schedule values will be specified as *reinforcer rates*.

In Herrnstein's (1961) experiment, a pair of VI schedules remained in effect until performance stabilized—usually about 30 daily sessions. Over the course of the experiment, different pairs of schedules, chosen so that the sum of the reinforcer rates programmed by the two schedules was constant, were arranged in successive conditions. When reinforcers could be obtained only after a brief delay from the first peck at either key following a peck at the other key—a so-called changeover delay or COD—the results were strikingly orderly: the proportion of pecks at each key approximately equalled the proportion of reinforcers obtained from that key. The data, shown in Figure 12–1, are well described by a simple equation, known as the matching law:

$$B_1/(B_1 + B_2) = r_1/(r_1 + r_2), \qquad (1)$$

where B_1 and B_2 represent the number of pecks emitted on keys 1 and 2, and r_1 and r_2 represent the number of reinforcers obtained by pecks on keys 1 and 2. This result and subsequent extensions provided the basis for Herrnstein's (1970) formulation of matching to relative reinforcement as a general law of behavior.

There are two features of concurrent VI VI schedules that must be appreciated in relation to the matching result. First, the probability of reinforcement for switching to an alternative increases with time spent away from it. Thus, as a subject continues to respond to the richer of the two schedules, at some time the probability of reinforcement for switching to the leaner schedule will be higher than for staying with the richer

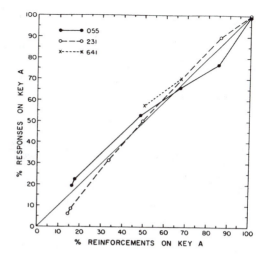

Figure 12–1. The proportion of responses made to one of two keys as a function of the proportion of food reinforcers received on that key, as arranged by concurrent VI VI schedules for three pigeons. The diagonal line indicates exact matching. From Herrnstein (1961).

schedule, thus encouraging responding to both alternatives. No such contingency operates in concurrent variable-ratio (VR) schedules: if the schedules differ, one alternative always has a higher probability of reinforcement than the other, and subjects usually respond exclusively to the richer alternative (Herrnstein & Loveland, 1975)—a result that is trivially compatible with Equation 1 because either B_1 and r_1 or B_2 and r_2 are zero.

Second, the high probability of reinforcement for switching on concurrent VI VI schedules makes switching very likely. When there was no COD in Herrnstein's (1961) experiment, the birds switched back and forth between the keys several thousand times in each session and distributed their pecks about equally between the two keys. The COD delayed reinforcement after each switch, thereby reducing switching rates and promoting independence of the two schedules. The role of the COD in concurrent-schedule performance is discussed at length in a comprehensive review of the matching law by Davison and McCarthy (1988).

An earlier experiment by Findley (1958), also using pigeons as subjects, arranged food reinforcers for pecks at a single key according to concurrent VI VI schedules. However, reinforcers could be obtained from only one schedule at a time, depending on the color of the food key. The pigeons could alternate between colors by pecking a second, "switching" key, and thus obtain all reinforcers from both schedules on the food key. The procedure is particularly well suited to measuring time spent engaged in one or the other alternative, defined by key-color time. Findley's paradigm has come to be known as the *switching-key* procedure, whereas Herrnstein's has been termed the *two-key* procedure for studying concurrent operants. By and large, the results of these two procedures are similar.

A third paradigm, introduced by Autor (1960/1969), separated choice between schedules of reinforcement from the behavior that obtains food reinforcers. In Autor's procedure, which is termed *concurrent-chain schedules*, identical concurrent VI VI schedules were arranged on two white keys, defining the initial links of the concurrent chains. The initial-link schedules were arranged as in Herrnstein's (1961) study, but without a COD. When a reinforcer was available on one key, a peck at that key produced a change of key color—to red, for example—instead of food, and the other key was darkened. Further pecks on the red key were reinforced with food according to a VI schedule. The red key and its correlated food schedule defined one terminal link; a different terminal link—correlated with green, for example—was produced by pecks at the other key during the initial links. The concurrent initial links were reinstated after food was presented; hence, the terminal links differed in the average delay to food. The reciprocal of delay is termed *immediacy,* and average immediacy is equivalent to rate of food presentation.

Concurrent chains may be viewed as two-key concurrent schedules of conditioned reinforcement, where the conditioned reinforcing values of the terminal-link stimuli depend on the immediacies of food reinforcement arranged by the VI schedules in their presence. Autor varied the terminal-link schedules over successive conditions and found that the distribution of initial-link key pecks matched the relative immediacy (or rate) of food in the terminal links. Thus, early research suggested that the matching law provided an excellent account of food-reinforced choice behavior of pigeons in three related paradigms.

Generality of Matching

The matching result for choice has remarkable generality. For example, matching to the relative duration of food provided by equal concurrent VI VI schedules has been observed with pigeons in the two-key and switching-key paradigms (Brownstein, 1971; Catania, 1963). Matching has also been obtained with rats, monkeys, and humans in experiments employing a variety of different responses and reinforcers, including electrical brain stimulation, drugs, and points exchangeable for money (for review, see Davison & McCarthy, 1988; de Villiers, 1977; Williams, 1988).

An experiment by Conger and Killeen (1974) is of special interest because it employed human subjects in a social setting. College undergraduates were studied one at a time in conversation with three "plants" designated E_1, E_2, and E_3. E_3 engaged the subject in conversation, and E_1 and E_2 provided verbal reinforcers such as "that's a good point" whenever a VI schedule, cued separately for E_1 and E_2 in such a way as to be hidden from the subject, had timed out and the subject had made some comment to E_1 or E_2. In the first half of the 30-minute session, E_1 provided 70% of the scheduled reinforcers while E_2 provided 30%; their roles were reversed for the second half of the session. The principal measure was the proportion of time that the subject spent talking to E_1 or E_2, who were, in effect, playing the roles of the two keys in Herrnstein's (1961) experiment described previously. When the results were pooled for all five subjects, Equation 1 was confirmed almost exactly. The data were more variable than those of Figure 12–1, probably because exposure to the schedules was so brief, but they strongly suggest that the matching law, which was identified for hungry pigeons pecking keys for food under tightly controlled conditions, appears to be equally valid for humans conversing in a relatively uncontrolled social setting.

Choice in Novel Combinations

Several investigators have asked whether matching holds for alternatives that have been trained separately. For example, suppose a pigeon has obtained food on a VI schedule by pecking a red key, and has also obtained food on a different VI schedule by pecking a green key, where the experimenter has presented red and green keys successively for fixed periods of time and there is no possibility of choice between them. This procedure is known as a *multiple* schedule, and each stimulus-schedule combination defines a multiple-schedule component. How would the bird's pecks be distributed when red and green are presented together for the first time?

Edmon, Lucki, and Grisham (1980) addressed this question by training pigeons on multiple-schedule components with different VI values on the left and right keys, where the components were presented in strict alternation for 1-minute periods. When baseline response rate in one component was expressed relative to the sum of rates in both components, the response-rate proportion was less extreme than the reinforcer-rate proportion—a common result in multiple schedules (see below). When the two keys were lighted simultaneously in choice probe tests, however, the allocation of responding was more extreme than predicted by matching. Herrnstein and Loveland (1976) also oberved overmatching in a novel-pairs probe test after training with various pairs of stimuli in concurrent schedules, and vom Saal (1972) obtained similar results in probe choice tests after training with a discrete-trial procedure. Thus, the matching law may systematically underestimate choice between alternatives that have been experienced separately.

Generalized Matching

Although matching is a common result for steady-state performance on concurrent VI VI schedules, choice allocation sometimes deviates from the strict matching relation of Equation 1 (see Baum, 1979, for review). Deviations from matching are well described by the expression:

$$B_1/B_2 = c(r_1/r_2)^a, \qquad (2)$$

where B_1 and B_2 represent the behavior allocated to alternatives 1 and 2, measured as pecks or time allocation and defined either by key position or the stimulus on the food key; r_1 and r_2 represent the reinforcers for the two alternatives; c represents a bias toward one alternative or the other, such as a position or stimulus preference that is constant across all reinforcement conditions; and a represents the sensitivity of the behavior ratio to the reinforcer ratio. Equation 2 is known as the *generalized matching law* (Baum, 1974), and it describes the relation between ratios of response and reinforcer rates in multiple as well as concurrent schedules (Davison & McCarthy, 1988; McSweeney, Farmer, Dougan, & Whipple, 1986).

The generalized matching law is often expressed in logarithmic form:

$$log\ (B_1/B_2) = log\ c + a\ log\ (r_1/r_2) \qquad (3)$$

because it is easy to estimate the parameters c and a by linear regression of log behavior ratios on log reinforcer ratios. The fitted slope estimates a, and the intercept, where the log reinforcer ratio is 0 (i.e., $r_1 = r_2$), estimates log c. If the ratio of responses exactly equals the ratio of reinforcers, the values of a and log c will be 1.0 and 0, respectively, and Equation 3 reduces mathematically to strict matching, as found by Herrnstein (1961). When a is 1.0 but log c deviates from 0, the result is known as *biased matching*. When a is reliably less than or greater than 1.0, the results are termed *undermatching* or *overmatching*, respectively. Some hypothetical data illustrating various values of c and a are shown in Figure 12–2.

The distinction between bias (c) and sensitivity (a) is especially important in applied situations that provide limited data. For example, suppose the experimenter arranges reinforcers in a 3:1 ratio for two alternative responses, and the subject re-

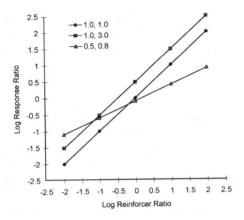

Figure 12–2. Hypothetical choice data illustrating different values of sensitivity and bias in a logarithmic expression of the generalized matching law, Equation 3. Exact matching results when both *a* and *c* are 1.0. When *a* is 1.0 and *c* is 3.0, the function is shifted upward, representing biased matching. When *a* is 0.5 and *c* is 0.8, the function is shallower and shifted downward from the origin (0,0), representing undermatching with a small bias.

sponds in a 2:1 ratio. From this result, one cannot determine whether response allocation is biased away from the more frequently reinforced response, or whether it undermatches the reinforcer ratio. At a minimum, response allocation must be measured at two different reinforcer ratios to estimate *c* and *a,* and at least five reinforcer ratios are customarily employed in basic research. When the parameters *c* and *a* are estimated reliably, they may be construed as higher-order dependent variables that characterize choice behavior under a given set of experimental conditions, and that may be related in an orderly way to quantifiable aspects of those conditions.

Some Determiners of Bias and Sensitivity in Research on Choice

A great deal of research, summarized by Davison and McCarthy (1988), has attempted to identify the determiners of *c* and *a* in Equation 2, and to evaluate their independence. A few examples will be reviewed here. In a two-response proce-

dure, pigeons' choice is strongly biased toward key pecking when the alternative response is lever pressing, although time allocation is less biased, perhaps because lever pressing is more awkward and time-consuming (Davison & Ferguson, 1978). Bias also depends on qualitative differences in the reinforcers provided by the alternatives (e.g., type of grain: Miller, 1976; food vs. brain stimulation: Hollard & Davison, 1971). The biasing effects of response type and reinforcer quality did not affect sensitivity in these examples.

In concurrent switching-key schedules, sensitivity increases when the stimuli defining the alternatives are made more distinctive (Alsop & Davison, 1991; Miller, Saunders, & Bourland, 1980). This is not surprising because, in the limit, sensitivity to reinforcer ratios must be zero when the alternatives are indistinguishable. The distinctiveness of the alternatives may also be enhanced by increasing the effort required to switch between them. For example, in a switching-key procedure, the allocation of time to an alternative became more extreme than matching (i.e., *a* > 1.0 or overmatching) when the number of responses required to switch between alternatives was increased (Pliskoff, Cicerone, & Nelson, 1978). Likewise, in a two-key procedure, strong overmatching (*a* >> 1.0) resulted when substantial distance and effort were required to travel between the food keys (Baum, 1982). It may be that any variable promoting separation between concurrent alternatives will enhance sensitivity to the reinforcer ratio and lead to overmatching.

Effects of Reinforcement Parameters

The matching law was extended to incorporate the effects of reinforcer amount and immediacy by Baum and Rachlin (1969) and Killeen (1972). A generalized version, in which each variable is expressed as a ratio and raised to a power that characterizes sensitivity to that variable, was suggested by Davison and McCarthy (1988):

$$B_1/B_2 = c(r_1/r_2)^a \, (m_1/m_2)^b \, (i_1/i_2)^d \qquad (4)$$

where m and i represent the amounts and immediacies of reinforcement, subscripted for the two alternatives. This equation implies that each dimension of reinforcement affects choice independently, and that they combine multiplicatively (or additively in a logarithmic version).

If reinforcer amounts and delays are unequal but remain constant while reinforcer rates are varied, they are mathematically equivalent to the bias term c. Thus, Equation 4 implies that sensitivity to reinforcer ratios, a, will be unaffected by other aspects of reinforcement, and conversely that sensitivity to other variables such as amount will be unaffected by reinforcer ratios.

Several findings have challenged this implication. For example, Davison (1988) found that sensitivity to reinforcer amount decreased as reinforcer rate increased. More generally, Equation 4 implies that choice allocation depends on the ratios of reinforcement variables and not their absolute values. However, Logue and Chavarro (1987) found that response ratios decreased when absolute amounts increased in a constant 3:1 ratio (with reinforcer rates held constant and equal), and that response ratios increased when total reinforcer rate increased with a fixed 3:1 reinforcer rate ratio. Alsop and Elliffe (1988) confirmed the latter result in a parametric study that varied both absolute and relative reinforcer rate: as absolute reinforcer rate increased, sensitivity to reinforcer ratios also increased. Therefore, a full account of choice behavior must consider absolute as well as relative values of reinforcer rate and amount. The achievement of such an account remains a challenge for the future.

Generalized Matching in Concurrent Chains

Systematic deviations from strict matching in concurrent chain VI VI schedules of the sort first studied by Autor (see above) were reported by Fantino (1969). His experiment varied the lengths of the two equal initial links with terminal-link delays of 30 and 90 seconds. Matching was obtained with initial links of moderate length, but when the initial links were very long,

initial-link choice approached indifference between the terminal-link schedules, and when the initial links were short, it approached exclusive preference for the richer terminal link. Thus, matching appears as a point on a continuum, depending on the temporal context in which the terminal links are set.

Grace (1994) has extended the generalized matching law to describe concurrent-chains performance. His model is:

$$B_{i1}/B_{i2} = c(r_{i1}/r_{i2})^{a_i} [(i_{t1}/i_{t2})(x_{t1}/x_{t2})]^{a_t(T_t/T_i)}, \quad (5)$$

where B_{i1} and B_{i2} represent responding in the initial links, r_{i1} and r_{i2} represent the rates of entry into the terminal links arranged by the initial-link schedules (which are usually equal), i_{t1} and i_{t2} represent the immediacies of food reinforcement in the terminal links, x_{t1} and x_{t2} represent other factors that influence terminal-link value such as reinforcer amount, T_t and T_i represent the average durations of the terminal and initial links, and a_i and a_t represent the sensitivities of initial-link allocation to the ratios of initial-link and terminal-link reinforcer rates, respectively. The exponent (T_t/T_i) captures the effects of relative initial-link and terminal-link length on initial-link preference reported by Fantino (1969). Grace (1994) showed that the model provided an excellent account of a wide range of published findings, and Grace (1995a) applied his equation to data on choice between terminal links that differed in both immediacy and amount of reinforcement to show that the effects of these variables were independent.

Is Matching Normative?

In view of all the empirically determined a-values that depart systematically from 1.0, it is hard to maintain the proposition that strict matching is truly general. Nevertheless, strict matching to the relative value of the alternatives may be normative for all situations, with deviations resulting from suboptimal selection of procedural variables by the experimenter or from failures of discrimination by the subject (Baum, 1979; Davison & Jenkins, 1985).

If strict matching is assumed, the parameters of the generalized matching law may be used to scale relative value. For example, consider a hypothetical experiment in which response ratios match reinforcer-rate ratios across a series of concurrent VI VI schedules for a given subject. Then, in the next phase of this hypothetical experiment, reinforcer rates are kept equal and constant while the amounts of food are varied independently for the two alternatives. If the ratio of responses is related to the ratio of reinforcer amounts according to Equation 4, with $b = 0.5$, one could argue that the subjects were matching their choices to the relative value of food, and that relative value is itself a power function of relative amount with an exponent of 0.5. This conjecture could be tested by arranging novel combinations of reinforcer rates and amounts, and using Equation 4 to predict response ratios (for a full discussion, see Killeen, 1972).

Relatedly, matching may be taken as an axiom for theory development. For example, the assumption of strict matching was used by Fantino (1969) to develop the delay-reduction theory of conditioned reinforcement, and thereby to explain the effects of relative initial-link and terminal-link length in concurrent chains (described above). Fantino assumed that subjects matched their initial-link choices to the relative reduction in delay to the reinforcer signaled by onset of the terminal-link stimuli. In equation form,

$$B_{i1}/B_{i2} = (T - t_1)/(T - t_2), \qquad (6)$$

where B_{i1} and B_{i2} represent initial-link responses to alternatives 1 and 2, t_1 and t_2 represent the average times from terminal-link onset to food, and T is the overall time between food reinforcers averaged over both links for both alternatives. Thus, $(T - t_1)$ and $(T - t_2)$ represent the reduction in delay to food signaled by the terminal-link stimuli, which Fantino has equated with their conditioned reinforcing value. Delay-reduction theory accounts well for performance in a wide variety of procedures involving signaled delays to reinforcement (see Fantino, Preston, & Dunn, 1993, for a recent review).

The predictions of delay-reduction theory are generally similar to those of Grace's (1994) model (Equation 5). However, delay-reduction theory implies that the conditioned reinforcing values of the terminal-link stimuli depend on the temporal context in which they appear, whereas Grace's model implies that conditioned reinforcing values depend only on the delays to reinforcement in their presence, with temporal context modulating preference between them. Grace's (1995b, Experiment 4) data generally support the independence of value from temporal context. Because applied work often relies on conditioned reinforcers, it is important to understand the determiners of their value.

Theoretical Explanations of Matching

Concurrent VI VI schedules may interact with behavior to produce matching as a byproduct of some more fundamental process. For example, if subjects follow the local probability of reinforcement as it changes through time spent on one or the other schedule (see above), they should switch between VI alternatives in a predictable pattern that closely approximates overall matching. Shimp (1966) examined sequential patterns of responding in a discrete-trial two-key choice experiment that mimicked this aspect of concurrent VI VI schedules, and found that his subjects tended to respond to whichever key had the momentarily higher probability of reinforcement. This pattern of responding, termed *momentary maximizing,* leads to matching on concurrent VI VI schedules (Shimp, 1966; Staddon, Hinson, & Kram, 1981). However, the pattern reported by Shimp has not always been found in related studies (e.g., Heyman, 1979; Nevin, 1969), so the empirical basis for momentary maximizing is less well established than the matching result it was supposed to explain.

Rachlin, Green, Kagel, and Battalio (1976) suggested a different account of matching known as *molar maximizing.* In concurrent VI VI schedules, subjects can obtain more reinforcers by responding to both alternatives than if they respond exclusively to either one; therefore, switching between alternatives tends to maximize total reinforcement. Some plausible assumptions about the relation between the allocation of responding to each alternative and the number of reinforcers obtained from that alternative, known as the *molar feedback function* for VI schedules (see below), lead theoretically to matching as the allocation that maximizes total reinforcement (e.g., Baum, 1981; Staddon & Motheral, 1978). However, experiments designed specifically to pit matching against molar maximizing have usually found that the allocation of behavior roughly matches relative obtained reinforcement even when matching leads to a substantial loss of total reinforcement (e.g., Mazur, 1981; Vaughan, 1981).

Herrnstein and Vaughan (1980) have proposed a third account of choice behavior, termed *meliorizing,* that emphasizes the local rates of reinforcement, defined as reinforcers obtained per unit time spent engaged in each alternative. Response allocation is assumed to shift toward the alternative with the greater local reinforcer rate, and becomes stable when neither alternative has a greater local reinforcer rate than the other, that is:

$$r_1/t_1 = r_2/t_2, \tag{7}$$

where t_1 and t_2 represent the times spent on the two alternatives. (Note that Equation 7 implies strict matching.)

Meliorizing accounts for performance on concurrent VR VR and VI VR as well as VI VI schedules. However, some predictions of meliorizing have been disconfirmed by Williams and Royalty (1989). They presented alternatives that differed in both local and overall reinforcer rates in probe tests with novel pairs, and found that response allocation was based on overall rather than local rates of reinforcement.

In a review of recent theoretical developments in the study of choice, Williams (1994) concluded that "none of the major theories can presently explain all of the available data" (p. 105). However, the failure of any theory to explain all of the data should not lead applied re-

searchers to dismiss the issues raised by theoretical analyses. For example, momentary maximizing theory calls attention to the importance of how choice behavior interacts with moment-to-moment schedule contingencies, and molar maximizing theory does likewise for long-term outcomes. Meliorizing provides a way to understand failures of molar maximizing and thus is directly relevant to real-world problems that involve some incompatibility between short-term satisfaction and long-term optimality. In effect, meliorizing subjects treat the alternatives as mutually exclusive and choose one or the other on the basis of current differences in their value, rather than choosing between different distributions of behavior to both alternatives on the basis of total value. Thus, meliorizing may help us to understand behavior in situations where choice of a small immediate reinforcer entails the loss of more highly valued but delayed outcomes—situations that are said to require "self-control" and have obvious relevance to many social and clinical problems (see Chapter 13).

Single-Alternative Choice

Many experimental analyses of operant behavior define only one response class, such as lever pressing or key pecking, and examine the rate of responding as a function of the schedule of reinforcement. Herrnstein (1970) suggested that even when only one defined response is eligible for reinforcement, the situation may still be construed as involving choice between that response and unmeasured activities (such as scratching or defecating), designated B_O, that are maintained by naturally occurring reinforcers (such as relief of discomfort), designated r_O. Herrnstein assumed that behavior was allocated between the experimentally defined response B, reinforced according to some schedule at a rate r, and B_O, maintained by r_O, so as to match relative obtained reinforcement. In the form of Equation 1,

$$B/(B + B_O) = r/(r + r_O). \tag{8}$$

Herrnstein further assumed that the sum of all available activities, $B + B_O$, was a constant, designated k and measured in units of the defined response. Inserting the assumed constancy into Equation 5 and rearranging,

$$B = kr/(r + r_0). \qquad (9)$$

According to Equation 9, which is known as Herrnstein's hyperbola or the relative law of effect, the rate of the defined response depends on the rate of reinforcers obtained by that response relative to all reinforcers, including unspecified reinforcers occurring in the situation.

As we have seen, many studies of concurrent operants have challenged the key assumption of strict matching, and several findings have challenged the constancy of k (e.g., McDowell & Wood, 1984). Also, Equation 9 breaks down at very high reinforcer rates or in long experimental sessions (Baum, 1993; McSweeney, 1992). However, it describes response rates maintained by VI schedules in studies with pigeons, rats, monkeys, and humans quite closely in most situations. It also accounts well for the effects of the magnitude of both positive and negative reinforcers in discrete-trial as well as free-operant procedures, and thus provides a good first approximation to a general law of behavior (see de Villiers, 1977, for review and discussion).

Expressions that are mathematically similar to Equation 9 can be derived from other sets of assumptions (e.g., Catania, 1973; Killeen, 1994; Staddon, 1977), but whatever its derivation, Equation 9 captures three important aspects of operant behavior. First, response rate is a monotonically increasing, negatively accelerated function of reinforcement rate or amount, exemplifying diminishing returns as response rate nears k, its asymptote. Second, the rate of approach to asymptote depends on the availability of other reinforcers in the situation. And third, response rate maintained by a given schedule may be increased or decreased by changing the rate of reinforcement from other sources. These features of Equation 9 are illustrated in Figure 12–3 and should be appreciated by anyone concerned with performance in clinical settings, schools, or the workplace.

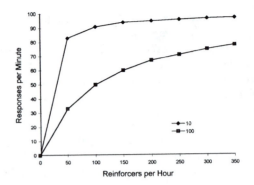

Figure 12-3. Hypothetical data showing the relation between response rate and reinforcer rate according to Herrnstein's hyperbola (Equation 9). When $r_O = 10$, the function reaches its asymptote at $k = 100$ more rapidly than when $r_O = 100$. Note that an increase in r_O from 10 to 100 reduces responding substantially more at low than at high rates of reinforcement.

Response Rate in Concurrent and Multiple Schedules

Equation 9 can be written separately to give the response rates of two concurrent operants, where experimentally specified reinforcers are arranged for each operant:

$$B_1 = kr_1/(r_1 + r_2 + r_0), \text{ and} \qquad (10)$$
$$B_2 = kr_2/(r_2 + r_1 + r_0).$$

If these separate expressions for response rate are divided, k and r_0 cancel out, leaving a ratio version of the matching law:

$$B_1/B_2 = r_1/r_2.$$

Thus, matching in concurrent schedules may be seen as the outcome of a process whereby the rate of each response is determined by the reinforcers for that response relative to all concurrently available reinforcers in the situation.

Herrnstein (1970) suggested that if two operants are arranged successively, as in the components of multiple schedules, Equation 10 may be written:

$$B_1 = kr_1/(r_1 + mr_2 + r_0), \text{ and} \qquad (11)$$
$$B_2 = kr_2/(r_2 + mr_1 + r_0),$$

where B_1 and B_2 represent response rates and r_1 and r_2 represent reinforcer rates in Components 1 and 2, r_0 represents the rate of unmeasured reinforcers, and m is a parameter taking values from 0 to 1.0 that characterizes the extent to which reinforcers in one component affect responding in the other component. Although Equation 10 fails in some situations (see Williams & Wixted, 1986, for review), it predicts that if $m < 1.0$, response-rate ratios undermatch reinforcer-rate ratios, which is the usual result. It also predicts, correctly, that response rate in one component of a multiple schedule depends on its rate of reinforcement relative to that in the alternated component (for summary, see Nevin, 1973). Thus, as for each alternative in a concurrent schedule, response rate in a multiple-schedule component depends on the context of reinforcement in which it is set.

RESISTANCE TO CHANGE

A Representative Experiment

Multiple schedules are especially useful for the study of resistance to change because components are presented at times and in an order chosen by the experimenter, independently of the subject's behavior, and two or more performances can be compared within subjects and sessions. For example, Nevin (1974, Experiment 1) trained pigeons to peck a single key for food reinforcers, where the key was lighted either red or green for 1-minute periods. When the key was red, a VI schedule arranged 60 reinforcers per hour, and when the key was green, an independent VI schedule arranged 20 reinforcers per hour. Components were separated by a 30-second time-out. After 30 sessions of baseline training, responding was disrupted in brief probe tests of resistance to change by presenting food at various rates, independently of responding, during the time-out periods between components. Response rates during resistance tests were expressed as proportions of baseline. The results are summarized in Figure 12–4, with proportions of baseline plotted on a logarithmic scale. This has the effect of mak-

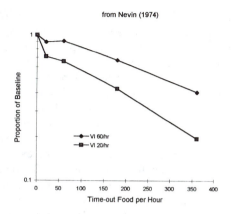

from Nevin (1974)

Figure 12–4. Average data for four pigeons trained on multiple VI schedules arranging 60 and 20 reinforcers per hour in two alternating components, showing the effects of presenting food during time-outs between components in probe tests. At every time-out food rate, response rate decreased less, relative to baseline, in the richer component. Note that the y-axis is logarithmic. Adapted from Nevin (1974, Experiment 1).

ing the functions roughly linear; the ratio of the slopes of these functions can be used to quantify relative resistance to change (Nevin, 1992b; Nevin, Mandell, & Atak, 1983). For present purposes, it suffices to note that at every time-out food rate, the decrease was smaller, relative to baseline, in the richer multiple-schedule component. Nevin (1974, Experiment 3) also found that resistance to time-out food was positively related to reinforcer duration in components with the same reinforcer rate. Thus, it appears that rate and amount of reinforcement have similar effects on resistance to change as well as on choice behavior.

Generality

When pigeons are trained on multiple schedules that differ in reinforcer rate or amount, and resistance to change is evaluated by applying some disruptor equally to the two components, response rate nearly always decreases less, relative to baseline, avoid reforming with the greater rate or amount of reinforcement. For example, Bouzas (1978) trained pigeons on multiple VI VI schedules yielding 60 and 15 reinforcers per hour in the two components and then introduced a VI schedule of punishment that superimposed 120 electric shocks per hour in both components. He found a smaller relative reduction in the richer component. The same result has been obtained with signaled unavoidable shocks (Lyon, 1963), with presession feedings (Eckerman, 1968) or variations in body weight (Herrnstein & Loveland, 1974), with increases in the number of responses required for reinforcement (Elsmore, 1971), and with the discontinuation of reinforcement in both components (extinction—Nevin, 1974, Experiment 2; Nevin, 1988; see Chapter 11). Comparable findings have been obtained with rats, monkeys, and humans (see below and Nevin, 1979).

Research with single schedules has yielded some similar results. For example, Church and Raymond (1967) trained one group of rats on a single VI schedule providing 300 reinforcers per hour, and another on a single VI schedule providing 18 reinforcers per hour. When response rates were disrupted by superimposing a VI schedule of 30 brief electric shocks per hour, there was a substantially smaller reduction, relative to baseline, for the group with the richer VI schedule, a result similar to that of Bouzas (1978) for pigeons on multiple schedules. However, there have been some failures to obtain the usual multiple-schedule results with single schedules. Cohen, Riley, and Weigle (1993; see also Cohen, Furman, Crouse, & Kroner, 1990) have reported consistent failures to find differences in resistance to response-independent food, prefeeding, or extinction in rats or pigeons trained on a variety of single schedules differing in reinforcer rate; indeed, they found that resistance to extinction was often greater for the leaner schedules. In related multiple-schedule experiments, however, they generally obtained greater resistance to change in the richer component. These findings suggest an important role for within-session alternation of stimuli signaling different conditions of reinforcement, and are especially important for applications designed to maximize resistance to change.

Two multiple-schedule experiments with human subjects have confirmed the usual find-

ings of greater resistance in the richer component. Mace, Lalli, Shea, Lalli, West, Roberts, and Nevin (1990) instructed adults with mental retardation to sort two colored sets of plastic dinnerware successively, and arranged a rich VI schedule of popcorn or coffee reinforcers for sorting one color and a lean VI schedule for sorting the other. In effect, the colors defined the components of a multiple schedule. There was no difference in baseline sorting rates, but when a television set was turned on, sorting was less disrupted for the color correlated with the richer schedule. Cohen, (1996) reported a similar result for college students typing at a computer terminal with points toward course credit as reinforcers. A rich VI schedule of points was arranged when the screen was one color, and a lean schedule when it was a different color. Again, there was no difference in baseline typing rates, but typing was more resistant to distraction by an alternative task (finding a cartoon character in a picture book) when the screen signaled the richer schedule. The results for representative individual human subjects are presented in the left column of Figure 12–5, together with results for a representative pigeon. Their similarity suggests that the findings of laboratory research on resistance to change with nonhuman subjects in tightly controlled conditions are valid also for humans in relatively natural settings.

Resistance to Change and the Matching Law

Nevin's (1974, Experiment 1) results, described above and shown in Figure 12–4, are consistent with Herrnstein's (1970) extension of the single-alternative matching law to multiple schedules, Equation 11. If r_{TO}, representing the rate of time-out food, is added to the denominator of the expression for each component, its decremental effect on response rate in a given component, relative to baseline, depends inversely on the rate of reinforcement in that component. More generally, Equation 11 can account at least ordinally for all the resistance findings summarized above if any disruptor reduces the rate of the measured response through increases

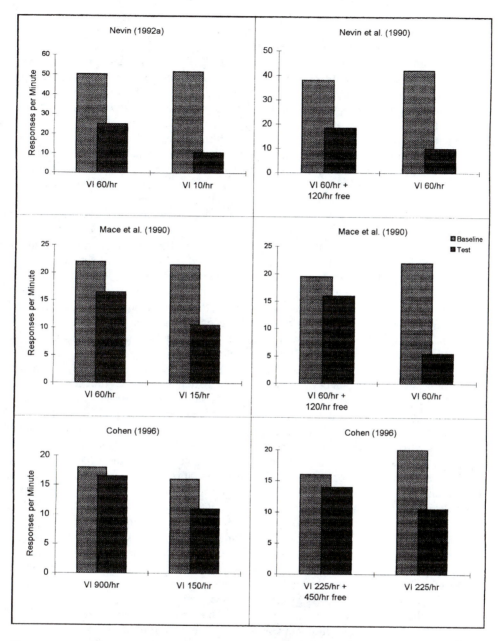

Figure 12–5. Baseline and resistance test data for individual subjects on multiple schedules of reinforcement. The top panels represent key pecking by two pigeons; the center panels represent sorting by S1, an adult with mental retardation; and the bottom panels represent typing by the median undergraduate in two experiments. The left column gives the data for baseline and resistance tests in multiple VI VI schedules where the components differ in VI reinforcer rate. The right column gives the data for baseline and resistance tests in equal multiple VI VI schedules, where free reinforcers have been added to one component. In every case, responding is more resistant to change in the component with the higher total reinforcer rate, regardless of whether all reinforcers were contingent on responding or the ordering of baseline response rates. Adapted from Nevin et al. (1990, Experiment 1); Nevin et al. (1992a, Experiment 2); Mace et al. (1990, Experiments 1 and 2); and Cohen (1996, Experiments 1 and 2).

in some other source of reinforcement, either measured (as in the case of time-out food) or unmeasured (as for punishment or prefeeding). The effects of extinction can be explained similarly by arguing that the relative value of unmeasured reinforcers increases with time since the termination of scheduled reinforcers. Thus, Herrnstein's (1970) formulation, suitably interpreted, can account for many aspects of resistance to change.

However, several findings argue for a separate account. Nevin, Tota, Torquato, and Shull (1990, Experiment 1) arranged identical VI schedules of food reinforcement for pigeons in two multiple-schedule components, and also provided response-independent food on variable-time (VT) schedules in one of those components throughout training. Baseline response rate in the component with added VT food was consistently lower than in the VI-only component, as predicted by Equation 9, since the VT food would contribute to reinforcement for behavior other than key pecking. Another way to explain the lower rate is that added VT food weakens the contingency between pecking and food, in that food is not uniquely contingent on pecking in the VI plus VT component. By contrast, added VT food strengthens the stimulus-reinforcer contingency, in that the stimulus for the VI plus VT component is better correlated with food than the stimulus for the VI-only component. Tests of resistance to prefeeding and to extinction showed that response rate was reduced less, relative to baseline, in the component with added VT food, even though its baseline response rate was lower. This result has been repeated with humans by Mace et al. (1990) and Cohen (1996) in the procedures described above, as shown in the right-hand column of Figure 12–5. These and related findings (Nevin, 1984; Nevin, Smith, & Roberts, 1987) strongly suggest that resistance to change depends on the correlation between stimuli and reinforcers in multiple schedules, independently of the response-reinforcer contingency and the resulting baseline response rate.

The independence of response rate and resistance to change is confirmed by comparing studies by Nevin, Mandell, and Atak (1983) and

Fath, Fields, Malott, and Grossett (1983). Both studies arranged different schedules in two components separated by a time-out. For Nevin et al., the schedules differed in reinforcer rate but maintained similar baseline response rates. For Fath et al., the reinforcer rates were the same, but high or low baseline response rates were established by differential reinforcement of short or long interresponse times in the two components. When resistance to change was tested by presenting time-out food in probe sessions, Nevin et al. found greater resistance in the component with the higher reinforcer rate, as in the results portrayed in Figure 12–4, even though baseline response rates were similar. By contrast, Fath et al. found that resistance to time-out food was similar in the two components, relative to baseline, even though baseline response rates differed markedly (see Nevin, 1992b, for summary of the average data).

Nevin (1992a) asked whether resistance to change depends on the context of reinforcement in the same way as response rate does, and at the same time tested the application of Herrnstein's account of response rate in multiple schedules (Equation 11) to resistance to change. Pigeons were trained on multiple VI VI schedules where the rate of reinforcement in one component was constant while the rate of reinforcement in the alternated component was either richer or leaner in different experimental conditions. Prefeeding and extinction tests showed that response rate in the constant component was more resistant to change when the alternated component was leaner than when it was richer; the average data for extinction are shown in Figure 12–6. This finding provides another instance of the effects of the context of reinforcement. It is also exactly opposite to the predictions of Equation 11 and related formulations, strongly suggesting the need for a separate account of resistance to change (see Nevin, 1992a, for the full argument).

Nevin's (1992a) resistance data are ordinally related to the stimulus-reinforcer contingency for the constant component, expressed as the ratio of the reinforcer rate in that component to the average reinforcer rate for the entire session (Gibbon, 1981). Nevin (1992b) reviewed a number of

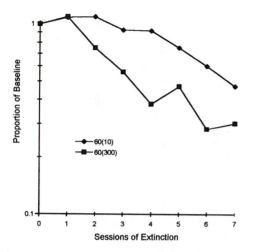

Figure 12–6. Average data for five pigeons trained on multiple VI VI schedules, showing the effects of extinction on responding in a component previously correlated with 60 reinforcers per hour after training in two conditions. Before extinction, there were 10 reinforcers per hour in the alternated component in one condition, and 300 reinforcers per hour in the second. Response rates are expressed as proportions of baseline. For all five subjects, extinction in the constant component progressed more rapidly when the alternated schedule had been rich than when it had been lean. Note that the y-axis is logarithmic. Adapted from Nevin (1992a, Experiment 1).

studies and found that the resistance ratio, measured as the inverse ratio of the slopes of the functions relating log response rate to the external disruptor in two multiple-schedule components, approximated a power function of the ratio of reinforcer rates in those components. The model is similar in mathematical form to the generalized matching law relating the ratio of steady-state response rates to the ratio of reinforcer rates (Equation 2), and to its extension to choice in concurrent chains (Equation 5).

Resistance to Change and Choice

The need for separate accounts of steady-state choice and resistance to change should not obscure the relations between them. In addition to their common mathematical description, initial-link preference in concurrent-chain schedules and relative resistance to change in multiple schedules depend on similar variables. For example, the terminal-link stimulus with the higher rate of reinforcement is preferred in concurrent chains, and response rate in the multiple-schedule component with the greater rate of reinforcement is more resistant to change, where both results are independent of response-reinforcer contingencies (Neuringer, 1969; Nevin et al., 1990). In a procedure that involved both concurrent-chain and multiple schedules, Grace and Nevin (1997) evaluated preference and resistance to change within subjects and sessions, and found a high correlation between these independent measures. Thus, preference and resistance to change may be convergent measures of the value of a signaled schedule of reinforcement.

THE METAPHOR OF BEHAVIORAL MOMENTUM

In classical physics, the momentum of a moving body is given by the product of its velocity and mass. When an external force is imposed, the change in velocity depends on mass according to Newton's second law:

$$\Delta v = f/m, \qquad (12)$$

which implies that for a given external force, the change in velocity is inversely related to mass.

In behavior analysis, reinforcement may endow responding with something analogous to momentum, where baseline response rate under constant conditions is analogous to velocity, and the resistance to change of that response rate is analogous to mass: the smaller the change in response rate when a disruptor is presented, the greater the behavioral mass.

In physics, the velocity and mass of a moving body are independent dimensions, and as we have seen, response rate and resistance to change are independently related to response-reinforcer and stimulus-reinforcer contingencies, respectively. Physical mass is independent of the magnitude of the imposed force, and Nevin et al. (1983) showed that relative behavioral mass in two multiple-schedule components was invariant with respect to the magnitude of the disruptor, and was internally consistent across three schedule pairs. The momentum metaphor may therefore be useful for quantifying the effects of signaled schedules of reinforcement, some of which may not be evident until behavior is challenged in some way.

Behavioral momentum—the product of baseline response rate and its resistance to change—captures some of the commonsense meaning of "learning." For example, a child is said to have learned arithmetic well if the child responds rapidly and accurately on arithmetic problems in class (high velocity), and also performs well at home while distracted by TV, or on an achievement test several years later (high mass). However, if the child performed poorly during distraction or on a subsequent test, one would not say that arithmetic was well learned no matter how rapidly and accurately the child performed in class.

Clinicians are often faced with the need to teach desirable behavior so that it occurs reliably during therapy and persists effectively in the client's natural world after therapy ends—that is, to establish a high level of momentum. Conversely, clients often engage in undesirable behavior that is remarkably persistent, suggesting a high level of momentum based on some combination of circumstances that may be identified through functional analysis (Neef & Iwata, 1994). The momentum metaphor, and an understanding of the separate determiners of behavioral velocity and mass, may therefore be valuable in clinical settings.

APPLICATIONS OF CHOICE AND MOMENTUM ANALYSES

Choice

One goal of applied work is to promote choice of socially desirable behavior over undesirable behavior. Laboratory research on choice is directly relevant to situations in the natural world where people engage in repeated choices between alternatives that are analogous to concurrent schedules. However, context effects of the sort described above are likely to complicate predictions in applied work, because both desirable and undesirable behavior may be reinforced outside the therapy setting.

Another difficulty for applied work is that real-world contingencies rarely mimic concurrent schedules in detail. However, they can at least be classified as ratio-like or interval-like by examining the relation (known as the molar feedback function) between the rate of responding and the resulting rate of reinforcement. For example, the number of berries obtained by searching in a rich patch increases in proportion to the rate of searching, even though searching does not always reveal berries. This is a ratio-like contingency. By contrast, fishing in a sparsely populated inlet is interval-like: one must cast at least occasionally to catch anything at all, but the total catch is limited by the stock of fish, regardless of how often the line is cast. The molar feedback functions for these types of situations are shown in Figure 12–7.

If both alternatives are ratio-like and lead to the same reinforcer (e.g., money), research and theory on choice behavior suggest that subjects will respond exclusively to the richer alternative. If they lead to qualitatively different reinforcers, though, subjects may switch between alternatives as their reinforcer preferences change. For example, smoking pays off on a very rich schedule—every puff brings smoke into the mouth and lungs. However, the decrease in enjoyment from smoking successive cigarettes, one right after another, ensures that even a heavy smoker will refrain from time to time and engage in some other behavior, such as going to a movie, even though it does not pay off so frequently or reliably.

If both alternatives are interval-like, some approximation to matching can be expected, with biases depending on a host of variables that may be difficult to evaluate in natural settings. Overmatching is likely if the alternatives have been experienced in separate contexts. Thus, the matching law may not always help to predict choice in natural situations.

In controlled situations, however, context effects can be avoided, and concurrent VI VI schedules with different responses and rein-

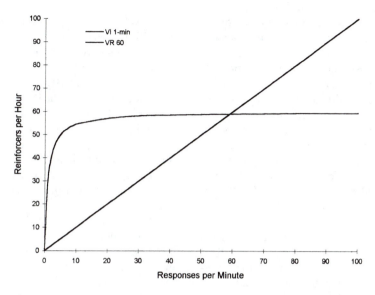

Figure 12–7. Molar feedback functions showing obtained reinforcer rate as a function of response rate. For a VI 1-minute schedule, obtained reinforcer rate rises rapidly toward its asymptote of 60 per hour and is essentially constant for all response rates above 20 per minute. By contrast, for a VR 60 schedule, reinforcer rate increases linearly with response rate.

forcers can be programmed explicitly. For example, Neef, Shade, and Miller (1994) arranged concurrent VI VI schedules with emotionally disturbed children for two sets of arithmetic problems to evaluate the effects of response effort, reinforcer delay, and reinforcer quality. They found large individual differences in the relative effectiveness of these dimensions, and the frequent occurrence of exclusive responding to one or the other problem set precluded quantitative assessments of bias, sensitivity, and independence of dimensions via the generalized matching law, Equation 2. In a similar study with teenagers in a special education program, Mace, Neef, Shade, and Mauro (1994) varied only the concurrent VI VI schedule values and obtained reasonably orderly undermatching. However, a variety of additional procedures was needed to prevent perseveration of response patterns when the schedule values changed. Thus, the practical value of concurrent schedules for quantifying factors that affect choice in individual clients may be limited.

On the other hand, clinical populations may exhibit consistent deviations from normal performance on concurrent schedules, and the generalized matching law can be used to identify and quantify them. For example, Oscar-Berman, Heyman, Bonner, and Ryder (1980) studied the performances of Korsakoff's patients and normal subjects on concurrent VI VI schedules, and observed that Korsakoff's patients were far less sensitive ($a \ll 1.0$ in Equation 2) to variations in reinforcer ratios. Reduced sensitivity to reinforcer ratios may indicate that the patients failed to discriminate the alternatives, or that they scaled reinforcer rate in a different way from normal individuals; either interpretation could contribute to the analysis of Korsakoff's syndrome.

Alternative Reinforcement

One of the difficulties in eliminating unwanted behavior is that the reinforcer may be unknown, or extremely difficult to discontinue. For example, a child's tantrums in a public place are virtually certain to attract parental attention. Therefore, a common procedure for reducing unwanted behavior is to arrange concurrent reinforcement for a desirable response, or to provide reinforcers if the undesired response does not occur for some time. Equation 9 implies that response rate goes down when alternative reinforcers are added to the denominator, whether or not they are contingent on any specified response. McDowell (1982) used this approach to decrease the oppositional behavior of an emotionally disturbed boy, and showed that the results were consistent with Equation 9.

On the basis of Equation 1 for strict matching and the feedback functions for the undesired and alternative responses, Myerson and Hale (1984) argued that to be most effective, the alternative reinforcer should be substitutable for that maintaining the undesired behavior and should be introduced on interval-like contingencies. However, the practical utility of these prescriptions for alternative reinforcement derived from basic research on steady-state choice behavior may be limited by considerations of behavioral momentum.

Resistance to Change

When alternative behavior is reinforced concurrently in order to reduce the frequency of an undesired response, there is likely to be a concomitant increase in the total rate of reinforcement in the situation. Because resistance to change increases with the total rate of reinforcement in a situation, reinforcing alternative behavior may inadvertently increase the persistence of undesired behavior. Mace (1991) explored two ways to reduce food stealing by a boy with mental retardation. When attempts to steal food were blocked (in effect, extinction of food stealing), the boy stopped trying to steal food within four sessions. However, a high rate of stealing recurred after blocking was discontinued. Mace then reinforced appropriate eating to decrease the rate of food stealing to a low level. When the effectiveness of this procedure was tested by discontinuing it and blocking further attempts to steal food, the boy persisted in theft attempts for over 30 sessions, in accordance with the predictions of behavioral momentum. The data are shown in Figure 12–8.

The increase in resistance to change produced by added reinforcement is, of course, advantageous if the behavior of interest is desirable. For example, Tota-Faucette (1991) used auditory biofeedback to teach children to relax in two distinctive stimulus situations that were presented alternately as components of a multiple schedule. In the first, the children received points that could be exchanged for toys contingent on meeting a relaxation criterion; in the second, there was an identical schedule of contingent points, and free points were awarded periodically. During training, relaxation levels were similar in the two situations, but relaxation was more resistant to extinction in the second (added free points) situation when auditory feedback and points were discontinued. Both Mace's and Tota-Faucette's studies show that persistence can be enhanced markedly by adding reinforcers that are not contingent on the response of interest.

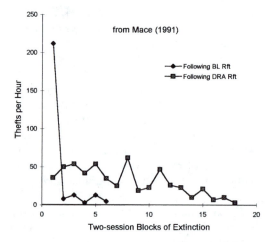

Figure 12–8. The rate of food-theft attempts by a boy with mental retardation when thefts were blocked after baseline (BL) and after differential reinforcement for appropriate mealtime behavior (DRA). Although DRA sharply reduced the theft rate, it also increased its persistence. From Mace (1991).

Behavioral Momentum and Compliance

All the research on behavioral momentum reviewed established a stable baseline in training before assessing resistance to change. However, the stable baseline may not be necessary. Skinner (1938) obtained substantial resistance to extinction after reinforcing a single response, and it may be that one or a few reinforcers are sufficient, metaphorically, to get behavior moving and endow it with enough mass to make its motion persist. Mace, Hock, Lalli, West, Belfiore, Pinter, and Brown (1988) applied this notion to the problem of noncompliance in adults with mental retardation. They presented a few requests that their clients were very likely to obey ("high-p commands," such as "Give me five"), and then issued a request that was normally resisted (a "low-p command" such as "Empty the trash"). They found much higher rates of compliance with low-p commands that followed immediately after a series of high-p commands than with low-p commands presented alone, suggesting that prompting and social reinforcement for easy instances of compliance generated some momentum for compliance in general. However, the effect was short-lived: there was no evidence of enhanced compliance if low-p commands were presented 20 seconds after the high-p command sequence.

The persistence of compliance with low-p commands can be enhanced by using food rather than praise to reinforce compliance with the preceding high-p commands (Mace, Mauro, Boyajian, & Eckert, 1997). Another variable that should be explored is the length of the high-p sequence: by analogy with the effects of length of training on resistance to free food in pigeons (Lentz & Cohen, 1980), low-p compliance should become even more persistent if high-p compliance was reinforced repeatedly. Finally, compliance with low-p commands might be especially persistent in an environment that included other reinforcers. For example, Davis, Brady, Hamilton, McEvoy, and Williams (1994) used the high-p command procedure to establish social interaction in children with autism, and found that the level of interaction was maintained after the procedure was discontinued, probably because of the natural reinforcers derived from interaction after it occurred reliably. Thus, extension of the behavioral momentum metaphor to compliance with requests has led to an effective method for establishing and maintaining desirable behavior (see Nevin, 1996, for a more comprehensive discussion).

FUTURE DIRECTIONS

Drug addiction is one of the most serious problems facing the United States and many other nations. Addiction leads to staggering social costs that result from lost productivity, poor health, crime, and personal tragedy. Therefore, the analysis and treatment of addictive behavior have a high priority.

Addiction involves repeated choices between two broad classes of behavior: seeking and using a drug, or engaging in activities that lead to nondrug reinforcers. Herrnstein and Prelec (1992) and Heyman (1996) have suggested that addiction can be understood as an instance of melioration—choosing the momentarily more valued alternative—even though that choice leads to a shifting mix of drug and nondrug reinforcers that is less than optimal, and ultimately catastrophic. Their analysis assumes that the value of any reinforcer is bitonic with the frequency of use: up to a point, value increases with frequency of engagement, as in learning to play a musical instrument, or skiing, or savoring a good wine. After some point, though, value diminishes with additional time spent practicing or skiing or wine-tasting. The same is true with drugs of abuse: with repeated consumption, tolerance develops and the absolute value of a given dose decreases. However, drugs differ from conventional reinforcers not only in their remarkable potency but also in that repeated drug use decreases the values of nondrug reinforcers derived through work, recreation, and social life. Thus, even as their absolute value decreases, the relative value of drugs increases with repeated use, and the addict eventually becomes trapped into the maximum possible frequency of drug-related behavior. The situation is functionally equivalent to that confronting a pigeon in a two-key procedure where each choice of the richer food schedule leads to a reduction in the overall availability of food (e.g., Vaughan, 1981): persistent meliorizing leads to the worst possible outcome in terms of the total rate of reinforcement.

Although the foregoing analysis is hypothetical, it accords well with the personal accounts of drug addicts (see Heyman, 1996, for review) and thus suggests that research on behavioral methods for bringing overall choice allocation under the control of its long-term consequences, rather than the momentary outcome of each successive choice, could be invaluable for the health and well-being of countless individuals. In applied work with nonaddicted drug users, one approach may involve training to limit the consumption of drugs — or any reinforcers, for that matter — and then to establish environment-reinforcer relations that make a pattern of moderation highly resistant to change.

For recovering addicts who are abstinent, and for those who have never used drugs, the goal is to make abstinence highly resistant to the temptations that abound in a drug-using society. Although a good deal is known about how to establish well-specified behavior so that it persists in the face of a disruptive challenge, much less is known about the persistence of the *non*occurrence of some class of behavior — metaphorically, establishing high inertial mass for refraining from some action. There is an urgent need for the extension of basic research on choice and momentum to help develop effective strategies for treating and preventing addiction.

ENDNOTE

The preparation of this chapter was supported in part by Grant IBN-9507584 from the National Science Foundation.

REFERENCES

Alsop, B. A., & Davison, M. (1991). Effects of varying stimulus disparity and the reinforcer ratio in concurrent-schedule and signal-detection procedures. *Journal of the Experimental Analysis of Behavior, 56*, 67–80.

Alsop, B. A., & Elliffe, D. (1988). Concurrent-schedule performance: Effects of relative and overall reinforcer rate. *Journal of the Experimental Analysis of Behavior, 49*, 21–36.

Autor, S. M. (1960). The strength of conditioned reinforcers as a function of frequency and probability of reinforcement. Unpublished doctoral dissertation, Harvard University; reprinted in D. P. Hendry (ed.) (1969), *Conditioned reinforcement*, 127–162. Homewood, Ill.: Dorsey.

Baum, W. M. (1974). On two types of deviation from the matching law: Bias and undermatching. *Journal of the Experimental Analysis of Behavior, 22*, 231–242.

Baum, W. M. (1979). Matching, undermatching, and overmatching in studies of choice. *Journal of the Experimental Analysis of Behavior, 32*, 269–281.

Baum, W. M. (1981). Optimization and the matching law as accounts of instrumental behavior. *Journal of the Experimental Analysis of Behavior, 36*, 387–403.

Baum, W. M. (1982). Choice, changeover, and travel. *Journal of the Experimental Analysis of Behavior, 38*, 35–49.

Baum, W. M. (1993). Performance on interval and ratio schedules of reinforcement: Data and theory. *Journal of the Experimental Analysis of Behavior, 59*, 245–264.

Baum, W. M., & Rachlin, H. (1969). Choice as time allocation. *Journal of the Experimental Analysis of Behavior, 12*, 861–874.

Bouzas, A. (1978). The relative law of effect: Effects of shock intensity on response strength in multiple schedules. *Journal of the Experimental Analysis of Behavior, 30*, 307–314.

Brownstein, A. J. (1971). Concurrent schedules of response-independent reinforcement: Duration of a reinforcing stimulus. *Journal of the Experimental Analysis of Behavior, 15*, 211–214.

Catania, A. C. (1963). Concurrent performances: A baseline for the study of reinforcement magnitude. *Journal of the Experimental Analysis of Behavior, 6*, 299–300.

Catania, A. C. (1973). Self-inhibiting effects of reinforcement. *Journal of the Experimental Analysis of Behavior, 19*, 517–526.

Church, R. M., & Raymond, G. A. (1967). Influence of the schedule of positive reinforcement on punished behavior. *Journal of Comparative and Physiological Psychology, 63*, 329–332.

Cohen, S. L. (1996). Behavioral momentum of typing behavior in college students. *Journal of Behavior Analysis and Therapy, 1*, 36–51.

Cohen, S. L., Furman, S., Crouse, M., & Kroner, A. L. (1990). Response strength in open and closed economies. *Learning and Motivation, 21,* 316–339.

Cohen, S. L., Riley, D. S., & Weigle, P. A. (1993). Tests of behavioral momentum in simple and multiple schedules with rats and pigeons. *Journal of the Experimental Analysis of Behavior, 60,* 255–291.

Conger, R., & Killeen, P. (1974). Use of concurrrent operants in small group research. *Pacific Sociological Review, 17,* 399–416.

Davis, C. A., Brady, M. P., Hamilton, R., McEvoy, M. A., & Williams, R. E. (1994). Effects of high-probability requests on the social interactions of young children with severe disabilities. *Journal of Applied Behavior Analysis, 27,* 619–637.

Davison, M. (1988). Concurrent schedules: Interaction of reinforcer frequency and reinforcer duration. *Journal of the Experimental Analysis of Behavior, 49,* 339–349.

Davison, M., & Ferguson, A. (1978). The effects of different response requirements in multiple and concurrent schedules. *Journal of the Experimental Analysis of Behavior, 29,* 283–295.

Davison, M., & Jenkins, P. E. (1985). Stimulus discriminability, contingency discriminability, and schedule performance. *Animal Learning and Behavior, 13,* 77–84.

Davison, M., & McCarthy, D. (1988). *The matching law.* Hillsdale, N.J.: Erlbaum.

de Villiers, P. A. (1977). Choice in concurrent schedules and a quantitative formulation of the law of effect. In W. K. Honig & J. E. R. Staddon (eds.), *Handbook of operant behavior,* 233–287. Englewood Cliffs, N.J.: Prentice-Hall.

Eckerman, C. (1968). *Deprivation conditions and chained schedule and multiple schedule performance.* Paper presented at the meeting of the American Psychological Association, San Francisco, Calif., August.

Edmon, E. L., Lucki, I., & Grisham, M. G. (1980). Choice responding following multiple schedule training. *Animal Learning and Behavior, 8,* 287–292.

Elsmore, T. F. (1971). Effects of response effort on discrimination performance. *Psychological Record, 21,* 17–24.

Fantino, E. (1969). Choice and rate of reinforcement. *Journal of the Experimental Analysis of Behavior, 12,* 723–730.

Fantino, E., Preston, R. A., & Dunn, R. (1993). Delay reduction: Current status. *Journal of the Experimental Analysis of Behavior, 60,* 159–169.

Fath, S. J., Fields, L., Malott, M. K., & Grossett, D. (1983). Response rate, latency, and resistance to change. *Journal of the Experimental Analysis of Behavior, 39,* 267–274.

Findley, J. D. (1958). Preference and switching under concurrent scheduling. *Journal of the Experimental Analysis of Behavior, 1,* 123–144.

Gibbon, J. (1981). The contingency problem in autoshaping. In C. M. Locurto, H. S. Terrace, & J. Gibbon (eds.), *Autoshaping and conditioning theory,* 285–308. New York: Academic Press.

Grace, R. C. (1994). A contextual model of concurrent-chains choice. *Journal of the Experimental Analysis of Behavior, 61,* 113–129.

Grace, R. C. (1995a). Independence of reinforcement delay and magnitude in concurrent chains. *Journal of the Experimental Analysis of Behavior, 63,* 255–276.

Grace, R. C. (1995b). *Temporal context and choice.* Unpublished doctoral dissertation, University of New Hampshire.

Grace, R. C., & Nevin, J. A. (1997). On the relation between preference and resistance to change. *Journal of the Experimental Analysis of Behavior, 67,* 43–65.

Herrnstein, R. J. (1961). Relative and absolute strength of response as a function of frequency of reinforcement. *Journal of the Experimental Analysis of Behavior, 4,* 267–272.

Herrnstein, R. J. (1970). On the law of effect. *Journal of the Experimental Analysis of Behavior, 13,* 243–266.

Herrnstein, R. J., & Loveland, D. H. (1974). Hunger and contrast in a multiple schedule. *Journal of the Experimental Analysis of Behavior, 24,* 107–116.

Herrnstein, R. J., & Loveland, D. H. (1975). Maximizing and matching on concurrent ratio schedules. *Journal of the Experimental Analysis of Behavior, 24,* 107–116.

Herrnstein, R. J., & Loveland, D. H. (1976). Matching in a network. *Journal of the Experimental Analysis of Behavior, 26,* 143–153.

Herrnstein, R. J., & Prelec, D. (1992). A theory of addiction. In G. Loewenstein & J. Elster (eds.), *Choice over time,* 331–360. New York: Russell Sage Foundation.

Herrnstein, R. J., & Vaughan, W., Jr. (1980). Melioration and behavioral allocation. In J. E. R. Staddon (ed.). *Limits to action: The allocation of individual behavior,* 143–176. New York: Academic Press.

Heyman, G. M. (1979). A Markov model description of changeover probabilities on concurrent variable-interval schedules. *Journal of the Experimental Analysis of Behavior, 31,* 41–51.

Heyman, G. M. (1996). Addiction: Choice or disease? *Behavioral and Brain Sciences.* In press.

Hollard, V., & Davison, M. (1971). Preference for qualitatively different reinforcers. *Journal of the Experimental Analysis of Behavior, 16,* 375–380.

Killeen, P. (1972). The matching law. *Journal of the Experimental Analysis of Behavior, 17,* 489–495.

Killeen, P. (1994). Mathematical principles of reinforcement. *Behavioral and Brain Sciences, 17,* 105–172.

Lentz, B. E., & Cohen, S. L. (1980). The effect of prior training on the contra-freeloading phenomenon. *Bulletin of the Psychonomic Society, 15,* 48–50.

Logue, A. W., & Chavarro, A. (1987). Effect on choice of absolute and relative values of reinforcer delay, amount, and frequency. *Journal of Experimental Psychology: Animal Behavior Processes, 13*, 280–291.

Lyon, D. O. (1963). Frequency of reinforcement as a parameter of conditioned suppression. *Journal of the Experimental Analysis of Behavior, 6*, 95–98.

Mace, F. C. (1991). *Recent advances and functional analysis of behavior disorders.* Paper presented at the meeting of the Association for Behavior Analysis, Atlanta, Ga., May.

Mace, F. C., Hock, M. L., Lalli, J. S., West, B. J., Belfiore, P., Pinter, E., & Brown, D. K. (1988). Behavioral momentum in the treatment of noncompliance. *Journal of Applied Behavior Analysis, 21*, 123–141.

Mace, F. C., Lalli, J. S., Shea, M. C., Lalli, E. P., West, B. J., Roberts, M., & Nevin, J. A. (1990). The momentum of human behavior in a natural setting. *Journal of the Experimental Analysis of Behavior, 54*, 163–172.

Mace, F. C., Mauto, B. C., Boyajian, A. E., & Eckert, T. L. (1997). Effects of reinforcer quality on behavior momentum: Coordinated applied and basic research. *Journal of Applied Behavior Analysis, 30*, 1–20.

Mace, F. C., Neef, N. A., Shade, D., & Mauro, B. C. (1994). Limited matching on concurrent-schedule reinforcement of academic behavior. *Journal of Applied Behavior Analysis, 27*, 585–596.

Mazur, J. E. (1981). Optimization theory fails to predict performance of pigeons in a two-response situation. *Science, 214*, 823–825.

McDowell, J. J. (1982). The importance of Herrnstein's mathematical statement of the law of effect for behavior therapy. *American Psychologist, 37*, 771–779.

McDowell, J. J., & Wood, H. M. (1984). Confirmation of linear system theory prediction: Changes in Herrnstein's *k* as a function of changes in reinforcer magnitude. *Journal of the Experimental Analysis of Behavior, 41*, 183–192.

McSweeney, F. K. (1992). Rate of reinforcement and session duration as determinants of within-session patterns of responding. *Animal Learning and Behavior, 20*, 160–169.

McSweeney, F. K., Farmer, V. A., Dougan, J. D., & Whipple, J. E. (1986). The generalized matching law as a description of multiple-schedule responding. *Journal of the Experimental Analysis of Behavior, 45*, 83–101.

Miller, H. L. (1976). Matching-based hedonic scaling in the pigeon. *Journal of the Experimental Analysis of Behavior, 26*, 335–347.

Miller, J. T., Saunders, S. S., & Bourland, G. (1980). The role of stimulus disparity in concurrently available reinforcement schedules. *Animal Learning and Behavior, 8*, 635–641.

Myerson, J., & Hale, S. (1984). Practical implications of the matching law. *Journal of Applied Behavior Analysis, 17*, 367–380.

Neef, N. A., & Iwata, B. A. (1994). Current research on functional analysis methodologies: An introduction. *Journal of Applied Behavior Analysis, 27*, 211–214.

Neef, N. A., Shade, D., & Miller, M. S. (1994). Assessing influential dimensions of reinforcers on choice in students with serious emotional disturbance. *Journal of Applied Behavior Analysis, 27*, 575–583.

Neuringer, A. J. (1969). Delayed reinforcement versus reinforcement after a fixed interval. *Journal of the Experimental Analysis of Behavior, 12*, 375–383.

Nevin, J. A. (1969). Interval reinforcement of choice behavior in discrete trials. *Journal of the Experimental Analysis of Behavior, 12*, 875–885.

Nevin, J. A. (1973). The maintenance of behavior. In J. A. Nevin & G. S. Reynolds (eds.), *The study of behavior,* 200–236. Glenview, Ill.: Scott, Foresman.

Nevin, J. A. (1974). Response strength in multiple schedules. *Journal of the Experimental Analysis of Behavior, 21*, 389–408.

Nevin, J. A. (1979). Reinforcement schedules and response strength. In M. D. Zeiler & P. Harzem (eds.), *Reinforcement and the organization of behaviour,* 117–158. Chichester, England: Wiley.

Nevin, J. A. (1984). Pavlovian determiners of behavioral momentum. *Animal Learning and Behavior, 12*, 363–370.

Nevin, J. A. (1988). Behavioral momentum and the partial reinforcement effect. *Psychological Bulletin, 103*, 44–56.

Nevin, J. A. (1992a). Behavioral contrast and behavioral momentum. *Journal of Experimental Psychology: Animal Behavior Processes, 18*, 126–133.

Nevin, J. A. (1992b). An integrative model for the study of behavioral momentum. *Journal of the Experimental Analysis of Behavior, 57*, 301–316.

Nevin, J. A. (1996). The momentum of compliance. *Journal of Applied Behavior Analysis, 29*, 535–547.

Nevin, J. A., Mandell, C., & Atak, J. R. (1983). The analysis of behavioral momentum. *Journal of the Experimental Analysis of Behavior, 39*, 49–59.

Nevin, J. A., Smith, L. D., & Roberts, J. (1987). Does contingent reinforcement strengthen operant behavior? *Journal of the Experimental Analysis of Behavior, 48*, 17–33.

Nevin, J. A., Tota, M. E., Torquato, R. D., & Shull, R. L. (1990). Alternative reinforcement increases resistance to change: Pavlovian or operant contingencies? *Journal of the Experimental Analysis of Behavior, 53*, 359–379.

Oscar-Berman, M., Heyman, G. M., Bonner, R. T., & Ryder, J. (1980). Human neuropsychology: Some differences between Korsakoff and normal operant performance. *Psychological Research, 41*, 235–247.

Pliskoff, S. S., Cicerone, R., & Nelson, T. D. (1978). Local response-rate constancy on concurrent variable-interval schedules of reinforcement. *Journal of the Experimental Analysis of Behavior, 29*, 431–446.

Rachlin, H., Green, L., Kagel, J. H., & Battalio, R. C. (1976). Economic demand theory and psychological theories of choice. In G. H. Bower (ed.), *The psychology of learning and motivation, Vol. 10*: 129–154. New York: Academic Press.

Shimp, C. P. (1966). Probabilistically reinforced choice behavior in pigeons. *Journal of the Experimental Analysis of Behavior, 9*, 443–455.

Skinner, B. F. (1938). *The behavior of organisms*. New York: Appleton-Century-Crofts.

Staddon, J. E. R. (1977). On Herrnstein's equation and related forms. *Journal of the Experimental Analysis of Behavior, 28*, 163–170.

Staddon, J. E. R., Hinson, J. M., & Kram, R. (1981). Optimal choice. *Journal of the Experimental Analysis of Behavior, 35*, 397–412.

Staddon, J. E. R., & Motheral, S. (1978). On matching and maximizing in operant choice. *Psychological Review, 85*, 436–444.

Tota-Faucette, M. E. (1991). *Alternative reinforcement and resistance to change*. Unpublished doctoral dissertation, University of North Carolina at Greensboro.

Vaughan, W., Jr. (1981). Melioration, matching, and maximization. *Journal of the Experimental Analysis of Behavior, 36*, 141–149.

vom Saal, W. (1972). Choice between stimuli previously presented separately. *Learning and Motivation, 3*, 209–222.

Williams, B. A. (1988). Reinforcement, choice, and response strength. In R. C. Atkinson, R. J. Herrnstein, G. Lindzey, & R. D. Luce (eds.), *Stevens' handbook of experimental psychology, 2nd ed., Vol. 2*: 167–244. New York: Wiley.

Williams, B. A. (1994). Reinforcement and choice. In N. J. Mackintosh (ed.), *Animal learning and cognition*, 81–108. New York: Academic Press.

Williams, B. A., & Royalty, P. (1989). A test of the melioration theory of matching. *Journal of Experimental Psychology: Animal Behavior Processes, 15*, 99–113.

Williams, B. A., & Wixted, J. T. (1986). An equation for behavioral contrast. *Journal of the Experimental Analysis of Behavior, 45*, 47–62.

CHAPTER 13

SELF-CONTROL

A. W. Logue

For many people, self-control is a laudatory goal to be achieved by virtue of substantial will-power. However, laboratory research, beginning about 30 years ago and continuing today, has given us a very different view. Laboratory research has provided extensive information about the causes and functions of self-control and about what will increase or decrease self-control. Much of this research has been conducted using nonhuman subjects while taking advantage of information from the fields of animal learning, motivation theory, and evolutionary theory. This chapter first describes some of this recent research on self-control—focusing on general, basic laboratory research—and then discusses self-control in specific problem situations. Because of length limitations, it will be possible to present only the highlights of much of this material.

DEFINITIONS

Laboratory researchers have defined self-control as choice of a larger but more delayed outcome over a smaller but less delayed outcome. Impulsiveness has been defined as the opposite (Ainslie, 1974; Logue, 1988, 1995; Rachlin & Green, 1972). For example, suppose you go to a restaurant and the waiter gives you a choice between tomato soup that is ready now and pumpkin soup (which you prefer) in half an hour. According to the present definitions of self-control and impulsiveness, if you choose the tomato soup, you will be demonstrating impulsiveness, and if you choose the pumpkin soup, you will be demonstrating self-control. This type of choice has also been described as a choice between immediate and delayed gratification.

Situations involving such choices occur frequently for both children and adults. Members of the general population are concerned with self-control and impulsiveness for their own, their friends', and their families' well-being. In addition, health, managerial, and law professionals want to know why people sometimes behave in ways that are not optimal in the long run, and how self-control can be increased.

Although it might appear that these definitions are for very specific kinds of choice behavior and not for the myriad behaviors that people tend to label self-control and impulsiveness, each type of behavior commonly termed self-control or impulsiveness can be described as choice between larger, more delayed outcomes and smaller, less delayed outcomes. For example, many people (including some clinicians) describe as self-control someone changing his or her own behavior through changing the influences that regulate that behavior, such as putting a finger under your nose to stop a sneeze (Goldfried & Merbaum, 1973; Skinner, 1953). This type of behavior can be described as choosing between a behavior that will result in a smaller, sooner reward (here this behavior is a sneeze) and a behavior that will prevent the first behavior and will result in the subject's behaving so as to obtain a larger reward later (here this behavior is putting a finger under your nose). Sneezing is the impulsive choice, and putting a finger under the nose so that the sneeze is suppressed is the self-control choice.

In addition to applying to a wide variety of prevalent behaviors, the present definitions of self-control and impulsiveness are useful in that they are operational definitions—definitions stated in terms of operations on the environment. Operational definitions are useful for laboratory research because they can be easily framed in terms of observable, verifiable laboratory events.

Thus, these definitions of self-control and impulsiveness are widely applicable and easily employed in laboratory research. Although common usage of the terms self-control and impulsiveness may seem to indicate that these terms refer to such concepts as willpower or the control by a homunculus over someone's behavior, such implications are not part of the present defini-

tions. The present definitions are useful for their objectivity and obvious applicability to many critical aspects of human behavior.

Note that the definitions of self-control and impulsiveness presented here are based on relative, not absolute, sizes of outcomes. The definitions talk about outcomes that are of smaller or larger sizes and shorter or longer delays. Whether a choice alternative is defined as self-control or impulsiveness depends on what other choices are available. For example, if someone has a choice between pumpkin soup that would not be ready for 30 minutes and immediately available tomato soup, and that person likes pumpkin soup more than tomato soup, choosing the pumpkin soup would be self-control. However, if the same person has a choice between pumpkin soup that would not be ready for 30 minutes and leek soup that would not be ready for an hour, and that person likes leek soup more than pumpkin soup, choosing the pumpkin soup would be impulsiveness. Thus, choosing the pumpkin soup, which would not be available for 30 minutes, is defined in one instance as self-control and in another as impulsiveness. The definitions depend on what other choices are available. The effects of context can help to explain why individuals' self-control can differ so markedly in different situations.

Every self-control choice can be described in terms of either positive or negative outcomes (see Figure 13–1). If a particular outcome is a positive one, then not having it (which happens when that outcome is not chosen) is a negative outcome. The reverse is also true; if a particular outcome is negative, then not having it (which happens when that outcome is not chosen) is a positive outcome. Therefore, any choice between a larger, more delayed outcome and a smaller, less delayed outcome is also a choice between a relatively small, less delayed loss and a relatively large, more delayed loss. For example, consider a choice between whether to study or whether to go to a movie. Framed as a choice between positive consequences, a student has a choice between going to a movie now or getting a good grade later. Framed as a choice between negative consequences, a student has a choice of missing

(a) Choice Between Positive Consequences

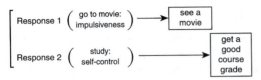

(b) Choice Between Negative Consequences

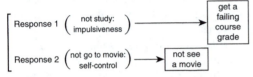

Figure 13–1. A self-control choice described both in terms of positive consequences (a) and negative consequences (b). In either case, the self-control choice is Response 2 (study, not go to movie), and the impulsive choice is Response 1 (go to movie, not study). A bracket indicates that a choice is available between the two responses.

the movie now or getting a failing grade later. No matter how this choice is described, to maximize actual overall positive consequences and minimize actual overall negative consequences, students should choose to study (i.e., they should choose to study and avoid getting a failing grade). Note that when a self-control choice is described in terms of negative rather than positive consequences, choosing the smaller, less delayed consequence (e.g., missing the movie) over the larger, more delayed consequence (e.g., getting a failing course grade) is now the self-control choice.

EVOLUTION, PHYSIOLOGICAL MECHANISMS, AND SELF-CONTROL

Consideration of how self-control and impulsiveness ultimately may or may not benefit the animal that exhibits them can help us understand how the demonstration of these behaviors may have evolved. Self-control and impulsive choices involve choosing between alternatives that differ in terms of their delay as well as their

size. The longer that an event is delayed, the less likely it is that that event will occur. For example, suppose that during a war there is very little food and grocery stores open sporadically, with people immediately grabbing whatever little food may be inside. If someone is waiting in front of a food store for the store to open, the longer that person has to wait, the more likely it is that the person will never get any food from that store. As the person waits, a bomb might destroy the store, some other people might get into the store first and take away all the food, or the person waiting might be killed by a sniper. Thus, if all else is equal, people will maximize their positive outcomes if they prefer less delayed over more delayed positive outcomes. Such preferences have been demonstrated repeatedly in the laboratory using both human and nonhuman subjects (Ainslie & Herrnstein, 1981; W. Mischel & Metzner, 1962; Schwarz, Schrager, & Lyons, 1983). These experiments are said to demonstrate that humans and other animals discount (in other words, value less) delayed events.

An analysis of the environment in which humans and other animals evolved suggests that animals may have evolved the tendency to discount delayed events. Humans used to live in an environment more similar to that of other animals, one in which future food sources and, in fact, any future events, were highly unpredictable (Kagel, Green, & Caraco, 1986). Approximately 1.4 million years ago, hominids were hunter-gatherers in Africa (Zihlman, 1982). Sometimes they hunted other animals, and sometimes they gathered roots, seeds, fruits, nuts and so on from the forests and fields. Food access at this time was fairly adequate and stable; the climate was fairly constant, natural disasters such as droughts and fires did not affect the food supply very much, there was a low population density, and the hunter-gatherers moved around a great deal to take optimal advantage of available food sources (Harlan, 1975). However, even though food access was fairly stable, life expectancy was much shorter than it is now because of increased death from disease and accidents. Approximately one million years ago, hunter-gatherers began to migrate out of Africa and away from the equator (Zihlman, 1982). As they did so, the weather became more variable, and access to food sources became more unstable. Therefore, in addition to the reasons listed above for the shorter lifespans of the African hunter-gatherers, these later humans had the additional reason of occasional starvation. About 10 thousand years ago, some hunter-gatherer societies began to settle in particular locations and to engage in agriculture. Natural disasters of various sorts could and often did wipe out a crop, and although these people learned how to store food and to trade, they still frequently lived on the edge of starvation (Harlan, 1975). Further, medical knowledge was very limited in most of these societies. Life expectancy was even shorter than it was for the hunter-gatherers (Cohen, 1987). Many early agricultural societies worshipped omnipotent nature gods, thus expressing their perceived inability to control future events (Harlan, 1975).

In these kinds of early human environments, a particular delayed event was not very likely to occur, and thus waiting for such events was not likely to result in any benefit (Kagel et al., 1986). In other words, in an environment in which future events are uncertain, impulsiveness, not self-control, is likely to maximize overall benefits. For example, if, as a result of frequent plagues, individuals are unlikely to live to the completion or even the beginning of their reproductive years, those individuals would have little reason to show self-control with regard to sexual behavior and pregnancy; sexual behavior resulting in pregnancy should be engaged in at every opportunity.

We know that impulsiveness is more likely than self-control to maximize overall benefits in an uncertain environment. We also know that humans and other animals were exposed to an uncertain environment over many, many generations during their evolutionary histories. Therefore, it is probable that during evolution, people and other animals that tended to value delayed outcomes less than immediate outcomes were more likely to survive in at least some situations.

This means that genes that contributed to impulsiveness probably increased an individual's inclusive fitness—the survival of that individual's biological relatives, who are the most likely carriers of that individual's genes (Barash, 1977; Hamilton, 1964a, 1964b; Maynard Smith, 1978) —resulting in an increased proportion of future animals possessing genes that tended to contribute to this delayed outcome discounting. For all of these reasons, it is likely that humans and other animals possess genes for delayed outcome discounting.

Discounting and impulsiveness differ according to the situation and the species (Forzano & Logue, 1994; Lejeune & Wearden, 1991; Real, 1991; Richelle & Lejeune, 1984; Timberlake, Gawley, & Lucas, 1987), and at least some of these differences may have an evolutionary basis. For example, in laboratory experimental sessions, when food rewards are used, hungry humans tend to be less impulsive than are pigeons (Tobin & Logue, 1994). This species difference may be related to the fact that, in nature, because of their high metabolic rates, pigeons need to forage continuously, whereas humans, with much lower metabolic rates, can eat in discrete meals.

The environment of the majority of the people in the United States is currently quite different from that of hunter-gatherers or early agricultural societies. First, for most people today, food of some sort is always available. Even if someone has no money for food, our culture has instituted food-stamp programs and soup kitchens. Second, our expected lifespan is considerably longer than that of evolving humans. Many diseases have been eradicated or are usually curable. At the same time, the chances of someone dying from a flood or a wild animal attack are quite small. Most people can expect to live long, relatively healthy lives. Third, in our culture, we have formalized the rules by which people must live; we have created laws along with ways in which those laws are enforced (tax collectors, police officers, district attorneys, etc.). Through printed and audiovisual media, as well as by word of mouth, there is extensive communication regarding the existence of these laws and the consequences for breaking them. Fourth, we simply have more knowledge now about the probability of the occurrence of certain future events, such as particular kinds of weather, demographic trends, and the usable life of a machine. Finally, even when someone does not know for sure what the consequences for a particular action might be, that person may be able to influence events to ensure that a particular outcome occurs. That might also have been true during, for example, hunter-gatherer times, but only if the person could expect to live long enough to exert the necessary and desirable influence—not as likely then as now. Together, these characteristics of our current society indicate that in our society the consequences for certain behaviors are often (although certainly not always) quite specific and quite certain.

Given that many future events in our current environment are now highly predictable, discounting of those events can be unadaptive (Ainslie, 1992). Discounting of delayed events that are virtually certain to occur can result in choices that are not the best overall strategy. Thus, evolution may have resulted in a mismatch between how we behave and our current environment. People persist in behaving as if many events almost certain to occur are unlikely or nonexistent, and therefore engage in unadaptive impulsiveness (such as cigarette smoking despite the long-term health risks).

The material presented in this section demonstrates that self-control is not necessarily "good" and impulsiveness is not necessarily "bad." If the goal is to maximize total received benefits, at least some situations exist in which demonstrating impulsiveness is more likely to reach that goal than is demonstrating self-control. Suppose someone is waiting beside a bush for the berries on that bush to ripen. If that person is very hungry, that person may become dangerously weak, or may even die, while waiting for the berries to ripen. The definitions of self-control and impulsiveness in use here do not take into account the likelihood of the chooser's actually receiving one or the other al-

ternative, nor do they take into account other circumstances that may affect the optimality of a particular choice. Thus, self-control is not always the goal of normal development (though children do tend to be more impulsive than adults). There are situations in which the best overall strategy is impulsiveness. People, and the professionals who assist those people, need to evaluate carefully the choices that are available, with less emotional baggage and with more consideration of the overall benefits of making a particular choice. All of us need to understand that, not only is impulsiveness sometimes the best strategy, but also, when someone is impulsive, that person is not inherently bad. Impulsiveness is part of our evolutionary heritage. What we should do is identify those situations in which self-control is more advantageous than impulsiveness, and then engage in whatever actions are necessary to ensure that self-control does indeed occur.

To increase self-control, it is necessary to understand precisely what physiological mechanisms and behavioral situations are responsible for people making self-control or impulsive choices. Some factors responsible for impulsiveness and self-control are fairly general and apply to most situations. Others, however, can differ depending on the particular situation. As yet, attempts to establish firmly a particular part of the brain as responsible for all cases of impulsiveness and self-control have proved unsuccessful. (Likely candidates have been the prefrontal cortex and the septum [Gorenstein & Newman, 1980; Grossman, 1967; Newman, Gorenstein, & Kelsey, 1983].) This is perhaps not surprising given that, although evolution may have shaped people and other animals so that they discount delayed events, different mechanisms may be responsible for this discounting in different situations. Natural selection acts on the function of a behavior, not on the physiological mechanism responsible for that behavior (Cosmides & Tooby, 1987). Therefore, a thorough understanding of a variety of influential factors will assist in our being able to modify self-control and impulsive behavior.

FACTORS AFFECTING SELF-CONTROL

Characteristics of an Outcome

At least three characteristics of an outcome affect whether or not someone will show self-control: outcome delay, outcome size, and outcome contingencies. The effects of each of these three characteristics are discussed in the following subsections.

Outcome Delay

Outcome delays appear to affect outcome value by discounting the physical value of an outcome: the greater the delay the greater the discounting. Impulsiveness occurs when delay discounts the physical value of a larger outcome to a degree that someone's perceived value of that outcome is less than that of a smaller, less delayed outcome (Logue, 1995). Therefore, changes in the perceived relative delays of the reinforcers can affect self-control. As an example, consider a situation in which someone who highly desires new clothes but does not have much money, and who can take only one day off in the next few weeks, perceives that he or she has available a choice between taking the day off today and buying one outfit and waiting to take the day off until after tomorrow's payday so as to be able to buy three outfits. In an extreme case, changing to a perceived choice between one outfit now and three outfits now will ensure choice of the three outfits. Similarly, changing to a perceived choice between one outfit tomorrow and three outfits tomorrow will also ensure choice of the three outfits. Making the perceived relative delays of the two alternatives appear more similar should result in greater choice of the larger outcome, and vice versa.

A large number of experiments have manipulated the physical values of the relative delays of the two outcomes in a variety of ways. As expected, greater relative delay to the larger outcome results in less self-control (Green, Fisher, Perlow, & Sherman, 1981; W. Mischel & Grusec, 1967). Other manipulations exist that, although they do not change the physical values of the relative outcome delays, they do change the perceived values of the relative outcome delays and thus also change self-control.

One example of such a manipulation consists of preexposing subjects to particular delays (Litrownik, Franzini, Geller, & Geller, 1977; Walls & Smith, 1970). Some researchers have argued that prior exposure to delays results in habituation to the frustration or aversiveness caused by delay, and thus should always result in at least some subsequent increased self-control (Eisenberger & Adornetto, 1986). Another view is that prior exposure should affect subsequent self-control behavior by causing contrast effects —that delays in a self-control paradigm seem shorter or longer than they really are because of previously exposing subjects to extremely long or short delays, respectively. A final view is that delay preexposure affects outcome expectancy (Grosch & Neuringer, 1981). Both of the latter two views correctly predict that delay preexposure should either increase or decrease self-control, depending on the relative lengths of the preexposed delays and the delays within the self-control choice (Eisenberger & Masterson, 1987; Grosch & Neuringer, 1981).

One particular kind of delay preexposure involves a fading procedure. In this procedure, subjects are first given a choice between equally delayed large and small outcomes. Then the delay to the small outcome is very gradually decreased, that is, faded until eventually the subject is choosing between a larger, more delayed outcome and a smaller, immediate outcome (alternatively, the delay to the large outcome can be very gradually increased). Both nonhuman (pigeon) and human (impulsive children) subjects exposed to this procedure have subsequently shown increased self-control (Logue, Rodriguez, Peña-Correal, & Mauro, 1984; Mazur & Logue, 1978; Schweitzer & Sulzer-Azaroff, 1988).

Perhaps because of its relationship to preexposure to outcome delay, preexposure to response effort can also increase self-control. In these experiments, self-control is defined as a choice between a smaller, easily available outcome and a larger, less easily available outcome, and demonstrating self-control involves actively maintaining a choice for a larger outcome over some period of time through some continued type of effort. This definition of self-control is actually very similar to the definition in use here, because greater effort often requires more time to exert than does less effort. Consistent with this interpretation, some researchers have stated that enduring a long delay is more effortful than enduring a short delay. Whatever the underlying mechanism, in children, rats, and pigeons, preexposure to effortful responding increases subsequent choices of a larger outcome requiring more effort (Eisenberger, Mitchell, & Masterson, 1985; Eisenberger, Weier, Masterson, & Theis, 1989; Mahoney & Bandura, 1972). More generally, past association of rewards with physical or cognitive effort can make the sensation of effort itself rewarding, resulting in a phenomenon that has been aptly named "learned industriousness" (Eisenberger, 1992).

One of the most commonly used methods for increasing self-control through manipulation of outcome delays involves manipulation of the perceived speed of the passage of time. Consider again the choice between one outfit available now and three outfits available tomorrow. If time is perceived as passing very quickly, then the perceived delay to the three outfits will be shorter, and self-control should increase. The opposite should also occur. Many experiments have examined what sorts of manipulations affect the perceived speed of the passage of time. Although more research is needed to determine these mechanisms, in general, it does appear that certain activities that seem to make time pass more quickly also increase self-control. For example, during the delay to the larger outcome, doing enjoyable activities, thinking enjoyable thoughts, or even having present some stimuli that have been previously associated with rewards, all increase self-control (Grosch & Neuringer, 1981; W. Mischel & Ebbesen, 1970; W. Mischel, Ebbesen, & Zeiss, 1972). Further, research has shown that a decrease in subjects' attention to the delay period

also increases self-control, possibly by means of a concurrent increase in the perceived speed of the passage of time. For example, one of the best ways for a subject to ensure maintenance of his or her self-control while waiting for the larger outcome is for the subject to completely remove any attention to the larger outcome's delay period by falling asleep (W. Mischel & Ebbesen, 1970). When people sleep, time seems to pass very quickly.

Outcome Size

Whether or not someone shows self-control is also a function of the sizes of the available outcomes. Making the perceived size of the larger outcome seem larger will, despite delay discounting, increase preference for the larger outcome.

One way to influence the relative sizes of the outcomes is simply to manipulate the perception that the outcomes are present. An outcome that is not and cannot be present has no size and will always be preferred less than an outcome that is or will be present, no matter what the size of the latter outcome. Experiments have attempted to manipulate outcome presence both by physical manipulations of the outcomes themselves and by manipulation of attention to the outcomes. Results show that, in general, for both children and pigeons, it is more difficult to wait for a larger outcome if the outcomes are physically present (Grosch & Neuringer, 1981; W. Mischel & Ebbesen, 1970; Yates & Revelle, 1979). Further, instructing children not to attend to the outcomes increases self-control (W. Mischel & Patterson, 1976; Patterson & Mischel, 1976). Researchers have postulated that people will be less impulsive if they control their attention or are distracted so that they do not think about the tempting situation; in such cases, time may seem to pass more quickly (Ainslie & Haslam, 1992).

One technique that may help people to increase self-control by increasing their awareness of the existence of the larger, more delayed outcome involves teaching people how to think about self-control situations in terms of cost-benefit rules. According to this method, people are taught to analyze a choice situation in terms of all of the possible costs and benefits associated with each possible choice, including what opportunities may be lost through making a particular choice (a type of cost). They are also taught to weigh carefully the relative net value of each outcome before making a decision. Instruction regarding this type of decision making does appear to increase choices of the alternative that provides the most benefit in the long term (Larrick, Morgan, & Nisbett, 1990).

Another way of helping people to increase self-control through increasing their awareness of the existence of the larger, more delayed outcome is the modeling of self-control (Bandura & Mischel, 1965; LaVoie, Anderson, Fraze, & Johnson, 1981). Watching someone else make a self-control choice and benefit by that choice can help to emphasize the availability of the larger, more delayed outcome. Modeling may also make the perceived time to the delayed outcome seem shorter. However, the precise mechanism by which modeling increases self-control is not yet known.

Changes in relative outcome size can be used to change self-control without going to the extreme of removing the presence of one or both of the outcomes. Simply making the relative size of the larger, more delayed outcome even larger will increase self-control. This can be done by increasing the physical or perceived size of the larger outcome, decreasing the physical or perceived size of the smaller outcome, or both. The relative size of an outcome can be manipulated by changing the volume of the outcome, the amount of timed access to the outcome, or the quality of the outcome. A number of experiments have demonstrated the usefulness of such strategies using both pigeons and humans (Fantino, 1966; Grusec, 1968; Herzberger & Dweck, 1978). In one experiment, human subjects were more likely to choose an alternative requiring more work (the self-control alternative) if that alternative yielded a reward of increased size (Blakely, Starin, & Poling, 1988).

The ways in which someone appears to think about the outcomes can also affect self-control, perhaps by influencing the perceived relative size

of the outcomes. Walter Mischel and his colleagues have shown in repeated experiments with children that if someone is told to think, or reports thinking, about the consummatory, motivational properties of outcomes (what Mischel calls "hot thoughts"), self-control decreases. However, if someone is told to think, or reports thinking, about the nonconsummatory, nonmotivational properties of outcomes (what Mischel calls "cool thoughts"), self-control increases (W. Mischel, Shoda, & Rodriguez, 1989). In a typical experiment, Mischel gives children a choice between one pretzel available now and three pretzels available if the child does not ring a bell until after a waiting period. Instructing the child to think about the taste of the pretzels and how crunchy they are decreases self-control. However, instructing the child to think about the shape and color of the pretzels increases self-control (W. Mischel & Baker, 1975). Although we are even less sure of a pigeon's than a child's thoughts, some comparable data appear to have been obtained in pigeons exposed to a self-control paradigm. Pigeons are less likely to wait for a larger amount of grain if the light in the hopper that delivers the grain is illuminated while they wait. This light, having been associated with the motivational properties of the grain, could serve the same stimulus function as Mischel's hot thoughts (Grosch & Neuringer, 1981).

A final way to increase the relative size of the self-control outcome in a self-control choice paradigm is to combine that outcome with another positive or negative outcome, thus increasing or decreasing, respectively, the net value of the self-control alternative. One way to do this is through delivering reward or punishment each time the self-control choice is made (Karniol & Miller, 1981; Little & Kendall, 1979). For example, parents can give their children cookies each time the children display self-control. Self-reward and self-punishment can also be used (Kanfer, 1971; O'Leary & Dubey, 1979). In self-reward, someone engages in a pleasurable activity (a reward) whenever that person has engaged in another specified activity. In self-punishment, an unpleasurable activity (a punisher) is used instead of the reward. Given that self-reward and self-punishment are not always manifested by changes in external behavior, it is not always possible to know when self-reward and self-punishment are occurring or what influences them. It is also not clear to what extent the concepts of self-reward and self-punishment are useful above and beyond knowing the subject's history with the external environment.

Outcome Contingencies

Someone can be aware that various outcomes exist that have specific delays and sizes but be unaware of what responses will or will not result in those outcomes. The relationships between responses and outcomes are called outcome contingencies. Certain outcome contingencies and the perceived presence of those contingencies can be used to increase self-control.

One outcome contingency that can affect self-control concerns whether or not the subject has the option to change his or her choice while waiting for the larger, more delayed outcome. In laboratory research, pigeons are less likely to end up actually receiving the larger, more delayed outcome if such a choice change is available (Elster, 1985; Logue & Peña-Correal, 1984). This may be because subjects in this situation have essentially repeated choices between an immediate, smaller outcome and a delayed, larger outcome before they receive the delayed, larger outcome.

Therefore, in this situation, the pigeons have more opportunities to be impulsive.

A related type of contingency that can also affect self-control is a precommitment contingency (Ainslie, 1975; Rachlin, 1974; see Figure 13–2). When this contingency is present, before having to make a choice between a self-control outcome and an impulsive outcome, an individual can make a (precommitment) response that will prevent a subsequent impulsive response. Not making the precommitment response results in the presentation of the usual self-control choice. An example of precommitment is our use of the alarm clock. In the morning, we have a choice between the larger, more delayed outcome of getting to school (or work) on time and the smaller, less delayed outcome of some extra sleep. The night before, we may precommit to making the self-control response the next morning by setting an alarm clock. When that alarm clock rings, it will essentially remove the response of continued sleep, and will make the only possible response that of getting to school (or work) on time (in some cases it may be necessary to use a very loud alarm clock located far from the bed). Precommitment responses have been demonstrated in human as well as nonhuman subjects, although there seem to be large individual differences in the ability to precommit (e.g., Rachlin & Green, 1972; Solnick, Kannenberg, Eckerman, & Waller, 1980). Precommit-

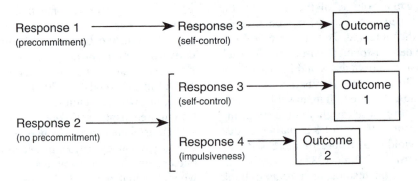

Figure 13–2. Diagram of precommitment (Response 1) and no precommitment (Response 2) choice alternatives.

ment responses are interesting to psychologists because they indicate that people's and other animals' preferences between the self-control and impulsive outcomes change as a function of time. When we set an alarm clock, we are demonstrating a preference for the larger, more delayed outcome of getting to school (or work) on time. However, the next morning, this preference often reverses. Precommitment strategies are an extremely useful, general self-control technique widely recognized in the popular culture.

Self-control can also be affected by knowledge of the outcomes to which different responses will lead. A person will not show self-control unless that person has learned that the self-control response will eventually lead to a larger outcome. Humans learn about the consequences for the choices in a self-control paradigm by making the responses and receiving the consequences, or by watching or speaking with other people who are involved in a similar choice or who have some knowledge about such a choice (Kendall, 1982; Kendall & Zupan, 1981). Monitoring—keeping careful track of one's own responses and the ensuing consequences, perhaps by some formal means such as keeping a list or drawing a graph —may assist in the recognition and memory of behavioral consequences and thus assist self-control (W. Mischel, 1990; Rachlin, 1974).

Sometimes self-control is hindered because the connection between the self-control response and its outcome seems tenuous or uncertain. As previously discussed, as the certainty of a future event decreases, the advantages accruing from waiting for that event also decrease. An example of this phenomenon concerns the trust that the chooser has in the person delivering the outcome (Shybut, 1968). If the chooser does not believe that the larger, more delayed outcome will be delivered, there is no point to the subject's demonstrating self-control. This may explain why it is that children are more likely to show self-control when tested by other children rather than by adults, and that African Americans are more likely to show self-control when tested by other African Americans rather than by Caucasians (Lew, 1982; Strickland, 1972).

Subjects' self-statements also appear to influence the subjects' perceptions of the response-outcome contingencies. Subjects who make statements during the waiting periods reminding themselves of what will happen if they wait, or of what they have to do to receive the larger reinforcer, are more likely to show self-control (Anderson & Moreland, 1982; Kendall, 1977; Meichenbaum & Goodman, 1971). In one experiment, young children aged 2.5 to 4 years had difficulty responding slowly in order to receive rewards. However, when they were taught to sing a song about responding slowly, they were able to respond slowly (Bentall & Lowe, 1987). Self-statements may increase self-control through providing stimuli ("reminders") associated with the response-outcome contingency. Similar stimuli can be provided to nonhuman subjects. When colored lights are present during delay periods, with the precise color used being identical to the color of the choice button that has been pecked, pigeons show more self-control than when such delay lights are not used (Logue & Mazur, 1981). Complex language behavior is not necessary for stimuli to function as reminders of the response-outcome contingencies and for self-control to be increased. Nevertheless, some research has shown that self-verbalization about the reinforcer contingencies is less effective than self-distraction at increasing self-control (described above; Anderson, 1978).

Characteristics of the Individual Person

Even though they are given the same choices, some people will show self-control and others will be impulsive. For example, much evidence suggests that, in general, self-control appears to increase as children age and become adults (Kopp, 1982; W. Mischel et al., 1989). More specifically, as children age, they are less affected by outcome delays and are able to take into account events that are in the distant future (Wilson & Herrnstein, 1985). This age-related change can be described as an increase in children's time horizon—the time period over which individuals integrate a series of events (Krebs & Kacelnik, 1984). Some evidence suggests that children progress through two stages in developing the adult pattern of self-control behavior. First, around the age of 6 years, children learn to wait for the more preferred outcome; they learn that it can be advantageous to wait for something rather than always to choose the immediate outcome. Then, around the age of 9 to 12 years, they learn when they should wait for the more preferred outcome; they learn that it is not always advantageous to wait for the more preferred outcome (Sonuga-Barke, Lea, & Webley, 1989a, 1989b). Apparently, as people age, they can develop abilities or learn strategies that will assist them in decreasing or removing the effects of discounting of delayed outcomes. These age-related traits and abilities may differ in degree among adults, and so may also be responsible for some of the differences in self-control seen among adults.

Many different traits and abilities exist that may be responsible for the increase in self-control that is generally seen as children age, and that may also be partly or wholly responsible for the differences in self-control that are often seen among adults. One example is the ability to discriminate time intervals. This ability appears to improve with age and to be associated with increased self-control (W. Mischel & Metzner, 1962). For example, in one experiment, boys who would work for a delayed, valuable outcome without any immediate benefit for doing so tended to estimate these times more accurately (Levine & Spivak, 1959).

Several different lines of research suggest that self-control is related to a variety of types of intellectual abilities (such as those measured by the Peabody Picture Vocabulary Test, SAT scores, and tests of expressive language behavior). In general, these studies indicate that a positive relationship exists between self-control and intellectual aptitude (Funder & Block, 1989; Golden, Montare, & Bridger, 1977; W. Mischel & Metzner, 1962; Rodriguez, Mischel, & Shoda, 1989). A positive relationship between verbal aptitude and self-control could help to explain the rela-

tively greater self-control seen in human than in nonhuman subjects (Logue, Peña-Correal, Rodriguez, & Kabela, 1986). The statements that human subjects make to themselves may help them to determine which choices will maximize total received positive outcomes, or may provide them with reminders to help make the long delay of a self-control choice seem shorter. Nevertheless, the data directly examining the role of language behavior in self-control in children are mixed. Some studies have found that language capacity or vocabulary are positively related to self-control (Kopp, 1982; Vaughn, Kopp, Krakow, Johnson, & Schwartz, 1986), but others have not (Kopp, 1982; Maitland, 1967). It is possible that what assists self-control is the ability to make certain kinds of verbalizations during delay periods, not language ability in general.

Given that self-control can sometimes involve withholding a response, it is possible that general activity level is related to the development of self-control. Children (especially those with attention-deficit hyperactivity disorder, or other subject populations with relatively high innate activity levels) might have particular difficulties withholding their responses within self-control situations. Younger children have trouble responding at a slow rate to obtain a reward (Bentall & Lowe, 1987). Further, pigeons, notoriously difficult to discourage from pecking, have difficulty showing self-control when the self-control response consists of not pecking (Lopatto & Lewis, 1985).

The learning of general strategies for increasing self-control can also contribute to the development of and individual differences in self-control. Around age five or six, children begin to learn what sorts of behaviors will make it easier to wait for a larger, more delayed outcome. For example, they learn that distracting themselves (such as by singing a song, playing a game, or falling asleep) or instructing themselves (such as by repeating to themselves that waiting will result in the larger reward) can help in the demonstration of self-control. In addition, somewhere between the third and sixth grades, children are able to report that thinking abstractly about the rewards and the task (such as thoughts about the shape of the rewards) rather than about the consummatory properties of the rewards (such as their taste) will also help in their demonstrating self-control (H. N. Mischel & W. Mischel, 1983; W. Mischel et al., 1989).

Investigation of any gender differences in self-control may also help provide explanations for individual differences in self-control. Studies using a variety of self-control paradigms and children of different ages have shown clearly that girls tend to demonstrate more self-control than boys (Kanfer & Zich, 1974; Logue & Chavarro, 1992; Maccoby & Jacklin, 1974; Sonuga-Barke et al., 1989a; Trommsdorff & Schmidt-Rinke, 1980). It is not at all clear what is responsible for these gender differences. However, it is known that differences in language ability between boys and girls are too small to explain the differences between them with regard to self-control (Hyde & Linn, 1988; Jacklin, 1989). Other, as yet unsubstantiated, hypotheses that could explain why girls show more self-control than boys include the different ways that girls and boys are socialized and differences in activity level between girls and boys (see, e.g., Funder, Block, & Block, 1983; Low, 1989). It is not yet clear whether or not men and women differ in terms of their tendencies to demonstrate self-control.

Finally, development of self-control may differ among different people depending on the culture in which they are raised. By definition, cultures vary in terms of the experiences they provide, experiences that may result in differing degrees of self-control. In the United States, there appear to be strong cultural tendencies for both self-control and impulsiveness. On the one hand, self-control and resistance to temptation have been part of America's Judeo-Christian heritage. However, in recent decades, there has been concern that this early emphasis on self-control may be dissipating. The baby boom children are now in their thirties and forties and are not saving as much money as their parents did when they were their age, and *we* hear repeated discussion of the recent me generation (Logue, 1995). In contrast, many people consider the Japanese culture to be virtually synonymous with self-control. From early childhood the Japanese stress consensus and cooperation. Individual gratification is valued much less than is advancement of the fortunes of the group, something that requires that each group member put aside personal desires in order to work for long-term societal goals. Japanese businesses and managers are known for taking a much more long-term view in their planning than are their Western counterparts. The Japanese are also noted for their high rate of savings (Christopher, 1983). However, just as in the United States, there is concern that self-control in Japan is decreasing. There has been a recent decrease in the rate of savings (Nasar, 1991). In addition, Japanese young adults now seem more inclined to feel that working hard should result in immediate rather than delayed rewards (Christopher, 1983). Thus, although the Japanese and American cultures have sometimes appeared to be significantly different with respect to self-control, the similarities between them may be increasing.

SPECIFIC PROBLEMS OF SELF-CONTROL AND IMPULSIVENESS

The preceding sections concerning different factors that affect self-control present many general strategies about how to increase or decrease self-control. These strategies include ways of influencing the effect of outcome delay, of outcome size, and of the response-outcome contingencies. However, the ability to understand and change self-control in particular situations may be dependent on specific aspects of a given situation. Thorough knowledge of what affects self-control in particular situations may assist in the development of specific techniques for changing self-control in those situations. Descriptions of some such situations and techniques follow.

Eating

A variety of problems associated with eating—that is, overeating, anorexia nervosa, and bulimia nervosa—can be seen as self-control problems. In all three cases, a person engages in a behavior that results in some relatively immediate positive outcome but in the long run is not beneficial to the person's health.

Overeating can be classified in two general types: overeating of all types of foods and overeating of specific types of food. Each type has a number of different causes and thus a number of different possible treatments. For example, overeating of all types of food can be caused by too many adipose (fat) cells in the body. People are hungry if their fat cells are not full of fat (Le-Magnen, 1985; Sjöström, 1978). The number of fat cells that a person has is significantly determined by that person's genes, and may increase if the person gains weight; the number can never decrease (Björntorp, 1987; Sjöström, 1978). In some people, impulsive overeating of all types of food can also be caused by exposure to stimuli that have been associated with food. Such a person is said to be externally responsive—encountering these stimuli increases the person's insulin level which, in turn, increases the person's hunger level and the tendency for any food consumed to be stored as fat (Rodin, 1985; Weingarten, 1983). Food variety can also increase overeating through avoidance of sensory-specific satiety effects, in which people and other animals satiate sooner when consuming only a limited set of gustatory and olfactory stimuli (Clifton, Burton, & Sharp, 1987; Rolls et al., 1981). Finally, for restrained eaters (people who do not ordinarily eat all that they wish), a belief that alcohol has been consumed also results in overeating of all types of food (Polivy & Herman, 1976).

Overeating of specific types of food can result from our genetic predispositions to prefer sweet foods, salty foods, and foods that we learn are high in calories (such as fatty foods). These preferences were adaptive in the environment in which we evolved. However, now most people in the United States have easy access to large amounts of sweet, salty, and fatty foods, and so we tend to overeat those foods (Logue, 1991; Simopoulos, 1987). Some people have a specific craving for carbohydrate foods. It has been hy-

pothesized that some such people (including some premenstrual women and people suffering from seasonal affective disorder—depression that tends to occur when the days are short) have insufficient amounts of the neurotransmitter serotonin stimulating their brains (Wurtman, 1981; Wurtman & Wurtman, 1984, 1988). It has been further hypothesized that serotonin is essential in animals' ability to tolerate delay—essentially that serotonin is involved in the suppression of impulsive behaviors (Mann & Stanley, 1986; Soubrié, 1986). In fact, self-control has been increased in rats by drugs that enhance serotonin functioning (Bizot, Thiébot, Le Bihan, Soubrié, & Simon, 1988; Thiébot, Le Bihan, Soubrié, & Simon, 1985). Given that consumption of a predominantly carbohydrate meal increases the amount of serotonin's chemical precursor, tryptophan (an amino acid), that enters the brain, people suffering from carbohydrate craving may be trying to increase the amount of serotonin in their brains (Logue, 1991). Finally, stress can also increase consumption of particular foods, especially palatable foods (Cantor, Smith, & Bryan, 1982; Rowland & Antelman, 1976).

These different causes of impulsive overeating suggest a number of different treatments. For example, precommitment procedures can be used to ensure that a person avoids stimuli that have been associated with food, meals containing a lot of different foods, alcohol consumption when food is present, sweet foods, salty foods, high-fat foods, situations in which stress is likely to occur with food present, or simply too many opportunities to eat. More specifically, when a person goes grocery shopping, that person can take only a limited amount of money. Then, unless the person is able to persuade someone at the store to provide a loan, it will be impossible for the person to buy large amounts of food. Practically speaking, of course, using precommitment procedures to avoid all of these different types of tempting situations is extremely difficult. More physiologically based treatments can also be used, such as giving carbohydrate cravers a drug that raises serotonin level. However, development of such drugs is still in its infancy.

Although a person with either anorexia nervosa or bulimia nervosa may feel that she or he is following an optimal strategy, just about everyone else views people suffering from these two disorders as engaging in behaviors that are not the best strategy the long run. Therefore, treating either disorder might be facilitated by making the long-term detrimental effects of these disorders seem closer in time. For example, perhaps speaking with people who have encountered some of the health problems caused by anorexia nervosa might be a useful part of treatment. At the same time, it might be helpful to try to decrease the value of being thin for the female by taking steps to convince her that, despite the media's depiction of attractive women as being extremely thin, people do not find her standard of thinness to be attractive. However, these treatment suggestions will certainly be insufficient by themselves. Anorexia nervosa and bulimia nervosa are notoriously difficult to treat and require a combination of treatments (see, e.g., Bemis, 1978; Garfinkel & Garner, 1982). For example, for bulimia nervosa, which is often associated with depression, antidepressants can be effectively used to ameliorate binging and purging (Agras, 1987; Hudson, Pope, & Jonas, 1984; Walsh et al., 1982).

Drug Abuse

People abuse many different kinds of drugs, including alcohol, cocaine, marijuana, nicotine, and caffeine. In all of these cases, taking the drug results in some short-term pleasure (including the removal of any withdrawal effects) but some long-term harm to health. Thus, drug abuse can be classified as impulsiveness. Further, there is some evidence that, in some cases, taking drugs such as alcohol and cocaine can increase impulsiveness in other situations. Thus, drug abuse can both be an example of impulsiveness and can itself cause impulsiveness (Logue, 1995).

Many successful methods for decreasing drug abuse exist that derive from a variety of perspectives. This section considers some possible treatments for drug abuse that are suggested by considering drug abuse within a self-control framework. One obvious way to decrease drug abuse is to decrease the relatively immediate rewards that result from taking a drug. For example, if the drug is an addictive one, it may be possible to eliminate the drug-taking reward of removing withdrawal symptoms by the use of some appropriate medication. Alternatively, the immediate positive value of taking an abused drug can also be decreased by following the drug's use with some immediate negative consequences. This is the principle behind the use of the medication Antabuse, which, if someone has taken it and then consumes alcohol, causes a profound physical reaction including "nausea, vomiting, tachycardia, marked drop in blood pressure, and other symptoms of massive autonomic arousal" (Litman & Topham, 1983, p. 172). Another method for decreasing the relatively immediate positive consequences that can follow use of an abused drug is to increase the value of other rewards present at the same time, thus making the rewards for drug taking seem relatively smaller. Precommitment, such as by the use of contingency contracts (Resnick & Resnick, 1984; Schelling, 1992), is another obvious method of treating impulsive drug abuse, one that is used by the majority of methadone maintenance clinics. Drug abusers sign such contracts when drugs are not currently available. The drug abusers agree that if they abuse drugs, they will receive certain negative consequences, and if they do not abuse drugs, they will receive certain positive consequences (Calsyn, Saxon, & Barndt, 1991; Nolimal & Crowley, 1990). Finally, another way to decrease impulsive drug abuse is to increase the value of the more delayed, larger rewards that result from not taking the drugs—either by directly increasing the value of those rewards or by making the delays to those rewards seem shorter. An example of how this could be done would be to show pregnant women a video clearly demonstrating how the blood supply in an umbilical cord is severely decreased if the mother consumes even a single drink of 100-proof whiskey (Altura et al., 1983).

Other Health-Related Behaviors

People engage in many other types of behaviors so as to obtain some immediate satisfaction, but at the expense of their long-term health. Thus, these are impulsive behaviors. Some examples are engaging in unprotected sexual activity (which can result in unwanted pregnancy and sexually transmitted diseases), being a couch potato (so that there is insufficient exercise to maintain health), not going to the doctor when a suspicious symptom occurs, and not taking your car for regular inspections (possibly resulting in a dangerous vehicle). In all of these cases, the consequence of a long, healthy life may be very delayed, and therefore its (discounted) value may play a small role when choices are being made between healthy and nonhealthy behaviors. The general self-control techniques described previously can be adapted so as to be very effective in particular health-related situations.

For example, many people (such as diabetics) are told by a medical care professional to engage in a specific treatment program. The treatment may have only long-term beneficial effects and consist of unpleasant behaviors (e.g., blood monitoring, changes in diet, and taking insulin shots or pills), and the underlying illness may have few, if any, currently debilitating symptoms. Under these circumstances, it is not surprising that many people have great difficulty adhering to the treatment program; they behave impulsively and do not maintain the treatment. Contingency contracting, a precommitment strategy, may be helpful in getting patients to adhere to their treatment programs, although the patients need to be sufficiently motivated and intelligent to use this self-control technique (Morgan & Littell, 1988).

Education, Management, and Money

Self-control plays a significant role in education. Whether or not teachers and students show self-control can affect how successful education is—how much students learn and how well-prepared they are for their future careers. Students must study rather than party in order to obtain good grades, and teachers must evaluate their students' work quickly rather than relax in order for the feedback to the students to be most useful. Some educators, those at institutions requiring scholarly work for raises and promotions, may have difficulty advancing in their careers when faced with the immediate rewards of teaching well and the delayed rewards of scholarly work. In addition, decisions concerning educational policy sometimes involve issues of self-control (weighing more immediate consequences against more delayed consequences).

When school careers are over and work careers have begun, workers need to manage their earnings, and self-control is again involved. For example, to have a fulfilling retirement, people need to give up some immediate, costly pleasures in favor of saving money. Sometimes people need to do less impulsive spending just to have sufficient funds to pay next month's bills. One consumer avoided the temptation to spend by literally freezing her credit cards in a six-inch block of ice (Kaplan, 1992). Many consumers, however, do not engage in such clever precommitment devices. Managers in organizations and businesses also need to take into account both short- and long-term consequences when making decisions, decisions that can affect the employees, clients, and/or neighbors of the organization or business. An example of such a decision is choosing an investment strategy (e.g., choosing between three-month treasury bills that pay all earnings to the investor within a few months of purchase of the treasury bills, and zero-coupon bonds, the earnings from which are not realized until after many years.) Sometimes, rather than choosing to earn money or good grades, people choose to cheat or to engage in gambling or theft, strategies likely to result in positive consequences only in the short term, at best.

Higher education administrators must also choose between self-control and impulsiveness. For example, college and university deans need to avoid making commitments against future funds, because new financial crises may arise making those funds difficult to obtain. As another example, Henry Rosovsky, for many years Dean of Arts and Sciences at Harvard University, offered a compelling analogy between universities and baseball teams that aptly illustrates some of the advantages and disadvantages of short- and long-term managerial strategies. According to Rosovsky, similar to a university, a baseball team has a choice between purchasing expensive star players (i.e., tenured faculty), who will give instant recognition to the team (but who may be past their prime), or devoting its energies to a farm system in which young players' talents are fostered for many years so that some (unfortunately, usually not all) of them will become star players (Rosovsky, 1990).

Getting Along With Yourself and Others

Issues of self-control are also involved in terms of how people and other animals interact with each other and how people feel about themselves. Such situations involve behaviors such as cooperation, lying, depression, suicide, and aggression.

Cooperation exists whenever two or more people work together to obtain something that they value. For example, some neighbors might cooperate in building a community swimming pool. Cooperation involves giving up something small now (some time, money, or effort) in return for almost certain receipt of a large something later.

Lying (deliberately providing false information) has been classified as both self-control and impulsiveness. Sometimes lying is self-control because it involves providing false information to obtain something in the sometimes very distant future (Alexander, 1989). Often, however, lying is impulsiveness because it is done to obtain some immediate reward without consideration of the long-term consequences if the lying should be discovered. An example of someone who engages in such lying is a researcher who is desperate for tenure and therefore fabricates some data. In this case, the immediate reward is

tenure, but should the lie be found out (and it often is), the researcher may find it impossible to get a grant or any sort of research position.

Depression has been associated with impulsiveness in that depressed people have less ability to feel pleasure and so large, delayed rewards do not seem so large to them. Similarly, because of their inability to concentrate and the ease with which they are distracted by immediate stimuli, depressed people can have difficulty waiting for a delayed reward. In some cases, depressed people may contemplate suicide (American Psychiatric Association, 1994) which, when its main function is to avoid short-term aversive stimuli, can be seen as impulsiveness. The possible connection between depression and impulsiveness is bolstered by results from experiments with children showing that children are more likely to show self-control when they are in a positive mood (Moore, Clyburn, & Underwood, 1976; Schwarz & Pollack, 1977). Depression and suicidal behavior can be exacerbated by drug abuse and also sometimes by low levels of serotonin. All of this research suggests that it may be possible to decrease depression and suicidal behavior by making delayed, large rewards seem closer. This could be accomplished by having people suffering from depression and suicidal tendencies speak with recovered depressives to hear about the rewarding aspects of life that can follow depression. Support groups can be helpful in this regard. Pharmacological treatments, such as the use of the medication Prozac, which enhances serotonin functioning, may also be useful. Finally, people who are depressed could use precommitment devices to avoid using drugs that can increase the risk of suicide (Logue, 1995).

In many cases, aggression results in the receipt of some immediate reward, such as the obtaining of some high-valued items. However, ultimately, the aggressor may lose his or her friends or job by such behaviors or may even end up in jail or the morgue. Thus, although aggression may result in the receipt of some immediate reward, the long-term consequences are often not positive ones, and aggression therefore should frequently be classified as impulsiveness. Much research has been devoted to the causes of aggression, with a variety of causes being identified (the influence of some, but not others, is quite easily modified by making changes in the environment). For example, consuming alcohol and having relatively high testosterone levels appear to be positively correlated with aggression (Beck, 1990; Hull & Bond, 1986). Many of the methods for decreasing impulsive aggression are similar to others previously mentioned in this chapter. People other than the aggressor—or the aggressor through use of precommitment techniques—can take steps to decrease the immediate rewards for aggression, increase the delayed rewards for nonaggression, or both. It may also be possible to decrease aggression by decreasing the perceived time to the rewards for nonaggression. One study showed that it was possible to increase self-control in young adult prisoners by having them observe peer models who held prestigious jobs within the prison, were soon to be released, and had a high tendency to delay rewards (Stumphauzer, 1972).

SUMMARY AND CONCLUSIONS

During the past 25 years, laboratory research on self-control has explored many different aspects of the nature and causes of this behavior. By operationally defining self-control as choice of a larger, more delayed outcome over a smaller, less delayed outcome, and impulsiveness as the opposite choice, it has been possible to study self-control under controlled laboratory conditions. Impulsiveness clearly results from the discounting of delayed events—a trait that most likely evolved and is sometimes adaptive, but probably less so now than originally. Self-control is not always good, and impulsiveness is not always bad. A starving person should not choose a banquet two weeks from now over some bread available today.

In general, self-control is influenced by the relative delays and sizes of the outcomes, whether or not a person can change his or her choice once it is made, and the chooser's understanding of the consequences of a particular choice. Further, self-control sometimes varies according to people's perceptual abilities, past experience, verbal and other intellectual abilities, gender, culture, and age. A self-control paradigm can be useful in understanding and changing behavior in situations involving eating disorders, drug abuse, sexual behavior, health-related behaviors, educational settings, earning and managing money, theft, cooperation, lying, administration, depression and suicide, and aggression.

Choices between outcomes of varying sizes and delays, and thus choices between self-control and impulsiveness, occur frequently and in many different contexts. However, although discounting of delayed events appears to occur for most species in most situations to some degree, the same mechanisms may not be responsible for these different cases of discounting. Therefore, understanding and modifying self-control and impulsiveness can differ according to the particular situation.

The kinds of choices that are made can have significant impact on people's health, career success, and ability to interact positively with others. Thus, the insights with respect to the nature and causes of self-control and impulsiveness afforded by laboratory research, including with nonhuman subjects, are extremely useful to clinical psychologists, physicians, lawmakers, educators, and the many others whose job it is to help people optimize their functioning.

REFERENCES

Agras, W. S. (1987). *Eating disorders: Management of obesity, bulimia, and anorexia nervosa.* New York: Pergamon.

Ainslie, G. (1975). Specious reward: A behavioral theory of impulsiveness and impulse control. *Psychological Bulletin, 82,* 463–496.

Ainslie, G. (1992). *Picoeconomics: The strategic interaction of successive motivational states within the person.* Cambridge, U.K.: Cambridge University Press.

Ainslie, G., & Haslam, N. (1992). Self-control. In G. Loewenstein & J. Elster (eds.), *Choice over time,* 177–209. New York: Russell Sage Foundation.

Ainslie, G., & Herrnstein, R. J. (1981). Preference reversal and delayed reinforcement. *Animal Learning & Behavior, 9,* 476–482.

Ainslie, G. W. (1974). Impulse control in pigeons. *Journal of the Experimental Analysis of Behavior, 21,* 485–489.

Alexander, R. D. (1989). Evolution of the human psyche. In P. Mellars & C. Stringer (eds.), *The human revolution: Behavioural and biological perspectives on the origins of modern humans,* 455–513. Princeton: Princeton University Press.

Altura, B. M., Altura, B. T., Carella, A., Chatterjee, M., Halevy, S., & Tejani, N. (1983). Alcohol produces spasms of human umbilical blood vessels: Relationship to fetal alcohol syndrome (FAS). *European Journal of Pharmacology, 86,* 311–312.

American Psychiatric Association. (1994). *Diagnostic and statistical manual of mental disorders* (4th ed.). Washington, D.C.: Author.

Anderson, W. H. (1978). A comparison of self-distraction with self-verbalization under moralistic versus instrumental rationales in a delay-of-gratification paradigm. *Cognitive Therapy and Research, 2,* 299–303.

Anderson, W. H., & Moreland, K. L. (1982). Instrumental vs. moralistic self-verbalizations in delaying gratification. *Merrill-Palmer Quarterly, 28,* 291–296.

Bandura, A., & Mischel, W. (1965). Modification of self-imposed delay of reward through exposure to live and symbolic models. *Journal of Personality and Social Psychology, 2,* 698–705.

Barash, D. P. (1977). *Sociobiology and behavior.* New York: Elsevier.

Beck, R. C. (1990). *Motivation: Theories and principles.* Englewood Cliffs, N.J.: Prentice-Hall.

Bemis, K. M. (1978). Current approaches to the etiology and treatment of anorexia nervosa. *Psychological Bulletin, 85,* 593–617.

Bentall, R. P., & Lowe, C. F. (1987). The role of verbal behavior in human learning: III. Instructional effects in children. *Journal of the Experimental Analysis of Behavior, 47,* 177–190.

Bizot, J. C., Thiébot, M. H., Le Bihan, C., Soubrié, P., & Simon, P. (1988). Effects of imipramine-like drugs and serotonin uptake blockers on delay of reward in rats. Possible implication in the behavioral mechanism of action of antidepressants. *The Journal of Pharmacology and Experimental Therapeutics, 246,* 1144–1151.

Björntorp, P. (1987). Fat cell distribution and metabolism. In R. J. Wurtman & J. J. Wurtman (eds.), *Human obesity,* 66–72. New York: New York Academy of Sciences.

Blakely, E., Starin, S., & Poling, A. (1988). Human performance under sequences of fixed-ratio schedules: Effects of ratio size and magnitude of reinforcement. *The Psychological Record, 38,* 111–119.

Calsyn, D. A., Saxon, A. J., & Barndt, D. C. (1991). Urine screening practices in methadone maintenance clinics: A survey of how the results are used. *The Journal of Nervous and Mental Disease, 179,* 222–227.

Cantor, M. B., Smith, S. E., & Bryan, B. R. (1982). Induced bad habits: Adjunctive ingestion and grooming in human subjects. *Appetite, 3,* 1–12.

Christopher, R. C. (1983). *The Japanese mind.* New York: Fawcett Columbine.

Clifton, P. G., Burton, M. J., & Sharp, C. (1987). Rapid loss of stimulus-specific satiety after consumption of a second food. *Appetite, 9,* 149–156.

Cohen, M. N. (1987). The significance of long-term changes in human diet and food economy. In M. Harris & E. B. Ross (eds.), *Food and evolution: Toward a theory of human food habits,* 261–283. Philadelphia: Temple University Press.

Cosmides, L., & Tooby, J. (1987). From evolution to behavior: Evolutionary psychology as the missing link. In J. Dupré (ed.), *The latest on the best: Essays on evolution and optimality,* 277–306. Cambridge: MIT Press.

Eisenberger, R. (1992). Learned industriousness. *Psychological Review, 99,* 248–267.

Eisenberger, R., & Adornetto, M. (1986). Generalized self-control of delay and effort. *Journal of Personality and Social Psychology, 51,* 1020–1031.

Eisenberger, R., & Masterson, F. A. (1987). Effects of prior learning and current motivation on self-control. In J. A. Nevin & H. Rachlin (eds.), *Quantitative analyses of behavior, Vol. 5: The effects of delay and of intervening events on reinforcement value,* 267–282. Hillsdale, N.J.: Erlbaum.

Eisenberger, R., Mitchell, M., & Masterson, F. A. (1985). Effort training increases generalized self-control. *Journal of Personality and Social Psychology, 49,* 1294–1301.

Eisenberger, R., Weier, F., Masterson, F. A., & Theis, L. Y. (1989). Fixed-ratio schedules increase generalized self-control: Preference for large rewards despite high effort or punishment. *Journal of Experimental Psychology: Animal Behavior Processes, 15,* 383–392.

Elster, J. (1985). Weakness of will and the free-rider problem. *Economics and Philosophy, 1,* 231–265.

Fantino, E. (1966). Immediate reward followed by extinction vs. later reward without extinction. *Psychonomic Science, 6,* 233–234.

Forzano, L. B., & Logue, A. W. (1994). Self-control in adult humans: Comparison of qualitatively different reinforcers. *Learning and Motivation, 25,* 65–82.

Funder, D. C., & Block, J. (1989). The role of ego-control, ego-resiliency, and IQ in delay of gratification in adolescence. *Journal of Personality and Social Psychology, 57,* 1041–1050.

Funder, D. C., Block, J. H., & Block, J. (1983). Delay of gratification: Some longitudinal personality correlates. *Journal of Personality and Social Psychology, 44,* 1198–1213.

Garfinkel, P. E., & Garner, D. M. (1982). *Anorexia nervosa.* New York: Brunner/Mazel.

Golden, M., Montare, A., & Bridger, W. (1977). Verbal control of delay behavior in two-year-old boys as a function of social class. *Child Development, 48,* 1107–1111.

Goldfried, M. R., & Merbaum, M. (eds.) (1973). *Behavior change through self-control.* New York: Holt, Rinehart and Winston.

Gorenstein, E. E., & Newman, J. P. (1980). Disinhibitory psychopathology: A new perspective and a model for research. *Psychological Review, 87,* 301–315.

Green, L., Fisher, E. B., Perlow, S., & Sherman, L. (1981). Preference reversal and self control: Choice as a function of reward amount and delay. *Behaviour Analysis Letters, 1,* 43–51.

Grosch, J., & Neuringer, A. (1981). Self-control in pigeons under the Mischel paradigm. *Journal of the Experimental Analysis of Behavior, 35,* 3–21.

Grossman, S. P. (1967). *A textbook of physiological psychology.* New York: Wiley.

Grusec, J. E. (1968). Waiting for rewards and punishments: Effects of reinforcement value on choice. *Journal of Personality and Social Psychology, 9,* 85–89.

Hamilton, W. D. (1964a). The genetical evolution of social behaviour. I. *Journal of Theoretical Biology, 7,* 1–16.

Hamilton, W. D. (1964b). The genetical evolution of social behaviour. II. *Journal of Theoretical Biology, 7,* 17–52.

Harlan, J. R. (1975). *Crops & man.* Madison, Wis.: American Society of Agronomy.

Herzberger, S. D., & Dweck, C. S. (1978). Attraction and delay of gratification. *Journal of Personality, 46,* 214–227.

Hudson, J. I., Pope, H. G., & Jonas, J. M. (1984). Treatment of bulimia with antidepressants: Theoretical considerations and clinical findings. In A. J. Stunkard & E. Stellar (eds.), *Eating and its disorders,* 259–273. New York: Raven Press.

Hull, J. G., & Bond, C. F. (1986). Social and behavioral consequences of alcohol consumption and expectancy: A meta-analysis. *Psychological Bulletin, 99,* 347–360.

Hyde, J. S., & Linn, M. C. (1988). Gender differences in verbal ability: A meta-analysis. *Psychological Bulletin, 104,* 53–69.

Jacklin, C. N. (1989). Female and male: Issues of gender. *American Psychologist, 44,* 127–133.

Kagel, J. H., Green, L., & Caraco, T. (1986). When foragers discount the future: Constraint or adaptation? *Animal Behaviour, 34,* 271–283.

Kanfer, F. H. (1971). The maintenance of behavior by self-generated stimuli and reinforcement. In A. Jacobs & L. Sachs (eds.), *The psychology of private events,* 39–59. New York: Academic Press.

Kanfer, F. H., & Zich, J. (1974). Self-control training: The effects of external control on children's resistance to temptation. *Developmental Psychology, 10,* 108–115.

Kaplan, M. (1992, September 14). Frozen assets. *New York,* p. 37.

Karniol, R., & Miller, D. T. (1981). The development of self-control in children. In S. S. Brehm, S. M. Kassin, & F. X. Gibbons (eds.), *Developmental social psychology: Theory and research,* 32–50. Oxford: Oxford University Press.

Kendall, P. C. (1977). On the efficacious use of verbal self-instructional procedures with children. *Cognitive Therapy and Research, 1,* 331–341.

Kendall, P. C. (1982). Individual versus group cognitive-behavioral self-control training: 1-year follow-up. *Behavior Therapy, 13,* 241–247.

Kendall, P. C., & Zupan, B. A. (1981). Individual versus group application of cognitive-behavioral self-control procedures with children. *Behavior Therapy, 12,* 344–359.

Kopp, C. B. (1982). Antecedents of self-regulation: A developmental perspective. *Developmental Psychology, 18,* 199–214.

Krebs, J. R., & Kacelnik, A. (1984). Time horizons of foraging animals. In J. Gibbon & L. Allan (eds.), *Timing and time perception,* 278–291. New York: New York Academy of Sciences.

Larrick, R. P., Morgan, J. N., & Nisbett, R. E. (1990). Teaching the use of cost-benefit reasoning in everyday life. *Psychological Science, 1,* 362–370.

LaVoie, J. C., Anderson, K., Fraze, B., & Johnson, K. (1981). Modeling, tuition, and sanction effects on self-control at different ages. *Journal of Experimental Child Psychology, 31,* 446–455.

Lejeune, H., & Wearden, J. H. (1991). The comparative psychology of fixed-interval responding: Some quantitative analyses. *Learning and Motivation, 22,* 84–111.

Le Magnen, J. (1985). *Hunger.* New York: Cambridge University Press.

Levine, M., & Spivak, G. (1959). Incentive, time conception and self control in a group of emotionally disturbed boys. *Journal of Clinical Psychology, 15,* 110–113.

Lew, M. B. (1982). Child and adult experimenters: Some differential effects. *Child Study Journal, 12,* 223–235.

Litman, G. K., & Topham, A. (1983). Outcome studies on techniques in alcoholism treatment. In M. Galanter (ed.), *Recent developments in alcoholism,* Vol. 1: 167–194. New York: Plenum.

Litrownik, A. J., Franzini, L. R., Geller, S., & Geller, M. (1977). Delay of gratification: Decisional self-control and experience with delay intervals. *American Journal of Mental Deficiency, 82,* 149–154.

Little, V. L., & Kendall, P. C. (1979). Cognitive-behavioral interventions with delinquents: Problem solving, role-taking, and self-control. In P. C. Kendall & S. D. Hollon (eds.), *Cognitive-behavioral interventions,* 81–115. New York: Academic Press.

Logue, A. W. (1988). Research on self-control: An integrating framework. *Behavioral and Brain Sciences, 11,* 665–709.

Logue, A. W. (1991). *The psychology of eating and drinking: An introduction* (2nd ed.). New York: Freeman.

Logue, A. W. (1995). *Self-control: Waiting until tomorrow for what you want today.* Englewood Cliffs, N.J.: Prentice-Hall.

Logue, A. W., & Chavarro, A. (1992). Self-control and impulsiveness in preschool children. *Psychological Record, 42,* 189–204.

Logue, A. W., & Mazur, J. E. (1981). Maintenance of self-control acquired through a fading procedure: Follow-up on Mazur and Logue (1978). *Behaviour Analysis Letters, 1,* 131–137.

Logue, A. W., & Peña-Correal, T. E. (1984). Responding during reinforcement delay in a self-control paradigm. *Journal of the Experimental Analysis of Behavior, 41,* 267–277.

Logue, A. W., Peña-Correal, T. E., Rodriguez, M. L., & Kabela, E. (1986). Self-control in adult humans: Variation in positive reinforcer amount and delay. *Journal of the Experimental Analysis of Behavior, 46,* 159–173.

Logue, A. W., Rodriguez, M. L., Peña-Correal, T. E., & Mauro, B. C. (1984). Choice in a self-control paradigm: Quantification of experience-based differences. *Journal of the Experimental Analysis of Behavior, 41,* 53–67.

Lopatto, D., & Lewis, P. (1985). Contributions of elicitation to measures of self-control. *Journal of the Experimental Analysis of Behavior, 44,* 69–77.

Low, B. S. (1989). Cross-cultural patterns in the training of children: An evolutionary perspective. *Journal of Comparative Psychology, 103,* 311–319.

Maccoby, E. E., & Jacklin, C. N. (1974). *The psychology of sex differences.* Stanford, Calif.: Stanford University Press.

Mahoney, M. J., & Bandura, A. (1972). Self-reinforcement in pigeons. *Learning and Motivation, 3,* 293–303.

Maitland, S. D. P. (1967). Time perspective, frustration-failure and delay of gratification in middle-class and lower-class children from organized and disorganized families. *Dissertation Abstracts, 27,* 3676-B.

Mann, J. J., & Stanley, M. (1986). *Psychobiology of suicidal behavior.* New York: New York Academy of Sciences.

Maynard Smith, J. (1978). Optimization theory in evolution. *Annual Review of Ecology and Systematics, 9,* 31–56.

Mazur, J. E., & Logue, A. W. (1978). Choice in a "self-control" paradigm: Effects of a fading procedure. *Journal of the Experimental Analysis of Behavior, 30,* 11–17.

Meichenbaum, D. H., & Goodman, J. (1971). Training impulsive children to talk to themselves. *Journal of Abnormal Psychology, 77,* 115–126.

Mischel, H. N., & Mischel, W. (1983). The development of children's knowledge of self-control strategies. *Child Development, 54,* 603–619.

Mischel, W. (1990). Personality dispositions revisited and revised: A view after three decades. In L. A. Pervin (ed.), *Handbook of personality: Theory and research,* 111–134. New York: Guilford.

Mischel, W., & Baker, N. (1975). Cognitive appraisals and transformations in delay behavior. *Journal of Personality and Social Psychology, 31,* 254–261.

Mischel, W., & Ebbesen, E. B. (1970). Attention in delay of gratification. *Journal of Personality and Social Psychology, 16,* 329–337.

Mischel, W., Ebbesen, E. B., & Zeiss, A. R. (1972). Cognitive and attentional mechanisms in delay of gratification. *Journal of Personality and Social Psychology, 21,* 204–218.

Mischel, W., & Grusec, J. (1967). Waiting for rewards and punishments: Effects of time and probability on choice. *Journal of Personality and Social Psychology, 5,* 24–31.

Mischel, W., & Metzner, R. (1962). Preference for delayed reward as a function of age, intelligence, and length of delay interval. *Journal of Abnormal and Social Psychology, 64,* 425–431.

Mischel, W., & Patterson, C. J. (1976). Substantive and structural elements of effective plans for self-control. *Journal of Personality and Social Psychology, 34,* 942–950.

Mischel, W., Shoda, Y., & Rodriguez, M. L. (1989). Delay of gratification in children. *Science, 244,* 933–938.

Moore, B. S., Clyburn, A., & Underwood, B. (1976). The role of affect in delay of gratification. *Child Development, 47,* 273–276.

Morgan, B. S., & Littell, D. H. (1988). A closer look at teaching and contingency contracting with Type II diabetes. *Patient and Education and Counseling, 12,* 145–158.

Nasar, S. (1991, September 24). Baby boomers fail as born-again savers. *The New York Times,* pp. A1, D5.

Newman, J. P., Gorenstein, E. E., & Kelsey, J. E. (1983). Failure to delay gratification following septal lesions in rats: Implications for an animal model of disinhibitory psychopathology. *Personality and Individual Differences, 4,* 147–156.

Nolimal, D., & Crowley, T. J. (1990). Difficulties in a clinical application of methadone-dose contingency contracting. *Journal of Substance Abuse Treatment, 7,* 219–224.

O'Leary, S. G., & Dubey, D. R. (1979). Applications of self-control procedures by children: A review. *Journal of Applied Behavior Analysis, 12,* 449–465.

Patterson, C. J., & Mischel, W. (1976). Effects of temptation-inhibiting and task-facilitating plans on self-control. *Journal of Personality and Social Psychology, 33,* 209–217.

Polivy, J., & Herman, C. P. (1976). Effects of alcohol on eating behavior: Influence of mood and perceived intoxication. *Journal of Abnormal Psychology, 85,* 601–606.

Rachlin, H. (1974). Self-control. *Behaviorism, 2,* 94–107.

Rachlin, H., & Green, L. (1972). Commitment, choice and self-control. *Journal of the Experimental Analysis of Behavior, 17,* 15–22.

Real, L. A. (1991). Animal choice behavior and the evolution of cognitive architecture. *Science, 253,* 980–986.

Resnick, R. B., & Resnick, E. B. (1984). Cocaine abuse and its treatment. *Psychiatric Clinics of North America, 7,* 713–728.

Richelle, M., & Lejeune, H. (1984). Timing competence and timing performance: A cross-species approach. In J. Gibbon & L. Allan (eds.), *Timing and time perception,* 254–268. New York: New York Academy of Sciences.

Rodin, J. (1985). Insulin levels, hunger, and food intake: An example of feedback loops in body weight regulation. *Health Psychology, 4,* 1–24.

Rodriguez, M. L., Mischel, W., & Shoda, Y. (1989). Cognitive person variables in the delay of gratification of older children at risk. *Journal of Personality and Social Psychology, 57,* 358–367.

Rolls, B. J., Rowe, E. A., Rolls, E. T., Kingston, B., Megson, A., & Gunary, R. (1981). Variety in a meal enhances food intake in man. *Physiology and Behavior, 26,* 215–221.

Rosovsky, H. (1990). *The university: An owner's manual.* New York: Norton.

Rowland, N. E., & Antelman, S. M. (1976). Stress-induced hyperphagia and obesity in rats: A possible model for understanding human obesity. *Science, 191,* 310–312.

Schelling, T. C. (1992). Self-command: A new discipline. In G. Loewenstein & J. Elster (eds.), *Choice over time,* 167–176. New York: Russell Sage Foundation.

Schwarz, J. C., & Pollack, P. R. (1977). Affect and delay of gratification. *Journal of Research in Personality, 11,* 147–164.

Schwarz, J. C., Schrager, J. B., & Lyons, A. E. (1983). Delay of gratification by preschoolers: Evidence for the validity of the choice paradigm. *Child Development, 54,* 620–625.

Schweitzer, J. B., & Sulzer-Azaroff, B. (1988). Self-control: Teaching tolerance for delay in impulsive children. *Journal of the Experimental Analysis of Behavior, 50,* 173–186.

Shybut, J. (1968). Delay of gratification and severity of psychological disturbance among hospitalized psychiatric patients. *Journal of Consulting and Clinical Psychology, 32,* 462–468.

Simopoulos, A. P. (1987). Characteristics of obesity: An overview. In R. J. Wurtman & J. J. Wurtman (eds.), *Human obesity,* 4–13. New York: New York Academy of Sciences.

Sjöström, L. (1978). The contribution of fat cells to the determination of body weight. In A. J. Stunkard (ed.), *Symposium on obesity: Basic mechanisms and treatment,* 493–521. Philadelphia: Saunders.

Skinner, B. F. (1953). *Science and human behavior.* New York: The Free Press.

Solnick, J. V., Kannenberg, C. H., Eckerman, D. A., & Waller, M. B. (1980). An experimental analysis of impulsivity and impulse control in humans. *Learning and Motivation, 11,* 61–77.

Sonuga-Barke, E. J. S., Lea, S. E. G., & Webley, P. (1989a). Children's choice: Sensitivity to changes in reinforcer density. *Journal of the Experimental Analysis of Behavior, 51,* 185–197.

Sonuga-Barke, E. J. S., Lea, S. E. G., & Webley, P. (1989b). The development of adaptive choice in a self-control paradigm. *Journal of the Experimental Analysis of Behavior, 51,* 77–85.

Soubrié, P. (1986). Reconciling the role of central serotonin neurons in human and animal behavior. *The Behavioral and Brain Sciences, 9,* 319–364.

Strickland, B. R. (1972). Delay of gratification as a function of race of the experimenter. *Journal of Personality and Social Psychology, 22,* 108–112.

Stumphauzer, J. S. (1972). Increased delay of gratification in young prison inmates through imitation of high-delay peer models. *Journal of Personality and Social Psychology, 21,* 10–17.

Thiébot, M.-H., Le Bihan, C., Soubrié, P., & Simon, P. (1985). Benzodiazepines reduce the tolerance to reward delay in rats. *Psychopharmacology, 86,* 147–152.

Timberlake, W., Gawley, D. J., & Lucas, G. A. (1987). Time horizons in rats foraging for food in temporally separated patches. *Journal of Experimental Psychology: Animal Behavior Processes, 13,* 302–309.

Tobin, H., & Logue, A. W. (1994). Self-control across species (*Columba livia, Homo sapiens,* and *Rattus norvegicus*). *Journal of Comparative Psychology, 108,* 126–133.

Trommsdorff, G., & Schmidt-Rinke, M. (1980). Individual situational characteristics as determinants of delay of gratification. *Archiv für Psychologie, 133,* 263–275.

Vaughn, B. E., Kopp, C. B., Krakow, J. B., Johnson, K., & Schwartz, S. S. (1986). Process analyses of the behavior of very young children in delay tasks. *Developmental Psychology, 22,* 752–759.

Walls, R. T., & Smith, T. S. (1970). Development of preference for delayed reinforcement in disadvantaged children. *Journal of Educational Psychology, 61,* 118–123.

Walsh, B. T., Stewart, J. W., Wright, L., Harrison, W., Roose, S. P., & Glassman, A. H. (1982). Treatment of bulimia with monoamine oxidase inhibitors. *American Journal of Psychiatry, 139,* 1629–1630.

Weingarten, H. P. (1983). Conditioned cues elicit feeding in sated rats: A role for learning in meal initiation. *Science, 220,* 431–433.

Wilson, J. Q., & Herrnstein, R. J. (1985). *Crime and human nature.* New York: Simon & Schuster.

Wurtman, J. J. (1981). Neurotransmitter regulation of protein and carbohydrate consumption. In S. A. Miller (ed.), *Nutrition and behavior,* 69–75. Philadelphia: Franklin Institute.

Wurtman, R. J., & Wurtman, J. J. (1984). Nutrients, neurotransmitter synthesis, and the control of food intake. In A. J. Stunkard & E. Stellar (eds.), *Eating and its disorders,* 77–86. New York: Raven Press.

Wurtman, R. J., & Wurtman, J. J. (1988). Do carbohydrates affect food intake via neurotransmitter activity? *Appetite, 11* (Supplement), 42–47.

Yates, J. F., & Revelle, G. L. (1979). Processes operative during delay of gratification. *Motivation and Emotion, 3,* 103–115.

Zihlman, A. L. (1982). *The human evolution coloring book.* Oakville, Calif.: Coloring Concepts, Inc.

CHAPTER 14

BEHAVIORAL ECONOMICS

Leonard Green
Debra E. Freed

REINFORCEMENT IN CONTEXT

It is a truism that certain responses when accompanied by certain events are subsequently more likely to occur. Likewise, certain responses when accompanied by certain events show no change in their subsequent likelihood of occurrence. The accompanying events that give rise to the increased likelihood of responding are referred to as reinforcers, and those having no effect on subsequent responding are nonreinforcers. Given these relations between responding and the occurrence of events accompanying responding, a logical next step might be to ask, "What makes some events reinforcers yet other events neutral with regard to their ability to influence the future likelihood of responding?"

This issue—namely, what makes an event a reinforcer—has a long and intellectually rich history. Wilcoxin (1969) has provided an excel-lent historical review of the "problem" of reinforcement. What is relevant to note is that in trying to understand the process by which reinforcement works (the *how* and *why* of reinforcement), the question of *what* makes a reinforcer a reinforcer engendered considerable discussion. Thorndike's (1911) statement of the Law of Effect clearly expressed one approach to this issue:

> The Law of Effect is that: Of several responses made to the same situation, those which are accompanied or closely followed by satisfaction to the animal will, other things being equal, be more firmly connected with the situation, so that when it recurs, they will be more likely to recur; those which are accompanied or closely followed by discomfort to the animal will, other things being equal, have their connections with that situation weakened, so that, when it recurs, they will be less likely to occur. The greater the satisfaction or discomfort, the greater the strengthening or weakening of the bond. (p. 244)

In an attempt to forestall the criticism that his law was too subjective, Thorndike defined satisfaction and discomfort in an operationally acceptable manner:

By a satisfying state of affairs is meant one which the animal does nothing to avoid, often doing such things as attain and preserve it. By a discomforting or annoying state of affairs is meant one which the animal commonly avoids and abandons. (p. 245)

Thorndike's Law of Effect was a theoretical statement. He posited connections between situations and responses (an S-R psychology) that were strengthened by some neural mechanism:

The connections formed between situation and response are represented by connections between neurones and neurones, whereby the disturbance or neural current arising in the former is conducted to the latter across their synapses. (p. 246)

Objections arose to a theoretical Law of Effect from many quarters. Some objected to what they still considered too-subjective a statement (i.e., the "satisfiers" and "annoyers"); others to the positing of reinforcement as necessary for the increased likelihood of the response; others to the hypothesized neural strengthening of S-R connections. Moreover, many were troubled by the apparent circularity inherent in the Law. Satisfiers (i.e., reinforcers) are those events that increase the future likelihood of a response, yet the way to define an event as a reinforcer is whether it increases the future likelihood of a response. How might a reinforcer be defined independently from its response-enhancing property? If positive reinforcers are "those stimuli which strengthen responses when presented" (Keller & Schoenfeld, 1950, p. 61), and the only way to know if an event is a reinforcer is to see if it leads to an increase in responding, then the circularity is obvious.

Skinner (1938) approached the issue from an empirical perspective. Not interested in the neural connections hypothesized to underlie the S-R connections, and distinguishing himself by his operant, non–S-R psychology, Skinner eliminated the theoretical trappings of the Law of Effect:

The operation of reinforcement is defined as the presentation of a certain kind of stimulus in a temporal relation with either a stimulus or a response. A reinforcing stimulus is defined as such by its power to produce the resulting change. There is no circularity about this; some stimuli are found to produce the change, others not, and they are classified as reinforcing and non-reinforcing accordingly. A stimulus may possess the power to reinforce when it is first presented (when it is usually the stimulus of an unconditioned respondent) or it may acquire the power through conditioning. (p. 62)

Skinner's confidence in disposing of circularity in the definition of a reinforcer, however, was not shared by all.

The most complete attempt to break out of the circularity of the Law of Effect was provided by Meehl's (1950) trans-situational reinforcement law. If an event is shown to be a reinforcer for a response in one situation, then it can be predicted that the event will reinforce any other learnable response. Thus, if food is shown to reinforce a rat's lever-pressing in a Skinner box, then one can now predict that food will likewise reinforce running in a maze, nose-poking, chain-pulling, etc.

The trans-situational reinforcement law may break out of the circularity in defining a reinforcer. Yet there remains the issue of what common properties inhere to all those events that are positive reinforcers. What properties distinguish positive reinforcers from negative reinforcers, and from events having no effect on the future likelihood of responding? After all, it does seem reasonable to assume that there are some events that are positive (e.g., food, sex, water, warmth), others that are negative (e.g., electric shock), and a third group of events that are neutral. What we need, then, is to discover those characteristics, properties, or components that distinguish one group from the others.

The most well-known example along such lines was that of Hull (1943). In his *Principles of Behavior,* Hull expressed his theoretical statement of the law of reinforcement:

Whenever an effector activity occurs in temporal contiguity with the afferent impulse, or the perseverative trace of such an impulse, resulting from the impact of a stimulus energy upon a receptor, and this conjunction is closely associated in time with the diminution in the receptor discharge characteristic of a need or with a stimulus situation which has been closely and consistently associated with such a need diminution, there will result an increment to the tendency for that stimulus to evoke that reaction. (p. 98)

The need- or drive-reduction theory of primary reinforcement, and the drive-stimulus reduction theory of secondary reinforcement, provide an incipient biological mechanism for reinforcement. Such an approach has its attraction. After all, now it could be known beforehand whether a given event would be reinforcing. The underlying biological mechanism of reinforcement could be sought. Unfortunately, it was not long before reinforcement effects were found in the absence of drive reduction; reinforcing effects were even obtained under conditions of drive-induction, that is to say, under conditions in which the reinforcing event increased drive or arousal (e.g., Harlow, 1953; Sheffield, 1966; Sheffield & Roby, 1950; Sheffield, Wulff, & Backer, 1951).

Against this historical background to the search for what makes an event a reinforcer, Premack's pre-potent response or relativity theory of reinforcement represents a major shift in the analysis of reinforcement. Premack (1965), rather than viewing reinforcers as stimuli that possess some property that makes them positive, negative, or neutral, demonstrated the relativity of reinforcement. His generalization was that "of any two responses, the more probable response will reinforce the less probable one" (Premack, 1965, p. 132). Thus, the reinforcement relation is reversible: "If the probability of occurrence of two responses can be reversed in order, so can the reinforcement relation between the two responses" (pp. 132–133). Clearly, there was nothing *within* the event that makes it reinforcing, punishing, or neutral. After all, the same event that under one situation is a positive reinforcer can, if the differential probability of occurrence changes, be a punisher (Premack, 1962).

Expansions and improvements on Premack's original analyses ensued. The response-deprivation hypothesis of Timberlake and Allison (1974) highlighted the important role that restriction of the contingent (reinforcing) event has on behavior: When under a schedule contingency an animal is deprived of its baseline amount of the contingent response, then there will be an increase in the instrumental behavior. Allison's conservation theory (Allison, Miller, & Wozny, 1979) proposed that the animal conserves between baseline and contingency conditions the total amount of a dimension (for example, work, energy, or utility) attributable to the instrumental and contingent responses. Thus, the animal will reallocate its distribution of responses under the contingency so as to expend the same total amount of energy engaging in the two responses as it did at baseline.

These conceptualizations, along with further refinements and advancements, begin to appreciate the context within which reinforcement occurs. Traditionally, analyses of the properties of reinforcers focused on the strengthening effects that individual reinforcers had on individual responses (e.g., Hull, 1943; Logan, 1960; Skinner, 1938), with little regard for other reinforcers or responses in the situation. The role of context in understanding the effects of reinforcement was unappreciated.

It was with Herrnstein's matching law (1961, 1970) that the importance of context was brought into sharp focus and incorporated directly into the law of effect. The matching law predicts that a given response is influenced not only by the reinforcers contingent upon it but also by other reinforcers within the situation. Thus, an animal is always choosing between reinforcement alternatives, and a given reinforcer's effect depends on the context of the other reinforcers in the situation. Consequently, the strengthening effect of a reinforcer will depend on its value relative to other reinforcers in the current situation. One formulation of the matching law can be expressed as follows:

$$B_x = kR_x / (R_x + R_o) . \qquad (1)$$

B_x represents allocation of behavior to alternative x, k is a constant representing the summation of all behaviors, R_x is the reinforcers obtained from alternative x, and R_o represents the reinforcers obtained from all other behaviors in the situation. The matching law thus states that behavior allocated to one alternative will be proportional to the reinforcers obtained from that alternative and inversely proportional to reinforcers obtained from other alternatives.

Herrnstein's matching law makes explicit that the effects of a reinforcer on behavior cannot be understood apart from other reinforcers in the situation and thus compels the study of reinforcer interactions. Studies of choice generally have investigated the interactions of reinforcers that differ with regard to their frequency, amount, delay, or probability (see Davison & McCarthy, 1988) but are otherwise qualitatively similar. For example, a typical choice experiment involves a hungry pigeon's choosing between identical food reinforcers that differ in their frequency. When the only parameters of reinforcement that vary are those such as frequency and amount, the results are well described by Baum's (1974) generalized matching law:

$$B_x/B_y = b\,(R_x/R_y)^s. \qquad (2)$$

As in Equation 1, B_x represents allocation of behavior to alternative x; B_y represents allocation of behavior to alternative y; R_x and R_y are the reinforcers produced by responding to those alternatives, respectively. The parameters b and s encompass bias and sensitivity. When the ratio of behavior as a function of the ratio of reinforcement is plotted in log-log coordinates, bias is evident as the y-intercept, and sensitivity is manifested as the slope of the line.

However, when other parameters of reinforcement are varied, such as the quality of the reinforcers in a situation or the type of constraint imposed on responding, then the domain of economics has been broached. Economics, after all, is the study of how consumers choose among scarce and different resources (respond under constraint), and explicitly acknowledges that commodities (reinforcers) interact in multiple

ways. The incorporation of economic principles in the experimental analysis of behavior thus represents a further progression in the understanding of reinforcement effects. The conjoining of economics and psychology into what is known as behavioral economics brings together the rigorous experimental techniques of operant psychology with the conceptual breadth of economics. Behavioral economics may provide for a richer understanding of reinforcement and for more encompassing theories of choice.

In this selective review of the (predominantly) animal literature that focuses on choices over different reinforcers, we hope to make apparent the utility of incorporating economic concepts into psychological theories of and experiments on choice. The value of such concepts is that they provide a broad understanding of reinforcer interactions, thereby extending our ability to predict choice in more realistic situations than is possible when variations only in the same or highly similar reinforcers are studied.

In the next section we show how several economic concepts have been operationalized and studied in the psychological laboratory. Our goal is not to provide a comprehensive review of all the research under the rubric of behavioral economics. Rather, we wish to show how the results from certain illustrative experiments that have incorporated economic principles in their design or interpretation can lead to a broader and more comprehensive understanding of behavior.

DEMAND

One of the crucial concepts for behavioral economics is that of *demand*. Demand refers to the amount of a commodity purchased at a given price. In economics, demand is studied by observing correlations between the price of a commodity and the amount of that commodity purchased by consumers. It might not seem immediately obvious how such a paradigm can be translated into behavioral psychology, but to do so is really quite straightforward. A commodity is the equivalent of a reinforcer. As Lea (1978, p. 443) noted, ". . . [R]einforcers and commodities are both classes of things that a subject will do something to get. . . ." Price, in economic terms, specifies the amount of money required to purchase a given amount of a commodity. In the operant chamber with nonhuman animals as "consumers," price is determined by the schedule of reinforcement. Different schedules do not establish price in the same way, however. A ratio schedule, in which a particular number of responses is required to obtain each reinforcer, is most directly analogous to price in the marketplace. An interval schedule, in which a minimum amount of time must elapse before a response will produce a reinforcer, specifies only a minimum price for each amount of reinforcer obtained; the maximum price is therefore limited only by an animal's ability to respond. Of course, if price is determined by a response requirement, then it must be the case that responses per se, rather than money, constitute the medium of exchange in behavioral economics experiments.

A consumer is said to obey the "law of demand" when changes in consumption are inversely related to changes in price. For example, as the price of a commodity increases, consumption of that commodity should decrease. Demand, then, is more properly understood as a function that relates changes in the amount of a commodity purchased to changes in its price. Such a function describes the demand *elasticity* for that commodity. Demand is *elastic* when changes in price produce greater-than-proportional changes in consumption; demand is *inelastic* when changes in price produce less-than-proportional changes in consumption. Demand curves plot consumption as a function of price in log-log coordinates, and the slope of the function represents the degree of elasticity. Two demand curves are depicted in Figure 14–1, illustrating elastic and inelastic demand. The absolute values of the slopes of such functions indicate the degree of elasticity. The absolute value of the slope of the inelastic function is less than unity, and the absolute value of the slope of the elastic function is greater than unity (Hursh & Bauman, 1987). For example, the price increase from 1 unit to 10 units illustrated in Figure 14–1 produces very little decrease in consumption

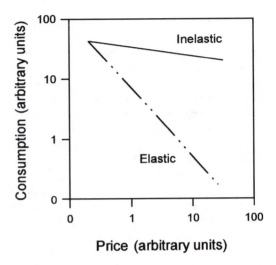

Figure 14–1. Elasticity of demand: Consumption as a function of price in log-log coordinates. Inelastic demand is represented by the solid line, which indicates small decreases in consumption as price increases. Elastic demand is represented by the broken line, which indicates large decreases in consumption over the same range of price increases.

when demand is inelastic (solid line) but drastic decreases in consumption when demand is elastic (broken line).

Own-Price Elasticity

Demand elasticity has been implicitly studied in an operant context for many years. The most obvious example is the extensive research conducted on schedules of reinforcement (e.g., Ferster & Skinner, 1957). The explicit inclusion of demand theory into behavioral psychology is apparent in experiments such as those of Foltin (1991), who studied the *own-price elasticity* of demand for food in baboons, that is, consumption of food as a function of changes in its own price. In 22-hour experimental sessions, six baboons each responded under a series of fixed-ratio (FR) schedules for food reinforcement. The only food provided outside the experimental situation was a daily ration of fresh fruit. The cost of food (i.e., the size of the ratio schedule) was progressively increased three times a week such that the range of schedules studied was FR 2 to FR 128. The FR values were experienced first in ascending order and then in descending order, followed by a replication of the ascending and descending order.

Figure 14–2 presents the food intake in grams for subject X-3639 (who showed the least variability across the four test series) at each FR value. Each consumption point represents an average of the four FR series, as determined by visual inspection of Foltin's (1991) Figure 1. Over most of the range of ratio values studied, demand for food was inelastic: increases in the price of food resulted in proportionally small decreases in food consumption. Only at the highest ratio values (i.e., FR 96 and 128) was demand for food elastic: increases in price produced large decreases in food consumption. This pattern of consumption, characterized by changes in demand elasticity across a range of prices, is termed *mixed elasticity*.

Lea and Roper (1977) demonstrated that demand for a commodity can also be influenced by changing the context in which that commodity is available. They studied rats' demand for food as a function of the quality of a concurrently available alternative food. In one com-

partment of a two-compartment chamber, hungry rats earned mixed-diet food pellets by responding on a fixed-ratio schedule. The schedule value (i.e., price) was increased from FR 1 to FR 16 across experimental conditions. In the second compartment of the chamber, an alternative food source (either the identical mixed-diet pellets or sucrose pellets) was sometimes made available according to an FR 8 schedule. This paradigm allowed Lea and Roper to determine the elasticity of demand for the mixed-diet pellets in the first compartment under three different conditions: when there was no alternative food source, when the alternative food source was the identical food, and when the alternative food source was qualitatively different (i.e., sucrose pellets).

Lea and Roper (1977) observed that demand for the mixed-diet pellets available in the first compartment was least elastic when there was no alternative food available, and most elastic when the alternative food was the identical mixed-diet pellets. These results are evident from the differences in the number of mixed-diet pellets earned per day from the first compartment as their FR requirement was increased. As shown in Figure 14–3, increasing the price of the mixed-diet pellets from FR 1 to FR 16 decreased consumption of that food by approximately 45% when there was no alternative food available, by about 63% when sucrose was concurrently available, and by nearly 80% when the identical food was available in the adjoining compartment.

An important contribution of demand theory to behavioral psychology is that it allows different reinforcers within a given context to be dissociated from each other, apart from their differences in value. Premack (1965) introduced the notion of ranking reinforcers along a unitary scale of value. The value of a given reinforcer was to be assessed from the amount of time an animal spent engaged with that reinforcer relative to the amount of time spent with other reinforcers under a free-baseline procedure. The more time spent in one activity relative to others, the greater its value.

Differences in demand elasticity may reveal an entirely different relationship between reinforcers than does relative value. For example,

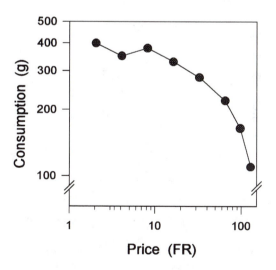

Figure 14–2. Estimated demand curve for subject X-3639 showing mixed elasticity. Over most of the range of FR values studied, the baboon's demand for food was inelastic, but at the highest FR values consumption of food decreased dramatically. Data are plotted on log-log coordinates. (From Foltin, 1991.)

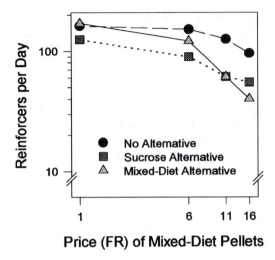

Figure 14–3. Rats' demand for mixed-diet food pellets as a function of the type of alternative reinforcer available. Demand is least elastic when no alternative is available, and most elastic when the identical food is the available alternative. Data shown are group means at each FR value, and are plotted on log-log coordinates. (From Lea & Roper, 1977.)

Hursh and Natelson (1981, Experiment 2) compared rats' demand for electrical stimulation of the brain (ESB) and food as the equally priced reinforcers were made uniformly more expensive. Food and ESB were available to rats living in the experimental chamber according to concurrent variable interval (VI) schedules. The schedule requirement for both reinforcers was increased from VI 3 seconds to VI 60 seconds across the conditions of the experiment. Hursh and Natelson confirmed the psychological lore with regard to the value of ESB (e.g., Gleitman, 1981; Kalat, 1995). That is, across the range of VI values, the rats preferred ESB over food in terms of number of reinforcers obtained and number of responses emitted.

The rats' consistent preference for ESB over food might lead one to expect that demand for ESB would be greater than that for food, that is, demand for ESB would be less elastic. However, as is evident from inspection of Figure 14–4, just the opposite was found. The demand curves indicate that demand for food was highly inelastic

whereas demand for ESB was highly elastic. That is, over the wide range of prices, food consumption was strongly defended, whereas the same increases in price produced large decreases in ESB consumption.

These results limit the utility of the concept of value as it has been commonly used—namely, as an indicator of what an animal will choose. After all, one might conclude that the value of ESB is greater than that of food because the rats chose ESB more frequently than food. But if we use value in this way, then we must in turn account for why the value of ESB changes as its price is increased, while the value of food does not change as its price is increased. The concept of demand takes into account how consumption and responding change as a function of price, and may thus provide additional insight into how best to conceptualize value.

The difference in elasticity found between different commodities as a function of equal increases in price has been used to identify luxuries and necessities. Commodities with inelastic de-

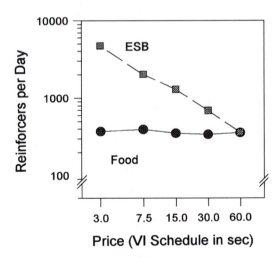

Figure 14–4. Rats' demand for food and electrical brain stimulation. Equal increases in price produced minimal changes in food consumption, indicating inelastic demand, but drastic changes in ESB consumption, indicating elastic demand. Data plotted on log-log coordinates are group means at each VI value. (From Hursh & Natelson, 1981, Experiment 2.)

mand are said to be necessities, whereas those with elastic demand are luxuries (Lea, 1978; Schwartz & Robbins, 1995). This interpretation can be applied to the results of an experiment by Elsmore, Fletcher, Conrad, and Sodetz (1980) in which baboons' demand for food and heroin was compared. At periodic intervals throughout a 24-hour session, two baboons could each choose between food reinforcement and heroin infusion. The prices of food and heroin, in terms of response requirement per reinforcer, were equal and were not expressly manipulated across conditions of the experiment. Rather, price was functionally increased by increasing the time interval between choice opportunities (thus decreasing the total number of choice trials per day). Such a manipulation effectively reduces the animals' *income* (total purchasing power). Decreasing income is tantamount to increasing all prices because the same prices now use up a greater percentage of the consumer's income (Hursh & Bauman, 1987). Figure 14–5 shows the number of food and heroin choices per day made by subject

P241 as the intertrial interval (ITI) was increased. Each point represents a visual estimation of the data presented in Elsmore et al.'s Figure 1. As is evident from the figure, as the intertrial interval increased from 2 minutes to 12 minutes across conditions, food consumption was defended while heroin consumption was drastically reduced, indicating inelastic demand for food but elastic demand for heroin.

Cross-Price Elasticity

The previous experiments have all examined own-price elasticity, that is, consumption of a particular commodity plotted as a function of changes in its own price. Demand theory also considers *cross-price elasticity*, or consumption of a particular commodity plotted as a function of changes in the price of another commodity available in the situation. Hursh's (1978) study of demand for food and water in baboons is representative. In his Experiment 1, he made available to each of two baboons (SM2 and SM3) a constant source of food and a constant source of water in 24-hour sessions. Both the food and water could be obtained by responding on independent VI 60-second schedules of reinforcement. In addition, an alternative source of food was sometimes concurrently available, according to a VI schedule whose value was varied across conditions.

Figure 14–6 shows the cross-price elasticity of the constant food and water for both subjects as a function of the price of the alternative food. The price of the alternative food indicated as ∞ refers to the condition in which no alternative food source was available. As can be seen, the baboons' demand for the constant food increased, while demand for water decreased slightly, as the price of the alternative food was increased. That is, when the alternative food became more expensive (i.e., as its VI schedule increased), the baboons increased consumption of the constant-priced food and decreased consumption of water. Thus, cross-price elasticity provides a framework for examining how responding for and consumption of reinforcers change as a function of

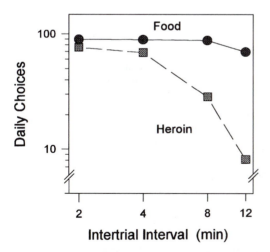

Figure 14–5. Estimated number of daily choices of food and heroin as a function of total income for subject P241. As income decreased (by increasing the time between choice trials), the baboon defended its consumption of food but decreased its consumption of heroin. Data are plotted on log-log coordinates. (From Elsmore et al., 1980.)

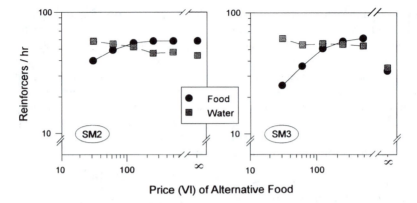

Figure 14–6. Cross-price elasticity: Baboons' demand for a constant source of food
and water as a function of the price of an alternative food source. As the price of
the alternative food was increased, demand for the constant food source increased
while demand for water decreased slightly. Data are plotted on log-log coordinates.
(From Hursh, 1978, Experiment 1.)

the degree of availability (i.e., price) of other reinforcers in the situation.

SUBSTITUTABILITY

Cross-price elasticity suggests a means of
looking at reinforcer interactions in a way similar to that of the matching law (Herrnstein, 1961,
1970). That is, manipulating the price of one
reinforcer in a situation affects not only consumption of that reinforcer, but also may affect
consumption of other reinforcers in the situation.
However, cross-price elasticity differs from the
matching law in that it allows for a broader conceptual range of reinforcer interactions. The various ways in which reinforcers can interact with
each other are described by the economic concept of *substitutability*. Substitutability delin-
eates a continuum of reinforcer interactions in
which perfect substitutability and perfect complementarity define the endpoints, with independence falling in between.

Substitutable reinforcers are generally those
that are functionally similar (Baumol, 1972), and
are frequently qualitatively similar (Rachlin,
1989). Thus, substitutable reinforcers are readily
"traded" for each other, to the extent that increasing the price of one will produce decreases

in its consumption and increases in consumption
of its substitute. Complementary reinforcers, on
the other hand, tend to be consumed in fairly
rigid proportion to each other; increasing the
price of one will produce decreases in consumption of both. Reinforcers are independent of each
other when changing the price of one does not influence consumption of the other. Some examples of these interactions may be Coke and Pepsi
(substitutes), hot dogs and hot dog buns (complements), umbrellas and compact discs (inde-
pendents). This range of interactions is not
readily accommodated by the matching law,
which implicitly assumes that all reinforcers are
substitutable: changing the rate of reinforcement
for one alternative is predicted to inversely
change responding for and consumption of other
reinforcers available in the situation. However, if
reinforcers can be demonstrated to interact in
other ways (i.e., as complements or indepen-
dents), then an economic conceptualization su-
persedes the matching law in descriptive and
predictive utility.

Substitutability and complementarity are evident in Hursh's (1978) experiment, described
previously. As can be seen in Figure 14–6, increases in the price of the alternative food increased consumption of the constant source of

food, demonstrating substitutability between the two foods. However, that same increase in the price of the alternative food caused decreases in consumption of the water, suggesting a complementary relationship between the water and the alternative food.

Commodity Choice

Although inferences about substitutability can be made from demand experiments such as Hursh's, substitutability can be studied directly. These direct tests are conducted by limiting the total number of responses an animal is permitted during an experimental session. This total is referred to as the animal's income. During the session, the animal may spend those responses on (usually) two concurrently available reinforcers, each of which can be "bought" for a certain number of responses. In subsequent conditions, the prices of the reinforcers are changed, and total income is adjusted so that the original consumption point can still be obtained. This *income-compensated price change* enables a substitution effect to be separated from an income effect: a change in consumption under the new set of prices and income reflects the nature of the interaction between the reinforcers and not a change necessitated by the fact that the animal's real income was changed.

This point may be illustrated more clearly by considering a human consumer's purchases of milk and soda. On an income of $500 a month a consumer might purchase five gallons of milk (at $2 per gallon) and two cases of soda (at $5 per case). If income remained constant at $500 a month while the price of milk increased to $5 per gallon, we might find that the consumer decreased consumption of milk and increased consumption of soda. Such a change in consumption might reflect substitution of soda for milk, but it might also reflect the fact that purchasing the same amount of milk and soda as previously would require a greater expenditure of income. That is, without an increase in income to compensate for the increased price of milk, real income (in terms of purchasing power) would be effectively reduced.

Figure 14–7 provides an illustration of the income-compensated price-change paradigm. The *x* and *y* axes represent, respectively, the amounts of reinforcer *X* and reinforcer *Y* that can be purchased or consumed, and points farther from the origin represent greater amounts of those commodities. The solid line defines the initial "budget," as determined by the total income allotted to the subject and the price of each reinforcer. The animal's consumption point is limited by that budget; the obtained combination of reinforcers must fall on the budget line (or below if the total income is not spent). The dashed line drawn through the hypothetical consumption point represents the new budget, in which the price of reinforcer *X* has been decreased, the price of reinforcer *Y* has been increased, and total income adjusted. Note that by adjusting total in-

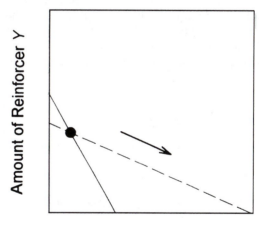

Figure 14–7. Representation of the income-compensated price change paradigm used to estimate substitution effects between two reinforcers. The solid line defines the initial budget condition and the filled circle a hypothetical consumption point under that budget. The dashed line specifies an income-compensated price change from the initial budget in which the price of reinforcer *X* is decreased, the price of reinforcer *Y* is increased, and total income is adjusted so that the original consumption point can still be obtained. Movement under the new budget in the direction of the arrow indicates increasing degrees of substitution of reinforcer *X* for reinforcer *Y*.

come so that the new budget line passes through the original consumption point, the package of reinforcers obtained under the original budget (i.e., the solid circle in Figure 14–7) can still be obtained under the new budget constraint. The degree to which consumption shifts in the direction of the arrow (i.e., toward the now-cheaper reinforcer) indicates the degree to which these reinforcers are substitutable for each other.

This paradigm was first used by Rachlin, Green, Kagel, and Battalio (1976). Rats' responses on one lever produced root beer, and responses on a second lever produced Tom Collins mix. Under the baseline budget constraint, the price of each reinforcer was an FR 1 for .05 ml of liquid, and income was limited to 300 responses per 24-hour session. The solid line in the left panel of Figure 14–8 shows this budget condition for one of the two rats studied. As indicated in the figure by the filled circle, when the reinforcers were equally priced, the rat preferred the root beer to the Tom Collins mix. In the next budget condition (indicated by the dashed line), the price of root beer was doubled (by halving the amount of liquid delivered per presentation), while the price of Tom Collins mix was halved (by doubling the amount of liquid delivered per presentation). Income was adjusted so that the rat's baseline package of root beer and Tom Collins mix could still be obtained under the new set of prices.

Even though the rat could still purchase the same combination of root beer and Tom Collins, there was a large change in consumption from the baseline condition. As shown by the solid square, consumption of the made-costlier root beer decreased while consumption of the made-cheaper Tom Collins mix increased. In another condition (shown as the dotted line) the price of root beer was made less expensive and that of Tom Collins mix more expensive (relative to baseline). Once again, consumption shifted in the direction of the now-cheaper commodity (the consumption point represented by the triangle). These consumption changes show that root beer and Tom Collins mix are highly substitutable reinforcers.

It is worth noting that the degree of substi-

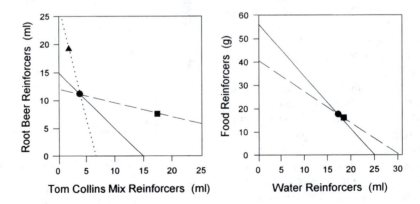

Figure 14–8. Income-compensated price changes reveal substitutable and nonsubstitutable reinforcers. The left panel shows estimated consumption of root beer and Tom Collins mix under three budget conditions for one rat. The solid line represents the baseline budget and the circle the approximate consumption of root beer and Tom Collins mix. Income-compensated price changes from the baseline are indicated by the broken lines, with changes in consumption shown by the square and triangle. The right panel shows estimated consumption of food and water for a different rat. The solid line and circle are the baseline budget and approximate consumption point, whereas the broken line shows the income-compensated price change and its corresponding consumption point. (From Rachlin et al., 1976.)

tutability found between these two reinforcers is not necessarily predicted by the rat's preference during the baseline condition. Even in the case of a second rat that chose root beer almost exclusively during baseline (data not presented), consumption of root beer decreased and that of Tom Collins increased significantly when, under an income-compensated price change, the price of root beer was doubled and the price of Tom Collins was halved. It is clear, then, that behavior is strongly influenced by economic factors (e.g., price and substitutability) and may not be predicted necessarily by a single scale of value in which the degree of preference under baseline predicts degree of modifiability.

Using the same paradigm, Rachlin et al. (1976) were also able to demonstrate a complementary relationship between reinforcers. In this experiment, rats could choose between food (5 pellets for every 10 presses on a lever) and water (0.1 ml for every 10 presses on a second lever) in a baseline condition with an income of 2,500 responses (the solid line in the right panel of Figure 8). In the subsequent condition, the price of food was increased 67% (10 presses now delivered 3 food pellets), the price of water was unchanged, and the rats' income was adjusted so that baseline quantities of food and water could still be obtained (the dashed line). Unlike the results of the Tom Collins/root beer experiment, the results with food and water suggest that these reinforcers are highly nonsubstitutable. Increasing the price of food decreased its consumption somewhat, but consumption of the relatively cheaper water increased only slightly (from that represented by the solid circle to that represented by the square in the right panel of Figure 14–8; compare these results with those in the left panel).

Results from studies of substitutability compel a broader conception of reinforcer interactions. For example, Green and Rachlin (1991) studied rats' choices between food and electrical stimulation of the brain (ESB), water and ESB, and food and water, under various income-compensated price changes. The results from their Rat A are depicted in Figure 14–9. The top two panels confirm Hursh and Natelson's (1981) findings of highly elastic demand for ESB: As the price of

ESB was increased and that of food or water decreased, consumption of ESB decreased while consumption of the now-cheaper reinforcer, whether food or water, increased. Not only do these results show demand for ESB to be highly elastic, but they also indicate that both food and water are largely substitutable for ESB. In the bottom panel of the figure are the results from the same rat from the conditions in which it chose between food and water. Note that, in this case, as the initially less-preferred reinforcer (i.e., water) was made considerably cheaper (as indicated by the dashed lines), consumption of water increased while consumption of the made-expensive food hardly changed. These results stand in marked contrast to those from the food versus ESB and water versus ESB situations.

If reinforcer interactions are transitive, then because food and water are each substitutable for ESB we would predict that food and water should be substitutable for each other. That is, if A = B and B = C, then A = C. However, as is evident from the bottom panel of Figure 14–9, food and water were not substitutable for each other; although A = B and B = C, A ≠ C.

Green and Rachlin's (1991) results in this regard provide an interesting counterpoint to those obtained by Miller (1976). Miller demonstrated that pairwise comparisons of three different reinforcers (wheat, buckwheat, and hemp) in pigeons yielded a unitary hedonic scale that could subsequently be used to predict the relative value of an unstudied pair. That is, the value of wheat to hemp and the value of wheat to buckwheat were first established. Then the value of hemp to buckwheat was well predicted, consistent with the view that reinforcer interactions are transitive. Green and Rachlin's results indicate that with nonsubstitutable reinforcers, however, it may not be possible to establish a unitary scale of value and that transitivity of interactions cannot be assumed.

Incorporating the concept of substitutability into psychological studies of choice also helps illuminate issues that might otherwise go unexplored or reveal relations that otherwise might not have been assumed. Previous studies assessing rats' preferences for fats (e.g., Ackroff, Vig-

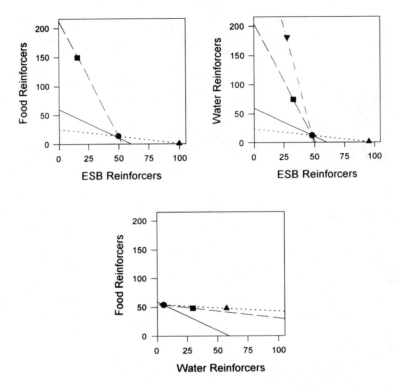

Figure 14–9. Consumption data from one rat under various budget conditions for food and ESB (top left panel), water and ESB (top right panel), and food and water (bottom panel). Although food and water were each substitutable for ESB, they were not substitutable for each other. (From Green & Rachlin, 1991.)

orito, & Sclafani, 1990) have typically relied on two-bottle preference tests in which an animal may drink from either of two bottles for a fixed period of time. Such studies demonstrate that rats have strong preferences for greasy/oily substances, even when those substances are nonnutritive (e.g., petrolatum, mineral oil). Such overwhelming preferences might suggest difficulty in modifying consumption of greasy/oily foods. Obviously, if preferences for fats are difficult to modify, and humans, like rats, show these preferences, then the incidence of heart disease and cancers from high-fat diets are not likely to decline very readily. However, our economic research indicates that initial preference, no matter how strong, does not necessarily predict what an animal will choose in the face of an economic constraint.

Figure 14–10 shows consumption of corn oil and sucrose, corn oil and mineral oil, and corn oil and water, under different budget constraints for a representative rat from an ongoing study in our laboratory. For each pair of reinforcers, a baseline budget defined by concurrent VR 20 VR 20 schedules and an income of 500 responses was implemented. This baseline is drawn as the solid line in each panel. The filled circle on these lines indicates the rat's baseline consumption point. The dashed lines drawn through those points establish income-compensated price changes from the baseline. In the case of corn oil versus sucrose (top left panel), the initially less-preferred corn oil was made cheaper (VR 10) while the more-preferred sucrose was made more expensive (VR 40); income was adjusted to allow the rat to obtain its baseline combination of sucrose

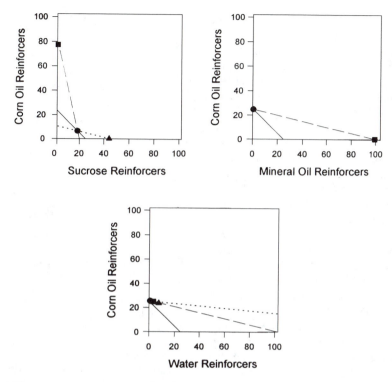

Figure 14–10. Consumption data from one rat under various budget conditions for corn oil and sucrose solutions (top left panel), corn oil and mineral oil solutions (top right panel), and corn oil solution and water (bottom panel). Both sucrose and mineral oil were substitutable for corn oil, but plain water was not.

and corn oil. In a third budget condition, the price of corn oil was increased from that at baseline (VR 40) while the price of sucrose was decreased (VR 10), and income was again adjusted. The same procedure was used to implement income-compensated price changes for the other commodity pairs. (The third budget in the corn oil versus water comparison decreased the price of water to VR 5, increased the price of corn oil to VR 50, and adjusted income.)

The data from our behavioral economic experiment show that both an equally caloric solution of sucrose as well as a noncaloric solution of mineral oil are highly substitutable for a 15% corn oil solution. However, plain water was not substitutable for corn oil. That is, the rat readily decreased consumption of corn oil in favor of a cheaper alternative when that alternative was sucrose or mineral

oil, but not when the alternative was plain water (as shown by a comparison of the three panels in the figure). Rats' preferences for fats appear to be readily modifiable depending on the economic conditions and the alternative reinforcer available. When a substitutable reinforcer is available, income-compensated price changes can produce substantial shifts in consumption.

Income-Leisure Choice

The fundamental assumption underlying both the matching law (Herrnstein, 1961, 1970) and consumer demand theory is that responding for a reinforcer (or purchasing a commodity) always occurs in the context of other reinforcers (commodities) that are available in the situation. One contribution of demand theory to operant psychology is that it formalizes the choice inherent in any instrumental situation, namely, the choice between responding and not responding (or in economic terms, the choice between income derived from working and leisure). That is, an animal can respond and earn its "income" of reinforcers according to a schedule of reinforcement. (Note that in this context, income refers to the number of reinforcers earned, rather than the total number of responses allotted.) In that same situation, the animal may also choose to forgo some of those reinforcers in exchange for leisure (i.e., all behaviors other than instrumental responding) obtained by not responding. Income and leisure, then, can be conceptualized as commodities in the same sense that more directly consumable reinforcers are. This conceptualization makes it possible to assess the interaction between the two and the influence of economic factors on their interaction.

The paradigm used to study income-leisure substitution is a slightly modified version of the income-compensated price change used by Rachlin et al. (1976). Figure 14–11 illustrates the paradigm. Both leisure and work are plotted on the x axis; because leisure encompasses all behaviors except for the instrumental work response, as the amount of work increases (points closer to the origin), leisure necessarily decreases. Income, or number of reinforcers obtained, is plotted on the y axis. The solid line specifies the baseline budget that constrains how much income and leisure may be obtained, and is determined by a ratio schedule of reinforcement (or wage rate, in economic terms). Ratio schedules produce a proportional relationship between work (responding) and income (reinforcement), and an inverse relationship between leisure and income. The prices of income and leisure can be manipulated by varying the ratio schedule requirement. Rich schedules (low ratio values) make income relatively cheap because many reinforcers can be obtained for little work—this same manipulation also makes leisure relatively expensive. Conversely, lean schedules (high ratio values) reduce the cost of leisure while increasing the cost of income because fewer rein-

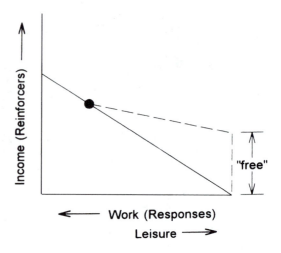

Figure 14–11. Representation of the paradigm used to study income-leisure substitution. The solid line specifies the constraint on reinforcers and responding imposed by a ratio schedule of reinforcement, and the circle indicates a hypothetical "package" of responding and reinforcement obtained. The broken line segments specify a new budget in which leisure is made cheaper and income is made more expensive by providing noncontingent ("free") reinforcers while increasing the ratio schedule. The extent to which the new consumption point moves rightward along the broken line indicates the extent to which leisure is substitutable for income.

forcers can be obtained for the same amount of work. Furthermore, income-compensated price increases can be arranged by increasing the ratio requirement above that at baseline while simultaneously introducing free (noncontingent) reinforcers.

This income-compensated price change is shown as the dashed-line segments in Figure 14–11. As in Figure 14–8, the new budget passes through the baseline consumption point of income and leisure; thus, the original combination of income and leisure can still be obtained. Assume, for example, that the baseline budget was determined by a ratio schedule requirement of 50, and that by making 5,000 responses, the subject obtained an income of 100 reinforcers (a combination of income and leisure represented by the filled circle). The new budget condition increases the price of income and decreases the price of leisure by doubling the ratio schedule requirement to 100; in addition, noncontingent reinforcers are delivered under this new budget condition equal to half those obtained at baseline. Thus, if the subject now made 5,000 responses (i.e., responded at its baseline rate), it would earn only 50 reinforcers. However, it would also receive 50% of its baseline reinforcers noncontingently, and therefore obtain another 50 reinforcers, totaling its baseline income. Movement of the consumption point along the new budget line, to a new package containing more leisure and less income than at baseline, indicates substitution of leisure for income when income becomes relatively more expensive and leisure becomes relatively cheaper.

A series of experiments by Green and his collaborators (Green, Kagel, & Battalio, 1982, 1987; Green & Green, 1982; Schrader & Green, 1990) assessed the substitutability of income and leisure in pigeons and rats. In one experiment (Green et al., 1982), pigeons' key pecks produced access to food in 40-minute sessions under four different baseline wage rates: random ratio (RR) 12.5, 25, 50, and 100. Each baseline condition was followed by an income-compensated change in which the ratio requirement was doubled and 50% of the reinforcers obtained at baseline were now delivered noncontingently at variable times throughout the session. Any decrease in responding under the price change would by necessity decrease the number of reinforcers earned (but not affect those delivered freely), and thus reduce total income. Therefore, the extent to which responding actually decreases under the price change reflects the degree to which income and leisure are substitutable.

Figure 14–12 shows the data from one representative pigeon. The solid line in each of the three panels indicates the constraint on work and income imposed by wage rates of RR 12.5 (top panel), RR 25 (middle panel), and RR 50 (bottom panel). The filled circles show the consumption points of income and work obtained under each baseline constraint. The dashed-line segments in each panel represent the price

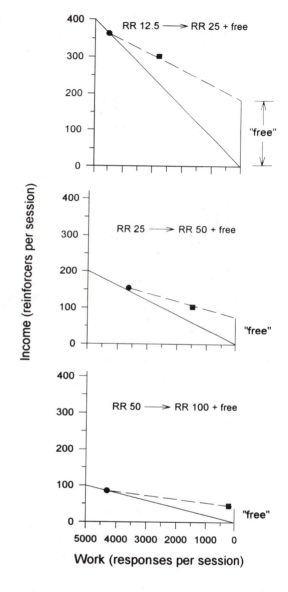

Figure 14–12. Substitution of leisure for income under three different income-compensated wage rates for Pigeon 47. As the wage rate decreased and income therefore became more expensive, the pigeon showed increasingly greater degrees of substitutability of leisure for income. (From Green et al., 1982.)

changes instituted by doubling the baseline ratio value and delivering 50% of the reinforcers earned at baseline freely throughout the session. As can be seen in the new consumption points represented by the filled squares, the income-compensated changes produced reductions in responding at each ratio value. Furthermore, there were greater decreases in responding and thus proportionally larger reductions in total earned food as income became more expensive (i.e., as the baseline ratio value increased).

The degree to which leisure is substituted for income was also shown by Green and Green (1982) to depend on the level of deprivation of the subjects. Pigeons studied under the same income-compensated procedure at 95% of their free-feeding body weights reduced responding more than did the same pigeons studied at 70% of their free-feeding weights. Taken together, these results indicate that the substitution of leisure for income depends on price and is, in addition, modified by an animal's "need." Analyses of work and need have been infrequently incorporated into the experimental analysis of behavior. Preliminary results from behavioral economic experiments point to their importance and prompt consideration of their implications.

NEW INDEPENDENT VARIABLES

The inclusion of concepts drawn from consumer demand theory into behavioral psychology, most notably that of substitutability, has been especially worthwhile in terms of providing a fuller understanding of reinforcer interactions. The conceptual breadth of economics has also precipitated empirical work that incorporates new (to psychology) independent variables. Some of the variables garnering recent attention include open/closed economies, income, and unit price. The inclusion of these variables in the analysis of behavior further expands our empirical investigations and theoretical analyses. There is also the potential for new applications to be derived from these laboratory-based, behavioral-economic results.

Open and Closed Economies

The distinction between open and closed economies has been addressed by Hursh (1980). He defined an *open economy* as one in which "the total daily consumption of [the commodities in question] was not the result of the subjects' interaction with the environment during the sessions, but was arbitrarily controlled by the experimenter" (p. 221). On the other hand, in a *closed economy*, ". . . total daily . . . consumption was determined solely by the subjects' interaction with the schedules of reinforcement . . ." (p. 222). In short, traditional operant experiments, by maintaining nonhuman subjects at approximately 80% of their free-feeding body weights through supplemental postsession feedings, have studied instrumental behavior under the conditions of an open economy. Several studies suggest a differential effect of economy type on instrumental responding. In particular, increasing the price of a commodity (usually food) produces increased responding in a closed economy but decreased responding in an open economy. Hursh and Bauman (1987) speculate that the postsession food provided in the typical open economy functions as a cheap, albeit temporally distant, substitute for the costly within-session food; however, a closed economy provides no such substitute, and responding must therefore increase to maintain intake. (See Timberlake & Peden, 1987, for an alternative explanation.)

The differential effect of economy type is demonstrated in Hursh's (1978) study, described earlier. His Experiment 1 assessed the influence of the price of one food source on consumption of an alternative food and water, under the conditions of a closed economy (see Figure 14–6). In that experiment, the two baboons obtained their daily rations of food and water by responding on variable-interval schedules of reinforcement in 24-hour sessions. Any reduction in responding therefore decreased total daily consumption. In Experiment 2, however, the baboons were assured a constant daily ration of food and water by terminating experimental sessions after a set number of reinforcers had been delivered. This open economy produced a different pattern of responding and consumption than did the closed economy of Experiment 1, as can be seen by comparing Figure 14–13 with Figure 14–6. Figure 14–13 shows the constant food and constant water reinforcers obtained per hour for both subjects as a function of the VI schedule for the alternative food source. Increases in the price of the alternative food had negligible effects on responding for either of the constant reinforcers. These results stand in contrast to the results from the closed economy (Figure 14–6), in which increases in the price of the alternative food produced increases in consumption of the constant food and decreases in consumption of the constant water.

More recently, Imam (1993) suggested that open and closed economies be viewed along a continuum that varies along the dimension of response-reinforcer independence. The "openness" of an economy can be calculated as the proportion of unearned food (both within- and post-session) to total daily food consumption. The greater the proportion of unearned food, the more the quotient reflects the degree of independence between responding and intake, and therefore the more open the economy. Consistent with Imam's independence quotient, an economy can be made more open not only by standard postsession feedings but also by the addition of non-session feedings but also by the addition of non-

contingent food within sessions. It is this implication that was empirically addressed.

Imam (1993) studied pigeons in either one-hour or four-hour experimental sessions. Postsession food was given only following the one-hour sessions, and the amount was based on the average food intake from the corresponding four-hour session. During both session durations, pigeons earned food according to an FR 50 schedule. In some conditions, food was conjointly earned with the FR schedule according to either a VI 60-second schedule or a VI 480-second schedule, thereby varying the overall reward density. In other conditions, noncontingent (unearned) food was concomitantly delivered with the FR schedule by either a VT 60-second or a VT 480-second schedule. The delivery of the noncontingent food has the effect of varying both total daily food and the independence quotient. Therefore, the economies ranged from completely closed, in which all food was earned within the session (the FR 50 conjoint VI schedules in the four-hour sessions), to various degrees of openness (conditions in which postsession and/or within-session unearned food was given). Imam estimated the independence quotient for each condition based on total food intake from earned and unearned sources. He found that decreasing the independence quotient (i.e., making

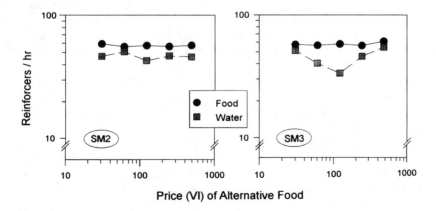

Figure 14–13. Baboons' demand for a constant source of food and water under an open economy as a function of the price of an alternative food source. Data are plotted on log-log coordinates. (From Hursh, 1978, Experiment 2.)

the economy less open) by decreasing the amount of within-session noncontingent food or by not providing post session food produced increases in instrumental responding, and, importantly, that the total response output was well predicted by the estimated independence quotients.

Income

Income can be defined as the limit on total daily intake, or overall rate of reinforcement. In this sense, income has not been incorporated as an independent variable in psychological models of choice. However, as Elsmore et al. (1980) demonstrated, income can strongly determine animals' choices between different reinforcers (Figure 14–5). More extensive investigations into the role of income in choice behavior have ensued. In one noteworthy example, Hastjarjo, Silberberg, and Hursh (1990) extended the pursuit of income effects to an "inferior" good. An inferior good is one for which consumption decreases over some range of increase in income. For example, as people's income increases, they may likely decrease consumption of retread tires or generic store-brand foods, because higher incomes now allow them to purchase higher-quality substitutes. Behavioral psychology has traditionally made use of "normal" goods, that is, reinforcers for which consumption increases as income is increased.

In Hastjarjo et al.'s Experiment 2, rats could choose between one standard food pellet and four quinine-adulterated (bitter-tasting) food pellets by pressing the corresponding lever. In phase 1 income was limited to 140 daily choice trials, and in phase 2 income was reduced to 100 daily choices. The result of this manipulation demonstrated that the quinine alternative was an inferior good. That is, consumption of the quinine pellets increased as income was reduced from 140 to 100 trials per day. When the price of the quinine pellets was then increased (by reducing the number of pellets per lever press from four to three) in the lower income phase, the rats chose and also consumed even more of the inferior good. This outcome establishes the quinine pellets as a

Giffen good (i.e., an inferior good whose consumption increases as its price increases), a result remarkable not only because it is counterintuitive, but also because a Giffen good has not been indisputably found in the human economy despite its long history in theory (Hastjarjo et al., 1990). As the authors note: "These results should also interest the behavior analyst, because . . . they establish a range of choice outcomes so broad as to complicate severely a popular behavior-analytic goal: creating a unitary model of choice" (p. 270). The experimental finding of a Giffen good is also of importance to economic theory because it demonstrates a nonobvious implication of consumer-choice theory (Kagel, Battalio, & Green, 1995).

Unit Price

Recent analyses (e.g., DeGrandpre, Bickel, Hughes, Layng, & Badger, 1993) have suggested that unit price may be the single variable underlying both reinforcer-magnitude and schedule-of-reinforcement effects. Unit price, in behavior analytic terms, is the cost-benefit ratio of schedule of reinforcement requirement divided by magnitude of reinforcement. Thus, unit price subsumes multiple independent variables into one and predicts that behavior may be a function of that unitary variable rather than its component parts per se. Consequently, whether unit price is doubled by halving the amount of reinforcement or by doubling the response reinforcement, the same effects on responding and consumption should be obtained.

In one such test, Hursh, Raslear, Shurtleff, Bauman, and Simmons (1988) varied four components of unit price for rats responding for food: fixed-ratio schedule, number of food pellets per delivery, response effort, and probability of reinforcement. The fixed-ratio value and the force required to make a lever-press response constituted the cost factors, whereas the number of food pellets and the probability of reinforcer delivery constituted the benefit factors of unit price. Unit price was defined as the product of the fixed ratio and the response effort, divided by the product of the number of pellets and reinforcer probability. Eight groups of rats were studied in a factorial design combining probability of reinforcement (1.0 or 0.5), number of food pellets (1 or 2), and response effort (0.265 or 0.530 N), and each group responded on FR schedules of 1, 15, 45, 90, 180, 360. These various combinations of factors yielded unit prices ranging from 0.1325 to 381.6. Hursh et al. found that across this range of unit prices, ". . . consumption by all groups appears to cluster about a single function . . ." (p. 426).

The evidence for a single function is apparent from the data presented in Figure 14–14. Shown is average consumption as a function of unit price for each of three groups of rats. Group 1 - 1.0 - high, represented by the circles, had its unit price determined by 1 pellet of food, probability of reinforcement equal to 1.0, and a high response effort (0.530 N). Group 1 - 0.5 - low, shown as the squares, had its unit price determined by 1 pellet

of food, 0.5 probability of reinforcement, and low response effort (0.265 N). Group 2 - 0.5 - high, shown as the triangles, had its unit price determined by 2 pellets of food, 0.5 probability of reinforcement, and high response effort. Note that the rats in these three groups, although differing in the number of pellets they received per reinforcer, the probability of reinforcement, and the effort required, all responded under the same unit price at each of the six FR values studied. Nonetheless, consumption at each of the FR values is essentially the same in all three groups when plotted as a function of unit price.

More recently, unit price has become a powerful means by which to examine and understand drug self-administration (see Bickel, DeGrandpre, & Higgins, 1995, and DeGrandpre & Bickel, 1996, for a review and reanalysis of drug self-administration research). With human cigarette smokers as subjects, Bickel, DeGrandpre, Hughes, and Higgins (1991) assessed whether consumption of nicotine would be comparable at equivalent unit prices. Participants were studied at several unit prices, ranging from 50 to 1,600, derived by combining a fixed-ratio schedule for cigarette puffs with number of puffs permitted per reinforcer. For example, for a unit price of 200, subjects responded in one condition on an FR 200 for 1 puff and in another condition on an FR 400 for 2 puffs. Bickel et al. (1991) found that, in general, subjects' consumption of cigarette puffs was roughly equivalent at a given unit price, regardless of how that unit price was derived. These results are important not only because they extend the generality of the unit-price concept to human cigarette smoking, but also because they reemphasize the usefulness of subsuming the interaction of response requirement and reinforcer magnitude effects under a single variable.

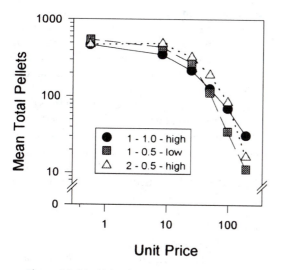

Figure 14–14. Unit price. Mean total food pellets consumed as a function of unit price for three groups of rats. A given unit price was determined by different combinations of cost (fixed-ratio requirement and response effort) and benefit (number of food pellets and probability of reinforcement) factors. Notice that a single function describes consumption across the three groups for whom unit price was equivalent. Data are plotted on log-log coordinates. (From Hursh et al., 1988.)

APPLICATIONS AND IMPLICATIONS

Herrnstein's matching law (1970), which describes choices among response alternatives, has many practical applications and potential uses in the realm of applied behavior analysis and behavior therapy (e.g., McDowell, 1981, 1982, 1988; Myerson & Hale, 1984; Winkler & Burkhard, 1990). The matching law as conceptualized in Equation 1 leads to the prediction that a target behavior, B_x, can be modified not only by directly changing the reinforcers it produces (R_x), but also by changing the other reinforcers available in the situation (R_o).

McDowell (1981), in a clinical intervention with an adult male who had mild retardation, demonstrated that an inappropriate behavior could be reduced by increasing the alternative reinforcers available. The man engaged in extreme oppositional behaviors (B_x) such as refusal to follow instructions and aggressiveness. These behaviors appeared to be reinforced by attention from his parents (R_x). Attention for these behaviors could not directly be decreased because such a decrease produced violent behaviors on the client's part. Consequently, a token-reinforcement system was implemented in which the client earned tokens that were exchangeable for money by engaging in other appropriate activities (e.g., reading and shaving). This token reinforcement contingency increases R_o and should, according to Equation 1, decrease oppositional behavior. Indeed, the client's oppositional behavior decreased by approximately 80% within the first few weeks of the intervention.

Although the matching law has given rise to many behavior-change applications, its ability to predict choice and suggest effective intervention strategies may prove limited in situations involving qualitatively different reinforcers. Consider the following example posited by Green and Freed (1993): A frazzled parent immediately gives in to a screaming child by dropping everything and playing with that child. This same parent also is quite indulgent and gives the child lots of toys for no reason in particular. Consider the target behavior, B_x, to be tantruming on the part of the child, and playing with the child to be the reinforcer that tantruming produces, R_x. The toys the parent provides can be considered other reinforcers available in the situation, R_o. According to the matching law, increasing the number of toys the child is given should decrease

tantruming. But also consider that toys (R_o) and playing (R_x) are likely to be complementary reinforcers, rather than substitutes, because they tend to be consumed together. If this is the case, then instead of reducing tantrums, noncontingent toys are likely to *increase* the child's tantrums.

In the absence of a behavioral-economic perspective, the matching law has difficulty in accounting for interactions between qualitatively different reinforcers, and it is for this reason that behavioral economics is receiving increasing attention in regard to its potential applications. In a case-study demonstration, Tustin (1994) conducted behavioral-economic analyses of responding for different types of reinforcers by three men with intellectual disability. For one of the men, brief presentations of visual stimuli (changing colors and patterns generated on a computer monitor) could be earned by pressing a button on a joystick according to an FR 5 schedule. In one condition, brief presentations of auditory stimuli (musical tones) were concurrently available, and in another condition, social attention (smiling at the subject, praising him, nodding at him) could concurrently be earned. In both conditions, the FR schedule for the alternative reinforcer varied from FR 1 to FR 20 across test sessions.

Although the relative price decrease for visual stimuli across sessions was the same in both conditions, the resulting increase in consumption of visual stimuli was not. When the alternative reinforcer was auditory stimulation, the number of visual stimuli earned changed much more rapidly and reached a higher absolute amount than when the alternative reinforcer was social attention. Tustin's results highlight the notion that considerations of changes in relative price alone are not sufficient for predicting the efficacy of a reinforcer in maintaining behavior; behavior modifiers must also consider the type of alternative reinforcer(s) available in the situation. (See also Neef, Mace, Shea, & Shade, 1992; Neef, Shade, & Miller, 1994.)

We discussed previously some of the experimental work on drug self-administration (see also Carroll, Carmona, & May, 1991; Epstein,

Bulik, Perkins, Caggiula, & Rodefer, 1991). In a compelling paper, Hursh (1991) explores the implications of using methadone in the treatment of heroin addiction. The use of methadone as a treatment is predicated on the assumption that methadone will effectively substitute for the addict's heroin. As Hursh noted, however, methadone is likely to be less than a perfect substitute because it is not available on demand, it is administered in doses designed to produce less of a euphoric state, and it is taken apart from the complex social ritual that often accompanies heroin administration.

Behavioral-economic concepts have also been employed in analyzing other complex human behaviors such as food choice (e.g., Lappalainen & Epstein, 1990; Smith & Epstein, 1991) and allocation of time to variously available activities such as candle-making and magazine reading (Bernstein & Ebbesen, 1978). Epstein, Smith, Vara, and Rodefer (1991) adopted a behavioral-economic approach to "determine environmental constraints under which vigorous activities would serve as substitutes for sedentary activities" (p. 311) in obese children. Two groups of children, averaging approximately 10 years of age and 60% overweight, first assessed their liking for several different sedentary and vigorous activities (e.g., reading comic books and riding an exercise bicycle, respectively). For each child, a most preferred sedentary activity was determined as well as a most preferred and least preferred vigorous activity. During the experiment proper, the children responded under concurrent variable ratio schedules. The schedules were embedded in a computer game, and the reinforcers earned were points later exchangeable for time to engage in the particular activity. Responding on one schedule, which was always a VR 2, earned the child points that could later be used to spend time engaging in a vigorous activity. Responding on the other schedule, which ranged from VR 2 to VR 16 across conditions, earned the child points that could later be used to spend time engaging in their most preferred sedentary activity. Two experimental groups were arranged. For one group the vigorous activity to be earned was

the child's most preferred one (HiVIG group), and for the second group the vigorous activity to be earned was the child's least preferred one (LoVIG group).

Figure 14–15 shows the resulting demand curves for both groups. Consumption of the sedentary activity decreased as its price increased (represented by the solid circles), while consumption of the vigorous activity increased (represented by the solid squares). However, the degree of elasticity is clearly affected by how much the children preferred the alternative vigorous activity. The HiVIG group's consumption of the sedentary activity was sensitive to all increases in price; the LoVIG group's consumption of the sedentary activity was only affected at the highest price. That is, as the price of the sedentary activity increased from VR 2 to VR 8, the LoVIG group showed no change in consumption of either reinforcer, maintaining its 2:1 preference for the sedentary activity over the vigorous activity. The HiVIG group, on the other hand, decreased consumption of the sedentary activity by almost 50% over this same range of price change. The implications of these results in the treatment of childhood obesity are clear. Obviously, one of the considerations in treatment design is getting overweight children to engage in more vigorous activities. An analysis such as Epstein et al.'s (1991) points the way to the implementation of more effective treatments.

A behavioral-economic approach may also provide an alternative perspective on research and treatment in areas that might not, at first glance, appear to lend themselves to such an approach. Social support is one of the most powerful yet most elusive forces in health care. For example, a major review concluded that the mortality attributable to lack of social support rivals that attributable to smoking cigarettes (House, Landis, & Umberson, 1988). A psychosocial support group for women with terminal breast cancer produced a near doubling in survival time (Spiegel, Bloom, Kraemer, & Gottheil, 1989). Yet numerous efforts to mobilize social support in health-promotion programs, such as those to encourage nonsmoking, have been unsuccessful

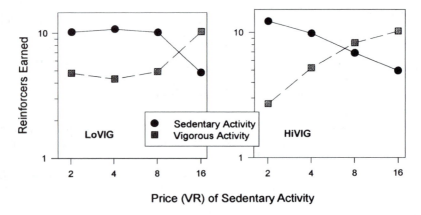

Figure 14–15. Obese children's demand for sedentary and vigorous activities as a function of increases in the price of the sedentary activity. Demand for the sedentary activity was much less elastic when the alternative reinforcer was the low-preferred (left panel) than when it was the high-preferred (right panel) of the vigorous activities. Data are plotted on log-log coordinates. (From Epstein et al., 1991.)

(e.g., Lichtenstein, Glasgow, & Abrams, 1986). In particular, a number of studies indicate that the benefits of social support fade after the support intervention is terminated.

Conventional models of social support view it as including instrumental, informational, and esteem-enhancing components (Cohen & Hoberman, 1983) that assist or aid instrumental performance. From the perspective that social support enhances instrumental performance, one would expect its benefits to persist beyond the end of treatment. The failure of social support's benefits to persist beyond treatment is then especially striking.

A behavioral-economic perspective may help articulate an alternative view of social support in which support is viewed as a commodity or reinforcer that is substitutable for other reinforcers. In the case of smoking, for example, social support may be substitutable for nicotine. When social support is readily available, consumption of nicotine should decrease, a prediction consistent with numerous studies indicating a lower likelihood of smoking and a greater likelihood of quitting among individuals with higher levels of social support (e.g., Graham & Gibson, 1971; Mermelstein, Cohen, Lichtenstein, Baer, & Ka-

marck, 1986). However, when support is withdrawn, as at the end of a treatment that emphasized it, behavior is again responsive to the other incentives in the situation; individuals return to smoking (Etringer, Gregory, & Lando, 1984). Fisher (1996) provides additional observations consistent with this behavioral-economic model of support as a reinforcer substitutable for other reinforcers rather than as an instrumental resource, and discusses its implications for improving interventions.

Such varied applications and implications of behavioral economics to individual behavior are just the tip of the iceberg. As Winkler and Burkhard (1990, p. 311) aptly stated, "Combining the efforts of behavior modification with the models provided through economics allows a more meaningful analysis of intervention effects and social policies."

CONCLUSIONS

Until quite recently, economics was held to be the domain only of (rational) humans. This is clearly not the case (Rachlin, 1980). As our review of selected behavioral-economic studies amply demonstrates, economic (rational) behavior is not the sole province of human beings. (See Rachlin, 1995, for further discussion of rationality in behavioral economics.) In fact, the study of economic behavior in nonhuman animals has already been successful in expanding behavior-analytic theories of choice, specifically Baum's generalized matching law (1974) as expressed in Equation 2. Rather than dispensing with the matching law because of the instances for which it does not account, some behavioral economists have chosen to incorporate the notion of substitutability into the exponent s (Rachlin, Battalio, Kagel, & Green, 1981). s takes on values close to unity for highly substitutable reinforcers, takes on values of zero for independent commodities, and approaches $-\infty$ for complementary reinforcers.

The study of economic behavior in nonhumans has also suggested applications to and implications for complex human behavior. Consider the area of drug use, for example. Analyses of substitutability have direct relevance to drug taking and addictions (see, e.g., Green & Kagel, 1996; Hursh, 1991). DeGrandpre and Bickel (1996) have argued that the economic concept of unit price provides a means of integrating the multiple independent variables in the drug self-administration literature (see also Foltin, 1994). Research from a behavioral-economic perspective provides new insights for the treatment of drug dependency and offers suggestions on public-policy issues related to illicit drug use (e.g., Bickel & DeGrandpre, 1996; Carroll, 1996; Hursh, 1991).

Although behavioral economics has made inroads in the domain of behavior analysis (see, for example, *Journal of the Experimental Analysis of Behavior*, November 1995, special issue on behavioral economics), it has not always been met with open arms. We have not addressed a fundamental assumption of economic theory—that consumers maximize utility. Behavior analysis certainly has its "maximizers," but there are also those who adamantly oppose maximizing as a mechanism underlying choice behavior. Indeed, this contentious issue has occupied a considerable place in the literature over the last several years (see, for example, Miller, Heiner, & Manning, 1990; Kagel et al., 1995; Rachlin et al., 1981, with commentaries; Vaughan & Herrnstein, 1987). However, as we have noted previously (Green & Freed, 1993), an opposition to maximization need not translate into an opposition to incorporating economic principles and theories into psychology. Not only is it possible for an animal's behavior to obey the demand law without maximizing utility (Allison, 1983), but it is also possible to derive the demand law without reference to utility at all.

So, too, there are those whose work falls within a behavioral-economic framework but who would not agree with all the issues we have raised nor with our interpretations. That is to say, those who do behavioral-economic research are not all cut from the same cloth. But they all would likely agree on the benefits that psychological research affords economics, including rigorous empirical testing and refinement of basic principles and theory (Hursh & Bauman, 1987; see Kagel et al., 1995), as well as the benefits that economic theory affords psychology, such as a broader conceptualization of factors that influence choice among different reinforcers and an expansion of our understanding of reinforcement.

The value of behavioral economics as a discipline is to be judged on its heuristic and predictive abilities, the breadth and scope of its focus, and ultimately the degree to which it enlarges our understanding of behavior—in short, its utility.

REFERENCES

Ackroff, K., Vigorito, M., & Sclafani, A. (1990). Fat appetite in rats: The response of infant and adult rats to nutritive and non-nutritive oil emulsions. *Appetite, 15,* 171–188.

Allison, J. (1983). Behavioral substitutes and complements. In R. L. Mellgren (ed.), *Animal behavior and cognition,* 1–30. New York: North-Holland.

Allison, J., Miller, M., & Wozny, M. (1979). Conservation in behavior. *Journal of Experimental Psychology: General, 108,* 4–34.

Baum, W. M. (1974). On two types of deviation from the matching law: Bias and undermatching. *Journal of the Experimental Analysis of Behavior, 22,* 231–242.

Baumol, W. J. (1972). *Economic theory and operations analysis* (3rd ed.). Englewood Cliffs, N.J.: Prentice-Hall.

Bernstein, D. J., & Ebbesen, E. B. (1978). Reinforcement and substitution in humans: A multiple-response analysis. *Journal of the Experimental Analysis of Behavior, 30*, 243–253.

Bickel, W. K., & DeGrandpre, R. J. (1996). Modeling drug abuse policy in the behavioral economics laboratory. In L. Green & J. H. Kagel (eds.), *Advances in behavioral economics, Vol. 3: Substance use and abuse*, 69–95. Norwood, N.J.: Ablex.

Bickel, W. K., DeGrandpre, R. J., & Higgins, S. T. (1995). The behavioral economics of concurrent drug reinforcers: A review and reanalysis of drug self-administration research. *Psychopharmacology, 118*, 250–259.

Bickel, W. K., DeGrandpre, R. J., Hughes, J. R., & Higgins, S. T. (1991). Behavioral economics of drug self-administration. II. A unit-price analysis of cigarette smoking. *Journal of the Experimental Analysis of Behavior, 55*, 145–154.

Carroll, M. E. (1996). Reducing drug abuse by enriching the environment with alternative nondrug reinforcers. In L. Green & J. H. Kagel (eds.), *Advances in behavioral economics, Vol 3: Substance use and abuse*, 37–68. Norwood, N.J.: Ablex.

Carroll, M. E., Carmona, G. G., & May, S. A. (1991). Modifying drug-reinforced behavior by altering the economic conditions of the drug and a non-drug reinforcer. *Journal of the Experimental Analysis of Behavior, 56*, 361–376.

Cohen, S., & Hoberman, H. M. (1983). Positive events and social supports as buffers of life change stress. *Journal of Applied Social Psychology, 13*, 99–125.

Davison, M., & McCarthy, D. (1988). *The matching law: A research review*. Hillsdale, N.J.: Erlbaum.

DeGrandpre, R. J., & Bickel, W. K. (1996). Drug dependence as consumer demand. In L. Green & J. H. Kagel (eds.), *Advances in behavioral economics, Vol. 3: Substance use and abuse*, 1–36. Norwood, N.J.: Ablex.

DeGrandpre, R. J., Bickel, W. K., Hughes, J. R., Layng, M. P., & Badger, G. (1993). Unit price as a useful metric in analyzing effects of reinforcer magnitude. *Journal of the Experimental Analysis of Behavior, 60*, 641–666.

Elsmore, T. F., Fletcher, G. V., Conrad, D. G., & Sodetz, F. J. (1980). Reduction of heroin intake in baboons by an economic constraint. *Pharmacology, Biochemistry, and Behavior, 13*, 729–731.

Epstein, L. H., Bulik, C. M., Perkins, K. A., Caggiula, A. R., & Rodefer, J. (1991). Behavioral economic analysis of smoking: Money and food as alternatives. *Pharmacology Biochemistry & Behavior, 38*, 715–721.

Epstein, L. H., Smith, J. A., Vara, L. S., & Rodefer, J. S. (1991). Behavioral economic analysis of activity choice in obese children. *Health Psychology, 10*, 311–316.

Etringer, B. D., Gregory, V. R., & Lando, H. A. (1984). Influence of group cohesion on the behavioral treatment of smoking. *Journal of Consulting and Clinical Psychology, 52*, 1080–1086.

Ferster, C. B., & Skinner, B. F. (1957). *Schedules of reinforcement*. Englewood Cliffs, N.J.: Prentice-Hall.

Fisher, E. B., Jr. (1996). A behavioral-economic perspective on the influence of social support on cigarette smoking. In L. Green & J. H. Kagel (eds.), *Advances in behavioral economics, Vol. 3: Substance use and abuse*, 207–236. Norwood, N.J.: Ablex.

Foltin, R. W. (1991). An economic analysis of "demand" for food in baboons. *Journal of the Experimental Analysis of Behavior, 56*, 445–454.

Foltin, R. W. (1994). Does package size matter? A unit-price analysis of "demand" for food in baboons. *Journal of the Experimental Analysis of Behavior, 62*, 293–306.

Gleitman, H. (1991). *Psychology* (3rd ed.). New York: Norton.

Graham, S., & Gibson, R. W. (1971). Cessation of patterned behavior: Withdrawal from smoking. *Social Science and Medicine, 5*, 319–337.

Green, J. K., & Green, L. (1982). Substitution of leisure for income in pigeon workers as a function of body weight. *Behaviour Analysis Letters, 2*, 103–112.

Green, L., & Freed, D. (1993). The substitutability of reinforcers. *Journal of the Experimental Analysis of Behavior, 60*, 141–158.

Green, L., & Kagel, J. H. (eds.) (1996). *Advances in behavioral economics, Vol. 3: Substance use and abuse*. Norwood, N.J.: Ablex.

Green, L., & Rachlin, H. (1991). Economic substitutability of electrical brain stimulation, food, and water. *Journal of the Experimental Analysis of Behavior, 55*, 133–143.

Green, L., Kagel, J. H., & Battalio, R. C. (1982). Ratio schedules of reinforcement and their relation to economic theories of labor supply. In M. L. Commons, R. J. Herrnstein, & H. Rachlin (eds.), *Quantitative analyses of behavior, Vol. 2: Matching and maximizing accounts*, 395–429. Cambridge, Mass.: Ballinger.

Green, L., Kagel, J. H., & Battalio, R. C. (1987). Consumption-leisure tradeoffs in pigeons: Effects of changing marginal wage rates by varying amount of reinforcement. *Journal of the Experimental Analysis of Behavior, 47*, 17–28.

Harlow, H. F. (1953). Learning by rhesus monkeys on the basis of manipulation-exploration motives. *Science, 117*, 466–467.

Hastjarjo, T., Silberberg, A., & Hursh, S. R. (1990). Quinine pellets an inferior good and a Giffen good in rats. *Journal of the Experimental Analysis of Behavior, 53*, 263–271.

Herrnstein, R. J. (1961). Relative and absolute strength of response as a function of frequency of reinforcement.

Journal of the Experimental Analysis of Behavior, 4, 267–272.

Herrnstein, R. J. (1970). On the law of effect. *Journal of the Experimental Analysis of Behavior, 13,* 243–266.

House, J. S., Landis, K. R., & Umberson, D. (1988). Social relationships and health. *Science, 241,* 540–544.

Hull, C. L. (1943). *Principles of behavior.* New York: Appleton-Century-Crofts.

Hursh, S. R. (1978). The economics of daily consumption controlling food- and water-reinforced responding. *Journal of the Experimental Analysis of Behavior, 29,* 475–491.

Hursh, S. R. (1980). Economic concepts for the analysis of behavior. *Journal of the Experimental Analysis of Behavior, 34,* 219–238.

Hursh, S. R. (1991). Behavioral economics of drug self-administration and drug abuse policy. *Journal of the Experimental Analysis of Behavior, 56,* 377–393.

Hursh, S. R., & Bauman, R. A. (1987). The behavioral analysis of demand. In L. Green & J. H. Kagel (eds.), *Advances in behavioral economics, Vol. 1:* 117–165. Norwood, N.J.: Ablex.

Hursh, S. R., & Natelson, B. H. (1981). Electrical brain stimulation and food reinforcement dissociated by demand elasticity. *Physiology & Behavior, 26,* 509–515.

Hursh, S. R., Raslear, T. G., Shurtleff, D., Bauman, R., & Simmons, L. (1988). A cost-benefit analysis of demand for food. *Journal of the Experimental Analysis of Behavior, 50,* 419–440.

Imam, A. A. (1993). Response-reinforcer independence and the economic continuum: A preliminary analysis. *Journal of the Experimental Analysis of Behavior, 59,* 231–243.

Journal of the Experimental Analysis of Behavior. (1995). Special issue on behavioral economics. *64(3).*

Kagel, J. H., Battalio, R. C., & Green, L. (1995). *Economic choice theory: An experimental analysis of animal behavior.* New York: Cambridge University Press.

Kalat, J. W. (1995). *Biological psychology* (5th ed.). Pacific Grove, Calif.: Brooks/Cole.

Keller, F. S., & Schoenfeld, W. N. (1950). *Principles of psychology.* New York: Appleton-Century-Crofts.

Lappalainen, R., & Epstein, L. H. (1990). A behavioral economics analysis of food choice in humans. *Appetite, 14,* 81–93.

Lea, S. E. G. (1978). The psychology and economics of demand. *Psychological Bulletin, 85,* 441–466.

Lea, S. E. G., & Roper, T. J. (1977). Demand for food on fixed-ratio schedules as a function of the quality of concurrently available reinforcement. *Journal of the Experimental Analysis of Behavior, 27,* 371–380.

Lichtenstein, E., Glasgow, R. E., & Abrams, D. B. (1986). Social support in smoking cessation: In search of effective interventions. *Behavior Therapy, 17,* 607–619.

Logan, F. (1960). *Incentive.* New Haven, Conn.: Yale University Press.

McDowell, J. J (1981). On the validity and utility of Herrnstein's hyperbola in applied behavior analysis. In C. M. Bradshaw, E. Szabadi, & C. F. Lowe (eds.), *Quantification of steady-state operant behaviour,* 311–324. Amsterdam: Elsevier.

McDowell, J. J (1982). The importance of Herrnstein's mathematical statement of the law of effect for behavior therapy. *American Psychologist, 37,* 771–779.

McDowell, J. J (1988). Matching theory in natural human environments. *Behavior Analyst, 11,* 95–109.

Meehl, P. E. (1950). On the circularity of the law of effect. *Psychological Bulletin, 47,* 52–75.

Mermelstein, R., Cohen, S., Lichtenstein, E., Baer, J. S., & Kamarck, T. (1986). Social support and smoking cessation and maintenance. *Journal of Consulting and Clinical Psychology, 54,* 447–453.

Miller, H. L., Jr. (1976). Matching-based hedonic scaling in the pigeon. *Journal of the Experimental Analysis of Behavior, 26,* 335–347.

Miller, H. L., Jr., Heiner, R. A., & Manning, S. W. (1990). Experimental approaches to the matching/maximizing controversy. In L. Green & J. H. Kagel (eds.), *Advances in behavioral economics, Vol. 2:* 253–287. Norwood, N.J.: Ablex.

Myerson, J., & Hale, S. (1984). Practical implications of the matching law. *Journal of Applied Behavior Analysis, 17,* 367–380.

Neef, N. A., Mace, F. C., Shea, M. C., & Shade, D. B. (1992). Effects of reinforcer rate and reinforcer quality on time allocation: Extensions of matching theory to educational settings. *Journal of Applied Behavior Analysis, 25,* 691–699.

Neef, N. A., Shade, D., & Miller, M. S. (1994). Assessing influential dimensions of reinforcers on choice in students with serious emotional disturbance. *Journal of Applied Behavior Analysis, 27,* 575–583.

Premack, D. (1962). Reversibility of the reinforcement relation. *Science, 136,* 255–257.

Premack, D. (1965). Reinforcement theory. In D. Levine (ed.), *Nebraska symposium on motivation,* 123–180. Lincoln: University of Nebraska Press.

Rachlin, H. (1980). Economics and behavioral psychology. In J. E. R. Staddon (ed.), *Limits to action: The allocation of individual behavior,* 205–236. New York: Academic Press.

Rachlin, H. (1989). *Judgment, decision, and choice: A cognitive/behavioral synthesis.* New York: Freeman.

Rachlin, H. (1995). Behavioral economics without anomalies. *Journal of the Experimental Analysis of Behavior, 64,* 397–404.

Rachlin, H., Battalio, R., Kagel, J., & Green, L. (1981). Maximization theory in behavioral psychology. *The Behav-*

ioral and Brain Sciences, 4, 371–417, includes commentaries.

Rachlin, H., Green, L., Kagel, J. H., & Battalio, R. C. (1976). Economic demand theory and psychological studies of choice. In G. H. Bower (ed.), *The psychology of learning and motivation, Vol. 10:* 129–154. New York: Academic Press.

Schrader, S. M., & Green, L. (1990). The economics of leisure in psychological studies of choice. In L. Green & J. H. Kagel (eds.), *Advances in behavioral economics, Vol. 2:* 226–252. Norwood, N.J.: Ablex.

Schwartz, B., & Robbins, S. J. (1995). *Psychology of learning and behavior* (4th ed.). New York: Norton.

Sheffield, F. D. (1966). A drive-induction theory of reinforcement. In R. N. Haber (ed.), *Current research in motivation,* 98–110. New York: Holt.

Sheffield, F. D., & Roby, T. B. (1950). Reward value of a non-nutritive sweet taste. *Journal of Comparative and Physiological Psychology, 43,* 471–481.

Sheffield, F. D., Wulff, J. J., & Backer, R. (1951). Reward value of copulation without sex drive reduction. *Journal of Comparative and Physiological Psychology, 44,* 3–8.

Skinner, B. F. (1938). *The behavior of organisms.* New York: Appleton-Century-Crofts.

Smith, J. A., & Epstein, L. H. (1991). Behavioral economic analysis of food choice in obese children. *Appetite, 17,* 91–95.

Spiegel, D., Bloom, J. R., Kraemer, H. C., & Gottheil, E. (1989). Effect of psychosocial treatment on survival of patients with metastatic breast cancer. *Lancet, 2(8668),* 888–891.

Thorndike, E. L. (1911). *Animal intelligence: Experimental studies.* New York: Macmillan.

Timberlake, W., & Allison, J. (1974). Response deprivation: An empirical approach to instrumental performance. *Psychological Review, 81,* 146–164.

Timberlake, W., & Peden, B. F. (1987). On the distinction between open and closed economies. *Journal of the Experimental Analysis of Behavior, 48,* 35–60.

Tustin, R. D. (1994). Preference for reinforcers under varying schedule arrangements: A behavioral economic analysis. *Journal of Applied Behavior Analysis, 27,* 597–606.

Vaughan, W., Jr., & Herrnstein, R. J. (1987). Stability, melioration, and natural selection. In L. Green & J. H. Kagel (eds.), *Advances in behavioral economics, Vol. 1:* 185–215. Norwood, N.J.: Ablex.

Wilcoxin, H. C. (1969). Historical introduction to the problem of reinforcement. In J. T. Tapp (ed.), *Reinforcement and behavior,* 1–46. New York: Academic Press.

Winkler, R. C., & Burkhard, B. (1990). A systems approach to behavior modification through behavioral economics. In L. Green & J. H. Kagel (eds.), *Advances in behavioral economics, Vol. 2:* 288–315. Norwood, N.J.: Ablex.

CHAPTER 15

OPTIMIZATION: SOME FACTORS THAT FACILITATE AND HINDER OPTIMAL PERFORMANCE IN ANIMALS AND HUMANS

Todd R. Schachtman
Phil Reed

THE CONCEPT OF OPTIMAL BEHAVIOR

The analysis of learned behavior is the study of changes in behavior. It is the analysis of behavioral differences. Organisms are different from one another in that they possess unique histories and distinctive features. They are constantly confronted with a variety of contexts and situations. Within each of these situations, they must choose among a variety of behaviors available to them at any given time. Each activity will bring its own consequence, and some consequences will be more adaptive or beneficial than others. The selection of a particular behavior may or may not be the most adaptive choice for that time and place. Adaptive choices may suggest advanced cognitive functioning. Indeed, some theorists have claimed that consciousness and attention in animals might be indicated by complex choice behavior (see Burghardt, 1991, for a discussion).

This chapter describes a number of different behaviors and situations in which subjects can be seen to produce reasonable or, in many cases, unreasonable behavior. Some of the behaviors considered are seen in humans, and others are found in animals. We discuss behaviors in animals and humans concurrently with the expectation that many of the processes resulting in optimization, or nonoptimization, apply equally well to both populations.

We will be using terms such as *rational, optimal,* and *maximizing* somewhat interchangably throughout this chapter, although the reader should realize that there are differences among them (see Lea, Tarpy, & Webley, 1987). The concept of rationality asks "how a well-informed person maximizes either objective value or subjective utility" (Lea et al., 1987, p. 87). Objective value refers to the value of an item or activity that is independent of the characteristics of the person or animal. A dollar has a particular value of exchange at a given time regardless of who possesses it. An ear of corn has a certain amount of nutrients regardless of who eats it. Subjective utility is the value of an item or activity that is based on characteristics of the individual. Subjective utility is derived from the subject's evaluation of the item. "Optimality is doing the best thing possible," whereas maximization means that some commodity is obtained to the largest extent possible (see Lea et al., 1987, p. 105). When all possible costs and benefits are being considered rather than merely being concerned with the maximization of a single commodity, optimization is the more appropriate expression.

Many of the instances of behavior discussed here are analyzed for the degree to which they are or are not optimal, yet we will also consider factors that influence whether the behavior *appears* optimal or reasonable to an observer or researcher. Since rapid learning is usually considered more adaptive than slow learning, learning will be considered optimal when it occurs rapidly even in situations where the learned response itself may not offer much benefit or adaptive value to the organism. A list of some of the issues discussed in the chapter is provided in Table 15–1, although the list is far from exhaustive.

The "reasonableness" of performance, or the extent to which performance can be considered "optimal," "ideal" or "rational," can vary depending on whether one is discussing the costs and benefits of one aspect of the situation or another and depending upon whether the focus is on the immediate situation or the long term. Even in a simple situation, such as an animal or person choosing to consume a particular food substance, one can analyze the optimal value of the behavior in a number of ways, including whether the food contains sufficient nutrients, whether it contains a reasonable amount of calories, whether it is the best-tasting food available, whether instead the animal expended too much energy bar pressing for food or

searching for and handling the food, whether the organism put itself in too much risk of predation by selecting this food source, whether the animal should share the food with its young or mate or siblings, whether the individual would be better off engaging in some other activity, such as mating or drinking fluid, and whether selecting this food substance will deplete this resource in the future, just to name a few considerations.

Evaluation of optimality based on one level of analysis may be erroneous if instead some other dimension of the behavior is considered (see Principle 1 in Table 15–1). Each feature asks a different question about whether the behavior can be considered optimal. Thus, optimal behavior can be discussed at many different levels, and infinite examples of behaviors exist that can be analyzed. Economists, psychologists, zoologists, biologists, and investigators from numerous other disciplines have been interested for a long time in the extent to which animals (including humans) behave most effectively in various situations. As a result, the analysis of optimal behavior has been examined in experiments on judgment, decision making, problem solving, concept formation, artificial intelligence, and conditioning.

This chapter focuses on some of the processes that can result in less than optimal behavior and describes some of the factors that can promote optimal behavior. Other issues related to the optimization of behavior can be found elsewhere in this book (see chapters on choice behavior by Logue and behavioral economics by Green & Freed). For the reasons suggested above, the topics covered in the present chapter are eclectic and varied, but they represent an attempt to address those issues we feel are of greatest interest and value to behavior therapists concerned with analyzing and modifying behavior. The diverse collection of topics selected for this chapter also attempts to portray some of the more exciting recent research developments in animal learning, memory, and conditioning.

Table 15–1.   Principles Summarizing Many of the Points Discussed in the Chapter

Principle 1:   Judgment of the optimality of behavior may estimate behavior as nonoptimal or optimal based on consideration of one dimension or consequence of the behavior. Consideration of alternative dimensions may produce a different judgment.

Principle 2:   Behavior can be seen as nonoptimal because outcomes rather than effects are measured (or vice versa).

Principle 3:   Behavior can be nonoptimal because of poor memory of information that is critical for deciding upon the appropriate behavior.

Principle 4:   Behavior can be nonoptimal because subjects do not use all of the probability information available in the contingency square (see Figure 15–1).

Principle 5:   Subjects can perform nonoptimally because of poor retention of individual event representations. Alternatively, subjects may perform poorly because the memory load from retention of individual event representations is large and disrupts efficient decision making, while retention of this information provides little utility.

Principle 6:   Judgment of the optimality of behavior may estimate behavior as nonoptimal because the value of nonresponding is underestimated.

Principle 7:   Behavior will not be optimal if the memory window is too long to contain currently accurate information or too short to accurately represent the prevailing circumstances.

Principle 8:   Developing a new adaptive behavior requires the costs of the trial and error process needed to develop the behavior. These initial costs may hinder optimal behavior in the short run, but the behavior may turn out to be optimal in the long run.

Principle 9:   Subjects may perform nonoptimally because their decisions were based on a trivial dimension. This principle differs from Principle 1 in that the former concerns use of an inappropriate dimension by the subject. Principle 1 refers to the dimension considered by the behavior analyst in judging the optimality of the behavior.

Principle 10:   Subjects may make poor choices deciding which situation requires a decision or some behavior change. These poor choices may hinder optimal behavior.

Principle 11:   Biological constraints can hinder optimal learning performance, since organisms are more prepared to learn some relationships than others.

Principle 12:   Behavior may not be optimal when resources and/or alternatives are so abundant that a confusion effect occurs and subjects obtain fewer resources than when resources or options are less plentiful.

Principle 13:   Behavior may not be optimal when subjects sample locations for resources that have been poor providers in the past in order to ensure that conditions have not changed.

Principle 14:   Behavior may not be optimal because organisms are members of a group or community and are expected to adhere to the rules and values of this group regardless of whether the behavior is personally advantageous.

Principle 15:   Stressful reactions to a problem can cause a person to choose poorly and behave nonoptimally.

Principle 16:   Nonoptimal behavior can arise because of our need to have a simple, organized, coherent, consistent view of the world. This can create distortions in the information.

Principle 17:   Errors occur when we try to reduce the complexity of the problem by abstracting it and integrating it into our existing schema.

Principle 18:   Some intransitivity in choice behavior is due to different attributes being compared in different situations.

Principle 19:   Subjects often cannot detect the relevant probabilities, and this can hinder rational behavior.

Principle 20:   Subjects will not perform optimally when objective value rather than subjective utility is considered, since the former does not take many factors into account, such as the law of diminishing returns, momentary preferences, and bliss points.

Principle 21:   Subjects do not perform optimally when the rules are changed and responding is based on the pre-shift contingencies.

STEPS USED IN OPTIMAL DECISION MAKING

Optimal behavior requires making reasonable decisions. Three steps in decision making are problem recognition, generating alternative choices, and evaluating choices (Mullen & Roth, 1991). Recognizing the problem is the person's realization that there is a challenge to the status quo and one or more of the outcomes stemming from this challenge may have more loss (or less benefit) than other outcomes. Generating choices obviously involves obtaining information about alternative courses of action. Evaluating choices is an important process in determining the optimal course of action. At this stage, a person determines the *outcomes* of the different courses of action and then evaluates what *effects* these outcomes will produce.

To distinguish between outcomes and effects, let's consider an example. You are trying to decide whether to play the lottery or not. We can say that you have two choices: to play or not. Playing involves paying one dollar for a ticket. You have a one-in-three million chance of winning the 10-million-dollar jackpot. If you do not play, you keep your dollar. What are the *outcomes* of the alternatives? If you play, you will either lose a dollar or win 10 million dollars. If you don't play, you keep your dollar with no chance at the 10 million. What are the *effects* of the alternatives? If you play, either you will have one dollar less to live on until your next payday, or you will be touring the Carribbean in your new yacht for the next several years without a financial care in the world. If you don't play, you will have that dollar to live on for the next month, but you can put your tourbook of the Carribbean away for the time being. Of course, we do not always have perfect knowledge of what the outcomes and effects of our decision will be, but we can try to perform optimally given the information that we have. Whether one analyzes behavior in terms of outcomes or effects can influence whether performance is optimal (see Principle 2 in Table 15–1).

THREE APPROACHES TO RATIONAL BEHAVIOR

The analysis of decision making can discuss behavior in terms of several dimensions. The first dimension is a *descriptive/normative* dimension, which involves a comparison between the behavior that actually occurs as well as its consequences (that is, the description of what does happen) and what should optimally happen. The second dimension concerns what decision is made versus the process of the decision making (*structural* approach versus analysis of the *process*). The third dimension concerns behaviors with an outcome that does not vary in probability (*riskless* behaviors) versus behaviors with outcomes that can vary in probability (*risky* behaviors). Optimization can be discussed with respect to any or all of these three perspectives or dimensions. The following subsections consider these three approaches in more detail.

Descriptive/Normative Dimension

It is common to analyze behavior with respect to how the experimenter's description of the subject's behavior matches up with the behavior that is believed to be optimal—the normative behavior that makes the greatest sense or maximizes utility. Hence, rational behavior can refer to the choice that is optimal regardless of the process that the subject goes through to make the choice (e.g., even if the subject chose randomly!). This issue plays a role in discussions of what choices are morally or ethically correct. Utilitarianism, as purported by Mill, claims that actions are morally correct if the net positive *effects* are larger than the alternative actions (Mullen & Roth, 1991). The action that benefits the greatest number of people most of the time is better than other alternatives. This form of utilitarianism is called consequentialism, in contrast to which, one can hold that some moral rules exist that "must be respected regardless of the consequences" (Mullen & Roth, 1991, p. 13). The latter viewpoint differs from the approach of studies examining the normative/descriptive dimension. In sum, the normative/descriptive dimension asks what the subject does and whether the behavior is the optimal thing to do.

Structural/Process Dimension

Behaving rationally or optimally can also refer to the process the subject goes through in making the choice. Hence, the person may be using a rational process even if the outcome of the decision ends up being nonoptimal (e.g., if a promised payoff is not delivered). When researchers analyze what processes are used to make optimal choices, the focus is on the cognitive activities used to detect the covariations of events (stimuli and responses) and their consequences, as well as the subject's integration of this information and the subject's evaluation of the consequences (Lea et al., 1987, p. 104). A great deal of debate has taken place as to what categories of probabilistic information are included in the judgments of covariation that subjects use. For example, for a single response and an outcome (such as a reward or punishment), subjects can use information regarding the probability of the outcome (O) occurring, given the target response (R), or $P(O/R)$. They also can use the probability of no outcome (noO) when the target response occurs, or $P(noO/R)$. These two values refer to the probabilites that are used in partial reinforcement training when it is compared to performance following consistent reinforcement (such as the partial reinforcement extinction effect, in which partial reinforcement leads to slower extinction than consistent reinforcement). When $P(noO/R) =$ zero, consistent reinforcement training occurs. Otherwise partial reinforcement training occurs —with "leaner" partial reinforcement schedules occurring with higher values of $P(noO/R)$.

Subjects can also, however, use information about the probability of the outcome when the target response is absent (noR)—that is, $P(O/noR)$— as well as when the likelihood of no outcome exists in the absence of the target response, $P(noO/noR)$. These latter values can be tricky to calculate, since they require that one decide how to

compute the number of "noRs" that occur so that the probabilities of $P(O/noR)$ and $P(noO/noR)$ can be determined. Figure 15–1 provides contingency diagrams for classical and instrumental conditioning. These contingency squares describe the rela-

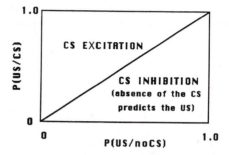

Classical Conditioning

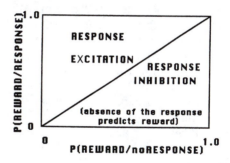

Instrumental Conditioning

Figure 15–1. Contingency squares for classical conditioning (top) and instrumental conditioning (bottom) adapted from Figure 1 of Gibbon et al. (1974). The diagonal represents zero contingencies with increasing densities of the noncontingencies occurring on the upper right portion of the diagonal. Values in the upper left corner represent cases in which the CS or response predicts the US, or reward, and these latter events rarely happen in the absence of the CS, or response. Values in the lower right corner represent cases in which USs, or rewards, happen frequently in the absence of the CS, or response, but rarely in the presence of these latter events. See p. 309 for definitions of the terms "CS" and "US."

tionship between the probability of outcomes, given the target event (CS or operant response), and the degree to which the target event becomes an excitatory predictor of the outcome or an inhibitory event that predicts when an outcome is less likely to occur.

A lot of discussion has taken place about how these units of information are combined to determine judgments of covariation and conditioning (e.g., Gibbon, Berryman, & Thompson, 1974; Miller & Schachtman, 1985; Rescorla, 1967; Wasserman, 1990). Once the covariation of events is calculated, the optimization process includes deciding which of the different (target) behaviors to select for performance. The process that the subjects experience while making such judgments and decisions has important ramifications for future learning and behavior. First, obviously the types of data used in the process—a combination of some or all of P(O/R), P(noO/R), P(O/noR), and P(noO/noR)—will determine the final outcome of the judgment process and thereby determine whether the behavior will occur (and possibly how frequent, vigorous, or enduring the response will be, as well as the topographic features of the behavior itself).

The process may also determine the information retained in memory from the experience. An example will help illustrate this point. A hungry rat is trained to press a lever for reinforcement such that, on the average, every other lever press produces food (a variable ratio 2, or VR2, schedule). The subject is exposed to P(food/lever press) = 0.5, P(food/no lever press) = 0, P(no food/lever press) = 0.5, and P(no food/no lever press). This fourth and final term also has some value, since the subject is not likely to press the lever continuously during the session. This training experience (and the processes it supposedly elicits) causes the subject to be highly likely to press the lever, and pressing is probably a reasonable thing for it to do, since doing so can provide food. What information does the subject retain from the experience that causes it to press the lever?

Associative learning theorists (e.g., Mackin-

tosh, 1983) claim that the training experience (and the probability information relevant to the target response) will cause the subject to form an association that includes the response, such as a response-reinforcer association during instrumental learning. A strong response-reinforcer association will be promoted by higher levels of P(food/lever press) and P(no food/no lever press), and low values of P(no food/lever press) and P(food/no lever press). Some theorists have claimed that subjects retain the individual pieces of data (individual probabilities). Subjects could also retain information based on the integration of these pieces of information. For example, the strength of the response-reinforcer association may be some kind of composite that includes these individual probabilities. Subjects might even retain the individual event occurrences or information about each event's frequency. (See Miller & Schachtman, 1985; Shanks, 1994; Shanks & Dickinson, 1986; Van Hamme & Wasserman, 1994; and Wasserman, 1990 for discussions of these issues). The retention of such information can be considered a multiple-trace cognitive process. Alternatively, the separate pieces of data may not be retained, and only the composite representation (e.g., a response-reinforcer association or some other composite value that is used to determine performance) that results from the integration of the information is retained. Shanks (1994) considered these possibilities as well as others, such as the view that subjects experience a heuristic or rule-learning process (see Holyoak, Koh, & Nisbett, 1989). Similar issues have been discussed with reference to the processes underlying concept formation (e.g., Medin & Schaffer, 1978; Rosch, 1975).

If retention of the individual component probabilities serves some advantage in assimilating future experiences with present and/or past events (perhaps allowing more accurate judgments), the multiple-trace process is optimal. Alternatively, if the retention of the individual component probabilities serves no purpose, the existence of this information in memory is potentially a misuse of cognitive resources. Other aspects of the processes underlying optimality are discussed later. Poor memory of important information can hinder the decision-making process and attenuate optimal behavior (see Principle 3 in Table 15–1). Moreover, subjects may perform poorly because they do not use all of the probability information in the contingency square assuming such information is important for optimal behavior choices (see Principles 4 and 5 in Table 15–1).

Risky/Riskless Dimension

Another distinction is that between risky and riskless behavior. Riskless decision making involves situations in which no uncertainty exists about whether or not a particular outcome will occur. An example would be deciding to buy one of two television sets available at a store. Many factors will influence your choice, but there is no uncertainty about the availability of the televisions. If you choose one, you will get it, and if you choose the other, you will bring that television home. In contrast, risky choice involves uncertainty. An obvious example of this is gambling.

FACTORS INFLUENCING OPTIMAL AND NONOPTIMAL BEHAVIOR

The school of functionalism in psychology produced an explicit focus on the role of behavior in enabling the organism to interact effectively with its environment. The effectiveness of the behavior is determined by the behavior's consequences. An important aspect of learning theory is the large emphasis the theory places on the way in which consequences of behavior influence the future occurrence of that behavior. The ability to make reasonable choices is clearly influenced by experience, and learning allows one to benefit from the experience. Hence, it is not surprising that a chapter that discusses animals' tendency to perform optimally focuses a great deal on learning. This section and the sections that follow describe a number of behaviors, many of them being learned behaviors or behaviors influenced by learning, in terms of optimality and the factors that influence optimal behavior.

The Process of Searching for Solutions Among Behavioral Alternatives

When an animal is confronted with a challenging environment, it will emit a behavior as an attempt to deal with the environment. If the behavior is unsuccessful, the animal will try another behavior and continue using this trial-and-error process until some behavior is successful (Bolles, 1970; Thorndike, 1898). Unsuccessful behaviors are discarded, and a useful behavior is retained because it is adaptive in the present circumstance, a process paralleling the operation of natural selection on the expression of alleles. It may take the organism many tries and a great deal of time before the most effective behavior is exhibited. Numerous alternatives may be sampled before optimal or maximal behavior occurs (Krebs, Kacelnik, & Taylor, 1978). Lea et al. point out that it "may cost time and money to find out where the cheapest source of supply is and to travel to the source once it has been identified" (1987, p. 105). As Shettleworth has claimed, sampling should be considered differently from producing errors because, while it may be nonoptimal, it may allow one to obtain information that might be useful in the future even though the animal does not appear to be "taking advantage of the currently best resources" (Shettleworth, 1994).

Nonresponding

It is also important to realize that nonresponding is an option that can have value. Behavior analysts must incorporate the value of nonresponding when estimating the optimal value of performance (see Principle 6 in Table 15–1). Obviously, nonresponding conserves energy, and it may also protect the animal from any injurious consequences that may result from behaving. Nonresponding or not working, that is, leisure, is an important variable in calculations and assessments of choice behavior (Rachlin et al., 1981).

The Temporal Window of Optimality

Another issue discussed by Shettleworth concerns how much of the past should be used as a source of information in making present decisions. Shettleworth (1994) states that the amount of the recent past included in the computation of the value of food patches (that is, places where food may be located) is called the "memory window" (see Cowie, 1977). The window must be long enough that the potentially unrepresentative events that occurred very recently are not weighted too much, but the window must be short enough to accurately reflect the existing conditions (see Principle 7 in Table 15–1).

It is also important to note that in some cases, there is a large cost in the short run (making the behavior seem nonoptimal) that may pay off in the long run, thereby being very optimal overall. Conversely, one can imagine cases where refraining from making such a change may provide a short-term benefit while incurring great expense (such as mortality) in the long run, thereby being less than optimal overall (see the discussion in the next main section and the chapter in this book by Logue). In all these cases, one may look at a behavior within the context of some time frame and view it as optimal or nonoptimal.

Change has a price. Moreover, since the environment is constantly changing, animals are constantly presented with the opportunity to change their current activity or, alternatively, to try to get by with the status quo. Some individuals acquire optimal behaviors rapidly, while others require more time and energy or more sampling experiences to locate or chance upon adaptive new solutions to the environmental change by trial and error (see Principle 8 in Table 15–1). The less astute animals may not live long enough to discover the solution. The quick acquisition of the behavior may occur by chance by stumbling onto the right solution quickly or because of superior ability to locate the solution (a normative/descriptive approach to optimal behavior would not need to distinguish between these possibilities). Either way, the one with the quick solution to the problem will appear more optimal to the behavior analyst.

The Value of the Immediate Situation

Another general and important issue in the study of optimization is the realization that not all circumstances are equally salient with respect to the need to change behavior or make a decision. Learning theorists have often examine changes in behavior in situations that are biologically relevant to the organism, such as situations that involve hunger and food, pain and relief from discomfort, thirst and fluid, and so on. Many learning textbooks state that the choice of such stimuli and circumstances by behavior analysts occurs because the subjects need biologically relevant events to produce an observable response (such as the unconditioned salivation produced by food for Pavlov's dogs or behaviors that will allow the animal to escape from a confining cage in Thorndike's early experiments). Observable behavior gives psychologists something to measure. Similarly, many philosophers, including Bain, Bentham, Mills, and Spencer, focused on the importance of hedonically relevant events on behavior because situations involving the need to approach pleasure and avoid pain are obviously of high priority to the organism's fitness.

The utility of behaviors is evaluated with respect to whether the behaviors produce the greatest good or pleasure, involve the least amount of loss or discomfort, or both. Those situations with the more pleasure or good available (or the greatest need to avoid aversiveness) are the most important for the subject to focus upon, and these circumstances will be carefully evaluated by the subject (see Principle 9 in Table 15–1). Katona (1975) claimed that the degree to which an individual will behave optimally depends on the importance of the situation to the organism (see Lea et al., 1987, p. 107). Decisions based on trivial dimensions can produce nonoptimal behavior because it is less important that such behaviors be ideal (see Principle 10 in Table 15–1).

Biological Constraints

The qualities that the organism brings to the situation may also influence whether optimal behavior occurs (Domjan & Burkhard, 1986). Each individual and species has its own shortcomings and strengths. To use instrumental conditioning examples, birds have a predisposition to associate peck responses with appetitive events like food but are not predisposed to peck to prevent the occurrence of an aversive event. Moreover, it is very easy to teach a bird to lift its wings to prevent the occurrence of an aversive event, but it is hard to teach a bird to lift its wings to receive food. Birds are predisposed to lift their wings to prepare to fly to avoid danger but not to receive food. It is easy to appreciate that if a bird must peck a stimulus to avoid a painful second stimulus, it will not learn or perform very optimally. Competing for resources with other organisms may be prepared for some species. Burghardt and Denny (1983) note instances of animals competing for food even when readily obtainable prey are lying around nearby (see Burghardt, 1991). Such examples remind us of a story about a young samarai novice who asks his teacher why, when a hungry lion runs full tilt, it may even pass right by prey as it runs across the field so swiftly, and the teacher says "because he is a lion" (Mishima, 1967). Biological constraints can hinder optimal learning and performance, and then the poor learning rate involving biologically irrelevant events is seen as nonoptimal (see Principle 11 in Table 15–1).

Classical conditioning is also influenced by event relevance. Stimulus relevance in classical conditioning (which presumably involves learning stimulus-stimulus associations) refers to the fact that stimuli may be better associated with some stimuli than with the alternatives. For example, a flavor that serves as a conditioned stimulus (CS), such as a sugar solution, is readily associated with illness as an unconditioned stimulus (US). Animals associate tastes with illness

very well, and the conditioned response (CR) to the taste is a conditioned avoidance response to the flavor (that is, the taste takes on anhedonic properties such that the animal won't consume the substance and often makes oral-facial movements that reflect this aversive reaction). However, tastes as CSs are not readily associated with USs that involve pain to the skin, such as stepping on a hot surface or an electric grid floor. In contrast to tastes, lights and tones as CSs are readily associated with USs such as pain to the skin, but are not readily associated with illness as a US. The effectiveness of a CS in producing conditioning depends on what US is used, and vice versa. This notion of belongingness or preparedness has received a great deal of attention (e.g., McNally, 1987)

The Confusion Effect and the Sampling of Poor Alternatives

Animals may perform poorly when alternatives or resources are so abundant that the subject is overwhelmed and makes poor choices (Landeau & Terborgh, 1986). This phenomenon has been referred to as the "confusion effect" (see Principle 12 in Table 15–1). Another instance of nonoptimal behavior stems from the subject's sampling from alternatives that have not been profitable in the past (Orians, 1981; Pyke, Pulliam, & Charnov, 1977; Royama, 1970). The subject may engage in such behavior to ensure that the conditions have not changed, even though such behavior may sacrifice short-term benefits (see Principle 13 in Table 15–1).

Social Influences on Optimality

A person will not perform optimally because he or she is a member of a group or community and is expected to adhere to the rules and values of this group regardless of whether such behavior is personally optimal or not (Mullen & Roth, 1991, p. 22, and see Principle 14 in Table 15–1). Also, people must attempt to make rational decisions as to what is optimal for themselves while interacting and perhaps competing with other people who are also trying to make rational decisions about their own well-being. This does not mean that optimal behavior is always selfish. Many of our decisions will influence the lives of other people, and the well-being of those people may be one of our goals. Hence, the value or utility of a choice will include the satisfaction of our goals as well as the well-being of others who are important to us (Mullen & Roth, 1991).

Alternatives that are selected because they maintain social order or maintain the social fabric of the culture may be considered adaptive although they do not bring any obvious, immediate, tangible benefit to the organism at the time of the behavior. People may show reciprocal altruism—that is, a type of cooperation—with an unrelated individual, and expend energy for the other's benefit when they can expect to benefit from that person at some time in the future (or to pay off someone for having assisted them in the past). This notion assumes that whoever reciprocates in the future remembers, or at least has learned something about his or her past interactions with other individuals (Shettleworth, 1994; Trivers, 1971).

There have been few, if any, demonstrations of true altruism in which an organism behaves as a means of benefiting another with an expected loss and no potential for future gain for the former behaving individual. Fortunately, there have also been few, if any, instances of true spiteful behavior in which an organism produces an expected loss for itself so as to produce a loss for another organism.

Behaviors that may appear irrational to an investigator may provide some nonobvious coping function to the individual. This point is illustrated nicely by G. F. Michel:

> [R]ather than seeing these mental faults as a means of coping with certain social problems, they are seen as preventing the individual from behaving rationally in certain situations. Of course, the coping strategies adopted by each of the people above may not be the best. However, because they have worked occasionally, they are difficult to change. Moreover, because they have bcome frequently used coping strategies, they no longer require conscious control for their utilization. (1991, p. 264)

Stress and Optimality

Mullen and Roth (1991) state that a person does not always perform optimally when confronted with a stressful situation (see Principle 15 in Table 15–1). Unpleasant stressful reactions to a situation can cause the person to choose poorly, perhaps as a means of alleviating the stressful dilemma as quickly as possible. Reynaud (1981, cited in Lea et al., 1987) claimed that people display different degrees of rationality depending on the different amounts of mental resources that are available to them at the time. When stress or other circumstances attenuate one's available resources, nonoptimal behavior may result. Stress or a shortage of cognitive resources can prematurely terminate the sequence of steps involved in information processing and can produce poor judgments. This effect of stress on processing can cause one to accept erroneous information (Gilbert, 1991).

It is interesting to note from an optimization point of view that some theories of stress claim that stress results from a threat to resources (Hobfall, 1989). According to Hobfall, our response to stress is to strive to minimize our loss of resources. When we are not experiencing stress, we are free to add to our existing resources. During stress we attempt to preserve what we have. According to other authors, stress is our reaction to an inability to attain a goal (Gutt, 1982). Depression and social withdrawal can occur as a means of stepping back and reassessing our resources and reconsidering our goals and goal attempts. Some individuals have found that depressed individuals do not very readily give up unattainable goals; that is, they show greater persistence (Bibring, 1953). However, such an idea appears to conflict with what we know about the low self-efficacy that often occurs for depressed individuals (Bandura, 1982).

Effects of Reorganizing Information on Optimality

Mullen and Roth also state that nonoptimal behavior can arise because of our need to have a simple, organized, coherent, consistent view of the world (see Principle 16 in Table 15–1). This notion is at least as old as the Gestalt psychologists who described the Law of Pragnanz as an organism's tendency to try to see the world as an organized, simple, and complete whole. Certainly the numerous and important developments in schema- and attribution-theory attest to the prevalence of such processes (e.g., Alba & Hasher, 1983). As Roth and Mullen claim, inconsistencies in our understanding will cause us to engage in irrational attempts to resolve the disequilibrium. Attempts will be made to retain our original perspective or to create a new perspective. Mullen and Roth also mention that errors occur when we try to reduce the complexity of the problem by abstracting it and integrating it into our existing schema of how the world works (see Principle 17 in Table 15–1). Given the few cases discussed thus far, it is clear that there are numerous instances of optimality and nonoptimality and a variety of factors that influence optimality. These factors pervade many of the phases of information processing.

THE PROCESS OF OPTIMAL DECISION MAKING AND RATIONALITY

Explanations for Optimal Behavior

Many processes exist that an organism might use to behave optimally. We have already mentioned rationality—the process by which organisms attempt to choose the alternative that maximizes benefits and minimizes losses. Lea et al. make this point clear when they mention that "almost every approach to psychology implies that something other than rationality determines behavior" (1987, p. 103). Lea et al. mention other ways that behavior may be governed. Subjects can behave randomly. Although the process may be utilized infrequently, it is likely that we have all used the proverbial (or not so proverbial) flip of a coin on occasion to make a decision. Second, conditioning and learning processes can also influence behaviors. As we will see, conditioning behaviors during instrumental contingencies—

that is, experience with different schedules of reinforcement—can influence behavior and cause behavior to be more or less optimal.

Third, Nobel laureate psychologist and economist Herbert Simon (1955, 1957) claimed that behavior need not always be optimal. Individuals will sometimes employ rules of thumb or heuristics that allow them to function effectively in most situations. Simon has claimed that "over the course of evolution or over the course of experience during our lifetimes, we have developed convenient, easy problem-solving methods that pretty much get us what we want ... we arrive at the best solution that we can under the circumstances" (Rachlin, 1989, pp. 58–59, based on Simon, 1978). Simon referred to this process as satisficing, meaning that the decision-making process will continue until some adequate (but not necessarily optimal) solution is discovered.

As mentioned earlier, Katona (1975) points out that people will use rational processes to the extent that the current situation is an important one for them. Hence, one can say that there are decisions to be made regarding which decision-making process to use. The importance of the decision to an animal's well-being could dictate whether a rational process is employed while making the decision (i.e., principle 10 in Table 15–1).

Evidence Against Rationality

As we mentioned earlier, the notion of rational decision making either proposes the view that organisms may behave optimally (descriptive/normative dimension) or suggests that they may use a rational process while making decisions (structural/process dimension). Despite the extensive influence of rational decision theory, most theorists realize that behavior is far from optimal or rational. Much evidence suggests that nonrational processes govern behavior even in situations lacking risk (i.e., situations in which the outcomes of the choice are certain).

Individuals show no absolute preferences for commodities (valuable items or opportunities) —an issue that we will discuss more fully when we describe Premack's Principle of reinforcement later in this chapter. In fact, preferences for commodities show some variability over time. This finding has been used to explain some intransitivity among individuals' preferences (Lea et al., 1987, pp. 113–114), although Tversky has said that some intransitivity is due to different attributies being compared in different situations, as Principle 18 in Table 15–1 describes (see Tversky, 1969; see also Alloy & Tabachnik, 1984; McGill, 1989). That is, commodity A may be preferred over commodity B and B over commodity C, but commodity C is preferred over A.

Similarly, subjects often cannot detect the relevant probabilities, and this can hinder rational behavior. Lotteries and insurance policies are based on the idea that people make nonrational decisions—lotteries and insurance companies make money since clients clearly pay more money into such endeavors than they can get out of the exchange (Lea et al., 1987, pp. 116–117). On one hand, one can conclude that subjects do not accurately assess the unlikely odds of a payoff in deciding whether to play the lottery or the unlikely need to use one's insurance company to pay off a mishap (see Principle 19 in Table 15–1). Alternatively, one can conclude that subjects do know the odds but fail to behave rationally given this knowledge.

Behavior is influenced by factors besides mere probabilities. Humans show an aversion to taking risk when choices are presented in terms of gains, but the subjects are risk-attracted when the same choice is phrased in terms of losses (Rachlin, Logue, Gibbon, & Frankel, 1986). For example, if subjects are told that an impending disease is expected to kill 600 people and they are given a choice of a solution in which 200 people will be saved versus a solution in which there is a 33% chance that 600 people will be saved, many more subjects choose the former option. This question is phrased in terms of "lives saved" or "gains," and subjects choose the low-risk, safer alternative (Tversky & Kahneman, 1981). If subjects are given a functionally identical question but one that is phrased in terms of losses, such as a solution in which 400

people die versus a solution that offers a 33% chance that no one will die, many more subjects choose the latter option. Since the question is phrased in terms of people dying or "losses," subjects chose the high-risk alternative.

It is interesting that animals are more risk-attracted when they are very low on resources (for example, hungry) but are less prone to risk when resources are abundant. However, when predation risk is high and danger is possible, subjects show risk aversion.

Even if subjects are not good at judging the odds or are not consistent in how they choose in certain probability situations, one can acknowledge, as Bernoulie pointed out long ago, that utility refers to subjective utility or subjective value, and wealth (as well as other commodities) truly does follow the law of diminishing returns (see Principle 20 in Table 15–1). This does not explain all the variation in choice behavior, but it does help explain some instances of choice behavior. Moreover, another view has been developed that does not require one to substitute objective costs and benefits with subjective utilities. This view is the subjective-probability approach, which states that estimates of probabilities by subjects do not always correspond with objective probabilities. We have many reasons to suspect that organisms are not rational. The next section examines additional processes that may generate this lack of apparent rationality.

Conditioning Can Produce Nonoptimality

Vicious-Circle Behavior and Negative Automaintenance

It has been known for many decades that some conditioning procedures produce nonoptimal behavior. Nonoptimal behavior can be readily produced by training subjects on one task and then switching around the contingency so that the subjects are performing poorly because they are using the old rule rather than the new rule to perform. One such example of self-punitive behavior is vicious-circle behavior (Brown & Cunningham, 1981), in which rat subjects are placed in a runway apparatus in the shape of a circle (i.e., like running around the circumference of a clock face) and given active avoidance training. The rats are initially taught that if they move from one segment of the circle to the next (say from the one o'clock location to the two o'clock location), they will avoid the shock that is about to occur at the first location. Subjects become very good at learning to move from one section of the circle runway to the next to avoid shock. In the next phase of the study, a passive-avoidance procedure is introduced in which subjects must stay at their existing location to avoid shock. This is actually a punishment contingency ("passive-avoidance" is really a misnomer that refers to a punishment contingency), since subjects will receive an aversive event if the response occurs. As might be expected, the subjects perform very poorly during this second phase of the study. They move to the next segment and get shocked. Despite the punishment contingency the shock promotes running. The more they receive shock, the more they are motivated to continue running, and this, of course, leads to more shock. Remaining still would prevent all shocks from occurring. Obviously, nonoptimal behavior can occur when the rules are changed and subjects behave according to the old rules (see Principle 21 in Table 15–1).

Another instance of nonoptimal behavior involves an autoshaping procedure with hungry birds using a long-box apparatus (Jenkins & Hearst, 1974). Autoshaping is a classical-conditioning procedure in which a CS (for example, a colored illuminated disc called a keylight) is presented for, say, five seconds and then is followed by a US (usually food that is presented for about five seconds). The learned response is approach and contact with the CS (sometimes referred to as "sign tracking," to distinguish it from "goal tracking," which is approach and contact with the US). When birds are presented with a bright keylight followed by food, they come to peck this light even though pecking is not required to obtain the food. In this so-called long box, the keylight CS was presented at one end of the long, narrow chamber, and then, after termination of the light,

food was presented at the other end of the chamber. The birds in this experiment first received these keylight-food pairings. They would see the light at one end of the chamber and then eat the food US at the other end. However, after such trials, the birds formed a light-food association and learned to approach and peck the keylight. However, because of the long distance, approach to the one end of the box where the light occurred meant that the subjects failed to obtain the food because they could not approach the light and then get to the other end of the long box in time for the food delivery. The learned response to approach the light CS was so strong that it caused the hungry bird to miss out on the food! Certainly this is not an adaptive behavior. Of course, missing out on the food caused the light-food association to extinguish, and the subjects ceased approaching the light and could eat the food presentations again and hence would receive CS-US pairings once again, and the cycle would continue.

A similar treatment uses a programmed negative contingency during instrumental conditioning. Subjects in a Skinner box received a keylight for five seconds followed by food. If the subject pecks the keylight, food is cancelled. Hence, it is a negative contingency—one referred to as an omission procedure (that is, when a response produces the omission of an appetitive event). Pecking causes the omission of food. Withholding pecking produces food. This procedure is called negative automaintenance (Williams & Williams, 1969). Note that with this procedure, when the subject does not respond on such a trial, it receives a keylight-food pairing. This is identical to a classical-conditioning autoshaping trial which, as mentioned above, promotes a CR of pecking. Clearly it is optimal for subjects to refrain from pecking during such training, and yet subjects do peck because of the strong forces of classical conditioning stemming from the keylight-food pairings.

Interval Schedules

Other schedules of reinforcements can produce nonoptimal performance. We know that behaviors are changed by their consequences.

Behavior followed by reward will increase the probability of the behavior's occurring in the future; that is, reinforcement strengthens behavior. When reinforcements follow the response frequently, the response occurs at a high rate. But schedules of reinforcement are really constraints on how often food will be delivered. Subjects respond rapidly on ratio schedules such that reward occurs every time the criterion number of responses occurs. On a ratio schedule, the relationship between the behavior and the outcome is one in which reinforcement frequency is directly related to response rate, and high response rates will lead to high reinforcement rates (Hursh, 1984; Williams 1994).

On some schedules of reinforcement, however, a high rate of responding is not optimal. On interval schedules, the time constraint means that reward cannot be delivered any more frequently than once per interval. For example, on a fixed-interval (FI) schedule, food will be delivered for the first response after the interval times out but will occur no faster than this rate no matter how much the subject responds. Subjects should not respond prior to the elapsing of the interval, and even if one can't expect subjects to perfectly detect, say, 60-second intervals on an FI 60-second schedule, this allowance still cannot explain the high levels of responding and short interresponse times that occur prior to the elapsing of the interval. Hence, as will be discussed later, response rate is not always a clear index of learning and the optimality of behavior.

Closed and Open Economies

In closed economies, the subjects receive the opportunity to eat when they make a response such as lever pressing. However, all the food they receive during the day will be obtained in this way. With closed economies, response rate is inversely related to the rate of reinforcement availability (Hursh, 1984). That is, as the temporal requirement used in, say, a variable interval schedule is increased (that is, reinforcement rate decreases), response rate increases.

In an open economy, however, subjects will receive food for lever pressing, but they also receive food without having to lever press for it in order to "hold reinforcement constant and independent of responding during the sessions" (Hursh, 1984). In an open economy, the greater the reward likelihood, the more the subject makes the target lever-press response. Therefore, whether a closed or open economy exists determines the relationship between response rate and reinforcement rate, and determines the degree to which the number of responses emitted is optimal for the number of reinforcers delivered.

Reward Magnitude and Contrast Effects

The magnitude of reinforcement can influence optimal behavior. Reed (1991) found that response rate increased with larger rewards on ratio schedules but decreased with larger rewards on interval schedules. At first glance, this might seem as though different things are occurring with the two schedules and give one the premature impression that the magnitude of reinforcement is improving optimal performance for one type of schedule and not the other. But remember that responding rapidly on ratio schedules is adaptive, since it will increase reinforcement rate, while decreases in response rate on interval schedules will generally eliminate inefficient responses and produce more optimal performance.

As we said, greater learning will occur with larger reward magnitudes. However, when an animal experiences a shift in reward magnitude, the experience with the previous reward size will influence the effectiveness of the later reward magnitude. Let's say rats are running through a maze to receive food at the end of the maze. One group receives a small amount of food (e.g., three pellets), and the other group receives a larger amount of food (e.g., five pellets). Now we may expect that the group that receives five pellets may perform a little better in the maze than the other group, but let's not concern ourselves with that difference. In a second phase of the study, all rats get five pellets. Hence, the one group is shifted from three pellets to five pellets while the other group continues to receive five pellets. The critical effect for the present purpose is that the group shifted from three to five pellets performs much better than the group that received five pellets all along. This effect is known as the *positive contrast effect.* Hence, this effect is the increase in performance that occurs when the subject experiences an upshift in the reward. It is surprising, since both groups receive five pellets in the second phase of the study, yet their performance in the maze is very different. One group is not performing optimally. It should also be noted that the shifted group is performing better than the nonshifted group in phase 2 even through it received *fewer* food pellets overall. The positive contrast effect shows that the effects of rewards are relative in that they depend on the animal's previous experience with reward.

The *negative contrast effect,* as one might guess, is the opposite of the positive contrast effect. Let's say that, just like the case above, we have one group that receives five pellets for running down the maze while another group receives three pellets. In phase 2, the group that had been receiving five pellets now receives three pellets while the other group continues to receives three pellets. In the second phase, the shifted group performs more poorly than the group that received three pellets all along. This is known as the negative contrast effect. Hence, this effect is the decrease in performance that occurs when the subject experiences a downshift in the reward. This difference occurs even though both groups receive the same number of pellets in phase 2 (three pellets), and the shifted group, despite receiving *more* pellets in phase 1, performs more poorly in phase 2. Whatever behavior might be considered optimal for a given level of reward, the behavior produced by the organism may be influenced by the individual's past history of reinforcement.

Measuring Response Strength

We should remind ourselves that if we are to consider optimal behavior rather than just merely reward maximization, other factors must be considered in our assessment about whether reasonable behavior occurs. Even the pauses in responding indicative of ratio strain that can occur with very lean ratio schedules (that is, with

lean ratios such as fixed ratio 1,000, the subject will respond quickly for a while as "bursts" of responses and then break for a while before continuing with another burst of responding) can still be considered adaptive in that one obviously wouldn't expect a subject to exhaust itself responding continuously.

The effectiveness of reinforcement has been described with respect to how well such reinforcement increases the probability or frequency of responding. The effects of reinforcement and, therefore, the strength of learning can in some cases be reflected in the frequency of responding. But the strength of the learning is not always manifested by analysis of response probability. Many cases exist in which response likelihood is not a useful or appropriate index of reinforcer effectiveness.

Response rate is not always indicative of learning (Williams, 1994, p. 82). Learning theorists have long acknowledged this point. Tolman's latent learning experiments from more than half a century ago revealed that animals do not always perform in a manner reflective of their knowledge. In Tolman's studies, animals learned about mazes while exploring them in the absence of food but had no reason to reveal this knowledge since, without food, there was little motivation to do so. While it is obvious that learning will not be assessed accurately when the subject lacks motivation or if the experimenter examines the wrong behavior, it may be less obvious that subjects may not exhibit knowledge that they possess but cannot retrieve at the time of testing (Miller, Kasprow, & Schachtman, 1986; Spear, 1978).

Nevin suggests that "resistance to change" might be a better measure of response strength than response rate (e.g., Nevin, 1992, and Nevin, this volume). Nevin has shown that the resistance to change is a valuable index of the strength of learning. Strong, well-learned responses will be slower to adjust to changes in the existing contingency. Behavioral momentum is an expression that has been used to describe a strong response that is not amenable to rapid change when the contingency is altered. Another measure of the strength of learning is to give the subjects a choice of responses. Choice can be used as a measure of the strength of association (Williams, 1994, p. 83; see Logue, and Green & Freed chapters in this book).

We might also note that the prevailing circumstances of the individual's situation can determine the way that the strength of the learning gets translated into behavior. Such circumstances can influence the form that the behavior takes as well as whether the response occurs at a high rate or a low rate. Interresponse times will vary for different schedules, and even the stimuli present during conditioning can vary the form that the response will take (Holland, 1983; Jenkins, 1977; Peele, Casey, & Silverberg, 1984).

The Value of the Behavior Relative to Other Behaviors

Every behavior can be viewed as a choice from among a number of available activities. As previously mentioned, since each behavior can have a different consequence and some consequences are preferred, some behavioral options are preferred. Premack (1965) stated that the outcomes of behavior can be viewed as behaviors themselves. That is, the consequence of a behavior is to engage in some other behavior. In a rewarding situation, a child who cleans his or her room is able to experience the eating of candy as the rewarding behavior. According to Premack, a lesser preferred behavior can be increased in frequency if it is followed by a consequent behavior of a higher preference. The child will increase the frequency of cleaning the room, since eating candy is more highly preferred than cleaning. A behavior will decrease in frequency if its consequence is a lesser preferred behavior. One might thus be less likely to wash the dishes if dishwashing causes one to vacuum, since vacuuming is less preferred than dishwashing. Hence, punishment is making an experience with a lesser preferred behavior contingent on performing a more preferred behavior. It will cause the likelihood of the more preferred behavior to decrease in the future.

Premack's ideas have provided a number of

new insights into the nature of reinforcement and punishment and the analysis of optimal behavior. First, Premack's view claims that the same behavior can be viewed as a reward (increases the frequency of a contingent behavior) or as a punisher (decreases the frequency of a contingent behavior) depending on the value of the event that serves as the behavior's consequence. Moreover, we can see that whether a behavior is considered optimal or not depends on whether its consequence is more or less preferred than the target behavior.

Premack also noted that individual differences will play a role in whether a behavior serves as a reward or as a punisher. Some people prefer broccoli over green beans, and others do not. Some people prefer vacuuming to dishwashing. Also, although I may usually prefer vacuuming to dishwashing, if I have been vacuuming all week, a chance to wash dishes for a change may actually serve as a reward for vacuuming. Similarly, and perhaps more obviously, drinking will reward other behaviors (i.e., drinking is preferred over the other behaviors) when the subject is thirsty but not at other times. Likewise, food will only increase the frequency of other behaviors when the subject is hungry.

A person's preferences can be assessed by placing the subject in a situation with the variety of behaviors available to the person. One can then observe the person's behaviors and see what behaviors the person engages in and how the person allocates his or her time among the different behaviors. Some individuals will spend the majority of their behavior on one task, thereby revealing that this behavior is highly preferred. Others will engage in another task instead. This distribution of behaviors is a person's "bliss point" or "set point" (Staddon, 1979). It reflects the person's optimal distribution of behaviors in the absence of any constraints beyond the fact that the subject can presumably engage in only one task at a time and the assessment period may have a set duration. Behavior analysts have used schedules of reinforcement to limit a subject's ability to engage freely in a behavior at its optimum or bliss-point level. The subject will then seek to attain this optimal level and will even work at some less desired task to engage in this target behavior at its optimal level. In other words, as we mentioned earlier, the target behavior can increase the probability of other responses, such as "work." The set-point notion stresses again that many factors must be considered when determining the utility of a commodity (i.e., a behavior). If a person is already at the set-point value for a given commodity, receiving additional units of the commodity may be aversive despite the fact that the commodity is appetitive in many other circumstances.

Maximizing Versus Matching

Other chapters of this book discuss the matching law and choice behavior in more detail, but we include brief mention of them in this section to highlight their importance in our discussion of optimality. The matching law applies to choice behavior (as well as single manipulandum situations) and claims that the distribution of responses will be proportional to the reinforcement rate of the alternatives (Herrnstein, 1961). An illustration will help bring the point closer to home. A subject has a choice between pressing on a lever that has a variable-interval (VI) 60-second schedule operating on it and pressing on a simultaneously available lever with a VI 30-second schedule on it. How would the subject distribute its responses? According to the matching law, the subject will distribute its performance based on the relative reinforcement rates. Since the VI-30 schedule on the second lever provides food twice as often as the schedule on the first lever, subjects should make 66.6% of their responses to the VI 30-second lever and 33.3% of their responses to the VI 60-second lever (Herrnstein, 1961). This way the subjects make twice as many responses to the one lever because food is twice as likely to occur on that lever.

As you can see, the matching law is a molar law of performance, since it predicts what should happen on an average over time and does not make specific predictions about which lever a subject should press at a particular moment or on

a particular trial. Also, this molar view does not specify what is controlling each individual response. At any given moment, an alternative's probability (a lever's probability) of receiving a response is the response's molar probability (for example, 66.6% on the second lever) (see Williams, 1994, p. 91).

Other approaches to the distribution of responses during concurrent-choice procedures have been explored as a means of explaining the matching of relative response rates to the corresponding reinforcement rates. One such approach uses the maximization theory (e.g., Rachlin et al., 1981), which states that the subject should perform a response at a particular moment on the alternative that maximizes the chance of obtaining reward. This view reflects the notions of optimality and rationality that we have been discussing in this chapter.

A great deal of support for the matching law stems from the use of concurrent variable-ratio (VR), variable-interval (VI) schedules, particularly if a temporal discounting factor is applied. With such a factor, the reinforcers gained on the VI schedule are discounted because they are distant in time from the behaviors on the VR that make them available (Williams, 1994, p. 92). A concurrent schedule is one in which there are two manipulanda present (e.g., two levers) and each manipulandum has a schedule of reinforcement available. Subjects may respond to one lever as a means of progressing through, say, a VI schedule (and the first response after the interval times out will produce reinforcement) or to the other lever to progress through, say, a VR schedule (and a certain number of responses is needed to obtain reinforcement).

Staddon (1992) claims that optimality theory explains such data nicely if the quantity being maximized is a decreasing of the average delay to reward rather than the quantity of reward (see Fantino, 1981, and Williams, 1994, for discussions). Reducing the delay to reward, producing the greatest probability of reward, and obtaining the largest magnitude of reward are all factors that should be considered in making choice decisions about various alternatives.

Before leaving our discussion of matching and maximizing, we should point out that other views of choice behavior have been developed. These relatively recent views include momentary matching, in which memory of the preceding trial is used in choice behavior, and melioration, in which the subject switches between alternatives such that the local rate of reinforcement is the same for the alternatives (Herrnstein & Vaughan, 1980; Vaughan, 1981). With melioration, the subject will have a much higher local rate of reinforcement on a VI 1-minute schedule on one lever than on a VI 5-minute schedule on the other lever, and so the subject will spend more time on the former lever. However, if the subject spends too much time on the former lever, it will end up with every response on the VI 5-minute schedule producing food (an extremely high local rate of reward), and this will cause the subject to shift back to the VI 5-minute lever (see Domjan & Burkhard, 1986, for a discussion). The subject will shift back and forth until the local rates of reinforcement are equal for the alternatives. This switching increases the local rate of reward and produces behavior that resembles matching. Another explanation of matching performance is momentary maximization (e.g., Shimp, 1978), which states that subjects will choose the alternative with the highest momentary probability of reinforcement, but this probability is computed with the use of information about the memory of the subject's recent responses (see Williams, 1994, for a discussion). According to Williams, maximizing, melioration, and momentary matching all have problems with some of the data explaining matching behavior (1994, pp. 101, 105; see also Baum, 1981; Heyman, 1983).

Effects of Contiguity on Optimality

Delay of reward typically slows learning (Renner, 1964; Tarpy & Sawabini, 1974). If rapid conditioned performance is considered optimal, then delay of reinforcement can be said to hinder optimal performance, since it can slow the learning of the target response. Renner (1964) and Tarpy and Sawabini (1974) summarized the effects of delays on instrumental learning. Delays of reinforcement often increase the number of errors, response times, and the number of trials to a criterion measure. Of course, it has been long known that some conditioning procedures can yield learning despite extremely long delays (e.g., Garcia, Ervin, & Koelling, 1966; Lett, 1975; Smith & Roll, 1967).

Response competition as a cause of the performance deficit arising from reinforcement delay has also been recognized for a long time (e.g., Spence, 1956). Responses elicited by events occurring during the delay may constrain the occurrence of conditioned target responses and may therefore attenuate the acquisition of the target association. However, a number of demonstrations of improved performance of the target behavior also exist as a result of the possibility of engaging in mediating behaviors during the delay (e.g., Grosch & Neuringer, 1981). The availability of such behaviors has pronounced beneficial effects on the degree of self-control displayed by humans (Mischel & Metzner, 1962) and pigeons (Grosch & Neuringer, 1981). Responses performed during the delay period will adversely affect performance to the degree that the delay interval behavior is dissimilar to the target behavior (Lattal & Crawford-Godbey, 1985). Hence, a chain of superstitiously reinforced responses occurring during the delay may not always facilitate responding by "bridging" the delay, especially if the component behaviors are very dissimilar. Other effects produced by reinforcement delay events are discussed in the following two sections.

Delay of reward slows extinction (Capaldi & Bowen, 1964; McCain & Bowen, 1967; Schoonard & Lawrence, 1962; Tombaugh, 1966). If resistance to change is considered an index of response strength and stronger response strength is considered optimal, then it can be said that delay of reward improves optimal performance during extinction. This assumes, of course, that the resistance-to-change concept applies to a change to an extinction condition. Alternatively, it is very reasonable to assume that performance appropriate to the existing contingency is optimal, and therefore, given the absence of reward during extinction, the subject should rapidly cease responding.

Other interesting findings regarding contiguity and instrumental performance exist aside from the findings that decreasing contiguity between the response and reward can attenuate performance. Thomas (1981) conducted an intriguing study in which he examined the influence of contiguity without manipulating the probability of reward. Subjects received the opportunity to eat food once every 20 seconds regardless of whether they responded. Hence, reward had the same likelihood regardless of whether responding occurred. If no response occurred, the subjects received food at the end of the 20-second interval. If the subject did make a response, food was delivered immediately. The subjects in this latter condition responded at a high rate relative to control subjects that received the same overall frequency of reward but with less contiguity between the response and reward. Clearly contiguity had a great influence on responding.

In a second experiment, Thomas pitted contiguity against the response-reward contingency. As in the previous experiment, subjects received food at the end of a 20-second period if no response occurred. If the subjects did respond during the interval, food was immediately delivered after the response for that interval, but the food during the next interval was cancelled. Hence, responding decreased the delay to reward but reduced the overall probability of food (i.e., optimality was reduced). In such a situation, subjects did learn to make the response showing that contiguity has a powerful influence on responding.

The Influence of Signals on Optimization: Response Attenuation

Signals Attenuate Response Rate

Signals for reward during brief delays of reinforcement can decrease conditioned performance. Many of the findings showing that signals for reward decrease response rate stem from studies that use interval schedules of rein-

forcement. Pearce and Hall (1978) examined the influence that external signals can have on the responding during schedules of reinforcement. The subjects in many of their experiments received a brief delay (e.g., 0.5 seconds) between the response that earned the reward and the delivery of that reward. They demonstrated that placing a signal (e.g., a tone) for each reward in a VI 60-second schedule will decrease response rate relative to a control condition that received the delay of reinforcement without the signal. These treatments can be seen in the top two conditions depicted in Figure 15–2. These treatments and the data to be described are from an experiment involving a within-subject design using a multiple schedule and food as reinforcement (Schachtman et al., 1987). Condition S-0.5 received a signal during a 500-millisecond delay of reinforcement, while condition U-0.5 did not. The data in Figure 15–3 reveal the poorer response rate by the condition that received the delay signal (condition S-0.5). Pearce and Hall argued that the decrement in responding found in the signaled condition in their earlier study was produced by the stimulus overshadowing the response, since the former was a more valid predictor of reinforcement than the latter. This instrumental overshadowing effect has been observed in many laboratories with a number of species and procedures (e.g., Iversen, 1981; Sizemore & Lattal, 1978; St. Claire-Smith, 1979; Williams & Heyneman, 1982). Hence, delays of reward can reduce responding, but signals during the delay will attenuate performance even more.

Sign Tracking

A number of hypotheses exist as to how a signal presented during a delay of reinforcement on variable interval schedules can attenuate performance. Iversen noted that subjects may orient toward the signal (a light or a tone) for reinforcement when it occurs. The subject may turn toward the speaker where a tone signal occurs or orient toward the lit bulb of the ceiling where the light signal occurs. These orienting responses or "sign-tracking behaviors" may then be superstitiously reinforced with the reinforcement that occurs shortly after the onset of the signal. The

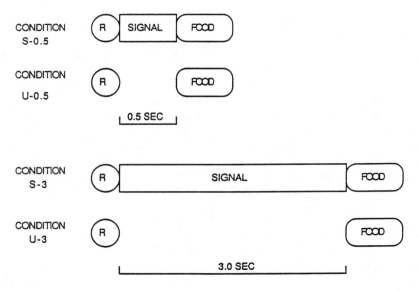

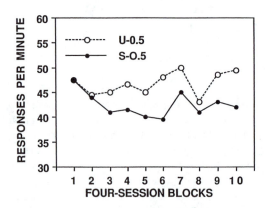

Figure 15–2. Procedure for producing instrumental overshadowing by presenting a signal during a 0.5-second delay of reinforcement (top conditions) and instrumental potentiation by presenting a signal during a 3.0-second delay of reinforcement. Time is represented horizontally, although events are not scaled correctly. The conditions that include the signal are the experimental conditions, and those without a signal are control conditions.

reinforcement and strengthening of such responses would then compete with the target response of, say, lever pressing or key pecking. The control condition without such a signal would not produce these orienting behaviors, and there-

Figure 15–3. Results of an experiment by Schachtman, Reed, and Hall (1987) examining the effects of signals for reinforcement on a VI 60-second schedule with a 0.5-second delay. The signal attenuated performance for the S-0.5 condition.

fore, these behaviors would not compete with the target behavior. Indeed, the occurrence of stereotypic responding during a signaled-delay period has been noted by Azzi et al. (1964) and by Silver and Pierce (1969), and these responses may influence performance of the target behavior. Although there has been some evidence against this sign-tracking explanation (see Hall, Channell, & Schachtman, 1987; Roberts, Tarpy, & Cooney, 1985), the possibilility that competing sign-tracking responses contribute in part to the instrumental overshadowing effect cannot be completely ruled out.

Reinforcement of IRTs

Williams and Heyneman (1982) and Sizemore and Lattal (1978) claimed that unsignaled delays of reinforcement on interval schedules encourage the reinforcement of bursts of responding—that is, reinforce responses with short interresponse times (IRTs)—while signals for reinforcement promote single occurrences of the response followed by a pause—that is, reinforcement of long IRTs. A subject makes its first response after the interval has timed out on the interval schedule. With unsignaled delays, the subject cannot know that this response produced food, and it continues to respond during the delay. When food comes, the reinforcement follows a burst of responses. With signaled delays, the signal informs the subject that food is about to be delivered, and the subject ceases responding and awaits the reinforcer. Food is delivered after one or few responses. Although there has been some lack of support for the hypothesis that the instrumental overshadowing effect is due to the differential reinforcement of response bursts (that is, reinforcement of different IRTs) (Hall, Channell, & Schachtman, 1987), this view remains a potential candidate.

Symmetry of Learning

Pearce and Hall (1978) described an associative view of instrumental overshadowing. They claimed that learning of response-outcome associations is formed during instrumental learning just like CS-US (or CS-outcome) associations are learned during classical conditioning. These two types of associations can compete for learning. Responses and signals can compete for becoming associated with outcomes. This view is sometimes called the "symmetry of learning" view because it claims that the associative learning that underlies instrumental and classical conditioning is similar and symmetrical (Mackintosh, 1983; Pearce & Hall, 1978; Reed & Reilly, 1990; Reilly, Schachtman, & Reed, 1996). The signal during the delay can overshadow the response and attenuate the development of the response-reinforcer (i.e., response-outcome) association, thereby decreasing responding.

Associative theories of the effects of instrumental overshadowing, as well as many of the views discussed, have difficulty with some of the findings of experiments that use signaled reward. As mentioned, with a short 0.5-second delay, responding is usually attenuated by signaling the onset of the delay (Hall, 1982; Lattal & Zeigler, 1982; Sizemore & Lattal, 1978). However, when the delay is 3 seconds or longer, signals increase response rates relative to control conditions (Meltzer et al., 1965; Schachtman et al., 1987;

Williams, 1982). This procedure is diagrammed in the lower part of Figure 15–2 in which a signaled 3-second delay condition is compared with a condition with a comparable but unsignaled delay. Food served as the reinforcement. Results from two conditions that produce potentiation of responding are described in Figure 15–4. Group S-3 received a signal throughout the 3-second delay of reinforcement, and Group U-3 did not. These results are from an experiment involving a within-subject design using a multiple schedule (Schachtman et al., 1987). These data show that signals improve performance with a 3-second delay.

A symmetry of learning notion can attempt to predict when signals will enhance and attenuate responding by suggesting that it depends on the strength of the response-reinforcer association. An associative account of the results above can suggest that a weak response-reinforcer association is ordinarily generated by a long delay used during a VI schedule and weak associations are potentiated by the presence of a stimulus (Revusky, 1971). An ordinarily strong response-reinforcer association would be produced by a short 0.5-second delay on a VI schedule without a reinforcement signal, and this strong association is overshadowed by the signal.

This explanation accounts for many of the delay effects using VI schedules, but it cannot ex-

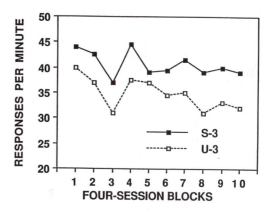

Figure 15–4. Results of an experiment by Schachtman, Reed, and Hall (1987) examining the effects of signals for reinforcement on a VI 60-second schedule with a 3.0-second delay. The signal enhanced performance for the S-3 condition.

plain findings stemming from the use of ratio and other schedules. As we will see in the next section, on a VR schedule, a signaled 0.5-second delay of reinforcement potentiates responding relative to control conditions not receiving a signal (Reed, Schachtman, & Hall, 1988a; but see Dickinson, Peters, & Shechter, 1984; Roberts, Tarpy, & Lea, 1984). Such ratio schedules with unsignaled delays produce high response rates, presumably reflecting a response-reinforcer association, and so overshadowing would be expected.

Other views of the attenuation of performance produced by a signal for reinforcement have been presented by Tarpy, Lea, and Roberts and by Reed and Schachtman. These views can be collectively referred to as "enhanced efficiency theories." We will suspend our discussion of them until the following section, because such views relate as much to the response-enhancing effects of signals for reward to as response-attenuation effects. To the extent that optimal behavior is seen as a high rate of responding, one must accept that signals for reinforcement can reduce this performance under some circumstances.

The Influence of Signals on Optimization: Performance Facilitation

While the above findings show that brief signals during reinforcement 0.5 second delays decrease response rate, other studies have found the opposite finding. Signals during delays of reinforcement help to partially offset the otherwise debilitating effects of delays on performance (Roberts, Tarpy, & Lea, 1984; Reed, Schachtman, & Hall, 1988a; Schachtman et al., 1987; Williams & Heyneman, 1982). When a signal is placed during a brief delay between a response that produces food (for example, the last response required by the ratio schedule) and the reinforcement, the signal enhances response rate relative to an unsignaled condition. This response-enhancing effect of the signal is referred to as instrumental potentiation. We saw such an effect in the results shown in Figure 15–4 with a 3-second delay of reinforcement.

Conditioned Reinforcment

Numerous theories have been suggested as to why events during delays of reward can improve performance. Some theorists have focused on the incentive value or conditioned reinforcing effects of events during the delay (Spence, 1956; Williams & Heyneman, 1982). Direct evidence that cues present during a delay period may act as secondary reinforcers comes from studies that have shown that such cues are capable of supporting new learning (Siegel & Milby, 1969) and from studies in which subjects are given a choice for signaled and unsignaled delayed reinforcement (e.g., Marcattilio & Richards, 1981; Wilkie, 1971).

Competing Responses

Other theorists have focused on competing nontarget responses becoming conditioned during unsignaled delays of reinforcement (responses that compete with and reduce the frequency of the target behavior). Signals during the delay may attenuate the development of these competing responses.

Temporal Placement of Signal During the Delay

Differences in signal placement during a delay may also determine the type and strength of the association formed. Williams (1982) placed a brief signal in different parts of the delay interval and obtained results that support the notion that the effect of a delay signal on behavior is dependent upon the temporal location of that stimulus within the delay interval. Williams argued that when the stimulus is relatively contiguous with the response that precedes it, conditioned reinforcement will be greatest. As the interval between the criterion response and the signal increases, the acquired strength of the conditioned reinforcing properties weakens (Tombaugh & Tombaugh, 1971). The greater the interval between the response and the signal, the more an attenuation of responding produced by the signal is due to interference with the response-reinforcer association. This overall pattern of findings is consistent with the marking hypothesis of signaling effects (e.g., Thomas, Lieberman, McIntosh, & Ronaldson, 1983), discussed later in the chapter. Of course, it should also be noted that a stimulus may acquire conditioned reinforcing properties to a larger extent when it is contiguous with the reinforcer (Fantino, 1977, 1981). However, if the stimulus is contiguous with the response rather than with the reinforcer, it may exert an influence as a brief discriminative stimulus.

Information Provided by the Signal

The occurrence of serially presented stimulus presentations during reinforcement delays can facilitate the subject's temporal estimation and fine-tune precise localization of the CR (that is, attenuate poorly timed anticipatory CRs) (Seger & Scheur, 1977; Williams, 1965). When serial CSs occur as signals for the US, it has been suggested that the initial CS signals whether the US will occur, and the later CS signals when the US will occur (Seger & Scheur, 1977). If a strong CR occurring near the time of the US is considered optimal with delays of reinforcement, serial CSs filling the delay can promote optimal responding.

Efficiency of Responding

Roberts, Tarpy, and Lea (1984) claimed that many of the instrumental signaling effects on time-based schedules, such as interval schedules, can be explained by noting that the signal for reinforcement improves the efficacy of the type of performance required by the schedule. Signals for reinforcement with brief delays on VI schedules typically decrease response rate. On VI schedules, a single response emitted after a pause from responding will be sufficient to obtain food if the timer has timed out and food is available. Responding rapidly in a small window of time is not an efficient use of energy resources on interval schedules. If signals for reward with brief delays on interval schedules promote a response-pause pattern of behavior, the signal is improving efficient performance by encouraging pauses after each response (albeit decreasing response rate at the same time). This lowering of response

rate does not cause an appreciable decrease in the number of rewards received; it merely reduces the amount of work expended to obtain reward. Unsignaled delays promote response bursts—a somewhat inefficient behavior on interval schedules. Therefore, signals for reinforcement improve efficient responding on interval-based schedules.

Tarpy and Roberts (1985) provided additional support for their view in showing that response rate is attenuated by a delay signal on differential-reinforcement of low rates of responding and increased on differential-reinforcement of high rates of responding. Like interval schedules, these schedules are time-based schedules. This is an important point, because the theory by Tarpy, Lea, and Roberts specifically stated that signals improve subjects' detection of temporal features of time-based schedules. Therefore, the theory does not predict an effect of signals on nontime-based schedules (although signals can influence behavior for reasons other than the enhanced-efficiency process the authors discuss in their model). Again, consistent with this view, the authors found little effect of signals on ratio schedules (Roberts et al., 1984).

Reed, Schachtman, and Hall (1988a, but see Dickinson, Peters, & Shechter, 1984, and Roberts et al., 1984) found that responding on ratio schedules was increased by signals for reinforcement presented during the delay. These findings and others (e.g., Reed, 1991; Reed & Schachtman, 1989; Schachtman & Reed, 1990, 1992) caused Reed and Schachtman to elaborate upon the notions by Tarpy, Lea, and Roberts in stating that signals for reinforcement increase the subject's sensitivity to the prevailing contingency, including time-based and nontime-based schedules. The increase in response rate on ratio schedules produced by signals for reinforcement is consistent with the view that signals improve the efficiency of responding. The more one responds on ratio schedules, the more food one obtains. According to Reed and Schachtman, signals for reinforcement improve optimal performance.

Figure 15–5 shows a facilitatory effect of a tone signal on responding in a VR 30-second

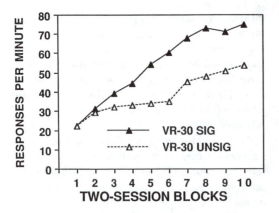

Figure 15–5. Results of an experiment by Reed, Schachtman, and Hall (1988a) examining the effects of signals for reinforcement on a VR 30-second schedule with a 0.5-second delay. The signal enhanced performance for the VR-30-SIG condition.

schedule (see Reed et al., 1988a, Experiment 1). These conditions were treated much like those depicted in the top two conditions presented in Figure 15–2 except that a VR schedule was used rather than a VI schedule. A 0.5-second delay of reinforcement was used with food as the reward. Condition VR-30-Sig received a tone during the 500-millisecond delay, while condition VR-30-Unsig did not. It is clear from the figure that the signal promoted higher levels of responding and hence significantly greater number of foods delivered. Although the work discussed in this section has been done with animal subjects, Reed has recently found that signaled delays also facilitate human contingency judgments (Reed, 1992).

Optimal Memory Retention

Memory, the retention of information over time, also plays a significant role in the optimization of behavior.

Rehearsal and Interference

As we have mentioned, delays of reinforcement hinder response rate, and signals can either enhance or attenuate responding depending on a number of factors, such as the existing schedule

of reinforcement and the specific parameters and stimuli employed (e.g., Reed, Schachtman, & Hall, 1988b, 1991). We have discussed some of the reasons why delays of reinforcement lower responding. Another view of the debilitating effects of reinforcement delay is that the events during the delay displace the target information from being rehearsed in active memory, that is, retroactive interference (Atkinson & Schiffrin, 1968; Lewis, 1979). The notion that target information resides for a limited period of time in memory is an old idea in learning theory (e.g., Hull, 1943). It ought to be noted, however, that trace decay/displacement theories are not without their shortcomings (e.g., Crowder, 1976, pp. 176–182; Grant, 1981). Despite such criticisms, the displacement/decay notions do provide an explanation of the poor conditioned responding with delayed reinforcement if the assumption is accepted that the delay events (e.g., signals), particularly if they follow closely after the target event, displace the target event from memory (or enhance the rate of the trace decay process).

There may, however, be more than one type of interference. For instance, Miller, Kasprow, and Schachtman (1986) distinguished between "processing" interference, in which competition occurs for use of a limited capacity processing system, and "similarity" interference, in which events of a qualitatively similar nature interfere with the retrieval of the target association. Miller, Greco, Marlin, and Balaz (1985) have suggested that these two sources of interference act independently (albeit often summating in their effects when similar events occur proximally in time) to degrade performance.

Revusky (1971), with his notion of situational relevance, suggested that disruption of target responding with delayed reinforcement will occur if events during the delay are relevant to the training situation, such as those that are a constituent of the training context, that is, are "situationally relevant," or if the events are qualitatively related to the target event and/or reinforcer, that is, "stimulus relevant." Optimal memory and, therefore, optimal performance, can be enhanced if such interference is minimized.

Marking Events in Memory: Signals Facilitate Performance "Revisited"

Lett (1973) proposed that interference is responsible for the poor performance typically observed in delayed-reward maze learning by rats. In reference to a T-maze task, Lett (1973; see also Revusky, 1977) asserted that delayed reward after entry into the goal box allows goalbox cues (that is, events that are situationally relevant, since they constitute part of the training apparatus/procedure) to interfere with learning about the instrumental contingency.

Cues present during the delay may serve to reactivate the representation of that target event and thereby facilitate later performance to the target. Lett (1973, 1975) has shown that good performance with long delays of reinforcement can be obtained by rats in a T-maze. This improved performance, relative to responding typically observed with long delays, was obtained if the subjects were removed from the maze (and therefore from the maze cues) immediately after the choice response. Following the delay, the subjects were placed in the start box, where reinforcement was presented if a correct response occurred on the previous run. Lett (1973) reasoned that the response may become associated with the apparatus cues, such that presentation of these cues reactivated the representation of the response that most recently occurred in the maze. Thus, the response representation would be reactivated when subjects were returned to the start box after a delay. Hence, reward or no reward would occur in the presence of the memory of the most recent response. Thus, in the framework of this explanation, contiguity is still regarded as paramount for conditioning, although the concept of contiguity is extended to cover events occurring in memory.

Lett (1975) has noted that performance is worse if subjects remain in the goal box following a response for even 15 or 60 seconds after responding relative to being immediately removed from the goal box. This has been interpreted (e.g., Revusky, 1977) as being a result of goal-box cues providing a source of interference if subjects are not removed from the presence of these cues during the delay because they are situationally relevant to the task.

Related to such phenomena, the "marking" hypothesis (e.g., Thomas et al., 1983; see also Lieberman, Davidson, & Thomas, 1985) states that performance is enhanced if a salient, unexpected stimulus is presented just before or just after the target event. The stimulus is said to "mark" the target event and can produce good learning with long delays of reinforcement. Such facilitated learning has been demonstrated to occur in maze learning by rats and autoshaping in pigeons. The marker allegedly promotes both promotes a backward search through memory for events that preceded and followed the marker and enhances attention to external events, which typically results in augmenting the processing of the target event. Lieberman, McIntosh, and Thomas (1979) noted that even the handling involved in removing the subject from the goal box after the choice response may mark the target response. Lieberman et al. suggest that marking produces enhanced performance and will be less effective the longer after responding the marker occurs. However, the marking hypothesis cannot readily account for the results of a study, by Barnes (reported in Revusky, 1977). In this study, all subjects were handled immediately after the choice response, but subjects that spent the delay interval prior to reinforcement in the home cage showed superior performance to subjects that spent the delay in the start box. The marking hypothesis cannot accommodate this result unless the home-cage experience somehow served as a more effective marker.

Signals may promote learning about not only single responses but also unitary sequences of behavior ("response units") appropriate to the schedule (Byrd & Marr, 1969; Reed, 1991; Reed, Schachtman, & Hall, 1991; Schachtman & Reed, 1992; Stubbs, 1971). Reed et al. (1991) and Schachtman and Reed (1992) found that signals improved the subject's ability to produce response sequences required to obtain reinforcement. One possibility for such findings is that the brief stimulus is functionally equivalent to a marking stimulus and encourages the subject's learning and/or retrieval of the target behavioral sequence, although some contribution of conditioned reinforcement provided by the signal remains plausible. Optimal responding (and presumably nonoptimal responding) can be enhanced by signals of reinforcement occurring during the reinforcement delay.

The Use of Memory Strategies

Some animals have a truly remarkable memory capability. Marsh tits, Clark's nutcracker, and many other birds store seeds in caches so that later in the year when food is scarce, the animals can gather and eat the seeds. Such birds have been shown to store as many as 6,000 seeds in as many as 2,000 caches (obviously more than one seed can be placed in each cache). The birds are able to remember where the seeds are hidden. Controlled experiments have shown that the birds truly remember the location of all these caches; it is not the case that the animals store all the seeds and then search randomly in hopes of uncovering some of them (e.g., Kamil & Balda, 1985). Other explanations that do not involve memory, such as being able to smell the hidden food, have also been ruled out.

Animals are clearly very good at remembering spatial locations where food has previously been available. Much of the laboratory work on this topic has used a type of maze called a "radial-arm maze," with rats as subjects. The maze consists of several (usually eight) long, narrow platforms called "arms" that extend out from a center circular platform. The radial arm maze is also raised above the ground so that if the animal wishes to travel down several of the arms, it must return to the center platform after visiting each arm.

Using this maze, experimenters place one pellet of food at the end of each arm at the start of each day's experimental session. Rats that are a little hungry will travel down the arms and eat the food pellet at the end of the arm. After they go down all the arms, they obtain all eight of the pellets. Once the rat eats the food from a particular arm, the arm will no longer have food present on

it during that session. Hence, rats will behave most efficiently during a session if they can obtain food from all eight arms while traveling down only eight arms, that is, by not making the mistake of visiting the same arm twice in a session.

Rats perform amazingly well at this task once they receive a few sessions so that they can learn that food is present at the end of each arm. They rarely make a mistake. The animals remember which arms they have visited during a session and which ones they have not visited. We should point out that the rats do not use a "non-memory" strategy of choosing a first arm and then traveling clockwise, so to speak, as a means of making sure that they do not make the error of repeating an arm. Moreover, the rats cannot see whether food is present at the end of the arm until they get to the end of the arm. Many other non-memory explanations have been ruled out.

Rats are very good at memorizing these spatial locations. However, experimenters have reduced the animal's memory performance by allowing the animals to choose, for example, four arms, then confining the animal for a period of time (for example, an hour) before it is allowed to resume traveling down the arms. Animals do poorly when an interval of several hours occurs during a session. This poor performance is likely the result of interference (see the discussion of interference earlier in this section).

A study by Cook, Brown, and Riley (1985) looked at animals' performance very carefully (including the types of errors that the animals make) during this type of procedure. The study discovered that when an animal was allowed to choose two arms before the interval occurred, then during the interval, the animal rehearsed which two arms it had already chosen. This is called "retrospective memory" because the animal rehearsed information about events it had encountered in the past during the session. However, if the animals were allowed to choose six arms before the interval, they rehearsed which two arms they had not yet chosen. This is called "prospective memory" because the animals were rehearsing information that they would encounter in the future. In other words, the animals appear to rehearse the information that provides the easiest memory load (two arms in both cases) to perform well. It appears that animals will use very efficient memory strategies.

Other Influences on Optimality

Self-Control

A detailed discussion of self-control is presented in another chapter of this book (see chapter by Logue). Nonetheless, a brief discussion here is warranted. Subjects have been shown to choose a smaller, immediate reward over larger, delayed rewards even when the larger, delayed rewards would seem optimal in such situations. Such behaviors are considered instances of interotemporal choice (Lea et al., 1987). Subjects can be said to behave impulsively in such situations; they lack the self-control that would allow them to tolerate a brief delay and obtain a larger reward. Some discounting factor for events in the future could explain the preference for immediate, small rewards (e.g., Herrnstein, 1990). But holding all other factors constant, moving the consequences of the choices later in time will improve self-control.

These choice procedures provide psychologists with an animal model of impulsive behavior that may reveal factors relevant to human eating disorders, drug abuse, gambling, and other applications in which self-control plays a role. A number of factors influence impulsive behaviors (see Logue, this volume). One treatment that facilitates self-control and therefore more optimal performance is the use of concurrent chain procedures in which subjects get an initial choice between alternative A and alternative B (Rachlin & Green, 1972). If subjects choose alternative A, they will be exposed to a period of time and will then receive a large, delayed reward. If subjects choose alternative B, a period of time will pass and the subjects will be given a choice between alternative C, in which an immediate, small reward will be delivered, and alternative D, in which a large, delayed reward will be delivered. Hence, if subjects initially choose alternative A, they do not get a

subsequent choice but are committed to a large, delayed reward. If they choose alternative B, they get a subsequent choice between a small, immediate reward (alternative C) and a large, delayed reward (alternative D). We know how subjects will behave with this latter choice—they will behave impulsively and will choose the small reward. However, training in this task produced an interesting result in that the subjects chose alternative A (relinquishing their opportunity to make a subsequent choice, eliminating their freedom to choose later in the trial) to commit to the large, delayed reward because choosing alternative B means that they will opt for a situation where they will have poor self-control and will behave nonoptimally (choosing alternative C over D).

Cognitive Style and Pathology

Learned helplessness can result from experience with uncontrollability and unpredictability. Its occurrence may depend on the subject's detection of a noncontingent relationship between the response and outcome (e.g., Garber & Seligman, 1980; Maier, 1989). If there is no relationship between responses and the outcome (the two events occur independently of each other), we say that a zero contingency exists between them. Many psychologists have claimed that depression and learned helplessness result from subjects experiencing a perceived absence of a contingency between their behavior and outcomes; subjects learning that their behavior is independent of the events that occur in their lives. Such a zero correlation between behavior and "outcomes" produces the feeling that one does not control events in one's environment. Learned helplessness can produce a number of behavioral, cognitive, and motivational-emotional disturbances and has consequences on neural processes, health, and immunity (Maier, 1989; Maier, Watkins, & Fleshner, 1994; Sklar & Anisman, 1981).

Factors that facilitate the detection of nonzero correlations may influence feelings of uncontrollability and unpredictability and may affect depression and anxiety (Mineka & Kihlstrom, 1978). Experience with prior contingent relationships is one factor that can greatly influence later exposure to contingencies. Alloy and Abramson (1982) found that prior experience with a contingent relationship between the response and outcome facilitated accurate judgments of a noncontingent relation between responding and a different outcome.

Abramson and Alloy (1980) found that subjects believe their behavior has control when the following conditions prevail: (1) good contiguity occurs between the response and outcome, (2) subjects have practice with the task, (3) subjects have foreknowledge about the contingency, (4) choice is involved in the task, (5) outcomes are desirable, and (6) events occur with high frequency.

Detection of contingency, judgments of cause and effect, and dispositional attributions are influenced by numerous biases and heuristics. Many of these biases and heuristics have been described by Kahneman, Tversky, Nisbett, Ross, Slovic and others (e.g., Kahneman, Slovic, & Tversky, 1982; Nisbett & Ross, 1980). We cannot discuss all of the biases and heuristics described in these reports. We will say that sometimes judgment processes lead to less than optimal choices and attributions. When a person is confronted with an event in the environment that is unexpected on the basis of the individual's current existing schema, the subject can either change its existing cognitive schematic structure so that the structure matches the events in the environment or distort its view of what is occurring in reality so that it does not have to alter its schema. Again, the choice that individuals make between these alternatives does not always appear optimal.

Characteristics of individuals can also influence judgments of covariation and contingency. Coppel and Smith (1980) noted that individuals with internal locus of control are biased to perceive response-reinforcer relationships more than CS-US relationships and perceive response-reinforcer relationships more than individuals with external locus of control. Similarly, those with external locus of control are more sensitive to CS-US associations than response-reinforcer

associations and are more likely to detect the former relations than individuals with internal locus of control.

Another characteristic of subjects that may influence detection of covariations and helplessness is the degree of attention devoted to events that the contingency comprises. Learned helplessness may occur in part from inattention to cues that are relevant to performing a task (Barber & Winefield, 1986; Maier, 1989). Providing extra cues can enhance processing of the target response and allow a "marking" of the target response in memory and may provide some benefit for individuals experiencing learned helplessness.

While affective disorders can influence and be influenced by processes of covariation detection, other forms of pathology can exert an influence as well. Mitchell, Channell, and Hall (1985) found that signals presented during delays of reinforcement facilitated performance on operant schedules for rats that had lesions of the basal ganglia, specifically, the caudate putamen. These lesions presumably provide an animal model of Parkinson's disease. The researchers reasoned that the improvement produced by the signals occurred because the signals provided valuable feedback about the production of the response that succeeded in producing food. It appears that signals for reinforcement may improve optimal performance in subjects with certain neuropathological afflictions.

SUMMARY

This chapter has focused on a number of diverse issues related to the occurrence and detection of optimal and nonoptimal behavior. Some of the factors described can provide tools for improving optimal behavior, and a few of them may allow some diagnostic information as to why existing behavior may not be taking complete advantage of resources available. Although the material covered in this chapter moved rather swiftly from findings and issues relevant to animal work to effects found in humans, and then quickly back again, it is our hope that such an interactionary approach to optimal behavior will continue to promote the cross-fertilization that benefits all relevant disciplines.

REFERENCES

Abramson, L. Y., & Alloy, L. B. (1980). Judgement of contingency: Errors and their implications. In A. Baum & J. Singer (eds.), *Advances in environmental psychology*, 111–130. Hillsdale, N.J.: Erlbaum.

Alba, J. W., & Hasher, L. (1983). Is memory schematic? *Psychological Bulletin, 93,* 203–231.

Alloy, L. B., & Abramson, L. Y. (1982). Learned helplessness, depression, and the illusion of control. *Journal of Personality and Social Psychology, 42,* 1114–1126.

Alloy, L. B., & Tabachnik, N. (1984). Assessment of covariation by humans and animals: The joint influence of prior expectations and current situational information. *Psychological Review, 91,* 112–149.

Arkes, H. R., & Hammond, K. R. (1986). *Judgment and decision making: An interdisciplinary reader.* New York: Cambridge University Press.

Atkinson, R. C., & Schiffrin, R. M. (1968). Human memory: A proposed system and its control processes. In K. W. Spence (ed.), *The psychology of learning and motivation,* Vol. 2: 89–105. San Diego, Calif.: Academic Press.

Azzi, R., Fix, D. S. R., Keller, F. S., Rocha e Silva, M. I. (1964). Exteroceptive control of response under delayed reinforcement. *Journal of the Experimental Analysis of Behavior, 7,* 159–162.

Bandura, A. (1982). Self-efficacy mechanism in human agency. *American Psychologist, 37,* 122–147.

Barber, J. G., & Winefield, A. H. (1986). Learned helplessness as conditioned inattention to the target stimulus. *Journal of Experimental Psychology: General, 115,* 236–246.

Baum, W. M. (1981). Optimization and the matching law as accounts of instrumental behavior. *Journal of the Experimental Analysis of Behavior, 12,* 387–403.

Bibring, E. (1953). The mechanism of depression. In P. Greenacre (ed.), *Affective disorders,* 13–48. New York: International Universities Press.

Bolles, R. C. (1970). Species-specific defense reactions and avoidance learning. *Psychological Review, 71,* 32–48.

Brown, J. S., & Cunningham, C. L. (1981). The paradox of persisting self-punitive behavior. *Neuroscience & Biobehavioral Reviews, 5,* 343–354.

Burghardt, G. M. (1991). Cognitive ethology and critical anthropomorphism: A snake with two heads and hog-nose snakes that play dead. In C. A. Ristau (ed.), *Cognitive ethology: The minds of other animals,* 53–90. Hillsdale, N.J.: Erlbaum.

Burghardt, G. M., & Denny, D. (1983). Effects of prey movement and prey odor on feeding in garter snakes. *Zeitschrift fur Tierpsychologie, 62,* 329–347.

Byrd, L. D., & Marr, M. J. (1969). Relations between patterns of responding and the presentation of stimuli under second order schedules. *Journal of the Experimental Analysis of Behavior, 12,* 713–722.

Capaldi, E. J., & Bowen, J. N. (1964). Delay of reward and goal box confinement time in extinction. *Psychonomic Science, 1,* 141–142.

Cook, R. G., Brown, M. F., & Riley, D. A. (1985). Flexible memory processing by rats: Use of prospective and retrospective information in the radial maze. *Journal of Experimental Psychology: Animal Behavior Processes, 11,* 453–469.

Coppel, D. B., & Smith, R. E. (1980). Acquisition of stimulus-outcome and response-outcome expectancies as a function of locus of control. *Cognitive Therapy and Research, 4,* 179–188.

Cowie, R. J. (1977). Optimal foraging in great tits *Parus major. Nature, 268,* 137–139.

Crowder, R. G. (1976). *Principles of learning and memory.* Hillsdale, N.J.: Erlbaum.

Dickinson, A., Peters, R. C., & Shechter, S. (1984). Overshadowing of responding on ratio and interval schedules by an independent predictor of reinforcement. *Behavioural Processes, 9,* 421–429.

Domjan, M., & Burkhard, B. (1986). *The principles of learning and behavior.* Pacific Grove, Calif.: Brooks/Cole.

Fantino, E. (1977). Conditioned reinforcement: Choice and information. In W. K. Honig & J. E. R. Staddon (eds.), *Handbook of operant behavior,* 313–339. Englewood Cliffs, N.J.: Prentice-Hall.

Fantino, E. (1981). Contiguity, response strength, and the delay-reduction hypothesis. In P. Harzem & M. H. Zeiller (eds.), *Advances in analysis of behavior, Vol. 2: Predictability, correlation, and contiguity,* 169–201. Chichester, England: Wiley.

Garber, J., & Seligman, M. E. P. (1980). *Human helplessness: Theory and application.* New York: Academic Press.

Garcia, J., Ervin, F. R., & Koelling, R. A. (1966). Learning with prolonged delay of reinforcement. *Psychonomic Science, 5,* 121–122.

Garrud, P., Goodall, G., & Mackintosh, N. J. (1981). Overshadowing of a stimulus-reinforcer association by an instrumental response. *Quarterly Journal of Experimental Psychology, 33B,* 123–135.

Gibbon, J., Berryman, R., & Thompson, R. (1974). Contingency spaces and measures in classical and instrumental conditioning. *Journal of the Experimental Analysis of Behavior, 21,* 585–605.

Gilbert, D. T. (1991). How mental systems believe. *American Psychologist, 46,* 107–119.

Grant, D. S. (1981). Short-term memory in the pigeon. In N. E. Spear & R. R. Miller (eds.), *Information processing in animals: Memory mechanisms,* 227–256. Hillsdale, N.J.: Erlbaum.

Grosch, J., & Neuringer, A. (1981). Self-control in pigeons under the Mischel paradigm. *Journal of the Experimental Analysis of Behavior, 35,* 3–21.

Gutt, E. (1982). Cause and function of the depressed response: A hypothesis. *International Review of Psychoanalysis, 9,* 179–189.

Hall, G. (1982). Effects of a brief stimulus acompanying reinforcement on instrumental responding in pigeons. *Learning and Motivation, 13,* 26–43.

Hall, G., Channell, S., & Schachtman, T. R. (1987). The instrumental overshadowing effect in pigeons: The role of response bursts. *Quarterly Journal of Experimental Psychology, 39B,* 173–188.

Herrnstein, R. J. (1961). Relative and absolute strength of response as a function of frequency of reinforcement. *Journal of the Experimental Analysis of Behavior, 4,* 267–272.

Herrnstein, R. J. (1990). Rational choice theory: Necessary but not sufficient. *American Psychologist, 45,* 356–373.

Herrnstein, R. J., & Vaughan, W. (1980). Melioration and behavioral allocation. In J. E. R. Staddon (ed.), *Limits to action: The allocation of individual behavior,* 143–176. New York: Academic Press.

Heyman, G. M. (1983). Optimization theory: Close but no cigar. *Behaviour Analysis Letters, 3,* 17–26.

Hobfoll, S. E. (1989). Conservation of resources: A new attempt at conceptualizing stress. *American Psychologist, 44,* 513–524.

Holland, P. C. (1983). Origins of behavior in Pavlovian conditioning. In G. H. Bower (ed.), *The psychology of learning and motivation,* Vol. 18: 129–174, Orlando, Fla.: Academic Press.

Holyoak, K. J., Koh, K., & Nisbett, R. E. (1989). A theory of conditioning: Inductive learning within rule-based default hierarchies. *Psychological Review, 96,* 315–340.

Hull, C. L. (1943). *Principles of behavior.* New York: Appleton-Century-Crofts.

Hursh, S. R. (1984). Behavioral economics. *Journal of the Experimental Analysis of Behavior, 42,* 435–452.

Iversen, I. (1981). Response interactions with signaled delay of reinforcement. *Behaviour Analysis Letters, 1,* 3–9.

Jenkins, H. M. (1977). Sensitivity of different response systems to stimulus-reinforcer and response-reinforcer relations. In H. Davis & H. M. B. Hurwitz (eds.), *Pavlovian-operant interactions,* 47–62. Hillsdale, N.J.: Erlbaum.

Jenkins, H. M., and Hearst, E. (1974). *Sign tracking: The stimulus-reinforcer relation and directed action.* Austin, Tex.: Psychonomic Society.

Kahneman, D., Slovic, P., & Tversky, A. (1982). *Judgment under uncertainty: Heuristics and biases.* New York: Cambridge University Press.

Kamil, A. C., & Balda, R. P. (1985). Cache recovery and spatial memory in Clark's nutcrackers (*Nucifraga columbiana*).

Journal of Experimental Psychology: Animal Behavior Processes, 11, 95–111.

Katona, G. (1975). *Psychological economics.* New York: Elsevier.

Krebs, J. R., Kacelnik, A., & Taylor, P. (1978). Test of optimal sampling by foraging great tits. *Nature, 275,* 27–31.

Landeau, L., & Terborgh, J. (1986). Oddity and the 'confusion effect' in predation. *Animal Behaviour, 34,* 1372–1380.

Lattal, K. A., & Crawford-Godbey, C. L. (1985). Homogeneous chains, heterogeneous chains, and delay of reinforcement. *Journal of the Experimental Analysis of Behavior, 44,* 337–342.

Lattal, K. A., & Zeigler, D. R. (1982). Briefly delayed reinforcement: An interresponse time analysis. *Journal of the Experimental Analysis of Behavior, 37,* 407–416.

Lea, S. E. G., Tarpy, R. M., & Webley, P. (1987). *The individual in the economy: A survey of economic psychology.* New York: Cambridge University Press.

Lett, B. T. (1973). Delayed reward learning: Disproof of the traditional theory. *Learning and Motivation, 3,* 237–246.

Lett, B. T. (1975). Long delay learning in the T-maze. *Learning and Motivation, 6,* 80–90.

Lewis, D. J. (1979). Psychology of active and inactive memory. *Psychological Bulletin, 86,* 1054–1083.

Lieberman, D. A., Davidson, F., & Thomas, G. V. (1985). Marking in pigeons: The role of memory in delayed reinforcement. *Journal of Experimental Psychology: Animal Behavior Processes, 11,* 611–624.

Lieberman, D. A,, McIntosh, D. C., & Thomas, G. V. (1979). Learning when reward is delayed: A marking hypothesis. *Journal of Experimental Psychology: Animal Behavior Processes, 5,* 224–242.

Mackintosh, N. J. (1983). *Conditioning and associative learning.* Oxford: Oxford University Press.

Maier, S. F. (1989). Learned helplessness: Event covariation and cognitive changes. In S. B. Klein & R. R. Mowrer (eds.), *Contemporary learning theory: Instrumental conditioning theory and the impact of biological constraints on learning,* 73–110. Hillsdale, N.J.: Erlbaum.

Maier, S. F., Watkins, L. R., Fleshner, M. (1994). Psychoneuroimmunology: The interface between behavior, brain, and immunity. *American Psychologist, 49,* 1004–1017.

Marcattilio, A. J. M., & Richards, R. W. (1981). Preference for signaled versus unsignaled reinforcement delay in concurrent-chain schedules. *Journal of the Experimental Analysis of Behavior, 36,* 221–230.

McCain, G., & Bowen, J. (1967). Pre- and postreinforcement delay with a small number of acquisition trials. *Psychonomic Science, 7,* 121–122.

McGill, A. L. (1989). Context effects in judgments of causation. *Journal of Personality and Social Psychology, 57,* 189–200.

McNally, R. J. (1987). Preparedness and phobias: A review. *Psychological Bulletin, 101,* 283–303.

Medin, D. L., & Schaffer, M. M. (1978). Context theory of classification learning. *Psychological Review, 85,* 207–238.

Meltzer, D., Maxey, G. C., & Merkler, N. L. (1965). The effect of delayed reinforcement on DRL conditioning. *Psychonomic Science, 2,* 331–332.

Michel, G. F. (1991). Human psychology and the minds of other animals. In C. A. Ristau (ed.), *Cognitive ethology: The minds of other animals,* 253–270. Hillsdale, N.J.: Erlbaum.

Miller, R. R., Greco, C., Marlin, N. A., & Balaz, M. A. (1985). Retroactive interference in animals: Independent effects of time and similarity of the intervening event with respect to acquisition. *Quarterly Journal of Experimental Psychology, 37B,* 33–48.

Miller, R. R., Kasprow, W. J., & Schachtman, T. R. (1986). Retrieval variability: Psychobiological sources and consequences. *American Journal of Psychology, 99,* 145–218.

Miller, R. R., & Schachtman, T. R. (1985). Conditioning context as an associative baseline: Implications for response generation and the nature of a conditioned inhibition. In R. R. Miller & N. E. Spear (eds.), *Information processing in animals: Conditioned inhibition,* 51–88. Hillsdale, N.J.: Erlbaum.

Mineka, S., & Kihlstrom, J. F. (1978). Unpredictable and uncontrollable events: A new perspective on experimental neurosis. *Journal of Abnormal Psychology, 87,* 256–271.

Mischel, W., & Metzner, R. (1962). Preference for delayed reward as a function of age, intelligence, and length of delay interval. *Journal of Abnormal and Social Psychology, 64,* 425–431.

Mishima, Y. (1967). *The way of the samurai.* New York: Perigee Books.

Mitchell, J. A., Channell, S., & Hall. G. (1985). Response-reinforcer associations after caudate putamen lesions in the rat: Spatial discrimination and overshadowing-potentiation effects in instrumental learning. *Behavioral Neuroscience, 99,* 1074–1088.

Mook, D. C. (1987). *Motivation: The organization of action.* New York: Norton.

Mullen, J. D., & Roth, B. M. (1991). *Decision making: Its logic and practice.* Savage, Md.: Rowman & Littlefield.

Nevin, J. A. (1992). An integrative model for the study of behavioral momentum. *Journal of the Experimental Analysis of Behavior, 57,* 301–316.

Nisbett, R., & Ross, L. (1980). *Human inference: Strategies and shortcomings of social judgment.* Englewood Cliffs, N.J.: Prentice-Hall.

Orians, G. H. (1981). Foraging behavior and the evolution of discriminatory abilities. In A. C. Kamil & T. D. Sargent (eds.), *Foraging behavior: Ecological, ethological, and psychological approaches,* 389–405. New York: Garland STPM Press.

Pearce, J. M., & Hall, G. (1978). Overshadowing the instrumental conditioning of a lever-press response by a more valid predictor of the reinforcer. *Journal of Experimental Psychology: Animal Behavior Processes, 4,* 356–367.

Peele, D. B., Casey, J., & Silverberg, A. (1984). Primacy of interresponse-time reinforcement in accounting for rate differences under variable-ratio and variable-interval schedules. *Journal of Experimental Psychology: Animal Behavior Processes, 10,* 149–167.

Premack, D. (1965). Reinforcement theory. In D. Levine (ed.), *Nebraska symposium on motivation,* Vol. 13: 123–180) Lincoln: University of Nebraska Press.

Pyke, G. H., Pulliam, H. R., & Charnov, E. L. (1977). Optimal foraging: A selective review of theory and tests. *Quarterly Journal of Biology, 52,* 137–154.

Rachlin, H. C. (1989). *Judgment, decision, and choice: A cognitive/behavioral synthesis.* New York: Freeman.

Rachlin, H. C., Battalio, R., Kagel, J., & Green, L. (1981). Maximization theory in behavioral psychology. *Behavioral and Brain Sciences, 4,* 371–417.

Rachlin, H., & Green, L. (1972). Commitment, choice, and self control. *Journal of the Experimental Analysis of Behavior, 17,* 15–22.

Rachlin, H., Logue, A. W., Gibbon, J., & Frankel, M. (1986). Cognition and behavior in studies of choice. *Psychological Review, 93,* 33–45.

Reed, P. (1989). Marking effects in instrumental performance on DRH schedules. *Quarterly Journal of Experimental Psychology, 41B,* 337–353.

Reed, P. (1991). Multiple determinants of the effects of reinforcement magnitude on free-operant response rates. *Journal of the Experimental Analysis of Behavior, 35,* 109–123.

Reed, P. (1992). Effect of a signalled delay between an action and outcome on human judgement of causality. *Quarterly Journal of Experimental Psychology, 44B,* 81–100.

Reed, P., & Reilly, S. 1990). Context extinction following conditioning with delayed reward enhances subsequent instrumental responding. *Journal of Experimental Psychology: Animal Behavior Processes, 16,* 48–55.

Reed, P., & Schachtman, T. R. (1989). Instrumental responding by rats on free-operant schedules with components that schedule response-dependent reinforcer omission: Implications for optimization theories. *Animal Learning & Behavior, 17,* 328–338.

Reed, P., & Schachtman, T. R. (1991). Instrumental performance on negative schedules. *Quarterly Journal of Experimental Psychology, 43B,* 177–197.

Reed, P., Schachtman, T. R., & Hall, G. (1988a). Overshadowing and potentiation of instrumental responding in rats as a function of the schedule of reinforcement. *Learning and Motivation, 19,* 13–30.

Reed, P., Schachtman, T. R., & Hall, G. (1988b). Potentiation of responding on a VR schedule by a stimulus correlated with reinforcement: Effects of diffuse and localized signals. *Animal Learning & Behavior, 16,* 75–82.

Reed, P., Schachtman, T. R., & Hall, G. (1991). The effect of signalled reinforcement on the formation of behavioral units. *Journal of Experimental Psychology: Animal Behavior Processes, 17,* 475–485.

Reilly, S., Schachtman, T. R., & Reed, P. (1996). Signaled delay of reinforcement: Effects of postconditioning manipulation of context associative strength on instrumental performance. *Learning and Motivation, 27,* 451–463.

Renner, K. E. (1964). Delay of reinforcement: A historical review. *Psychological Bulletin, 61,* 341–361.

Rescorla, R. A. (1967). Pavlovian conditioning and its proper control procedures. *Psychological Review, 74,* 71–80.

Revusky, S. H. (1971). The role of interference in association over a delay. In W. K. Honig & P. D. R. James (eds.), *Animal memory,* 155–213. New York: Academic Press.

Revusky, S. H. (1977). The concurrent interference approach to delay learning. In L. Barker, M. Best, & M. Domjan (eds.), *Learning mechanisms in food selection,* 319–366. Waco, Tex.: Baylor University Press.

Reynaud, P-L. (1981). *Economic psychology.* New York: Praeger.

Roberts, J. E., Tarpy, R. M., & Cooney, N. (1985). The effects of signaled reward on sign tracking and response rate. *Animal Learning & Behavior, 13,* 13–17.

Roberts, J. E., Tarpy, R. M, & Lea, S. E. G. (1984). Stimulus response overshadowing: Effects of signalled reward on instrumental responding as measured by response rate and resistance to change. *Journal of Experimental Psychology: Animal Behavior Processes, 10,* 244–255.

Rosch, E. (1975). Cognitive representations of semantic categories. *Journal of Experimental Psychology: General, 104,* 192–233.

Royama, T. (1970). Factors governing the hunting behavior and selection of food by the great tits (*Parus major L.*). *Journal of Animal Ecology, 39,* 619–668.

Schachtman, T. R., & Hall, G. (1990). Potentiation and overshadowing of instrumental responding by pigeons: The role of behavioral contrast. *Learning and Motivation, 21,* 85–95.

Schachtman, T. R., & Reed, P. (1990). The roles of response-reinforcer correlation in signalled reinforcement effects. *Animal Learning & Behavior, 18,* 51–58.

Schachtman, T. R., & Reed, P. (1992). Reinforcement signals facilitate learning about early constituents of a response sequence. *Behavioural Processes, 26,* 1–11.

Schachtman, T. R., Reed, P., & Hall, G. (1987). Overshadowing and potentiation of instrumental responding by pigeons on a VI schedule of reinforcement. *Journal of Experimental Psychology: Animal Behavior Processes, 13,* 271–279.

Schaub, R. E., Bugelski, B. R., & Horowitz, L. (1968). The conditions governing secondary reinforcers. *Psychonomic Science, 12,* 224.

Schoonard, J., & Lawrence, D. H. (1962). Resistance to extinction as a function of the number of delay of reward trials. *Psychological Reports, 11,* 275–278.

Seger, K. A., & Scheur, C. (1977).The informational properties of S1, S2, and the S1–S2 sequence on conditioned suppression. *Animal Learning & Behavior, 5,* 39–41.

Shanks, D. R. (1994). Human associative learning. In N. J. Mackintosh (ed.), *Animal learning and cognition.* 335–374. San Diego, Calif.: Academic Press.

Shanks, D. R., & Dickinson, A. (1986). Associative accounts of causality judgement. In G. H. Bower (ed.), *The psychology of learning and motivation,* Vol. 21: 229–261. San Diego, Calif.: Academic Press.

Shettleworth, S. J. (1994). Biological approaches to the study of learning. In N. J. Mackintosh (ed.), *Animal learning and cognition,* 185–220. San Diego, Caif.: Academic Press.

Shimp, C. P. (1978). Memory, temporal discrimination, and learned structure in behavior. In G. H. Bower (ed.), *The psychology of learning and motivation,* Vol. 12: 39–76. New York: Academic Press.

Siegel, P. S., & Milby, J. B. (1969). Secondary reinforcement in relation to shock termination: Second chapter. *Psychological Bulletin, 72,* 146–156.

Silver, M. P., & Pierce, C. H. (1969). Contingent and non-contingent response rates as a function of delay of reinforcement. *Psychonomic Science, 14,* 231–232.

Simon, H. A. (1955). A behavioral theory of rational choice. *Quarterly Journal of Economics, 69,* 99–118.

Simon, H. A. (1957). *Models of man.* New York: Wiley.

Simon, H. A. (1978). Information processing theory of human problem solving. In W. K. Estes (ed.), *Handbook of learning and cognitive processes,* 271–296. Hillsdale, N.J.: Erlbaum.

Sizemore, O. J., & Lattal, K. A. (1978). Unsignalled delay of reinforcement in variable-interval schedules. *Journal of the Experimental Analysis of Behavior, 30,* 169–175.

Sklar, L. S., & Anisman, H. (1981). Stress and cancer. *Psychological Bulletin, 89,* 369–406.

Smith, J. C., & Roll, D. L. (1967). Trace conditioning with X-rays as an aversive stimulus. *Psychonomic Science, 9,* 11–12.

Spear, N. E. (1978). *Processing of memories: Forgetting and retention.* Hillsdale, N.J.: Erlbaum.

Spence, K. T. (1956). *Behavior theory and conditioning.* New Haven, Conn.: Yale University Press.

Staddon, J. E. R. (1979). Operant behavior as adaptation to constraint. *Journal of Experimental Psychology: General, 108,* 48–67.

Staddon, J. E. R. (1992). Rationality, melioration, and law-of-effect models for choice. *Psychological Science, 3,* 136–141.

St. Claire-Smith, R. (1979). The overshadowing of instrumental conditioning by a stimulus that predicts reinforcement better than the response. *Animal Learning & Behavior, 7,* 224–228.

Stubbs, D. A. (1971). Second order schedules and the problem of conditioned reinforcement. *Journal of the Experimental Analysis of Behavior, 16,* 289–313.

Tarpy, R. M., & Roberts, J. E., (1985). Effects of a signalled reward in instrumental conditioning: Enhanced learning on DRL and DRH schedules of reinforcement. *Animal Learning & Behavior, 13,* 6–12.

Tarpy, R. M., & Sawabini, F. L. (1974). Reinforcement delay: A selective review of the last decade. *Psychological Bulletin, 81,* 984–997.

Thomas, G. V. (1981). Contiguity, reinforcement rate, and the law of effect. *Quarterly Journal of Experimental Psychology, 33B,* 33–43.

Thomas, G. V., Lieberman, D. A., McIntosh, D.C., & Ronaldson, P. (1983). The role of marking when reward is delayed. *Journal of Experimental Psychology: Animal Behavior Processes, 9,* 401–411.

Thorndike, E. L. (1898). Animal intelligence: An experimental study of the associative processes in animals. *Psychological Review Monographs, 2,* Whole No. 8.

Tombaugh, J. W., & Tombaugh, T. N. (1971). Effects on performance of placing a visual cue at different temporal locations within a constant delay interval. *Journal of Experimental Psychology, 87,* 220–224.

Tombaugh, T. N. (1966). Resistance to extinction as a function of the interaction between training and extinction delays. *Psychological Reports, 19,* 791–798.

Trivers, R. L. (1971). The evolution of reciprocal altruism. *Quarterly Review of Biology, 46,* 35–57.

Tversky, A. (1969). Intransitivity of preferences. *Psychological Review, 76,* 31–48.

Tversky, A., & Kahneman, D. (1981). The framing of decisions and the rationality of choice. *Science, 221,* 453–458.

Van Hamme, L. J., & Wasserman, E. A. (1994). Cue competition in causality judgments: The role of nonpresentation of compound stimulus elements. *Learning and Motivation, 25,* 127–151.

Vaughan, W., Jr. (1981). Melioration, matching, and maximizing. *Journal of the Experimental Analysis of Behavior, 36,* 141–149.

Wasserman, E. A. (1990). Detecting response-outcome relations: Toward an understanding of the causal texture of the environment. In G. H. Bower (ed.), *The psychology of learning and motivation,* Vol. 26: 27–82. San Diego, Calif.: Academic Press.

Wilkie, D. M. (1971). Delayed reinforcement in a multiple schedule. *Journal of the Experimental Analysis of Behavior, 10,* 233–239.

Williams, B. A. (1982). Blocking the response-reinforcer association. In M. L. Commons, R. J. Herrnstein, & A. R. Wagner (eds.), *Quantitative analysis of behavior: Acquisition,* Vol. 3: 427–448. New York: Ballinger.

Williams, B. A. (1994). Reinforcement and choice. In N. J. Mackintosh (ed.), *Animal learning and cognition,* 81–109. San Diego, Calif.: Academic Press.

Williams, B. A., and Heyneman, N. (1982). Multiple determinants of "blocking" effects on operant behavior. *Animal Learning & Behavior, 10,* 72–76.

Williams, D. R. (1965). Classical conditioning and incentive motivation. In W. F. Prokasy (ed.), *Classical conditioning,* 340–357. New York: Appleton-Century-Crofts.

Williams, D. R., & Williams, H. (1969). Automaintenance in the pigeon: Sustained pecking despite contingent non-reinforcement. *Journal of the Experimental Analysis of Behavior, 12,* 511–520.

CHAPTER 16

ADJUNCTIVE BEHAVIOR: APPLICATION TO THE ANALYSIS AND TREATMENT OF BEHAVIOR PROBLEMS

John L. Falk
Anne S. Kupfer

CHARACTERIZING PROBLEM BEHAVIOR

All cultures have problem behaviors; they differ in how they handle them. Societies spend considerable time and resources dealing with problem behaviors. They try to avert them (prevention), and if the behaviors occur, they try to get rid of them (therapeutics). For example, inappropriate, chronic spitting could be viewed as something that just shouldn't be done, as a simple problem of an unwanted bit of behavior. But most cultures would ask in addition: Why does this person persist in inappropriately spitting? This is a question of origins, of asking: What factor(s) is this behavior a function of? Is the person possessed by an innate demon, cursed by witchcraft, or unusually blessed with the power of spit-inspired divination? Except in the last instance, most cultures would want people to

change their behavior by not doing all that spitting.

How are they induced to change their behavior? Telling them verbally to stop is one way. But for behavior that already has become a problem, simple requests are usually ineffective. Verbal exhortations to change, such as "Just say no!" are fatuous. Usually, unwanted behavior is punished by formal and informal social agencies. Sometimes this is effective; often it is not. One can attempt to identify the variables maintaining problematic behavior. In traditional cultures, oracles do this by applying divination techniques. Functionally, divination and subsequent curing rituals often come down to sorting out and remedying social relations. In traditional psychoanalysis, there may be a search for critical early-life events that need to be recalled and resolved. Behavior analytic techniques also seek to move from dealing simplistically with the form of problematic behavior, its topography, to its function. But with function the question becomes: What variables is this behavior a function of; what changes its probability? The more traditional methods ask: What purpose does the aberrant behavior serve? It is not that behavior analysis is uninterested in acquiring such information, but it does not assume that strong, persistent, unwanted behavior is present because it serves some crucial purpose. That is treated as an empirical question rather than as a guiding assumption.

An important assumption shared by all clinical and experimental approaches to behavior problems is that pathological behavior is determined by lawful, not unlawful, processes. One may argue whether disturbed behavior is primarily (1) an abnormal response to a normal situation, or (2) a normal response to an extreme or deranged situation. The same considerations occur in interpreting pathological changes in clinical medicine: (1) Is the pathological change the result of an abnormal response to a normal physiological signal (the result of an inherently defective organic system), or (2) is it a normal response to an extreme stimulus (a normal system reacting to a chronically exceptional stimulus)? Although recent interpretations have placed increasing emphasis on inherently flawed systems (genetic and/or neurochemical defects), much current behavior analysis continues to search for, and locate, the sources of disturbed behavior in reactions to current and historic environmental contexts. This latter orientation views behavioral problems as essentially normal reactions to historic paths of environmental contingencies that have channeled behavior into dysfunctional patterns. The position was delineated clearly, with telling experimental examples, 35 years ago by Sidman in an article titled "Normal Sources of Pathological Behavior" (Sidman, 1960).

In animal research the origins and current determinants of behavior are delineated by parametrically varying several values of the relevant variables. This strategy has proved to be more informative than one that assumes an animal's behavior is invariably done in the service of some evident or assumed purpose. The evolutionary origins of behavior have displaced analyses framed in terms of purpose or God's design. A distinct advantage of working with animal species is that the relevant variables can be manipulated quite freely. With humans, scientific delineation is more restricted. But as the behavior of all species, including humans, is the product of evolutionary processes, considerable overlap and generalization occur with respect to the principles of behavior, and animal studies have been of enormous help in clarifying these general principles.

ANIMAL BEHAVIOR AND HUMAN BEHAVIOR THERAPY: RELEVANCE?

What does an examination of animal behavior have to contribute to human behavior therapy? The relation was eagerly pursued in the 1940s and 1950s. Proponents of experimental psychology's "learning theory," at least in the United States, sought to expand the scope of its considerations by reductively including the behavioral phenomena described by psychoanalysis into learning theory's existing explanatory system. For example, Dollard and Miller (1950) substituted the principle of reinforcement for the Freudian pleasure principle, learned drives and skills for ego strength, and the processes of response inhibition and generalization for repression and transference. The overt assumption was that disturbed human behavior could be described in terms of the rigorous principles of learning theory as explicated in laboratory experiments with animals. The practical aim was to understand psychopathology in objective, learning-theory terms so that dysfunctional learned behaviors (neuroses) could be changed therapeutically by applying the same behavioral principles. Learning new solutions would supplant neurotic patterns.

The general skepticism most clinicians felt, expressed by their quiet neglect of learning theory, perhaps could be traced to their discernment that clinical phenomena, and their dramatic and practical engagement with behavior, had more to offer to learning theory than did learning theory to psychopathology. With a few exceptions, working clinical psychologists applied a variety of conceptual schemes to their therapeutic tasks, from Gestalt psychology to client-centered therapy, that made little use of the tenets of learning theory. These schemes took human behavior as their starting point, and derived explanations from considerations of these observations, rather than from laboratory data on animal learning. As comprehensive orientations, they may have owed more to literature and the social-philosophic orientation of the therapist than to scientific elegance, but perhaps they offered most clinicians more immediately interpretable frameworks for viewing the problems they confronted. With respect to the relevance of the "animal neurosis" literature to clinical practice, most clinicians quietly demurred. In retrospect, their reluctance to close ranks with learning theorists is not surprising. Learning theory presented itself as an all-but-completed system. Clinicians were invited to use the theory to reinterpret the syndromes they were charged with correcting, and reap the implied benefits. The practical impact of this program, in our opinion, was modest.

But challenges to learning-theory accounts also came from within the ranks of those studying animal behavior. The human "psychopathologies" of excessive territorial acquisition, patriarchal domination, and aggression were analyzed from a sociobiological standpoint as consequences of our evolutionary and genetic heritages. Perhaps there was more to the biology of maladjusted behavior than could be accounted for by primal scenes, toilet training, and the inadequate acquisition of ego strength, with or without the assistance of learning theory. Fundamental predicaments of social life had been considered seriously by Freud (1930/1961), if not by many Freudians or learning-theory interpretations of Freud. Furthermore, the rise of biological psychiatry, with its successful application of a range of therapeutic drugs to behavioral problems, provided the alternative reductive scheme embodied in neuropsycho-

pharmacology, a discipline with far greater current cachet than animal-conditioning science could muster. The Pavlovian cum neo-Hullian foray into the realm of human psychopathology survives mainly within specific applications, rather than as a body of general interpretive and predictive theory. These applications function as stand-alone fragments, less ambitious in aim and scope than the parent enterprise. As breakaway applications, they have carried away their own specialized mini-theory constructs, for example, opponent-process theory (Solomon, 1980), learned helplessness (Seligman, 1975), reciprocal inhibition (Wolpe, 1958), and conditioned-reflex theories (Wolpe, Salter, & Reyna, 1964). It is not our aim to evaluate the success of these applications. Most are serious endeavors aimed at using selected principles gained from laboratory research to advance therapeutic practice. A few suffer from a lack of appreciation of the basic principles and what operations might constitute their application. For example, in a chapter dealing with reconditioning and disinhibition applied to a claustrophobic client, Salter (1961) describes succinctly his approach:

> We dispose of his childhood in a few minutes. . . . There is often no point in going into the background of the case. We see the malconditioned dog before us, and his problem tells us all we need to know about the kennel from which he came. (Salter, 1961, p. 62)

Salter can hardly be faulted for an intellectualized approach.

At about the time the application of learning theory to clinical phenomena started to fragment into less ambitious but focused efforts, the principles of operant conditioning began to be utilized for the analysis and amelioration of behavior problems. The impetus for this development came mainly from experimental psychologists trained in animal research who now found themselves working principally in clinical settings. Operant analysis easily melded animal and human behavior, for not only had this been its intent from the outset, but complex human activities were addressed early in its development (e.g., Skinner, 1957). A key aspect of the operant analysis of behavior made it particularly attractive to clinicians: its preference for analyzing individual behavior, as opposed to treating group data with inferential statistics. The power of individual analysis, both in practical and methodologic terms, became quickly apparent (Barlow & Hersen, 1984; Kazdin, 1982) and continues to prove itself in a variety of clinical and educational contexts. The application of behavioral principles derived from animal research was no longer simply a speculative academic exercise.

What we hope to accomplish here is not to present a comprehensive framework for behavior therapy; the aim is modest, and in keeping with the more limited aspirations of most animal-behavior enterprises in their applications to human clinical problems (e.g., opponent-process, learned helplessness). We identify a set of environmental conditions that can induce problematic behavioral excesses, indicate their varied manifestations, and suggest how such situations may be modified to diminish dysfunctional behavior.

ADJUNCTIVE BEHAVIOR: ITS VARIETY AND GENERATING CONDITIONS

This section describes the phenomenon of schedule-induced behavior, and the main variables that determine its appearance and magnitude. The initial generation and observation of schedule-induced behavior occurred as an unexpected outcome of an experimental arrangement. The following situation may seem an inauspicious one for yielding anything of clinical interest, for it involves normal rats, food deprivation, a rather simple schedule of reinforcement, and little else—hardly the rich, varied, and complex life-history trajectory one thinks of in connection with behavioral deviations and excesses. The experimental situation was an ordinary one, even 35 years ago. A food-deprived rat was placed in a chamber for about 3 hours each day and obtained food contingent upon pressing a lever (Falk, 1961a). Small food pellets were made available on a variable-interval 1-minute

schedule, wherein a lever-press delivered a pellet on the average once per minute during these daily sessions. The only nonstandard feature of this arrangement was that water was freely available from a drinking tube during these sessions, and the water intake was measured. Note that the animals were never deprived of water, for it was available in an animal's home cage during the 21 hours it was not in the lever-pressing situation. The variable-interval food schedule produced the expected moderate and rather steady rate of lever-pressing. But what was unexpected, and most curious, was that animals drank relatively huge amounts of water during sessions. And they did this unabated every day during sessions. When they obtained each pellet, they quickly ate it, drank a draught of water, and then returned to lever-pressing. Thus, these 200-g animals drank about 90 ml to 100 ml of water in 3 hours, about one-half their body weight.

It is not unusual for an animal to drink while eating. What was unusual was the consistently excessive amount. Control experiments indicated that if the animals were given the amount of food that would be delivered in the course of a 3-hour session all at once as a single ration at the beginning of a 3-hour observation period, then drinking amounted to only about 10 ml, rather than 100 ml (Falk, 1967). The excessive drinking (polydipsia) persisted during each daily session; it did not occur when the animals returned to their home cages. Thus, the polydipsia is a behavioral phenomenon, not a physiological one.

The excessive drinking was shown not to depend upon pellet delivery's being an unpredictable event, nor was lever-pressing a required feature, nor was the drinking adventitiously, that is, "superstitiously" (Skinner, 1948), reinforced by pellet delivery (Falk, 1961b; 1969). The principles of neither operant nor classical conditioning seem able to account for schedule-induced polydipsia or other schedule-induced behaviors to be described (Falk, 1971).

As thus far discussed, there would be no compelling reason for a clinical psychologist to have more than a passing interest in this arcane bit of rat psychopathology. But we hope to show that there is sufficient reason, for the phenomenon has considerable generality: it is not just about overdrinking and about rats. Schedule-induced excessive behaviors are not confined to a single species, response topography, or kind of behavior. They are not a general reaction to "stress." To use a contemporary political rallying phrase: "It's the economy, stupid!" We shall return to this point.

In addition to polydipsia, a variety of behaviors and physiological consequences can occur as excessive adjuncts to schedules of reinforcement. Some are of interest to the clinician: aggression (Frederiksen & Peterson, 1974; Kelly & Hake, 1970; Looney & Cohen, 1982); hyperactivity (Killeen, 1975; Levitsky & Collier, 1968; Muller, Crow, & Cheney, 1979); stereotyped behaviors (Miller & Gollub, 1974; Wieseler, Hanson, Chamberlain, & Thompson, 1988); chronic, fixed hypertension (Falk, Tang, & Forman, 1977); excessive drug-taking (Falk, 1993); defecation (Rayfield, Segal, & Goldiamond, 1982; Wylie, Layng, & Meyer, 1993; Wylie, Springis, & Johnson, 1992); eating (Bellingham, Wayner, & Barone, 1979; Cantor, Smith, & Bryan, 1982); and pica (Roper, Edwards, & Crossland, 1983; Villarreal, 1967). Most of these have been investigated in more than one species, and some in a variety of species.

Schedule-induced behavior has been studied in several rat and mouse strains; in the pigeon; in rhesus, Java macaque, and squirrel monkeys; in the guinea pig; in the Mongolian gerbil; in the chinchilla; in the chimpanzee; and in humans.

The major variables determining the occurrence and magnitude of schedule-induced behavior are not difficult to describe. They have been most completely delineated for polydipsia and attack behavior in several species. Although other schedule-induced behaviors have been less thoroughly explored (e.g., hyperactivity and stereotyped behaviors), enough is known about their excessive and persistent occurrence under schedule-induction conditions to safely infer that the same determining variables and functional relations are operative. First, the excessive behaviors that occur are not new or unusual behaviors in the situations in which they manifest. What is unusual about them is their intensity and/or frequency. Drinking is not in itself unexpected during feeding, but polydipsia is. And this is true of many persistently maladjustive acts. Such conduct comes to clinical attention, or is a personal problem, not because it exists, but because it dominates the behavioral domain and interferes with more appropriate behavior. Household cleanliness is normal and expected; obsessive-compulsive cleansing is not.

Briefly, it is the confluence of two general conditions that generates schedule-induced behavior: the presence of a highly valued commodity (e.g., food for a food-deprived organism) and a degree of intermittence in the availability of such a commodity, that is, a limited schedule of access. The functional relations that describe how these two conditions combine to determine the degree of excessive behavior are straightforward, but not entirely intuitive. Most of the animal research has used food deprivation to create a commodity that is highly valued: small food pellets. Roughly speaking, the amount of schedule-induced behavior generated by an appropriate intermittent schedule of commodity availability is a direct function of the state of deprivation with respect to that crucial commodity. For example, in such a situation, the degree of polydipsic drinking or of attack behavior is an increasing, direct function of the degree of steady-state reduction in body weight (Falk, 1981).

However, a deprivation state that engages regulatory functions is not a necessary condition for the induction of adjunctive excesses. For example, schedule-induced polydipsia occurred in nondeprived rhesus monkeys under fixed-interval schedules of reinforcement when sucrose-flavored pellets were used (Grant & Johanson, 1988). (In contrast to this nondeprivation condition, when sucrose or glucose pellets replaced balanced-diet pellets in schedule-induction sessions with deprived rats, there was a marked reduction in polydipsia [Christian, 1976; Christian & Schaeffer, 1973; Falk, 1967]. Sugar pellets are apparently better motivational items for the nondeprived organism, and balanced pellets are more efficacious for the deprived. Think of trying to make a meal out of a bag of sugar, in contast to savoring a few chocolates after dinner, and the differing results are not surprising.)

The second, and necessary, determining factor, commodity intermittency, operates by a slightly more complex function to induce excessive behavior. The function is a bitonic one. Thus, if small amounts of a valued commodity are delivered either closely in time, or quite infrequently, then little or no schedule-induced behavior is generated. But when commodity provisioning occurs at a middle range of intermittency, excessive adjunctive behavior can be generated. In the rat polydipsia example, if inter-pellet durations are systematically explored in separate sessions, polydipsic intake progressively increases as the time between pellets is lengthened up to about 2 minutes, but with longer times it progressively decreases, until at 5- or 10-minute inter-pellet times the drinking is at normal levels. Although the middle range of intermittency values on the bitonic function is most effective for generating excessive, adjunctive behaviors, the important factor is not so much the time between commodity-delivery episodes but the overall rate at which the crucial commodity is being acquired. To continue our example, commodity acquisition is a joint function of inter-pellet time and pellet size (portion magnitude): at the 1-minute value of intermittency, increasing portion magnitude will decrease session polydipsia, whereas under the 5-minute intermittency condition, increasing the magnitude will increase it (Falk, 1969). Thus, increasing the portion magnitude shifts the entire bitonic function (degree of adjunctive behavior as a function of inter-commodity delivery duration) to the right. This portion-magnitude shift in the bitonic relation even holds for the rhesus monkey with respect to the way the portion magnitude of a reinforcing drug available for intravenous self-injection determines the amount of adjunctive saline self-injected (Grant & Johanson, 1990).

To summarize the main conditions that generate schedule-induced behavior: (1) Deprivation of a crucial commodity alone does not induce excessive behavior. Deprivation by itself does not give rise to increased drinking or aggression. Deprivation simply ensures that a standard food pellet becomes a commodity of high value. (2) It is not just that a low rate of provisioning of a crucial commodity induces excessive behavior. "Stress" and "frustration" should be maximal at very low rates of commodity acquisition, or when reinforcing events are no longer delivered, but such conditions do not generate the behavioral excesses (Christian, Schaeffer, & King, 1975, pp. 65–68; McCoy & Christian, 1976). It is the middle range of commodity acquisition, not too rich or too lean, that induces exaggerated behaviors. It is these factors acting in concert: the presence of a commodity that has become crucial, and its rate of acquisition within an effective (medium) range, that generate chronically excessive behavior. The exaggerated behavior persists for as long as the generating conditions for it persist.

The quantitative relations governing schedule-induced behavior have been confirmed across animal species, so that, for example, the schedule-induced polydipsia bitonic function occurs for rhesus (Allen & Kenshalo, 1976) and Java macaque (Allen & Kenshalo, 1978) monkeys, and for aggression in squirrel monkeys (De-Weese, 1977). But what is the experimental evidence that adjunctive behavior occurs in humans? There are a number of laboratory studies that have imposed commodity-scheduling conditions on humans and measured schedule-induced behavior (for a brief review, see Falk, 1994). Experiments have scheduled access to monetary gain and opportunities to gamble or to solve mazes, and found greatly increased locomotor activities and bodily movements in humans in comparison with activity and movement under unscheduled-access conditions (e.g., Muller et al., 1979; review: Falk, 1994). In addition to hyperactivity, humans show schedule-induced increases in fluid intake (Doyle & Samson, 1988; Kachanoff, Leveille, McLelland, & Wayner, 1973), eating (Cantor, Smith, & Bryan, 1982), stereotyped behavior (Hollis, 1973; Wieseler,

Hanson, Chamberlain, & Thompson, 1988), aggression (Frederiksen & Peterson, 1974; Kelly & Hake, 1970), grooming (Cantor, Smith, & Bryan, 1982), and smoking (Cherek, 1982; Cherek & Brauchi, 1981; Wallace & Singer, 1976).

WHY ADJUNCTIVE BEHAVIOR OCCURS

There is no discernible reason, in terms of satisfying a pressing requirement for food, why overdrinking should occur. Drinking does not produce food delivery, nor is it associated adventitiously with food delivery. In fact, an organism short on energy supplies can only lose more calories by drinking a large quantity of water, heating it to body temperature, and excreting it. Nevertheless, the ubiquity of adjunctive behaviors—their occurrence in a variety of species, under the control of the same set of determinants—suggests the evolution of an adaptive behavioral mechanism of some generality. The adaptive significance of adjunctive behaviors in terms of the theory of evolution has been presented previously (Falk, 1977, 1986) and will not be recapitulated here. Only a brief indication of the argument as it applies to the persistence of puzzling behavior in animals (Falk, 1977) and humans (Falk, 1986; Falk & Feingold, 1987) will be given.

First, it is important to note that schedule-induced escape from various schedules of positive reinforcement occurs in rats, pigeons, squirrel monkeys, and rhesus monkeys (e.g., for a brief review, see Falk, 1984; Brown & Flory, 1972; Lydersen, 1992, 1994; Lydersen, Perkins, Thome, & Lowman, 1980). Animals will engage in operant behavior that repeatedly terminates a positive-reinforcement schedule with a time-out period. The amount of time-out taken during a session usually varies as an increasing, direct function of the degree of schedule intermittency (i.e., the leaner the schedule, the greater the escape from the schedule). Thus, although it is an unexpected finding, animals do escape from schedules of positive reinforcement. Furthermore, although food-deprived animals are clearly in need of the food, the amount of escape was actually found to increase when body weight was allowed to decrease (Dardano, 1973). Such escape behavior may occur owing to an aversive property of positive schedules that increases as a direct function of their meagerness.

The combination of the functional relations governing two opposing vectors forms the condition that generates the bitonic function already described as characteristic of adjunctive behavior. Recall that when a commodity is of crucial importance and environmental conditions constrain the rate of access to it within a middle range, so that the rate is neither too rich nor too lean, then excessive adjunctive behavior will be generated. This is the bitonic functional relation. As the rate of access to limited portions of an important commodity is varied from high to low, the rate at which that commodity is consumed is forced to decline. As noted above, in parallel with this decrease in the rate of acquisition of a commodity there is an equivalent increase in an escape vector, that is, schedule-induced escape increases. The inverse of the difference between the consummatory and escape vectors generates the bitonic function (Figure 16–1, shaded portion). The vectors are in opposition, so when they are equal and in balance, the maximum adjunctive behavior is generated. If the rate of commodity acquisition is allowed to increase from the balanced midpoint, then escape decreases and so does adjunctive behavior. If the rate of commodity acquisition is allowed to decrease from the midpoint, then escape increases and adjunctive behavior decreases. Hence, at the midpoint, when neither vector dominates the situation, the vectors are in balance and ambivalence or conflict is maximal—and so is adjunctive behavior.

Another way of stating this relation is that adjunctive behavior is maximal when the situation is maximally equivocal. This has a possible evolutionary origin and may possess a current adaptive significance. Briefly, life presents many situations characterized by pairs of vectors in opposition. There are important activities crucial for

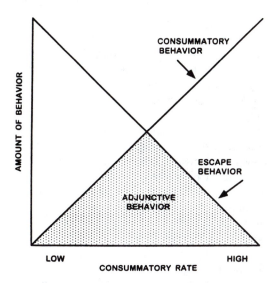

Figure 16–1. Amount of adjunctive behavior as the inverse of the difference between two functions: the rate of generator schedule consummatory behavior, and the probability of escape behavior.

survival, such as feeding, mating, territorial defense and parental care. But physical and social environments can pose problems for maintaining suitable engagement with these activities: A food source may become inoperative or depleted. Mating may involve competition from others and degrees of rejection from potential mates. Territorial maintenance may require constant defense against competitors. Parental behavior may be in opposition to other attractions. All such cases can be viewed as predicaments comprising an appetitive vector for a crucially important activity, which is opposed by an escape vector (e.g., patch depletion, competitive threat). If the appetitive vector is strong because the environment effectively supports engagement in the relevant behavior (a rich schedule of reinforcement), then the individual remains in such situations to feed, mate, defend territory, or care for offspring. But if the respective environments only poorly support any of these activities (schedule too lean), then the best course of action may be to move on —to escape. The most interesting cases are those

in which the pair of opposing vectors are of approximately equal strength. Such a predicament constitutes an unstable equilibrium, and anything producing a slight advantage for one of the vectors unbalances the flow of behavior in its direction—precipitously and often irreversibly.

Once escape begins, the situation has been fatefully decided and escape cascades: the feeding situation, mate, territory, or young are abandoned. If a feeding patch is abandoned, a threat or competitor fled from, or a territory relinquished, reacquisition or reestablishment is improbable. Under maximally equivocal circumstances (midpoint of Figure 16–1), the optimal course of action would be to refrain from a precipitous choice until the situation clarifies. A decision based on a momentary, small change in the strength of a vector may be based on inadequate information and be fatefully disadvantageous. The best course of action would be to delay committing to either action, and wait for additional information to produce clarification. For that to occur, if behavior were to come under the stimulus control of some other feature of the environment, the behavioral-vector domain would become diversified and thereby protected from precipitous choice. This occurs in ethologic situations for animals when conflicts give rise to displacement activities (e.g., feeding or aggressive acts, sleep postures, sexual displays). Fateful decisions are delayed until situational clarification occurs. The conflict situations described constitute generator conditions inducing adjunctive behavior. In terms of evolutionary processes, the adaptive function of adjunctive behavior is to delay commitment to either engaging a situation or escaping from it until one or the other vector becomes clearly ascendant.

BEHAVIORAL PROBLEMS FROM THE PERSPECTIVE OF ADJUNCTIVE BEHAVIOR

Human studies in which adjunctive behaviors were generated in the laboratory were indicated briefly above. But what happens when, unlike most generator conditions occurring in laboratory studies of humans, or in ethologic settings for animals, the inducing situation is a more permanent, endemic feature of a person's social and economic niche? Crucially important reinforcing events typically are available intermittently, rather than continuously, whether simple biological or subtle social events are considered. This is especially the case when the reinforcing events are delayed products of complex, operant behavior, a circumstance common in modern life. Some unwanted, excessive behavior may be profitably considered as both originating and persisting owing to the perpetuating environmental conditions embodied in intermittent reinforcement. These conditions constitute predicaments of marginality, wherein the acquisition of important reinforcers is in a range of intermittency such that adjunctive behavior is induced chronically. Again, marginality predicaments are not those characterized by extremely sparse schedules of reinforcement. Such minimal rates of reinforcement generate little adjunctive behavior (escape vectors dominate).

On the other side of the bitonic function (see Figure 16–1) are situations providing a rich flow of desirable commodities and activities, situations that also do not generate adjunctive behavior (consummatory behavior dominates). It is the middle range of access rates that generates adjunctive behavioral excesses (the conflicting reinforcement-schedule vector and the escape vector are of equal strength). Although adjunctive behavior can be innovative and creative activities, the major portion may consist of chronic actions that are either wasteful distractions (e.g., television viewing, loquacious talking, all-consuming hobbies) or frankly deleterious conduct (e.g., aggressive comportment, substance abuse, obsessive or compulsive routines).

Goffman (1967) described several occupations that are characterized by intermediate rates of reinforcement, and in which a person continually faces "problematic consequentiality." Such occupations are "where the action is." They are often risky ones in which crucially important decisions must be made that involve the possibility of intermittently gaining powerful reinforcers,

along with the concurrent possibility that quite aversive consequences may occur in place of the positive reinforcers. Strong and competing approach-escape vectors are in continuous play in the control of behavior, an ideal environment for generating adjunctive behavior. These sorts of conditions permeate the lives of commodity-market speculators, prospectors, treasure hunters, salvage seekers, test pilots, astronauts, high-construction workers, commission salesmen, entertainment promotors, politicians, performing artists, athletes, and street criminals. As a consequence, these pursuits are associated with increased liabilities for a variety of excessive behavior disturbances: violence, drug abuse, sexual misconduct, unwise gambling, and sociopathic functioning. As indicated previously, not all adjunctive behavior generated in the course of such activities is necessarily deleterious. Behavioral excesses can be unusual, creative, and even possess practical utility. In addition, it is easy to overlook the less dramatic, "quiet-desperation" adjunctive behaviors of professionals. The creative writer, fearful that any pause in literary output presages burnout, may actuate the self-fulfilling prophesy of writer's block (self-imposed time-out), for if one does not write, then one does not experience the onset of a pause in writing. Put in terms of adjunctive behavior analysis, if the creative acts occur as brief, but spaced, bouts, and at considerable effort (response cost), one of the consequences may be escape behavior. Escape by the author while remaining within his or her study is not-writing behavior. Escaping spatially from the study may be distracting, but it also may set the occasion for writing in a new locus, for at least that locus has not been experienced as a marginal-creation context. The scientist, living from one barely adequate, soft-money, competitive federal grant to the next may evidence a variety of distracted (time off task) behaviors. A good deal of adjunctive behavior may present as general anxiety, the sources of which the clinician should be prepared to discern. An assessment of a client's rates of reinforcement with respect to commodities and activities deemed of crucial importance may reveal the generating conditions for unwanted, excessive behavior.

Incidents in which reinforcement intermittency is occurring along with motivational exigency may illuminate how episodes of excessive, undesirable behavior are induced. Assaultive or abusive episodes may result from circumstances that appear to provide a flow of reinforcing events. But the rate of flow, or the magnitude of the reinforcers, may be in a range that generates adjunctive behavior. For example, diadic, social reinforcers exchanged on a date may induce adjuncts such as giddy laughter, humorous banter, or episodic silences (micro-escapes). But a lean or awkward flow of interactional reinforcement also may induce unplanned drinking, aggressive driving, or date rape.

Beside particular occupational or social pursuits that may favor the induction of adjunctive behavior, more prosaic but nonetheless potent environmental contexts may predispose individuals to develop adjunctive behaviors deleterious to their overall adjustment in society. Consider the plight of young people developing in a poor urban ghetto. Their opportunities for substantial and persisting reinforcement are limited. Not only are legitimate employment opportunities sparse and low-paying, but substandard educational institutions may not provide the skills required to compete for better positions if they do become available. Petty crimes, such as drug dealing, pay well in the short run. Conventional opportunities and satisfactions may be difficult to find in this environment, but there are potential reinforcers that receive peer-group approval and require minimal skills to engage in, for example, drug dealing, drug taking, and petty crime. The combination of sparse and unstable conventional reinforcement opportunities, together with the ready availability of ones that are easy, brief, but destabilizing, constitutes a set of conditions that favor the development and maintenance of the deleterious adjunctive behaviors. It is not surprising that drug abuse, violence, and poor parenting are overrepresented activities under such conditions.

This is not to imply that distinctly privileged circumstances cannot also induce disruptive behavioral adjuncts. A young person may be sent to a fine boarding school, that provides good individual attention and facilities for education. Although the parents expect superior performance to be a consequence of this environment, they may have little time or occasion to provide their offspring with direct social reinforcement. They are important and busy people; the young person, at this stage, is not. The lean schedule of parental social reinforcement, together with high expectations and the often competitive social interactions within such a school, may afford the young person only a sparse schedule of social reinforcement. The student's migrant, but relatively confined, status may isolate the student from easily attaining other satisfying social contacts. Access to a high, disposable income may permit easy adjunctive indulgence in illegal drugs or other unfortunate activities, with minimal risk of legal consequences. A variety of "acting-out" behaviors may be induced adjunctively under a schedule of high demands and marginal social reinforcement. Acting-out (e.g., class clown, bully, or daredevil) may originate as adjunctive behavior and then evolve into a social operant resulting in the attainment of local power and status. Knowledge of the generating conditions may aid in the remediation of behavior that presents as sociopathic, or as sustained by "bad companions."

THERAPEUTIC AND PREVENTION EXAMPLES

A corollary thread running through the above discussion is that if a midrange of reinforcing events induces undesirable, adjunctive behavior, then either more acceptable adjunctive behavior should be substituted, or the generating situation should be manipulated to attenuate the induction. Traditionally, symptom substitution has been viewed as a poor therapeutic outcome because it does not resolve what may be an underlying problem. However, the replacement of dysfunctional activities by adjustive or creative behavior may be the shorter, more directly effective solution. On the other hand, if the generator conditions can be altered to alleviate the induction of unwanted behavior, then that might be the more desirable course. Often this will require an enrichment of the generator condition: for the commodity in question, more frequent and/or greater magnitude of reinforcing events.

It is not always possible to effect changes in generator conditions. A person's avocation, or socioeconomic niche, may not be easily subject to change. Furthermore, life is fraught with intermittent reinforcement with respect to its most powerful reinforcers. If dysfunctional adjunctive behavior is thereby generated, then more benign or creative behavior could be substituted for the less desirable, or a reevaluation of the generator context should be a therapeutic end. For example, if the message of contemporary society is that "you can't be too rich or too thin," then no respective financial increment or body weight decrement will move a person out of the pernicious generator conditions driving excessive acquisitive or dietary behavior. Behavioral insatiability—conditions under which a person is always deemed not rich enough, thin enough, loved enough, or famous enough—presents challenges to therapeutics, as well as to prevention.

From a clinical perspective, dysfunctional behavior presents with one or more of three general characteristics: it may be deficient (repertoire is absent or weak), excessive (too much of it), or out of context (intrusive, i.e., unexpected and counterproductive). Adjunctive behavior in animals and humans clearly shows the latter two characteristics: it appears as both excessive and out of context. But analysis of the conditions determining adjunctive behavior, as well as consideration of its evolutionary lineage, indicate that its excessive features and intrusive details follow as normal responses to the marginal conditions entailed by certain intermittent schedules of reinforcement (cf. the first section of this paper: Characterizing Problem Behavior). For example, collateral aggression within, or escape from, certain situations affording positive reinforcement, which might seem irrational as well as dysfunctional, are revealed as orderly, pre-dictable reactions (e.g., Flory, 1969; Lydersen et al., 1980; Webbe, DeWeese, & Malagodi, 1974).

It is important to note that although ingestive and aggressive behavior have been the focus of much schedule-induction research, the particular adjunctive behavior manifesting in a situation can be quite varied. It is a function of what current facilitating stimuli are present in the environment and the behavioral history individuals bring to the situation (e.g., Falk, 1971; Tang & Falk, 1986, 1988; Tang, Williams, & Falk, 1988; Williams, Tang, & Falk, 1992). Adjunctive behavior is neither contingently maintained by the delivery of the generator schedule's reinforcing event, nor is it an unconditioned response elicited by that event. This is why, in the light of classical and operant analyses of behavior, adjunctive behavior has seemed both empirically and theoretically so puzzling. But it is neither unpredictable nor out of control. In fact, a consideration of various psychopathological phenomena, such as obsessive-compulsive behavior, may be clarified by analysis in terms of schedule induction (e.g., Altemus, Glowa, Galliven, Leong, & Murphy, 1996; Rapoport, Ryland, & Kriete, 1992; Woods et al., 1993).

There are dynamic features in how adjunctive behavior manifests that are worth considering from a clinical point of view. One is its course of development. It often develops rapidly, but since it is not elicited behavior, it is not evident instantaneously. Sometimes it develops over a considerable period, manifesting only gradually over many weeks or months (e.g., Looney & Dove, 1978; Magyar & Malagodi, 1980). Thus, the development of some dysfunctional behavior may not be the result of a concurrent change or deterioration in a person's life situation. It simply may take a long time for the adjunctive behavior to develop under long-standing inducing conditions.

A second feature concerns the point at which episodes of adjunctive behavior occur in relation to the generator schedule. In many studies, an adjunctive bout occurs in the period immediately following each delivery of a reinforcing event (Figure 16–2). This is not an invariant feature,

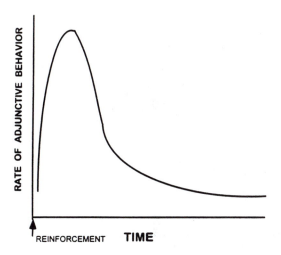

Figure 16–2. Rate of adjunctive behavior as a function of time since delivery of a reinforcing event.

for if the postreinforcement occurrence of adjunctive behavior is specifically prevented, it usually appears in alternative temporal loci (for a brief review, see Falk, 1994). A sudden bout of dysfunctional behavior immediately following a reinforcing event seems odd and, from a therapeutic point of view, perhaps disappointing. Consider the following case.

Client L.H., a blind, nonverbal 18-year-old male, was institutionalized for most of his life with a diagnosis of severe mental retardation. He engaged in several kinds of self-injurious behaviors (S.I.B.), which included rubbing his chin with his hands and/or shoulders, producing severe tissue damage. Owing to the extent of damage from his S.I.B., he was kept in five-point restraint for most of the day, as well as during the night. In order to determine whether his S.I.B. might be adjunctive behavior, he was given a small bite of ice cream every 2 minutes. The 2-minute interval was divided into five consecutive 24-second bins, and the number of chin rubs by any part of his arm was recorded within these bins. Interobserver reliability for these data was 95%. Each session presented 15 bites, and thus lasted 30 minutes. The distribution of chin rubs within the consecutive bins was similar to the temporal distribution commonly observed for adjunctive behavior (Figure 16–2). Figure 16–3 shows that the bin with the greatest number of chin rubs was almost always the first bin (immediately after a bite of ice cream was taken). This pattern of behavior developed quickly and was complete by the fourth day. Although the experiment may only suggest that the severe chin-rubbing had its historic origin as an adjunctive behavior, it does implicate generator-schedule events in its exacerbation and maintenance. One may unwittingly increase, or even initiate, unwanted adjunctive behavior when attempting to promote adjustive behavior by differentially reinforcing instances of a desired behavior. An understanding of the adjunctive phenomenon occurring, and its probable determining variables, allows the behavior therapist to adjust remedial efforts in an informed and creative fashion. If schedule induction initiates or exacerbates dysfunctional behavior, such as chin-rubbing, then the generator schedule probably should be adjusted toward shorter interreinforcement intervals (i.e., be enriched).

Although a previous section outlined the major variables inducing adjunctive behavior, two additional factors are worth discussing because they can influence the strategy and efficacy of therapeutic efforts. The first of these is response requirement. The rate at which a crucial commodity is acquired is the main determinant of the degree of adjunctive behavior induced (cf. the bitonic function), so that induced behavior occurs whether or not operant behavior is required for the intermittent delivery of the commodity. However, if operant behavior is required, the induced behavior may be greater and more frequent than if the commodity is delivered noncontingently on an intermittent basis. For example, fixed-interval and fixed-ratio schedules of food presentation produced schedule-induced attack in pigeons (Flory, 1969; Gentry, 1968) and monkeys (Cherek, Thompson, & Heistad, 1973; DeWeese, 1977; Hutchinson, Azrin, & Hunt, 1968), with large fixed-ratio requirements producing more attack than either equivalent, intermittent, noncontingent food delivery (Cherek et al., 1973; Flory & Everist,

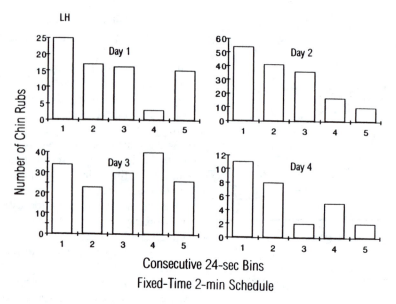

Figure 16–3. Amount of adjunctive behavior (chin rubs) for client L.H. as a function of time since delivery of ice cream bite on fixed-time 2-minute schedule, Days 1–4.

1977; Sicignano [Kupfer], 1981) or short, fixed ratios (Allen, Sicignano [Kupfer], Webbe, & Malagodi, 1981; Hutchinson et al., 1968; Knutson, 1970; Lyon & Turner, 1972).

The determination that response requirements, particularly large requirements, can exacerbate an already excessive adjunctive behavior may be related to findings that inappropriate behaviors, such as S.I.B. and aggression, occur at greater levels under task conditions in which there is either some demand or an increased level of task difficulty (Carr & Durand, 1985; Carr, Newsom, & Binkoff, 1976, 1980; Weeks & Gaylord-Ross, 1981). Additionally, Iwata, Dorsey, Slifer, Bauman, and Richman (1982) reported that a surprisingly higher percentage of subjects' S.I.B. was maintained under conditions in which S.I.B. produced escape from the demands of adults than under conditions in which S.I.B. produced attention from adults. Taken together, these findings suggest that demanding situations may engender higher levels of inappropriate behavior. Although some researchers have concluded that these inappropriate behaviors are maintained by

escape or task-avoidance functions, an alternative view is possible. As noted, greater levels of adjunctive aggression often occur under response-dependent than under response-independent schedules of reinforcement. Thus, demand situations may generate greater levels of adjunctive behavior, and once generated, this behavior may intersect an environmental contingency affording either escape or attention, which then further exacerbates a behavior that was initially simply adjunctive.

In addition to the factor of "response requirement," the efficacy of periodic versus aperiodic generator schedules in inducing adjunctive behavior requires comment. Intuitively, one might guess that reinforcing events occurring somewhat unpredictably would induce more adjunctive behavior than would predictable events. The evidence, however, is in the other direction. Briefly, when an alternative schedule was available by responding on a changeover key, pigeons preferred variable-ratio to fixed-ratio schedules (Sherman & Thomas, 1968). In agreement with this finding, higher levels of attack occurred under fixed-ratio compared with equivalent variable-ratio schedules (Webbe et al., 1974). These studies have a clear implication for the clinician attempting to change behavior. If the institution or maintenance of a performance is to be accomplished by using a schedule of intermittent reinforcement, the risk of inducing an unwanted adjunctive behavior would be lessened by using a variable, rather than a fixed, schedule. This is illustrated by the following cases.

J.O. was a verbal 14-year-old male diagnosed as having moderate mental retardation, with several behavior problems. His most dysfunctional behavior was aggression, which consisted of two or more of the following: repeated aggression against others, aggression against objects (e.g., tables), and bites at his own hand. The frequency of aggressive episodes was recorded daily and summarized weekly. Each occurrence of an aggressive episode resulted in J.O.'s being removed from his regular classroom activities into a hallway (a time-out [T.O.] procedure) until he exhibited a 1-minute calm period. Additionally, he was given a premium of his choice (a small edible or praise) every 15 minutes as long as no aggressive behavior was occurring at the moment the premium was scheduled to be delivered. This fixed-time schedule of premium

delivery, in conjunction with the T.O. procedure, was eventually sufficient to reduce the frequency of aggressive episodes from about 15 per week to about 6 per week. These differing rates of aggressive behavior remained stable at the respective frequencies for substantial periods of time (Figure 16–4). When the fixed-time schedule was changed to a variable-time schedule in which a premium was delivered only on the average once every 15 minutes, the aggressive episodes decreased to about 2 per week, and this rate too remained stable.

B.S. was a 24-year-old male diagnosed with moderate mental retardation and behavior disorder (Vought, 1996). B.S.'s dysfunctional behavior included S.I.B., which consisted of slapping his head, banging his head against objects, and biting himself. He also had episodes of aggression against others as well as property destruction. The severity of these episodes required one-to-one staffing at all times and complete social isolation. When he first entered the program, an activity schedule was instituted that included toileting every hour, dinner at 6 P.M., and a van ride at 7:30 P.M. This schedule maintained his S.I.B. and aggressive behaviors at manageable levels so that B.S. was able to be in the proximity of others without constant supervision. Ob-

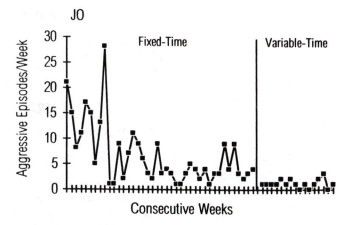

Figure 16–4. Number of aggressive episodes per week for client J.O. under baseline, fixed-time, and variable-time conditions of premium delivery (see text).

servation revealed that his problematic behaviors occurred reliably in association with toileting, dinner, and van rides. His schedule remained fixed for 30 days and was then changed to a variable-time schedule (V.T.). Toileting was placed on a V.T. 1-hour schedule, dinner varied within a 1-hour time block between 5 and 6 P.M. on alternate days, and the van ride varied within a half-hour time block between 7 and 7:30 P.M. on alternate days. This V.T. schedule resulted in further decreases in all his dysfunctional behaviors (Figure 16–5). Figure 16–5 also shows that a follow-up after six months, during which the V.T. schedule was maintained, produced further

decreases, with no S.I.B. associated with toileting and no aggression associated with van rides.

CONCLUDING STATEMENT

Some years ago, Foster (1978) indicated that human adjunctive behavior in clinical settings received scant consideration. Since then, little has improved in this regard. Foster remarked that

> . . . authors of "how-to" textbooks and workshops on behavior modification have devoted little or no time to alerting consumers to the existence of adjunctive phenomena extrinsic to *and* intrinsic to treatment programs. As a result, this writer has observed numerous cases where professionals and paraprofessionals devoted strenuous, shortsighted, and futile efforts at directly modifying apparently adjunctive behaviors by imposing medications or consequences on them. (Foster, 1978, p. 545)

It is not that medication, punishing emission of the adjunctive behavior, or reinforcing alternative behavior, cannot impact these kinds of nonadjustive activities. Perhaps they can. But knowing the environmental variables that maintain and exaggerate these sorts of behavior indicates that there may be more direct and efficacious ways to prevent and alleviate dysfunctional adjunctive behavior.

ENDNOTE

Preparation of this chapter was supported by the National Institute on Drug Abuse, Grant K05 000142.

REFERENCES

Allen, J. D., & Kenshalo, D. R., Jr. (1976). Schedule-induced drinking as a function of interreinforcement interval in the rhesus. *Journal of the Experimental Analysis of Behavior, 26*, 257–267.

Allen, J. D., & Kenshalo, D. R., Jr. (1978). Schedule-induced drinking as functions of interpellet interval and draught size in the Java macaque. *Journal of the Experimental Analysis of Behavior, 30*, 139–151.

Allen, R. F., Sicignano (Kupfer), A., Webbe, F. M., & Malagodi, E. F. (1981). Induced attack during ratio schedules of reinforcement: Implications for measurement of

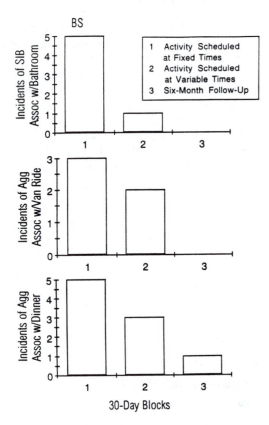

Figure 16–5. Number of self-injurious or aggressive episodes under fixed-time and variable-time care regimen schedules (data from Vought, 1996; see text).

adjunctive behaviors. In C. M. Bradshaw, E. Szubadi, & C. F. Lowe (eds.), *Quantification of steady-state operant behavior,* 385–388. Amsterdam: Elsevier/North-Holland Biomedical Press.

Altemus, M., Glowa, J. R., Galliven, E., Leong, Y.-M., & Murphy, D. L. (1996). Effects of serotonergic agents on food-restriction-induced hyperactivity. *Pharamacology, Biochemistry and Behavior, 53,* 123–131.

Barlow, D. H., & Hersen, M. (1984). *Single case experimental designs: Strategies for studying behavior change* (2nd ed.). New York: Pergamon.

Bellingham, W. P., Wayner, M. J., & Barone, F. C. (1979). Schedule induced eating in water deprived rats. *Physiology and Behavior, 23,* 1105–1107.

Brown, T. G., & Flory, R. K. (1972). Schedule-induced escape from fixed-interval reinforcement. *Journal of the Experimental Analysis of Behavior, 17,* 395–403.

Cantor, M. B., Smith, S. E., & Bryan, B. R. (1982). Induced bad habits: Adjunctive ingestion and grooming in human subjects. *Appetite, 3,* 1–12.

Carr, E. G., & Durand, V. M. (1985). Reducing behavior problems through functional communication training. *Journal of Applied Behavior Analysis, 18,* 111–126.

Carr, E. G., Newsom, C. D., & Binkoff, J. A. (1976). Stimulus control of self-destructive behavior in a psychotic child. *Journal of Abnormal Child Psychology, 4,* 139–153.

Carr, E. G., Newsom, C. D., & Binkoff, J. A. (1980). Escape as a factor in the aggression of two retarded children. *Journal of Applied Behavior Analysis, 13,* 101–117.

Cherek, D. R. (1982). Schedule-induced cigarette self-administration. *Pharmacology, Biochemistry and Behavior, 17,* 523–527.

Cherek, D. R., & Brauchi, J. T. (1981). Schedule-induced cigarette smoking behavior during fixed-interval monetary reinforced responding. In C. M. Bradshaw, E. Szubadi, & C. F. Lowe (eds.), *Quantification of steady-state operant behavior,* 389–390. Amsterdam: Elsevier/North-Holland Biomedical Press.

Cherek, D. R., Thompson, T., & Heistad, G. T. (1973). Responding maintained by the opportunity to attack during an interval food reinforcement schedule. *Journal of the Experimental Analysis of Behavior, 19,* 113–123.

Christian, W. P. (1976). Control of schedule-induced polydipsia: Sugar content of the dry food reinforcer. *The Psychological Record, 26,* 41–47.

Christian, W. P., Jr., & Schaeffer, R. W. (1973). Effects of sucrose concentrations upon schedule-induced polydipsia on a FFI 60-sec dry-food reinforcement schedule. *Psychological Reports, 32,* 1067–1073.

Christian, W. P., Schaeffer, R. W., & King, G. D. (1975). *Schedule-induced behavior: Research and theory.* Montreal: Eden Press.

Dardano, J. F. (1973). Self-imposed timeouts under increasing response requirements. *Journal of the Experimental Analysis of Behavior, 19,* 269–287.

DeWeese, J. (1977). Schedule-induced biting under fixed-interval schedules of food or electric-shock presentation. *Journal of the Experimental Analysis of Behavior, 27,* 419–431.

Dollard, J., & Miller, N. E. (1950). *Personality and psychotherapy.* New York: McGraw-Hill.

Doyle, T. A., & Samson, H. H. (1988). Adjunctive alcohol drinking in humans. *Physiology and Behavior, 27,* 419–431.

Falk, J. L. (1961a). Production of polydipsia in normal rats by an intermittent food schedule. *Science, 133,* 195–196.

Falk, J. L. (1961b). The behavioral regulation of water-electrolyte balance. In M. R. Jones (ed.), *Nebraska symposium on motivation,* 1–33. Lincoln: University of Nebraska Press.

Falk, J. L. (1967). Control of schedule-induced polydipsia: Type, size, and spacing of meals. *Journal of the Experimental Analysis of Behavior, 10,* 199–206.

Falk, J. L. (1969). Conditions producing psychogenic polydipsia in animals. *Annals of the New York Academy of Sciences, 157,* 569–593.

Falk, J. L. (1971). The nature and determinants of adjunctive behavior. *Physiology and Behavior, 6,* 577–588.

Falk, J. L. (1977). The origin and functions of adjunctive behavior. *Animal Learning and Behavior, 5,* 325–335.

Falk, J. L. (1981). The environmental generation of excessive behavior. In S. J. Mulé (ed.), *Behavior in excess: An examination of the volitional disorders,* 313–337. New York: Macmillan.

Falk, J. L. (1984). Excessive behavior and drug-taking: Environmental generation and self-control. In P. K. Levison (ed.), *Substance abuse, habitual behavior, and self-control,* 81–123. Boulder: Westview Press.

Falk, J. L. (1986). The formation and function of ritual behavior. In T. Thompson & M. D. Zeiler (eds.), *Analysis and integration of behavioral units,* 335–355. Hillsdale, N.J.: Erlbaum.

Falk, J. L. (1993). Schedule-induced drug self-administration. In F. von Haaren (ed.), *Methods in behavioral pharmacology,* 301–328. Amsterdam: Elsevier.

Falk, J. L. (1994). Schedule-induced behavior in humans: A reply to Overskeid. *The Psychological Record, 44,* 45–62.

Falk, J. L., & Feingold, D. A. (1987). Environmental and cultural factors in the behavioral action of drugs. In H. Y. Meltzer (ed.), *Psychopharmacology: The third generation of progress,* 1503–1510. New York: Raven Press.

Falk, J. L., Tang, M., & Forman, S. (1977). Schedule-induced chronic hypertension. *Psychosomatic Medicine, 39,* 252–263.

Flory, R. K. (1969). Attack behavior as a function of minimum inter-food interval. *Journal of the Experimental Analysis of Behavior, 12,* 825–828.

Flory, R. K., & Everist, H. D. (1977). The effect of a response requirement on schedule-induced aggression. *Bulletin of the Psychonomic Society, 9,* 383–386.

Foster, W. S. (1978). Adjunctive behavior: An under-reported phenomenon in applied behavior analysis? *Journal of Applied Behavior Analysis, 11,* 545–546.

Frederiksen, L. W., & Peterson, G. L. (1974). Schedule-induced aggression in nursery school children. *The Psychological Record, 24,* 343–351.

Freud, S. (1930/1961). *Civilization and its discontents.* New York: Norton.

Gentry, W. D. (1968). Fixed-ratio schedule-induced aggression. *Journal of the Experimental Analysis of Behavior, 11,* 813–817.

Goffman, E. (1967). *Interaction ritual.* Garden City, N.Y.: Anchor Books.

Grant, K. A., & Johanson, C. E. (1988). The nature of the scheduled reinforcer and adjunctive drinking in nondeprived rhesus monkeys. *Pharmacology, Biochemistry and Behavior, 29,* 295–301.

Grant, K. A., & Johanson, C.-E. (1990). The generation of adjunctive behavior under conditions of drug self-administration. *Behavioural Pharmacology, 1,* 221–234.

Hollis, J. H. (1973). "Superstition": The effects of independent and contingent events on free operant responses in retarded children. *American Journal of Mental Deficiency, 77,* 585–596.

Hutchinson, R. R., Azrin, N. H., & Hunt, G. M. (1968). Attack produced by intermittent reinforcement of a concurrent operant response. *Journal of the Experimental Analysis of Behavior, 11,* 489–485.

Iwata, B. A., Dorsey, M. F., Slifer, K. J., Bauman, K. E., & Richman, G. S. (1982). Toward a functional analysis of self-injury. *Analysis and Intervention in Developmental Disabilities, 2,* 3–20.

Kachanoff, R., Leveille, R., McLelland, J. P., & Wayner, M. J. (1973). Schedule induced behavior in humans. *Physiology and Behavior, 11,* 395–398.

Kazdin, A. E. (1982). *Single-case research designs: Methods for clinical and applied settings.* New York: Oxford University Press.

Kelly, J. F., & Hake, D. F. (1970). An extinction-induced increase in an aggressive response with humans. *Journal of the Experimental Analysis of Behavior, 14,* 153–164.

Killeen, P. (1975). On the temporal control of behavior. *Psychological Review, 82,* 89–115.

Knutson, J. F. (1970). Aggression during the fixed-ratio and extinction components of a multiple schedule of reinforcement. *Journal of the Experimental Analysis of Behavior, 13,* 221–231.

Levitsky, D., & Collier, G. (1968). Schedule-induced wheel running. *Physiology and Behavior, 3,* 571–573.

Looney, T. A., & Cohen, P. S. (1982). Aggression induced by intermittent positive reinforcement. *Neuroscience and Biobehavioral Reviews, 6,* 15–37.

Looney, T. A., & Dove, L. D. (1978). Schedule-induced attack as a function of length of exposure to a fixed-time 90-sec schedule. *Bulletin of the Psychonomic Society, 12,* 320–322.

Lydersen, T. (1992). Timeout induced by differential reinforcement of low rate schedules. *Behavioural Processes, 28,* 1–12.

Lydersen, T. (1994). Schedule-induced timeout: Effects of timeout-contingent delayed reinforcement. *Behavioural Processes, 31,* 323–336.

Lydersen, T., Perkins, D., Thome, S., & Lowman, E. (1980). Choice of timeout during response-independent food schedules. *Journal of the Experimental Analysis of Behavior, 33,* 59–76.

Lyon, D. O., & Turner, L. (1972). Adjunctive attack and displacement preening in the pigeon as a function of ratio requirement for reinforcement. *The Psychological Record, 22,* 509–514.

Magyar, R. L., & Malagodi, E. F. (1980). Measurement and development of schedule-induced drinking in pigeons. *Physiology and Behavior, 25,* 245–251.

McCoy, J. F., & Christian, W. P. (1976). Schedule-induced drinking and reinforcement omission. *Physiology and Behavior, 17,* 537–539.

Miller, J. S., & Gollub, L. R. (1974). Adjunctive and operant bolt pecking in the pigeon. *The Psychological Record, 24,* 203–208.

Muller, P. G., Crow, R. E., and Cheney, C. D. (1979). Schedule-induced locomotor activity in humans. *Journal of the Experimental Analysis of Behavior, 31,* 83–90.

Rapoport, J., Ryland, D., & Kriete, M. (1992). Drug treatment of canine acral lick: An animal model of obsessive-compulsive disorder. *Archives of General Psychiatry, 49,* 517–521.

Rayfield, F., Segal, M., & Goldiamond, I. (1982). Schedule-induced defecation. *Journal of the Experimental Analysis of Behavior, 38,* 19–34.

Roper, T. J., Edwards, L., & Crossland, G. (1983). Factors affecting schedule-induced wood-chewing in rats: Percentage and rate of reinforcement, and operant requirement. *Animal Learning and Behavior, 11,* 35–43.

Salter, A. (1961). *Conditioned reflex therapy* (2nd ed.). New York: Capricorn Books.

Seligman, M. E. P. (1975). *Helplessness: On depression development and death.* San Francisco: Freeman.

Sherman, J. A., & Thomas, J. R. (1968). Some factors controlling preference between fixed-ratio and variable-ratio schedules of reinforcement. *Journal of the Experimental Analysis of Behavior, 11,* 689–702.

Sidman, M. (1960). Normal sources of pathological behavior. *Science, 132,* 61–68.

Sicignano (Kupfer), A. (1981). *Examination of the role of the response requirement as a determinant of schedule-induced behavior.* Unpublished master's thesis, University of Florida, Gainesville.

Skinner, B. F. (1948). "Superstition" in the pigeon. *Journal of Experimental Psychology, 38,* 168–172.

Skinner, B. F. (1957). *Verbal behavior.* New York: Appleton-Century-Crofts.

Solomon, R. L. (1980). The opponent-process theory of acquired motivation: The cost of pleasure and the benefits of pain. *American Psychologist, 35,* 691–712.

Tang, M., & Falk, J. L. (1986). Ethanol polydipsic choice: Effects of alternative fluid polydipsic history. *Alcohol, 3,* 361–365.

Tang, M., & Falk, J. L. (1988). Preference history prevents schedule-induced preferential ethanol acceptance. *Alcohol, 5,* 399–402.

Tang, M., Williams, S. L., & Falk, J. L. (1988). Prior schedule exposure reduces the acquisition of schedule-induced polydipsia. *Physiology and Behavior, 44,* 817–820.

Villarreal, J. (1967). *Schedule-induced pica.* Paper read at Eastern Psychological Association, Boston, April.

Vought, J. (1996). [The effects of fixed versus variable activity schedules on inappropriate behavior.] Unpublished raw data.

Wallace, M., & Singer, G. (1976). Adjunctive behavior and smoking induced by a maze solving schedule in humans. *Physiology and Behavior, 17,* 849–852.

Webbe, F. M., DeWeese, J., & Malagodi, E. F. (1974). Induced attack during multiple fixed-ratio, variable-ratio schedules of reinforcement. *Journal of the Experimental Analysis of Behavior, 22,* 197–206.

Weeks, M., & Gaylord-Ross, R. (1981). Task difficulty and aberrant behavior in severely handicapped students. *Journal of Applied Behavior Analysis, 22,* 187–206.

Wieseler, N. A., Hanson, R. H., Chamberlain, T. P., & Thompson, T. (1988). Stereotypic behavior of mentally retarded adults adjunctive to a positive reinforcement schedule. *Research in Developmental Disabilities, 9,* 393–403.

Williams, S. L., Tang, M., & Falk, J. L. (1992). Prior exposure to a running wheel and scheduled food attenuates polydipsia acquisition. *Physiology and Behavior, 52,* 481–483.

Wolpe, J. (1958). *Psychotherapy by reciprocal inhibition.* Stanford, Calif.: Stanford University Press.

Wolpe, J., Salter, A., & Reyna, L. J. (1964). *The conditioning therapies: The challenge in psychotherapy.* New York: Holt, Reinhart & Winston.

Woods, A., Smith, C., Szewczak, M., Dunn, R., Cornfeldt, M., & Corbett, R. (1993). Selective serotonin reuptake inhibition decreases schedule-induced polydipsia in rats: A potential model for obsessive-compulsive disorder. *Psychopharmacology, 112,* 195–198.

Wylie, A. M., Layng, M. P., & Meyer, K. A. (1993). Schedule-induced defecation by rats during ratio and interval schedules of food reinforcement. *Journal of the Experimental Analysis of Behavior, 60,* 611–620.

Wylie, A. M., Springis, R., & Johnson, K. S. (1992). Schedule-induced defecation: No-food and massed-food baselines. *Journal of the Experimental Analysis of Behavior, 58,* 389–397.

CHAPTER 17

LEARNED HELPLESSNESS

J. Bruce Overmier
V. M. LoLordo

The term *"learned helplessness"* has achieved considerable currency in psychology today and is used to describe and account for a wide range of phenomena (see Mikulincer, 1994; Peterson, Maier, & Seligman, 1993). *PsycINFO* includes some 2,000 records under "Learned Helplessness," with the studies ranging across CNS monoamine sensitivity, animal learning, human reactions to selected environmental contingencies, children's learning styles and teacher efficacy constructs, dependency in old age and interventions with Alzheimer's patients, and psychosomatic vulnerability. Just what is learned helplessness, what has given rise to all this interest, and how do these diverse topics all relate to one another? It is these questions we address.

The label "learned helplessness" is properly applied to three scholarly/scientific domains: (1) in reference to the basic phenomena as initially reported by Overmier & Seligman (1967), who

called the phenomena "learned helplessness," (2) the broad theories proposed by Seligman and his associates that extend the conceptualization of the basic phenomenon into an account of human behavior and referred to as the "learned helplessness theory of depression" (Abramson, Seligman, & Teasdale, 1978; Seligman, 1975); and (3) the extensions of the basic research paradigm searching for collateral consequences of the operations initially observed to induce learned helplessness or experiments designed as tests of inferences derived from the theory and best referred to as "learned helplessness *paradigm* research."

This review will reveal some central points that we wish to illustrate: (1) basic psychological research with animals continues to yield novel findings, (2) these findings stimulate new theory, (3) the findings and theory are relevant to clinical phenomena and provide bases for principled understanding and management of clinical phenomena, and (4) all three taken together stimulate new basic research that initiates a new cycle of discovery and application. It is well beyond this review to address the full evidentiary basis for the construct of learned helplessness, its extensions, the underlying mechanisms, or the challenges to any claims. We can but hint at these as we tell the story. But let us begin.

A LITTLE HISTORY

The origin of this research is only very indirectly rooted in concern for clinical phenomena. Rather it rises most directly out of the tenets of the basic two-process theory of avoidance learning proposed by Mowrer (1947) that were being tested in the animal laboratory of Richard Solomon. Now, it is true that Mowrer proposed the two-process theory of avoidance based upon his understanding of classical conditioning of fear and his interests in understanding how fear and anxiety modulate human behaviors, but the theory was in fact illustrated and tested in the arena of animal learning (Mowrer, 1950). The paradox of avoidance learning as Mowrer saw it was how the nonoccurrence of an event could function as a reinforcer. The essence of the two-process account is that avoidance behavior depends first upon a classical conditioning of a fear state that has aversive motivational properties to an antecedent stimulus and then upon instrumental learning of behavior that is reinforced by termination of the elicited fear. Mowrer argued that although these two learning processes in nature normally proceeded sequentially, with the second building on the first, the two processes were in principle separable and independent. And, indeed, Solomon and Turner (1962), using a novel *transfer of control* paradigm, showed that control of an instrumental avoidance response independently trained in response to a visual cue in one apparatus could immediately be transferred to a new auditory stimulus if in another apparatus that auditory stimulus had separately and independently been established as a classically conditioned signal eliciting fear.

The principles of separability and independence can be taken, however, to imply more, for example, that the *order* of the two experiences in the transfer-of-control paradigm is irrelevant. It was this implication that Overmier and Leaf (1965) set out to test by comparing the degree of transfer of control that was observed when the order of experiences was classical conditioning followed by instrumental training as opposed to instrumental avoidance learning followed by classical conditioning. The researchers did observe good transfer of control of the original avoidance behavior to the separately established CS for both orders, but the degree of discriminative performance and persistence of the transferred control were substantially less when the classical conditioning occurred first. Additionally observed but unreported in their published paper because it was noticed only later was that the latencies of the escape response on the initial instrumental escape/avoidance training trials were substantially longer in the group of animals for which the classical conditioning treatment occurred first. So, although the basic tenets of two-process theory were substantially correct insofar as transfer occurring, there were important consequences of inverting the order of events: When classical conditioning occurred first, it somehow proactively interfered with the later instrumental behavior. This raised three questions: What exactly were the consequences? What were the critical features of the classical conditioning that caused these consequences? And, most importantly, what were the broad implications for behavior theory?

THE BASIC PHENOMENON

Overmier guessed that it was the initial experiences with aversive events (electric footshocks) within the aversive classical conditioning that caused the proactive interference, because Brookshire, Littman, and Stewart (1961) and others (e.g., Pearl, Walters, & Anderson, 1964) had shown special persisting effects of prior shocks. This led him to take animals that, by virtue of their being subjects in another experiment asking quite a different experimental question (see

Church, LoLordo, Overmier, Solomon, & Turner, 1966), had been exposed to uncontrollable—the hallmark of USs in classical conditioning—footshocks of somewhat greater number and greater duration than used in the original transfer-of-control experiment. Overmier found that those animals that had had a prior exposure to an extended series of shocks a day before, even in a different environment, simply did not learn an instrumental escape/avoidance task well, if at all.[1] The prior series of stressful shocks impaired the animals' ability to cope with a new stressful challenge.

In their seminal paper, Overmier and Seligman (1967) systematically followed up this observation under a variety of parametric conditions and confirmed that prior exposure to an extended series of uncontrollable aversive events of modest duration dramatically impaired the animals. What they observed was that the previously "traumatized" animals showed three kinds of deficits composing a *syndrome:* (1) the animals failed to reliably initiate escape responses in the presence of shocks—a motivational deficit, (2) they failed to show learning after having experienced a reinforced escape response—an associative or cognitive deficit, and (3) they showed passivity during the shocks—an affective/emotional deficit. Both the nature and the magnitudes of the deficits were dramatic. Overmier and Seligman (1967) characterized this as "learned helplessness."

Following up on a suggestion in the Overmier and Seligman paper, Seligman and Maier (1967) conducted an experiment that involved three groups: an untreated control group, a master group that received shocks that it could escape, and a yoked group that received shocks that were matched in some way to the master group. This design has come to be called the "triadic design" and is now common in this area. Any difference—physiological, behavioral, cognitive, or emotional—that obtains between the master and the yoked groups in a subsequent test is then attributed to operational differences associated with the differences in controllability of the stress. Seligman and Maier found that inescapable shocks resulted in marked deficits in a subsequent escape learning test, but escapable shocks of matched durations did not. Thus, it was the *uncontrollability* of the shocks that was critical; the phenomenon is not merely the result of exposures to aversive, stressful shocks. The phenomenon was quickly perceived as likely to be important, and within a few years, it had been demonstrated in a wide variety of species, including slugs, cockroaches, goldfish, mice, rats, gerbils, cats, dogs, and humans, across dozens of laboratories (see Brown, Davenport, & Howe, 1994; Eisenstein & Carlson, 1996; Maier & Seligman, 1976, for sets of references) and a variety of induction and test conditions (e.g., Altenor, Kay, & Richter, 1977).[2] That this phenomenon is ubiquitous may imply that the underlying mechanism involves cellular processes, and very recent research into the mechanism is consistent with this speculation (Minor, Winslow, & Chang, 1994)

An analysis of the kind of learning that might underlie this learned helplessness phenomenon was provided by Maier, Seligman, and Solomon

---

[1]Although it is not much discussed, it is generally necessary that the duration of the experience be "substantial" for both animals and humans. If it is brief, in animals sometimes facilitation is observed (Anisman & Waller, 1972), while in humans the phenomenon of "reactance" (Wortman & Brehm, 1975) may be observed. But all that is another story.

[2]In virtually all animal studies, the index of learned helplessness-induced interference is impaired escape behavior. This is a stringent criterion, because electric footshocks directly elicit movements. Overmier (1968) showed that the proactive interference was as great or greater and detectable after longer periods of time if one used a pure avoidance task in the second phase. See also Overmier, Patterson, and Wielkiewicz (1980, p. 9 and Fig. 2). In addition, parallel proactive interference phenomena can be detected when appetitive conditions are used in the induction treatment, the test treatment, or both (e.g., Goodkin, 1976; Mineka, Gunnar, & Champoux, 1986). The escape learning task most commonly used in demonstrating learned helplessness in the **rat** is an FR-2 shuttlebox escape response in which the rat must cross from side A to side B and then back to side A to escape. This is because if only a single crossing (FR-1) is used, the inescapably shocked rats do not differ from escapably shocked or unshocked rats in escaping.

(1969) and Seligman, Maier, and Solomon (1971). The researchers proposed that the dogs learned (acquired the belief or expectation) that their responses and shock termination were independent and that this belief generalized to new situations involving shocks or similar events, and perhaps even more broadly than that. This, then, constitutes the learned helplessness hypothesis that, based upon systematic replication of the phenomenon in humans, broad integrative analysis, and clinical intuitions, Seligman (1975) later elaborated into the learned helplessness theory of depression.

LEARNED HELPLESSNESS HYPOTHESIS

Upon its formal presentation (Maier & Seligman, 1976), the learned helplessness hypothesis evoked a storm of rebuttals among learning theorists (e.g., Levis, 1976; see Maier, 1989, for a keen analytic review of this controversy). The controversy arose because (a) a new kind of learning was proposed—learning of independence or zero-contingency relations, and (b) the learning was represented cognitively as an expectation or belief about the responses and outcomes. Both of these challenged then current neobehavioristic metatheory of learning—especially for animals. And despite an enormous amount of generally confirmatory research, there is still some dissatisfaction with the principles embodied in the learned helplessness hypothesis. Moreover, this does not even include the controversy over whether the learned helplessness phenomenon is a model for depression or the concerns over the learned helplessness theory of depression. In all events, these ideas have proved one source of stimulation for research on the determinants of judgments of control, contingency, and causality (e.g., Alloy & Tabachnik, 1984; see Matute and Miller, this book) and of response-outcome expectations (Dickinson & Balleine, 1994) as determiners of behavior.

Controversies

Naturally enough, alternative hypotheses were proposed. These counter-hypotheses focused upon only the first deficit of the syndrome, the response initiation deficit. When hypotheses are pitted experimentally one against the other by committed scholars, resolution often requires detailed arguments about procedure and nuances of data and theory. We do not want to get buried in such here, and so we offer to you only sufficient surface structure for grasping the issues and the flavor of the debates. We do direct you to sources of critical analyses should you want to pursue the issues in more depth.

Physiological

One alternative to the learned helplessness hypothesis of the proactive interference with the phase-two learning of an escape/avoidance response was reductionistic and emphasized a physiological process. Because the learned helplessness phenomenon appeared to be time bound and to dissipate within 48 hours, Miller and Weiss (1969) suggested that it might reflect stress-induced neurochemical depletion and recovery.[3] The idea was that the first-phase treatment depleted neurochemicals critical for the initiation of responses. This neurochemical depletion hypothesis is especially interesting, as it can be viewed in two ways: (1) as an alternative mechanism to that proposed by the learned helplessness hypothesis, or intriguingly, and (2) as a physiological mechanism of learned helplessness —and hence, to the extent that learned helplessness is an account of depression, as a physiological mechanism of depression! After all, surely every instance of learning (or cognition or belief or psychoneurosis) involves some change(s) in physiology (e.g., in animals: Kraemer, Ebert, Lake, & McKinney, 1984; in humans: Pandey, Pandey, Dwivedi, & Sharma, 1995).

A long and important series of experiments was initiated by Weiss (e.g., Weiss, Stone, &

---

[3]Whether in fact the learned helplessness phenomenon dissipates within a relatively short time of 48 to 168 hours is disputed. The observed time course seems to be dependent upon the behavioral index used (e.g., Overmier, 1968) and the history of the animals (Seligman & Groves, 1970).

Harrell, 1970) to test the hypothesis that CNS changes in neurotransmitter levels were causally involved in the learned helplessness phenomenon. The strategy was to replicate in rats the behavioral phenomenon of interference with escape behavior and show that this was exactly paralleled by appropriate changes in brain chemistry and that appropriate alternative manipulations of brain chemistry could either relieve or induce the behavioral effects (see Weiss, Glazer, & Pohorecky, 1976; and Weiss, Goodman, Losito, Corrigan, Charry, & Bailey, 1981, for reviews; see also the interchange between Seligman and Weiss edited by Weinraub and Schulman, 1980). Weiss, his colleagues, and others (e.g., Anisman, 1975) focused upon brain monoamines, and norepinephrine in particular, presumably because motor behavior is dependent upon noradrenergic function (Herman, 1970) and Maynert and Levi (1964) had previously shown that exposure to inescapable shock induces a time-dependent disruption of noradrenergic function—although according to their data, recovery occurs within a few hours.

Using the triadic design of matched triplets of animals (in identical chambers), one of which was trained to escape shocks to the tail and hence had controllable shocks, one of which received identical shocks but uncontrollable—the so-called yoked procedure, and one of which received no shocks, Weiss, et al. did indeed demonstrate that a very long series of intense inescapable shocks results in depletion of norepinephrine (primarily in hypothalamus and locus coeruleus) in the uncontrollably shocked, yoked animals relative to animals that had control and to the unshocked animals, which did not differ. This proved to be an important, seminal finding— that there were significant CNS changes resulting not just from stress but only from uncontrollable stress! Moreover, Weiss et al. showed that if they tested these rats for new escape/avoidance learning at the time when the neurochemicals were low—say 30 minutes after the shocks—the animals were impaired in their performance. They also showed that a drug-induced depletion of central norepinephrine impaired performance in

the absence of prior experience with uncontrollable shocks. Finally, they showed that infusion of a monoamine oxidase inhibitor into locus coeruleus *during* the initial inescapable stress prevented the proactive interference with later coping behavior (Simson, Weiss, Ambrose, & Webster, 1986). Perhaps more important, considering that learned helplessness phenomenon was by this time being proposed as a model for depression, Leshner, Remler, Biegon, and Samuel (1979) showed that if inescapably shocked rats were treated daily for a week *after* the stress with a tricyclic antidepressant that blocks reuptake of norepinephrine and serotonin, the learned helplessness was relieved, while placebo treatment had no such beneficial effect.

Concurrently, Weiss (1968) observed in similar triplets that there were somatic changes that paralleled the CNS and behavioral phenomena: the rats exposed to the uncontrollable shocks, and only those, showed gastric ulcerations—a finding that suggests possible linking of learned helplessness to psychosomatics (see Murison & Overmier, 1993).

The possibility of interrelating physiology, behavior, and perhaps even cognition stimulated substantial continuing research of a variety of sorts. Many studies explored further the links between stress—uncontrollable stress in particular —and monoaminergic function (e.g., Anisman, 1978; Tsuda & Tanaka, 1985). Serotonin was also added to the list of monoamines studied in this stress-helplessness paradigm (Hellhammer, Hintgen, Wade, Shea, & Aprison, 1983; Petty & Sherman, 1983). This is important because when the learned helplessness theory of depression gained currency, this finding of serotonin depletion contributed to the development of specific serotonin reuptake inhibitors (SSRIs, such as Prozac) as treatments for depression.

A major difficulty for the monoamine depletion hypothesis, however, was the issue of temporal pattern. Immediately after uncontrollable shocks, the norepinephrine level is reduced by about 75%, but 24 hours later it is reduced by only 20%, yet the magnitude of the learned helplessness effect is virtually constant over this or longer intervals (Seligman, Rosellini, & Kozak, 1975; Smith, Cohen, & Turner, 1968). That is, the degree of manifest helplessness did not seem to be correlated with the degree of monoamine depletion at the time the testing was initiated. This difficulty was surmounted when it was found that once an animal had experienced sufficient inescapable stress to deplete monoamines, subsequent exposure to a new stressor—one usually inadequate in itself to have such an effect—will institute a new depletion of the monoamines (e.g., Anisman & Sklar, 1979; Petty, Chae, Kramer, & Jordan, 1994)). Indeed, even mere *signals* for uncontrollable stressors were found sufficient to initiate such redepletion (Cassens, Kuruc, Roffman, Orsulak, & Schildkraut, 1981). These findings, then, offer a resolution to the problem of the temporal discrepancies by allowing even moderate test phase stress to initiate monoamine depletion contingent upon having previously experienced depletion caused by severe uncontrollable stress. This appears to be a kind of biochemical "flashback" process, and one cannot help being struck by the possibility that a similar process will mediate the memorial flashbacks common in PTSD, of which depression is a major component.

These findings of redepletion are consistent with the idea that alterations in monoamines underlie the learned helplessness phenomenon. What is not resolved is whether these monoamine levels merely directly disrupt behavior initiation in some mechanistic way or, rather, represent and/or mediate the brain's encoding of the cognition/expectancy of uncontrollability that underlies the learned helplessness hypothesis.

Behavioral

The most common counter-proposal emphasized a behavioral process—that of simple stimulus-response (S→R) incompatibility. The essence of the idea is simply that during the first phase of exposure to the uncontrollable aversive events, some response is learned according to well-accepted S-R principles, and this response occurs in the second phase, interfering with the escape behavior required by the test task (e.g.,

Levis, 1976). Now, in fact, Overmier and Seligman had explicitly addressed this possibility by treating animals in the first phase with a curare-like drug that blocked the myoneural junction, making motor responses impossible and hence making response learning during the first phase quite unlikely. But, apparently, not as unlikely as S-R psychologists thought was the acquiring a belief that two events are independent or uncorrelated (so-called zero-contingency).

An alternative form of the stimulus-response incompatibility hypothesis that the curare experiment does not address is whether the incompatible response learned is one of "inactivity." This possibility, too, had already been addressed by Maier (1970) through a different strategy. In the first phase for one group, Maier actually arranged to train a passive response of "holding still" to escape shocks that was directly incompatible with the later-to-be-learned active escape/avoidance behavior. A second group received matched uncontrollable aversive events. Maier found that only those animals that experienced uncontrollable events persistently failed to learn to escape later while those that had explicitly learned the incompatible response showed some transient interference but ultimately learned to escape as well as the untreated controls! Many critical details of a variety of experiments pro and con the incompatible response hypothesis have been carefully detailed by Maier and Seligman (1976), who concluded that this hypothesis does not account fully for the data. Nonetheless, this incompatible response account persisted (Anisman, deCatanzaro, & Remington, 1978; Glazer & Weiss, 1976)—and persists today (e.g., Anderson, Crowell, Torrez, DePaul, & McEachin, 1995).

Now, there is nothing in the learned helplessness hypothesis that requires that it be the *only* mechanism causing proactive interference. And indeed, one would expect that incompatible responses or holding still, if learned, could cause at least some transient proactive interference with later learning. This makes it all the more surprising that Maier found training to hold still did not yield a lasting effect similar to learned helplessness. On the other hand, some experiments have shown that rats that are trained to hold still for very long times are later very slow to learn an active escape response, indeed slower even than inescapably shocked ones (Anderson, Crowell, Cunningham, & Lupo, 1979). However, as Lo-Lordo (in press) reviews, the current research relating the development of reduced responding across the series of shocks in phase one to the degree of subsequent deficit in learning to escape in phase two fails to provide a definitive account (e.g., Crowell & Anderson, 1979; Lawry, Lupo, Overmier, Kochevar, Hollis, & Anderson, 1978). So the controversy continues, and the facts are being established (Balleine & Job, 1991, versus Prabhakar & Job, in press), but to the learned helplessness theorists, it seems a strained argument.

As is apparent, the counter-hypothesis of an incompatible-response (or incompatible "nonresponding") focuses only on the first—albeit possibly the most dramatic—component deficit of the learned helplessness syndrome, that of failures of response initiation.[4] It generally ignores the other component deficits—the associative/cognitive deficit and the emotional deficit. One way of providing evidence against the incompatible-response hypothesis would be to look at the associative and emotional deficits. In fact, that is what was done; researchers turned from simple unitary escape tasks and began looking at phase-two learning as assessed in choice tasks. This is because such choice tasks use *accuracy* as the dependent measure and, hence, are relatively insensitive to the latency of response initiation and motivational factors that characterize the first deficit.

Rats' choice behavior was studied in a small Y-maze after the rats had previously received uncontrollable shocks or not, according to the triadic design (Jackson, Alexander, & Maier, 1980). The rats' task in this *response* choice test phase was to escape from footshock by making a turn in a particular direction (say left), which resulted in termination of the shock. Choice of turning in the wrong direction required the animal to choose again, and the shock went off only when the rat turned left. The researchers found that the uncontrollably shocked rats learned a correct turning response more slowly, making more errors than the other two groups made, implying a response-outcome associative/cognitive deficit. The differences could not be accounted for in terms of differences in initial accuracy or numbers of successful choices; these were equivalent. Jackson et al. further demonstrated that the response initiation deficit (seen in the shuttlebox as above) and the associative/cognitive deficit in this maze were independent of each other by showing that while the former disappeared after 2 to 3 days, the latter persisted undiminished for at least a week.

Left unresolved as yet is the exact nature of this second form of proactive interference. Is it attributable to reducing the organism's attention to response-produced cues and increasing attention to irrelevant aspects of the test situation (Lee & Maier, 1988)? Alternatively, is it perhaps attributable to reducing the reinforcement efficacy of the response-dependent shock termination? If the latter, does it arise from a disruption of the central reinforcement mechanisms (known to be related to monoaminergic function, e.g., Wise & Rompre, 1989) or from reduced perceived severity of the footshocks being escaped? Or, possibly, all of these are involved.

Indeed, consistent with an attentional mecha-

---

[4]The fact that when only a single crossing (FR-1) is used the inescapably shocked rats do not differ from escapably shocked or unshocked rats in escaping could by itself be taken as evidence against the incompatible-response hypothesis. In addition, however, the commonly used FR-2 task can be seen not only as increasing behavioral demands but also as increasing associative/cognitive complexity (Maier & Testa, 1975; see, Maier 1989). It is uncertain whether this is the reason that learned helplessness appears under the FR-2 contingency or whether it is because of some other correlated feature. For example, if the first crossing does not terminate the shock, the rat is in fact being punished for that response. Hollis and Overmier (1973) demonstrated that dogs exposed to prior uncontrollable shocks are much more sensitive to even brief punishments—an increased sensitivity that is also seen in depressed individuals (Lewinsohn, Lobitz, & Wilson, 1973).

nism, Maier, Jackson, and Tomie (1987) showed that providing extra feedback for each shuttle response to inescapably shocked rats substantially reduced or eliminated the usual learned helplessness. On the other hand, consistent with the alternative of reduced severity, Maier and associates have also shown, using the triadic design, that exposure to uncontrollable shocks does activate an endogenous opioid-based analgesia to a greater degree than does exposure to controllable ones (see Maier, Drugan, Grau, Hyson, MacLennan, Moye, Madden, & Barchas, 1983). Importantly, the uncontrollable shock-induced analgesia can be reinstated by later "mild" stress (Jackson, Coon, & Maier, 1979). One might be tempted to jump at this point to the conclusion that such opioid analgesia "explains" the learned helplessness. However, if this were so, there should be a within-groups correlation between the extent of analgesia and the degree of manifest helplessness, and the two should be modulated similarly by similar physiological interventions. Alas, this is not the case! For example, injections of dexamethasone that block the stress-induced release of ACTH and beta-endorphin from the pituitary. When dexamethasone is given before inescapable shocks, it completely eliminates the long-term analgesia that otherwise results from those shocks, but it has no effect on the escape learning deficit (MacLennan, Drugan, Hyson, Maier, Madden, & Barchas, 1982; Maier, Sherman, Lewis, Terman, & Liebeskind, 1983).

One needs to consider, in contrast to the reduced severity hypothesis, another explanatory possibility. Because the learned helplessness effect is a result of prior uncontrollable aversive experiences, while comparable controllable ones do not have the same effect, some scholars explored the possibility that the uncontrollability renders the experiences more aversive (Mineka, Cook, & Miller, 1984). Many experiments have now confirmed this. So, one might also consider the possibility that the inescapable shock series results in greater fear when the organism is exposed to a later challenge and that this augmented fear impairs learning, performance, or both. Rats that have been inescapably shocked on the previous day are indeed more fearful at the start of escape testing than yoked controls. Moreover, the former group shows a larger increase in fear in response to the first few escapable shocks (e.g., Maier, 1990; Minor, 1990). The positive correlation between increased fear and the escape learning deficit raises the question of whether the former causes the latter. However, again, experiments that measured fear and the shuttlebox escape learning deficit concurrently showed that the two effects can be dissociated (Maier, 1990). Diazepam administered just before the escape learning test reduced both pre-shock and post-shock fear to control levels but had no effect on the escape deficit. On the other hand, the opiate antagonist naltrexone had no effect on fear-induced freezing but wiped out the escape deficit (also see Maier, Grahn, Kalman, Sutton, Wiertelak, & Watkins, 1993; Minor, Chang, & Winslow, 1994). Thus, the more intense fear in the test situation resulting from prior inescapable shocks appears neither necessary nor sufficient for the shuttlebox escape deficit.

Conceptual

One point is clear from discussions of the different deficit symptoms of the learned helplessness phenomenon: the symptoms are not always highly correlated. For example, one can observe an associative/cognitive deficit in the absence of a motivational deficit (e.g., Maier & Minor, 1993; we also note that in depression, as well, not all symptoms co-occur). Such dissociations may occur only under special circumstances, but they nonetheless have important implications for the learned helplessness hypothesis that invokes a single mediating state as the cause of a multidimensional learned helplessness syndrome (singular). The dissociations clearly imply that there are at least partially independent symptoms. How are we to understand this?

One possibility is that the learned mediating state is itself multidimensional. Overmier (1985) proposed exactly this based upon a reanalysis of the helplessness induction procedures. He noted that not only are the shocks uncontrollable but also the *onsets* of the shocks are commonly unpredictable. This suggested that perhaps, just as one could learn independence between responses and outcomes (and believe that responses are irrelevant), one could learn independence between signal events and the occurrences of hedonically important events (and believe that potential signals are irrelevant). These two kinds of relations are operationally independent. An example is that in classical conditioning, a CS predicts the US, but the US is uncontrollable. On this view, one might expect the two operational dimensions to have different loci of effect and to induce different kinds of deficits. This possibility is illustrated in Figure 17–1.

One implication of the conceptualization in Figure 17–1 is that manipulation of degree of predictability could modulate test task performance in particular ways. In the basic learned helplessness phenomenon, external predictability of shock onsets is held constant and low, while the degree of controllability is varied, thus revealing a deficit symptom that is reflected substantially in response initiation and response-outcome learning. But imagine holding constant and low the degree of controllability and varying the degree of predictability of onsets. This should reveal a deficit symptom that is reflected substantially in stimulus-response and/or stimulus-stimulus associative learning. Using a triadic design modified for manipulation of degree of predictability, it was demonstrated that animals preexposed to a series of *unpredictable* uncontrollable shocks learned a conditional discriminative choice avoidance task slower than those preexposed to *predictable* uncontrollable shocks —just as suggested by Figure 17–1 (Overmier & Wielkiewicz, 1983). The groups did not differ on the response initiation components of the task, just on the accuracy. (It remains to be seen whether similar results would be obtained in a simple choice task like a *T*-maze.)

Perhaps the most pure assessment for stimulus-stimulus associative learning is classical conditioning, and this too is impaired by prior exposure to a treatment of explicitly unrelated CSs and USs, relative to periodic USs only or no CSs or USs, even when the CSs are different from those used in the final classical conditioning test (Dess & Overmier, 1989; Linden, Savage, & Overmier, 1997). This kind of *general*

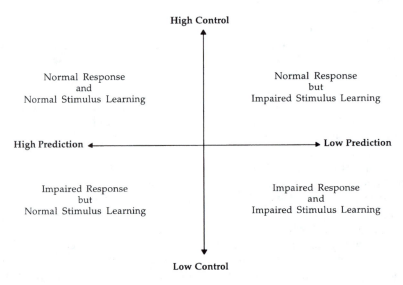

Figure 17–1. Dimensional space for contingencies and its relation to response and stimulus learning

learned irrelevance interfering with later associative classical conditioning involving different CSs could be seen as an exact analog phenomenon to *general* learned helplessness interfering with later instrumental training with different responses.

The proposal to treat controllability and predictability as separate orthogonal dimensions gains support from a number of other experiments. For example, when controllability and predictability of shocks are manipulated independently and the effects measured in terms of experienced stress as indexed by amount of circulating corticosterone either during the shock series or later in a signaled-escape test task, the two factors both reduced stress but had different loci of effect. Only controllability reduced stress during the shock series, and only prior predictability reduced stress in the signaled-escape test task (Dess, Linwick, Patterson, & Overmier, 1983; see Mineka & Henderson, 1985, for a review of related work).

Although controllability and predictability are operationally independent, they may not always be conceptually independent—especially as regards the ending of aversive events. For example, one possible reason that controllable shocks do not have the same effects as uncontrollable ones is that it is possible to conceive of the response (or its feedback) as a signal for a period free from shock—a so-called safety signal (see Moscovitch & LoLordo, 1968). Hence, it could be that responses have their effect not through some construct of controllability but rather through predictability of a period free from shock. Indeed, there are empirical demonstrations that stimuli presented at the end of inescapable shocks serve to reduce the effective severity of those shocks just as would responses (e.g., Overmier, Murison, Skoglund, & Ursin, 1985), a result that increases the viability of the argument.

The question of how control exerts its influence has stimulated extensive research and theorizing on the modulators of conditioning of fear (e.g., in animals: Anderson, Crowell, Torrez, DePaul, & McEachin, 1995; Minor, Trauner, Lee, & Dess, 1990; see Minor, Dess, & Overmier, 1991, for an analysis; in humans: Averill, 1973; Miller, 1980).

One line of research motivated by the question involved experiments in which backward CSs, which began when shocks ended and lasted for a few seconds, were added to the inescapable shocks in an effort to mimic the effects of an escape contingency. This treatment at least partially attenuated the deficit in subsequent escape learning (Maier & Warren, 1988; Volpicelli, Ulm, & Altenor, 1984). However, exposure to inescapable shocks followed by backward CSs did not mimic another effect of exposure to escapable shocks—the ability to immunize the animal against the effects of subsequent inescapable shocks (Maier & Warren, 1988). The argument that the effects of adding escapability can be mimicked by adding a stimulus took a new turn when Minor, Trauner, Lee, and Dess (1990) examined the effects of cessation signals, that is, stimuli that are present only during the last few seconds of each shock and thus might come to signal the end of shock. The addition of cessation signals to inescapable shocks partially alleviated the escape learning deficit and also produced some immunization against the effects of subsequent inescapable shocks. The effects of such signals upon choice learning deficits are yet to be studied. Such an experiment could have important implications for the mechanisms of the a sociative/cognitive deficit.

THE LEARNED HELPLESSNESS THEORY OF DEPRESSION

Empirical demonstrations of the learned helplessness phenomenon in humans were sought within a few years of the first published reports in animals. The first phase "inducing" treatments in them used uncontrollable shocks and noises and, as conceptual analogues, unsolvable problems. The tests, too, varied from simple escape tasks to solving anagrams. Essentially, the same "learned helplessness" phenomenon was observed: prior exposure to uncontrollable and unsolvable tasks interfered with later successful performances on new, different tasks (e.g., Hiroto & Seligman

1975). In overview, given appropriate design and procedures, the learned helplessness effect in humans is a substantial and reliable effect (see Villanova & Peterson, 1991).

One might here critically comment that the effects seen in laboratory experiments with humans seem rather more modest than should be the case for something that we wish to expand into a theory for a psychopathology. But in response, we reply that it is in fact rather remarkable—and indeed a tribute to the devastating power of experiencing uncontrollable and unpredictable events—that the 1- to 2-hour experiments reveal any effects at all, especially given that (1) the experiments are typically conducted with students who have a remarkable amount of prior sustained response-dependent-outcome experience that might immunize them against the laboratory manipulations, and (2) the participants are commonly instructed (by law in the USA) that they may leave the experiment without penalty at any time—that is, *they retain ultimate control throughout,* which subverts the principal condition for the experience of "uncontrollability"! Having this possibility of ultimate control is in fact known to dramatically reduce the impact of the arranged uncontrollability (Geer, Davison, & Gatchel, 1970; Miller, 1980; see Peterson, Maier, & Seligman, 1993, for a discussion of the difficulties in instantiating in human subjects those conditions explored in the animal model). Nonetheless, it is clear that essentials of the basic behavioral phenomena demonstrated in animals find their parallels in humans—and that the participants also reported alterations in feelings and mood. It was from these parallels, then, that a basis for a learned helplessness theory of depression emerged.

Reviewing numerous similarities between the operational/behavioral features of the learned helplessness phenomenon seen in animals and causal/symptomatic features of "reactive" depression led Seligman (1974) to propose that learned helplessness in animals might serve as a model for reactive depression in humans. Seligman's analysis followed four lines of evidence: (1) behavioral and physiological symptoms, (2)

etiology, (3) cure, and (4) prevention. Careful attention to the nature of the modeling process, the formal structure of models, and the rules of evidence in models is critical to such an evaluation (see Overmier & Patterson, 1988, for a presentation), and Seligman generally adhered to these rules. The process was made difficult because with respect to each of the four lines of evidence, not every instance of either learned helplessness or depression manifests the full array of possible features. For one example, consider the "characteristics" of depression; depression has a long list of symptoms—a constellation of motor retardation, low responsiveness, anhedonia overlaid with a general sadness, anorexia, disturbed sleep, negative cognitive set, reduced aggression, and so on—consistent with the diagnosis but none of which is critical to the diagnosis.

Numerous similarities or analogies can be noted between the learned helplessness phenomenon and depression (e.g., both typically show reduced behavioral output in the face of challenge) and several parallels can be noted between causal processes (e.g., monoamine restoration or ECS treatment produce symptom relief); some of them are shown in Table 17–1.

One important feature of the modeling process emphasized by Seligman was that relations empirically known in one domain but as yet uninvestigated in the other constituted hypotheses for future research to test. Indeed, this very strategy has been—and continues to be—highly productive of new research with both animals (e.g., Dorworth & Overmier, 1977; Overmier, Murison, Taklo, & Esplid, 1994) and humans (e.g., Hiroto, 1974).

Seligman's (1974) initial insights were later amplified and expanded in his intuitive 1975 book, *Helplessness: On Depression, Development and Death,* recently reissued. It is this book to which one should turn to get a sense of the analytic style of its author and a perspective on the range of applications Seligman saw for the learned helplessness theory of depression. And in a very real sense, as seen in the nearly 2,000 technical articles and chapters on learned helplessness in the *PsycINFO* database, Seligman's

Table 17–1. Some Parallels Between Learned Helplessness and Depression

CAUSAL FACTORS	HELPLESSNESS UNCONTROLLABLE TRAUMA	DEPRESSION UNCONTROLLABLE NEGATIVE LIFE EVENTS
Symptoms		
• Behavioral	Response initiation deficit	Unresponsiveness, psychomotor retardation
• Cognitive	Associative deficit Reinforcement ineffective	Disrupted thinking
		Negative expectations Sadness
	Attentional shifts Emotional passivity Augmented recall of aversive events Reduced aggression Reduced food intake	Emotionally flat Ruminations Anorexia
• Physiological	NE depletions Dexamethasone nonsuppression	Monoamine dysfunction Dexamethasone nonsuppression
Treatments	Antidepressants ECT Forced escape Time	Antidepressants ECT Behavioral efficacy training Time

vision has been validated. However, one should not be lulled into thinking that all research has been confirmatory or that the learned helplessness theory has been accepted by all. Indeed, serious criticisms both empirical and conceptual have been posed (e.g., Costello, 1978; Linden, 1988). And Seligman and his associates have responded with revisions of the theory (e.g., Abramson, Seligman, & Teasdale, 1978).

The original learned helplessness theory of depression was formally identical to the learned helplessness hypothesis of the animal phenomenon, with some shifts in language to accommodate the differences between the lives of humans and the lives of other animals and the fact that humans can report their feelings. Serial combinations of personal experiences such as loss of job as a result of corporate takeover, accidental death of a child or spouse, loss of one's house by fire, being forced to move to a new, strange city — or other combinations of such events over

which one seemingly has little control—may lead individuals to perceive that one is powerless and doomed and that nothing one tries can change one's deteriorating world for the better as additional threats loom. The resulting cognitive state, a feeling of "nothing I try seems to matter," can be anticipated to interfere with future efforts to meet the challenges of the now poorer-quality life, to interfere with learning new coping skills, and to produce persistent feelings of sadness/crying, loss of interest in sex, weight loss, and increased susceptibility to flu or other illness that in turn amplifies the inability to feel well and/or to function constructively—in short, reactive depression. That is, sufficient exposure to uncontrollable events (typically aversive but not necessarily—indeed, Seligman mentions "success depression") leads to an altered set of expectations about self-efficacy that impair later coping in the face of challenge. Of course, some individuals may be more vulnerable than others because of either their genetic makeup (perhaps in pituitary-adrenal reactivity; e.g., Gulley & Nemeroff, 1991) or their past personal history of success or failure experiences. But it is the case that a substantial percentage of depressive episodes can in fact be traced to a set of life disruptions as suggested (Holmes & Rahe, 1967; Paykel et al., 1969; see Anisman & Zacharko, 1982, and Paykel & Hollyman, 1984, for overviews from different perspectives).

Upon presentation of the theory, practitioners had two reactions: (1) a sense of fresh perspectives and new insights and (2) a sense of concern that the theory missed the essence of depression. The theory offered new perspectives on cognitive therapy and indeed suggested new variations and themes to be developed in the course of the therapy, themes emphasizing ability to control events and the restricted contexts of prior failures and losses. It suggested that a behavioral treatment of "putting through"—guiding the client in achieving behavioral success—and reinforcing active behaviors (e.g., Burgess, 1969) could be therapeutic, as had been demonstrated in animals (Seligman, Marer, & Geer, 1968; Williams & Maier, 1977). That helpless animals showed alterations in monoamine status made clear to practitioners *why* monoamine oxidase inhibitors and tricyclic antidepressants, which also modulate monoamine status, were useful adjuncts to therapy. Indeed, helplessness-like animal paradigms have become standard screening models for new antidepressant drugs (e.g., Henn, Edwards, & Anderson, 1986; Katz & Sibel, 1982; Porsolt, 1989) and in combination with study of the cellular mechanisms of learned helplessness in animals may yield new classes of drug treatments as well (Minor, Chang, & Winslow, 1994).

What were the concerns? One was that the learned helplessness theory of depression seemed to restrict itself to one form of depression—reactive depression—while ignoring so-called endogenous depression. But data suggest that all forms of depression may be related to negative life events and that the distinction between endogenous and reactive depressions, rather than

being truly qualitative, may be more a reflection of degree of genetically determined functional disturbance or hyper-reactivity in a neurochemical system (see Paykel & Hollyman, 1984). Thus, it might be better to think of two dimensions, one of biologically induced vulnerability and the other of environmental-contingency-induced vulnerability (Lloyd, 1980a, 1980b), both of which vary over time so that when the combination exceeds some threshold, a depressive episode ensues. This stress X diathesis concept is illustrated in Figure 17–2. (See Banks & Kerns, 1996; Bebbington, 1987; Pucilowski, Overstreet, Rezvani, & Janowski, 1993, for an empirical illustration of the relation in animals, and Monroe & Simons, 1991, for analysis of stress-diathesis modeling.)

A second concern was that as originally presented, the theory predicted that whenever persons experienced an appropriate series of uncontrollable events, they should develop cognitions and expectancies of uncontrollability, and these in turn should induce the syndrome of deficits in performance, learning, and emotions. Yet, it is observed that similar uncontrollable traumatic experiences differ in their consequences across individuals. They differ in (a) whether the objective uncontrollability induces perceptions of uncontrollability and (b), even if it does induce such perceptions, whether some form of helplessness ensues. The latter could be accounted for by the stress X diathesis hypothesis.

Alternatively, the differential consequences may be attributable to individual differences in cognitions—which may or may not be rooted in biological differences. For example, even when events are uncontrollable, normal people are biased toward perceiving that they have more control than they do, at least for some period (Alloy & Abramson, 1979), and such "illusions of control" are known to have functional value in reducing stress (Geer, Davison, & Gatchel, 1970). Such biases—positive or negative—can be learned over time, even by animals (e.g., Alloy & Ehrman, 1981). Or, individuals may correctly perceive that they have no control at a given moment but do not consider it a personal failure and

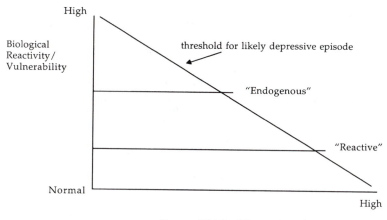

Figure 17–2. Illustration of the possible interaction of sources of vulnerability and levels of on each as predictors of likelihood of depressive episode. There are also implications for optimal treatment access via drug or behavioral manipulation in terms of which is initially closer to baseline (normal).

hence do not internalize it. Or, even if they do internalize it, they may not see it as either a lasting situation or generally representative of their world. These possibilities were addressed by revising the learned helplessness theory of depression to incorporate biases and attributions as intermediate cognitive stages in the development of the act-outcome expectancies that underlie the learned helplessness phenomenon (Abramson, Seligman, & Teasdale, 1978; see Abramson, Metalsky, & Alloy, 1989, for even further refinements, although the following comments generally apply to it as well). A representation of the reformulated conception is presented in Figure 17–3.

In essence, Abramson et al. argued that whether or not particular experienced environmental contingencies induced learned helplessness depended upon (a) perceptions that may or may not be veridical *plus,* critically, (b) the causal attributions that the individual makes about the perceived situation. They argued that for a state of learned helplessness to ensue, the individual had

to make the attributions that (1) the perceived uncontrollability was due to their own inability/failing ("internal"), (2) their inability would persist ("stable"), and (3) it was a general characteristic for everything in their life ("global") — a pessimistic attributional style. Thus, the particular pattern of causal attributions could well account for variations in patterns of symptoms or any degree of functional impairment, task or situation-limited impairment, or even no impairment at all. This reformulated theory of learned helplessness could even account for how an experience of control-misperceived as one of no control—could result in an outcome of learned helplessness!

Indeed, this potential for predicting varied outcomes is exactly the problem for this reformulated theory: it breaks the direct causal link between objective experience and empirical outcomes. Thus, in the absence of rather explicit knowledge about the cognitive processes underlying perceptual biases, perceptions, and each of the causal attributions, one can no longer make

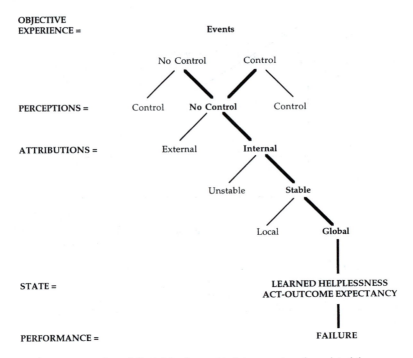

Figure 17–3. "Causal Chain" for learned helplessness in reformulated theory

scientific predictions, while the opportunity for clinically based insights is opened wide. This is not to suggest that the reformulation is in any way inappropriate or unscientific. It is likely that the reformulated theory does better capture the clinical realities, but it also poses new challenges to scholars.

The reformulated theory directs research in wholly new directions. Now, before one can assess the validity of the learned helplessness theory of depression, one first needs to develop methods for identifying, specifying, and measuring a variety of hypothesized cognitive states and to identify and specify the modulators of the cognitive processes that lead to these states. That is, in essence, what is needed is a developed science of the causes of the causal attributions! Also needed is an account of how these attributions determine the behavioral, associative, and emotional symptoms that compose the syndrome

we began with. It is no easy task, but it is exciting for some to pursue. The initial urge is merely to ask the individuals about these things, but we know that such reports—at least about causes and processes, if not about states—are notoriously suspect (e.g., Nisbett & Wilson, 1977). Nonetheless, somehow, ask we must. Most scholars involved in the task are wary of the all too subtle difficulties.

Importantly, this new direction was not an unexplored direction. Rotter, for example, had already proposed the construct "locus of control" (internal versus external) as a learned expectational state that modulates behavior and illustrated techniques for assessing such constructs and their role in behavior (see Lefcourt, 1966). One should not jump quickly here on the basis of common words to identify Rotter's construct as the internal-external causal attribution of the reformulated learned helplessness theory of depression, although the two surely are related. The point here is merely to note that the new research demanded by the reformulated learned helplessness theory of depression has models to guide it.

Experiments have been pursued with the goal of demonstrating that after objective experiences, the particular set of attributions made by an individual can be related to the individual's later performances in other tasks (e.g., Alloy, Peterson, Abramson, & Seligman, 1984). Global, "pessimistic" style was predictive of poor performance. The number of such experimental studies is, in fact, limited. However, a number of correlational studies reliably relate the pessimistic attributional style to reported symptoms of depression (see Sweeney, Anderson, & Bailey, 1986).

The specific pattern of three causal attributions made also seems to be generally characteristic of the individual such that individuals might be characterized as having particular attributional styles—a higher-order construct. These characteristic styles are actually manifest in the ways individuals explain both situations and their behavior in them. In fact, Peterson and Seligman (1984) called this integrated construct "explanatory style" and devised reasonable, reliable, stable ways of assessing it (e.g., Peterson, Semmel, von Baeyer, Abramson, Metalsky, & Seligman, 1982).

Given where all this research started, explanatory style appears to be at least as important as the objective experiences of the individuals. Explanatory style has been related not only to risk for depression (Peterson & Seligman, 1984), as would be expected from the reformulated theory, but also to outcomes ranging from social/business/competitive performance (Peterson, 1990; Seligman & Schulman, 1986) to risk for physical illness (Peterson, 1988). Does this mean that the objective experiences so prominent in the animal model play little or no role in the human depression? No, not at all (e.g., Robins & Block, 1989). Indeed, explanatory style is but one risk factor; physiological/biological status (possibly, genetically biased) is another (Depue,

1979), and recent experiences are still another (Paykel & Hollyman, 1984). Importantly, the organism's longer-term cumulative life history experiences certainly are at least partial determiners of both causal attributional/explanatory style (Dweck, Goetz, & Strauss, 1980; Jackson & Tessler, 1984) and biological status (Kraemer, 1988). This, then gives the cumulative life experiences a double role. In the long term, these experiences contribute to the shaping of causal attributions and explanatory style and to biological vulnerability (Lloyd, 1980a), while in the short term, they provide the environmental challenge (Lloyd, 1980b; Paykel, 1983) that may serve as the precipitating events for the reactive depression for which learned helplessness is a model.

One of the important extensions of this line of work on learned helplessness is to look beyond the global/pessimism-failure relation to a global/optimism-success relation. This obverse of learned helplessness has been dubbed "learned optimism" (Seligman, 1991) or "learned mastery," and, intriguingly, it, too, has antecedents in the animal literature (Volpicelli, Ulm, Altenor, & Seligman, 1983). Attention to this obverse phenomenon may in fact make positive contributions to solving numerous social problems and aid us in making our children competent and resilient to the myriad negative influences threatening their future as productive citizens (Chicchetti & Garmezy, 1993; Dweck & Licht, 1980; Garmezy & Masten, 1986).

REFERENCES

Abramson, L. Y., Seligman, M. E. P., & Teasdale, J. (1978). Learned helplessness in humans: Critique and reformulation. *Journal of Abnormal Psychology, 87,* 49–74.

Abramson, L. Y., Metalsky, G., & Alloy, L. B. (1989). Hopelessness depression: A theory-based subtype of depression. *Psychological Review, 96,* 358–372.

Alloy, L. B., & Abramson, L. Y. (1979). Judgment of contingency in depressed and nondepressed students: Sadder but wiser? *Journal of Experimental Psychology: General, 108,* 441–485.

Alloy, L. B., & Ehrman, R. N. (1981). Learning about response reinforcer contingencies affects subsequent acquisition of stimulus reinforcer contingencies. *Learning & Motivation, 12,* 109–132.

Alloy, L. B., Peterson, C., Abramson, L. Y., & Seligman, M. E. P. (1984). Attributional style and the generality of learned helplessness. *Journal of Personality and Social Psychology, 46,* 681–687.

Alloy, L. B., & Tabachnik, N. (1984). Assessment of covariation by humans and animals: The joint influence of prior expectations and current situational information. *Psychological Review, 91,* 112–149.

Altenor, A., Kay, E., & Richter, M. (1977). The generality of learned helplessness in the rat. *Learning & Motivation, 8,* 54–61.

Anderson, D. C., Crowell, C. R., Cunningham, C. L., & Lupo, J. V. (1979). Behavior during shock exposure as a determinant of subsequent interference with shuttlebox escape-avoidance learning in the rat. *Journal of Experimental Psychology: Animal Behavior Processes, 5,* 243–257.

Anderson, D. C., Crowell, C. R., Torrez, J., DePaul, M., & McEachin, J. (1995). Punishment intensification and fixed-duration shocks: Nullification with brief pre- or post-treatment shocks. *Psychobiology, 23,* 329–344.

Anisman, H. (1975). Time dependent variations in aversively motivated behaviors: Nonassociative effects of cholinergic and catecholaminergic activity. *Psychological Review, 82,* 359–385.

Anisman, H. (1978). Neurochemical changes elicited by stress: Behavioral correlates. In H. Anisman & G. Bignami (eds.), *Psychopharmacology of aversively motivated behavior,* 119–172. New York: Plenum.

Anisman, H., deCatanzaro, D., & Remington, G. (1978). Escape performance following exposure to inescapable shock: Deficits in motor response maintenance. *Journal of Experimental Psychology: Animal Behavior Processes, 4,* 197–218.

Anisman, H., & Sklar, L. (1979). Catecholamine depletion in mice upon reexposure to stress: Mediation of the escape deficits produced by inescapable shock. *Journal of Comparative & Physiological Psychology, 93,* 610–625.

Anisman, H., & Waller, T. G. (1972). Facilitative and disruptive effect of prior exposure to shock upon subsequent avoidance performance. *Journal of Comparative & Physiological Psychology, 78,* 113–122.

Anisman, H., & Zacharko, R. M. (1982). Depression: The predisposing influence of stress. *Behavioral & Brain Sciences, 5,* 89–137.

Averill, J. R. (1973). Personal control over aversive stimuli and its relation to stress. *Psychological Bulletin, 80,* 286–303.

Balleine, B., & Job, R. F. S. (1991). Reconsideration of the role of competing responses in demonstrations of the interference effect (learned helplessness). *Journal of Experimental Psychology: Animal Behavior Processes, 17,* 270–280.

Banks, S. M., & Kerns, R. D. (1996). Explaining high rates of depression in chronic pain: A diathesis-stress framework. *Psychological Bulletin, 119,* 95–110.

Bebbington, P. (1987). Misery and beyond: The pursuit of disease theories of depression. *International Journal of Social Psychiatry, 33,* 13–20.

Brookshire, K. H., Littman, R. A., & Stewart, C. N. (1961). Residua of shock-trauma in the white rat: A three factor theory. *Psychological Monographs, 75,* No. 10 (Whole No. 514).

Brown, G. E., Davenport, D. A., & Howe, A. R. (1994). Escape deficits induced by a biologically relevant stressor in the slug. *Psychological Reports, 75,* 1187–1192.

Burgess, E. (1969). The modification of depressive behavior. In R. Rubin & C. Franks (eds.), *Advances in behavior therapy, vol. 1 (1968):* 193–200. New York: Academic Press.

Cassens, J., Kuruc, A., Roffman, M., Orsulak, P. J., & Schildkraut, J. J. (1981). Alterations in brain norepinephrine metabolism and behavior induced by environmental stimuli previously paired with inescapable shock. *Behavioural Brain Research, 2,* 387–407.

Chicchetti, D., & Garmezy, N. (1993). Prospects and promises in the study of resilience. *Development & Psychopathology, 5,* 497–502.

Church, R. M., LoLordo, V. M., Overmier, J. B., Solomon, R. L., & Turner, L. H. (1966). Cardiac response to shock in curarized dogs: Effects of shock intensity and duration, warning signal, and prior experience with shock. *Journal of Comparative & Physiological Psychology, 62,* 1–7.

Costello, C. G. (1978). A critical review of Seligman's laboratory experiments on learned helplessness and depression in humans. *Journal of Abnormal Psychology, 87,* 21–31.

Crowell, C. R., & Anderson, D. C. (1979). Shuttle interference effects in the rat depend upon activity during prior shock: A replication. *Bulletin of the Psychonomic Society, 14,* 413–416.

DeCola, J. P., Rosellini, R. A., & Warren, D. A. (1988). A dissociation of the effects of control and prediction. *Learning & Motivation, 19,* 269–282.

Depue, R. A. (ed.) (1979) *The psychobiology of the depressive disorders.* New York: Academic Press.

Dess, N. K., Linwick, D., Patterson, J., & Overmier, J. B. (1983). Immediate and proactive effects of controllability and predictability on plasma cortisol responses to shocks in dogs. *Behavioral Neuroscience, 97,* 1005–1016.

Dess, N. K., & Overmier, J. B. (1989). General learned irrelevance: Proactive effects on Pavlovian conditioning in dogs. *Learning & Motivation, 20,* 1–14.

Dickinson, A., & Balleine, B. (1994). Motivational control of goal directed action. *Animal Learning & Behavior, 22,* 1–18.

Dorworth, T., & Overmier, J. B. (1977). On learned help-lessness: The therapeutic effects of electroconvulsive shocks. *Physiological Psychology, 5,* 355–358.

Dweck, C. S., Goetz, T. E., & Strauss, N. (1980). Sex differ-ences in learned helplessness: IV. An experimental analy-sis and naturalistic study of failure generalization and its mediators. *Journal of Personality and Social Psychology, 38,* 441–452.

Dweck, C. S., & Licht, B. G. (1980). Learned helplessness and intellectual achievement. In J. Garber & M. E. P. Seligman (eds.), *Human helplessness: Theory and appli-cations,* 197–221. New York: Academic Press.

Eisenstein, E. M., & Carlson, A. D. (1996). *A comparative approach to the behavior called learned helplessness.* Manuscript in submission.

Garmezy, N., & Masten, A. S. (1986). Stress, competence, and resilience: Common frontiers for therapist and psy-chopathologist. *Behavior Therapy, 17,* 500–521.

Geer, J., Davison, G. C., & Gatchel, R. J. (1970). Reduction of stress in humans through nonveridical perceived control of aversive stimulation. *Journal of Personality and Social Psychology, 16,* 731–738.

Glazer, H. I., & Weiss, J. M. (1976). Long-term interference effect: An alternative to "learned helplessness." *Journal of Experimental Psychology: Animal Behavior Processes, 2,* 202–213.

Goodkin, F. (1976). Rats learn the relationship between re-sponding and environmental events: An expansion of the learned helplessness hypothesis. *Learning & Motivation, 7,* 382–394.

Gulley, L. R., & Nemeroff, C. B. (1991). The neurobiologi-cal basis of mixed depression-anxiety states. *Journal of Clinical Psychiatry, 54,* 16–19.

Hellhammer, D. H., Hintgen, J. N., Wade, S. E., Shea, P. A., & Aprison, M. H. (1983). Serotonergic changes in specific areas of rat brain associated with activity-stress gastric le-sions. *Psychosomatic Medicine, 45,* 115–122.

Henn, F. A., Edwards, E., & Anderson, D. (1986). Receptor regulation as a function of experience. *NIDA Research Monographs Series,* Monogr. #74, 107–116.

Herman, Z. (1970). The effects of noradrenalin on rats' be-havior. *Psychopharmacologia, 16,* 369–374.

Hiroto, D. S. (1974). Locus of control and learned helpless-ness. *Journal of Experimental Psychology, 102,* 187–193.

Hollis, K. L., & Overmier, J. B. (1973). Effect of inescapable shock on efficacy of punishment of appetitive instrumen-tal responding by dogs. *Psychological Reports, 33,* 903–906.

Holmes, T. H., & Rahe, R. H. (1967). The social readjust-ment scale. *Journal of Psychosomatic Research, 11,* 213–218.

Jackson, M. E., & Tessler, R. C. (1984). Perceived lack of control over life events: Antecedents and consequences in a discharged patient sample. *Social Science Research, 13,* 287–301.

Jackson, R. L., Alexander, J. H., & Maier, S. F. (1980). Learned helplessness, inactivity, and associative deficits: The effects of inescapable shock on response choice es-cape learning. *Journal of Experimental Psychology: Ani-mal Behavior Processes, 6,* 1–20.

Jackson, R. L., Coon, D. J., & Maier, S. F. (1979). Long term analgesic effects of inescapable shock and learned helplessness. *Science, 206,* 91–94.

Katz, R., & Sibel, M. (1982). Animal model of depression: Tests of three structurally and pharmacologically novel antidepressant compounds. *Pharmacology, Biochemistry, & Behavior, 16,* 973–977.

Kraemer, G. W. (1988). Speculations on the developmental neurobiology of protest and despair. In P. Simon, P. Soubrie, & D. Widlocher (eds.), *Animal models of psychi-atric disorders, Vol. 2: An inquiry into schizophrenia and depression,* 110–139. Basel: Karger.

Kraemer, G. W., Ebert, M. H., Lake, C. R., & McKinney, W. T. (1984). Cerebrospinal fluid measures of neurotransmit-ter changes associated with pharmacological alteration of the despair response to social separation in rhesus mon-keys. *Psychiatry Research, 11,* 303–315.

Lawry, J. A., Lupo, V., Overmier, J. B., Kochevar, J., Hollis, K., & Anderson, D. C. (1978). Interference with avoidance behavior as a function of qualitative properties of in-escapable shocks. *Animal Learning & Behavior, 6,* 147–154.

Lee, R. K. K., & Maier, S. F. (1988). Inescapable shock and attention to internal versus external cues in a water escape discrimination task. *Journal of Experimental Psychology: Animal Behavior Processes, 14,* 302–311.

Lefcourt, H. M. (1966). Internal versus external control of re-inforcement: A review. *Psychological Bulletin, 65,* 206–220.

Leshner, A. I., Remler, H., Biegon, & Samuel, D. (1979). The antidepressant desmethylimipramine (DMI) counteracts learned helplessness in rats. *Psychopharmacology, 66,* 207–208.

Levis, D. J. (1976). A reply and an alternative S-R interpre-tation. *Journal of Experimental Psychology: General, 105,* 47–65.

Lewinsohn, P. M., Lobitz, W. C., & Wilson, S. (1973). "Sen-sitivity" of depressed individuals to aversive stimuli. *Jour-nal of Abnormal Psychology, 81,* 259–263.

Linden, D. R., Savage, L. M., & Overmier, J. B. (1997). Gen-eral learned irrelevance: Pavlovian analog to learned help-lessness. *Learning & Motivation, 28,* 230–247.

Linden, M. (1988). Clinical usefulness and limits of the help-lessness model of depression. In P. Simon, P. Soubrie, & D. Widlocher (eds.), *Animal models of psychiatric disor-ders, Vol. 2: An inquiry into schizophrenia and depression,* 203–207. Basel: Karger.

Lloyd, C. (1980a). Life events and depressive disorder reviewed: I. Events as predisposing factors. *Archives of General Psychiatry, 37,* 529–539.

Lloyd, C. (1980b). Life events and depressive disorder reviewed: II. Events as precipitating factors. *Archives of General Psychiatry, 37,* 541–548.

LoLordo, V. M. (in press). Desesperanza aprendida: El estado actual de la investigacion con animales. In A. M. Perez, R. Ardila, W. Lopez, R. Quilones, & F. Reyes (eds.), *Advances in the study of behavior.* Siglo XXI: Madrid (in Spanish).

MacLennan, A. J., Drugan, R., Hyson, R., Maier, S. F., Madden, J., & Barchas, J. D. (1982). Hypophysectomy and dexamethasone block the analgesic but not the shuttlebox escape learning consequences of inescapable shock. *Journal of Comparative & Physiological Psychology, 96,* 904–912.

Maier, S. F. (1970). Failure to escape traumatic electric shock: Incompatible skeletal-motor responses or learned helplessness. *Learning & Motivation, 1,* 157–169.

Maier, S. F. (1989). Learned helplessness: Event covariation and cognitive changes. In S. B. Klein & R. R. Mowrer (eds.), *Contemporary learning theories: Instrumental conditioning theory and the impact of biological constraints on learning.* Hillsdale, N.J.: Erlbaum.

Maier, S. F. (1990). The role of fear in mediating the shuttle escape learning deficit produced by inescapable shock. *Journal of Experimental Psychology: Animal Behavior Processes, 16,* 137–150.

Maier, S. F., Drugan, R., Grau, J. W., Hyson, R., MacLennan, A. J., Moye, T., Madden IV, J., & Barchas, J. D. (1983). Learned helplessness, pain inhibition, and endogenous opiates. *Advances in Analysis of Behavior, 3,* 275–323.

Maier, S. F., Grahn, R. E., Kalmar, B. A., Sutton, L. C., Wiertelak, E. P., & Watkins, L. R. (1993). The role of the amygedala and dorsal raphe nucleus in mediating the behavioral consequences of inescapable shock. *Behavioral Neuroscience, 107,* 377–378.

Maier, S. F., Jackson, R. L., & Tomie, A. (1987). Potentiation, overshadowing, and exposure to inescapable shock. *Journal of Experimental Psychology: Animal Behavior Processes, 13,* 260–270.

Maier, S. F., & Minor, T. R. (1993). Dissociation of interference with the speed and accuracy of escape produced by inescapable shock. *Behavioral Neuroscience, 107,* 139–146.

Maier, S. F., & Seligman, M. E. P. (1976). Learned helplessness: Theory and evidence. *Journal of Experimental Psychology: General, 105,* 3–46.

Maier, S. F., Seligman, R. L., & Solomon, R. L. (1969). Pavlovian fear conditioning and learned helplessness: Effects on escape and avoidance behavior of (a) the CS-US contingency and (b) the independence of US and voluntary responding. In B. A. Campbell & R. N. Church (eds.),

Punishment and aversive behavior, 299–342. New York: Appleton-Century-Crofts.

Maier, S. F., Sherman, J. E., Lewis, J. W., Terman, G. W., & Liebeskind, J. C. (1983). The opioid/nonopioid nature of stress-induced analgesia and learned helplessness. *Journal of Experimental Psychology: Animal Behavior Processes, 9,* 80–90.

Maier, S. F., & Testa, T. J. (1975). Failure to learn to escape by rats previously exposed to inescapable shock is partly produced by associative interference. *Journal of Comparative and Physiological Psychology, 88,* 554–564.

Maier, S. F., & Warren, D. A. (1988). Controllability and safety signals exert dissimilar proactive effects on nociception and escape performance. *Journal of Experimental Psychology: Animal Behavior Processes, 14,* 18–25.

Maynert, E. W., & Levi, R. (1964). Stress release of norepinephrine and its inhibition by drugs. *Journal of Pharmacology & Experimental Therapeutics, 143,* 90–95.

Miller, N. E., & Weiss, J. (1969). Effects of somatic or visceral responses to punishment. In B. A. Campbell & R. M. Church (eds.), *Punishment and aversive behavior,* 343–372. New York: Appleton-Century-Crofts.

Mikulincer, M. (1994). *Human learned helplessness.* New York: Plenum.

Miller, S. (1980) Why having control reduces stress: If I can stop the roller coaster, I don't want to get off. In J. Garber & M.E.P. Seligman (eds.), *Human helplessness: Theory and applications,* 71–95. New York: Academic Press.

Mineka, S. (1985) The frightful complexity of the origins of fears. In F. R. Brush & J. B. Overmier (eds.), *Affect, conditioning, and cognition: Essays on the determinants of behavior,* 55–73. Hillsdale, N.J.: Erlbaum.

Mineka, S., Cook, M., & Miller, S. (1984). Fear conditioned with escapable and inescapable shock: Effects of a feedback stimulus. *Journal of Experimental Psychology: Animal Behavior Processes, 10,* 307–323.

Mineka, S., Gunnar, M., & Champoux, M. (1986). Control and early socioemotional development: Infant rhesus monkeys reared in controllable versus uncontrollable environments. *Child Development, 57,* 1241–1256.

Mineka, S., & Henderson, R. W. (1985). Controllability and predictability in acquired motivation. *Annual Review of Psychology, 36,* 495–529.

Minor, T. R. (1990). Conditioned fear and neophobia following inescapable shock. *Animal Learning & Behavior, 18,* 212–226.

Minor, T. R., Chang, W., & Winslow, J. L. (1994). Stress and adenosine: I. Effect of methylxanthine and amphetamine stimulants on learned helplessness in rats. *Behavioral Neuroscience, 108,* 254–264.

Minor, T. R., Dess, N. K., & Overmier, J. B. (1991). Inverting the traditional view of "Learned Helplessness." In M.

R. Denny (ed.). *Fear, avoidance, and phobias: A fundamental analysis,* 87–134. Hillsdale, N.J.: Erlbaum.

Minor, T. R., Trauner, M. A., Lee, C., & Dess, N. K. (1990). Modeling signal features of escape response: Effects of cessation conditioning in "Learned Helplessness" paradigm. *Journal of Experimental Psychology: Animal Behavior Processes, 16,* 123–136.

Minor, T. R., Winslow, J. L., & Chang, W. (1994). Stress and adenosine: II. Adenosine analogs mimic the effect of inescapable shock on shuttle-escape performance in rats. *Behavioral Neuroscience, 108,* 265–276.

Monroe, S. M., & Simons, A. D. (1991). Diathesis-stress theories in the context of life stress research: Implications for depressive disorders. *Psychological Bulletin, 110,* 406–425.

Moscovitch, A., & LoLordo, V. M. (1968). Role of safety in the Pavlovian backward conditioning procedure. *Journal of Comparative & Physiological Psychology, 66,* 673–678.

Mowrer, O. H. (1947). On the dual nature of learning — A reinterpretation of "conditioning" and "problem solving." *Harvard Educational Review, 17,* 102–148.

Mowrer, O. H. (1950). *Learning theory and personality dynamics.* New York: Ronald Press.

Murison, R., & Overmier, J. B. (1993). Parallelism among stress effects on ulcer, immunosuppression, and analgesia: Commonality of mechanisms? *Journal of Physiology* (Paris), *87,* 253–259.

Nisbett, R. E., & Wilson, T. D. (1977). Telling more than we can know: Verbal reports and mental processes. *Psychological Review, 84,* 231–259.

Overmier, J. B. (1968). Interference with avoidance behavior. *Journal of Experimental Psychology, 78,* 340–343.

Overmier, J. B. (1985). Towards a reanalysis of the causal structure of the learned helplessness syndrome. In F. R. Brush & J. B. Overmier (eds.), *Affect, conditioning, and cognition: Essays on the determinants of behavior,* 211–227. Hillsdale, N.J.: Erlbaum.

Overmier, J. B., & Hellhammer, D. (1988). The learned helplessness model of human depression. In P. Simon, P. Soubrie, & D. Widlocher (eds.), *Animal models of psychiatric disorders, Vol. 2: An inquiry into schizophrenia and depression,* 177–202. Basel: Karger.

Overmier, J. B., & Leaf, R. C. (1965). Effects of discriminative Pavlovian fear conditioning upon previously or subsequently acquired avoidance responding. *Journal of Comparative & Physiological Psychology, 60,* 213–217.

Overmier, J. B., Murison, R., Skoglund, E. J., & Ursin, H. (1985). Safety signals can mimic responses in reducing the ulcerogenic effects of prior shocks. *Physiological Psychology, 13,* 243–247

Overmier, J. B., Murison, R., Taklo, T., & Esplid, R. (1994). Effects of traumatic stress on defensive burying: An alternative test of the learned helplessness model of depression and enhanced retrieval of unpleasant memories. *Biological Psychiatry, 36,* 703–704.

Overmier, J. B., & Patterson, J. (1988). Animal models of human psychopathology. In P. Simon, P. Soubrie, & D. Widlocher (eds.), *Animal models of psychiatric disorders, Vol. 1: Selected models of anxiety, depression, & psychosis,* 1–35. Basel: Karger.

Overmier, J. B., Patterson, J., & Wielkiewicz, R. M. (1980). Environmental contingencies as sources of stress in animals. In S. Levine & H. Ursin (eds.), *Coping and health,* 1–38. New York: Plenum.

Overmier, J. B., & Seligman, M. E. P. (1967). Effects of inescapable shock upon subsequent escape and avoidance learning. *Journal of Comparative & Physiological Psychology, 63,* 28–33.

Overmier, J. B., & Wielkiewicz, R. M. (1983). On unpredictability as a causal factor in learned helplessness. *Learning & Motivation, 14,* 324–337.

Pandey, G., Pandey, S., Dwivedi, Y., & Sharma, R. (1995). Platelet serotonin-2A receptors: A potential biological marker for suicidal behavior. *American Journal of Psychiatry, 152,* 850–855.

Paykel, E. S. (1983). Recent life events and depression. In J. Angst (ed.), *The origins of depression,* 91–106. Heidelberg: Springer.

Paykel, E. S., & Hollyman, J. A. (1984). Life events and depression — A psychiatric view. *Trends in Neuroscience, 7* (12), 478–481.

Paykel, E. S., Myers, J. K., Dienell, M. N., Klerman, G. L., Lindenhal, J. J., Pepper, M. P. (1969). Life events and depression — A controlled study. *Archives of General Psychiatry, 21,* 753–760.

Pearl, J., Walters, G. C., & Anderson, D. C. (1964). Suppressing effects of aversive stimulation on subsequently punished behaviour. *Canadian Journal of Psychology, 18,* 343–355.

Peterson, C. (1988). Explanatory style as a risk factor for illness. *Cognitive Therapy & Research, 12,* 117–130.

Peterson, C. (1990). Explanatory style in the classroom and on the playing field. In S. Graham & V. S. Folkes (eds.), *Attribution theory: Applications to achievement, mental health and interpersonal conflict.* 53–75. Hillsdale, N.J.: Erlbaum.

Peterson, C., Maier, S. F., & Seligman, M. E. P. (1993). *Learned helplessness: A theory for the age of personal control.* New York: Oxford University Press.

Peterson, C., & Seligman, M. E. P. (1984). Causal explanations as a risk factor for depression: Theory and evidence. *Psychological Review, 91,* 347–374.

Peterson, C., Semmel, A., von Baeyer, C., Abramson, L. Y., Metalsky, G. I., & Seligman, M. E. P. (1982). The attributional style questionnaire. *Cognitive Therapy & Research, 6,* 287–299.

Petty, F., Chae, Y-L., Kramer, G., & Jordan, S. (1994). Learned helplessness sensitizes hippocampal norepinephrine to mild stress. *Biological Psychiatry, 35,* 903–908.

Petty, F., & Sherman, A. D. (1983). Learned helplessness induction decreases in vivo cortical serotonin release. *Pharmacology, Biochemistry, & Behavior, 18,* 649–649.

Porsolt, R. D. (1989). Modeles animaux de maladies mentales: Apport de la psychopharmacologie. *Confrontations Psychiatriques, No. 30,* 151–163.

Prabhakar, T., & Job, R. F. S. (1996). The effects of order of shock durations on helplessness in rats. *Animal Learning & Behavior, 24,* 175–182.

Pucilowski, O., Overstreet, D. H., Rezvani, A. H., & Janowski, D. S. (1993). Chronic mild stress-induced anhedonia: Greater effect in genetic rat model of depression. *Physiology & Behavior, 54,* 1215–1220.

Robins, C. J., & Block, P. (1989). Cognitive theories of depression viewed from a diathesis-stress perspective: Evaluations of the models of Beck and Abramson, Seligman, & Teasdale. *Cognitive Therapy & Research, 13,* 297–313.

Seligman, M. E. P. (1874). Depression and learned helplessness. In R. J. Friedman & M. M. Katz (eds.), *The psychology of depression.* Washington, D.C.: Winston.

Seligman, M. E. P. (1975). *Helplessness: On depression, development, and death.* San Francisco: Freeman.

Seligman, M. E. P. (1991). *Learned optimism.* New York: Knopf.

Seligman, M. E. P., & Groves, D. (1970). Non-transient learned helplessness. *Psychonomic Science, 19,* 191–192.

Seligman, M. E. P., & Maier, S. F. (1967). Failure to escape traumatic shock. *Journal of Experimental Psychology, 74,* 1–9.

Seligman, M. E. P., Maier, S. F., & Geer, J. (1968). The alleviation of learned helplessness in the dog. *Journal of Abnormal Psychology, 73,* 256–262.

Seligman, M. E. P., Maier, S. F., & Solomon, R. L. (1971). Unpredictable and uncontrollable events. In F. R. Brush (ed.), *Aversive conditioning and learning,* 347–400. New York: Academic Press.

Seligman, M. E. P., Rosellini, R. A., & Kozak, M. J. (1975). Learned helplessness in the rat: Time course, immunization, and reversibility. *Journal of Comparative & Physiological Psychology, 88,* 542–547.

Seligman, M. E. P., & Schulman, P. (1986). Explanatory style as a predictor of productivity and quitting among life insurance agents. *Journal of Personality and Social Psychology, 50,* 832–838.

Simson, P. G., Weiss, J. M., Ambrose, J., & Webster, A. (1986). Infusion of monoamine oxidase inhibitor into the locus coeruleus can prevent stress induced behavioral depression. *Biological Psychiatry, 21,* 724–734.

Smith, J. A., Cohen, P. S., & Turner, L. M. (1968). Short-term interference effects of inescapable shocks upon acquisition of subsequent escape-avoidance responding. *Proceedings of 76th Annual Convention of the American Psychological Association,* 145–146.

Solomon, R. L., & Turner, L. H. (1962). Discriminative classical conditioning under curare can later control discriminative avoidance responses in the normal state. *Psychological Review, 69,* 202–219.

Stolk, J. M., Conner, R. L., Levine, S., & Barchas, J. D. (1974). Brain norepinephrine metabolism and shock induced fighting behavior in rats: Differential effects of shock and fighting on the neurochemical response to a common footshock stimulus. *Journal of Pharmacology & Experimental Therapeutics, 190,* 193–209.

Sweeney, P. D., Anderson, K., & Bailey, S. (1986). Attributional style in depression: A meta-analytic review. *Journal of Personality and Social Psychology, 50,* 974–991.

Tsuda, A., & Tanaka, M. (1985). Differential changes in noradrenaline turnover in specific regions of rat brain produced by controllable and uncontrollable shocks. *Behavioral Neuroscience, 99,* 802–817.

Volpicelli, J. R., Ulm, R. R., & Altenor, A. (1984). Feedback during exposure to inescapable shocks and subsequent shock-escape performance. *Learning & Motivation, 15,* 279–286.

Volpicelli, J. R., Ulm, R. R., Altenor, A., & Seligman, M. E. P. (1983). Learned mastery in the rat. *Learning & Motivation, 14,* 204–222.

Villanova, P., & Peterson, C. (1991). Meta-analysis of human helplessness experiments. Unpublished manuscript, Northern Illinois University. Cited in Peterson, Maier, & Seligman, 1993.

Weinraub, M., & Schulman, A. (eds.) (1980). Coping behavior: Learned helplessness, physiological change, and learned inactivity—An interchange between Martin E. P. Seligman and Jay Weiss. *Behaviour Research & Therapy, 18,* 457–512.

Weiss, J. (1968). The effects of coping responses on stress. *Journal of Comparative & Physiological Psychology, 65,* 251–260.

Weiss, J. M., Glazer, H. I., & Pohorecky, L. A. (1976). Coping behavior and neurochemical changes: An alternative explanation for the original "learned helplessness" experiments. In G. Serban & A. Kling (eds.), *Animal models in human psychobiology,* 232–269. New York: Plenum.

Weiss, J. M., Goodman, P. A., Losito, B. G., Corrigan, S., Charry, J. M., & Bailey, W. H. (1981). Behavioral depression produced by an uncontrollable stressor: Relationship to norepinephrine, dopamine, and serotonin levels in rats. *Brain Research Reviews, 3,* 167–205.

Weiss, J. M., Stone, E. A., & Harrell, N. (1970). Coping behavior and brain norepinephrine level in rats. *Journal of Comparative & Physiological Psychology, 72,* 153–160.

Weiss, J. M., Sundar, S. K., Becker, K. J., Cierpial, M. A. (1989). Behavioral and neural influences on cellular immune responses: Effects of stress and interlukin-1. *Journal of Clinical Psychiatry, 50,* 43–53.

Williams, J. L., & Maier, S. F. (1977). Transituational immunization and therapy of learned helplessness in the rat. *Journal of Experimental Psychology: Animal Behavior Processes, 3,* 240–252.

Wise, R. A., & Rompre, P-P. (1989). Brain dopamine and reward. *Annual Review of Psychology, 40,* 152–156.

Wortman, C., & Brehm, J. W. (1975). Response to uncontrollable outcomes: An integration of reactance and the learned helplessness model. *Advances in Experimental Social Psychology, 8,* 278–336.

CHAPTER 18

THE APPLIED IMPLICATIONS OF RULE-GOVERNED BEHAVIOR

Steven C. Hayes
Winifred Ju

I felt a Funeral, in my Brain,
And Mourners to and fro
Kept treading—treading—till it seemed
That Sense was breaking through—

And when they all were seated,
A Service, like a Drum—
Kept beating—beating—till I thought
My Mind was going numb—

And I heard them lift a Box
And creak across my Soul
With those same Boots of Lead, again,
The Space—began to toll,

As all the Heavens were a Bell,
And Being, but an Ear,
And I, and Silence, some strange Race
Wreaked, solitary, here—

And then a Plank in Reason, broke,
And I dropped down, and down—
And hit a World, at every plunge,
And Finished knowing—then—
—Emily Dickinson (1830–1886)

Verbal behavior is a dominant aspect of human life. Humans talk to each other and to themselves, they talk both in the presence of and in the absence of an audience, and they talk both overtly and covertly. Education, religion, government, and psychotherapy all largely involve people's altering the behavior of people through language.

People learn both by contacting events first hand and by being told about these events. They change their behavior in the presence of both nonverbal and verbal stimuli. In behavioral terms, we can say that actions can be both contingency-shaped and rule-governed (Skinner, 1969).

Behavior analysts have discovered a number of properties of antecedent verbal stimuli, or "rules," that have important implications for clinicians with respect to the therapeutic strategies they utilize. These findings suggest that rule-governance is not an innocuous procedure—that it has notable properties that indicate times when verbal stimuli should and should not be used to guide clinically significant behavior change.

THE BEHAVIOR ANALYTIC LITERATURE ON RULES: A BRIEF REVIEW OF EMPIRICAL FINDINGS

Two main strategies have been used to assess the relative contributions of verbal stimuli and programmed contingencies to the modification of behavior. The first approach has been to observe the impact of rules on behavior patterns in single schedules of reinforcement (Buskist, Bennett, & Miller, 1981; Buskist & Miller, 1986; Kaufman et al., 1966).

Schedules Are in Part What You Say They Are

Behavior under schedule control is often highly predictable; therefore, alternations from typical patterns can be traced to the effects of verbal stimuli. This strategy was particularly popular in the early behavior analysis work on rules. The fixed interval (FI) schedule was frequently used because it is a well-established finding that adult human FI performance often differs significantly from responding on an FI by other organisms (e.g., Leander, Lippman, & Meyer, 1968; Lippman & Meyer, 1967; Weiner, 1964, 1965, 1969). Nonhumans tend to show "break-and-run" or scalloped patterns when exposed to an FI schedule, while adult humans tend to show either high, steady rates or very low rates of responding. Human infants initially show nonhuman-like performances (Lowe, Beasty, & Bentall, 1983); then, as they grow older, there is a gradual transition to adult performances from approximately age 2 to age 7 (Bentall, Lowe, & Beasty, 1985). In adults, response patterns more like those of nonhumans are produced on an FI when steps are taken to reduce counting, such as requiring concurrent mental math or reading aloud (e.g., Laties & Weiss, 1963; Lowe, Harzem, & Hughes, 1978) or using a response-produced clock (Lowe, Harzem, & Bagshaw, 1978; Lowe, Harzem, & Hughes, 1978).

The basic conclusion derived from this line of research is that humans tend to generate self-rules regarding schedules of reinforcement, and these rules, ultimately, have a role in behavior. For example, adult humans tend to show high, steady rates on an FI when they formulate a rule that specifies *rate* as the relevant variable ("You just need to keep responding and eventually it will work"); and they show very low rates of responding with one or two responses at the end of the interval when *time* is formulated as the relevant variable ("This works every 10 seconds"). Speaking simply, responding to schedules of reinforcement can be in part rule-governed.

Rule-Induced "Insensitivity"

In the second approach, rule-governed behavior is exposed to changes in programmed contingencies of reinforcement, such as occur in multiple schedules (Baron, Kaufman, & Stauber, 1969; Hayes, Brownstein, Zettle, Rosenfarb, & Korn, 1986b), or unannounced period of extinction (Hayes, Brownstein, Haas, & Greenway,

1986a; Shimoff, Catania, & Matthews, 1981). In this case, the relative sensitivity to changes in programmed contingencies is what is at issue.

It turns out that when behavior is controlled by verbal rules, it tends to be relatively insensitive to changes in contingencies that are not contacted by the rule itself, in comparison with behavior that is directly shaped or established by minimal instructions (Hayes et al., 1986; Matthews, Shimoff, Catania, & Sagvolden, 1977; Shimoff et al., 1981; see Catania, Shimoff, & Matthews, 1989, and Hayes, Zettle, & Rosenfarb, 1989 for recent reviews). Instructed subjects (e.g., subjects who were told how to respond to maximize reinforcement) show less behavior change than uninstructed subjects in response to several different types of schedule changes: (a) changes that result in no potential increase in consequence delivery (Shimoff et al., 1981), (b) changes that result in a great potential increase in consequences (Shimoff et al., 1981), (c) changes that allow for a substantial decrease in responding with no change in the rate of consequence delivery (Galizio, 1979), and (d) changes that totally remove all programmed consequences (Hayes et al., 1986; Matthews et al., 1977).

This so-called *insensitivity* effect has excited clinical behavior analysts in part because many forms of clinically significant behavior seem to exemplify the same overall pattern: the persistence of particular patterns of responding persist despite their directly experienced or potential negative consequences. Others have argued that these findings have implications for treatment as well, since many popular forms of clinical intervention rely heavily on rules and thus may inadvertently be establishing therapeutically undesirable forms of insensitivity (e.g., Azrin & Hayes, 1984).

Altering the Range of Behavior

Rule-governed behavior has other attributes as well. Rules can readily alter the range and topography of behavior that is available to contact natural consequences. This property means that some rules can *increase* contact with natural contingencies, while other rules *decrease* such contact. This was first shown by Hayes et al. (1986). Button-presses moved a light through a matrix according to a multiple fixed-ratio (FR = 18)/differential-reinforcement-of-low-rate (DRL 6-seconds) schedule, with components alternating every 2 minutes. Points worth chances on money prizes were awarded for successfully moving the light through the matrix. Subjects were told to "Go fast" when one light was on and to "Go slow" when a different light was on. The presentation of instruction lights was varied within three conditions. In one condition only the Go Fast light was on, in a second only the Go Slow light was on, and in a third the lights alternated each minute (twice as fast as the alternating of schedules). This manipulation ensured that some subjects had a full range of behavior available to contact these two rate-relevant contingencies, while the others had a narrow range of behavior available. In all cases the instruction light within each condition was only accurate half the time, but out of those subjects with instructions that produced a narrow range of behavior, only one of the two schedules was likely to lead to points. After some time being exposed to these conditions, half the subjects had all instruction lights turned off. In general, subjects followed the rules whenever the instruction lights were on. This meant, for example, that subjects shown only the Go Slow light received points on the DRL 6, but not the FR 18. The opposite was true for the Go Fast subjects. But when the instruction lights were turned off, subjects given narrow ranges of behavior continued to show control only by one schedule, while subjects who were presented with the alternating Go Fast–Go Slow instruction lights immediately showed schedule-appropriate behavior in both components. Subjects in the latter condition displayed a wide range of behavior that had contacted the contingencies—when the instructions were removed, they "knew what to do."

Several other researchers have shown similar findings (Joyce & Chase, 1990). The relevance of added contingencies for rule-following in determining the effects of explicitly programmed consequences modified considerably the meaning of rule-induced insensitivity. It is not literally that rules are insensitive to contingencies; rather, rules alter how programmed contingencies are contacted. They also add important new contingencies, a fact seen in the next section.

Increased Social Control

Rules greatly amplify social regulatory processes in two ways. First, rules can be stored in the form of permanent products available to influence the behavior of others removed by time or space from the speaker. For example, the reader of this book is responding to ink on paper given a long social and educational history that establishes such control. But the writer is not sitting next to the reader. The writer may now be insane, dead, or in another profession. This property of human verbal behavior enormously amplifies the importance, pervasiveness, and indirect relevance of the social community in human affairs. Second, the social community can often discriminate whether or not a rule has been followed and can deliver socially mediated consequences accordingly. In other words, rule-following can be entirely conventional. Much more will be said about this quality later.

Altered Motivation

Verbal stimuli do not just direct the form of behavior. They can also lead to the initial establishment of consequences (Hayes et al., 1987; Hayes, Kohlenberg, & Hayes, 1991; Hayes, Brownstein, Devany, Kohlenberg, & Shelby, 1987). Suppose, for example, you are told for the first time that *bon* in French is the same as *bueno* in Spanish, and that *bueno* in Spanish is the same as *bra* in Swedish, and that *bra* in Swedish is the same as *good* in English. If *good* already functions as a reinforcer, this rule alone may make it possible to teach new skills by consequating effective performances with *bon, bueno,* or *bra.* In addition, rules can change the

effectiveness of existing consequences (Hayes & Ju, in press). In the presence of the words *Finger-lickin' good,* for example, the effectiveness of fried chicken as a reinforcer for responding may be greater than in the absence of such words.

Together, these processes allow the verbal creation of highly abstract consequences. Initially, generalized social reinforcers (such as *good*) may be established through fairly direct processes (e.g., pairing with other reinforcers), but *good* is in turn modified by many kinds of verbal relations. There are kinds of goods, conditions for particular goods, attributes that are said to be good, and so on. Highly abstract verbal concepts such as justice, egalitarianism, or sincerity can be used as consequences ("you are so just") as a result. We will attempt a theoretical account of such effects later.

Indirect Alteration of Functions of the Nonverbal Environment

Probably one of the most important effects of rules is that they can alter the functions of the nonverbal environment. If a nonverbal stimulus enters into a verbal relation, functions attributed to the verbal term will, under some contextual condition, transfer to the nonverbal stimulus (Hayes & Hayes, 1992). Let us say, for example, that a child is taught that the printed word *DOG* goes with the sound "dog," and is also taught that the printed word *DOG* goes with actual dogs. The two directly trained relations are: *DOG* to actual dogs and *DOG* to the sound, "dog." Let us, then, say that on a separate occasion, the child plays with an actual dog and is bitten. Through classical conditioning, actual dogs may thus come to elicit pain sensations, feelings of anxiety, and feelings of fear. On some future occasion, upon hearing the sound "dog," the child may suddenly start to cry and engage in avoidance responses even though no dog is actually present and the child has had no direct history of reinforcement for any of these activities in response to the sound "dog." It is through this process that verbal rules give the nonverbal world new meaning (cf. Schlinger & Blakely, 1994, 1987).

Summary

Rules are powerful events. They permit a remarkably indirect, conventional, and specific form of stimulus control. Rules allow the establishment of remote social contingencies and a rapid modification of the range of behaviors available to make contact with the environment. But rules are not all positive. They can produce rigidity. They can make other important sources of control over behavior ineffective.

Due to the decreased ability to manipulate the environment directly, many outpatient therapeutic interventions are based heavily on verbal exchanges as a form of intervention. Much of clinical psychology works by the establishment of verbal rules. Understanding rule-governance is thus a matter of critical importance to empirical clinical psychology and its development.

TYPES OF RULE-FOLLOWING

Rules are verbal antecedents. We take "verbal" stimuli to be stimuli that have their effects because they participate in equivalence classes (see Tierney & Bracken, this volume) or other derived stimulus relations (Hayes & Hayes, 1989). A full account of this definition is beyond the scope of the present chapter (see Hayes & Hayes, 1992); however, for all practical purposes, a detailed account of this kind is not necessary. A common-sense definition will work almost as well.

Understanding a rule and actually following the rule are two different behaviors, however (Hayes, 1991; Hayes, Zettle, & Rosenfarb, 1989), and for clinical purposes it is important to see why rules are followed in the first place.

Most rules seem to evoke rule-following because they engage direct contingencies. *Pliance*, or rule-governed behavior under the control of a history of socially mediated consequences for a correspondence between the rule and relevant

behavior, is one type. Another type of rule-following is *tracking*, or rule-governed behavior under the control of a history of a correspondence between the rule and the contingencies engaged entirely by the exact form of the behavior in that particular situation—what we call "natural" contingencies (Hayes & Wilson, 1993; Hayes, Zettle, & Rosenfarb, 1989). When behavior is under the control of natural contingencies (i.e., contingency-shaped), the consequences of an action are determined completely by the topography of the action in a given situation (Hayes, Zettle, & Rosenfarb, 1989). In this case, the consequences that are contacted have nothing to do with whether a person acted "maliciously," "intentionally," or "unknowingly." For example, if a Shao-Lin priest brands himself with a hot iron, the burn he receives is still a burn whether he accidentally touched the branding iron or did so voluntarily. Conversely, branding himself "by not watching where he was going" versus "to demonstrate the intensity of his faith" will have different socially mediated consequences. With behavior that is contingency-shaped, the likelihood of touching a hot iron should, eventually, decrease. The red glow should function as a discriminative stimulus (Skinner, 1938) in the presence of which touching is punished or avoidance is reinforced. However, if the branding iron were being used as part of an elaborate ritual, avoidance would likely produce aversive socially mediated consequences, such as castigation by fellow believers.

To illustrate the distinction further, suppose an adult tells a child, "Dress warmly, dear, it's cold outside." If the child then puts on a jacket because of a history of possible praise or punishment from the adult for following the rule, then the behavior is pliance. Conversely, if the child puts on a jacket to get warm, under the control of a history of such rules accurately describing natural contingencies, then the behavior is tracking.

The distinction between plies and tracks is functional, not formal. A rule can be in obvious track form and still evoke pliance. Similarly, behavior that is rebellious or resistant may still be pliance, so long as the function of the rule is dependent upon a history of socially mediated consequences for a correspondence between the rule and relevant behavior. A teenage girl accurately told, "Your friends will get you in trouble," may respond by angrily trying to keep her parents from controlling what she does. In this instance, the rule is probably functioning as a ply—as if consequences for following or not following the rule are arbitrary and social—rather than as a description of natural consequences. The resistance shown by the teenager (i.e., *counterpliance*) has probably been consequated, in part, by the social withdrawal of the parent or other rule-giver.

Augmenting is a different kind of rule, in which the antecedent verbal stimuli do not indicate or change contingencies—rather, they change the effectiveness or importance of consequences. Say, for example, that a person who often drinks Gatorade hears a radio advertisement announcing: "Gatorade! The thirst quencher!" This statement is unlikely to function as a ply since the social community is not likely to discriminate whether or not the rule had been given and, then, differentially reinforce the purchase of Gatorade accordingly. It may function as a track in that drinking Gatorade may actually decrease thirst. However, it does not signal a contingency since the commercial may be heard during times of thirst as well as satiation. In other words, the probability of natural reinforcement is no higher in the presence of the rule than in its absence. Instead, what may be involved is the verbal equivalent of reinforcer sampling (cf. Allyon & Azrin, 1968): as we talk about Gatorade we may also be able to picture it and taste it (i.e., some of the perceptual functions associated with the drink may be present). In technical terms, the stimulus functions of one member of an equivalence class transfer to another member. This transfer, in turn, may function motivationally (see Hayes & Ju, in press).

Two different types of augmentals have been distinguished in the behavior analytic literature. When a rule establishes consequential functions for the first time through a verbal rule, it is a *for-*

mative augmental. This process has been shown empirically in several studies (e.g., Hayes et al., 1987; Hayes, Kohlenberg, & Hayes, 1991).

The term *motivative augmentals* refers to antecedent verbal stimuli that temporarily alter the degree to which previously established consequences function as reinforcers or punishers. The Gatorade example is of this type.

Many of the consequences of importance to humans are remote, improbable, or abstract. The verbal processes involved in augmenting may help explain how such consequences come to be important. Formative augmentals may lead to the establishment of such abstract verbal consequences as liberty, justice, and equality, while motivative augmentals may support the importance of achievement, respect, understanding, and other consequences so important to a civilized society.

EVIDENCE FOR THE PLIANCE-TRACKING DISTINCTION

The research on augmenting is just beginning, but there is a substantial literature relevant to the pliance-tracking distinction. This literature is important for our purposes because it links the literature on rule-governance directly to applied interventions.

Tracking can be social since some natural contingencies are social—but pliance is necessarily social and in an unusual fashion. Only a social community can differentially detect and reinforce control by a rule as distinct from delivering consequences based on the *form* of the behavior seen. Because of this inherent quality of socially monitored correspondence, pliance requires that the social community have access both to the rule and to the relevant behavior controlled by the rule. If either is certainly removed—where by "certainly" we mean as viewed by the rule-follower—then pliance should be unlikely.

This distinction suggests an effective way of assessing whether an instance of rule-following is pliance or tracking: compare rule-following in a public context, in which both the rule and the relevant behavior are accessible to potential mediators, with that seen in a private context in which either the rule and/or the relevant behavior are apparently not at all accessible. Such public/private comparisons have been made in the social psychology literature on compliance, obedience, and related social influence processes (see Hayes et al., 1989 for a review), and in the human operant literature as well (e.g., Barrett, Deitz, Gaydos, & Quinn, 1987). But the relevance of this to applied work is most direct in a research literature on the processes through with such clinical interventions as coping self-statements or self-control procedures operate.

Almost all psychotherapies are conducted in a social context. Clients are presented with verbal material by the therapist, and corresponding client behavior is examined. These conditions satisfy the core requirements for a pliance contingency. To what degree can clinical changes seen in psychotherapeutic interventions be said to be due to pliance? This question has been examined with some widely used interventions.

In an initial study in this area, Zettle and Hayes (1983) compared the efficacy of coping self-statements in the reduction of speech anxiety. Speech-anxious college students were randomly assigned to a control group, or to one of two kinds of coping self-statement interventions. Both of the coping conditions received a self-statement like those commonly used clinically. Subjects selected a statement from a container that they were told held different types of statements. They were asked to repeat this statement to themselves both before and during speeches.

In actuality, all the statements in the container were identical. The difference between the two coping conditions was that in the private version, subjects simply returned the statement to the container after reading it, while in the public condition, the statement was shared with the therapist.

Results obtained on both self-report and behavioral measures of anxiety showed that the public coping self-statement group improved performance over the control condition. The private group did not. Thus, coping "self-statements" may work through social means. In this study at least, coping self-statements established pliance, not tracking. Speaking loosely, clients improved because they knew that the therapist knew they were supposed to follow a particular rule.

Coping statements were examined in a second study focusing on pain tolerance using a cold-pressor task (Hayes & Wolf, 1984). A very similar design to the earlier study was used. Once again, only subjects in the public coping self-statement group improved their tolerance of a cold-pressor task longer than those in an attention-placebo condition. Private self-statements had no effect.

Rosenfarb and Hayes (1984) examined this issue using children and expanded the finding to disinhibitory modeling. Children who were very fearful of the dark were randomly assigned to one of two treatment conditions (coping self-statement or disinhibitory modeling) or to one of two control groups (one controlling for time and the other controlling for the content of the coping statements by using neutral statements from children's books). Children in the coping self-statement group listened to a tape (they were told it was a "radio show") in which they were instructed in self-statements that previous research had shown to be quite effective in decreasing fear of the dark in children (Kanfer, Karoly, & Newman, 1975). The children picked their own "radio show" by punching one of many buttons on a panel. In actuality, regardless of the button pushed, the same tape was played. The public/private manipulation was as follows: half of the subjects (in the "public" condition) showed the experimenter the button they would push, the other half did not (in the "private condition"). The experimenter then left the room, the child pushed the button, and the "radio show" was played. The disinhibitory modeling conditions had the identical public and private manipulations, except that subjects watched a videotape of a same-gender coping model entering a dark room while saying aloud the same self-statements used in the self-statement groups.

Coping self-statements and modeling both increased dark tolerance equally well in these fearful children compared with the control conditions, but this was true *only* when the treatments were public. If the children thought that no one —not even the experimenter—could know what they listened to or watched, the treatment effects disappeared entirely. This was true even though the private groups remembered and reported using the interventions just as well as the public groups. These findings show fairly clearly that these interventions work by setting a kind of social standard against which performance can be subsequently evaluated. Put another way: these interventions work by pliance, not tracking; they work by social persuasion, not by information. The same type of results have been shown with self-control procedures and with goal-setting (Hayes, Rosenfarb, Wulfert, Munt, Korn, & Zettle, 1985).

These results are important because practitioners of many forms of cognitive and behavioral therapy talk about their procedures in largely nonsocial terms. Cognitive therapists talk more about what the client thinks than about what the therapist apparently could think about what the client thinks. As a result, little careful thought has been given to ways in which pliance might be increased in cognitive therapy.

IMPLICATIONS OF RULE-GOVERNANCE FOR APPLIED PROBLEMS

The literature on rule-governance suggests many ways that applied problems can emerge and be treated. It suggests new approaches, provides theoretical concepts for the interpretation of existing approaches, and presents new areas of caution.

Clinical Problems in Rule-Governed Terms

In some cases, increasing rule control of certain kinds may be helpful, such as when rule generation and following are too weak. Behavior occurring under such conditions may be labeled as impulsive, lazy, antisocial, or immoral. Rules

introduce new forms of social regulation that allow greater resistance to extinction or to short-term immediate consequences. Individuals can function as both speaker and listener, and a person can listen to his or her own talk. Thus, self-rules can participate in the control of other behavior. The difference between following self-rules and rules made by others, however, is that when a person is listening to his or her own speech, the social contingencies involved in pliance do not operate in the same manner as when the person is listening to someone else. The socially mediated consequences for following or not following a self-rule are indirect (i.e., based on derived stimulus relations)—since the self-rule may occur at a very subtle level—and the "natural" consequences may be temporally noncontiguous (i.e., delayed).

Disorders in rule generation or following may occur in several ways: individuals may fail to formulate rules in situations requiring them to do so; they may formulate inaccurate, unrealistic or ineffective rules; they may fail to follow rules that lead to beneficial outcomes; or they may follow rules that lead to harmful consequences (Hayes, Kohlenberg, & Melancon, 1989). Most of the strategies incorporated into cognitive therapy can be interpreted as attempts to teach individuals proper rule-formulation (Schilling & Poppen, 1983; Zettle & Hayes, 1983): therapists encourage their clients to bring verbal behavior under the control of direct contact with experienced events (i.e., natural contingencies) rather than under states of reinforceability (e.g., worries and fears) or audience control (e.g., pleasing others). The formulation of inaccurate or unrealistic rules can also occur at the level of the verbal community at large. For example, a television commercial promoting the rule "You can never be too rich or too thin" is encouraging rule-following that could aversely affect an individual's health and well-being. In fact, many advertisers cater to the effects of immediate contingency control (e.g., feeling elated, aroused, relaxed, etc.). But for these commercials to have an impact, audiences must be able to both understand and follow the rules to which they are exposed.

Rule-following, in this sense, involves both the understanding of the rule and the verbal activation of behavioral functions in terms of the rule (Hayes et al., 1989). Most adolescents already know who Joe Camel is and what product he promotes. To encourage the purchase of Camel cigarettes, advertisers need only establish the product name as an effective reinforcer; thus, Camel cigarettes become related to *cool* in much the same manner that *bon* becomes related to *good*. Once Camel cigarettes are functioning as formative augmentals, the immediate social contingencies and the immediate effects of the nicotine itself may draw the teenager into a pattern of smoking. Recent community intervention projects (Biglan, 1995) have focused on promoting rule-following that might compete effectively with the destructive effects of these kinds of immediate contingency control. The rule "Don't smoke—smoking is for losers" is meant to establish an insensitivity to these direct contingencies. However, before such rules will have an impact, a sufficiently strong pattern of rule-following must first be established. Synanon, for example, is an invasive drug-treatment program that emphasizes intense social control for the purposes of establishing pliance with regard to house rules. Strong and consistent social contingencies are provided for rule-following in the hopes that a greater degree of insensitivity to destructive immediate contingencies will result.

At the other end of the continuum, when rule-generation and rule-following are too strong, behavior may be described as obsessive, anxious, overcompliant, insensitive or rigid. In these cases, targeting proper rule formulation or increasing insensitivity to direct contingencies may actually compound the problem. Instead, avoiding or decreasing rule control of certain kinds may be more helpful. Individuals diagnosed with obsessive-compulsive behavior disorder, for example, may not benefit from directive interventions, such as rational emotive therapy (Ellis, 1962). The replacement of the client's rules with the therapist's rules does not attenuate excessive rule-following. Conversely, the more traditionally nonempirical approaches,

such as Gestalt (Perls, 1969) and Morita (Morita, 1929/1984), may be more consistent with the basic behavioral literature on rule-governance. These historically "non-behavioral" therapies emphasize the experiential aspects of learning by minimizing direct therapist instruction, by increasing the use of nonvocal experiential exercises, by making use of metaphor, and by applying paradoxical techniques with the purpose of diminishing the insensitivity-producing effects of verbal control (Hayes, Kohlenberg, & Melancon, 1989).

Because rule-governance is so central to human action, an almost unlimited number of applied implications could be developed. In many ways, the field of applied psychology is about the issue of rule-governance. We will limit our examples to a small set.

Developing Rule Control: The Example of Moral Behavior

The distinction between pliance, tracking, and augmenting provides a working model of moral development (Hayes, Gifford, & Hayes, in press). Six basic kinds of moral behavior emerge from the pliance/tracking/augmenting distinction. Those from the point of view of the listener are moral pliance, moral tracking, and moral augmenting. Those from the point of the view of the speaker are social concern for pliance, social concern for tracking, and social concern for augmenting. These can be arranged into a usual sequence based on their complexity.

Moral pliance involves following rules about what is good or proper because the verbal community differentially consequates rule-following per se. Moral pliance involves the implicit (and often explicit) rule "Do it because I said so." It makes sense that pliance is most basic because it adds new reinforcers and punishers to those contingencies already present, and because it is in the direct interest of speakers. A parent shouting "stop it!" will have that behavior negatively reinforced by termination of crying, and the children will often be presented with direct and immediate reasons to stop.

Moral tracking involves following rules about what best produces existing reinforcers and punishers for the individual. An example of a moral track might be "People won't like you if you lie." This type of rule-following is more complex than pliance. The consequences referred to in the rule are often probabilistic or remote, and the track does not add new, immediate consequences to the situation.

Moral augmenting involves the acquisition of and motivation to obtain increasingly abstract reinforcers and punishers, based on systems of verbal relations. Formative augmentals are the more important kind in the area of morality, because they establish new consequential functions through verbal means. This form of behavior is more difficult than the others because it is such a verbal process.

Social concern for pliance is moral behavior oriented toward the establishment of pliance in others or in the social group as a whole. It is involved with such issues as "How can we establish law and order?" or "How I get my children to mind me?" a concern over pliance, while much more evolved and complex than pliance from the point of view of the listener, is still a rather basic behavior, since pliance can remove very direct and aversive events from the immediate environment of the speaker.

Social concern for tracking is moral behavior oriented toward the establishment of tracking in others or in the social group as a whole. It is concerned with such issues as "How can we eliminate self-destructive behavior in our youth?" or "How can we get people to think in terms of the long-term consequences?" This is the first type of moral behavior that is quite subtle and difficult to achieve, because the reinforcers for the speaker are long term and indirect.

Social concern for augmenting is moral behavior oriented toward the establishment of verbal consequences in others or in the social group as a whole and increasing the motivation of others to work toward abstract consequences. It is concerned with such issues as "How can we establish a society that seeks justice?" This is the most difficult kind of morality to establish since

self-interest for the speaker is least obviously involved.

This approach to morality helps explain why parenting practices that give rise to pliance (e.g., clear rules, careful monitoring, consistent consequation of behavior) are so important to children. It also explains why helping children come into contact with natural consequences is important, and why abstract ends taught in the form of religion or ethics are crucial to socialization.

Avoiding Rule Control: The Example of Social Shaping

If one of the side effects of verbal control is an insensitivity to direct contingency control, then rule-based therapies should be used primarily when behavioral rigidity is desirable (e.g., for problems such as smoking, weight control, impulsive behavior, aggressive outbursts). When such rigidity might be detrimental (e.g., in "spontaneous" or "socially sensitive" behavior), the research on rule-governance suggests that instruction-based intervention strategies may not be as effective as experiential approaches.

Social-skills training provides a prime example of the ineffectiveness of rule-based treatment models. Proponents of this training model make the assumption that socially ineffective people have specific deficits in particular skill areas that can be identified and described in detail sufficient that the therapist will be able to instruct behavior change and provide feedback on the degree to which role-played performances approximate the instructed ideal (Devany & Nelson, 1986). This model has been pursued for decades by dozens, even hundreds, of researchers, and yet there is still no useful list of the specific components of "social skill" (Ciminero, Calhoun, & Adams, 1977; Conger & Conger, 1982; Rosenfarb, Hayes, & Linehan, 1989).

Social behavior involves many thousands of specific and subtle response forms (facial expressions, gestures, voice intonation, movements, and so on) that are very much a function of such factors as the audience, setting, timing, and so on. Social interactions involve acts that may be highly variable in form and their effects depend entirely upon the context in which they occur. Solutions to such questions as, "Why can't I get women to fall in love with me?" cannot be readily attained with an instruction book of behavioral topographies. Several minutes at a calculator can confirm that even a few dozen response forms and contextual factors can lead to billions of specific combinations and sequences. It seems unlikely that such a collection could be learned by rules.

But even if this problem could be solved, the basic literature on rule-governance suggests that rule-governed social behavior might be less sensitively modified by natural contingencies than social behavior that is contingency-shaped. Rule-governed social behavior could well seem rigid or artificial. There is no reason why social behavior could not be shaped directly, however, by presenting and amplifying its consequences (Hayes, Kohlenberg, & Melancon, 1989).

The first study of this kind (Azrin & Hayes, 1984) focused on cues of social interest displayed in heterosocial interactions. The rationale for using level of interest was that cues of this sort may be one of the major modulating events in a heterosocial interaction. Male subjects were asked to view a videotape of a female (no audio) conversing with an off-screen male, and then to rate, each minute, how interested they thought she was in the unseen male. In the original taping, the female had also given interest ratings each minute, and by using these as a criterion, the male subjects' ratings could be assessed for accuracy. Treatment consisted simply of giving subjects feedback on the accuracy of their guesses. Thus, this strategy allowed both assessment and training of sensitivity to social interest cues, even though we had no idea what these cues were (as we would need to if we were developing a rule-based intervention).

The results showed that with feedback, subjects improved in their ability to discriminate social interest, that this ability generalized to previously unviewed females and led to improvements in actual social skills in subsequent role-play situations.

In another study (Rosenfarb, Hayes, & Linehan, 1989), experiential and instructional social-skills training were compared in the treatment of adults with social-interaction difficulties. In this study, subjects repeatedly role-played social situations. The experiential intervention consisted of the therapist's stating his "gut reaction" about the overall quality of the role-played performance without any description of the behaviors the therapist liked or disliked. In the instructional-intervention condition, therapists and clients generated rules about effective social behaviors.

The results of this study suggested that subjects receiving experiential feedback improved more than subjects that did not. In addition, subjects in the experiential-feedback condition were more likely to generalize improvements to novel situations outside the therapeutic setting. Instructions did not improve overall performance.

The research on contingency-shaped social competence has begun to increase in popularity. More recent studies have made use of computer technology that provides more immediate feedback to subjects and, at the same time, minimizes the demand characteristics of the experimenter (Follette, Dougher, Dykstra, & Compton, 1992). In sum, the work on rule-governance undermines the need for the generation of instructions for clinical intervention. The accumulating research on contingency-shaped treatments demonstrates that instructional approaches are not necessary for behavior change to occur.

Avoiding Rule Control: Psychotherapy as Shaping

Within the last decade, an increasing number of applied psychologists have begun to develop treatment techniques that consciously attempt to undermine the effects of verbal control. Kohlenberg and Tsai (1991) have endeavored to provide a theoretical account of the improvements shown by some clients during intense client-therapist relationships and to delineate the steps therapists can take to facilitate these intense and curative relationships. The result is *functional analytic psychotherapy* (FAP), a radical behavioral treatment in which the client-therapist relationship is at the core of the change process. The approach seems to fit well within the current literature on rule-governance.

FAP theory indicates that, in general, the therapeutic process is facilitated by a caring, genuine, sensitive, and emotional client-therapist relationship. The assumption FAP makes is that therapeutic interventions often emphasize contrived reinforcers (i.e., reinforcers that are unlikely to occur outside of a therapeutic setting), and for that reason, the effects of this intervention may not generalize to the natural environment. By this line of reasoning, following a client's angry outburst with "I hear you saying that you're angry" may not teach that client how to interact effectively with others in daily life. In addition, therapists frequently diminish the effectiveness of praise due to overuse, and the deliberate use of consequences can be viewed by clients as manipulative or aversive, thereby producing counterpliance.

FAP therapists argue that such countertherapeutic situations can be avoided by structuring therapy such that the therapist's genuine reactions to the client's behavior naturally reinforce improvements as they happen. Such a process is most likely to occur when the client's presenting problem is evoked in the actual therapeutic situation. Thus, rather than formulating rules of conduct and relying on verbally constructed futures, the therapist can directly shape the client's behavior as it occurs. For example, instead of instructing a client seeking help for intimacy problems to "do three behavioral exchanges with your partner," an intense and emotional therapist-client relationship might naturally evoke withdrawal responses. The therapist in this situation can then directly reinforce improvements as they occur.

Client behaviors of most interest to FAP clinicians are those that occur during the therapy session and are called *clinically relevant behaviors* (CRBs). These CRBs include: daily-life problems that occur during the session (CRB1), improvements that occur during the session (CRB2), and clients' interpretations of their own behavior (CRB3).

Techniques or guidelines for therapists to follow are aimed at evoking, noticing, reinforcing, and interpreting the client's behavior at the time of occurrence. FAP therapists are trained to follow five strategic rules of therapeutic technique: watch for CRBs, evoke CRBs, reinforce CRB2s, observe the potentially reinforcing effects of therapist behavior in relation to client CRBs, and give interpretations of variables that affect client CRBs.

Kohlenberg and Tsai's major hypothesis is that, the more proficient a therapist is at observing CRBs, the more enhanced the therapeutic outcome. In other words, a therapist who is skilled at observing instances of clinically relevant behavior as they occur is more likely to naturally reinforce, punish, and extinguish client behaviors in ways that foster the development of behavior useful in daily life.

Due to the problem of contrived versus natural reinforcement, it is generally advisable to avoid procedures that attempt to stipulate the topography of therapist reactions in advance. Conjuring up a reinforcing reaction (e.g. "that's terrific" or "great") without relating it to the specific client-therapist history can result in reactions that seem manipulative and insincere. In terms of the issues in this chapter, rules for the therapist that specify topographies are likely to produce insensitivity. Rather, the rules regarding the conduct of FAP are general and strategic. For example, they urge the therapist to observe his or her spontaneous private reactions to client behavior and bring these into the room.

Empirical data supportive of the FAP approach are still limited. We use this example, however, because there are few psychotherapeutic approaches that are so clear in their attempt to shape behavior and to avoid certain kinds of rule-governed behavior. The rule-governance literature provides good conceptual support for its claims. FAP is one of a small but growing number of behavioral techniques offered as an alternative to instruction-oriented intervention strategies.

Developing Rule Control: The Didactic Psychotherapies

Clinical radical behaviorists have often been accused by cognitive therapists of ignoring the role of cognition in human psychopathology (Bandura, 1977; Mahoney, 1974). According to these critics, the focus of behavior analysis on identifying environmental variables, of which behavior is a function, is overly simplistic and incomplete unless supplemented by a consideration of cognitive control. Bandura (1995), for example, argues that certain cognitions (e.g., self-efficacy expectations) reveal "functional dependencies" with performance.

The differences between cognitive and behavioral perspectives, however, are more based upon basic philosophical differences with respect to the goals of science, the nature of truth, and the ontological or pragmatic status of causes (Hayes & Wilson, 1995). From a behavioral point of view, thinking is behaving, and thus a causal account in cognitive terms boils down to behavior causing behavior. Because of their interest in behavioral influence (not just prediction) behavior analysts object to such nonmanipulable causes (for more extended discussions on this point see Hayes, 1993; Hayes & Brownstein, 1986; Hayes & Hayes, 1992, Hayes, Hayes, & Reese, 1988; Hayes & Wilson, 1993).

Despite these philosophical differences, the language of rule-governance provides tools for the analysis of cognitive therapy. Thinking can be viewed as the human act of formulating and then follow one's own rules. In technical terms, self-rules are verbal stimuli that have some of their psychological functions as a result of their participation in derived stimulus relations. The formulation of self-rules is a function of one's interaction with a social-verbal community that repeatedly questions its members about past, present, and future actions and about the variables of which their behavior is a function (Zettle, 1990).

Cognitive therapists attempt to change the impact of cognition in several ways. Behavior that is largely contingency-shaped can become more rule-governed by evoking rules in the client and reinforcing individuals for a correspondence between their actions and the rules that are stated. Similarly, if the relevant behavior is already rule-governed the underlying rules can be evoked and selectively modified through pliance or tracking.

For example, an advocate of rational emotive therapy might teach the client to formulate a rule linking antecedent conditions and relevant actions even in cases in which the behavior was dominantly contingency-shaped. It is not uncommon to have clients at first deny that their behavior was guided by a rule—irrational or otherwise. Once the behavior is cast in rule terms, however, the therapist can selectively respond to the form of the rule or to the client's behavior with regard to it.

Changing a client rule or the behavior controlled by it can be done in many ways, but we will consider both pliance and tracking. In the case of pliance, the therapist uses therapist-mediated consequences to establish client rules of particular forms ("You should not say *should*") and to then respond to behavior in those terms. We have already cited literature showing that many cognitive interventions operate by pliance (see Hayes, Zettle, & Rosenfarb, 1989 for a review). It is also possible to change client rules through tracking. In this approach, the therapist arranges for the natural consequences of client rules to be contacted. For example, the use of homework that "tests" cognitions, as in Beck's cognitive therapy, can be thought of in these terms.

Thinking of cognitive therapy in rule-governed terms focuses change on the actual context that supports or weakens rule control. This context includes aspects of the relationship between the client and the therapist, as well as the natural environment in which clients live.

Undermining Rule Control: The Paradoxical and Transformational Therapies

It is possible not just to avoid rule control, as in shaping-based approaches, or to use it, as in cognitive approaches, but also to undermine it and transform it. Our own *acceptance and commitment therapy* (ACT) is an intervention of this kind, and we will examine it in some detail. ACT is a functional contextualistic treatment approach designed to address issues of emotional avoidance, excessive literal response to cognitive content, and the inability to make and keep commitments to behavior change (Hayes, 1987; Zettle & Hayes, 1983; Hayes & Melancon, 1989; Hayes, Kohlenberg, & Melancon, 1989). It is a treatment that is especially oriented toward the chronic, severe, treatment-resistant and multiply-disordered client.

In traditional cognitive-behavioral approaches, undesirable emotions or thoughts are believed to produce undesirable patterns of living. On that basis, aversive thoughts or emotions are targeted for change, control, or elimination. Conversely, rather than trying to change private events or self-rules, ACT attempts to recontextualize them so as to alter their function without altering their form or frequency. It does this by establishing a verbal community of two in which literal meaning and reason-giving are deemphasized, emotional and cognitive acceptance is encouraged (the competing context of control is described below), the necessary link between private and other behaviors is undermined, and goal-setting and achievement are approached directly.

In the first stage of ACT, an attempt is made to establish a state of "creative hopelessness" in which the client begins to see former "solutions" as impossible to implement. In effect, the client's rules of behavior change are challenged fundamentally. When all solutions are no longer solutions, the client has no change rules to follow. The client feels hopeless, but it is a creative hopelessness because fundamentally new approaches are possible when old approaches have been abandoned.

ACT then seeks to define emotional and cognitive control as the core problem. By the time the client comes to therapy, he or she has been well trained by the social-verbal community to view control of private events as important, and rules of life change are usually entirely cast in these terms. The social-verbal community re-quires people to give verbal explanations for their behavior, even if its sources are unknown or obscure (Semin & Manstead, 1981). Many of these explanations point to the need for emotional and cognitive control (e.g., "I felt so anxious I just couldn't go"), and thus most clients apply their behavior-change efforts to this target. Unfortunately, these targets are not readily rule-governed. Thus, people are led to apply verbally mediated solutions to targets that are dominantly unresponsive to such approaches.

For example, consider an obsessive person who is trying not to think something. This person is applying a rule about cognitive control to thought elimination ("I don't like thinking X, so I need to get rid of that thought"). Unfortunately, thought elimination is not readily rule-governed. Rules about thought elimination tend to elicit the thoughts they nominally are designed to eliminate because they specify their targets (e.g., "I don't like thinking X" specifies "X"). ACT therapists point to this kind of paradox and to the overarching principle: Rules about emotional and cognitive control are notoriously unsuccessful.

In order to weaken unhealthy forms of verbal control, ACT attempts to undermine literal meaning itself. Words are often used as if they mean or are the things to which they refer. In more technical terms, derived stimulus relations can come to dominate over directly contacted stimulus functions. A word and the situation to which it refers can easily be confused, and many functions that would adhere to the situation become present with regard to the words. For example, a person may think, "This is awful." The person may then act as if the person is in an awful situation, not in a situation in which he or she is having the thought, "This is awful." This context of literality establishes functions for thought that would be appropriate to the situations constructed, but may not be appropriate for the thought itself. A variety of experiential and metaphorical techniques are used to weaken these derived stimulus relations. For example, clients may be asked to repeat words hundreds of times, until all their "meaning" disappears. Similarly, clients are taught to adopt a particular verbal style in therapy that emphasizes the nature of verbal processes (e.g., saying, "I'm having the thought that I can't go to the mall" as opposed to simply stating, "I can't go to the mall").

Emotional-exposure exercises further weaken rules about the necessity of emotional and cognitive control. Imaginal and in vivo exercises are used to elicit some of what the client most fears, and the reactions that then occur are contacted in deconstructed form.

In the final stages of ACT, clients work on their values and commitment action linked to those values. In essence, having weakened socially conventional forms of rule-control that are oriented toward private events, ACT seeks to support verbal control targeted toward valued behavior change. Verbal commitments are made and practiced. ACT tries to establish a discrimination between self-rules that cannot be followed effectively (i.e., rules of emotional avoidance) and self-rules that can be followed effectively and, when followed, can lead to positive consequences (e.g., commitments to behavior change).

Several clinical outcome studies have been conducted on ACT, and the data are supportive (see Hayes, Strosahl, & Wilson, in press, for a review). Our interest in ACT in the context of the present chapter, however, is with the way ACT seeks to alter rule control. ACT suggests that more empirical therapies could be built around attempts to undermine or transform rule control, rather than simply to use it or to work around it.

Application of Rules to Psychopathology: The Example of Suicide

Understanding how rules alter behavior can be useful for an analysis of psychopathology as well as treatment. Suicide will be our example, though many others present themselves (e.g., see Hayes, Wilson, Gifford, Follette, & Strosahl, 1996).

The purposeful act of taking one's own life is an instance of rule-governed behavior based on derived relations involving time (Hayes, 1994) and the verbal construction of expected consequences of action. Temporal relations are a part of a class of relations that have to do with change, such as cause-effect, if . . . then, or before-after. Based on a history of derived temporal sequences among events, a person is able to respond in the present by constructing a sequential relation between at least two events. For example, "death" can participate in if . . . then verbal relations with many other events that have acquired desirable functions both directly and through the transformation of stimulus functions tied to direct events, such as, "If I am dead, I will no longer suffer, everyone will be happier, they will all be sorry for what they've done to me, I will finally be at peace," and so on.

In technical terms, "death" enters into formative and then motivative augmentals, such that it becomes a verbal consequence of importance (Hayes & Wilson, 1993). Thus, as a verbal action, suicide is a kind of rule-governed behavior. Once personal death becomes a verbal consequence of importance, rules can be followed that give rise to it. The motivating conditions behind more than half of actual or attempted suicides involve an attempt to escape from aversive states of mind such as guilt or anxiety (Baumeister, 1990; Smith & Bloom, 1985). However, the impact of such rules as "If I die, then I will be at peace" depends upon the degree to which they conflict with other functional rules, such as "Suicide is an offense against God." It is for this reason that the psychotherapies and religious institutions around the world strive to create meaning, values, and purpose in the lives of individuals.

This analysis makes sense of the great pervasiveness of suicide in human civilization, especially when contrasted with the arguable absence of this behavior in nonhumans. By this analysis, suicide is not the product of a diseased mind; it is an outgrowth of normal verbal processes. Stated another way, the issue shifts from why people kill themselves to the more important question of why they do not.

CONCLUSION

Humans live in a verbal world. All attempts to change human behavior have to address this simple fact in some ways. Thus, the study of verbal regulation bears upon every applied technique in psychology. In the present chapter we have shown how verbal regulation bears on our clinical understanding, and how methods can be used to establish, avoid, transform, or undermine different kinds of verbal control. By consciously examining how techniques deal with issues of verbal regulation, the rule-governed literature might suggest modifications or innovations for many therapeutic procedures.

REFERENCES

Allyon, T., & Azrin, N. H. (1968). Reinforcer sampling: A technique for increasing the behavior of mental patients. *Journal of Applied Behavior Analysis, 1,* 13–20.

Azrin, R., & Hayes, S. C. (1984). The discrimination of interest within a heterosexual interaction: Training, generalization, and effects on social skills. *Behavior Therapy, 15,* 173–184.

Bandura, A. (1977). Self-efficacy: Toward a unifying theory of behavioral change. *Psychological Review, 84,* 191–215.

Bandura, A. (1995). Comments on the crusade against causal efficacy of human thought. *Journal of Behavior Therapy and Experimental Psychiatry, 26,* 179–190. Special issue: Cognition, behavior and causality: A broad exchange of views stemming from the debate on the causal efficacy on human thought.

Baumeister, R. F. (1990). Suicide as escape from self. *Psychological Review, 97,* 90–113.

Baron, A., Kaufman, A., & Stauber, K. A. (1969). Effects of instructions and reinforcement-feedback on human operant behavior maintained by fixed-interval reinforcement. *Journal of the Experimental Analysis of Behavior, 12,* 701–712.

Barrett, D. H., Deitz, S. M., Gaydos, G. R., & Quinn, P. C. (1987). The effects of programmed contingencies and social conditions on response stereotypy with human subjects. *Psychological Record, 37(4),* 489–505.

Beck, A. T., Rush, A. J., Shaw, B., & Emery, G. (1979). *Cognitive therapy for depression.* New York: Guilford.

Bentall, R. P., Lowe, C. F., & Beasty, A. (1985). The role of verbal behavior in human learning: II. Developmental differences. *Journal of the Experimental Analysis of Behavior, 43(2),* 165–180.

Biglan, A. (1995). *Changing cultural practices: A contextualist framework for intervention research.* Reno, Nev.: Context Press.

Buskist, W. F., & Miller, H. L. (1986). Interaction between rules and contingencies in the control of human fixed-interval performance. *Psychological Record, 36(1),* 109–116.

Buskist, W. F., Bennett, R. H., & Miller, H. L. (1981). Effects of instructional constraints on human fixed-interval performance. *Journal of the Experimental Analysis of Behavior, 35(2),* 217–225.

Catania, C., Shimoff, E., & Matthews, B. A. (1989). An experimental analysis of rule-governed behavior. In S. C. Hayes (ed.), *Rule-governed behavior: Cognition, contingencies, and instructional control,* 119–152. New York: Plenum.

Ciminero, A. R., Calhoun, S. K., & Adams, H. E. (1977). *Handbook of behavioral assessment.* New York: Wiley.

Conger, J. C., & Conger, A. J. (1982). Components of heterosocial competence. In J. P. Curran & P. M. Monti (eds.), *Social skills training,* 313–347. New York: Guilford.

Devany, J. M., & Nelson, R. O. (1986). Behavioral approaches to treatment. In H. C. Quay & J. S. Werry (eds.), *Psychopathological disorders of childhood,* 523–557. New York: Wiley.

Ellis, A. (1962). *Reason and emotion in psychotherapy.* Secaucus, N.J.: Stuart.

Follette, W. C., Dougher, M. K., Dykstra, T. A., & Compton, S. N. (November 1992). *Teaching complex social behaviors to subjects with schizophrenia using contingent feedback.* Paper presented at the meeting of the Association for Advancement of Behavior Therapy, Boston.

Galizio, M. (1979). Contingency-shaped and rule-governed behavior: Instructional control of human loss avoidance. *Journal of the Experimental Analysis of Behavior, 31(1),* 53–70.

Hamilton, M. (1967). Development of a rating scale for primary depressive illness. *British Journal of Social and Clinical Psychology, 6,* 278–296.

Hayes, S. C. (1987). A contextual approach to therapeutic change. In N. S. Jacobson (ed.), *Psychotherapists in clinical practice: Cognitive and behavioral perspectives,* 327–387. New York: Guilford.

Hayes, S. C. (1991). A relational control theory of stimulus equivalence. In L. J. Hayes & P. N. Chase (eds.), *Dialogues on verbal behavior,* 29–40. Reno, Nev.: Context Press.

Hayes, S. C. (1993). Analytic goals and varieties of scientific contextualism. In S. C. Hayes, L. J. Hayes, H. W. Reese, & T. R. Sarbin (eds.), *Varieties of scientific contextualism,* 11–27. Reno, Nev.: Context Press.

Hayes, S. C. (1994). Verbal relations, time, and suicide. In S. C. Hayes, L. J. Hayes, M. Sato, & K. Ono (eds.), *Behavior analysis of language and cognition.* Reno, Nev.: Context Press.

Hayes, S. C., & Brownstein, A. J. (1986). Mentalism, behavior-behavior relations and a behavior analytic view of the purposes of science. *The Behavior Analyst, 9,* 175–190.

Hayes, S. C., Brownstein, A. J., Devany, J. M., Kohlenberg, B. S., & Shelby, J. (1987). Stimulus equivalence and the symbolic control of behavior. *Mexican Journal of Behavior Analysis, 13,* 361–374.

Hayes, S. C., Brownstein, A. J., Haas, J. R., & Greenway, D. E. (1986a). Instructions, multiple schedules, and extinction: Distinguishing rule-governed from schedule controlled behavior. *Journal of the Experimental Analysis of Behavior, 46,* 137–147.

Hayes, S. C., Brownstein, A. J., Zettle, R. D., Rosenfarb, I., & Korn, Z. (1986b). Rule-governed behavior and sensitivity to changing consequences of responding. *Journal of the Experimental Analysis of Behavior, 45,* 237–256.

Hayes, S. C., Gifford, E. V., & Hayes, G. J. (in press). Moral development as the development of verbal regulation. *The Behavior Analyst.*

Hayes, S. C., & Hayes, L. J. (1989). The verbal action of the listener as a basis for rule-governance. In S. C. Hayes (ed.), *Rule-governed behavior: Cognition, contingencies, and instructional control,* 153–190. New York: Plenum.

Hayes, S. C., & Hayes, L. J. (1992). Verbal relations and the evolution of behavior analysis. *American Psychologist, 47,* 1383–1395.

Hayes, S. C., Hayes, L. J., & Reese, H. W. (1988). Finding the philosophical core: A review of Stephen C. Pepper's *World Hypotheses. Journal of the Experimental Analysis of Behavior, 50,* 97–111.

Hayes, S. C., & Ju, W. C. T. (in press). Seeing the light: A behavioral analysis of religious beliefs and practices. *The Behavior Analyst.*

Hayes, S. C., Kohlenberg, B. S., & Hayes, L. J. (1991). Transfer of consequential functions through simple and conditional equivalence classes. *Journal of the Experimental Analysis of Behavior, 56,* 119–137.

Hayes, S. C., Kohlenberg, B. S., & Melancon, S. M. (1989). Comprehensive distancing, paradox, and the treatment of emotional avoidance. In M. Ascher's (ed.), *Paradoxical procedures in psychotherapy,* 184–218. New York: Guilford.

Hayes, S. C., Strosahl, K., & Wilson, K. G. (in press). *Acceptance and commitment therapy: Understanding and treating human suffering.* New York: Guilford.

Hayes, S. C., & Wilson, K. G. (1993). Some applied implications of a contemporary behavior-analytic account of verbal events. *The Behavior Analyst, 16,* 283–301.

Hayes, S. C., & Wilson, K. G. (1995). The role of cognition in complex human behavior: A contextualistic perspective. *Journal of Behavior Therapy and Experimental Psychiatry, 26,* 214–248.

Hayes, S. C., Wilson, K. G., Gifford, E. V., Follette, V. M., & Strosahl, K. (1996). Experiential avoidance and behavioral disorders: A functional dimensional approach to diagnosis and treatment. *Journal of Consulting and Clinical Psychology, 64,* 1152–1168.

Hayes, S. C., & Wolf, M. R. (1984). Cues, consequences and therapeutic talk: Effects of social context and coping statements on pain. *Behaviour Research and Therapy, 22(4),* 385–392.

Hayes, S. C., Zettle, R. D., & Rosenfarb, I. (1989). Rule-following. In S. C. Hayes (ed.), *Rule-governed behavior: Cognition, contingencies, and instructional control,* 191–220. New York: Plenum.

Joyce, J. H., & Chase, P. N. (1990). Effects of response variability on the sensitivity of rule-governed behavior. *Journal of the Experimental Analysis of Behavior, 54(3),* 251–262.

Kanfer, F. H., Karoly, P., & Newman, H. (1975). Reduction of children's fear of the dark by competence-related and situational threat-related verbal cues. *Journal of Consulting and Clinical Psychology, 43,* 251–258.

Kaufman, A., Baron, A., & Kopp, R. E. (1966). Some effects of instructions on human operant behavior. *Psychonomic Monograph Supplements, 1,* 243–250.

Kohlenberg, B. S., Hayes, S. C., & Tsai, M. (1993). Radical behavioral psychotherapy: Two contemporary examples. *Clinical Psychology Review, 13,* 579–592.

Kohlenberg, R. J., and Tsai, M. (1991). *Functional analytic psychotherapy.* New York: Plenum.

Laties, V. G., & Weiss, B. (1963). Effects of concurrent task on fixed-interval responding in humans. *Journal of the Experimental Analysis of Behavior, 6,* 431–436.

Leander, J. D., Lippman, L. G., & Meyer, M. M. (1968). Fixed interval performance as related to subjects' verbalizations of the reinforcement contingency. *The Psychological Record, 18,* 469–474.

Lippman, L. G., & Meyer, M. M. (1967). Fixed interval performance as related to instructions and to subjects' verbalization of the contingency. *Psychonomic Science, 8,* 135–136.

Lowe, C. F., Beasty, A., & Bentall, R. P. (1983). The role of verbal behavior in human learning: Infant performance on Fixed Interval schedules. *Journal of the Experimental Analysis of Behavior, 39,* 157–164.

Lowe, C. F., Harzem, P., & Bagshaw, M. (1978). Species differences in temporal control of behavior. II: Human performance. *Journal of the Experimental Analysis of Behavior, 29,* 351–361.

Lowe, C. F., Harzem, P., & Hughes, S. (1978). Determinants of operant behavior in humans: Some differences from animals. *Quarterly Journal of Experimental Psychology, 30,* 373–386

Mahoney, M. J. (1974). *Cognition and behavior modification.* Cambridge, Mass.: Ballinger.

Matthews, B. A., Shimoff, E., Catania, C., & Sagvolden, T. (1977). Uninstructed human responding: Sensitivity to ratio and interval contingencies. *Journal of the Experimental Analysis of Behavior, 27,* 453–467.

Morita, S. (1984). *Shinkeishitsu no hontai to ryoho (Nature and treatment of nervosity)* (26th ed.). Tokyo: Hakuyosha (in Japanese).

Perls, F. S. (1969). *Gestalt therapy verbatim.* Lafayette, Calif.: Real People Press.

Rosenfarb, I., & Hayes, S. C. (1984). Social standard setting: The Achilles' heel of informational accounts of therapeutic change. *Behavior Therapy, 15,* 515–528.

Rosenfarb, I. S., Hayes, S. C., & Linehan, M. M. (1989). Instructions and experiential feedback in the treatment of social skills deficits in adults. *Psychotherapy, 26 (2),* 242–251.

Schilling, D. J., & Poppen, R. (1983). Behavioral relaxation training and assessment. *Journal of Behavior Therapy and Experimental Psychiatry, 14(2),* 99–107.

Schlinger, H. D., Jr., & Blakely, E. (1987). Function-altering effects of contingency-specifying stimuli. *The Behavior Analyst, 10,* 41–45.

Schlinger, H. D., Jr., & Blakely, E. (1994). A descriptive taxonomy of environmental operations and its implications for behavior analysis. *The Behavior Analyst, 17 (1),* 43–58.

Semin, G. R., & Manstead, A. S. (1981). The beholder beheld: A study of social emotionality. *European Journal of Social Psychology, 11(3),* 253–265.

Shimoff, E., Catania, C., & Matthews, B. A. (1981). Uninstructed human responding: Sensitivity of low-rate performance to schedule contingencies. *Journal of the Experimental Analysis of Behavior, 36,* 207–220.

Skinner, B. F. (1938). *The behavior of organisms.* Englewood Cliffs, N.J.: Prentice-Hall.

Skinner, B. F. (1969). *Contingencies of reinforcement: A theoretical analysis.* New York: Appleton-Century-Crofts.

Smith, G. W., & Bloom, I. (1985). A study in the personal meaning of suicide in the context of Baechler's typology. *Suicide and Life-threatening Behavior, 15,* 30–13.

Weiner, H. (1964). Conditioning history and human fixed-interval performance. *Journal of the Experimental Analysis of Behavior, 7,* 383–385.

Weiner, H. (1965). Conditioning history and maladaptive human operant behavior. *Psychological Reports, 17,* 935–942.

Weiner, H. (1969). Human verbal persistence. *Psychological Record, 20,* 445–456.

Zettle, R. D. (1990). Rule-governed behavior: A radical behavioral answer to the cognitive challenge. *The Psychological Record, 40,* 41–49.

Zettle, R. D., & Hayes, S. C. (1983). Dysfunctional control by client verbal behavior: The context of reason giving. *The Analysis of Verbal Behavior, 4,* 30–38.

Zettle, R. D., & Raines, J. C. (1989). Group cognitive and contextual therapies in treatment of depression. *Journal of Clinical Psychology, 45,* 438–445.

CHAPTER 19

STIMULUS EQUIVALENCE AND BEHAVIOR THERAPY

Kevin J. Tierney
Maeve Bracken

A BRIEF ACCOUNT OF STIMULUS EQUIVALENCE

Over the past number of years, the analysis of emergent behavior has generated a great deal of experimental research. The bulk of this research has been conducted using the matching-to-sample paradigm (Sidman, 1971). Matching-to-sample training is a form of training that is employed to teach a series of conditional discriminations to a participant.

In the simplest variant of the procedure, a person is trained to match stimulus A with stimulus B and then trained to match stimulus B with stimulus C. Given this, the person may show the ability to produce several "matching responses" that have not actually been trained. The person may show reflexivity (ability to match A with A, B with B, and C with C), symmetry (ability to match B to A, and C to B), and, most interest-

ingly, transitivity (matching A to C) (Hayes, 1989). Where all these matching phenomena occur, a stimulus equivalence class including A, B, and C is said to have been formed because each member of the class is treated equivalently (Sidman, 1971, 1986).

Much everyday learning presumably involves the development and modification of stimulus equivalence classes, and it has been suggested as a paradigm for explaining the emergence of comprehension and reading skills (Sidman & Cresson, 1973) and, more controversially, the development of language itself (Devany, Hayes, & Nelson, 1986). A striking feature of stimulus equivalence classes is that as the number of members (stimuli) in the class increases, the number of matching responses that emerge increases dramatically. For example, training 2 relationships (A to B and B to C) produces a three-member class (i.e., a class incorporating the stimuli A, B, and C) with a further 7 matching relationships emerging (A to A, B to B, C to C, B to A, C to B, A to C, C to A), a total of $3^2 - 2 = 7$), but training 4 relationships (A to B, B to C, C to D, D to E) produces a five-member class (A, B, C, D, E) with a further 21 matching relationships emerging ($5^2 - 4 = 21$). Thus, training two additional relationships produces 14 further matching relationships. Natural stimulus equivalence classes may have very many members with a huge number of emerging matching relationships.

PROCEDURAL ISSUES

The conventional procedure for training stimulus equivalence classes involves training several (typically, three) A to B relationships concurrently using a matching-to-sample procedure. On a trial either A1, A2, or A3 is presented as a sample, and then B1, B2, and A3 are presented simultaneously. Feedback is presented on correct choices (which will be B1 following A1, B2 following A2, and B3 following B3). Once criterion performance is reached on the matching-to-sample task, a second training phase begins in which either B1, B2, or B3 is presented as a sample and then C1, C2, and C3 are presented simultaneously. Correct choices will be C1 following B1, C2 following B2, and C3 following B3. Again, training continues until a performance criterion is reached. Typically, the stimuli used (such as the picture of an object, the object's spoken name, and the object's written name) are arbitrary (or meaningless in relation to each other) or form a class familiar to the language-competent community but not known by language-disabled or developmentally retarded individuals.

A test is required to demonstrate that the three stimulus equivalence classes have been formed (the classes will be A1, B1, and C1; A2, B2, and C2; A3, B3, and C3). This is achieved by presenting C1, C2, or C3 as samples and then A1, A2, and A3 simultaneously as choices. "Correct" choices (that is, choices indicating that equivalence classes have been formed) will be A1 following C1, A2 following C2, and A3 following

C3. Success indicates that reflexivity, symmetry, and transitivity are all present (Hayes, 1989). In language-competent humans, correct performance occurs spontaneously in a very high proportion of individuals, provided the criteria for performance in the two earlier training phases of the experiment are sufficiently severe. Interestingly, other species do not readily form stimulus equivalence classes (Dugdale & Lowe, 1990).

According to Sidman (1990), because all derived relations must emerge before it can be said that an equivalence class has been formed, there are certain consistencies that must follow:

1. If the individual tests for reflexivity, symmetry, and transitivity prove positive, so also must the combined symmetry and transitivity test. This latter test is sometimes referred to as an equivalence test.
2. If the equivalence test proves negative, one or more of its components must also prove negative; that is, reflexivity, symmetry, and/or transitivity must be absent.
3. If one of these properties is not absent and the test for equivalence is negative, we must attribute this result to another factor.
4. If the test for equivalence is positive, so also must all tests for its components be positive.

To date most published research has been concerned with the necessary and sufficient conditions of training procedures, the structure of stimulus equivalence classes, and the role of language competence in successful performance on the task.

RELEVANCE TO EVERYDAY LIFE

Much of our everyday behavior can be better understood when we consider how stimuli come to be treated equivalently. For example, a child speaks the word "*ball*" and gets a particular response from an adult, such as pointing to the child's ball. When the child sees a picture of the ball, the child soon learns that this image represents the toy that is "ball." Eventually, when the child is asked the question "Where is your ball?", the child will point to the ball in the physical presence of the ball or to the ball in the picture.

In this example, we have three very different stimuli, and yet each one has come to elicit the same response from the child. The three stimuli also fulfill the requirements for equivalence, that is, reflexivity, symmetry, and transitivity. These stimuli have therefore formed a stimulus equivalence class.

Fields, Reeve, Adams, and Verhave (1991) have argued that equivalence classes in combination with stimulus generalization can provide a plausible mechanism for the formation of natural categories. Fields et al. (1991) trained five undergraduate subjects to match A1(2) to B1(2), and B1(2) to C1(2), respectively. The A1(2) and B1(2) stimuli consisted of nonsense syllables, while the C1(2) stimuli consisted of contiguous horizontal strings of ASCII character 177 (a square). Each stimulus comprised a different number of this character in a horizontal line. Each character was 3mm wide and 5mm high on the computer screen. Class 1 (C1) included lines 2 through 7 characters long. Class 2 (C2) included lines 19 through 24 characters long. The remaining 13 lines were reserved for tests of the generalization of equivalence. The stimuli were presented using a microcomputer with a monochrome monitor. Subjects were trained to match A to B and were then tested for symmetry, that is, B1 to A1, and B2 to A2. Following this, B-C was trained with six variants of C1 and C2. Testing took place for C1(x) to B1 and C2(x) to B2, where x represents the different line lengths. At this stage, subjects were tested for all of the emergent relations as well as the trained ones. In the generalization testing stage, the A stimuli served as comparisons, and the intermediate line lengths served as samples, that is, C8 through C18. All five subjects were able to form the required equivalence classes. As the lines increased for C8 to C18, the likelihood of choosing A1 decreased.

These stimuli became members of an equivalence class, not through training but rather through their close relation to a stimulus that had been trained. Fields et al. (1991) suggested that this combination of equivalence class formation and generalization can be used as a model of natural categories that we observe in the real world.

THE ORIGINS OF EQUIVALENCE RESPONDING

Not surprisingly, the issue of the origin of equivalence classes is one that has received some attention in the literature. As a starting point, it might be assumed that logic is the source of equivalence responding (Sidman & Tailby, 1982). However, this view is not sustainable. Using the relation "is parallel to," the stimuli A, B, and C fulfill all requirements necessary to form an equivalence class when A is parallel to B, and B is parallel to C. This relation is reflexive, as each stimulus is parallel to itself. It is also symmetric, as B is parallel to A, and C is parallel to B. Finally, it is transitive, as A is also parallel to C. This equivalence relation follows mathematic logic, supporting the view that logic is the source of equivalence.

Not all logical relations are necessarily equivalent, however. For example, the relation "is greater than" does not possess the properties of equivalence. If A is greater than B, and B is greater than C, then A is greater than C. This is a transitive relation. However, this relation is neither symmetric nor reflexive. B is not greater than A, C is not greater than B, and no stimulus is greater than itself. Unlike an equivalence relation, this relation does not require all three properties and yet it is still a logic relation. As equivalence does not demand logic, logic therefore cannot be its source (Sidman, 1990).

Other researchers prefer to argue that equivalence stems from naming. Naming has been described as "a symbolic skill that involves bidirectionality . . . (or) an arbitrary verbal response which is symmetrically related to its controlling stimulus" (Dugdale & Lowe, 1990; p. 132). The stimulus and verbal response are symmetric, because the stimulus elicits the particular verbal response and the verbal response controls behaviors that are related to the stimulus.

Equivalence has been demonstrated in children as young as two years old. Using three groups of children, Devany, Hayes, and Nelson (1986) demonstrated that stimulus equivalence and language development are indeed closely related. The first group were normally developing preschoolers recruited from the child-care center in the University of North Carolina. These children had speech skills consistent with their chronological age. Groups 2 and 3 consisted of retarded children. Group 2 spoke incomplete but brief sentences when prompted and had some voluntary speech. Children who were able to use sign language were also included in this group. Group 3 was classified as the no-language group. The children failed to spontaneously use word signs or picture-boards and were lacking in functional language skills and sign language. The three groups were matched for mental age on the basis of an individual intelligence test.

Each child was taught four conditional discriminations: if A, then B; if D, then E; if A, then C; if D, then F. The stimuli used were animal-like figures colored with markers. The stimuli were presented on sheets of white paper, with a sample at the top of the page and two comparisons on the bottom of the page. The left-right position of the comparisons was randomized to prevent choice of position rather than stimulus. During training, the children were prompted when necessary to select the correct stimulus. As the child made the correct choice, the prompting was faded.

Results showed that the normal child group and the retarded/language group required fewer trials on the conditional discrimination tasks than the retarded/no-language group. During the testing stage, the performance of language-able children was consistent with the formation of equivalence classes, whereas the language-disabled group performed at chance level only. These findings support the view that a close link exists between language development and the formation of equivalence classes.

The authors maintained, however, that it was not possible to determine whether stimulus equivalence class formation was a necessary requirement for language development or whether language was necessary for the formation of equivalence classes.

A number of authors have supported the view that giving each stimulus a name makes it easier to treat the stimuli equivalently (Beasty, 1987). In a series of experiments conducted by Lowe and Beasty (1987), it was demonstrated that children who failed an equivalence task, and were then taught to give the stimuli names, later succeeded on the same equivalence test. The children were taught to match A (vertical line sample) to B (green comparison), and A (vertical line sample) to C (triangle comparison). Tests were then conducted to assess whether the subjects could form an equivalence class with B and C. Subjects who failed this test were then taught to name the stimuli; that is, when presented with the A-B relation, they were told to say "up-green" and "up-triangle" when presented with the A-C relation. When the subjects were retested, they immediately formed the B-C and C-B relations.

Crowther, Dugdale, and Lowe (1993) carried out an experiment with 13 two- to five-year old children. The experiment consisted of two stages. Initially, a procedure was developed to ensure rapid learning on arbitrary matching tasks without the use of instructions such as "A goes with B." The stimuli consisted of three-dimensional wooden shapes. Those who failed to learn the task were taught to vocalize labels for the A stimuli, and if they failed yet again, they were taught a label for the B stimuli. There were two different types of labeling training. After picking up a stimulus, the children were told: "That is Omni/Delta," or the experimenter simply said, "Omni/Delta." Those who failed to learn the labels were taught to point to the appropriate stimulus while saying the words. After learning the A-B task, the children were tested on a symmetry test (B-A).

1. Nine of the children learned the A-B task without any labeling interventions and passed the symmetry test.
2. Two children learned the A-B task but failed on the symmetry test. These children were

then given labeling training. One was told, "That is Omni/Delta," whereas the other was told, "Say Omni/Delta." The first child learned the correct labels in 32 trials but failed the symmetry test again. He was then taught the labels for the B stimuli and subsequently passed the test. The second child required 96 trials to learn the labels. She also applied the labels to the corresponding B stimuli and passed the symmetry test.

3. Two children failed to learn the A-B task before labeling took place. The first child was then given the relational instruction "That is." He responded 100% correctly on the A-B task but failed the symmetry test. He then learned the labels for the B stimuli and went on to pass the test. The second child was given the "Say" instruction but still failed to learn the labels. Pointing was then introduced. After a total of 196 labeling trials, she learned the A-B relation and reached criterion after 48 trials. She then passed the symmetry test.

The results indicate that the learning of labels facilitates the learning of conditional discriminations.

Another way to assess the role of naming in equivalence class formation is to assess nonhumans on similar tasks. McIntire, Cleary, and Thompson (1987) reported that a group of monkeys, that they had trained displayed all the defining characteristics of equivalence. Hayes (1989) and Saunders (1989), however, argued that these results could be attributed to the extensive training received by the subjects in all the tested relations (i.e., there were no derived relations). If there are no derived relations, there is no possibility of an equivalence class.

The results of a study by Savage-Rumbaugh, Rumbaugh, Smith, and Lawson (1980) seemed much more promising in relation to emergent behaviors in nonhumans. Savage-Rumbaugh et al. taught two chimpanzees (Sherman and Austin) lexigram names for a number of food and tool objects. A food and a tool item were put as a set into each of three bins. The chimps were then re-

inforced for putting the two remaining sets of tool and food items into the appropriate bins. Once they had accomplished this, they were required to put one of the items into a bin and label it with a food or tool lexigram. They eventually learned to label the food and tool items without the use of the bins. They were then presented with five food items and five tool items that they had previously learned the lexigram names for but had not classified as food or tool items. Austin correctly categorized all the items, and Sherman incorrectly categorized one.

In the second stage, photographs of the three foods and tools used in the initial categorization were taped to the corresponding objects, and the chimps had to label them as foods or tools. Following this, they labeled the photographs alone. Then they were presented with photographs of four tools and five foods that they had learned the lexigram names for but had not labeled foods or tools. Sherman labeled them all correctly, but Austin had to rotate the photos before labeling them correctly.

In the final stage, the three food and tool lexigrams used in training were taped onto photos of corresponding objects, and the chimps had to label the objects in the photos as foods or tools. When they succeeded on this task, the photos were removed, and the chimps labeled the lexigrams. Sherman labeled 15 out of the 16 presented to him, and Austin labeled 17 out of 17.

According to Cerutti and Rumbaugh (1993), "Once the foods and tools could be individually named, sorted by concept class, and named by concept class, the names of foods and tools could also be named by concept class" (p. 817).

This derived relation could be said to be an equivalence relation. To fully describe these stimuli as members of an equivalence class, further tests for symmetry and transitivity would have to be conducted. It still remains to be seen whether Sherman and Austin were treating each member equivalently.

Schusterman and Kastak (1993) examined the possibility that a California sea lion could pass tests for equivalence. Rio was a three-year-old

California sea lion when the study began. Training took place in outdoor pools at Long Marine Laboratory in Santa Cruz, California.

The matching-to-sample apparatus consisted of a set of wooden boards containing three window-fronted boxes in which the stimuli were placed. The middle board housed the sample stimulus, with the comparison stimuli on the outer boards. The stimuli were placed in the boxes by two assistants, who received their instructions via headphones from the experimenter. The comparison stimuli were placed in the boxes simultaneously so that the subject would not make a choice based upon the order of placement. Pieces of fresh fish were given to Rio as reinforcement for correct responses.

Thirty potential equivalence classes were trained. The stimuli for the first 8 were three-dimensional "junk" objects made of wood, steel, or plastic. They were painted black and were presented against a white background. Stimuli for the next 22 classes consisted of black shapes painted on a white background on pieces of plywood. After the sample and comparisons were presented, the subject was expected to make a choice by pressing her nose to the board containing one of the comparisons. Rio learned the first 2 A-B relations by trial and error, the next 6 by exclusion, and the last 22 by trial and error again. After each problem had been learned, it was incorporated into the baseline of previously learned stimuli. Rio was then tested on 12 B-A relations, and if they were successfully accomplished, training began on B-C relations. These were taught by trial and error, and when they had been learned, they were also incorporated in the baseline of previously learned stimuli. Following training, Rio was tested on C-B symmetry, A-C transitivity, and C-A equivalence.

On the B-A symmetry test, Rio passed 8 out of 12 problems. On the C-B symmetry tests, she passed 10 out of 12 problems, which was statistically above chance. On the A-C transitivity test, she had a score of 11 out of 12, and on the C-A test she passed 14 out of 18 tests. Because Rio passed all the necessary tests for equivalence

without the use of labeling, naming, or instruction, it would appear that language is indeed unnecessary for the formation of equivalence classes. If this is the case, the origin of stimulus equivalence class formation is left unresolved.

Sidman (1990) suggested that equivalence may not have a source as such but that it may be a given or a "fundamental stimulus function." As children grow, they are taught to say a particular word in response to the presentation of a particular stimulus. They are also taught to do the reverse, that is, point out the stimulus when the word is spoken. Children receive a great deal of reinforcement for this type of behavior (which is called symmetry in equivalence terms) and subsequently engage in it frequently. As this type of emergent behavior is continuously reinforced, other forms of similar behavior may also emerge as a natural consequence. Emergence of equivalence may be facilitated by, but not dependent upon, the emergence of symmetrical behavior through the reinforcement of "naming." Whether equivalence is a phenomenon in its own right or is dependent on language, it seems clear that normally developing language-able humans possess the ability to form equivalence classes, usually with the minimum of effort.

SOME APPLICATIONS

Having outlined the basic phenomena of equivalence class formation, we will now attempt to indicate the relevance of some of this literature for behavior therapy.

Anxiety Disorders

As a starting point, we will consider an old but enduring objection to a conditioning theory of anxiety disorders (Rachman, 1977). One of the objections raised by Rachman is that many individuals who suffer from anxiety disorders, including phobias, cannot recall having had an unpleasant or aversive experience in the presence of a feared stimulus. For this reason, many authors have resorted to cognitive explanations and have emphazised the role of beliefs and expectations as the cause of phobias. A related issue is the failure of anxiety responses to extinguish over time.

There is a growing literature on the transfer of functions through equivalence classes that is of particular relevance to this issue and may provide an alternative explanation to the cognitive accounts that many authors have resorted to in dealing with the problematic observations reported above. Transfer of function refers to the phenomenon whereby a discriminative response trained to one member of an equivalence class transfers to other members without further training. There are numerous examples of transfer of discriminative function in the literature. Hayes, Kohlenberg, and Hayes (1991) have demonstrated transfer of conditional reinforcement and punishment functions through equivalence classes. Barnes and Keenan (1993) have demonstrated a transfer of control through equivalence classes of complex, time-based schedule responding. They used two different schedules. One was similar to a ratio schedule and generated high rates of responding by participants. The other was similar to a D.R.L. schedule and generated low rate responding. Hayes, Devany, Kohlenberg, Brownstein, and Shelby (1987) demonstrated transfer of control of clapping and hand waving. Other forms of responding that have been shown to transfer in this manner are conditional matching (Gatch & Osborne, 1989) and simple simultaneous discriminations (de Rose, McIlvane, Dube, & Stoddard, 1988).

The study that is of most relevance to present considerations, however, is a study by Dougher, Auguston, Markham, Greenway, and Wulfert (1994). In this study, two experiments were reported in which volunteer college students served as participants. In experiment 1, two four-member equivalence classes were established using a standard matching-to-sample training. This was followed by classical conditioning in which a member of one class of stimuli served as a CS+ for delivery of an electric shock and a member of the second class served as a CS–. Although there was some variability in responding,

transfer of conditioning was demonstrated to other members of the equivalence class involving the stimulus used as a CS+. The response measure used was skin conductance. In experiment 2, it was demonstrated that extinction functions transferred to all other members of an equivalence class when one member of the class was presented in an extinction procedure.

Taken in conjunction with the general literature on transfer of function, these findings provide an initial response to one of the oldest and most enduring problems for a contingency-based account of an important clinical disorder. However, as Dougher et al. (1994) have argued, the strength and stability of the responses used in their study are not comparable to those in clinical conditions. Consequently, some caution must be exercised in extrapolating from these results.

Another common objection to behavioral accounts of the acquisition of phobias is derived from the observation that stimuli do not appear to have an equal potential to become conditioned fear stimuli (Seligman, 1971). Seligman has proposed that certain stimulus-response connections are biologically "prepared." It is argued that such connections are of biological significance, easily conditioned, and slow to extinguish. The traditional behavioral counterargument to this position is that ontogenic and not phylogenic processes account for such nonequipotentiality of stimuli. That is, to explain why some stimuli appear to be prepared and others do not, behaviorists have sometimes argued that unobserved experiences within the lifetime of the individual have produced the two categories of stimuli. For example, McAllister and McAllister (1995) argued that experiments that purport to demonstrate preparedness often fail to rule out the effects of pseudoconditioning and sensitization as alternative sources of preparedness. However, this argument is rather weak because it relies on individuals having direct experience of all potential stimuli to prime them as easily conditioned or difficult-to-condition stimuli. In practical terms, this route to preparedness seems cumbersome and unlikely. Although there is no research that impinges directly on this issue, it is easy to envisage how equivalence classes might provide a more efficient and plausible ontogenic mechanism to preparedness. For example, it is possible that a natural category incorporating potentially phobic stimuli could be formed via a combination of a naturally occurring analogue of matching-to-sample training and stimulus generalization, as outlined by Fields et al. (1991). Subsequently, an unpleasant experience with one member of this class might be sufficient to prime all other members of that class as easily conditioned stimuli.

Clinical Tests

A second application of the equivalence class literature is based on the assumption that the failure of verbally competent human beings to form equivalence classes, using experimental procedures known to generate equivalence, tells us something about their existing stimulus classes and prior experiences. The relevant findings come from studies that employed nonarbitrary stimuli.

In keeping with a long tradition in behavior analysis, the stimuli employed in most studies of stimulus equivalence to date have been arbitrary and have had no intended prior relationship to each other. They have usually been arbitrary visual stimuli (e.g., Devany et al., 1986), although more recently they have been drug states (de Grandpre, Bickel, & Higgins, 1992) and haptically perceived stimuli; that is, stimuli whose shapes were perceived by manual wielding (Tierney, De Largy, & Bracken, 1995) have all been used successfully. However, the history of behavior analysis teaches us that occasional deviations from this time-honored practice may be informative. For example, the landmark experiment published by Garcia and Koelling (1966) on taste aversion learning that used nonarbitrary stimuli had important implications for the study of associative processes.

An early study that employed nonarbitrary stimuli in an equivalence experiment was reported by Watt, Keenan, Barnes and Cairns, (1991), who found that if nonarbitrary stimulus elements were used, some Northern Irish Protestant subjects failed a test of stimulus equivalence class formation. This occurred when A-elements were Catholic names (e.g., Patrick O'Hagen), B-elements were nonsense syllables (e.g., zid), and C-elements were Protestant symbols (e.g., orange order). In contrast, English subjects presumably without the same lengthy experience of prior learning about Catholic names and Protestant symbols did show stimulus equivalence class formation. This result suggests that stimulus equivalence class formation may be systematically disrupted by prior experiences with the stimuli.

An analogous experiment reported by Leslie, Tierney, Robinson, Keenan, Watt, and Barnes (1993) used the methodology in a similar manner. However, the subjects used by Leslie et al. were general anxiety patients, and the stimuli were anxiety-related stimuli. The experiment used nine patients who were being treated for general anxiety and a matched control group. The first stage of training established links between stimulus words that described anxiety-provoking situations (e.g., a job interview) and nonsense syllables. When these links were established, subjects were taught to match the same nonsense syllables to stimulus words that described pleasant outcomes. All subjects were then tested to determine whether the transitive link between the threatening situations and the pleasant outcomes had emerged. These transitive links were observed for eight out of the nine control subjects but for only two of the general anxiety patients. Furthermore, there was less overlap between the two groups on the emergence of transitive links than there was for their scores on the Speilberger State-Trait Anxiety Inventory (Speilberger, Gorsuch, & Lushene, 1970). Thus, the equivalence test appeared to provide a more powerful method for discriminating between the two groups than a test that is routinely used in clinical practice for that purpose. Obviously, these findings will need to be replicated with larger groups of subjects before the methodology can be employed as a diagnostic tool in clinical practice. However, the initial indications are promising. Furthermore, it may be possible to extend this rationale to other clinical problems.

Reading

Some additional applications of the equivalence literature stem from some early experiments that examined the basic phenomenon. Sidman (1971) was initially interested in reading comprehension in children with learning difficulties. He viewed the earliest conditional discrimination training experiments as simplified versions of standard reading comprehension tasks.

According to Sidman and Tailby (1982), the findings from experiments on matching-to-sample training are of relevance in three ways. First, the observation that the number of emergent relations can greatly exceed the number of trained relations means that the procedure is an extremely efficient form of training. In an early experiment (Sidman, 1971), retarded adolescents learned to select pictures (A) conditionally upon 20 dictated picture names (B). Subsequently, they learned to select printed names (C) conditionally upon the same 20 dictated names. Sidman and Tailby then demonstrated that A-B and A-C were equivalence relations by testing for symmetry and transitivity. Subjects demonstrated an ability to correctly select an appropriate picture conditionally upon presentation of a printed word (C-B) and also to select an appropriate printed word conditionally upon presentation of a picture. These were untrained or emergent responses that were not evident prior to training. The training of the 40 conditional relations had given rise to 80 new performances, as oral naming of pictures (B-A) and printed words (C-A) was also observed. A later experiment (Sidman & Tailby, 1982) added an additional member to the stimulus class, yielding a two- to fivefold increase in teaching efficiency.

Second, Sidman argued that there are formal similarities between the types of responding observed in equivalence experiments and reading. For example, matching auditory to visual stimuli corresponds to simple auditory comprehension; matching visual stimuli to each other corresponds to reading comprehension, and naming textual stimuli corresponds to simple oral reading. These formal similarities are sufficient to suggest that matching-to-sample training might constitute an efficient teaching method.

Furthermore, Sidman (1994) has demonstrated that matching auditory words to pictures and to printed words is a sufficient prerequisite for the emergence of reading comprehension and oral reading. He has urged the development of automated programs to teach reading comprehension via purely receptive auditory-visual training. Such an application would constitute a direct practical application of his and others' experimental findings to an important educational issue.

Third, linguists have challenged behavior analytic accounts of language by arguing that unreinforced utterances are a common feature of language (e.g., Chomsky, 1965). The equivalence paradigm provides a mechanism for the emergence of apparently unreinforced matching-to-sample and oral naming and exposes the potential source of reinforcement for such behaviors. Although the account requires further elaboration, it is at least a small step in the direction of addressing this outstanding objection by Chomsky.

Generalization

A possible further application of the equivalence paradigm to behavior therapy stems from some recent work by I. Taylor and M. O'Reilly (personal communication, December 1995), whose study involved training young adults with mental disability in the skills required to shop in a supermarket. In common with many attempts to teach skills to such individuals, Taylor and O'Reilly were concerned with the failure to generalize acquired skills to new settings. They evaluated two methods to improve generalization. One technique involved training multiple exemplars; that is, they trained participants in a range of supermarket settings. The second method involved equivalence training using photographs of different supermarkets. Both methods were observed to be moderately successful in facilitating generalization of the acquired skills to new settings.

GENERAL COMMENTS

Some deficiencies have manifested in traditional behavioral explanations of clinical problems and other complex behaviors. At a general level, these difficulties stem from an inability of behaviorists to specify plausible sets of historical antecedents that can accommodate all that is known about the nature, distribution, and complexity of such behaviors. The response of many behavior analysts has been to adopt more cognitively oriented approaches (Latimer & Sweet, 1984).

In this chapter, we have tried to show how the growing literature on stimulus equivalence can help to address some of these difficulties by enabling us to specify the sorts of historical antecedents that can address some of the perceived deficiencies in a number of functional explanations. We are optimistic that the growing literature will extend the plausibility of such explanations and will provide insights into other problems of interest to behavior therapists. Furthermore, we have shown how the approach can be of practical use in the treatment of some clinical problems. Again, we are confident that future research will reveal techniques of even wider clinical utility.

REFERENCES

Barnes, D., & Keenan, M. (1993). A transfer of functions through derived arbitrary and nonarbitrary stimulus relations. *Journal of the Experimental Analysis of Behavior, 59,* 61–81.

Beasty, A. (1987). *The role of language in the emergence of equivalence relations: A developmental study.* Unpublished Ph.D thesis, University of Wales.

Cerutti, D. T., & Rumbaugh, D. M. (1993). Stimulus relations in comparative primate perspective. *The Psychological Record, 43,* 811–821.

Chomsky, N. (1965). *Aspects of the theory of syntax.* Cambridge, Mass.: MIT Press.

Crowther, L. M., Dugdale, W., & Lowe, C. F. (1993). *How does naming promote stimulus equivalence?* Paper presented at the annual conference of the Experimental Analysis of Behavior Group, London, England, U.K.

de Grandpre, R. J., Bickel, W. K., & Higgins, S. T. (1992). Emergent equivalence relations between introceptive (drug) and exeroceptive (visual) stimuli. *Journal of the Experimental Analysis of Behavior, 58,* 9–18.

de Rose, J. C., McIlvane, W. J., Dube, W. V., & Stoddard, L. T. (1988). Stimulus class formation and functional equivalence in moderately retarded individuals' conditional discriminations. *Behavioral Processes, 17,* 167–175.

Devany, J. M., Hayes, S. C., & Nelson, R. O. (1986). Equivalence class formation in language-able and language-disabled children. *Journal of the Experimental Analysis of Behavior, 46,* 243–257.

Dougher, M. J., Auguston, E., Markham, M. R., Greenway, D. E., & Wulfert, E. (1994). The transfer of respondent eliciting and extinction functions through stimulus equivalence classes. *Journal of the Experimental Analysis of Behavior, 62,* 331–351.

Dugdale, N., & Lowe, C. F. (1990). Naming and stimulus equivalence. In D. E. Blackman & H. Lejeune (eds), *Behavior analysis in theory and practice: Contributions and controversies,* 115–138. Brighton, U.K.: Erlbaum.

Fields, L., Reeve, K., Adams, B. J., & Verhave, T. (1991). Stimulus generalization and equivalence classes: A model for natural categories. *Journal of the Experimental Analysis of Behavior, 55,* 305–312.

Garcia, J., & Koelling, R. A. (1966). Relation of cue to consequence in avoidance learning. *Psychonomic Science, 4,* 123–124.

Gatch, M. B., & Osborne, J. G. (1989). Transfer of contextual stimulus function via equivalence class development. *Journal of the Experimental Analysis of Behavior, 51,* 369–378.

Hayes, S. C. (1989). Nonhumans have not yet shown stimulus equivalence. *Journal of the Experimental Analysis of Behavior, 51,* 385–392.

Hayes, S. C., Devany, J. M., Kohlenberg, B. S., Brownstein, A. J., & Shelby, J. (1987). Stimulus equivalence and symbolic control of behavior. *Revista Mexicana de Analisis de la Conducta, 13,* 361–374.

Hayes, S. C., Kohlenberg, B. S., & Hayes, L. J. (1991). The transfer of general and specific consequential functions through simple and conditional equivalence relations. *Journal of the Experimental Analysis of Behavior, 56,* 119–137.

Latimer, P. R., & Sweet, A. A. (1984). Cognitive versus behavioural procedures in cognitive behaviour therapy: A critical review of the evidence. *Journal of Behaviour Therapy and Experimental Psychiatry, 15,* 9–22.

Leslie, J. C. Tierney, K. J., Robinson, C. P., Keenan, M., Watt, A., & Barnes, D. (1993). Differences between clinically anxious and non-anxious subjects in a stimulus equivalence training task involving threat words. *Psychological Record, 43,* 153–161.

Lowe, C. F., & Beasty, A. (1987). Language and the emergence of equivalence relations: A developmental study. *Bulletin of the British Psychological Society, 40,* A42.

McAllister, W. R., & McAllister, D. E. (1995). Two-factor fear theory: Implications for understanding anxiety based clinical phenomena. In W. O'Donohue & L. Krasner (eds.), *Theories of behavior therapy: Exploring behavior change.* Washington, D.C.: American Psychological Association.

McIntire, K. D., Cleary, J., & Thompson, T. (1987). Conditional relations by monkeys: Reflexivity, symmetry and transitivity. *Journal of the Experimental Analysis of Behavior, 51,* 279–285.

Rachman, S. J. (1977). The conditioning theory of fear acquisition: A critical examination. *Behaviour Research and Therapy, 15,* 375–387.

Saunders, K. J. (1989). Naming in conditional discrimination and stimulus equivalence. *Journal of the Experimental Analysis of Behavior, 51,* 379–384.

Savage-Rumbaugh, E. S., Rumbaugh, D. M., Smith, S. T., & Lawson, J. (1980). Reference: The linguistic essential. *Science, 210,* 922–924.

Schusterman, R. J., & Kastak, D. (1993). A California sea lion *(Zalophus Californianus)* is capable of forming equivalence relations. *The Psychological Record, 43,* 811–821.

Seligman, M. E. P. (1971). Phobias and preparedness. *Behavior Therapy, 2,* 307–320.

Sidman, M. (1971). Reading and auditory-visual equivalences. *Journal of Speech and Hearing Research, 14,* 5–13.

Sidman, M. (1986). Functional analysis of emergent verbal classes. In T. Thompson & M. D. Zeiler (eds.), *Analysis and integration of behavioural units,* 213–245. Hillsdale, N.J.: Erlbaum.

Sidman, M. (1990). Equivalence relations: Where do they come from? In D. E. Blackman & H. Lejeune (eds.), *Behaviour analysis in theory and practice: Contributions and controversies,* 93–114. Hillsdale, N.J.: Erlbaum.

Sidman, M. (1994). *Equivalence relations and behavior: A research story.* Boston: Authors Cooperative, Inc.

Sidman, M., & Cresson, O., Jr. (1973). Reading and cross-modal transfer of stimulus equivalences in severe retardation. *American Journal of Mental Deficiency, 77,* 515–523.

Sidman, M., & Tailby, W. (1982). Conditional discrimination vs. matching-to-sample. An expansion of the testing paradigm. *Journal of the Experimental Analysis of Behavior, 37,* 5–22.

Speilberger, C. D., Gorsuch, R. L., & Lushene, R. E. (1970). *Manual for the State-Trait Anxiety Inventory.* Palo Alto, Calif.: Consulting Psychologists Press.

Tierney, K. J., De Largy, P., & Bracken, M. (1995). Formation of an equivalence class incorporating haptic stimuli. *The Psychological Record, 45,* 431–437.

Watt, A., Keenan, M., Barnes, D., & Cairns, E. (1991). Social categorisation and stimulus equivalence. *Psychological Record, 41,* 35–50.

CHAPTER 20

ORIGINS OF NEW BEHAVIOR

Peter D. Balsam
James D. Deich
Tatsuya Ohyama
Patricia D. Stokes

As one of us was riding the New York subway last week, there was a man reciting disorganized passages from the works of Shakespeare in a very loud voice. Most passengers left the subway car after a minute or two. It was clear that for most people this was very bizarre behavior. This anecdote illuminates the dimensions along which behavior is judged to be adaptive by others. For behavior to be successful, it must occur in an appropriate place and at an appropriate time, it must fit the stimulus situation, and it must be appropriate in its form. The psychological mechanisms that underlie the timing and situational control of behavior have been widely studied (Balsam, 1988). In contrast, the mechanisms that underlie the production of new behavior have not generated as much research activity. This is surprising in that the induction of new behavior is a basic question in all areas of psychology.

For example, a fundamental question in the study of development is why one response form gives way to another as the organism gets older. Babies go from crawling to walking, or from suckling to feeding. New forms emerge, *de novo,* as when a child's first words are uttered. Similarly, creative problem solving is a topic of study in cognitive psychology. In the study of learning, it is not yet understood why shaping induces new behavior. In education, one is constantly concerned with the teaching of new responses, and successful psychotherapy often requires that clients learn new ways of reacting. It is clear that when we understand the principles that underlie the generation of new behavior, we will have information that is useful across the range of practical problems that psychologists have addressed.

In this chapter, we review some of our own work on the origins of new behavior. We have studied this problem in three domains. We have researched how a rat is shaped to press a bar, how a young bird learns to eat a piece of seed, and how humans learn a novel sequence of simple actions. This research, along with research from other laboratories, is used to illustrate the operation of principles that underlie the generation of new behavior. We then consider some applications of these principles to practical problems. The applications are speculative, but we hope that those more familiar with applied problems will see the power of the principles we articulate and experiment with them in the practical world.

RESPONSE VARIATION AND SELECTION

A conceptual framework that we have found useful for analyzing changes in response form comes from the evolutionary metaphor proposed by Staddon & Simmelhag (1971). In this view, one must understand both the origins of new behavior (principles of variation) and changes in the relative frequency of behavior (principles of selection). Existing response forms are differentially selected by reinforcement. Forms that are most strongly selected by reinforcement contingencies are those that come to dominate. Exactly how reinforcement affects the future occurrence of behavior is a topic of considerable research, and one that has reached a highly sophisticated level of discourse (see Williams, 1988). The bulk of this paper focuses on principles of variation, but first we need to consider some assumptions that underlie our analysis of behavior.

Before discussing where new behavior comes from, we must consider two views of the nature of behavior. First, let us consider how new behavior could come about if behavior is considered to be continuous in space and time. In Skinner's (1953) classic view of how new response forms are acquired through shaping, differential reinforcement is said to shape responses in the way that a sculptor shapes clay. Behavior is continuously malleable. Evidence in support of this view comes largely from studies involving the shaping of response location, duration, and force (see Galbicka [1988] and Stokes & Balsam [1991] for reviews). Animals learn *where* and *when* to per-

form a response through differential reinforcement of behavior by selection of variants that continuously change in time and space.

However, we do not think the continuous view of behavior change is a complete model of how animals learn *what to do*. Behavior is organized into discrete components or packets (Timberlake, 1983; Timberlake & Lucas, 1989). Support for this point of view comes from developmental and neurophysiological analyses of many types of motor behavior (Berridge, 1994; Fentress, 1983; Gallistel, 1980; Golani & Fentress, 1985), including operants (Teitelbaum, 1977). If one considers a particular action to be a sequence of components, then learning to do something new may come from a change in these components themselves or in their sequential organization.

We have no reason to believe that our analysis of behavioral variation does not apply equally well to variation in components and component sequences as well as to continuous variations of behavior in space and time, but it is worth keeping the distinction in mind. It is possible that different processes underlie these different kinds of variation and/or that there is an order in which different types of variants are induced. We now return to the discussion of the origins of new behavior.

SOURCES OF BEHAVIORAL VARIATION

When teaching our students how to shape a rat to press a bar, we tell them to begin by rewarding the rat for approaching the bar. We tell them that once the rat reliably approaches the bar, they should reward it only for making contact with the bar. Then reward the rat only for moving the bar, and finally reward it only for pressing the bar. These vague instructions usually result in a room full of bar-pressing rats. In our human keyboard task, we first reward subjects for hitting the "enter" key. Then we reward them for hitting an alpha key followed by the enter key. Then we reward them for hitting the space bar followed by some number of alpha keys and then the enter key. This usually results in a room full of key-pressing college students.

In both these tasks, there is so much constraint

on the way in which one approximation leads to the next that the training procedures are quite effective. In both cases, we make implicit use of these constraints to get our experiments to work. The effective therapist, teacher, or coach has an implicit understanding of the constraints in the tasks that each teaches. They use these constraints in designing programs of behavior change, though they often cannot articulate why the technique works. In this chapter, we describe some of the mechanisms that underlie the emergence of new behavior. We have chosen to organize this work in a scheme similar to the one developed in Segal's (1972) seminal paper on the origins of operant behavior.

Structural Class

Strengthening one response may lead to the induction of responses that are linked structurally to the original response. Members of a structural class are linked to each other by a neuroanatomical substrate. We will illustrate how structural class might be involved in the performances of our human subjects in the keyboard task. In those experiments, subjects are presented with a standard keyboard that is masked so that only the space bar, the enter key, and eight alpha keys are accessible. In our standard procedure (Stokes, Mechner, & Balsam, submitted), subjects are shaped to start a sequence with the space bar, press any of the alpha keys at least 10 times, and then press the enter key. Correct sequences are rewarded with points. We then measure the number of presses in each sequence, the exact key locations that are hit, and the time between key presses. We can therefore measure variation in the number, location, and timing of presses.

We keep the particular keys that are accessible to subjects constant, and we ask them to use only one hand while doing the task. We also have them sit directly in front of the keyboard, which rests on a counter top. All these aspects of the procedure have a profound effect on the subjects' behavior. If we were to allow the use of two hands, or if we fixed the hand in a different location than the one chosen by the subject, we would induce different behavior. It seems likely that

changing these aspects of the task would contact the structural constraints of key pressing in different ways, and that we would see changes in the sequences of keys that are pressed and in the timing of the presses. It is because of the structural properties of the effectors (e.g. fingers, wrists, and arms) and the constraints of the task that particular variants are induced rather than others (see Deich & Balsam, 1994, for a detailed consideration of how the fit between effectors and the task constrains the development of new behavior).

Functional Class

Skinner (1938) defined operants in terms of their consequences. All responses leading to a common outcome are members of the same functional class. It is thus possible to have behaviors that are very different from each other in form or topography be members of the same functional class. Consequently, strengthening one member of the class may induce other members of the class that are not at all similar to the original response. For example, if we reward a child's polite request for a cookie, other "cookie-getting" behavior may also appear, some of it perhaps not so polite. Figure 20–1 shows that although subjects need make only 10 responses to satisfy the reinforcement contingency in the keyboard task, they continue to produce many variants throughout the experiments. This group of subjects continued to make about a dozen different run lengths, even after hundreds of trials. Subjects show sustained variation in the location and timing of presses as well. Thus, strengthening one response leads to the induction of a large class of behavior.

When we acquire skilled movements, we need not learn all possible variants of the response. For example, when we learn to grasp objects, new variants of that response are emitted the first time we encounter objects of sizes or shapes that we have not previously encountered. There is considerable experimental evidence showing that continuous response dimensions can come under the control of continuous stimulus dimensions without having to explicitly learn the correspondence between every variant on both dimensions (Koh & Meyer, 1991; Wildeman, 1978).

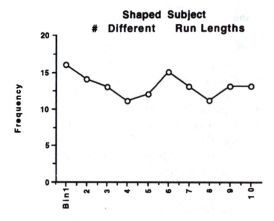

Figure 20–1. The mean number of different run lengths is shown in blocks of 25 trials. Subjects were required to make at least 10 presses. The figure shows that throughout the experiment, subjects averaged around 12 different run lengths in each block of trials.

Contingencies on Variability or Novelty

One can reward novelty (Goetz & Baer, 1973; Holman, Goetz, & Baer, 1977; Pryor, Haag, & O'Reilly, 1969). Pryor, Haag, and O'Reilly (1969) rewarded dolphins for doing a new trick each day. Soon the dolphins exhibited behavior that the trainers had never before seen. Similarly, Neuringer and his students (Neuringer, 1986) have a number of elegant demonstrations showing that rewarding people for being variable will produce the appropriate behavior. Figure 20–2 shows a replication of this basic finding, which we conducted with the help of our students Tucker McElroy and Anthea Paterniti. At the start of the experiment, a 6-by-6 matrix with a white square in the upper left-hand corner (the starting position) and a yellow square in the lower right-hand corner (the target position) appeared on the screen. The remaining 34 squares in the matrix were red. Subjects were instructed to use two directional keys (arrow down and arrow right) to move the white square through the grid in any way necessary to earn points. Points appeared on the screen after each correct

sequence of five right and five down presses. If subjects pressed either directional key more than five times, the screen went black, the white box returned to the upper left-hand corner of the screen, and no points were earned.

Each subject was exposed to four conditions. In the Lag0 condition, any sequence of five right and five down presses was correct. In the Lag2 condition, points were earned only if a current sequence differed from two prior ones. The Lag10 condition required a sequence that differed from 10 previous sequences, and the Lag25 a difference from 25 prior sequences. We often use an uncertainty metric as a measure of response variability. When there is low variability, sequences are very predictable, and there is little uncertainty. Figure 20–2 shows mean sequential uncertainties (for a discussion, see Stokes, 1995). Variability increased as the lag requirement increased. It is thus possible to modulate variability by using variability as a criterion for reward.

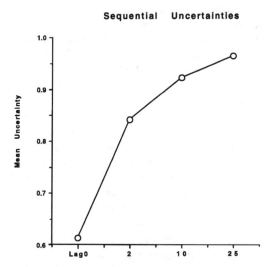

Figure 20–2. The mean sequential uncertainty is shown as a function of the lag requirement. Subjects were rewarded for sequences that were different from the previous 0, 2, 10, or 25 sequences as specified in the lag requirement. Sequential uncertainty is a measure of the variability in the sequences.

Induction by Disappointment

It has long been known that extinction increases variability. The classic account of shaping claims that it is the nonreinforced occurrence of a previous approximation that induces the closer approximation. The increase in variability during extinction has been experimentally demonstrated in location (Antonitis, 1951; Eckerman & Lanson, 1969), duration (Margulies, 1961; Millenson & Hurwitz, 1961; Millenson, Hurwitz, & Nixon, 1961), displacement (Herrick, 1965; Herrick & Bromberger, 1965), latency (Stebbins & Lanson, 1962), force (Notterman, 1959), and specific topography (Stokes, 1995) of responding. Figure 20–3 shows the results of a study conducted with the help of Karen Zechowy. In that study, we examined the effect of extinction on variability in the number of responses between the space bar and enter key in the keyboard task. Subjects were reinforced for making at least 10 presses for 200 trials followed by an extinction session lasting for 15 minutes. As in other procedures, extinction increases response variability.

We wondered what underlies this increase in variability. There is much evidence in the study of Pavlovian conditioning that learning occurs when outcomes are surprising or unexpected (Kamin, 1969; Rescorla & Wagner, 1972; Wagner & Brandon, 1989). We asked if the increased variability in operant behavior was the result of extinction or the result of surprise. To answer this question, we shaped three groups of subjects to respond on the keyboard task. At the end of each correct sequence, subjects earned 10 points. After subjects were performing the task steadily, they received a block of 10 trials in which the number of points changed. In the extinction group, subjects earned no points for 10 trials. In the downshift group, subjects earned only 1 point for the 10 trials, and in the upshift group, subjects earned 100 points for the 10 trials. If surprise produces variability, then all groups should have increases in variability. If nonreward produces variability, then only the extinction group should have increases in variability. Finally, if disappointment increases variability, then both the extinction and downshift groups should have increases in variability.

Figure 20–4 shows that both groups that received a decrease in reward increased in variability. Variability in the upshift group remained unchanged. Thus, disappointment, not surprise or extinction, increases variability.

Elicitation

Another source of new behavior arises from the mere presentation of a stimulus. Some have suggested that the conditioned response may emerge from the unconditioned response. The concordance between the form of the conditioned and unconditioned responses in operant procedures raises the possibility that the conditioned response arises from the unconditioned one (Segal, 1972). Responses may also be elicited by all the stimuli present in a given situation, including those we usually think of as the response manipulandum. Bindra (1974) suggested that all responses are elicited in this way. In his view, the role of reinforcement is to get the subject to pay attention to the stimuli that evoke the correct response.

Our experimental analysis of the origins of the rat's bar press have led us to conclusions similar to Bindra's. In one experiment we exposed a group of rats to several conditions and observed what

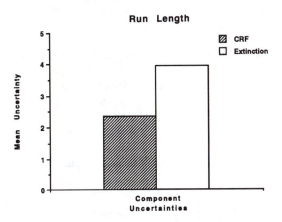

Figure 20–3. The average uncertainty for run length is shown during continuous reinforcement and during extinction. Uncertainty is a measure of variability in run lengths.

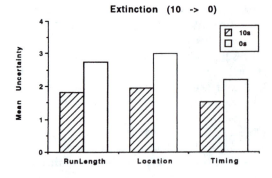

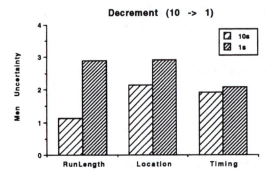

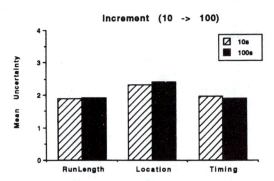

Figure 20–4. The average uncertainty in run length, location, and timing of key presses is shown for the three experimental groups. In all groups, the average uncertainty for the 10 trials prior to a shift in outcome is plotted next to the uncertainty for the 10 trials of the shifted outcome condition. All subjects earned 10 points for each correct sequence prior to the shift. The top row shows the group shifted to extinction in which no points were earned. The middle row shows the decrement group in which correct responses earned only 1 point after the shift. The bottom row shows the increment group in which correct sequences earned 100 points after the shift.

topographies were generated by those conditions. We have developed a coding scheme for characterizing the rat's bar press topography (Stokes, 1995; Stokes & Balsam, 1991). The categories of interacting with the bar include touching the bar with the right or left paw, grasping it with both paws, nosing it, biting it, and so on. First, we observed nondeprived rats interact with the bar. We then deprived them and again observed how they interacted with the bar. We observed the bar-directed behavior of deprived rats during dipper training in which the dipper was presented regardless of what the rat was doing on a variable-time 30-second schedule. Finally, the rats were shaped to press a bar, and their terminal behaviors were coded. Figure 20–5 shows the average frequency of the different topographies in the different conditions. Shaping the rat to press the bar does change the frequency of the components, but generally speaking, rats do the same things to bars prior to shaping as they do to bars after they have "learned" to respond. The components of the bar press are elicited by bars prior to shaping.

Stimulus Compounding

Another way in which new behavior arises is from the interaction of simultaneously presented stimuli. There are examples in the ethological literature in which blends of distinct behavior patterns occur when the releasing stimuli for different patterns are presented simultaneously. For example, Leyhausen (1956) carefully described the behavioral blends of aggression and fear that can be found in the cat under conditions that evoke both reactions. When novel compounds are presented, novel blends of behavior may emerge.

Similarly, one would expect this kind of blending to be a source of new behavior even when the stimulus control is learned rather than unconditioned.

Sensitization and Emotional Induction

The repeated presentation of reinforcers may also give rise to new behavior. When sensitization occurs, the presentation of a stimulus, par-

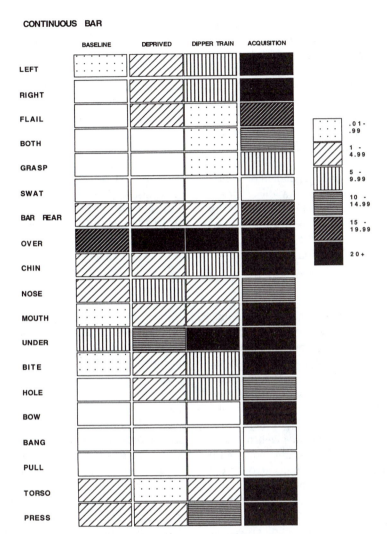

Figure 20–5. The frequency of different components of bar contact are shown for all the experimental conditions. In the baseline phase, subjects were observed in the experimental chamber. In the next condition, subjects were water-deprived and all interactions with the bar were recorded. Deprived subjects were then dipper-trained and finally shaped to press the bar.

ticularly a strong one, results in the enhanced ability of the cue to elicit a new response. Sometimes the potentiated response is a stronger version of the elicited response (Lipsitt & Kaye, 1965). Sometimes the potentiated response is different from the one originally elicited by a cue. For example, in the sea slug Aplysia, elicitation of the gill-withdrawal response by me-

chanical stimulation of the gill makes the defensive inking response more likely. If a strong stimulus is presented periodically, so-called schedule-induced behaviors may be potentiated (Staddon, 1977; Wetherington, 1979). The behavior that tends to occur following reinforcer presentation depends on the environmental supports available during these periods. For example, following periodic food presentation, rats will drink excessively, chew on wood chips, run in a wheel, or be aggressive toward a conspecific following food presentation depending on which stimuli are present (cf. Staddon, 1977). Like sensitization, the response evoked by a cue is facilitated by the presentation of a strong stimulus. However, a defining feature of this class of phenomena is that multiple reinforcer presentations are required to produce the facilitation. The strength of the facilitation is dependent on the interval between reinforcer presentations. Perhaps general arousal produces the enhanced reactivity (Killeen, 1984). Again, the induced responses may bear no resemblance to the responses previously observed in that situation.

Habituation/Extinction

The repeated presentation of a stimulus may result in a diminution of the response controlled by that cue. If we know the response to be conditioned, we call the procedure *extinction*. If we believe the response to be an unconditioned response, we call the procedure *habituation*. In either case, new responses may emerge from the operation. If a response has multiple components, such as aggressive or courtship displays, repeated presentations of a releasing stimulus may cause different components to habituate at different rates. Such differential habituation could result in significant changes in the organization of response components. Alternatively, the habituation of one response may disinhibit other weaker response tendencies. Fear induced by separation from parents may inhibit feeding. The onset of independent feeding in some species may be a concomitant of habituation of the fear response. As Galef (1977) has shown, rat pups will generally avoid new foods. However, feeding responses will emerge if pups are exposed to the odor of specific foods. Interestingly, in rats older than 21 days, this odor exposure must occur in a social context (Galef & Kennett, 1987). In both cases, the emergence of the feeding response depends on exposure to the odor. Thus, the first occurrence of independent feeding may depend on habituation of the neophobic response.

Our own studies of the ontogeny of pecking in ring doves suggest that the extinction of feeding responses directed at parents may be an important step in the development of independent feeding. In ring doves, squabs are completely dependent on their parents for food until they are nearly 3 weeks old (see Balsam, Deich, & Hirose, 1992 for a review). The parents initially feed the squabs "crop-milk," a cheeselike substance produced by the crop, and gradually mix in more seed, which they feed the squabs by regurgitation. Squabs begin pecking at about 2 weeks of age but do not ingest seed until they are 16 to 18 days old. Squabs can be weaned at 3 weeks of age and reach adult levels of feeding efficiency after approximately 4 weeks post-hatch.

Initially, regurgitative feedings are initiated by the parents, but by the time the young leave the nest on about postnatal day 10, the squab beg vigorously to obtain parental feeding. The begging consists of the squab's thrusting its beak at the parent's beak while making very rapid fluttering motions with its wings. The begging is sometimes accompanied by a high-pitched whistle. Until around day 14, parents respond to the begging by feeding the young. After day 14 the parents become more and more likely to withdraw from the young when they beg. Parental feeding of young begins to decline near the end of the third week and ceases by the end of the fourth week posthatch. The extinction of the begging response may be important for allowing squab to be exposed to and have the experiences necessary to induce the adult feeding response (Hirose & Balsam, 1995).

Pavlovian Conditioning

Pavlovian conditioning may also produce discontinuous change in response forms. When a cue is paired with a primary reinforcer, an entire behavior system is conditioned (Hogan, 1974, 1994; Timberlake & Lucas, 1989). Thus, when a conditioned stimulus is paired with a noxious stimulus, the whole defensive system is conditioned; when paired with a sexual outcome, the whole reproductive system is conditioned; and when paired with food, an entire feeding system is conditioned. In the prototypical Pavlovian learning experiment the conditioned response (CR) is similar to the unconditioned response (UR). However, cases in which CR and UR resemble each other are common to the psychology laboratory but probably fairly uncommon in nature. Even in laboratory studies of Pavlovian conditioning it is clear that the form of the CR is not invariably similar to that of the UR (Holland, 1984). For example, if a brief key light is paired with grain, pigeons will come to peck at the key light with a peck topography that is quite similar to the feeding topography (Jenkins & Moore, 1973; LaMon & Zeigler, 1988). However, if general contextual cues signal food presentation, the CR is an increase in locomotor activity (Mustaca, Gabelli, Papini, & Balsam, 1991). CR topographies are influenced by the reinforcer type (Jenkins & Moore, 1973; Pavlov, 1927), reinforcer frequency (Innis, Simmelhag-Grant, & Staddon,

1983), antecedent stimulus type (Holland, 1984; Timberlake & Grant, 1975), and stimulus duration (Holland, 1980), as well as by properties of the learning and test context (Balsam, 1985). It is clear that the response that emerges as learned does not necessarily resemble any previously observed response to the unconditioned stimulus or any previously experienced conditioned stimulus.

Pavlovian processes seem to play an essential role in the development of pecking in the doves. We found that if we reared ring doves without exposure to seed, the squabs' initial unconditioned thrusts at seed quickly habituated (Balsam, Graf, & Silver, 1992). Figure 20–6 shows data taken from several experiments that illuminate the conditions necessary for the facilitation and maintenance of pecking at seed. All subjects were reared on a powder mixture so that they never experienced seed except during experimental sessions.

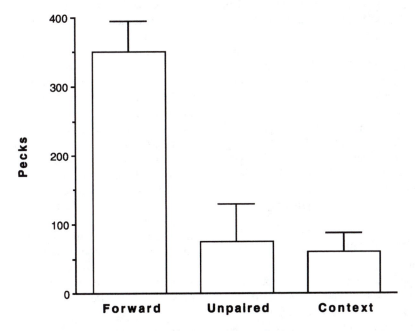

Figure 20–6. The mean frequency of pecking is shown for three experimental groups. In the forward group, squab were fed immediately following a 20-minute visual exposure to seed for the week prior to testing. In the unpaired group, subjects were fed 2 hours after exposure to seed. In the context group, squab were fed immediately after exposure to the empty test context. All groups were tested with access to seed on the day following the last treatment.

All groups were given experimental treatments on days 14 to 20, and on day 21 they were tested in an arena with seed spread across the floor. Subjects in the paired group were allowed to look at seed for 20 minutes and were then immediately fed by the experimenter. Subjects in the unpaired group were allowed to look at seed and fed by the experimenter 2 hours after the seed exposure. Subjects in the context group were exposed to the context alone (without any seed to look at) and fed immediately after the exposure. Figure 20–6 shows the mean level of pecking in each of the groups when they were tested with free access to seed. Only subjects that received the Pavlovian pairings show a high level of pecking. Thus the Pavlovian contingency may be essential to the emergence of the adult feeding response. Consistent with this view, Hirose & Balsam (1995) found that these pairings are embedded in the normal interaction of parents and squabs during the third and fourth weeks after hatching.

Pavlovian influences on response form may be quite pervasive, as Pavlovian contingencies are embedded in all operant procedures (see Allan, this volume). In fact, Moore (1973) suggested that shaping may only be effective because of the implicit Pavlovian contingencies in the procedure. When we shape a pigeon to peck a key, we are really pairing the sight of the key light with seed. Such pairings are sufficient for generating key-pecking (Brown & Jenkins, 1968). In any operant procedure the manipulandum is paired with the reinforcer (Timberlake & Lucas, 1989). Thus the potential for Pavlovian influences on response form is inherent in all operant procedures.

Induction by Chaining

New responses may be induced by chaining. This will happen when the occurrence of one response brings the subject into contact with stimuli that control a different response. This was the machinery that Hull (1935) suggested could account for creative problem solving.

This mechanism turned out to play a crucial role in the development of pecking in the doves. The earliest thrusts at seed are frequently not accompanied by gaping, the opening of the beak. As

squab get older, gaping becomes more likely and then becomes tightly coordinated with head movement in adults. It turned out that the Pavlovian contingency was necessary to increase thrusting at seed, but that experience by itself did not seem to produce a coordinated gape (Deich & Balsam, 1994). Deich and Balsam (1994) found that gapes are four times more likely to occur in proximity to a head thrust at seed than they are when the birds are not pecking. We hypothesized that there may be a specific eliciting stimulus for gaping. It seemed plausible that the visual, kinesthetic, or vestibular cues produced by movement of a squab toward the substrate induces gaping. To investigate this possibility, we have recently conducted some experiments with the help of our students Manu Saluja and Emily Wall. In these studies, the experimenter moved the bird toward the substrate. In our first experiment we showed that at about 2 weeks of age it is sufficient to move the bird to induce gaping. Figure 20–7 shows some data from our subsequent analyses of which movement-produced-stimuli elicit gaping. One group of subjects was moved toward the substrate. A second group of subjects was moved toward the substrate while blindfolded, and the third group of subjects remained stationary while the floor was raised toward them. The results indicate that it is the movement-produced cues, not the visual cues, that trigger the gaping.

The emergence of the skilled adult peck seems to depend on at least three processes for its emergence. Pavlovian associations between seed and ingestional consequences induce the thrusting movement toward the ground. This movement brings the squab into contact with the movement-produced-stimuli that elicit gaping. The initial thrust-gape coordinations are produced by this chaining. Subsequently, the thrust-gape coordinations that are successful at obtaining seed are selected by reinforcement.

Imitation

Imitation also provides a means for acquiring new response forms. Animals of many species are capable of imitation (Whiten & Ham, 1992). Though there are few examples of imitation that

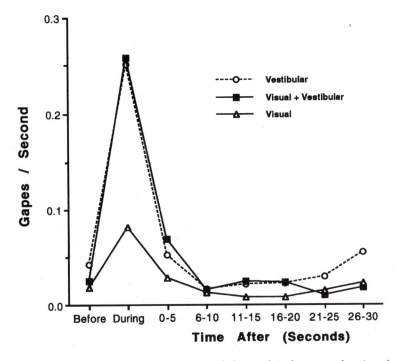

Figure 20–7. The mean number of gapes made by squab is shown as a function of time since stimulus exposure. One group of squab (visual + vestibular) was moved by the experimenter toward the substrate. A second group of squab (vestibular) was blindfolded when the experimenter moved them. The third group of subjects (visual) was held above the substrate and the surface was moved toward them.

are unassailably instances of copying the behavior of a model (Galef, 1990), there are some seemingly well-controlled demonstrations of this phenomenon (Heyes & Dawson, 1990; Mineka, this volume; Palameta & Lefebvre, 1985). One has the impression that imitation is a ubiquitous way in which humans learn new responses. It would seem to be an effective means of inducing new responses even if only by focusing attention on new stimuli.

APPLICATIONS

Response Class

When we reward a particular response, we are strengthening other members of the structural and functional response classes to which that response belongs. The practical application of this understanding requires knowledge about existing response structures in the individual. For most of us, reaching for and asking for an object are members of the same functional class, but we cannot always rely on common cultural history to understand class membership. Carr (1988), for example, has found that for some children, aggression is a means of obtaining objects, whereas for others it is a means of getting adult attention, or a means of requesting that another child play with them. When Carr is able to teach the children to achieve the same ends with a nonaggressive response, the aggression declines. The success of the intervention depends on understanding the function of the aggression and inducing new, more appropriate class members. Similarly, Schroeder and his colleagues (see Schroeder & MacLean, 1987) have found that in children with autism, punishment of one type of self-injurious behavior may result in the decrease of several types of self-injurious behavior. Again, if one could know the membership of response classes, one could design very efficient interventions for dealing with multiple response problems. This would be particularly true in cases where it might be easier to measure, record, or react to some class members than to others.

The adaptability of new learning will depend on the range of responses that are in the repertoire to deal with new situations that are similar to the original situation but require a variant of the original response requirement. For example, our subjects in the keyboard experiment would have no trouble adapting to a change in contingency that required them to make at least 12 responses per trial rather than the original 10 responses. This is because the original contingency generated variants that would be successful under the changed contingency. In any educational or clinical intervention, enough variants must be induced during training (treatment) so that the behavior will be sustained under the constantly changing conditions of the natural environment.

Indeed, one aspect of expert performance has to do with the nature of the variants that are produced when a particular response fails. The expert must have large functional classes relevant to the area of expertise. For example, the skilled mechanic will have many ways of removing a difficult nut. Therefore, if the initial attempts to remove the nut fail, the other relevant variants will be induced. Training of expert performances necessarily requires the establishment of broad functional classes.

In the clinical domain, Kazdin (1982) has described the importance of response covariation in designing and assessing interventions. Decreasing one member of a class may decrease other members of a class. Some of the decrease may be desired, as in the case of the self-injurious behavior of the child with autism, but some of the decreases may be undesirable, such as a suppression of speaking following punishment for aggression.

On the other hand, suppressing one member of a class may sometimes lead to increases in other members of a response class. This might occur when the motivation to achieve a particular outcome remains high. In this case, unpunished or unextinguished members of the response class may increase in frequency. At least some instances of what is sometimes referred to as *symptom substitution* may reflect this type of interaction within response classes.

What is needed to make the most of this knowledge is to develop techniques for quickly assessing response-class membership. We wonder how much more effective interventions might be if the therapist first assessed the relation of a target response to other responses in the client's repertoire. However, even in the absence of a general tool for assessing response interactions, it might be quite important to consider these interactions in all therapies. This would require a full initial assessment of all of a client's behavior, and repeated assessments throughout therapy. This inclusive type of assessment seems necessary in order to see how the whole repertoire of behavior changes as a result of therapy. In this way, indirect changes in behavior that might be either helpful or damaging will be detected and considered. These assessments can be done directly in circumstances that involve hospitalization, by a pencil and paper assessment aimed at the patient, by interview, or possibly with the help of family members.

Sustained Variability

Sometimes it is desirable to generate highly reliable or even stereotyped behavior, for example when children are learning to count, or when adults are executing dangerous procedures. Other times, greater variation is more advantageous. High variability is positively correlated with skill acquisition in young children (Seigler, 1995). Effective application of skills as diverse as social interactions and mathematical computation depends on being able to vary in ways that meet the demands of a current and changing situation. Creative problem solving depends on high levels of variability, as exhibited by acclaimed artists and scientists in their areas of expertise (Gardner, 1993; Wallace & Gruber, 1989).

It is well established that variability can be maintained by use of explicit variability contingencies (Machado, 1989; Neuringer, 1986, 1993). Variability levels are also maintained without explicit reinforcement. For example, during skill acquisition, individuals may substitute more efficient strategies for less efficient ones, but even after the skill is acquired, they do not use fewer strategies (Carpenter & Moser, 1982; Seigler, 1994).

Recent work in our laboratory indicates that sustained variability levels are influenced by an individual's early training history. Shaping rats to bar-press with more stringent topographic requirements results in higher variability than do less stringent shaping contingencies (Stokes, 1995). Shaping often results in a more variable terminal performance in humans than do verbal instructions (Joyce & Chase, 1990). In our work with the keyboard task, we have found that shaping procedures that involve a big jump in a response requirement early in shaping generate more variable terminal performances than do other patterns of changing response requirements (Stokes, Mechner, & Balsam, submitted). Perhaps when we learn what to do, we also learn how differently to continue doing it.

Disappointment

The fact that a disappointing outcome will generate variability might be useful to the teacher and clinician. While one would not want to consistently convey to either students or clients that they were failures, it might be strategically useful to reduce rewards for particular responses. For example, following the establishment of a new response, one may wish to have that response fail to produce an expected outcome. Once variability is induced, the reward contingency can be reinstated. In this way, enough variants may be generated so that behavior can adapt to a range of conditions. Furthermore, in a social context, stereotypy in social exchange may be relatively ineffective in the long run. It seems useful to consider whether a terminal performance ought to be variable and how to induce that variability. With humans it may be sufficient to do this imaginally. Perhaps one of the reasons why techniques that involve consideration of the consequences of failure are effective is that consideration alone may potentiate alternate ways of responding to a situation.

Elicitation

One obvious application of this concept would be to design tools so that the responses generated by the objects facilitated the tool use. Ergonomic design is of course a highly desirable goal, and a better understanding of the biophysical constraints on behavior would be useful.

In a similar vein, athletic coaches often employ a tacit understanding of how to induce a proper movement through elicitation. The one of us that has an effective tennis serve learned the movement by practicing overhand strokes with a weighted towel. The characteristics of the towel and weight only allow for a particular set of movements. In this way, the proper arm and body motion is induced.

In a traditional clinical setting, the presentation of stimuli that induce strong emotional reactions is often seen as useful for understanding the existing behavior patterns of a client. Our analysis suggests that this kind of experience may be additionally useful if it induces new responses that can be used to modify inappropriate reactions.

Blending

Arranging unusual conjunctions of stimuli is a common technique in creativity training. Finke, Ward, & Smith (1992), for example, had subjects create novel combinations of simple shapes to create novel objects. Similarly, attribute listing is sometimes used to generate new combinations that lead to invention. In the creation of new behavior, similar processes may be at work. One reason why "getting away for a while" might be of some therapeutic value is that novel environments may provide for new stimulus conjunctions and lead to new behavior. The therapist might consider creating unusual stimulus conditions as a way of generating new behavior patterns. An understanding of what types of combinations might be most effective in a given set of circumstances will require additional analysis.

Sensitization

The presentation of a strong stimulus to induce new responses is certainly used in folk psychology. When someone says, "I did it to shake them up," it usually refers to doing something that evokes a strong reaction in the hopes of inducing behavioral change. A research program that studies the nature of things that "shake people up" and the variants induced by this operation would be useful in a broad range of applied settings.

Schedule-induced or adjunctive behavior has previously been suggested as a model of excessive behavior. It has been suggested that alcoholism may sometimes originate as a schedule-induced response (Falk, 1994; Riley & Weatherington, 1989). Periodic reinforcer presentations have been shown to induce eating (Cantor, Smith, & Bryan, 1982), drinking (Porter, Brown, & Goldsmith, 1982), smoking (Cherek, 1982), and aggression (Robinson, Flory, & Dunahoo, 1990; Roper, 1981).

It may be worthwhile for therapists to keep in mind that a problem behavior may be meliorated simply by changing the reinforcement schedule. Adjunctive behavior is an inverted U-shaped function of the reinforcer rate. Thus it may be useful to either increase or decrease reinforcer frequency to see whether that modulates a problem behavior or even to see what new behaviors might be induced.

Habituation

Exposure to stimuli has long been used as a means of fear or anxiety reduction. One might wonder what effects this procedure might have on the behaviors that occur in the formerly fear-provoking setting. Mere exposure to any cue seems to increase preferences for that object, and perhaps there are concomitant changes in the behavior that occurs in the presence of the object as a result of the exposure. Forced exposure to family members might produce some interesting changes in interactions. Again, perhaps even imagined exposure could produce some behavioral changes.

Pavlovian Conditioning

As mentioned earlier, the form of the conditioned response is determined by both the nature of the unconditioned stimulus and the nature of the conditioned stimulus. An intriguing therapeutic possibility arises from this principle. Perhaps one could change the behavior emitted in a given situation by pairing that situation with new reinforcers. One could try to eliminate problematic behavior as well as induce new behavior with this procedure. Again, it is possible that imaginal or vicarious pairings might have some effectiveness in humans (Mineka, this volume).

Chaining

We are constantly relying on chaining to bring about new behavior when we say that people should expose themselves to new things. The skilled teacher, therapist, or coach has the tacit knowledge of what behaviors bring people in contact with the conditions that induce a more effective form of behavior. In each domain, making those connections explicit would result in a much more effective behavioral technology.

CONCLUSIONS

We have described a number of processes that underlie the production of new behavior and speculated about how these processes might be exploited to solve practical problems. The experimental analysis allows us to isolate these processes, but in the real world multiple processes are engaged by simple operations. It should be clear that when one person reinforces the behavior of another, all the mechanisms we have discussed have the potential to influence responding. The presentation of the reinforcer allows for habituation, sensitization, elicitation, Pavlovian conditioning, chaining, and imitation to influence response forms. Parametric studies of the individual processes as well as studies of how these processes interact are needed in each practical domain.

Thus far we have proposed only one role for

stimuli in the emergence of new behavior: to induce or elicit such behavior, probably via the activation of endogenous motor programs. However, from a practical perspective one must also consider the discriminative roles stimuli play that are essential for behavior to be effective. Once a particular induced behavior occurs, it may be either successful or unsuccessful in leading to an adaptive outcome, and this success may depend upon the details of circumstances in the environment that are associated with this success or failure. Let's consider a real-world example to see how such discriminative stimulus effects may be important in controlling the behavioral variants that occur in a particular situation.

The failure of a mechanic to remove a bolt will lead to the induction of new responses and variants via disappointment. However, as the mechanic gains skill, he or she is likely to focus on more detailed aspects of the particular failure and to select a response variant based on this stimulus information. The mechanic will recognize not simply a failure to remove a bolt, but a more specific type of failure. For example, the bolt may be rusted in place or have a head that is badly worn. The skillful mechanic will have acquired appropriate responses under the control of each specific situation: For the rusted bolt, apply oil or a solvent, tap with a hammer, and try again. For the bolt with the worn head, use a tool that more securely grasps the head or grasps it with more force and try again. Two solutions for a general case such as "failure to remove a bolt" are often not interchangeable, and in fact, trying the solution that is inappropriate for the particular failed situation may make things worse: the novice may try to remove the rusted bolt with a forceful gripping device that may destroy its weakened head, necessitating a more complex repair.

The view proposed here is that once responses are induced by any mechanism, they come under refined discriminitive control as the individual acquires a new behavior. Eventually the new response may become largely independent of the mechanism that initially induced it, coming instead under the control of specific environmental stimuli. In a sense, then, it is ultimately not just new behaviors that are learned, but rather new controlling relations between stimuli and behavior. This view suggests that the success of any intervention will depend on establishing numerous and specific connections between stimuli and specific members of response classes. An expert in a particular domain is likely to have more numerous, yet more specific, controlling relations between stimuli and responses than a novice. This allows the expert to deal effectively with a broad range of situations in that domain.

Perhaps the biggest challenge in developing a technology of new response forms will be to articulate the behavioral grammar that underlies response linkages. The articulation of principles that underlie the connections between responses will require a great deal of data, but the payoff will be worth it. We can imagine discovering very robust pathways for bringing about new behaviors. In the same way that all ring dove squab come to handle grain in highly stereotyped and efficient ways as a result of experience, it is possible that one will discover pathways to effective social behavior or robust pathways to teaching a variety of verbal and motor skills. If we can explicate these pathways, we will have enormously effective techniques for behavior change.

ENDNOTES

We thank the following for their substantial contributions to the project reported here: Lynn Aronson, Roseanne Benjamin, Alice Deich, Katharine Iskrant, Katherine Kao, Chris Kozma, Angelika Landrigen, Amy Lazev, Elizabeth Pierson, Anat Reschke, Manu Saluja, Jenine Tankoos, Elizabeth Tolin, Wendy Tunick, Emily Wall, Octavia Wong, Jordana Zanger, and Karen Zechowy. This work was supported by funds from the Samuel R. Milbank Chair to P.B.; a grant from the Cambridge Center for Behavioral Studies to P.B. and P.S.; and National Science Foundation grants BNS-8919231 and IBN 9222891 to P.B. and J.D.

REFERENCES

Antonitis, J. J. (1951). Response variability in the white rat during conditioning, extinction, and reconditioning. *Journal of Experimental Psychology, 42,* 273–281.

Balsam, P. D. (1985). The functions of context in learning and performance. In P. Balsam & A. Tomie (eds.), *Context and learning,* 1–21. Hillsdale, N.J.: Erlbaum.

Balsam, P. D. (1988). Selection, representation and equivalence of controlling stimuli. In R. C. Atkinson, R. J. Hernstein, G. Lindzey and R. D. Luce (eds.), *Steven's handbook of experimental psychology, 2nd ed, Vol. 2: Learning and cognition,* 111–166. New York: Wiley.

Balsam, P. D., Deich. J. D., & Hirose, R. (1992). The roles of experience in the transition from dependent to independent feeding in ring doves. *Annals of the New York Academy of Sciences, 662,* 16–36.

Balsam, P. D., Graf, J. S., & Silver, R. (1992). Operant and Pavlovian contributions to the ontology of pecking in ring doves. *Developmental Psychobiology, 25,* 389–410.

Berridge, K. C. (1994). The development of action patterns. In J. A. Hogan & J. J. Bolhuis (eds.), *Causal mechanisms of behavioural development,* 147–180. Cambridge, Mass.: Cambridge University Press.

Bindra, D. (1974). A motivational view of learning, performance, and behavior modification. *Psychological Review, 81,* 199–213.

Brown, P. L., & Jenkins, H. M. (1968). Auto-shaping of the pigeon's key-peck. *Journal of the Experimental Analysis of Behavior, 11,* 1–8.

Cantor, M. B., Smith, S. E., & Bryan, B. R. (1982). Induced bad habits: Adjunctive ingestion and grooming in human subjects. *Appetite, 3,* 1–12.

Carpenter, T. P., & Moser, J. M. (1982). The development of addition and subtraction problem-solving skills. In T. P. Carpenter, J. M. Moser, & T. A. Romberg (eds.), *Addition and subtraction: A cognitive perspective,* 9–24. Hillsdale, N.J.: Erlbaum.

Carr, E. G. (1988). Functional equivalence as a mechanism of response generalization. In R. H. Horner, G. Dunlap, & R. L. Koegel (eds.), *Generalization and maintenance: Lifestyle changes in applied settings,* 221–241. Baltimore: Paul H. Brookes Publishing Co.

Cherek, D. R. (1982). Schedule-induced cigarette self-administration. *Pharmacology, Biochemistry, and Behavior, 17,* 523–527.

Deich, J., & Balsam, P. (1994). Development of prehensile feeding in ring doves (*Streptopelia risoria*): Learning under organismic and task constraints. In M. Davies & P. Green (eds.), *Perception and motor control in birds,* 160–181. Heidelberg: Springer-Verlag.

Eckerman, D. A., & Lanson, R. N. (1969). Variability of response location for pigeons responding under continuous reinforcement, intermittant reinforcement, and extinction.

Journal of the Experimental Analysis of Behavior, 12, 73–80.

Falk, J. L. (1994). Schedule-induced behavior occurs in humans: A reply to Overskied. *The Psychological Record, 44,* 45–62.

Finke, R. A., Ward, J. B., & Smith, S. M. (1992). *Creative cognition: Theory, research, and applications.* Cambridge, Mass.: MIT Press.

Fentress, J. C. (1983). Ethological models of species-specific behavior. In P. Teitelbaum & E. Satinoff (eds.), *Handbook of behavioral neurobiology,* Vol. 6: 185–234. New York: Plenum.

Galbicka, G. (1988). Differentiating the behavior of organisms. *Journal of the Experimental Analysis of Behavior, 50,* 343–354.

Galef, B. G., Jr. (1977). Mechanisms for the social transmission of acquired food preferences from adult to weanling rats. In L. M. Barker, M. R. Best, & M. Domjan (eds.), *Learning mechanisms in food selection,* 123–148. Waco, Tex.: Baylor University Press.

Galef, B. G., Jr. (1990). The ecology of weaning: Parasitism and the achievement of independence by altricial mammals. In M. Beckoff & D. Jamieson (eds.), *Interpretation and explanation in the study of behavior,* Vol. 1: 74–95. Boulder, Colo.: Westview Press.

Galef, B. G., Jr., & Kennett, D. J. (1987). Different mechanisms for social transmissions of diet preferences in rat pups of different ages. *Developmental Psychology, 20,* 209–215.

Gallistel, R. (1980). *The organization of action: A new synthesis.* Hillsdale, N.J.: Erlbaum.

Gardner, H. (1993). *Creating minds.* New York: Basic Books.

Goetz, E. M., & Baer, D. M. (1973). Social control of form diversity and the emergence of new forms in children's block building. *Journal of Applied Behavior Analysis, 6,* 209–217.

Golani, I., & Fentress, J. C. (1985). Early ontology of face grooming in mice. *Developmental Psychobiology, 18,* 529–544.

Herrick, R. M. (1965). Lever displacement under a fixed-ratio schedule and subsequent extinction. *Journal of Comparative and Physiological Psychology, 59,* 263–270.

Herrick, R. M., & Bromberger, R. A. (1965). Lever displacement under a variable ratio schedule and subsequent extinction. *Journal of Comparative and Physiological Psychology, 59,* 392–398.

Heyes, C. M., & Dawson, G. R. (1990). A demonstration of observational learning in rats using a bidirectional control. *Quarterly Journal of Experimental Psychology, 42B,* 59–71.

Hirose, R., & Balsam, P. (1995). Parent-squab interaction during the transition from dependent to independent feeding in the ring dove (*Steptopelia risoria*). *Animal Behaviour, 50,* 595–606.

Hogan, J. A. (1974). Responses in Pavlovian conditioning studies. *Science, 186,* 156–157.

Hogan, J. A. (1994). Development of behavior systems. In J. Hogan & J. Bolhuis (eds.), *Causal mechanisms of behavioral development,* 242–264. Cambridge, Mass.: Cambridge University Press.

Holland, P. C. (1980). CS-US interval as a determinant of the form of Pavlovian appetitive conditioned responses. *Journal of Experimental Psychology: Animal Behavior Processes, 6,* 155–174.

Holland, P. C. (1984). Origins of behavior in Pavlovian conditioning. In G. H. Bower (ed.), *The psychology of learning and motivation,* Vol. 18: 129–174. Orlando, Fla.: Academic Press.

Holman, J., Goetz, E., & Baer, D. M. (1977). The training of creativity as an operant and an examination of its generalization characteristics. In B. C. Etzel, J. M. LeBlanc & D. M. Baer (eds.), *New developments in behavioral research: Theory, method and application,* 441–471. New York: Wiley.

Hull, C. L. (1935). The mechanism of the assembly of behavior segments in novel combinations suitable for problem solution. *Psychological Review, 42,* 219–245.

Innis, N. K., Simmelhag-Grant, V. L., & Staddon, J. E. R. (1983). Behavior induced by periodic food delivery: The effects of interfood interval. *Journal of the Experimental Analysis of Behavior, 39,* 309–322.

Jenkins, H. M., & Moore, B. R. (1973). The form of autoshaped reinforcers. *Journal of the Experimental Analysis of Behavior, 20,* 163–181.

Joyce, J. H., & Chase, P. N. (1990). Effects of response variability on the sensitivity of rule-governed behavior. *Journal of the Experimental Analysis of Behavior, 54,* 251–262.

Kadzin, A. E. (1982). Symptom substitution, generalization, and response covariation: Implications for psychotherapy outcome. *Psychological Bulletin, 91,* 349–365.

Kamin, L. J. (1969) Selective associations and conditioning. In N. J. Mackintosh & W. K. Honig (eds.), *Fundamental issues in associative learning,* 42–64. Halifax: Dalhousie University Press.

Killeen, P. (1884). Incentive Theory III: Adaptive clocks. In J. Gibbon & L. Allen (eds.), *Timing and time perception,* 515–527. New York: New York Academy of Sciences.

Koh, K., & Meyer, D. E. (1991). Function learning: Inductions of continuous stimulus-response relations. *Journal of Experimental Psychology: Learning, Memory, and Cognition, 17,* 811–836.

LaMon, B., & Zeigler, H. P. (1988). Control of response form in the pigeon: Topography of ingestive behaviors and conditioned keypecks with food and water reinforcers. *Animal Learning & Behavior, 16,* 256–267.

Leyhausen, P. (1956). Verhaltensstudien bei Katzen. *Z. Tierpsychol., Beiheft,* 2.

Lipsitt, L. P., & Kaye, H. (1965). Changes in neonatal response to optimizing and non-optimizing suckling stimulation. *Psychonomic Science, 2,* 221–222.

Machado, A. (1989). Operant conditioning of behavioral variability using a percentile reinforcement schedule. *Journal of the Experimental Analysis of Behavior, 52,* 155–166.

Margulies, S. (1961). Response duration in operant level, regular reinforcement, and extinction. *Journal of the Experimental Analysis of Behavior, 4,* 317–321.

Millenson, J. R., & Hurwitz, H. M. B. (1961). Some temporal and sequential properties of behavior during conditioning and extinction. *Journal of the Experimental Analysis of Behavior, 4,* 97–106.

Millenson, J. R., Hurwitz, H. M. B., & Nixon, W. L. B. (1961). Influence of reinforcement schedules on response duration. *Journal of the Experimental Analysis of Behavior, 4,* 243–250.

Moore, B. R. (1973). The role of directed Pavlovian reactions in instrumental learning in the pigeon. In R. A. Hinde & J. Stevenson-Hinde (eds.), *Constraints on learning,* 159–189. New York: Academic Press.

Mustaca, A. E., Gabelli, F., Papini, M. R., & Balsam, P. D. (1991). The effects of varying the interreinforcement interval on appetitive contextual conditioning in rats and ring doves. *Animal Learning & Behavior, 19,* 125–138.

Neuringer, A. (1986). Can people behave "randomly"? The role of feedback. *Journal of Experimental Psychology: General, 115,* 62–75.

Neuringer, A. (1993). Reinforced variation and selection. *Animal Learning & Behavior, 21,* 83–91.

Notterman, J. M. (1959). Force emission during bar pressing. *Journal of Experimental Psychology, 58,* 341–347.

Notterman, J. M., & Mintz, D. E. (1965). *Dynamics of response.* New York: Wiley.

Palameta, B., & Lefebvre, L. (1985). The social transmission of a food-finding technique in pigeons: What is learned? *Animal Behaviour, 33,* 892–896.

Pavlov, I. P. (1927). *Conditioned reflexes.* New York: Dover Publications.

Porter, J. H., Brown, R. T., & Goldsmith, P. A. (1982). Adjunctive behavior in children on fixed interval food reinforcement schedules. *Physiology and Behavior, 28,* 609–612.

Pryor, K. W., Haag, R., & O'Reilly, J. (1969). The creative porpoise: Training for novel behavior. *Journal of the Experimental Analysis of Behavior, 12,* 653–661.

Rescorla, R. A., & Wagner, A. R. (1972). A theory of Pavlovian conditioning: Variations in the effectiveness of reinforcement and nonreinforcement. In A. H. Black & W. F. Prokasy (eds.), *Classical conditioning II: Current research and theory,* 64–99. New York: Appleton-Century-Crofts.

Riley, A. L., & Wetherington, C. L. (1989). Schedule induced polydipsia: Is the rat a small furry human? (An analysis of an animal model of human alcoholism). In S. B. Klein & R. R. Mowrer, (eds.), *Contemporary learning theories: Instrumental conditioning theory and the impact of biological constraints on learning,* 205–238. Hillsdale, N.J.: Erlbaum.

Robinson, J. K., Flory, R. K., & Dunahoo, C. L. (1990). The effects on schedule-induced attack of covarying meal size and spacing. *Physiology & Behavior, 47,* 259–263.

Roper, T. J. (1981). What is meant by the term "schedule-induced," and how general is schedule-induction? *Animal Learning and Behavior, 9,* 433–440.

Schroeder, S. R., & MacLean, W. (1987). If it isn't one thing, it's another: Experimental analysis of covariation in behavior management data of severe behavior disturbances. In S. Landesman, P. M. Vietze, & M. J. Begab (eds.), *Living environments and mental retardation,* 315–336. Washington, D.C.: American Association on Mental Retardation.

Segal, E. F. (1972). Induction and the provenance of operants. In R. M. Gilbert & J. R. Millenson (eds.), *Reinforcement: Behavioral analyses,* 1–34. New York: Academic Press.

Seigler, R. S. (1994). Cognitive variability: A key to understanding cognitive development. *Current Directions in Psychological Science, 3,* 1–5.

Seigler, R. S. (1995). How does change occur? A microgenetic study of number conservation. *Cognitive Psychology, 28,* 225–273.

Skinner, B. F. (1938). *The behavior of organisms: An experimental analysis.* Englewood Cliffs, N.J.: Prentice-Hall.

Skinner, B. F. (1953). *Science and human behavior.* New York: Free Press.

Staddon, J. E. R., & Simmelhag, V. L. (1971). The "superstition" experiment: A reexamination of its implications for the principles of adaptive behavior. *Psychological Review, 78,* 3–43.

Staddon, J. E. R. (1977). Schedule-induced behavior. In W. K. Honig & J. E. R. Staddon (eds.), *Handbook of operant behavior,* 125–152. Englewood Cliffs, N.J.: Prentice-Hall.

Stebbins, W. C., & Lanson, R. N. (1962). Response latency as a function of reinforcement schedule. *Journal of the Experimental Analysis of Behavior, 5,* 299–304.

Stokes, P. D. (1995). Learned variability. *Animal Learning and Behavior, 23 (2),* 164–176.

Stokes, P. D., & Balsam, P. D. (1991). Effects of reinforcing preselected approximations on the topography of the rat's barpress. *Journal of the Experimental Analysis of Behavior, 55,* 213–231.

Stokes, P. D., Mechner, F., & Balsam, P. D. (submitted). Effects of initial conditions on response variability and topography.

Teitelbaum, P. (1977). Levels of integration of the operant. In W. K. Honig & J. E. R. Staddon (eds.), *Handbook of operant behavior,* 125–152. Englewood Cliffs, N.J.: Prentice-Hall.

Timberlake, W. (1983). Rats' response to a moving object related to food or water: A behavior systems analysis. *Animal Learning and Behavior, 11,* 309–320.

Timberlake, W., & Grant, D. (1975). Autoshaping in rats to the presentation of another rat predicting food. *Science, 175,* 690–692.

Timberlake, W., & Lucas, G. A. (1989). Behavior systems and learning: From misbehavior to general principles. In S. B. Klein & R. R. Mowrer (eds.), *Contemporary learning theories,* pp. 237–274. Hillsdale, N.J.: Erlbaum.

Tolman, E. C. (1932). *Purposive behavior in animals and men.* New York: Appleton-Century-Crofts.

Wagner, A. R., & Brandon, S. E. (1989). Evolution of a structured connectionist model of Pavlovian conditioning (AESOP). In S. B. Klein & R. R. Mowrer (eds.), *Contemporary learning theories: Pavlovian conditioning and the status of learning theory,* 149–189. Hillsdale, N.J.: Erlbaum.

Wallace, D. B., & Gruber, H. E. (1989). *Creative people at work.* New York: Oxford University Press.

Wetherington, C. L. (1979). Schedule-induced drinking: Rate of food delivery and Herrnstein's equation. *Journal of the Experimental Analysis of Behavior, 32,* 323–333.

Whiten, A., & Ham, R. (1992). On the nature and evolution of imitation in the animal kingdom: Reappraisal of a century of research. *Advances in the Study of Behavior, 21,* 239–283.

Wildeman, D. G. (1978). Continuous repertoires: Multiple-response control by a continuous stimulus dimension. *Psychological Reports, 43,* 63–68.

Williams, B. A. (1988). Reinforcement, choice, and response strength. In R. A. Atkinson, R. J. Hernstein, G. Lindsay & R. P. Luce (eds.), *Steven's handbook of experimental psychology,* 2nd ed., Vol. 2: *Learning and cognition,* 167–244. New York: Wiley.

CHAPTER 21

OBSERVATIONAL AND NONCONSCIOUS LEARNING

Susan Mineka

Souhir Ben Hamida

The original theory dating back to Pavlov (1927) and Watson and Rayner (1920) that emotional as well as attitudinal responses (e.g., Eagly & Chaiken, 1993; Levey & Martin, 1987; Martin & Levey, 1987) are often acquired through a process of direct classical conditioning has certainly proved to be useful in explaining the acquisition of many individuals' emotional and attitudinal responses. According to this theory, conditioned stimuli (CSs) that are originally neutral acquire the capacity to elicit conditioned responses (CRs) when they are repeatedly paired with an unconditioned stimulus (US) that elicits an unconditioned response (UR). Although our understanding of how this process of classical conditioning occurs has changed dramatically in recent decades (e.g., Mackintosh, 1983; Rescorla, 1988), it is known to be a robust way to condition emotional and attitudinal responses to formerly neutral stimuli. Nevertheless, it is also equally clear that direct classical conditioning is not the only way through which people acquire emotional and attitudinal responses. Indeed, as

this chapter will document, there are at least two other forms of learning that are also sources of acquisition of emotional and attitudinal responses to formerly neutral stimuli. The first is observational conditioning of emotional and attitudinal responses, and the second is nonconscious learning of such responses. Moreover, there is also evidence that once certain types of fears are acquired, the fear can be elicited by CSs that are presented outside a person's awareness, thus helping to account for the irrationality of some emotional responses.

OBSERVATIONAL CONDITIONING OF EMOTIONAL RESPONSES

Background

In the field of learning there has been a long-standing interest in whether nonhuman animals could acquire a variety of new responses simply through watching other animals perform those responses (see Galef, 1988, 1996, for reviews).

Part of the interest in this topic centered around issues regarding the mental faculties of animals and how similar they were to the mental faculties of humans. The presumption was that humans could learn through observation alone, and demonstration that animals could do this as well would support Darwin's proposal regarding the continuity of mental faculties in humans and nonhumans. Much of this research has centered around the demonstration that observer animals can learn through imitation alone, novel motor responses made by other demonstrater animals (see Galef, 1996; Zentall & Galef, 1988, for two volumes on this topic). There is little doubt that human children and adults are capable of such learning as well (e.g., Bandura, 1969, 1986).

Relatively less attention has been paid to the topic of observational learning of emotional responses and preferences—a topic of more central interest to researchers in clinical psychology. Clinical theorists and researchers have been interested in this topic because of the shortcomings of the original model of acquisition of fears and phobias through direct traumatic conditioning put forth by Pavlov (1927) and Watson and Rayner (1920). A variety of shortcomings of this model have been uncovered in the past 25 to 30 years (e.g., Mineka, 1985a, 1985b; Mineka & Zinbarg, 1991, 1996; Rachman, 1977, 1978, 1990), with one of the most frequently discussed shortcomings being how to account for the acquisition of fears and phobias when there is no prior history of traumatic conditioning. For years there has been speculation that observational or vicarious conditioning may play an important role in the cases of acquisition where there is no direct traumatic conditioning history (e.g., Bandura, 1969; Marks, 1969; Rachman, 1977, 1978).

Although evidence for the possiblity of vicarious conditioning of emotional responses dates back to at least Berger's (1962) classic experiments with humans, many would claim that the evidence from human research was not wholly convincing for several reasons. First, of several dozen studies using variants on Berger's paradigm reviewed by Green and Osborne (1985),

what was shown was simply that human subjects could acquire conditioned responses, indexed solely through autonomic measures such as skin conductance or heart rate, when they watched an observer exhibit an emotional fear response, ostensibly after receiving a shock US in the presence of some CS. However, from such studies one can not conclude that strong, persistent phobic-like fears can be acquired through observation alone. For example, phobic-like fears are manifested not only in autonomic arousal but also in self-report and behavior (Lang, 1968, 1971). In addition, the emotional responses that were conditioned in this way were always very mild and transient, as is necessary because of ethical constraints that would prohibit the conditioning of strong and persistent fears in human subjects. Yet by definition, human fears and phobias are exhibited and elicited in multiple response systems and are strong and persistent (see Mineka, Davidson, Cook, & Keir, 1984). Other evidence for the acquisition of fears and phobias through observation alone was also unconvincing, because it came simply through anecdotal reports of people who claimed to have acquired fears in this way. What was needed was strong empirical documentation that such fears can be acquired observationally.

Observational Conditioning of Snake Fear in Monkeys

Between 1984 and 1993, Mineka and Cook and colleagues published a series of about 10 experiments using a primate model of phobic fears documenting that strong and persistent phobic-like fears can indeed be learned through observation alone. In conducting this series of experiments, Mineka and Cook capitalized upon earlier observations that wild-reared rhesus monkeys that had been born in India but had lived in the indoor Wisconsin Primate Laboratory for 15 to 25 years demonstrated an intense phobic-like fear of snakes that was also extraordinarily resistant to extinction using flooding-like extinction procedures (Joslin, Fletcher, & Emlen, 1964; Mineka, Keir, & Price, 1980). By contrast, laboratory-reared monkeys who had lived their entire lives in the indoor Wisconsin Primate Laboratory exhibited no such fear of snakes. The presumption was that the lab-reared monkeys lacked the requisite learning experiences that the wild-reared monkeys would have had during their first few years of living in the wild in India. Furthermore, it did not seem likely that all of the wild-reared monkeys had had direct traumatic conditioning experiences with snakes, but rather that many or most of them had probably acquired their fear through observing other monkeys behaving fearfully in the presence of snakes. Yet this hypothesis that acquisition of a phobic-like fear of snakes could occur through observation alone was only an hypothesis until Mineka et al. (1984) set out to test it directly.

In the first experiment on observational conditioning of snake fear, Mineka et al. (1984) attempted to maximize the likelihood of obtaining observational conditioning of fear by using wild-reared parent monkeys as models and their own lab-reared adolescent offspring as the observers. Fear was measured in two different ways. First, all monkeys (models and observers) were trained to reach rapidly across an open Plexiglas box to obtain a food treat (such as a marshmallow) when the box contained a neutral wood object. This was done to obtain a stable baseline of nonfearful behavior. When a toy or live snake (boa constrictor) was placed in the box, the wild-reared monkeys exhibited their intense fear of the snake by refusing to reach over the snake for the food treat. Nonfearful lab-reared observer monkeys continued to reach rapidly for the food treat even when a real or toy snake was present, thereby demonstrating their lack of fear of snakes. Second, during each trial, which lasted 40 to 60 seconds, the model monkey's behavior in the presence of snake and neutral stimuli was scored. The experimenters had been trained to score reliably 13 different fear behaviors that monkeys tend to exhibit in such circumstances when frightened. Wild-reared monkeys showed high levels of such fear behaviors in the presence of snake but not neutral stimuli, whereas before observational conditioning, lab-reared observers showed minimal levels of fear behavior in the presence of either snake or neutral stimuli.

During observational conditioning, the lab-reared observer monkeys watched wild-reared fearful model monkeys (from a few feet away) behaving fearfully in the presence of real and toy snakes and nonfearfully in the presence of neutral objects—a discriminative observational fear-conditioning procedure. After six sessions of such observational fear conditioning (involving a total of 24 minutes of exposure to the wild-reared models behaving fearfully in the presence of real and toy snakes), the lab-reared monkeys were tested by themselves to determine whether they had acquired a fear of snakes. The results were very striking: Five out of six lab-reared monkeys now showed an intense fear of snakes that was nearly as strong as that of their parents who had served as models. In this and subsequent experiments, it was shown that significant acquisition of fear occurs with only one or two sessions of observational fear conditioning involving only 4 to 8 minutes of exposure to a fearful model (see also Mineka & Cook, 1993). Moreover, it was not at all necessary for the models and observers to be genetically related (as they were only in the Mineka et al., 1984, study) or even acquainted for such robust observational conditioning to occur. In addition, observers who had acquired the fear through these procedures could even pass the fear on to other unrelated observers (e.g., Cook, Mineka, Wolkenstein, & Laitsch, 1985). Finally, Cook and Mineka (1990) showed that observer monkeys even acquired this snake fear observationally when they observed the model behaving fearfully toward snakes on videotapes (that is, without any experience with a live model). These results have particularly fascinating implications for the potential that the mass media have for becoming the source of observationally acquired fears in humans.

Two other features of these experiments are particulary noteworthy. First, the observer monkeys exhibited fear of snakes not only in the same context in which they had acquired it but also in a completely different context using an additional index of fear (e.g., Cook et al., 1985; Cook & Mineka, 1990; Mineka, 1987; Mineka & Cook, 1988, 1993; Mineka et al., 1984). Second, the observationally acquired fear was also very persistent. In each of the experiments just described, observer monkeys were tested again three months following acquisition and showed perfect retention of the fear even though they had no additional contact with models' behavior in the presence of snakes in the interim period. Thus, these results provide a convincing primate model for the acquisition of phobic-like fears through observation alone in that the fear was exhibited in multiple fear response systems, was nearly as intense as that of the wild-reared models, was not context specific, and was very persistent. Indeed, they provide the strongest empirical support yet available for the hypothesis that human fears and phobias undoubtedly can be acquired not only through direct traumatic conditioning but also through vicarious acquisition.

Immunization Against the Acquisition of Snake Fear

Another criticism of the earlier conditioning models was that not everyone who undergoes a traumatic conditioning experience acquires a fear. Rachman (1978, 1990) has been one of the leading critics of early conditioning models on this and other grounds. Fortunately, this criticism can be seen as applying only to traditional and outmoded models of conditioning (Mineka, 1985b; Mineka & Zinbarg, 1991, 1996). What this criticism fails to consider is that there is a host of known variables that affect the amount of conditioning that will accrue to a CS during a given traumatic or observational fear-conditioning experience. For example, it is well known that prior exposure to a CS by itself will reduce the subsequent amount of conditioning that accrues to that CS when it is finally paired with a US. This phenomenon is known as latent inhibition (Lubow, 1973; see also Lubow this volume); familiarity with a stimulus reduces its conditionability. So for example, a child who had had prior exposure to snakes before observ-

ing a parent or peer behaving fearfully with snakes would be less likely to acquire a fear of snakes than would a child for whom the snake was a totally novel object during an observational fear-conditioning experience.

Mineka and Cook (1986) asked the further important question of whether prior exposure to a nonfearful model behaving nonfearfully with some object such as a snake would produce an even more potent interference with observational conditioning of snake fear than is seen with the simple latent inhibition paradigm just described. To examine this question, they exposed three groups of observer monkeys to one of three preconditioning experiences before receiving the traditional observational fear-conditioning paradigm. The Immunization group first watched nonfearful model monkeys behaving *nonfearfully with snakes* for six sessions; the Latent Inhibition group first spent an equal amount of time by themselves with snakes for six sessions (no nonfearful model was present); the Pseudoimmunization group first spent six sessions watching nonfearful model monkeys behaving *nonfearfully with neutral objects* (a control procedure). Subsequently, all three groups of observer monkeys spent six sessions watching fearful models behaving fearfully with snakes and nonfearfully with neutral objects -- our traditional discriminative observational fear-conditioning procedure. As expected, observers in the Pseudoimmunization group showed the expected rapid acquisition of an intense fear of snakes, and those in the Latent Inhibition group also showed significant acquisition of fear, although the trend was for the acquired fear levels to be lower than in the Pseudoimmunization group. Especially striking were the results of the Immunization group: Of eight monkeys in this group, six showed no acquisition of snake fear whatsoever. In other words, their prior exposure to nonfearful models behaving nonfearfully with snakes effectively immunized them against the later acqusition of snake fear when they were exposed to fearful models behaving fearfully with snakes.

Extrapolating from this study to what goes on

in human observational fear conditioning, one would expect that children who had extensive prior exposure to a nonfearful peer, sibling, or parent behaving nonfearfully with some object might well be immunized against the possible later effects of being exposed to a fearful model behaving fearfully in the presence of that object. This in turn may help account for why the objects of children's fears are not more highly correlated with their parents' fears (see Emmelkamp, 1982; Marks, 1987, for reviews), because many children may have had additional experiences by themselves or with nonfearful models prior to being exposed to a fearful parent behaving fearfully to that object. It also suggests that parents who want to be sure that they do not pass on their fears and phobias to their children should make sure their children have some experience with their feared objects in the presence of nonfearful models. Moreover, for certain kinds of especially common fears (such as to snakes and spiders and some insects), school programs designed to familiarize children with such objects by having models exhibiting nonfearful behavior might be very effective in preventing the acquisition of such fears for a good majority of the children.

Preparedness and the Nonrandom Distribution of Fears and Phobias

Yet another criticism of earlier conditioning models was that they do not appear to account adequately for the often observed nonrandom distribution of fears and phobias (e.g., Marks, 1969; Seligman, 1971). In his classic paper on preparedness and phobias, Seligman (1971) theorized that humans may be especially likely to acquire fears of objects or situations that may once have posed a threat to our early ancestors. The idea was that there may have been a selective advantage in the struggle for existence for those humans who rapidly acquired such fears relative to their conspecifics who did not. Later, de Silva, Rachman, and Seligman developed a rating system for assessing the preparedness of both the content and the behaviors associated

with phobias. For example, a rating of 5 was "given to objects or situations that were probably dangerous to pretechnological man under not uncommon circumstances," whereas a rating of 1 was "given to objects or situations that were very unlikely to have ever been dangerous to pretechnological man." Similarly, for behaviors, a rating of 5 was "given to actions that probably defended against danger for pretechnological man under not uncommon circumstances," whereas a rating of 1 was "given to actions that were very unlikely to have ever defended against danger for pretechnological man" (1977, p. 67). These ratings were made for 69 cases of phobia. As expected, the researchers found that the content of a great majority of phobias was rated as quite highly prepared (see Mineka & Zinbarg, 1996, for further discussion of these results).

A substantial body of human research also exists that is consistent with the idea that we more readily acquire fears of prepared or fear-relevant objects such as snakes and spiders or angry faces than of other more unprepared or fear-irrelevant objects such as flowers, mushrooms, or happy faces (e.g., Öhman, 1986, 1993, 1996; Öhman, Dimberg, & Öst, 1985, for reviews). In a long and impressive series of experiments, Öhman and his colleagues have demonstrated superior conditioning of electrodermal responses (galvanic skin responses) when fear-relevant stimuli are paired with mild electric shocks relative to fear-irrelevant stimuli. The superior conditioning is usually indexed by heightened resistance to extinction for the fear-relevant stimuli that have been paired with shocks relative to the fear-irrelevant stimuli that have been paired with shocks. Nevertheless, these experiments by themselves have the same limitation as those previously reviewed regarding the human experiments on observational conditioning of electrodermal responses. Specifically, the "fear" response is usually manifested in only one response system (although some experiments have also employed self-report evaluative response measures), and the conditioned responses are mild and transitory relative to what is seen in real human fears and phobias, which are obviously manifested in multiple response systems and are notoriously persistent.

To circumvent these limitations of the human experiments on preparedness and phobias, Mineka and Cook decided to address this question using their primate model for the acquisition of fears through observational conditioning. As already noted, the stimulus object used in most of these experiments had been snakes (which are clearly fear-relevant stimuli) because that was a naturally occurring fear in wild-reared rhesus monkeys, and so models for the fear were readily available. However, the question remained whether naive observer monkeys would acquire a fear of other more fear-irrelevant objects as readily as they acquired a fear of snakes.

To test this idea it was necessary to equate the model's fear performance in the presence of a fear-relevant object with that in the presence of a fear-irrelevant object. This is because the major determinant of the observer's level of acquired fear is the amount of fear shown by the model during observational conditioning, and this varies across trials and days in ways that cannot be controlled by the experimenter (see Mineka & Cook, 1993; see also below). Because it was not at all clear that the experimenters could condition model monkeys to show the same level of fear to fear-irrelevant objects such as artificial flowers or a toy rabbit that they showed to fear-relevant objects such as toy snakes or a toy crocodile, it was necessary to harness the wonders of modern videotechnology to pursue this question. As discussed earlier, the experimenters had already demonstrated that observer monkeys could acquire a fear of snakes simply through watching videotapes of model monkeys behaving fearfully with snakes. This meant that they could use modern editing techniques to make it appear as if the model were reacting with fear to any stimulus they chose—fear-relevant or fear-irrelevant. In this way, it was possible to equate precisely the amount of fear shown by models to fear-relevant and fear-irrelevant stimuli and then determine whether observer monkeys showed superior conditioning with the fear-relevant as opposed to the fear-irrelevant stimuli.

The first experiment in this series included two groups of naive observer monkeys (Cook & Mineka, 1990, Experiment 2). The SN+FL– group watched videotapes of model monkeys behaving fearfully with toy snakes and nonfearfully with brightly colored artificial flowers; the FL+SN– group watched videotapes of model monkeys behaving fearfully with the flowers and nonfearfully with the toy snakes. Again, the fear performance exhibited by the models was identical; only the stimulus to which the monkeys were responding differed. Results indicated that the SN+FL– group acquired a fear of real and toy snakes, but the FL+SN– group did not acquire a fear of flowers. Another experiment showed that these differences in fear conditionability for snakes and flowers were not simply due to differences in the salience of the flowers versus snakes (Cook & Mineka, 1990, Experiment 3; Mineka, 1992). If salience were the critical difference, then monkeys should also acquire an *appetitive* discrimination more easily with snakes than with flowers. However, the experimenters demonstrated that monkeys acquired a complex appetitive discrimination as easily with flowers as the discriminative stimuli as with toy snakes as the discriminative stimuli. In this paradigm, one of two toy snakes (or one of two flowers) served as a discriminative stimulus signaling availibility of food, and the second stimulus signaled that food was not available.

Yet another experiment (Cook & Mineka, 1989, Experiment 2) extended the generality of these findings by showing that similar results applied when different fear-relevant and fear-irrelevant stimuli were used. For this experiment, the fear-relevant stimulus was a toy crocodile (CR) and the fear-irrelevant stimulus was a toy rabbit (RA). The edited videotapes were identical to those used in the SN+ FL–/ FL+ SN– experiment except for the stimuli to which the models appeared to be responding with fear. The results paralleled those for the snake/flower experiment, with observer monkeys in the CR+RA– group showing acquisition of a fear of the toy crocodile but observer monkeys in the RA+ CR– group not showing acquisition of fear to the toy rabbit.

The results of this series of experiments thus strongly support the proposition originally made by Seligman (1971) that human and nonhuman primates may have a phylogenetically-based predisposition to more readily acquire a fear of certain objects or situations that may have once posed a threat to their early ancestors than a fear of objects or situations that posed no such threat. The results extend those of Öhman and colleagues in two important ways (Cook & Mineka, 1991; Mineka, 1992). First, they show that the phenomenon still occurs when robust and persistent fears that are manifested in more than one response system are examined, rather than simply relatively fragile conditioned electrodermal responses. Second, they provide stronger support for the proposition that such differences in conditionability to fear-relevant as opposed to fear-irrelevant objects are likely to stem from phylogenetic or evolutionary factors rather than from ontogenetic or developmental factors. This question cannot be addressed in the human experiments on this topic, because all human subjects entering into these experiments have had prior experiences with the objects used in the experiments. Thus, it is possible that preexisting associations to, for example, snakes versus flowers are more responsible than evolutionary or phylogenetic factors as posited by Seligman and Öhman for the differences shown in fear conditionability. Yet in the monkey experiments, none of the observer monkeys (which had spent their entire lives in the Wisconsin Primate Laboratory) had any prior exposure to any of the stimulus objects used in any of the experiments. This makes it much more likely that the observed differences in fear conditionability to the toy snakes or toy crocodiles were due to phylogenetic or evolutionary factors than to ontogenetic factors.

Mechanisms of Observational Conditioning of Fear

Thus far, we have discussed observational conditioning of fear as if it were a separate and distinct pathway from direct traumatic conditioning for fear acquisition, as Rachman (1977,

1978, 1990) has done (see also, Öst & Hugdahl, 1981). For example, observational conditioning might occur through a cognitive, social inference process in which a naive observer who sees a model reacting fearfully to some object may infer that this object must be dangerous and that he or she also should be afraid. However, at least within the paradigm discussed here, the mechanisms of observational conditioning seem very similar, if not identical, to those involved in direct classical conditioning. This proposal is similar to that of Bandura (1969), who argued that "both direct and vicarious conditioning processes are governed by the same basic principle of associative learning, but they differ in the source of the emotional arousal" (p. 167). As discussed at length by Mineka and Cook (1993), the model's fear response or fear performance seems to act as an unconditioned stimulus (US) that elicits a fear response in the observer (UR). The formerly neutral stimulus for the observer (the CS is the snake) is repeatedly paired with this US and soon acquires the capacity to elicit a conditioned fear response in the observer (CR).

As noted earlier, the single biggest determinant of how much fear the observer acquires is how much fear the model exhibits during observational conditioning. Moreover, the observational fear-conditioning process is a highly emotional one, with observers exhibiting fear behaviors as they watch the models behaving fearfully in the presence of snakes. Indeed, across 42 observer monkeys that participated in this long series of experiments, the correlation between the model's level of fear and the observer's level of fear during the observational conditioning sessions was 0.82. The level of acquired fear the observers showed following conditioning also correlated 0.69 with the level of fear exhibited by the models during conditioning. These very high correlations show that observational conditioning of fear is not a "cold," cognitive social inference process but rather a highly emotional one. These and other results discussed by Mineka and Cook (1993) strongly support the view that the mechanisms of observational fear conditioning seem highly similar to those in direct traumatic conditioning, where it is well known that the intensity of a US is a major determinant of the the level of conditioning that will accrue to a CS (Mackintosh, 1974, Chapter 2).

NONCONSCIOUS LEARNING

Background

Thus far we have discussed the many cases in which direct or observational conditioning seems to be able to account for the acquisition of emotional and attitudinal responses. However, sometimes an individual does not recall any experience of acquisition (either a direct or an observational conditioning experience). It is not uncommon, for example, for an individual to not have a clear recollection of when certain symptoms began or what triggered their onset (e.g., Lazarus, 1971). Similarly, it is not uncommon to find that individuals may volunteer an answer to the question of what caused their fear but feel uncertain about their answer's validity. It may seem surprising that if learning is indeed involved, as we usually believe it is, the process or circumstances of acquisition would not have gone unnoticed or have been forgotten. However, this does seem to happen.

Rimm and colleagues found that of 45 female undergraduates reporting a specific fear, nearly 50% (22) were unable to recall plausible learning experiences associated with the development of their fears (Rimm, Janda, Lancaster, Nahl, & Dittmar, 1977). In the same sample, 23 were able to recall a plausible account that most often involved a direct learning experience. A study of clinically diagnosed animal phobics, social phobics, and claustrophobics showed higher rates of recall (Öst & Hugdahl, 1981). The researchers found that 57.5% of individuals recalled direct conditioning experiences and 17% reported vicarious experiences, whereas another 10% recalled informational or instructional experiences. However, 15% of the entire sample were not able to recall experiences of any kind. Of the three categories of phobics studied, the 31 social

phobics were the most likely to recall no learning experience whatsoever. More than a quarter (26%) reported no direct traumatic or observational experiences, compared with 10% and 11% of animal phobics and claustrophobics, respectively. Townsley, Turner, Beidel, and Calhoon (1995) also compared the traumatic recollections of social phobics to those of normals. They found that 44% of the socially anxious sample recalled traumatic conditioning experiences compared to 20% of the control sample. Interestingly, when the anxious sample was subdivided into specific and generalized social phobia, the former group was found to show a higher percentage of traumatic experiences than the latter group (56% vs. 40%). The relatively high rates of trauma recall for specific social phobics in this study are very similar to those of Öst and Hugdahl (1981), leading some theorists to speculate that the subjects in this study were mostly specific social phobics (Mineka & Zinbarg, 1995). Given these results, it is conceivable that traumatic memories are stronger in cases when the fear is more closely associated with a specific stimulus or situation (as in specific social phobia). Furthermore, recollections may be more common when the fears that develop are more intense (i.e., full-blown phobias) than when they are mild (Öst & Hugdahl, 1981). In a study of agoraphobics, 10% recalled no specific onset circumstances (Öst & Hugdahl, 1983). Öst and Hugdahl (1981) suggested that this may be due to difficulty in recall, but they also mentioned the possibility that their data point to another, yet unknown method of fear acquisition other than direct, observational, or instructional learning.

Clearly, a proportion of phobic individuals does not have a definite traumatic memory; this proportion may be as high as 50% in some studies (Rimm et al., 1977) or as low as 10% to 15% in others (Öst & Hugdahl, 1981, 1983). Moreover, it is possible that such figures are somewhat misleading. For example, one could argue that of those individuals who do report a traumatic memory, some may be expressing their efforts at making sense of a problem that seems to have assailed them out of the blue and remains uncontrollable to them. In other words, as Nisbett and Wilson (1977) warned, people may be unaware of what actually affects their mental processes, and yet they may not hesitate to report their convictions about what they think affects or affected them. Individuals with anxiety disorders and other psychological conditions in which learning may have had a potent influence may simply provide inaccurate reports when asked about the causes of their behaviors. These inaccuracies may implicate events that were not necessarily causal or contributory but were simply salient or consistent with post hoc theories of what can cause such behaviors. As Chapman and Chapman's classic studies showed, individuals may detect a covariation where none exists if they are suspecting or expecting it (Chapman, 1967; Chapman & Chapman, 1967, 1969). For example, Murray and Foote suggested that some of the traumas reported by their snake phobic and snake-fearful subjects may not have been conditioning events but rather were "experiences that may have been frightening because of a pre-existing general fear of snakes" (Murray & Foote, 1979, p. 492).

Moreover, individuals may detect in the researcher or clinician's question an implicit assumption that a clear causal agent can or should be recalled. This "clinician-induced demand," together with the need to make sense of one's own problems, could lead to a bias to report traumatic events even when no clear, convincing recollection exists. Thus, it remains possible that some of the individuals who recall traumas may be reporting incidents that were not actually significant to the acquisition process. Clinicians, therefore, should take individuals' causal accounts of their problems with some skepticism, bearing in mind that these inaccuracies do not usually involve voluntary misleading of the therapist but rather involve naturally occurring cognitive distortions.

That some individuals do not seem to recall traumatic events could conceivably be seen as a blow to the learning accounts of some disorders.

However, there are two possible explanations for what has happened in such situations, and both involve learning. First, we have previously argued that in some such instances, the fear may be based on second-order conditioning, with the first-order CS having been long extinguished (Mineka, 1985a). In second-order conditioning, a first-order CS (CS_1) is paired directly with a US, and after it has acquired the capacity to elicit CRs, it is paired with a second-order CS (CS_2—which is never paired directly with a US). The CS_2 gradually acquires the capacity to elicit CRs, and its ability to do so is maintained even if CS_1 is extinguished (Rizley & Rescorla, 1972).

Second, it is possible that such learning occurs automatically, unintentionally, and without the person's conscious awareness, a type of learning referred to as nonconscious learning. Such nonconscious processing is to be distinguished from the psychodynamic unconscious (Kihlstrom, 1987). The latter involves a hypothesized vast portion of our psyche characterized by its own goals, intentions, and desires separate from those of the conscious mental components (e.g., Freud, 1933). This is to be contrasted with the more contemporary concept of nonconscious processing, a product of modern cognitive psychology (Kihlstrom, 1987; Lewicki 1986a). Note that we do not say "the nonconscious" but rather refer to it as an adjective describing a certain kind of information processing or learning.

Nonconscious Versus Conscious Learning

In cognitive psychology, nonconscious learning is differentiated from conscious learning in that the former is faster and can cover a larger quantity of complex information (Lewicki, 1986a). Unlike conscious learning, neither nonconscious learning nor the use of the information thus acquired is amenable to voluntary control (Lewicki, 1986a; Lewicki & Hill, 1989; Öhman, 1986). A study by Lewicki, Czyzewska, and Hoffman (1987) in which subjects seemed to have little control over whether they learned or whether they used the information processed nonconsciously supports this hypothesis. Nonconscious learning is thought to be insensitive to rational thinking and cognitive arguments (Lewicki, 1986a) and to be separate and independent from conscious learning mechanisms (Reber, 1989).

Unfortunately, views about nonconscious learning remain heavily divided despite the fact that most researchers agree that such learning is different from conscious learning in important ways. Some researchers have no doubt that such learning is completely nonconscious and indeed wonder why cognitive psychologists—who routinely study automatic processes of which their subjects are not expected to be aware—still have suspicions about the existence of such learning (e.g., Reber, 1989). On the other hand, others believe that what is referred to as nonconscious learning does not occur entirely without awareness (Brody, 1989; Holender, 1986; Perruchet & Pacteau, 1990). The position we take here is that regardless of whether this learning is truly nonconscious, these minor distinctions should not detract us from the essential characteristics that differentiate it from conscious learning. As already noted, most investigators in the field agree that nonconscious learning is more automatic, is faster, can cover a greater amount of information, and is difficult to influence by mere conscious thought or intention (Jacoby, Lindsay, & Toth, 1992; Lewicki, 1986a; Lewicki, Hill, & Czyzewska, 1992; Öhman, 1986; Reber, 1989). Indeed, a large number of rigorous experiments using different methodologies support the existence of nonconscious learning with these characteristics (Lewicki, 1986a, 1986b; Lewicki et al., 1987; Lewicki, Hill, & Bizot, 1988; Lewicki, Hill, & Sasaki, 1989; Reber, 1967, 1989; Reber, Kassin, Lewis, & Cantor, 1980; Stadler, 1989). We will briefly describe only one of these experiments because of space limitations; therefore, the reader is directed to the literature on nonconscious learning for detailed treatment (see Reber, 1989, for a review; Lewicki et al., 1992).

A typical nonconscious learning experiment involves a learning phase during which certain stimuli are presented in a pattern for which the covariation is too complex or subtle to be processed consciously. Following this, subjects may be given a distracting task during which consolidation of any information learned is thought to occur. A testing phase then verifies and measures the subjects' implicit knowledge of the covariation. This can be done by eliciting "intuitive judgments" about novel stimuli or by having the subjects engage in a task on which above-chance performance can only imply that the covariation has been learned.

In one experiment (Lewicki et al., 1989, Experiment 1), undergraduates were told that the study investigated people's intuitive understanding of digitized brain scans. During the learning phase, subjects were shown 36 of these scans (computer graphics characters assembled in the shape of a brain). Each brain scan was accompanied by a brief description (presumably written by a psychologist) of the person whose brain had been allegedly scanned. The descriptions focused on the person's intelligence. Subjects were then instructed to rate each person's intelligence based on the scan and the description. These stimuli contained a subtle covariation between the relative frequency of a particular computer graphic character in the scan and whether the person was described as intelligent. During the testing phase, subjects were shown 80 other brain scans unaccompanied by descriptions. They were asked to rate the intelligence of the persons whose scans they were viewing by using their "intuitions" and "initial impressions."

The results showed that as the testing phase progressed, subjects became more accurate in judging the intelligence of the persons whose scans they were viewing in accordance with the nonsalient covariation. The subjects rated scans with a higher frequency of the particular computer graphic as coming from more intelligent individuals and those with a lower frequency as coming from less intelligent indivudals. Extensive post-experimental interviews of subjects showed that no one mentioned anything that was even slightly relevant to the actual covariation presented. Even those subjects who reported having intuitions could not specify their nature. It seems that these subjects learned a covariation nonconsciously, used it to make judgments that were increasingly correct as the number of trials progressed, but remained unaware of its nature. In addition, Lewicki et al. (1989) suspect that the knowledge that was biasing these subjects' judgments was, in some sense, self-perpetuating.

Although we have made a clear distinction between conscious and nonconscious learning, we believe that a subset of learning that occurs nonconsciously may be later "recognized" and then recalled consciously. As Chapman and Chapman's research demonstrates, individuals may not notice strong covariations when they do not suspect or expect them (Chapman, 1967; Chapman & Chapman, 1967, 1969). Conversely, theories leading one to expect a covariation may well facilitate one's recognition of the covariation that one has already acquired. We speculate that clinicians or researchers, by asking about situations in which there could have been direct, observational, or nonconscious learning in the individual's past, may be providing just that implicit theory: that prior learning has led to the fear.

The Relevance of Nonconscious Learning to Clinical Conditions

We will focus on how nonconscious learning could potentially shed light on observational learning relevant to clinical conditions. However, a similar analysis can be made for direct learning also, probably with as much benefit. In observational learning, the emotional expressions and behavior of the model are crucial. In many cases, however, people attempt to suppress embarrassing or otherwise socially inappropriate emotions such as fear, anxiety, and disgust. Social etiquette and the taboo associated with being "too emotional," particularly if the models recognize the irrationality of their fear, may sometimes minimize models' overt, florid expressions of fear and other negative emotions. Such concealment may be particularly successful when such emotions are not intense. Of course, some observers have a keen eye and can consciously detect a model's camouflaged emotional expressions, although this is not always an easy task. As lie detection experts know, anxiety signals can be very skillfully disguised when there is motivation to do so (Ekman & Frank, 1993).

Studies of observational conditioning in monkeys have shown that the intensity of fear acquired by an observer is highly correlated with the intensity of the model's expressions of fear (Mineka & Cook, 1993). Although this sensitivity to the intensity of the model's fear seems adaptive, it it is also possible that the observer will acquire low levels of fear even at subdued levels of the model's emotional expression. Thus, we speculate that individuals may show nonconscious learning of associations between suppressed fear or other masked emotional expressions of the model and certain stimuli or events. For example, a model could react to a stimulus by exhibiting what Ekman would call "micro-expressions"—subtle facial expressions that last a mere fraction of a second and are often very quickly camouflaged by larger, more neutral or socially appropriate facial expressions (Ekman & Friesen, 1969). Similarly, a model can react to a stimulus with understated bodily movements, posture changes, or voice intonations. Such subtle manifestations of emotion, particularly anxiety, are difficult to notice, especially in the presence of salient stimuli that compete for the observer's attention. Although conscious attention may be diverted toward prominent stimuli or ongoing tasks, the covariation between the model's suppressed expressions of fear and the stimuli to which the model is reacting could potentially have been nonconsciously acquired by the observer. This would be an adaptive, though more conservative mechanism by which individuals could potentially benefit from information about potential danger in the environment even when there are competing demands for attention.

One example of subtle covariations may occur when passive avoidance is the emotional expression in the model's fear repertoire. Nonbehaviors (such as passive avoidance) are clearly less salient than overt fear behaviors (Nisbett & Wilson, 1977). A model's declining to go into locations where a feared stimulus may be found, for example, or the model's systematic engagement in alternate activities when the stimulus is present may provide more subtle indications of fear. Passive avoidance actually prevents the observer from ever noticing full-fledged fear expressions and escape reactions by the model. It may be that when a model's fears are primarily expressed through less salient passive avoidance, the observer is more likely to learn the covariation through a nonconscious processing mechanism. The coping mechanism of avoidance itself could potentially be transmitted in this manner; observers may not even recall themselves displaying fear reactions toward the stimulus because they have always kept away from it. Only future research can clarify the nature and extent of these processes.

Nonconscious learning may also help explain another phenomenon that involves the association of a stimulus with behaviors often too covert to be consciously processed: the immunization against the acquisition of a specific fear. The prior experiences of an observer with a stimulus have been shown to be influential in later acquisition of fear of that stimulus. For example, three quarters of the observer monkeys previously exposed to a nonfearful model behaving nonfearfully with a snake, compared to subjects not so exposed, were immunized against the later effects of being exposed to a fearful model behaving fearfully (Mineka & Cook, 1986). In modeling nonfearful behavior, human and primate nonfearful models probably often engage in subtle "nonbehaviors" such as neutral facial expressions and relaxed body postures. These nonverbal behaviors that make up the model's confident approach toward a stimulus such as a snake may provide an observer with an opportunity to learn a potent covariation between the safety information a model conveys and an otherwise potentially fear-arousing stimulus. And it would seem likely that at least sometimes this occurs nonconsciously.

In addition, nonconscious learning may have some important implications for our understanding of individual differences in the acquisition of fears. Individuals with a predisposition for the acquisition of fears because of having an anxious temperament (e.g., Biederman, Rosenbaum, Chaloff, & Kagan, 1995) could potentially be more efficient at acquiring nonconscious covariations between threat and environmental stimuli. We are currently replicating and extending an experiment by Lewicki (1986a) to test the hypothesis that socially anxious individuals are more prone to nonconscious learning of covariations between a neutral stimulus and preattentively processed social threat cues.

Nonconscious Learning of Attitudes and Social Rules

We have so far focused on the vicarious acquisition of fears and anxiety reactions. However, nonconscious learning may be helpful to our understanding of a broad range of behaviors, attitudes, and implicit rules acquired in social contexts. Psychologists from a variety of orientations often refer to behaviors or attitudes as being culturally acquired. Nevertheless, little attention has been paid to the fact that the information acquired is often far too intricate to have been acquired explicitly. For instance, as with complex grammatical rules and their irregularities, social rules are also often extremely sophisticated. Yet both categories of rules are acquired at an age too young for higher level analysis. Furthermore, as with linguistic rules, social rules are often learned despite their never having been explicitly explained or taught by individuals in the child's environment.

As a case in point, let us consider the social rules regarding eye contact. When do we make eye contact? When do we refrain from making eye contact? For how long do we do it? With whom? In what context? What does prolonged eye contact mean, with whom, and when? Finally, how do we know when and whether any of these rules are transgressed? These rules are extremely potent; most people know them at a young age, at least by late adolescence, and most people are fairly proficient in using them. Even if they are unable to articulate these rules, most people would be able to indicate when the rules have been transgressed. Furthermore, many people are able to detect individual and cultural differences and, with some familiarity, take them into account in their judgments regarding whether the rules have been transgressed. Clearly, we have acquired this eye-contact vocabulary from our social environment. It is likely, given the complexity of the rules and their implicit transmission, that most of us have acquired them nonconsciously and only later been made aware of their existence and content. However, some individuals with a variety of mental disorders seem not to have acquired such rules. Determining ways to teach them through explicit learning is often one of the difficult tasks that behavior therapists face.

If nonconscious processing can help us acquire quickly and effortlessly such crucial rules for social survival without distracting us from important tasks, it can confer an important evolutionary advantage. We are social animals, and much of our learning occurs in a social context (Bandura, 1969, 1986, 1992). Our social environment provides us with important information about the external world as well as about where we stand in our social network. As Bandura observed, modeling provides rules for the observer to utilize in generating its own behavior. Modeling also provides predictive information. A mechanism that allows us to maximize our learning from complex social interactions without requiring conscious effort, intention, or inhibition (Öhman, 1986) would clearly be advantageous. It is likely that future research will show that it is in part through nonconscious observational learning that we acquire rules, attitudes, and

habits from our family of origin and our culture. Anxious or relaxed attitudes toward sexuality, compulsive or lax attitudes toward cleanliness, cautious or reckless attitudes toward money and resources, as well as the ensuing behavioral products of these attitudes, may all have been learned over the years, insidiously, without our awareness, from exposure to how others act in our social environment.

Preparedness and Nonconscious Conditioning

The concept of preparedness (Seligman, 1971) applies not only to overt acquisition through direct or observational fear-conditioning paradigms, as discussed earlier, but also to nonconscious acquisition and elicitation of phobic responses. Experiments with electrodermal responses to fear-relevant and fear-irrelevant stimuli have shown that phobic subjects react physiologically to prepared phobic stimuli even when presented subliminally (out of awareness) (Öhman & Soares, 1994). Furthermore, conditioned electrodermal responses (where the conditioning occurred under conditions allowing awareness) were slower to extinguish when the subliminal stimuli presented were fear-relevant than when they were fear-irrelevant (Öhman & Soares, 1993). That is, following conditioning to fear-relevant or fear-irrelevant stimuli that were presented supraliminally (allowing awareness), the CSs were presented in extinction for only 30 msec followed by a backward mask (preventing awareness). Only subjects conditioned with fear-relevant stimuli showed conditioned responses to the masked stimuli. These and many other findings from Öhman's laboratory show that prepared or fear-relevant stimuli somehow facilitate nonconscious or preattentive processing more than unprepared or fear-irrelevant stimuli (Öhman, 1986, 1993, 1996). They also help to account for part of the irrational quality to phobic responses in that subjects may show activation of the physiological response system (preparing them for fight or flight) even before there is conscious awareness of the phobic stimulus (Öhman, 1996; Öhman & Soares, 1993). Moreover, such findings may also help to explain the persistence of phobic responses in the face of rational arguments.

In addition, a recent very important series of experiments from Öhman's laboratory has demonstrated that with prepared or fear-relevant stimuli, but not with unprepared or fear-irrelevant stimuli, subjects will even show *acquisition* of a conditioned response when the CSs used during acquisition are masked and therefore not consciously perceived. For example, Esteves, Dimberg, Parra, and Öhman (1994) compared conditioning to masked angry faces (fear-relevant) with that to masked happy faces (fear-irrelevant). During extinction, the masks were removed, allowing conscious awareness of the CSs. Results during extinction indicated that significant conditioning had occurred to the masked angry faces but not to the masked happy faces. Moreover, the experiments were elegantly designed to rule out possible pseudoconditioning effects. Öhman and Soares (1995) subsequently replicated the same basic effect using snakes and spiders as fear-relevant stimuli and flowers and mushrooms as fear-irrelevant stimuli. They also showed that the subjects were not aware of the fear-relevant (or fear-irrelevant) masked stimuli used during acquistion (that is, their recognition was at chance levels). These results are surprising from the standpoint of contemporary conditioning theory, where the prevailing consensus has been that conditioning occurs only with awareness (Dawson & Schell, 1985; Wagner, 1981). With prepared or fear-relevant stimuli, this clearly seems not to be the case in that masked stimuli that subjects cannot identify at above-chance levels nevertheless can become effective conditioned stimuli (Öhman, 1996).

Although the vast bulk of research on the preparedness effect has involved fear-conditioning paradigms, the concept certainly applies to other domains of life that are crucial to survival and reproduction (Seligman, 1970; Seligman & Hager, 1972). For example, rats and humans clearly acquire aversions to tastes paired with gastroin-testinal illness much more readily than they acquire associations to visual or auditory cues associated with gastrointestinal illness (Garcia & Koelling, 1966; Logue, 1979). It is also quite possible that we acquire familial and cultural attitudes and behaviors that are relevant to certain domains more readily than others. Attitudes toward treatment of relatives, of children, of partners, as well as attitudes toward sexuality, cleanliness, resource management, and social status, may well be more easily acquired from our social environment than attitudes concerning other, less evolutionarily relevant domains. For example, Nielsen and Sarason (1981) found that sexually relevant material intruded into awareness more easily than other types of material. Possibly, information from such evolutionarily important domains is also more easily processed automatically. Social status in female rhesus monkeys seems to be learned from their mothers (de Waal, 1989). In humans, behaviors and attitudes that communicate social status may also be transmitted socially, at times through subtle nonverbal channels. This would certainly be consistent with Öhman and colleagues' extensive work showing that angry faces serve as fear-relevant cues relative to happy and neutral faces. Attitudes from domains that are less evolutionary relevant, such as those toward music, art, and politics, are obviously also socially transmitted. However, the learning in such domains may be less automatic and more amenable to change and to conscious manipulation.

Nonconscious Attitude Formation

Nonconscious learning may also be involved in the formation of the many attitudes and preferences that we seem to begin developing early on in our lives. Research on attitude and preference formation suggests that the mechanism is often automatic. For instance, in a typical experiment, subjects are asked to sort randomly ordered stimulus cards according to how much they like them (e.g., Levey & Martin, 1975; Martin & Levey, 1978). After this, subjects are asked to assign a numerical rating of like/dislike to each stimulus card. The typical result is that neutral cards become either more or less liked, depending on the cards with which they had been associated during the rank-ordering task (Levey & Martin, 1987). A neutral card that was associated with a liked card gains more positive ratings, for instance. Although subjects seem to notice changes in their attitudes toward the neutral stimuli, they do not seem aware of the direction of the change. Levey and Martin call the phenomenon "evaluative conditioning," but their research seems to have striking similarities to that of nonconscious learning. For instance, the instructions to subjects to provide "first impressions," subjects' apparent lack of insight, and the at times extremely low stimulus exposure intervals that preclude awareness, are all reminiscent of nonconscious learning studies. Research on nonconscious learning of preferences and attitudes is an exciting field that may prove to have profound implications on the sources of individual differences, psychological and behavioral problems, and even societal issues such as stereotyping.

Implications for Treatment

The automatic and nonconscious acquisition of fear and other emotional and attitudinal responses could potentially render conscious cognitive change as attempted during insight therapies, a less than ideal therapeutic option. More active behavioral techniques, such as exposure therapy, systematic desensitization, and modeling, may, in turn, derive their effectiveness by acting directly on nonconsciously as well as consciously acquired covariations. Treatment devised to act specifically on nonconscious processing may also prove to be fruitful. For instance, in one intriguing study, agoraphobics showed ameliorated symptoms when subliminally exposed to agoraphobia scenes (Lee, Tyrer, & Horn, 1983). Perhaps subliminal exposure therapy might be a promising, albeit more technically demanding, treatment procedure, particularly in cases in which individuals are reluctant to comply with exposure because of intense anxiety.

Spontaneous remission has always been a mystery to psychology, yet it has received very little attention from researchers, perhaps because it occurs relatively rarely. However, when it occurs, some cases of spontaneous remission of fear could possibly be attributed to nonconscious invalidation of certain previously learned covariations. Here again, individuals are left wondering after the fact about the causes of their new, more adaptive reactions.

Nonconscious or automatic processing has been extensively implicated in the maintenance of fears. Attentional biases toward specific threat stimuli when a mixture of threat and nonthreat cues are available have been reported in individuals suffering from a variety of anxiety disorders (e.g., MacLeod & Mathews, 1991; Mathews, 1993). Moreover, individuals who are highly trait anxious, but at subclinical levels, have been shown to have a greater tendency to have their attention automatically drawn to threatening material (MacLeod & Mathews, 1988; Mogg, Mathews, & Bird, 1990). Researchers who study these attentional biases suspect that they are implicated in maintaining anxiety by creating hypervigilance toward the presence of the threatening stimuli. Because they are automatic, these biases are probably unresponsive to rational argument or voluntary control.

CONCLUSIONS

This chapter has reviewed the evidence that observational and nonconscious learning undoubtedly play an important role in the origins of many emotional and attitudinal responses that behavior therapists attempt to help their clients' change in the course of behavior therapy. Empirical evidence that observational conditioning of phobic levels of fear can indeed occur is now very strong, based on the results of a long series of studies using a primate model for the observational conditioning of fear by Mineka, Cook and colleagues. Strong evidence also exists that nonconscious learning can occur in humans. At present, the majority of this evidence regarding nonconscious learning derives from complex cognitive paradigms using nonemotional stimuli. However, we believe it is quite likely that similar learning occurs within the emotional and attitudinal domains. And indeed, very recent evidence from Öhman's laboratory shows that nonconscious conditioning of emotional responses does occur with prepared or fear-relevant stimuli (e.g., Öhman, 1996; Öhman & Soares, 1995). Moreover, Levey and Martin (1987) have also reviewed evidence that evaluative conditioning is often involved in the formation of attitudinal responses and that it seems to occur nonconsciously. In the future, learning theorists and behavior therapists should attend more carefully to the roles that observational and nonconscious learning may play in the origins of their clients' emotional and attitudinal responses as well as to possible roles they may play in treatment.

REFERENCES

Bandura, A. (1969). *Principles of behavior modification.* New York: Holt, Rinehart and Winston.

Bandura, A. (1986). *Social foundations of thought and action: A social cognitive theory.* Englewood Cliffs, N.J.: Prentice-Hall.

Bandura, A. (1992). Social cognitive theory and social referencing. In M. S. Feinman (ed.), *Social referencing and social construction of reality in infancy,* 175–208. New York: Plenum.

Berger, S. (1962). Conditioning through vicarious instigation. *Psychological Review, 69,* 450–466.

Biederman, J., Rosenbaum, J. F., Chaloff, J., & Kagan, J. (1995). Behavioral inhibition as a risk factor for anxiety disorders. In S. John & E. March (eds.), *Anxiety disorders in children and adolescents,* 61–81. New York: Guilford.

Brody, N. (1989). Unconscious learning of rules: Comment on Reber's analysis on implicit learning. *Journal of Experimental Psychology: General, 118,* 236–238.

Chapman, L. J. (1967). Genesis of popular but erroneous diagnostic observations. *Journal of Abnormal Psychology, 72,* 193–204.

Chapman, L. J., & Chapman, J. P. (1967). Illusory correlation in observational report. *Journal of Verbal Learning and Verbal Behavior, 6,* 151–155.

Chapman, L. J., & Chapman, J. P. (1969). Illusory correlation as an obstacle to the use of valid psychodiagnostic signs. *Journal of Abnormal Psychology, 74,* 271–280.

Cook, M., & Mineka, S. (1989). Observational conditioning of fear to fear-relevant versus fear-irrelevant stimuli in rhesus monkeys. *Journal of Abnormal Psychology, 98,* 448–459.

Cook, M., & Mineka, S. (1990). Selective associations in the observational conditioning of fear in monkeys. *Journal of Experimental Psychology: Animal Behavior Processes, 16,* 372–389.

Cook, M., & Mineka, S. (1991). Selective associations in the origins of phobic fears and heir implications for behavior therapy. In P. Martin (ed.), *Handbook of behavior therapy and psychological science: An integrative approach,* 413–434. New York: Pergamon.

Cook, M., Mineka, S., Wolkenstein, B., & Laitsch, K. (1985). Observational conditioning of snake fear in unrelated rhesus monkeys. *Journal of Abnormal Psychology, 94,* 591–610.

Dawson, M., & Schell, M. (1985). Information processing and human autonomic classical conditioning. *Advances in Psychophysiology, 1,* 89–165.

de Silva, P., Rachman, S., & Seligman, M. (1977). Prepared phobias and obsessions: Therapeutic outcomes. *Behaviour Research and Therapy, 15,* 65–78.

de Waal, F. (1989). *Peacemaking among primates.* Cambridge, Mass.: Harvard University Press.

Eagly, A., & Chaiken, S. (1993). *The psychology of attitudes.* Fort Worth, Tex.: Harcourt Brace.

Ekman, P., & Frank, M. G. (1993). Lies that fail. In M. Lewis & C. Saarni (eds.), *Lying and deception in everyday life,* 184–200. New York: Guilford.

Ekman, P., & Friesen, W. V. (1969). Nonverbal leakage and clues to deception. *Psychiatry, 32,* 88–106.

Emmelkamp, P. (1982) *Phobic and obsessive-compulsive disorders: Theory, research, and practice.* New York: Plenum.

Esteves, F., Dimberg, U., Parra, C., & Öhman, A. (1994). Nonconscious associative learning: Pavlovian conditioning of skin conductance responses to masked fear-relevant facial stimuli. *Psychophysiology, 31,* 375–385.

Freud, S. (1933). *New introductory lectures on psychoanalysis.* New York: Norton.

Galef, B. G. (1988). Imitation in animals: History, definition, and interpretation of data from the psychological laboratory. In T. Zentall & B. G. Galef (eds.), *Social learning: Psychological and biological perspectives,* 3–28. Hillsdale, N.J.: Erlbaum.

Galef, B. G. (1996). Introduction. In C. M. Heyes & B. J. Galef (eds.), *Social learning in animals: The roots of culture,* San Diego, Calif.: Academic Press.

Garcia, J., & Koelling, R. (1966). Relation of cue to consequence in avoidance learning. *Psychonomic Science, 4,* 123–124.

Green, G., & Osborne, J. (1985). Does vicarious instigation provide support for observational learning theories? A critical review. *Psychological Bulletin, 97,* 3–17.

Holender, D. (1986). Semantic activation without conscious identification in dichotic listening, parafoveal vision, and visual masking: A survey and appraisal. *Behavioral and Brain Sciences, 9,* 1–66.

Jacoby, L. L., Lindsay, D. S., & Toth, J. P. (1992). Unconscious influences revealed. *American Psychologist, 47,* 802–809.

Joslin, J., Fletcher, H., & Emlen, J. (1964). A comparison of the responses to snakes of lab- and wild-reared rhesus monkeys. *Animal Behavior, 12,* 348–352.

Kihlstrom, J. F. (1987). The cognitive unconscious. *Science, 237,* 1445–1452.

Lang, P. J. (1968). Fear reduction and fear behavior: Problems in treating a construct. In J. Schlein (ed.), *Research in psychotherapy, Vol. 3:* 90–103. Washington, D.C.: American Psychological Association.

Lang, P. J. (1971). The application of psychophysiological methods to the study of psychotherapy and behavior modification. In A. Bergin & S. Garfield (eds.), *Handbook of psychotherapy and behavior change: An empirical analysis,* 75–125. New York: Wiley.

Lazarus, A. A. (1971). *Behavior therapy and beyond.* New York: McGraw-Hill.

Lee, I., Tyrer, P., & Horn, S. (1983). A comparison of subliminal, supraliminal and faded phobic cine-films in the treatment of agoraphobia. *British Journal of Psychology, 143,* 356–361.

Levey, A. B., & Martin, I. (1975). Classical conditioning of human "evaluative" responses. *Behaviour Research and Therapy, 13,* 221–226.

Levey, A. B., & Martin, I. (1987). Evaluative conditioning: A case for hedonic transfer. In H. Eysenck & I. Martin (eds.), *Theoretical foundations of behavior therapy,* 113–132. New York: Plenum.

Lewicki, P. (1986a). *Nonconscious social information processing.* Orlando, Fla.: Academic Press.

Lewicki, P. (1986b). Processing information about covariations that cannot be articulated. *Journal of Experimental Psychology: Learning, Memory, and Cognition, 12,* 135–146.

Lewicki, P., Czyzewska, M., & Hoffman, J. (1987). Unconscious acquisition of complex procedural knowledge. *Journal of Experimental Psychology: Learning, Memory, and Cognition, 13,* 523–530.

Lewicki, P., & Hill, T. (1989). On the status of nonconscious processes in human cognition: Comment on Reber. *Journal of Experimental Psychology: General, 118,* 239–241.

Lewicki, P., Hill, T., & Bizot, E. (1988). Acquisition of procedural knowledge about a pattern of stimuli that cannot be articulated. *Cognitive Psychology, 20,* 24–37.

Lewicki, P., Hill, T., & Czyzewska, M. (1992). Nonconscious acquisition of information. *American Psychologist, 47,* 796–801.

Lewicki, P., Hill, T., & Sasaki, I. (1989). Self-perpetuating development of encoding biases. *Journal of Experimental Psychology: General, 118,* 323–337.

Logue, A. W. (1979). Taste aversion and the generality of the laws of learning. *Psychological Bulletin, 86,* 276–296.

Lubow, R. E. (1973). Latent inhibition. *Psychological Bulletin, 79,* 398–407.

Mackintosh, J. (1974). *The psychology of animal learning.* London: Academic Press.

Mackintosh, N. (1983). *Conditioning and associative learning.* New York: Oxford University Press.

MacLeod, C., & Mathews, A. (1988). Anxiety and the allocation of attention to threat. *Quarterly Journal of Experimental Psychology, 40,* 653–670.

MacLeod, C., and Mathews, A. M. (1991). Cognitive-experimental approaches to the emotional disorders. In P. Martin (ed.), *Handbook of behavior therapy and psychological science,* 116–150. New York: Pergamon.

Marks, I. (1969). *Fears and phobias.* London: Academic Press.

Marks, I. (1987). *Fears, phobias, and rituals: Panic, anxiety, and their disorders.* New York: Oxford University Press.

Martin, I., & Levey, A. (1978). Evaluative conditioning. *Advances in Behavior Research and Therapy, 1,* 57–102.

Martin, I., & Levey, A. (1987). Knowledge, action, and control. In H. Eysenck & I. Martin (eds.), *Theoretical foundations of behaviour therapy.* 133–152. New York: Plenum.

Mathews, A. (1993). Anxiety and the processing of emotional information. In L. Chapman, J. Chapman, & D. Fowles (eds.), *Models and methods of psychopathology: Progress in experimental personality and psychopathology research,* 254–280. New York: Springer.

Mineka, S. (1985a). Animal models of anxiety-based disorders: Their usefulness and limitations. In J. Maser & A. Tuma (eds.), *Anxiety and the anxiety disorders,* 199–244. Hillsdale, N.J.: Erlbaum.

Mineka, S. (1985b). The frightful complexity of the origins of fears. In J. B. Overmier & F. R. Brush (eds.), *Affect, conditioning, and cognition: Essays on the determinants of behavior,* 55–73. Hillsdale, N.J.: Erlbaum.

Mineka, S. (1987). A primate model of phobic fears. In H. Eysenck & I. Martin (eds.) *Theoretical foundations of behavior therapy,* 81–111. New York: Plenum.

Mineka, S. (1992). Evolutionary memories, emotional processing and the emotional disorders. In D. Medin (ed.), *The psychology of learning and motivation,* Vol. 28: 161–206. New York: Academic Press.

Mineka, S., & Cook, M. (1986). Immunization against the observational conditioning of snake fear in rhesus monkeys. *Journal of Abnormal Psychology, 95,* 307–318.

Mineka, S., & Cook, M. (1988). Social learning and the acquisition of snake fear in monkeys. In T. Zentall & B. G. Galef (eds.), *Comparative social learning,* 51–73. Hillsdale, N.J.: Erlbaum.

Mineka, S., & Cook, M. (1993). Mechanisms involved in the observational conditioning of fear. *Journal of Experimental Psychology: General, 122,* 23–38.

Mineka, S., Davidson, M., Cook, M., & Keir, R. (1984). Observational conditioning of snake fear in rhesus monkeys. *Journal of Abnormal Psychology, 93,* 355–372.

Mineka, S., Keir, R., & Price, V. (1980). Fear of snakes in wild- and lab-reared rhesus monkeys. *Animal Learning and Behavior, 8,* 653–663.

Mineka, S., & Zinbarg, R. (1991). Animal models of experimental psychopathology. In C. E. Walker (ed.), *Clinical psychology: Historical and research foundations,* 51–86. New York: Plenum.

Mineka, S., & Zinbarg, R. (1995). Conditioning and ethological models of social phobia. In R. Heimberg, M. Liebowitz, D. Hope, & F. Schneier (eds.), *Social phobia: Diagnosis, assessment and treatment,* 134–162. New York: Guilford.

Mineka, S., & Zinbarg, R. (1996). Conditioning and ethological models of anxiety disorders: Stress-in-dynamic-context anxiety models. In D. Hope (ed.), *Nebraska symposium on motivation, Vol. 43. Perspectives on anxiety, panic, and fear,* 135–211. Lincoln: University of Nebraska Press.

Mogg, K., Mathews, A., & Bird, C. (1990). Effects of stress and anxiety on the processing of threat stimuli. *Journal of Personality and Social Psychology, 59,* 1230–1237.

Murray, E. J., & Foote, F. (1979). The origins of fear of snakes. *Behaviour Research and Therapy, 17,* 489–493.

Nielsen, S. L., & Sarason, I. G. (1981). Emotion, personality, and selective attention. *Journal of Personality and Social Psychology, 5,* 945–960.

Nisbett, R. E., & Wilson, T. D. (1977). Telling more than we can know: Verbal reports on mental processes. *Psychological Review, 84,* 231–259.

Öhman, A. (1986). Face the beast and fear the face: Animal and social fears as prototypes for evolutionary analyses of emotion. *Psychophysiology, 23,* 123–145.

Öhman, A. (1993). Stimulus prepotency and fear: Data and theory. In N. Birbaumer & A. Öhman (eds.), *The organization of emotion: Cognitive, clinical and psychophysiological perspectives,* 218–239. Toronto: Hogrefe.

Öhman, A. (1996). Preferential preattentive processing of threat in anxiety: Preparedness and attentional biases. In R. Rapee (ed.), *Current controversies in the anxiety disorders,* 253–290. New York: Guilford.

Öhman, A., Dimberg, U., & Öst, L.-G. (1985). Animal and social phobias: Biological constraints on the learned fear response. In S. Reiss & R. Bootzin (eds.), *Theoretical issues in behavior therapy,* 123–175. New York: Academic Press.

Öhman, A., & Soares, J. J. F. (1993). On the automatic nature of phobic fear: Conditioning electrodermal responses to masked fear-relevant stimuli. *Journal of Abnormal Psychology, 102,* 121–132.

Öhman, A., & Soares, J. J. F. (1994). "Unconscious anxiety": Phobic responses to masked stimuli. *Journal of Abnormal Psychology, 103,* 231–240.

Öhman, A., & Soares, J. J. F. (1995). *Unconscious emotional learning: Conditioning of skin conductance response to masked phobic stimuli.* Manuscript submitted for publication.

Öst, L. G., & Hugdahl, K. (1981). Acquisition of phobias and anxiety response patterns in clinical patients. *Behaviour Research and Therapy, 16,* 439–447.

Öst, L. G., & Hugdahl, K. (1983). Acquisition of agoraphobia, mode of onset and anxiety response patterns. *Behaviour Research and Therapy, 21,* 623–631.

Pavlov, I. (1927). *Conditioned reflexes.* London: Oxford University Press.

Perruchet, P., & Pacteau, C. (1990). Synthetic grammar learning: Implicit rule abstraction or explicit fragmentary knowledge? *Journal of Experimental Psychology, 119,* 264–275.

Rachman, S. (1977). The conditioning theory of fear acquisition: A critical examination. *Behaviour Research and Therapy, 15,* 375–388.

Rachman, S. (1978). *Fear and courage.* San Francisco: Freeman.

Rachman, S. (1990). *Fear and courage.* New York: Freeman.

Reber, A. S. (1967). Implicit learning of artificial grammars. *Journal of Verbal Learning and Verbal Behavior, 77,* 317–327.

Reber, A. S. (1989). Implicit learning and tacit knowledge. *Journal of Experimental Psychology: General, 118,* 219–235.

Reber, A. S., Kassin, S. M., Lewis, S., & Cantor, G. W. (1980). On the relationship between implicit and explicit modes in the learning of a complex rule structure. *Journal of Experimental Psychology: Human Learning and Memory, 6,* 492–502.

Rescorla, R.A. (1988). Pavlovian conditioning: It's not what you think it is. *American Psychologist, 43,* 151–160.

Rimm, D. C., Janda, L. H., Lancaster, D. W., Nahl, M., & Dittmar, K. (1977). An exploratory investigation of the origin and maintenance of phobias. *Behaviour Research and Therapy, 15,* 231–238.

Rizley, R. C., & Rescorla, R. A. (1972). Associations in second-order conditioning and sensory preconditioning. *Journal of Comparative and Physiological Psychology, 81,* 1–11.

Seligman, M. (1970). On the generality of the laws of learning. *Psychological Review, 77,* 406–418.

Seligman, M. (1971). Phobias and preparedness. *Behavior Therapy, 2,* 307–320.

Seligman, M., & Hager, J. (eds.) (1972). *Biological boundaries of learning.* New York: Appleton-Century-Crofts.

Soares, J. J. F., & Öhman, A. (1993). Backward masking and skin conductance responses after conditioning to non-feared but fear-relevant stimuli in fearful subjects. *Psychophysiology, 30,* 460–466.

Stadler, M. A. (1989). On learning complex procedural knowledge. *Journal of Experimental Psychology, 15,* 1061–1069.

Townsley, R., Turner, S., Beidel, D., & Calhoun, K. (1995). Social phobia: An analysis of possible developmental factors. *Journal of Abnormal Psychology, 104,* 526–531

Wagner, A. R. (1981). SOP: A model of automatic memory processing in animal behavior. In N. Spear & R. Miller (eds.), *Information processing in animals: Memory mechanisms,* 5–47. Hillsdale, N.J.: Erlbaum.

Watson, J. B., & Rayner, R. (1920). Conditioned emotional reactions. *Journal of Experimental Psychology, 3,* 1–14.

Zentall, T., & Galef, B. G. (eds.) (1988). *Social learning: Psychological and biological perspectives.* Hillsdale, N.J.: Erlbaum.

CHAPTER 22

OBJECT CONCEPTS: BEHAVIORAL RESEARCH WITH ANIMALS AND YOUNG CHILDREN

Suzette L. Astley
Edward A. Wasserman

For many years, psychologists have recognized the importance of categorization for adaptive behavioral functioning. The focus of our chapter will be on object categories or concepts that presumably allow human adults to group the hundreds of stimuli we encounter daily into a smaller and more tractable number of functional equivalents. Functional equivalents are stimuli that may, for practical purposes, be treated as the same because they are used in the same way or lead to common consequences. When we come across an individual object we have never seen before, for example, our categorization of it as a *chair* or a *telephone* allows us to use it in familiar ways. Thus, categories may permit us to function more efficiently; we need not learn to respond to each new entity we encounter, but instead we may exhibit familiar responses to unfamiliar stimuli when they belong to familiar categories.

Many theorists believe that categorization must be a central behavioral capacity. Younger and Cohen (1985) argue that:

> Categorization is an essential perceptual-cognitive activity enabling the reduction of the enormous diversity in the world to a manageable level. Through our categories, we relate new experiences to old; the unfamiliar becomes familiar. Each object and event in the world is perceived, remembered, and talked about, not as unique, but rather as a member of a category or concept that we already know something about. Category structures give meaning to incoming stimulation. Faced with a new situation, we are not confronted with a bewildering array of novel entities, but rather with lamps, clocks, tables, and chairs. (p. 211)

Furthermore, our ability to learn about naturally occurring predictive relationships in the world may be facilitated by our ability to categorize. Thus, a person able to distinguish the category of *fruit* from that of *foliage* may more rapidly learn that the eating of fruit is followed by reinforcing consequences, whereas the eating of foliage is followed by punishing consequences. Treating objects as members of categories may facilitate learning the relationships between one object category and another or between an object category and a reinforcing or punishing consequence. If one groups apples and pears together as fruit, for example, the experience of reinforcing consequences following the eating of apples and pears may not function as separate learning trials. Treating apples and pears as members of the same category may cause separate learning experiences with them to accumulate as though to a single stimulus, or nearly so. Thus, the effects of reinforcement contingencies with respect to one member of a category may generalize to other members to the extent that these other stimuli are seen as part of the same category.

Because of this within-category generalization, it may be important for behavior therapists to make special efforts to promote category formation early in therapy. A behavior-therapy client may not initially treat perceptually different objects as members of the same category, even though they are. Thus, experiences with one object will not spontaneously generalize to other members of the category in a manner that would be therapeutically useful. Alternatively, a client might initially treat two perceptually similar objects as the same, even though they are from different ontological categories. This client is likely to inappropriately generalize responses from one object to a similar-apppearing object from a different category. Explicit categorization training early in therapy with those categories most relevant to and useful in the daily world of the client might forestall later problems related to inappropriate generalization.

One area where this approach may be helpful is in the treatment of fears and phobias. A fearful or phobic client may discriminate between related stimuli, such as distinguishing streets from bridges or cars from planes. One aspect of therapy might be to establish related fear-producing and non–fear-producing stimuli as a stimulus class. The therapist, for example, might initially establish streets and bridges as part of a common stimulus category. To the extent that therapy has been successful in establishing streets and bridges as members of the same stimulus class, reinforcement of street crossing might generalize to bridge crossing.

As another example, categorization might have an important role to play in helping children or developmentally disabled adults determine whether or not to approach an adult in a novel situation. Parents and guardians are naturally concerned about safety in such situations, and they may wish to teach a set of rules to guide the child or developmentally disabled adult in contacts with adults. It may first be necessary, however, to establish two different stimulus classes: one containing adults with whom a child is familiar and another containing those with whom the child is not familiar. Once such a discrimination is firmly established, a child may be better able to follow rules about when to approach and when not to approach an adult in a novel situation.

A BEHAVIORAL ANALYSIS OF CONCEPTS

Keller and Schoenfeld (1950) broke important ground in describing a behavioral approach to concepts. They noted that we should not ask what a concept is. Instead, we should ask what type of behavior is called *conceptual*. They proposed that "when a group of objects gets the same response, when they form a class the members of which are reacted to similarly, we speak of a concept" (p. 154). Keller and Schoenfeld focused on the familiar behavioral processes of generalization and discrimination in defining concepts. "Generalization *within* and discrimination *between* classes—this is the essence of concepts" (p. 155).

In our own program of research, we have tried to follow Keller and Schoenfeld's lead in resisting the tendency to hypothesize higher-level cognitive or mental structures (unless our data were to provide overwhelming evidence in support of their existence, of course). This behavioral approach contrasts with the essentialist approach to categories that has been dominant among developmental psychologists in recent years. Essentialists propose complicated cognitive structures, and they show very little interest in examining the processes through which the structures might have developed or the ways that experience might affect them. (See Astley & Wasserman, in press, for a more thorough discussion of problems with the essentialist view.) Instead, we concentrate on the better-understood principles of generalization and discrimination in categorization behavior in animals and in young children. We, and the researchers we will cite in this chapter, have focused on the stimulus situation and training procedures so that we might better understand how experience and perception interact in creating categorization behavior.

SIMILARITY RELATIONS WITHIN AND BETWEEN CATEGORIES

Some commentary on terminology and on perceptual relations among stimuli seems in order prior to our review of research. A common or "lay" view of object categories is that they are distinguished by defining features. This notion has a long history that can be traced to Aristotle; thus, it is labeled the *classical view* (Smith & Medin, 1981). According to the classical view, object categories are characterized by a set of necessary and collectively sufficient defining features. When one acquires categorization behavior, therefore, one learns what the defining features are and varies behavior accordingly. This approach might account for what are called *well-defined categories,* such as geometric shapes. However, many types of categories, especially those termed natural kinds (Quine, 1969), seem to defy characterization through defining features shared by all members of the class. Many people, for example, list "able to fly" as an attribute of birds; the same individuals accept flightless penguins and ostriches, however, as members of the category *bird.*

After discussing well-defined concepts, Keil (1989) writes,

A great many other concepts, however, refer to classes of things that occur in the world independently of human activities. Such classes of things are known as "natural kinds," because they cohere in nature as groups of entities that are governed by a common set of laws. There is no simple definition for natural kinds, but they are commonly thought to include such things as animals and plants, as well as elements and compounds. (p. 25)

Even human artifacts and inventions may defy definition in terms of defining features shared by all exemplars. Wittgenstein (Pitcher, 1966) said:

Consider for example the proceedings that we call "games." I mean board-games, card-games, ball-games, Olympic games, and so on. What is common to them all?—Don't say: "There must be something common, or they would not be called "games"—but *look* and *see* whether there is anything common to all.— For if you look at them you will not see something that is common to *all,* but similarities, relationships, and a whole series of them at that. To repeat: don't think, but look!—Look for example at board-games, with their multifarious relationships. Now pass to card-games; here you find many correspondences with the first group, but many common features drop out, and others appear. When we pass next to ball-games, much that is common is retained but much is lost—Are they all "amusing"? Compare chess with noughts and crosses. Or is there always winning and losing, or competition between players? Think of patience. In ball-games there is winning and losing; but when a child throws his ball at the wall and catches it again, this feature has disappeared. Look at the parts played by skill and luck; and at the difference between skill in chess and skill in tennis. Think now of games like ring-a-ring-a-roses; here is the element of amusement, but how many other characteristic features have disappeared! And we can go through the many, many other groups of games in the same way; can see how similarities crop up and disappear. (pp. 188–189)

To account for the relationships among exemplars within a category, Rosch and Mervis (1975) discussed "family resemblance," a notion they attribute to Wittgenstein (1953). According to this view, the exemplars within natural kind categories have one or more features from among the attributes typical for that category. Few exemplars have all of the typical features. Generally, each exemplar has a somewhat different subset of them. The term *family resemblance* comes from the similarity that can often be seen among biologically related family members. Each family member may exhibit a different set of the family-characteristic attributes, but their overall resemblance makes individuals recognizable as members of a family. Rosch and Mervis proposed a similar mechanism to account for the apparent coherence of many object categories as well. Thus, having feathers and wings, singing, being able to fly, laying eggs, and building nests are commonly cited as characteristics of birds. Diverse exemplars will still carry the label *bird* even though they demonstrate different subsets of these attributes.

Rosch and her colleagues also noted that our linguistic labeling system for objects has a hierarchical quality. Rosch, Mervis, Gray, Johnson, and Boyes-Braem (1976) studied the hierarchical or taxonomic nature of category labels. "A *taxonomy* is a system by which categories are related to one another by means of class inclusion. . . . Each category within a taxonomy is entirely included within one other category (unless it is the highest level category) but is not exhaustive of that more inclusive category" (p. 383). Categories such as tree, table, and car are at what is called the basic level. Nested within the basic level, and thus more narrowly defined, are so-called subordinate categories; groupings such as oak tree, kitchen table, and sports car are subordinate categories. Inclusive of several basic-level categories, and thus more broadly constituted than the basic level, are so-called superordinate categories; categories such as plant, furniture, and vehicle are considered to be at the superordinate level. Rosch et al. (1976) found that adult humans who were shown representations of individual objects or living things were most likely to report a label at the basic level. When shown a picture of a robin, for example, people were most likely to call it a bird rather than to say it was an animal or a robin.

It has been suggested that the tendency of people to name objects with basic-level labels (as described above), and for basic-level labels to emerge developmentally earlier than subordinate- or superordinate-level categories (Rosch et al., 1976), are due to the greater diagnosticity of cues for the basic level. According to this argument, basic-level categorization of exemplars is useful because one exemplar is likely to share many features with exemplars of the same basic-level category, and relatively few features with other exemplars of other basic-level categories within the same superordinate category. More concretely, a particular robin is likely to share many features with other individual members of the basic-level category *bird,* but to share many fewer features with individual members of the basic-level category *fish.* Thus, categorization at the basic level is a relatively easy and efficient way to divide up a complex world. On the other hand, according to this view, subordinate classification is less useful, because an individual exemplar is likely to share a very large number of attributes with other exemplars of the same subordinate category, but also to share a large number of attributes with exemplars of other subordinate categories. Thus, an individual robin is likely to resemble other robins closely, but is likely also to share many features with blue jays and swallows. Subordinate classification does not divide the world as neatly and easily into discriminable categories as does basic-level classification.

Rosch et al. (1976) also view superordinate categorization as less useful than basic-level categorization. Because superordinate categories encompass basic-level groupings, some of which may be rather well differentiated from one another, there are few attributes that are shared by a large proportion of the exemplars within the superordinate category. Human subjects, for example, can list few characteristics shared by most musical instruments or most vehicles, but they can name a number of attributes common to guitars or to cars (Rosch et al., 1976).

About the superiority of the basic level, Rosch et al. conclude that ". . . the basic categorization is the most general and inclusive level at which categories can delineate real-world correlational structures" (p. 384).

EXPERIMENTAL RESEARCH ON OBJECT CONCEPTS OR CATEGORIES

Introductory Comments

As the intent of this book is to summarize basic research done within the learning-theory tradition, our review will focus on research with animal subjects. Much behaviorally oriented work on categorization and conceptualization has been conducted with animals. We will occasionally cite work with human subjects, however, where data are available and relevant.

Prior to the 1960s, discriminative behavior was extensively studied with animal subjects; but in general, few studies used stimuli with the complexity or variability seen in the exemplars constituting most linguistic categories. In this chapter, we will concentrate on studies that used naturalistic representations (such as photographs) of objects and living things rather than simple stimuli that vary in only a few dimensions. We will cite research with simpler stimuli, however, when it will help to elucidate underlying processes.

Because the techniques for teaching object categories are likely to be of special interest to behavior therapists, we will organize the first main portion of this review according to the different methods that have been used to study basic-level categorization behavior in animals. We will also separately describe work with pigeon subjects and with primates, the two sorts of animals with which categorization studies have most often been conducted.

We begin with a discussion of the earliest work on categorization with animal subjects that used go/no go, or successive, discrimination training. This section includes an extended description of a study by Edwards and Honig (1987) that raises important issues relating to memorization of exemplars and to appropriate control and test conditions for studies of categorization. Next, we describe projects that used a two-choice simultaneous discrimination. In this section, we detail a study by Siegel and Honig (1970) that compared simultaneous with successive discrimination. Finally, we consider studies conducted in our laboratory using a four-choice simultaneous discrimination procedure.

We will not cover work on what are called polymorphous categories (e.g., Huber & Lenz, 1993; Jitsumori, 1993; Lea & Harrison, 1978; Lea, Lohman, & Ryan, 1993) because of space limitations and because we believe that a consideration of this research would not be as useful to behavior therapists as would the work cited here. Polymorphous categories are constructed by selection from among a set of features via an m-out-of-n rule. Jitsumori (1993), for example, studied polymorphous categorization in pigeons with stimuli that varied in three two-valued features (color, shape, and background color). One value of each feature was defined as positive, and one was defined as negative. In Jitsumori's Experiment 1, stimuli with two positive and one negative value were associated with reinforcement, and stimuli with two negative and one positive value were not associated with reinforcement. Readers who wish to know more about the work on polymorphous categories are advised to consult the sources we have cited.

In the second main portion of this work, we describe studies using procedures that have proved effective in teaching animals and young children to form nonsimilarity-based stimulus classes, that may be analogous to superordinate conceptual categories.

We end this chapter with a summary and suggestions for how behavior therapists might use these findings with their clients.

Given that our audience may comprise many behavior therapists, returning to a specific clinical example we mentioned earlier may serve as an effective preface to the description of specific experiments. Consider a client who avoids bridges but approaches other types of walkways (such as sidewalks). According to the conceptual framework presented here, the client who avoids bridges but not sidewalks is essentially making a categorical discrimination that can be understood through the learning principles of generalization and discrimination. The studies cited below explore the role of these processes in the organization of stimulus classes.

Go/No Go and Successive Discrimination Experiments

Pigeon Studies

An early study of categorization in animal subjects that used naturalistic representations (photographs) of real objects was conducted by Herrnstein and Loveland (1964). The stimuli were photographs projected onto a screen in the pigeon's experimental chamber, and the operant response was pecking at an adjacent key. This study used a go/no go discrimination technique. With this procedure, pecks to half of the stimuli (hereafter called the the positive discriminative stimuli or S+s) were intermittently reinforced, and pecks to the other half of the stimuli (hereafter referred to as the negative discriminative stimuli or S–s) were not reinforced. The 80 or 81 photographs in each daily session were chosen from a set of 1,200. Each day, approximately 40 of the photographs contained people, and pecks to these slides were intermittently reinforced; the other approximately 40 slides did not contain human beings, and pecks to these slides were not reinforced. The pigeons rapidly acquired discriminative responding in the presence of the pictures, pecking at high rates during positive discriminative stimuli and at low or zero rates during negative discriminative stimuli. This result may not be suprising, as subjects may simply have learned to respond appropriately to the individual stimuli that appeared during more than one training session. For that reason, tests were given in which never-before-seen photographs from the positive and negative categories were substituted for the training exemplars. The pigeons responded differentially to these stimuli as well. Herrnstein, Loveland, and Cable (1976) replicated this result in experiments in which photographs of water, trees, or a specific person

served as positive stimuli. Generalization to novel exemplars from the positive and negative stimulus sets was observed in these experiments, too.

Cerella (1979) studied a concept discrimination in which one or more silhouettes of white oak leaves served as the positive stimulus class, and silhouettes of non-oak leaves served as the negative stimulus class. Operant responding was measured via a key adjacent to the screen on which the pictures of leaves were presented. Cerella found discrimination learning to be more rapid when positive trials used repetitions of a single exemplar than when the trials used 40 different exemplars (Experiments 1 and 2). A common set of 40 non-oak silhouettes served as negative exemplars in both of these experiments. Tests of generalization to novel exemplars from the positive class disclosed approximately equal levels of generalization for the subjects trained with one positive exemplar and for those trained with 40 different positive exemplars. Experiment 3 demonstrated generalization to novel exemplars from the negative class after training with 40 different oak silhouettes as positives and 40 different non-oak silhouettes as negatives. In Experiment 4, training was given with only a single positive exemplar and no negative exemplars. The tendency to peck novel oaks nearly equaled that to the training stimulus; however, there was little tendency to peck novel non-oaks. In Experiment 5, pigeons were required to discriminate between a single white oak leaf and 40 other white oak leaves. These pigeons performed poorly, even when they were given 12 times as many training sessions as other pigeons given the oak/non-oak discriminations; two failed to discriminate, and another two discriminated at subcriterial levels. The strong generalization to novel exemplars from the oak leaf set in Experiments 1–5 thus may have been due to the pigeons' inability to discriminate between different exemplars. If, in fact, the pigeons could not distinguish the oak leaves from one another, then the pigeons' behavior in these experiments could not be characterized as conceptual. Wasserman, Kiedinger, and Bhatt (1988) point out that generalization among exemplars does not demonstrate conceptualization when generalization is due to the rather more obvious and trivial matter of a failure to discriminate exemplars from one another.

Discrimination of natural categories need not depend on prior experience with the component categories. This fact was demonstrated in a study by Herrnstein and deVilliers (1980). In this study, and in those remaining in this section, pecks directly to the projection screen in the experimental chamber were measured as operant responses. The discriminative stimuli were underwater photographs taken by a scuba diver, stimuli the pigeons could not have experienced before. The positive class for the experimental subjects comprised 20 photographs containing fish, and the negative class comprised 20 photographs not containing fish. Many of the non-fish pictures contained other underwater creatures. The control-group subjects were given what is called a *pseudocategory discrimination,* in which both the positive and negative stimulus classes contained equal numbers of fish and non-fish photographs; presumably, subjects in this condition could solve the discrimination only by memorizing the specific exemplars in the positive and negative stimulus sets, because no single cue or set of cues reliably distinguishes them. The experimental subjects learned to respond differentially to the photographs nearly twice as rapidly as did the control-group subjects. Experimental subjects continued their discriminative performance in test sessions with novel stimuli, although overall discrimination to the novel exemplars was lower than that to the training exemplars.

A more recent study (Astley & Wasserman, 1992) using the go/no go procedure supports the notion that perceptual similarity underlies much of the pigeons' categorization behavior in the research described earlier. These experiments also examined the effects of varying the number of training exemplars and generalization to exemplars from both the positive and negative sets. In Experiment 1, pigeons learned a successive go/no go discrimination in which all subjects were given the same set of 48 S– stimuli: 12 dif-

ferent people, 12 different flowers, 12 different cars, and 12 different chairs. Each of the four pigeons was given a single positive exemplar, however, from a different conceptual category: one pigeon viewed a person, another viewed a flower, a third viewed a car, and the fourth viewed a chair. Reinforcement for the positive stimulus was arranged via a Fixed-Interval (FI) 30-second schedule, and the trial ended after the presentation of the reinforcer. Responding on this procedure should be a function of the similarity of the members of the four negative classes to the positive stimulus. If the positive stimulus is equally similar to all the negative stimuli, then responding across categories of negative stimuli should be approximately equal. If, however, the positive stimulus is more similar to the same-category negative stimuli than it is to the different-category negative stimuli, then response rates should be significantly higher to the same-category negatives than to the others. Experiment 1 obtained only weak support for this hypothesis. The overall proportion of erroneous pecks to the same-category negative stimuli rose from .24 (very close to the .25 expected by chance) to an average of only .30 over the 12 days of discrimination training.

A second set of pigeons experienced the same procedure described above, except that the positive set for these subjects comprised 12 different exemplars from a single category, each seen once in a daily session (Astley & Wasserman, 1992, Experiment 2). This latter discrimination was learned more slowly than was the discrimination in Experiment 1 with only a single positive exemplar. It took only 6 days for pigeons given the discrimination with only 1 positive to respond an order of magnitude more to the positive than the negatives, whereas the pigeons given the discrimination with 12 positives took 11 days to attain the same level of performance. The latter discrimination also entailed a higher proportion of within-category errors to the negatives. Over 16 days of successive discrimination training, a mean of 43% of all errors were committed to stimuli from the same category; this proportion is significantly different from the 25% expected by chance. The highest mean daily proportion of within-category errors for pigeons given a single positive was 48%, whereas the proportion for pigeons given a dozen positives was 57%. Note that these data demonstrate within-category generalization *and* within-category discrimination. The above-chance level of responding to the same-category exemplars demonstrates within-category generalization, while the fact that the level of responding to within-category negatives was significantly less than that to the positive stimuli demonstrates within-category discrimination. Thus, unlike in Cerella's studies of oak leaves, the categorical generalization observed here cannot be due simply to a failure to discriminate exemplars within a conceptual category from one another.

Test sessions were given in which novel exemplars from the three categories different from the positive category were substituted in order to examine the potential role of generalized inhibitory tendencies following training with 12 positive exemplars. Negatives for only a single category were substituted in each test session.[1] The mean response rates to the original positive and negative stimuli averaged 3.33 and 0.11 pecks per second, respectively. The mean response rate to novel stimuli from the three negative categories averaged 0.69 pecks per second. This score was significantly below the rate to the positive stimuli, but significantly above the rate to the original negative stimuli. The latter difference presumably reflects an inhibitory analog of the excitatory generalization decrement found in the Herrnstein and deVilliers (1980) study.

An earlier series of experiments by Edwards and Honig (1987) had raised serious questions about the role of exemplar memorization in the typical category-discrimination paradigm and the informational value of stimuli associated with reinforcement and nonreinforcement in

generalization tests. These experiments used photographs to conduct a person present/person absent discrimination with pigeon subjects. In Experiment 1, training for two experimental groups was conducted with 20 matched pairs of photographs, such that one exemplar was a photo of a person and the other was a photo of the same scene without a person in it. For one experimental group (the human positive group), responses to exemplars from the person-present set were intermittently reinforced; for the other experimental group (the human negative group), responses to exemplars from the person-absent set were intermittently reinforced. A pseudocategory control group (called a *memorization control group*) experienced positive and negative sets, each made up of exemplars from the person-present and person-absent categories. Performance was measured by a discrimination ratio of pecks to the positive stimuli divided by total pecks; thus, scores could range from .5 to 1.0. Discrimination with the matched exemplars was presumably difficult, as the representations in the positive and negative sets were as nearly identical as possible —except for the presence of a person. Nevertheless, the human positive subjects performed significantly better than did those in the memorization control group. Subjects in the human negative group, however, performed very similarly to subjects in the memorization control group, whose performance remained near chance over 16, 40-trial sessions.

Probe tests substituted novel exemplars for the photographs with persons or for those of the background scenes, for the human positive and the human negative subjects. The human positive subjects showed transfer, with a slight decrement, of discriminative behavior to novel stimuli. Subjects in the human negative group continued to show poor discrimination performance on the probe trials with novel stimuli. To provide a further test of the generality of the performance of

---

[1]Novel exemplars from the category shared by the positives and by one set of the negative exemplars were not given. Because responses to some of the exemplars from this category were reinforced and responses to others were not, it would have been difficult to distinguish the relative contribution of excitatory and inhibitory tendencies to novel stimuli from this category.

the human positive subjects and to examine whether the human negative subjects' poor performance was dependent on the matched training stimuli, novel unmatched stimuli were substituted for all exemplars in a later acquisition test. Subjects in the human positive and the human negative conditions acquired the discrimination at a similar rate and to similar asymptotes. This result implies that the poor performance of the human negative subjects on the matched discrimination and on probe trials may have been due to a tendency to peck at features that characterize positive discriminative stimuli and to withhold pecks to features that characterize negative discriminative stimuli. In the human negative discrimination, the presence of a person characterized the negative set, and the presence of the background cues characterized both the positive and negative stimulus sets; pecks to the background features on both person-present and person-absent slides would have produced near-chance levels when discriminative performance was measured by a peck ratio, and may have been responsible for the poor performance of the human negative subjects.[2] This interpretation of the Experiment 1 data is supported by the results of Experiment 4, which obtained comparable and high discriminative performance for the human negative and the human positive discriminations with unmatched stimuli.

Edwards and Honig's Experiment 3 was an attempt to learn whether the failure of the memorization control group to learn the discrimination in Experiment 1 was due to a general inability of pigeons to memorize such a large set of exemplars, or was instead due to the fact that the positive and negative sets were matched. In Experiment 3, training with the matched pairs continued. Every other day, however, training was also given with a set of unmatched stimuli, divided so that the positive set and negative set contained equal numbers of human-present and human-absent photographs. The memorization control pigeons made only very modest gains in discriminative performance to the matched slides, but they quickly acquired discriminative performance to the unmatched stimuli—rivaling that observed with the human positive discrimination of Experiment 1. This result indicates that pigeons can indeed memorize a set of 40 stimuli rather rapidly when the stimuli are not constituted from matched pairs.

Although the results reported above seem to demonstrate acquisition of a concept and extension of that concept to novel exemplars, other of Edwards and Honig's results require us to question this interpretation. As noted above, in Experiment 3 subjects in the memorization control group from Experiment 1 were given additional training with matched slides. The additional training raised the level of discriminative behavior to the matched stimuli to .61. At this point, probe transfer tests were given in which either *all* of the negative stimuli or *all* of the positive stimuli were replaced for a session. Performance transferred virtually without decrement to the novel positive exemplars and to the novel negative exemplars on probe tests with the matched stimuli. Because the positive and negative sets for the memorization control group were made up of equal numbers of person-present and person-absent representations, transfer of discriminative behavior to novel stimuli could only have been accomplished through the informativeness of the stimuli that were *retained* during the test. About this result, Edwards and Honig wrote, "Experiment 3 also showed that birds may categorize visual stimuli on the basis of their reward value and/or the pattern of responding associated with reward versus extinction. This last finding raises the possibility that the probe test performance for Group Human Positive in the first phase of Experiment 2 may have been based on the reward value of the remaining slides, rather than transfer of a category-based response rule" (p. 251).

---

[2]Pecking to the positive features and withholding of pecks to the negative features would, alternatively, have led the human positive group to excellent discriminative responding.

This finding also calls into question the generalization test results of Cerella's (1979) Experiments 1–3. There, generalization was measured via tests that substituted novel exemplars for *all* of the positive stimuli or for *all* of the negative stimuli. In more abstract terms, we might consider discrimination training in Cerella's Experiments 1–3 and in Edwards and Honig's Experiments 2–4 to have established two sets of stimuli, *A* and *B,* through the imposition of different contingencies for each set. In generalization tests, novel exemplars were substituted for all of the *A*s or for all of the *B*s. A high level of generalization to novel exemplars may be produced in this procedure by the reward or informational value of the familiar stimuli that continue to be presented during the test sessions. That is, when all of the *A*s continue during the test, pigeons may treat the novel stimuli as *B*s simply because they are not *A*s. Conversely, when all of the *B*s continue during the test, pigeons may treat the novel stimuli as *A*s simply because they are not *B*s. Thus, when generalization tests are conducted in a manner that substitutes novel exemplars for either all of the positive stimuli or all of the negative stimuli, as Cerella did, we must view the generalization test results with caution. The reinforcement contingencies to the positive or negative stimuli that were retained during the test sessions may have produced the virtually undecremented transfer to novel exemplars seen in Cerella's Experiments 1–3.

Generalization to novel exemplars due to the reinforcement contingencies to the training stimuli that appear in test sessions is not a concern in any of the other studies described in this chapter. These other studies either substituted novel exemplars for both positive and negative stimuli (e.g., D'Amato & Van Sant, 1988, described below; Herrnstein & deVilliers, 1980; Herrnstein & Loveland, 1964) or substituted only a small portion of the exemplars within the positive or negative sets (e.g., Astley & Wasserman, 1992).

Primate Studies

D'Amato and Van Sant (1988) studied the person concept with monkeys *(Cebus apella)* using the go/no go procedure. Photographic stimuli were projected onto a frosted panel in the experimental chamber, and responding to a lever below the screen was the operant. In Experiment 1, training was given with a set of 10 photographs containing one or more people and a set of 10 photographs not containing people. For one of the monkeys in this experiment, the positive set comprised photographs containing people, and for the other monkey it comprised photographs not containing people. Training was given with a single pair of one positive and one negative exemplar until subjects responded at over 75% correct on that pair of stimuli, and then training was given on the next pair of stimuli. A response on the operant lever within 5 seconds of the onset of a positive stimulus constituted a correct response and led to food delivery; failure to respond within 5 seconds of the onset of the positive stimulus constituted an incorrect response, and terminated the stimulus and initiated the intertrial interval (ITI). Withholding a response for 5 seconds following the onset of a negative stimulus constituted a correct response, and terminated the stimulus and initiated the ITI; responses within 5 seconds of the onset of a negative stimulus were punished by continuation of the negative stimulus for an additional 15 seconds. Once subjects had met the criterion on all 10 of the pairs, they began transfer tests. Transfer test sessions comprised 20 trials with the stimuli on which the monkeys had been trained and 20 trials with novel photographs, 10 of which contained people and 10 of which did not. The regular reinforcement contingencies applied to all stimuli during testing sessions, and sessions continued until the subjects met the criterion of 75% correct. There were four additional transfer tests, each of which used 20 completely novel exemplars intermixed with 20 exemplars from the training set or earlier transfer tests. Transfer Tests 4 and 5 used matched pairs of novel stimuli. Because responses to the novel stimuli were differentially reinforced, special attention was given to the monkeys' performance on first exposure to stimuli in the transfer sessions. The two monkeys both exceeded chance on the first exposures to the novel stimuli in the third transfer test session, after they had received training on 30 person and 30 nonperson slides.

Experiments 2 and 3 were conducted similarly to Experiment 1. In Experiment 2, however, training was conducted with matched pairs of stimuli to heighten the salience of the features of the positive set. In Experiment 3, a 60-second time-out was given for responses to the negative stimuli, and the training set included only fair-skinned Caucasian people whereas the transfer set included some African American and other dark-skinned people. The transfer results of Experiments 2 and 3 resembled those of Experiment 1, except that responding was somewhat more variable across the five subjects in the latter two experiments. Over Experiments 1–3, D'Amato and Van Sant's subjects required training with an average of 40 exemplars before showing significant transfer on the first exposure to novel stimuli.

D'Amato and Van Sant examined the slides on which monkeys in the three experiments persistently made errors, and found a tendency to respond to irrelevant features (i.e., features that do not characterize humans, such as patches of red) that were nonetheless common among the human slides. In addition, they found a tendency for several monkeys not to respond to a slide of a human that other humans would easily recognize, but that was unlike other slides used in training. D'Amato and Van Sant concluded that their subjects were responding to the novel slides on the basis of their resemblance to slides seen earlier in training, and not based on any abstract "person concept."

General Comments

The studies described in this section provide several pieces of information that may be important for understanding basic processes of category learning. They suggest that even pigeons can easily and quickly discriminate stimulus classes that correspond to human object concepts. Learning was faster and reached higher levels when the exemplars were divided according to human conceptual categories than when they were not. When the exemplars were divided according to human conceptual categories, learning was faster with only one positive exemplar than with several. Discriminative behavior generalized to novel exemplars from both the positive and the negative stimulus classes, and it generalized better when multiple exemplars were given in training than when only a single exemplar was used.

The ability of pigeons to discriminate object classes that correspond to human conceptual categories does not depend on prior experience with the objects. Pigeons are able to discriminate fish from non-fish in underwater scenes that they could not have experienced before. In addition, the ability to discriminate human object concepts was not dependent on aspects of the photo other than the target object, as pigeons in Edwards and Honig's Experiment 1 were able to discriminate photographs that were identical except for the human target.

Both the pigeon and the monkey results are consistent with the notion that category discrimination and generalization are based on perceptual similarity, ideas that are discussed more fully later in this chapter.

Finally, the go/no go discrimination procedure might be judged to be particularly effective in a therapeutic or applied setting where the fundamental goal is to help the client discriminate situations in which a particular response is appropriate from those in which the response is not appropriate. Children, for example, need to learn to discriminate a number of factors in order to learn when it is safe and when it is not safe to cross the street. A treatment program designed to teach safe street-crossing might include go/no go training with exemplar scenarios that embody a variety of factors, such as the presence or absence of cars, a walk signal, or a crossing guard.

Two-Choice Simultaneous Discrimination

Pigeon Studies

Malott and Sidall (1972) studied concept discrimination with a procedure in which photographs were pasted to cubes and the pigeon had to peck the appropriate cube to obtain reinforcement in a reservoir under it. The S+ set comprised pictures containing people, and the S– set comprised pictures containing objects (and no people). A single S+ and S– were presented simultaneously, and pigeons were required to continue training with a particular problem (pair of exemplars) until they met a criterion of five consecutive correct choices with it. In different phases of the study, pigeons were required to learn discriminations in which the S+ class was composed of human faces, human torsos, or groups of humans. Training with these discriminations continued until pigeons showed mastery of each one by choosing correctly on the first exposure of five consecutive problems with a type of discrimination. Malott and Sidall were interested in how many problems the pigeons would have to complete before mastering a discrimination. The researchers found that the minimum number of problems to mastery was between 3 and 17 (not including the trials that demonstrated mastery) across pigeons and problems. The torso/object discrimination was mastered more quickly, on average, than either the face/object or multiple people/object discriminations. Performance across earlier and later discriminations suggested little positive transfer due to experience. A control group of subjects received training on a pseudocategory discrimination. The control group pigeons failed to master the discrimination within 20 to 25 problems.

Siegel and Honig (1970) compared performance on a person present/person absent discrimination both when the positive and negative stimuli were presented successively and when they were presented simultaneously. The positive stimuli used in training consisted of photographs containing people, and the negative set consisted of photographs of landscapes, animals, and inanimate objects. Photographs were projected onto a split screen in front of the pigeon, and responding to keys centered below the screen on each half of the split served as operant responses. One group of pigeons was given simultaneous training in which a positive stimulus and a negative stimulus appeared at once, each on a different

half of the split screen. Pigeons in this condition were reinforced on a VI 37.5-second schedule for pecks to the key under the positive stimulus, and the trial ended after the reinforced peck; pecks to the key under the negative stimulus incurred a 5-second delay in the availability of reward. Another group of pigeons was given successive training in which only a single positive or negative stimulus appeared at a time, on only one side of the split screen. Responses to positive stimuli were reinforced on a VI 37.5-second schedule, and positive and negative stimulus presentations were each 60 seconds in duration. Each exemplar was seen approximately five times during training. In test sessions, novel stimuli were substituted from the positive and negative classes. On test trials, one positive and one negative stimulus were presented simultaneously. Both the pigeons trained with simultaneous presentation of stimuli and those trained with successive presentation of stimuli maintained the discrimination during simultaneous tests with novel stimuli. The discriminations were even maintained when the photographs were rotated 180 degrees. In addition, discriminations were maintained when tests were given with scenes matched except for the presence of a human, and were also maintained when mannequins were substituted for humans in the matched photographs. The discrimination was degraded, however, when the photographic images were defocused.

Primate Studies

Schrier, Angarella, and Povar (1984) studied acquisition of person and monkey concept discriminations in two separate experiments using a spatial discrete-trial choice procedure with stumptailed monkeys *(Macaca arctoides)* as subjects. Pictures were projected on a screen in the experimental chamber, and monkeys were reinforced for pressing the correct key in a two-choice task. In Experiment 1, daily sessions included three trials with each of 40 photographs containing humans and 40 not containing humans or animals. Daily sessions in Experiment 2 were the same as those of Experiment 1, except that one set of slides included monkeys and the other set did not, but sometimes included other animals. Once a monkey's discrimination performance on the first discrimination had stabilized, it was given exposure to a completely new set of 80 stimuli as a transfer test. In Experiment 1, each monkey was then given training on a pseudocategory discrimination for a test of individual stimulus memorization. In the fourth phase of Experiment 1, individual people and backgrounds were varied in pairs of discriminations to examine the ability of the monkeys to learn to discriminate individual people or backgrounds when the other aspect of the display was held constant. Finally, monkeys were returned to the person/non-person discrimination prior to testing with exemplars selected by the human experimenters for their similarity to the slides in earlier training to which the monkeys did well or poorly.

The monkeys in the Schrier et al. study learned both the person and the monkey discriminations with the choice procedure, and the monkey discrimination was learned more rapidly. On the person discrimination, individual subjects first exceeded 80% correct slightly before Day 30 of training. On the monkey discrimination, the two subjects first exceeded 80% correct on Day 8 and Day 12, respectively. Both experiments found modest positive transfer to novel exemplars in the first session of training with them. Performance to the novel exemplars on the first test day for the human discrimination averaged 10 percentage points above that on the first day of training; performance to the novel exemplars on the first 5 days of the monkey discrimination averaged 14 percentage points above that on the first 5 days of training. The subjects in Experiment 1 learned the pseudocategory discrimination nearly as rapidly as they learned the true discrimination. Schrier et al. found the monkeys to be better at discriminating different backgrounds when the person on them was held constant than at discriminating different individual people when the background was held constant. Finally, the tests with slides selected by the human experimenters for their similarity to ex-

emplars supporting good or poor discriminative performance found more accurate performance to the novel stimuli identified as potential good exemplars than to those identified as potential poor exemplars.

Schrier et al. (1984) noted that their subjects' learning rate was much slower than had been exhibited by pigeons in studies using similar stimuli. One difference between their studies and those with pigeons that had been published to that point was that the former used a discrete-trial choice procedure and the latter used a go/no go discrimination procedure. Experiment 3 constituted a go/no go version of the Schrier et al. choice studies. The operant was pressing a single key centered under the projection screen. A monkey that had served in Experiment 1 was first given the person discrimination under the a go/no go paradigm, and once stability of the discrimination had been attained, the monkey was transfered to completely novel stimuli. The subject was then given the monkey discrimination of Experiment 2 under the go/no go paradigm, and again it was transfered to novel stimuli with that discrimination. Although it had been given 45 days of training on the person discrimination under the choice paradigm, the subject in this experiment began the go/no go paradigm at chance levels. However, it quickly attained a high level of discrimination on both the person and the monkey discriminations. Initial performance to novel exemplars, however, was only a few percentage points higher than that seen at the beginning of training in each of the discriminations; thus, transfer here was no better than that obtained with the choice procedure.

One other possible factor that may have led to only moderate rates of generalization to novel exemplars in the Schrier et al. (1984) studies was that subjects were trained with only a limited set of exemplars (80). It may be that with a limited set of exemplars, subjects may memorize the individual stimuli, and that this stimulus memorization reduced generalization to novel exemplars. To examine this possibility, Schrier and Brady (1987, Experiment 1) conducted a study that used 1,124 different slides with humans and an equivalent number of slides without humans. Slides were presented in pairs; one slide of the pair contained humans and the other slide contained no humans. A pellet of food followed a press to the panel on which the slide with humans was projected; the intertrial interval immediately followed a press to the panel on which the slide without humans was projected. Eighty trials were given per session. The subjects were nine rhesus monkeys *(Macaca mullata)*. Seven of the monkeys showed rapid development of high levels of choice accuracy, whereas two showed more moderate gains. The "good learners" averaged over 80% correct by Day 6 of training and slightly exceeded 90% on the last day of training (Day 14), even though no slide was ever repeated. The most rapid gains were made in the first five days of training. Schrier and Brady concluded that use of a procedure that precluded learning about individual slides increased their monkeys' ability to categorize exemplars on the first exposure to them.

Four-Choice Categorization Studies

In this section of the chapter, we discuss research conducted in our laboratory using a four-choice categorization procedure. This method was developed in an attempt to more closely model the ways in which humans seem conceptually and linguistically to divide the world. Our conceptual categories do not often consist simply of "A" and "not-A." Instead, our conceptual categories are of the form "A," "B," "C," and so on. When viewing a scene, for example, we are not likely to say, "That is a human being and those other things are not human beings." Instead, we are likely to say, "That is a human being, that is a car, that is a tree, and that is water." The four-choice categorization procedure better reflects this noncomplementary division of the world.

In the four-choice procedure, pigeons were required to discriminate, concurrently, slide images from four different basic-level categories (from four different superordinate classes). Slides were projected individually onto a viewing screen in the front panel of the experimental chamber. At each of the four corners of the screen was a response key. When operational, each key was illuminated by a different colored light. Trials began when a slide depicting an exemplar from one of the four categories was projected onto the screen. Once the pigeon had completed 30 pecks to the screen, the four corner keys were illuminated. A single choice response was permitted. If it was to the correct key for the category of the exemplar depicted on the screen, then reinforcement was given and the trial ended; if it was to one of the three incorrect keys for that category, then no reinforcement was given and the illumination of the four keys ended. A correction trial began immediately after an incorrect choice, and correction trials continued until the pigeon chose the correct key. Responses to correction trials were not scored. Across quartets of subjects, a different response key was correct for each of the four object categories used.

Bhatt, Wasserman, Reynolds, and Knauss (1988, Experiment 1B) used the discrimination procedure described above. The stimuli were presented via photographic slides taken of 10 exemplars each from the categories of cats, flowers, cars, and chairs. Because Herrnstein (1985) had reported difficulty in getting pigeons to discriminate human artifacts from one another, Experiment 1B included both natural and artifact categories. Choice accuracy rose rapidly in training from the chance level of 25% to nearly 80% within 30 days. Two test sessions were given in which novel stimuli were substituted for half of the exemplars in each category. Accuracy to the familiar slides in these tests averaged 81%, and to the novel exemplars it averaged 64%. There was no indication here, or in any of our other studies described below, that learning was more rapid or that generalization was more complete to the natural than to the artifact categories.

Wasserman, Kiedinger, and Bhatt (1988, Experiment 2) conducted a comparison of the speed of learning the four-choice categorization task described above with the speed of learning a four-choice pseudocategory discrimination. In the four-choice pseudocategory discrimination, an equal number of exemplars from the four categories was associated with each of the four keys —that is, the upper-left key was correct for one fourth of the cats, one fourth of the flowers, one fourth of the cars, and one fourth of the chairs, and so on for the other three keys. The pigeons given the true category task averaged 79% correct over Days 37 through 40 of training, whereas the pigeons given the pseudocategory task averaged only 44% correct.

The more rapid acquisition of a true category task than a pseudocategory task implies that stimuli within a category are perceptually similar. Wasserman et al. (1988, Experiment 1) further examined this possibility in a split-category study. Daily sessions included trials with 20 exemplars each from two of the four categories (cats, flowers, cars, and chairs). Each session included trials with a different pair of categories. The correct responses to each category were "split" between two different keys. For one pigeon, for example, one half of the cat slides required a peck to one key (R1), and the other half of the cat slides required a peck to another key (R2) for reinforcement; one half of the flower slides required a peck to a third key (R3), and the other half of the flower slides required a peck to yet a fourth key (R4) for reinforcement. (Cat-chair, car-flower, and car-chair sessions were similarly constructed, with different pigeons having different category-key assignments). If the cat slides in the first set of 10 were equivalently discriminable from all the other 30 slides in a session, then errors should be randomly distributed to R2, R3, and R4; if, however, the cat slides in the first set of 10 were more similar to the second set of 10 cat slides than to the 20 flower slides, then there should be more R2 errors than R3 or R4 errors. The pigeons' errors of commission were clearly consistent with the latter possibility. Over Days 105 to 112 of training, a mean of 56% of all errors were within-category in nature as compared with the chance level of 33% to each of the three incorrect possibilities.

The split-category experiment also answered

an important question concerning the novel stimulus tests of the initial four-choice categorization experiment (Bhatt et al., 1988, Experiment 1B). Did pigeons in the earlier study generalize to new exemplars from the four categories because the new exemplars were indistinguishable from the exemplars in training? The split categories in the newer study corresponded with the training and novel sets of Experiment 1B of Bhatt et al.; thus, this question could be decisively answered. Over Days 105 to 112, the pigeons' split categorization accuracy averaged 72%, significantly greater than chance (25%). So, the training and novel generalization test stimuli of Bhatt et al.'s Experiment 1B were in fact discriminable from one another. The generalization observed in that study was not due to an inability of the pigeons to discriminate photographs in the training set from those in the testing sets (cf. Cerella, 1979).

A later series of studies examined parametric aspects of learning on the four-choice procedure. Bhatt (1988, see also Wasserman & Bhatt, 1992) systematically varied the number of different exemplars from the categories—cats, flowers, cars, and chairs—given during training. One group of subjects was trained with 1 exemplar from each of the four categories (each shown 12 times daily), another was trained with 4 exemplars (each shown 3 times daily), and yet another was trained with 12 exemplars (each shown once daily). The speed of learning was an inverse function of the number of exemplars shown per category. The mean numbers of days to reach a criterion of 70% accuracy on 2 successive days of training were 6 for Group 1, 11 for Group 4, and 22 for Group 12. Generalization tests were given with 8 novel exemplars from each of the four categories. The degree of generalization was a direct function of the number of different exemplars given during training. The mean percentage correct was 27% for Group 1, 45% for Group 4, and 62% for Group 12. Thus, although increasing the number of exemplars raised the difficulty of learning the discrimination, it heightened the generalization to novel exemplars. The heightened generalization with a larger number of training exemplars may be due to the increased likelihood that the novel exemplars will resemble one or more training exemplars with a larger training set.

Whether stimulus repetition is necessary for categorization learning to take place was examined by Bhatt et al. (1988, Experiment 3). A library of 2,000 photographs was created: 500 photographs each of people, flowers, cars, and chairs. People were substituted for cats because of the difficulty in obtaining such a large sample of cat photographs. Fifty sessions each comprising 40 trials were given so that no exemplar was ever shown twice. Discrimination accuracy rose to a mean level of 70% over Days 41 to 50 of training. On Day 51, pigeons were tested with a mixture of 20 slides shown on Day 50 and 20 novel slides. Accuracy to the slides seen on Day 50 averaged 79%, and to the novel slides accuracy averaged 75%. There was no significant difference between discrimination of the familar and the novel slides. This result, however, was in the correct direction to show that training exemplars are remembered and that repetition improves performance.

Bhatt et al.'s Experiment 4 with different pigeons more systematically examined the role of repetition on discrimination performance. Forty slides (10 each of people, flowers, cars, and chairs) were randomly chosen from those used in Experiment 3. Four-choice categorization training with these repeating slides was given on alternate days. On the other days, training was given in a nonrepeating fashion with the slides remaining from the pool of 2,000. Accuracy of responding increased faster and attained higher ultimate levels to the repeating slides over the 96 days of training. From a mean of 29% in the first 4-day block, responding to the repeating set ultimately rose to 85% in the last 4-day block. From a mean of 26% in the first 4-day block, responding to the nonrepeating set ultimately rose to 66% in the last 4-day block. The higher level of discrimination of repeating stimuli over nonrepeating stimuli was statistically significant.

General Comments

Research with the two- and four-choice categorization procedures is congruent with that using the go/no go procedure in showing that perceptual similarity can play an important role in the formation of object categories. In the research cited above, the effectiveness of the two-choice procedure in training a category discrimination was demonstrated in pigeons and primates, and the effectiveness of the four-choice procedure was demonstrated in pigeons. As discussed above, the four-choice categorization task may better reflect the noncomplementary nature of human conceptual categories than the two-choice or go/no go procedures.

Studies with both pigeons and primates showed that repetition of a small set of exemplars may promote their memorization, and that this memorization may lead to lessened generalization to novel exemplars.

Taken as a whole, the results cited above suggest two factors that behavior therapists should consider when implementing a treatment program involving the training of categories. First, the therapist should consider whether go/no go or choice procedures are best suited for the problem at hand. The go/no go procedure is best suited to situations where the problem requires a response in the presence of one category of stimuli and the withholding of the response in the presence of other categories of stimuli. The choice procedure, however, is best suited for problems where one active response is required to one category of stimuli and a different active response is required to another category of stimuli. The choice of go/no go versus choice procedures may, in addition, depend on the client. Some clients may have difficulty withholding responses; in this case, the choice procedure might be best, because the client is required to make a different active response in the presence of stimuli from different categories.

A second factor the therapist should consider is the number of exemplars used in training. The Bhatt (1988) experiment that varied the number of exemplars in training found faster learning with a smaller set of training exemplars, but poorer generalization to novel exemplars. Thus, the behavior therapist must balance the speed-of-learning advantage afforded by training with a small set of exemplars against the greater generalization to novel situations afforded by training with a larger set of exemplars.

NONSIMILARITY-BASED CATEGORIES

Although perceptual similiarity can go far toward accounting for many of the results described above (Astley & Wasserman, 1992), it cannot fully explain all of human taxonomic categorization. As should have been apparent from our earlier discussion of superordinate categories, perceptual similarity alone cannot explain their coherence. Casual reflection about familar superordinates supports this notion. Chairs and lamps, for example, are generally quite dissimilar even though they are both members of the class *furniture*. Rosch et al. (1976) systematically studied the taxonomic nature of concepts with human subjects and found superordinate categories to have few reported characteristic features or motor programs and little in common in the way of overall shape.

It may be that perceptual similarity is not all there is even for basic-level or subordinate categories. Other processes may contribute to those aggregations as well. Past experiences with and behavior toward objects in basic-level categories may help tie them together. Rosch et al. (1976), for example, did find subjects to report similar typical actions in the presence of objects in basic level categories. Furthermore, in the view of a number of theorists, to be classified as conceptual or categorical in nature, behavior must exhibit a coherence that goes *beyond* perceptual similarity (e.g., Herrnstein, 1990; Lea, 1984; Murphy & Medin, 1985; Wattanabe, Lea, & Dittrich, 1993). Lea (1984) proposed that a true concept comprises stimuli that are tied together by relations that are not based solely on perceptual similarity. He argued that if responses learned to

some members of a category transfer to others and if such transfer is based only on perceptual similarity, then the very idea of a concept becomes superfluous; primary stimulus generalization alone can completely explain transfer from some category members to others.

Herrnstein (1990) developed a five-level scheme of categorization in which the higher levels represent greater levels of abstraction. The research described above is consistent with classification at Herrnstein's Level 2, *open-ended categories,* where similarity is the primary mechanism for category coherence. Herrnstein reserved the term *concept* for relations that have achieved Level 4. For a class of stimuli to qualify as a concept, changes in response tendencies to one member of the class must propagate rapidly to all other members of the class "more than can be accounted for by similarities among members of the set" (p. 150). Rather than perceptual similarity as the basis for concept formation, Herrnstein proposed mediated generalization and mediated association (e.g., Osgood 1953; Underwood, 1966), notions that have fallen into disuse in recent years.

> The terms were used to describe transfer of conditioning across stimuli too different to be attributed to common features or attributes. The theoretical notion was that the stimuli may have had no stimulus elements in common, but, presumably because of past conditioning, they evoked overlapping responses. The overlapping responses provided the bridge for transfer. (Herrnstein, 1990, p. 150)

As an example, due to a common response (chairs and lamps are both called "furniture") and/or a common context (chairs and lamps are both sold in furniture stores and are found in homes) and/or a common use (a chair and lamp may be used together in reading), perceptually dissimilar stimuli may come to be classed together. Hull (1943) referred to generalization between stimuli based on mediating associations as secondary stimulus generalization. The limitations of a similarity-based approach were also noted years ago by Keller and Schoenfeld (1950), who asserted that mediated generalization plays an important role in human conceptual behavior. A similar analysis of conceptualization was proposed by Goldiamond (1966).

Some of our own earlier work failed to find evidence of mediated or secondary generalization (Bhatt & Wasserman, 1989). Other work, however, has succeeded in showing that there are techniques whereby pigeons *can* demonstrate secondary generalization among complex natural exemplars. Vaughan (1988) found that after several discrimination reversals, pigeons came to treat members of each of two 20-items slide sets as functional equivalents of one another. Importantly, all 40 slides shown to the pigeons depicted trees; thus, the 20 items in each set were random assortments, with no obvious perceptual "glue" holding them together and distinguishing them from items in the other set.

Further Studies of Mediated Generalization

Urcuioli, Zentall, Jackson-Smith, and Steirn (1989) provided evidence of mediated generalization in pigeons using a different procedure. Their Experiment 2 entailed a three-phase design. Pigeons first learned a many-to-one matching-to-sample task, in which a vertically striped comparison key was correct when the sample was red (R) or vertically striped (V), and a horizontally striped comparison key was correct when the sample was green (G) or horizontally striped (H). Then the R and G samples were associated with circle (C) and dot (D) comparison stimuli. Finally, transfer of training for the remaining samples (V and H) to the new comparison stimuli was assessed. For the consistent group, the V sample again had the same correct comparison stimulus as the R sample, and the H sample again had the same correct comparison stimulus as the G sample. For the inconsistent group, the V sample now had a different correct comparison from the R sample, and the H sample now had a different correct comparison from the G sample. If training in Phase 1 had established equivalence between the R and V samples and between the G and H samples by connecting

them to common comparisons, respectively, then the consistent group should learn the new discrimination significantly faster than the inconsistent group. The data supported this prediction. (For related results, see Zentall, Steirn, Sherburne, and Urcuioli [1991].)

Recent research we have conducted with pigeons and young children has used a three-phase choice procedure like that of Urcuioli et al. (1989), except that the training procedure was simpler than matching-to-sample and the stimuli were more complex and naturalistic. The procedure for the study by Wasserman, DeVolder, and Coppage (1992) is schematically depicted in Figure 22–1. This study used photographic representations of exemplars from four different basic-level categories from four different superordinate categories. The assignment of categories to the designations C1, C2, C3, and C4 was counterbalanced across subjects. In original training, 12 diverse exemplars from each of two categories were associated with one common response (R1), and 12 diverse exemplars from two other categories were associated with another common response (R2). In reassignment training, the exemplars from C1 and C3 were associated with new responses (R3 and R4, respectively), and the exemplars from C2 and C4 were withheld. Dur-

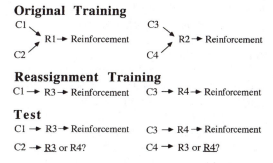

Original Training

Reassignment Training

Test

Figure 22–1. A schematic diagram of the design of the Wasserman, DeVolder, and Coppage (1992) experiment. The designations C1, C2, C3, and C4 represent separate classes of stimuli, and R1, R2, R3, and R4 represent different responses. Outcomes consistent with a mediational outcome in test sessions are indicated by underlining.

ing testing, performance of R3 versus R4 was measured to the exemplars from C1, C2, C3, and C4. Reinforcement contingencies were the same as in reassignment training for C1 and C3 exemplars, but responses were nondifferentially reinforced to exemplars from C2 and C4. For ease of explaining the results of these and later studies, responding to the C2 and C4 exemplars that accorded with the expectations of a mediational analysis will be called "correct," even though all responses in the presence of these stimuli were reinforced.

If original training bound the C1/C2 and C3/C4 combinations into higher-order categories, then exemplars from C2 should predominately occasion R3, and those from C4 should predominately occasion R4, even though these stimulus-response combinations were *never* trained. The results were consistent with this hypothesis: after several blocks of original training, each followed by a block of reassignment training, responses in accord with reassignment training were significantly above chance to the reassigned categories (C1 and C3, 87%) *and* to the nonreassigned categories (C2 and C4, 72%). Both percentages significantly exceeded the chance accuracy score of 50%, and the percentage correct to the reassigned stimuli significantly exceeded that to the nonreassigned stimuli. These results clearly show that the three-phase procedure is one by which pigeons are able to form categories of functionally equivalent but perceptually different stimuli, even when the component categories themselves comprised complex and multidimensional stimuli.

A parallel project was undertaken with preschool children, who performed a photograph-sorting task. DeVolder, Lohman, and Wasserman (reported in Wasserman & DeVolder, 1993) followed the logic and plan of the earlier study with pigeons. The children in this project were four or five years of age. Five rectangles were drawn on the response board: one in the center and one at each corner of the center rectangle. Only two diagonally located peripheral rectangles were available in each phase of the study; the two unavailable rectangles were

marked with large Xs. The rectangles corresponding with R1 and R2 were available during original training, and the rectangles corresponding with R3 and R4 were available during reassignment and testing. Stimuli were photographs made from the slides used in the pigeon study. During original training, photographs from C1, C2, C3, and C4 were singly placed in the center rectangle to begin a trial. The child was asked to place the photograph on one of the two available rectangles. As in the pigeon study, R1 was correct in the presence of C1 and C2 exemplars and R2 was correct in the presence of C3 and C4 exemplars. In all phases of the study, correct responses were verbally reinforced ("That is correct") and incorrect responses were verbally punished ("That is not correct"). No correction trials were given. During reassignment, training was given only with C1 and C3 stimuli. In reassignment, R3 was correct in the presence of C1 exemplars, and R4 was correct in the presence of C3 exemplars. Again, as in the pigeon study, test trials were given with each of the exemplars from C1, C2, C3, and C4, and differential reinforcement was given only for responses to C1 and C3 exemplars. Responses to C2 and C4 were nondifferentially reinforced, that is, all were followed by "That is correct." During testing, the children averaged 99% correct to the C1 and C3 exemplars and 80% correct to the C2 and C4 exemplars. The accuracy to both the reassigned C1 and C3 exemplars and to the nonreassigned C2 and C4 exemplars exceeded chance accuracy. The drop in accuracy from reassigned to nonreassigned exemplars was again statistically significant.

The two studies described above establish that response mediation can forge a class of functionally equivalent but perceptually diverse stimuli. If a mediational approach is to provide an effective model for human categorization behavior, however, response mediation must extend to novel exemplars from the component categories joined in original training. Human conceptual categories are open sets; we not only apply the terms *table* and *cat* to familiar tables and cats, but also to novel tables and cats. We extend the superordinate designations *furniture* and *animals,* respectively, to these novel stimuli.

The next step in our research program was to use the three-phase procedure to examine transfer of discriminative responding to novel exemplars. We also sought to replicate the DeVolder, Lohman, and Wasserman experiment with different experimental stimuli. We wanted the images to be naturalistic, but also to vary from one another in systematic ways. So we chose to study simulated human faces. This study was conducted by the first author and Paul Norwood and is reported in Astley and Wasserman (in press).

The 24 simulated faces were black line drawings on a white background. There were 6 faces in each of four "families" that corresponded to the C1, C2, C3, and C4 of Figure 22–1. The members of each family had the same hair and chin, but the individuals had unique eyebrows, eyes, noses, and mouths; no other face shared those specific features. All of the faces had the same ears. Four faces in each family were used in the training phases of the study, and 4 were withheld for novel stimulus tests. The stimuli were presented on an 11-inch black-and-white computer monitor. The children were asked to respond to the faces by pointing directly at a location on the screen. The response locations were represented by four different-appearing houses placed at the four corners of the box where the faces appeared. Two houses, those on one diagonal, appeared during original training, and the other two houses, on the other diagonal, appeared during reassignment and test. Children were told that they were playing a game in which their job was to help the boys in the pictures get home for dinner. Correct pointing responses were followed by auditory feedback from the computer: a cartoonlike voice said, "I'm home, what's for dinner?" Incorrect choices were followed by the same voice saying, "Oh-oh, this isn't my home." The experimenter also verbally emphasized the correctness or incorrectness of the children's choices.

The participants were children between the ages of four and seven. Briefly, original training was intended to create mediating responses to the C1/C2 and C3/C4 pairs. In reassignment, new responses were trained to the C1 and C3 exemplars. Testing examined transfer of the newly learned responses to the stimuli withheld during reassignment and to novel stimuli that were interspersed during the test session. Two exposures to original training and two exposures to reassignment were given before the testing session. If association with a common response in original training had created an effective mediator, then we expected predominant choice of R3 in the presence of C2 exemplars and predominant choice of R4 in the presence of C4 exemplars.

The primary group of interest in our assessment of mediation includes those children who performed at high levels of accuracy in both original and reassignment training, as only they would have a good chance of having learned the requisite mediating responses and of demonstrating the new responses in the testing session. These children averaged 99.6% correct to the reassigned C1 and C3 exemplars during testing, and they averaged 93.8% to the nonreassigned C2 and C4 exemplars. Responding on trials with novel exemplars followed a similar pattern; participants averaged 100.0% correct to the novel C1 and C3 exemplars and 88.9% to the the novel C2 and C4 exemplars. All these effects were significantly different from the 50% expected by chance.

The Astley and Norwood study left several questions unanswered. No 4-year-olds in that study reached sufficient levels of discrimination accuracy during training to proceed to test. In addition, faces may be stimuli with unique characteristics for human subjects. To see whether our results would extend to younger children and to know whether we could produce the mediated generalization effect with stimuli other than faces, we undertook a study using silhouettes of leaves as stimuli and gave longer exposure to original and reassignment training. This study was completed by the first author and Brent Finger, and is described in Astley and Wasserman (in press).

Silhouettes of maple, pine, willow, and nut leaves were counterbalanced across the designations C1, C2, C3, and C4 for different subjects. Four exemplars from each category were used in original and reassignment training, and two were reserved for novel stimulus test sessions. Four differently patterned boxes served as response locations. Verbal praise and an ascending series of tones served as positive reinforcers, and a comment about the incorrectness of the response and a descending series of tones served as punishers. Training proceeded as described for the Astley and Norwood study, but training and testing were conducted over 2 consecutive days, and stimuli were gradually introduced during original training to facilitate learning of that discrimination. In addition, the children were questioned during testing to determine whether they recognized the familiar exemplars as ones they had seen before and novel exemplars as ones they had not seen before. Four- to six-year-old children participated.

Our attempts to help 4-year-olds to reach criterion were modestly successful; 3 of the 20 participants who reached criterion during training were 4 years of age. The overall results for those meeting criterion were as predicted by the mediation hypothesis. Responding averaged 94.4% to the the reassigned C1 and C3 exemplars and 80.6% correct to the nonreassigned C2 and C4 exemplars; both percentages were significantly greater than chance. Responding to the novel C1 and C3 exemplars averaged 63.7% correct, and to the novel C2 and C4 exemplars it averaged 68.7% correct; again, both percentages were significantly greater than chance. The participants were, in addition, very accurate in their determination of which of the exemplars they had or had not seen earlier in training. The children correctly identified 89.6% of the familiar exemplars as having been seen before and 87.8% of the novel exemplars as not having been seen before. These effects were significantly greater than chance.

The studies described above collectively demonstrated response-mediated generalization in pigeons and in young children. This phenomenon was demonstrated with photographs, simulated human faces, and leaf silhouettes. Mediation linked entities that were themselves whole classes of objects; they were, in fact, basic-level categories in the two earliest studies. Accuracy levels were generally higher to the stimuli that received direct reassignment training than to those that benefited from mediation only; the decrement from the reassigned to the nonreassigned stimuli appears to be a secondary generalization analog of primary generalization decrement. In addition, the latter two studies demonstrate primary generalization to novel exemplars from both the reassigned and the nonreassigned component categories. The last study described in this section importantly demonstrates that this generalization will occur even when the subjects recognize that the exemplars are novel.

SUMMARY COMMENTS AND SUGGESTIONS FOR APPLICATION

What are the implications of the results described above for the practices of behavior therapists? How might therapists use the information we have provided concerning basic behavioral research on object concepts in animals and young children? Clearly, practicing therapists will have the most effective notions about how these findings might be used in actual practice, so our insights will be humbly offered. Our suggestions will be organized around some of the most important phenomena that emerged in our own research and in that of others.

Some of the coherence in basic-level categories comes from the perceptual similarity of the objects within them. For this reason, behavior therapists could adopt procedures that highlight the natural differences between categories. It might be possible to teach distinctions between basic-level categories and different superordinates first so that therapy begins with the easiest discriminations. Alternatively, the therapy might begin with the most clearly discriminated cases and proceed to cases in which the positive instance and the negative instance are less distinct. In teaching appropriate street crossing, for example, the therapist might teach a child to discriminate a situation with a "walk" light from one with a "don't walk" light. The therapy might later proceed to much subtler discriminations involving aspects such as the distance of approaching cars.

In addition, several aspects of the training procedure can speed learning and promote broader generalization to novel exemplars. The research cited above amply demonstrates faster acquisition of an object concept discrimination when training uses only a few exemplars per category. Thus, therapy might begin with only a few exemplars. As training progresses, however, the pool of exemplars should be quickly expanded. Expansion of the pool of exemplars in training will promote wider generalization of the category to newly encountered exemplars. In addition, continued training with only a few exemplars might promote memorization of the already learned exemplars, as was seen in Edwards and Honig's Experiment 3.

The four-choice discrimination studies indicate that it might also be desirable to train several object concepts concurrently. This sort of concurrent discrimination corresponds more closely with the way that humans ordinarily acquire and use object concepts. The studies of the second author and his collaborators at the University of Iowa demonstrate that pigeons can form four-choice discriminations relatively quickly and easily when the classes correspond to human object categories. It it likely that most behavior-therapy clients could complete a similar discrimination within a far shorter time period than was taken by the pigeons.

Ultimately, however, human conceptual categories and our labels for them have a hierarchical nature. Perceptual similarity has its limits as an explanatory mechanism, especially regarding higher-level or superordinate categories. Whatever process or mechanism creates such

categories in "normal" human development, our three-stage procedure has shown that response mediation can create nonsimilarity-based categories in both pigeons and young children. Thus, once basic-level aggregations have been firmly established, behavior therapists might give special attention to providing language or other behavioral codes that might help their clients form higher-level connections. Stokes and Baer (1977) suggest that language cues might produce mediated generalization in a therapeutic setting. Self-generated instructions (e.g., "I will share my toys") might facilitate transfer of behavior learned in the counselor's office to a novel situation. The verbal responses might also provide an effective discriminative stimulus to facilitate transfer of behavior across stimulus situations.

The procedures used in the studies with animals that were described above may be particularly useful in many approach-avoidance situations. The therapist can teach correct responses across a wide range of exemplars in therapy and then test for generalization to novel situations in a controlled manner. This process is likely to facilitate generalization of the therapy to naturally occurring situations. Categorization training can establish a rule for behavior and at the same time help establish generalization within a set of category exemplars and discrimination between exemplars from different categories.

We hope we have shown the importance of object concepts or categories for behavioral functioning, and that both perceptual factors and associative experience play an important role in the coherence of object categories. Our research on the role of mediation in the formation of nonsimilarity-based aggregations is continuing. Issues we plan to explore further include generalization to novel exemplars in animal subjects and whether mediators other than differential responses can join basic-level categories. We hope this research will give us an even wider window on the processes by which perceptually dissimilar classes might be linked and provide further information helpful to behavior therapists.

ENDNOTES

The preparation of this manuscript was supported by National Institute of Mental Health Grant MH51562. We thank David Wacker and Janet Drew for providing several very specific and helpful suggestions concerning behavior therapy applications.

Correspondence concerning this article should be addressed to Suzette L. Astley, Psychology Department, Cornell College, 600 First St. W., Mt. Vernon, IA 52314-1098.

REFERENCES

Astley, S. L., & Wasserman, E. A. (in press). Mediating associations, essentialism, and nonsimilarity-based categorization. In T. Zentall & P. Smeets (eds.), *Stimulus class formation.* Amsterdam: North Holland Publishers.

Astley, S. L., & Wasserman, E. A. (1992). Categorical discrimination and generalization in pigeons: All negative stimuli are not created equal. *Journal of Experimental Psychology: Animal Behavior Processes, 18,* 193–207.

Bhatt, R. S. (1988). *Categorization in pigeons: Effects of category size, congruity with human categories, selective attention, and secondary generalization.* Doctoral dissertation, University of Iowa, Iowa City.

Bhatt, R. S., & Wasserman, E. A. (1989). Secondary generalization and categorization in pigeons. *Journal of the Experimental Analysis of Behavior, 52,* 213–224.

Bhatt, R. S., Wasserman, E. A., Reynolds, W. F., Jr., & Knauss, K. S. (1988). Conceptual behavior in pigeons: Categorization of both familiar and novel examples from four classes of natural and artificial stimuli. *Journal of Experimental Psychology: Animal Behavior Processes, 14,* 219–234.

Cerella, J. (1979). Visual classes and natural categories in the pigeon. *Journal of Experimental Psychology: Human Perception and Performance, 5,* 68–77.

D'Amato, M. R., & Van Sant, P. (1988). The person concept in monkeys *(Cebus apella). Journal of Experimental Psychology: Animal Behavior Processes, 14,* 43–55.

Edwards, C. A., & Honig, W. K. (1987). Memorization and feature selection in the acquisition of natural concepts in pigeons. *Learning and Motivation, 18,* 235–260.

Goldiamond, I. (1966). Perception, language, and conceptualization rules. In B. Kleinmutz (ed.), *Problem solving: Research, method, and theory,* 183–224. New York: Wiley.

Herrnstein, R. J. (1985). Riddles of natural categorization. *Philosophical Transactions of the Royal Society, B308,* 129–144.

Herrnstein, R. J. (1990). Levels of stimulus control: A functional approach. *Cognition, 37,* 133–166.

Herrnstein, R. J., & de Villiers, P. A. (1980). Fish as natural category for people and pigeons. In G. Bower (eds.), *The psychology of learning and motivation,* 59–95. San Diego, Calif.: Academic Press.

Herrnstein, R. J., & Loveland, D. H. (1964). Complex visual concept in the pigeon. *Science, 146,* 549–551.

Herrnstein, R. J., Loveland, D. H., & Cable, C. (1976). Natural concepts in pigeons. *Journal of Experimental Psychology: Animal Behavior Processes, 2,* 285–302.

Huber, L., & Lenz, R. (1993). A test of the linear feature model of polymorphous concept discrimination with pigeons. *The Quarterly Journal of Experimental Psychology, 46,* 1–18.

Hull, C. L. (1943). *Principles of behavior.* New York: Appleton-Century-Crofts.

Jitsumori, M. (1993). Category discrimination of artificial polymorphous stimuli based on feature learning. *Journal of Experimental Psychology: Animal Behavior Processes, 19,* 244–254.

Keil, F. (1989). *Concepts, kinds, and conceptual development.* Cambridge, Mass.: MIT Press.

Keller, F. S., & Schoenfeld, W. N. (1950). *Principles of psychology.* New York: Appleton-Century-Crofts.

Lea, S. E. G. (1984). In what sense do pigeons learn concepts? In H. L. Roitblat, T. G. Bever, & H. S. Terrace (eds.), *Animal cognition,* 263–276. Hillsdale, N.J.: Erlbaum.

Lea, S. E. G., & Harrison, S. N. (1978). Discrimination of polymorphous stimulus sets by pigeons. *Quarterly Journal of Experimental Psychology, 30,* 521–537.

Lea, S. E. G., Lohman, A., & Ryan, C. M. E. (1993). Discrimination of five-dimensional stimuli by pigeons: Limitations of feature analysis. *The Quarterly Journal of Psychology, 46,* 19–42.

Malott, R. W., & Sidall, J. W. (1972). Acquisition of the people concept in pigeons. *Psychological Reports, 31,* 3–13.

Murphy, G. L., & Medin, D. L. (1985). The role of theories in conceptual coherence. *Psychological Review, 92,* 289–316.

Osgood, C. E. (1953). *Method and theory in experimental psychology.* New York: Oxford University Press.

Pitcher, G., (ed.) (1966). Wittgenstein: *The philosophical investigations.* New York: Anchor Books.

Quine, W. V. (1969). Natural kinds. In N. Rescher (ed.), *Essays in honor of Carl G. Hempel,* 5–23. Dordrecht, Holland: D. Reidel.

Rosch, E., & Mervis, C. B. (1975). Family resemblances: Studies in the internal structures of categories. *Cognitive Psychology, 7,* 573–605.

Rosch, E., Mervis, C. B., Gray, W. D., Johnson, D. M., & Boyes-Braem, P. (1976). Basic objects in natural categories. *Cognitive Psychology, 8,* 382–439.

Schrier, A. M., Angarella, R., & Povar, M. L. (1984). Studies of concept formation by stumptailed monkeys: Concepts humans, monkeys, and the letter "A." *Journal of Experimental Psychology: Animal Behavior Processes, 10,* 564–584.

Schrier, A. M., & Brady, P. M. (1987). Categorization of natural stimuli by monkeys *(Macaca mulatta)*: Effects of stimulus set size and modification of exemplars. *Journal of Experimental Psychology: Animal Behavior Processes, 13,* 136–143.

Siegel, R. K., & Honig, W. K. (1970). Pigeon concept formation: Successive and simultaneous acquisition. *Journal of the Experimental Analysis of Behavior, 13,* 385–390.

Smith, E. E., & Medin, D. L. (1981). *Categories and concepts.* Cambridge, Mass.: Harvard University Press.

Stokes, T. F., & Baer, D. (1977). An implicit technology of generalization. *Journal of Applied Behavior Analysis, 10,* 349–367.

Underwood, B. J. (1966). *Experimental psychology.* New York: Meredith Publishing Company.

Urcuioli, P. J., Zentall, T. R., Jackson-Smith, P., & Steirn, J. N. (1989). Evidence for common coding in many-to-one matching: Retention, intertrial interference, and transfer. *Journal of Experimental Psychology: Animal Behavior Processes, 15,* 264–273.

Vaughan, W., Jr. (1988). Formation of equivalence sets in pigeons. *Journal of Experimental Psychology: Animal Behavior Processes, 14,* 36–42.

Wasserman, E. A., & Bhatt, R. S. (1992). Conceptualization of natural and artificial stimuli by pigeons. In W. K. Honig & J. G. Fetterman (eds.), *Cognitive aspects of stimulus control,* 203–223. Hillsdale, N.J.: Erlbaum.

Wasserman, E. A., & DeVolder, C. L. (1993). Similarity- and nonsimilarity-based conceptualization in children and pigeons. *Psychological Record, 43,* 779–793.

Wasserman, E. A., DeVolder, C. L., & Coppage, D. J. (1992). Nonsimilarity-based conceptualization in pigeons via secondary or mediated generalization. *Psychological Science, 3,* 374–379.

Wasserman, E. A., Kiedinger, R. E., & Bhatt, R. S. (1988). Conceptual behavior in pigeons: Categories, subcategories, and pseudocategories. *Journal of Experimental Psychology, 14,* 235–246.

Wattanabe, S., Lea, S. E. G., & Dittrich, W. H. (1993). What can we learn from experiments on pigeon concept discrimination? In H. P. Zeigler & H. J. Bischof (eds.), *Vision, brain, and behavior in birds,* 351–390. Cambridge, Mass.: MIT Press.

Wittgenstein, L. (1953). *Philosophical investigations.* New York: Macmillan.

Younger, B. A., & Cohen, L. B. (1985). How infants form categories. In G. H. Bower (ed.), *The psychology of learning and motivation,* 211–247. New York: Academic Press.

Zentall, T. R., Steirn, J. N., Sherburne, L. M., & Urcuioli, P. J. (1991). Common coding in pigeons assessed through partial versus total reversals of many-to-one conditional and simple discriminations. *Journal of Experimental Psychology: Animal Behavior Processes, 17,* 194–201.

CHAPTER 23

MEMORY RETRIEVAL PROCESSES

Russell E. Morgan
David C. Riccio

Historically, the term *memory* has generally been avoided in the empirical study of animal behavior. Despite common use of the term in popular culture dating back to at least the time of the ancient scholars, most behavioral scientists working with animals considered the term too mentalistic for use in empirically based scientific textbooks and journals. This historical belief that memory was not an important construct in the study of behavior had both an experimental and a theoretical basis. Early studies of discrimination learning with animals (Skinner, 1950) suggested that little, if any, forgetting was to be found. Thus, if learning was relatively permanent, there was no further reason to investigate processes collectively referred to as *memory*.

On a theoretical basis, the study of memory was discouraged by the dominance of the associationistic/behavioristic view that learning simply required the establishment of associations between specific stimuli and responses. Performance that might have been considered to indicate imperfection in memory was instead understood to result from failure to reproduce the exact stimulus circumstances to which the organism originally responded. In other words, once learning took place, so-called forgetting could only be a matter of loss of stimulus control. As a result of this view, sometimes referred to as the "correspondence assumption" or "epistemic correlation" (Roitblat, 1982; Spear & Riccio, 1994), there was no need to consider that a mentalistic representation or "memory" mediated between the process of learning and the act of remembering. The stimulus-response connection was both an objective and a sufficient account of the processes of learning and remembering.

The behavioristic stimulus-response orientation served the young discipline of psychology well throughout the first half of the twentieth century by both stimulating a vast amount of research and, probably of greater importance, helping establish psychology as an empirically based scientific discipline. However, it was ultimately the results of these empirical investigations, along with the human verbal memory research that stemmed from the early work of Ebbinghaus (1885), that led to the need for consideration of memory mechanisms—and, more generally, cognition—in the study of both animal and human behavior.

In the thirty years since the beginning of this "cognitive era," the study of both human and animal memory has grown rapidly. Although much is yet to be explained regarding the phenomenon of memory, researchers generally agree that memory is not simply a permanent, unchanging record of events, as once thought. Rather, memory is a malleable record of one's experiences that is subject to alterations based on interactions with both past and future experiences. As we will see, memory availability and strength are also thought to depend strongly on the conditions under which remembering is attempted (e.g., similarity of training and test environments).

With the increased interest in memory research during the past 30 years, a number of specialized fields of memory research have emerged. For instance, some research has focused on how representations of experience are stored in memory (McGaugh & Herz, 1972; Miller & Springer, 1973), on the nature of such representations (Honig, 1978; Roitblat, 1980; Spear, 1978), on memory-encoding mechanisms (Craik & Tulving, 1975; Lewis, 1979), and on models of memory retrieval (Miller & Springer, 1973; Riccio & Richardson, 1984; Spear, 1973, 1978; Tulving & Thompson, 1973). Other research has focused on distinctions between different types of memories, such as working versus reference and declarative versus procedural memories (Olton, Becker, & Handelmann, 1979; Sherry & Schacter, 1987; Squire, 1992), and on the biological basis for such memory distinctions (Eichenbaum, 1994; McClelland, McNaughton, & O'Reilly, 1995; Mishkin & Appenzeler, 1987; Squire & Zola-Morgan, 1991).

The diversity of this research and the vast amount of literature that now exists preclude addressing many of the important issues of concern to memory researchers in a chapter this size. Therefore, the remaining portion of this chapter will focus on a relatively specific yet fundamental issue in memory research: the processes and variables involved in retrieval (remembering) of memories in both humans and other animals.

IMPORTANCE OF RETRIEVAL PROCESSES OVER CONSOLIDATION/STORAGE OF MEMORIES

Though numerous memory models have been proposed, most all address, in some form or another, three basic stages deemed necessary for normal memory functioning: encoding, retention (storage), and retrieval (remembering). As mentioned previously, the focus of this chapter is on mechanisms of memory retrieval. However, to understand these mechanisms we must first examine the means by which memories are encoded and stored.

A very fruitful method of examining the stages of memory processing has involved investigation of memory impairments, in particular, naturally occurring and experimentally induced amnesias. In trying to understand the normal functions of a complex process such as memory, researchers have often resorted to observing the characteristics of memory deficits. Beginning with the report by Duncan (1949) that administration of electroconvulsive shock (ECS) to rats soon after avoidance training resulted in impaired acquisition of avoidance behavior, memory researchers soon began to realize the potential knowledge that could be gained by manipulating, more or less independently, the encoding, storage, and retrieval of acquired representations.

Although it is now common to refer to three phases of memory processing, early theories and research focused solely on encoding/storage of information. The research that supported these theories, generally referred to as "consolidation theories," was originally encouraged by the classic text *The Organization of Behavior* (Hebb, 1949), which speculated that recently received information was initially encoded in a short-term store in the form of "transient neural reverberatory circuits." It was the uninterrupted activation of these proposed neural circuits, following the learning episode, that would eventually result in long-term structural changes responsible for long-term memory storage. Support for this theory was found in numerous studies indicating that experimentally induced instances of retrograde amnesia (RA), produced by procedures such as ECS, hypothermia, protein synthesis inhibition, and drug administration, were most profound when administered immediately after training (Duncan, 1949; Madsen & McGaugh, 1961; Overton, 1964; Quartermain, McEwen, & Azmitia, 1970; Riccio, Hodges, & Randall, 1968). Newly acquired information was shown to become progressively less susceptible to these amnestic agents as the interval between training and their administration was increased, a phenomenon commonly referred to as the "temporal-gradient of retrograde amnesia." As described by McGaugh (1966), these temporally graded instances of RA seemed to indicate that the processes involved in long-term memory storage continued well after the initial coding of the information.

The consolidation view fit nicely with Hebb's suggestion that encoding of new information initiated transient neuronal activity in the central nervous system (CNS) designed to create long-term structural changes. Agents that produced RA were thought to disrupt the reverberatory circuits necessary for consolidation by creating electrochemical interference in the CNS. However, if activation of these circuits was allowed to continue uninterrupted for some unspecified time, the neurochemical changes initiated by the learning episode were believed to result in permanent structural changes. Once this consolidation process was completed, the memory was no longer susceptible to disruption by amnestic agents.

One important implication of the consolidation view is that memory disruption is permanent. Because amnesia is attributed to originally failing to consolidate or store the target information, no possibility exists of later recovering the memory without further learning. This issue of permanency is now considered to be the primary shortcoming of consolidation-based theories. As Miller and Springer (1973) and Spear (1971, 1973) first suggested, the consolidation view can be seriously challenged in regard to any specific type of amnesia by simply demonstrating a single instance in which memory recovery occurs. Any example of recovery from amnesia, provided it occurs without the benefit of further learning, indicates that consolidation had originally occurred.

Although the validity of consolidation theories was originally questioned following reports of spontaneous recovery from amnesia (Zinkin & Miller, 1967), weakening of amnestic effects following familiarization with the amnestic agent (Jenson & Riccio, 1970; Lewis, Miller, & Misanin, 1969), and delayed onset of RA following amnestic treatment (Geller & Jarvik, 1968; Hinderliter, Webster, & Riccio, 1975; Mactutus & Riccio, 1978; McGaugh & Landfield, 1970; Miller & Springer, 1971), findings regarding the issue of permanency eventually posed the most direct challenge to the consolidation view.

Although reports of amnesic patients demonstrating receding or "shrinking" RA over time had existed for many years, their memory recovery was often attributed to new learning obtained as a result of patients' friends and family instructing them as to what they had forgotten. However, in experimental studies as early as 1966, Braun, Meyer, and Meyer showed that memory loss for a brightness discrimination task following posterior decortication in rats could be reversed by administration of amphetamine. Moreover, many subsequent studies have demonstrated recovery from experimentally induced amnesias through various means, all of which presumably preclude the possibility of new learning. These memory-recovery treatments include reexposure to the amnestic treatment prior to retention testing (Hinderliter et al., 1975;

Overton, 1978; Richardson, Riccio, & Morilak, 1983; Thompson & Neely, 1970) or reexposure to the discrete training stimuli (CS or UCS) in a noncontingent manner (Gordon & Mowrer, 1980; Mactutus, Ferek, & Riccio, 1980; Miller & Springer, 1972). In some instances, even a short exposure to the learning context alone can result in memory recovery (Miller & Springer, 1972; Sara, 1973).

Further evidence against the traditional consolidation view comes from the finding that retrograde amnesia for old, well-established memories can be obtained by simply "reactivating" that memory trace prior to administering the amnestic agent. Originally demonstrated by Misanin, Miller, and Lewis (1968) with ECS as the amnestic treatment, the finding that established memories can become susceptible to disruption following reactivation has since been replicated with a number of different learning tasks and amnestic agents (Gerson & Henderson, 1978; Howard, Glendenning, & Meyer, 1974; Howard & Meyer, 1971; Mactutus, Ferek, George, & Riccio, 1982; Mactutus, Ferek, & Riccio, 1980; Robbins & Meyer, 1970). These studies have carefully demonstrated that the performance deficit is not the result of extinction resulting from the reactivation treatments and, furthermore, that these reactivated memories may actually be more vulnerable than new learning to disruption (Mactutus et al., 1982). Elaborating on the importance of these findings, Lewis (1976, 1979) has suggested that the state of activity rather than the age of a memory may determine the memory's susceptibility to disruption.

The evidence just reviewed indicates that consolidation and storage are typically not major determinants of memory loss. Rather, accessibility to a memory may reflect the interaction of the memory's state of activity with post-learning experiences. Although processing of new information and updating of old information surely occurs in the time soon following new learning,

there is little reason to deny that some type of long-term engram (i.e., a stored record of the information) is created immediately upon learning. Even retrieval-oriented explanations of the temporally graded RA phenomenon acknowledge that new information is likely to remain in an active or semiactive state for some time after the learning episode. Hence, what was previously believed to be a "window" of memory susceptibility soon after learning may instead be interpreted as a time when the memory is being both elaborated upon and associated with the existing contextual environment. As indicated by Hinderliter et al. (1975), there appears to be a short time following learning during which contextual components (i.e., internal and external environmental cues) of a learning episode are assimilated to the memory trace (see also Boller & Rovee-Collier, 1994; Gordon et al., 1981, updating studies). Following administration of an amnestic agent, this elaborative process is believed to continue, but with the memory now being redintegrated[1] with the new contextual environment. That the memory does not become associated with the usual contextual environment may result in its not being assimilated into the existing network of memories, subsequently making it less readily retrieved. Accessibility to the memory then becomes dependent upon the availability of retrieval cues from the distinctive, new context.

This proposed process of elaborating and updating memories into an existing network of associations may be an important link between retrieval-based theories of amnesia and the numerous studies that have implicated medial-temporal lobe (i.e., hippocampus and surrounding cortical areas) damage with memory impairments (see Squire, 1992, for review). Although basic representations may be formed independent of these medial-temporal systems, as demonstrated by intact learning of avoidance, choice, and other procedural tasks following me-

---

[1]"Redintigration" refers to the concept that when reactivated a memory can be updated or reconstructed so as to include new learning acquired subsequent to forming the original memory. See William James (1890, p. 536) for an early, enlightening discussion.

dial-temporal ablations, retrieval of more complex/relational learning is generally believed to require these systems.

Several investigators have noted, however, that during conflict in which the same stimuli specify competing behaviors (e.g., reversal learning, transfer of training), hippocampus-damaged subjects typically demonstrate an inability to dissociate contextual conditions related to the separate task requirements (Shapiro & Olton, 1994; Weiskrantz & Warrington, 1975; Winocur & Olds, 1978). Furthermore, these apparently interference-induced deficits can be reduced by enhancing the salience of task-related contextual cues (Winocur & Bindra, 1976; Winocur & Breckenridge, 1973; Winocur & Olds, 1978). Although further research needs to be conducted to investigate this relationship between medial-temporal damage and use of contextual cues, the existing research does suggest that investigators should consider the possibility that a memory trace is formed despite medial-temporal impairment. However, the memory may not be fully accessible as a result of impairments in the subjects' ability to use contextual stimuli as retrieval cues or to assimilate the memory trace into an existing network of contextual associations.

FORGETTING AS A RETRIEVAL IMPAIRMENT

So far we have focused on induced instances of memory loss (e.g., retrograde amnesia) as a means of demonstrating how forgetting can occur. In doing so, we have suggested that amnesia does not typically occur as a result of storage disruption. Rather, we have implicated retrieval deficits as a major source of induced memory loss. With this background, the remainder of the chapter will focus on explanations of the normal, everyday forgetting that occurs in generally healthy individuals.

The work of Spear (1973, 1978; Kraemer & Spear, 1993) and others (Miller & Springer, 1973; Riccio & Richardson, 1984; Schachtman, Brown, Gorgon, Catterson, & Miller, 1987) has

suggested that the locus of much forgetting may be found in the "retrieval" phase of memory. Whether explicitly stated or not, a consistent notion among the retrieval-based theories is that once learning is encoded (perceived), it is immediately stored in memory. As previously discussed in relation to induced memory deficits, further processing and assimilation of the memory are believed to continue for some time, but the actual engram is thought to be stored immediately. The ease with which the target memory can later be retrieved is then determined by two major factors: (1) interference existing between the target memory and other acquired information and (2) the similarity of internal and external contextual cues encoded along with the information and those cues present at the time of attempted retrieval. These two factors are believed to act both independently and in conjunction as determinants of the retrievability of a memory in any given circumstance.

ROLE OF INTERFERENCE

The study of interference in remembering has a long, active history in psychology dating back to its origins as an explanation for the forgetting of lists of paired verbal associates (McGeoch, 1932). The basic notion of interference is that information or associations are most readily remembered if similar, competing information or associations are not available. As originally described by McGeoch (1942), this competition among associations is typically revealed at the time of memory retrieval.

In the years since McGeoch's (1942) classic text, many researchers (e.g., Postman, 1976; Underwood, 1957) have attempted to specify the important variables controlling interference-induced forgetting. For instance, as opposed to McGeoch's original emphasis, proactive interference (the loss of a target memory as a result of previous learning) rather than retroactive interference (forgetting caused by conflicting memories acquired subsequent to the target memory) is now considered the more important determinant of forgetting. This emphasis on proactive interference arose from the work of Underwood (1957) who, in an early forerunner of the now popular meta-analysis technique, examined many experiments involving repeated list learning and found that the amount of forgetting typically seen over a 24-hour period was strongly predicted by the number of previous associations learned (see Figure 23–1). This finding and the work that followed from it (Barnes & Underwood, 1959; Postman, 1976; Underwood, 1969; Wickens, 1972) helped to clarify a number of discrepant findings regarding the importance of interference to forgetting by demonstrating the importance of considering what has been ac-

quired both prior to and following the target information.

Although comparisons of memory interference in humans and animals have sometimes proven difficult, variations in the temporal relationships between the interfering information, the information to be remembered, and the retention test similarly influence the likelihood of a specific type of interference occurring across species. Retroactive interference has been shown to be more likely with a short interval between the second learning episode and the test, whereas proactive interference is more likely with a long delay before testing and a short interval between the two learning episodes. However, as with virtually any instance of potential interference, similarity between learning episodes and the retention test context can drastically increase interference of either type (Spear, 1978; Spear & Riccio, 1994).

Although many similarities exist regarding interference phenomena across species, potentially important differences have been noted. In some situations, animals have been found to be more susceptible than humans to nonspecific interference (e.g., Wickens, Tuber, Nield, & Wickens 1977). Much of this increased susceptibility appears to be due to animals' reliance on contextual cues (stimuli) to guide behavior. Whereas humans typically rely on verbal cues, animals must rely on contextual/environmental cues to provide them with instructions on what contingencies are in effect and how they should act. As suggested by Spear and Riccio (1994), the context in which learning occurs may be thought of as a superordinate stimulus within which the specific training cues are presented. Should more than one set of training cues become associated with a given context, the likelihood of confusion or interference among these memories increases. (See Holland's 1986 description of occasion setters for a similar description of the instructional role of context.)

A series of studies by Spear and colleagues has helped clarify the instructional or discriminative role of context in ambiguous situations (Spear, 1971; Spear, Gordon, & Chiszar, 1972;

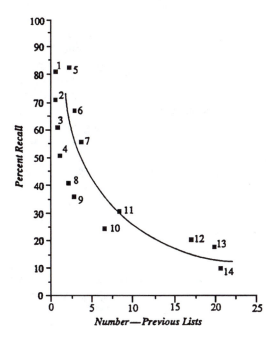

Figure 23–1. Rate of forgetting of verbal materials found after a 24-hour retention interval is shown for each of 14 experiments that differed in the number of lists of verbal units the subjects had learned in the laboratory prior to learning the critical list for which retention was tested. This dramatic suggestion that rate of forgetting of verbal units in the laboratory might be impaired by prior learning in the laboratory (proactive interference) subsequently was corroborated in a variety of direct experimental tests (adapted from Underwood 1957, and Spear and Riccio, 1994).

Spear, Smith, Bryan, Gordon, Timmons, & Chiszar, 1980). In each of these experiments, rats were first trained on a task requiring them to inhibit responding to avoid punishment (i.e., passive-avoidance), then trained on an opposing task requiring them to actively respond to avoid punishment (i.e., active-avoidance), and then tested for retention, all in the same apparatus. Testing indicated that animals' behavior (passive or active avoidance) was controlled by incidental contextual stimuli presented during each training phase. These contextual stimuli included internal drug stimuli (e.g., pentobarbital), exteroceptive environmental stimuli (a constantly sounding buzzer), and training in different experimental rooms. Although these cues were incidental to learning the basic avoidance tasks, it became clear during testing, which occurred under various cueing conditions, that performance was controlled by the contextual stimuli. (See DeKeyne & Deweer, 1990; Spear, 1978; Thomas, McKelvie, Ranney, & Moye, 1981, for further review.)

DIRECT ROLE OF CONTEXT IN RETRIEVAL

Besides demonstrating the important role of similarity in memory retrieval, the studies mentioned earlier by Spear et al. (1972, 1980) and DeKeyne and Deweer (1990) highlight the second significant role of context in memory: that of serving as a retrieval cue. Both human and animal research have shown that seemingly irrelevant contextual or environmental cues present at the time information is processed can later serve as important cues for memory retrieval. Moreover, alterations or removal of such cues can often impair memory. For example, a study by Riccio, Urda, and Thomas (1966) demonstrated that pecking by pigeons to an illuminated disk for reward could be reduced by simply tilting the floor of the apparatus 30 degrees from its training position. The pigeons had been trained with the floor either horizontal or angled but were given no discrimination training. Studies such as this one are particularly informative about the

general importance of context since responding was found to be contextually controlled without the need for any form of discrimination training. That is, the pigeons were never trained to perform one response in context A and another in context B, but they nonetheless learned about the environment in which training occurred.

A study by Gordon, McCracken, Dess-Beech, and Mowrer (1981) examining the effects of altering static background cues on retention of an instrumental avoidance response further demonstrates this retrieval role for context. In this study, rats were trained to avoid footshock by escaping from a white chamber and entering a black chamber within 5 seconds after the onset of a light stimulus (CS). The contextual manipulations were conducted by training the rats in either of two distinctively different training rooms using two seemingly identical but different avoidance chambers. The two training rooms differed in terms of size, illumination, odor cues, and background noise. Twenty-four hours after the completion of training, each rat received an avoidance retention test in either the original training room or the alternate training room. Mean avoidance latency for the rats tested in the original context (training room) was 4 seconds, but those tested under different conditions had a mean latency between 12 and 13 seconds. Performance was thus clearly impaired by the change in incidental background cues.

The memory impairment demonstrated above has proven to be a robust phenomenon, having been found with a vast array of different learning procedures, including autoshaping experiments with pigeons (Honey & Hall, 1990), free-operant appetitive tasks (Thomas, 1981), and appetitive and aversively motivated maze tasks (Chiszar & Spear, 1969; Perkins & Weyant, 1958). This so-called context change effect has also been demonstrated with classically (Pavlovian) conditioned responses, such as CS-shock induced suppression of ongoing responding in the conditioned emotional response (CER) task (Balaz, Capra, Hartl, & Miller, 1981) and taste-aversion learning (Archer, Sjoden, & Nilsson, 1984).

One important issue that should be briefly

considered when examining the effect of incidental contextual cues on memory retrieval is the potential role of novelty. Initially recognized by Bindra (1959) and Spear (1978), the issue of novelty effects refers to the fact that the typical context change finding of impaired retention in the different context may indeed reflect the retrieval-cue value of the training context, but it may also reflect interfering behaviors resulting from the novelty of the new test context. However, in a recent experiment with pigeons, the retrieval-cue value of visual contextual stimuli was demonstrated while concurrently controlling for the effects of novelty (Thomas & Morrison, 1994). Responding was found to be similarly impaired whether the test context was novel or familiar, indicating that the training context did, at least in this task, serve as a retrieval cue.

A retrieval role for context has also been demonstrated for human verbal memory. In a particularly elaborate set of studies by Smith and colleagues (Smith, 1979; Smith, Glenberg, & Bjork, 1978), subjects who learned verbal materials in a salient environmental context (i.e., a distinctively colored, shaped, and sized room) tended to remember the information much better when tested in that same room (also see Godden & Baddeley, 1975; Greenspoon & Ranyard, 1957; for contradictory findings see Fernandez & Glenberg, 1985). Subjects' internal context has also been found to influence retention, as demonstrated by studies such as Lowe (1983) in which student subjects who learned verbal materials either in or out of an intoxicated state later recalled the information better under the same state conditions (also see Eich, Weingartner, Stillman, & Gillin, 1975; Overton, 1985; Weingartner, Miller, & Murphy, 1977). Furthermore, verbal memories have been demonstrated to be context-dependent when the "context" refers to the specific words accompanying the target information (Tulving & Osler, 1968) or the semantic context in which the verbal information is presented (Morris, 1978).

The view that a memory is retrieved when some subset of the attributes associated with the target episode are present leads to a consideration of the contribution of internal cues. Thus, not only the attributes of the CS or US but also the internal states elicited by them and related events might permit accessing of the memory. In this connection, Haroutunian and Riccio (1977, 1979) found that administration of stress-linked hormones, epinephrine or ACTH, in conjunction with exposures to the conditioned fear stimulus, enhanced the CS reinstatement effect in immature rats. Because these hormones in the absence of the CS did not produce a similar outcome, they suggested that mimicking the arousal of the training state under relatively weak reminder conditions (CS only) facilitated retrieval of the target memory, thus augmenting the reinstatement effect.

Conceptually similar outcomes have been obtained in other paradigms as well. For example, administration of ACTH at testing alleviates what has been termed the "Kamin effect," that is, the retention deficit obtained at intermediate intervals (4 to 6 hours) following active avoidance training (Klein, 1972). In this case, the exogenously delivered hormone presumably provides cues that are otherwise unavailable because of a negative feedback system inhibiting the release of ACTH. Furthermore, the memory loss produced by experimentally induced amnesia is also reversed or attenuated by exogenous ACTH at testing (Mactutus, Smith, & Riccio, 1980; Rigter, Van Riezen, & deWied, 1974). Consistent with the notion that stimuli associated with ACTH dissipate relatively quickly, the duration of memory recovery was transient. However, when ACTH administration was combined with exposure to conditioned fear cues, substantial recovery from amnesia was found to persist for several days, a finding not unlike that obtained with reinstatement by Haroutunian and Riccio (1977).

In addition to resulting in "spontaneous" and induced forgetting, extinction exposures result in reduced responding. This type of performance decrement has also proven reversible by recreating internal stimulus states associated with conditioning. Following extinction of either passive avoidance (punishment) or active avoidance learning (Ahlers, Richardson, West, & Riccio, 1989; Richardson, Riccio, & Devine, 1984), test performance is enhanced by administering ACTH. Since the two tasks have opposite response requirements, improvement cannot be due to simple changes in motor performance. One puzzling feature of these studies, however, was that the recovery from extinction was also obtained with long intervals between the hormone administration and testing (Richardson & Riccio, 1991).

In addition to serving the role of internal states that act as retrieval cues in producing recovery of memory, these stimuli may mediate the transfer of learning to other stimuli. In one study (Concannon, Riccio, & McKelvey, 1980), rats initially received a series of noncontingent footshocks in a neutral apparatus. Later, they received epinephrine injections while being exposed to a distinctive place cue (black chamber). When subsequently given a spatial avoidance test, these subjects showed more aversion to the distinctive compartment than saline-injected controls. Moreover, in the absence of the aversive episode ("trauma"), pairing epinephrine with the cues had no discernible effect. Concannon et al. (1980) suggested that the initial repeated shocks resulted in endogenous release of epinephrine that became linked with further shocks. The exogenous epinephrine injection then presumably served to redintegrate the representation of that noxious event, which then became associated the contemporary environmental cues of the black chamber.

Taken together, these various findings suggest that internal stimuli could well contribute to the development and maintenance of clinically relevant behaviors. Conversely, they have potentially interesting implications for therapeutic situations focusing on retrieval of memories.

FACILITATION OF RETRIEVAL: METHODS AND ISSUES

The evidence reviewed thus far indicates that associative interference and contextual change are prominent sources of normal forgetting in both humans and other animals. Of course, these are by no means mutually independent processes; rather, both most likely contribute to typical instances of forgetting. Given some potential understanding of the processes through which forgetting occurs, the next question of interest concerns how we might overcome, or at least minimize, these forgetting processes.

The literature concerning associative interference and context effects strongly suggests that learning involving salient, multifaceted, or easily discriminable stimuli should help facilitate memory retrieval (DeKeyne & Deweer, 1990; Spear, 1978). This suggestion comes from the belief that such stimuli should decrease interference by being distinct and at the same time increase the likelihood of retrieval by supplying a large number of attributes that could act as potential retrieval cues. Therefore, one means of improving retrieval may be to conduct training in the presence of salient or novel cues whenever possible. This suggestion likely holds true for the contingent stimuli directly involved in learning as well as the incidental contextual cues, since it is well known that saliency and, more generally, ability to procure attention are important characteristics influencing the associability of stimuli (Lubow, 1973; Rescorla & Wagner, 1972). However, a potential problem with this solution is that by increasing the saliency of contextual cues present during acquisition, the likelihood of a stimulus generalization decrement following contextual change could increase. In other words, if an event occurs in the presence of very potent or distinct cues, information about this event may be very difficult to retrieve should these same cues not be available during testing.

Possibly a more practical solution to facilitate memory retrieval would be to include some form of contextual generalization training during acquisition. For example, Rovee-Collier and colleagues (Amabile & Rovee-Collier, 1991; Boller & Rovee-Collier, 1992; Rovee-Collier & DuFault, 1991) have suggested that the dependence of memory retrieval on the original encoding context can be overriden by explicit training subjects in multiple contexts. In their work,

Rovee-Collier et al. found that infants trained to respond to the same mobile in two different contexts subsequently recognized the mobile in a third, novel context. Such training may facilitate retrieval by increasing the sheer number of contextual stimuli that could serve as cues for retrieval. Much like the student who studies in numerous locations and then has no trouble remembering information in the test location, training in multiple contexts should help overcome the context change effect.

A similar issue has been discussed with regard to exposure therapies used to treat anxiety disorders (Bouton, 1988). Exposure therapies typically involve extensive exposure to the fear-evoking stimulus itself as a means of extinguishing fear/avoidance behavior. However, to what extent this "fear extinction" generalizes to conditions other than those present during the exposure therapy has been questioned (Bouton, 1988). For instance, in what is referred to as the "renewal effect," Bouton and his colleagues (Bouton & Bolles, 1979; Bouton, Ricker, & Sean, 1994; Bouton & Swartzentruber, 1991) have demonstrated repeatedly that fear extinction that occurs within a specific context does not generalize to previously fearful situations. Apparently, returning the subject to a previously fearful situation/environment has the effect of removing the contextual cues that encourage retrieval of the CS-NoUS (extinction) training. However, it is conceivable that extinction training conducted in multiple contextual situations might generalize to more diverse conditions, resulting in a decreased potential for "renewal" of extinguished fear.

MEMORY FOR STIMULUS ATTRIBUTES

While the potential facilitative effects of conditioning in multiple contexts are as yet unclear, Riccio and colleagues have suggested that similar generalization of contextual cues may occur normally as a fundamental type of memory loss (Gisquet-Verrier & Alexinsky, 1986; Riccio, Ackil, & Burch-Vernon, 1992; Riccio, Rabi-nowitz, & Axelrod, 1994; Riccio, Richardson, & Ebner, 1984). This memory loss, which has received less attention than the impairments of performance or response deficits described above, has been termed the *forgetting of stimulus attributes*. In this case, subjects remember quite well *what* to do but forget the specific features of the stimulus situation or stimulus to which they should respond. Thus, with the passage of time, perceptually discriminable cues are no longer differentiated, and as a consequence, responding tends to occur to a broader array of stimuli.

Historically, investigation of this form of memory loss in animals developed out of research on variables influencing stimulus generalization gradients. An early and illuminating study by Perkins and Weyant (1958) showed that changing the color of the training runway severely disrupted an appetitive approach response in rats when the shift was instituted shortly after acquisition. However, with a one-week interval between training and testing, subjects performed about as well in the novel as in the original runway. This shift in the pattern of responding, *flattening of the generalization gradient,* as it is termed, has subsequently been obtained in aversive as well as appetitive tasks, with free operant and discrete trial paradigms and with changes in contextual, discriminative, and conditioned stimuli (e.g., McAllister & McAllister, 1963; see also Riccio, Rabinowitz, & Axelrod, 1994; Riccio, Richardson, & Ebner, 1984, for reviews). Importantly, the flatter gradients with delayed testing reflect an increase in responding to nontarget cues, not a failure to respond or floor effect. As Perkins and Weyant noted, "Forgetting the color of the runway occurs more rapidly than does the general tendency to run" (1958, p. 599). Thus, as organisms forget the precise features of the stimuli controlling their behavior, target and nontarget (generalized) stimuli become more functionally interchangeable. In effect, the number of retrieval cues increases.

The principle that as memory for attributes decreases, the level of responding increases ("when less is more") has a number of conceptual and methodological implications (Riccio, Ackil, &

Burch-Vernon, 1992; Riccio, Rabinowitz, & Axelrod, 1994). Of particular interest here is the application to the analysis of "incubation of anxiety." As McAllister and McAllister (1967) pointed out some years ago, little evidence exists that the absolute level of conditioned fear to a CS increases over time, but substantial support exists for the proposition that more (nontarget) stimuli come to elicit fear. Thus, the forgetting of specific features of a CS can result in "incubation" in the sense that fear occurs to a wider range of environmental cues.

Another conceptual implication relates to the role of exemplars in person perception and similar phenomena. Exemplar models emphasize that one remembers concrete instances of people (or events) actually encountered rather than abstracted prototypes. If a new target stimulus matches with this retrieval representation, a host of associated characteristics are activated that influence inferences about the new person. Anderson and Cole (1990) have demonstrated how memory representations of significant others can bias inferences about traits of newly encountered individuals and have noted that this exemplar-based activation of attributes could served to mediate various forms of transference, including those involved in the therapeutic situation. But if the individuating features of exemplars, like other target stimuli, become less discriminable over time, a wider array of newly encountered persons may be viewed as "matching" the exemplar and result in perceptions of the person in accordance with that match.

How we explain our own behavior is clearly a fundamental aspect of personality, yet evidence exists that shifts in self-attributions occur with the passage of time and that these changes may reflect the forgetting of stimulus characteristics. In a study with college students, Moore, Sherrod, Liu, and Underwood (1979) found that self-assessments of behavior shortly after an event were likely to be ascribed to situational variables (e.g., "the microphone made me nervous"; "the exciting challenge made me talkative"). However, after a delay interval of several weeks, the same behaviors came to be attributed to dispositional (trait) factors (e.g., "I'm an anxious person"; "I

tend to talk a lot"). These subjects also showed poorer memory for situational details after the long interval, an outcome consistent with the view that forgetting of stimulus features contributes to the shift in attributional biases.

The methodological importance of loss of attribute memory stems from the fact that a change in the stimulus is often used as a probe to evaluate some aspect of associative processes. For brevity, we consider only one example of a wide class of paradigms: The development of tolerance to morphine, long considered a purely pharmacological effect, has been demonstrated to depend on conditioning processes (Siegel, 1975, 1989). One central finding is that tolerance is disrupted when subjects are tested in an environmental context distinctively different from the one associated with the prior morphine administrations. Presumably, the context comes to serve as a conditional stimulus to elicit a compensatory CR; shifting the context effectively removes those cues. In one study, Feinberg and Riccio (1990) replicated the shift effect when the change occurred shortly after tolerance exposure but, consistent with the forgetting of attributes, obtained no disruption of tolerance when the stimulus change was initiated after a long delay. The failure of subjects to remember and discriminate contexts led to an outcome that, taken alone, would have incorrectly appeared to support a pharmacological interpretation of tolerance; that is, the lack of a context shift effect.

MEMORY FOR EARLY EXPERIENCES

Contemporary research on animal memory has generated a number of interesting findings, many of which have potential relevance for clinical phenomena. Consider, for example, the typical absence of memory for childhood events prior to the age of 4 or 5 and characterized by Freud as "infantile amnesia." While few subscribe to Freud's psychodynamic interpretation of infantile amnesia, laboratory research has demonstrated that the phenomenon is robust and pervasive. An important study by Campbell and Campbell (1962) found that retention of learned fear in rats improved as a function of age: Preweanlings showed substantial forgetting, while adults still expressed strong fear after several weeks. A methodological nicety of their study was that the degree of original learning was largely equated for all age groups. Thus, differences in memory could not be attributable to weaker or impoverished learning in the younger subjects. A number of studies from various labs have subsequently replicated and elaborated on this ontogenetic change in memory (see Campbell & Spear, 1972; Spear & Riccio, 1994, for reviews). Of particular interest is the work by Rovee-Collier and her colleagues (see Rovee-Collier, 1990, for review), who use a simple motor conditioning task (leg kicking) in human infants only a few months old. When leg kicking is rewarded by activation of a mobile suspended over the infant, the rate of kicking increases, as is characteristic of operant conditioning. The conditioned response decreases as a function of increasing retention intervals, and this forgetting is more rapid in 3-month-olds than in 6-month-olds or older children.

So, while Freud's explanation for infantile amnesia is almost surely incorrect, it appears that rapid forgetting in immature organisms reflects a fundamental psychobiological process. The relatively poor memory in immature organisms also poses a paradox, however, as it would seem to undermine widely held assumptions about the significance of "early experience" for later behavior: If information is not retained during development, how do early events continue to have an impact in adulthood? While several resolutions of this dilemma can be suggested, we will focus on one involving other counteracting memory retrieval processes. The basic phenomenon is called "reinstatement," first described by Campbell and Jaynes (1966), in whose study, immature rats, following fear conditioning, were exposed once a week to a very abbreviated version of the training sessions. In marked contrast with retention controls, these animals showed virtually no loss of fear after 1 month. Moreover, this reinstatement (or maintenance) of memory was not based upon new learning during the periodic exposures, as untrained controls receiving

only the reinstatements showed little if any fear at testing.

The phenomenon of reinstatement suggests one important way in which early experiences persist over time. Because organisms are likely to occasionally encounter at least an abbreviated or similar version of the original episode, the memory is maintained. This possibility is made even more plausible by the finding that brief exposure to the conditioned fear cues alone (i.e., without the fearful US) can also produce the reinstatement effect (Silvestri, Rohrbaugh, & Riccio, 1970). Thus, minimal repetitions of a traumatic event or even exposure to cues associated with the event can reduce or prevent the forgetting that might otherwise occur. These findings suggest that the consequences of single traumatic episodes may be maintained merely by occasional reencounters with the elements of the episode rather than by full-blown recurrences.

Reinstatement is not the only way in which memory loss in immature organisms can be alleviated. In recent years, extensive research by N. E. Spear (using rats) and Rovee-Collier (using human infants) has investigated the conditions under which early learning can be "reactivated" at a later time. Basically, brief exposure to the training episode (or elements thereof) prior to testing can reverse or attenuate the ontogenetically related retention loss. While the reactivation procedures are not unrelated to those of reinstatement, the major distinction is that the reactivation treatment is typically given just once, shortly prior to the test session. Not all components of the training situation are equally effective as reminder cues. Moreover, the effectiveness of a particular cue may vary with the retention interval (Miller, Jagielo, & Spear, 1991), an outcome also reported by Gisquet-Verrier and Alexinsky (1988) with other sources of forgetting. Some intriguing evidence also exists that a reactivated memory may be more persistent than newly acquired information at that same age (Miller et al., 1991). For example, subjects who are trained at 18 days and receive a reactivation exposure a few days later show better retention than other subjects given all their training at an older age.

MALLEABILITY OF INACCESSIBLE (REPRESSED) INFORMATION

Memory is often described as a pictorial representation or record of our experiences as we have perceived them. Yet, upon further reflection, we frequently find that memories are generally not very precise representations or records of these experiences. Various sources of forgetting can result in memories that contain less information than we originally encoded or even more information as a result of phenomena such as the "forgetting of attributes" described previously. This characteristic malleability of human memory has been demonstrated by numerous investigators (Bartlett, 1932; Boller & Rovee-Collier, 1992; Hertel & Ellis, 1979; Loftus, 1979).

This memory malleability can potentially have numerous implications for memory retrieval. For instance, in studies of human eyewitness memory, when misleading postevent information is presented to adults, retrieval of the original memory is frequently impaired (Chandler, 1991; Loftus, 1979, 1981). Such applied instances of retroactive interference in human memory have been used in courts of law to demonstrate the dynamic characteristics of episodic (event-specific) memories.

The susceptibility of memory to change over time may also be relevant to current therapeutic and courtroom issues involving reactivation of "repressed" memories. If we assume that such inaccessible or amnestic memories do exist, an important question becomes: Are inaccessible memories somehow protected from the influence of subsequent learning, or are they subject to malleability and distortion in much the same manner as available memories? Because instances of inaccessible memory being recovered have commonly involved traumatic experiences from an individual's remote past, the accuracy of these memories has been difficult to verify. Attempts to experimentally model these circumstances in humans have also proven to be quite limited (Loftus, 1993).

Although it is difficult to conceive of an experimental model of repressed memory, recent findings regarding the potential influence of new information (learning) on inaccessible memories

may offer some insight concerning the accuracy of recovered memories. For instance, a study by Morgan and Riccio (1994) used hypothermia exposure to produce anterograde amnesia (AA) for memory of passive-avoidance training in rats. Following a return to normal body temperature, some of the subjects were given various durations of "extinction exposure" by retaining them in the presence of the previously fearful training cues without providing further training. Although the extinction exposure did not reactivate the avoidance memory (see Initial Test Latency in Figure 23–2), the subsequent extent of memory recovery following recooling—a procedure known to reactivate hypothermia-induced amnesia (Richardson, Guanowsky, Ahlers, & Riccio, 1984)—diminished as a function of increased extinction duration. Thus, the extinction exposure apparently modified the memory of avoidance training despite the target memory remaining inaccessible prior to recooling.

Another study examined the issue of changes in memory for inaccessible information with regard to the previously described phenomenon of forgetting of stimulus attributes. As previously described with accessible memories, discriminable stimuli tend to become more equivalent or interchangeable in controlling responding after a delay interval. However, it is not clear whether such changes occur to the stimulus generalization gradients when a memory remains inaccessible during the retention interval. But a study by Morgan and Riccio (1992) found that memory for contextual stimuli was susceptible to forgetting despite the inaccessible state of the information. As in the study described above, rats given passive-avoidance training while hypothermic later displayed anterograde amnesia for this task unless recooled shortly prior to testing. However, in the present study, rats were tested following recooling in either the original context or a set of discriminatively different contextual cues. As displayed in Figure 23–3, when the target memory was reactivated and tested one day after training, subjects displayed strong fear (avoidance) only when tested in the original context (Groups Hypo-shift and Hypo-same at 1-day delay). However, when reactivation and testing

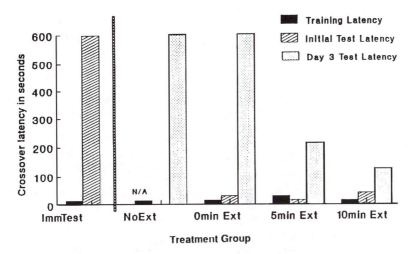

Figure 23–2 Median latency to crossover from the white (safe) to the black (fear) compartment of a two-chambered passive-avoidance (PA) apparatus during training, an initial retention test, and a final (Day 3) retention test. Long latencies are indicative of strong retention. To test the extent of learning while hypothermic, Group ImmTest was tested for retention immediately following training while still hypothermic. Initial Test Latencies for all remaining groups reflect 24-hour post-training performance in a normothermic state. Day 3 Test Latencies indicate performance following a group's respective extinction treatment and reinstatement of hypothermia (adapted from Morgan and Riccio, 1994).

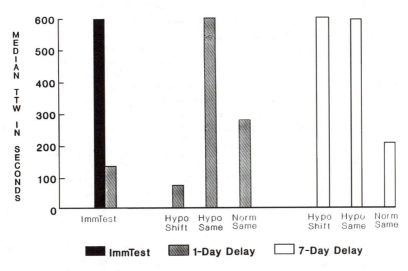

Figure 23–3. Median total-time-in-white (safe compartment) scores for animals tested immediately, 1 day, or 7 days after passive-avoidance training. The first term in each two-term group designation indicates subjects' temperature at testing, and the second term indicates whether subjects were tested in the environmental context in which they had been trained (SAME) or not (DIFF).

were delayed for 1 week, subjects were fearful in both sets of test contexts (Groups Hypo-shift and Hypo-same at 7 day delay). Thus, the inaccessible memory apparently underwent modification in the form of forgetting of the precise attributes of the training context during the delay interval.

Alteration of an inaccessible memory has also been demonstrated recently in human infants. Using the previously mentioned operant kicking task, Boller, Rovee-Collier, Borovsky, O'Conner, and Shyi (1990) found that at 6 months of age, treatments used to reactivate memory after normal infantile forgetting ("infantile amnesia") do not result in access or expression of the memory until at least 1 hour after the reactivation treatment. In a subsequent study (Boller & Rovee-Collier, 1994), 6-month-olds were exposed to a novel context immediately after receiving a memory reactivation treatment. Retention testing then indicated that the original training memory had been modified to include information about the novel context despite this target memory's remaining inaccessible during the novel exposure period. As these authors suggested: "The present experiment demonstrates that a reactivated memory need not have become accessible (i.e., returned to working memory) in order to be modified" (p. 253).

These studies indicate that a history of memory inaccessibility should not necessarily be taken to imply that a memory has remained encapsulated or protected over time. The retroactive influence of subsequently acquired information, and possibly proactive influences, should be strongly considered in attempting to determine the accuracy of recovered memories. Furthermore, it should be noted that even if a memory were to remain completely intact over time, subsequently acquired information and contextual changes may be expected to alter interpretation and perception of the information at the time of recovery.

ENDNOTES

Preparation of this chapter was supported in part by National Institute of Mental Health Grant MH37535 to David C. Riccio, National Institutes of Health Grants DA07559 and ES07475 to Barbara J. Strupp (Cornell University), and EPA Superfund Grant P42–ES05950 to B. J. Strupp.

REFERENCES

Ahlers, S. T., Richardson, R., West, C., & Riccio, D. C. (1989). ACTH produces long-lasting recovery following partial extinction of an active avoidance response. *Behavioral and Neural Biology, 51,* 102–107.

Amabile, T. A., & Rovee-Collier, C. (1991). Contextual variation and memory retrieval by at six months. *Child Development, 62,* 1155–1166.

Anderson, S. M., & Cole, S. W. (1990). "Do I know You?": The role of significant others in general social perception. *Journal of Personality and Social Psychology, 59,* 384–399.

Archer, T., Sjoden, P. O., & Nilsson, L. G. (1984) The importance of contextual elements in taste-aversion learning. *Scandinavian Journal of Psychology, 2,* 251–257.

Balaz, M. A., Capra, S., Hartl, P., & Miller, R. R. (1981). Contextual potentiation of acquired behavior after devaluing direct context-CS associations. *Learning and Motivation, 12,* 383–397.

Barnes, J. M., & Underwood, B. J. (1959). "Fate" of first-list associations in transfer theory. *Journal of Experimental Psychology, 58,* 97–105.

Bartlett, F. C. (1932). *Remembering: A study in experimental and social psychology.* New York & London: Cambridge University Press.

Bindra, D. (1959). Stimulus change, reactions to novelty, and response decrement. *Psychological Review, 66,* 96–103.

Boller, K., & Rovee-Collier, C. (1992). Contextual coding and recoding of infants' memories. *Journal of Experimental Child Psychology, 53,* 1–23.

Boller, K., & Rovee-Collier, C. (1994). Contextual updating of infants' reactivated memories. *Developmental Psychobiology, 27,* 241–256.

Boller, K., Rovee-Collier, C., Borovsky, D., O'Conner, J., & Shyi, G. C. (1990). Developmental changes in the time-dependent nature of memory retrieval. *Developmental Psychology, 26,* 770–779.

Bouton, M. E. (1988). Context and ambiguity in the extinction of emotional learning: Implications for exposure therapy. *Behavior Research and Therapy, 26,* 137–148.

Bouton, M. E., & Bolles, R. C. (1979). Contextual control of conditioned fear. *Learning and Motivation, 10,* 445–466.

Bouton, M. E., Ricker, S. T., & Sean, T. (1994). Renewal of extinguished responding in a second context. *Animal Learning & Behavior, 22,* 317–324.

Bouton, M. E., & Swartzntruber, (1991). Sources of relapse after extinction in Pavlovian and instrumental conditioning. *Clinical Psychology Review, 11,* 123–140.

Braun, J. J., Meyer, P. M., & Meyer, D. R. (1966). Sparing of a brightness habit in rats following visual decorticating. *Journal of Comparative and Physiological Psychology, 61*, 79–82.

Campbell, B. A., & Campbell, E. B. (1962). Retention and extinction of learned fear in infant and adult rats. *Journal of Comparative and Physiological Psychology, 55*, 1–8.

Campbell, B. A., & Jaynes, J. (1966). Reinstatement. *Psychological Review, 73*, 478–480.

Campbell, B. A., & Spear, N. E. (1972). Ontogeny of memory. *Psychological Review, 79*, 215–236.

Chandler, C. C. (1991). How memory for an event is influenced by related events: Interference in modified recognition tests. *Journal of Experimental Psychology: Learning, Memory, and Cognition, 17*, 115–125.

Chiszar, D. A., & Spear, N. E. (1969). Stimulus change, reversal learning, and retention in the rat. *Journal of Comparative and Physiological Psychology, 69*, 190–195.

Concannon, J. T., Riccio, D. C., & McKelvey, J. (1980). Pavlovian conditioning of fear based upon hormonal mediation of prior aversive experience. *Animal Learning & Behavior, 8*, 75–80.

Craik, F. I. M., & Tulving, E. (1975). Depth of processing and the retention of words in episodic memory. *Journal of Experimental Psychology: General, 104*, 268–294.

DeKeyne, A., & Deweer, B. (1990). Interaction between conflicting memories in the rat: Contextual pretest cuing reverses control of behavior by testing context. *Animal Learning & Behavior, 18*, 1–12.

Duncan, C. P. (1949). The retroactive effect of electroshock on learning. *Journal of Comparative and Physiological Psychology, 42*, 32–44.

Ebbinghaus, H. (1885). *Memory: A contribution to experimental psychology.* Translated by H. A. Ruger & C. E. Bussenues, 1913. New York: Teachers College, Columbia University.

Eich, J., Weingartner, H., Stillman, R., & Gillin, J. (1975). State-dependent accessibility to retrieval cues and retention of a categorized list. *Journal of Verbal Learning and Verbal Behavior, 14*, 408–417.

Eichenbaum, H. (1994). The hippocampal system and declarative memory in humans and animals: Experimental analysis and historical origins. In D. L. Schacter & E. Tulving (eds.), *Memory systems 1994.* Cambridge, Mass.: MIT Press.

Feinberg, G., & Riccio, D. C. (1990). Changes in memory for stimulus attributes: Implications for tests of morphine tolerance. *Psychological Science, 1*, 265–267.

Fernandez, A., & Glenberg, A. M. (1985). Changing environmental context does not reliably affect memory. *Memory and Cognition, 13*, 333–345.

Geller, A., & Jarvik, M. E. (1968). The time relations of ECS induced amnesia. *Psychonomic Science, 12*, 169–170.

Gerson, R., & Henderson, R. W. (1978). conditions that potentiate the effects of electroconvulsive shock administered 24 hours after avoidance training. *Animal Learning & Behavior, 6*, 346–351.

Gisquet-Verrier, P., & Alexinsky, T. (1986). Does contextual change determine long-term forgetting? *Animal Learning & Behavior, 14*, 349–358.

Gisquet-Verrier, P., & Alexinsky, T. (1988). Time-dependent fluctuations of retention performance in an aversively motivated task. *Animal Learning & Behavior, 16*, 58–66.

Gisquet-Verrier, P., DeKeyne, A., & Alexinsky, T. (1989). Differential effects of several retrieval cues over time: Evidence for time-dependent reorganization of memory. *Animal Learning & Behavior, 17*, 394–408.

Godden, D. R., & Baddeley, A. D. (1975). Context-dependent memory in two natural environments: On land and underwater. *British Journal of Psychology, 66*, 325–331.

Gordon, W. C., McCracken, K. M., Dess-Beech, N., & Mowrer, R. R. (1981). Mechanisms for the cueing phenomenon: The addition of the cueing context to the training memory. *Learning and Motivation, 12*, 196–211.

Gordon, W. C., & Mowrer, R. R. (1980). An extinction trial as a reminder treatment following electroconvulsive shock. *Animal Learning & Behavior, 8*, 363–367.

Greenspoon, J., & Ranyard, R. (1957). Stimulus conditions and retroactive inhibition. *Journal of Experimental Psychology, 53*, 55–59.

Haroutunian, V., & Riccio, D. C. (1977). Effect of arousal conditions during reinstatement treatment upon learned fear in young rats. *Developmental Psychobiology, 10*, 25–32.

Hebb, D. O. (1949). *The organization of behavior.* New York: Wiley.

Hertl, P. T., & Ellis, H. C. (1979). Constructive memory for bizarre and sensible sentences. *Journal of Experimental Psychology: Human Learning and Memory, 5*, 386–394.

Hinderliter, C. F., Webster, T., & Riccio, D. C. (1975). Amnesia induced by hypothermia as a function of treatment-test interval and recooling in rats. *Animal Learning and Behavior, 3*, 257–263.

Holland, P. C. (1986). Temporal determinants of occasion setting in feature positive discriminations. *Animal Learning & Behavior, 14*, 111–120.

Honey, R. C., & Hall, R. C. (1990). Context-specific conditioning in the conditioned-emotional-response procedure. *Journal of Experimental Psychology: Animal Behavior Processes, 3*, 271–278.

Honig, W. K. (1978). Studies of working memory in the pigeon. In S. H. Hulse, H. Fowler, & W. K. Honig (eds.), *Cognitive processes in animal behavior*, 211–247. Hillsdale, N.J.: Erlbaum.

Howard, R. L., Glendenning, R. L., & Meyer, D. R. (1974). Motivational control of retrograde amnesia: Further explorations and effects. *Journal of Comparative and Physiological Psychology, 86*, 187–192.

Howard, R. L., & Meyer, D. R. (1971). Motivational control of retrograde amnesia in rats: A replication and extension. *Journal of Comparative and Physiological Psychology, 74,* 37–40.

James, W. (1890/1983). *The principles of psychology.* Cambridge, Mass: Harvard University Press.

Jenson, R. A., & Riccio, D. C. (1970). Effects of prior experience upon retrograde amnesia produced by hypothermia. *Physiology and Behavior, 5,* 1291–1294.

Kamin, L. J. (1969). Selective association in conditioning. In N. J. Mackintosh & W. K. Honig (eds.), *Fundamental issues in associative learning.* Halifax, Nova Scotia: Dalhousie University Press.

Klein, S. B. (1972). Adrenal-pituitary influence in reactivation of avoidance-learning memory in the rat after intermediate intervals. *Journal of Comparative and Physiological Psychology, 79,* 341–359.

Kraemer, P., & Spear, N. E. (1993). Retrieval processes and conditioning. In T. R. Zentall (ed.), *Animal cognition: A tribute to Donald A. Riley.* Hillsdale, N.J.: Erlbaum.

Lewis, D. J. (1976). A cognitive approach to experimental amnesia. *American Journal of Psychology, 89,* 51–80.

Lewis, D. J. (1979). Psychobiology of active and inactive memory. *Psychological Bulletin, 86(5),* 1054–1083.

Lewis, D. J., Miller, R. R., & Misanin, J. R. (1969). Selective amnesia in rats produced by electroconvulsive shock. *Journal of Comparative and Physiological Psychology, 69,* 136–140.

Loftus, E. F. (1979). The malleability of human memory. *American Scientist, 67,* 312–320.

Loftus, E. F. (1981). Mentalmorphosis: Alteration in memory produced by the bonding of new information of old. In J. Long & A. Baddeley (eds.), *Attention & performance IX,* 417–437. Hillsdale, N.J.: Erlbaum.

Loftus, E. F. (1993). The reality of repressed memories. *American Psychologist, 48(5),* 518–537.

Lowe, G. (1983). Alcohol and state-dependent learning. *Substance & Alcohol Actions/Misuse, 4,* 273–282.

Lubow, R. E. (1973). Latent inhibitor. *Psychological Bulletin, 79,* 398–407.

Mactutus, C. F., Ferek, J. M., George, C. A., & Riccio, D. C. (1982). Hypothermia-induced amnesia for newly acquired and old reactivated memories: Commonalities and distinctions. *Physiological Psychology, 10,* 79–95.

Mactutus, C. F., Frank, J. M., & Riccio, D. C. (1980). Amnesia induced by hypothermia: An unusually profound, yet reversible, memory loss. *Behavioral and Neural Biology, 30,* 260–277.

Mactutus, C. F., & Riccio, D. C. (1978). Hypothermia-induced retrograde amnesia: Role of body temperature in memory retrieval. *Physiological Psychology, 6,* 18–22.

Mactutus, C. F., Riccio, D. C., & Ferek, J. M. (1979). Retrograde amnesia for old (reactivated) memory: Some anomalous characteristics. *Science, 204,* 1319–1320.

Mactutus, C. F., Smith, R. L., & Riccio, D. C. (1980). Extending the duration of ACTH-induced memory reactivation in an amnesic paradigm. *Physiology and Behavior, 24,* 541–546.

Madsen, M. C., & McGaugh, J. L. (1961). The effects of ECS on one-trial avoidance learning. *Journal of Comparative and Physiological Psychology, 54,* 522–523.

McAllister, D. E., & McAllister, W. R. (1967). Incubation of fear: An examination of the concept. *Journal of Experimental Research in Personality, 2,* 180–190.

McAllister, W. R., & McAllister, D. E. (1963). Increase over time in the stimulus generalization of acquired fear. *Journal of Experimental Psychology, 65,* 576–582.

McClelland, J. L., McNaughton, B. L., & O'Reilly, R. C. (1995). Why are there complementary learning systems in the hippocampus and neocortex?: Insights from the successes and failures of connectionist models of learning and memory. *Psychology Review, 102,* 419–457.

McGaugh, J. L. (1966). Time-dependent processes in memory storage. *Science, 153,* 1351–1358.

McGaugh, J. L., & Herz, M. J. (1972). *Memory consolidation.* San Francisco: Albion.

McGaugh, J. L., & Landfield, P. W. (1970). Delayed development of amnesia following electroconvulsive shock. *Physiology and Behavior, 5,* 1109–1113

McGeoch, J. A. (1932). Forgetting and the law of disuse. *Psychological Review, 39,* 352–370.

McGeoch, J. A. (1942). *The psychology of human learning: An introduction.* New York: Longmans, Green.

Miller, J. S., Jagielo, J. A., & Spear, N. E. (1991). Differential effectiveness of various prior-cuing treatments in the reactivation and maintenance of memory. *Journal of Experimental Psychology: Animal Behavior Processes, 17,* 249–258.

Miller, R. R., & Springer, A. D. (1971). Temporal course of amnesia in rats after electroconvulsive shock. *Physiology and Behavior, 6,* 229–234.

Miller, R. R., & Springer, A. D. (1972). Induced recovery of memory in rats following electroconvulsive shock. *Physiology and Behavior, 8,* 645–651.

Miller, R. R., & Springer, A. D. (1973). Amnesia, consolidation, and retrieval. *Psychological Review, 80,* 69–79.

Misanin, J. R., Miller, R. R., & Lewis, D. J. (1968). Retrograde amnesia produced by electroconvulsive shock after reactivation of a consolidated memory trace. *Science, 160,* 554–555.

Mishkin, M., & Appenzeler, T. (1987). The anatomy of memory. *Scientific American, 256,* 80–89.

Moore, B. S., Sherrod, D. R., Liu, T. J., & Underwood, B. (1979). The dispositional shift in attribution over time. *Journal of Experimental Social Psychology, 15,* 553–569.

Morgan, R. E., & Riccio, D. C. (1992, May). *Forgetting of stimulus attributes in an amnestic memory paradigm.*

Paper presented at the annual meeting of the Midwestern Psychological Association, Chicago.

Morgan, R. E., & Riccio, D. C. (1994). Extinction of an amnestic memory in rats: Evidence for the malleability of "inaccessible" information. *Learning and Motivation, 25,* 431–446.

Morris, C. D. (1978). Acquisition-test interactions between different dimensions of encoding. *Memory and Cognition, 6,* 354–363.

Olton, D. S., Becker, J. T., & Handelmann, G. H. (1979). Hippocampus, space, and memory. *Behavioral and Brain Sciences, 2,* 313–365.

Overton, D. A. (1964). State-dependent or "dissociate" learning produced with pentobarbital. *Journal of Comparative and Physiological Psychology, 57,* 3–12.

Overton, D. A. (1978). Major theories of state dependent learning. In B. T. Ho, D. W. Richards III, & D. L. Chute (eds.), *Drug discrimination and state dependent learning,* 283–318. New York: Academic Press.

Overton, D. A. (1985). Contexual stimulus effects of drugs and internal states. In P. D. Balsam & A. Tomie (eds.), *Context and learning,* 357–384. Hillsdale, N.J.: Erlbaum.

Perkins, C. C., & Weyant, R. G. (1958). The interval between training and test trials as determiner of the slope of generalization gradients. *Journal of Comparative and Physiological Psychology, 51,* 596–600.

Postman, L. (1976). Interference theory revisited. In J. Brown (ed.), *Recall and recognition,* 157–181. Bath, England: Wiley.

Quartermain, D., McEwen, B. S., Azmitia, E. C. (1970). Amnesia produced by electroconvulsive shock or cycloheximide: Conditions for recovery. *Science, 169,* 683–686.

Rescorla, R. A., & Wagner, A. R. (1972). A theory of Pavlovian conditioning: Variations in the effectiveness of reinforcement and nonreinforcement. In H. H. Black & W. F. Prokasy (eds.), *Classical conditioning II: Current research and theory.* New York: Appleton-Century-Crofts.

Riccio, D. C., Ackil, J. K., & Burch-Vernon, A. (1992). Forgetting of stimulus attributes: Methodological implications for assessing associative phenomena. *Psychological Bulletin, 122,* 433–445.

Riccio, D. C., & Haroutunian, V. (1979). Some approaches to the alleviation of ontogenetic memory loss. In B. A. Campbell & N. E. Spear (eds.), *Ontogeny of learning and memory,* 289–309. Hillsdale, N.J.: Erlbaum.

Riccio, D. C., Hodges, L. A., & Randall, P. K. (1968). Retrograde amnesia produced by hypothermia in rats. *Journal of Comparative and Physiological Psychology, 66,* 618–622.

Riccio, D. C., Rabinowitz, V. C., & Axelrod, S. (1994). Memory: When less is more. *American Psychologist, 49(11),* 917–926.

Riccio, D. C., & Richardson, R. (1984). The status of memory following experimentally induced amnesias: Gone, but not forgotten. *Physiological Psychology, 12,* 59–72.

Riccio, D. C., Richardson, R., & Ebner, D. L. (1984). Memory retrieval deficits based upon altered contextual cues. *Psychological Bulletin, 96,* 152–165.

Riccio, D. C., Urda, M., & Thomas, D. R. (1966). Stimulus control in pigeons based on proprioceptive stimuli from floor inclination. *Science, 153,* 434–435.

Richardson, R., Guanowsky, V., Ahlers, S. T., & Riccio, D. C. (1984). Role of body temperature in the onset of, and recovery from hypothermia-induced anterograde amnesia. *Physiological Psychology, 12,* 125–132.

Richardson, R., & Riccio, D. C. (1991). Memory processes, ACTH, and extinction phenomena. In L. Dachowski & C. F. Flaherty (eds.), *Current topics in animal learning: Brain, emotion, and cognition,* 1–23. Hillsdale, N.J.: Erlbaum.

Richardson, R., Riccio, D. C., & Devine, L. (1984). ACTH-induced recovery of extinguished avoidance behavior. *Physiological Psychology, 12,* 184–192.

Richardson, R., Riccio, D. C., & Morilak, D. (1983). Anterograde memory loss induced by hypothermia in rats. *Behavioral and Neural Biology, 37,* 76–88.

Rigter, H., Van Riezen, H., & deWied, D. (1974). The effects of ACTH- and vasopressin-analogues on CO_2-induced retrograde amnesia in rats. *Physiology and Behavior, 13,* 381–388.

Robbins, M. J., & Meyer, D. R. (1970). Motivational control of retrograde amnesia. *Journal of Experimental Psychology, 84,* 220–225.

Roitblat, H. L. (1980). Codes and coding processes in pigeon short-term memory. *Animal Learning & Behavior, 8,* 341–351.

Roitblat, H. L. (1982). The meaning of representation in animal memory. *Behavioral and Brain Sciences, 5,* 353–406.

Rovee-Collier, C. (1990). The "memory system" of prelinguistic infants. *Annals of the New York Academy of Sciences, 608,* 517–536.

Rovee-Collier, C., & DeFault, D. (1991). Multiple contexts and memory retrieval at three months. *Developmental Psychobiology, 24,* 39–49.

Sara, S. J. (1973). Recovery from hypoxia and ECS induced amnesia after a single exposure to the training environment. *Physiology and Behavior, 9,* 85–89.

Schachtman, T. R., Brown, A. M., Gordon, E. L., Catterson, D. A., & Miller, R. R. (1987). Mechanisms underlying retarded emergence of conditioned responding following inhibitory training: Evidence for the comparator hypothesis. *Journal of Experimental Psychology: Animal Behavior Processes, 13,* 310–322.

Shapiro, M. L., & Olton, D. S. (1994). Hippocampal function and interference. In D. L. Schacter & E. Tulving (eds.), *Memory systems 1994.* Cambridge, Mass.: MIT Press.

Sherry, D. F., & Schacter, D. L. (1987). The evolution of multiple memory systems. *Psychological Review, 94,* 439–454.

Siegel, S. (1975). Evidence from rats that morphine tolerance is a learned response. *Journal of Comparative and Physiological Psychology, 89,* 498–506.

Siegel, S. (1989). Pharmacological conditioning and drug effects. In A. J. Goudie & M. Emmett-Oglesby (eds.), *Psychoactive drugs,* 115–180. Clifton, N.J.: Humana Press.

Silvestri, R., Rohrbaugh, M., & Riccio, D. C. (1970). Conditions influencing the retention of learned fear in young rats. *Developmental Psychology, 2,* 389–395.

Skinner, B. F. (1950). Are theories of learning necessary? *Psychological Review, 57,* 193–216.

Smith, S. M. (1979). Remembering in and out of context. *Journal of Experimental Psychology: Human Learning & Memory, 5,* 460–471.

Smith, S. M., Glenberg, A., & Bjork, R. A. (1978). Environmental context and human memory. *Memory and Cognition, 6,* 342–353.

Spear, N. E. (1971). Forgetting as retrieval failure. In W. K. Honig & P. H. R. James (eds.), *Animal memory.* San Diego, Calif.: Academic Press.

Spear, N. E. (1973). Retrieval of memory in animals. *Psychological Review, 80,* 163–194.

Spear, N. E. (1978). *The processing of memories: Forgetting and retention.* Hillsdale, N.J.: Erlbaum.

Spear, N. E., Goldon, W. C., & Chiszar, D. A. (1972). Interaction between memories in the rat: Effect of degree of prior conflicting learning on forgetting after short intervals. *Journal of Comparative and Physiological Psychology, 78,* 471–477.

Spear, N. E., & Riccio, D. C. (1994). *Memory: Phenomena and principles.* Boston: Allyn & Bacon.

Spear, N. E., Smith, G. J., Bryan, R. G., Gordon, W. C., Timmons, W. C., & Chiszar, D. A. (1980). Contextual influences on the interaction between conflicting memories in the rat. *Animal Learning & Behavior, 8,* 273–281.

Squire, L. R. (1992). Memory and hippocampus: A synthesis from findings with rats, monkeys, and humans. *Psychological Review, 99,* 195–231.

Squire, L. R., & Zola-Morgan, M. (1991). The medical temporal lobe memory system. *Science, 253,* 1380–1386.

Thomas, D. R. (1981). Studies of long-term memory in the pigeon. In N. E. Spear & R. R. Miller (eds.), *Information processing in animals,* 257–290. Hillsdale, N.J.: Erlbaum.

Thomas, D. R., & Lopez, L. J. (1962). The effects of delayed testing on generalization slope. *Journal of Comparative and Physiological Psychology, 55,* 541–544.

Thomas, D. R., McKelvie, A. R., Ranney, M., Moye, T. B. (1981). Interference in pigeons' long-term memory

viewed as a retrieval problem. *Animal Learning & Behavior, 9,* 58–586.

Thomas, D. R., & Morrison, S. K. (1994). Novelty versus retrieval cue value of visual contextual stimuli in pigeons. *Animal Learning & Behavior, 22,* 90–95.

Thompson, C. I., & Neely, J. E. (1970). Dissociated learning in rats produced by electroconvulsive shock. *Physiology and Behavior, 5,* 783–786.

Tulving, E., & Osler, S. (1968). Effectiveness of retrieval cues in memory for words. *Journal of Experimental Psychology, 77,* 493–601.

Tulving, E., & Thomson, D. M. (1973). Encoding specificity and retrieval processes in episodic memory. *Psychological Review, 80,* 352–373.

Underwood, B. J. (1957). Interference and forgetting. *Psychological Review, 64,* 49–60.

Underwood, B. J. (1969). Attributes of memory. *Psychological Review, 76,* 559–573.

Weingartner, H., Miller, H., & Murphy, D. L. (1977). Mood-state-dependent retrieval of verbal associations. *Journal of Abnormal Psychology, 86,* 276–284.

Weiskrantz, L., & Warrington, E. K. (1975). The problem of the amnesic syndrome in man and animals. In K. H. Pribram & R. L. Issacson (eds.), *The hippocampus,* Vol. 2. New York: Plenum.

Wickens, D. D. (1972). Characteristics of word encoding. In A. W. Melton & E. Martin (eds.), *Coding processes in human memory.* Washington, D.C.: Winston.

Wickens, D. D., Tuber, D. S., Nield, A. F., & Wickens, C. (1977). Memory for the conditioned response: The effects of potential interference introduced before and after original conditioning. *Journal of Experimental Psychology: General, 106,* 47–70.

Winocur, G., & Bindra, D. (1976). Effects of additional cues on passive avoidance learning and extinction in rats with hippocampal lesions. *Physiology and Behavior, 17,* 915–920.

Winocur, G., & Breckenridge, C. B. (1973). Cue-dependent behavior of hippocampally-damaged rats in a complex maze. *Journal of Comparative and Physiological Psychology, 82,* 512–522.

Winocur, G., & Olds, J. (1978). Effects of context manipulation on memory and reversal learning in rats with hippocampal lesions. *Journal of Comparative and Physiological Psychology, 92,* 312–321.

Zinkin, S., & Miller, A. J. (1967). Recovery of memory after amnesia induced by electroconvulsive shock. *Science, 155,* 102–104.

CHAPTER 24

DETECTING CAUSAL RELATIONS

Helena Matute
Ralph R. Miller

Sometimes humans perceive causal relations that do not really exist (as in superstitious behavior, illusions of control, and various clinical problems); sometimes we do *not* perceive causal relations that do exist (as in cases in which our belief that minority people cause crime *blocks* our identifying poverty amidst wealth as a major cause of crime); yet at other times we show extreme accuracy in detecting causal relationships. The question of why (and how) we attribute causal roles to some events but not to others has interested psychologists and philosophers for many years (e.g., Hume 1739/1964). Within psychology, problems related to causal attribution have been studied in areas as diverse as social (Heider, 1958), clinical (e.g., Alloy & Abramson, 1979), developmental (Piaget & Inhelder, 1951), perception (Michotte, 1963), and information processing (Kahneman, Slovic, & Tversky, 1982).

In this chapter, we will focus on causal judgment in the framework of associative learning. This perspective bridges animal and human research in its study of how organisms process causal information. The basic idea underlying this approach is that conditioned responding (CR) occurs in animals under conditions analogous to those that would lead a human subject to conclude that a causal relationship exists between the conditioned stimulus (CS), or cause, and the unconditioned stimulus (US), or effect (see, e.g., Dickinson, 1980; Rescorla, 1988). That is, in contrast to more traditional theories of conditioning (e.g., Pavlov, 1927) that focused on the CS as directly eliciting or causing the CR, in current conditioning research the focus is generally on the subject's learning that the CS (e.g., light, tone, etc.) is a cause or a predictor of the US or effect (usually food, foot shock, or sex object), and hence, the occurrence of a CR is usually seen merely as evidence that the animal has learned that the CS signals the US. Similarly, in instrumental conditioning, the subject's response is frequently viewed as the cause of the outcome (e.g., the delivery of reinforcement, see e.g., Dickinson & Shanks, 1995).

The straightforward prediction following from this approach is that conditioning phenomena are replicable in human causal learning situations, both in laboratory experiments and in real life. More specifically, the conditions that affect animal conditioning, and that have been extensively studied over many years, should also affect causal attribution in human judgment. Recent reviews by Allan (1993), Shanks (1993), Wasserman (1990a, 1993), and Young (1995) provide summaries of the basic findings in this area from the theoretical and experimental perspectives (see also the recent volume edited by Shanks, Holyoak, & Medin, 1996). In this chapter we discuss the conditions that favor the detection (and nondetection) of causal and noncausal relations and show how these findings can be applied for the better understanding and treatment of clinical problems.

BASIC RESEARCH ON CAUSAL LEARNING AS A BRIDGE BETWEEN CONDITIONING EXPERIMENTS AND REAL-WORLD APPLICATIONS WITH HUMANS

Behavior therapists have known for many years that the results of conditioning research with animals can be applied to the understanding of human behavior. However, our point of view, as well as that of many other researchers currently studying basic associative learning in humans, is that the gap between animal conditioning experiments and human applications is enormous and needs to be filled with intermediate steps at the level of basic human research. More specifically, we need experiments showing exactly how human subjects (and not only animals) process and respond to causal information.

As an example of the gap between animal research and human applications, consider learned helplessness, a phenomenon that was developed in the field of animal conditioning (Overmier & Seligman, 1967; Seligman & Maier, 1967) and has been applied to almost all areas of human problems (see Peterson, Maier, & Seligman, 1993 for a recent review). According to learned helplessness theory (Abramson, Seligman, & Teasdale, 1978), when subjects are exposed to response-independent outcomes, they learn that outcomes are uncontrollable. This, in turn, may lead them (if certain attributions are made), to expect that outcomes will remain uncontrollable in the future. If this expectation takes place, subjects become helpless. This may manifest as depression, anxiety, and several other symptoms.

However, if we analyze the available data on learned helplessness, we can see that for several reasons, some additional experiments on human causal learning would be necessary in order to draw such conclusions. First, the theory was initially developed from animal conditioning experiments. Thus, the central assumption that subjects detect that outcomes were response-independent could only be inferred from the animal's behavior. Second, most applied settings in which this theory has been used to explain subjects' problems (e.g., depression) represent conditions in which the symptom is already there by the time the researcher begins the investigation. Thus, the assumption that it was caused by the subject's detection of the absence of a causal relation between responses and outcomes is again an inferred one.[1] Third, laboratory experiments on learned helplessness in humans have generally focused on the attributional component that, according to the theory, takes place *once subjects have already detected* that outcomes are response-independent (Abramson et al., 1978). Consequently, learned helplessness researchers frequently inform subjects that they are not controlling the outcome (see e.g., Abramson & Alloy, 1981), and by giving this information, researchers are able to investigate the subsequent attributions and potential deficits. However, by

---

[1]Note that the difficulty of detecting the etiology of a real-world problem is not constrained to the area of learned helplessness, but is a well-known problem in clinical psychology.

using this strategy, the assumption that subjects can detect response-outcome independence remains untested. As noted by Abramson and Alloy (1981, p. 438), "with uncontrollability so transparent, it is no wonder that [nondepressives] detect noncontingency accurately." But what if subjects were unable to detect noncontingency by themselves (Schwartz, 1981a, 1981b)? Obviously, subjects would make no attributions concerning uncontrollability if they were not able to detect it, nor would they develop any of the subsequent potential deficits. Experiments that actually test whether subjects exposed to uncontrollable outcomes are able to detect the absence of a causal relation between their responses and the occurrence of the outcomes (and if so, how and in which conditions) are a necessary intermediate step between animal learned helplessness experiments and applications of learned helplessness theory to human real-world domains. Below we consider this and other related areas of basic research in human causal learning, and analyze in which cases and to which extent are applications justified.

DIFFICULTY IN DETECTING CAUSALITY WHEN CONTIGUITY IS WEAK

One of the best-known facts from animal and human conditioning is that the CS (cause) and the US (effect) must occur in temporal and spatial proximity for the animal to learn a predictive relationship between them (i.e., for conditioning to take place). In general, as the CS-US delay increases, conditioned responding becomes weaker (Pavlov, 1927). The same applies to the response-outcome contiguity in instrumental learning.

This impact of contiguity upon behavior (human and animal) is well known in behavior therapy (e.g., the problem of the long delay between going on a diet and losing weight). The interesting thing for our present purposes is that exactly the same general rule applies to human causal learning. For example, Shanks, Pearson, and Dickinson (1989) reported several causal judgment experiments with humans in which they manipulated the temporal delay between the

potential cause (the subject's response [R] in a computer keyboard) and the effect (the appearance of a visual outcome [O] on the computer screen). Subjects experienced this relationship during several learning trials and were asked to rate the degree to which their own response was the cause of the appearance of the outcome. In all conditions, increasing the R-O delay produced lower judgments of causality, all other things being equal. Similarly, Wasserman and Neunaber (1986) showed that subjects tended to perceive a causal R-O relation when the response advanced the occurrence of the outcome but not when the response postponed the occurrence of the outcome.

Thus, contiguity affects not only behavior, but also the causal attributions that subjects make. If contiguity is weak, subjects may fail to detect a causal relation that does exist. As an example, consider a patient's difficulty in recognizing the beneficial effects of a therapy with a necessary long delay before a beneficial outcome occurs. Not surprisingly, many patients may prefer pharmacological over behavioral therapy, due to the differential response-outcome intervals.

Thus, if we aim to change a patient's attribution of causality, one of the aspects we ought to consider manipulating is contiguity and the factors that affect it. For example, we might think of "filling the gap" between the response and the outcome by introducing a signaling stimulus when contiguity is weak (e.g., Kaplan & Hearst, 1982). According to some authors (e.g., Young, 1995), this establishes a causal chain that enhances the likelihood that the response be perceived as the ultimate cause for the distant outcome (see Rescorla, 1982, for a different interpretation). This result has been observed in several human causal learning experiments that used weak R-O contiguity (e.g., Reed, 1992; Shanks, 1989, Experiment 2): The insertion of a CS during the delay period enhanced the perception of a causal relation between the response and the delayed outcome. Applications may include recognizing the several steps (mood changes, etc.) the patient may experience during the delay period as part of the causal chain leading to the distant outcome.

So far, we have focused our discussion on the difficulty in detecting a causal relation when contiguity is weak. The symmetrical problem is that high R-O contiguity favors the perception of a causal relation even if the relationship occurs by pure chance. We discuss this prediction in the next section.

EXPOSURE TO UNCONTROLLABLE OUTCOMES: HELPLESSNESS OR SUPERSTITION?

Consider a patient who has been diagnosed as having a serious illness and has decided to follow some "newly discovered" therapeutic exercises that are claimed to produce incredible improvements. The patient is indeed experiencing some recovery. Should this recovery be attributed to the exercises? Of course, in order to know whether or not a relationship is causal, the subject needs to know, in some way or another, two things. First, what is the probability of the outcome's occurring in the *presence* of responding, p(O|R), and second, what is the probability of the outcome's occurring in the *absence* of responding, p(O|noR) (see Allan, 1993; Shanks, 1993 for discussions on how this learning may take place). If p(O|R) is greater than p(O|noR), then the subject may conclude that performing the response increases the likelihood of the outcome occurring. By contrast, if p(O|noR) is greater, then the subject should refrain from responding in order to obtain the outcome. These two cases represent contingent conditions in which the response (or its absence) affects the occurrence of the outcome. Finally, if p(O|R) equals p(O|noR), then the response does not influence the outcome; hence, the outcome is said to be response-independent because it occurs with the same probability whether or not the subject responds.

Many researchers have examined whether subjects are actually sensitive to these event contingencies and can discriminate contingency (conditions in which the response affects the outcome, that is, p[O|R] < or > p[O|noR]) from ad-

ventitious contiguity (p[O|R] = p[O|noR]). The results of these experiments are somewhat mixed. Whereas some researchers have reported that animal and human subjects are sensitive to response-outcome independence and can learn that they do not have control over the outcomes (e.g., Seligman, 1975), others have shown that subjects exposed to response-independent outcomes tend to think they are controlling the outcome (i.e., illusion of control) and to behave superstitiously (e.g., Alloy & Abramson, 1979; Langer, 1975; Matute, 1994; Skinner, 1948; Wright, 1962). What evidence supports each of these discrepant views?

The seminal paper on the exposure to response-independent outcomes was published by Skinner in 1948. Skinner exposed a group of pigeons to uncontrollable (free) food on a fixed time schedule and observed that pigeons tended to develop repetitive patterns of behavior as if they "thought" their behavior was causing the reinforcer to occur. This was proposed as a model for human superstitious behavior, which according to Skinner would take place in much the same way as superstitious behavior in the pigeon. That is, even if the response is not the cause of the outcome, the response is adventitiously reinforced through R-O contiguity; thus, the response will tend to occur more frequently in the future. Several researchers replicated Skinner's findings in human subjects (e.g., Catania & Cutts, 1963; Wright, 1962). However, these views were neglected, in part because of a very convincing article by Staddon & Simmelhag (1971) that explained "superstition in the pigeon" in terms of reinforcers predisposing subjects toward certain temporally and reinforcer-specific responses, rather than randomly selecting ongoing behavior as suggested by Skinner. Additionally, Skinner's ideas were contrary to the intuitive view that organisms (especially humans) are sensitive to causal relations and can distinguish them from spurious correlations.

Learned helplessness theory (Abramson et al., 1978; see Overmier & LoLordo in this volume for a current review) was then developed, based on the view that animal and human subjects exposed to noncontingency between responses and outcomes were able to learn that their behavior did not control (i.e., cause) reinforcement. According to Abramson et al., learning that outcomes were uncontrollable could lead, if certain attributions were made, to several deficits that are collectively termed the *learned helplessness* effect (Overmier & Seligman, 1967).

The proposal that subjects were able to learn response-outcome independence was contrary to traditional views (e.g., Skinner, 1948) that subjects learn by simple contiguity, regardless of whether reinforcement was controllable or not. This difference was not only relevant at the theoretical level, but it had important implications for clinical problems as well. For instance, according to some traditional models of behavior therapy, depression was caused by an overall absence of reinforcers. In contrast, according to learned helplessness theory, it was not the absence of reinforcers that caused depression, but the subject's perception (and later expectations) that reinforcers were occurring independently of her or his behavior (see Maier, 1989; Overmier & LoLordo, this volume; Seligman, 1975).

However, most of the evidence seemingly supporting learned helplessness theory has been obtained under conditions in which subjects are exposed to "failure feedback," and consequently is open to alternative interpretations. That is, in a typical learned helplessness experiment (e.g., Hiroto & Seligman, 1975), subjects are either (a) told that they gave the wrong answer each time they finish a cognitive problem, or (b) exposed to uncontrollable reinforcement (noise termination) but told, after each trial, that they failed to stop the noise (see Abramson & Alloy, 1981; Hiroto & Seligman, 1975, for procedural details commonly used in human learned helplessness research; Matute, 1994, for further discussion of methodological issues). Consequently, alternative explanations such as failure exposure (e.g., Buchwald, Coyne, & Cole, 1978), egotism (Frankel & Snyder, 1978), or even extinction due to the continuous failure to get the desired event may be more relevant to these results than

learned helplessness theory. As acknowledged by Abramson and Alloy (1981), these experiments do not test whether the subjects detect response-reinforcer independence (see also Peterson et al., 1993, for a current discussion of alternative theories).

One solution to this problem is to eliminate the failure feedback used in the typical manipulation. That is, subjects can be exposed to uncontrollable reinforcement (noise termination) in the absence of failure feedback. However, we found not one reference reporting a true learned helplessness effect in the absence of failure feedback. For example, among the very few human experiments that have not used failure feedback, Thornton & Jacobs (1971) found that the behavior of the "helpless" group in a subsequent test phase did not differ from that of the control group. Kofta and Sedek (1989) were able to obtain an effect, but this effect was interpretable by an alternative mechanism (Sedek & Kofta, 1990). Moreover, when failure feedback is eliminated from the typical learned helplessness procedure, subjects do not detect response-outcome independence. On the contrary, they ordinarily develop an illusion of control and superstitious behavior (Matute, 1994, 1995), similar to what was previously described by Alloy and Abramson (1979), Langer (1975), Skinner (1948), Wright (1962), and many others. Indeed, many subjects (as well as some patients) adopt a suspicious attitude if they are subsequently informed that their behavior was not causing the outcome.

Even though "true" learned helplessness (i.e., deficits unambiguously attributable to the perception and expectations of uncontrollability) has not yet been demonstrated in human subjects, and even though "pure" uncontrollability (i.e., in the absence of failure feedback) seems to lead to the opposite outcome (i.e., illusion of control and superstitious behavior), learned helplessness and superstitious behavior could simply represent opposite ends of the same continuum. Consider, for example, the patient who has been diagnosed as having an incurable illness. This patient may take either of two courses of action.

First, she or he may realize that outcomes (e.g., transient improvements) are response-independent (i.e., therapy-independent), that nothing can really change the outcome, and consequently may become depressed. Second, this patient may try all types of therapies, including the most superstitious ones (e.g., witchcraft), and associate transient recoveries with some of those "therapies." This behavior may be called superstitious, but the pejorative name notwithstanding, it may be preventing depression.

It is not unusual to observe those two opposite patterns of responding to uncontrollable outcomes in different individuals in real life. Under desperate situations people may tend to either superstition or depression. The finding by Alloy and Abramson (1979) that nondepressed subjects are more prone to illusions of control than are depressed subjects is consistent with this hypothesis. A clear implication (see Alloy & Abramson, 1988; Alloy & Clements, 1992) is that, in cases in which the outcome is uncontrollable, letting subjects keep their illusions and superstitions, or even favoring the development of new ones, can have prophylactic effects against depression and other problems.

ACCURATE DETECTION OF CAUSAL AND NON-CAUSAL RELATIONS

We have argued that in many uncontrollable situations, subjects do not realize that they lack control over the outcome. But is this always true? Thus, an important remaining problem is to identify the conditions that lead to the perception of response-outcome independence because these conditions will ultimately determine, among other things, whether learned helplessness may occur (Maier & Seligman, 1976).

Even though these conditions have not been well identified in the learned helplessness literature, there are several experiments conducted on the judgment of causality as well as in animal learning that indicate under which conditions response-outcome dependence and independence will be perceived. In general, results have been quite consistent. In contingent conditions—that is, conditions in which outcomes do depend on the subject's active or passive responding—animal subjects learn to respond differentially to different event contingencies (e.g., Hallam, Grahame, & Miller, 1992; Rescorla, 1968) and the causal ratings of human subjects reflect that they too can accurately detect the actual event contingencies (see Shanks & Dickinson, 1987; Wasserman, 1990a for reviews). The results are also consistent with respect to detection of noncontingent conditions (those in which the effect is independent of the cause), provided that the potential cause is an exogenous event (i.e., not a subject's response, e.g., Baker & Mackintosh, 1977; Rescorla, 1968).

Moreover, within the laboratory, causal judgment data indicate that humans are able to perceive, *at least under ideal conditions,* when their response does not cause an outcome to occur (see Shanks & Dickinson, 1987; Wasserman, 1990a for reviews). It should be noted, however, that these experiments are more theoretically oriented than the experiments on superstition and learned helplessness. That is, subjects in these causal judgment experiments are informed that their goal is to find out how much control they have over a certain outcome (e.g., a triangle flashing on the computer's monitor). They are also often told that the best strategy they can use in order to find out how much control is possible is to respond on about 50% of the trials so that they can be equally exposed to both p(O|R) and p(O|noR). Thus, what these experiments show is that, at least under these ideal laboratory conditions, human subjects do have the capacity to learn that outcomes are response-independent. The problem is that this "scientific behavior" (i.e., responding on 50% of the trials to test both p[O|R] and p[O|noR]) does not seem to occur spontaneously in more naturalistic conditions (e.g., learned helplessness experiments) in which subjects are exposed to aversive outcomes and are trying to escape. For example, Matute (1996) observed that in their attempts to escape, most subjects exposed to uncontrollable aversive conditions responded at almost every opportunity.

Therefore, no matter how uncontrollable reinforcement (termination of the aversive stimulus) was, it tended to occur in the presence, rather than in the absence, of responding. Thus, subjects could not learn that the outcome would have occurred with the same probability if they had not responded. This in turn caused subjects to believe that their response was controlling the outcome, which led to an illusion of control.

Going back to our previous example of the patient diagnosed as having a serious illness and who acted at a very high rate (trying witchcraft and all other possible types of therapy), most transient recoveries would probably be contiguous with his or her acting rather than being passive. Thus, it would not be surprising if this patient continued to use superstitious therapies rather than becoming helpless or depressed. Only if this patient stops responding (perhaps because of a lack of reinforcement during a prolonged interval) will some eventual reinforcement occur in the absence of responding thereby allowing the subject to learn that his or her behavior did not influence the temporary recovery.

In summary, we have seen that subjects do have the capacity to detect response-outcome independence, but they tend toward illusions of control and superstitious behavior in naturalistic conditions in which they are trying to obtain a valued outcome that occurs noncontingently. The subjects' probability of responding, $p(R)$, appears to be an important modulating factor: subjects responding at high rates (e.g., subjects responding at every opportunity to escape an aversive situation) tend toward stronger illusions of control than subjects responding at lower rates (probably because a higher percentage of responses become reinforced—in a partial schedule—as the subject's $p[R]$ approaches 1). According to this view, conditions that reduce $p(R)$, such as fatigue, punishment, depression, extinction (lack of reinforcers), or any other source for a low (passive) response rate can lead to a detection of response-outcome independence by allowing subjects to be exposed to both $p(O|R)$ and $p(O|noR)$. Consequently, learned helplessness effects, rather than superstitious behavior,

could potentially be observed under those conditions.

One more factor that could reduce the illusion of control (and perhaps favor depression in some cases) is the availability of an alternative cause (different from the subject's response) to which the outcome could be attributed. For example, early people's illusion that they caused rain by dancing probably disappeared when science provided an alternative, competing cause for rain. Of course, this process of discounting one potential causal factor on the basis of the availability of alternative causes is not constrained to the illusion-of-control problem and has received considerable attention on its own right. The rest of the chapter addresses these findings.

DISCOUNTING POTENTIAL CAUSES: THE INFLUENCE OF PRIOR (AND SUBSEQUENT) KNOWLEDGE

Let us consider a totally different example: people suffering from sleep disorders who are given both hypnotics *and* relaxation training sometimes attribute their improvement to the drug rather than to their new relaxation abilities (Davison, Tsujimoto, & Glaros, 1973). Why? We cannot claim the effects of contiguity (nor contingency) in this case. The patient falling asleep after having consumed a hypnotic *and* having performed a relaxation exercise is exposed to similar contiguity (and contingency) between each of the two potential causes and the reinforcer. We may claim, however, that prior knowledge (perhaps through earlier sharing of information by others, perhaps through the initial sessions in which the relaxation abilities were poor) tells the subject that the drug alone is sufficient to induce sleep. Consequently, the subject discounts relaxation as a therapeutic factor.

This effect is called *forward blocking* and is well documented in animal (e.g., Kamin, 1968) and human (e.g., Shanks, 1985) research. In a typical animal experiment, the subjects may be exposed, during Phase 1, to several trials in which a light CS is followed by a foot-shock US.

Then, in Phase 2, the light is presented simultaneously with a tone and followed again by a foot shock. That is, the experiment takes the form of A→E (A followed by E) in Phase 1, and AX→E in Phase 2. Then at test, X (the tone in our example) is presented alone to see if it produces fear of the foot shock US, which is equivalent to asking the subject whether X predicts that E will occur. In general, X is not perceived as a predictor of the foot shock (experimental subjects do not show fear of X). In contrast, control animals that lack the critical prior knowledge provided by the A→E pairings in Phase 1 perceive X as a predictor of E. The usual explanation is that in the experimental group, prior learning that A predicts E *blocks* the attribution of a causal role to X if X is trained in the presence of A. A similar result has been observed in many instrumental animal experiments in which a CS predicting reward caused a decrement in instrumental responding (e.g., Pearce & Hall, 1978; Williams, 1975). (As a real-world example, consider also the differential causal explanations given to a clinical case by therapists coming from different theoretical perspectives).

Competition between potential causes has also been demonstrated in the human laboratory. For example, Shanks (1985) and Hammerl (1993) have shown that humans reduce the causal role that they attribute to their own behavior if an additional potential cause (a CS) for the outcome is present.

Other human experiments on competition between causes (e.g., Wasserman, 1990b) have frequently used a medical diagnostic situation in which subjects are shown the records of fictitious patients who have consumed some allergens (which are analogous to potential causes or CSs) and then developed some allergies (analogous to potential effects [E] or USs). Subjects are subsequently asked about the degree of causal relation between the target allergen X and the allergic reaction. As in the animal experiments described above, human subjects tend to discount the potential causal role of allergen X if the competing allergen A has a stronger association to the allergic reaction. Whether this deficit in at-

tributing a causal role to X is due to the subjects' not having learned the X→E relationship (e.g., Rescorla & Wagner, 1972) or to their subsequent discounting (even though they learned it) the influence of X on the basis of the stronger A→E relation (e.g., Miller & Matzel, 1988; Shanks & Dickinson, 1987) is a matter of current theoretical debate.

This debate, despite its theoretical nature, has important implications. For example, suppose a patient has been exposed to several A→E episodes in which A caused effect E (e.g., alcohol→sexual impotence). Then A (alcohol) begins to occur simultaneously with X (e.g., disturbing thoughts) and is also followed by E (i.e., AX→E). According to the results of many experimental reports with both animals and humans, this person will probably discount the potential causal role of X (the disturbing thoughts in our example). But what if this were also an important causal factor? The patient's behavior would be more adaptive if the X→E relation were learned, and in some way stored, even if X were discounted as a causal factor, than if the X→E relation had never been encoded. In other words, if the information about the relationship between X and E had not initially been acquired due to competition from the stronger A→E association (e.g., "Because I know that A is the cause of E, I do not need to pay attention to X"), then the attribution could never be reversed. In contrast, if the information about X had been processed and stored, though discounted as a causal factor, then this attribution would be available to be reversed if necessary.

On the one hand, traditional associative theories (e.g., Rescorla & Wagner, 1972) posit that competition between causes occurs during acquisition (if one association is very strong, the other one is not learned) and thus it is not subject to reevaluation. On the other hand, comparator theories of learning (e.g., Miller & Matzel, 1988; Shanks & Dickinson, 1987) posit that subjects acquire associations concerning all potential causes present on a given situation. According to this view, discounting effects take place at a postlearning (i.e., reasoning or attributional) stage, and the information is there to be reevaluated if necessary (see also Van Hamme & Wasserman, 1994, for an explanation of retrospective evaluation as learning, rather than postlearning, process; and Miller & Matute, 1996, for difficulties with such a model).

Many experiments have been conducted to investigate whether information is subject to retrospective reevaluation. For example, consider the following design: AX→E in Phase 1 followed by A→no E in Phase 2. That is, the subjects first learn that A and X, presented together, lead to E, and then they learn that A by itself does not lead to E (e.g., they first learn that the combination of two therapeutic techniques produces an improvement, and then they learn that technique A, when used by itself, does not produce the effect). Will learning that A does not lead to E enhance the causal attribution to X that occurred during Phase 1? The two approaches already mentioned address this question in different ways. Traditional associative theories (e.g., Rescorla & Wagner, 1972) predict that during Phase 1, subjects learn about both A and X, and then further learning during Phase 2 that A by itself does not cause E has no impact on what subjects had initially learned about X during Phase 1. Comparator theories (Miller & Matzel, 1988; Shanks & Dickinson, 1987), on the other hand, predict that learning in Phase 2 that A does not produce the effect will prompt subjects to reexamine their attribution and give a stronger causal role to X. That is, subjects would conclude that the therapeutic technique X was more effective than they had initially thought. This prediction has been confirmed in several experiments (e.g., Dickinson & Charnock, 1985; Kaufman & Bolles, 1981; Matzel, Schachtman, & Miller, 1985). Similarly, many other experiments have also demonstrated that other types of posttraining manipulations (variations of the Phase 2 training in this example) result in subjects' (animals and humans) reexamining their initial attribution and giving a second, modified, conditioned (or attributional) response (Chapman, 1991; Cole, Barnet, & Miller, 1995; Shanks, 1985; Van Hamme & Wasserman, 1994). Thus, we can conclude

that people can reevaluate their initial attributions of causality, but of course a careful examination of the conditions under which retrospective processing takes place is important. These are discussed below.

STRONGLY VALENCED CAUSES ARE NOT DISCOUNTED

Consider now a patient who attributes her or his success at business meetings to two causes, (A) preparing for the meeting, and (X) performing a ritual of obsessive (superstitious?) behaviors. Thus, in Phase 1 we have AX→E. Then, you try to convince this patient that being prepared is sufficient to be successful (A→E) and that, therefore, the ritual (X) is superfluous. Will the patient finally accept the hypothesis that X was not a causal factor based exclusively on the A→E information? Or will some additional therapy (e.g., extinction of X) be necessary?.

This is called *backward blocking* because the traditional two phases of a forward blocking design (see above) are reversed (i.e., the compound phase is here presented as Phase 1 rather than Phase 2). Based on what we have already discussed, we would expect that A→E training in Phase 2 would result in subjects' discounting the potential causal role they may have attributed to X during Phase 1. This prediction has been confirmed in several human causal learning studies (e.g., Chapman, 1991; Shanks, 1985) but has resisted the attempts of animal researchers for many years (Miller, Hallam, & Grahame, 1990; Schweitzer & Green, 1982). Thus, this type of retrospective evaluation is a potential difference in information processing between animals and humans, suggesting that sometimes, even in simple laboratory tasks, humans perform differently than animals.

However, this is not necessarily so. Miller and Matute (1996) noted an important difference between the experiments that attempted to obtain this effect in animal subjects and those that had obtained it in human subjects. In animal experiments, the effect E was always an event of high biological significance (usually a foot-shock

US), whereas the effect E used in human experiments was always a neutral, fictitious event occurring on a computer screen (e.g., a fictitious allergy developed by a fictitious patient). Thus, Miller and Matute ran rats as subjects in a procedure as similar as possible to the one that had been used with human subjects. Specifically, they used neutral tones, rather than biologically relevant stimuli, as both causes and effects. (Only after completion of the two phases of backward blocking was the effect made biologically significant through pairing it with a foot-shock US, in order to provide the motivation needed to assess responding in a subsequent test phase.)

The results showed a retrospective processing effect in animals using the backward blocking design (i.e., AX→E; A→E; Test X). Rat subjects demonstrated that they, like humans, can reconsider the causal role attributed to X during Phase 1 (i.e., AX→E) if they later learn that A alone is sufficient to produce E (i.e., A→E). Compared with that of control rats that had not received the critical A→E training in Phase 2, the response of the experimental subjects to X was substantially weakened.

Thus, whereas traditional attempts to obtain backward blocking in animals using biological significant USs as effects had failed, studies using neutral stimuli that are known to yield backward blocking in humans produced backward blocking in animals. This suggests that, whereas organisms can discount the role of potential causes in neutral settings, this discounting process is less apt to occur in valenced settings.

The conditions under which backward blocking was obtained in this experiment as compared with previous attempts are of potential importance when considering applications to behavior therapy. For example, increasing the biological significance of the US (nausea) or the alcohol concentration and taste in aversion therapy with alcoholics should increase the efficacy of these techniques by reducing the likelihood that the patients discount alcohol as the cause of their sickness. Moreover, if the business success of our previously discussed patient is a biologically

significant event (those that are important for the well-being of the organism) we should predict that this patient will not be able to discount the role of the obsessive ritual as a causal factor in producing success.

This prediction was further supported in the laboratory by Miller and Matute (1996), who observed that even forward blocking, which is commonly observed in animal subjects (e.g., Kamin 1968), failed to occur if the auditory stimuli used as potential causes were of high intensity (and thus, presumably, of higher biological significance than neutral stimuli commonly used as CSs in conditioning experiments). That is, when X was biologically significant (e.g., very intense), subjects did not discount its potential causal role as is usually the case. Moreover, Denniston, Miller, and Matute (1996) observed that the influence of biological relevance on backward blocking was not constrained to cases in which biological significance was a feature inherent to the stimulus (e.g., high intensity). Rather, neutral stimuli (e.g., moderate intensity sounds) can also become biologically significant, and thus protected from discounting processes, if they are previously associated with a significant event (e.g., foot-shock US). In this study, E→US (Phase 1), followed by AX→E (Phase 2), A→E (Phase 3), and E→US (Phase 4), did not produce backward blocking when X was presented alone during the subsequent test phase. (Rats showed fear of X, thus suggesting that they had not discounted X as a causal factor in producing E, and thus, the US foot-shock.) However, when Phase 1 (E→US) was eliminated (i.e., X was a neutral event not associated with a US), rats did discount X as a causal factor producing E (rats showed little fear of X). This suggests that an important factor in modulating the occurrence of these selective attribution effects is whether the potential causes are biologically significant (either because of their inherent properties or because they have been previously conditioned through pairings with a significant event.)

Most situations of interest for applied psychology involve valenced conditions that are important to the well-being of the subject, either because the effect is inherently significant or because it has been associated to significant events (USs) during the patient's history. Consequently, we anticipate that backward blocking will probably be difficult to obtain in applied situations. Thus, if patients have experienced causes A and X followed by a significant US effect in the past, they will probably be reluctant to discount X as the cause of the US, no matter how many times we show them that A is the cause of the US. According to this view, extinction of X, rather than (or in addition to) showing that A alone was the cause of the US, will probably be necessary (recall our obsessive business person above; or the difficulty in eliminating stereotypes).

PREDICTING EFFECTS AND DIAGNOSING CAUSES

We have seen that animals exposed to A→E during Phase 1 and AX→E during Phase 2 do not expect E (foot-shock) at test when X is presented alone; and that the patient who is exposed to hypnotics in Phase 1 and hypnotics plus relaxation in Phase 2 does not anticipate sleep when relaxation alone is used.

Now imagine that A usually precedes (causes) symptom E (A→E), but that later on you see new patients who have developed the symptoms E and X simultaneously after being exposed to A (i.e., A→EX). That is, here, instead of having two potentially competing causes we have two potentially competing effects. In the future, would you tend to view these two symptoms, E and X, as competing cues for diagnosing that cause A has occurred? That is, would you discount the potential diagnostic value of X as a result of the initial A→E pairings? Or in contrast, would you interpret those two syndromes as cumulative evidence that cause A has occurred?

Waldmann and Holyoak (1992) predicted this later possibility as the only possible outcome of such a scenario. That is, they posited that collaboration rather than competition between effects would occur in human subjects exposed to multiple potential effects of a common cause. In-

deed, their results, which were replicated by Van Hamme, Kao, and Wasserman (1993), seemed to confirm this hypothesis. However, there is also considerable evidence indicating that if a certain effect or symptom has a strong diagnostic value, other effects tend to be ignored as potential diagnostic cues both in human (Chapman, 1991; Matute, Arcediano, & Miller, 1996; Price & Yates, 1993; Shanks & Lopez, 1996) and animal subjects (Esmoris-Arranz, Miller, & Matute, 1997). Apparently, effects compete in some situations as diagnostic cues and collaborate in other situations. Matute et al. (1996) investigated which conditions yielded competition between effects and which ones did not. They studied several conditions and concluded that the wording of the question used for assessment of the causal attribution plays an important role in determining whether effects compete or collaborate among themselves. That is, when subjects are asked whether each of the effects is an "effect of the cause," effects seem to collaborate with each other (subjects accept all potential effects of the cause in a noncompetitive manner); however, when subjects are asked about the "diagnostic value" of each of the effects, effects seem to compete among themselves (i.e., accepting effect A as a good diagnostic cue tends to lower the diagnostic value of effect X.) Thus, for example, a patient may view just one symptom as *the* diagnostic cue to recognize when an illness has come back (when is time to go back into therapy); but on the other hand, once the illness is present, the patient will probably predict all possible symptoms. As in the multiple-causes conditions described above, these attributions concerning multiple effects should also be subject to reevaluation under some conditions if the initial attributions prove wrong. However, research on competition and collaboration between effects has just started, and there is much to be done before the conditions under which reevaluation occurs in diagnostic settings can be identified.

Finally, note that this discussion of competition versus collaboration between effects also raises the issue of whether causes, which have traditionally been assumed to compete among themselves for predictive value (see previous section), could also collaborate among themselves in some cases. Indeed, collaboration between causes has been described in several different settings (e.g., Leddo, Abelson, & Gross, 1984). As an example, knowledge of a history of childhood abuse and of a history of mental illness in kin can collaborate, rather than compete, as predictors of mental illness in a patient. Based on available evidence, causes and effects do not appear to substantially differ in their susceptibility to competition or collaboration. Effects compete for diagnostic value just as causes compete for predictive value, but only when demand characteristics foster competition among the relevant stimuli.

CONCLUSIONS

We have tried to bring together research performed with animal and human subjects in the field of causal learning and to show some avenues through which this approach can benefit clinical psychology. In doing so, we have attempted (a) to call the attention of the reader to some points that, in our view, are not yet fully developed in basic research and to which we recommend caution if they are going to be applied, and (b) to suggest potential applications of those aspects that have been more thoroughly elaborated in basic research.

In summary, basic research on causal learning has revealed four important principles. First, causal judgments are sensitive to both contiguity and contingency between cause and effect. Thus, enhancing these two factors should prove beneficial when we want our patients to detect a causal relation between, say, a therapy and a beneficial effect.

Second, many laboratory experiments have shown that exposure to uncontrollable outcomes may result in superstitious behavior and illusion of control instead of resulting in learned helplessness and depression, as had been generally assumed within clinical psychology. Indeed, much of the human data that apparently support

learned helplessness theory can be explained by alternative theories such as exposure to failure feedback or an absence of reinforcers. On the other hand, the conditions that led to the perception of uncontrollability (and that could lead, therefore, to unambiguous helplessness deficits) are not yet well established. But it seems that conditions leading to passivity and reduced responding (e.g., fatigue, punishment, extinction) probably favor subjects' detection of response-outcome independence, and thus the development of learned helplessness over superstitious behavior. Additionally, the existence of some alternative potential cause for the outcome (other than the subject's behavior) may also reduce the illusion of control. Nevertheless, it is possible that superstitious behavior and illusion of control may prevent the development of helplessness and depression. Thus, in many situations they should be encouraged when possible.

Third, the process of selective attribution and discounting of potential causes allows subjects to select the most likely cause for an outcome. This process readily explains why subjects may attribute their improvement to some (but not all) of the components of a given therapy (e.g., "What makes me sleep is the pill, not the relaxation exercise"). Additionally, it has been shown that subjects can reconsider these selective attributions should they receive new information suggesting that the initial attribution was in error. However, these selective attribution processes seemingly occur only in situations with relatively neutral events; biologically significant events (those that are important to the well-being of the organism) are apparently protected from discounting processes. For example, would it be possible to discount the role of a potential cause if this cause is a very significant event in the patient's life (e.g., the loss of a loved one)? Probably not. Discounting procedures in applied situations would *probably* require the addition of extinction (or other) procedures if the to-be-discounted cause is of inherent or acquired biological significance.

Finally, causes and effects do not appear to be substantially different in their susceptibility to competition. That is, under analogous conditions, multiple effects seem to compete or collaborate for diagnostic value just as multiple causes compete or collaborate for predictive value. As we mentioned, a patient may pay attention to just one symptom as *the* diagnostic cue indicating that the illness is coming back, but may also predict that, once the illness is established, all other possible symptoms will occur. These attributional biases sometimes may prove adaptive, and sometimes may not (e.g., the patient may be using a wrong diagnostic cue). The patient's recognizing that selective attributions can occur, and that under some conditions they can be rather biased, might prove helpful in obtaining more accurate and complete judgments of the actual causal factors.

ENDNOTES

Support for the preparation of this chapter was provided by Dirección General de Investigación Científica y Técnica (Spain) Grant PB95-0440, Grant PI96-6 from the Basque Government, and National Institute of Mental Health (USA) Grant 33881. We thank Pilar Antón, José Cáceres, Pilar Castro, and Ane Uribe for illuminating conversations suggesting potential clinical applications of phenomena that we described in an earlier draft, and for their critical comments that helped us turn that draft into a chapter that we hope will be more relevant to behavior therapy.

REFERENCES

Abramson, L. Y., & Alloy, L. B. (1981). Depression, nondepression, and cognitive illusions: Reply to Schwartz. *Journal of Experimental Psychology: General, 110,* 436–447.

Abramson, L. Y., Seligman, M. E. P., & Teasdale, J. D. (1978). Learned helplessness in humans: Critique and reformulation. *Journal of Abnormal Psychology, 87,* 49–74.

Allan, L. G. (1993). Human contingency judgments: Rule based or associative? *Psychological Bulletin, 114,* 435–448.

Alloy, L. B., & Abramson, L. Y. (1979). Judgment of contingency in depressed and nondepressed students: Sadder but wiser? *Journal of Experimental Psychology: General, 108,* 441–485.

Alloy, L. B., & Abramson, L. Y. (1988). Depressive realism: Four theoretical perspectives. In L. B. Alloy (ed.), *Cognitive processes in depression,* 223–265. New York: Guilford.

Alloy, L. B., & Clements, C. M. (1992). Illusion of control: Invulnerability to negative affect and depressive symptoms after laboratory and natural stressors. *Journal of Abnormal Psychology, 101,* 234–245.

Baker, A. G., & Mackintosh, N. J. (1977). Excitatory and inhibitory conditioning following uncorrelated presentations of CS and US. *Animal Learning and Behavior, 5,* 315–319.

Buchwald, A. M., Coyne, J. C., & Cole, C. S. (1978). A critical evaluation of the learned helplessness model of depression. *Journal of Abnormal Psychology, 87,* 180–193.

Catania, A. C., & Cutts, D. (1963). Experimental control of superstitious responding in humans. *Journal of the Experimental Analysis of Behavior, 6,* 203–208.

Chapman, G. B. (1991). Trial order affects cue interaction in contingency judgment. *Journal of Experimental Psychology: Learning, Memory and Cognition, 17,* 837–854.

Cole, R. P., Barnet, R. C., & Miller, R. R. (1995). Effect of relative stimulus validity: Learning or performance deficit? *Journal of Experimental Psychology: Animal Behavior Processes, 21,* 293–303.

Davison, G. C., Tsujimoto, R. N., & Glaros, A. G. (1973). Attribution and the maintenance of behavior change in falling sleep. *Journal of Abnormal Psychology, 82,* 124–133.

Denniston, J. C., Miller, R. R., & Matute, H. (1996). Biological significance as a determinant of cue competition. *Psychological Science, 7,* 325–331.

Dickinson, A. (1980). *Contemporary animal learning theory.* Cambridge: Cambridge University Press.

Dickinson, A., & Charnock, D. J. (1985). Contingency effects with maintained instrumental reinforcement. *Quarterly Journal of Experimental Psychology, 37B,* 397–416.

Dickinson, A., & Shanks, D. R. (1995). Instrumental action and causal representation. In D. Sperber, D. Premack, & A. J. Premack (eds.), *Causal cognition: A multidisciplinary debate,* 5–25. Oxford: Clarendon Press.

Esmoris-Arranz, F. J., Miller, R. R., & Matute, H. (1997). Blocking of subsequent and antecedent events. *Journal of Experimental Psychology: Animal Behavior Processes, 23,* 145–156.

Frankel, A., & Snyder, M. L. (1978). Poor performance following unsolvable problems: Learned helplessness or egotism? *Journal of Personality and Social Psychology, 36,* 1415–1423.

Hallam, S. C., Grahame, N. J., & Miller, R. R. (1992). Exploring the edges of Pavlovian contingency space: An assessment of contingency theory and its various metrics. *Learning and Motivation, 23,* 225–249.

Hammerl, M. (1993). Blocking observed in human instrumental conditioning. *Learning and Motivation, 24,* 73–87.

Heider, F. (1958). *The psychology of interpersonal relations.* New York: Wiley.

Hiroto, D. S., & Seligman, M. E. P. (1975). Generality of learned helplessness in man. *Journal of Personality and Social Psychology, 31,* 311–327.

Hume, D. (1964). *Treatise on human nature* (ed., L. A. Selby-Bigge). London: Oxford University Press. (Originally published 1739.)

Kahneman, D., Slovic, P., & Tversky, A. (eds.) (1982). *Judgment under uncertainty: Heuristics and biases.* Cambridge, UK: Cambridge University Press.

Kamin, L. J. (1968). "Attention-like" processes in classical conditioning. In M.R. Jones (ed.), *Miami symposium on the prediction of behavior: Aversive stimulation,* 9–31. Miami, Fl.: University of Miami Press.

Kaplan, P. S., & Hearst, E. (1982). Bridging temporal gaps between CSs and USs in autoshaping: Insertion of other stimuli before, during, and after CS. *Journal of Experimental Psychology: Animal Behavior Processes, 8,* 187–203.

Kaufman, M. A., & Bolles, R. C. (1981). A nonassociative aspect of overshadowing. *Bulletin of the Psychonomic Society, 18,* 318–320.

Kofta, M., & Sedek, G. (1989). Repeated failure: A source of helplessness or a factor irrelevant to its emergence? *Journal of Experimental Psychology: General, 118,* 3–12.

Langer, E. J. (1975). The illusion of control. *Journal of Personality and Social Psychology, 32,* 311–328.

Leddo, J., Abelson, R. P., & Gross, P. H. (1984). Conjunctive explanations: When two reasons are better than one. *Journal of Personality and Social Psychology, 47,* 933–943.

Maier, S. F. (1989). Learned helplessness: Event covariation and cognitive changes. In S. B. Klein & R. R. Mowrer (eds.), *Contemporary learning theories: Instrumental conditioning theory and the impact of biological constraints on learning.* Hillsdale, N.J.: Erlbaum.

Maier, S. F., & Seligman, M. E. P. (1976). Learned helplessness: Theory and evidence. *Journal of Experimental Psychology: General, 105,* 3–46.

Matute, H. (1994). Learned helplessness and superstitious behavior as opposite effects of uncontrollable reinforcement in humans. *Learning and Motivation, 25,* 216–232.

Matute, H. (1995a). Human reactions to uncontrollable outcomes: Further evidence for superstitions rather than helplessness. *Quarterly Journal of Experimental Psychology, 48B,* 142–157.

Matute, H. (1996). Illusion of control: Detecting response-outcome independence in analytic but not in naturalistic conditions. *Psychological Sciences, 7,* 289–293.

Matute, H., Arcediano, F., & Miller, R. R. (1996). Test question modulates cue competition between causes and between effects. *Journal of Experimental Psychology: Learning, Memory, and Cognition, 22,* 182–196.

Matzel, L. D., Schachtman, T. R., & Miller, R. R. (1985). Recovery of an overshadowed association achieved by extinction of the overshadowing stimulus. *Learning and Motivation, 16,* 398–412.

Michotte, A. (1963). *The perception of causality.* New York: Basic Books.

Miller, R. R., Hallam, S. C., & Grahame, N. J. (1990). Inflation of comparator stimuli following CS training. *Animal Learning & Behavior, 18,* 434–443.

Miller, R. R., & Matute, H. (1996). Biological significance in forward and backward blocking: Resolution of a discrepancy between animal conditioning and human causal judgment. *Journal of Experimental Psychology: General, 125,* 370–386.

Miller, R. R., & Matzel, L. D. (1988). The comparator hypothesis: A response rule for the expression of associations. In G. H. Bower (ed.), *The psychology of learning and motivation,* Vol. 22: 51–92. San Diego, Calif.: Academic Press.

Overmier, J. B., & Seligman, M. E. P. (1967). Effects of inescapable shock upon subsequent escape and avoidance learning. *Journal of Comparative and Physiological Psychology, 63,* 28–33.

Pavlov, I. P. (1927). *Conditioned reflexes.* London: Clarendon Press.

Pearce, J. M., & Hall, G. (1978). Overshadowing the instrumental conditioning of a lever-press response by a more valid predictor of the reinforcer. *Journal of Experimental Psychology: Animal Behavior Processes, 4,* 356–367.

Peterson, C., Maier, S. F., & Seligman, M. E. P. (1993). *Learned helplessness: A theory for the age of personal control.* New York: Oxford University Press.

Piaget, J., & Inhelder, B. (1951). *La genese de l'ideé de hasard chez l'enfant* [The origin of the idea of chance in the child]. Paris: Presses Université France.

Price, P. C., & Yates, J. F. (1993). Judgmental overshadowing: Further evidence of cue interaction in contingency judgment. *Memory & Cognition, 21,* 561–572.

Reed, P. (1992). Effect of a signalled delay between an action and outcome on human judgment of causality. *Quarterly Journal of Experimental Psychology, 44B,* 81–100.

Rescorla, R. A. (1968). Probability of shock in the presence and absence of CS in fear conditioning. *Journal of Comparative and Physiological Psychology, 66,* 1–5.

Rescorla, R. A. (1982). Effect of a stimulus intervening between CS and US in autoshaping. *Journal of Experimental Psychology: Animal Behavior Processes, 8,* 131–141.

Rescorla, R. A. (1988). Pavlovian conditioning: It's not what you think it is. *American Psychologist, 43,* 151–160.

Rescorla, R. A., & Wagner, A. R. (1972). A theory of Pavlovian conditioning: Variations in the effectiveness of reinforcement and nonreinforcement. In A. H. Black & W. F. Prokasy (eds.), *Classical conditioning II: Current research and theory,* 64–99. New York: Appleton-Century-Crofts.

Schwartz, B. (1981a). Does helplessness cause depression, or do only depressed people become helpless? Comment on Alloy and Abramson. *Journal of Experimental Psychology: General, 110,* 429–435.

Schwartz, B. (1981b). Helplessness, illusions and depression: Final comment. *Journal of Experimental Psychology: General, 110,* 448–449.

Schweitzer, L., & Green, L. (1982). Reevaluation of things past: A test of the "retrospective hypothesis" using a CER procedure in rats. *Pavlovian Journal of Biological Science, 17,* 62–68.

Sedek, G., & Kofta, M. (1990). When cognitive exertion does not yield cognitive gain: Toward an informational explanation of learned helplessness. *Journal of Personality and Social Psychology, 58,* 729–743.

Seligman, M. E. P. (1975). *Helplessness.* San Francisco: Freeman.

Seligman, M. E. P., & Maier, S. F. (1967). Failure to escape traumatic shock. *Journal of Experimental Psychology, 74,* 1–9.

Shanks, D. R. (1985): Forward and backward blocking in human contingency judgment. *Quarterly Journal of Experimental Psychology, 37B,* 1–21.

Shanks, D. R. (1989). Selectional processes in causality judgment. *Memory & Cognition, 17,* 27–34.

Shanks, D. R. (1993). Human instrumental learning: A critical review of data and theory. *British Journal of Psychology, 84,* 319–354.

Shanks, D. R., & Dickinson, A. (1987). Associative accounts of causality judgment. In G. H. Bower (ed.), *The psychology of learning and motivation,* Vol. 21: 229–261. San Diego, Calif.: Academic Press.

Shanks, D. R., Holyoak, K. J., & Medin, D. L. (eds.) (1996). *The psychology of learning and motivation, Vol. 34: Causal judgment.* San Diego, Calif.: Academic press.

Shanks, D. R., & Lopez, F. J. (1996). Causal order does not affect cue selection in human associative learning. *Memory & Cognition, 24,* 511–522.

Shanks, D. R., Pearson, S. M., & Dickinson, A. (1989). Temporal contiguity and the judgment of causality by human subjects. *Quarterly Journal of Experimental Psychology, 41B,* 139–159.

Skinner, B. F. (1948). Superstition in the pigeon. *Journal of Experimental Psychology, 38,* 168–172.

Staddon, J. E. R., & Simmelhag, V. L. (1971). The "superstition" experiment: A reexamination of its implications for the principles of adaptive behavior. *Psychological Review, 78,* 3–43.

Thornton, J. W., & Jacobs, P. D. (1971). Learned helplessness in human subjects. *Journal of Experimental Psychology, 87,* 367–372.

Van Hamme, L. J., Kao, S-F., & Wasserman, E. A. (1993). Judging interevent relations: From cause to effect and from effect to cause. *Memory & Cognition, 21,* 802–808.

Van Hamme, L. J., & Wasserman, E. A. (1994). Cue competition in causality judgments: The role of nonpresentation of compound stimulus elements. *Learning and Motivation, 25,* 127–151.

Waldmann, M. R., & Holyoak, K. J. (1992). Predictive and diagnostic learning within causal models: Asymmetries in cue competition. *Journal of Experimental Psychology: General, 121,* 222–236.

Wasserman, E. A. (1990a). Detecting response-outcome relations: Toward an understanding of the causal texture of the environment. In G. H. Bower (ed.), *The psychology of learning and motivation,* Vol. 26: 27–82. San Diego, Calif.: Academic Press.

Wasserman, E. A. (1990b). Attribution of causality to common and distinctive elements of compound stimuli. *Psychological Science, 1,* 298–302.

Wasserman, E. A. (1993). Comparative cognition: Toward an understanding of cognition in behavior. *Psychological Science, 4,* 156–161.

Wasserman, E. A., & Neunaber, D. J. (1986). College students' responding to and rating of contingency relations: The role of temporal contiguity. *Journal of the Experimental Analysis of Behavior, 46,* 15–35.

Williams, B. A. (1975). The blocking of reinforcement control. *Journal of the Experimental Analysis of Behavior, 24,* 215–225.

Wright, J. C. (1962). Consistency and complexity of response sequences as a function of schedules of noncontingent reward. *Journal of Experimental Psychology, 63,* 601–609.

Young, M. E. (1995). On the origin of personal causal theories. *Psychonomic Bulletin & Review, 2,* 83–104.

CHAPTER 25

LEARNING AND EATING

T. L. Davidson
Stephen C. Benoit

What determines when humans and other animals will eat or refrain from eating? How do we choose which foods to consume? What factors are involved with the termination of a meal? Customarily, researchers have looked to physiology and appealed to motivational concepts when they have attempted to address these and other questions related to food intake. For example, much work has been guided by the idea that depletion of critical energy stores gives rise to physiological cues that signal departure from homeostasis (see Friedman, 1990; Kissileff & Van Itallie, 1982; LeMagnen, 1984). These signals work in combination with food-related exteroceptive cues to stimulate food intake until homeostasis is restored. Within this general framework, regulatory psychobiologists and other neuroscientists have sought to identify the neurohormonal origins of these internal cues, the neural locus of their receptors, the pathways in-

volved in the transmission of energy state information, and the neural structures involved with the integrative processing of this type of information (see Mogenson, 1976).

Specification of the physiological controls of food intake continues to be the goal of a great deal of research and theory. However, in recent years, investigators have come to recognize that eating is also subject to control by learning mechanisms. That is, meal initiation, termination, and food selection represent learned behaviors that can be understood in terms of the operation of the same learning principles that have been used to explain other types of behavior. The objectives of this chapter are to (a) describe the basic features of a learning analysis, (b) review how this analysis has been applied to the study of food intake and, (c) consider the implications of this approach for understanding disordered eating behavior in humans.

BASICS OF A LEARNING ANALYSIS

What Are the Stimuli?

A logical first step in a learning analysis of a given behavior is to specify the sensory events that the animal (human or infrahuman) learns about. This is not usually a problem in most laboratory experiments, because these events are typically selected by the experimenter. For example, the experimenter may program a discrete auditory or visual stimulus to occur shortly before the presentation of some biologically relevant event such as a morsel of food or a shock. In this case, the discrete stimuli, the biologically relevant cues, and their temporal arrangement are chosen according to the experimenter's wishes.

In contrast, a number of important stimuli that seem to be involved with normal food intake are not usually programmed by an experimenter. Hungry animals locate and consume food that gives rise to distinct postingestive consequences. Various researchers have proposed that in addition to responding to conventional types of stimuli, animals learn about interoceptive (e.g., hunger) stimuli that are present prior to and for some time after meal initiation, about the sensory aspects of food (e.g., its taste, texture, aroma, and visual features), and about interoceptive cues that are produced as a consequence of food intake (e.g., Capaldi, 1992; Davidson, 1993; Sclafani, 1990). Although it is possible to arrange conditions in which one or more of these sources of stimuli are brought under at least partial experimental control, normally the occurrence of these cues and their temporal relations to one another does not depend on experimental intervention.

What Types of Experiences Produce Learning?

The most fundamental thing that can be learned about a stimulus is that it exists (Rescorla, 1988). Assessment of this form of learning typically involves presenting a given stimulus at one time and then measuring behavior in the presence of that stimulus at another time. A commonly studied effect of exposure to a single stimulus is *habituation* (see Thompson, Donegan, & Lavond, 1988, for review). Habituation is exhibited when the capacity of a stimulus to evoke a behavioral reaction decreases with repeated exposures (Peeke & Petrinovich, 1984). This refractory-like effect does not appear to be a consequence of fatigue, as it is specific to the habituating stimulus. That is, response decrements equal to those occurring to the habituated stimulus are not observed for other stimuli that are also capable of evoking that same response (Whitlow, 1975). Furthermore, inserting a novel stimulus (e.g., a light) in the regular temporal interval following one presentation of a habituated stimulus (e.g., a tone) increases the strength of the response to the next presentation of the habituated cue. This finding argues against the idea that decreased responsiveness is the result of sensory adaptation (see Wagner, 1979; Whitlow, 1975).

Habituation has been observed in a wide variety of species and has been implicated in the function of a number of behavioral systems, including ingestion (see Peeke & Petrinovich, 1984; Thompson et al., 1988). For example, a basic fact of food intake is that the strength or vigor of ingestive behavior typically decreases over the course of a meal. Although this effect is usually attributed to changes in the postingestive consequences of intake, it has been proposed that at least part of the reduction in eating that leads to meal termination is based on habituation to oral stimuli that accompany the ingestion of food (see Swithers & Hall, 1994).

Experience provides the opportunity to learn about more than the existence of individual events. Animals must also learn about how events in their environment are related to other events. One procedure that seems to be quite effective at establishing relations among different stimuli is simple *Pavlovian conditioning* (Pavlov, 1927; see also Kehoe & Macrae this volume). Many readers will be familiar with the idea that in first-order Pavlovian conditioning, the presentation of a biologically relevant unconditioned stimulus (US) is preceded by the occurrence of a more biologically neutral event known as a conditioned stimulus (CS). The CS (e.g., a tone or light) acquires the ability to evoke conditioned responses (CRs) to the extent that it signals or predicts the delivery of the US (e.g., a shock or a morsel of food).

Associative relations can also be formed between two different neutral stimuli. For example, animals can learn that a light predicts the occurrence of a tone. Evidence for the establishment of this association is often absent during the course of training. Instead, learning is revealed when behavior in the presence of the light is modified by subsequently establishing the tone as a signal for a US (see Rescorla, 1984). A variation of this procedure establishes the tone as a signal for the US (i.e., first-order conditoning) prior to training the light as a signal for the tone (i.e., second-order conditioning). With this arrangement, the tone is treated like a surrogate US during the second-order conditioning phase of the experiment. Evidence for association formation is provided to the extent that the light comes to directly evoke conditioned responses as a consequence of its relationship to the tone (see Rescorla, 1984).

Recent analyses describe eating behavior as a Pavlovian conditioning phenomenon (e.g., Capaldi, 1992; Sclafani, 1990; Tordoff, 1991; Weingarten, 1983). When animals eat, associations form between the sensory properties of food (e.g., tastes, aromas, and visual features) and the postingestive consequences of eating. As a result of this learning, the occurrence of a food CS gains the capacity to evoke ingestive behavior. What is known as flavor-nutrient learning is an example of this type of conditioning. This form of conditioned responding may be revealed in nonhomeostatic food intake, or eating that occurs when food is presented in the absence of any obvious physiological need for food. It is also the case that associations can be formed between the sensory aspects of different foods. For example, in flavor-flavor conditioning, the flavor of one food can be associated with that of another food, thereby enabling manipulations that affect the preference for one flavor to also affect preference for the other.

Some types of Pavlovian conditioning involve learning relations among more than two stimuli.

For example, whether or not a CS will be followed by a US can be made dependent on the presentation of yet another cue. This is illustrated by a simple experiment in which a tone CS signals delivery of a US under one condition (e.g., when a light is on) but not under another (e.g., when the light is removed). Animals show that they are sensitive to this conditional relationship by exhibiting more conditioned behavior when the tone is presented in conjunction with the light than when the tone is presented by itself (e.g., Davidson & Rescorla, 1986; Rescorla, 1985).

It has also been suggested that cues involved with food intake are embedded in this type of conditional relationship. This suggestion is based on the assumption that the occurrence of a postingestive US depends on the conjoint presentation of both a food CS and interoceptive cues produced by the physiological need for food. That is, an appetitive postingestive US typically will not occur if the animal is hungry but there is no food or if there is food but the animal is not hungry. Both hunger cues and food cues need to be present for eating to be followed by positive postingestive consequences (e.g., Davidson, 1993; Gibson & Booth, 1989).

What Is Learned?

According to a number of contemporary views, learning about one event (e.g., habituation), learning simple relations between two events (e.g., simple Pavlovian conditioning), and learning conditional relations involving more than two events (e.g., conditioned modulation) all involve the operation of representational processes (e.g., Konorski, 1967; Rescorla, 1985; Wagner & Brandon, 1989). For example, it is now commonly assumed that once a stimulus is detected by a sensory apparatus, it becomes part of a memory system that enables important features of that stimulus to be mentally represented. This system is usually conceived of as a network of representational nodes or units. The knowledge structure of an animal (i.e., what it has learned) can be thus defined with respect to activation of events that are represented within this network.

From this perspective, the transient form of

habituation previously discussed is based on changes in the level of activation of the representation of the habituated stimulus. According to Wagner (e.g., 1979; Whitlow & Wagner, 1984), habituation occurs because the first presentation of a stimulus in an iterative series activates its memorial representation to a greater extent than do subsequent presentations.[1] When a stimulus is presented, it provokes an initial state of representational activity that, if strong enough, can result in the evocation of an unconditioned response. The weaker the level of this activation, the weaker the response-evoking capacity of the represented stimulus.

Pavlovian conditioning can be viewed as a procedure that establishes linkages between different memory nodes, such that the activation of one node (e.g., that representing the CS) will result in the activation of another (e.g., that representing the US). A given US representation can be activated by many different CS representations. In addition, different CS nodes can combine to form a single representation that is perceptually distinct from its consituent representations. This configural unit can then be linked to the representation of a US (e.g., Rescorla, 1973). Furthermore, there is no requirement that associative linkages involve US representations. Representations of two or more behaviorally neutral events can also be linked together. However, because such stimuli are weak elicitors of responding on their own, special testing techniques are usually needed to obtain evidence for such linkages (Rescorla, 1984).

Conditioned modulatory stimuli, unlike simple excitatory CSs or configural cues, do not appear to influence behavior based on the ability to directly activate a US representation (see Swartzentruber, 1995, for review). Although ideas have differed somewhat about just how modula-

tion takes place (e.g., Holland, 1991a; Rescorla, 1985; Wagner & Brandon, 1989), our own data (e.g., Davidson, Aparicio, & Rescorla, 1988; Davidson & Rescorla, 1986; Jarrard & Davidson, 1991), as well as data from other laboratories (Bouton & Swartzentruber, 1986; Holland, 1991b), favor the view that modulators influence conditioned responding by modulating the threshold for activation of the memorial representation of the US (see Rescorla, 1985). The presence of the modulator decreases the threshold for activation of the US, making it easier for the US memory to be evoked by presentation of its associated target. In the absence of the modulator, the memory of the US is below threshold for activation. Consequently, the target CS-US relation will be ineffective, and little conditioned responding should be observed.

As previously noted, habituation, simple Pavlovian conditioning, and conditioned modulation have each been postulated to occur as a consequence of ingestive behavior. Thus, considering what is learned as a consequence of these types of experiences may help elucidate basic processes involved in the control of eating.

THE LEARNED CONTROLS OF EATING

Habituation and Meal Termination

The palatability or hedonic quality of a food or drink decreases as it is consumed. This was demonstrated in humans by Cabanac (1971), who reported that the pleasantness ratings of sucrose solutions declined gradually as small amounts of the solutions were ingested over a short period of time. In rats, taste reactivity responses to the slow infusion of sucrose into the oral cavity change from highly appetitive (e.g., numerous

---

[1]The process underlying this difference in activation can be described as follows: After the physical stimulus is terminated, elements of its memorial representation begin to decay, first entering an intermediate state before becoming inactive. Whitlow and Wagner (1984) proposed that elements in this intermediate state cannot be restored directly to the state activated by presentation of the stimulus. Therefore, if a stimulus is presented while elements of its representation reside in the refractory-like intermediate state, these elements will be unavailable for activation by the subsequent presentation of the stimulus. The response weakens with repeated presentations of the habituating stimulus because fewer elements of that cue are returned to the representational state that evokes the unconditioned response.

tongue profusions and licks) to neutral (e.g., allowing the infusate to passively drip out of the mouth) or aversive (e.g., headshakes and gapes) during the course of continuous infusion (see Grill & Berridge, 1985).

To account for his findings, Cabanac (1971) proposed that the sensory qualities of food become less pleasant as physiological need for food is decreased, and he referred to this relationship as "negative alliesthesia." However, it is now clear that this type of declining responsiveness to food stimuli is not solely a function of decreasing need for food. Rather, experience with the sensory aspects of food can contribute to meal termination independent of any reduction of physiological need that is produced by that experience (e.g., LeMagnen 1956). This point has been confirmed in rats and humans (LeMagnen, 1956; Mook, 1990; Rolls, 1990). For example, hungry rats will eat a substantial meal of laboratory chow before they voluntarily stop feeding. If the rats are offered the same laboratory chow a short time later, they either eat little more or refrain from eating. However, if they are offered a glucose solution, they ingest a second meal that can be calorically equal to or greater than the first. This is not simply a consequence of the greater palatability of the glucose solution relative to the lab chow. If glucose solution is consumed during the first meal, lab chow is eaten and glucose solution is ignored during the second meal. Thus, rats do not become satiated for calories per se but become less responsive to some specific quality of the food consumed first. This quality does not appear to be related to the nutritional composition of the two foods. Rats that will consume no more sucrose solution will nonetheless ingest a large meal of powdered sucrose. These data suggest that rats can become satiated for specific tastes, textures, odors, or other sensory properties of food (e.g., see Mook, 1990, for review).

This type of "sensory-specific satiety" (LeMagnen, 1956) has also been observed in studies of human eating. In the first of a series of experiments by Rolls and her associates (see Rolls, 1990, for review), subjects were asked to taste and provide preference ratings for several foods

(e.g., potato chips, yogurt, bananas, cheese and crackers). Next, the subjects were given a meal of one of these foods which they ate to apparent satiation. Finally, they rated all the foods again. The pleasantness ratings of the food they ate in the meal decreased significantly more than the ratings of the other foods. Another manipulation involved giving the subjects a surprise second meal shortly after they had completed the first meal. If the food given in the first and second meals were the same, intake during the second meal dropped sharply. If the foods given during each meal were different, intake during the first and second meals was about the same (Rolls, 1990; Rolls, Rolls, Rowe, & Sweeney, 1981). Thus, eating a given food did not reduce either intake or the perceived pleasantness of other foods. Rather, the reduction in amount eaten and pleasantness was apparently specific to the food that was eaten.

This form of satiety is apparently based on the sensory aspects rather than on only the caloric or nutritive content of the eaten food. In one experiment, pleasantness ratings were measured for foods with different caloric contents but similar sensory qualities (Rolls, Laster, & Summerfelt, 1989). Subjects ate as much of either the high- or low-calorie version of the food as they wanted during a test meal. The decrease in pleasantness ratings that occurred after this meal were not affected by the number of calories consumed. Moreover, varying the sensory properties of foods appears to increase intake even when the foods' nutritive composition and caloric content are held constant (Rolls & Hetherington, 1989). For example, giving subjects successive courses of three distinctively flavored cream cheese sandwiches enhanced intake relative to when subjects were given only their favorite flavor (also see Treit, Spetch, & Deutsch, 1982). This effect of varying the sensory features of food is not limited to flavor. Giving subjects successive courses of three different shapes of pasta also promoted intake compared to a condition in which only the subject's favorite shape of pasta was available (Rolls, Rowe, & Rolls, 1982). Thus, variations in the appearance or texture of food can also influence intake.

These findings with humans and other animals make it clear that repeated experience with the sensory qualities of food reduces behavioral responsivity (in the form of pleasantness ratings or intake) to those qualities. Furthermore, little decrement is typically observed in responding to the sensory properties of foods that have not been experienced recently. Because these features of sensory-specific satiety are also defining characteristics of habituation, some have suggested that sensory-specific satiety is a form of habituation that is based on experience with food (e.g., Booth, 1990; Swithers & Hall, 1994).

Habituation of ingestive behavior based on oral experience has recently been the subject of direct experimental investigation. In most studies of eating, including those examining specific satieties, the duration of and interval between exposures to food stimuli are largely determined by the subject. In contrast, demonstrations of habituation with conventional cues typically bring the duration and temporal pattern of stimulus presentation under explicit experimental control. Swithers and her associates (see Swithers & Hall, 1994, for review) attempted to employ this type of explicit control in their studies of the role of habituation in the control of food intake. This was accomplished by providing young rats with brief intraoral infusions of small amounts of sweet solutions through indwelling cannula. This technique, which modifies procedures developed previously to assess taste reactivity (Grill & Norgren, 1978), allows experimenters to program the initiation, duration, temporal pattern, and volume of infusate delivery. The effects of different types and patterns of oral experience can then be assessed by recording changes in mouthing movements (i.e., jaw or tongue movement) evoked in response to oral stimulation. In other words, each infusion provided an oral experience with a diet and also served as a test of responsivity to that experience.

The changes in mouthing movements that occurred with repeated oral infusions closely resembled the behavioral changes produced by repeated stimulation in other response systems. Most notably, oral responsivity declines with repeated oral stimulation. This response decrement was observed for noncaloric diets, for diets with nutritive contents that could not be absorbed by young rats, and with volumes of infusate that produced minimal levels of gastric fill. In addition, the decrement in oral responding could be observed for as long as 3 hours after the last of a series of repeated stimulations. Furthermore, the decline in oral responsiveness was diet specific. Changing the taste of the infusate could reinstate mouthing activity to levels at or near those observed prior to the beginning of oral stimulation. It is difficult to attribute these findings to the postingestive consequences of the infusions. Interpretations in terms of fatigue or sensory adaptation also seem implausible. Rather, the results suggest the operation of a habituation process much like that observed for other behavioral systems. Swithers-Mulvey and Hall (1992) also reported that habituation to repeated, brief oral infusions suppressed normal ingestion (from a cup on the floor of the test apparatus) of the infused substance even when compared to a control condition that received the same number and volume of infusions intragastrically rather than intraorally. These results provide additional support for the idea that habituation to oral sensations contributes to normal meal termination.

Eating Behaviors as Pavlovian Conditioned Responses

Whereas habituation to oral stimulation may contribute to meal termination, typically, other types of experiences have been implicated in the initiation of eating and the development of food preferences. Many, if not most, of these experiences can be viewed as examples of simple Pavlovian conditioning. This section briefly overviews the role of Pavlovian conditioning mechanisms in the formation of learned food preferences. An extensive review of this topic has been provided recently by Capaldi (1992).

Conditioned Food Preferences

One way for a particular flavor or taste to become liked is to associate it with another flavor that is already liked. Conversely, a flavor that is liked will be liked less to the extent that is is associated with another flavor or taste that is disliked. A form of Pavlovian conditioning that could produce such likes and dislikes is *flavor-flavor learning* (e.g., see Capaldi, 1992). Several researchers have shown that ingestive behavior evoked by relatively neutral flavors (i.e., those that normally elicit neither strong ingestion nor avoidance) may be modified by this type of conditioning, For example, Holman (1975) combined cinnamon flavor with a highly preferred saccharin solution and wintergreen flavor with a less preferred saccharin solution. Rats trained with those solutions showed increased preference for cinnamon over wintergreen even when both flavors were presented without saccahrin during testing. Because saccharin contains no calories, preference for cinnamon must have been based on association with saccharin's sweet taste rather than its caloric consequences. Furthermore, presenting a neutral flavor in solution with quinine (a bitter substance that is normally rejected by rats and humans) reduces the preference shown by rats for that flavor (Fanselow & Birk, 1982). In addition, Breslin, Davidson, and Grill (1990) showed that taste reactivity responses to dilute solutions of either quinine or hydrochloric acid could be changed from aversion to acceptance by establishing oral infusion of these normally rejected tastes as signals for the oral infusion of sucrose solution. Because these rats were not food deprived during training, it is unlikely that this shift in preference was based on a reduction in the physiological need for food.

Animals can also learn to associate the sensory properties of food with postingestive consequences. An animal that suffers intragastric malaise after eating a food will avoid consuming that food after it has recovered from the illness. This is known as a conditioned taste aversion (see Domjan, 1980, for review). However, food preferences also result when flavors are associated with the positive postingestive aftereffects of consuming highly caloric or nutritious foods. This is known as "flavor-nutrient learning" (see Capaldi, 1992).

Preliminary evidence for flavor-nutrient learning was provided by Booth (1972). In one series of experiments, Booth fed rats two different flavored meals that also differed in caloric content. After several exposures to each flavor/calorie combination, the rats were given a choice test between the two flavors. During testing, each flavor was presented in a diet that was equated for calories at a density midway between the two training diets. The rats preferred the flavor that had been previously combined with the high-calorie diet (Booth & Davis, 1973). Of course, it is possible that diets containing different amounts of calories give rise to distinctive orosensory stimuli. If so, the conditioned preference shown by Booth's rats could have been based on flavor-flavor learning. In other words, maybe the rats learned to prefer the flavor that was associated not with the postingestive aftereffects of the high-calorie diet but with flavor of that diet.

Subsequent research confirmed that flavor-nutrient learning occurs independently of flavor-flavor learning. As pointed out elsewhere (e.g., Capaldi, 1992; Tordoff, 1991), flavor stimulation that accompanies intake is confined mainly to the time when the ingested flavor is in contact with sensory receptors in the mouth, nose, and throat. In contrast, the caloric or nutritive consequences of ingestion are presumed to persist long after the flavor stimulation has dissipated. Therefore, associating a flavor with caloric or nutritive postingestive consequences (flavor-nutrient learning) should occur over longer delays than would support the formation of associations between two different flavors (flavor-flavor learning). Consistent with this hypothesis, Capaldi, Campbell, Sheffer, and Bradford (1987) showed that flavor preference learning over a delay is an increasing function of the caloric content of a distinctively flavored consequent solution and does not occur at all if the consequent solution contains no calories (also see Holman, 1975; Lavin, 1976).

Additional evidence for flavor-nutrient learning was provided by Sclafani, and his co-workers (see Sclafani 1990, for review). These researchers developed an intragastric infusion preparation that allows flavors and their nutritive postingestive consequences to be dissociated during voluntary feeding in nondeprived rats. The rats were given two different flavors of water, one each on alternate days. As they drank one flavor, a nutrient solution (carbohydrate or fat) was automatically infused into the stomach (approximately 1.3 ml of solution was infused for each 1 ml that was consumed orally). Plain water was infused into the stomach as the rats drank the other flavor. After several of these training trials, the rats were given access to both flavors simultaneously. They showed an overwhelming preference for the flavor that was followed by intragastric infusion of nutrients. They also preferred this flavor to water, indicating that they had acquired a preference for the flavor paired with nutrients rather than only an aversion for the flavor that was paired with plain water infusions. Thus, conditioned flavor preference is observed even if the delivery of the consequent solution completely bypasses the oral cavity. This provides strong evidence that positive post-ingestive consequences of eating produce a US that is capable of supporting learning about the sensory features of food.

Flavor preferences have also been conditioned in humans (e.g., Booth, Mather, & Fuller, 1982; Zellner, Rozin, Aron, & Kulish, 1983). One study (Birch, McPhee, Steinberg, & Sullivan, 1990) presented young children (under age 5) with two novel flavors mixed in solutions of different caloric densities. By the end of eight training trials with each flavor, the children gave increased preference ratings (relative to a pretest) to the flavor presented with the high-calorie solution, whereas no change in ratings occurred for the flavor presented in the low-calorie solution. Birch et al. (1990) related these results to earlier findings (e.g., Birch & Marlin, 1982) that "mere exposure" could reduce the tendency of children to reject or avoid novel foods (i.e., neophobia). They suggested that an association of a novel flavor with the positive post-ingestive consequences of calories is formed with repeated exposures to the flavor. Development of this association contributes to a reduction in neophobia by promoting intake. A similar mechanism may account for the increased liking

for piquant flavors with repeated exposure (Stevenson & Yeomans, 1995).

Another basis for the establishment of conditioned food preferences involves the social transmission of information about food. For example, Birch (1980) reported that preschool children prefer foods that are chosen by their peers or have been approved by their teacher or other significant adult (Birch, Zimmerman, & Hind, 1980). The development of preferences for piquant foods, such as chili peppers, also seems to be strongly influenced by observing older siblings or parents consume this type of food (see Rozin, 1990).

Social factors also appear to influence the development of food preferences in rats. Galef (see 1988 for review) produced strong food preferences in "observer" rats by exposing them to a "demonstrator" rat that had already consumed the novel target food. For example, following eight 30-minute exposures to two equipalatable diets, observer rats preferred the diet that was fed previously to a demonstrator (Galef, 1989). Such preferences can persist for more than a month after exposure to a demonstrator. Furthermore, simple exposure to a target diet, without exposure to a demonstrator that had eaten the diet, fails to enhance preference. Lasting preference, even for a mildly aversive diet (one flavored with cayenne pepper), can also be produced by exposing rats to demonstrators that had eaten the diet. Moreover, there is evidence that if a demonstrator rat eats more of one flavored food than of another, observer rats will also eat the two foods in the same relative quantities (Galef & Whiskin, 1995).

Preferences of this type have been attributed to a Pavlovian process known as *evaluative conditioning* (Martin & Levey, 1978; Rozin, 1990). According to this view, the evaluation of one event (e.g., a flavor) can be made more positive by associating it with another event that is already positively evaluated. With respect to food preferences, a novel food or flavor is viewed as a CS that is paired with a US in the form of a positive social event. In children, the CS may become more attractive by virtue of being associated with the approval of peers or respected adults. In rats, preference for a flavor CS may increase by being associated with olfactory cues on the breath of demonstrator rats (Galef, Mason, Preti, & Bean, 1988).

Conditioned Meal Initiation

Traditionally, the initiation of eating and behavior instrumental to obtaining food has been attributed to the activation of physiological mechanisms concomitant with departure from energy homeostasis. However, recent views recognize that learning can also contribute to the control of these behavioral functions. Although most of these views assume that physiological and learned factors interact to control eating behavior (e.g., Bindra, 1978; Toates, 1981, 1994), some favor learning as the primary, if not the preeminent, mechanism. For example, Woods and Strubbe (1994) proposed that learning about environmental and temporal cues allows eating behavior to occur in anticipation rather than as a consequence of departure from energy homeostasis.

The phenomenon of "resistance to satiation" provided some initial evidence for conditioned eating (see Morgan, 1974, for a review). Following food-rewarded training when hungry, rats and other animals will continue to eat and make food-rewarded responses when they are tested after food satiation. Capaldi and Myers (1978) showed that the continuation of responding during satiated testing is under strong stimulus control. For example, they trained rats to eat food pellets when hungry in one context (i.e., a straight alley runway) before satiating them with pellets in another context (i.e., the homecage) to the point where eating no longer occurred. However, pellet eating resumed as soon as the rats were returned to the original training context. These findings indicated that stimuli conditioned to elicit eating behavior when the rats were hungry continued to elicit eating when the rats were food sated. Later, Weingarten (1983) reached this same conclusion in a study that employed discrete cues (tone and light) rather than contexts as conditioned stimuli.

Conditioned meal initiations have also been demonstrated in humans (Birch, McPhee, Sullivan, & Johnson, 1989). Hungry children who were approximately 3 to 4 years of age ate snacks in the presence of one set of cues (CS+) but not in the presence of a different set (CS−). Following 10 pairs of these training trials, the children were given the opportunity to eat to satiety, and then food intake was measured during separate presentations of CS+ and CS−. During satiated testing, differences were small when relatively discrete cues served as CS+ and CS−. However, CS+ appeared to evoke much more eating than CS− when different contexts (i.e., rooms in different locations) were employed as discriminative stimuli.

The learned control of eating behavior was demonstrated more dramatically by Capaldi, Davidson, and Myers (1981). In one experiment, a group (group P) of food-deprived rats were allowed to eat small amounts of food pellets in the homecage. These rats were then trained on a discrimination problem while food sated. In this problem, food pellets like those the rats were given in the homecage, were placed in the goal cup of one runway (a black or white alley), whereas no pellets were placed in the goal cup of another runway. A control group (group A) was treated the same as group P except that it did not receive food pellets in the homecage.

Only group P learned to run faster in the alley that contained the pellets than in the alley that did not. Indeed, the speed of running in the alley with the pellets increased markedly with training for group P but not for group A. Thus, the rats in group P, but not those in group A, learned the discrimination while satiated. Furthermore, all the rats in group P consumed the pellets in the goal cup. Only 2 of 10 rats in group A ate any pellets in the alley. The performance of group A indicated that the food pellets were not inherently rewarding under satiation. The performance of group P indicated that for the pellets to be rewarding they had to be consumed when the rats were food deprived. Additional controls showed that consuming the pellets in the homecage as part of ad lib feeding is not sufficient to enable the pellets to reinforce discriminative responding when rats are food satiated. The pellets must be consumed when the rat is hungry if they are to promote eating and behavior leading to food when the rat is satiated.

This pattern of results is readily interpreted within a Pavlovian conditioning framework. Eating food when hungry enables the sensory features of the food to be associated with positive postingestive US. Conditioned eating behavior emerges as this association is formed. This is flavor-nutrient learning (Capaldi, 1992), which can be seen as a basic type of Pavlovian first-order conditioning. Once flavor-nutrient conditioning occurs, other stimuli, such as exteroceptive context or discrete cues, can be associated with the flavor stimulus and thereby elicit conditioned eating even if the flavor is no longer followed by a positive postingestive US. This represents Pavlovian second-order conditioning. In other words, it appears that eating food when hungry establishes the sensory properties of food as a CS for a postingestive US. Other cues (e.g., contextual stimuli, discrete cues) acquire the ability to evoke second-order conditioned eating and food approach responses to the extent that they signal the occurrence of a food (e.g., flavor) CS that previously predicted the occurrence of a postingestive US.

Learning About Interoceptive Cues

Based on the preceding discussion, there seems to be little doubt that Pavlovian conditioning makes an important contribution to the control of food intake. Part of that control is based on associations between the sensory properties of food (i.e., food cues) and the postingestive aftereffects of eating. In addition, eating behavior is influenced by associations among different food cues and among food cues and other types of exteroceptive stimuli. This section explores the possibility that the influence of interoceptive signals of energy need (i.e., hunger cues) on eating behavior is also based, at least in part, on learning mechanisms.

The idea that interoceptive sensory stimuli are produced as a consequence of departure from energy homeostasis is central to many theories of the physiological control of food intake (see Friedman, 1990, for review). Accordingly, a great deal of research has been and continues to be directed at identifying the physiological origins of these "hunger" cues. For example, Cannon's (see Carlson, 1916) early claim that hunger is a sensation originating in the stomach was followed by more recent suggestions that changes in metabolic (e.g., Tordoff, Rawson, & Friedman, 1991) or neuropeptide activity (e.g., Leibowitz, 1992) or in the availability and/or utilization of glucose (e.g., Campfield & Smith, 1990; Louis-Sylvestre & Le-Magnen, 1980) or lipids (e.g., Langhans & Scharrer, 1987; Ritter & Taylor, 1989) contributed to the production of signals of energy need.

Although most physiological theories assume that hunger cues promote eating behavior, the mechanisms that actually link physiological change to behavioral change are not usually specified. However, like exteroceptive food cues, the influence of interoceptive hunger stimuli on eating may depend on learning. It has been shown that animals can learn about signals arising from their state of energy need when these cues are explicitly programmed as discriminative stimuli (e.g., Capaldi, Viveros, & Davidson, 1981). A common tactic is to train rats under conditions where response A (e.g., turn left in a maze or press left manipulandum) leads to food only when the animal is highly food deprived and response B (e.g., turn right in a maze or press right manipulandum) leads to food only when the animal is under a lower level of food deprivation (Corwin, Woolverton, & Schuster, 1990; Jenkins & Hanratty, 1949; Schuh, Schaal, Thompson, Cleary, Billington, & Levine, 1994). However, we have shown that rats can learn to use cues produced by different degrees of food deprivation as discriminative signals for the presence or absence of electric shock (Davidson, 1987; Davidson & Carretta, 1993; Davidson, Flynn, & Jarrard, 1992). This assures that behavior is controlled by deprivation state and not by some extraneous factor associated with the food or ingestion (e.g., food palatability or incentive motivation). Moreover, we have shown that discriminative control of conditioned freezing by food deprivation intensity stimuli generalizes to cues produced by physiological manipulations, such as adminstration of insulin, glucose antimetabolites, nutritive stomach loads, or cholecystokinin, all of which are known to either promote or reduce food intake (Benoit & David-son, 1996; Davidson, 1987; Davidson & Carretta, 1993; Davidson, Flynn, & Grill, 1988). These data indicate that interoceptive deprivation cues rather than external cues arising from the deprivation regimen control behavior in our situation.

Findings that rats can learn about their hunger cues in experimental situations encourage the idea that what animals learn about their hunger cues may be an important determinant of their eating behavior in general. Questions about the nature of this learning and about the conditions that produce it have been addressed within three distinct conceptual frameworks:

1. *Stimulus-response (S-R) theory.* A number of early theorists, (e.g., Estes, 1958; Guthrie, 1935; Hull, 1943) proposed that internal "hunger" stimuli are directly associated with feeding and responses that are successful in obtaining food. This S-R association is formed because the hunger cues are present when feeding and food-gathering responses are reinforced by the positive consequences of ingestion. As a result of association formation, these internal stimuli acquire the capacity to directly elicit feeding behavior.

2. *Configural learning.* According to Booth and his collaborators (Booth, 1992; Gibson & Booth, 1989), the occurrence of an appetitive postingestive US is predicted by the joint occurrence of internal hunger stimuli and "dietary" cues related to the sensory aspects of food. The combination of hunger and food stimuli give rise to a unique configural stimulus with perceptual features that are different from either of its constituent elements. This configural stimulus acts as a Pavlovian CS in that its capacity to elicit eating responses depends on the strength of its direct association with the postingestive US.

3. *Conditioned modulation.* Recently, we proposed an alternative to the idea that hunger cues enter into the learned control of eating through their involvement in simple direct associations with either food USs or food-reinforced responses (Davidson, 1993; Davidson & Benoit, 1996). From our perspective, ani-mals use their interoceptive hunger cues to solve the problem of whether to eat or refrain from eating. This problem takes the general form of B→A+, B–, A–, where A represents food cues, B represents hunger cues, and + represents an appetitive postingestive US. With this arrangement, hunger cues signal that food cues will be followed by an appetitive postingestive US (B→A+). Neither food cues in the absence of hunger cues (A–) nor hunger cues in the absence of food cues (B–) are followed by that US.

Consistent with analyses of what is learned when conventional auditory and/or visual stimuli are embedded in B–A+, B–, A– or related (e.g., B–A+, A–) arrangements (see Swartzentruber, 1995, for review), we proposed that hunger cues "modulate" the capacity of food cues to elicit conditioned eating responses. The hunger cues accomplish this by lowering the threshold for activation of the memorial representation of the postingestive US (e.g., Davidson & Rescorla, 1986; Rescorla, 1985; Swartzentruber & Rescorla, 1994). In other words, interoceptive hunger cues increase the likelihood that an animal will remember the postingestive US when it encounters food or a cue related to food. This would in turn increase the capacity of food and food-related cues to elicit feeding responses. In the absence of hunger signals, the threshold for activation of the US representation may be too high to be activated by the presence of food-related stimuli with which it is associated. If so, little or no eating behavior would occur. According to this framework, food deprivation cues have little capacity to directly elicit feeding behavior. Although deprivation cues make it easier for food cues to retrieve memories of the positive postingestive consequences of food intake, deprivation stimuli have little ability to activate those memories on their own.

Choosing Among These Interpretations

Some findings that pose problems for the S-R and the configural learning views appear to be interpretable within the conditioned modulation framework. Holland and Rescorla (1975) gave food-deprived rats Pavlovian first-order (e.g., tone-food) followed by second-order (e.g., light-tone) conditioning, Next, they assessed the effects of satiation on the capacity of first- and second-order stimuli to evoke conditioned responses. They reported that compared to controls that remained food deprived, satiated rats showed dramatic reductions in first-order conditioned responding but virtually no decrement in second-order conditioned responding. Based on S-R theory, hunger cues should have been associated with both first- and second-order conditioned responses during training when the rats were food deprived. Thus, removing hunger cues by food sating the rats should have disrupted both first- and second-order performance.

In addition, consider again the results of Capaldi, Davidson, & Myers (1981). In phase 1, rats that ate pellets in the homecage when food deprived learned a new response in phase 2 to obtain those pellets when they were food satiated. Recall that phase 1 training would promote first-order (food-postingestive US) conditioning, whereas phase 2 training would promote Pavlovian second-order (alley-food) learning. With respect to Booth's configural learning account, in phase 1, hunger cues would combine with food cues to produce a unique configural stimulus that was directly associated with the postingestive US. Yet, because the rats received alley training while food sated in phase 2, the configural cue emerging from the combination of hunger and food pellets would not be present to reinforce learning about alley stimuli. Thus, it is not clear how a configural view would account for Capaldi et al.'s findings.

The conditioned modulation view seems to account for the results of both of these studies. Hunger cues are presumed to modulate eating

behavior by signaling when food cues are followed by a positive postingestive US. In first-order conditioning, hunger cues accomplish this by lowering the threshold for activation of the US representation, thereby making it easier for conditioned food cues to activate that representation. However, hunger cues are not usually informative about when second-order conditioned stimuli (e.g., tones, alley cues) are followed by food cues. Thus, the capacity of second-order CSs to evoke conditioned responses would not depend on the presence of hunger cues. Therefore, removing hunger cues would have a much greater disruptive effect on first-order than on second-order conditioned responding.

The S-R, configural learning, and conditioned modulation hypotheses were directly compared in a recent experiment conducted in our laboratory (Davidson & Benoit, 1996). In this experiment, we trained rats to use food-deprivation cues as discriminative signals for a mild shock, and then we used various transfer tests to assess what the rats learned during this training.

The design of our discriminaton problem took the general form B→A+, B−, A−, described earlier. The arrangement of stimuli in our design, the arrangement used to study conditioned modulation with conventional cues (e.g., Davidson & Rescorla, 1986), and the arrangement of cues that we postulate to underlie eating behavior are depicted in Table 25–1. As shown in the table, although the identity of the relevant stimuli differs across situations, the set of stimulus-event relations that produce learning is fundamentally the same.

In our experiment, rats were trained in a distinctive context (context A) under conditions in which their level of food deprivation at the time

Table 25–1. Comparsion of Hypothetical Stimulus-Event Relations in Three Settings

GENERAL FORM	B→A+	B−	A−
Conventional Cues	Light→Tone +[a]	Light-	Tone-
Normal Eating	Hunger→Food+[a]	Hunger−	Food−
Deprivation Discrimination	Hunger→Context+[b]	Hunger−	Context−

[a]Appetitive US.
[b]Aversive US.

of training alternated between 0-hour (free access to food for the preceding 24 hours) and 24-hour (no food for the preceding 24 hours) food deprivation. One group (group 24+) was shocked following 24-hour but not 0-hour food deprivation. Another group (group 24–) received the opposite deprivation level-shock contingency. A control group (+/–) received shock in a manner uncorrelated with level of food deprivation. Incidence of conditioned freezing (i.e., skeletal muscle immobility) during the first 2 minutes of each 4-minute session served as the index of learning.

Figure 25–1 shows that by the end of training, groups 24+ and 24– froze more under their shocked than under their nonshocked level of food deprivation. Group +/– showed nondifferential freezing under each deprivation level. Thus, each group appeared to be appropriately sensitive to its particular deprivation level-shock contingency. Figure 25–2 compares the freezing behavior of each group on the last block of training under 24-hour food deprivation and during subsequent transfer testing. The leftmost panel of

Figure 25–2 shows that during the last block of training, 24-hour food deprivation produced less freezing for group 24– than for group 24+, whereas the level of freezing for group +/– did not differ from Group 24+. Next, control of conditioned freezing by 24-hour food-deprivation stimuli was assessed in a novel transfer context (context B) that had not been associated previously with shock. Figure 25–2 (center-left panel) shows that despite the existence of group differences and relatively high levels of freezing at the end of training, almost no freezing was observed for any group in novel context B. This indicated that hunger cues did not control freezing in context A, based solely on their direct association with the shock US.

The rats were then trained in another novel context (context C) when they were 19-hour water deprived but not food deprived. The purpose of this procedure was to associate context C with the shock US in the presence of interoceptive states signals different from those existing under the 0- and 24-hour food-deprivation con-

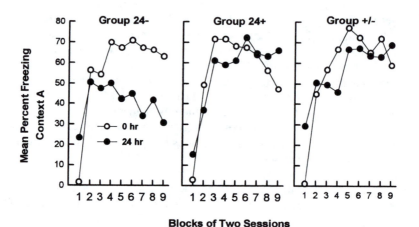

Blocks of Two Sessions

Figure 25–1. Mean percent freezing in context A. The closed circles represent data for sessions after 24-hour food deprivation. Open circles show data for sessions after 0-hour food deprivation. The far left panel shows results for group 24–, which received a brief foot shock after 0– but not 24-hour food deprivation. The middle panel shows data for group 24+, which received the reverse contingency between shock and food deprivation. The far right panel shows data for Group +/–, which received foot shocks uncorrelated with either level of food deprivation.

ditions employed during original training. After all groups exhibited a comparable, high level of conditioned freezing as a result of training in context C (center-right panel in Figure 25–2), freezing in context C was tested after the rats were returned to 24-hour food deprivation.

The rightmost panel of Figure 25–2 shows that freezing during this test varied with the deprivation cue-shock contingencies that had been established during original training in context A. Food deprivation promoted freezing for group 24+ relative to the uncorrelated control and inhibited freezing for group 24– relative to that control. This outcome indicated that freezing behavior was not based on the formation of a direct association involving the shock US and a "configural" CS that could have emerged from the compound of deprivation and exteroceptive contextual stimuli. Because food deprivation cues never occurred in context C when shock was delivered, the rats had no opportunity to learn such a configural association. Instead, the finding that 24-hour food-deprivation cues controlled freezing in context C supports the idea that these signals served to modulate the activation of the memorial representation of the shock US. For group 24+, hunger cues lowered the threshold for activation of the US representation, thereby enhancing the capacity of stimuli associated with that US (contexts A and C) to elicit conditioned freezing. For group 24–, 24-hour food deprivation signaled that shock would not be delivered. For this group, hunger cues may have increased the threshold for activation of the US representation, thereby making it more difficult for that representation to be activated by contextual stimuli. Overall, the results of this experiment were inconsistent with the views that behavioral control by hunger stimuli was based on either S-R or configural learning. Instead, our findings provided evidence that food-deprivation cues can in principle serve as conditioned modulatory stimuli.

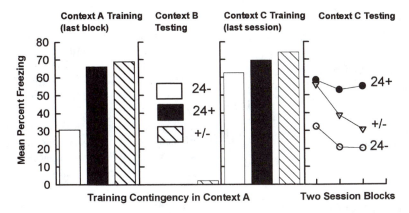

Figure 25–2. Mean percent freezing under 24-hour food deprivation in contexts A, B, and C. Open bars and circles show freezing data for group 24–, which received foot shock after 0– but not 24-hour food deprivation in context A. Filled bars and circles show data from group 24+, which received the reverse contingency between shock and food deprivation in context A. Striped bars and triangles show data for group +/–, which received uncorrelated pairings of deprivation and shock in context A. The far left panel shows data for all groups during the last session of training in context A. The left-middle panel shows data for all groups during context B testing. The right-middle panel shows data for all groups at the end of context C shock training under 19-hour water deprivation. The far right panel shows two-session blocks of transfer testing under 24-hour food deprivation for all groups.

Summary

The picture that emerges from this analysis integrates the sensory properties of food, the postingestive aftereffects of food intake, and internal signals of energy need in the learned control of eating behavior. In this picture, traditional distinctions between homeostatic and nonhomeostatic controls of intake are blurred. Eating in response to exteroceptive cues and eating that is stimulated by metabolic depletion are both viewed as crucially dependent on learning mechanisms.

LEARNING AND DISORDERED EATING

If normal eating behavior depends on the integration of learning about food cues, postingestive USs, and modulatory hunger stimuli, it makes sense to consider the possibility that disordered patterns of eating involve changes in conditions that produce learning and in what is learned about these stimuli. Although several important syndromes of maladaptive eating have been identified, we will focus our—admittedly speculative—discussion on anorexia nervosa (AN). The defining behavioral feature of this disorder is severe, self-imposed, restriction of food intake that continues in the face of strong medical contraindications (e.g., Strober, 1986). This disorder is of particular interest not only because of its pernicious symptoms but also because it has been especially resistant to experimental and theoretical analysis.

Variations in the Conditions That Produce Learning

As mentioned previously, a highly effective way to reduce subsequent intake of a particular food is to follow ingestion of that food with gastric illness (see Domjan, 1980). If the sensory properties of a food are followed by aversive rather than by pleasing postingestive consequences, reduction in the intake of that food will likely ensue. This phenomenon is known as conditioned taste aversion (CTA), which has been implicated in cancer cachexia (Bernstein & Borson, 1986), tumor anorexia (e.g., Bernstein & Meachum, 1990), and anorexias resulting from dietary deficiencies (Cannon, Crawford, & Carrell, 1988; Rozin & Rodgers, 1967). However, a basic problem with using CTA as a model for AN, is that CTA is usually confined to the specific food that is associated with illness, whereas in AN almost all foods are rejected. For CTA to be a viable model of AN, some mechanism is needed to describe how the representation of an aversive postingestive US can be activated by food in general.

It may be that for AN, ingestion of food, any food, is what evokes the production of an aversive postingestive US. Marrazzi and Luby (1986) hypothesized that severe dieting produces an endogenous opiate-based high that serves to reinforce continued starvation. Given evidence that tolerance builds up to the analgesic effects of repeated exposures to 24-hour food deprivation (Davidson, McKenzie, Tujo, & Bish, 1992), it is possible that this reinforcing high also grows weaker at a given level of caloric restriction. This could influence eating behavior in at least two ways. First, the buildup of tolerance at lower levels of dietary restriction might provoke more severe dietary restrictions aimed at reinstating the original opioid aftereffects. Second, if refraining from eating results in tolerance to endogenous opiates, eating may provoke unpleasant or aversive withdrawal effects. This aversive US would presumably occur as a general consequence of food intake, with the magnitude of the aversive afteraffect dependent on the food's caloric content. Thus, not eating would be negatively reinforced by avoiding the experience of an aversive postingestive US.

Variations in What Is Learned

Eating behavior involves not only overt behavioral responses but also various physiological reactions that occur in anticipation of food. For example, food and cues associated with food can be conditioned to evoke cephalic phase responses (e.g., Powley & Berthoud, 1985), which include salivation, insulin release, and increased gastric motility. These responses are presumed to prepare the animal for incoming food by priming the physiological mechanisms involved with the transport, digestion, and storage of metabolic fuels.

A model formulated by Jansen (1994), although saying little about the conditions that precipitate AN, has implications for how AN might be perpetuated. The capacity of food cues to elicit cephalic phase and other anticipatory responses is presumably based on the association of food cues with the representation of the postingestive US. It follows that one way to extinguish the performance of such anticipatory CRs would be to present food cues without the occurrence of the postingestive US. Anorexia nervosa may involve this type of extinction treatment.

People with AN characteristically obsess about food without eating it (Cooper & Fairburn, 1984). It may be that this form of cognitive exposure to food cues in the absence of food intake is necessary to extinguish cephalic phase responses. Consistent with this idea are reports that AN patients have weaker cephalic phase responses to food cues than patients who do not severely restrict their food intake (LeBoff, Leichner, & Spigelman, 1988; but see Broberg & Bernstein, 1989). The extinction of cephalic phase responses would reduce the ability of people with AN to prepare physiologically for the arrival of food. Woods (1991) argued that the ingestion of food in the absence of these preparatory responses has highly unpleasant postingestive aftereffects. Thus, once preparatory responses are extinguished in people afflicted with AN, food cues could become associated with an aversive US. This association would then contribute to the reduction of food intake.

Finally, people with AN do not eat despite self-reports of undiminished hunger (e.g., Blundell & Coscina, 1992; Garfinkel & Garner, 1982). Thus, AN seems to involve an abnormal response to hunger cues. Benoit (unpublished manuscript) points out that hunger cues can be established as signals for the occurrence of aversive as well as appetitive USs. This is confirmed by findings that 24-hour food-deprivation cues can be trained as signals for when exteroceptive cues will be followed by shock (e.g., Davidson, 1987; Davidson & Benoit, 1996). Benoit suggested that hunger cues may also modulate the capacity of exteroceptive food cues to activate the representations of other types of aversive USs. For example, hunger may come to signal that food will be followed by consequences such as guilt, obesity ideation, or social disapproval. If these consequences are less likely when food occurs without hunger or when hunger occurs without food, hunger cues should come to modulate the activation of these aversive US representations. Eating behavior would be disrupted to the extent that hunger cues come to make it easier for food cues to evoke memories of aversive rather than positive postingestive USs.

It is also possible that the modulatory influence of hungers cues could be overshadowed by other types of learning. For example, social cues or cultural stereotypes related to eating may be directly associated with aversive US representations (e.g., ideation of obesity or social disapproval) and may therefore be capable of activating those representations whether or not the person is hungry. The activation of these aversive representations may be enough to counteract any eating behavior evoked by activation of positive US representations associated with food cues.

REFERENCES

Benoit, S. C., & Davidson, T. L. (1996). Interoceptive sensory signals produced by 24-hr food deprivation, pharmacological glucoprivation and lipoprivation. *Behavioral Neuroscience, 110*, 168–180.

Bernstein, I. L., & Borson, S. (1986). Learned food aversion: A component of anorexia syndromes. *Psychological Review, 93*, 462–472.

Bernstein, I. L., & Meachum, C. L. (1990). Food aversion learning: Its impact on appetite. In E. D. Capaldi & T. L. Powley (eds.), *Taste, experience, and feeding*, 170–178. Washington, D.C.: American Psychological Association.

Bindra, D. A. (1978). How adaptive behavior is produced: A perceptual-motivational alternative to response-reinforcement. *The Behavioral and Brain Sciences, 7*, 41–91.

Birch, L. L. (1980). The effects of peer model's food choices and eating behaviors on preschooler's food preferences. *Child Development, 51,* 489–496.

Birch, L. L., & Marlin, D. W. (1982). I don't like I, I never tried it: Effects of exposure on two-year-old children's food preferences. *Appetite, 3,* 353–360.

Birch, L. L., McPhee, L., Steinberg, L., & Sullivan, S. (1989). Conditioned flavor preferences in young children. *Physiology & Behavior, 47,* 501–505.

Birch, L. L., McPhee, L., Sullivan, S., & Johnson, S. (1989). Conditioned meal initiation in young children. *Appetite, 13,* 105–113.

Birch, L. L., Zimmerman, S. I., & Hind, H. (1980). The influence of social-affective context on the formation of children's food preferences. *Child Development, 51,* 856–861.

Bloomberg, R., & Webb, W. B. (1949). Various degrees within a single drive as cues for spatial learning in the white rat. *Journal of Experimental Psychology, 39,* 628–636.

Blundell, J. E., & Coscina, D. V. (1992). Integration of signals responsible for eating patterns. In G. H. Anderson & S. H. Kennedy (eds.), *The biology of feast and famine: Relevance to eating disorders,* 93–101, New York: Academic Press.

Booth, D. A. (1972). Conditioned satiety in the rat. *Journal of Comparative and Physiological Psychology, 81,* 457–471.

Booth, D.A. (1985). Food-conditioned eating preferences and aversions with interoceptive elements: Learned appetites and satieties. *Annals of the New York Academy of Sciences, 443,* 22–37.

Booth, D. (1990). Learned role of tastes in eating motivation. In E. D. Capaldi & T. L. Powley (eds.), *Taste, experience, and feeding,* (179–208). Washington, D.C.: American Psychological Association.

Booth, D.A. (1992). Acquired ingestive motivation and the structure of food recognition. *Sixth Workshop of the International School of Ethology.* Erice: Sicily, June.

Booth, D. A., & Davis, J. D. (1973). Gastrointestinal factors in the acquisition of oral sensory control of satiation. *Physiology & Behavior, 11,* 23–29.

Booth , D. A., Mather, P., & Fuller, J. (1982). Starch content of ordinary foods associatively conditions human appetite and satiation, indexed by intake and pleasantness of starch-paired foods. *Appetite, 3,* 163–184.

Bouton, M. E., & Swartzentruber, D. (1986). Analysis of the associative and occasion-setting properties of contexts participating in a Pavlovian discrimination. *Journal of Experimental Psychology: Animal Behavior Processes, 12,* 333–350.

Breslin, P. A. S., Davidson, T. L., & Grill, H. J. (1990). Conditioned reversal of reactions to normally-avoided tastes. *Physiology & Behavior, 47,* 535–538.

Broberg, D. J., & Bernstein, I. L. (1989). Cephalic insulin release in anorexic women. *Physiology & Behavior, 45,* 871–874.

Cabanac, M. (1971). Physiological role of pleasure. *Science, 173,* 1103–1107

Campfield, L. A., & Smith, F. J. (1990). Systemic factors in the control of food intake. In E. M. Stricker (ed.), *Handbook of behavioral neurobiology,* Vol. 10: 183–206. New York: Plenum.

Cannon, D. S., Crawford, I. L., & Carrell, L. E. (1988). Zinc deficiency conditions food aversions in rats. *Physiology & Behavior, 42,* 245–247.

Capaldi, E. D. (1992). Conditioned food preferences. In D. Medin (ed.), *The psychology of learning and motivation,* Vol. 28: 1–33. New York: Academic Press.

Capaldi, E. D., Campbell, D. H., Sheffer, J. D., & Bradford, J. P. (1987). Conditioned flavor preferences based on delayed caloric consequences. *Journal of Experimental Psychology: Animal Behavior Processes, 13,* 150–155.

Capaldi, E. D., Davidson, T. L., & Myers, D. E. (1981). Resistance to satiation: Reinforcing effects of food and eating under satiation. *Learning and Motivation, 12,* 171–195.

Capaldi, E. D., & Myers, D. E. (1978). Resistance to satiation of consummatory and instrumental performance. *Learning and Motivation, 9,* 197–201.

Capaldi, E. D., Viveiros, D. M., & Davidson, T. L. (1981). Deprivation stimulus intensity and incentive factors in the control of instrumental responding. *Journal of Experimental Psychology: Animal Behavior Processes, 7,* 140–149.

Carlson, A. J. (1916). *The control of hunger in health and disease.* Chicago: University of Chicago Press.

Cooper, P. J., & Fairburn, C. G. (1984). Cognitive behavior therapy for anorexia nervosa: Some preliminary findings. *Journal of Psychosomatic Research, 28,* 493–499.

Corwin, R. L., Woolverton, W. L., & Schuster, C. R. (1990). Effects of cholecystokinin, d-amphetamine and fenfluramine in rats trained to discriminate 3 from 22 hr of food deprivation. *Journal of Pharmacology and Experimental Therapeutics, 253,* 720–728.

Davidson, T. L. (1987). Learning about deprivation intensity stimuli. *Behavioral Neuroscience, 101,* 198–208.

Davidson, T. L. (1993). The nature and function of interoceptive signals to feed: Toward integration of physiological and learning perspectives. *Psychological Review, 100,* 640–657.

Davidson, T. L., Aparicio, J., & Rescorla, R. A. (1988). Transfer between Pavlovian facilitators and instrumental discriminative stimuli. *Animal Learning & Behavior, 16,* 285–291.

Davidson, T. L., & Benoit, S. C. (1996).The learned function of food deprivation cues: A role for conditioned modulation. *Animal Learning & Behavior, 24,* 46–56.

Davidson, T. L., & Carretta, J. C. (1993). Cholecystokinin, but not bombesin, has interoceptive sensory consequences like 1-hr food deprivation. *Physiology & Behavior, 53,* 737–735.

Davidson, T. L., Flynn, F. W., & Grill, H. J. (1988). Comparison of the interoceptive sensory consequences of CCK, LiCl, and satiety in rats. *Behavioral Neuroscience, 102,* 134–140.

Davidson, T. L., Flynn, F. W., & Jarrard, L. E. (1992). Potency of food deprivation intensity cues as discriminative stimuli. *Journal of Experimental Psychology: Animal Behavior Processes, 18,* 174–181.

Davidson, T. L., McKenzie, B. R., Tujo, C. J., and Bish, C. K. (1992). Development of tolerance to endogenous opiates activated by food deprivation. *Appetite, 19,* 1–13.

Davidson, T. L., & Rescorla, R. A. (1986). Transfer of facilitation in the rat. *Animal Learning & Behavior, 4,* 380–386.

Domjan, M. (1980). Ingestional aversive learning: Unique and general processes. In J. S. Rosenblatt, R. A. Hinde, C. Beer, & M. C. Busnel (eds.), *Advance in the study of behavior,* Vol. II: 275–336. New York: Academic Press.

Estes, W. K. (1958). Stimulus-response theory of drive. In M. R. Jones (ed.), *Nebraska symposium on motivation,* 35–68. Lincoln: University of Nebraska Press.

Fanselow, M., & Birk, J. (1982). Flavor-flavor associations induce hedonic shifts in taste preference. *Animal Learning & Behavior, 10,* 223–228.

Friedman, M. I. (1990). Making sense out of calories. In E. M. Stricker (ed.), *Handbook of behavioral neurobiology,* Vol. 10: 513–529, New York: Plenum.

Galef, B. G., Jr. (1988). Communication of information concerning distant diets in a social central-place foraging species: *Ratus norvegicus.* In T. Zentall & B. G. Galef, Jr. (eds.), *Social learning: A comparative approach,* 119–140. Hillsdale, N.J.: Erlbaum.

Galef, B. G., Jr. (1989). Enduring social enhancement of rats' preferences for the palatable and the piquant. *Appetite, 13,* 81–92.

Galef, B. G., Jr., Mason, J. R., Preti, G., & Bean, N. J. (1988). Carbon disulfide: A semiochemical mediating socially-induced diet choices in rats. *Physiology & Behavior, 42,* 119–124.

Galef, B. G., Jr., & Whiskin, E. E. (1995). Learning socially to eat more of one food than of another. *Journal of Comparative Psychology, 109,* 99–101.

Garfinkel, P. E., & Garner, D. M. (1982). *Anorexia nervosa: A multidimensional perspective.* New York: Brunner/Mazzel.

Gibson, E. L., & Booth, D. A. (1989). Dependence of carbohydrate-conditioned flavor preference on internal state in rats. *Learning and Motivation, 20,* 36–47.

Grill, H. J., & Berridge, K. C. (1985). Taste reactivity as a measure of the neural control of palatability. In J. M. Sprague & A. N. Epstein (eds.), *Progress in psychobiology,* 1–62. San Diego, Calif.: Academic Press.

Grill, H. J., & Norgren, R. (1978). The taste reactivity test, II: Mimetic responses to gustatory stimuli in chronic thalamic and chronic decerebrate rats. *Brain Research, 143,* 281–297.

Guthrie, E. R. (1935). *The psychology of learning.* New York: Harper.

Holland, P. C. (1991a). Occasion setting in Pavlovian conditioning. In D. L. Medin (ed.), *The psychology of learning and motivation,* Vol. 28: 69–125. San Diego, Calif.: Academic Press.

Holland, P. C. (1991b). Acquisition and transfer of occasion setting in operant feature positive and feature negative discriminations. *Learning and Motivation, 22,* 366–387.

Holland, P. C., & Rescorla, R. A. (1975). The effects of ways of devaluing the unconditioned stimulus after first- and second-order appetitive conditioning. *Journal of Experimental Psychology: Animal Behavior Processes, 1,* 355–363.

Holman, E. W. (1975). Immediate and delayed reinforcers for flavor preferences in rats. *Animal Learning & Behavior, 6,* 91–100.

Hull, C. L. (1943). *Principles of behavior.* New York: Appleton-Century-Crofts.

Jansen, A. (1994). The learned nature of binge eating. In C. R. Leg & D. Booth (eds.), *Appetite: Neural and behavioral bases,* 193–211. Oxford: Oxford University Press.

Jenkins, J. J., & Hanratty, J. A. (1949). Drive intensity discrimination in the white rat. *Journal of Comparative and Physiological Psychology, 42,* 228–232.

Kissileff, H. R., & Van Itallie, T. B. (1982). Physiology of the control of food intake. *American Review of Nutrition, 2,* 371–418.

Konorski, J. (1967). *Integrative activity of the brain: An interdisciplinary approach.* Chicago: University of Chicago Press.

Langhans, W., & Scharrer, E. (1987). Role of fatty acid oxidation in the control of meal pattern. *Behavioral and Neural Biology, 47,* 7–16.

Lavin, M. J. (1976). The establishment of flavor-flavor associations using a sensory preconditioning training procedure. *Learning and Motivation, 7,* 173–183.

Leboff, D. B., Leichner, P., & Spigelman, M. N. (1988). Salivary response to olfactory stimuli in anorexics and bulimics. *Appetite, 11,* 15–25.

Leibowitz, S. F. (1992). Neurochemical-neuroendocrine systems in the brain controlling macronutrient intake and metabolism. *Trends in Neuroscience, 15,* 491–498.

LeMagnen, J. (1956). Hyperphagie provoquee chez le rat blanc par l'alteration du mechanisme de satiete peripherique. *Comptes Rendus de la Societe de Biologie, 147,* 1753–1757.

LeMagnen, J. (1984). Ingestive behavior in the homeostatic control of internal environment. *Appetite, 5,* 159–168.

Louis-Sylvestre, J., & LeMagnen, J. (1980). A fall in blood glucose precedes meal onset in free-feeding rats. *Neuroscience and Biobehavioral Reviews, 4,* 13–15.

Marrazzi, M. A., & Luby, E. D. (1986). An auto-addiction opiod model of chronic anorexia nervosa. *International Journal of Eating Disorders, 5,* 191–208.

Martin, I., & Levey, A. B. (1978). Evaluative conditioning. *Advances in Behavior Research & Therapy, 1,* 57–102.

Mayer, J. (1955). Regulation of energy intake and body weight. The glucostatic theory and the lipostatic hypothesis. *Annals of the New York Academy of Sciences, 63* (article 1), 15–43.

Mogenson, G. J. (1976). Neural mechanisms of hunger: Current status and future prospects. In D. Novin, W. Wyricka, & G. Bray (eds.), *Hunger: Basic mechanisms and clinical implications,* 473–485. New York: Raven Press.

Mook, D. G. (1990). Satiety, specifications, and stop rules: Feeding as voluntary action. *Progress in Psychobiology and Physiological Psychology, 14,* 1–65.

Morgan, M. J. (1974). Resistance to satiation. *Animal Behavior, 22,* 449–466.

Pavlov, I. P. (1927). *Conditioned reflexes.* Oxford: Oxford University Press.

Peeke, H. V. S., & Petrinovich, L. (1984). Approaches, constructs, and terminology for the study of response change in the intact organism. In H. V. S. Peeke & L., Petrinovich (eds.), *Habituation, sensitization, and behavior,* 1–16. Orlando, Fla.: Academic Press.

Powley, T. L., & Berthoud, H. R. (1985). Diet and cephalic phase insulin responses. *American Journal of Clinical Nutrition, 42,* 991–1002.

Rescorla, R. A. (1973). Evidence for a unique-cue account of configural conditioning. *Journal of Comparative and Physiological Psychology, 85,* 331–338.

Rescorla, R. A. (1984). Comments on three Pavlovian paradigms. In D. L. Alkon & J. Farley (eds.), *Primary neural substrates of learning and behavioral change,* 25–45. New York: Cambridge University Press.

Rescorla, R. A. (1985). Facilitation and inhibition. In R. R. Miller & N. E. Spear (eds.), *Information processing in animals: Conditioned inhibition,* 299–326. Hillsdale, N.J.: Erlbaum.

Rescorla, R. A. (1988). Behavioral studies of Pavlovian conditioning. *Annual Review of Neuroscience, 11,* 329–352.

Ritter, S., & Taylor, J. S. (1989). Capsaicin abolishes lipoprivic but not glucoprivic feeding in rats. *American Journal of Physiology, 474,* R1232–R1239.

Rolls, B. J. (1990). The role of sensory-specific satiety in food intake and food selection. In E. D. Capaldi & T. L. Powley (eds.), *Taste, experience, and feeding,* 179–208. Washington, D.C.: American Psychological Association.

Rolls, B. J., & Hetherington, M. (1989). The role of variety in eating and body weight regulation. In R. Shepard (ed.), *Handbook of the psychophysiology of human eating,* 57–84. Chichester, England: Wiley.

Rolls, B. J., Laster, L. J., & Summerfelt, A. (1989). Hunger and food intake following consumption of low-calorie foods. *Appetite, 13,* 115–127.

Rolls, B. J., Rolls, E. T., Rowe, E. A., & Sweeney, K. (1981). Sensory specific satiety in man. *Physiology & Behavior, 27,* 137–142.

Rolls, B. J., Rowe, E. A., & Rolls, E. T. (1982). How sensory properties of food affect human feeding behavior. *Physiology & Behavior, 27,* 137–142.

Rozin, A. (1990). The importance of social factors in understanding the acquisition of food habits. In E. D. Capaldi & T. L. Powley (eds.), *Taste, experience, and feeding,* 255–269. Washington, D.C.: American Psychological Association.

Rozin, P., & Rodgers, W. (1967). Novel diet preferences in vitamin-deficient rats and rats recovered from vitamin deficiency. *Journal of Comparative and Physiological Psychology, 63,* 421–428.

Schuh, K. J., Schaal, D. W., Thompson, T., Cleary, J. P., Billington, C. J., & Levine, A. S. (1994). Insulin, 2-deoxy-d-gluocse, and food deprivation as discriminative stimuli in rats. *Pharmacology, Biochemistry, and Behavior, 47,* 317–324.

Sclafani, A. (1990). Nutritionally based learned flavor preferences in rats. In E. D. Capaldi & T. L. Powley (eds.), *Taste, experience, and feeding,* 139–178. Washington, D.C.: American Psychological Association.

Stevenson, R. J., & Yeomans, M. R. (1995). Does exposure enhance liking for the chili burn? *Appetite, 24,* 107–120.

Stricker, E. M. (1990). Homeostatic origins of ingestive behavior. In E. M. Stricker (ed.), *Handbook of behavioral neurobiology,* Vol. 10: 45–60. New York: Plenum.

Strober, M. (1986). Anorexia nervosa: History and psychological concepts. In H. D. Brownell & J. P. Foryet (eds.), *Handbook of eating disorders,* 231–246. New York: Basic Books.

Swartzentruber, D. (1995). Modulatory mechanisms in Pavlovian conditioning. *Animal Learning & Behavior, 23,* 123–143.

Swartzentruber, D., & Rescorla, R. A. (1994). Modulation of trained and extinguished stimuli by facilitators and inhibitors. *Animal Learning & Behavior, 22,* 309–316.

Swithers, S. E., & Hall, W. G. (1994). Does oral experience terminate ingestion? *Appetite, 23,* 113–138.

Swithers-Mulvey, S. E., & Hall, W. G. (1992). Control of ingestion by oral habituation in rat pups. *Behavioral Neuroscience, 106,* 710–717.

Thompson, R. F., Donegan, N. H., & Lavond, D. G. (1988). The psychobiology of learning and memory. In R. C. Atkinson, R. J. Herrnstein, G. Lindzey, & R. D. Luce (eds.), *Steven's handbook of experimental psychology,* Vol. 2: 245–347. New York: Wiley.

Toates, F. M. (1981). The control of ingestive behavior by internal and external stimuli — A theoretical review. *Appetite, 2,* 35–50.

Toates, F. M. (1986). *Motivational systems.* Cambridge: Cambridge University Press.

Toates, F. M.. (1994). The learned nature of binge eating. In C. R. Leg & D. Booth (eds.), *Appetite: Neural and behavioral bases,* 305–327. Oxford: Oxford University Press.

Tordoff, M. G. (1991). Metabolic basis of learned food preferences. In M. I. Friedman, M. G. Tordoff, & M. R. Kare (eds.), *Chemical senses,* Vol. 4: 239–260. New York: Marcel Dekker.

Tordoff, M. G., Rawson, N., & Friedman, M. I. (1991). 2,5-Anhydro-D-mannitol acts in liver to initiate feeding. *American Journal of Physiology, 363,* R283–287.

Treit, D., Spetch, M. L., & Deutsch, J. A. (1982). Variety in the flavor of food enhances eating in the rat: A controlled demonstration. *Physiology and Behavior, 30,* 207–211.

Wagner, A. R., & Brandon, S. E. (1989). Evolution of a structured connectionist model of Pavlovian conditioning (AESOP). In S. B. Klein & R. R. Mowrer (eds.) *Contemporary learning theories: Pavlovian conditioning and the status of traditional learning theory,* 149–189. Hillsdale, N.J.: Erlbaum.

Wagner, R. R. (1979). Habituation and memory. In A. Dickinson & R. A. Boakes (eds.), *Mechanisms of learning and motivation.* Hillsdale, N.J.: Erlbaum.

Weingarten, H. P. (1983). Conditioned cues elicit feeding in sated rats: A role for learning in meal initiation. *Science, 220,* 431–433.

Weingarten, H. P. (1985). Stimulus control of eating: Implications for a two-factor theory of hunger. *Appetite, 6,* 387–401.

Whitlow, J. W. (1975). Short-term memory in habituation and dishabituation. *Journal of Experimental Psychology: Animal Behavior Processes. 104,* 189–206.

Whitlow, J. W., & Wagner, A. R. (1984). Memory and habituation. In H. V. S. Peeke & L. Petrinovich (eds.) *Habituation, sensitization, and behavior,* 103–153. Orlando, Fla.: Academic Press.

Woods, S. C. (1991). The eating paradox: How we tolerate food. *Psychological Review, 98,* 488–505.

Woods, S. C., & Strubbe, J. H. (1994). The psychobiology of meals. *Psychonomic Bulletin & Review, 1,* 141–155.

Zellner, D. A., Rozin, P., Aron, M., & Kulish, D. (1983). Conditioned enhancement of human's liking for flavors by pairing with sweetness. *Learning and Motivation, 14,* 338–350.

CHAPTER 26

DRUG CONDITIONING AND DRUG-SEEKING BEHAVIOR

Christopher L. Cunningham

One hallmark of addiction to alcohol and other drugs is a pattern of behavior that produces a progressive increase over time in the frequency of exposure to an abused substance. Indeed, many diagnostic criteria for substance-related disorders include this feature among the primary benchmarks for identifying affected individuals (e.g., American Psychiatric Association, *DSM-IV*, 1994). An understanding of the factors contributing to such behavior patterns is essential for designing therapeutic strategies to reduce or eliminate those behaviors. Information about processes that affect drug-seeking behavior is also critical for reducing the likelihood of relapse following treatment.

Contemporary theories of addiction generally emphasize three broad categories of influence on drug-seeking behavior: biological, psychological, and sociocultural (Chaudron & Wilkinson, 1988; Jaffe, 1992). Within the categories of biological and psychological influences, interest has fo-

cused on the rewarding and aversive effects of abused drugs and on the phenomena of tolerance, sensitization, and dependence (e.g., Tabakoff & Hoffman, 1988). An underlying premise of most biopsychological approaches to addiction is that drug-seeking behavior is best viewed as an instance of *learned* instrumental behavior, that is, a behavior that is importantly influenced by its consequences. In general, it is assumed that positive or rewarding effects of drugs tend to promote an increase in drug-seeking behavior, whereas negative or aversive effects tend to decrease such behavior. It is the balance between a drug's positive and negative effects that determines whether response-contingent exposure to drug is reinforcing, that is, whether there will be an increase in the frequency of the behavior that produced the drug. Individual differences in the intensity and quality of a drug's motivational effects are generally attributed to variation in: (a) genotype (e.g., genetically determined differences in sensitivity

518

to drug effects or in susceptibility to develop tolerance, sensitization, dependence); (b) environmental conditions before, during, or after exposure to the drug; and (c) experiential factors including prior drug exposure (i.e., tolerance, sensitization, dependence) and previous learning. Presumably, these kinds of individual differences explain, in part, why only a subset of the population of substance users develops the excessive drug-seeking behavior patterns that characterize the addict.

This chapter focuses on the potential contribution of learning to drug-seeking behavior and the role that such learning might play in causing relapse to drug-taking after treatment or a period of abstinence. Special emphasis will be placed on the learning that results from the predictive relationship between stimuli (interoceptive or exteroceptive) that signal delivery of a drug and its effects. This learning, which can be viewed as a form of Pavlovian conditioning, is believed to be important in drug-seeking behavior for several reasons. First, it can produce changes in physiological or behavioral responses, motivational states (e.g., craving), or expectancies that affect the probability or vigor of drug-seeking behavior. Second, it can alter (enhance or depress) unconditioned drug effects, thus changing the intensity and perhaps the quality of the outcomes that normally maintain or strengthen instrumental drug-taking behavior. Several examples of these types of Pavlovian changes from the drug-conditioning literature will be presented, along with descriptions of the various theories implicating such learning in the acquisition, maintenance, and relapse of drug-seeking behavior. Finally, potential implications of such data and theories for treatment of human substance abusers will be considered.

DRUGS AS UNCONDITIONED STIMULI

An underlying premise of the present analysis is that a drug experience can function as an *unconditioned stimulus* in much the same way as other events (e.g., food, electric shock) that have

served in this role in Pavlovian conditioning paradigms. Indeed, Pavlov (1927/1960) himself was among the first to recognize the US properties of drug administration when he reported the results of Krylov's experiments showing that environmental stimuli that regularly signaled injection of morphine acquired the ability to increase salivary secretion and other effects normally induced by morphine itself. Although contemporary views of Pavlovian conditioning have changed considerably since Pavlov's time (Rescorla, 1988), a wide variety of findings have continued to provide support for the notion that drugs can function as USs in Pavlovian conditioning paradigms in both animals and humans (e.g., Childress et al., 1992; Cunningham, 1993; Goudie & Demellweek, 1986; Lynch, Stein, & Fertziger, 1976; Stewart & Eikelboom, 1987; Siegel, 1989; Wikler, 1968).

Typical laboratory demonstrations of Pavlovian drug conditioning involve a positive contingency between exposure to a distinctive stimulus and delivery of a drug. The signaling stimulus is labeled the *conditioned stimulus* (CS), whereas drug administration serves as the *unconditioned stimulus* (US). Exposure to CS-drug contingencies has been shown to produce dramatic changes in responses evoked by the CS (i.e., *conditioned responses* or CRs) as well as in responses evoked by the US (i.e., *unconditioned responses* or URs). When CRs are measured in the same response system(s) activated by the US, the CR sometimes resembles the UR but in other cases may be opposite in direction to the UR (Eikelboom & Stewart, 1982; Stewart & Eikelboom, 1987). In other instances, the effect of conditioning is recorded in an entirely different response system (Cunningham, 1993). Although theories differ in the significance attached to these various types of CRs, all have been hypothesized to play a role in influencing drug-seeking behavior.

The relationship between the CR and drug UR has assumed a prominent role in many of the theoretical discussions relating Pavlovian drug conditioning to self-administration and relapse. In recent years, two major theoretical models have emerged, one emphasizing the hypothesized negative motivational properties of drug-opposite CRs and another focusing on the hypothesized positive motivational properties of drug-like CRs. The first model, which has elements similar to earlier views presented by Wikler (1948, 1965, 1968, 1973), attributes the conditioning of drug-opposite CRs to an adaptive homeostatic process that compensates for drug-induced perturbations in normal behavioral or physiological processes (Siegel, 1975, 1989, 1990). These compensatory CRs are assumed to be responsible, at least in part, for producing drug tolerance, that is, a reduction in the magnitude of the drug UR. Furthermore, because the symptoms of drug withdrawal are also often opposite to drug URs, elicitation of drug-compensatory CRs is thought to produce an aversive motivational state. In fact, it has been suggested that these withdrawal-like drug-compensatory CRs may be an overt manifestation of the subjective state of drug *craving* (Hinson & Siegel, 1980). Presumably, this aversive state will motivate instrumental behaviors that have been successful in obtaining drugs in the past. Drug administration will then negatively reinforce those instrumental behaviors by alleviating the conditioned aversive state. Drug administration will also strengthen the Pavlovian learning process that underlies the compensatory CRs, creating a vicious circle reminiscent of those characterizing other forms of maladaptive behavior (Brown & Cunningham, 1981). Thus, this model predicts relapse to drug-seeking behavior if the individual is reexposed to drug-paired CSs, even after long periods of abstinence when all signs of physical dependence have subsided.

The major alternative model focuses instead on positive-incentive motivational effects produced by drug conditioning (Lynch et al., 1973; Stewart et al., 1984). According to this model, exposure to a drug-paired CS evokes drug-like CRs that establish a positive motivational state that enhances the incentive value of drug-related stimuli. Thus, by eliciting conditioned effects resembling the original drug effect, the CS is thought to promote renewed drug-taking in much the same way as a small dose of drug reinstates

self-administration after extinction (de Wit & Stewart, 1981, 1983). Such conditioning may also contribute to sensitization, that is, enhancement of the drug UR. Thus, drug-seeking could be further increased by a drug-paired CS because it augments the reinforcing value of the drug experience (Stewart et al., 1984). In contrast to the compensatory-response model, this model assumes that drug-taking is positively reinforced by the appetitive, rewarding effects of the drug, and gives little weight to negative reinforcement produced by alleviation of withdrawal. However, both models are similar in their emphasis on reexposure to a drug-paired CS as providing impetus for relapse in the absence of exposure to the drug itself. Additional implications of these and other theoretical models will be addressed after consideration of several recent studies illustrating various effects of drug conditioning on behavior during the CS and during the US.

DRUG CONDITIONING: EFFECTS ON BEHAVIOR DURING THE CS

Historically, one of the most intriguing aspects of Pavlovian conditioning has been the acquired ability of the CS to elicit or control a *new* response in the absence of the US previously associated with the CS. This alteration in the functional properties of the CS by conditioning not only illustrates a remarkable adaptation to environmental conditions, but it also has strong implications for the way one thinks about the consequences of drug exposure. Specifically, the existence of such conditioning offers a plausible yet relatively simple mechanism for explaining how a drug's influence on individuals can extend well beyond the period of time in which the drug is in direct contact with brain receptors or other tissues mediating its unconditioned effects.

This section contains several different examples of conditioned changes in behavior measured during the CS in the absence of the drug US after a period of training involving multiple exposures to CS-US pairings. This presentation is not intended to provide a comprehensive review of the Pavlovian drug-conditioning literature. Rather, these examples were chosen to illustrate the general types of findings reported in the literature, the kinds of responses that have been studied, and a few of the parametric determinants of Pavlovian drug conditioning.

Morphine-Induced Conditioned Hyperthermia

Most of the commonly abused drugs elicit unconditioned changes in body temperature (Schönbaum & Lomax, 1991). Moreover, repeated drug exposure can produce changes in the unconditioned thermal response to drugs and result in development of conditioned thermal responses to CSs paired with those drugs (Cunningham et al., 1990). The results of two recent experiments reporting conditioned increases in body temperature after exposure to morphine are shown in Figure 26–1. Both experiments used rats in an experimental protocol designed to minimize possible influences of stress or extraneous stimulation on the learning or expression of conditioned responses. Subjects were surgically implanted with an intravenous cannula for remote delivery of drug and with a telemetry device for automated, continuous recording of body temperature. Furthermore, animals remained in the recording chamber 24 hours per day during the conditioning phase. Once per day, experimental (paired) subjects were exposed to a 15-minute CS consisting of a white noise and houselight that was paired with intravenous infusion of a 5 mg/kg dose of morphine (US). This dose initially produced a large increase in body temperature (about 1.5 degrees C or more), and repeated exposure accelerated the onset of hyperthermia (Broadbent & Cunningham, 1996; Schwarz & Cunningham, 1990). This dose presumably also had significant effects on various other physiological and behavioral responses (e.g., heart rate, activity, pain sensitivity), although these other effects were not measured in these particular experiments.

In the experiment depicted in the upper panel of Figure 26–1 (Schwarz & Cunningham, 1990), paired subjects were infused with morphine beginning 30 seconds after the CS was turned on.

For control subjects, the CS and drug US were unpaired, that is, the US was delivered more than an hour after termination of the CS. Thus, controls were matched for any nonassociative effects of exposure to the CS and US, but were not

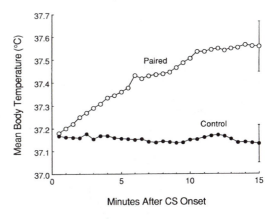

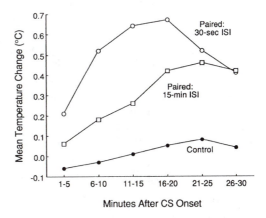

Figure 26–1. Conditioned hyperthermia induced by CS-morphine pairings in rats. Both panels show the outcome of drug-free tests conducted after a series of drug-conditioning trials. *Top panel:* The Paired group had previously received IV infusions of morphine beginning 30 seconds after onset of a 15-minute noise-light CS; the CS and morphine were explicitly unpaired in the Control group (Adapted from Schwarz & Cunningham, 1990). *Bottom panel:* The Paired groups differed in the time delay (interstimulus interval or ISI) between onset of the 15-minute noise-light CS and administration of morphine; the Control group received explicitly unpaired exposures to CS and morphine. (Adapted from Broadbent & Cunningham, 1996.)

expected to develop a CR. The top panel shows data from special tests conducted in the absence of morphine infusion to allow measurement of the CR without the confounding thermal influence of morphine itself. As can be seen, test presentation of the CS without drug produced a reliable increase in body temperature in paired subjects, but little change in control subjects. Thus, in this instance the CR and UR were in the same direction (hyperthermia). Furthermore, conditioned hyperthermia was evident after only seven conditioning trials, suggesting that this kind of learning occurs relatively rapidly. Given that body temperature is normally very tightly regulated in rodents (Gordon, 1993), the magnitude and rapidity of the thermal response observed in these studies is quite remarkable.

The lower panel of Figure 26–1 illustrates the results of a subsequent experiment in which the effect of the time interval between onset of the CS and delivery of the drug US was examined (Broadbent & Cunningham, 1996). For one group of experimental subjects, CS onset preceded drug delivery by 30 seconds as in the previous example. For the second experimental group, however, CS onset preceded drug delivery by 15 minutes. As in the earlier example, control subjects received unpaired exposures to CS and US. The experimental question of interest was whether lengthening the delay (i.e., interstimulus) interval between CS onset and US delivery would have the same detrimental effect on drug conditioning as found with more conventional forms of Pavlovian conditioning (Mackintosh, 1974, 1983). As expected, the results of the drug-free test shown in the lower panel revealed a negative relationship between length of the delay interval and strength of conditioned hyperthermia.

The latter finding clearly illustrates the sensitivity of organisms to temporal relationships in drug conditioning. Such findings are important because of their potential implications for identifying which of the various cues that precede a drug experience are most likely to gain control over conditioned physiological or behavioral responses. Of particular interest in this regard are

the results of a follow-up experiment (Broadbent & Cunningham, 1996; Experiment 2) that also compared groups that differed in the time interval between CS onset and US delivery (30 seconds versus 15 minutes), but were matched for the duration of overlap between the CS and the onset of morphine's effects following infusion. In this experiment, as long as the short and long interstimulus interval groups both had at least 15 minutes of overlap with the initial effects of the drug (i.e., by extending the CS for at least 15 minutes after drug infusion), the detrimental effects of the long delay were eliminated (data not shown). These observations suggest that analyses of the Pavlovian conditioning hypothesized to occur during drug self-administration should focus more on the role played by stimuli that overlap the drug's action rather than on stimuli that terminate as drug administration begins. CSs that overlap drug effects may be more likely to acquire control over CRs that can affect subsequent drug-seeking behavior. Such stimuli may also deserve greater attention in the design of learning-based therapeutic interventions aimed at extinguishing drug-induced conditioned responses. For example, an item of drug paraphernalia that continues to be used during drug intoxication (e.g., a crack pipe) may be a more effective CS than an item that is no longer present after onset of a drug's effects.

Morphine-Induced Conditioned Tachycardia

The cardiovascular system, like the thermoregulatory system, is also strongly influenced by abused drugs and shows sensitivity to Pavlovian CS-drug contingencies. For example, administration of intravenous morphine to unrestrained rats produces an initial decrease in heart rate, the magnitude and duration of which are positively related to morphine dose (Schwarz, Peris, & Cunningham, 1987). This bradycardia is followed by a longer-lasting increase in heart rate (tachycardia) that is also positively related to drug dose. When infusion of morphine was signaled 30 seconds earlier by onset of a noise-light CS using an experimental preparation similar to that described earlier, the CS acquired the ability to evoke a conditioned increase in heart rate in anticipation of drug infusion (Schwarz-Stevens & Cunningham, 1993). Because heart rate has a relatively short response latency (compared with body temperature), it was possible to monitor acquisition of heart rate conditioning on a trial-by-trial basis. This acquisition process is illustrated in Figure 26–2, which depicts the mean change in heart rate (from a pre-stimulus baseline period) recorded during the last 5 seconds of the interstimulus interval (i.e., just before drug infusion) on successive conditioning trials. As can be seen, experimental and control subjects displayed an equivalent mild tachycardia on initial conditioning trials. With repeated CS-US pairings, experimental subjects showed a progressive increase in magnitude of tachycardia, whereas the response of control subjects decreased toward baseline. Thus, in contrast to the previous example of thermal conditioning, the direction of the CR (tachycardia) was *opposite* to the initial UR to morphine

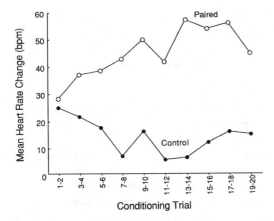

Figure 26–2. Acquisition of conditioned tachycardia induced by CS-morphine pairings in rats. The Paired group received IV infusions of morphine beginning 30 seconds after onset of a noise-light CS on each trial; the CS and morphine were explicitly unpaired in the Control group. The figure depicts mean heart rate change from baseline during the 5-second interval just before delivery of drug. (Adapted from Schwarz-Stevens & Cunningham, 1993.)

(bradycardia). However, the biphasic nature of the heart rate UR complicates this conclusion because one might also argue that the CR was similar to the subsequent tachycardia component of the morphine UR.

As in the case of thermal conditioning with morphine, these data suggest that morphine-induced conditioning occurs relatively rapidly, within six to eight trials. Furthermore, they clearly illustrate the expected positive relationship between number of conditioning trials and strength of the CR. Finally, in physiological terms, the conditioned response produced a sizable change in the cardiovascular system, representing an increase exceeding 10% of baseline heart rate.

Alcohol-Induced Conditioned Activation

The next few examples of drug conditioning extend the phenomenon to one of the most commonly abused drugs, alcohol. The first example also extends drug conditioning to a different species, the mouse. Exposure to low alcohol doses often produces an initial increase in locomotor activity in mice (Phillips & Crabbe, 1991), an effect that has been hypothesized to serve as an animal model of the reinforcing effects of drugs (Wise & Bozarth, 1987). In the study depicted in Figure 26–3, experimental mice received alternate-day intraperitoneal (IP) injections of an activating dose of ethanol (2 g/kg) paired with 5 minute exposure to a distinctive test chamber (Cunningham & Noble, 1992). Thus, in this experiment, the test chamber itself served as the CS. General activity measured on these conditioning trials was substantially higher after ethanol injection than after a control injection of saline (data not shown). Ethanol-treated control subjects received identical injections of drug, but these injections were unpaired with the test chamber (i.e., injections were given 1 hour later in the home cage). Drug-naive control subjects received only saline injections during the training phase. To assess the CR in the absence of the confounding influence of ethanol, all mice were given a saline injection just before placement in the test chamber. This test showed a higher level of activity in the paired group than in either of the control groups, which did not differ (Figure 26–3). Thus, as in the case of morphine-induced conditioned hyperthermia, the CR was in the same direction as the UR (hyperactivity). Because paired and control groups treated with ethanol were matched in terms of their exposure to the test chamber and to ethanol injection, the activity difference measured during the saline test was presumably due to the contingent relationship between CS and US on conditioning trials. The lack of difference between the ethanol-treated control and drug-naive groups suggests that unpaired exposure to the US had no nonspecific effects on general activity in this case. It has been suggested that the learning processes involved in mediating such conditioned-activity responses are the same as those mediating the development of a conditioned preference for the drug-paired CS (Cunningham & Noble, 1992).

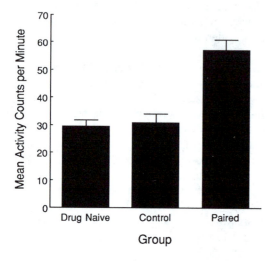

Figure 26–3. Conditioned activity induced by CS-alcohol pairings in mice. The Paired group had previously received injections of alcohol paired with five-minute exposure to a distinctive test chamber (CS+); Control mice received alcohol in the home cage one hour after exposure to the CS. These data were collected during a test exposure to the CS after injection of saline. (Adapted from Cunningham & Noble, 1992.)

Alcohol-Induced Conditioned Hyperthermia

On the basis of the preceding examples, one might be tempted to hypothesize that either the target response system or the nature of the US drug determines whether the CR will be in the same direction as the UR. However, the literature does not support this conclusion, and the next example is intended to help dispel that notion. In this example, rats were exposed to a discriminative conditioning procedure in which distinctive environmental cues were differentially paired with injection of a moderate dose of ethanol (1.4 g/kg IP) or injection of saline (Mansfield & Cunningham, 1980). In one environment, rats were placed in standard metal cages (similar to the home cage) in a large, well-illuminated laboratory room. In the other environment, rats were placed in plastic cages with wood chips in a darkened enclosure with a flashing light and the scent of orange peel. All rats were exposed to both environments on alternating days, consistently receiving ethanol injection paired with one environment (CS+) and saline with the other environment (CS–) (counterbalanced). After 14 exposures to each environment, subjects were given a series of tests to evaluate the effects of conditioning on rectal temperature.

Figure 26–4 shows the outcome of tests designed to assess whether the ethanol-paired environment had acquired the ability to evoke a thermal CR in the absence of ethanol. For this test, rats were exposed to either the CS+ or CS– environment after injection of saline. As shown in the figure, this test yielded an outcome similar to that described earlier for morphine-induced conditioning in the same response system, that is, subjects displayed a conditioned hyperthermia in the paired (CS+) environment relative to the control (CS–) environment. Moreover, the thermal response of experimental rats in the CS– environment was nearly identical to that of drug-naive control rats.

Although the directions of the thermal CRs induced by ethanol and morphine are similar, the relationship of those CRs to their URs is not. As noted earlier, the morphine-induced thermal CR and UR were in the same direction (both hyper-

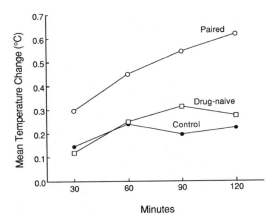

Figure 26–4. Conditioned hyperthermia induced by CS-alcohol pairings in rats. Drug-treated animals were previously exposed to a within-subject discriminative conditioning procedure that paired a distinctive environment with injections of ethanol (CS+); a second environment was consistently paired with saline injections (CS–). The figure depicts mean rectal temperature change from baseline during postconditioning tests with saline injection in either the CS+ (Paired) or CS– (Control) environments. (Adapted from Mansfield & Cunningham, 1980.)

conditioning is inferred from the effect of the CS on behaviors that occur only under unique testing conditions (cf. Cunningham, 1993). Such studies have tested the ability of a drug-paired CS to: (a) alter the unconditioned response to a probe stimulus (e.g., tail-flick or paw-lift to painful stimulation), (b) change learned behaviors established by contingencies not involving the drug (e.g., bar-pressing for food), or (c) reinforce or punish contingent behaviors (e.g., taste aversion, conditioned reinforcement, place preference). In most of these studies, the exact relationship between CR and UR is unknown because these responses are not directly measured. Nevertheless, these studies have provided strong evidence of drug-induced Pavlovian conditioning and have played a critical role in theorizing about the possible impact of such conditioning on drug self-administration and relapse.

One example of this general type of conditioning procedure will be described here. This particular example, which involves the conditioned place-preference paradigm, was selected because of its potential implications for understanding the influence of drug-induced conditioned motivational changes on drug-seeking behavior (Carr et al., 1989; Swerdlow et al., 1989). During the first phase of a place-conditioning study, subjects receive pairings of the drug US with a set of distinctive environmental stimuli (e.g., a box with unique visual or tactile cues). Often, these trials are matched by exposure to an alternative set of stimuli paired with injection of a control solution (e.g., saline) as part of a discriminative conditioning procedure. The effects of this training are evaluated in a second phase when subjects are offered a spatial choice between a location containing the drug-paired stimuli and one or more alternative locations containing different stimuli. Typically, no drug is given during this test. In essence, the second phase can be viewed as an instrumental learning task that assesses the conditioned reinforcing (or punishing) properties of the drug-paired CS. A greater amount of time spent in contact with the drug-paired CS (relative to an appropriate control) is generally interpreted as indicating that the unconditioned motivational effects of the

thermia). However, the direction of the thermal CR induced by ethanol (hyperthermia) was opposite to the UR produced by ethanol (hypothermia). Thus, the target response system alone cannot be used to predict whether the CR will resemble the UR. It should also be clear from the preceding examples that the nature of the US drug cannot be used to predict the direction of the CR. Each of the two drugs described here (morphine, ethanol) was shown to be capable of inducing a CR that either resembled the UR or was opposite to the UR, depending on the target response system.

Alcohol-Induced Conditioned Place Preference

All of the foregoing examples have involved assessment of Pavlovian drug conditioning in experiments where the CR and UR have been measured directly in the same response system. However, a large part of the drug-conditioning literature consists of studies in which the impact of drug are rewarding. Conversely, a relatively lower amount of time spent in contact with the CS is presumed to reflect aversive motivational effects of the drug US. Thus, interpretation of results from this procedure is most often based on the assumption that conditioned motivational effects are in the *same* direction as unconditioned motivational effects of the drug US.

Figure 26–5 shows the outcome of the place-preference test from an experiment in which mice initially received four pairings of ethanol with 30-minute exposure to a chamber containing distinctive tactile (floor) cues (Cunningham et al., 1992). Subjects were also exposed equally often to an alternative tactile stimulus after saline injections. These tactile cues were originally selected on the basis of previous studies indicating that drug-naive mice spent about half their time on each stimulus during choice tests. In this particular experiment, experimental groups differed in magnitude (dose) of the drug US given on each

conditioning trial (1, 2, 3 or 4 g/kg IP). As shown in the figure, percent time on the drug-paired floor during drug-free testing was positively related to drug dose during conditioning. Furthermore, the direction of the conditioned effect was consistent with the conclusion that ethanol had a positive motivational effect at all but the lowest dose, which appeared to produce no conditioning.

The implications of studies like this appear to be greatest for theories emphasizing the positive-incentive motivational properties acquired by CSs paired with abused drugs (Stewart, 1992). Furthermore, because testing occurred long after the acute effects of alcohol had subsided, one can easily draw an analogy between the approach response established by the ethanol-paired CS in this study and the relapse to drug-seeking behavior that is hypothesized to result from reexposure to Pavlovian drug-paired CSs following long periods of abstinence or treatment for addiction.

DRUG CONDITIONING: EFFECTS ON BEHAVIOR DURING THE US

In addition to studying the influence of drug conditioning on behavior measured during the CS, one can also assess conditioning effects on the drug-induced UR. In fact, such studies are of special interest in the analysis of drug-seeking behavior because of their potential implications for understanding the role played by learning in the development of drug tolerance and sensitization. This section describes two studies that evaluated the effect of an alcohol-paired CS on two different URs elicited by alcohol: locomotor activation and hypothermia. In one case, conditioning enhanced the UR, whereas in the other case, conditioning reduced the UR.

Alcohol-Induced Activation

The first example comes from the same conditioned-activity experiment described earlier in which experimental mice received four pairings of a distinctive test chamber with injection of ethanol during the conditioning phase (Cunning-

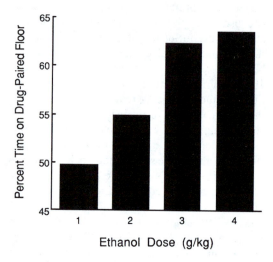

Figure 26–5. Conditioned preference for a spatial location containing stimuli previously paired with alcohol in mice. Animals were exposed to a within-subject discriminative conditioning procedure that paired a distinctive tactile stimulus with one of several doses of alcohol (CS+); a second tactile stimulus was consistently paired with saline injections (CS–). The figure depicts percent time spent on the alcohol-paired floor during a choice test between CS+ and CS–. (Adapted from Cunningham et al., 1992.)

ham & Noble, 1992). One control group was exposed to the test chamber equally often, but always received an unpaired injection of ethanol 1 hour later in the home cage. A second control group never received ethanol during the conditioning phase. During the critical UR test, all three groups were injected with the training dose of ethanol and placed into the test chamber. As can be seen by comparing Figures 26–3 and 26–6, overall activity rates were much higher during the UR test (Figure 26–6) than during the CR test (Figure 26–3), reflecting the general activating effect of ethanol in mice at this test dose (2 g/kg IP). More important, the activity response to ethanol was significantly higher in the paired group than in either of the two control groups, which did not differ. Thus, in the case of locomotor activity, conditioning enhanced the ethanol UR, that is, produced *sensitization*. In fact, in this particular instance, conditioning appeared to explain all of the sensitization to ethanol because the control group that had received unpaired ethanol

exposures showed no sensitization relative to the drug-naive control group.

Alcohol-Induced Hypothermia

The other example of a conditioning effect on the drug UR comes from the previously described study in which rats were exposed to ethanol and saline injections in a conditioning procedure using different laboratory environments as the CS+ and CS– (Mansfield & Cunningham, 1980). During the UR test, rats were placed in both environments (on different days) and given an injection of ethanol. Figure 26–7 shows the outcome of this test. As expected, drug-naive rats showed a pronounced hypothermia after ethanol injection. In contrast, ethanol-treated rats tested in the paired (CS+) environment showed a marked reduction in hypothermia, consistent with the development of tolerance. Of special interest, when

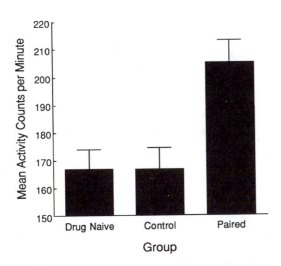

Figure 26–6. Conditioned increase in the locomotor activating effect of alcohol in mice. The Paired group had previously received injections of alcohol paired with five-minute exposure to a distinctive test chamber (CS+); Control mice received alcohol in the home cage one hour after exposure to the CS. These data were collected during a test exposure to the CS after injection of alcohol. (Adapted from Cunningham & Noble, 1992.}

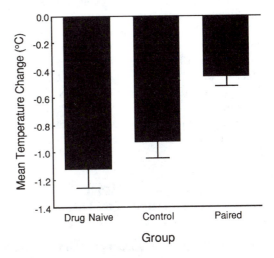

Figure 26–7. Conditioned decrease in the hypothermic effect of alcohol in rats. Drug-treated animals were previously exposed to a within-subject discriminative conditioning procedure that paired a distinctive environment with injections of ethanol (CS+); a second environment was consistently paired with saline injections (CS–). The figure depicts mean rectal temperature change from baseline measured 60 minutes after alcohol injection during postconditioning tests in either the CS+ (Paired) or CS– (Control) environments. (Adapted from Mansfield & Cunningham, 1980.)

those same rats were tested in the control (CS–) environment, most of their tolerance dissipated, yielding an enhanced hypothermia that was very similar to that shown by drug-naive rats receiving ethanol for the first time. Thus, for body temperature, presentation of the CS appeared to mediate *tolerance* to the ethanol UR.

In both this example and the preceding one, separate tests of the CR yielded outcomes that might lead one to explain these examples of conditioned sensitization and conditioned tolerance in terms of a summation of the CR and UR. That is, conditioned sensitization of ethanol-stimulated activity could be described as a summation of the hyperactivity CR (Figure 26–3) and hyperactivity UR (Figure 26–6) whereas conditioned tolerance to ethanol-induced hypothermia could be attributed to summation of a hyperthermia CR (Figure 26–4) and a hypothermia UR (Figure 26–7). Although that may be a plausible interpretation for these and certain other findings in the literature, such findings are not ubiquitous. The literature offers several examples in which drug-paired CSs evoke robust CRs that do not appear to affect the drug UR (e.g., Broadbent & Cunningham, 1996) or in which drug-paired CSs affect the drug UR in the absence of a CR (e.g., Tiffany et al., 1983; Zelman et al., 1985). Various methodological and theoretical reasons have been presented to explain such dissociations between CR and UR (e.g., Baker & Tiffany, 1985; Siegel, 1989).

EFFECTS OF DRUG CONDITIONING ON DRUG-TAKING: AN EXAMPLE

Like all the preceding examples, most of the drug-conditioning literature consists of studies in which drug exposure is controlled by the experimenter rather than self-administered by the subject. Moreover, few studies have ever attempted to relate frequency of drug self-administration to conditioned responses induced by self-administration. Recently, however, an experiment using a signaled self-administration paradigm has yielded interesting new data on the ability of a discriminative stimulus for ethanol to

evoke conditioned thermal responses that appear to modulate the reinforcing effect of ethanol (Cunningham, 1994). Rats trained to bar-press for sweetened ethanol were exposed to a within-subject differential conditioning procedure in which brief periods of access to ethanol on an operant schedule (FR8) were either unsignaled or signaled 15 minutes earlier by a light or noise stimulus. Bar-pressing was reinforced on unsignaled (Blank+) trials and on one of the two signaled trials (CS+); bar-pressing was not reinforced on the other signaled trial (CS–) (see Figure 26–8). The bar was retracted and ethanol was not available between trials. Body temperature was monitored

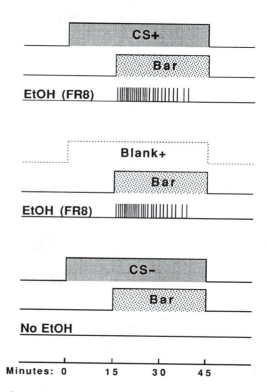

Figure 26–8. Event diagram of trial contingencies in a signaled self-administration experiment. Rats were exposed to all three trial types during daily 16-hour sessions. Bar-pressing was reinforced by access to sweetened alcohol (EtOH) on a fixed-ratio 8 (FR8) schedule of reinforcement on CS+ and Blank+ trials, but not on CS– trials. A white noise and light served as CS+ and CS–, respectively; no stimulus was present on Blank trials. (From Cunningham, 1994.)

continuously from surgically implanted telemetry devices.

Figure 26–9 depicts body-temperature change (from a pretrial baseline) during each of the three trial types after several weeks of training. In general, body temperature increased on reinforced trials (CS+ and Blank+), but remained at baseline on nonreinforced trials (CS–). Of greater interest, however, was the finding that the body-temperature increase on CS+ trials began during the 15-minute signal period before the bar was inserted into the operant chamber and exceeded the thermal response recorded on Blank+ trials. Because there were no differences in body temperatures measured on the initial conditioning trials, the response differences shown in Figure 26–9 appeared to develop as a result of exposure to the differential conditioning procedure. The anticipatory hyperthermia was therefore interpreted as evidence of a Pavlovian thermal CR similar to that produced in experiments involving experimenter-administered drug exposure (see Figures 26–1 and 26–4).

The most interesting finding from this study, however, was the effect of CS+ on self-administration of ethanol and the relationship between conditioned hyperthermia and self-administration. Specifically, total responding for ethanol was greater on CS+ trials than on Blank+ trials (bars in Figure 26–9). Moreover, there was a significant positive correlation ($r = +.77$) between temperature change measured during the 5-minute interval just before access to the bar and bar-press response total on CS+ trials. The finding that a drug-paired CS enhanced drug self-administration is consistent with previous data indicating that environmental cues paired with an experimenter-administered drug will increase drug intake (Hinson et al., 1986; Krank, 1989). However, the finding of a relationship between frequency of self-administration and a specific conditioned response is relatively unique and appears to offer strong support for theories postulating a role for Pavlovian conditioning in drug-seeking behavior.

Given the earlier examples of drug conditioning, one aspect of the data shown in Figure 26–9 deserves special comment. In contrast to studies showing that injection of ethanol produces hypothermia (e.g., see Figure 26–7), self-adminis-

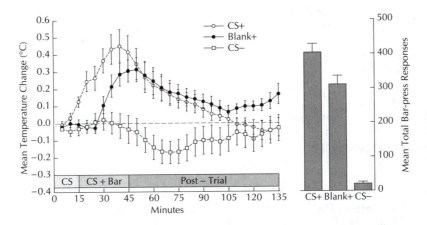

Figure 26–9. Conditioned hyperthermia induced by signaled self-administration of alcohol in rats. Subjects received several weeks of training with the trial contingencies shown in Figure 26–8. The curves depict mean change in body temperature recorded from implanted biotelemetry devices during and after each conditioning trial. The bars depict mean total bar-press responses for sweetened ethanol during each of the three types of conditioning trials. (Adapted from Cunningham, 1994.)

tration of ethanol did not produce an absolute decrease in body temperature during any phase of this experiment. In fact, body temperature was generally elevated above baseline during reinforced trials and remained elevated for more than an hour after the trial ended. This elevation was interpreted as a summation of conditioned hyperthermia (elicited by the CS+ and sight of the bar), unconditioned hyperthermia produced by the activity involved in bar-pressing on the FR8 schedule, and unconditioned hypothermia elicited by ethanol (Cunningham, 1994). Whether or not this interpretation is correct, these findings illustrate the potential difficulty in determining whether one should categorize a drug-induced CR as drug-like or drug-opposite. In this case, one can only infer that the hyperthermia CR was opposite the ethanol UR by appealing to results of studies involving experimenter-administered ethanol and assuming that the same thermoregulatory systems that produce body temperature decreases in those studies were engaged by self-administered ethanol in this study. Additional consideration will be given to this issue in a later discussion of theoretical implications of the Pavlovian drug-conditioning literature for understanding drug self-administration and relapse.

DRUG CONDITIONING IN HUMANS

Before concluding this brief review of empirical findings from the drug-conditioning literature, it is important to note that the literature contains an increasing number of studies that provide clear evidence of drug conditioning in humans. Although these studies have not always used the same rigorous control procedures found in animal studies (see reviews by Robbins & Ehrman, 1992; Glautier & Tiffany, 1995), they suggest that the same general phenomena observed in animal studies of drug conditioning also occur in humans that are repeatedly exposed to abused drugs. In some cases, investigators have examined the development of conditioning to CSs that are paired with drug in the laboratory (e.g., Cascella et al., 1989; Dafters & Anderson,

1982; Glautier et al., 1994; Newlin, 1986), while in other cases the effects of stimuli thought to signal drug in the natural environment have been assessed (e.g., Childress et al., 1988; Newlin, 1985; Ehrman, Robbins, et al., 1992). As in the animal studies described earlier, both types of studies have yielded evidence of drug-like and drug-opposite CRs (Glautier & Remington, 1995). Furthermore, drug-paired CSs have been found to alter the UR to drug (e.g., Ehrman, Ternes, et al., 1992; Shapiro & Nathan, 1986). Such studies are critical both for identifying the types of behavioral and physiological CRs induced by drugs in humans and for learning more about the range of stimuli capable of serving as CSs for drugs. Overall, these studies provide strong support for the conclusion that knowledge derived from animal drug-conditioning studies is important in improving our understanding of the role played by conditioning in modulating drug-seeking behaviors of humans.

CONDITIONING EFFECTS ON BEHAVIOR DURING THE CS AND US: THEORETICAL IMPLICATIONS

Although the examples in the previous sections represent only a small subset of the available literature on drug conditioning, they illustrate several features of that larger literature. For example, they show that drug conditioning can occur quite rapidly, that it can be produced by different classes of drugs, and that it can be observed in different species. Furthermore, they show that drug conditioning is sensitive to many of the parameters known to influence other forms of Pavlovian conditioning, including number of trials, interstimulus interval, and US magnitude. They also demonstrate that the CR produced by drug conditioning is sometimes in the same direction as the drug UR and sometimes in the opposite direction. Finally, these studies show that drug-paired CSs can sometimes enhance the drug UR and sometimes reduce the drug UR.

As mentioned earlier, much of the recent research in the area of drug conditioning has been interpreted in terms of two theoretical models, one emphasizing the negative motivational (withdrawal-like) properties of drug-opposite CRs (e.g., Siegel, 1989) and another emphasizing the positive motivational (incentive) properties of drug-like CRs (e.g., Stewart et al., 1984). To date, efforts to provide definitive evidence in support of one model over the other have not been successful, although some reviewers have found greater support for the incentive model over the compensatory response model (e.g., Niaura et al., 1988; Rohsenow et al., 1990–1991). As illustrated earlier, the literature offers clear evidence that both drug-like and drug-opposite responses can be conditioned, and both outcomes can actually be produced in the same organism as a result of exposure to a single type of drug (e.g., Schwarz-Stevens & Cunningham, 1993). However, because both drug-like and drug-opposite CRs are thought to be affected similarly by conditioning variables (e.g., number of trials, interstimulus interval, US magnitude, etc.), it has been difficult to identify manipulations that allow one to vary one type of CR while holding the other constant. Tests of these models, therefore, have typically relied on attempts to correlate each type of CR with drug-taking or with self-report measures intended to assess hedonic state that may or may not be predictive of drug-taking (e.g., mood state, urge to use, craving). A further complication in the interpretation of such studies is the difficulty that sometimes arises in trying to decide whether the measured CR should be considered drug-like or drug-opposite. For example, in the morphine heart-rate conditioning experiment described earlier, the tachycardia CR was opposite to the early phase of the heart UR but similar to its later phase. Thus, it is not immediately clear whether one should expect the tachycardia CR to be accompanied by an aversive, withdrawal-like motivational state or an incentive-enhancing positive motivational state.

The signaled ethanol self-administration study described earlier (Cunningham, 1994) offers general support for a role of Pavlovian conditioning in drug-seeking behavior, but its impli-
cations for distinguishing between these two theoretical models are unclear. On the one hand, one might characterize the conditioned hyperthermia observed in that study as a drug-compensatory CR that increased bar-pressing by inducing an aversive motivational state that was alleviated by the ethanol reinforcer. Also, drug-compensatory CRs may have produced tolerance to certain effects of ethanol, which could have increased bar-pressing by reducing an ethanol effect that normally impeded or suppressed performance (e.g., ataxia) or by reducing the reinforcing efficacy of ethanol and thereby requiring greater intake to achieve the same effect. The difficulty with this analysis has already been mentioned. That is, the absence of a hypothermia UR weakens the conclusion that the anticipatory CR was compensatory. On the other hand, one might argue that the hyperthermia CR indexed an incentive motivational process that enhanced self-administration through appetitive priming mechanisms. Furthermore, this same process might have sensitized the drug UR, thereby increasing its reinforcing efficacy. A third possibility, not yet discussed, is that the hyperthermia CR represents a relatively nonspecific conditioned arousal response that may not depend at all on the direction of the UR (Cunningham & Schwarz, 1989). This interpretation receives support from studies like those described earlier in which a hyperthermia CR is observed both when the UR is hyperthermia (Broadbent & Cunningham, 1996; Schwarz & Cunningham, 1990) and when it is hypothermia (Mansfield & Cunningham, 1980). Presumably, evocation of a conditioned arousal response could energize previously learned instrumental drug-seeking behaviors and alter the reinforcing efficacy of the drug experience.

Before ending this discussion of theoretical models, it should be noted that there are at least two other prominent models implicating Pavlovian conditioning in drug-seeking behavior that do not emphasize the CR or CR-UR interaction in the same way as the preceding models. In a theory developed primarily to explain morphine tolerance, Baker and Tiffany (1985) have described a mechanism derived from Wagner's (1981) associative theory of habituation that explains how a drug-paired CS can reduce the drug UR even though it may not acquire the ability to elicit a compensatory CR. Thus, this theory expects changes in drug-seeking behavior induced by a CS in the presence of the drug, but does not address CS-related behavioral changes in the absence of drug. In contrast, the incentive-sensitization theory proposed by Robinson and Berridge (1993) emphasizes the role of associatively mediated changes in the incentive salience of drug-paired CSs and explicitly posits a dissociation between the processes governing incentive sensitization and those determining the rewarding components of the drug UR. Although aspects of this theory are similar to Stewart et al.'s (1984) incentive motivation theory, the important effects of conditioning are not attributed to the ability of the CS to evoke drug-like CRs or to an interaction between such CRs and the UR. Rather, conditioning is viewed as a process that focuses exaggerated "wanting" (craving) specifically onto drug-paired stimuli. Because CSs previously paired with drug can acquire the ability to trigger attribution of incentive salience in the absence of drug, the incentive-sensitization theory can readily explain relapse and other changes in drug-seeking behavior that occur after long periods of abstinence.

Although this brief theoretical review has not yielded a single model that can encompass all of the available data, it does reveal some common themes that appear to be useful when analyzing effects of Pavlovian drug conditioning on drug-seeking behavior. Although differing in their details, most of the theoretical models described above can explain relapse, in part, based on the acquired ability of the CS to evoke a motivational process or state that increases the likelihood of instrumental drug-seeking behaviors in the absence of drug. Most of these models also provide a mechanism for understanding how conditioning might change the future probability of drug-seeking by altering the drug UR after an individual has relapsed (or during maintenance of self-administration). The significance of sim-

ilarity or dissimilarity between the CR and drug UR in the explanation of drug-seeking behavior is currently unresolved. Our understanding of the relative importance of drug-like and drug-opposite CRs will depend on future research that provides a more complete picture of the variables affecting each type of CR and their underlying neurobiological mechanisms, thereby allowing a more detailed examination of their relationship to drug-seeking behavior. At the same time, it is important to realize that information about the CRs evoked by a drug-paired CS offers at best an incomplete picture of the overall learning produced by Pavlovian contingencies (Rescorla, 1988).

CLINICAL IMPLICATIONS

Cue Reactivity and Cue Exposure Therapy

Findings and theories derived from the Pavlovian drug-conditioning literature have influenced clinical practice and research for many years. However, it is only during the past 10 years that clinical interests in conditioning-based treatments have coalesced under the broad heading of "cue exposure therapy" (Drummond et al., 1995a; Niaura et al., 1988; Marlatt, 1990; Rohsenow et al., 1990–1991). Although the conceptual bases for cue exposure therapy extend well beyond Pavlovian conditioning, the specific therapeutic strategies encompassed by cue exposure therapy reveal a strong appreciation for the major tenets of the conditioning model (Drummond et al., 1995b). A general approach has been to measure "cue reactivity" to various exteroceptive or interoceptive stimuli that are known or thought to have a significant impact on drug-seeking behavior. Assessment of cue reactivity typically involves self-report measures (e.g., craving, urges, mood), and/or the recording of specific psychophysiological responses (e.g., skin temperature, skin conductance, heart rate, blood pressure, salivation) or behaviors related to drug use in the presence of drug-associated stimuli (Glautier & Tiffany, 1995). Measurements of cue reactivity can be viewed as analogous to the measurement of a CR in Pavlovian conditioning studies, although responses recorded in cue-reactivity studies may not be uniquely attributable to conditioning processes. Therapy is then directed toward cue exposure manipulations intended to reduce reactivity to stimuli associated with drug-seeking. The rationale for this approach can be traced directly to the conditioning principle of extinction (see Falls, this volume). The traditional conditioning literature provides strong evidence that repeated exposure to a CS in the absence of its original US will produce a decrement in the CR (Mackintosh, 1974). Presumably, a reduction in the CR evoked by a drug-paired CS will reduce the ability of that CS to engage motivational processes that enhance drug-seeking behavior or to alter the drug UR.

The literature on extinction of Pavlovian conditioned drug responses is relatively sparse. Although several examples of extinction produced by nonreinforced CS exposure can be found in animal studies (e.g., Mansfield & Cunningham, 1980; Siegel, 1975; Siegel et al., 1979), much more effort has been devoted to studying acquisition of drug-induced CRs than to studying their elimination. Human studies have shown that repeated nonreinforced cue exposure can be effective in reducing reactivity to drug-associated stimuli (e.g., Childress et al., 1987; Powell et al., 1993). However, there are still relatively few studies offering information on the long-term therapeutic impact of cue exposure on drug-seeking behaviors in humans addicted to alcohol or other drugs (for recent reviews, see Brandon et al., 1995; Dawe & Powell, 1995; Rohsenow et al., 1990–1991, 1995).

Decremental Manipulations in Pavlovian Conditioning

Given the paucity of data from the drug-conditioning literature with direct implications for treatment, the remainder of this chapter will be devoted to a relatively general discussion of phenomena from the non-drug Pavlovian conditioning literature that may have important implications in the development of therapies designed to reduce drug-seeking behavior. In particular, this discussion will focus on manipulations that are known to produce decrements in Pavlovian CRs. The most well-known of these manipulations, extinction through nonreinforced CS exposure, has already been introduced. Although extinction can be effective in reducing CRs, the conditioning literature indicates that extinction is also quite vulnerable in the sense that a variety of influences can result in reappearance of the CR after extinction (Bouton & Swartzentruber, 1991). These findings, many of which are described in later sections, have supported the conclusion that nonreinforced CS exposure does not eliminate the original CS-US association or the CS's ability to evoke a CR under certain conditions (Bouton, 1991, 1993; Bouton & Swartzentruber, 1991; Rescorla, 1979; see Falls, this volume). This conclusion suggests that clinicians using extinction-based therapies such as cue exposure must be especially sensitive to variables that can reverse the decremental effects of nonreinforced CS exposure. Furthermore, strong consideration should be given to other approaches known to produce CR decrements and to strategies that may strengthen resistance to or prevent "relapse of the CR." To foster a greater appreciation for these issues, several of the major decremental manipulations in Pavlovian conditioning will be briefly described in the following sections.

Cue Removal

One of the potentially most effective ways to eliminate the influence of drug-induced CRs is simply to remove drug-associated stimuli from the drug-user's environment (or to remove the drug user from those stimuli). Indeed, several examples from the clinical literature support the therapeutic value of this approach. For example, one might argue that the positive relationship between frequency of attendance at self-help meetings (e.g., Alcoholics Anonymous) and treatment success (Baekeland et al., 1975) is indicative of an overall reduction in frequency of exposure to drug-associated CSs. A similar conclusion about the value of cue removal can be derived from studies that have examined the effects of residence relocation on drug use in opiate addicts (Maddux & Desmond, 1982; Ross, 1973). In one study (Maddux & Desmond, 1982), percentage of time abstinent was much higher when individuals were in relocated residences (54%) than in their original residences (12%), an outcome consistent with the suggestion that a new location is less likely to present CSs previously associated with drug use. The unusually high remission rates seen in heroin-addicted Vietnam veterans after their return to the United States (Robins et al., 1975) has also been cited as an example of the beneficial impact of cue removal in reducing relapse (Siegel, 1990).

Although the conceptual basis for incorporating cue removal into treatment for addiction is straightforward, there are several potential limitations on this approach. First, complete removal of individuals from their current environments may not always be practical or possible. Second, given the many opportunities for pairing drug with a wide variety of CSs over the lifetime of an addict, it may be very difficult to identify even a majority of the cues that have gained control over drug-induced CRs. Finally, many of the effective CSs for such CRs may be interoceptive (e.g., mood states; cf. Greeley & Ryan, 1995), raising the possibility that the CS will relocate along with the individual despite major changes in the external environment. Although such considerations suggest that cue removal may not be completely effective in eliminating drug-related CRs, a strong case can nevertheless be made in favor of therapeutic strategies that include efforts to minimize contact with stimuli previously associated with drug (e.g., cue-avoidance training).

Extinction

An obvious limitation of the cue-removal approach is that it really offers no protection against the effects of "accidental" reexposure to drug-paired CSs. Thus, most conditioning-based therapies have utilized repeated nonreinforced presentations of the CS as a means of reducing or eliminating CRs through the process of extinction (i.e., nonreinforced cue exposure). Presumably, after CRs established by drug conditioning have been reduced in this way, reexposure to the controlling CSs will be less likely to trigger relapse by arousing motivational states that activate drug-seeking behavior.

Research on treatment outcomes produced by cue exposure in individuals addicted to alcohol, nicotine, cocaine, or opiates is still in its infancy. Although promising results have been reported, the data are mixed, and well-controlled clinical trials showing long-term outcomes are lacking (Brandon et al., 1995; Dawe & Powell, 1995; Rohsenow et al., 1995). In this context, one issue that deserves greater attention in the cue exposure literature is the vulnerability of extinguished CRs to relapse. As mentioned earlier, a variety of findings suggest that repeated nonreinforced exposure to a CS may not completely eliminate its potential to elicit a CR. Pavlov (1927/1960) originally described two conditioning phenomena that clearly illustrate the lability of extinguished CRs. The first is the phenomenon of *disinhibition,* which refers to the ability of a novel or intense event to reestablish the CR to an extinguished CS. The implication of this phenomenon for therapy is the possibility that an unexpected or emotionally intense experience not previously associated with drug-taking (e.g., automobile accident, death of loved one, physical violence) may disinhibit extinguished CRs, thereby engaging the learned motivational processes that lead to renewed drug-taking. The other relevant phenomenon described by Pavlov is *spontaneous recovery,* which refers to the observed increase in CR magnitude that occurs as a function of time after nonreinforced exposure to the CS (e.g., Rescorla & Cunningham, 1978). An implication of this phenemenon is that the effects of cue exposure may "wear off" over time after initial treatment unless the treatment is periodically repeated.

The contemporary conditioning literature offers other evidence that the CR decrements produced by extinction are not permanent. Several studies have shown, for example, that separate exposure to the US after extinction (signaled or unsignaled) will produce *reinstatement* of an extinguished CR (e.g., Rescorla & Cunningham, 1977, 1978; Rescorla & Heth, 1975). Although such reinstatement is relatively short-lived and disappears rapidly with additional nonreinforced CS exposure, this phenomenon implies that reexposure to a drug after extinction could enhance the ability of the CS to evoke a motivational CR, even though the CS was not directly paired with the US again. Thus, reinstatement of drug-seeking behavior caused by "priming" injections of a drug reinforcer (e.g., de Wit & Stewart, 1981, 1983) might be explained in terms of reinstatement of extinguished Pavlovian CRs that modulate instrumental drug-seeking behaviors. Similarly, exposure to certain types of drugs (e.g., alcohol containing medications, analgesics) after cue exposure treatment may cause relapse via reinstatement of extinguished CRs.

Contextual Control of Extinction

Recent studies from the Pavlovian literature indicate that one of the most powerful determinants of CR expression following extinction is the "context" in which the CS is presented (Bouton, 1991, 1993; see Bouton, this volume). In laboratory studies, context is often defined operationally as the experimental apparatus in which a subject is tested. At a more general level, context has been used to refer to any stimulus that modulates the control exerted by other stimuli (Balsam, 1985). Explicit manipulation of context in Pavlovian conditioning studies appears to have greater impact on an extinguished CR than on an intact CR. That is, a change in context seems more likely to allow a CS to reevoke an extinguished CR than to degrade expression of an established CR. For example, Bouton and King (1983) found equivalent expression and extinction of conditioned fear in rats that were given nonreinforced CS exposures either in the same context used for original conditioning (Context A) or in a different context (Context B). Although rats showed nearly a complete loss of conditioned fear after extinction in Context B, a substantial CR was elicited when the CS

was once again presented in Context A. This phenomenon, labeled the *renewal* effect, has been demonstrated in both appetitive and aversive tasks across several different response systems (Bouton & Swartzentruber, 1991).

Consideration of the role played by context in Pavlovian extinction has strong implications for cue exposure therapy. Although the nature of the stimuli that function as effective contexts for human substance abusers is not known, one might speculate that all of the following are potential contexts: home, workplace, school, recreational sites (e.g., concert hall, sports stadium, bowling alley), drug-use locations (e.g., restaurant, tavern, drug house), hospital or treatment facility. Because CS-drug pairings are more likely to have occurred in all but the last of these contexts, cue exposure (e.g., exposure to drug paraphernalia) given in a treatment facility may substantially reduce the CR evoked by the CS in that context (Context B), but not eliminate the ability of that CS to evoke its CR in other contexts (Context A). That is, when the individual returns to other contexts after cue exposure in a treatment facility, there may be renewal of the extinguished CR along with its influence on drug-seeking behavior. One obvious, though daunting, solution to this problem is to conduct cue exposure in as many different contexts as possible. Overall, data from the conditioning literature suggest that cue exposure therapy must be sensitive to the possibility that removal of the extinction context can precipitate relapse via renewal of extinguished CRs.

Conditioned Inhibition

Historically, Pavlovian extinction has been closely linked with the concept of inhibitory conditioning (Rescorla, 1979). Conditioned inhibition is generally viewed as a learning process that endows CSs with the ability to reduce excitatory CRs (i.e., CRs produced by exposure to positive CS-US contingencies) (Rescorla, 1969). Thus, conditioned inhibition is a Pavlovian decremental manipulation with potential implications for therapies designed to reduce drug-seeking behavior. The development of conditioned inhibition appears to depend on nonreinforcement of the to-be-conditioned inhibitory CS in the presence of some conditioned excitatory stimulus, a situation that often occurs when there is a negative contingency between presentation of the CS and US (LoLordo & Fairless, 1985). For example, intermixed presentations of a reinforced CS (A) with nonreinforced exposures to a compound CS consisting of A and another CS (i.e., AX–) will endow the added CS (X) with inhibitory properties. Not only will X reduce CRs normally evoked by A, it will also reduce CRs evoked by other excitatory CSs in transfer tests (e.g., Rescorla & Holland, 1977).

The ability to establish inhibitory stimulus control over Pavlovian CRs has intriguing implications for conditioning-based therapies. First, it is quite reasonable to suppose that many stimuli in the drug user's natural environment have acquired conditioned inhibitory properties. For example, there may be certain situations or circumstances in which drug use once occurred but no longer does. Conceivably, distinctive stimuli correlated with the absence of drug in these settings (e.g., wearing a particular article of clothing) may acquire the properties of a conditioned inhibitor (CI). Thus, when analyzing drug-use patterns to identify excitatory CSs as targets for cue-exposure therapy, attention should also be given to identifying stimuli that may have become CIs for drug-related CRs. One reason for knowing about such stimuli is to prevent exposure to them during extinction of the target CS because CIs can interfere with extinction of excitatory CSs (a phenomenon known as "protection from extinction"; Soltysik, 1985). More important, these natural CIs could be exploited in the therapeutic process, for example, by teaching individuals to use these stimuli to suppress excitatory CRs that would normally activate drug-seeking behavior. In addition, one might actually establish novel stimuli as explicit CIs during therapy and then train individuals to self-administer CIs as part of their strategy for coping with situations that are normally associated with drug-taking. Because CIs appear to retain their inhibitory properties when context is changed

(Bouton & Nelson, 1994), this approach may help overcome some of the problems that can be caused by renewal of Pavlovian CRs after removal of the cue-exposure therapy context (see previous section).

On the basis of the foregoing analysis, one might be tempted to explain the earlier examples of context-shift effects on extinguished CRs in terms of conditioned inhibition to the extinction context. Although there is evidence that novel stimuli combined with an excitatory CS during extinction acquire inhibitory properties (Cunningham, 1979, 1981; Rescorla, 1979), it does not appear that context-shift effects after extinction can be attributed to removal of a conditioned inhibitory context (Bouton, 1991). As an alternative, Bouton (1993) has offered a memory-retrieval model of these effects. Interestingly, research in support of this model has yielded a finding that encourages use of a therapeutic strategy like that derived from consideration of the role played by CIs. Specifically, a novel cue correlated with extinction was found to facilitate transfer of extinction across contexts (i.e., attenuate renewal), even though that cue did not acquire inhibitory properties (Brooks & Bouton, 1994). This outcome was attributed to the ability of the cue to facilitate retrieval of the memory of extinction outside the extinction context. The clinical implications of this finding are similar to those described above for an explicit CI established during therapy. That is, one might establish novel stimuli as retrieval cues during extinction in the therapeutic setting and then train individuals to self-administer those cues as extinction reminders in their natural environment.

Decremental Manipulations Involving a Second US

Thus far, discussion has focused on operations that decrement the Pavlovian CR by changing the relationship between the CS and its original US. However, the contemporary Pavlovian-conditioning literature also includes two decremental operations that involve a second US whose motivational valence is typically opposite that of the original US. In the first case, a CS (A) that has previously been associated with one US (US_1) is subsequently associated with a different US (US_2). The result is a reduction in the original CR and the acquisition of a new CR that reflects the influence of the new US (e.g., Bouton & Peck, 1992; Krank, 1985; Peck & Bouton, 1990; Scavio, 1974). If US_1 and US_2 activate opposing motivational systems (i.e., appetitive versus aversive), the motivational state aroused by the CS will presumably be reversed by this procedure. In the second case, the original US (US_1) itself is paired with a motivationally opposite US (US_2) in a procedure that is sometimes referred to as *counterconditioning* or *revaluation*. This procedure, which has been extensively used to support representational theories of Pavlovian conditioning, often reduces CRs evoked by CSs previously associated with US_1 (Delamater & LoLordo, 1991).

Therapeutic strategies involving operations similar to those just described have had a long history in the behavioral treatment of substance abuse under the label *aversion therapy* (Childress et al., 1985; Elkins, 1975). Aversion therapy has been most frequently used to treat alcoholism and typically involves pairing various alcohol-related stimuli (e.g., sight, smell, taste) with an aversive event (US) such as chemically-induced nausea and emesis, painful electric stimulation, drug-induced respiratory arrest, or unpleasant imagery (Elkins, 1975). Because of the risks associated with stressful chemical and electrical stimuli and the potential for high dropout rates, contemporary applications of aversion therapy often rely more on the use of imagery (covert sensitization; cf. Rimmele et al., 1989). Although it has been difficult to isolate the impact of aversion therapy per se in extant treatment-outcome studies, it is nevertheless viewed as a potentially useful element of multidimensional treatment approaches (Frawley, 1995; Rimmele et al., 1989).

In general, the aversion-therapy literature has not distinguished between the two decremental operations involving a second US described

earlier. Although the literature indicates that both operations can be effective in reducing an established CR, the conceptual bases for those reductions and their broader implications vary between these two approaches. The major difference is in the expected impact of treatment on CRs evoked by other CSs associated with the same drug. This difference can be illustrated by considering the situations depicted in Figure 26–10. In both panels, it has been assumed that separate associations are formed between the drug (US_1) and at least two different CSs (A and B). This assumption appears quite reasonable in the case of addicted individuals with long histories of drug exposure in various situations. In the case of Alternative Outcome Training (upper panel), if only one of those CSs

Original Learning	Alternative Outcome Training	Expected Change in Original CR
$A \rightarrow US_1$		$\downarrow CR_A$
	$A \rightarrow US_2$	
$B \rightarrow US_1$		$\circ CR_B$

Original Learning	Outcome Revaluation Training	Expected Change in Original CR
$A \rightarrow US_1$		$\downarrow CR_A$
	$US_1 \rightarrow US_2$	
$B \rightarrow US_1$		$\downarrow CR_B$

Figure 26–10. Two examples of Pavlovian decremental manipulations involving a second US. The upper panel depicts Alternative Outcome Training in which a CS (A) previously paired with US_1 is subsequently paired with a different US (US_2). This training is expected to reduce the CR originally evoked by CS_A, but to have no effect on CRs evoked by other CSs paired with US_1 during original learning. The lower panel depicts Outcome Revaluation Training in which the original US (US_1) is paired with a motivationally opposite US (US_2) after conditioning with US_1. The potential outcome is a reduction in all CRs originally induced by conditioning with US_1. See text for further explanation.

($_A$) is paired with an unpleasant outcome (US_2) during aversion therapy, one can only expect to produce a decrement in the CR evoked by CS_A, not that evoked by CS_B. This decrement occurs because Alternative Outcome Training degrades the predictive relationship between CS_A and US_1 at the same time as it establishes the new relationship between CS_A and US_2. In contrast, Outcome Revaluation Training (lower panel), has the potential to reduce drug-related CRs evoked by *all* CSs previously associated with the drug (US_1).

For the most part, aversion therapy appears to have been implemented as Alternative Outcome Training in that the aversive event (US_2) has been paired with stimuli predictive of the drug's effects (i.e., CSs) rather than the drug state itself. From a theoretical perspective, the advantages of this approach are that it directly reduces the original CR and endows the CS with aversive motivational properties that should discourage subsequent contact with that CS. The main disadvantage, as illustrated in Figure 26–10, is that these effects will be limited to CSs that are paired with alternative outcomes during treatment. It is unclear from the literature how often aversion therapy is implemented as Outcome Revaluation Training instead of Alternative Outcome Training. In principle, use of antabuse (disulfiram) in aversion therapy for alcoholism might be expected to more closely resemble Outcome Revaluation Training because individuals would experience alcohol intoxication in conjunction with the adverse consequences of altering ethanol metabolism.

Theoretically, the main advantage of Outcome Revaluation Training is its potential to have a widespread impact on CRs evoked by any CS previously associated with the original drug. There are, however, several possible disadvantages. First, because the CS is never presented during treatment, the treatment would not be expected to change the ability of the CS to activate a memory of the drug US. Thus, any post-treatment experience that restored the value of the drug US could conceivably reestablish the abil-

ity of all previously associated CSs to evoke their original CRs. A second disadvantage is suggested by studies showing that the impact of outcome revaluation may vary as a function of the target response system (Holland & Straub, 1979). A third potential disadvantage is suggested by studies indicating that pairing of drug states with aversive outcomes may have the unexpected outcome of reducing the aversive properties of the drug state (Revusky et al., 1979; Cunningham & Linakis, 1980). However, the latter outcome has only been shown in tests of new learning with US_1, not in tests of previously established associations. Although these considerations argue against a treatment strategy that relies exclusively on Outcome Revaluation Training, they should not discourage consideration of its potential in combination with other decremental manipulations.

Increasing the Efficacy of Cue Exposure Therapy

Assuming that a broad goal of cue exposure therapy is to reduce or eliminate CRs elicited by CSs that have previously been associated with administration of drug, the list of manipulations that might be useful in this effort extends well beyond simple extinction. Figure 26–11 summarizes the various Pavlovian decremental manipulations that have been or could be applied in behavior therapies designed to weaken drug-related CRs. Although laboratory investigations of these manipulations have rarely examined the joint effects of two or more of these manipulations, it seems quite reasonable to expect that the combined application of several of these manipulations would be more effective in reducing CRs than any single manipulation.

Another possibility for consideration is the use of pharmacological agents that accelerate extinction. One example of this possibility was recently provided in a study of the effects of the opiate antagonist naloxone on conditioned place preference induced by ethanol. Although naloxone had no effect on the learning or initial

Summary of Pavlovian
Decremental Manipulations

Cue Removal

Cue Exposure (Extinction)

Multiple Context Extinction

Conditioned Inhibition Training

Extinction Reminder Training

Alternative Outcome Training

Outcome Devaluation Training

Figure 26–11. Summary of procedures known to produce decrements in Pavlovian CRs. See text for additional explanation.

expression of conditioned preference, it facilitated extinction of that preference (Cunningham et al., 1995). These findings are of particular interest in light of recent clinical trials suggesting that a similar, longer-lasting opiate antagonist (naltrexone) is a useful adjunct in the treatment of alcoholism (O'Malley et al., 1992; Volpicelli et al., 1992). Although it is clearly too soon to recommend this particular drug for widespread use in cue exposure therapy, findings such as these encourage further research on its potential and that of other pharmacological agents that might alter extinction. One possible complication in this approach is that a drug introduced at the time of extinction may serve as a context whose removal leads to renewal of the extinguished CR (e.g., Cunningham, 1979; Bouton et al., 1990). However, this effect clearly does not occur in every instance of extinction in the presence of a drug state (Cunningham et al., 1995).

SUMMARY AND CONCLUSIONS

This chapter has addressed the empirical and theoretical bases as well as possible clinical implications of the suggestion that stimuli associated with administration of abused drugs influence drug-seeking behavior in part through Pavlovian conditioning mechanisms. A brief, selective review of several studies illustrated several common findings in the drug-conditioning literature. In particular, these studies showed that drug conditioning can occur rapidly, that it can be produced by different classes of drugs, and that it can be observed in several different species, including humans. Moreover, these studies indicate that drug conditioning is affected by many of the same parameters known to influence conditioning induced by non-drug USs, including number of trials, interstimulus interval, and US magnitude. Pavlovian drug conditioning will produce robust behavioral and physiological changes (CRs) that can often be measured during the CS in the absence of the drug US. In some cases, these CRs are in the same direction as the drug-induced UR, while in other cases the CR and UR are in the opposite direction. The factors determining the relationship between CR and UR are still unknown, although it does not appear to be determined simply by drug class or target response system. Pavlovian drug conditioning will also produce changes in the drug UR measured in the presence of the CS. Thus, conditioning may contribute to drug tolerance or drug sensitization.

Theories relating Pavlovian drug conditioning to instrumental drug-seeking behavior have focused on the hypothesized ability of drug-paired CSs to engage motivational systems or states that activate drug-seeking or on the ability of those CSs to alter the reinforcing efficacy of self-administered drugs. According to these theories, relapse to drug-seeking behavior after treatment or long periods of abstinence is caused by reexposure to CSs previously associated with drug that elicit CRs with motivational implications for drug-seeking. The compensatory-conditioned-response theory emphasizes the aversive, withdrawal-like properties of drug-opposite CRs, whereas the incentive-motivational theory accentuates the positive motivational effects that accompany drug-like CRs. Efforts to provide definitive evidence in favor of one theory over the other have not been successful, and the significance of similarity or dissimilarity between the CR and drug UR is still unresolved.

Although the various drug-conditioning theories differ in the specific details of how Pavlovian CRs might influence drug-seeking behavior, they all lead to a similar conclusion for treatment of addiction. That is, most conditioning theories suggest that manipulations designed to reduce or eliminate the drug-related CR should be useful in reducing the likelihood of relapse after treatment. This implication of conditioning theory is already well-recognized in cue exposure therapies derived from the principle of Pavlovian extinction. The rationale for this approach is that repeated exposure to a CS in the absence of its drug US should eventually eliminate the CR evoked by that CS, thereby removing a source of motivation for renewed drug-seeking behavior. The conditioning literature, however, indicates that a variety of influences can reestablish extinguished CRs. These influences include disinhibition, spontaneous recovery, reinstatement, and renewal. Given this vulnerability of CRs weakened by simple extinction, it was suggested that strong consideration should be given to utilizing other Pavlovian decremental manipulations in combination with extinction (Figure 26–11).

Overall, these findings from the basic learning literature and clinical literature encourage greater attention to the potential influence of Pavlovian conditioning on drug-seeking behavior. Additional research is needed on determinants of drug-induced CRs and the exact nature of the relationship between specific types of CRs and drug-taking. There is also a need for more basic research on manipulations that decrement drug-induced CRs and the effects of combinations of those manipulations on the ability of drug-paired CSs to precipitate relapse. Such research efforts should aid in long-term efforts to refine behavioral therapies to reduce substance abuse and addictive behavior.

ENDNOTES

Preparation of this chapter and most of the original research described here was supported by grants from the National Institute on Alcohol Abuse and Alcoholism (AA07702, AA08621, AA07468) and the National Institute on Drug Abuse (DA03608, DA07262). Thanks are extended to the students, research assistants and colleagues who contributed to this research. Thanks are also extended to Nancy Bormann, Julie Broadbent, Julia Chester, John Crabbe, Shelly Dickinson, and Nicholas Grahame for helpful comments on an earlier draft of this chapter.

REFERENCES

American Psychiatric Association (1994). *Diagnostic and statistical manual of mental disorders, fourth edition (DSM-IV)*. Washington, D.C.: American Psychiatric Association.

Baekeland, F., Lundwall, L., & Kissin, B. (1975). Methods for the treatment of chronic alcoholism: A critical appraisal. In R. J. Gibbins, Y. Israel, H. Kalant, R. E. Popham, W. Schmidt, & R. G. Smart (eds.), *Research advances in alcohol and drug problems,* Vol. 2: 247–327. New York: Wiley.

Baker, T. B., & Tiffany, S. T. (1985). Morphine tolerance as habituation. *Psychological Review, 92,* 78–108.

Balsam, P. D. (1985). The functions of context in learning and performance. In P. D. Balsam & A. Tomie (eds.), *Context and learning,* 1–21. Hillsdale, N.J.: Erlbaum.

Bouton, M. E. (1991). Context and retrieval in extinction and in other examples of interference in simple associative learning. In L. Dachowski & C. F. Flaherty (eds.), *Current topics in animal learning: Brain, emotion, and cognition,* 25–53. Hillsdale, N.J.: Erlbaum.

Bouton, M. E. (1993). Context, time, and memory retrieval in the interference paradigms of Pavlovian learning. *Psychological Bulletin, 114,* 80–99.

Bouton, M. E., Kenney, F. A., & Rosengard, C. (1990). State-dependent fear extinction with two benzodiazepine tranquilizers. *Behavioral Neuroscience, 104,* 44–55.

Bouton, M. E., & King, D. A. (1983). Contextual control of the extinction of conditioned fear: Tests for the associative value of context. *Journal of Experimental Psychology: Animal Behavior Processes, 9,* 248–265.

Bouton, M. E., & Nelson, J. B. (1994). Context-specificity of target versus feature inhibition in a feature-negative discrimination. *Journal of Experimental Psychology: Animal Behavior Processes, 20,* 51–65.

Bouton, M. E., & Peck, C. A. (1992). Spontaneous recovery in cross-motivational transfer (counterconditioning). *Animal Learning & Behavior, 20,* 313–321.

Bouton, M. E., & Swartzentruber, D. (1991). Sources of relapse after extinction in Pavlovian and instrumental learning. *Clinical Psychology Review, 11,* 123–140.

Brandon, T. H., Piasecki, T. M., Quinn, E. P., & Baker, T. B. (1995). Cue exposure treatment in nicotine dependence. In D. C. Drummond, S. T. Tiffany, S. Glautier, & B. Remington (eds.), *Addictive behavior: Cue exposure theory and practice,* 211–227. Chichester, England: Wiley.

Broadbent, J., & Cunningham, C. L. (1996). Pavlovian conditioning of morphine hyperthermia: Assessment of interstimulus interval and CS-US overlap. *Psychopharmacology, 126,* 156–164.

Brooks, D. C., & Bouton, M. E. (1994). A retrieval cue for extinction attenuates response recovery (renewal) caused by a return to the conditioning context. *Journal of Experimental Psychology: Animal Behavior Processes, 20,* 366–379.

Brown, J. S., & Cunningham, C. L. (1981). The paradox of persisting self-punitive behavior. *Neuroscience and Biobehavioral Reviews, 5,* 343–354.

Carr, G. D., Fibiger, H. C., & Phillips, A. G. (1989). Conditioned place preference as a measure of drug reward. In J. M. Liebman & S. J. Cooper (eds.), *Neuropharmacological basis of reward,* 264–319. New York: Oxford University Press.

Cascella, N., Muntaner, C., Kumor, K. M., Nagoshi, C. T., Jaffe, J. H., & Sherer, M. A. (1989). Cardiovascular responses to cocaine placebo in humans: A preliminary report. *Biological Psychiatry, 1989,* 285–295.

Chaudron, C. D., & Wilkinson, D. A. (1988). *Theories on alcoholism.* Toronto: Addiction Research Foundation.

Childress, A. R., Ehrman, R., Rohsenow, D. J., Robbins, S. J., & O'Brien, C. P. (1992). Classically conditioned factors in drug dependence. In J. H. Lowinson, P. Ruiz, & R. B. Millman (eds.), *Substance abuse: A comprehensive textbook,* 2nd ed., 56–69. Baltimore: Williams & Wilkins.

Childress, A. R., McLellan, A. T., Ehrman, R. N., & O'Brien, C. P. (1987). Extinction of conditioned responses in abstinent cocaine or opioid users. In L. S. Harris (ed.), *Problems of drug dependence,* 189–195. Rockville, Md.: NIDA Research Monograph 76.

Childress, A. R., McClellan, A. T., Ehrman, R., & O'Brien, C. P. (1988). Classically conditioned responses in opioid and cocaine dependence: A role in relapse? In B. A. Ray (ed.), *Learning factors in substance abuse,* 25–43. Rockville, Md.: NIDA Research Monograph 84.

Childress, A. R., McLellan, A. T., & O'Brien, C. P. (1985). Behavioral therapies for substance abuse. *International Journal of the Addictions, 20,* 947–969.

Cunningham, C. L. (1979). Alcohol as a cue for extinction: State dependency produced by conditioned inhibition. *Animal Learning & Behavior, 7,* 45–52.

Cunningham, C. L. (1981). Association between the elements of a bivalent compound stimulus. *Journal of Experimental Psychology: Animal Behavior Processes, 7,* 425–436.

Cunningham, C. L. (1993). Pavlovian drug conditioning. In F. van Haaren (ed.), *Methods in behavioral pharmacology,* 349–381. Amsterdam: Elsevier.

Cunningham, C. L. (1994). Modulation of ethanol reinforcement by conditioned hyperthermia. *Psychopharmacology, 115,* 79–85.

Cunningham, C. L., Crabbe, J. C., & Rigter, H. (1990). Pavlovian conditioning of drug-induced changes in body temperature. In E. Schönbaum & P. Lomax (eds.), *Thermoregulation: Physiology and biochemistry,* 101–127. New York: Pergamon.

Cunningham, C. L., Dickinson, S. D., & Okorn, D. M. (1995). Naloxone facilitates extinction but does not affect acquisition or expression of ethanol-induced conditioned place preference. *Experimental and Clinical Psychopharmacology, 3,* 330–343.

Cunningham, C. L., & Linakis, J. G. (1980). Paradoxical aversive conditioning with ethanol. *Pharmacology Biochemistry & Behavior, 12,* 337–341.

Cunningham, C. L., Niehus, D. R., Malott, D. H., & Prather, L. K. (1992). Genetic differences in the rewarding and activating effects of morphine and ethanol. *Psychopharmacology, 107,* 385–393.

Cunningham, C. L., & Noble, D. (1992). Conditioned activation induced by ethanol: Role in sensitization and conditioned place preference. *Pharmacology Biochemistry & Behavior, 43,* 307–313.

Cunningham, C. L., & Schwarz, K. S. (1989). Pavlovian-conditioned changes in body temperature induced by alcohol and morphine. *Drug Development Research, 16,* 295–303.

Dafters, R., & Anderson, G. (1982). Conditioned tolerance to the tachycardia effect of ethanol in humans. *Psychopharmacology, 78,* 365–367.

Dawe, S., & Powell, J. H. (1995). Cue exposure treatment in opiate and cocaine dependence. In D. C. Drummond, S. T. Tiffany, S. Glautier, & B. Remington (eds.), *Addictive behavior: Cue exposure theory and practice,* 197–209. Chichester, England: Wiley.

de Wit, H., & Stewart, J. (1981). Reinstatement of cocaine-reinforced responding in the rat. *Psychopharmacology, 75,* 134–143.

de Wit, H., & Stewart, J. (1983). Drug reinstatement of heroin-reinforced responding in the rat. *Psychopharmacology, 79,* 29–31.

Delamater, A. R., & LoLordo, V. M. (1991). Event revaluation procedures and associative structures in Pavlovian conditioning. In L. Dachowski & C. F. Flaherty (eds.), *Current topics in animal learning: Brain, emotion, and cognition,* 55–94. Hillsdale, N.J.: Erlbaum.

Drummond, D. C., Tiffany, S. T., Glautier, S., & Remington, B. (eds.) (1995a). *Addictive behavior: Cue exposure theory and practice.* Chichester, England: Wiley.

Drummond, D. C., Tiffany, S. T., Glautier, S., & Remington, B. (1995b). Cue exposure in understanding and treating addictive behaviours. In D. C. Drummond, S. T. Glautier, & B. Remington (eds.), *Addictive behavior: Cue exposure theory and practice,* 1–17. Chichester, England: Wiley.

Ehrman, R. N., Robbins, S. J., Childress, A. R., & O'Brien, C. P. (1992). Conditioned responses to cocaine-related stimuli in cocaine abuse patients. *Psychopharmacology, 107,* 523–529.

Ehrman, R., Ternes, J., O'Brien, C. P., & McLellan, A. T. (1992). Conditioned tolerance in human opiate addicts. *Psychopharmacology, 108,* 218–224.

Eikelboom, R., & Stewart, J. (1982). Conditioning of drug-induced physiological responses. *Psychological Review, 89,* 507–528.

Elkins, R. L. (1975). Aversion therapy for alcoholism: Chemical, electrical, or verbal imaginary? *International Journal of the Addictions, 10,* 157–209.

Frawley, P. J. (1995). Aversion Therapy. In N. S. Miller (ed.), *Topics in addiction medicine,* Vol. 1: 1–8. Chevy Chase, Md.: American Society of Addiction Medicine.

Glautier, S., Drummond, C., & Remington, B. (1994). Alcohol as an unconditioned stimulus in human classical conditioning. *Psychopharmacology, 116,* 360–368.

Glautier, S., & Remington, B. (1995). The form of responses to drug cues. In D. C. Drummond, S. T. Tiffany, S. Glautier, & B. Remington (eds.), *Addictive behavior: Cue exposure theory and practice,* 21–46. Chichester, England: Wiley.

Glautier, S., & Tiffany, S. T. (1995). Methodological issues in cue reactivity research. In D. C. Drummond, S. T. Tiffany, S. Glautier, & B. Remington (eds.), *Addictive behavior: Cue exposure theory and practice,* 75–97. Chichester, England: Wiley.

Gordon, C. J. (1993). *Temperature regulation in laboratory rodents.* New York: Cambridge University Press.

Goudie, A. J., & Demellweek, C. (1986). Conditioning factors in drug tolerance. In S. R. Goldberg & I. P. Stolerman (eds.), *Behavioral analysis of drug dependence,* 225–285. Orlando, Fla.: Academic Press.

Greeley, J., & Ryan, C. (1995). The role of interoceptive cues for drug delivery in conditioning models of drug dependence. In D. C. Drummond, S. T. Tiffany, S. Glautier, & B. Remington (eds.), *Addictive behavior: Cue exposure theory and practice,* 119–136. Chichester, England: Wiley.

Hinson, R. E., & Siegel, S. (1980). The contribution of Pavlovian conditioning to ethanol tolerance and dependence. In H. Rigter & J. C. Crabbe (eds.), *Alcohol tolerance and dependence,* 181–199. Amsterdam: Elsevier/North-Holland Biomedical Press.

Hinson, R. E., William, T., Cappell, H., & Poulos, C. X. (1986). Pavlovian conditioning and addictive behavior: Relapse to oral self-administration of morphine. *Behavioral Neuroscience, 100,* 368–375.

Holland, P. C., & Straub, J. J. (1979). Differential effects of two ways of devaluing the unconditioned stimulus after Pavlovian appetitive conditioning. *Journal of Experimental Psychology: Animal Behavior Processes, 5,* 65–78.

Jaffe, J. H. (1992). Current concepts of addiction. In C. P. O'Brien & J. H. Jaffe (eds.), *Addictive states,* 1–21. New York: Raven Press.

Krank, M. D. (1985). Asymmetrical effects of Pavlovian excitatory and inhibitory transfer on Pavlovian appetitive responding and acquisition. *Learning and Motivation, 16,* 35–62.

Krank, M. D. (1989). Environmental signals for ethanol enhance free-choice ethanol consumption. *Behavioral Neuroscience, 103,* 365–372.

LoLordo, V. M., & Fairless, J. L. (1985). Pavlovian conditioned inhibition: The literature since 1969. In R. R. Miller & N. E. Spear (eds.), *Information processing in animals: Conditioned inhibition,* 1–49. Hillsdale, N.J.: Erlbaum.

Lynch, J. J., Fertziger, A. P., Teitelbaum, H. A., Cullen, J. W., & Gantt, W. H. (1973). Pavlovian conditioning of drug reactions: Some implications for problems of drug addiction. *Conditional Reflex, 4,* 211–223.

Lynch, J. J., Stein, E. A., & Fertziger, A. P. (1976). An analysis of 70 years of morphine classical conditioning: Implications for clinical treatment of narcotic addition. *Journal of Nervous and Mental Disease, 163,* 47–58.

Mackintosh, N. J. (1974). *The psychology of animal learning.* New York: Academic Press.

Mackintosh, N. J. (1983). *Conditioning and associative learning.* New York: Oxford University Press.

Maddux, J. F., & Desmond, D. P. (1982). Residence relocation inhibits opioid dependence. *Archives of General Psychiatry, 39,* 1313–1317.

Mansfield, J. G., & Cunningham, C. L. (1980). Conditioning and extinction of tolerance to the hypothermic effect of ethanol in rats. *Journal of Comparative and Physiological Psychology, 94,* 962–969.

Marlatt, G. A. (1990). Cue exposure and relapse prevention in the treatment of addictive behaviors. *Addictive Behaviors, 15,* 395–399.

Newlin, D. B. (1985). The antagonistic placebo response to alcohol cues. *Alcoholism: Clinical and Experimental Research, 9,* 411–416.

Newlin, D. B. (1986). Conditioned compensatory response to alcohol placebo in humans. *Psychopharmacology, 88,* 247–251.

Niaura, R. S., Rohsenow, D. J., Binkoff, J. A., Monti, P. M., Pedraza, M., & Abrams, D. B. (1988). Relevance of cue reactivity to understanding alcohol and smoking relapse. *Journal of Abnormal Psychology, 97,* 133–152.

O'Malley, S. S., Jaffe, A. J., Chang, G., Schottenfeld, R. S., Meyer, R. E., & Rounsaville, B. (1992). Naltrexone and coping skills therapy for alcohol dependence: A controlled study. *Archives of General Psychiatry, 49,* 881–887.

Pavlov, I. P. (1927/1960). *Conditioned reflexes.* New York: Dover Publications.

Peck, C. A., & Bouton, M. E. (1990). Context and performance in aversive-to-appetitive and appetitive-to-aversive transfer. *Learning and Motivation, 21,* 1–31.

Phillips, T. J., & Crabbe, J. C. (1991). Behavioral studies of genetic differences in alcohol action. In J. C. Crabbe & R. A. Harris (eds.), *The genetic basis of alcohol and drug actions,* 25–104. New York: Plenum.

Powell, J. H., Gray, J. A., & Bradley, B. (1993). Subjective craving for opiates: Evaluation of a cue exposure protocol for use with detoxified opiate addicts. *British Journal of Clinical Psychology, 32,* 39–53.

Rescorla, R. A. (1969). Pavlovian conditioned inhibition. *Psychological Bulletin, 72,* 77–94.

Rescorla, R. A. (1979). Conditioned inhibition and extinction. In A. Dickinson & R. A. Boakes (eds.), *Mechanisms of learning and motivation: A memorial volume to Jerzy Konorski,* 83–110. Hillsdale, N.J.: Erlbaum.

Rescorla, R. A. (1988). Pavlovian conditioning: It's not what you think it is. *American Psychologist, 43(3),* 151–160.

Rescorla, R. A., & Cunningham, C. L. (1977). The erasure of reinstated fear. *Animal Learning & Behavior, 5,* 386–394.

Rescorla, R. A., & Cunningham, C. L. (1978). Recovery of the US representation over time during extinction. *Learning and Motivation, 9,* 373–391.

Rescorla, R. A., & Heth, C. D. (1975). Reinstatement of fear to an extinguished conditioned stimulus. *Journal of Experimental Psychology: Animal Behavior Processes, 104,* 88–96.

Rescorla, R. A., & Holland, P. C. (1977). Associations in Pavlovian conditioned inhibition. *Learning and Motivation, 8,* 429–447.

Revusky, S., Taukulis, H. K., Parker, L. A., & Coombes, S. (1979). Chemical aversion therapy: Rat data suggest it may be countertherapeutic to pair an addictive drug state with sickness. *Behavior Research and Therapy, 17,* 177–188.

Rimmele, C. T., Miller, W. R., & Dougher, M. J. (1989). Aversion therapies. In R. K. Hester & W. R. Miller (eds.), *Handbook of alcoholism treatment approaches,* 128–140. New York: Pergamon.

Robbins, S. J., & Ehrman, R. N. (1992). Designing studies of drug conditioning in humans. *Psychopharmacology, 106,* 143–153.

Robins, L. N., Helzer, J. E., & Davis, D. H. (1975). Narcotic use in Southeast Asia and afterward. *Archives of General Psychiatry, 32,* 955–961.

Robinson, T. E., & Berridge, K. C. (1993). The neural basis of drug craving: An incentive-sensitization theory of addiction. *Brain Research Reviews, 18,* 247–291.

Rohsenow, D. J., Monti, P. M., & Abrams, D. B. (1995). Cue exposure treatment in alcohol dependence. In D. C. Drummond, S. T. Tiffany, S. Glautier, & B. Remington (eds.), *Addictive behavior: Cue exposure theory and practice,* 169–196. Chichester, England: Wiley.

Rohsenow, D. J., Niaura, R. S., Childress, A. R., Abrams, D. B., & Monti, P. M. (1990–1991). Cue reactivity in addictive behaviors: Theoretical and treatment implications. *International Journal of the Addictions, 25,* 957–993.

Ross, S. (1973). A study of living and residence patterns of former heroin addicts as a result of their participation in a methadone treatment program, *Proceedings of the fifth National Conference on Methadone Treatment,* 554–561. New York: National Association for the Prevention of Addiction to Narcotics.

Scavio, M. J. (1974). Classical-classical transfer: Effects of prior aversive conditioning upon appetitive conditioning in rabbits. *Journal of Comparative and Physiological Psychology, 86,* 107–115.

Schönbaum, E., & Lomax, P. (eds.) (1991). *Thermoregulation: Pathology, pharmacology, and therapy.* New York: Pergamon.

Schwarz, K. S., & Cunningham, C. L. (1990). Conditioned stimulus control of morphine hyperthermia. *Psychopharmacology, 101,* 77–84.

Schwarz, K. S., Peris, J., & Cunningham, C. L. (1987). Effects of restraint and naltrexone on the biphasic heart rate response to morphine in rats. *Alcohol and Drug Research, 7,* 327–339.

Schwarz-Stevens, K. S., & Cunningham, C. L. (1993). Pavlovian conditioning of heart rate and body temperature with morphine: Effects of CS duration. *Behavioral Neuroscience, 107,* 1039–1048.

Shapiro, A. P., & Nathan, P. E. (1986). Human tolerance to alcohol: The role of Pavlovian conditioning processes. *Psychopharmacology, 88,* 90–95.

Siegel, S. (1975). Evidence from rats that morphine tolerance is a learned response. *Journal of Comparative and Physiological Psychology, 89,* 498–506.

Siegel, S. (1989). Pharmacological conditioning and drug effects. In A. J. Goudie & M. W. Emmett-Oglesby (eds.), *Psychoactive drugs: Tolerance and sensitization,* 115–180. Clifton, N.J.: Humana Press.

Siegel, S. (1990). Classical conditioning and opiate tolerance and withdrawal. In D. J. K. Balfour (ed.), *Psychotropic drugs of abuse,* 59–85. New York: Pergamon.

Siegel, S., Hinson, R. E., & Krank, M. D. (1979). Modulation of tolerance to the lethal effect of morphine by extinction. *Behavioral and Neural Biology, 25,* 257–262.

Soltysik, S. S. (1985). Protection from extinction: New data and a hypothesis of several varieties of conditioned inhibition. In R. R. Miller & N. E. Spear (eds.), *Information processing in animals: Conditioned inhibition,* 369–394. Hillsdale, N.J.: Erlbaum.

Stewart, J. (1992). Neurobiology of conditioning to drugs of abuse. *Annals of the New York Academy of Sciences, 654,* 335–346.

Stewart, J., de Wit, H., & Eikelboom, R. (1984). Role of unconditioned and conditioned drug effects in the self-administration of opiates and stimulants. *Psychological Review, 91,* 251–268.

Stewart, J., & Eikelboom, R. (1987). Conditioned drug effects. In L. L. Iversen, S. D. Iversen, & S. H. Snyder (eds.), *New directions in behavioral pharmacology,* Vol. 19: 1–57. New York: Plenum.

Swerdlow, N. R., Gilbert, D., & Koob, G. F. (1989). Conditioned drug effects on spatial preference: Critical evaluation. In A. A. Boulton, G. B. Baker, & A. J. Greenshaw (eds.), *Psychopharmacology (Neuromethods)* Vol. 13: 399–446. Clifton, N.J.: Humana Press.

Tabakoff, B., & Hoffman, P. L. (1988). A neurobiological theory of alcoholism. In C. D. Chaudron & D. A. Wilkinson (eds.), *Theories on alcoholism,* 29–72. Toronto: Addiction Research Foundation.

Tiffany, S. T., Petrie, E. C., Baker, T. B., & Dahl, J. L. (1983). Conditioned morphine tolerance in the rat: Absence of a compensatory response and cross-tolerance with stress. *Behavioral Neuroscience, 97,* 335–353.

Volpicelli, J. R., Alterman, A. I., Hayashida, M., & O'Brien, C. P. (1992). Naltrexone in the treatment of alcohol dependence. *Archives of General Psychiatry, 49,* 876–880.

Wagner, A. R. (1981). SOP: A model of automatic memory processing in animal behavior. In N. E. Spear & R. R. Miller (eds.), *Information processing in animals: Memory mechanisms,* 5–47. Hillsdale: N.J.: Erlbaum.

Wikler, A. (1948). Recent progress in research on the neurophysiologic basis of morphine addiction. *American Journal of Psychiatry, 105,* 329–338.

Wikler, A. (1965). Conditioning factors in opiate addiction and relapse. In D. M. Wilner & G. G. Kassebaum (eds.), *Narcotics,* 85–100. New York: McGraw-Hill.

Wikler, A. (1968). Interaction of physical dependence and classical and operant conditioning in the genesis of relapse. In A. Wikler (ed.), *The addictive states,* 280–287. Baltimore: Williams and Wilkins.

Wikler, A. (1973). Dynamics of drug dependence: Implications of a conditioning theory for research and treatment. In S. Fisher & A. M. Freedman (eds.), *Opiate addiction: Origins and treatment,* Vol. 38: 7–21. New York: Wiley.

Wise, R. A., & Bozarth, M. A. (1987). A psychomotor stimulant theory of addiction. *Psychological Review, 94,* 469–492.

Zelman, D. C., Tiffany, S. T., & Baker, T. B. (1985). Influence of stress on morphine-induced hyperthermia: Relevance to drug conditioning and tolerance development. *Behavioral Neuroscience, 99,* 122–144.

CHAPTER 27

THE FUTURE DIRECTION OF BEHAVIOR THERAPY: SOME APPLIED IMPLICATIONS OF CONTEMPORARY LEARNING RESEARCH

Amy E. Naugle
William O'Donohue

Behavior therapy and applied behavior analysis traditionally have reflected and incorporated the experimental findings of learning theory. It was believed that the findings from the basic laboratory supporting accounts of learning and conditioning could then be extrapolated to understanding human behavior and, more specifically, to understanding the development and maintenance of behavior disorders. Initially, behavior therapists and applied behavior analysts used experimentally derived principles to provide a framework for developing effective interventions to treat specific clinical problems. As an alternative to psychological hypotheses that arose largely out of the psychoanalytic tradition, behavior therapists applied conditioning techniques and directly manipulated environmental contingencies as a way of modifying disordered behavior. O'Donohue (Chapter 1) refers to the development of these early behavioral interventions as first generation of behavior therapy. In his introductory chapter, O'Donohue enumerates the shared characteristics of early learning researchers and their research and offers an explanation for why these characteristics are less evident in the field of behavior therapy today. Although the goal of this book is to provide accounts of contemporary learning theory and research that in turn offer implications for promoting what O'Donohue refers to as third-generation behavior therapy, many of the chapters offer a thoughtful reminder of the strengths and goals of the research and researchers responsible for the rise of first-generation behavior therapy.

With the deviation from first-generation behavior therapy to what has been termed second-generation behavior therapy, the gap between the experimental setting and the applied environment broadened. The consequence of this widening gap was twofold. First, behavior therapists became more and more distanced from research on basic learning processes and began developing and testing interventions that arose directly from their work in the therapy setting. Second, many animal learning researchers became more detached from applied concerns and explicated the implications for human learning in a manner less accessible to behavior therapists working exclusively in an applied setting. Although an ideal solution would be for learning researchers and the deliverers of behavioral interventions to be one and the same, as was clearly the case in first-generation behavior therapy, there are other amenable solutions as well. The responsibility thus falls on the shoulders of both those engaged in basic experimental research and those involved in delivering psychological interventions. When potentially relevant, animal research on basic learning processes needs to be presented in a fashion that is accessible to behavior therapists and offers direct implications for human learning. Behavior therapists who are not directly involved in the experimental laboratory similarly have an obligation to be regular and thoughtful consumers of the research and to implement the findings into their applied work.

In this chapter we attempt to integrate relevant and important points from the previous chapters and provide suggestions to clinicians regarding how to incorporate both early learning theory and the more contemporary accounts outlined by the authors in this book into their clinical work. We also propose that the basic research conducted with animals in the laboratory be extended to experimental designs that directly investigate these same basic processes in humans. Basic research with human subjects will lead us to developing more sophisticated models that reflect the complexity of the environments with which we interact.

THE IMPORTANCE OF A BACKGROUND IN LEARNING RESEARCH

The term *behavior therapist* today can have a variety of meanings. Clinicians trained in a number of different psychological paradigms may implement techniques derived from early learning research to treat specific clinical problems with little regard for or understanding of the principles and experimental research that yielded the technique. For example, a psychodynamic clinician may understand problems in living as the result of inadequate attachment to a significant figure in the early stages of development. Yet, the same clinician may still use an exposure-based strategy for treating a client who, in addition to having other clinical problems, presents for therapy to address his fear of flying in an airplane. The clinician may implement a systematic desensitization hierarchy in conjunction with relaxation to treat the phobia but be unable to explain why the client experienced a panic attack while checking his baggage at the airport and subsequently canceled his vacation. The clinician may simply see behavior therapy as a set of techniques that "work" with little regard for the underlying theory and research. In fact, there is data to support the drift within applied behavior analysis to becoming primarily a technical effort with less emphasis on conceptual issues (Hayes, Rincover, & Solnick, 1980).

A cognitive-behavior therapist who has a familiarity with and appreciation for the learning principles from which exposure-based interventions are derived may find himself or herself in the same predicament. Behavior therapists may be trained primarily as technicians with little familiarity with the findings that emerge from basic learning research. In this case, the behavior therapist can describe the basic Pavlovian principles that account for the development and maintenance of the phobia and can modify the specific intervention consistent with the principles. However, the therapist may still be unable to explain the ineffectiveness of the intervention or how to subsequently modify it to reduce or eliminate the phobic response. Both of these examples illustrate the importance of staying familiar with the findings and implications that emerge from the basic laboratory.

Being well versed in the basic experimental literature on learning theories has several advantages for behavior therapists in the 1990s. First, contemporary learning theories may explain more comprehensively why and how traditional behavioral techniques are ineffective in impacting problematic behavior that is generally responsive to such interventions. That is, careful consideration of more contemporary conditioning research may both explain treatment failures and offer suitable remedies. Behavior therapists who continue to implement techniques that come largely out of 1960s learning theory may overly attend to their treatment successes and ignore these treatment failures. Or they may rely on alternative interventions not grounded in any basic experimental work in an attempt to augment where behavioral techniques fall short. Both of these options represent what can happen as behavior therapists move further away from new developments in basic learning research. Outdated behavior therapy supports the widespread belief among clinical psychologists that the work of basic learning researchers provides an inadequate and incomplete paradigm for the broad set of clinical problems of clients that present for therapy.

In addition to explaining and remedying treatment failures and making existing interventions more effective, contemporary learning research can guide behavior therapists in delivering effective interventions more efficiently and in strengthening treatment effects. The changing nature of the health care delivery system, the emphasis on empirically validated treatments (Task Force on Promotion and Dissemination of Psychological Procedures, 1995), and the push to minimize the length of treatment may be the impetus for behavior therapists specifically and all therapists more generally to turn to the laboratory and to current basic experimental research.

A third advantage of contemporary learning theory concerns the level of sophistication that differentiates it from earlier learning theory and research. Historically, behaviorism has been criticized for its simplicity and lack of application to complex human behavior. Therefore, while first-generation behavior therapy showed great promise in constructing interventions for a circumscribed set of behavior problems (e.g., phobias, skills deficits in the developmentally disabled, enuresis), it was more difficult to see the relevance for more complex psychological or behavioral problems (e.g., depression, long-standing interpersonal difficulties). The learning research summarized in the preceding chapters addresses this criticism by elaborating upon traditional Pavlovian and operant principles of conditioning and offering experimentally supported models that have implications for understanding and effectively treating complex disorders of behavior.

THE ROLE OF CONTEXT IN LEARNING THEORY AND THE IMPLICATIONS FOR BEHAVIOR THERAPY

The one significant addition that pervades most of the contemporary learning research presented in the preceding chapters is the attention given to the role of context (Branch & Hackenberg, Chapter 2; Kehoe & Macrae, Chapter 3; Bouton & Nelson, Chapter 4; Williams, Johns & Norton, Chapter 5; Lubow, Chapter 6; Allan, Chapter 8; Nevin, Chapter 12; Green & Freed, Chapter 14; Schachtman & Reed, Chapter 15; Morgan & Riccio, Chapter 23). Contemporary models of classical conditioning are especially attentive to incorporating an understanding of the complex interaction between contextual variables and other stimuli in the conditioning process. Traditional Pavlovian models concentrated on manipulating the presentation of a single conditioned stimulus and paid less attention to how additional variables impact the generalizability of conditioning trained in one context to another context. The additional emphasis on context shows an appreciation for how conditioning that occurs in the natural environment diverges from the more fundamental findings from the controlled laboratory environment. The rich environment in which human behavior problems both develop and maintain requires more careful consideration of the important contingencies that control such behavior. Acknowledging the complexity of the context in which learning occurs has important implications for behavior therapists.

Assessment

One implication involves how behavior therapists gather information during the assessment phase of therapy. When a client presents for therapy for help with a specific problem, behavior therapists are compelled to comprehensively and efficiently assess the contingencies responsible for the development and maintenance of the problematic behavior. Typically, behavior therapists rely heavily on the client's verbal descriptions of the controlling variables and implement their intervention based exclusively on this information. The summary provided by Branch and Hackenberg (Chapter 2) suggests that relying heavily on verbal reports of contingencies provided by the client is problematic. The authors refer to experimental research that illustrates how the behavior of human subjects comes under the control of explicitly arranged contingencies in the absence of accurate verbal hypotheses regarding the variables that are controlling their behavior. Thus, there is evidence to support the notion that clients may not aptly identify the environmental conditions that give rise to their behavior. It is also the case that while a client may accurately explain a subset of variables that control a particular behavior, the subset is not likely comprehensive. The caution for therapists is to recognize that a client's description of contingencies may operate as a heuristic for both the therapist and the client that prevents the identification of other important causal variables (Matute & Miller, Chapter 24). In their chapter on detecting causal relationships, Matute and Miller discuss strategies for facilitating the judgments humans make about cause and effect.

Similarly, it may be that the client is unable to verbally describe any possible events responsible for the development of a clinical problem. In an attempt to provide a parsimonious explanation for the client's presenting problem, the therapist may inadvertently focus on revealing a single salient event that initially elicited the problematic behavior. However, the idea that fear reactions or phobic responses develop only as the result of a single salient event is inconsistent with contemporary learning research. There is evidence supporting how strong conditioned associations can occur without exposure to a single salient event (Kehoe & Macrae, Chapter 3). Therefore, describing a chain of episodes that led to conditioned aversion to a particular stimulus or set of stimuli may be especially problematic for clients.

Behavior therapists must therefore continue to utilize assessment strategies other than self-report to generate a thorough conceptualization of the problematic behavior clients present within therapy. One option is for behavior therapists to conduct their assessment and subsequently implement their interventions in more naturalistic settings. Naturalistic behavioral observation can provide more accurate and relevant information concerning the client's presenting problem than can be gleaned from a therapy room. Oftentimes behavior therapists operate from the assumption that they can identify a single stimulus or class of stimuli that elicits fear or a phobic response and that further exposure to the conditioned stimulus in therapy will produce a response similar in form and magnitude regardless of how similar the therapy context is to the context in which the phobic response usually occurs. More thorough and naturalistic assessment strategies would allow therapists to more accurately discern the context-specific nature of conditioned fear. Observing and interacting with the client within his or her natural environment provides the therapist access to how variations in client behavior are influenced by multiple factors that are present in a richer environment than a traditional clinical setting can offer.

An alternative option to going into a client's natural environment is for behavior therapists to develop and utilize behavior assessment strategies within session that are more analogous to the real-world environment. For example, technological advances such as interactive video and virtual reality technologies provide opportunities for therapists to expose clients to a broader set of stimuli than those the client identifies as fear inducing. Such innovative methods may make it possible for behavior therapists to identify and describe the relationship between variables and how the presence of additional contextual variables impacts conditioned performance.

Regardless of whether the assessment is conducted in the natural environment or in an analogue situation, it is imperative for the behavior therapist to organize information regarding the relationship between particular environmental events and target behaviors. One strategy offered by Williams, Johns, & Norton (Chapter 5) demonstrates the use of a contingency space to plot the relations between unconditioned stimuli and conditioned stimuli. Use of this tool in the clinical setting would allow the behavior therapist to more accurately determine the probability of the disordered behavior and quantitatively document how the manipulation of other contextual factors impacts the probability of responding in a given way.

Treatment

A second implication of attending to additional contextual variables is that it may encourage therapists to more carefully consider the setting in which treatment is delivered. The experimental work on the role of context offers useful information regarding how treatment effects generalize outside of therapy. Therefore, the therapy setting must be sensitive to both the environmental conditions in which original training may have occurred (to the degree that this is possible) and the setting in which treatment effects need to be maintained. We first discuss the impact that contextual variables have on initial conditioning and then turn to discussing generalizability issues in exposure-based interventions.

The basic research on latent inhibition has important implications for both primary prevention and tertiary intervention for a variety of common clinical problems. An abundance of research demonstrates that preconditioned exposure to a stimulus impacts the likelihood of the same stimulus becoming an effective conditioned stimulus (see Lubow, Chapter 6). Preconditioning makes a particular stimulus more familiar than stimuli that the subject has never been exposed to. Therefore, familiar cues are less likely to form a conditioned

association when paired with an unconditioned stimulus; they are less likely to control anxiety disorders or problematic behaviors associated with drug use (Bouton & Nelson, Chapter 4), particularly when presented in a familiar context. Additionally, experimental manipulations that precede the pairing between the unconditioned stimulus and the conditioned stimulus with the presentation of the conditioned stimulus alone provide evidence that first learning generalizes better across contexts. The subsequent US-CS association is more context specific than learning that occurs to the conditioned stimulus alone.

While behavior therapists are primarily involved in secondary intervention to treat problems after they have arisen, the research on latent inhibition introduces the need for a stronger emphasis on primary prevention. Bouton and Nelson (Chapter 4) suggest that we should devote more attention to developing and supporting environmental conditions that promote healthy learning in the first place. Such initial learning experiences would generalize more readily across multiple contexts and leave conditioning experiences that lead to maladaptive behavior as "the context-specific, second learned exceptions to the rule."

Lubow (Chapter 6) offers a number of suggestions for how the experimental literature on latent inhibition applies to the prevention of specific clinical problems. The applications of latent inhibition procedures to the realm of behavior medicine are numerous. Lubow discusses strategies for reducing the side effects of radiation and other chemical therapies, specifically with regard to preventing taste aversions from developing. Applied research has also been done that explores the influence of preconditioning exposures in the development of dental phobias. The implication is that a child who has a number of positive or neutral experiences during his or her visits to the dentist is less likely to develop a conditioned phobic response during future dental visits that involve painful procedures. Preexposure to other potential fear-inducing situations may have a similar effect in preventing fearful or avoidance behavior from being conditioned. Children who are given the opportunity to become acquainted with an unfamiliar school environment and form a positive association with the environment before being left at school without a parent may be less fearful of the school environment and more eager to return to school each day than children without preexposure. Much of the research done on latent inhibition, however, has been retrospective in nature. As suggested by Lubow (Chapter 6), it may be advantageous to identify specific target populations at risk for acquiring specific problematic behaviors (e.g., phobic responses) and identify target stimuli that may elicit such behavior to prevent clinical problems from developing in the first place.

Direct preexposure to the to-be-conditioned stimulus is not the only way to prevent the development of fears. Research on modeling immunization (see Mineka & Hamida, Chapter 21) suggests that watching others interact with a target stimulus is effective in preventing the development of fear when the subject is subsequently exposed to the stimulus. This research is similar to the concept of vicarious learning. Children may strongly benefit from watching a parent interact in a nonfearful way with a novel stimulus. A child who observes his or her parent approaching a dog and petting the dog, according to the modeling immunization research, will be less likely to develop a phobic response.

The effect of latent inhibition depends on a number of factors. The number of stimulus preexposures strongly impacts the effectiveness of preexposure in preventing future acquisition of fear to the same stimulus. Therefore, one preexposure visit to the dentist or to the classroom will be less likely than will more exposures to prevent fear acquisition. Similarly, the intensity of the preexposed stimulus plays a role in the magnitude of the latent inhibition effect. Sitting in the waiting room of the dentist's office while a sibling is in the examining room will have a less powerful inhibiting effect than being allowed to sit in the dentist's chair, examine the tools, and talk with the dentist. A third factor that may influence the strength of inhibition is the interval between stimulus preexposure and subsequent

exposure to the target stimulus. There is mixed evidence on the impact of the temporal relationship between preexposure and acquisition, and additional research is needed.

Generalizability: Extinction and Reacquisition

Several clinical interventions, particularly exposure-based therapies, are based on the principle of extinction. Consideration of how contextual factors influence the generalizability of extinction or interference strategies is crucial in implementing exposure-based therapies. It is clear from the research employing classical conditioning models that extinction is not unlearning. Rather, the original association is largely preserved (Kehoe & Macrae, Chapter 3), and reacquisition is largely dependent on the contexts in which the original association and newly formed associations between stimuli occur. Therefore, it is imperative that the context in which exposure-based therapies occur closely resembles the context in which treatment effects need to be maintained. There are a number of additional considerations for maximizing the generalizability of treatment results in exposure-based interventions as well as for understanding relapse.

After intensive therapy designed to decrease the frequency and ultimately eliminate the occurrence of a target behavior, the potential for relapse remains (e.g., Marlatt, 1992). The most obvious reason for the reacquisition of a target behavior is reexposure to the unconditioned stimulus. Consider the young man who experiences a number of frightening reactions after experimenting with PCP. The young man subsequently begins avoiding situations directly associated with the context in which the drug-induced reactions occurred. Therapy with the young man involves a series of exposure exercises in which the young man develops alternative associations with the contextual cues that previously elicited panic attacks. The intervention appears to be successful, and the client resumes his previous level of social interactions and is no longer avoiding contextual variables associated with the drug-conditioned experience. To the dismay of the therapist, the client calls to request a session before his 3-month follow-up session, reporting the recurrence of panic symptoms. The client explains that he had acquiesced to smoking marijuana at a party several nights before and again experienced hallucinogenic effects similar to what he experienced when experimenting with PCP. The reexposure to the unconditioned stimulus (marijuana laced with PCP) explains the client's relapse.

Relapse may also take place when the extinction training occurs in a markedly different context than the context in which either the original conditioning took place or to which treatment effects should generalize. Consider again the previous clinical example. Imagine that the most-feared conditioned stimulus for the young man is hearing loud music and that prior to treatment he avoids situations where he might be exposed to loud music. One intervention strategy might involve using systematic desensitization to reduce avoidance of situations where loud music is likely to occur (i.e., pubs and restaurants). Systematic desensitization may not be the most effective treatment strategy for impacting lasting behavioral change for two reasons. First, systematic desensitization procedures typically include an element of imagined exposure. Exposure to an *imagined* pub or restaurant is neither the context in which the fear was acquired nor the situation to which the therapist is ultimately interested in having treatment effects generalize. Therefore, direct exposure to loud music in the context where the CS–US association occurred and where the client wishes to interact will maximize treatment efficacy. Second, systematic desensitization also involves exposing the client to the feared CS in conjunction with relaxation training. This counterconditioning strategy makes responding to the CS highly context dependent. Once the contextual variables associated with relaxation are removed (e.g., a relaxation tape), relapse can occur.

An additional caveat for behavior therapists worth considering and attending to is the extent to which the therapist becomes an important contextual factor in maintaining the effects of behavioral interventions. Even in taking precautions to ensure that the extinction context is similar to the real-world environment in which the client must interact, a therapist might overlook the role he or she plays in the extinction context. Since the therapist himself or herself may be an important cue in extinguishing fear, he or she must work with the client to establish safety cues outside of therapy that mimic the safety cue provided by the presence of the therapist.

OPERANT CONDITIONING AND CHOICE

Stimulus Control: Context and Operant Conditioning

The preceding section has focused primarily on the role of context in contemporary models of respondent conditioning. We believe it is worth briefly mentioning the role of context in an operant conditioning paradigm. Allan (Chapter 8) elaborates on the distinction between operant and respondent conditioning by specifying the contingencies that influence the probability of responding. The distinction outlined by Allan suggests that respondent conditioning is under the control of events that precede the behavior and that the future probability of an operant response is influenced by consequences that follow the response. However, in a traditional three-term contingency operant analysis, the discriminative function of stimuli plays a significant role in the effectiveness of consequences in affecting behavior. Discriminative stimuli set the occasion for when a response will be reinforced. Therefore, an operant analysis of clinical problems, in addition to assessing the relative effectiveness of particular reinforcers under the different conditions, must address whether a target behavior occurs more often in the presence of one set of stimuli than another.

The clinical problem of depression has been conceptualized as the result of inadequate contact with positive events that may serve as reinforcers for an individual's behavior (e.g., Lewinsohn, 1974). It may be that the depressed individual's environment provides an insufficient number of reinforcing stimuli. Alternatively, it may be that the depressed individual's behavior is under inappropriate stimulus control. That is, the individual does not recognize feedback from the environment as either reinforcing or punishing and subsequently does not adjust his or her behavior appropriately (Compton & Follette, 1996).

Consider the middle-aged woman who presents for therapy complaining of depression and social isolation. The woman has a family and works in an environment that provides many opportunities to interact with others. However, the woman is ineffective in establishing relationships and no longer initiates contact with her co-workers. After a comprehensive assessment of the woman's presenting complaint and interpersonal skills, the therapist begins with the hypothesis that inappropriate stimulus control is the most fitting conceptualization to explain the woman's depression. The goal of therapy would then be to bring the woman's behavior under the control of a different set of contingencies. Stimulus discrimination procedures involve arranging the therapy environment so that the woman learns to discriminate when particular interpersonal behaviors will be reinforced. However, the client must first properly orient herself to the therapist so that the discriminative function of particular cues from the therapist will evoke the client's behavior to be reinforced.

Identifying and Delivering Reinforcers

The effectiveness of a stimulus as a reinforcer depends on a number of factors. To identify the effectiveness or reinforcing value of a particular stimulus or set of stimuli, we must first make the stimulus a consequence of responding. All too often behavior therapists a priori identify stimuli as reinforcers without first establishing their effectiveness in altering the probability of behavior. The outcome is that the stimuli do not actually function as an effective reinforcer. Identifying reinforcers on the basis of empirical investigation is crucial.

An additional problem is that reinforcers determined independently of their influence on behavior are often arbitrary rather than natural reinforcers (Ferster, 1972). It is the distinction made between natural and arbitrary reinforcement that emphasizes the limitations of applying animal research in the laboratory to complex human behavior in the natural environment. Natural reinforcement relies less delivery by a second party than arbitrary reinforcement and is more likely to be available outside of therapy. While some behavioral interventions require a therapy milieu that more closely resembles traditional laboratory procedures in modifying behavior, other types of clinical problems may be more effectively treated in a therapy environment that matches the client's natural environment. Functional analytic psychotherapy (FAP; Kohlenberg & Tsai, 1991) is an interpersonal approach to therapy based on behavior analytic principles that underscores the importance of natural reinforcement in impacting client behavior.

Maximizing the effectiveness of consequences on altering the future probability of behavior depends on a number of factors, including the type of schedule, the frequency of delivery, and the duration between the emitted response and arrival of the consequence. The most important reminder for behavior therapists involves taking into consideration the latter issue of contiguity. Longer delays between behavior and its consequences decrease the effect of the consequence as a reinforcer or punisher. The importance of immediacy in the delivery of reinforcement is reflected in behavioral interventions for building complex social skills. Establishing complex social behavior requires that the therapist first build the necessary component skills. In shaping more effective social skills, a behavior therapist may use a variety of techniques, including behavioral rehearsal using a variety of social situations. The shaping process requires that the therapist provide immediate contingent feedback to the client regarding the client's performance in the role-played scenarios. With regard to how contiguity impacts the effectiveness of a reinforcer, behavioral rehearsal strategies are more effective than soley instructing the client to practice skills between sessions and report back to the therapist the degree of success of the out-of-session interactions.

Before moving on to a discussion of the relativity of reinforcement, we believe it is necessary to discuss strategies that facilitate the behavior therapist's ability to identify reinforcers. One strategy is to institute a free-operant analysis for determining both what events function as reinforcers and the relative occurrence of behaviors in a free-operant environment. Such a strategy would allow the behavior therapist to identify how deprivation of high-probability responses or other environmental events can be used to alter the frequency of occurrence for some target response. Contemporary operant research such as Timberlake's (1995) causal system model clarifies these additional conditions that impact reinforcement necessary for behavior therapists to incorporate into their clinical work.

Choice

Both the Premack principle (Premack, 1965) and Herrnstein's matching law (Herrnstein, 1961) provide a basis for useful and interesting models for understanding the relativity of consequences. The matching law simply says that the relative rate of responding is directly proportional to the frequency of reinforcers produced by a response. Herrnstein's work on matching law again brings to the forefront of behavior therapy the important role that context plays in understanding behavior. The allocation of behavior is influenced by reinforcers contingent on the target behavior as well as other reinforcers present in the environment. A clinical example demonstrating matching law is shown in how time allocated in session impacts the client's compliance with out-of-session homework. In this clinical example, the therapist instructs the client to monitor his or her daily mood, including subjective level of anxiety and depression. When the therapist allocates time in session to talking about the mood ratings and inquiring about situational factors that impact that mood, the therapist provides reinforcement for carrying out

homework assignments. When the therapist forgets to ask about the homework or shifts the discussion away from the homework when the client raises the issue, the client's continued completion of homework will match the schedule of the reinforcement that is delivered. That is, clients will be less compliant with completing homework assignments when reinforcement in session is contingent on client behavior other than homework completion.

Green and Freed (Chapter 14) provide an account of behavioral economics that makes explicit the implications of matching law. The contribution of the theory and experimental work of behavioral economics is underutilized and underappreciated by behavior therapists. Behavioral economics enriches our understanding of principles of reinforcement by allowing us to predict choice in situations that more closely resemble the rich complexity of the environments in which relative responding occurs. In developing an intervention to impact the problems in living identified by a client, the behavior therapist must formulate an understanding of how an individual chooses among different events available in the environment. Specifying the complex interactions of reinforcers allows the behavior therapist to make more precise predictions about the occurrence of specific behaviors of interest.

In their discussion of behavioral economics, Green and Freed (Chapter 14) also refer to Premack's elucidation of the relativity of reinforcement. The Premack principle emphasizes that events are not inherently reinforcing or punishing. Premack expands the concept of relativity of reinforcement by providing evidence that responses with a lower probability of occurrence increase in frequency when more probable events are made contingent on their occurrence.

One example of how the Premack principle is utilized clinically is demonstrated in Linehan's dialectical behavior therapy (Linehan, 1993) for treating individuals diagnosed with borderline personality disorder. Consider a client who presents for therapy with a number of clinical problems, including parasuicidal behavior, a child with behavior problems, and difficult interpersonal relationships. In the early stages of therapy, the therapist establishes the frequency of time the client allots to these different areas and notes that the client allocates most of the in-session time to talking about her difficult child and her interpersonal interactions at work. In doing so, the client devotes relatively little time to exploring and talking about the circumstances that contribute to her self-injury. Linehan outlines a hierarchy in her treatment approach that provides guidelines for how to distribute time contingently. Given that self-injury interferes with the client's functioning and is potentially life threatening, it is imperative that the therapist and client work together to develop strategies to decrease the occurrence of such behavior. Therefore, it is necessary to spend time in the therapy session developing an analysis of the contingencies that maintain parasuicidal behavior so that the therapist and client can develop strategies for reducing this behavior outside of session. Talking about quality-of-life issues (i.e., the client's frustrations as a parent and interpersonal encounters in the workplace) is a higher probability response in session than talking about self-injury. Thus, the therapist can impact the probability of talking about self-injury in session (which is necessary for impacting change in this area) by making talking about the quality-of-life issues contingent on discussing self-injury.

A last issue related to choice is reflected in Logue's chapter on self-control (Chapter 13). Self-control is a concept that illustrates how organisms choose between a smaller immediate reward and larger delayed rewards. In addition, some problematic behavior may have powerfully reinforcing consequences in the short term but result in longer-term negative consequences (Dinsmoor, Chapter 10). Safeguarding an individual from distal aversive consequences may be promoted by developing strategies for exercising self-control in the short term. Decreasing high-risk sexual behavior such as engaging in unprotected sex and having multiple sexual partners that places individuals at risk for contracting HIV is an example of this concept.

Whether an instance of behavior is an example of self-control versus impulsiveness is again determined by the context; that is, it is functionally defined. Behavior that is defined as impulsive under one set of contingencies may be an instance of self-control in another context. Targeting an impulsive behavior for intervention first involves identifying situations where it is advantageous for self-control to occur and then developing strategies to increase the likelihood that self-control will occur. The decision of a client to utilize psychotherapy versus relying on other strategies for solving problems illustrates this concept of self-control. A client who presents for therapy to deal with depression may report that one effective strategy for impacting his mood is to drink a couple of beers. The therapist informs the client that one of the requirements of therapy is that the client discontinue drinking alcohol while he is in therapy. The client then makes a choice between the smaller, immediate outcome of continuing to drink as a problem-solving strategy and the larger delayed outcome that would likely result from utilizing psychotherapy as a more lasting strategy for decreasing his level of depression.

Logue outlines three factors that affect self-control, and consideration of these factors may be beneficial to the therapist for maximizing the likelihood of the client's choosing psychotherapy over drinking, that is, increasing self-control. Delay of the outcome is the first factor. A longer latency in the impact of therapy on mood will decrease the likelihood of the client's staying in therapy. Therefore, it is crucial to maximize therapeutic effects early in therapy. It may be beneficial for the behavior therapist to schedule more frequent sessions in the early stages of therapy as a strategy for decreasing the length of delay. A second consideration in increasing self-control is the size of the outcome. The behavior therapist's emphasis on the broad implications of effective therapy and its benefits over drinking may increase the perceived outcome for the client and secure the client's commitment to therapy. A final factor that impacts self-control concerns what Logue refers to as outcome contingencies. One specific outcome contingency that increases self-control is making a precommitment to making a self-control response. Contracting with the client for a set number of sessions at the end of which the therapist and client agree to reevaluate therapy may be one way of influencing self-control responding in this example.

VERBAL BEHAVIOR AND COMPLEX HUMAN PROBLEMS

The previous sections of this chapter outline possible applications for some of the contemporary learning theory and research presented in the preceding chapters. One of the difficulties in applying what is in large part animal research conducted in the laboratory to the therapy setting is directly related to the role verbal behavior plays in complex human interactions. Outpatient behavior therapy is in large part characterized as a verbal enterprise. As such, the verbal behavior that occurs in the context of the therapeutic setting is of significant interest. Fortunately, one of the important developments in the field of contemporary learning theory centers on exploring basic verbal processes. The contemporary work in this area extends beyond the traditional Skinnerian analysis of language (Skinner, 1957), which essentially understood verbal behavior similar to other operants, behavior under the control of a particular set of contingencies. While contemporary analyses of verbal behavior extend beyond a basic operant analysis, behavior therapists remain well served by having a knowledge of traditional behavior analytic models of verbal behavior.

Verbal Behavior as an Operant

Most verbal behavior is dependent on reinforcement from a social-verbal community. In psychotherapy, the social-verbal community is provided by the client and therapist, who mutually reinforce the verbal behavior of each other. Branch and Hackenberg (Chapter 2) point out that this process of mutual reinforcement that occurs between the client and therapist is influenced not only by the immediate verbal interaction but also by the established speaker and listener repertoires of each. Part of what occurs in the early stages of therapy is that the aspects of both the client's listener and speaker repertoires are made explicit to the therapist. Just as it imperative for the therapist to identify the contingencies that give rise to other operant behavior, so is it necessary to identify the variables that control a client's verbal behavior. By defining the stimulus conditions and available reinforcers that support particular verbal operants, the therapist gains awareness of how his or her own behavior, verbal or otherwise, impacts what the client talks about and under what set of conditions.

Early research on verbal conditioning (e.g., Krasner, 1958) provides evidence of how it is the behavior of the listener that explicitly shapes verbal behavior on the part of the speaker. In part, we encourage behavior therapists to become familiar with this literature as a caution. The behavior of the therapist strongly influences how the verbal behavior of clients gets shaped and subsequently what gets focused on in session. Therefore, the client verbal behavior that gets reinforced by the therapist may not be what is most significant to the client or what offers the most useful information in terms of determining and implementing an effective intervention. For example, a therapist may overly attend to childhood experiences of trauma reported by the client that may or may not have direct relevance to the client's presenting complaint or primary clinical issue. When a therapist talks with the client about these historical experiences, it is important for the therapist to recognize that what is potentially being shaped is the client's verbal behavior rather than any improvements related to the target problem.

Before moving on to a discussion of more contemporary theories of verbal processes, we would like to also note that shaping client verbal behavior in session can have important implications for impacting out-of-session target behaviors. While we offer caution regarding the influence the therapist has on client verbal behavior, the caution is really a reminder for therapists to systematically identify how client verbal behavior comes under the control of the therapy context. As Hayes and Ju discuss in their chapter on rule-governed behavior (Chapter 18), a client's behavior is often under the control of his or her verbal descriptions of contingencies. Therefore, shaping clients in session to accurately describe the contingent relationship between environmental events and their behavior may be an effective strategy for maximizing the maintenance of clinical improvements outside of therapy.

Stimulus Equivalence and Derived Relational Responding

The research on stimulus equivalence and derived relations (Hayes & Ju, Chapter 18; Tierney & Bracken, Chapter 19) has interesting implications for understanding the role of language in psychotherapy. This contemporary analysis of language provides a framework for understanding how verbal behavior alters the function of environmental events and changes how people respond to contingencies. In verbal organisms, the functions of particular stimuli can be derived without being directly trained (e.g., Devany, Hayes, & Nelson, 1986; Lipkens, Hayes, & Hayes, 1993) and therefore are not adequately accounted for in traditional accounts of stimulus generalization. Events may take on stimulus properties of other events that are part of the same verbally derived equivalence class or stimulus relation; that is, the stimulus function transfers from one event to another. For example, an individual may experience a panic attack while shopping at a large department store. Following the attack, the person avoids shopping at the department store, consistent with a respondent model of understanding fear and anxiety. However, the individual also begins avoiding trips to the grocery store and is fearful of driving even though he or she has never experienced a panic attack in either of these situations. In this example, the fear-evoking function of these new events was not directly trained. Stimulus equivalence and derived rela-

tional responding provides a model for understanding how it is that these new events take on a particular stimulus function as part of a stimulus relation. (For a comprehensive account of stimulus relations and relational frame theory, see Hayes, Gifford, & Wilson, in press.)

This contemporary verbal analysis may also be useful for understanding at a general level how the verbal exchange that occurs between the client and the therapist can bring about lasting change. As an example, Follette, Naugle, and Callaghan (1996) apply a verbal analysis consistent with stimulus equivalence and relational frame theory that explains how it is that the therapist becomes an important and effective source of reinforcement such that his or her behavior increases effective responding on the part of the client.

CONCLUSION

In the tradition of first-generation behavior therapy, it is essential that behavior therapists remain active consumers of and contributors to the experimental work investigating basic processes of learning. Doing so will lead to a more sophisticated understanding of complex human problems and will allow behavior therapists to develop and implement more effective interventions. In this chapter we attempt to narrow the gap between the applied arena of behavior therapy and contemporary learning theory by illustrating some clinical applications of the research emerging from the laboratory. The examples provided in this chapter are only the tip of the iceberg. The preceding chapters in this book abound with ideas for further research, both basic and applied, and have numerous implications for the growth and effectiveness of behavior therapy.

REFERENCES

Compton, S. N., & Follette, W. C. (1996). *An analysis of the ablility of depressed subjects to evaluate the impact of their social behavior.* Unpublished Master's Thesis, University of Nevada, Reno.

Devany, J. M., Hayes, S. C., & Nelson, R. O. (1986). Equivalence class formation in language-able and language-disabled children. *Journal of the Experimental Analysis of Behavior, 46,* 243–257.

Ferster, C. B. (1972). Clinical reinforcement. *Seminars in Psychiatry, 4,* 101–111.

Follette, W. C., Naugle, A. E., & Callaghan, G. M. (1996). A radical behavioral understanding of the therapeutic relationship in effecting change. *Behavior Therapy, 27,* 623–641.

Hayes, S. C., Gifford, E. V., & Wilson, K. G. (in press). Stimulus classes and stimulus relations: Arbitrary applicable relational responding as an operant. In T. Zentall & P. Smeets (eds.), *Stimulus class formation.*

Hayes, S. C., Rincover, A., & Solnick, J. V. (1980). The technical drift of applied behavior analysis. *Journal of Applied Behavior Analysis, 13,* 275–285.

Herrnstein, R. J. (1961). Relative and absolute strength of response as a function of frequency of reinforcement. *Journal of the Experimental Analysis of Behavior, 4,* 267–272.

Kohlenberg, R. J., & Tsai, M. (1991). *Functional analytic psychotherapy.* New York: Plenum.

Krasner, L. (1958). Studies of the conditioning of verbal behavior. *Psychological Bulletin, 55,* 148–170.

Lewinsohn, P. M. (1974). A behavioral approach to depression. In R. J. Friedman & M. M. Katz (eds.), *The psychology of depression: Contemporary theory and research.* New York: Wiley.

Linehan, M. M. (1993). *Cognitive-behavioral treatment of borderline personality disorder.* New York: Wiley.

Lipkens, G., Hayes, S. C., & Hayes, L. J. (1993). Longitudinal study of derived stimulus relations in an infant. *Journal of Experimental Child Psychology, 56,* 201–239.

Marlatt, G. A. (1992). Substance abuse: Implications of a biopsychosocial model for prevention, treatment, and relapse prevention. In J. Grabowski & G. R. VandenBos (eds.), *Psychopharmacology: Basic mechanisms and applied intervention,* 127–162. Washington, D.C.: American Psychological Association.

Premack, D. (1965). Reinforcement theory. In D. Levine (ed.), *Nebraska symposium on motivation,* Vol. 13: 123–180. Lincoln: University of Nebraska Press.

Skinner, B. F. (1957). *Verbal behavior.* New York: Appleton-Century-Crofts.

Task Force on Promotion and Dissemination of Psychological Procedures (1995). Training in and dissemination of empirically-validated psychological treatments: Report and recommendations. *The Clinical Psychologist, 48,* 3–23.

Timberlake, W. (1995). Reconceptualizing reinforcement: A causal-system approach to reinforcement and behavior change. In W. O'Donohue & L. Krasner (eds.), *Theories of behavior therapy,* 59–96. Washington, D.C.: American Psychological Association.

INDEX